# 1 MONTH OF
# FREE
# READING

## at
## www.ForgottenBooks.com

By purchasing this book you are eligible for one month membership to ForgottenBooks.com, giving you unlimited access to our entire collection of over 1,000,000 titles via our web site and mobile apps.

To claim your free month visit:
www.forgottenbooks.com/free890701

ISBN 978-0-265-79605-4
PIBN 10890701

*James Raine* HISTORY, *by the Will of*

# DIRECTORY & GAZETTEER

*James* OF THE *Gordon*

# County of York;

WITH A VARIETY OF

COMMERCIAL, STATISTICAL, AND PROFESSIONAL
INFORMATION:

ALSO COPIOUS LISTS OF THE

### Seats of the Nobility and Gentry

*Of Yorkshire.*

BY EDWARD BAINES.

THE DIRECTORY DEPARTMENT BY W. PARSON.

VOL. II.

EAST AND NORTH RIDINGS.

*ILLUSTRATED BY MAPS, PLANS, &c.*

Printed and Published

BY EDWARD BAINES, AT THE LEEDS MERCURY OFFICE;

AND SOLD BY

HURST AND ROBINSON, 90, CHEAPSIDE, LONDON,

AND ALL OTHER BOOKSELLERS.

1823.

# CONTENTS OF THIS WORK.

## VOL. I.

## VOL. II.

# INDEX OF SUBJECTS.

# INDEX OF PLACES,

EXHIBITING A VIEW OF ALL THE PARISHES IN THE EAST AND NORTH RIDINGS OF YORKSHIRE, OF THE AINSTY OF YORK, AND OF THE LIBERTY OF ST. PETER'S, WITH THE TOWNSHIPS IN THE RESPECTIVE PARISHES, AND THE POPULATION OF EACH ACCORDING TO THE OFFICIAL RETURNS OF THE 28TH OF MAY, 1821, TAKEN BY ORDER OF PARLIAMENT.

The first column contains the Folio where each Place is to be found in this Volume; the other three columns relate to the Population: first, the return of 1821; second, the total numbers in each Parish according to that return; and third, the returns of 1811, from which the Increase or Decrease during the last 10 years may be ascertained.

All the Towns, Villages, and Hamlets in the East and North Ridings and Ainsty will be found alphabetically arranged in their proper places, though only such as are Parishes or Townships are inserted in this Index.

## (EAST RIDING.)

Those marked thus * are partly in the Liberty of St. Peter of York.

| Names of Parishes and Townships. | Page | POPULATION. In 1821 | Parish Totals | In 1811 |
|---|---|---|---|---|
| Acaster Malbis, | 137 | | | |
| (pt. of) Naburn | 376 | 366 | | 346 |
| *Acklam with | 149 | | | |
| Barthorpe ... | 149 | 389 | | 310 |
| *Leavening ... | 362 | 294 | 788 | 225 |
| Aldbrough ...... | 149 | 802 | | 687 |
| Newton East | 373 | 38 | | 39 |
| Newton West | 373 | 158 | 998 | 147 |
| *Allerthorpe ... | 150 | 132 | | 132 |
| Waplington ... | 397 | 19 | 151 | 14 |
| Argam........... | 150 | 35 | 35 | 20 |
| Atwich, Arram, | 151 | | | |
| and Skirlington | 389 | 326 | 326 | 286 |
| Aughton ........ | 151 | 269 | | 247 |
| Cottingwith E. | 191 | 308 | | 392 |
| Laytham .... | 362 | 125 | 702 | 104 |
| Bainton........ | 152 | 300 | 300 | 237 |
| Barmston ...... | 152 | 205 | 205 | 206 |
| Beeford ...... | 154 | 620 | | 524 |
| Dunnington .. | 199 | 76 | | 49 |
| Lissett ...... | 363 | 95 | 791 | 94 |
| Bempton ...... | 155 | 231 | 231 | 241 |
| Bessingby ..... | 155 | 83 | 83 | 82 |
| Birdsall ........ | 168 | 240 | 240 | 242 |
| *Bishop Wilton | 400 | | | |
| with *Belthorpe | 155 | 570 | | 454 |
| *Bolton ...... | 168 | 112 | | 94 |
| *Youlthorpe | 402 | | | |
| with *Gowthorpe ...... | 211 | 111 | 793 | 124 |
| Blacktoft ...... | 168 | 278 | | 241 |
| Scalby ..... | 385 | 179 | 457 | 97 |
| Boynton ...... | 169 | 123 | 123 | 109 |
| Brandesburton .. | 169 | 562 | | 509 |
| Moor Town .. | 370 | 29 | 591 | 40 |
| Brantinghum .. | 170 | 174 | | 132 |
| Ellerker...... | 201 | 249 | 423 | 209 |

| Names of Parishes and Townships. | Page | POPULATION. In 1821 | Parish Totals | In 1811 |
|---|---|---|---|---|
| Bridlington and Quay ........ | 170 | 4275 | | 3741 |
| Buckton .... | 182 | 147 | | 162 |
| Easton ...... | 200 | 21 | | 24 |
| Grindall .... | 212 | 107 | | 69 |
| Hilderthorp... | 218 | 51 | | 51 |
| Sewerby and Marton ...... | 386 | 317 | | 246 |
| Speeton...... | 390 | 116 | 5034 | 127 |
| *Bubwith ...... | 182 | 540 | | 477 |
| Breighton .. | 170 | 179 | | 146 |
| Foggathorpe.. | 206 | 137 | | 100 |
| Gribthorpe | 211 | | | |
| and Willitoft | 400 | 145 | | 132 |
| Harlethorpe.. | 212 | 93 | | 74 |
| Spaldington .. | 390 | 361 | 1455 | 331 |
| *Bugthorpe .... | 183 | 281 | 281 | 260 |
| Burnby ........ | 183 | 95 | 95 | 113 |
| Burstwick-cum-Skeckling .... | 183 / 387 | } 436 | | 360 |
| Ryhill and Cammerton ... | 384 | 315 | 751 | 264 |
| Burton Agnes ... | 183 | 321 | | 267 |
| Gransmoor .. | 211 | 85 | | 73 |
| Haysthorp .. | 214 | 109 | | 111 |
| Thornholm .. | 395 | 94 | 609 | 82 |
| Burton Bishop.. | 183 | 534 | 534 | 515 |
| Burton Cherry.. | 188 | 417 | 417 | 358 |
| Burton Fleming, or North .... | 184 | 386 | 386 | 300 |
| *Burton Pidsea | 184 | 378 | 378 | 299 |
| Burythorpe .... | 184 | 216 | 216 | 202 |
| Carnaby ..... | 185 | 130 | 130 | 132 |
| Catton Low .... | 185 | 177 | | 145 |
| High..... | 185 | 198 | | 181 |
| Kexby .. | 359 | 149 | | 145 |

| Names of Parishes and Townships. | Page | POPULATION. | | | Names of Parishes and Townships. | Page | POPULATION. | | |
|---|---|---|---|---|---|---|---|---|---|
| | | In 1821 | Parish Totals | In 1811 | | | In 1821 | Parish Totals | In 1811 |
| Bulkholme ...... | 152 | 106 | | 89 | Londesborough | 364 | 244 | 244 | 215 |
| Barnby on the Marsh ......... | 153 | 525 | | 476 | Lowthorp ...... | 364 | 149 | 149 | 171 |
| Belby ......... | 154 | 49 | | 38 | Lund ......... | 364 | 357 | 357 | 327 |
| Cotness ........ | 191 | 29 | | 26 | *Mappleton and | 365 | | | |
| Kilpin ......... | 360 | 318 | | 243 | *Rowiston ... | 383 | 187 | | 191 |
| Knedlington... | 361 | 118 | | 90 | Cowdons..... | 192 | 146 | | 113 |
| Laxton ......... | 362 | 268 | | 271 | Hatfield Great | 213 | 127 | 460 | 130 |
| Metham ........ | 369 | 45 | | 41 | Marfleet ......... | 365 | 127 | 127 | 121 |
| Saltmarsh .... | 384 | 179 | | 168 | *Market-Weighton and Arras | 151 | 1724 | | 1506 |
| Skelton ........ | 388 | 221 | | 166 | *Shipton ...... | 387 | 369 | 2093 | 356 |
| Thorpe ........ | 395 | 53 | | 52 | Middleton..... | 369 | 441 | 441 | 406 |
| Yokefleet...... | 402 | 199 | 4443 | 161 | *Millington...... | 370 | 282 | 282 | 205 |
| Huggate .. ..... | 224 | 413 | 413 | 362 | Muston ........ | 370 | 350 | 350 | 275 |
| Humbleton ...... | 357 | 136 | | 111 | Nafferton ..... | 371 | 917 | | 804 |
| Danthorpe ..... | 192 | 25 | | 47 | Wansford .... | 397 | 344 | 1261 | 368 |
| Elsternwick ... | 201 | 154 | | 119 | New Village, extra P........ | 372 | 149 | 149 | 141 |
| Fitling ...... | 204 | 119 | | 129 | Norton ........ | 373 | 1017 | | 710 |
| Flinton ..... | 206 | 125 | 586 | 111 | Sutton........ | 393 | 87 | | 94 |
| Hunmanby ...... | 357 | 1018 | 1018 | 963 | Welham...... | | 64 | 1168 | 45 |
| Hutton Crans-wick ........ | 358 | 917 | | 748 | Nunbarnholme | 374 | 203 | | 152 |
| Rotsea ....... | 383 | 23 | | 18 | Thorp in the Street ......... | 395 | 37 | 240 | 16 |
| Sunderland-wick ........ | 392 | 60 | 1000 | 27 | Nunkeeling with Bewholme ... | 374 167 | 243 | 243 | 198 |
| Reik Little, extra P. ......... | 359 | 51 | 51 | 19 | Ottringham .... | 374 | 637 | 637 | 522 |
| Reingham ...... | 358 | 639 | 639 | 550 | Owthorn........ | 375 | 143 | | 74 |
| *Kilham ....... | 359 | 971 | 971 | 789 | Frodingham S. | 906 | 71 | | 68 |
| Kilnsea, with Spurn ......... | 360 | 196 | 196 | 122 | Rimswell..... | 382 | 139 | | 107 |
| Kimwick......... | 360 | 236 | | 203 | Waxholme...... | 397 | 72 | 415 | 66 |
| Bewick ...... | 155 | 192 | | 154 | Patrington ...... | 375 | 1244 | 1244 | 1016 |
| Bracken ...... | 169 | 30 | | 22 | Paul or Paghill | 376 | 486 | | 574 |
| Lockington, Part of......... | 363 | 124 | 576 | | Thorngumbald | 395 | 259 | 745 | 215 |
| Kilnwick Percy | 360 | 43 | 43 | 60 | Pocklington .... | 377 | 1962 | | 1539 |
| Kirby Grindalythe | 361 | 178 | | 166 | Meltonby...... | 369 | 78 | | 79 |
| Duggleby..... | 199 | 154 | | 102 | Owsthorpe ... | 375 | 9 | | 12 |
| Thirkleby ..... | 394 | 44 | 376 | 43 | Yapham .... | 402 | 114 | 2163 | 122 |
| Kirby Underdale | 361 | 335 | 335 | 293 | *Preston ...... | 880 | 828 | | 799 |
| Kirkburn ...... | 361 | 119 | | 115 | Lelley ...... | 363 | 119 | 947 | 123 |
| Eastburn ...... | 200 | 12 | | 16 | Reighton......... | 381 | 217 | 217 | 175 |
| Southburn ..... | 390 | 103 | | 87 | *Riccall ........ | 381 | 599 | 599 | 518 |
| Tibthorp ...... | 395 | 221 | 455 | 168 | Rillington .... | 381 | 683 | | 561 |
| Kirkham, extra P | 361 | 7 | 7 | 14 | Scampston..... | 385 | 200 | 883 | 180 |
| *Langtoft ...... | 361 | 416 | | 353 | Rise ......... | 382 | 221 | 221 | 203 |
| *Cotham ...... | 188 | 16 | 432 | 15 | Riston Long.... | 382 | 361 | 361 | 328 |
| Langton ........ | 362 | 280 | | 233 | Roos ........ | 383 | 442 | 442 | 365 |
| Kennythorpe | 359 | 83 | 363 | 59 | Routh ......... | 383 | 124 | 124 | 128 |
| Leaven ........ | 362 | 658 | | 574 | Rowley ........ | 383 | 425 | | 370 |
| Flemholme .. | 217 | 93 | 751 | 74 | Wauldby .... | 397 | 44 | 469 | 50 |
| Leckonfield....... | 368 | 302 | 302 | 290 | Rudston .......... | 383 | 477 | 417 | 375 |
| Lockington..... | 368 | 367 | | 429 | Ruston Parva.. | 384 | 140 | 140 | 113 |
| †Aike is partly in St. John of Beverley ...... | 149 | 59 | 426 | 84 | Saneton and Houghton.... | 384 | 334 | | 297 |
| | | | | | Cliff North.. | 186 | 89 | 423 | 99 |
| | | | | | Scorborough..... | 385 | 88 | 88 | 86 |
| | | | | | Scrayingham .. | 385 | 157 | | 131 |

| Names of Parishes and Townships. | Page | In 1821 | Parish Totals | In 1811 |
|---|---|---|---|---|
| Dunnington (part of) .......... | 199 | 551 | | 494 |
| Gate Helmsley... | 455 | 209 | 209 | 212 |
| Haxby ........-- | 451 | 417 | | 396 |
| Heslington, (part of) Parish Heslington ...... | 217 | 221 | | 152 |
| Husthwaite (P.) Carleton .... | 423 | 169 | | 153 |
| Husthwaite .. | 459 | 324 | 493 | 322 |
| Kirkby Wharfe, part of) Parish Ulleskelfe, WR. | 626 | 426 | | 402 |
| Kirkdale, (part of) Parish Nawton with Wombleton ... | 493 / 566 | 218 | | 210 |
| Mary, St. Bishops-hill, sen. (part of) Dringhouses | 142 | 156 | | 154 |
| Michael St. le Belfrey (partof) and St. Olaves, parishes: Clifton (part of) | 426 | 200 | | 223 |
| Minster yd. with Bedern, (extra parochial) ... | 62 | 924 | 924 | 882 |
| Newbald parish, Newbald N.... | 371 | 543 | | 553 |
| Newbald S. ... | 372 | 179 | 722 | 153 |
| Osbaldwick (P.) Murton......... | 492 | 134 | | 128 |
| Osbaldwick ... | 500 | 176 | 310 | 135 |
| Overton, (part of) parish, Skelton | 542 | 86 | | 112 |
| Salton parish, Brawby ......... | 418 | 188 | | 139 |
| Salton .......... | 523 | 148 | 336 | 137 |
| South Cave, (part of) parish, Faxfleet ...... | 203 | 163 | | 180 |
| Stillington parish | 549 | 698 | 698 | 691 |
| Strensall parish | 554 | 378 | 378 | 424 |
| Warthill (part of) parish, Warthill ............ | 569 | 115 | | 95 |
| Wheldrake, (part of) parish, Langwith, ... | 362 | 39 | | 37 |
| The Ainsty of the City of York. | | | | |
| Acaster Malbis (part of)...... | 137 | 291 | | 286 |
| Acomb parish, Acomb,...... | 138 | 733 | | 655 |

| Names of Parishes and Townships. | Page | In 1821 | Parish Totals | In 1811 |
|---|---|---|---|---|
| Knapton .... | 143 | 137 | 870 | 120 |
| Askham Bryan | 139 | 377 | 377 | 382 |
| Askham Richard | 140 | 249 | 249 | 190 |
| Bilbrough (P.) | 140 | 260 | 260 | 235 |
| Bilton parish, Bickerton .... | 140 | 149 | | 133 |
| Bilton ... .. | 140 | 223 | | 211 |
| Tockwith .... | 147 | 436 | 808 | 419 |
| Bishopthorpe (P.) | 141 | 301 | 301 | 262 |
| Bolton Percy parish, Appleton Roebuck .... | 139 | 585 | | 514 |
| Bolton Percy | 141 | 238 | | 230 |
| Colton ...... | 141 | 148 | | 137 |
| Steeton ...... | 145 | 83 | 1054 | 91 |
| Helaugh (P.) , . | 142 | 191 | 191 | 208 |
| Kirkhammerton (part of) parish, Wilstrop | 148 | 95 | | 85 |
| Long Marston parish Angram | 139 | 66 | | 77 |
| Hutton ...... | 143 | 125 | | 143 |
| Long Marston | 143 | 388 | 579 | 397 |
| Mary, St. Bishops-hill, sen. (pt.of) Middlethorpe | 143 | 44 | | 71 |
| Mary, St. Bishops-hill, jun. (part of) Copmanthorpe | 142 | 281 | | 250 |
| Holgate .... | 143 | 83 | | 80 |
| Poppleton Upper............ | 144 | 346 | | 323 |
| Moor Monkton (P.) Hessay .. | 142 | 161 | | 146 |
| Moor Monkton | 143 | 269 | 430 | 260 |
| Poppleton Nether, (P.) ...... | 144 | 254 | 254 | 217 |
| Rufforth, (P.) .. | 145 | 295 | 295 | 273 |
| Stillingfleet (part of) parish, Acaster Selby | 138 | 188 | | 191 |
| Tadcaster (part of) parish, Catterton .... | 141 | 63 | | 73 |
| Oxton .... | 144 | 66 | | 65 |
| Tadcaster, WR. | 411 | 775 | | 775 |
| Thorp Arch, (P.) | 145 | 343 | 343 | 398 |
| Walton, (P.).... | 148 | 247 | 247 | 235 |
| Wighill, (P.).... | 148 | 250 | 250 | 214 |
| Borough of Beverley, and Liberties.* | | | | |
| Kingston-upon-Hull, town and county of the town.† | | | | |

* See page 159.    † See page 256.

| Names of Parishes and Townships. | Page | POPULATION. In 1821 | Parish Totals | In 1811 | Names of Parishes and Townships. | Page | POPULATION. In 1821 | Parish Totals | In 1811 |
|---|---|---|---|---|---|---|---|---|---|
| Acklam ......... | 403 | 105 | 105 | 105 | Burrill & Cowling ............ | 421 | 113 | | 120 |
| Ainderby Steeple | 403 | 266 | | 280 | Crakehall...... | 430 | 550 | | 519 |
| Morton ...... | 491 | 240 | | 202 | Firby .......... | 440 | 76 | | 52 |
| Thrintoft ... | 566 | 165 | | 102 | Langthorne ... | 471 | 135 | 2631 | 132 |
| Wharlaby ... | 569 | 97 | 768 | 69 | Birkby ......... | 414 | 90 | | 85 |
| Allerston......... | 405 | 401 | 401 | 344 | Hutton Bonville | 460 | 107 | | 135 |
| *Alne ............ | 405 | 386 | | 365 | Smeaton Little | 545 | 64 | 261 | 78 |
| *Aldwark ... | 405 | 163 | | 146 | Bossall......... ... | 416 | 31 | | 50 |
| *Flawith ...... | 440 | 94 | | 101 | Butter-crambe | 422 | 235 | | 165 |
| *Thorlthorp·· | 564 | 238 | | 187 | Claxton ...... | 426 | 135 | | 93 |
| *Tollerton ... | 566 | 481 | | 481 | *Flaxton-on-the- | | | | |
| Youlton ...... | 590 | 56 | 1418 | 55 | Moor ......... | 440 | 299 | | 245 |
| Ampleforth ...... | 405 | 214 | | | Harton.......... | 450 | 190 | | 165 |
| .*Ampleforth·· | 405 | 192 | | 152 | Sand Hutton | 461 | 202 | 1092 | 174 |
| Oswald Kirk·· | | | | | Bowes ............ | 417 | 1095 | | 773 |
| Quarter ...... | 501 | 176 | 582 | 139 | Boldron······ | 415 | 168 | | 172 |
| Appleton-le-street | 406 | 173 | | 146 | Gilmonby ···· | 442 | 175 | 1438 | 93 |
| Amotherby ... | 405 | 249 | | 223 | Brafferton ···· | 417 | 178 | | 164 |
| Broughton ... | 420 | 94 | | 93 | Thornton Bridge ······ | 565 | 43 | 221 | 46 |
| Hieldenley ... | 456 | 23 | | | Bransby with | | | | |
| Swinton ...... | 556 | 334 | 873 | 282 | Stearsby ······ | 417 | 277 | 277 | 208 |
| Appleton-upon-Wisk ......... | 406 | 492 | 492 | 400 | Brignall·········· | 418 | 216 | 216 | 189 |
| Arkengarthdale | 407 | 1512 | 1512 | 1529 | Brompton Patrick ········· | 502 | 158 | | 142 |
| Arncliffe Ingleby | 462 | 331 | 331 | 290 | Arrathorne ... | 407 | 64 | | 74 |
| Aysgarth ......... | 408 | 293 | | 293 | Hunton ······ | 459 | 496 | | 424 |
| Abbot side High ......... | 403 | 641 | | 585 | Newton-le-Willows······ | 494 | 250 | 968 | 266 |
| Abbot side Low............ | 403 | 181 | | 195 | Brompton······ | 419 | 516 | | 435 |
| Askrigg ...... | 407 | 765 | | 745 | Sawdon ······ | 524 | 130 | | 125 |
| Bainbridge ... | 410 | 872 | | 813 | Snainton ···· | 545 | 603 | | 525 |
| Bishopdale ... | 415 | 95 | | 79 | Troutsdale ·· | 568 | 45 | 1303 | 60 |
| Burton with Walden ...... | 421 | 478 | | 453 | Brotton ········ | 419 | 332 | | 384 |
| Carperby ...... | 423 | 283 | | 262 | Kilton ······ | 464 | 100 | | 101 |
| Hawes ......... | 450 | 1408 | | 1185 | Skinningrave | 543 | 60 | 492 | 68 |
| Newbiggin ... | 493 | 126 | | 130 | Bulmer ········ | 420 | 339 | | 293 |
| Thoralby ...... | 564 | 342 | | 310 | Henderskelf ·· | 455 | 159 | | 137 |
| Thornton Rust | 565 | 135 | 5621 | 120 | Welburn ···· | 569 | 352 | 850 | 221 |
| Ayton Great...... | 409 | 1023 | | 922 | Burniston ······ | 420 | 298 | | 253 |
| Ayton Little... | 410 | 68 | | 41 | Carthorp ···· | 424 | 301 | | 311 |
| Nunthorpe ... | 499 | 110 | 1201 | 128 | Exelby, Leeming, & Newton | 438 | 562 | | 553 |
| Barningham ... | 411 | 384 | | 350 | Gatenby ···· | 441 | 88 | | 65 |
| Hope ......... | 458 | 44 | | 43 | Theakstone ·· | 557 | 87 | 1326 | 65 |
| Scargill ...... | 538 | 136 | 564 | 117 | Byland Old ···· | 422 | 133 | 133 | 126 |
| Barton St. Mary | 412 | 436 | | 414 | Carleton ······ | 423 | 260 | 260 | 230 |
| Newton Morrell | 494 | 31 | 467 | 32 | Catterick ······ | 424 | 561 | | 541 |
| Barton-in-the-street ......... | 412 | 176 | | 159 | Appleton ······ | 406 | 87 | | 89 |
| Butterwick ... | 422 | 50 | | 62 | Bolton-on-Swale········ | 416 | 100 | | 76 |
| Coneysthorpe | 427 | 160 | 386 | 156 | Brough ······ | 420 | 98 | | 97 |
| Bedale............ | 412 | 1137 | | 1078 | Colbourne···· | 427 | 133 | | 139 |
| ·iskew.......... | 404 | 620 | | 511 | | | | | |

| Names of Parishes and Townships. | Page | POPULATION. | | | Names of Parishes and Townships. | Page | POPULATION. | | |
|---|---|---|---|---|---|---|---|---|---|
| | | In 1821 | Parish Totals | In 1811 | | | In 1821 | Parish Totals | In 1811 |
| Ellerton | 437 | 140 | | 111 | Easington, | 434 | 507 | | 445 |
| Hipswell | 457 | 273 } | | | Liverton, | 474 | 251 | 758 | 244 |
| St. Martin's, | 484 | 23 } | | {266 | Easingwold, | 434 | 1912 | | 1576 |
| Hudswell, | 459 | 305 | | 253 | Raskelf, | 507 | 440 | 2352 | 383 |
| Killerby, | 464 | 48 | | 53 | Ebberston, | 436 | 505 | 505 | 437 |
| Kiplin, | 465 | 100 | | 94 | Edstone Great, | 436 | 156 | 156 | 137 |
| Scorton, | 538 | 496 | | 449 | Ellerburn, | 437 | | | |
| Scotton, | 539 | 128 | | 98 | Wilton, | 585 | 203 | 203 | 209 |
| Tunstall, | 568 | 253 | | 213 | Egton, | 437 | 1037 | 1037 | 1026 |
| Uckerby, | 568 | 52 | | 50 | Felix Kirk, | 439 | | | |
| Whitwell, | 585 | 99 | 2888 | 71 | Boltby, | 415 | 403 | | 363 |
| Cayton | 425 | 447 | | 343 | Sutton | 554 | 325 | | 303 |
| Osgodby, | 500 | 72 | 519 | 70 | Thirlby, | 557 | 167 | 884 | 166 |
| Easby, | 426 | 147 | 147 | 124 | Filey, | 904 | | | |
| Coverham, | 428 | | | | Gristhorpe, | 444 | 212 | | 181 |
| Aggelthorpe, | 403 | 131 | | 140 | Lebberston, | 472 | 143 | 355 | 128 |
| Caldbridge, | 422 | 103 | | 68 | Finghall, | 439 | 196 | | 152 |
| Carlton, | 423 | 280 } | | {578 | Aikber, | 403 | 43 | | 29 |
| Carlton H. D. | 423 | 398 } | | | Burton, | 422 | 204 | | 205 |
| Melmerby, | 487 | 112 | | 111 | Hutton Hang, | 461 | 25 | 308 | 32 |
| ScraftonL.&W | 539 | 146 | 1170 | 131 | Forcett, | 440 | 86 | | 128 |
| Cowsby, | 428 | 91 | 91 | 93 | Barforth, | 411 | 141 | | 126 |
| Cowton East, | 428 | 338 | 338 | 302 | Carkin, | 423 | 24 | | 47 |
| Coxwold, | 429 | 348 | | 326 | Ovington, | 501 | 166 | 417 | 148 |
| AngramGrange | 406 | 29 | | 26 | Foston, | 440 | 91 | | 70 |
| Birdforth, | 414 | 42 | | 4? | Thornton | 565 | 173 | 964 | 157 |
| Byland | 422 | 372 | | 358 | Fylingdales, | 441 | 1702 | 1702 | 1559 |
| Newbrough, | 493 | 162 | | 109 | Gilling, | 442 | 921 | | 795 |
| Oulston, | 501 | 225 | | 228 | Cowton N. | 428 | 270 | | 322 |
| Thornton | 565 | 70 | | 78 | Cowton S. | 429 | 148 | | 152 |
| Wilden Grange | 585 | 29 | | 23 | Eppleby, | 436 | 157 | | 158 |
| Yearsley, | 590 | 170 | 1447 | 163 | Eryholme, | 438 | 177 | 1673 | 139 |
| Crambe, | 430 | 152 | | 138 | Gilling, | 442 | 168 | | 176 |
| Barton L. W. | 412 | 188 | | 175 | Cawton, | 425 | 105 | | 87 |
| Whitwell | 535 | 182 | 522 | 162 | Grimston, | 444 | 56 | 329 | 47 |
| Crathorne, | 431 | 330 | 330 | 304 | Glasedale, | 443 | 1043 | 1043 | 877 |
| Croft, | 431 | 368 | | 339 | Grinton, | 444 | 889 | | 649 |
| *Dalton | 432 | 167 | | 131 | Melbecks, | 487 | 1726 | | 1586 |
| Stapleton, | 548 | 113 | 648 | 93 | Muker, | 491 | 1425 | | 1339 |
| Rundall, | 432 | | | | Reeth, | 510 | 1460 | 5300 | 1394 |
| Fawdington, | 439 | 39 | 39 | | Guisborough, | 444 | 1912 | | 1834 |
| Rundall& Leckby | 472 | 170 | | 180 | Commondale. | 427 | 86 | | 79 |
| Norton-le-Clay | 499 | 142 | 312 | 139 | Hutton L. C. | 461 | 56 | | 70 |
| Cuthbert St. | | | | | Pinchinthorpe | 506 | 80 | | 68 |
| Heworth | 456 | 146 | 146 | 100 | Tocketts | 566 | 46 | 2180 | 43 |
| Dalby, | 432 | 169 | 169 | 129 | Hackness, | 448 | 143 | | 174 |
| Danby, | 432 | 1373 | 1373 | 1145 | Broxa | 420 | 61 | | 67 |
| Danby on Wiske | 433 | 328 | | 273 | Harwood dale | 450 | 235 | | } 91 |
| Yafforth, | 587 | 149 | 477 | 129 | with Silphoe | 541 | 96 | | |
| Ownholme, | 433 | 113 | | 225 | Suffield | 554 | 97 | 632 | 98 |
| Allerton Abbey | 437 | 47 | | | Harlesey, E. | 449 | 420 | 420 | 305 |
| Stainton, | 547 | 54 | | {91 | HawkwellE.&W. | 451 | 176 | | 144 |
| Walburn, | 569 | 37 | 251 | 53 | Barden, | 411 | 106 | | 124 |
| ...by, | 433 | 105 | | 113 | Garriston | 441 | 52 | 334 | 63 |
| Aske, | 407 | 109 | | 83 | Hawnby, | 451 | 286 | | 203 |
| Brompton | 419 | 388 | | 379 | Arden | 406 | 139 | | 127 |
| Easeby, | 542 | 163 | 765 | 147 | Bilsdale W.side | 414 | 127 | | 128 |

b

| Names of Parishes and Townships | Page | POPULATION. In 1821 | Parish Totals | In 1811 |
|---|---|---|---|---|
| Borrowby, ... | 416 | 64 | | 50 |
| Ellerby, ...... | 437 | 80 | | 65 |
| Hutton Mulgv. | 461 | 90 | | 90 |
| Mickleby, ... | 488 | 147 | | 174 |
| NewtonMulgv. | 494 | 134 | | 139 |
| Ugthorpe, ... | 568 | 275 | 2194 | 276 |
| Malton New, ... | 477 | | | |
| St. Leonards, | | 2339 | | 2203 |
| St. Michael,... | | 1666 | 4005 | 1510 |
| Malton Old, ... | 482 | 1064 | 1064 | 961 |
| Mansfield, ...... | 483 | 440 | | 352 |
| Cliffe, ......... | 426 | 53 | 493 | 64 |
| Marrick,......... | 483 | 621 | 621 | 499 |
| Marske, ...... | 483 | 576 | | 479 |
| Redcar,...... | 508 | 673 | 1249 | 411 |
| Marske, ...... | 484 | 290 | 290 | 247 |
| Marton, ...... | 484 | 397 | 397 | 361 |
| Marton ......... | 485 | 164 | 164 | 179 |
| *Masham,...... | 485 | 1171 | | 1014 |
| Burton-on-Ure | 422 | 170 | | 164 |
| *Ellingstring, | 438 | 204 | | 139 |
| *Ellingtons,.. | 438 | 152 | | 123 |
| Fearby,...... | 439 | 214 | | 216 |
| Healey ...... | 452 | 413 | | 354 |
| Ilton with Pott | 463 | 266 | | 209 |
| Swinton ...... | 555 | 177 | 2767 | 182 |
| Melsonby,...... | 487 | 440 | 440 | 377 |
| Middleham,.... | 488 | 880 | 880 | 714 |
| *Middlesbrough | 489 | 40 | | 35 |
| Linthorp, .... | 474 | 196 | 236 | 177 |
| Middleton, .... | 489 | 247 | | 229 |
| Aislaby, .... | 404 | 147 | | 153 |
| Cawthorne, ... | 425 | 22 | | {313 |
| Cropton, ...] | 431 | 321 | | |
| Hartoft, ...... | 450 | 134 | | 104 |
| Lockton, ...... | 474 | 324 | | 252 |
| Rosedale E. side | 522 | 339 | | 308 |
| Wrelton,...... | 587 | 193 | 1737 | 173 |
| Middleton Tyas, | 490 | 569 | | 506 |
| Moulton,...... | 491 | 236 | 805 | 179 |
| Myton-on-Swale | 492 | 185 | 185 | 125 |
| Newton,......... | 494 | 119 | 119 | 137 |
| Newton-ou-Ouse | 494 | 495 | | 415 |
| Beningbrough, | 414 | 99 | | 98 |
| Linton-on-Ouse | 474 | 268 | 862 | 291 |
| Normanby,...... | 495 | 191 | | 148 |
| Thornton- Risebro', ...... | 565 | 32 | 223 | 34 |
| Northallerton,... | 495 | 2626 | | 2234 |
| Brompton, ... | 418 | 1223 | | 1012 |
| Deighton, ... | 433 | 134 | | 125 |
| Romanby, ... | 522 | 294 | | 251 |
| Worsall High, | 596 | 154 | 4431 | 105 |
| Nunnington, ... | 499 | 418 | 418 | 339 |
| *Olave St. ...... | 62 | 666 | | 626 |
| *Clifton, part of | 426 | 969 | | 183 |
| *Rawcliffe(pt.of) | 506 | 57 | 992 | 61 |
| Ormesby ...... | 500 | 349 | | 399 |

| Names of Parishes and Townships | Page | POPULATION. In 1821 | Parish Totals | In 1811 |
|---|---|---|---|---|
| Eston........ | 438 | 272 | | 303 |
| Morton, ...... | 490 | 26 | | 22 |
| Normanby ... | 495 | 122 | | 110 |
| Upsall ......... | 568 | 16 | 785 | |
| Osmotherley ... | 500 | 755 | | 878 |
| Ellerbeck...... | 437 | 81 | | 76 |
| Harlesey West | 449 | 51 | | 82 |
| Thimbleby .. | 557 | 200 | 1087 | 190 |
| Oswaldkirk ...... | 501 | 212 | 212 | 210 |
| Otterington N. | 501 | 44 | | 49 |
| Thornton L. B. | 565 | 247 | | 208 |
| ThorntonL.M. | 565 | 294 | 565 | 259 |
| Otterington S.... | 501 | 201 | 201 | 155 |
| Overton ......... | 501 | 59 | | 56 |
| *Shipton ...... | 541 | 377 | | 364 |
| *Skelton...... | 542 | 187 | 623 | 174 |
| Pickering........ | 502 | 2746 | | 2332 |
| Goathland.... | 443 | 335 | | 270 |
| Kingthorpe ... | 465 | 52 | | 44 |
| Marrishes .... | 483 | 210 | | 193 |
| Newton ...... | 494 | 212 | 3555 | 168 |
| Pickhill ......... | 506 | 334 | | 352 |
| Ainderby- Quernhow.... | 403 | 99 | | 86 |
| Holme ...... | 457 | 102 | | 86 |
| Howe......... | 459 | 32 | | 31 |
| Sinderby .... | 542 | 86 | | 75 |
| Swainby .... | 555 | 33 | 686 | 42 |
| Richmond ...... | 511 | 3546 | 3546 | 3056 |
| Rokeby&Egleton | 521 | 222 | 222 | 201 |
| Romaldkirk .... | 521 | 377 | | 302 |
| Cotherstone .. | 427 | 706 | | 689 |
| Holwick ...... | 457 | 201 | | 182 |
| Hunderthwaits | 459 | 313 | | 390 |
| Lartington ... | 471 | 243 | | 231 |
| Lunedale ...... | 476 | 265 | | 283 |
| Mickleton ... | 488 | 356 | 2461 | 337 |
| Rouncton W. ... | 522 | 217 | 217 | 190 |
| Rudby............ | 522 | 76 | | 88 |
| Hutton ......... | 460 | 919 | | 762 |
| Middleton .... | 490 | 111 | | 100 |
| Rouncton E. | 522 | 135 | | 102 |
| Skutterskelfe | 544 | 32 | | 35 |
| Sexhow ...... | 541 | 38 | 1311 | 34 |
| Scalby ......... | 524 | 446 | | 454 |
| Burniston ... | 421 | 347 | | 260 |
| Cloughton ... | 426 | 366 | | 335 |
| Newby ...... | 493 | 40 | | 56 |
| Staintondale... | 547 | 294 | | 269 |
| Throxenby ... | 566 | 66 | 1559 | 58 |
| Scarborough ... | 524 | 8188 | | 6710 |
| Falsgrave.... | 569 | 345 | 8533 | 357 |
| Seawton ...... | 538 | 154 | 154 | 150 |
| Scruton ......... | 539 | 411 | 411 | 374 |
| Seamer ......... | 540 | 596 | | 485 |
| Ayton East ... | 410 | 353 | | 397 |
| Irton ......... | 463 | 105 | 1034 | 94 |
| Seamer ......... | 540 | 226 | 23 | |

| Names of Parishes and Townships. | Page | POPULATION. | | | Names of Parishes and Townships. | Page | POPULATION. | | |
|---|---|---|---|---|---|---|---|---|---|
| | | In 1821 | Parish Totals | In 1811 | | | In 1821 | Parish Totals | In 1811 |
| Sessay | 541 | 364 | | 303 | Thormanby | 564 | 118 | 118 | 135 |
| Hutton Sessay | 461 | 129 | 493 | 81 | Thornton Dale | 564 | 879 | | 805 |
| Sheriff Hutton | 461 | 756 | | 664 | Farmanby | 439 | 403 | 1282 | 366 |
| Cornbrough | 427 | 63 | | 63 | Thornton-le-st. | 565 | 131 | | 127 |
| Farlington | 439 | 170 | | 169 | Kilvington N. | 464 | 68 | 199 | 66 |
| Lilling Ambo | 474 | 208 | | 149 | Thornton Stwrd. | 565 | 265 | 265 | 229 |
| Stittenham | 549 | 81 | 1278 | 82 | Thornton Watls. | 566 | 180 | | 160 |
| Sigston Kirby | 541 | 131 | | 122 | Clifton-on-Ure | 426 | 50 | | 38 |
| Sowerby | 546 | 53 | | 59 | Rookwith | 522 | 76 | | 73 |
| Winton | 585 | 138 | 322 | 139 | Thirn | 557 | 126 | 432 | 98 |
| Silton over | 542 | 94 | | 92 | *Topcliffe | 567 | 659 | | 573 |
| Kepwick | 463 | 170 | 264 | 169 | Aisenby | 404 | 230 | | 188 |
| Sinnington | 542 | 343 | | 299 | Baldersby | 411 | 241 | | 207 |
| Edstone Little | 437 | 16 | | 14 | Catton | 425 | 99 | | 113 |
| Marton | 484 | 255 | 614 | 206 | Dalton | 432 | 235 | | 215 |
| Skelton | 542 | 791 | | 717 | Dishforth | 433 | 340 | | 323 |
| Moorsome | 490 | 353 | | 383 | Elmyre | 438 | 78 | | 74 |
| Stanghow | 548 | 91 | 1235 | 107 | Marton-le-moor | 485 | 201 | | 189 |
| Slingsby P. | 544 | 548 | 548 | 464 | Rainton | 507 | 347 | | 342 |
| Smeaton Great | 545 | 250 | | 218 | Skipton | 544 | 110 | 2540 | 109 |
| Hornby | 458 | 238 | 488 | 211 | Upleatham | 568 | 239 | 239 | 312 |
| Sneaton | 546 | 251 | 251 | 167 | *Warthill | 569 | 38 | 38 | 34 |
| *Spennythorne | 546 | 249 | | 225 | Wath, | 569 | 186 | | 193 |
| Bellerby | 414 | 407 | | 549 | Melmerby, | 487 | 258 | | 226 |
| Harnby | 449 | 194 | 850 | 202 | Middleton | 490 | 102 | | 91 |
| Stainton | 547 | 356 | | 311 | Norton Conyrs. | 499 | 87 | 633 | 62 |
| Hemlington | 455 | 72 | | 77 | Welbury, | 570 | 257 | 257 | 243 |
| Ingleby Barwick | 462 | 175 | | 114 | Well, | 570 | 370 | | 332 |
| Maltby | 476 | 168 | | 155 | Snape, | 545 | 689 | 1059 | 616 |
| Thornaby | 564 | 197 | 968 | 149 | Wensley, | 570 | 317 | | 273 |
| Stanwick St. John | 549 | 59 | | 51 | Bolton Castl., | 415 | 278 | | 265 |
| Aldbrough | 404 | 544 | | 443 | Leyburn, | 473 | 810 | | 593 |
| Caldwell | 422 | 188 | | 170 | Preston, | 507 | 378 | | 345 |
| Layton East | 471 | 137 | 928 | 120 | Redmire, | 510 | 399 | 2182 | 393 |
| Sturtforth | 549 | 460 | 460 | 569 | Westerdale, | 571 | 281 | 281 | 248 |
| *Sockburn | | | | | Whenby, | 571 | 129 | 129 | 101 |
| Dinsdale over | 433 | 66 | | 70 | Whitby, | 571 | 8697 | | 6969 |
| Girsby | 442 | 85 | 151 | 93 | Aislaby, | 404 | 253 | | 216 |
| Stockton | 550 | 357 | 357 | 263 | Askdaleside, | 438 | 395 | | 364 |
| Stokesley | 550 | 1897 | | 1439 | Hawsker with | 450 | | | |
| Bushby Gt. & Lt. | 422 | 117 | | 82 | Stainsacre, | 547 | 634 | | 519 |
| Easby | 434 | 124 | | 101 | Newholme | 493 | 259 | | 326 |
| Newby | 493 | 152 | 2290 | 137 | Ruswarp, | 523 | 1918 | | 1498 |
| Stonegrave | 553 | 177 | | 136 | Ugglebarnby, | 568 | 428 | 12584 | 383 |
| Ness East | 493 | 59 | | 75 | Whorlton, | 585 | 583 | | 510 |
| Ness West | 493 | 65 | | 56 | Faceby, | 439 | 178 | | 139 |
| Newton East | 494 | 72 | 373 | 60 | Pottoe, | 507 | 207 | 968 | 185 |
| Sutton on Forest | 554 | 443 | | 457 | Wigginton, | 585 | 309 | 309 | 286 |
| Huby | 459 | 497 | 940 | 434 | Witton East, | 585 | | | |
| Fanfield West | 556 | 709 | 709 | 670 | Within, | 586 | 444 | | 393 |
| Ferrington and | 556 | | | | Without, | 586 | 303 | 747 | 302 |
| *Wigginthorpe | 585 | 617 | | 545 | Witton West, | 586 | 519 | 519 | 439 |
| Ganthorpe | 441 | 106 | 723 | 96 | Wycliffe, | 587 | 152 | 152 | 140 |
| Thirkleby | 557 | 293 | 293 | 293 | Wykeham, | 587 | 582 | 582 | 511 |
| Thirsk | 557 | 2533 | | 2155 | Yarm, | 588 | 1504 | 1504 | 1431 |
| *Carleton Min. | 423 | 221 | | 205 | Bis. of Durham. | | | | |
| Hutton Sand | 461 | 273 | | 244 | Craike & Castle, | 429 | 538 | 538 | 453 |
| | 546 | 748 | 3775 | 685 | | | | | |

# ADDITIONS AND ALTERATIONS.

*In the First and Second Volumes.*

## LEEDS.

Aldam William, mert. h. South Parade
Andrews, J. & J. bacon & butter factors, 7, George street
Armistead John, Water Lodge
Atkinson J. jun. solicitor ; h. Albion street
Bacchus S. J. attorney, Wellington road
Barr Charles, banker ; h. Commercial st.
Bedford Chas. bricklayer, &c. Templar st.
Bennet James, foreign wool, oil, indigo, &c. merchant, Albion street
Benson Jervas, gent. Park row
Bentley James, stuff and shawl manufacturer, 5, Saddle yard, Briggate
Benyon Thos. merchant ; h. Headingley
Beverley John & Son, wrought iron & steel mfrs. & merchants, Back of Shambles
Bolland C. & C. attornies, Park square
Bowes & Kilham, flax spinners, patent thread, linen & canvas mrfs. Steander
Bradley John, draper, &c. Cross Parish
Braithwaite John, iron monger, nail mfr. and bar iron merchant, Market place
Briggs Wm. stuff merchant. Vicar lane
Broadbent Joseph, hatter, &c. 30, Briggate
Broadhead John, linen draper, Bridge end
Brown John, mert ; h. Farfield cottage
Brown J. jun. stuff mert, Boar ln, h. West st
Brownless George, brush manufacturer, and salt merchant, Simpson's-fold
Bruce, Dorrington, & Walker, stuff merchants, Albion street
Bruce Wm. merchant ; h. Well-close-place
Burland T. wire worker, 58, St. James st
Carr John, merchant ; h. 41, Park square
Child & Bulmer, painters, &c. Briggate
Cradock James, stuff mfr. Hill house, Bank
Cradock Thos. stuff mfr. Timble bridge
Crawford Rev. Samuel, Sunny Bank
Crosland, coach proprietor, Brunswick pl.
Cross John, merchant, &c. Meadow lane
Crossley and Robinson, woollen cloth printers, School close
Crossland Charles, drysalter, Meadow ln.
Davy Wm. consular office, 45, Albion st.
Davy Josiah & Co. merts. 45, Albion st
Day Wm. woolstapler, Albion street
Dewhirst B. letter press printer, New st
Dickinson Jonathan, brush manufacturer, and salt merchant, Water lane
Dorrington Rt. stuff mert. h. Camp row
Eagland Thomas, corn-factor, Warehouse hill ; house, Water lane
Feather J, H. vict. Old George, Briggate
Fieldhouse Wm. ironmonger, (wholesale) 75, Kirkgate
Francis John, vict. Fleece, Briggate
Fryer Wm. jun. watch maker, Templar st.
Furbank Rev. Thomas, Upperhead row
Galloway Thos. painter, Bridge end
Gledhill Richard, gent. Old Church yard
Greenwood Henry, Esq. banker ; h. boar ln
Greenwood J. music preceptor, Park row
Hall Wm, jun. woolstapler, Bank street
Hallewell Benjamin, British wine manufacturer, under the White Cloth Hall
Hamilton Rev. R. W. Albion street
Hardwick and Brown Bricklayers and builders, Skinner lane
Hardy J. Esq. Recorder, Little Woodhouse

Harrison & Tooth, oil merts, Hunslet lane
Hatter Jey Robert, grocer, Bridge end
Heaps John, agent to the Yorkshire milled lead and patent pipe Co. 45, Kirkgate
Hill Beverley, merchant, Park square
Hirst John, paper warehouse, Mill hill
Hobson Abm. gent. Wellington st. Park ln.
Hobson F. bookseller, Back of Shambles
Holroyd Joshua, gent. Clay Pit lane
Holt J. Wheat Sheaf, Back of Shambles
Houseman Mrs. Wellington road
Howard Jas. W. surgeon, 2, Templar st
Humble Misses, gentlewmn, South parade
Illingworth Jerm mert. house, Knostrop
Jackson Rev. Miles, Burley
Jackson Mrs. gentlewoman, Trafalgar street
Johnson James, baconfactor, 72, Kirkgate
Kirkbride John, currier 81, Kirkgate
Kirlew Rd. agent for Vessels to Gun and Shot Wharf, London ; Warehouse hill
Lancaster John, operative chemist and druggist, corner of St. Peter's square
Lawson & Walker, brass founders, Mabgt.
Lee Wm. ironmonger, 72, Briggate
Le Resche Mrs. lodgings, Wellington road
Lewes John, draper, &c. Lowerhead row
Linley John, house, sign, and ornamental tillot and shield painter, Bridge end
Mabon, Brown, and Mabon, cloth mfrs. Mill Garth
Maddy Wm. linen draper, Cross Parish
Malleson Rev. J. P. day school, Park row
Marshall John, mert ; h. Chapel Allerton
Masterman R. Horse & Jockey, Bond street
Mawson John, gent. Park lane
Midgley Robt. plumber, &c. Meadow lane
Milnes Wm. merchant ; h. Wellington pl.
Morris Thomas gentleman, South Parade
Neesom Jas. wholesale tea dlr. and hop mert. near Salem chapel, Hunslet ln.
Nell Mrs. gentlewoman, East Parade
Newlove Geo. wine merchant, West street
Noble James, surgeon, Top of Park row
North B. B. Harewood Arms, Old square
Orange John, gent. Littlewoodhouse
Palmer Thomas, ironmonger, whitesmith, and bellhanger, 21, Briggate
Pape Thomas, druggist, Lowerhead row
Payne, R. E. solicitor, Albion street
Peacock, Richardson, and Co. merchants and linen mfrs. Sterne's Buildings
Pearson Wm. grocer, 28, Lowerhead row
Poole Mrs. and Miss Parsons ladies seminary, Woodhouse hall
Priestley C. T. agent, Coburgh street
Pryce John and Co. drysalters & wh. tea dlrs.—agent, Wm. Percival, Swinegate
Ramsden J. plumber, St. James's street
Rimington Mrs. Elis. gentlewmn. Park pl.
Robson Mrs. South parade
Royce M. gentlewmn. Hunslet lane
Scholes and, Askey, cabinet makers and dealers in mahogany, White Horse yd.
Sheepshanks Wm. & John, merchants, and mfrs. New Road end & Sheepscar lane
Sherwood Wm. supervisor, Simpson's fold
Simpson J. and J. tobacconists, Water ln.
Spencer Frederick, druggist, 33, Vicar l-
Stott Harriot, gentlewoman, Park sq

Taylor Edward, gent. Park quare
Thompson Mrs, La. seminary, Cobourg st.
Threlfall Jas. linen draper, 8 Market place
Tiffany C. T. & Co. brush mfrs. 47, Kirkgate
Turnbull T. White Horse Tavern, Boar ln.
Turtle Thos. vict. Bay Horse, Cross Parish
Wailes Geo. Esq. barrister, Post-office
Wainhouse Edw. & Ch. merts. Annslet ln.
Walker Robert, mercht.; b. Park square
Walker John, gent. Park place
Walker Thos. coach builder; b.Park square
Walker Mr. and Mrs. ladies' boarding
  school, Park square
Ward Benj. merchant; house, Park row

Watson John, timber and raff merchant,
  (hard wood) Great Waterloo street
Watson Miss, gentlewmn. South parade
Wells James, currier, &c. Lady lane
Whittenbury E. W. cloth mfr. 25, back of
  Park row ; counting-house, Trinity la.
Williamson James, M. D. Park square
Wood James, gent. St. Peter's square
Wood Richard, merchant, Trafalgar street
Wood Mrs. gentlewmn. Park Buildings
Woodcock and Harrison, machine makers,
  Meadow lane
Wrigglesworth J. grocer, Lowerhead row
Young John and Co. woollen mfrs. and com-
  mission merts. Albion st; h. Meadow ln

*Addingham.*
Trees&Dyson,worsted spnrs
Wall Rd. Golden Fleece
*Almondbury,*
Broughton Jonah, cloth
  dresser and merchant
Coates Rev. John, master of
  grammar school
Jones Rev. ——, curate
Smith John, drysalter
Walker Wm. cloth dresser
*Adwalton,*
Barraclough Isaac, grocer
Birket Wm. grocer
Blakey Richard, grocer
Bower J. vict. Unicorn Inn
Maltby Widow, grocer
Mann James, grocer
Sugden Wm. vict. New Inn
Whitelegg Wm. White Hart
*Armin,*
Woodhead Rt. yeoman
*Armley,*
Nicholls W. tanner, Hill top
Wainman Wm. woollen mfr.
*Askwith,*
Land Wm. farmer
*Badsworth,*
Hepworth Joshua, Esq.
Fisher Rev. Joseph, curate
Froggatt John,schoolmaster
*Baildon,*
Brown John, grocer, &c.
Holmes and Gill, worsted
  manufacturers
*Barnoldswick,*
Barnard Rev. M.
Dean Henry, gent. Park ln.
*Barnsley,*
Blackburn Thos. wh. grass-
  seeds dealer, Old mill
Bradley Wm. steel wire
  drawer, Sough bridge
Naylor and Co. flax spin-
  ners, Barnsley Old mill
Porter J. propr. of the Hope
  Calender works, Town end
*Batley Carr,*
Elliss James and Son, wool-
  len manufacturers
Elliss, Smith, and Co. mill
  owners
Fozard Abraham, cloth mfr.
Naylor James, cloth mfr.
Smith, Elliss, and Co. car-
  pet manufacturers

Stapleton F. blanket mfr.
Stapleton T. blanket mfr.
*Beal, or Beaghall,*
Dickson William, maltster
*Brierley,*
Mayor,
Thomas Hull, Esq. M.D.
  Capital Burgesses,
John B. Arden
Charles Ross
John Jackson
Matthew Chalmers
Robert Stabler
James Thompson
Christopher Muschamp
W. Brigham
David Pinder
Robert Fishwick
Thomas Ramshaw
William Richardson
John Myers

Ingle James, surveyor, tan-
  ner, fellmonger, glue and
  starch mfr. Beck side
*Bierley North,*
Holdforth Jas. cotton mfr.
Marshall, Leigh, and Co.
  ironfounders
Clough Saml. book-keeper
*Bingley,*
Ellis James, corn miller
Longbottom Joseph, grocer
*Birstwith,*
Snow Thos. clock &c.maker
*Bishop Monkton,*
Emmett Thos. flax dresser
Wilks John, flax dresser
*Bolton, near Bradford,*
Hodgson Thos. worsted mfr.
*Bolton Abbey,*
Benson Mrs.Margt. Riddings
Pickup Henry, agent
Scott Wm. agt to the Duke of
  Devonshire, Strid Cottage
*Booth Ferry,*
Wells Wm. vict. Ship Inn
*Bowling,*
Paley J. G. Esq.
*Bradford,*
Audsley Squire, oil mercht.
Lister Robt. woollen draper
Marshall Thos. and William
  worsted spinners & mfrs.
Thackray Joseph, Woodhall
Wittam and Co. worsted
  spinners and mfrs.

Wood John, jun. worsted
  spinner & mfr. Union mills
Wood John and Son, comb
  manfrs. Bridge street
*Bramham,*
Smyth John, Esq.
*Bramley,*
Stead Thos. woollen mfr.
Stead John, woollen mfr.
Young James, woolstapler
*Bretton,*
Taylor Rev. Jas. domestic
  chaplain toCol. Beaumont,
  & master of grammar schl.
Raine Wm. agent to Col.
  Beaumont
*Bretton Monk,*
Hartison John, farmer
Hirst Richard, whitesmith
  & gunsmith
*Burnt Yates,*
Cockshot Wm. schoolmaster
Jennings M. Prince of Wales
*Campsall,*
Foljambe John, Esq
Myers Richard, maltster
*Chapel Allerton,*
Bickerdike John, maltster
*Clayton West,*
Dalby J.
Pickles John, fancy mfr.
*Cleckheaton,*
Dickson M.
Eyre Joseph, gentleman
Eyre E. & T. woollen mfrs.
*Colne Bridge,*
Haigh Thos. cotton spinner
*Cowling,*
Watson Emmett, grocer,&c.
*Darley,*
Newman C. Esq.
*Darrington,*
Crament Wm. gardener to
  Hon. E. Petre
*Darton,*
Hall & Co. manfrg. chemists
*Deighton Kirk,*
Greaves Robert, yeoman
*Deighton North,*
Hannam Robert, farmer
Mawson Eliz. farmer
Snowden Richard farmer
*Denholme,*
Atkinson Wm. worsted mfr.
Knowles Jonth. vict. Gate

Ogden Joseph, coal mercht. and woollen manfr.
Ogden Thos. coal merchant

*Dewsbury,*
Howgate Joseph, vict. Bull

*Dodworth,*
Rintcliffe Godfrey, cooper & machine maker
Gillott John, wood agent
Handey Mrs. H. gentlewmn.
Hirst George, gent.
Milnes Joseph, yeoman
Rooke Daniel, gent.
Shaw & Dent, hat manfrs.
Wadsworth Jonth. wood agt.

*Dodworth Bottoms,*
Rooke S. & E. gentlemen
Shaw G. & J. lath merchants

*Doncaster,*
Sturges John, Esq.
Swire John, Esq. South parade
Harrop Geo. builder
Ibbeson M.

*Drighlington,*
Boys Eli, woollen manfr.
Mitchell Thos. sizeing boiler

*Earlsheaton,*
Illingworth Joseph, malt and flour dealer and grocer

*Eccleshill,*
Blaymires John, schoolmstr.
Bolton John, vict. Hart
Edmondson Christr. butcher
Gaunt Edw. surgeon
Hare Saml. worsted mfr.
Hare Thos. worsted mfr.
Hodgson Richard, maltster
Thomas Isaac, fulling miller
Yewdale Benj. worsted mfr.

*Elmsall South,*
Booth George, gent.
Haigh Geo. yeoman

*Farnley,*
Hodgson Geo. stone mercht.
Holdsworth Jas. stone mert.
Newton John, gent.
Rawson John, Esq. mill
Robinson Leonard, jun. mfr.

*Farsley,*
Wood T. I. and J. scribbling millers and woollen mfrs.
Roberts Wm. sen. woollen mfr. & land measurer

*Featherstone,*
Cheesebrough Rev. Joseph
Smith Mrs. gentlewoman
Whitley Jonath. schoolmstr.

*Fewston,*
Graham Joseph, bookkeeper,
King Joseph, surgeon
Robinson Michael, superintendant to Chippendale & Co.
Ward Thos. parish clerk

*Follyfoot,*
Allison Richd. & Son, stone masons & bridge builders
Bears Miss Penelope, gentwn.
Birch John, Harewood Arms
Bragg and Wagstaff, linen bleachers, Aketon

Cass Joseph, linen mfr.
Collingworth Jas. corn dlr.
Hatteraley Wm. and Son, millwrights

*Goldsbrough,*
Hon. Edw. Stourton, hall

*Greenhow Hill,*
Hunter John, Miner's Arms
Wilson Wm. schoolmaster

*Grewelthorpe,*
Jackson Wm. gent.

*Grimstone,*
Jackson John, gent.

*Halifax,*
Dean Saml. gent. Causeway
Nicholl Francis & Co. brass and iron founders
Priestley Jones & Co. bombazine & Norwich crape mfrs.
Slade Captain, Aked's lane
Thompson Mrs. Lord street
Wigglesworth James, commissioner for taking affidavits in the courts in Ireland

*Hammerton Green,*
Vickers John, vict. George Inn, posting house

*Hammerton Kirk,*
Thompson Wm. Esq.
Atkinson Thomas, yeoman
Stead Thomas, joiner

*Hampsthwaite,*
Rinder John, carpenter
Skirrow Saml. yeoman

*Hanlith,*
Preston Robt. gent. & agent to L. R. Sargeantson, Esq.

*Havercroft,*
Watson John, yeoman

*Haworth,*
Moore John, grocer &c.

*Headingley,*
Wood Thomas, corn miller Oil mill

*Heck,*
Blyth Thos. yeoman
England Geo. yeoman

*Hiendley South,*
Earnshaw Rawdon, boarding school

*Highfield.*
Hodgson R. Esq.

*High Town,*
Lister Wm. bookbinder, &c.
Lister M. druggist & grocer

*Holbeck,*
Ogle James, woollen mfr.

*Holme,*
Bearnell Chas. cloth dresser

*Holmfirth,*
Balmforth Rev. Tho. academy
Crutwell Rev. Richard,

*Hook,*
Boynton Kendall, brewer

*Hopton,*
Barker Wm. woollen mfr.
Hunton Paul, woollen mfr.
Smith John, woollen mfr.

Staincliffe and Hinchlie, woollen mfrs.

*Horton Great,*
Booth Daniel, vict. 4 Ashes
Hudson Wm. Primrose hill

*Horton Little,*
Baxter Jph. vict. Red Lion

*Howden,*
Schofield, Clarkson & Clough, bankers, on Spooner & Co. London

*Hoyland High,*
Wigfield Thos. nail maker

*Hoyland Swaine,*
Armitage John, yeoman
Dyson John, yeoman
Shaw, Giles & Isaac, cattle dealers
Swift Joseph, cloth mfr.
Waine Jesse, farmer

*Huddersfield,*
Lockwood John, mercht. & mfr. Cowersby
Stocks Wm. jun. chief constable

*Hunslet,*
Brook J. and E. merchants

*Hull,*
Alderson John, solicitor, clerk of the Court of Requests
Beilby W. T. 1st clerk at Trinity House
Cunningworth William, vict. Jolly Sailor, 37, Blanket row
Jervas Joseph, vict. Turk's Head, 33, Myton gate
Laidlaw Alex. tanner, fellmonger, & leather dresser, 37, High street; house Wilmington
Picard J. K. Son, & Co. white lead and paint mfrs. Old Dock side

*Ilton, (N. R.)*
Exelby J. classical academy

*Ingbirchworth,*
Waite George, farmer

*Keighley,*
Crabtree Elijah, schoolmaster

*Killinghall,*
John Williamson, Esq. magistrate, Hollings
Farnell John, tailor & draper
Northorp Cornelius, plumber

*Kirkby-cum-Netherby,*
Harland Benjamin, farmer, Barrowby Grange

*Kirkby Malzeard,*
Bulmer Rd. classical academy
Teasdale Jane, gentlewmn.

*Kirkby Overblow,*
Hon and Rev. Jacob Marsham, D. D. Rector
Rev Geo. Webb, curate

*Kirkstall,*
Burneston Wm. vict. Kirkstall Hotel
Dickinson C. woollen mfr.
Eddison John, woollen mfr.
Fox Rev. James

A 2

Spink James, gent.
Watson Jonas, fellmonger
Wood John, woollen mfr.

**Knaresborough,**
Taylor & Conyers, solicitors

**Knottingley,**
Long S. M. maltster

**Leathley,**
Simpson Thomas, corn dlr.

**Linthwaite,**
Broughton J. cloth dresser

**Linton,**
Groves William, farmer
Pattison Wm. yeoman

**Lockwood,**
Abley Thomas, corn dealer
Armitage Jph. blacksmith
Ellis John, joiner, &c.
Kingston John, joiner, &c.
Quarmby Thos. blacksmith
Rushworth Wm. joiner, &c.
Wadsworth Joseph, cooper

**Longwood,**
Robson Thos. cloth mercht.

**Low Moor,**
Worsnop James, stuff mfr.

**Malton,**
J Cumber and not J. Snowball, agent to the Atlas fire office.

**Marsden,**
Armitage E. & D. merchts.
Lumb Thos. vict. Rain
Taylor E. and J. ironfounders

**Middleton,**
Hudson Matthias, butler

**Minskip,**
Thompson Joseph, yeoman,

**Mirfield,**
Barker Jph. woollen mfr.
Buckley Benj. woollen mfr.
Eastwood Wm. woollen mfr.
Hirst Geo. woollen mfr.
Hirst Joseph, schoolmaster
Holt John, woollen mfr.
Micklethwaite Jas. maltster
Oxley John, woollen mfrs.
Rangeley John, woollen mfr.
Sheard John, woollen mfr.
Stancliffe J. mercht. & mfr.
Stancliffe Wm. coal owner
Turner Wm. attorney
Turner Charles, coal owner
Webster Abm. woollen mfr.
Webster Geo. woollen mfr.
Wheatley J. mercht. & mfr.
Wheatley Chas. coal owner
Wheatley Thos. coal owner

**Notton,**
Holt Elias, agent
Marshall Mrs. A.
Peaker Richard, corn miller

**Nun Monkton,**
Beckwith Rev. Thos. curate

**Osmundthorpe,**
Lasseys and Co. coal merts

**Ossett,**
Greaves Thos. mill owner
Hanson Wm. cotton spinner
Megson Joshua, card maker
Mitchell Mark, card maker
— oss T. & Sons, machine mkrs

**Oxnop,**
Cousins J Shoulder of Mutton

**Ouslethwaite,**
Elmhurst Robt. attorney

**Pateley Bridge,**
Ashworth John, linen draper
Kirkby Henry, flax spinner
Kirkby Grange and Co. flax spinners
Wilson Rev. John

**Pontefract,**
Dunhill Thos. gent.
Firth T. refined liquorice dealer, Market place
Rawson Bev. M.

**Pool, near Otley,**
Lockton T. pasteboard mfr.

**Pudsey,**
Farrar John, woollen mfr.
Hunter Thos. bailiff
Lonsdale W. H. grocer, draper, and ironmonger

**Purston Jackling,**
Buchanan Robert, yeoman,

**Rawcliffe,**
Beechell Wm. yeoman

**Reedness,**
Sheppard J. C. shopkeeper

**Ripley,**
Williamson J. Esq. Hollings
Broadbent S. Hare & Hounds
Wood G. Star, (excise office)

**Ripon,**
Farrer Wm. Esq. Mayor.
Bishop Wm. tallow chandler

**Rodley,**
Hardaker John, clock maker

**Roksby.**
Bowness Rev. Geo. rector

**Roseberry Topping,**
In a part of the impression of the N. & E. Riding map the altitude of *Roseberry Topping* is stated at 1022, instead of 1488 feet.

**Saddleworth,**
Kenworthy J. surg. Dobcross
Kenworthy James, dyer, Grass Croft, Clough
Shaw Joseph, guardian of the poor, Woodhouse
Whitehead A. and W. coal merchants, High moor
Winterbottom J. surg. Delph
Wright James, merchant & manfr. Grass croft, Clough

**Selby,**
M'Clellan T. linen &c, drpr

**Settle,**
Carr Wm. High constable
Woods George, paper mfr.

**Sheffield,**
Fenton Francis, Esq. American Consular agent
Bishop L. razor mfr Broco st.

**Silkstone,**
Clark R. Esq. Noble Thorp

**Skipton,**
Armstrong J.

**Staincross,**
Shaw John, Esq.

**Stanningley,**
Rodgers John, brass founder
Sykes Thos. grocer
Watkinson J. doffin plate mkr

**Sutton, near Keighley,**
Gregson George, tailor &c.

**Swillington,**
Wilks and Co. Pottery

**Tankersley,**
Newton, & Co. coal merts and iron founders

**Thornhill Lees,**
Sanderson Abraham, maltster

**Thornton, near Bradford,**
Craven Joseph, worsted mfr.

**Thornton near Skipton,**
Barnard Rev. Wm. Mordaunt,

**Wakefield,**
Cogswell J. & Co.'s vessels to Liverpool, M. W. & Fri
Shaw J. iron mert. Westgate
Walker Miss, ladies' boarding school, St. John's

**West End,**
Scaife Wm. joiner, &c.

**Whiston.**
Hartley & Co. machine mkrs

**Whixley,**
Binks Thos. yeoman
Daniels T. & W. tanners

**Wilsden,**
Nicholls & Skirrow, worsted spinners, mfrs. and merts. 12, Maiden lane, London

**Winksley,**
Thompson & Son, flax spars

**Woodhouse Carr,**
Whittaker John, cloth dresser

**Woodhouse Great,**
Rawling Francis, dyer,

**Woodthorpe,**
3 miles W. of Sheffield.
Parker Hugh, Esq. hall

**Woodthorpe, nr Wakefield**
Wood Rev. W.

**Woolley,**
Moor John, Esq.

**Wortley Lower, nr. Leeds,**
Cliffe John, fire brick mfr.
Stead Wm. woollen mfr.

**Wragby,**
Simpson Rev. John

**York,**
Cockburn Rev. Wm. M. A. Dean of the Cathedral
Baines Rev. John, M. A. vicar of St. Trinity

*Errata at Page 288. Mr. Chantry was born at Norton, 4 miles from Sheffield, & 2¼ miles within the Derbyshire border, so that the honour of having given birth to this eminent sculptor, belongs to Derbyshire, and not to Yorkshire. Leggit was his mother's maiden name, but he was baptized Francis only.*

Pontefract Sessions 1st Mon. after Easter Week, not Mon. in Easter week.

# YORKSHIRE;

## East and North Ridings.

## CONTENTS OF THE INTRODUCTORY CHAPTER.

THE first volume of this publication was confined principally to matter relating to the West-Riding of Yorkshire; and the present volume, which completes the Topographical History and Directory of this large division of the kingdom, comprehends the CITY AND AINSTY OF YORK, THE EAST RIDING, AND THE NORTH-RIDING of this County. The extent and jurisdiction of the Ainsty are described with precision at page 136 of the present volume; it remains, therefore, only to take a general view of the distinguishing features of the East and North Ridings.

The East-Riding is divided into seven wapentakes,* namely—

| | |
|---|---|
| Buckrose, | Howdenshire, |
| Dickering, | Ouse & Derwent, |
| Harthill, | and the Town and |
| Holderness, | County of Hull. |

The North-Riding is divided into twelve wapentakes, namely—

| | |
|---|---|
| Allerton, | Hang East, |
| Birdforth, | Hang West, |
| Bulmer, | Langbargh, |
| Gilling East, | Pickering Lythe, |
| Gilling West, | Ryedale, and |
| Hallkeld, | Whitby Strand. |

The North-Riding is bounded on the north by the river Tees; on the east by the German ocean; on the south by the Ainsty of York and the East and West-Ridings; and on the west by the county of Westmoreland. The boundaries of the East-Riding are, the Derwent to the north; the Ouse to the west; the Humber to the south; and the German ocean to the east.

In tracing the Roman roads of Yorkshire, the course of the great road, called Watling-street, running from south to north, has already been described,† and shown to

* The wapentakes of the West-Riding are enumerated at page 653, Vol I.

At page iii. Vol. I.

extend from Bawtry, where it enters the county of York, to the Tees, where it crosses into the county of Durham.— Another military road, running east and west, from Manchester to York, has also been described. This road, proceeding still eastward, advanced to Malton, where it was divided into two branches, the first called Wade's causeway, leading to Dunsley Bay, the *Dunus Sinus of Ptolemy*; and the other to Scarborough and Filey. The straight course of a Roman road may be traced over the high grounds of the Wolds, from York to Bridlington Bay, the *Gabrantovicorum Sinus Portiosus*, or *Salutaris*; a branch of this road has also been discovered, tending towards Hunmanby.— Another line may also be followed in a direction to Patrington, *(Praetorium)* and the Spurn point, which appears to be the *Ocellum Promontorium of Ptolemy*, and where was once the noted seaport of Ravenspurn, now engulphed in the ocean.— From Lincoln a Roman road may be traced to the south bank of the Humber, near Wintringham, where are still seen vestiges of the station *ad Abum*. On the north bank Brough indicates the position of another ancient station, from which it is probable that a branch of road communicated with York. From this sketch it will appear that the military roads of the Romans converged in every direction, from the extremities of the province of Eboracum to York, their common centre, which, as will be seen from the subjoined history of that ancient city, was so long the head quarters of the Roman army.

The East-Riding of Yorkshire, although it displays a great variety of aspect, is far less conspicuously marked with the bold features of nature than the other parts of the county; but if it contains no scenery that can be called truly romantic, some parts of the Riding are beautifully picturesque, and afford very extensive and

A 3

even magnificent prospects, especially when the sea or the Humber enters into view.— From its topographical appearance, this Riding may be considered as three different districts, the Wolds forming one of them, and the other two lying, one to the east and the other to the west, of that elevated region. The wolds consist of an assemblage of chalky hills, extending from the northern to the southern extremity of the East-Riding. The soil is commonly a free and rather light loam, with a mixture of chalky gravel, in some parts very shallow; it also contains a deeper and more kindly loam, and a light sandy mixture. On the Wolds very extensive improvements have taken place during the last forty years, and a district, which, in the middle of the last century, was a complete waste—fit only for the production and support of rabbits, by the encouragement given to agriculture between the years 1790 and 1815, has been brought into a state of prosperous cultivation. The eastern division, above referred to, extends from Filey to Spurn Head; in some parts of this extensive tract, particularly between Filey and Bridlington, the face of the country is much diversified, and throughout the whole district clay and loam are the predominant soils. The improvements in agriculture have here also been very extensive, and a judicious system of drainage has accomplished wonders. The third natural division of the East-Riding extends from the western foot of the Wolds to the boundaries of the North and West-Ridings; this tract of land is called Levels, and, as its name imports, it is every where flat and unpicturesque, but by no means unproductive.

In the North-Riding the face of the country is much more diversified. Along the coast, from Scarborough to Cleveland, it is hilly and bold, the cliff being generally from 60 to 150 feet high, and in some places, as at Stoupe Brow, seven miles from Whitby, it rises to the stupendous height of 893 feet. From the cliff the country rises in most places very rapidly, and a little further inland successive hills rising one above another, form the elevated tract of the Eastern Moorlands. The cultivated dales situated amongst these moors are pretty extensive, some of them containing from five to ten thousand acres, and Eskdale and Bilsdale much more. The level lands at the bottom of the vallies are seldom more than two or three hundred yards in breadth, but the land is generally cultivated to a considerable distance up the sides of the hills.— Most of the dales partake more or less of the following soils;—a black moor earth upon clay; a sandy soil, in some places inter-

mixed with stones; and a light loam upon a grit rock. In some instances, as in the neighbourhood of Hackness, there is on the side of the hills a stiff loam upon limestone, and a deep sandy loam upon a whinstone; and in the bottom a light loam upon gravel or freestone. The interior parts of the Eastern Moorlands present a bleak and dreary aspect, and little wood is to be seen, except in the dales or on the declivities of some of the more fertile of the hills. Passing into Cleveland, the country is lightly featured with hills, and the soil is generally clay; in some cases a clayey loam, and in others a fine red sandy soil. The vale of York, more in the interior, is not confined within any determinate boundaries, but is rather marked out by the face of the country.— This extensive vale has, from the river Tees, a general slope, though interrupted by some irregularities of surface, and some bold swells, as far as York, where it sinks into a perfect flat. The northern part of this tract has the Eastern Moorlands on one side, and the Western Moorlands on the other. The soil in that part of the vale of York which lies within the North-Riding is described by Mr. Tuke, in his survey, to be of different degrees of fertility, and to be very differently composed; generally it is a clayey loam, and few parts of the country can excel this celebrated vale in fertility.— The Western Moorlands differ greatly from those in the eastern part of the Riding. They are generally calcareous, and although their altitude is considerably higher, they are much more fertile than the eastern Moorlands, which consist mainly of grit-stone and free-stone rock. Many of the dales which intersect the western Moorlands are extremely fertile; of these Wensleydale may be ranked as the first, both in extent and fertility. On the south several small dales open into the dale of Wensley. The soil of this master dale, on the banks of the river, is generally a rich loamy gravel, and on the sides of the hills a clayey loam upon a substratum of limestone. Swaledale is little inferior to Wensley in extent, though it falls far short of it in beauty, but by some it is esteemed more romantic, and by all it must be admired. In fertility it is pretty much upon a par with its neighbours. The smaller dales, which are very numerous, are in general similar to these in appearance and production. Even the mountains here, some of which are of considerable altitude, as will be seen from the Map of the East and North Ridings, seldom exhibit marks of unconquerable sterility, but are many of them covered to their summits with fine sweet grass, bent or rushes.[*]

[*] Tuke's Agricultural Survey.

The east MOORLANDS of the North-Riding form a peculiar feature in the country, being wholly detached from the mountains in the west. Some points of the east MOORLANDS rise nearly 900 feet above the level of the sea; but the most remarkable summit of the whole is Roseberry Topping, described at page 522 of this volume.—By its detached position and superior elevation, it commands in all directions a prospect at once extensive and interesting. The hill rests on a basis of alum rock, interspersed with iron-stone, and its pinnacled summit indicates to the surrounding country the approaching change in the weather, as expressed in the following metrical proverb:—

"When Roseberry Topping wears a cap,
"Let Cleveland then beware of a clap."

Along the whole length of the North-Riding, from west to east, the country is bounded by the river Tees. This river, rising in the mountains of Westmoreland and Cumberland, pursues a very direct course into the German ocean, below Stockton, where it spreads out into the estuary of Redcar, three miles in breadth.—The Tees is navigable for ships of 60 tons burthen, up to Stockton, but the channel is serpentine and intricate, and the current rapid. A few inconsiderable streams from the western mountains fall into the river Tees, but the great body of the waters of Yorkshire flow in the opposite direction, and their course, from their rise to their termination in the Humber, is described in pages vii and viii of the first volume of this work. The Derwent rises in the eastern moors of the North-Riding, at about four miles from the sea, and after taking a southerly direction through the romantic valley of Hackness, runs in a line almost parallel with the coast, till it comes to the foot of the Wolds; it then takes a westerly direction, and having received the Rye, from Helmsley, passes by the borough of Malton, to which it is navigable for vessels of twenty-five tons burthen. It is the boundary between the North and East-Ridings, from its junction with the small river Hertford, till it approaches Stamford-Bridge, where it enters the East-Riding, and falls into the Ouse, near the village of Barmby, about three miles and a half above Howden. In the east Moorlands of the North-Riding rises the Eske, which, after watering the dale to which it gives name, forms the inner harbour of Whitby, and is there lost in the German Ocean. The small river Hull traverses the East-Riding from north to south, visiting Driffield and Beverley in its course, and at its influx into the Humber contributes to

form the secure harbour of Kingston, which, from this river, is generally called Hull.

The sea coast of the North and East-Ridings of Yorkshire is very extensive, and affords several secure harbours:—The harbours of Hull, Scarborough, Whitby, and Bridlington, are described under their appropriate heads in this volume, to which may be added the Bay of Filey and Robin Hood's Bay.

The Minerals of the North-Riding consist chiefly of the alum Mines, on the coast of Whitby, as mentioned at pages 416 and 574 of this volume, and the lead mines in Swaledale, and the neighbouring vallies, as described at page 554. About the middle of the last century copper of good quality was produced near Middleton Tyas, but the works have been for some years discontinued. Copper was also discovered, about five and twenty years ago, at Richmond, but it does not appear that the discovery has ever yet tended to any profitable result. The same observation applies to the iron-stone, which may be found in the east Moorland; though it should seem, from ancient records, that as early as the 13th century, iron was wrought and forged in Rosedale; Ayton is the only place in the North-Riding where forges have been established in modern times, and even these have now totally disappeared, from the difficulty of procuring fuel. Various parts of this Riding produce coal, particularly the plain between Easingwold and Thirsk, and the west Moorlands; but the latter is of an inferior quality, and fit only for the burning of lime. Good free-stone for building, appears in many parts of the Riding; and stone-quarries are worked both in the neighbourhood of Scarborough and Whitby, from whence are drawn the massive blocks used in the construction of the piers at these ports. Lime-stone, and a species of marble, not inferior to that of Derbyshire, are found in the vale of the Greta, near Rokeby, and large blocks of red granite are seen on the surface, in certain parts of the west Moorlands.

In the East-Riding chalk is the principal mineral substance.—Near the coast it extends from Hessle, on the banks of the Humber, its southern extremity, to Reighton, ten miles south of Scarborough, its northern boundary. The chalk rocks always contain large quantities of water, which may be had by boring or sinking, even at a considerable distance from the hills. Many large springs break out along the eastern edge of the chalk, generally in the gravel which covers it. The river Hull is formed by the united waters of a number of these springs; and at Spring Head, from which the town of Hull is supplied with water, 240,000 gallons are raised daily; this water contains a small portion of carbonate of lime and iron, which is separated by exposure to the atmosphere in a course of three miles. The intermitting spring at *Keldgate*, near Cottingham, described at page 189 of this volume, rises upon the gravel, but it is not far distant from the chalk. In the gravel beds on the chalk are found the remains of large animals, some of them in a state of great perfection; *vertebræ*, eighteen feet in length, and from 8 to 10 inches in diameter, have been dug up in these beds, and teeth, measuring 8 or 10 inches in circumference, are frequently discovered here. At Hull, the gravel depository of the animal remains is about ninety feet from the surface, and the workmen employed in boring for water near the north bridge described their tools to have smelt as if they had been cutting fish, so that it is probable not only the bones but also the fleshy part of the animal remains. The coast, from Spurn to Bridlington, forms a section of all the beds above the chalk, and as it is not in the line of dip, two beds are generally seen at the same time. A bed of dark red clay commences at Kilnsea, containing round boulders*, mixed with pebbles, both of which are composed of Granite, Gneiss, Mica slate, Porphyry, Grauwacke, Quartz, Mountain Limestone, containing organic remains, all the sand-stones and coal-shales, coal, fuller's-earth, chalk, and flint. In this bed the chalk pebbles are in the greatest quantity. On the western side of Holderness, along the edge of the chalk hills, a very extensive tract of rich land has been formed, in the course of ages, called *Warp Land*, which consists of the clay and sand deposits of the Humber. The greatest breadth of this tract is from Hull to Hedon, a distance of nine miles, and its length, from Hull to Lowthorp, a distance of twenty miles. A narrow piece of newly-formed warp extends from Hedon to Spurn, including Sunk Island, and is called the Marshes. How long this operation of land making has been proceeding in this quarter, human penetration and local records are alike incapable of determining, but that its date is of many centuries is obvious, as Drypool, which stands upon the present bank of the Humber, is mentioned in the Domesday survey, and a causeway, extending from Beverley to the newly-built town of Hull, at nearly its present level, existed in the time of Edward I. The depth of the warp

* Fragments of rock.

at Hull is forty-eight feet; beneath it is a bed of moor land, consisting principally of peat earth, two feet in thickness. The warp land extends beyond Driffield, but it is there much shallower than at Hull, and its width does not exceed four miles. That this moor, now covered with warp, was formerly upon the surface, is shown by the nature of its composition, being evidently peat, which could not be formed in any other situation; and that it is extended across the Humber into Lincolnshire is proved by pieces of wood, exactly the same as those found in the moor, having been washed up at Hessle after a high wind.

The Wolds consist of one extensive mass of indurated chalk, the surface of which is very curious; broken by a vast number of deep dales and sudden depressions, most of them, if not all, taking a direction towards some general outlet to the east or the southeast of Yorkshire. It may be observed, however, as a peculiarity, that the whole of the extreme edge or margin of the Wolds, to the north and to the west, with one exception, continues in a regular and entire state along the surface, without any of those depressions which take place at a very little distance within. The depression that breaks through the margin is at Market Weighton, and a small canal, upon Foulton's plan might, at an easy expense, be directed from hence to the navigable river Hull, near Beverley, with great public advantage to this part of the country. In France and in America canals of this description are becoming very general, and prove highly advantageous. It is very probable that the Wolds have been the last deposit of all the great masses of simple and homogeneous matter in this part of the world. There are scattered all over this elevated tract nodules of pyrates, of a round form, composed of iron and sulphur, which the country people call *bullets*; there are also great quantities of loose fragments of sand-stones, which are perfectly foreign to the calcareous matter of which the Wolds are formed, and they have, doubtless, been brought here by the action of the sea, after the chalky stratum had been deposited and hardened, or they would have sunk into the pulp.

All along the eastern side of the Wolds from Bridlington to Beverley, and from thence to Hessle, by the Humber side, the sand-stone, and the chalk which rests upon it, dip and vanish under an extensive bed of alluvial soil, which forms the whole of Holderness. On the north and west the Wolds exhibit a bold and striking front, resembling a marine cliff, which is entirely surrounded by an extensive plain of alluvial deposit, spreading to the north, the west, and the south, and terminating in a circular form, with the following towns and villages upon its outskirts : Christhorp, Liberston, Cayton, Seamer, Ayton, Brompton, Wycomb, Snainton, Thornton, Pickering, and thence in a right line towards Hamilton Hill. Stretching westward it terminates at or near Knottingley, Monkfryston, Tadcaster, Wetherby, Knaresbro', and Aldborough, at each of which places is found a bed of limestone, in a sloping direction, dipping under the alluvial deposit towards the Wolds. This limestone covers in an unconformable manner the extensive sand-stone and coal series of the West Riding. The sand stone, rising from under the Tadcaster bed of lime, extends to Bradford, at which place beautiful impressions of Euphorbium, Bamboo Cane, and other tropical productions are to be seen; and in the neighbourhood of Bradford an alum shale is found, which might probably be worked with advantage, both from the ample supply of coal, and the ready demand for the alum when manufactured. At a little distance from Knaresbro', near the river side, and almost opposite to the mansion of Sir Thos. Slingsby, Bart. is a bed of Strontian earth, which is very rare, if not unique, in this kingdom.

The Manufactures of the North and East Ridings are upon a very circumscribed scale. The commerce of these divisions of the county is principally confined to the ports of Hull, Whitby, and Scarborough, and its nature and extent will be appreciated by a reference to the history of each of those places contained in this volume.

Yorkshire is rich in Antiquities; every division in the following pages will be found to abound with them, but they are too numerous to be recapitulated, except in the general indexes to these volumes, from which their description in the work may be referred to. The city of York in particular is a mass of antiquity, and the brief but comprehensive history of that venerable city, with its cathedral and other public buildings and institutions, will be read with a lively interest, and may be implicitly relied upon, being drawn from the best authorities.

It has already been observed* that the

* See Volume I. Page xii.

Ecclesiastical affairs of this County are under the superintendence of the Archbishop of York, the Primate of England, and that they are chiefly administered by the Archdeacons. In Yorkshire there are four Archdeaconries, namely, York, East Riding, Cleveland, and Richmond; these are divided into sixteen Deaneries, which are thus arranged :—

ARCHDEACONRY OF YORK *alias* THE WEST RIDING.†
Deanery—City and Ainsty of York,
Craven,
Doncaster,
Pontefract.
ARCHDEACONRY OF EAST RIDING.
Deanery—Buckrose,
Dickering,
Harthill and Hull,
Holderness.
ARCHDEACONRY OF CLEVELAND.
Deanery—Bulmer,
Cleveland,
Ryedale,
Ripon,
Ripon-cum-Masham, a peculiar jurisdiction.
ARCHDEACONRY OF RICHMOND.
Deanery—Boroughbridge,
Catterick,
Richmond.

This archdeaconry extends into Lancashire, Cumberland, and Westmoreland. The parishes of Yorkshire amount to 563, and the Townships and Chapelries, exclusive of the parishes, to no fewer than 1310.

At the period of the publication of the first volume of this work, the population returns of the whole county, up to the 26th of May, 1821, were not fully completed, but they are now printed, and in our possession. In the first volume were given the returns of all the places in the West Riding under the head of an "INDEX OF PLACES," and the returns for the Ainsty, the East Riding, and the North Riding are given with the same particularity in this volume, thereby completing the population returns of the whole county, distinguishing the parishes and the townships within each; and to render this return still more full and comprehensive, a summary of the population in all the wapentakes, liberties, and separate jurisdictions of Yorkshire, is here subjoined :—

† THE WEST RIDING CHARITABLE SOCIETY is a benevolent Institution of great utility, and has for its object the relief of the Widows, Orphans and distressed Families of the Clergy, within the Archdeaconry of York. For some time this Institution did not receive that support to which, by its merits, it is entitled, but latterly, from the zeal of its officers, public beneficence has flowed more freely into this channel, and during the last year the sum of £725 was distributed among 37 different families, of which sum £640 was appropriated to the Widows and Daughters of Clergymen. The Treasurer and Secretary for the City and Ainsty of York, and for the Deanery of Craven, is the Rev. Joseph Swaine, of Beeston, near Leeds; and for the Deaneries of Doncaster and Pontefract, the Rev. Samuel Sharp, of Wakefield.

# Population of Yorkshire,

SHEWING THE NUMBER OF FAMILIES, THE PROPORTION OF PERSONS OCCUPIED IN AGRICULTURE, TRADE, &c. AND THE NUMBER OF INHABITANTS.

## EAST RIDING.

| Wapentakes, &c. | FAM. By how many Families occupied. | OCCUPATIONS. Families chiefly employed in Agriculture. | Families chiefly employed in Trade, Manufactures, or Handicraft. | Other Families not comprised in the preceding classes. | PERSONS. Males. | Females. | Total of Persons. |
|---|---|---|---|---|---|---|---|
| Buckrose .................. | 2080 | 1425 | 360 | 295 | 5839 | 5347 | 11,186 |
| Dickering.................. | 3372 | 1598 | 1093 | 681 | 8255 | 8206 | 16,461 |
| Harthill ................. | 8790 | 4048 | 3407 | 1335 | 20,659 | 21,342 | 42,001 |
| Holderness, .............. | 5563 | 3132 | 1480 | 951 | 13,862 | 13,566 | 27,428 |
| Howdenshire, ........... | 1649 | 970 | 433 | 246 | 3863 | 3942 | 7805 |
| Ouse and Derwent, ...... | 1563 | 1147 | 242 | 174 | 3957 | 3952 | 7909 |
| Liberty of St. Peter's York | 2045 | 1025 | 690 | 330 | 4565 | 4639 | 9204 |
| Ainsty of York, ........ | 1734 | 1206 | 371 | 157 | 4290 | 4450 | 8740 |
| York City, .............. | 4412 | 288 | 3333 | 791 | 9547 | 11,240 | 20,787 |
| Beverley Liberty, ........ | 1718 | 295 | 753 | 670 | 3494 | 4009 | 7503 |
| Town and County of Hull | 7573 | 346 | 4475 | 2752 | 14,430 | 16,995 | 31,425 |
| Total East Riding. | 40,499 | 15,480 | 16,637 | 8,382 | 92,761 | 97,688 | 190,449 |

## NORTH RIDING.

| Allertonshire .......... | 1811 | 1165 | 563 | 83 | 4370 | 4389 | 8759 |
| Birdforth .................. | 2430 | 1549 | 726 | 155 | 5916 | 5784 | 11,700 |
| Bulmer...................... | 3059 | 1953 | 623 | 483 | 7790 | 7722 | 15,512 |
| Gilling East .............. | 1558 | 779 | 341 | 438 | 3536 | 3644 | 7180 |
| Gilling West.............. | 3499 | 1467 | 1215 | 817 | 9176 | 8666 | 17,842 |
| Halikeld .................. | 1307 | 947 | 245 | 115 | 2945 | 3013 | 5958 |
| Hang East.................. | 2192 | 906 | 678 | 608 | 4918 | 5196 | 10,114 |
| Hang West .............. | 3127 | 1304 | 714 | 1109 | 7271 | 7436 | 14,707 |
| Langbargh .............. | 6547 | 2584 | 2213 | 1750 | 14,416 | 15,442 | 29,858 |
| Pickering Lythe ......... | 3060 | 1796 | 659 | 605 | 7690 | 7542 | 15,332 |
| Ryedale .................. | 3892 | 1710 | 1170 | 1012 | 9737 | 9787 | 19,500 |
| Richmond Borough ...... | 760 | 24 | 615 | 121 | 1875 | 1971 | 3846 |
| Scarborough Borough ... | 2022 | 87 | 734 | 1201 | 3877 | 4656 | 8533 |
| Whitby Strand............ | 3467 | 466 | 1074 | 1927 | 6936 | 7980 | 14,916 |
| Total North Riding. | 38,731 | 16,737 | 11,570 | 10,424 | 90,153 | 93,228 | 183,381 |

## WEST RIDING.

| Agbrigg .................. | 30,492 | 3341 | 23,067 | 4084 | 77,579 | 76,712 | 154,291 |
| Barkston Ash .......... | 4314 | 2561 | 1205 | 548 | 10,218 | 10,554 | 20,772 |
| Claro .................... | 8055 | 3612 | 2404 | 2039 | 20,153 | 19,713 | 39,866 |
| Morley .................. | 36,706 | 2237 | 31,834 | 2635 | 92,231 | 93,537 | 185,768 |
| Osgoldcross .............. | 6383 | 3202 | 1702 | 1479 | 15,016 | 15,262 | 30,278 |
| Skyrack .................. | 7396 | 2104 | 4487 | 805 | 18,629 | 18,467 | 37,096 |
| Staincliff and Ewecross... | 12,673 | 3915 | 7235 | 1523 | 32,067 | 32,744 | 64,811 |
| Staincross .............. | 6346 | 1953 | 3644 | 749 | 16,960 | 15,952 | 32,912 |
| Strafforth and Tickhill... | 26,721 | 6786 | 16,154 | 3781 | 63,709 | 64,200 | 127,909 |
| Ripon Liberty ........... | 2517 | 825 | 980 | 712 | 6008 | 6123 | 12,131 |
| Doncaster Borough ...... | 1798 | 307 | 1184 | 307 | 3857 | 4687 | 8544 |
| Doncaster Soke ........ | 229 | 160 | 55 | 14 | 583 | 600 | 1183 |
| Leeds Town and Liberty | 17,836 | 610 | 14,890 | 2336 | 40,532 | 43,264 | 83,796 |
| Total, West Riding ... | 161,466 | 31,613 | 108,841 | 21,012 | 397,542 | 401,815 | 799,357 |
| East Riding ... | 40,499 | 15,480 | 16,637 | 8382 | 92,761 | 97,688 | 190,449 |
| North Riding ... | 38,731 | 16,737 | 11,570 | 10,424 | 90,153 | 93,228 | 183,381 |
| Total of the County ... | 240,696 | 63,830 | 137,048 | 39,818 | 580,456 | 592,731 | 1,173,187 |

# HISTORY OF YORK.

## CONTENTS.

# HISTORY

OF THE

# CITY OF YORK.

YORK or EBORACUM is situated at the confluence of the rivers Ouse and Foss, near the centre of Great Britain, and in one of the most rich and extensive vallies in England. It is the capital of the great county to which it gives name, the see of an Archbishop, who is primate and metropolitan of England, and the second city in rank in the kingdom. This city is placed at the point of Junction, though independent of them all, of the three Ridings or districts into which the shire is subdivided. Antiquarians, into whose researches and conjectures it is not the business of this history deeply to enter, hold that, it was built by Ebraucus, the son of Mempricius, a British king, the third from Brute, and called from its founders Kaer-ebrawc, or the city of Ebraucus, in the year of the world, 2983, about the time when David reigned in Judea, and Gad, Nathan, and Asaph prophesied in Israel. Of king Ebraucus, it is recorded, that he also built Aclud,[*] supposed by some to be Aldborough, and by others Carlisle, and also Mount Agnea, the capital of Scotland; that he reigned sixty years, and by twenty wives had twenty sons and thirty daughters, and dying at York, was interred[*] in a temple, dedicated to Diana, which he had erected, and of which the ancient church of St. Helen's, at the junction of Blakestreet and Davygate, now forms the remains. Another conjecture is, that a colony of Gauls having seated themselves in Spain and Portugal, were driven from thence by the Romans into mid-England, and took up their head station at York, to which they gave the name of Eboracum, from Ebora, a town in Portugal, or Ebura, in Andalusia.[†] Leyland and Camden consider the name as derived from the situation of the city on the river Eure, to which the

Romans might add the termination cum, or the Saxons wic, a place of refuge: and if the point was clear, which it is not, that the Ouse was anciently called Eure, as low as York, it would go far towards settling the etymology of this ancient city. In Domesday book, York is called, Civitas Eborum, and Eurwic. Humphrey Lhuyd, the learned Welsh antiquarian, in mentioning the Brigantine towns that are in Ptolemy's Geography, says, Eboracum is well known to be the very same city that the Britons called Caer-Effroc, and is now contracted into York. Drake, the historian of York, in his Eboracum, gives several other conjectures upon this subject, which serve only to show how futile is the attempt to solve a difficulty involved in the obscurity of upwards of twenty centuries. After the death of Ebraucus, little but the names of their kings is mentioned by British historians, for thirty successions, except, that Geofry of Monmouth, says, that Elidurus having driven his brother Artogal from his throne, met one day, in hunting, his deposed sovereign in the woods, and as he had long secretly repented of the injustice he had done him, he took him home secretly and concealed him in his bed chamber; then feigning to be sick, he assembled all his nobles from various parts of the kingdom, whom he admitted into his chamber one by one, and cut off the heads of every one of them that would not promise again to submit to the rule of Artogal. The agreement for his restoration being ratified, Elidurus conducted his brother to York, where in the presence of the assembled people he took the crown from his own head and placed it upon his brother's. Artogal being thus restored to his kingdom reigned for ten years in peace and equity, when he died, and was buried at York, and was again succeeded by Elidurus.

Alcuin a native of this city, who wrote near a thousand years ago, says, that York

* Geofry of Monmouth.
† Sir Thomas Widdrington's MSS.

B

was built by the Romans, and he has left his testimony on this subject in the following lines:—

> *Hanc* Romana *manus muris, & turribus, altam,*
> *Fundavit primo——*
> *Ut fieret ducibus secura potentia regni:*
> *Et decus imperii, terrorque hostilibus armis.*

> This city, first, by *Roman* hand was form'd,
> With lofty towers, and high built walls
>     adorn'd;
> It gave their leaders a secure repose;
> Honour to th' empire, terror to their foes.

This was no doubt the traditional account in his day, and the resemblance which York bears to the form of ancient Rome gives countenance to the opinion: The plan of Rome left by Fabius, represents it in the form of a bow, of which the Tyber was the string, as the Ouse may be said not unaptly to be the bow-string of York. Both these rivers runs directly through the cities which they water, and have contributed to their ancient splendour and present consequence. Drake is of opinion, that York was first planted and fortified by Agricola, and it is certain that when the emperor Adrian came into this island, in the year 124, he took up his station at York. Adrian brought into Britain to aid in the conquest of Caledonia, the Sixth Roman Legion, styled *Legio Sexta Victrix;* in the year 150 Eboracum was the most considerable Roman station; and Antoninus in his itinerary mentions it with the addition of "Legio VI. Victrix." Marcus Aurelius Lucius, a British king, is said to have been the first crowned head in the world that embraced christianity, and it is highly probable that this monarch was born in York, as it is recorded of his father, Coilus, that he lived, died and was buried here.[*] In the reign of Commodus, the Caledonians, encouraged by the lax discipline of the Roman soldiers, made a successful irruption into England, and after cutting in pieces the Roman army, ravaged the country, as far as York.[†] Marcellus Ulpius, aided by the Ninth Legion drove back the Caledonians within their own borders, and thus for a short time rescued the country from the terrible visitation of the northern invaders, but as the sword had placed the Romans in Britain, nothing but force could sustain them there.

Tradition now gives place to genuine history.[‡] The Roman power began to totter in their widely extended colonies. The banished Britons had become so bold as to ad-

[*] Geofry of Monmouth, and Historiæ August.

[†] Rapin.

[‡] Vide Eutropii hist. Roman.

vance to York, and under Fulgenius to undertake the siege of that city. Virius Lupus, the Propraetor in Britain, feeling his perilous situation wrote to the emperor Severus, "informing him of the insurrection and inroad of the Barbarians (as the native inhabitants were called) to beg that he might have either a greater force, or that the emperor would come over in person." Severus chose the latter; attended by his two sons, Caracalla and Geta, and by a numerous army, he arrived in Britain, in 207, and fixed his station at York. The invaders on his arrival retired to the north, and took up their stand in their fortresses beyond Adrian's Wall, extending from Newcastle to Carlisle. This did not satisfy the emperor: Though suffering under the combined influence of age and infirmity, and obliged to be carried in a horse litter, he marched from York against the Caledonians, penetrated to the extremity of the island, and subdued this hitherto fierce and unconquered nation. His next care was to build a stone wall about 80 miles in length, and of great strength, in the place where his predecessor Adrian had thrown up ramparts of earth; and thus the conquest seemed complete, but according to Dion it was not purchased without the loss of fifty thousand men. Severus having left his son Caracalla in the north, to superintend and facilitate the building of the wall, returned to York, where he struck coin, on which he designated himself, Britanicvs Maximvs, as conqueror of the island. For more than three years he lived and held his imperial court in the Prætorian palace of this city,[§] frequently giving judgment in judicial cases; and a rescript of his is still preserved in the Roman code, issued by the emperor, and dated from this city, on the 3d of the nones of May, in the consulate of Fustinus and Rufus, corresponding to the year 211, relating to the recovery of the right of possession of servants, or rather of slaves. At this period York shone forth with meridian splendour. The concourse of tributary kings, says Drake, of foreign ambassadors, and Roman nobles which crowned the courts of the sovereigns of the world, when the Roman empire was in its prime, elevated Eboracum to the height of sublunary grandeur. Before the time of Severus, a temple dedicated to Bellona, the goddess of war, was erected at York, and it is probable that its site, was without Bootham bar, near the place on which the Abbey of St. Mary's now

[§] The ground on which the imperial palace is supposed to have stood extends from Christ's church, to Aldwark, comprehending the site of all the houses, and gardens, on the east side of Goodramgate, and of St. Andrewgate.

stands. On the return of Severus from his northern conquest, he sought a temple to sacrifice to the gods who had crowned him with success, when he was led by an ignorant soothsayer to the temple of Bellona; this was looked upon as the presage to the emperor's death, and might in that superstitious age hasten the event. Before the death of Severus, but when his end was drawing nigh, the Caledonians again took up arms and attacked the Roman garrisons on the borders. The revival of this spirit of revolt threw the emperor into a fury, and he sent out his legions to put every man, woman, and child amongst the insurgents to the sword. These orders were given at York, and their character has been expressed in two Greek verses, which may be rendered thus—

" Let none escape you ; spread the slaughter
    wide ;
" Let not the womb the unborn infant hide
" From slaughter's cruel hand."

Before this bloody purpose could be fully executed, death overtook the emperor himself. His last words to his sons whom he left joint emperors, displayed the policy of a military tyrant, they were these—" I leave you, Antonines *(a term of affection)* a firm and steady government, if you will follow my steps and prove what you ought to be; but weak and tottering if otherwise. Do every thing that conduces to each others good; cherish the soldiery; and then you may despise the rest of mankind, A disturbed and every where distracted republic I found it, but to you I leave it firm and quiet —even the Britons. I have been all—and yet I am now no better for it." Then turning to the urn which was to hold his ashes he said—" Thou shalt hold what the whole world could not contain !" He then breathed his last.* His funeral obsequies were celebrated at a short distance from the city; his body was brought out in military array by the soldiers habited in his general's costume, and laid on a magnificent pile, erected for the purpose. His sons applied the lighted torch, and his remains being reduced to ashes, were placed in a porphyrite urn to be carried to Rome. On their arrival in the imperial city they were deposited in the monument of the Antonines, and the extraordinary ceremony of deification was conferred upon the deceased emperor by the senate and the people who valued military renown as the perfection of imperial virtue, That the memory of this great captain might survive in Britain, his grateful army with infinite labour raised three large hills or tumuli in the place where his funeral rites were per-

* On the 5th of February, 212.

formed, near the city of York, and which to this day bear the name of Severus's Hills. This is the opinion of Mr. Drake, but other historians maintain that the hills are natural elevations in the face of the country, and merely received their name from the funeral obsequies having been here performed.

On the death of Severus his two sons jointly assumed the imperial purple, but Caracalla, the elder, murdered his brother Geta in his mother's arms, and put to death at least 20,000 persons of both sexes, under the vague charge that they were " the friends of Geta." After disgracing Eboracum, with these and other abominable crimes, this monster returned to Rome, and afterwards repaired to Syria, where he was assassinated at the instigation of Opilius Macrinus, by Martialis, a desperate soldier, who had been refused the rank of centurion. During the century of repose which succeeded the departure of Caracalla, the Roman soldiers greatly improved the country by cutting down woods, draining marshes, and forming those noble roads and streets which to this day are called Roman.† It is worthy of remark, that Eboracum is the principal city in all their itinera or routes, and it is the only point from whence antiquaries can with certainty fix any Roman station in the North of England. In the next century Carausius himself, a Briton, landed in this island and procured himself to be proclaimed emperor at York. Under his usurpation, Britain, destined in a future age to obtain the empire of the sea, already assumed its natural and respectable station as a maritime power. Carausius fell by the hands of, and was succeeded by, Alectus, who reigned until the Roman emperor Constantius, surnamed Chlorus, landed in Britain, by whom Alectus was slain, and the province reduced to its former obedience. Of Carausius and Alectus it is observed, that they were both of plebeian origin, and that Alectus who had been a smith was slain by a sword of his own fabrication.

Constantius, who had many years before visited this island in the capacity of Roman Propraeter, when Aurelian was emperor, had married a British princess named Helena, the issue of which marriage was Constantine, surnamed the Great, born at York, in the year 272.‡ Constantius afterwards assumed the purple, and his last expedition into Britain was in the year 305. Two years after his arrival, the emperor was seized

† For the Roman roads of Yorkshire, see Vol. I. West-Riding History, page iii. and Vol. II. East and North-Riding Histories, page 5.

‡ Eumenius inter Panegy. Veteres,

with a mortal disease, and his son Constantine, who had been left at Rome in the hands of his colleagues Dioclesian and Galerius, as a pledge of his father's fidelity, abruptly quitted the imperial capital and repaired to York, to receive the commands of his dying parent. The sight of his eldest and best beloved son so revived the emperor, that raising himself in bed, and embracing him closely, he gave thanks to the gods for this unexpected favour, and said he could now die in peace, as he could leave his yet unaccomplished actions to be performed by him. Then gently lying down, he disposed of his affairs to his own mind, and taking leave of his children of both sexes, who, says Eusebius, like a choir stood and encompassed him, he expired, having previously delivered over to the hands of his eldest son, the imparial dominion.

Immediately upon the death of Constantius, his son and successor Constantine, was invested with the purple robe in his father's own place. The inauguration of this great monarch, in the city where he drew his first breath, serves to shed an additional lustre on Eboracum, and has procured for this ancient city the name of Altera Roma. The British soldiers in the pay of Rome saluted their illustrious countryman, emperor at York, and presented him with a *tufa*, or golden globe as a symbol of his sovereignty over the island of Britain. This emblem he highly-prized, and upon his conversion to Christianity, he placed a cross upon it and had it carried before him in all his processions. Since the time of Constantine, the tufa has become the usual sign of majesty, and is considered a part of the royal regalia. According to the Latin authors, Britain remained in peace during the long reign of Constantine, though the country was by no means free from the irruptions of the Picts and Scots. The emperor not only left York, but he afterwards quitted Italy and removed the seat of empire from Rome to Byzantium or Constantinople. The faith of the emperor had undergone a change, and in the year 312, according to Eusebius, he forsook the dark and barbarous superstitions of Paganism and embraced the Christian faith; on the same authority it is recorded, that the conversion of Constantine, is to be ascribed to the miraculous sign of a cross which was displayed in the heavens, while he meditated and prepared the Italian expedition. Before this extraordinary change took place he was a worshipper of the sun, and his filial piety had increased the council of Olympus, by the solemn apotheosis or deification of his father, Constantius.

Soon after the conquest of Italy, in the emperor made a solemn and authen declaration of his sentiments by the celebrated edict of Milan, which restored peace to the catholic church, and promulgated, truly christian principle of religious liberty, leaving every man to follow that religion which his own conscience dictated, and signing for this universal toleration these weighty reasons—first, that in this way peace and happiness of the people were consulted; and second, that by such a conduct, the Deity, whose seat is heaven, would be best propitiated. Britain did not with this change, though the native imperial potentate of York was the greater actor in scene.

From the departure of Constantine, ancient residence of " the Lords of the Universe" began to decline, and the materials British history, subsequent to that period, so scanty, that little more is known than naked fact, that the Romans, after an occupation of four hundred years, quitted island. During the greatest part of the period of occupation, the sixth legion of Roman army, and sometimes the ninth, latter of which merged into the former) sided at York. This legion consisted of six to seven thousand troops, of which one-tenth part was horse, and the remaining foot soldiers. The antiquities indicative of the long residence of the Romans here, less numerous than might have been supposed, if we did not take into the consideration, that fire, sword, ignorance, and superstition, have all contributed their assistance the devouring hand of time, to erase the monuments which the imperial power served to erect. It may seem strange, we have not to show any temples, theatres or palaces, which edifices must have made Eboracum shine with distinguished lustre; but the wonder will cease when in the following pages of this history we trace such horrid destruction of every thing both sacred and profane. To Christian ancestors we owe much of this destruction; their holy zeal rendered them anxious to eradicate every vestige of paganism, and the Roman altars and votive monuments were naturally enough consigned destruction under their Gothic hands. Still however, there are many Roman remains to be found here, and great quantities of coins, signets, fibulæ, urns and sarcophagi have been dug up and recovered through a period of fifteen centuries. The coins are all of the emperors, from Augustus to Gratian, and the catalogue of them as well as many other Roman antiquities found in this city, is preserved in the Appendix to Drake's Eboracum. The antiquaries, Camden, Burton, Thoresby, Drake, and others, have searched out and described some of the most remarkable of them. Nearly two centuries ago, a *theca* or repository for urns of a Roman family, was dug up here, but it was so little regarded at York, that in time it found its way to Hull, where it served as a trough for watering horses at a public inn! The inscription was partly obliterated, but it amounted to this— That Marcus Verecundus Diogenes, a native of Bury, in Gascoigny, overseer of the highways of the colony of York, died there; who, while living, made this monument for himself. In digging the foundation for a house on Bishop-hill the elder, in the year 1638, a small, but elegant urn, with figures in *basso relievo*, of sacrificing instruments, &c. on the sides* was found, which was presented to Charles I. when at York, by Sir Ferdinando Fairfax. The altar bears a heathen inscription, which may be thus translated—To the great and mighty Jupiter, and to all gods and goddesses, household and peculiar, *Publius Aelius Marcianus*, prefect of Cohort, for the preservation of his own health and that of his family, dedicated this altar to the great preserver.

The most remarkable sepulchral monument that has, in these latter ages, been discovered at York, is that of the standard bearer of the Ninth Roman Legion, dug up in the year 1688, in Trinity Gardens, near Micklegate, and described by our northern antiquary, the venerable Thoresby, in his Ducatus Leodiensis. The stone is about six feet high, and two feet in breadth, rising to the top with an angle: near the bottom of the stone is the inscription L. DVCCIVS. LVOFRVFJ. NVS. VIEN SIGNFLEG VIII. NN XXIIX. HSE. above which stands the figure of a Roman soldier, with the ensign of a cohort or manipulus in his right hand, and a corn meter in his left. This ancient relic was happily rescued by Bryan Fairfax, Esq. from demolition, by the workmen who had broken it in the middle, and were preparing to make use of it for two *troughs*, as they are called, to bind together a stone wall which they were erecting. By Mr. Fairfax's direction it was walled upright with the inscription and effigies in front, and was afterwards removed to Ribston, near Wetherby, by Sir Henry Goodrick, who first placed it in his own garden, and subsequently removed it to the more appropriate situation of the chapel yard.†

* Dr. Martin Lister's communication to the Royal Society.

† See Ribston, vol. i. page 580.

A part of a wall is yet standing in York, which is undoubtedly of Roman erection, and which probably served as an interior fortification to the city. It is the south wall of the Mint-yard, formerly the hospital of St. Laurence. This erection consists of a multangular tower, which leads to Bootham-bar, and a wall which ran the length of Coney or Coning-street, and Castlegate to the Foss. The outside, to the river, is faced with small *saxum quadratum*, of about four inches thick, and laid in rows like our modern brick work, but the length of the stones is irregular; from the foundation twenty courses of these small stones are laid, and after these five courses of bricks, which are succeeded by other twenty-two courses of stones, on which five more courses of Roman bricks are laid, beyond which the wall is imperfect and cap'd with modern building. The Roman bricks are about seventeen inches long, eleven inches broad, and two and a half inches thick, and the cement is so hard as to be almost imperishable. The tower is the same on the inside as the out, and has a communication with Bootham-bar, under the vallum or rampart that hides it in that way.— In the year 1716, a curious and antique bust, five inches high by four in breadth, representing the head of a beautiful female, was found in digging the ruins near St. Mary's Abbey, and is supposed to represent the head of Lucretia, the Roman Matron, whose wrongs expelled the Tarquins. The last specimen of antiquity mentioned by Drake, under this head of the history of York, is a noble Roman arch of the Tuscan order, standing in a principal gate of the city, facing the great road to the Metropolis, by way of Calcaria or Tadcaster. This arch, which is the chief in Micklegate-bar, is a triplit, and supports a massy pile of Gothic turrets. In Clifton-fields out of Bootham-bar, about three hundred yards from the city, several sarcophagi or stone coffins, and a great quantity of urns of different colours and sizes have been found. Campus Martius, anciently without the city of Rome, was the place where the funeral piles were lighted to consume the deceased Romans, and the presumption is, that Clifton-fields formed the Campus Martius of Eboracum. Almost all the memorials of the Romans which have presented themselves in this city, have been found by digging: Few of them have been found above ground, and it may be justly said, that modern York stands upon ancient Eboracum.

For a description of the Roman remains found previous to the year 1700, we are indebted to the indefatigable and elaborate historian of York; and for the descrition of those discovered during the last and the preceding century, as well as for much other interesting information, we have to offer our acknowledgments to Mr. William Hargrove's modernised edition of the Eboracum. From this latter source, we derive the following information relating to the Roman antiquities found in York since Mr. Drake's time :—In 1734, a small figure of a household god (Saturn) was found by a person digging a cellar in Walmgate; the composition of which the image is formed is a mixture of metal, and the workmanship exhibits all the elegance of a Roman mould. Into whose hands this relic has fallen is not known. Six years afterwards two curious Roman urns were dug up near the Mount without Micklegate-bar, one of them of glass coated with a silver-coloured substance called *electrum*, the other of lead, which falling into the hand of an ignorant plumber, was consigned to the melting-pot. A pedestal of grit with a short Roman inscription, was also found the same year, near Micklegate bar.

A Roman sepulchre, of singular form, was found in the year 1768, by some labourers who were preparing a piece of ground for a garden, near the city walls west of Micklegate-bar, and is described with the elaborate precision of an admirer of ancient Romans, by Dr. William White, in the transactions of the Antiquarian Society. The sepulchre was formed of Roman tiles, built up in the form of a roof, and making a triangle with the ground below. On the top was a covering of semi-circular tiles, of small diameter, so close as to prevent the least particle of earth from falling into the cavity, and each end of the dormitory was closed with a tile on which was inscribed LEG. IX. HIS. being doubtless the burying-place of a soldier of the *Legio nona Hispanica*. Two years afterwards, part of the foundation of a temple of Roman brick-work was discovered two feet below the surface, in Friars' Gardens, near Toft-green, beneath which was a flat grit stone with a Roman inscription, indicating that this was a temple, sacred to the Egyptian god SERAPIS, and was erected at the cost of Claudius Heronymianus, lieutenant of the Sixth Conquering Legion. In the same year was found on the banks of the Ouse, about a mile and a half east from the city, a number of ancient remains, consisting of pieces of pateræ (goblets) and urns, a stratum of oyster shells, with a number of bones of cattle strewn in various directions, collectively favouring the opinion that a Roman temple had stood here, and that these were the remains of idolatrous sacrifices offered in the dark ages of pagan idolatry. A massive

brass flaggon was also turned up by the plough, in a field near York, weighing 17lb. 4½oz. and calculated to contain five modern pints. This vessel stood on three legs, and the top of the lid exhibited a head or face apparently connected with the Heathen Mythology.

A small Roman votive altar of stone, six inches high and six inches in breadth at the base, bearing a Roman inscription somewhat impaired by time, but from which it appears that this relic was dedicated by a soldier of the Sixth Legion, to the mother of the Emperor Antonius Pius, was found in Micklegate, by the workmen, while digging a drain in the middle of the street, and after remaining for some years in the possession of Mrs. Mildred Bourchier, is now deposited in the Minster Library. Several other Roman remains were found with this altar, about eight or ten feet below the surface; and the workmen met with two or three firm pavements of pebbles one below another, beneath which were several fragments of beautiful red glazed pateræ, adorned · with figures of gods, birds, and vines, and one of them inscribed *tanuf*; there were also several small altars, and an earthen lamp with some Roman coins of Constantine the Great.

The following remains have been found in the present century, and for ages yet to come the inexhaustible mines of antiquarian wealth, on which the city of York stands, will doubtless, yield their contributions to the cabinets of the curious. In June, 1802, the workmen, while digging for the foundations of the New Gaol, near the site of the Old Bastile Hill, found about one hundred silver pennies of William the Devastator in good preservation, though it is probable that they have lain in the ground nearly eight centuries. According to Leland, a castle anciently stood on this site. The most venerable sepulchral remains which have been presented to the antiquary for many years, were discovered in September, 1804, by the workmen while digging a large drain in the Minster-yard, from south to west of the cathedral. After passing through a stratum of human bones under which were two coffins, hollowed out of the solid stone, the workmen came to eleven or twelve coffins, each formed of stone (apparently brought from the quarries of Malton) loosely placed together, without cement or fastening. Each of these coffins was covered with a rough flag four inches thick, under which skeletons were found laid on the bare earth, the coffins being without bottoms. The situation being wet, some of the coffins contained a quantity of clear water, through which the skeletons appeared entire, but when the water was removed and the bodies exposed to the air, they crumbled into dust. The singular form of these coffins, the rough manner in which they were constructed; and their depth in the earth, prove their great antiquity, and confirm the belief that they are vestiges not merely of Roman or Saxon times, but that they contain remains of our Aboriginal ancestors. On Monday, the 17th of August, 1807, while the workmen were preparing the foundations for a building near Barstow's Hospital, in the suburbs of York, a Roman vault presented itself about four feet from the surface, which was eight feet long by five feet wide, and six feet high, built of stone and arched over with Roman brick. A coffin of rag stone grit, about seven feet long, occupies nearly the whole of the vault, and in the coffin is a human skeleton entire, with the teeth complete, supposed to be the remains of a Roman lady, consigned to the mansions of the dead fourteen centuries ago. Near the skull, which is remarkably small, was found a lachrimatory, in which vessels the ancients deposited the tears they shed for their departed friends. The workmen also found at the same time, not far from the vault, a large red coloured urn, in which were ashes, and the partially burnt bones of a human body. The whole collection is preserved for the inspection of the curious, and may be seen in the place where they have lain undisturbed, while upwards of forty generations of men have passed over the stage of human existence. In a field without Bootham bar, two Roman stone coffins were dug up in March, 1813, each containing a skeleton entire, with the teeth, the most imperishable part of man when dead, and the most liable to decay when living, entire. These coffins are now deposited in the cathedral amongst other sepulchral antiquities, as objects of interest to the curious. In May in the same year, two stone coffins seven feet in length, and three feet wide, cut out of a solid block of stone which was left six inches thick, were dug up in a gravel pit near Fulford church, in each of which was a human skeleton, and a small quantity of a white substance resembling lime saturated with grease. These remains are now in the possession of R. Simpson, Esq. of Bootham. Several conjectures have been formed as to the identity of the occupants of these masonic encasements, and as one of them had evidently undergone decapitation, from his skull having been found on the breast, it was erroneously imagined that this was Archbishop Scroope, the ardent reformer of the fifteenth century, who was treacherously seized by the Earl of Westmoreland, and afterwards beheaded. At Aldbrough, the

site of ancient Isurium, numerous specimens of tesselated pavements have often been found, but it was not till the year 1814, that any remains of this kind were ever discovered at York. In the month of March in that year, a beautiful specimen of this Mosaic work was discovered adjoining the rampart within Micklegate bar, which has been cleared and enclosed, and is, along with a number of other Roman remains, preserved for the inspection of the curious.

The decline of the Roman power obliged them to abandon their distant conquests, and in the reign of Theodosius the younger, the empire sunk so fast, that Britain, and of course York, the city of the Brigantines, as it was called, was no longer a residence for the " lords of the universe." Rome and York both declined together, and to them might be applied the reflection of the old poet, on the fall of Carthage:

Unhappy men! to mourn our lives' short date,
When cities, realms, and empires share our fate.

During the period between the evacuation of Britain by the Romans, and the conquest of this island by the Normans, the city of York partook largely in the vicissitudes to which the country was exposed. The Picts and the Scots, the Saxons and the Danes, each in succession, erected their standards before its gates, and obtained possession of the city. The general history of Northumbria, during these early ages, is already sketched in this work, under the head of YORKSHIRE;[*] and it will suffice here, to remark of this epoch, that York, though shorn of that splendour which imperial Rome conferred, still maintained a distinguished rank as a metropolitan city, and as the centre of commercial attraction. The celebrated instructor of Charlemagne, who wrote in the ninth century, thus speaks of York :—

" Quo variis populis et regnis undique lecti,
Spe lucri venunt quærentes divite terra,
Divitias, sedem sibimet lucrumque laresumque."

" Hither for gain from various foreign ports
Come trading people, seeking opulence,
And a secure abode in wealthy land."

At this period, York was the seat not only of trade, but of letters; she was, indeed, the Athens of that dark age, and the library collected by Archbishop Egbert, and placed in the cathedral, ranked amongst the first in Christendom. Alcuin, in one of his letters to his royal pupil, Charlemagne, re-

* See vol. 1. page iv.

quests that scholars may be sent from France, to copy the works deposited here, " that the garden of letters may not be shut up in York; but that some of its fruits may be placed in the paradise of Tours."[*] William, of Malmsbury, speaking of this library, says, " it is the noblest repository and cabinet of arts and sciences in the whole world."

Among the most celebrated of the British monarchs before the conquest, was King Arthur. This monarch expelled the Saxons from York, and almost from the Island, in the year 520, by the sanguinary battle of Baden Hills, in which 90,000 of the enemy were slain. Arthur, after the defeat of the Saxons, undertook an expedition into Scotland, with a determination to destroy that ancient seat of enmity from one end to the other. From this purpose he was dissuaded by the Bishops. The Scots had just received the gospel, and it was represented to the King, by his spiritual guides, in the true spirit of that religion which he professed, that Christians ought not to spill the blood of Christians—a maxim, that has unfortunately for the world, not been sufficiently inculcated in modern times. Arthur, after his expedition to Scotland, returned to York, where he convened an assembly of the clergy and people, to heal the divisions, and to regulate the affairs of the church. At this time, this great monarch, and his clergy, with the nobility, and the soldiers, kept their Christmas in York. This was the first festival of the kind ever celebrated in Britain, and from which, all those ever since held have taken their model. " The latter end of December," says the historian,[†] "was spent in mirth, jollity, drinking, and the vices that are too often their consequences, so that the representations of the old heathenish feasts, dedicated to Saturn, were here again revived. Gifts were sent mutually from one to another, frequent invitations passed between friends, and domestic offenders were not punished. All this was to celebrate the nativity of Christ, then, as they say, born." Arthur, after all his glory, had the misfortune to be slain in a rebellion of his own subjects, and by the hands of his own nephew. From his death, violent dissentions arose among the British princes, and the Saxons again so completely prevailed, as to gain an entire conquest over the whole kingdom. Those Britons, who would not submit to pass under the Saxon yoke, sought shelter in the Cambrian moun-

* Epist. Alcuini ad Carolum Regem. Coll. I. page 399.
† Buchanan.

tains, where their posterity, according to Welsh history, have ever since maintained their station.

It does not belong to this work to trace the events of the Heptarchy, of which period it has been observed, with some justice, that if " the old wives' tales and friars' dreams" be expunged, this volume of history will be reduced to a page. But it is proper to record, that in the year 867, the Danes, who had long envied the happiness of their neighbours, the Saxons, in the possession of the greatest and the wealthiest island in Europe, fitted up a mighty fleet, and entered the Humber in the spring, with a strong invading army, under the command of Hinguar and Hubba. Their first operation was against York, where a sanguinary battle was fought in the midst of the city, and the two Saxon kings, Osbert and Ella, being slain in the engagement, the city fell into the hands of the Danish invaders. In the conflict, York was reduced to a heap of ruins, by the enraged barbarians, who spared neither palace nor cottage, age, or sex. " Matrons and virgins," says Hoveden,[*] were ravished at pleasure. The husband and wife either dead or dying, were tossed together. The infant snatched from its mother's breast was carried to the threshold, and there left butchered at its parents' door, to make the general cry more hideous." For some ages the struggle was maintained in England between the Saxons and the Danes, but in the year 1010 the power of the former was extinguished. The Danes, under Sweyn, their sovereign, advanced into Northumbria, with a powerful army, and pitched their tents on the banks of the Ouse. To this place, Ethelred, the Anglo-Saxon monarch, with an army strengthened by a number of Scots, marched to give them battle. The engagement, which took place near York, was bloody and well contested. Ethelred fought to retain, and Sweyn to obtain a kingdom. Victory at length declared for the Danes, and Ethelred, with a few of his followers, seising a boat, passed over the Ouse, and fled into Normandy, leaving his crown and his kingdom to the conqueror. The Danish viceroys, or Comites Northumbriæ, took up their residence at York, while their sovereigns not unfrequently made this city the royal residence. The death of Sweyn, who breathed his last at Gainsborough, took place in the year 1014, and he was succeeded by his son, Canute, the most powerful monarch of his time. The reproof given by this King to his fawning courtiers, is so just and impressive, that its memory has survived through eight centuries. Some of these flatterers breaking out in expressions of admiration of his power and grandeur, exclaimed, that to him, every thing was possible. Upon which, Canute ordered his chair to be placed upon the sea-shore, while the tide was rising; as the waters approached, he commanded them with a voice of authority to retire, and to obey the lord of the ocean. For some time he feigned to sit in expectation of their submission, but the sea still advanced towards him, and began to wash him with its billows; on which he turned to his courtiers, and said, " Behold how feeble and impotent is man. Power resideth in one Being alone, in whose hands are the elements of nature, and who alone can say to the ocean—Thus far shalt thou go and no farther, and who can level with his nod the most towering piles of pride and ambition."

On the death of Canute, in 1035, Harold, his second son, surnamed Harefoot, succeeded to his British dominions; this monarch was succeeded by Hardicanute, a licentious tyrant, who died two years after his accession, at the nuptials of a Danish lord. Edward, the Confessor, though not the hereditary descendant, was raised to the throne by the voice of the people, to the exclusion of Sweyn, the Danish claimant, and was the last of the Saxon line who ruled in England. Harold, the son of Godwin, succeeded Edward, but was opposed by his brother Tosti, at whose instance, Harfager, the King of Norway, undertook the invasion of this kingdom, with a numerous and well appointed army, embarked on board a kind of Norwegian armada. This mighty armament entered the Humber, in the autumn of 1066, and the ships sailed up the Ouse, as far as Riccall, within ten miles of York; where they were moored. Having landed their forces, the invaders marched to York, which city they took by storm, after a desperate conflict, fought at Fulford, on the eve of St. Matthew, with Morcar, the governor, and Edwin, Earl of Chester. Harold no sooner heard of the arrival of the Norwegians, than he marched to York, at the head of a powerful army. On his approach, the invaders quitted the city, and took up a strong position to the East of York, having the Derwent in front, the Ouse to the right, and their navy on the left. Harold, disregarding the advantageous position of the enemy, determined to cross the wooden bridge which passed over the river, and to attack them in their trenches. His army was put in motion early in the morning, but an impediment, as the historians say, was interposed by a champion, in the Norwegian army, who placing himself on the bridge, kept by his own individual prowess the whole British army at bay for three hours! This hero being at length slain by a dart, the English army passed the bridge, and attacking the enemy in their trenches, sword in hand, victory declared on the side of Harold. The King of Norway and Tosti were both slain; and their army, which consisted of sixty thousand men, suffered so complete an overthrow, that though from five to six hundred vessels were necessary to bring them to England, twenty vessels were sufficient to carry back the miserable remains that survived the slaughter. This battle, which commenced at sun rise, and did not terminate till three o'clock in the afternoon, was fought at Stamford Bridge,* on the 23d of September, 1066. The spoil taken by the victors was immense, and it is represented, that the gold alone which the Norwegians left behind them, was as much as twelve men could carry on their shoulders.† Harold's triumph was of short duration. Returning to York, on the night of the battle, he gave orders for solemn feasts and rejoicings to begin the next day. Scarcely had these demonstrations of public joy commenced, when a messenger arrived from the South, and announced to Harold, as he sat in state, at a magnificent entertainment, that Duke William of Normandy, had landed with a mighty army, at Pevensey, in Sussex. The recently acquired victory of Harold, though great and honourable, proved in the main prejudicial to his interests, and may be regarded as the immediate cause of his ruin. He had lost many of his bravest officers and soldiers in the action; and he had disgusted the survivors, by refusing to distribute among them the Norwegian spoils. On receiving the intelligence of the arrival of William, the King marched at the head of his army, through London, to Sussex, in order to expel the invaders. Here the sanguinary battle of Hastings was fought, only nine days after the battle of Stamford Bridge, and here Harold lost both his kingdom and his life.

During the heptarchy, York was reduced from the capital of a kingdom, to the capital of an earldom. In this state it remained till the reign of Edward, the Confessor, in whose time it suffered a still greater revolution: for though it is the generally received opinion, that Alfred first divided England into counties, shires, or shrievalties, towards the close of the ninth century, and appointed a chief officer to govern them, called a Shire-reve, or Sheriff, yet it does not appear that this change took

* See Stamford Bridge in this volume.
† Camden.

place in the north, earlier than the middle of the eleventh century, when the ancient kingdom of Northumbria, which extended from the Humber to the Tweed, and from the German ocean to the Irish sea, was split into shires under the designation of 𝕰𝖚𝖗𝖊𝖜𝖎𝖈𝖐𝖘𝖈𝖎𝖗𝖊, 𝕽𝖎𝖈𝖍𝖒𝖚𝖓𝖉𝖊𝖘𝖊𝖎𝖗𝖊, 𝕷𝖔𝖓𝖈𝖆𝖘𝖙𝖗𝖊𝖘𝖊𝖎𝖗𝖊, 𝕮𝖆𝖕𝖑𝖆𝖓𝖉𝖊, since called the 𝕭𝖎𝖘𝖍𝖔𝖕𝖗𝖎𝖈𝖐 𝖔𝖋 𝕯𝖚𝖗𝖍𝖆𝖒, 𝖂𝖊𝖘𝖙𝖒𝖊𝖗𝖎𝖑𝖔𝖓𝖉𝖊 & 𝕮𝖚𝖒𝖇𝖗𝖊𝖑𝖔𝖓𝖉𝖊,

No sooner was William the Conqueror, established on the English throne, than he showed that his policy was to root out the ancient nobility, and to degrade the native inhabitants of the humbler classes, to the situation of miserable slaves. In the North, where the spirit of liberty and independence has always been cherished, the tyrant was determined to rivet his chains. For this purpose, Robert, the Norman, was sent down to Durham, with a guard of 700 men; but the inhabitants rose upon the governor, and exterminated both him and his guard. William once more drew his conquering sword, which he was not soon inclined to sheathe. He marched into York, at the head of a powerful army, and the city with its two castles, were speedily garrisoned with Norman soldiers. The Saxon nobles in this city had manifested a disposition to shake off the Norman yoke, and on the arrival of William, they fled into Scotland, where they were joined by Malcolm, the Scottish king. The Danes soon after united in the confederacy, and arrived in the Humber with a powerful army, under the command of Osbern, brother to the Danish king. Their first operation was against York, which they carried on the 19th of September, 1069, sword in hand, in the midst of flames, enkindled by the Normans, to prevent the suburbs from being made useful to the besiegers. In this fire, the invaluable library of the cathedral was, to the irreparable injury of learning, totally destroyed. William no sooner heard that the garrison of York had been taken by his enemies, and that three thousand of his troops had been put to the sword, than he hastened, at the head of a powerful army, into the North: and on his march thither was often heard to swear, " by God's splendour," which was his favourite oath, that he " would not leave a soul of them alive." On his arrival in Yorkshire, he had the address to corrupt Osbern, the Danish general, and to induce him to quit the country with his army, leaving his allies to the vengeance of the ruthless tyrant. For six months the siege of York was prosecuted with all the means which the Conqueror could command. During this time, Waltheof the governor, and his troops displayed prodigies of valour and constancy; but at length famine began to rage in the city with so much violence that the garrison was obliged to capitulate. At first the Conqueror affected to display some degree of forbearance, but it was only the better to secure his victims; a pretence was soon found to dispatch the gallant Waltheof, by the hand of the executioner; and, it is said, that he was the first nobleman ever beheaded in England. Upon the ancient kingdom of Northumbria, the Norman looked as the nest of rebellion. Under this impression, and in order to gratify his own blood-thirsty nature; he razed the city of York to the ground, and with it fell all the principal nobility and gentry in the North, and a large portion of the inhabitants. The garrison, which consisted of English and Scotch troops, notwithstanding the articles of capitulation, all perished, " and this noble city," says William, of Malmsbury, himself a Norman, " was wasted by famine, fire, and sword to the very roots." Nor did the tyrant stop here: he laid the whole country waste, from the Humber to the Tweed, and rendered it so complete a scene of desolation, that for nine years neither the plough nor the spade was put into the ground; and such was the wretched state of the inhabitants who escaped the sword, that they were forced to eat dogs and cats, horses, and even human flesh, to preserve their miserable existence. This account is confirmed by Roger Hoveden, and Simeon of Durham, as well as by the concurrent testimony of all the historians of those times, and from that day to this, York has never regained its ancient splendour. Before the Norman conquest the city of London was inferior to York,* and the author of the Polychronicon writes, that before it was burnt by William, York seemed as fair as the city of Rome, and was justly enough, by William Harrison, stiled, *Altera Roma*. According to Leland, the suburbs at this time extended to the towns a mile round the city.

Conscious of the detestation in which he was held, William entertained a perpetual jealousy of the English people. In the wantonness of power he obliged them every night to extinguish their fires and candles, at the ring of a bell, called " The Curfew:" he also caused a survey to be made of all the lands in the kingdom, which were unregistered in the Domesday book, many of the estates of the nobles in Yorkshire, as in other

* J. Hardynge.

parts of the kingdom, he wrested from their rightful owners and bestowed upon his rapacious followers.

For half a century the history of York is almost a blank; but in the reign of Stephen, in the year 1137, it appears once more to have reared its head, when it was again destroyed by an accidental fire, which burnt down the cathedral, the abbey of St. Mary's, with thirty-nine parish churches in the city, and Trinity church in the suburbs. At this awful juncture, David, king of Scotland entered England, at the head of a powerful army, and ravaged and laid waste the country to the very gates of the city of York. Roused into energy by these accumulated disasters, Thurstan, the archbishop, who acted as Stephen's viceroy in the north, summoned the neighbouring barons, and exhorted them to repel the enemy. Enraged to see their country desolated by the invaders, they each of them in their district collected a considerable force, which assembled at Northallerton, and totally defeated the Scotch in the famous *Battle of the Standard.*

For seven centuries York had exhibited a series of sanguinary wars, and repeated desolations; from this period it enjoyed, for some ages, the blessings of peace, and again rose to wealth and importance. In less than fifty years after the terrible conflagration in the reign of Stephen, Henry II. under pretence of raising money for the holy wars, imposed upon his subjects a contribution of one-tenth of their moveables, and demanded from the city of York, one-half of the sum that he required from London. At that period York was eminent for trade, and in the 27th year of the reign of Edward III. the staple trade of wool, which had before been at Bruges, in Flanders, was fixed in this city. Many of the merchants of York were members of "the corporation of the staple," established at Calais, and the woollen manufacture flourished in York so late as the reign of Henry VIII. In that reign an act was passed regarding one branch of the manufacture, the preamble of which sets forth, that "Whereas the city of York being one of the ancientest and greatest cities within the realm of England, before this time hath maynteyned and upholden by divers and sundry handicrafts there used, and most principally by making and weaving coverlets and coverings for beds, and thereby a great number of the inhabitants and people of the said city and suburbs thereof, and other places within the city of York, have been daily set on work in spinning, dyeing, carding, and weaving of the said coverlets," &c.

* See Northallerton.

This trade continued to prevail for some ages afterwards, but in the year 1736, when the author of the Eboracum published his book, York was no longer a manufacturing city, nor has the staple trade, which has made the West-Riding its principal seat, ever returned to this ancient capital.

In the ages following the Norman conquest, York was often visited by the kings of England. Henry II. held the first parliament ever mentioned in history by that name, in this city, in the year 1160, in which Malcolm, king of Scotland, appeared, and did homage for the territories which he held of the English crown. Eleven years afterwards, the same king called another parliament, or convention of the bishops and barons at York, to which he summoned William the successor of Malcolm, to do homage for the kingdom of Scotland; on which occasion the Scotch king deposited on the altar of St. Peter, in the cathedral church, his breast plate, spear, and saddle, in memorial of his subjection.

At the commencement of the reign of Richard I. York became the scene of a horrible persecution and massacre, which will be ever memorable in the annals of this city. The prejudices of the age had stigmatised the lenders of money on interest with the odious name of *usurers*, and the crusades to the holy land to rescue Jerusalem from the hands of the Saracens, had enflamed the zeal of the nation against every body of men not bearing the name of christian. The Jews were a people first introduced into England, by William the Conqueror, and in York, where a number of them settled soon after the conquest, they might be viewed with some portion of that horror which the bloody deeds of the tyrant so naturally excited. These accumulated causes of hostility engendered in the minds of the people an implacable hatred towards them, and the claims which they had upon the estates of those to whom they had lent money aggravated the public hostility. To obtain popular favour, the king, who was crowned with great pomp at Westminster, strictly enjoined and commanded that no Jew whatever should appear at his coronation. Notwithstanding this order two of the principal Jews in York, of the names of Benedict and Jocenus went from hence to London, with a pompous retinue in order to meet their brethren, and to present presents to the king, as a peace-offering, at his coronation. On the day of the ceremonial, many of the Jews mixed in the crowd, and the populace, with a savage ferocity, commenced a general massacre upon them in London, plundered their property, burnt down their houses, and destroyed numbers of their wives and children. The king issued forthwith a proclamation to stop these proceedings, but the example of the metropolis spread into various parts of the country, and similar scenes, though on a smaller scale, were transacted at Norwich, Lynn, Stamford, and York. Benedict and Jocenus, the York Jews, were attacked on their way to the coronation, and Benedict being grievously bruised and wounded, was dragged into a church, where he was forced to renounce Judaism, and to submit to the ceremony of baptism. This conversion, the heroic Israelite, with the zeal of a Daniel, steadily disclaimed, and when brought the next day into the presence of the king, and asked whether he was a christian or no, he answered, no! he was a Jew, and should die in that faith. To the honour of the king he was restored to his friends, but to the reproach of his brutal assailants he died shortly after of his bruises. Jocenus returned to York, where a still more awful fate awaited him. Either by accident or design, the city of York took fire, in the midst of a boisterous night, and the flames spread in all directions. This calamity was seized upon to renew the persecution against the Jews, and while the citizens were engaged in extinguishing the flames, the house of Benedict was violently entered by the lawless rabble, who murdered the wife and children of the deceased Jew, and applied to their own use all the property on which they could lay their rapacious hands. Jocenus, alarmed for his own safety, sought refuge in the castle, to which he removed his family and effects, and his example was followed by nearly all the other Jews in the city. The governor of the castle having some business without its walls, left it for a short time in the hands of the Jews, who, under an apprehension that he might have joined in the conspiracy with their enemies, refused to re-admit him on his return. The high sheriff, a man more under the guidance of his passions than of his judgment, enraged by this indignity, issued his writ of *posse comitatus* to raise the country to besiege and take the castle. And now, says Hemingford, the canon of Gisburgh, was shown the zeal of a Christian populace. An innumerable company of armed men, as well from the city as from other parts of the county, rose simultaneously, and begirt the fortress. The high sheriff began to repent of his inconsiderate order, and the wiser and better sort of the citizens stood aloof from a flood that might soon overwhelm themselves. A great many of the clergy, however, joined the besiegers, and a certain fanatical friar, clad in a white vesture, was every where seen crying out—"the enemies of Christ must be destroyed." This zealot was amongst the first to suffer the destruction he announced, for in his endeavour to fix the battering engines against the walls, a large stone fell upon his head, and dashed out his brains. Driven to extremities, the Jews held a council, and offered, as Hoveden says, a mighty sum of money to be allowed to escape with their lives, but this offer was rejected. On which, as M. Paris observes, a certain foreign rabbin, or doctor of their law, stood up amongst them and said,— "Men of Israel, our creator has commanded that we should at any time be ready to die for our law; when he gave us life he enjoined that with our own hands, and of our own accord, we should devoutly restore it to him again, rather than submit to the cruelty of our enemies." This invitation to imitate the example of the followers of Josephus, in the cave of Jotapata, was embraced by many of the Jews, but others chose rather to try the victors' clemency. Before the self-devoted victims began to execute the sentence upon each other, they set fire to the castle, and committed all their property to the flames, to prevent it from falling into the hands of their enemies. The rabbin then directed that the husbands should cut the throats of their own wives and children, and Jocenus began the execution first, by applying the knife to the throats of Anne, his wife, and his five children! The example was speedily followed by the other masters of families, and afterwards, as a mark of peculiar honour, the Rabbin cut the throat of Jocenus himself! The last of the victims, was the self-devoted adviser of the deed, who probably was the only actual suicide. At dawn the next morning, the survivors announced the horrid catastrophe which had befallen their brethren, to the besiegers, casting the dead bodies of the victims over the wall, to convince them of the reality of their story. At the same time they supplicated for mercy, with an assurance, that if it was granted to them, they would all become Christians. The merciless Barbarians pretending to compassionate their sufferings, obtained admission into the castle. No sooner was this effected, than they flew upon the poor Jews, and slew every one of them, though to the last they cried out for baptism. With their hands reeking with blood, the murderers hastened to the cathedral, where the bonds, which the Christians had given to the Jews, (money lenders) were deposited. These documents they took out of the chests, and committed to the flames, thus freeing themselves and others from their obligations. This massacre happened at York, on the 11th of March, 1189; and it is estimated, that no fewer than from fifteen hundred to two thousand Jews in York, fell victims to the sanguinary persecution. When the news of these deeds of blood reached the king, who had embarked for the holy land, he sent orders to his chancellor and regent, the Bishop of Ely, to go down into Yorkshire, and execute strict justice upon the offenders; but the regent ill discharged the trust confided to him, for he contented himself by the imposition of a few mulcts and fines upon the inhabitants, and not a single individual was executed, though the crime might have been brought home to numbers, not only amongst the citizens, but also amongst persons of the military and ecclesiastical orders. Notwithstanding the horrors of this sanguinary persecution, a new colony of Jews settled in York in the same reign, and remained in this city till the time of Edward I. and Jubbergate and Jewberry, probably both derive their names from having been the favourite seats of their residence.

In the reign of King John, a convention was held at York between the English and Scotch kings and their nobles, in which an existing difference was settled by an agreement that the two sons of the former should marry the two daughters of the latter. In the last year of the troublous reign of king John, the northern barons laid siege to York, but retreated from before its walls, on receiving one thousand marks from its inhabitants.

The marriage of the daughter of Henry III. king of England, to Alexander, the third son of the king of Scotland, took place in the cathedral church of this city amidst very splendid festivities in the year 1230.

In 1298, another parliament sat at York, when the English barons attended, and the king's confirmation of Magna Charta, and also Charta de Forresta, was read to them. During this reign of Edward I. the courts of justice were removed from London to York, where they remained for several months, till the king's return after the famous battle of Falkirk. York, then ranked amongst the English ports, but Hull had already begun to rise into fame as a maritime town, and soon absorbed a large share of the commerce which was formerly confined to this city.

In this reign the flame broke out, which for nearly a century involved England and Scotland in that general conflagration, with the vents of which every reader of English history is familiar. The Scots marched into England in great force, and having laid the country waste to the gates of York, retired. The archbishop fired with indignation, raised an army of priests, monks, and others, to the amount of ten thousand men, with which he pursued the spoilers, and overtook them at Myton-upon-Swale, in the neighbourhood of Boroughbridge, where he attacked them with more fury than skill, and where he suffered a signal defeat.[*]

The reign of Edward III. which shines with so much lustre in the annals of England, constitutes a splendid period in the history of York. In the year 1327, the first year of his reign; that monarch ordered his whole army to rendezvous in this city, in order to oppose Robert Bruce, king of Scotland, who, with an army of twenty thousand horse was ravaging the northern part of the kingdom. While Edward lay at York preparing for this expedition, there came to his aid John, Lord Beaumont, of Hainault, one of the bravest knights of the age, accompanied with other gallant knights and gentlemen, who, with his retinue composed a band of five hundred, or according to Knighton, of two thousand men. Most of these foreigners were lodged in the suburbs; but to Lord John himself the king assigned the abbey of White Monks in the city. The king with the queen's mother, lodged in the monastery belonging to the Friars Minors, which must have been an extensive and stately building, since each of them kept a separate court, and that of the king was very magnificent. For six weeks, Edward had his court at York, with an army of sixty thousand men, which, notwithstanding its numbers, was well supplied with provisions, of which the citizens felt no lack. The foreigners too had reason to be satisfied with their entertainment, but jealousies arose between them and the English, which were not terminated without bloodshed. On Trinity Sunday, the king gave a magnificent entertainment at the monastery. To his usual retinue of five hundred knights, he added sixty more; and the queen's mother had in her suite sixty ladies of the highest rank and greatest beauty in England. At night was given a splendid ball, but while the courtiers were in the midst of their amusement " a strange and hideous noise interrupted them and alarmed the whole court." A contest had arisen between the foreign auxiliaries and a body of English archers, who lodged with them in the suburbs; and hostilities being once begun abettors successively came in on both sides, till near three thousand of the archers were collected. Many of the Hainaulters were slain, and the rest were obliged to retire and fortify themselves in their quarters. During the quarrel, part of the city took fire, and it was with equal dif

[*] See Myton, Vol. II.

ficulty that the king was able to subdue the flames and to restrain the fiery spirits with which he had to contend. The foreigners breathed nothing but vengeance, and on the night following, headed by their officers, they fell upon the Lincolnshire and North-amptonshire archers, and slew about three hundred of them. This rash act induced about six thousand of the English to combine, and to take the desperate resolution to sacrifice every soul of the Hainaulters to the manes of their countrymen. By the firmness and wise precautions of the king, this catastrophe was arrested and the tranquillity of the city was ultimately restored. During these transactions ambassadors arrived in York from Scotland to treat for peace, but after some weeks the negociations broke off, and the king with all his barons marched at the head of his whole army against the Scots, in all the martial pomp of those chivalrous times. It is not the province of this history to follow Edward through his campaigns; suffice it to say, that after a keen pursuit the Scotch army was at last overtaken and couped up by the English in Stanhope-park, from which they were suffered to escape by the treachery of Lord Mortimer, at the moment when they were ready to surrender from the cravings of famine. Edward, chagrined at the loss of his prey, when it seemed within his grasp, returned to York and afterwards to London, having previously dismissed Lord John of Hainault, to the Continent, bounteously rewarded for his services. The next year Lord John, returned with his niece Philippa, the most celebrated beauty of the age, and with a great retinue conducted her to York, where the court then was, in order to her marriage with the king in this city. On the Sunday before the eve of St. Paul's conversion in the year 1329, the marriage was publicly solemnised in the cathedral, by the archbishop. Upon these happy nuptials, says Froissart, the whole kingdom teemed with joy, and the court at York expressed these feelings in a more than ordinary manner; for three weeks the feastings were continued without intermission, there were nothing but justs and tournaments in the day time, and maskings, revels, and interludes with songs and dances in the night. The Hainault soldiery, actuated by a licentious and revengeful spirit, took advantage of this carnival to treat the inhabitants with outrage and violence, and to such an excess did they carry their misconduct, that they ravished several of the wives, daughters, and maid servants of the inhabitants, and set fire to the suburbs of the city, by which a whole parish was nearly destroyed. The citizens scandalized by those proceed-

ings, challenged the Hainaulters to battle; this challenge was accepted, and the battle was fought in a street called Watling-gate, with such desperate fury that five hundred and twenty-seven of the foreigners were slain or drowned in the Ouse, and two hundred and forty-two fell of the English. During the wars in France, in which Edward and his renowned son, the Black Prince, gained the memorable victories of Crecy and Poictiers, and rendered captive the French king. David Bruce, the competitor of John Baliol, king of Scotland, undertook to invade England, which was then left to the sole government of the queen. Bruce penetrated to the gates of York, and burnt part of the suburbs, having laid waste the country through which he passed with fire and sword. Philippa, the queen regent, then at York, having collected a powerful army, repulsed the invaders, and pursued them to Neville's cross, in the county of Durham, where, on the 17th of October, 1347, she gained a signal victory, having slain fifteen thousand of the Scots, and taken Bruce prisoner. The victorious queen having rescued her country from the hands of these cruel invaders, returned to York, and subsequently presented king David to her husband and sovereign.

The unfortunate reign of Richard II. was extremely favourable to the citizens of York. That monarch visited the city several times, and granted the citizens many charters, immunities, and privileges. On his visit to York, in the year 1389, to adjust a dispute between the archbishop and the dean and chapter, the king took his sword from his side, and gave it to be borne before William de Selby, who was then dignified with the title of Lord Mayor, which is retained to the present day by the first magistrate of this city.* In this reign Edmund

* A maximum upon the necessaries of life was fixed in the reign of Edward I. which continued for many years with certain modifications, and in the year 1393, an ordinance for the price of victuals and drink was proclaimed in a full court at York, "by the advice and consent of our lord the king's justices" in manner following:—

| | |
|---|---|
| Good wheaten bread 4 loaves per | i |
| Strong beer per gallon .................. | ⅓ |
| Claret wine per gallon .................. | viii |
| Red wine, the best .................. | viii |
| A carcase of choice beef ............ xx | iv |
| A Scotch cow .................. | x |
| A carcase of mutton .................. | xx |
| ———— of the best veal ......... ii | vi |
| ———— a lamb ......... ......... | viii |
| A hog, the best ......................... iii | iv |
| A capon .................. | iv |
| A hen .................. | i |
| A fat goose.......................... | iv |
| A fresh salmon, the largest & best ii | |
| Oats per bushel.................. | i⅓ |

Langley, the fifth son of Edward III. was created the first Duke of York. A contagious distemper, of the nature of a plague, raged with great violence throughout England, of which malady there died, in the city of York alone, in the years 1390 and 1391, twelve thousand souls. In the nineteenth year of the king's reign two sheriffs were appointed instead of three bailiffs, and the city of York was erected into a county of itself.

The inhabitants of York were not unmindful of these benefactions and royal concessions, and they took the first opportunity to manifest their gratitude to Richard, even after the deposition and murder in Pontefract castle. Henry Percy, Earl of Northumberland, having lost his brother and son in the battle of Shrewsbury, Richard Scroop, Archbishop of York, whose brother the king (Henry IV.) had beheaded, and Thomas Mowbray, Earl Marshal of England, whose father died in exile, united with Lords Falconberg, Bardolf, Hastings, and others, in a conspiracy to depose the occupier of Richard's throne. The archbishop's impatience precipitated the disclosure of the plot. Scroop framed several articles of impeachment against the King, which he caused to be fixed upon the doors of the churches in his own diocese, and sent them in the form of a circular into other counties in the Kingdom, inviting the people to take up arms to reform abuses. To strengthen this call he preached a sermon to three congregations assembling for religious worship in the cathedral, and roused 20,000 men suddenly to arms, who joined his standard at York, on which was painted the five wounds of our Saviour.— To subdue this rebellion Henry sent an army of 30,000 men into Yorkshire, under the command of the Earl of Westmoreland and the Prince John, on the arrival of the king's forces at York, they found the archbishop encamped out of the gates of the city, on the forest of Galtres, so advantageously, that it was not judged advisable to attack them. The wily Earl, affecting to favour the views of the insurgents, solicited an interview with the archbishop, who took with him the Earl Marshal. Having got them into his toils, and plied them well with wine, he arrested them on the spot for high treason, and their lives paid the forfeit of their precipitancy and misplaced confidence. In 1408 the Earl of Northumberland again appeared in arms, and was defeated and slain on Bramham Moor, by Sir Thomas Rokesby, High-sheriff of Yorkshire. Henry soon after came to York, and completed his revenge by the execution of several of the insurgent citizens, and the confiscation of their estates.

Henry VI., the hero of Agincourt, being engaged during the principal part of his reign in the wars with France, made only one visit to York, when he and his queen went to perform their devotions at the venerable shrine of St. John of Beverley.

During the civil wars between the rival houses of York and Lancaster, this city was the rendezvous of armies, and the theatre on which was displayed the memorials of royal vengeance. After the battle of Wakefield, in which Richard, Duke of York met his fate,[*] the head of that nobleman was placed upon Micklegate bar, as were also the heads of a number of his followers. The sanguinary battle of Towton changed the fortune of the two roses,[†] and the victorious Edward IV. caused the head of his father and of his adherents to be taken from Micklegate bar, and the heads of the Lancastrian nobles, Devon and Kime, to take their places.

When Edward departed this life, his brother Richard was at York, and had a funeral requiem performed in the cathedral of that city for the repose of his soul.— After Richard III. had usurped the sovereign power, and had been crowned in London, he came to York, where the ceremony of his coronation was performed a second time, in the cathedral, by Archbishop Rotherham. Tournaments, masques, and other diversions, together with the most luxurious feasting followed the coronation, and by their immense costs exhausted the public treasury.[‡] Richard distinguished the city of York by various marks of royal munificence; and the citizens showed their gratitude by a steady adherence to his interests.

After the battle of Bosworth field had placed the crown on the head of Henry VII. the people of Yorkshire and Durham refused to pay a land-tax imposed for the purpose of defraying the expenses of the army. The Earl of Northumberland was the reputed adviser of this measure, which rendered him so unpopular, that the populace assailed his house, and slew the Earl, with many of his servants. The sword being thus drawn, they threw away the scabbard, and chose for their leader Sir John Egremont, a man greatly disaffected to the house of Lancaster, and John a Chambre, a man of humble birth, but possessed of a vast share of popular in-

[*] See Vol. i. page 422.
[†] See Vol. i page 411.
[‡] Except the treasury was very scantily supplied it could not have been easily exhausted by purchasing the necessaries of life, for it appears, that about this time wheat sold for 2s. a quarter, barley for 1s. 10d. and oats for 1s. 2d.

fuence. Thomas Earl of Surrey being sent against the insurgents, he defeated their principal band, and made John a Chambre with several of his followers prisoners. The rest of the malcontents fled to York, and afterwards dispersed, while Sir John Egremont found an asylum in Flanders, under the protection of Margaret Duchess of Burgundy. John a Chambre, less fortunate, was brought to trial, and executed at York, with great solemnity, upon a high gallows, with a number of his adherents suspended around him.

From this period the annals of York contain scarcely any important transaction, till the year 1536, the 27th of Henry VIII. when the suppression of the monasteries and the progress of the reformation excited a great sensation in the northern counties.— The suppression of the religious houses, inflicted a terrible blow on the grandeur of York. In the reign of Henry V. this city contained, besides the cathedral, 41 parish churches, 17 chapels, 16 hospitals, and 9 religious houses; including the noble abbey of St. Mary, without Bootham Bar. No sooner, says Drake, was the word given, than down fell the monasteries, priories, chapels, and hospitals in this city, and with them, for company, I suppose, 18 parish churches, the materials and revenues of all being converted to secular uses. The lame, sick and old people were turned out of hospitals, and priests and nuns out of religious houses, to starve or beg their bread. The natural consequence of such sweeping and indiscriminate reforms was to excite a spirit of rebellion, and in Yorkshire a formidable insurrection was raised by Robert Aske, a gentleman of considerable fortune, who possessed great influence in the country. The other chief persons concerned were Sir Robert Constable, Sir John Bulmer, Sir Thomas Percy, Sir Stephen Hamilton, Nicholas Tempest, and William Lumley, Esqrs. Their enterprise they called "the pilgrimage of grace, and they swore that they were moved by no other motive than their love to God, their care of the king's person and issue, their desire to purify the nobility, to drive base-born persons from about the king, to restore the church, and to suppress heresy. Allured by these fair pretensions, about 40,000 men, from the counties of York, Durham, and Lancaster, flocked to their standard, and their zeal, no less than their numbers inspired the court with apprehensions. When the army was put in motion, a number of priests marched at their head in the habits of their order, carrying crosses in their hands; in their banners — was woven a crucifix, with the representa-

tion of a chalice, and the five wounds of Christ:[*] and they wore on their sleeve an emblem of the five wounds with the name of Jesus wrought in the middle. The rebels succeeded in taking both Hull and York, and laid siege to Pontefract Castle, in which the Archbishop and Lord Darcy, at the head of a body of the King's troops had thrown themselves. The castle speedily surrendered, and the prelate and nobleman joined the insurrection. The Duke of Norfolk, at the head of a small army of 5000 men, was sent against the rebels, and the king issued a proclamation, in which he told them that they ought no more to pretend to give a judgment with regard to government, than a blind man with regard to colours:— " and we," he added, " with our whole " council, think it right strange that ye who " are but brutes and inexpert folks, do take " upon you to appoint us, who be meet or not " for our council." The Duke of Norfolk encamped near Doncaster, where he entered into a negotiation with the rebels, which was protracted till the Pilgrims of Grace, reduced almost to a state of famine, and dispirited by the sudden rising of the Don, at two different times, when they meditated an attack, began, to disperse, and suffered their leaders to be taken prisoners. Some of them, with the abbots of Fountains, Jervaux, and Rivalx, were executed at Tyburn, Sir Robert Constable was hanged in chains over Beverley gate, at Hull; Lord Darcy was beheaded on Tower Hill; and Aske, the leader of the insurrection, was suspended from a tower, probably Clifford's Tower, at York. In August 1541, Henry VIII. in order to tranquilize the minds of his subjects, made a tour into the north : On his arrival at Barnsdale, in the West-Riding of this county, he was met by two hundred gentlemen in velvet coats and suitable accoutrements, with four thousand tall yeomen and three hundred clergymen, who, on their knees, made submission to his Majesty, and presented him with £600. From thence the king repaired to York, where he spent 12 days, and returned to London by way of Hull, crossing the Humber, into Lincolnshire. Five years after this visit Henry died, leaving behind him the terrible character that throughout his reign he neither spared man in his anger nor woman in his lust.— The first printing press was erected in York in his reign by Hugo Goes, the son of an ingenious printer at Antwerp. The site of this infant establishment was in the Minster-yard, near St. William's college, where the royal printing press was afterwards placed in 1642, while Charles I. was at York.

* Fox, vol. ii. page 992.

In the reign of Edward VI., on the 15th of April, 1551, began that terrible distemper, called *the Sweating Sickness*. This disease, which first manifested itself in sudden chillness, was succeeded by a violent sweat, which brought on sleep, and terminated in death, spread throughout the kingdom, and produced a great mortality in York.

Yorkshire, during the reign of Mary, surnamed the bloody, enjoyed repose, and it does not appear, that this ancient city was the scene of any of her persecutions.

The long and splendid reign of Elizabeth affords few materials for the historian of York. In her reign, a rebellion broke out in the North, headed by Thomas Percy, Earl of Northumberland, and Charles Nevil, Earl of Westmoreland, the object of which was to restore the Roman Catholic religion. The failure of this enterprise involved many of the conspirators in ruin; and on Good Friday, the 27th of March, 1570, Simon Digby, of Askew, and John Fulthorpe, of Isebbeck, Esqrs. with Robert Pennyman, of Stokesley, and Thomas Bishop, of Pocklington, gentlemen, were drawn from the Castle of York, to Knavesmire, and there " hanged, headed, and quartered." To strike terror into the inhabitants, their heads with four of their quarters, were placed on the four principal gates of the city, and the other quarters were set up in different other parts of the country. The Earl of Westmoreland found means to escape out of the country, but Northumberland was taken, and being attainted by Parliament, was beheaded, August 22, 1572, on a scaffold, erected in the Pavement, at York, and his head set on a high pole on Micklegate-bar. This was the last open attempt made to restore the Roman Catholic religion in this kingdom.

James I. visited York, in the year 1603, on his way from Scotland to London, and was received by the Lord Mayor and citizens, with great magnificence and splendid demonstrations of loyalty. In the year 1617, this monarch, with his nobles and knights, both English and Scotch, again passed through York, in his way to Scotland, and met with a reception equally cordial. During his residence, this *sagacious* prince, the Solomon of the North, *touched* about 70 persons afflicted with the King's Evil.— In the second year of his reign, York was once more visited by a plague, of which 3512 persons died. To prevent the spread of the contagion, stone crosses were erected in various parts of the vicinity of York, where the country people, without coming into the city, met the citizens, and sold them provisions. Several of these memorials of the last plague, which ever prevailed here, remain to this day. In 1697, there was a frost of such severity and continuance, that the Ouse became almost a solid body of ice, and a horse race was run on the river, from the Tower, at the end of Marygate, under the great arch of the bridge, to the crane, at Skeldergate postern. Seven years afterwards, there was so heavy a fall of snow, during a frost of about seven weeks, that when it was dissolved by a thaw, the waters of the Ouse so much inundated North-street and Skeldergate, that the inhabitants were obliged to quit their habitations, and to seek safety in more elevated situations.

The contests between the prerogatives of the Crown, and the privileges of Parliament, in the reign of Charles I. shook York to its centre; and it is a little remarkable, that the same county which afforded the scene of action for the battle which decided the fate of the house of Lancaster, on the field of Towton, should have witnessed the overthrow of the house of Stuart, on the field of Marston. Eight years after Charles had mounted the British throne, and before evil advisers had embroiled him with his Parliament and people, he visited the city of York, on his way from Scotland to London, and received a loyal and cordial welcome. Six years afterwards, on the 30th of March, 1639, the Scots having broken out into open rebellion, the King came down to York, on an expedition against the insurgents. During the king's residence in York, he kept the festival, called " *Maunday Thursday*," in the Cathedral; when the Bishop of Ely washed the feet of thirty-nine poor aged men, in warm water, and dried them with a linen cloth. Afterwards, the Bishop of Winchester washed them over again in white wine, and dried, and kissed them. This part of the ceremony being over, the king gave to each of them several articles of apparel, a purse of money, and a quantity of wine and provisions. To add to the royal condescension, his Majesty on the day following, being Good Friday, touched two hundred persons, in the Minster, for the King's Evil; but with what success, the historian very discreetly chooses not to disclose. Having spent a month in York, his Majesty and his nobles, at the head of the army marched towards Scotland. On his approach the Scotch laid down their arms, and swore allegiance; but the very next year, when the king had disbanded his army, Lesley, Earl of Leven, and the Marquis of Montrose, entered England, at the head of a Scotch army. To arrest the progress of the invaders, the

c 3

King left London, and came to York, where he convened a great council of all the Peers of England, to meet and attend his Majesty there. This proceeding naturally spread an alarm through the country that the king intended to lay aside one of the three estates of Parliament, and to govern the nation without a House of Commons.—— Petitions poured in upon his Majesty, beseeching him to call a parliament, and the gentry of Yorkshire pressed this measure upon him with much earnestness. On the 24th of September, 1640, the great assembly of Peers met in the Deanery, at York, the hall of which was richly hung with tapestry, and the king's chair of state was placed upon the half-pace of the stairs, at the upper end of the hall, from whence his Majesty delivered a speech, in which he announced his intention to call a parliament in the course of the present year; his majesty asked council, at the same time, of the Peers in what way to treat a petition for a redress of grievances which he had received from the Scotch invaders, and how his army should be kept on foot and maintained until the supplies from Parliament might be had for that purpose. While the sitting of the Peers continued, which was from the 24th of September till the 16th of October, commissioners were employed in negociating a peace with the Scotch, at Ripon; but these negociations produced merely a cessation of hostilities, till the meeting of Parliament. The accumulated evils of thirty years of mis-government, had now brought the kingdom to the verge of a great revolution. The long Parliament assembled on the 3rd of November, 1640; and their two first acts were to vote down the council court of York, and to impeach Strafford and Laud, the King's chief advisers. The government, which in the hands of Charles had assumed the character of an absolute monarchy, soon became democratical, to a degree incompatible with the spirit of the constitution. Lieutenants and Deputy Lieutenants of counties, who had exercised powers for the national defence, not authorised by statute, were declared delinquents. Sheriffs who had been employed to assess ship money, and the Jurors and Officers of the Customs, who had been employed in levying tonnage and poundage, as well as the holders of monopolies by patents, were brought under the same vague charge, and the latter were expelled from the House of Commons. The Judges, who had given their votes against Hampden, in the trial of ship-money, were accused before the Peers, and in a few weeks such a revolution was produced in the government, by the House

of Commons, seconded by the Peers, that the kingly power which had been almost omnipotent, was in danger of being reduced to insignificance. These measures naturally placed the Parliament at issue with the King, and the differences between the conflicting authorities continued to increase during the years 1640 and 1641, till an open rupture became unavoidable. In the early part of 1642, the King, with his son Charles, Prince of Wales, the Duke of York, and several noblemen left London: and on the 18th of March arrived at York where he was received by the nobility and gentry of the North, with suitable demonstrations of loyalty. His Majesty's first care, on his arrival in Yorkshire, was to secure the vast magazines in the fortress of Hull, consisting of all the arms and ammunition of the forces levied against the Scots; with this view he repaired to that port in person, and required Sir John Hotham, the governor, who had received his commission from the Parliament to deliver up the possession. Sir John, perceiving that matters were drawing to a crisis, shut the gates, and refused to admit the King, though he requested leave to enter with twelve persons only. Charles, being thus repulsed, slept that night at Beverley, and the next day returned to York, having previously declared Hotham a traitor. Civil war seemed now inevitable. The armies which had been raised for the service of Ireland were openly enlisted by the Parliament for their own purposes, and the command of them was given to the Earl of Essex. The Queen, on the other hand, departed the kingdom, and sold the crown jewels, in Holland, to purchase a cargo of arms and ammunition. The King still remained at York, where he employed himself with great activity in rousing his adherents to arms. His unhappy predilection for arbitrary power, had raised him a host of enemies, while his moral virtues, which adorned his station, had procured him a great body of zealous supporters. Negociations still proceeded, and Parliament presented for his acceptance, nineteen propositions, in which the privileges of Parliament so far out-weighed the prerogatives of the Crown that they were deemed wholly inadmissible:—" Should I grant these demands," said the King in reply, " I may be waited on bare-headed; I may have my hand kissed; the title of Majesty may be continued to me; and *the King's authority signified by both Houses*, may still be the style of your commands;' I may have swords and maces carried before me; and please myself with the signs of a crown and a sceptre; but as to true and real power, I should remain but the outside, but the picture, but the sign of a King." Charles accordingly resolved to support his authority by arms. His towns, he said, were taken from him; his ships, his arms, his money; but there still remained to him a good cause, and the hearts of his loyal subjects, which, with God's blessing, he doubted not, would recover all the rest. Having constituted the Earl of Cumberland supreme commander of his forces, and appointed Sir Thomas Glemham governor of York; his Majesty, after a residence of five months in this city, took his departure for the South, and erected his royal standard at Nottingham, on the 25th of August.

Sir Thomas Fairfax, of Denton, and Captain Hotham, son of the governor of Hull, at the head of a body of forces in the service of Parliament, advanced from the West, so far towards York, as to fortify Tadcaster and Wetherby, and twice repulsed Sir Thomas Glemham, in two vigorous assaults which he made on their forces, in the latter of these places. The success of the parliamentarians induced the loyal party in Yorkshire to solicit succour from the Earl of Newcastle, who had raised a considerable force in the North. The Earl immediately marched to their assistance, and on the 30th of November arrived at York, with 6000 men and 10 pieces of artillery. The Earl of Cumberland then resigned his commission to the Earl of Newcastle, who, after having staid only three days in York, to refresh his troops, marched out with 4000 men and 7 pieces of cannon, to attack the enemy at Tadcaster. At the same time, the Earl sent his Lieutenant-general, the Earl of Newport, with 1000 men to attack Wetherby. In both these expeditions, the loyalists were successful, and the King's affairs in this quarter began to wear a more promising aspect. At the beginning of the year 1643, Leeds, Wakefield, Skipton, and Knaresbro', were all in the hands of the loyalists; and Bradford, which had stood a siege, surrendered to them after the battle of Adwalton. On the 22d of February the Queen landed at Bridlington Quay, with 38 pieces of cannon, and 10,000 stand of small arms. The Lord-general, as the Earl of Newcastle was called, on receiving intelligence of her arrival, set out from York, and conveyed her Majesty, with the military stores to this city, where she remained three months. For this service he was created a Marquis. Early in the following year, Sir Thomas Fairfax, having gained a considerable victory over the royalist force near Selby, was joined by the Scotch general, the Earl of Leven; and these two commanders,

with their united forces, commenced the blockade of York, on the 19th of April. The parliamentary army not being sufficiently numerous to invest the city, the Northern side remained open; and the Earl of Newcastle, having between four and five thousand cavalry in the place, could, by means of a bridge over the Ouse, transport them to either side of the river, and attack any corps that he might see divided from the rest. The Earl of Manchester, however, soon after arrived with his troops, consisting of 6000 foot and 3000 horse, provided with 12 field pieces, took a position near Bootham bar, towards Clifton, and thus completely invested the city. The siege of York was now vigorously prosecuted by the three parliamentary generals, Fairfax, Leven, and Manchester, with an army of from twenty to thirty thousand men; several batteries were opened against the place, and particularly one on a hill, near Walmgate bar, from whence four pieces of cannon played incessantly on the tower, castle, and city, while the garrison and armed inhabitants, from their different platforms, kept up a heavy fire on the works of the besiegers. The siege was pressed forward with great spirit, and with various success, till the 30th of June, in the evening of which day, the besiegers, to their surprise and consternation, received information that Prince Rupert, with an army of twenty thousand men, was advancing to the relief of the city, and would that night take up his quarters at Knaresbro' and Boroughbridge. The parliamentary general, having called a council of war, resolved to raise the siege. Accordingly, on the 1st of July, they drew off from their entrenchments before the city, and marched to Hessaymoor, 6 miles West of York. His Royal Highness, aware of this movement, caused only a body of horse to face the enemy, at Skipbridge, and interposing the Ouse between him and the adverse army, safely joined his forces to those of the Marquis of Newcastle. His arrival in York produced the most unfeigned demonstrations of joy, and a council of war was immediately called, in which the Marquis of Newcastle, having received intelligence that dissensions prevailed amongst the parliamentarian generals, who were about to separate, and expecting at the same time a further reinforcement of 5000 men, under Colonel Clavering, gave it as his decided opinion, that it was unnecessary and inexpedient at the present moment to hazard an engagement. To this reasoning, Prince Rupert, whose martial ardour was not sufficiently tempered with prudence, insisted upon the propriety of an immediate attack, and strengthened his reasons by asserting, that he had positive orders from the King to bring the enemy to action. Fairfax, and the other generals of the parliamentary army, were divided in their opinions. "The English," says Fairfax, in his Memoirs, "were for fighting; the Scots for retreating, to gain, as they alleged, both time and place of more advantage. This being resolved on, we marched away for Tadcaster, which made the royalists advance the faster. Lieutenant-general Cromwell, Lesly, and myself, were appointed to bring up the rear. We sent word to the Generals that it was necessary to make a stand, or else, the enemy having this advantage, might put us in some disorder; but by the advantage of the ground we were on, we hoped to make it good, till they came back to us, which they did. The place was Marston fields,* which afterwards gave name to this battle." "This action," says Hume, fought on the 2nd of July, 1644, " was obstinately disputed between the most numerous armies that were ever engaged during the course of these wars; nor were the forces on each side much different in number. Fifty thousand British troops were led to mutual slaughter; and the victory seemed long undecided between them. Prince Rupert, who commanded the right wing of the royalists, was opposed to Cromwell, who conducted the choice troops of the parliament, inured to danger under that determined leader, animated by zeal, and confirmed by the most rigid discipline. After a short combat, the cavalry of the royalists gave way; and such of the infantry as stood near them were likewise borne down, and put to flight. Newcastle's regiment alone, resolute to conquer or to perish, obstinately kept their ground, and maintained by their dead bodies the same order in which they had at first been ranged. In the other wing, Sir Thomas Fairfax and Colonel Lambert, with some troops, broke through the royalists; and transported by the ardour of pursuit, soon reached their victorious friends, engaged also in the pursuit of the enemy. But after that tempest was passed, Lucas, who commanded the royalists in this wing, restoring order to his broken forces, made a furious attack on the parliamentary cavalry, threw them into disorder, pushed them upon their own infantry, and put the whole wing to route. When ready to seize on their carriages and baggage, he perceived Cromwell, who was now returned from the pur-

\* Marston Moor, the scene of this memorable battle is near the highway, between Wetherby and York, from each of which places it is about 7 miles distant.

suit of the other wing. Both sides were not a little surprised to perceive that they must renew the combat; for that victory which each of them thought they had already obtained. The front of the battle was now exactly counter-changed; and each army occupied the ground which had been possessed by the enemy at the beginning of the day. This second battle was equally furious and desperate with the first; but after the utmost efforts of courage by both parties, victory wholly turned to the side of the parliament. The Prince's train of artillery was taken, and the whole royalist army pushed off the field of battle." This battle sealed the fate of the royal cause. The day after the battle, the brave Marquis of Newcastle resolved to quit the kingdom; and Prince Rupert drew his army from the city of York and marched into Lancashire.

In this state of desertion, Sir Thomas Glemham, the governor, was reduced to the painful necessity of surrendering the city; which he did, thirteen days after the battle of Marston Moor, on the most honourable terms. The siege of York had continued nearly thirteen weeks, during which time the city had sustained twenty-two assaults, and between four and five thousand of the enemy had perished before its walls. On its surrender, the parliamentary generals entered the city in solemn procession, and went directly to the Cathedral, where a psalm was sung, and the following day was observed as a day of general thanksgiving. York, being thus subjected to the parliament, Lord Ferdinando Fairfax was made its governor; and he, and his son, the General, surnamed the hero of the commonwealth, received commissions to reduce all the garrisons in this county, that still held out for the King—a commission which, in a short time, they effected. After the whole kingdom was brought under subjection to the parliament, York was dismantled of its garrison, with the exception of Clifford's tower, of which the Lord Mayor was appointed governor, and continued to hold that commission for several years.

York has little share in the annals of the Protectorate. Cromwell does not appear to have been ever in this city, except at the time of its capture after the battle of Marston Moor; and another time on his way into Scotland, when the royal arms were displaced to substitute those of the existing government; when he partook of the Lord Mayor's hospitality at a public dinner, and the day following he pursued his journey northward. One of the assises at York during the Commonwealth, was rendered remarkable by the attendance of that extraordinary instance of human longevity, Henry Jenkins. The cause was heard in the year 1667, and was between the vicar of Catterick and William and Peter Mawbank, wherein the witness deposed that the tithes of wool, lamb, &c. had been paid, to his knowledge, one hundred and twenty years or more! Jenkins had appeared at York two years before, to prove the existence of an ancient road to a mill far one hundred and twenty years. He remembered the dissolution of the monasteries, and said that great lamentation was made on that occasion. In early life he was butler to Lord Conyers, of Hornby castle, and was often at Fountain's Abbey during the residence of the last abbot, who, he said, frequently visited his lord, and drank a hearty glass with him. He was been at Ellerton-upon-Swale, in this county, before parish registers were in use; but Bishop Lyttleton communicated to the Society of Antiquarians, on the 11th of December, 1766, a paper copied from an old household book of Sir Richard Graham, Bart. of Norton Conyers, the writing of which says, that upon his going to live at Bolton, Jenkins was said to be about one hundred and fifty years old, that he had often examined him in his sister's kitchen, where he came to beg alms, and found facts and chronicles agree in his account. He was then one hundred and sixty-two or one hundred and sixty-three years of age; and said that he went to Northallerton, with a horse load of arrows for the battle of Flodden field, with which a bigger boy went forward to the army, under the Earl of Surrey, King Henry being at that time at Tournay, and he believed himself then eleven or twelve years old. This was in 1513, and four or five people of the same parish, said to be one hundred years old or near it, declared Jenkins to have been an old man ever since they knew him. He died in December, 1670, at the place of his birth, aged one hundred and sixty-nine years, where a monument is erected to his memory, the epitaph of which was composed by Dr. Thomas Chapman, master of Magdalen College, Cambridge.* Jenkins was cotemporary with Thomas Parr, the patriarchal Shropshireman, of whom it is recorded that he was born in 1483, and lived in the reign of ten kings and queens; that the general habits of his life were temperate and frugal, that he was able, even at the age of one hundred and thirty to do husbandry work; and that at the age of one hundred and five, he did penance in Alderbury church, for lying with Katherine Milton, and getting her with child,† that he died in 1635, aged one hun-

* See Ellerton-upon-Swale.
† Oldys's M.S. notes on Fuller's Worthies.

dred and fifty-two years and nine months; and that his remains rest among the eminent dead in Westminster Abbey.

The county of York was well disposed to promote the restoration, and General Monk, on his arrival here in 1659, found the public disposition so favourable to the royal cause, that he was for some time in a state of suspense, whether he should not proclaim the king in this city. A secret correspondence had for some time been maintained between the General and Lord Fairfax, who had imbibed the same principles, and on the 11th of May, 1660, Charles II. was proclaimed with great solemnity at York. On the 5th of August, 1665, the Duke and Duchess of York visited this city, and were received with every demonstration of loyalty and affection; but in the year 1679, when the bill of exclusion was brought forward in parliament, the Duke in passing through York on his way to Edinburgh, was received here with much less cordiality. This defect of ceremony drew on the magistrates the resentment of the court; they received a severe reprimand from the secretary of state, and the city being afterwards considered disaffected, its charter was in the year 1684 suspended. This year the notorious Jefferys attended at York as one of the Judges of Assize.

On the death of Charles II. his brother James, Duke of York, succeeded to the throne; and on the petition of the citizens restored their charter, which was received with the greatest solemnity, and nothing was omitted to display their joy on the occasion. The inhabitants of York continued to show their gratitude and loyalty to this infatuated monarch, till the moment of his abdication, after which, this city followed the example of the rest of the kingdom, by recognising the Prince of Orange as sovereign of the kingdom, under the title of William III.

From this period to the rebellion in 1745, the annals of York are not marked by any extraordinary transactions; but at that momentous crisis, the city, as well as the county, gave the most unequivocal proofs of its loyalty and attachment to the reigning dynasty,·and to the reformed religion. On the 23d of July, 1746, his Royal Highness the Duke of Cumberland, on his return to London from the defeat of the rebels at Culloden, visited York, and was received with the honours due to his illustrious rank and eminent services. In 1757, the new regulations for levying the militia produced a spirit of insubordination in Yorkshire, and a vast body of farmers, labourers, and artisans, from upwards of thirty parishes, assembled at York, and demolished two houses, without Monk bar, in one of which the deputy-lieutenants were expected to assemble, to receive the constable's returns. Since the reign of Charles I. York, which was in former times the residence of Emperors and Kings, has not been visited by any English sovereign; though it has often been honoured with the presence of different branches of the royal family.

In our own times, the present sovereign of these realms, while Prince of Wales, visited the city of York, accompanied by his royal brother who derives his title from this ancient metropolis. On Monday, the 24th of August, 1789, in the race week, their Royal Highnesses arrived on the race ground, in their carriage, and alighted at some distance from the Grand Stand, whence they rode about on horseback, to gratify public curiosity by a sight of their persons. When the day's sport was over, they repaired to the carriage of Earl Fitzwilliam, whose guests they were, and entered the city amidst the congratulations of the populace. The following day, the corporation presented the Heir-apparent with the freedom of the city in an elegant gold box; and on Thursday, in the race week, he dined at the Mansion-House, in company with a large assemblage of the nobility and gentry of the county. On the following Saturday, the Prince of Wales and the Duke of York proceeded to Castle Howard, having previously ordered Lieutenant Colonel St. Leger to pay into the hands of Walter Fawkes, Esq. High-Sheriff of the county, two hundred guineas, for the relief of debtors in the castle. In 1791, Charles James Fox visited York at the races, a grand dinner was given him and many noblemen and gentlemen at the Mansion-House, and he was presented with the freedom of the city in a gold box, accompanied by a copy of a resolution passed by the corporation, in which he was complimented on "the constant and beneficial exertions of his abilities in support of the British Constitution, upon the true principles of the glorious revolution; of the rights of every degree of citizens; and of the peace, liberty, and happiness of mankind." In November, 1795, Prince William Frederick of Gloucester, on his return from Scarborough to the South, spent some time in York, and was presented with the freedom of the city, in a gold box. In 1805, the Right Hon. John Earl St. Vincent, whose courage and talents as a naval commander are so well known, honoured this city with a visit, and received its freedom, in a box of "heart of oak."

On the 26th of August, 1822, while his Royal brother and Sovereign, George IVth, was in Scotland, his Royal Highness the Duke of Sussex honoured this city with a visit, and partook of the hospitalities of the Corporation, at the Mansion-house, where a public dinner was given to his Royal Highness, on which occasion the freedom of the city was presented to him in a gold box, accompanied by an address expressive of the admiration of that "splendid career of useful beneficence and spirited patriotism which gave a brilliant lustre to his exalted birth."

The city of York, as it now stands, is nearly two miles and three quarters in circuit. There are no existing records to show when the walls were built. They were, no doubt, in existence in the time of the Saxons and Danes, as well as during the Roman government; and they were re-edified, if not actually re-built in the reign of Edward I., to protect the city against Scotch invaders, who penetrated to its gates. After the siege of York, in 1644, the walls stood in great need of repairs, and the three following years were employed in that necessary duty. The coroding hand of time has ever since been at work, and they are now falling rapidly into decay. In several places the delightful promenade formed by them is already interrupted, and if the hand of reparation does not alter for the better, what time changes for the worse, it is not difficult to foresee what will be the end.

The entrance into the city is by four principal gates or bars, and five posterns, or smaller entrances; the gates are, MICKLEGATE-BAR, to the South-West, adorned with lofty turrets, finely embattled; over the Roman arch, already described, hangs a large shield, bearing the arms of England and France; and on each side, one of less size, decorated with the city arms: this is at the entrance from Tadcaster. BOOTHAM-BAR, to the North-West, on the road leading to Edinburgh, is an ancient structure, built almost wholly of grit; but though the materials are Roman, the architecture is Gothic. MONK-BAR, to the North-East, on the entrance from Malton and Scarborough, is a stately gate, bearing the arms of France quartered with those of England, on the battlements. And WALMGATE-BAR, on the South-East, leading to Beverley and Hull: the foundations of this bar are formed of large blocks of grit, but the arches are modern, having undergone a thorough repair, in 1648, after the gate had been almost demolished by the siege.

The Posterns are, North-street-postern, Skeldergate - postern, Castlegate - postern, Fishergate-postern, Layerthorp-postern, and Longwalk - postern. There are also six bridges, the New Ouse bridge, built under the direction of Mr Peter Atkinson, architect. The first stone of this bridge was laid with considerable pomp, on the 10th of December, 1810, and the work was completed in March, 1820; The Right Hon. George Peacock, filling at both these periods the office of Lord Mayor. The old bridge, after having existed for six centuries, was then removed, and gave place to this handsome modern erection. A new bridge, over the Foss, leading into Walmgate, cotemporary with the new Ouse bridge, and built by the same architect, at the expense of the corporation, serves to mark the public spirit of the present age. The other bridges, which are all over the Foss, at different points, claim no particular observation,

This city is divided into four districts, which take their names from the four gates, and are called Micklegate-ward, Bootham-ward, Monkgate-ward, and Walmgate-ward. Micklegate-ward, in the South West part of the city, is incompassed on one side by the city walls, and on the other, by the river Ouse. It contains six parishes, namely, Bishop-hill, the elder and younger; Trinity; St. Martin's; St. Johns; and All Saints'. Bootham-ward occupies the North West angle of the city, and has in its district, the parishes of Belfrey's; St. Helen's; and St. Martin's. Monk-ward is the North East part, and comprises Trinity; St. Cuthbert's; St. Saviour's; Christ's; and St. Sampson's. Walmgate-ward is on the North East, and contains seven parishes, namely, St. Margaret's; St. Dennis; St. George; Crux; All Hallow's; St. Mary's; and St. Michael's. These four divisions comprise the whole city, within the walls, except the close of the cathedral.

York, the archiepiscopal see, like most other ancient cities, is remarkable for the number of its sacred edifices, and in enumerating and describing the churches of York, in which religious services are still performed, the CATHEDRAL, that " Chief of houses, as the rose of flowers," claims the precedency.

It has always been observed,* that on the introduction of Christianity into this kingdom, about the year 625, Edwin, King of Northumbria, himself a convert from Paganism, elevated Paulinus, a Roman missionary, to the dignity of first archbishop of York. The residence of this King was York, but at so low an ebb was religion, that there was not found a temple within his metropolis suitable for the performance of the ceremony of baptism. A small oratory of wood, was in consequence erected for the

occasion, on the site of the present cathedral, which was dedicated, as is the present edifice, to St. Peter, and on Easter Day, in the year 627, the King, with his two sons, Osfrid and Edfrid, along with a number of the nobles, were solemnly baptised in this primitive erection. The ceremony over, says Bede, the prelate took care to acquaint the King, that since he had become a Christian, he ought to build a House of prayer, more suitable to the divinity he now adored; and by the bishop's direction, he began to build a magnificent fabric of stone, in the midst of which was inclosed the oratory already erected. Under the influence of that zeal which inspired the Royal convert, the building proceeded with great spirit; but scarcely were the walls ready to receive the roof, when the King was slain in battle, and Paulinus was obliged to quit the country. For some years the church lay neglected, but in 632, Oswald, a successor of Edwin, undertook to complete the building, which he had no sooner finished, than he was killed by Penda, the Pagan king of Mercia, and the newly-erected structure was almost destroyed. In this ruinous condition it was found by archbishop Wilfred, the munificent patron of Ripon,† who, about the year 674, repaired the walls, fixed on the roof, and restored it to its former grandeur. " And now, by the hand of providence," says Drake, " the church stood an flourished under the successive beneficence of its spiritual governors, for near 400 years, during which period it received the valuable donation of archbishop Egbert's library; upon which Alcuin, the Gamaliel of his age, who had drank freely at this spring of erudition, has bestowed so high an eulogium.‡ In the year 1069, as has been already seen, the native inhabitants, aided by the Danes, in their attempt to throw off the yoke of the conquerer, set fire to the suburbs, which spreading to the city, communicated to the cathedral, and involved them all in one common ruin. William, on entering the city, seised upon the revenues of the church; but he soon after elevated Thomas, his chaplain and treasurer, to the Archbishopric, and by him the cathedral was restored to its former splendour. In 1136, a casual fire again burnt down this edifice, along with St. Mary's Abbey, and thirty-nine parish churches. For four and thirty years the cathedral lay in ruins; but, in the year, 1171, during the episcopacy of Roger, archbishop of this province, the choir with its vaults were re-built, and the South part of the cross isle of the church, was added in the time of Walter Grey.

Roger's successor, in the early part of the reign of Edward I. John le Romain, father of the archbishop, began and finished the North transepts, with a handsome steeple in the midst; and John, his son, with his own hand, laid the foundation of the nave, from the west and eastward, on the 7th of April, 1291, invoking the grace of the Holy Ghost. The materials for this part of the cathedral were contributed by Robert de Vavasour, from his quarry near Tadcaster; and by Robert de Percy, Lord of Boulton, from his Woods at that place. William de Melton was the next founder, in 1390, and with the aid of indulgences of relaxation, sold to " the charitable," he finished the west end with the steeples, as it remains at this day. But the great benefactor of the cathedral was archbishop John Thoresby; this prelate conceiving that the choir, built by Roger, did not correspond with the west end of the church lately erected, and that there was no place in this church of York " where our Lady's mass, the glorious mother of God, could decently be celebrated," himself contributed one thousand eight hundred and ten pounds, towards building a new choir, and consummating this fabric. All the machinery for raising public contributions to the church was also put in motion: indulgences of relaxation were granted to the liberal; letters mandatory were addressed to the clergy, enjoining them; under pain of the greater excommunication, to suffer their collectors to gather the alms of the charitable, and the old hall and chambers of the archbishop's manor of Shireburn were demolished to provide stone and materials for the erection of the new choir, the first stone of which was laid by the archbishop, on the 29th of July, 1361. The wages of workmen about this time were three-pence a day to a master mason or carpenter, and three-half-pence to their " knaves," as their journeymen were then called;* A pound's worth of silver then was a pound weight, which is equal to four pounds of our present money, and one penny then would purchase as much corn as twenty-pence now, bringing the artisan's wages to the rate of 2s. 6d. a day, or 15s. a week. The contribution of the archbishop was of course most munificent, and amounted to not less a sum in our money than 36,000l. !

Fleetwood's Chronicon Pretiosum.

In addition to the means already mentioned for raising the supplies, a bull apostolical was issued by Pope Urban VI. and a kind of income tax of five per cent. was imposed on ecclesiastical benefices for three years, for the necessary repairs and re-edification. By these means a vast sum was collected; which being augmented by a munificent donation from Archdeacon Skirlaw, the choir was finished, and the structure completed by the taking down of the old lantern steeple, and the erection of a new one in its stead, A. D. 1370. Thus within the space of less than 200 years, reckoning from the period in which the south transept was begun by Walter de Grey, the superb cathedral of York was completed in the forms and dimensions in which it appears at this day, exhibiting a splendid monument of the piety of former times, and an interesting combination of Gothic architecture through five successive ages. Of all the different parts of this magnificent structure the chapter house is the only one of which the date is totally unknown. No records now extant give any account of the time of its erection; but from the style of architecture, Drake conjectures that it is to be ascribed to Walter de Grey.—— The pavement of the cathedral is of recent date; anciently it consisted of the grave-stones of bishops and other ecclesiastics, but in the year 1696, the old pavement was removed, under the direction of the Earl of Burlington, when several curious rings of ruby and saphire, set in gold, belonging to those whose mortal remains had mixed with their parent dust, were discovered, and are now shewn in the vestry. The stone for the new pavement was given by Sir Edward Gascoigne, of Parlington, from his quarry at Huddlestone, and the marble was obtained by sawing the old grave-stones into dies suitable for the purpose of this mosaic work.—— The expense of the workmanship, which amounted to £2500, was defrayed by a subscription raised for the purpose, among the nobility, clergy, and gentry of the city and county of York. The archbishops of York, since the introduction of Christianity, in the time of the Heptarchy, to the present period, amount to eighty three in number, and their names in numerical order, with the dates when each of them entered upon the see, is subjoined:—

## ARCHBISHOPS OF YORK FROM 625 TO 1822.

| 1 Paulinus | 625 | 6 Wilfred II | 718 | 12 Wymondus | 831 | 18 Athelwold | 971 |
|---|---|---|---|---|---|---|---|
| 2 Cedda | 664 | 7 Egber | 731 | 13 Wilferus | 854 | 19 Oswald | 971 |
| 3 Wilfred | 666 | 8 Adelbert | 767 | 14 Adelbald | 900 | 20 Adulf | 992 |
| 4 Bosa | 677 | 9 Eanbald | 780 | 15 Rewardus | 921 | 21 Wulstan II | 1002 |
| 5 St. John of Beverley | 692 | 10 Eanbald II | 797 | 16 Wulstan | 930 | 22 Afric Pullesk | 1023 |
| | | 11 Wulsius | 812 | 17 Oskitell | 955 | 23 Kinsius | 1050 |

| | | | |
|---|---|---|---|
| 24 Aldred········1060 | 39 Henry de Newark········1298 | 53 Lawren.Bothe 1476 | 69 Rich. Neile...1631 |
| 25 Thomas ······1070 | 40 Thomas Corbridge ····1299 | 54 Thos. de Rotherham ····1480 | 70 John Williams 1641 |
| 26 Gerard·········1100 | 41 Wm. de Greenfield ·······1305 | 55 Thos. Savage 1501 | 71 Accep.Frewen 1660 |
| 27 Thomas II....1109 | | 56 Chpr. Bainbridge ····1508 | 72 Rhd. Sterne··1664 |
| 28 Thurstan.....1114 | 42 Wm.deMelton1315 | 57 Thos. Wolsey 1514 | 73 John Dolben 1683 |
| 29 Henry Murdac1140 | 43 Wm. de la Zouch ····1340 | 58 Edward Lee··1531 | 74 Thos. Lamplugh········1688 |
| 30 St. William...1153 | 44 John Thoresby 1352 | 59 Rbt. Holgate..1544 | 75 John Sharp...1691 |
| 31 Roger·········1154 | 45 Alex. Neville 1374 | 60 Nich.Heath....1555 | 76 Sir.W. Dawes 1713 |
| 32 Geoffry Plantagenet·······1190 | 46 Thos.Arundel 1388 | 61 Thos. Young 1561 | 77 Lancelot Blackburne·······1754 |
| 33 Walter deGrey1216 | 47 Rbt.Waldby·· 1396 | 62 Edm. Grindal 1570 | 78 Thos.Herring 1742 |
| 34 Sewal ······1256 | 48 Rhd. Scroope 1398 | 63 Edwin Sandys 1576 | 79 Mth. Hutton 1747 |
| 35 Godfrey de Ludham ...1258 | 49 Henry Bowet 1407 | 64 John Piers....1588 | 80 John Gilbert.. 1757 |
| 36 Walter Giffard 1265 | 50 John Kemp...1426 | 65 Mthw.Hutton 1594 | 81 R.Drummond1761 |
| 37 W.Wickwane 1279 | 51 Wm. Bothe...1452 | 66 Tob.Matthew 1606 | 82 W. Markham 1777 |
| 38 John le Romaine ····1285 | 52 Geo. Neville...1464 | 67 Geo.Montaign 1628 | 83 Edw. Venables |
| | | 68 Saml. Harsnet 1629 | Vernon ····1808 |

. The Archbishop of York is Primate of England, and to him attaches the honour of crowning the Queen. According to Dr. Heylin, the archbishopric of York is the most ancient metropolitan See in England, having been so constituted in the reign of King Lucius, in the year 180. As has been already seen, this see was, on the conversion of the Saxon Edwin, elevated to its former honour, when Paulinus was made archbishop, and then each metropolitan had twelve suffragan bishops; at present York only retains Durham, Carlisle, Chester, and Sodor and Man, though formerly its archbishop was metropolitan of Scotland. Warm and repeated contentions have existed for ecclesiastical supremacy between this See and Canterbury, which all terminated in this, that the Archbishop of York stiles himself " Primate of England; and He of Canterbury, " Primate of all England; and the former has still precedency of all Dukes who are not of the royal blood, and of all great officers of state, the Lord Chancellor alone excepted.* The yearly tenths of the Archbishop of York, as returned in the survey made by the commissioners appointed by the Crown, in the reign of Henry VIII. on the eve of the reformation, were valued at £161, and the value of the living, as stated in the King's books, of the same date, at £1610. In Northumberland, the Archbishop of York has the power of a Palatine. The Right Reverend Father in God, the Hon. Edward Venables Vernon, L.L.D. is the present archbishop, and was translated to the archiepiscopal See from the bishopric of Carlisle, in 1808.

The Cathedral of York is one of the largest sacred structures in England, as the following comparative table, copied from Hargrove's History of York, will serve to demonstrate, and its magnificence corresponds with its magnitude :—

| COMPARATIVE Table. | York. | St. Paul's. | Winchester. | Canterbury. | Ely. | Lincoln. | Westminster. | Salisbury. |
|---|---|---|---|---|---|---|---|---|
| | ft. | ft. | ft. | ft. | ft. | ft. | ft. | ft. |
| Length from E. to W. ............ | 524 | 500 | 554 | 514 | 517 | 498 | 489 | 452 |
| ———— west door to the choir.. | 264 | 306 | 247 | 214 | | | 130 | 236 |
| ———— of the Choir ............... | 162 | 165 | 138 | —— | 101 | —— | 152 | 140 |
| ———— of the space behind the altar | 69 | —— | 93 | | | | | |
| ———— of the cross aisles from N. to S. | 222 | 248 | 208 | low 124 up 154 | 178 | 227 | 190 | 210 |
| Breadth of the Body and side aisles .. | 100 | 107 | 86 | 74 | 73 | 83 | 96 | 76 |
| Height of the vaulting of the nave.... | 96 | 88 | 78 | 88 | —— | 83 | 101 | 81 |
| Height of the two western towers or steeples ................... | 196 | 221 | n.w. 133 | s. w. 130 n.w. 100 | 270 | 270 | | 400 |
| ———— of the lantern tower.......... | 235 | —— | —— | 235 | 113 | 288 | —— | 400 |

* Dugdale, Vol I. fol. p. 290.

In surveying the EXTERIOR of the Cathedral, one of the first feelings that forces itself upon the mind of the visitor is, regret that so stately an edifice should be inclosed within so circumscribed an area. Advancing from the *South* by the usual approach, the best situation for a general view of this structure is between the foot road, or passage into the Minster yard, and the Deanery, nearly opposite to the South transept. Over the clock, which is above the spacious flight of stone steps, is a large Gothic window of painted glass, and still higher, a circular window of exquisite masoury and richly variegated glass, in imitation of the Marygold flower, sometimes called St. Catharine's wheel. The summit is crowned with neat and elegant turrets. In this transept are seen a number of narrow and acutely pointed arches, with slender pillars, crowned with plain or slightly ornamented capitals. The windows are comparatively small, and their ornaments exhibit a marked difference from those which are seen in other parts of the building. Between this part and the western towers arise six small pinnacles, originally intended for buttresses to the tower part of the nave. In the niches are ancient statues, supposed to represent Christ, the four Evangelists, and Archbishop St. William. The South side of the choir presents an appearance peculiarly striking; the massy columns finely decorated with a variety of figures, and terminating in richly ornamented pinnacles, the windows large and displaying a beautiful tracery, a small transept of the tower with its superb light, and the screen work before the three furthest windows of the upper tier, all concur to render this part of the structure strikingly beautiful and magnificent.

The *Western* or principal front, with its two towers or steeples, excels those parts already described; human skill could scarcely have produced any thing more complete in this style of architecture. This front has been cloistered for statuary, but many of the niches are divested of the valuable productions with which they were formerly adorned. The top of each of the towers is surmounted with eight pinnacles, and in the south tower is a peal of ten bells, unequalled, it is said, by any in the kingdom. At this front there are three entrances, the centre of which is by massy folding doors. Over the principal door-way is the figure of William de Melton, and on each side the figures of Vavasour and Percy, the benefactors of the church. The expulsion of Adam and Eve from Paradise is pourtrayed upon the arch in fine tracery, and the liberality and taste of the present Archbishop, and the Dean and Chapter, are contributing to repair the depredations which time and fanatical zeal have inflicted upon the statuary and the other ornaments.

The *Eastern* or choir end, begun by Archbishop Thoresby, is more modern than those parts already described, and displays a more florid style of architecture, crowned with niches and airy pinnacles. Over one of the finest windows in the world is seen the statue of the venerable founder of the choir, mitred and robed, sitting in his archiepiscopal chair, and holding in his left hand a representation of the church, while his right seems to point at the window. At the basis of the window are the heads of Christ and his apostles, with that of a King, supposed to be Edward III. In the niches of the buttresses again appear the statues of Vavasour and Percy. The great tower, or lantern steeple, is supported in the inside by four large and massy columns, forming four arches, and is finished in a style very much superior, though not inappropriate to that of the towers in the western front.

The *Northern* side of the Cathedral is not less superb than its Southern front. The transept and nave present a spectacle highly interesting to the eye of curiosity and taste. Here also may be observed the exterior form and style of architecture of the Chapter-House, of which the wonderous buttresses and other decorations seem to indicate the age of its completion to have been nearly the same as that of the building of the choir; such is their appearance by day. - By moon-light, the effect here, as on all large masses of architecture, is truly sublime ; a kind of optical delusion of the most impressive kind takes place, and the towers and pinnacles of the Cathedral " acquire a degree of lightness so superior to that which is shown under the meridian sun, that they no longer appear of human construction."\*

The INTERIOR of the Cathedral corresponds in every particular with the magnificence of the exterior. The cross aisle displays a most superb specimen of the style of architecture which prevailed in the latter part of the reign of Henry III. The circular arch, that at that time was not entirely laid aside, still appears in the upper part, inclosing others of the pointed form. The pillars which support the larger arches are of an angular shape, encompassed by slender columns, a little detached; and the rich leafy capitals of all the columns unite to form a foliated wreath round the head of the pillar. The windows are long, narrow, and pointed, consisting of one light, or divided into several by unramified mullion,

\* Dallaway.

and variously decorated on the sides by slender free-stone, or marble shafts. Between the upper arches appear the quatre-feuille and cinque-feuille ornaments, afterwards transferred to the windows, and there forming the first steps towards the beautiful tracery which is displayed in the nave and choir. The windows in the South end are arranged in three tiers; the uppermost composed of two concentric circles of small arches, is admired as a fine piece of masonry, and has a noble appearance; the first window of the second tier exhibits a representation of Archbishop St. William; the second consists of two lights, one of which is decorated with the portrait of St. Peter, and the other with that of St. Paul, each with his proper insignia. In the next window appears Archbishop Wilfred. The four figures of Abraham, Solomon, Moses, and Peter, that occupy the windows on the lowermost tier, are of modern workmanship, and form an honourable memorial of the skill and liberality of Peakitt, a native artist. In the corner, on the left of the south entrance, is a small door, which leads by 273 winding stone steps to the top of the lantern steeple. Few persons in health and strength visit the Cathedral, without at some time enjoying the prospect which this eminence commands, from which the surrounding country, lying stretched as on a map, presents the eye with a field of observation at once rich, extensive, and gratifying.

The North transept displays the same style of architecture as the South. The windows are here disposed in two tiers; the lowest of which consists of five noble lights, each about 50 feet high, and 5 in breadth. These lights are designated by the name of the "Five Sisters," from a tradition, not very well supported, that five maiden sisters were at the expense of their erection. The rich stained glass represents embroidery, and there is a small border of stained glass round the edge. The baptismal font of the Cathedral, formed of dark shell variegated marble, stands in the western aisle.

Architecture perhaps never produced, nor can imagination easily conceive a vista of greater magnificence and beauty, than that which is seen at the western entrance of the Cathedral The best point of observation is under the central tower, or lantern steeple. Here may at once be seen the statuary screen, the several painted windows, and the lengthened aisles and lofty columns. The screen which separates the nave from the choir, rising only just high enough to form a support for the organ, does not intercept the view of the eastern end of the church with its columns, its arches, and its superb window. Tracery of the richest kind appears in the windows, especially in that which occupies a large portion of the western front, and when illuminated by the rays of the declining sun, exhibits a grandeur surpassing the power of description. The figures of the first eight archbishops decorate the lowermost compartments, and above are represented eight saints. The escutcheons of Edward II. and the Saxon Prince, Ulphus, are placed under this window; and the upper windows, though less sumptuously decorated, are elegantly adorned with imagery and escutcheons. Under these runs an open gallery, in which, exactly over the pointed arches, formerly stood images of the tutelary saints of the several nations of Christendom; but most of them have been displaced, except the figure of St. George, and his combatant, the grim visaged dragon.

The screen which separates the nave from the service choir is a curious and elaborate piece of workmanship, the history of which is not precisely known. The style of decoration refers it to the age of Henry VI. whose statue, tradition reports, once filled the place next to his predecessor. After his death, it is said, Henry, whose misfortunes the people commiserated, became an object of adoration, and his statue was therefore ordered to be removed; but it is more probable, that it was his successor, Edward IV. who, being then the sun of the political firmament, became the object of adoration, and that to him the homage of courtly devotion was offered, by removing the statue of his rival. For some ages the place remained unoccupied, but on the visit of James I. to York, he was complimented by being placed in the empty cell. Another conjecture is, that this screen originally belonged to the Abbey of St. Mary, at the manor, and that King James I. presented it to the Cathedral, in compliment to whom the Dean and Chapter placed his statue in the niche which was formerly occupied by the unfortunate Henry. In the course of the judicious repairs which this screen has undergone, the statue of James has been transferred to Ripon Minster, and a well executed figure of Henry VI. by Mr. Michael Taylor, a sculptor of considerable eminence in York, is placed in the station originally enjoyed by that monarch.

The organ is now placed over the entrance into the choir, which was its original situation. At the instance of Charles I. who contributed £1000 for the erection of an organ, and for other purposes, it was placed opposite the bishop's throne, to afford a more complete view of the east window from the body of the nave; but in the year of

the revolution it was removed back to its
ancient situation which it now occupies,
and by its solemn peals, swelling through
the lofty arches, gives to the devout mind
some faint conception of the celestial choir.

In the architecture of the choir a variation from that of the nave is perceptible.
The roof displays more tracery; an elegant
kind of festoon work descends from the
capitals of the pillars from which the vault-
ing springs; through every part is seen a
great profusion of ornaments; and the
whole exhibits a near approach to the
highly florid style which prevailed before
the end of the 15th century. The ancient
wood work of the choir yet remains. It is
carved with pinnacles of different heights,
and pedestals, whereon, probably, once
were images of wood for greater decoration;
if so, they have disappeared. Behind these
are galleries, and regular pews; and under
the front of them are the stalls for the
canons and other ecclesiastical officers, beginning with the Dean's stall to the right,
and the Precentor's to the left. The Cathedra, or throne of the archbishop, is situated
at the end of the prebendal stalls, on the
south side, and the pulpit is placed opposite.
On the left of the throne the Lord Mayor
and Aldermen have their seats, and the
Judges of assize sit opposite them, near the
pulpit. In the middle of the area there is a
small pillar of brass, supported by four
lions, on the top of which is an eagle of the
same metal, standing upon a globe, and
which, with expanded wings, receives the
service Bible for the lessons.

The ascent from the nave through the
choir to the high altar is by a flight of fifteen
steps. Here a stone screen of excellent
Gothic architecture, about forty-nine feet
long by twenty-eight feet high, presents itself.
This screen was formerly obscured by a
wooden screen and gallery, which were
swept away in the year 1726, by order of
Dean Finch, by whose direction the screen,
which had before been covered with tapestry,
was glazed with plate glass protected by copper bars. Under the altar is a vault, commonly called the Crypt, with an entrance from
the north and south aisles by iron grated
doors. While exploring this ancient subterraneous chantry we survey part of the old minster, and are carried back to the time of King
Edwin, the first royal Northumbrian convert
to Christianity. The windows of the choir
shed their richly varied light through the
numerous figures of kings, prelates, and
saints. Those of the small transepts are remarkable for their height and elegance,
reaching almost to the roof and divided into
one hundred and eight compartments, each

of which depicts a portion of scripture history. But the eastern window is the master-
piece, and perhaps stands unrivalled for
magnitude, beauty, and magnificence.
This window is nearly the full breadth and
height of the middle choir, and is seventy-
five feet high and thirty-five wide. The
upper part exhibits a piece of ample and
beautiful tracery. Below are one hundred
and seventeen compartments occupied with
representations of the Supreme Being, of
monarchs, priests, and saints, and of most of
the principal events in the scripture records.
The glazing of this window was commenced
in the year 1405, at the cost of the dean and
chapter, by John Thornton, of Coventry,
who, in consideration of his superior skill
and application, was to receive the weekly
sum of four shillings, with the further payment of one hundred shillings a year, for his
labour, which was completed in less than
three years! To the south of this magnificent window is exhibited in painted glass the
Annunciation; or, the meeting of Mary and
Elizabeth, from the design of Sebastian del
Piombo in figure as large as life. This
window was originally brought from the
church of St. Rouen, in Normandy, and was
presented to the dean and chapter of York,
in the year 1804, by the Earl of Carlisle,
whose arms, garter, coronet, and crest, fill up
the compartments, above and below, and
perpetuate the remembrance of the noble
donor's munificence.

The present religious services performed
in the Cathedral, are the morning prayers
daily at seven o'clock, in the vestry, in which
the ecclesiastical courts are held. The cathedral service is performed in the choir at
ten o'clock in the forenoon, when an anthem
is sung, unless there be a sermon or litany.
The evening prayers are performed every
day in the week, at three o'clock in the afternoon in winter, and four o'clock in summer,
in which an anthem is performed. On Sunday the service commences at ten o'clock in
the morning, when a sermon is preached,
and at four in the afternoon, when an anthem is sung. On Wednesdays and Fridays
in Advent and Lent, and during the whole of
Passion week, the choral service and singing
are intermitted both morning and evening.

The chapter-house is a magnificent
structure. Its form is an octagon of sixty-
three feet in diameter, and, reckoning to the
centre knot in the roof, sixty-seven feet ten
inches in height. This vast space is not interrupted by a single pillar, the roof being
wholly supported by a single pin geometri-
cally placed in the centre. The stalls for the
canons, forty-four in number, ranged along
the sides, are highly finished in stone, and

curiously wrought canopies are supported by small and elegant columns of Petworth marble. Over these runs a narrow gallery, which extends quite round the building. The capitals of the columns have a great variety of carved fancies upon them, with ludicrous, and not always chaste conceits, of the witty artists of the thirteenth century. The entrance from the north transept is in the form of a mason's square. Every other side of the octagon is adorned with a window rich in tracery and figured glass, rising from the part first above the stalls, and reaching to the roof. Of this edifice, particularly of the chapter-house, Æneus Sylvanus, afterwards Pius II. said—" It is famous all over the world for its magnificence and workmanship, but especially for a fine lightsome chapel, with shining walls and small thin-waisted pillars quite round;" and an old monkish verse, with a free translation of which this history of the Cathedral is introduced, bestows upon it this encomium :—

" Ut Rosa flos florum
" Sic est domus ista domorum."

The vestries, which are situated on the south side of the choir, contain several curiosities, which are shown and explained by the vergers ; but the most important of these relics is a large ancient horn, presented by Prince Ulphus, and bearing the following inscription, in capital letters :—

CORNU HOC, ULPHUS, IN OCCIDENTALI PARTE
DEIRÆ PRINCEPS UNACUM OMNIBUS TERRIS
ET REDDITIBUS SUIS OLIM DONAVIT.
AMISSUM VEL ABREPTUM
RENEBI. DOM. FAIRFAX DEMUM RESTITUIT,
DEC. ET CAPIT, DE NOVO ORNAVIT
A. D. MDCLXXV.

By this horn, which is made of an elephant's tooth, curiously carved, and was originally mounted with gold, the church of York holds several lands of great value, a little to the eastward of the city, which are called " Terræ Ulphi." About the time of the reformation this antique vessel disappeared, till soon after the restoration. A large and elegant bowl, originally presented by Archbishop Scroope, in 1398, to the company of Cordwainers of this city is preserved here. In the middle of the bowl is the Cordwainers' arms, richly embossed—it is edged with silver double gilt, and stands upon three silver feet; round the rim, in the old English character, is the following inscription :—

Richarde Arche beschope Scrope grant unto all those that drinkis of this cape I Uti dapis to pardon. Robert Gobson beschope mesm grant in same forme aforesaide I

Uti dapis to pardon. Robert Strensal.

On the dissolution of the Cordwainers' Company, in the year 1806, this cup was presented by the fraternity to Mr. Sheriff Hornby, of York, as a mark of their esteem, and he soon afterwards generously presented it to the Cathedral to swell the number of the curiosities. There is also shown here a state canopy of gold tissue, given by the city in honour of James I. on his first visit to York. Three silver chalices and several ancient rings found in the graves of the archbishops are exhibited ; together with a wooden head, found near the grave of Archbishop Rotherham, who, having died of the plague, was interred here in effigy. There is also a superb pastoral staff of silver, about seven feet long, with the figure of the Virgin and the infant placed under the crook. This staff was given by Catharine, of Portugal, queen dowager of England, to her confessor, when he was nominated to be catholic archbishop of York, by James II. in 1689; and it is said, that when he marched in procession to the minster, the Earl of Darnley wrested it from him, and deposited it in the hands of the dean or chapter, in whose possession it has ever since remained. An antique chair, as old as the cathedral, and in which several of the kings of England have been crowned, is still preserved here, and placed within the altar rails, when the archbishop officiates, for his use. These, with some less important relics, form the curiosities at present exhibited in the vestries.

Adjoining to the council room is the ancient treasury, which, before the reformation, contained wealth of inestimable value. At that period all its wealth was seized and converted to secular uses. The library was formerly in a room adjoining the western side of the south transept, but it is now removed to a building which was anciently a chapel belonging to the archiepiscopal palace, situated at a small distance from the north-west corner of the cathedral, and having undergone a complete repair, under the judicious direction of the very reverend the Dean, exhibits a fine specimen of the early age of Anglo-Normanic architecture. The destruction of the ancient library by repeated fires left this cathedral without so important an appendage, till the early part of the seventeenth century, when Mrs. Matthews, relict of the right reverend the archbishop of that name, presented her husband's valuable collection of books, consisting of upwards of three thousand volumes. To these has since been added a small, but select collection, bequeathed by the will of Mrs. Fothergill, relict of the Reverend

Marmaduke Fothergill, which, with several late purchases, gifts, and bequests, form together a valuable library.

The number of persons of rank and distinction, whose mortal remains are deposited in this ancient temple, is very considerable. The head of Edwin, the first christian king of Northumberland, was interred in the cathedral at York, and his body in the monastery at Whitby. History also records, amongst the persons interred here, the names of Eadbert and Eanbald, kings of Northumberland; Swein, king of Denmark; Tosti, brother of king Harold; William de Hatfield, second son of Edward III.; Thomas Mowbray, Duke of Norfolk, and Sir J. Lamplugh, both beheaded for their loyalty to the house of York; and a very large proportion of the archbishops, who have presided over this See, from the introduction of Christianity into this province to the present day. Amongst the monuments still in existence to the memory of illustrious laymen, is chiefly to be noticed that of Charles Howard, Earl of Carlisle, privy councillor to Charles II. The sepulchral monument of the Earl of Stafford, who died in 1695, and that of the honourable Thomas Watson Wentworth, third son of Edward Lord Rockingham. Amongst those of modern days, that which public esteem and affection have erected to the memory of that distinguished friend of his country and of mankind, Sir George Savile, claims the regard of all those who can appreciate extensive benevolence and distinguished patriotism.

Of the Clergy of the Cathedral of St. Peter, at York, at present, the following forms a complete list:—

The Right Hon. and Most Rev. Edward Venables Vernon, D.C.L. Archbishop of York, Primate of England, &c. &c. palace at Bishopthorpe.

The very Rev. William Cockburn, M.A. Dean of York.

#### CANONS RESIDENTIARY.

Archdeacon Markham, M.A. Wetwang.
Archdeacon Eyre, M.A. Apesthorpe.
Rev. Robert Croft, M.A. Stillington.
Rev. G. Deaneth Kelly, M.A. Ampleford.
PRECENTOR—The Hon. and Rev. E. Rice, D.D. Driffield.
CHANCELLOR OF THE CHURCH—Rev. H. F. Mills, M.A. Laughton.
SUBDEAN—Rev. Geo. Cuthbert, M.A.
SUCCENTOR OF THE CANONS—Rev. W. S. Willes, M.A.

#### ARCHDEACONS.

York—Rev. Robert Markham, M.A.
Nottingham—Rev. John Eyre, M.A.
East-Riding—Rev. R. D. Waddilove, D.D.
Cleveland—Rev. F. Wrangham, M.A. F.R.S.

#### PREBENDARIES.

Wm. Abbott, B.D. Fridaythorpe.
Robert Affleck, M.A. Tockerington.
Richard Carey, M.A. Knaresbrough.
Hon. A. H. Cathcart, M.A. Langtoft.
J. J. Coneybeare, M.A. Warthill.
E. A. H. Drummond D.D. Husthwaite.
John Dolphin, M.A. Riccall.
John Ellis, B.A. Barnby Moor.
R. P. Goodenough, M.A. Fenton.
W. R. Hay, M.A. Dunnington.
Hon. T. A. Harris, M.A. Osbaldwick.
Lamplugh Hird, M.A. Botevant.
Henry Kitchingman, M.A. Bole.
Edward Otter, M.A. Ulleskelfe.
W. Preston, M.A. Bilton.
Hon. John Lumley Savile, M.A. South Newbold.
Samuel Smith, D.D. Grindall.
Wm. V. Vernon, M.A. North Newbold.
Robert Darley Waddilove, D.D. Dean of Ripon, Wistow.
Henry Watkins, M.A. Givendale.
James Webber, B.D. Strensall.
W. S. Willes, M.A. Holme.
John Wingfield, D.D. Weighton.
T. B. Woodman, M.A. Bugthorpe.

#### COLLEGE OF VICARS.

Rev. Richard Forrest, Sub-Chanter.
Rev. James Richardson, M.A.
Rev. Wm. Bulmer, M.A.
Rev. James Dallin, M.A.
Rev. Henry A. Beckwith, M.A.
ORGANIST—Mr. Matthew Camidge.
ASSISTANT-ORGANIST—John Camidge, Musical Doctor.

1 Clerk of the Vestry, 8 singing men and 8 boys, 3 Vergers.

REGISTRAR—William Mills, Esq.

#### Officers of the Ecclesiastical Court.

CHANCELLOR AND COMMISSARY—Granville Venables Vernon, Esq. M.A.
DEPUTY-REGISTRAR—Joseph Buckle, Esq.

#### PROCTORS.

Mr. Wm. Mills.          Mr. F. W. Storry.
Mr. Wm. Askwith.        Mr. J. R. Mills.
Mr. Geo. Lawton.        Mr. Thos. Dewst.
Mr. Thos. Wilson.       Mr. J. R. Fryer.

APPARITORS—Messrs. Wm. & John Jackson. The court is held in the cathedral. Office, Minster yard—open from nine in the morning to five in the evening.

Formerly the Archbishop had a palace close to the cathedral, on the north side of that edifice, erected by Archbishop Thomas I. but it was dismantled by Archbishop Young, whose cupidity was tempted to make this spoliation by the lead which covered its roof.

The chapel of St. Sepulchre formerly stood not far from the site of the archiepiscopal palace. This chapel was built and amply endowed by Roger, Archbishop of York, and had, at the reformation, a revenue amounting to £192. 16s. 6d. After the edifice had ceased to answer the purpose originally intended, part of it was converted into a public house, and from an opening at the end of a dungeon, with which the chapel was provided, the publican named his house "The Hole in the Wall." In the year 1816, the public house became ruinous, and was taken down, when, on removing the materials, the workmen came to a subterraneous prison, some feet below the surface of the earth, which had no doubt been used, in the dark ages of cruelty and superstition, as a dungeon, for the purpose of immuring ecclesiastical delinquents. In the following year a rude piece of Saxon sculpture, cut upon a stone, which, it is conjectured, formed the base of the arch over the doorway leading into this dungeon, was found, which pourtrays a man in the agonies of death, surrounded by demons, who are tormenting his body, and seizing his departing spirit. This singular relic is deposited in the Minster library.

Not far from the dungeon is the prison and the "Hall of Pleas," for the Liberty of St. Peter. The prison, kept by Thomas Harrison, is used for offenders within the liberty, and there is a small court room in the upper story, where causes in common law arising within this jurisdiction are tried. The Liberty of St. Peter comprehends all those parts of the city and county of York which belong to the church of St. Peter, and an enumeration of which will be found in the population returns prefixed to this volume. Henry John Dickens, Esq. barrister-at-law, is the steward, and Christopher Newstead, Gentleman, of York, is the Clerk of the Peace and Under Steward for this liberty, of which Mr. John Brook is the Chief Bailiff, and Thomas Harrison the Constable. The jurisdiction is separate and exclusive, and it has its own Magistrates, Steward, Bailiff, Coroners, and Constables. Amongst its privileges, the inhabitants, men, and tenants of this liberty, are exempt from the payment of all manner of tolls throughout England, Ireland, and Wales, on the production of a certificate, which the under steward is always ready to supply. Four general quarter sessions are held for this liberty, at the sessions-house, in the Minster-yard, on the Saturday in each week appointed by statute for holding the general quarter sessions, to inquire into "all manner of felonies, poisonings, inchantments,

sorceries, arts magic, trespasses, &c."[*] And a court is held in the hall every three weeks, where pleas in actions of debt, trespass, replevin, &c. to any amount whatever, arising within the liberty, are heard. There is also a court leet and view of frank-pledge for the whole liberty, held twice a year, namely, on Wednesday in Easter week, and the first Wednesday after new Michaelmas day.

The Register Office, or the Archbishop's Prerogative Court, as it is sometimes called, is held in an old building at the east end of the cathedral, in which the registration of wills and the granting of licenses for the general diocese of York take place. The Dean and Chapter have also a distinct office, in which secular business is transacted for the inhabitants of the Liberty of St. Peter's.

The Deanery house of this cathedral is situated in the Minster-yard, and was erected in the year 1090. At the reformation the yearly tenths were valued at 30l. 17s. 0½d. and the living, which is in the gift of the king, at 307l. 10s. 7½d. The present dean is the Right Reverend William Cockburn, M.A. who was created dean in 1823. The deanery has the rectories of Pocklington, Pickering, and Kilham, of which the dean is patron and ordinary; he likewise presents to Thornton, Ebberston, Ellerburne, Barnby-Moor, Givendale, and Hayton vicarages.— He appoints also the residentaries, but must choose them out of the prebendaries, and the first prebendary he sees after a vacancy, has a right to claim the residentaryship.— The dean and the four residentaries constitute the chapter; and the value of a residentiaryship is estimated, in Bacon's Liber Regis, at 209l. per annum.

There are yet considerable remains of an ancient building erected here to the honour of St. William, Archbishop of York, called "St. William's college," for the parsons and chantry priest of the college to reside in, it being deemed contrary to the honour and decency of the church for them to live in houses of laymen and women, as heretofore. Belfrey's church is situated in the Minster-yard, but as it will be enumerated amongst the churches where service is still performed, it is unnecessary to dwell upon it here. Besides this church there were formerly two other parish churches within the Cathedral close, namely,

* The time appointed by statute for holding the General Quarter Sessions in England is—
Christmas—in the 1st week after Epiphany.
Easter—in the 1st week after the close of Easter.
Midsummer—in the 1st whole week after St. Thomas-a-Becket.
Michaelmas—in the 1st whole week after the 11th of October.

"St. Mary ad Valvas," and "St. John del Pike." The first of these edifices was removed in the year 1365, and the latter in 1585.

The Beddern was a college of vicars choral, belonging to the cathedral; and the choral was first ordained in 1252. Though standing in Goodramgate, and consequently not within the close of St. Peter's, it is always classed with that district, on account of its original connexion. The vicars choral were formerly 36, agreeing in number with the prebendal stalls in the cathedral, and besides attending to their duty in the choir, one officiated for each canon, receiving for their services the annual sum of forty shillings each. The chantries and obits, from which the vicars choral derived their chief support, being dissolved, their number is greatly diminished, and in the vicissitude of human events, the Beddern, once the seat of imperial grandeur, and subsequently of ecclesiastical pride, is now the abode of poverty, and a scene of dilapidation. The Beddern chapel, which was founded in 1348, is no longer used for the general services of the sanctuary, but is confined to the christening of children and the churching of women.—— These several appendages formerly surrounded the cathedral, and were detached from the city by walls, closed in by four large pair of gates, which were shut every night. Those gates, of which there are still some remains, were placed, the first to open into Petergate, opposite Little Blake-street; the second into Petergate, opposite Stonegate; the third at the end of College-street, opposite the Beddern; and the fourth into Uggleford.—— The circumference of the Cathedral close, with its district, is nearly three quarters of a mile, and when in its meridian glory, it formed a little ecclesiastical world of its own.

In addition to the Cathedral, there are in York twenty-three other churches, in which divine service is statedly performed.* They are——

The Church of ALL HALLOWS,* commonly called ALL SAINTS, a discharged rectory, in the gift of the crown, valued in the king's books at 5l. 16s. 10½d.§ and stated in Bacon's Liber Regis to be of the clear yearly value of 65l. 3s. 9d.‡ The Rev. Wm. Flower is the present incumbent. The church stands

* In the churches marked thus* there is only divine service on the Sunday morning, which commences at ½ past 10 o'clock; thus
† in the afternoon, at ½ past 2 o'clock; thus
‖ both morning and afternoon, at ½ past 10 and ½ past 2.
§ These books were made by commissioners appointed by the crown for that purpose, in the reign of Henry VIII. on the eve of the reformation.
‡ Published in 1786.

partly in High Ousegate, but principally in the Pavement. It is a very ancient structure, and, according to Drake, is built on the ruins of Eboracum. The body of the church and part of the steeple exhibit a very antique appearance; but the edifice is chiefly remarkable for a more modern erection of exquisite Gothic workmanship, on the old steeple. This tower is finished lantern-wise, and tradition says, that anciently a large lamp hung in it, which was lighted in the night time, as a mark for travellers to aim at, in their way to York, over the immense forest of Galtres. There is still the hook or pully on which the lamp hung in the steeple, and iron bars cross the windows, in which the glass might be fixed. This lantern, it is conjectured, was built in the fifteenth century, and there are here several old monuments cotemporary with the supposed erection of the tower. Part of the present burial ground was formerly used as a herb and fish market, but in 1782-3, the churchyard was enlarged, and the chancel being then taken down, the ground on which it stood was applied to enlarge the market-place. At the same time the whole fabric underwent a thorough repair.

ALL-SAINTS, North-street; an ancient rectory, valued in the king's books at 4l. 7s. 11d. and in Bacon's Liber Regis at 44l. 17s. 2d. The present rector is the Rev. Wm. Lea. Pickard, M.A. and the king is the patron. The service is on alternate Sundays, both morning and afternoon. In early times this rectory belonged to the priory of St. Trinity, in Micklegate, to which it was granted by the Conqueror, and confirmed by the bull of Pope Alexander II. The principal object in this church worthy of the stranger's attention, is the ancient painted glass in the windows, and a mutilated piece of Roman monumental sepulchre in the south wall.

ST. CRUX, or Holy Cross,† in the Shambles, is a rectory in the gift of the king, valued in the king's books at 6l. 16s. 8d. and in Bacon's Liber Regis 78l. 6s 9d. The Rev. John Overton, M.A. is the present incumbent. The year 1424, is the supposed date of this church, which was given by Nigell Fossard, lord of Doncaster, to St. Mary's Abbey. The steeple is of brick, ornamented with a small dome, and, like the steeple at Chesterfield, seems to have lost its perpendicular line.

ST. CUTHBERT's Church† is a rectory, and stands near the postern at the end of Peaseholm-green; the living is valued in the king's books at 5l. 10s. 10d. and in Bacon's Liber Regis at 88l. 2s. 6d.; the king is the patron, and the Rev. Thomas Henry Yorke, M.A. is the rector. There is an annual distribution of 2l. 10s. to the poor, made at this church on Martinmas Day, in virtue of a bequest made by Sir Martin Bowes, a native of York, but Lord Mayor of London, in 1545. Many ancient remains have been found in digging here, and amongst others a sepulchral tile inscribed LEG. IX. HISP.

ST. DENNIS, in Walmgate; this church is a rectory, of which the Rev. James Serjeantson, M.A. is the incumbent, and the king the patron. In the king's books it is valued at 4l. 0s. 10d. and in Bacon's Liber Regis at 31l. 17s. Divine service is performed once a fortnight, at half-past two o'clock in the afternoon. Tradition represents this church to have been originally a Jewish Synagogue or Tabernacle, but the tradition seems to rest on no sufficient authority. In the year 1796, in consequence of an injury suffered by the foundations, the west end of this edifice was taken down, and the size of the church thereby considerably reduced. At the same time, the neat and lofty spire which was perforated by a shot during the last siege of York, was taken down, and a square tower, not in good taste, substituted. The ancient porch was then also removed, but the carved door-way remains, and would grace a more entire and handsome edifice.

ST. HELEN's Church, in the Square bearing that name, was formerly a rectory, appropriated to the nunnery of Moxeby, but in the reign of Henry V. it was ordained a vicarage; the value of this living in the king's books is 4l. 5s. 5d.; in Bacon's Liber Regis, it is valued at 46l. 4s. 6d.; the Rev. John Acaster, clerk, is the vicar. Tradition says, that upon the site of this church there anciently stood an heathen temple dedicated to Diana. In the year 1743, the church-yard belonging to this church was appropriated to the public use, and a plot of land in Davygate, appropriated to the interment of the dead instead of it. In 1700, the York Tavern was erected on part of this land. Prior to these alterations, the area bore the opprobrious name of Cuckold's Corner, but after the improvement, it became St. Helen's Square, by which name it is now called. Near the entrance to the church is a large Saxon Font, in which it is conjectured that adults were formerly baptised by emersion.

The Church of ST. JOHN the Evangelist,† near Ouse-bridge, appertains to the dean and chapter of York, and though mentioned in the Liber Regis, has no value affixed to the living. The Rev. James Richardson, M.A. is the curate. In this church are interred the remains of Sir Richard Yorke, of York, Knight, mayor of the staple at Calais, and Lord Mayor of York, in 1469, and 1482. The steeple was blown down by

a high wind in 1551, and has never been rebuilt. In consequence of the recent improvements near Ouse-bridge, the burying-ground has been materially contracted, and the street made more spacious in front of the church.

The Church of ST. LAWRENCE, in Walmgate, was anciently a rectory, but is now a vicarage, of which the dean and chapter of York are the patrons. It is valued in the king's books at 5l. 16s., and in Bacon's Liber Regis at 13l. 4s. 10d. The Rev. Wm. Wright Layng, A.B. is the vicar, and divine service, which is performed once a day on alternate Sundays, commences at half-past ten in the morning. At the siege of York this church was nearly destroyed, and it remained in ruins till 1669, when it was repaired partially; but in the year 1817 it was thoroughly repaired and enlarged.

ST. MARGARET's Church,* on the north side of Walmgate, is a rectory, in the gift of the king, valued in the books at 4l. 9s. 9½d. and in Bacon's Liber Regis at 27l. 8s. 5d. The living is enjoyed by the Rev. John Overton, A.M. In 1672, the steeple of this church fell down and injured the roof, which, owing to the then poverty of the parish, was not repaired till twelve years afterwards. The porch of St. Margaret's exhibits an extraordinary specimen of Saxon sculpture and architecture, and is said to have been brought from the dissolved hospital of St. Nicholas, without the neighbouring bar. It comprises four united circular arches (ornamented with figures) below and within each other. The arches are supported by a light round column. The top of the porch is crowned with a small stone crucifix, and the effect is altogether antique and interesting.

ST. MARTIN's Church,* Micklegate, is a rectory, vested in trustees, valued in the king's books at 5l. 16s. 3d. and in Bacon's Liber Regis at 46l. 4s. 6½d. The Rev. Montagus John Wynyard is the rector. The painted glass in the windows of this church is very beautiful, and in the wall of the church yard there are several curious pieces of defaced Roman sculpture.

The Church of ST. MARTIN, the Bishop,‡ in Coney-street, is an ancient edifice, noticed in Domesday-book. The living is a vicarage, valued in the king's books at 4l. and estimated in Bacon's Liber Regis at the clear yearly value of 21l. 16s. 9d. The patrons are the dean and chapter of York, and the Rev. William Bulmer, M.A. vicar, is the present incumbent. The appearance of the exterior of the church is improved by a tower steeple, and it is rendered remarkable by a clock which projects into the street.

also a prayer meeting at 6 o'clock on Sunday morning, and at five in summer and 6 in winter on the Tuesday and Friday mornings. The other chapel is of still more recent date; it was built in the year 1816, in Albion-street, and is, from its situation, called *Albion Chapel*, and the services are at half past ten in the morning, 6 in the evening on Sundays, at 7 o'clock on Thursday evenings. This building is about half the size of the other Methodist chapel. They are both supplied with preachers from the conference in connexion with the late Reverend John Wesley.

The Calvinistic Chapel, in Grape-lane, is now occupied by the Primitive Methodists, their Sunday service is at half-past 10 in the morning: prayers at 6 in the morning and 8 in the evening: Monday and Friday services at half-past 7 in the evening: Saturday evening prayers at 8 in the evening.'

The Independents, though formerly scarcely known in York, have of late become a numerous body, and will, probably, under the ministry of the zealous and eloquent young preacher, lately called to preside over them, still further increase. Their chapel, which is eligibly situated in Lendal, and thence called " *Lendal Chapel*," was built in the year, 1814, at a cost of 3000l. and will accommodate a congregation of 1000 persons. The Rev. James Parsons is the minister; and the Sabbath services, of which there are three, commence at half past ten in the morning, half-past two in the afternoon, and half-past 6 o'clock in the evening. There is also a lecture on Thursday, and a prayer meeting on Monday, each of which services commences at 7 o'clock in the evening.

The Sandemanians, a sect of seceders from the Scotch church, founded by the Rev. John Glass, have a chapel in Grape-lane, with a small burial ground annexed. Owing to the smallness of their numbers, they have no stated pastor, but this congregation assembles for divine service every Sabbath morning at half-past 10, and again in the afternoon at 2 o'clock.

The religious community, so long the lords of the ascendant, both in this city and in this country, but now ranked as dissenters, occupy, in place of the stately Cathedral, a neat brick-built chapel, of modern erection, in Little Blake street. The Rev. Benedict Rayment is the pastor of this congregation. The morning services commences in the chapel on Sundays and Holidays, at 10 o'clock in the morning, and the evening service at 3 o'clock in the afternoon, except in the two mid-winter months of December and January, when the evening service begins an hour earlier. Every Sunday morning a musical high mass, accompanied by a sweet and full toned organ, (recently built at an expense of 500l.) is celebrated here; and in Lent and Advent public lectures are given in the evening, every Sunday, Tuesday, and Thursday, which commence at 7 o'clock.

In the suburbs of the city, without Micklegate Bar, is a large and handsome brick building, called " *The Nunnery*," which has been used since the year 1686, as a boarding school for ladies of the Roman Catholic persuasion. The assistants in this seminary having quitted the world, and devoted themselves entirely to the instruction of youth, are popularly denominated nuns, each of them constantly wears a large black veil; and exhibits other tokens of monastic peculiarity. At present the establishment consists of sixty young ladies, some of them sent from a considerable distance, for the purpose of education, more than twenty nuns, and about twelve lay-sisters, with an officiating clergyman, (the Rev. James Newham,) and four domestic servants. Mrs. Coyney is the Rev. Mother Superior of the convent. On the premises is a small chapel, in which the prayers are read every morning at eight o'clock, and on the Sabbath day also, at two o'clock in the noon. These services are open to the public. Over the general entrance is a gallery, in which several of the nuns take their station to accompany the organ during divine service, and the effect of the music may not be inaptly styled seraphic.

There are in York 30 churches and chapels, and ten monasteries and religious houses which have gone to decay. Three of the decayed churches have been already mentioned in the history of the cathedral and appendages; the others are St. Bridget, St. Nicholas, in Micklegate; St. Clement without Skeldergate Postern; St. Gregory near Micklegate; St. Peter the Little, Peter-lane; St. Clement's, nearly opposite Merchant's Hall; St. George, near New lane; St. Andrew, in Fishergate; St. Peter in the Willows, at the upper part of Layerthorpe Close: these ancient edifices were all in the ward of Walmgate. In Monk-ward the decayed churches are St. Mary's, Layerthorpe, and St. Maurice, Monkgate. In Bootham ward, St. Andrew, St. Stephen, and St. John the Baptist, in Hungate; St. Wilfrid, near Blake-street. In the suburbs there are St. George's chapel, St. George's close; St. Helen's and the church of All Saints, near Fishergate postern; St. Edward and St. Michael, Watlingate; St. Giles, in Gillygate; and the chapel of St. Mary Magdalene, near the boundary stone of the city.

The monasteries and religious houses, were the abbey of St. Mary, situated behind the Manor-house; the monastery of the Begging Friars, anciently a Roman temple sacred to the heathen god Serapis, situated in Friar's gardens; the convent of black or Dominican Friars, near Micklegate bar; the monastery of the Friars Minor, on the banks of the Ouse, formerly the occasional residence of the kings of England; the monastery of the Friars Carmelites, which in the days of its glory, occupied a principal part of the ground from Whipmawhapmagate to the river Foss; and the monastery of the Crouched Friars, at the corner of Barker-hill. In Beggargate-lane stood the nunnery of St. Clement, founded by Henry I., in 1145, for the nuns of the Benedictine order; in Stone-wall-close, the priory of St. Andrews, founded in 1202, by Hugh Murdac, for twelve canons of the order of Sempingham; the priory of St. Nicholas, Watlingate, a royal foundation, established under the patronage of the kings of England, for a select number of both sexes; and the priory of St. Trinity, in Trinity gardens, Micklegate.

The greater part of these edifices have totally disappeared; but the ruin of St. Mary's Abbey, formerly one of the glories of York, and still,

"Great in ruin, noble in decay,"

remains a monument of departed splendour. This once noble and magnificent monastery, is situated on the North side of the city, and the land gently slopes from without Bootham bar to the Ouse. The site is a fine spot of ground, nearly square, and comprehends a circuit of 1280 yards. In the Abbey wall were two principal gates, one to the East, opening into Bootham, near the gate of the city, and the other into Marygate. A spacious piece of rich ground to the North of this street, running down to the river, was used by the monks for their fat cattle, and called Almry-garth. According to Ingulphus, there was a monastery here before the conquest, in which Siward, the valiant Earl of Northumberland was interred. And tradition has placed upon this site, the temple of Bellona, from which the Emperor Severus received the presage of his death. The monastery was then dedicated to St. Olave, and its name was not changed to that of St. Mary, till the time of William Rufus, who was one of its distinguished patrons. In the year 1270, this Abbey was totally destroyed by fire, but under the direction of Simon de Warwick, the then Abbot, who laid the first stone of the new erection, it again raised its head, and in two and twenty years the identical fabric, of which we this day see the venerable remains, was completed. From this time the munificence and piety of princes and nobles, enriched the Abbey of St. Mary, and on the dissolution of the religious houses, in the reign of Henry VIII. its annual revenue, according to Speed, amounted to £2085. 1s. 5¼d. The privileges of this monastery were as remarkable as its opulence. The abbot had the honour to be mitred, and enjoyed a seat in parliament, with the title of Lord Abbot. Our eighth Henry, whose cupidity was a great deal less equivocal than his love of reformation, seised upon the revenues of the dismantled monastery, and ordered a palace to be built out of its ruins, which was called the King's Manor. This palace, however, sunk into decay, and though James I. gave orders to have it repaired, and rendered fit for a royal residence, it has, in some degree, shared the fate of the Abbey, and the whole is now in the possession of the Grantham family. Time and depredation have reduced even the walls of this venerable fabric within narrow limits; at present, the greatest part of the inclosure is a pasture; the rest is leased for gardens; and such parts of the palace as are habitable, are let in humble tenements; at which, the mitred lord abbots, in the plenitude of their power, would have cast a glance of disdain. The Manor-house is occupied as a boarding school for young ladies', for which purpose it is well adapted. Sufficient yet remains of the ruins of the Abbey, to carry the mind back to other times, and to indicate the labours and the resting place of Stephen de Whitby, whose supposed tomb-stone, thus inscribed, is seen in a small court, now a stable yard, at the East end of the cloisters: HIC: JACET: STEPANO: AB. B: ISPN. It has long been a matter of surprise and regret, that a ruin, so picturesque, and in a situation so inviting, should be disfigured with the unsightly nuisances which incumber this ancient Abbey; and it is much to be wished, that either the noble proprietor of the venerable domain, or the corporation of York, with his Lordship's permission, would so far act the part of public benefactors, as to render this an attractive scene, as it is so capable of being made, both to the inhabitants themselves, and to every man of taste and lover of antiquity that visits this ancient city

The *Red Tower*, another of the ancient buildings of York, is so called from being built of brick; it is situated not far from Walmgate bar, on the South bank of the Foss, and when York was a commercial city, commanded the Foss island. This ancient edifice, the antiquity of which can-

E

not be precisely fixed, is supposed to be nearly coeval with the period of the residence of the Romans in this country. The manufacture of brimstone in the interior of this building has aggravated the dilapidations of time, and its present appearance conveys but a very imperfect idea of the stately square structure, through the loop holes of which the engines of war were pointed to protect the navy of the port of York from hostile attack.

Behind Trinity Gardens, in the South East corner of the city, is an ancient mound, the origin of which is not known. In ancient deeds and histories it is called, *vetus ballium*, or *Old Bayle*, signifying a place of security, and probably forms the platform, as Leland and Camden suppose, of an ancient ruined castle. The mound is ornamented with a small plantation of trees, and exactly corresponds with that on which Clifford's tower is erected, on the opposite side of the river. This point commands a fine view of York, and of the rich country by which it is surrounded.

Adjoining to the wall of the Castle yard, at the South West extremity of Castlegate, stands a round tower, built by William the Conqueror, as a keep to the Castle, and called *Clifford's Tower*, a name derived from the Lords, who were anciently its wardens, and which family probably from that circumstance, claims the right of carrying the sword before the king in York. In Leland's time it was "al in ruine," and in that state it continued till the contests between Charles I. and his parliament, when it was repaired and strengthened with fortifications and a draw-bridge, a deep moat being supplied from the waters of the Foss. After the surrender of the city to the parliamentary generals, Thomas Dickinson, the Lord Mayor, a zealous supporter of the popular cause, was made governor of this tower. But in the year 1683, Sir John Reresby was appointed governor by Charles II., and in the following year, on the festival of St. George, about ten o'clock at night, the magazine took fire, and reduced the tower to a ruin, in which state it remains to this day. The cause of the fire was never correctly ascertained, but the destruction is supposed to have been intentional, and to have proceeded from that jealousy of military control, which English citizens so justly entertain, and which the presence of a fortress, commanding the city, was so well calculated to excite. At that time a popular toast in York was, "the demolition of the mince-pie," and the garrison, apparently aware of the approaching catastrophe, all escaped unhurt. At the entrance into the

keep is a square tower, the wall of which is ten feet thick; and near to it is a draw-well of excellent water, nearly twenty yards deep. The sides of the gigantic mount at which the building stands are planted with trees and shrubs, and the moat which formerly surrounded it is now so completely filled up, that the entire space, comprising about three acres, forms a beautiful garden and pleasure grounds. The property is held with other lands near the city, by grant from James I. to Babington and Duffield; the present owner is Samuel Wilks Wassk Esq. of Camblesford, near Selby, and it is occupied by Lady Grant.

York is celebrated for the number and variety of its benevolent institutions, which may be enumerated under the following heads;—Hospitals—Asylums—Schools, and other charities.

The *Hospital of St. Anthony*, was founded from three to four centuries ago, by Sir John Langton, Knt. nine times Mayor of York, for the brethren of St. Anthony. After the dissolution of the religious houses it fell into the hands of a fraternity, consisting of a master and eight keepers, who gave a feast every three years, probably out of the remaining revenues of the old hospital; but in 1625, this feast was discontinued, and the fellowship dissolved. The legendary story of St. Anthony, of Padua, and his pig, says Drake, is represented in one of the windows of the church of the Saviour. The brethren of this mendicant house used to go a begging in the city and elsewhere, and were generally well rewarded for St. Anthony's sake. But if they were not relieved every time with a full alms, they grumbled, said their prayers backwards, and told the people that St. Anthony would plague them for it. There is an inflammatory cutaneous disease, called St. Anthony's fire: this the brethren made the people believe the Saint would inflict upon them if they disobliged him, or would cure them of it, if they merited a cure. In this they had such an ascendency here, and the patron of this hospital was held in such esteem, that when any person's sow pigged, one was set apart, and fed as fat as they could make it, to give to the brethren of St. Anthony, that they might not be tormented by the fiery disease; and hence came the proverb, *As fat as an Anthony pig*. In 1646, the whole of the building in which the brethren met was re-edified, and it is now appropriated chiefly for the use of the charity school.

*Agar's Hospital* is situated near the county hospital, and is occupied by six poor aged widows, each of whom receive

14l. 18s. 4d. half yearly towards their maintenance, paid by the feoffees of Mr. Alderman Agar, the founder, out of land which now forms part of the estate of Lord Middleton.

Of Barstow's Hospital, in the suburbs of York, little is known with certainty, except that it consists of six miserable cottages, appropriated to persons of both sexes, who each receive about forty shillings a-year. The donation, it is said, was given about a hundred years ago, and the donors are supposed to have been two maiden sisters, of the name of Barstow.

The Spital, (a contraction for hospital of St. Catharine, is situated near the Mount, at the entrance to the city. This was anciently a house of entertainment for poor travellers or pilgrims, who could not afford to pay for lodgings in the town. Buildings of this kind were usually placed, extramuros, on the side of the highway, and this was a Xenodochium of that kind. In Drake's time it was kept up, and repaired at the city's expense, as a habitation for poor widows, though it was then hardly deserving of the name of a charity; but we collect from Hargrove's History, that by the successive donations of various benefactors within the last century, it now affords residences for four ancient widows, each of whom derives an income from the charity, amounting to 18l. 3s. per annum.

Colton's Hospital, is situated in Tanner row, and derives its name from the founders, Dr. Colton, and Mary his wife by whom it was provided, in the year 1717, for the occupation of "eight poor women." At present, the funds which are produced from lands at Cawood and Thorp Willoughby, yield to each of the eight inmates about six pounds a-year.

Ingham's Hospital was founded by Sir Arthur Ingham, a senior Alderman of York, in the year 1640, and endowed with five pounds a-year for each of the ten poor women, its inmates, who have also a new gown every two years. The endowment also provides, twenty nobles for "an honest able man to read prayers in the chapel," payable out of certain lands at Sheriff Hutton. The buildings forming this hospital are situated in Bootham, and consist of ten cottages, of two rooms each, with a chapel in the centre. The badge of these widows is, a silver cock gilt, the crest of the Irvin family, of Temple Newsam, of which family Sir Arthur was the founder. The patronage of this hospital is now in the Dowager Marchioness of Hertford, the eldest daughter of the late Lord Irvin, and one of the lineal descendants of Sir Arthur.

St. Leonard's Hospital is an ancient foundation, which existed before the conquest, and when in the meridian of its usefulness, supported thirteen brethren, four secular priests, eight sisters, thirty choristers, two schoolmasters, twenty-six bead men, and six servitors; but by the consent of the brotherhood, it was surrendered in the 31st year of Henry VIII. and the revenue, amounting to 362l. 11s. 1½d. placed at the disposal of the king.

The Spital of St. Loy, like that of St. Catherine, was built for the accommodation of poor travellers and pilgrims, in Catholic times; it stood on the East side of the Monk bridge, but not a vestage of it now remains.

Maison Dieu was founded in White Friar's lane, Layerthorpe, by Edward IV. whence it is natural to infer, that there must anciently have been here a monastery of White Friars also, from which the name has arisen. But on this subject, we can only conjecture; as there are no remains of either building, and, even the name of the lane itself is now no longer retained.

Mason's Hospital, in Colliergate, was founded by a widow of that name, in 1732, for the use of six poor widows, who have an annual income from the original benefactress of one pound a-year, and from the benevolent Countess of Conyngham, of fifty shillings, producing to each of them yearly, three pounds ten shillings.

Middleton's Hospital, in Skeldergate, is a monument of the piety and benevolence of Dame Ann Middleton, who bestowed by will two thousand pounds for its erection and endowment. In this hospital, twenty widows of poor freemen in York, have dwellings, with an income of five pounds sixteen shillings a-year each; three pounds sixteen shillings of which is derived from the funds of the original benefactress, and two pounds from an augmentation bequeathed by Thomas Norfolk, gent. A full length effigy of Dame Middleton is placed in a niche, over the front entrance, with an inscription, partly obliterated, enumerating her charities.

A little beyond Bootham row, and nearly opposite to Marygate, is an alms-house that few ladies in the early part of life would claim as their inheritance, called "The Old Maids' Hospital." The founder of this institution was Mrs. Mary Wandesford, of the city of York, spinster, who by will dated the 4th of Nov. 1725, bequeathed an estate at Brumpton-upon-Swale, near Richmond, with a mortgage of 1200l. and 1200l. South-Sea stock in trust, "for the use and benefit of ten poor gentlewomen, who were never married," members of the established church.

" who shall retire from the hurry and noise of the world into a house of protestant retirement, with 10*l.* per annum to a reader. Since this time the funds of the Old Maids' Hospital, have been considerably augmented by other bequests, and each of the inmates now receives 16*l.* 17*s.* 4*d.* annually, which Mr. Hargrove, from whom we quote, and who has displayed a very laudable zeal in investigating the affairs of the charities of York, intimates should be still further increased from the improved value of land within a period of nearly a hundred years. The Maiden Testator, does not in her will fix at what time of life ladies may become candidates for this charity, but the Court of Chancery, by a decree of the date of 1739, has fixed the age at fifty years. The present steward of this establishment is Mr. John Mills, with a salary of 6*l.* a-year, and the Rev. W. Bulmer, with a stipend of 15*l.* annually, is the reader or chaplain. Every Wednesday and Friday morning at eleven o'clock, duty is performed in the chapel.

Without Micklegate bar, at the principal entrance to the city on the left, is an antique stone building, called St. Thomas' Hospital, erected for the fraternity of *Corpus Christi*, incorporated by letters patent, the 6th of November, in the 37th of Henry VI. This hospital was originally instituted for a master and six priests, who were bound to keep a solemn procession every year, on the Friday after Corpus Christi day, and the day after to have a solemn mass or dirge, to pray for the prosperity of brothers and sisters living, and for the souls departed; and further to keep yearly ten poor folks, having every of them towards their living 3*l.* 6*s.* 8*d.* a-year, with a further provision that they should find eight beds for poor people being strangers. In addition to this hospitality, the fraternity found entertainment of another kind for the citizens, and once in every year, namely, on the Thursday after Trinity Sunday, they performed the play of Corpus Christi, in aid of which, every trade in the city was obliged to furnish a pageant. At that time the building was far more extensive than at present; but in the time of Henry VIII. it felt the shock of all other similar institutions, and in 1683, it was inhabited only by ten poor widows, to whom mendicity afforded the means of subsistence. In 1787, the hospital underwent considerable alterations and improvements, and the number of inmates were increased to twelve. In the year 1791, Mr. Luntley, a glover in Blakestreet, left by will 1000*l.* to this institution, the interest of which, yields nearly four guineas per annum to each of the inhabitants, and Lady Conyngham, augmented their in-

come to upwards of 6*l.* by leaving 25. a-year to be divided in equal parts among them.

Near Merchants' Hall, in Fosgate, stands an ancient Spital, called *Trinity Hospital*, founded in 1373, by John de Rawcliff, and endowed with lands worth 10*l.* a-year for the sustentation of a priest or master, and for the brethren and sisters of the same. The priest was to pray for the founder, and for the king, as well as for all christian souls, and to pay weekly to thirteen poor folks and to two poor scholars resident in the hospital, four-pence in silver each. In the 3rd of Edward VI. this hospital was dissolved, and the land was given to the king; but the hospital and chapel were kept standing, and the Merchants' Company of this city perpetuated the charity by their liberality, and at present ten poor persons—five of each sex, live in the house, and receive a stipend of 5*l.* each per annum.

The *Hospital of Sir Robert Watter*, Knight, twice Lord Mayor of York, is situated in Neutgate-lane. Sir Robert, by his will proved June 15, 1612, appointed that a hospital should be erected out of his houses in " Nowtgate, which should be for the perpetual maintenance of ten persons; to consist of a governor or reader with 3*l.* per annum, and certain brothers and sisters, to each of whom 2*l.* per annum, was to be allowed out of the lordship of Cundale. From some cause not explained, this charity has been suffered to deteriorate: the number of dwellings is only seven, and instead of ten there are only seven inmates; the reader, probably from the smallness of the stipend, does not exist, and only 14*l.* is paid to the institution, instead of twenty guineas annually.

In St. Dennis Church-lane, stands an alms-house, founded, as is supposed, by the Company of Cordwainers, and intended as an asylum for poor aged and decayed persons of that craft. This building had anciently a cupola and bell, which was tolled on the death of any of its members, and from the religious services performed in the hospital, it obtained the name of " *The Maison Dieu* —or the House of God. The Cordwainers' Company, after existing for several centuries, certainly not less than four, was dissolved in the year 1808, parliament having in that year repealed the act, on which they grounded their right to regulate the markets and their trade in general. On the dissolution of the Company, the entire patronage of the Maison Dieu, with the archieves of the fraternity were transferred to Mr. Hornby, of York, one of the principal members, and by the liberality of that gentleman, the hospital, which had sunk into a state of dilapidation, was taken down and re-built at his own cost.

This hospital now consists of four comfortable dwellings, appropriated to the use of as many decayed shoe-makers, who pay to their benefactor an annual acknowledgment of one penny. This establishment presents a favourable field for the exercise of benevolence, and we venture to recommend that some charitable person should endow it with a small portion of land, from the rents whereof the successive inmates of the Maison Dieu, who are now nearly destitute of income, may through all time have the evening of their days brightened by a humble competency.

The law of Mortmain has wisely kept the endowment of hospitals and religious houses within very moderate limits; and in more modern times the legislature† has instituted a security against death-bed charitable bequests, by providing that no lands or tenements shall be given for, or charged with, any charitable use whatsoever, unless by deed indented, executed in the presence of two witnesses twelve calendar months before the death of the donor, and enrolled in the Court of Chancery within six months after its execution, and unless such gift be made to take effect immediately, and be without power of revocation.

*Wintershelf's Hospital*, nearly opposite St. Margaret's Church, in Walmgate, was founded by Perceval Wintershelf, gentleman, early in the last century, and forms accommodation for six poor aged persons, who enjoy a revenue of from 7l. to 8l. a year.

The ladies of York have contributed essentially to swell the number of the public charities of this city, and their benevolence has in several instances embraced more than one institution. In addition to the names of pious memory already enumerated, Mrs. Wright, Dame Hewley, Mrs. Wilson, and Lady Conyngham's, remain to be mentioned :—

Mrs. Jane Wright, of the city of London, widow, left by will, in 1675, 1000l. in money, with the residue of her property, amounting to about 550l. more, to be devoted to the purpose of placing out as apprentices, as many poor boys and girls, who are natives and inhabitants of "the parish of Goodramgate, near the Minster, in the city of York, being the parish, as she says, in which I was born," as the minister, churchwardens, and vestry-men of the said parish may think proper—the residue of the income, if any, to be applied to the relief of poor widows and housekeepers in the parish, and to the assistance of the apprentices at the expiration of their apprenticeships, in commencing business. The trustees very judiciously ex-

pended the sum which they realised, in the purchase of a house in Gondramgate, and lands in Rufforth and Water Poppleton, which now together yield for the purpose of the charity 363l. a year, and which sum is distributed half-yearly, according to the will of the testatrix. By a decision of the Court of Chancery, two-thirds of this ample income is distributed in the parish of St. Trinity, and one-third in the parish of St. John del Pyke.

Lady Hewley's charities comprehend an hospital and a liberal annual contribution towards "teaching the children of the poor to read and write." The hospital is a neat brick building, situated in Tanner Row, in which ten poor women, of the Unitarian persuasion, find a comfortable asylum.* Originally, the annual stipend was only 6l. each, but from the nature of the property, under the provident management of the trustees, it is now swelled to 15l. a year, which is paid in monthly instalments by the Rev. Charles Wellbeloved. In 1700, " Dame Sarah Hewley," as she is styled, paid into the Exchequer 1000l. thereby purchasing an annuity of 63l. 10s. for ninety-nine years, to be applied to the purpose of teaching the children of the poor to read and write." For thirteen years; namely, between 1780 and 1793, the payment of the annuities was suspended for want of new trustees to fill the places of those who were deceased : but, by the zeal and public spirit of Robert Driffield, Esq. the payment of the annuity was resumed, and the arrears refunded, the effect of which has been, that the capital stock is swelled to 1650l. four per cents. and that fund is rendered permanent, which would have expired in the year 1807. The annual income from this stock is now devolved, in compliance with the will of the testatrix, to the support of free schools, in York and its vicinity, at the discretion of the trustees, John Rawdon, Esq., the Rev. Charles Wellbeloved, and George Palmes, Esq.

*Wilson's Hospital*, situated at Fossbridge, was founded in 1717, by Mrs. Dorothy Wilson, spinster, for the reception of ten poor women, each of whom has a room to herself, and for their maintenance the donor left certain lands at Skipwith and Nun-Monkton, from which each of them receives 15l. per annum. The same lands were also

---

* Dame Hewley, (whose maiden name was Wolridge) when a spinster, was a ward in chancery, and tradition says, we believe truly, that she eloped with Mr., afterwards Sir John Hewley, upon a matrimonial expedition, she riding before and he behind, on the same horse, thinking thereby to protect her intended husband from the censure of the Lord Chancellor, by alleging, that she ran away with him, and not he with her :

† By the act 9th George II. c. 36.

made subject to the following payments :—Twenty pounds per annum to a schoolmaster for teaching twenty boys, and reading prayers twice a day to them, and to the hospitalers. The boys are also to be provided with new clothes annually, and 6*l.* a year appropriated to placing three of them out as apprentices. The yearly sum of 2*l.* each is applied to three blind people; and the same sum to a schoolmistress for teaching six children in the parish of Dennis to read. Owing to the increased value of the estate, the allowance to the inmates of the hospital has advanced from 6*l.* 10*s.* to 15*l.* per annum each : the schoolmaster's salary has advanced from 20*l.* to 30*l.* and the schoolmistress's stipend is doubled. The property is vested in seven trustees, none of whom are to be aldermen of the city! The hospital has been twice taken down and re-built, the first time in 1765, and the latter in 1812, and it now forms a neat brick building of modern appearance, very convenient to the inmates, and rather ornamental than otherwise, to the part of the town in which it stands.

Amongst the most munificent of the benefactors to the city of York, may be placed the Right Honourable Ellen Countess Dowager Conyngham, who, by will dated 13th of August, 1814, bequeathed the sum of 8000*l.* in 3 per cents. consolidated Bank Annuities, for the purpose of paying certain annuities to her servants out of the dividends, but as the said annuitants died, to be paid in annuities of 20*l.* each, to poor indigent and distressed widows of poor deceased clergymen of, or who reside in the county of York. The same lady bequeathed the sum of 6666*l.* 13*s.* 4*d.* of 3 per cent. reduced Bank Annuities, the dividends therefrom to be distributed to ten poor clergymen, who should respectively be in the possession of only one living, under the yearly value of 100*l.* which living is to be situated in the county of York : the archbishop, dean, and recorder for the time being, to elect both to this and the foregoing charity. The executors to her ladyship, are also ordered to transfer 2000*l.* of 3 per cent. consolidated Bank Annuities, and to distribute the annual dividends thereof in annuities of 10*l.* each, to six poor indigent widows or unmarried women, being fifty years of age or upwards, residing in York, and not respectively possessed of 50*l.* a year, to be elected by the trustees. Her ladyship also left 3000*l.* of 3 per cent. Old South Sea Annuities, to appropriate the dividends thus—To St. Thomas' Hospital, near Micklegate bar, twenty-five pounds; to St. Catherines', ten pounds; to Middleton's, forty pounds; and to Mason's, fifteen pounds. From all which it appears, that this lady applied to charitable purposes nearly 20,000*l.* stock, to be distributed either in York, or by persons in high situations, resident in or connected with this city.

Mr. John Allen having acquired a moderate competency by his profession as a dancing-master, in this city, bequeathed by will, dated January 9, 1747, the following benefactions to its public charities :—

To the York County Hospital......300*l.*  
To the Blue Coat Boys' and Grey  
    Coat Girls' School...............300*l.*  
To the Minister of St. Michael le  
    Belfrey, for the Poor............ 40*l.*  
To light the Minster with candles  
    sooner than hitherto.. .........200*l.*  

And a sum for the erection or endowment of a hospital, which amounts to about 140*l.* a year, from which fund twelve poor old men receive each 12*l.* annually, towards their support and house rent.

The hospitals in this city, for affording medical aid to the indigent, are—The County Hospital, the Dispensary, the Lunatic Asylum, and the Retreat.

*The County Hospital* is situated in Monkgate, and owes its origin to the benevolent Lady Hastings, who, in the year 1740, bequeathed a legacy of 500*l.* for the relief of the diseased poor in the county of York, which fund being augmented by other contributions, the present edifice was soon after erected. Every person who is a benefactor of 20*l.* or a subscriber of two guineas annually, is a governor of this institution, and intitled to recommend one out or one inpatient at a time; a subscriber of three guineas annually may recommend one out and one in-patient at a time; and an annual subscription of a guinea intitles the subscriber to recommend one out-patient, and no more. Since the commencement of this establishment, on the 4th of April, 1740, to May 1st, 1822, 45,650 patients have been admitted, of whom 31,313 have been discharged cured, and 9,320 relieved. It is much to be lamented, that owing to the inadequacy of the funds, one of the large wards of this excellent institution has been entirely closed for some years, a circumstance the more to be regretted, since, with the exception of the Hull Infirmary, this is the only charity of the kind for the North and East Riding, and for the county of the city of York.—The Cow-pox inoculation is performed here gratuitously every Tuesday and Saturday mornings, from ten to eleven o'clock; and two fever wards have lately been erected in the garden of the hospital, by a separate fund raised for the purpose. The officers of the County Hospital are—William Gray, Esq. treasurer; Dr. Lawson and Dr. Wake, physicians; Mr. James Atkinson and Mr. George Champney, surgeons; the Rev. James Richardson, chaplain; Mr. Hewley Graham, steward and secretary; and Mr. Ward, apothecary. The house is visited by two gentlemen among the contributors resident in York, and, by a late regulation, the Female wards are visited by ladies.

The *Dispensary* is a small building, situated in St. Andrewgate, of the same nature as the County Hospital, though unconnected with it. Its objects are to dispence gratuitously advice, medicine, and surgical assistance, to those who are unable to pay for them. This establishment, which was opened on the 28th of March, 1788, has continued to flourish through a period of four and thirty years, and has, out of 42,488 patients, effected cures upon 29,851 of them.* The expense of this establishment last year amounted to 433*l.* and the number of patients admitted and remaining on the books was 2054, exclusive of 648 children inoculated without cost for the Cow-pox.† The officers are Dr. Beckwith Dr. Wake, and Dr. Goldie, physicians; Mr. Atkinson, Mr. Drake, and Mr. E. Wallis, surgeons; Mr. Allen, treasurer; and Mr. Wilson, apothecary.

The *Lunatic Asylum*, out of Bootham Bar, was built by general subscription, in 1774, from a plan prepared by Mr. Alderman Carr, and the building, as an edifice, is worthy of the architect. The original object of this insitution was to provide an asylum for pauper lunatics, or such as belonged to indigent families. The plan subsequently underwent a change, and it was then determined to admit opulent patients, upon the plea that the profits from the payments of the rich would contribute to the support of the poor. This change led to enormous abuse, continued through a long series of years, and it required the benevolent interference of Mr. S. Tuke, and the intrepid and persevering scrutiny of Godfrey Higgins, Esq. to clean this Augean stable, and to restore the institution to its original benevolent purpose. These salutary reforms were commenced in 1813. While the investigations were proceeding, one wing of the asylum was discovered to be on fire, and

before the flames could be extinguished, damage was done to the building and property amounting to 2,392*l.* and four patients perished in the conflagration! This disastrous event took place on the 28th of December, 1813, and served to shut out from all mortal eyes proofs of mal-administration, at which the imagination shudders. The investigation, however, continued to be prosecuted, and it terminated in the dismissal of all the servants of the house, and the resignation of Dr. Best, the physician.— From this time the whole system underwent a complete renovation: the treatment of kindness succeeded to that of coercion, and the consequence has been, that the establishment has ever since been rising in public estimation. Considerable additions have been since made to the building, an extensive new erection for females only was opened towards the end of the year 1817.— The present officers of this institution are, Dr. Wake, physician; Mr. William Allen,‡ superintendent; Mrs. Birkett, matron; and twenty keepers. There are in the house an average of about 130 lunatics, consisting chiefly of those who neither receive nor require any aid from the funds of the institution. The buildings and offices of this noble asylum occupy about three acres of ground, and there are also attached to it about two acres of garden ground. The charge for pauper patients is 8*s.* per week, and the payments of the other patients are partly regulated by their circumstances. The intention of the founders of this asylum was to confine its benefits to the county of York, but that regulation is now sometimes relaxed.

There is, at the distance of about a mile from York, near the delightful village of Healington, an establishment called the "*Retreat*, for persons afflicted with disor- "ders of the mind," founded in the year 1796, by the Society of Friends, popularly called Quakers. This establishment owes its origin to the severe treatment and death of a quaker lunatic patient in another asylum, and adds another to the multitude of instances, which are daily occurring, where good arises out of evil. The venerable William Tuke was the projector of " the Retreat," and his efforts were seconded and essentially aided by Mr. Lindley Murray, the distinguished English Grammarian of the present age. The structure consists of a centre and four wings, to which was added,

---

* Medical and chirurgical attendance are given every Monday, Wednesday, and Friday, at eleven o'clock, and medicines dispensed gratis to all proper objects, recommended by an annual subscriber of half-a-guinea or upwards, or by a donator of ten guineas or upwards. Patients incapable of attending in person are visited at their own houses.
† The hour of attendance for vaccination is Tuesday morning, between nine and ten o'clock.

‡ The spirit which actuates this gentleman may be discovered from a work, recently written by him, entitled, " Lectures on the Temper and Spirit of the Christian Religion."

in the year 1819, a new building, called, "the Lodge," for the accommodation of patients of the higher class of either sex.— The quantity of ground appropriated to this institution is twelve acres, and both the exterior appearance and the internal management are such as to discard every appearance of gloom and melancholy. The concurrent testimony of all those who have visited this institution, for the purpose of acquainting themselves with its economy and management, confirm the opinion, that it is one of the best regulated establishments in Europe, either for the recovery of the insane, or for their comfort where they are in an incurable state. "The Retreat," including "the Lodge," is capable of accommodating, and generally contains, about sixty patients, of which about two-fifths are men, and three-fifths women. This institution receives all classes of patients, and the lowest sum paid for board, washing, and medical assistance, is 4s. a week; the next class pay 8s. and the gradation is continued according to the circumstances of the patient, till, in some instances, it amounts to several guineas a week. Great stress is laid here upon the benefit of the early removal of the patients to the asylum after the first decisive symptoms of insanity have appeared, and, as an inducement to the friends of the patients to pursue this course, an abatement of 4s. a week is made in the payment for the first year, for such patients as are sent within six months after the first appearance of the disorder.— This institution, since its first establishment, has been attended with an expense of 12,000l. to the religious community with whom it originated. Its benefits are extended on the recommendation of "a quarterly meeting, donor, or annuitant," to Quakers, and to those who are not strictly members of this society, Dr. Belcombe, a physician eminent in his profession, at York, presides over the medical department, and Mr. G. Jepson is the superintendent. Neither the physician, nor any other officer or servant of this institution receives any fee, but all have fixed salaries for their services. The general management is in a Court of Directors; and visitors, both male and female, are appointed to inspect the institution. Some years ago there was a branch of this establishment formed in a building adjoining Walmgate Bar, called "the Appendage,"* in which there were, during the last year, ten patients, seven of whom were females.

* Persons wishing to become more intimately acquainted with the economy and management of this establishment, may consult with advantage, Mr. S. Tuke's "Description of the Retreat," published in 1813.

The Free Schools and Charity Schools, like the hospitals of York, are numerous;—

The *Free Grammar School* within the Close of the Cathedral, was erected by Robert Holgate, D. D. Archbishop of York, in 1546, and endowed with 12l. a year for a master, to attend daily, "to read and teach grammar, and other good authors and works, generally to all scholars thither resorting to learn the same." This is a chartered school under the designation of "the Free School of Robert Holgate;" the Archbishop is patron, and the Rev. George Graham, A. B. is the present master.

The free grammar school in that part of the city, called, "*Le Horse ayer*," is the remains of a large hospital, founded by Robert *de* Pykering, Dean of York, in 1330. On its suppression, the hospital, with all its possessions, was annexed to the Dean and Chapter of York, who, by a grant from Philip and Mary, founded a grammar school, and perpetually endowed the master with the lands; in addition to which Robert Dallison, Chanter of the cathedral church of Lincoln, granted to the Dean and Chapter of York an annuity of four pounds, issuing out of the manor of Hartesholm, in the county of Lincoln, which was appropriated to this school. The appointment of the master is in the Dean and Chapter of York, by whom the number of scholars is regulated, and that number seldom exceeds 23.— The present master is the Rev. J. Grayson. The dilapidated church of St. Andrew's has undergone strange mutations—it has been now a house of prayer, then a den of thieves; and at present part of it is used as a stable, and the other part as the free grammar school.

Three Free Schools of a minor description were erected and slenderly endowed by the late Mr. John Dodsworth, an ironmonger, in York, the first of them near the church of St. Lawrence, in Walmgate, erected in 1798, for teaching twenty poor boys to read and write, of the parishes of St. Lawrence with St. Nicholas, St. Peter-le-Willows, St. Margaret, and St. Dennis, to be chosen in equal numbers by the parishioners, in vestry assembled; the second of Mr. Dodsworth's schools is on Bishophill, for twenty poor children, from the six parishes on that side of the river, in proportion to their size; this school was opened on the first of January, 1804; and they have each an endowment of 10l. a year, bequeathed by the founder. The other school, which is in Friar Walls, is also for 20 children. The present masters of Dodsworth's Schools are, Walmgate-bar, George Brotherton; Friar Walls, James Smithies; Bishophill, John Forth.

Amongst the noblest of the York charities may be placed the *Blue Coat Boys* and the *Grey Coat Girls Schools*. On the 14th of June, 1705, a school was opened in St. Anthony's Hall, for forty boys, to be clothed, fed, and taught. The out-fit was made at the cost of the Corporation, and the fund for defraying the annual expenses arose out of voluntary subscriptions, which amounted, at the first opening of the school, to £190 per annum. That income has since been increased in more than a ten-fold degree, and it appears, from a joint report of the two schools, published in 1832, that the expenses of these establishments, from the 10th of October, 1820, to the 10th of October, 1821, amounted to £2000 15s. 3d. which sum was furnished by annual subscriptions, amounting to 476l.; permanent annual receipts, from interest of money and rents of estates, 1425l.; children's labour, 14l.; and an annual collection at St. Belfrey's church, 71l. The boys, which now amount to sixty in number, are taught to weave as well as to read, write, and cast accounts; and the girls, of whom there are forty-four, are taught to read, write, cast accounts, spin, wash, and knit, and are, under the matron's directions, qualified for good useful servants. The increase in the number of scholars took place in 1820, in consequence of a noble legacy of 4000l. bequeathed by Thomas Wilkinson, Esq. of Highthorne, late an alderman of the city. The ample funds of this charity, which, as has been already stated, was designed originally for boys only, induced the benefactors to extend the benefit of the institution to the children of the other sex, and their school house was at first in Marygate, till the year 1784, a building was erected for the purpose, in Monkgate, which is still occupied in that way.— Children are not admitted into either of these schools till they have attained their ninth year, and when they are of a proper age, the boys are put out apprentices for seven years, to sea, husbandry, manufacturing trades, or handicraft businesses, at the discretion of the committee—1007 boys have been bound apprentices since the establishment of the charity. The girls are placed out to household service, under the regulations of that school, and 311 girls have received the benefit of the institution since its first establishment in 1775. Annual subscribers of 10s. and benefactors of 10l. become trustees. The gentlemen have the direction of the boys, and the ladies the direction of the girls, and by each of them, in their respective schools, visitors are nominated to superintend the same. Mr.

Robert Davies is treasurer, steward, and secretary of both schools; Mr. Thomas Crosby and his wife are master and mistress of the boys; Mrs. Milner is matron, Mrs. Catharine Collier sewing, knitting, writing, and reading mistress; and Mr. John Peckitt secretary to the girls' school.

*Haughton's Charities* entitle the donator to a distinguished rank amongst the benefactors of this city. Mr. William Haughton, the founder of the charity school which bears his name, was originally a dancing master in York, but had removed to London, where he died in the year 1773, bequeathing 1300l. for educating twenty poor children of the parish of St. Crux, in York, to read and write English, with an addition of 900l., payable on the demise of certain annuitants. A school house has been erected near the church of St. Crux, and the Rev. John Overton is the present master, with a stipend of 200l. derived from this institution. Mr. Haughton also left the interest of 500l. to be devoted to paying the rents of poor widows in the parish of St. Crux; and he bequeathed for forty tradesmen, or other persons, ten in each ward, by way of loan without interest, 1000l. but which sum was reduced to 232l. 6s. in litigation to establish the will of the testator.

The *Spinning School*, at York, is an establishment set on foot by two excellent ladies—the late Mrs. Cappe and Mrs. Gray, in 1782. In this school sixty girls are instructed in reading, knitting, and sewing; for though it was originally intended to employ the children in spinning worsted, that design was abandoned soon after the night school was given up, and a day school established in its place. The school, which is situate in St. Andrewgate, consists of two divisions—one half the children being taught to read and knit in the junior school, on the ground floor, and the other half taught to read and sew on the second story. The children of this school are principally clothed at the cost of their benefactors, who, in addition to gratuitous learning, supply them with milk to breakfast. The present mistress of the sewing school is Mary Gladdin, and of the knitting school Hannah Robinson. Connected with this establishment, and with the Girls Grey Coat School, there is a *Female Society*, principally consisting of honorary and benefitted members, established in 1788, for the relief, in sickness, of those who have been educated at these schools. There is also a private fund formed by the contributions of the ladies, for the further relief of the benefitted members of the Female Friendly Society and others; and an annuity fund, for affording annuities of forty shillings a year, for life, to such benefitted members as have attained the age of fifty-five years. The number of members of the York Benefit Society amount to about 300, of which about one-third are honorary and two-thirds benefited members. Upon the subject of these institutions, and about female charities in general, both for children and adults, Mrs. Cappe's "observations on Charity Schools and Female Benefit Societies," published in 1805, may be consulted with much advantage.

The *Central Diocesan Society*, at York, established on the 13th of March, 1812, under the patronage of the Archbishop, for promoting the education of the poor in the principles of the Church of England, have two schools in this city, one in a spacious apartment under the Banqueting Room, at the Manor, containing 485 boys, and another in Merchant Taylor's Hall, containing 250 girls. It appears from the last annual report that there are at present, in connexion with this Diocesan Society, 131 schools, and that they have under tuition 15,377 children of both sexes, of whom 8911 are boys and 6466 girls. Mr. Samuel Danby is the master of the boys' school at York, for which duty he receives one hundred guineas a year; and Mrs. Ann Danby of the girls' school, with a stipend of forty pounds a year.

A school, partly on the *Lancasterian* plan of education, was established in Newtgate, in 1813, and removed into St. Saviourgate in 1816, where 120 girls, of all religious denominations, are instructed in reading, writing, and accounts, at the charge of one penny a week. The deficiency in the funds is made up by annual subscriptions and donations, to which the Society of Friends are the principal contributors.— Treasurer, Mrs. Hannah Catton; mistress, Hannah Wilkinson.

At the *Catholic School*, in Castlegate, of which Mr. Thomas Bolland is master, sixty boys are educated gratuitously in reading, writing, and arithmetic; and particular regard is had to instruct them in their religious and moral duties.

The York *Sunday Schools*, belonging to the Established Church, were begun in the year 1786, and are under the direction of a committee, consisting of the clergy and several laymen. At present there are in these schools between six and seven hundred children. The school-room for the boys is situate at the Merchants' Hall, Fossgate, on Bishophill, and in Bootham; and those for girls on Bishophill, in Coppergate, Bootham, Walmgate, and Bedderu. Several ladies take an active part in the conduct-

ing of these schools. Ninety bibles, the gift of Lord Wharton's trustees, are annually distributed amongst the scholars.— Every scholar to be entitled to one of these bibles has to say by heart the Church catechism, and the 1st, 15th, 25th, 91th, 101st, 113th, and 145th psalms, and to be well acquainted with the principles of the Christian religion. In these schools the National system of education has been lately adopted with considerable success.— There is a Sunday school for boys, belonging to the parish of All Saints, North-street, under the direction of the worthy rector, the Rev. W. L. Pickard, but it is quite unconnected with the Sunday school committee. The Sunday school committee also superintend the schools established by the late John Dodsworth, Esq. and also the concerns of the Charitable Society.

The *Methodist Sunday Schools* in York contain 600 scholars, of whom 333 are girls, and 268 are boys: of this number 220 girls and 210 boys receive instruction at the schools in Fossgate, of which there are two; and 113 girls and 58 boys are taught in the chapel in Albion-street. The *Primitive Methodists* have a small Sunday school in Grape-lane, consisting of twenty-five boys and the same number of girls.

In the *Sunday School of Lendal Chapel* held in a spacious room in the basement story of that edifice, 390 Sunday school scholars receive instruction from twenty-five teachers.

The *York Emanuel* is an institution without any building attached to it, established in the years 1781-2, for the benefit of ministers of all denominations, and the wives, widows, and children of ministers in any part of the kingdom, labouring under the misfortune of blindness or idiocy, who appear to the governors to be proper objects.— The term *blindness* is construed literally, and such a deprivation of sight as disables the candidate from performing the usual duties of life, renders him or her eligible; idiocy is such a deprivation of reason as is not deemed lunacy. Persons applying for relief transmit a statement of their case in writing to the secretary, (Richard Townend, Esq.) previous to the general meeting, held in York half-yearly, on the second Thursday in April and October, authenticated by one justice of the peace and two neighbouring ministers. The annuities granted fluctuate between fifteen and fifty pounds.— This institution owes its origin to the distressed situation of a clergyman of the name of Daniel Hall, of Leven, in the East Riding, who, at the age of sixty-five, was obliged to perform the duties of three cur-cies for ninety pounds per annum, and who, in a declining state of health, had no other means of supporting a wife and ten children, five of whom were blind. To provide an annuity of fifteen or twenty pounds a year for each of those blind children, a subscription was set on foot, and the appeal made to the benevolent on their behalf produced a sum of £4000. With the surplus which this subscription afforded the York Emanuel originated, and at the period of the publication of the last report, the fund for its maintenance was swelled by the contributions of the benevolent to £10,000 stock in the three per cent. consolidated annuities.

The other charitable institutions of York are :—The Charitable Society for the relief of the distressed actually resident in York ; and the Benevolent Society, for the relief of strangers in casual distress, both which societies visit those they relieve. The Lying-in Society ; the Bible Society ; the Church Missionary Society ; the Religious Tract Society ; the Hibernian Society ; and the Society for the Conversion of the Jews. The Clothing Society ; the Faithful Female Servant Society ; and the Society for the Suppression of Vice and Immorality, the main object of which is to co-operate with the Hull Penitentiary, and to send unfortunate females who wish to relinquish their vicious courses, to that asylum. There is also a Vagrant Office, in Little Shambles, by which vagrancy is checked and the distressed traveller relieved. Formerly there was in this city a Society called the Humane Society, for the recovery of drowned persons, &c. on the plan of the Royal Humane Society in London. The York institution now no longer exists, but as the directions of those establishments for relieving the apparently dead, cannot be too generally promulgated, they are here subjoined :—

## DIRECTIONS.

### WHAT THOU DOEST——DO QUICKLY.

On the alarm of any person being DROWNED, SUFFOCATED, &c., send to the nearest RECEIVING-HOUSE ; and also, if it can be done, send another person for medical assistance.

The RECEIVING-HOUSE will instantly prepare the couch, light a fire in the room, and provide two or three gallons of boiling water.

The BODY, in the mean-time, must be conveyed gently to the Receiving - House, wrapt in a blanket, coat, or other warm covering, with the head raised.

Not more than *four* or *five* persons, besides the medical assistants, to be allowed, on any account, to enter the room where the body is placed.

When the body is in the room, strip and dry it ; clean the mouth and nostrils ; lay it on the couch, in cold weather near the fire, and cover it with a warm blanket ; and gently rub it with warm flannels.—In summer, expose the body to the rays of the sun ; and in hot close weather, air should be freely admitted.

YOUNG CHILDREN to be put between two persons, in a warm bed.

If MEDICAL ASSISTANTS do not speedily arrive, then let the body, if DROWNED, be gently rubbed with flannel sprinkled with spirits or flour of mustard, and a heated warming-pan, covered, may be lightly moved over the back and spine.

To RESTORE BREATHING—Press or pinch the mouth or nostrils exactly close, for the space of half a minute, or a minute, then let them free ; but if no perceptible sign of life appears, then introduce the pipe of a bellows (when no apparatus is at hand) into one nostril ; the *other*, and the mouth being closed, *blow into or inflate the lungs*, till the breast be a little raised ; the mouth and nostrils must then be let free.—Repeat this process till life appears.

TOBACCO-SMOKE, or the SMOKE of MYRRH or FRANKINCENSE, is to be thrown gently into the fundament, with a proper instrument, or the bowl of a pipe covered, so as to defend the mouth of the assistant.

The BREAST to be fomented with *hot spirits*—hot bricks or tiles, covered, &c. to be applied to the soles of the feet, and palms of the hands.

If no signs of life appear, the body is to be put into the warm bath.

Electricity is recommended to be early employed by the medical assistants, or other judicial practitioners.

IN CASES OF INTENSE COLD. Rub the body with *snow, ice*, or *cold water*. —Restore warmth by slow degrees ; and, after some time, if there be no appearance of life, the above means for restoring the drowned must be employed.

HANGING. A FEW OUNCES of BLOOD may be taken from the jugular vein, or the arm ;—Cupping glasses may be applied to the head and neck ;—Leeches also to the temples. The other methods of treatment, the same as recommended for the apparently drowned.

SUFFOCATION, BY NOXIOUS VAPOURS or LIGHTNING. COLD WATER to be repeatedly thrown upon the face, &c., drying the body at intervals.—IF THE BODY FEELS COLD, employ gradual *warmth*, and the above process for restoring the drowned.

INTOXICATION. The BODY is to be laid on a bed, with the head a little raised; the neck-cloth, &c. removed. Obtain immediately MEDICAL ASSISTANCE, as the *modes of treatment must be varied* according to the circumstances of the patient.

GENERAL OBSERVATIONS. ON SIGNS OF RETURNING LIFE, a tea-spoonful of warm water may be given; and, if swallowing be returned, warm wine or diluted brandy.

The patients must be put into a warm bed, and, if disposed to sleep, they will generally awake perfectly restored.

The MEANS above recommended, are to be used for THREE OR FOUR HOURS. It is an absurd and vulgar opinion to suppose persons irrecoverable, because LIFE does not soon make its appearance.

*Bleeding and Salt never to be employed, unless by the direction of the Medical Assistants.*

Benevolent persons, by immediately pursuing and persevering in the above directions, have restored many lives.

At the same time, it is proper always to recommend the attendance of the Faculty, as their professional knowledge will induce them to direct and vary the above means of restoring life, according to accidental circumstances.

The commercial and trading establishments of York are numerous, amongst which the Banks naturally take the precedency: There are here three banking establishments exclusive of the Savings' Bank, namely,

Messrs. Raper, Swann, Clough, Swann, Bland, and Raper, Coney-street, who draw on Sir R. C. Glyn, Bart. Mills, Halifax, Glyn and Co. No. 12, Birchin-lane, London.

Messrs. Wilson, Tweedy, and Wilson, High Ousegate, who draw on Sir William Curtis, Bart. Robarts, and Curtis, 15, Lombard street, London.

Messrs. Wentworth, Chaloner, Rishworth, and Co. Low Ousegate, who draw on Messrs. Wentworth, and Co. No. 25, Threadneedle street, London.

All the York Banks open at nine, and close at four o'clock.

The Savings' Bank, established in 1816, in New street, is in a flourishing situation, and has investments to the amount of 70,923*l.* 0*s.* 1*d.* made by 1854 depositors, consisting chiefly of servants and labouring persons.— Mr. Francis Carbutt is the secretary, and the hours of business are from 12 to 1 on Tuesdays, and from 11 to 1 on Saturdays.

There are four newspapers published in York:—

The *Courant*, published in Coney street, on Tuesday, by Mr. Henry Cobb.— This is the senior paper in York, and being

established in 1720, is of course upwards of a century old. Its present politics are favourable to the Whig principles.

The *Chronicle*, published on Thursday, in Coppergate, by Mr. Wm. Blanchard, was established by Mr. Christopher Etherington, on the 18th of December, 1772. The politics of this paper are Tory, but not...

The *Herald*, published in the Pavement, on Saturday, by Messrs. Hargrove, Gawthorp, and Hargrove. This paper was established on the 1st of January, 1790. Messrs. Wilson, Spence, and Mawman, was afterwards published by Mr. Alexander Bartholoman, (who had been many years the overseer of their printing office,) and has always been decidedly a Whig publication.

The *Yorkshire Gazette*, published in the Minster yard, on Saturday, by Messrs. Wolstenholme and Co. This paper was established on the 24th of April, 18.. and is a decided Tory publication.

*Pick's Racing Calendar* was begun in 1786, and has been yearly continued to the present time. Mr. Thomas Sotheran, bookseller, is the proprietor and publisher. ... also produces annually, in March, the ... *Companion.*

A new *Racing Calendar* was commenced in 1821, by Mr. Robert Johnson, and will continue to be issued from his press, generally early in March.

In this city there are nominally three market days, namely, Tuesday, Thursday, and Saturday, but the principal market on Saturday. There is also a market for Swine, held every Wednesday, near Fossbridge.

The merchants of the staple have long since ceased to reside in York, the trade in wool in this city was for some ages discontinued; but on the 6th of May, in the year 1706, the wool market was revived, and there is now a wool fair, as it is called, held in Peaseholme green, every Thursday, from Lady-day to Michaelmas, which is well attended, and at which the growers from the North and from the East, meet the consumers from the West to sell their fleeces. There is also a leather fair, held in ... street, on the first Wednesday in March, June, September, and December, which, though so recently established as 1818, is become a mart of considerable consequence.

These flourishing branches of trade serve to compensate for the declension of business at the "Butter Stand" in Micklegate. Formerly great quantities of this article was brought to York, and after being weighed here by officers appointed for the purpose, was purchased by contractors, and shipped to London. Thirty years ago 80,000 firkins of butter were annually received at this office; now the quantity does not exceed one-sixth part of that amount.

The Fairs held in this city are numerous: In Peaseholme green there is a Line Fair on the Saturdays before Michaelmas Day, Martinmas Day, Christmas Day, Lady Day, St. Peter's Day, and Lammas Day, (all old style) as well as on Whit Monday. The line or flax is brought from the neighbourhood for sale, and the fair, which commences about nine o'clock in the morning, is over by eleven.— The three great Cattle and Horse fairs of York are held on the grounds out of Bootham Bar, called the Horse Fair, on Whit Monday, St. Peter's Day, and Lammas Day.— Besides these, there are several minor fairs, for horses, horned cattle, &c. held in Walmgate, Fossgate, the Pavement, and Petergate.

The Merchant Tailors' Company assemble quarterly in their hall, in Aldwark, to transact their business; but the concerns of the fraternity not requiring much room, they have very laudably awarded a considerable part of their premises to the use of charitable institutions. The master of this guild is Mr. Wm. Whitehead; and the wardens are Messrs. H. Stephenson, J. Wade, George Knowles, and John Hollins; the searchers are Messrs. John Nicholson and Geo. Vause.

The MERCHANTS' COMPANY of York, for the encouragement of trade, is of considerable antiquity, and has outlived the commerce of the city. Their hall is situated in Fossgate; and the old stone archway by which it is entered is surmounted by the arms of the Merchants of the Staple. The officers are chosen triennially, and consist at present of Mr. J. Hodgson, governor; Mr. Seth Agar, deputy-governor; Messrs. C. J. Hanson and H. Stead, wardens; and Mr. Thomas Ward, secretary. On the ground floor of the hall there is a chapel, and a hospital called "Trinity Hospital," endowed by the Company, in which five aged men and five aged women live, and are allowed each 5l. annually.

The offices for the distribution of stamps for the West and North Ridings are held in this city; that for the West-Riding in Petergate, of which Wm. Gray, Esq. is distributor; and the North-Riding office is in New street, of which Wm. Hale, Esq. is distributor. The East-Riding stamp office is at Hull.

The Post-Office is in Lendal, near the Mansion-house and the York Tavern, close to St. Helen's square. William Oldfield, Esq. is the post-master; and a comprehensive scale, communicating a considerable body of information relating to that establishment, will be found at page 107, in the present volume; after which will also be found copious details relating to the carriers and coaches to and from this city.

The commerce and traffic carried on upon and through the medium of the Ouse, though now much less than in remote times, is still very considerable. Regular trading vessels between London and York, of the burden of from 110 to 180 tons, navigate its waters, and vessels of about half that burden are constantly passing between Hull and this city, from which goods are conveyed by water into the interior of the county, as far as Boroughbridge and Ripon. There is also a packet boat from Newton-on-Ouse, and another from Selby and Cawood, which arrive and return every Saturday, as well as a steam-packet from thence to Gainsbro'.— York is amply supplied with coal, brought up the Ouse in barges from Flockton, Haigh Moor, and Silkstone, all in the West-Riding: and the inhabitants are supplied with water by the Water Works Company, from the works in Lendal, of which Mr. Ransley is the managing clerk, under the direction of a committee. On the Foss there is a navigable communication from the junction of that river with the Ouse, to the parish of Stillington, in the North-Riding.

The Hawkers' and Pedlars' Office is situated in the Mint-yard, and is kept by Mr. George Burnell. From this office licences are issued yearly, on the 1st of August.

The Excise-Office is in Spurriergate, and is open from 8 o'clock in the morning to 5 o'clock in the afternoon. Thos. Hall, Esq. of Bishop-hill, is the collector; Mr. Wm. Simpson, of Fowler's court, Spurriergate, is clerk; and Mr. Thos. Bushby, of Spurriergate, the supervisor. There are also attached to this establishment eight officers of division, and three for the different rides, exclusive of two permit writers & an office keeper.

The manufactories of York are neither numerous nor upon a large scale; there are, however, some establishments of this nature which claim attention.—The white and red lead manufactory of Messrs. Charles Liddell and Co. in Newtgate-lane, is an extensive concern in that line, and the process attracts a good deal of notice in York. The glass manufactory of Messrs. Prince and Prest, in the Suburbs near Fishergate Bar, was established in 1797, and is chiefly employed in the fabrication of Flint glass, vessels and glass phials. The wholesale book concern of Messrs. Wilson and Sons, in High Ousegate, ranks among the first establishments of the kind out of the metropolis. This city has also manufactures of carpets, linen, stuffs, flax, cordage, agricultural implements, combs, gloves, paper hangings, articles in chemistry, musical instruments, and jewellery, and the art sculpture is practised with considerable

F

cess. In this, as in the other principal cities of England, there is an incorporated Goldsmiths' Company, which is authorised and directed by Act of Parliament to elect two wardens yearly, and to appoint an assay master or assayer. The Assay Office in York is situated in Feasgate, and the assay days are Tuesday and Friday in every week. Mr. William Greaves North is the present assayer. The persons forming the Goldsmiths' Company are those who have served a regular apprenticeship to the trade, are free of, and inhabitants of the city, and by them all elections and appointments relating to their corporation are made.

The population of York, within the last ten years, has increased about seventeen per cent. upon the population of 1811; in that year the return was 19,099, it is now 22,529, as appears from the following

## POPULATION RETURN

OF THE SEVERAL PARISHES OF THE CITY OF YORK, MADE TO PARLIAMENT ON THE 28TH OF MAY, 1821.

| | |
|---|---|
| All Saints, North street | 910 |
| All Saints, Pavement | 554 |
| All Saints, Peaseholme | 223 |
| Andrew St. | 185 |
| Castle of York | 152 |
| Crux St. | 327 |
| Cuthbert St. | 209 |
| Dennis St. | 1093 |
| Giles St. | 681 |
| Helen St. Stonegate | 678 |
| Helen St. on the Walls | 398 |
| John St. Delpike | 367 |
| John St. Evangelist, Micklegate | 938 |
| Lawrence St. | 799 |
| Margaret St. | 808 |
| Martin St. Coney street | 610 |
| Martin St. Micklegate | 562 |
| Mary St. Bishop hill, jun. | 767 |
| Mary St. Bishop hill, sen. | 681 |
| Mary St. Castlegate | 939 |
| Maurice St. | 798 |
| Michael St. le Belfrey | 1343 |
| Michael St. Spurriergate | 593 |
| Mint yard | 133 |
| Olave St. Marygate | 666 |
| *Peter St. Liberty | 994 |
| Peter St. the Little | 680 |
| Peter St. le Willows | 418 |
| Sampson St. Patrick Pool | 1041 |
| Saviour St. | 987 |
| Trinity, Goodramgate | 527 |
| Trinity King's Court | 557 |
| Trinity, Micklegate | 845 |
| Wilfred St. | 227 |
| Total | 22,529 |

* That part within the City or Suburbs.

The places of public amusement and relaxation in this city are the theatre, the assembly rooms, the concert rooms, the race course, the cock pit, and the bowling green; with the public baths, walks, and rooms, and other places of less importance.

The *Theatre Royal* is conveniently situated in the spacious opening at the upper part of Blake street. The present building was erected by Mr. Joseph Baker, in 17— in the early part of the theatrical career of Tate Wilkinson, Esq. who, in 1769, became manager, under a patent from the Crown. This edifice has just undergone very considerable improvements; the square form of the interior is changed for the semi-circular and instead of the row of boxes there, now two entire tiers, with very handsome lobbies; but the most material of the alterations consists in the improved entrance. Formerly it was through a narrow tortuous passage, where the visitants to the boxes, pit, and gallery, indiscriminately pressed together—now, on the contrary, the entrance to the gallery is through the Mint yard, and a spacious hall in front receives the frequenters of the boxes and pit upon their first entrance into the theatre, but they immediately separate; the former turning to the left, ascend two capacious flights of stone steps, and the latter proceed straight forward through the hall of entrance to the pit. The whole of this part of the building is fire proof. Upon attaining the summit of the first lobby on the left, an elegant saloon presents itself, where confectionaries and other refreshments may be had by the company. The house is lighted with wax, supported by handsome glass chandeliers, and the embellishments in the pannels round the theatre, which are in *basso relievo*, reflect great credit upon Mr. Rhodes, of Leeds, the artist, by their chaste and classical effect. The cost of these improvements has been defrayed out of a fund raised for the purpose by voluntary contributions, towards which Mr. Mansel, the present spirited manager, was a large contributer, the corporation subscribing 200L.; and the city of York can now boast of as beautiful a theatre as any in the kingdom. The theatrical season here is from the beginning of March to the latter end of May, and during the assize and race weeks. The house is calculated, at the ordinary prices of 4s. boxes, 2s. pit, and 1s. gallery, to hold 200l. It is only justice to the York stage to add, that it has had the honour to furnish more talent for the metropolitan boards than any other provincial establishment in these islands.

The *Assembly Rooms* are in Blake street, near the theatre. The edifice formed by this suite of gay apartments was erected by subscription, in shares of 5l. and 50l. each, in the year 1730, from a design by the celebrated Lord Burlington. The vestibule, or entrance room, is 32 feet by 21 wide, and 21 feet high. The assembly room is an antique Egyptian 112 feet long, 40 feet broad, and 40 This room consists of two orders, lower part exhibiting forty-four columns, rich capitals, on which the wall above raised up, and an elegant cornice combine the Corinthian order; the upper part is after the composite, decorated with festoons, in imitation of acorns and oak leaves, surmounted with a beautiful cornice, enriched with curious ornaments. From the ceiling are suspended thirteen lustres of crown glass, each holding eighteen wax candles. On the right is the lesser assembly room, measuring 66 feet by 22, the ceiling of which is adorned with beautiful antique fret-work. In the assize and race weeks these rooms are open for concerts and assemblies, and at other times frequently display an assemblage of fashion and splendour, which serve to revive the recollection of the days when our Edwards and Henries held their courts in this our ancient city. During the winter there are five subscription concerts in these rooms, which usually commence in January; and four benefit concerts, with a separate subscription for quadrille dances and card parties, called " the York Winter Assemblies." The managers of the concerts are, Dr. Camidge and Mr. P. Knapton.

The *Yorkshire Amateur Concerts*, established at Sheffield, in 1806, for the gratification of a musical taste and the promotion of social intercourse amongst the lovers of harmony in this county, is held at York triennially. The performance which is annual in succession at Sheffield, Leeds, and York, continues for two days, and affords one of the richest musical treats that is to be enjoyed in any part of the kingdom.

Next to New Market, York Races bear the first rank upon the English turf—and if in England, then in the world. In Camden's time horse racing was a favourite amusement in the surrounding forest of Galtres, and as a golden bell, which was tied on the forehead of the winning horse, was the prize, hence the phrase arose of " bearing away the bell." In latter times Clifton's Ings were the scene of generous strife, but in the year 1709, Knavesmire, so called from being the swampy pasture of the poor householders' cattle, has been used for this purpose.[*] In 1713, the King's gold cup, for which one hundred guineas has since been substituted,

[*] Knave, the Anglo-Saxon term for a man of low condition. On the last day of the August Meeting, in 1804, a four mile race was run upon this course, which will be long memorable in the annals of the turf. The match was between Mrs. Thornton, backed by the Colonel, and Mr. Flint; and the attractive novelty of the scene was so great, that 50,000 spectators were that day drawn to Knavesmire. In the early part of the contest the fair jockey rode with great spirit and dexterity, but while running the third mile her horse, Vingarillo, broke down, and she of course lost the race. York has long been famous for its attachment to racing, both equestrian and pedestrian. In the winter of 1773, Powell, the pedestrian, undertook for a considerable wager, to go from London to York and back again in six days. On Monday, the 29th of November, he commenced his task, early in the morning, and at half-past two o'clock in the afternoon of Wednesday, he arrived in York, attended by a vast concourse of spectators. After an hour and a half's repose, he again resumed his labour, and arrived at Hick's Hall, London, at half past six o'clock on Saturday night, amidst the congratulations of 500 horsemen, and an innumerable multitude of pedestrians, who had gone out to Barnet to meet him. Fuller, in his " Worthies," mentions an equestrian feat of a Yorkshireman, not less extraordinary. John Lepton, Esq. of York, a gentleman in the service of James I. for a considerable wager, undertook to ride, on horseback, three times from London to York, and three times from York to London, in six days, being a journey of nearly two hundred miles each in six successive days. On Monday, the 20th of May, 1606, he commenced his journey, from Aldersgate, and arrived in York before it was dark at night. The next day he travelled from York to London; and this he did successively every day in the week, " to the greater praise of his strength in acting," says our author, than " to his discretion in undertaking the task." William Nevison, the notorious highwayman, whom Charles II. used to call *Swift Nick*, after committing a robbery near London, about sun rise, rode his mare to York in the course of the day, and appeared upon the Bowling Green in that city, before sun-set. From this latter circumstance, when brought to trial for the offence, he established an *alibi*, to the satisfaction of the Jury, though he was in reality guilty—and thus was indebted for his life rather to the fleetness of his horse than to the integrity of his conduct. But a career of flagitious crime generally terminates in ignominious punishment. Nevison, though he escaped this time, was afterwards brought to trial for another robbery, of which he was found guilty, and executed for the offence.

F 2

was procured for these races, and has ever since been run for on the first day of the August meeting. The course is at a distance of about a mile from York, to the left of the London road, and the accommodation both for the company and the racers is of the first order. The meetings are in May and August, in each successive year. Mr. Robert Rhodes is the clerk of the course, and Mr. Parkinson the steward of the Grand Stand. "The Stand" and the "Round House," were both built by subscription, and are open to subscribers, and non-subscribers are admitted to them during each meeting on paying a guinea.

The salubrious recreation of the *Bath* may be taken in York at any period of the year. Near the New Walk there is a very eligibly situated cold bath, with two convenient dressing rooms, one for ladies and the other for gentlemen; and at Lendal Tower, adjoining to the water works, there is a suite of baths, hot, tepid, and cold.

The prisons in York are the Castle, the New Gaol, the new House of Correction, and St. Peter's prison. *The Castle* is situated at the end of Castlegate, near the confluence of the Foss and the Ouse. Formerly the waters of the Foss were drawn in a deep moat round the Castle, and in the early part of the last century, this prison was inaccessible, except by two draw-bridges; but the moat is now entirely filled up, and the access is by folding doors, and a postern lodge, from Castlegate. According to Drake, there was a castle in York before the time of William I. at the place called "the Old Bayle;" but that fortress has now disappeared, and the present Castle was, as our historian conjectures, built on a Roman tower, by the Conqueror, and made of unusual strength to keep the citizens and the Northumbrians in awe of their tyrant. For some ages after the conquest this was the constant residence of the High Sheriff of the county in succession, as the Mansion-house is now the residence of each successive Lord Mayor: it was likewise the storehouse for the king's magazines, and the treasury for such part of his revenue as was kept in the North. It was then a fortress, in which however, the Assizes were held; but towards the end of the seventeenth century, it was converted into a prison, to which purpose it has been ever since appropriated. Though the Assizes for the three Ridings are held here, the Castle is not within any of them, nor is it in the jurisdiction of the city; it is extra parochial, though it is assessed, and bears charges with the parish of St. Mary, Castlegate. The extent of the city's liberties are within twenty-nine yards

of the Castle gate, and the boundary is marked by the city arms, of five lions, cut in stone, and placed in the wall on each side of the street.* The Castle, with its appendages, occupies about four acres of ground; the walls are 1100 yards round, and within the walls, in front of the Castle, is an area, called the Castle yard, of the size of about an acre, in which the county meetings for the election of knights of the shire, and other public business, are held.

The buildings, which form three sides of a square, consist of the County Gaol, in front, the Record Office, &c. to the East; and the County Hall, to the West of the Castle yard; the wall to the North, which, with the lodge, completes the square, is built at the foot of the mound, formed by the ruins of Clifford's tower. The *County Gaol* occupies the site on which the towers of the Castle anciently stood. These towers having sunk into a ruinous state during a lapse of six centuries, they were taken down in the year 1701, and the present structure was raised in their stead. The funds for this public work were obtained by a tax of three-pence in the pound on all lands, &c. within the County; and, at the time of its erection, it was considered an edifice "so noble and complete, as to exceed all others of the kind in Britain, perhaps in Europe." This building consists of two wings, divided by the felons' court yard. The right wing is a prison for debtors, ascended by a large double series of steps, and contains twenty-two rooms, sixteen feet square, and nearly twelve feet high, with apartments for the use of the governor; which office is at present, and has been for many years filled, much to the public satisfaction, by Mr. Wm. Staveley.† In a room at the entrance to this wing, is a large closet or recess, occupied by the under gaoler, Wilson, in which the curiosities of the Castle, quaintly called "the King's plate," consisting of the deadly weapons, and heavy chains of the most notorious offenders, are deposited and exhibited. In the left wing of this building is a chapel, used for divine service, and ascended by

---

* The city arms were formerly argent, with only a cross gules. The five Lions were afterwards added by William the Conqueror, in honour of the five brave magistrates, Clifford, Housegate, Talbot, Lascelles, and Errington, who so valiantly defended the city against his arms, in 1070, until obliged to surrender through famine.

† This is considered a situation of great trust and responsibility, and the Governor has a salary of £700. a year, besides the prison fees, which amount to a considerable sum annually.

steps, corresponding to those on the right. The Rev. William Flower, jun. is the present Chaplain, and the Rev. James Richardson, is the Lecturer. The felons' cells in the rear of the court yard, are in general about seven feet square, and eight feet high. The building on the East side of the Castle yard contains apartments for the Clerk of Assize, the county record, an indictment office, hospital rooms, (attended by Mr. George Champney, the surgeon,) and cells for the female prisoners; it was erected in the year 1780, and considerably enlarged three years afterwards. The whole length of this building is 150 feet, and its front is adorned with an elegant colonnade, with four Ionic pillars, corresponding to the County-hall.— The County-hall, or Basilica, on the West side of the area, was built in 1763, at the charge of the County, John Ramsden, of Byrom, Esq. being then High Sheriff. In 1777, it was rebuilt in a more modern style of architecture, with a portico entrance of six Ionic columns, thirty feet high, surmounted by an elegant statue of Justice, and other emblematic devices. The length of this building is 150 feet, and its breadth 44 feet. Here the business of the various courts is transacted through the year, and the Lent and Lammas Assizes are held in the crown court to the left, and the *nisi prius* court to the right of the entrance. Near the Grand Jury room, in the rear of the building, with an aspect to the Ouse, is the New Drop, used for the execution of criminals. Formerly, the last and most awful sentence of the law was executed on a gallows, out of Micklegate bar, at a place called Tyburn, about a mile from the city; but, in 1802, the present platform was erected, and on the 28th of August, in that year, the first execution in this situation took place. Since that time, to August, 1822, seventy-three malefactors have been executed here, making an average sacrifice in this county alone, of nearly four lives a year to the criminal laws. The county of York is in that judicial division of the kingdom, called the Northern Circuit; and the High Sheriff for the County, for the year 1823, is Walter Fawkes, Esq. of Farnley Hall.

The *New Gaol*, for the City and Ainsty of York, is a handsome and commodious stone building, of modern erection, begun in the year 1802, and completed in 1807. This structure occupies part of the site of the ancient castle, called "the Old Bayle," near Skeldergate postern. The outer wall, which is of brick, incloses about three quarters of a square mile, in the centre of which stands the prison, with a neat court yard in front, adorned with a cupola and vase, which are seen in various parts of the city and its neighbourhood. The building consists of three stories, part of which is occupied by felons, and the second and third by debtors. The office of governor is filled by Mr. George Rylah, who has a salary of 150*l.* a-year, exclusive of gaol fees; his apartments form an outshot building behind the prison, in the attic story of which is a chapel, in which the Rev. William Flower, sen. the Chaplain, preaches a sermon every alternate Sunday, and reads prayers every Thursday evening to the prisoners. Mr. George Champney discharges the duties of surgeon to this prison. The executions here are happily very rare; during the last fifteen years there have been no more than two, and when they take place, a scaffold is erected without the wall, next to the Old Bayle hill.

The Gaol for the imprisonment and correction of " lesser criminals," was formerly a part of St. Anthony's hall, on Peaseholme green; but in the year 1814, a structure was completed on Toft-green, under the direction of Mr. Peter Atkinson, architect, and city steward, which may rank amongst the best constructed prisons in the kingdom. The expense attendant upon the erection of this prison, like that for the building of the city gaol, was defrayed by a joint assessment on the City and on the Ainsty, for the use of both of which it is intended, the former contributing three-fifths, and the latter two-fifths. The governor is Mr. John King; the Rev. Wm. Flower, sen. is the Chaplain, and performs service once every alternate Sunday, and reads prayers every Tuesday evening. This establishment, which admits of the classification of prisoners, may serve as a model to those who may be engaged in the erection or management of prisons.

The Courts of Justice in York are the Castle, for the County, (as has been already explained); Guild-hall for the City; and the Court of Pleas, for the liberty of St. Peter's. The Ecclesiastical Court is held in the Minster-yard, and the list of its officers will be found appended to that of the Cathedral Clergy.

The government of the City of York, like the government of the kingdom of Great Britain, is in three estates—the Lord Mayor, as Sovereign; the Aldermen and body of twenty-four, as a house of Lords; and the Common-council, corresponding in some degree to the House of Commons. The members and officers of the Corporation, for the year 1823, are :—

The Right Hon. THOMAS SMITH, Lord Mayor, (2d Time.)

(Whose Office will expire on the 3d of February, 1824.)

Robert Sinclair, Esq. *Recorder.*

John Pemberton Heywood, and W. S. Nicholl, Esqrs. City Counsel.

## ALDERMEN.

| | | |
|---|---|---|
| †Thomas Wilson, Esq. and father of the City | †George Peacock, Esq. | *W. H. Hearon, Esq. |
| †William Hotham, Esq. | †Right Hon. Lord Dundas | *John Dale, Esq. |
| †William Ellis, Esq. | †Isaac Spencer, Esq. | *R. Chaloner, Esq. M. P. |
| *John Kilby, Esq. | *William Dunslay, Esq. | *James Saunders, Esq. |

Those marked thus † have served the office of Lord Mayor twice.
Those marked thus * have served the office once.

## SHERIFFS.

John Cobb, Esq.     |     Charles Liddell, Esq.

Whose offices expire on the 3d of September, 1823.

Richard Townend, Esq. Town Clerk.

Gentlemen who have served the office of Sheriff, called the Twenty-four.

| | | | |
|---|---|---|---|
| George Healey, gent. | Gen. Dodsworth, gent | Joseph Agar, gent. | Robert Cattle, gent. |
| Stephen Hartley | William Hornby | Edmund Gill | John Hodgson |
| John Sutcliffe | James Shepherd | Thomas Beal | William Blanchard |
| George Darbyshire | Robert Lakeland | G. W. Wentworth | Thomas Rayson |
| William Bilton | William Cooper | William Oldfield | Cook Taylor |
| George Fettes | John Jackson | George Wilkinson | John Wormald |
| Joseph Volans | George Cressey | Thomas Cattley | WmStephensonClerk |
| Christopher Cattle | | | |

CHAMBERLAINS—Whose offices expire the 3d of February, 1824.

| | | |
|---|---|---|
| Mr. Peter Armistead | Mr. John Rigg | Mr. George Jennings |
| Mr. George Bell | Mr. William Dawson | Mr. Richard Burdekin |

## COMMON COUNCILMEN.

| *Walmgate Ward.* | Mr. Wm. Dalton | Mr. Wm. Robinson |
|---|---|---|
| Mr. Thomas Bewlay, Foreman of the Commons | Mr. Emanuel Siddall | Mr. Robert Pulleyn |
| Mr. Matthew Browne | Mr. John Benson | Mr. Wm. Hargrove |
| Mr. Joseph Davis | Mr. Robert Gibson | Mr. Edward Jackson |
| Mr. Wm. Cartwright | Mr. John Lawton | Mr. Robert Jennings |
| Mr. Joseph Wood | Mr. Richard Hornby | Mr. Wm. Storry |
| Mr. Thomas Fowler | Mr. Thomas Wilkinson | |
| Mr. John Ward | Mr. John Pearson | *Micklegate Ward.* |
| Mr. Thomas Sanderson | Mr. Wm. Cowling | Mr. Wm. Stead |
| Mr. Francis Richardson | Mr. Henry Cobb | Mr. Matthew Walker |
| Mr. John James Baker | Mr. Wm. Pearson | Mr. Wm. Coates |
| Mr. George Ellis | Mr. Wm. Hubie | Mr. Edward Seagrave |
| Mr. Thomas Benson | Mr. Joseph Smith | Mr. Wm. Ferrand |
| Mr. James Day | *Bootham Ward.* | Mr. John Kirlew |
| Mr. Wm. Peacock | Mr. George Burnill | Mr. Wm. Stead, jun. |
| Mr. John Ickeringill | Mr. Thomas Brearey | Mr. Wm. Chapman |
| Mr. John Slater | Mr. Samuel Knapton | Mr. Richard Rawdon |
| Mr. Wm. Blanchard | Mr. Wm. Judson | Mr. Leonard Overend |
| Mr. Wm. Evers | Mr. Wm. Hudson | Mr. Thomas Rayson, jun. |
| *Monk Ward.* | Mr. Richard Williamson | Mr. Henry Cave |
| Mr. John Hurwood | Mr. John Walker | Mr. Thomas Peacock |
| Mr. Richard Kilner | Mr. James Barber | Mr. Francis Calvert |
| Mr. James Whitwell | Mr. Richard Brown | Mr. Michael Varvill |
| Mr. Wm. Ingram | Mr. Wm. Cattell | Mr. Christopher Watson |
| Mr. Wm. Scawin | Mr. George Ellis | Mr. Henry Steward |
| | Mr. Joseph Marshall | Mr. John Simpson |

Prothonotary, John Seymour, Esq.—City Steward, Mr. Peter Atkinson.
Esquires to the Lord Mayor—Mr. William Baynes and Mr. William Eadon.
Chaplain, Rev. William Flower, sen.
Four Officers at Mace, viz. Thomas Kimber, Francis Burr, John Sanderson, and Wm. Bell.
Chief Constable for the City, Mr. William Baynes, Petergate.
Chief Constable for Ainsty, Mr. Thos. Beal, Dring Houses, & Mr. Geo. Steward, Blossom st.
Porter to Lord Mayor, Geo. Land; Police Officer, Wm. Pardoe; City Informer, Jas. Pardoe.
The Coroners for the City and Ainsty, are Messrs. Samuel Cawling, Davygate, and Robert Ellison, Castlegate; and for the Liberty of St. Peter's, Mr. John Plowman, of Munby, and Mr. John Richardson, of Collingate, York.

The Mayor of York, by ancient prescription, assumes the title of Lord, which peculiar honour, as we have already seen, was conferred on this Chief Magistrate, by Richard II. in 1389. The same sovereign, in 1393, presented Robert Scroope, the then Lord Mayor, with a large gilt mace, to be borne before him, and a cup of maintenance to the sword-bearer. The Lord Mayor is the King's Lieutenant in his absence; he takes the chair in the presence of the Judge of Assize, who sits on his right hand: at the Sessions he 's supreme; and no act or law for the gove nment of the city can be valid without h's presence. This officer is annually chos n on the 15th of January, and on the 3d f February, the Lord Mayor elect, as he 's called during the interval, enters upon his office. If the Lord Mayor be married, his wife is dignified with the title of Lady Mayoress, and in addressing her, the t rm "My Lady," is applied. In Drake's time, though the husband parted with both honour and title at the time he was divested of office, yet by the courtesy of York, in favour of the fair sex, her ladyship still enjoyed her title, by no other right perhaps, but that of an old rhyming proverb, which says—

" He is a lord for a year and a day,
" But she is a lady for ever and for ay."

This courtesy towards the Lady Mayoress has, however, now ceased; and at the expiration of her husband's year of office, the term My Lady is dropped, unless she was previously entitled to it by marriage, or in her own right.

The residence of the Lord Mayor is the Mansion-house, a stately edifice, built in the year 1756, and which stands at the north end of Coney street, near Lendal, and occupies the site of the ancient chapel of the Guild of St. Christopher. The revenue of the Lord Mayor was formerly derived chiefly from the toll of corn coming to the market, but that toll in 1784, was liberally relinquished by the corporation, and this mansion is the scene of his hospitalities. The state-room, where the chief magistrate gives his entertainments, is 40 feet 6 inches in length, and 27 feet 9 inches in breadth, and is lighted in front by a double tier of windows. There are here eight valuable portraits in excellent preservation : of his present Majesty, presented by him to the Corporation; King William III.; George II.; the late Marquis of Rockingham; Sir John Lister Kaye, M. P. and Lord Mayor, in 1737; Lord Bingley, M. P. and Lord Mayor in 1757, (when George Lane Fox, Esq.); Sir Wm. M. Milner, M. P. and Lord Mayor in 1797 and 1798; Lord Dundas, Lord Mayor in 1811, (when the Hon. Lawrence Dundas, M. P.) and in 1821, when Lord Dundas, and the only English Peer ever Lord Mayor of York. It is worthy of remark, that York had the honour to set the Corporation of London the example of erecting a Mansion-House for their Lord Mayor.

The Guild-hall is situated behind the Mansion-house, and was built in the year 1446. In this fine Gothic Hall, which is ninety-six feet long, by forty-three feet wide, the Assizes for the city are held, and it is then formed into two courts, the Crown Court at the end of the Hall, and the Nisi Prius Court near the entrance. The elections for members of parliament are also held here, and it may be proper in this place to mention, that the city of York is at present represented in parliament by Marmaduke Wyvill and Robert Chaloner, Esqrs. who, like the corporation of the city they represent, are both of the whig party. Three times a week, namely, on Tuesday, Thursday, and Saturday, the Lord Mayor, and at least one alderman, sit at the Guild-hall, for the administration of justice; and the business of the Quarter Sessions for the city is also transacted in this place. At the end of this hall are several rooms for the grand and petit juries, one of which is called the Inner Room, in which the County Court, for the recovery of debts in the County, not exceeding Five Pounds, consolidated with the Sheriff's Turn Court, and the Court of Common Pleas, is held weekly, usually on the Tuesday.

The Council Chambers is a building of modern erection, adjoining the Guild-hall. When the old Council Chambers of the city upon Ouse-Bridge were taken down in 1810, these chambers were built adjoining: the Inner Room, & the Lower House, namely, the Common Council, hold their deliberations in one of them, while the *Upper House*, consisting of the Lord Mayor, Recorder, City Council, Aldermen, Sheriffs, and the Gentlemen of the Twenty-four assemble in the Upper Chamber.

Amongst its other public institutions York enjoys the advantage of an excellent Subscription Library, containing about ten thousand volumes in the various branches of science and literature. This institution was commenced in the year 1794, but it was not till the year 1811, that the present Library Room, which is very eligibly situated in St. Helen's Square, was built. The number of members at present amounts to four hundred and seventy-seven; the mode of admission is by ballot, and the terms are ten guineas entrance, and an annual subscription of twenty-six shillings, paid in advance. Mr. Joseph Shepherd is the Librarian. There are in York some other Libraries, Subscription and Circulating, the principal of which is, the Select Subscription Library, in Lady Peckett's yard, Pavement.

On the ground floor, under the York Subscription Library, in St. Helen's Square, there is a Subscription News Room, handsomely fitted up, and furnished with the London and country newspapers. Subscribers are admitted by ballot, and the members of the room have each the privilege of introducing a friend, not resident in York, for one month, on registering his name in a book kept for that purpose. The annual subscription is one guinea, and the admission fee ten shillings and sixpence. There are also two other Subscription News Rooms, one at the York Tavern, and the other, called the York Club Room, at Etridge's Hotel.

The Cavalry Barracks, erected in 1796, are situated at a distance of about a mile S. W. of the city, on the Fulford road. The cost of these erections, with the twelve acres of ground appropriated to the purpose, has been little short of 30,000*l.* and the accommodation they afford is for three field officers, five captains, nine subalterns, four quarter-masters, two hundred and forty non-commissioned officers and privates, and 266 horses. The parade ground is very extensive, and in front of the range appropriated to the officers is a large grass plot, for the accommodation of the numerous and fashionable company who frequently attend to hear the fine martial band which plays upon the parade. Mr. Anthony Lefroy is the barrack master.

York has produced several characters eminent in history, and a still larger number eminent in the ages in which they lived. Amongst the former of these may be mentioned CONSTANTINE THE GREAT, the first

Christian Emperor; FLACCUS ALBANUS, the pupil of Bede and the mentor of Charlemagne; and WALTHEOF, Earl of Northumberland, and son of the gallant Siward. Amongst the latter we find the names of ROBERT FLOWER, the hermit of Knaresborough, usually called St. Robert, born in 1190; JOHN LE ROMAINE, the thirty-eighth Archbishop of York, and the natural son of John Romaine, a priest and treasurer of the cathedral; JOHN WALDBY, and ROBERT his brother, two eminent scholars, who flourished about the middle of the fourteenth century, the former of whom was the forty-seventh archbishop of this province; JOHN ERGHOM, a friar Eremite; and JOHN BATE, a friar Carmelite; both profound expositors of the holy scriptures, and authors of celebrity in the fifteenth century; VALENTINE FREES and his WIFE, rendered memorable by having, according to Fox, died for religion at the stake in the year 1531, and of whom Fuller says, that they were, according to his recollection, the only man and his wife ever thus married together in martyrdom; EDWARD FREES, the brother of Valentine, born also at York, who, for having *heretically* painted some passages of scripture on the borders of several pieces of cloth, was committed to prison by John Stoaksley, Lord Bishop of London, and there, according to Fox, was fed with *manchet* made of *sawdust*, and kept in prison till the flesh of his wrists grew over his irons, his reason having in the mean time so far forsaken him that when brought for examination before his persecutor, he said, " My Lord is a good man !" GEORGE TANKERFIELD, another martyr, was born in York; Sir Thomas Widdrington says he was a cook in London, and was, by Bishop Bonner, antichrist's great cook, roasted and burnt to death.— THOMAS MORTON, the son of a mercer in York, born in the Pavement, in the year 1564, rose by his merit successively to the bishopricks of Chester, Lichfield, and Coventry, and lastly to Durham: when he was a parish priest, and rector of Marston, the plague raged in York with so much fury that a number of infected persons were sent out of the city to Hob-Moor, where tents were erected for their accommodation, on which occasion this intrepid disciple of his divine master visited them daily, and administered alike to their spiritual wants and to their temporal necessities.* HENRY SWINBURNE,

* The writer of this prelate's life says, that he was school fellow, at York, with *Guy Faux*, the famous popish incendiary, who is said to have been born at Bishopthorp, and educated in this city.

an eminent doctor of civil law, was born at York about the middle of the sixteenth century, and educated at the Free Grammar School in this city. As his contemporary and countryman, Gilpin, was called *the apostle of the north*, so Swinburne was styled *the northern advocate*—the one being famous for his learning in divinity, and the other in the civil law. SIR THOMAS HERBERT, son of Mr. Thomas Herbert, merchant and alderman of York, was born in this city in 1606, and educated here till he was admitted a commoner of Jesus College, Oxford, in 1621. Having completed his studies, he travelled for some years through Africa and Asia, under the patronage of William Earl of Pembroke, his kinsman.— On his return home he waited on the Earl, and was invited to dine with him the next day, but the Earl dying suddenly that very night his hopes of preferment from that quarter were blasted, and he again left England to visit various parts of Europe.— Upon finishing his travels he settled in his native country, and in the time of the civil wars adhered to the cause of the Parliament. By the persuasion of Philip Earl of Pembroke, he became one of the commissioners to treat with the King's officers for the surrender of Oxford to the Parliamentary army. Subsequently he was put upon the King as one of his menial servants, along with others, in the place of several of his own servants; while in this situation he became a convert to the royal cause, and continued with his Majesty till he was brought to the block. Charles II. immediately upon the restoration, rewarded his faithful service to his father in the two last years of his life by creating him a baronet in 1660, which honour he enjoyed for upwards of twenty years, and died at his house in York on the first of March, 1681.— CHRISTOPHER CARTWRIGHT, a profound scholar, stiled *Vir eruditissimus*, was born at York, and is known to the learned world for his Annotations on Genesis and Exodus. JOHN EARLE was born at York in 1601, and admitted of Merton College, Oxford, in 1620. His younger years, says Antony Wood, his biographer, were adorned with oratory, poetry, and witty fancies, and

his elder with quaint preaching and subtle disputes. He rose successively from the Deanery of Westminster to the Bishoprick of Worcester, and ultimately to that of London; and dying at Oxford, in 1665, was buried near the high altar in Merton College Church, in that city. MARMADUKE FOTHERGILL, born in 1652, in the house called Pevey's Inn, in the parish of St. Dyon's, Walmgate, was a divine of great learning and piety, and in ecclesiastical antiquity stood almost unrivalled. By his last will he left a fine collection of books as a library to the parish of Skipwith, of which he had been minister, on condition that the parishioners should build a proper room for them at their own cost; but this charge they parsimoniously refused to incur, and the library was, by his widow, presented to the Dean and Chapter of York, to swell the Minster collection. FRANCIS DRAKE, the venerable and learned historian of York, was the son of the Rev. Francis Drake, rector of Hemsworth and vicar of Pontefract. Though not born in this city, he settled here in early life, and practised as a surgeon with considerable reputation.— Having married Mary, the youngest daughter of John Woodyeare, Esq. of Crook-hill, he devoted himself principally to his literary pursuits, and in the year 1736 published his *Eboracum*, a work which will serve to confer immortality on the history and antiquities of that city, and which will, in its turn, hand down his name to the latest posterity.

In this brief but faithful history of ancient and modern York, the contrast between the imperial city—the residence of Emperors and of Kings, and the decayed capital of a northern county, forces itself strongly upon the mind, and serves to exhibit the vicissitudes to which the affairs of places, as well as of persons, are subject.— But York—though shorn of some of its brightest beams—though three times razed to the ground by invaders, [*] in remote periods —and though deprived of its commerce by Hull, and of its manufactures by Leeds, in more modern times, is still an interesting and venerable city ; of which it may be said, in the lines of Sir Thomas Widdrington :—

York's not so great as Old York was of yore,
Yet York it is, though wasted to the core :
It's not that York which Ebrank built of old ;
Nor yet that York which was of Roman mould ;
York was the third time burnt, and what you see
Are York's small ashes of antiquity.

[*] First by the Saxons, second by the Danes, and third by the Normans.

# An Alphabetical List

OF THE

# STREETS, SQUARES, COURTS, LANES,

&c. &c.

# IN THE CITY OF YORK.

Albion row, North street, Bar walls
Albion street, Skeldergate
Aldwark, St. Andrewgate
Anderson's court, Stonegate
Archbishop's court, Monkgate
Artichoke yard, Micklegate
Atkinson's cout, Micklegate
Atkinson's yard, Walmgate
Baggergate lane, without Walmgate bar
Bakehouse passage, Shambles
Baker's lane, Micklegate
Ball yard, Skeldergate
Barker hill, Monk bar without
Barker lane, Micklegate
Bay Horse yard, Walmgate
Bean's passage, Walmgate
Bearpark's passage, North street
Beddern, Goodramgate
Beedam's yard, Skeldergate
Bell's yard, Petergate
Bennington's passage, Walmgate
Bishop hill, Fetter lane
Bishop hill lane, Skeldergate
Black Bull lane, Walmgate
Black Horse passage, Fossgate
Blake street, St. Helen's square
Blossom street, Micklegate bar
Blue Ball yard, Skeldergate
Blue Bell passage, Micklegate
Blue Bell passage, Walmgate
Bootham bar, end of Petergate
Bootham row, Bootham
Bootham square, Bootham row
Brearey's court, St. Helen's square
Bridge street, Back lane, North street
Brunswick place, Peaseholm green
Butcher's yard, Walmgate
Butler's yard, Walmgate
Cade's yard, Wellington row
Caroline row, Walmgate

Carr's lane, Skeldergate
Castlegate, High Ousegate
Castlegate postern, Castle lane
Castle lane, Castlegate
Castlemills, Castlegate postern
Cattle's buildings, Barker hill
Chapel yard, Grape lane
Church lane, bottom of Shambles
Church lane, Coney street
Church lane, Walmgate
Church lane, North street
Clarkson's passage, Walmgate
Clark's yard, Wellington row
Clementhorp, Skeldergate postern
Coach yard, Thursday market
Coate's yard, Tanner row
Coates's buildings, Skeldergate
Coffee yard, Stonegate
College street, Goodramgate
College yard, College street
Colliergate, near the Pavement
Common hall lane, St. Helen's square
Coney street, Spurriergate
Copley's court, Coney street
Coppergate, Pavement
Cordukes's yard, Petergate
Coupland's yard, Gillygate
Costant passage, Coney street
Cragg's waggon yard, Coppergate
Crosser's yard, Micklegate
Cumberland row, Coney street
Davygate, Thursday market
Dawson's passage, Walmgate
Dawson's yard, Fossgate
Dodsworth's yard, Walmgate
Dougleby's passage, Davygate
Dundas street, Palmer lane
Dunning's yard, Fossgate
Elliott's yard, without Walmgate bar
Etby's buildings, Walmgate

Far Water lane, Castlegate  
Feasegate, Peter lane  
Fentiman's passage, North street  
Fetter lane, Skeldergate  
Finkle street, Thursday market  
First water lane, Castlegate  
Fishergate, Castlegate postern without  
Fletcher & Sesar's yard, North street  
Foot of Pavement, Fossgate  
Fossgate, Pavement  
Foss lane, Walmgate  
Foundry yard, Walmgate  
Fowler's court, Spurriergate  
Fowler's yard, Aldwark  
Fraser's passage, Davygate  
Friargate, Castlegate  
Friar Walls, Far water lane  
Garnet's yard, Walmgate  
Gibson's passage, North street  
Gibson's yard, Micklegate  
Gill's passage, Shambles  
Gillygate, Bootham bar  
Girdlergate, Petergate  
Globe passage, Shambles  
Glover's passage, Goodramgate  
Goodramgate, Petergate  
Grape lane, Petergate  
Great Stonegate, Petergate  
Green lane, Hungate  
Hackett's yard, Petergate  
Harcourt yard, Thursday market  
Harker's yard, Micklegate  
Haxby's passage, Skeldergate  
Hay market, end of Colliergate  
Heworth moor, Monk bar without  
Hill's yard, Walmgate  
Hilston's buildings, Marygate  
Hirst's yard, Walmgate  
Holgate lane, without Micklegate bar  
Holme's passage, Haymarket  
Hornport lane, Petergate  
Hospital yard, Walmgate  
Hover lane, Hungate  
Howgate lane, Walmgate  
Hudson's passage, Stonegate  
Hungate, St. Saviourgate  
Jackson's passage, Walmgate  
Jewbury, Layerthorp postern  
Johnson's yard, Walmgate  
Jubbergate, Spurriergate  
Judges' old lodgings yard, Coney street  
King's Staith, E. Side New bridge  
Kirby's yard, without Walmgate bar  
Knowles's yard, Mount  
Lady Peckett's yard, Pavement  
Lambert's yard, Tanner row  
Layerthorp postern, Peaseholm green  
Lazenby's passage, Jubbergate  
Lendal, St. Helen's square  
Leopard yard, Coney street  
Leopard yard, Pavement  
Little Blake street, Blake street  

Little Stonegate, Great Stonegate  
Little Swinegate, Swinegate  
Long close, Walmgate  
Lord Mayor's walk, Monk bar  
Love lane, Barker hill  
Low buildings, Hungate  
Magpie corner, Goodramgate  
Manor house, Marygate  
Manor shore, Marygate  
Manor yard, Bootham bar without  
Marygate, Bootham bar  
Masindues, St. Dennis lane, Walmgate  
Melrose's yard, Walmgate  
Merchant's hall yard, Fossgate  
Meynell's yard, Petergate  
Micklegate, Ouse bridge  
Micklegate bar, Micklegate  
Micklegate bar lane, out of Micklegate bar  
Middleton's passage, Skeldergate  
Middle water lane, Castlegate  
Minster gates, Petergate  
Minster yard, Petergate and College street  
Mint yard, Little Blake street  
Monk bar, Goodramgate  
Monkgate, without Monk bar  
Monk street, Monk bar  
Moore's court, Stonegate  
Mount Pleasant, Blossom street  
Mucky Peg lane, Thursday market  
Mush's yard, Goodramgate  
Naylor's yard, Aldwark  
Near Water, Castlegate  
Nessgate, High Ousegate  
New bridge street, Ouse bridge  
Newgate, Shambles  
New racket, Petergate  
New street, Coney street  
Newtgate, Walmgate  
New walk, Tower street, Castlegate  
Nightingale's yard, Fossgate  
North street, bottom of Micklegate  
Noton's yard, Stonegate  
Nunnery lane, without Micklegate bar  
Ogleforth, Goodramgate  
Ogleforth lane, Minster yard  
Old racket, Petergate  
Old Wharf, Skeldergate  
Otley's yard, Aldwark  
Ouse bridge, Ousegate  
Ousegate High, Pavement  
Ousegate Low, Ouse bridge  
Pack Horse yard, Skeldergate  
Palmer lane, Hungate  
Parapet buildings, Micklegate bar  
Parsonage house, Coney street  
Patrick Pool, Swinegate  
Pavement, High Ousegate  
Paviour lane, Walmgate  
Peaseholm green, St. Saviourgate  
Petergate, Haymarket  
Peter lane, High Ousegate  
Pipe maker's yard, Gillygate

Posterns, see page 34.
Pound lane, Hungate
Powell's yard, Tanner row
Precenter's court, Minster yard
Priestman's lane, Marygate
Prince's court, Coney street
Pullan's passages, North street
Pump yard, Micklegate
Pump yard, Newgate
Queen's staith, W. side New bridge
Rawdon's yard, Micklegate
Rayson's buildings, North street
Red Lion yard, Micklegate
Rosemary lane, Skeldergate postern
Sampson's square, Thursday market
Scawin's yard, Petergate
School yard, Ogleforth
Seagrave court, Micklegate
Seller's yard, Pavement
Shambles great, Pavement
Shambles little, Great Shambles
Shepherd's court, Gillygate
Silver street, Jubbergate
Skeldergate, bottom of Micklegate
Skelderdgte posterns, Skeldergate
Smith's yard, Skeldergate
Spen lane, St. Saviourgate
Spurriergate, Ousegate
St. Andrewgate, Colliergate
St. Dennis lanes, Walmgate
St. George street, Newgate, Walmgate
St. Helen's square, Coney street
St. John's yard, North street
St. Margaret's church lane, Walmgate
St. Martin's lane, Micklegate
St. Mary's row, Bishop hill the elder
St. Mary's square, Bishop hill
St. Michael's church lane, Spurriergate
St. Saviourgate, Colliergate
St. Saviour row, St. Saviourgate
Staker's yard, Thursday market
Starcourt lane, Thursday market

Stonebow lane, Pavement
Stonegate, St. Helen's square
Straker's yard, Feasgate
Swinegate, Girdlergate
Tanner row, North street
The Groves, Lord Mayor's walk
Thomas passage, Skeldergate
Thompson's passage, Walmgate
Thief lane, Micklegate bar without
Thursday market, Feasgate
Toft green, Tanner row
Tower street, Castle street
Trinity lane, Micklegate
Trout's passage, Walmgate
Union court, Bishop hill
Union court, St. Martin's lane
Union place, Fishergate
Union street, Peaseholm green
Waite's buildings, Walmgate
Wakefield court, Micklegate
Walker's lane, Thursday market
Walker's yard, Skeldergate
Walmgate, Feasgate
Walmgate bar, end of Walmgate
Ward's passage, Gillygate
Waterloo place, Coney street
Water's yard, Walmgate
Watson's court, Stonegate
Wellington row, North street
Wellow's yard, Walmgate
West's yard, Walmgate
Whipmawhapma gate, Pavement corner
Whip's yard, Goodramgate
Whip's old yard, Goodramgate
White Horse yard, Skeldergate
Whitwell's entry, Colliergate
Wilberforce's yard, Walmgate
Willow street, Walmgate bar
Winterskell hospital, Walmgate
Wood's yard, Tanner row
Wrightson's yard, Walmgate

# DIRECTORY

## CITY OF YORK.

—◆—

It will be observed that Abbreviations are occasionally used, but they have been introduced only where unavoidable; and, it is presumed will be quite intelligible without any particular explanation.

The Alphabetical List of Streets, Courts, &c. will be found greatly to facilitate the search for those in retired situations.

---

Abbey Eliz. gentlewmn. North street
Abbey Wm. gent. Dundas street
Abershaw Mrs. Elizabeth, North st.
Acaster Rev. J. Monkgate
Adams David, wood turner, Silver st.
Addiual James, hutter & barn factor, cooper, and vict. Golden Barrel, Walmgate
Addy Ann, shopkeeper, Petergate
Adselts John, brush mkr. Tanner row
Agar Mrs. gentlewoman, Marygate
Agar Joseph, gent. High Ousegate
Agar, Seth, & Co. grocers, Stonegate
Agar Mary, gentlewoman, Castlegate
Agar Thos. attorney, Little Stonegate
Agar Edward, grocer, Micklegate
Agar J. & B. curriers, High Ousegate
Agar Isaac, joiner, Walmgate
Agar Thos. hogs dlr. Peaseholme gn.
Agar Wm. shopkeeper, Peter lane
Agar Richard, victualler, Lord Nelson, Goodramgate
Alderson Jacob, cooper and cheesemonger, Fossgate
Alexander Wm. and Son, printers, booksellers, binders, stationers, & agents to the Suffolk and General County fire office, Castlegate
Alexander David, St. George street
Allen John, law stationer, Bootham
Allen Oswald, apothecary, Colliergate
Allen Matthew, apothecary and superintendant of the Lunatic Asylum, Bootham
Allen Caroline, dress maker, Micklegt.
Allen Geo. boarding school for young gentlemen, Beddern
Allen Wm. grocer, Girdlergate
Allen & Neltborp, bricklyrs. Aldwark

Allen Joseph, basket maker, Middle Water lane
Allinson H. B. wire worker, Fossgate
Allison John, cabinet mkr. Mint yard
Allison Henry, verger, Goodramgate
Almand Thos. cabinet mkr. Hungate
Almond Christr. joiner, Walmgate
Ambler Abraham, woolstapler, Peaseholme green
Ambler John, shopkeeper, Tanner row
Ambler John, joiner, College street
Ambrose B. artificial flower manufacturer, Far Water lane
Anderson R. H. solicitor, Stonegate
Anderson Rich. grocer, Low Peter gt.
Anderson Richard, gardener, Atkinson's court, Micklegate
Anderson Wm. butcher, Walmgate
Anderson Wm. gardener, Walmgt. bar
Ann Mrs. George, Micklegate
Appleyard John, bricklayer, First Water lane
Aray R. tobacco pipe mkr. Feasegt.
Archbell Rbt. bacon & butter factor, Micklegate
Ardington William, gardener, &c. Castlegate lane
Armatage Abia, dress and stay maker, North street
Armistead Peter, butcher, Micklegate
Armstrong J. H. grocer, and agent to the London Genuine Tea Company, Foss bridge, Walmgate
Arnett Richard, St. Andrewgate
Arundel Mary, city cook, Waterloo place
Arthur Thomas, flour dealer & bricklayer, Hungate
Ashton Thos. joiner, Albion street

G

Askwith William, proctor, Gillygate
Aspinall Jas. straw hat mfr. Coney st.
Aspinall Edmund, Holgate lane
Asquith Wm. painter, Dunning's yard
Astley William, Low Jubbergate
Atkinson Peter,architect; h. Micklegt.
Atkinson and Sharp, architects, Fetter lane
Atkinson James, surgeon, Lendal
Atkinson James, woollen draper, Coppergate
Atkinson Wm. rag merchant, Middle Water lane
Atkinson & Blenkarn, oats shelling mill, Walmgate
Atkinson Sarah, vict. Malt Shovel, Fossgate
Atkinson Wm. horse hirer, Fossgate
Atkinson Robert, farmer and cowkeeper, Layerthorp
Atkinson Miss Jane, Little Stonegate
Atkinson John, bookbinder, Micklegt.
Atkinson Thos. butcher, Fetter lane
Atkinson Geo. shoemaker, Fetter lane
Atkinson Susannah; dress maker, near Ouse bridge
Atlay Christ. exciseman, Gillygate
Atlay Matthew, farmer, Mount
Audner Robert, painter and paper hanger, St. Andrewgate
Audner Geo. house and sign painter, St. Andrewgate
Autherson Richard, fishmonger, Great Shambles
Aveson Rd. shoemaker, Goodramgate
Aveson Michael, boot mkr. Dundas st.
Awmack Mary, gentwmn. Walmgate
Awmack Joseph, grocer, Fossgate
Ayer John, land agent and surveyor, Castlegate
Backhouse Jas. keeper of the Lunatic Asylum, Gillygate
Backhouse Mrs. gentlwmn. Micklegt.
Backhouse Thomas & James, nursery and seedsmen, Tanner row
Bainbridge & Woodall, woollen drapers, Low Ousegate
Bainbridge Wm. bricklayer, Pavement
Bainbridge John, miller, Walmgate
Baines Geo. coal mercht. Blossom st.
Baines Mrs. cowkpr. St. Saviour's row
Baines John, vict. Odd Fellows, Hungt.
Baines John, cut nail maker, Hungate
Baines Thos. shoemaker, Castle mills
Baines Joseph, shoemkr. Goodramgt.
Baines Henry, poulterer, without Castlegate postern
Baker Mrs. gentlewoman, Coney st.
Baker J. J. chemist & druggist, High Ousegate
Baker George, paper stainer, & agent to the Norwich Union Fire office, St. Helen's square
Bakes John, shoemaker, Marygate

Balfour Walter, Esq. Micklegate
Banks Timothy, shoemaker, Lord Mayor's walk
Banks Robert, miniature painter, Harker's yard, Micklegate
Banks Catharine, straw hat manufacturer, Fossgate
Banks Christopher, Fossgate
Bannister David, mason, College st.
Barber Mrs. Grace, gentwn. Castlegt.
Barber and Whitwell, working goldsmiths, jewellers, silver plate manufacturers, watch makers and engravers, Coney street
Barber Jas. Black Swan Inn, (Clark's Hotel & posting house) Coney st.
Barber Thos. shoemaker, Walmgate
Barber Wm. ladies' shoemkr. Coney st.
Barclay A. and W. booksellers and stationers, 2, New Bridge street
Bardon Wm. butcher, Goodramgate
Barker David, chorister, Monkgate
Barker Rev. Thomas, Spen lane, St. Saviourgate
Barker Geo. bookbinder, Pavement
Barker Anne, poulterer, Little Smbla.
Barker Edward, agent to Deacon, Harrison & Co. carriers, Swinegt.
Barker John, copper plate printer and engraver, Low Ousegate
Barker M. R. overlooker, Bishop hill.
Barker Ralph, plane mkr. Fetter lane
Barker Geo. Middle Water lane
Barker Geo. joiner, St. Mary's row
Barker Wm. cowkeeper, Holgate ln.
Barker John, shoemaker, Church lane, Coney street
Barlow Mrs. Mary, Bootham
Barmby Saml. shoemaker, Swinegate
Barnard Wm. shoemaker, Petergate
Barnby G. & W. shoemkrs. Girdlergt.
Barnett John, optician, glass cutter and stainer, College street
Barnett Thos. shoemaker and animal preserver, Barker ln. Micklegate
Barr Wm. army and hunting saddler, Coney street
Barr Jane, dress maker, Gillygate
Barra George, plumber and glazier, Goodramgate
Barra James, plumber, glazier and painter, High Petergate
Barra James, plumber, glazier and painter, Low Petergate
Barrett Richd. brick maker, Baker hill
Bartcliffe James, cowkeeper, without Walmgate bar
Bartholoman Mary, gentlewoman, Castlegate
Bartholoman Thomas, vict. Stanhope Press, Swinegate
Bartley Joseph, Walmgate bar
Barwick Mary, gentlewoman, Rosemary lane, Skeldergate

Bashforth John, foreman at Gibson's foundry, Walmgate
Bateson Wm. shoemaker, Fetter lane
Batteridge Wm. gent. Barker hill
Batty Thos. vict. George and Dragon, Pavement
Batty Elizabeth, silk & muslin dyer, Fossgate
Batty Edward, gardener, without Walmgate bar
Bayldon Wm. Esq. Bootham
Bayne Geo. bookkeeper, Tanner row
Baynes William, vict. Baynes' Hotel, Petergate
Baynes Geo. vessel owner, Blossom st.
Beadle and Perfect, house, sign, and furniture painter, Micklegate
Beal T. & G. upholsterers and cabinet makers, Stonegate
Beal Richard, wool comber, Walmgt.
Beal John, joiner, Middle Water lane
Bean James, vict. portrait and house painter, Canteen, Barrack yard
Bean Richd. butcher, Thursday market
Bean William, vict. Three Jolly Butchers, Girdlergate
Bean Wm. gentleman, Walmgate
Bean Samuel, joiner and carpenter, Davygate; house, Gillygate
Bean John, wheelwright, Patrick pool
Bean William, umbrella maker and wholesale spirits dealer, Stonegt.
Bean Wm. tailor, Coffee yd. Stonegt.
Bean Thos. plane maker, Waterloo pl.
Bean Wm. currier, Jubbergate
Bean John, shopkeeper, Walmgate
Bearpark B. J. & G. gardeners, nursery and seedsmen, Bootham
Bearpark Miss Sally, milliner & dress maker, High Petergate
Bearpark William, victualler, White Horse, Bootham
Bearpark Robert, jun. gardener, Lord Mayor's walk
Beck William, tanner, Walmgate
Beckwith Stephen, M. D. Coney st.
Beckwith Ann, gentlewmn. Castlegt.
Beckwith John, Esq. Micklegate
Bedford David, schoolmaster, Blossom street
Bedford John, flax dresser, Walmgt. bar
Beedham Elizabeth, gentlewoman, Beedham's yard, Skeldergate
Beedham John, cabinet maker, Fetter lane
Beedham Wm. joiner & cabinet maker, Beedham's yard, Skeldergate
Beilby Varley, Esq. Mount, Micklegate bar
Belcombe Wm. M. D. High Petergate
Bell Thos. gentleman, Haymarket
Bell and Rigg, boot and shoemakers, Haymarket
Bell Geo. currier, Marygate

Bell John, tobacco and snuff dealer, Stonegate
Bell David, shoemaker, Fossgate
Bell Eliz. gentlewoman, Gillygate
Bell David, hair dresser, Walmgate
Bell Anthony, butcher, Gt. Shambles
Bell David, whitesmith and gunsmith, Walmgate
Bell Thos. flour dealer, Walmgate
Bell Thomas, victualler, Sun Inn, Blossom street
Bell Sarah, vict. Blue Bell, Walmgt.
Bell John, cabinet maker, Dundas street, Hungate
Bell Richard, grocer and druggist, Thursday market
Bell John, victualler, Wellington, Goodramgate
Bell Mrs. C. gentlewoman, Gillygate
Bell J. grocer, Jubbergate
Bell Eliz. pastry cook, Little Blake st.
Bell Thomas E. cutler, Gillygate
Bell Thomas, milk dealer, Walmgate
Bell Thomas, joiner, Walmgate
Bell Jane, shopkeeper, Great Shambles
Bell Henry, blacksmith, Hungate
Bell Thos. butcher, Thursday market
Bell William, Lord Mayor's officer, Gillygate
Bell Michael, mustard dealer, Monkgt.
Bell Thos. tailor and clothes cleaner, Little Swinegate
Bell John, roper, flax dresser, draper, &c. Walmgate
Bellerby Thomas, joiner and cabinet maker, Bishop hill
Bellerby John, upholsterer, cabinet maker & undertaker, Micklegate
Bellerby Henry, cheesemonger and flour dealer, Stonegate
Bellerby Edw. baker, Peaseholme grn.
Bellerby John, bricklayer, Pump yard
Bellerby Robert, fruiterer, Stonegate
Bellerby Wm. cowkeeper, Bishop hill
Belt Thomas, victualler, Royal Oak, Goodramgate
Belt Thos. vict. Horse Shoe, Coppergt.
Belwood Mrs. Ann, Minster yard
Bennett Col. John, Mount, without Micklegate bar
Bennett and Flintoft, sculptors and masons, St. Andrewgate
Bennett Thos. sculptor, &c.; house, Ogleforth
Bennington Jas. bricklayer, Walmgt.
Bennington James, shoemaker, Black Horse passage, Fossgate
Bennington Francis, cowkpr. Walmgt.
Benson Mrs. gentlwmn. Micklegate
Benson John, wine & spirit merchant Hungate; house, St. Saviourgate
Benson Mrs. Johanna, gentlewoman, St. Saviourgate
Benson Mrs. Martha, Monkgate

Benson Thos. chain mfr. and saddlers ironmonger, Green lane, Hungate
Benson George, billiard table keeper, Low Ousegate
Benson Jeremiah, coach proprietor & livery stables keeper, Lit. Blake st.
Benson Thomas, joiner and carpenter, St. Saviourgate
Benson John, Gillygate
Benson Wm. St. Andrew's Church yd.
Benson Francis, shoemkr. Blossom st.
Berry Robert, wholesale confectioner, St. Helen's square
Bewlay Robert, brick manufacturer, Heworth moor
Bewlay Thos. tobacco manufacturer, Low Ousegate
Bewlay A. butcher, Great Shambles
Bickerdike Robert, shopkeeper, High Jubbergate
Bickers and Sowerby, milliners and dress makers, Spurriergate
Bickers John, vict. and spirit dealer, Turk's Head, College street
Bickers Mrs. Little Stonegate
Bigland Geo. Esq. Blake street
Bilbrough John, tailor, North street
Bingley Joseph, shoemkr. Girdlergate
Bingley Wm. butcher, High Petergate
Bingley Thomas, baker & flour dealer, Swinegate
Binning Sarah, fruiterer, Stonegate
Binnington Mrs. C. Bootham row
Birbeck John, cowkeeper, Walmgate
Birbeck James, flour dealer, Walmgt.
Birch Thos. boat builder, Clementhorp
Birch Mary, shopkeeper, Goodramgate
Birdsall Richard, Methodist preacher, Spurriergate
Birkenshaw Geo. fruiterer, Feasegate
Birks Thomas, straw hat maker, Colliergate
Birks Wm. tea dealer, Swinegate
Birks John, coach maker, Grape lane
Birkwood Rt. schoolmaster, Walmgt.
Black William, victualler, Sycamore Tree, Minster yard
Blackburn John, butcher, Gt. Shambles
Blackstone Geo. linen and woollen draper, & tailor, Low Jubbergate
Blake Bartholomew, gardener and seedsman, Tanner row
Blakey John, cabinet mkr. Tanner row
Blanchard Mrs. H. gentlewoman, St. Saviourgate
Blanchard John, solicitor, 1, New Bridge street
Blanchard William, hatter and hosier, High Ousegate
Blanchard Wm. printer & publisher of the Chronicle, Thursdays, Coppergate; house, Coney street
Blanchard Robert, vict. Golden Slipper, Far Water lane

Bland Henry, Esq. banker; house, Garrow hill
Bland Geo. shopkeeper, Gillygate
Bleckly Wm. linen draper, tea dealer, & general accountant, 3, Low Ousegate
Bleckly John, grocer and tea dealer, Thursday market
Blenkarn Matthew, miller, Walmgate
Blythe John, victualler, Bay Horse, Walmgate
Blythe John, joiner, Fossgate
Bolland Thomas, sen. schoolmaster, Castlegate
Bolland Thomas, jun. bookseller, stationer & bookbinder, Spurriergate, and agent to the London Genuine Tea Company, 23, Ludgate hill
Bolland & Hall, mesdames, lodginghouse, Little Blake street
Bollans Robert, brasier & tin plate worker, Great Shambles
Bollans Francis, joiner, cabinet maker, & furniture broker, Low Petergt.
Bolton Wm. stone mason, Wellington row
Bolton Mary, schoolmistress, Fossgate
Boocock John, shoemaker, Great Shambles
Boocock Geo. hair dresser, Walmgate
Booker William, Lambert's yard, Tanner row
Bootland Matthew, shopkeeper, Low Jubbergate
Bootley Wm. shopkeeper, Micklegate
Bore Mrs. Mary, St. Saviourgate
Borrows Elizabeth, straw hat manufacturer, High Petergate
Bothamley John, plane maker, Tanner row
Bott Jonathan, stocking mfr. Colliergt.
Botterill Matthew, gent. Monkgate
Botterill James, saddler, Goodramgt.
Botterill Joseph, bacon dlr. Feasegate
Bottomley Saml. shopkpr. North st.
Bowes Sarah, straw hat manufacturer, Walmgate
Bowes John & Son, bricklayers, Dunning's yard, Fossgate
Bowes A. dress maker, Skeldergate
Bowman Wm. baker & flour dealer, Green lane, Hungate
Bowman John, shoemkr. Aldwark
Bowman Wm. Goodramgate
Bowman Wm. cowkpr. Barker hill
Bownas & Co. milliners and dress makers, Little Blake street
Bownas John, Little Blake street
Bowser Wm. vict. Black Boy, North st.
Bowser Ann, ladies' nurse, North st.
Boyes & Fowler, glass & china dealers, Walmgate
Boyes James, shopkpr. Coppergate
Boyle John, confectioner, Hungate

Boynton Wm. tailor, Goodramgate
Brabiner Thomas, vict. Black Swan, Peaseholme green
Bradley Thos. coach builder & harness maker, High Jubbergate
Bradley Luke, woollen draper, Fossgt.
Bradley Wm. bricklayer, Lambert's yd.
Bradley John, joiner, Hungate
Bradley John, Walmgate bar
Bradley Saville, painter, Beddern
Braithwaite Richard, tailor, Lord Mayor's Walk
Braithwaite Richd. broker, Swinegate
Braithwaite Thos. shoemaker, Little Blake street
Braithwaite John, hair dresser, Goodramgate
Braithwaite Abraham, spirit dealer, Spurriergate
Bramley Mrs. Ann, Skeldergate
Bramley & Dent, boot & shoemakers, Blake street
Bramley John, butcher, Gt. Shambles
Bramley Ambrose, butcher, Fossgate
Bramley Wm. Smith's yd. Skeldergt.
Brassington Richard, bookbinder and paper ruler by machine, Waterloo place; house, Bishop hill
Brayshaw Eleanor, grocer & tea dlr. High Petergate
Breary & Myers, coach builders, harness makers, &c. Little Stonegate & Davygate
Brewis J. W. linen draper & tea dealer, Peter lane
Bridgewater Chpr. bricklayer, North st.
Bridgewater John, Ogleforth
Bridgewater Thos. joiner, L. Shambles
Briggs Rev. Geo. Ogleforth
Briggs Geo. vict. Crown and Anchor, Low Jubbergate
Briggs Rd. (sexton) St. Saviourgate
Brigham Margaret, drawer of ladies' breasts, Sampson's square
Briscomb Robert, cooper, Walmgate
Britton & Co. grocers, &c. Spurriergt.
Britton Wm. whitesmith, Aldwark
Broadley Mrs. C. E. Mint yard
Broadmead Richard, vict. Jubbergate
Brocklebank Thomas, leather cap mfr. Micklegate
Brodell Lawrence, Bootham square
Brodie Mrs. Mary, St. Andrew's church yard
Bromley James, coal and lime merchant, Fossgate
Brook Mrs. Ann, gentwmn. Gillygate
Brook John, solicitor; h. Petergate
Brook & Bulmer, solicitors, New st.
Brook Richard, shoemkr. Walmgate
Brook Thomas, musician, Gillygate
Brookbank John, ironmonger, hardware dealer, and house and sign painter, Coney street

Brookbank Miss, gentwn. Gillygate
Brotherton Geo. mathematical school, without Walmgate bar
Broughton James, tape dealer, Butcher's yard, Walmgate
Brown George, surgeon, Castlegate
Brown Wm. confectioner, Coney st.
Brown & Jennings, linen drapers, Pavement
Brown Matthew, gent. Blossom st.
Brown Christopher, musical preceptor, Micklegate
Brown Richard, confectioner and tea dealer, Coney street
Brown John, woollen dpr. Skeldergt.
Brown & Hopps, grocers and flour dealers, Great Shambles
Brown Wm. gent. Gillygate
Brown Richd. hair dresser, Micklegate
Brown John & Co. painters, Davygate
Brown & Kirlew, coach, sign & house painters, Davygate
Brown Robert, lace and fringe maker, Bootham square
Brown Thos. stay maker, Thursday market
Brown Geo. bookkpr. Peaseholm grn.
Brown Geo. tailor, Peter lane
Brown Thos. broker, High Jubbergt.
Brown Matthew, auctioneer, Gillygt.
Brown James, shoemkr. Ogleforth
Brown Wm. fireman, Walmgate
Brown Richard, without Walmgt. bar
Brown William, joiner, Union court, Trinity lane
Brown Jane, dress maker, Union ct. Trinity lane
Brown Hannah, keeper of ferry, North street, Postern
Brown & Wilks Misses, M. & B. ladies' day school, Skeldergate
Brownridge Robert, tea dealer and perfumer, Stonegate
Bruce John, flax dresser, Walmgt. bar
Brumfitt Edward, mail guard, Parapet buildings
Brunton Rbd. gunmaker, Stonegate
Buchanan Ann, Leopard yd. Pavemt.
Buck John, vict. Horse and Groom, Mint yard
Buckland Mrs. Mary, Castlegate
Buckland Misses, M. A. & E. ladies' boarding school, Castlegate
Buckle Joseph, proctor & deputy registrar of the Archbishop's court; house, Monkgate
Buckle Marmaduke, woolstapler, coal merchant, and tea dealer, St. Saviour's row
Buckle Wm. shopkeeper, Micklegate
Buckle A. dress maker, Boo ham row
Buckley Joseph, glass & china dealer, & stone mason, Coppergate
Buckley Lieut. Frederick, Fishergate

Buckley Thos. chorister, Ogleforth
Budd Eliz. shopkeeper, Goodramgate
Bullivant Isaac, cutler, Newgate
Balmer Francis, sen. merchant, Precentor's court
Bulmer Geo. solicitor ; h. Coney st.
Bulmer Rev. Wm. M.A. Coney street
Bulmer James, land agent & surveyor, Precentor's court
Bulmer Francis, jun. butter, ham, cheese & seed mert. Tanner row
Bulmer J. A. grocer and tea dealer, Hay market
Bulmer Richard, tailor & habit maker, Aldwark
Bulmer Geo. cooper, Girdlergate
Bulmer Mrs. widow, Aldwark
Burdekin Richard, bookseller, stationer & binder, Pavement
Burdon Wm. commercial and mathematical academy, Skeldergate
Burdsall Wm. whitesmith, Dunning's yard, Fossgate
Burdsall Rd. Fowler's ct. Spurriergt.
Burgess Mrs. Sarah, Albion street
Bingley Mrs. gentlewoman, without Micklegate bar
Burnell Geo. hop & spirit merchant, Mint yard, Little Blake st.
Burniston John, joiner and cabinet maker, Walmgate
Burniston Hannah, widow, Lord Mayor's walk
Burr Francis, broker, Peter lane
Burrell John, Micklegate
Burrill Hannah, butcher, Silver st
Burrill Mary, china, glass & earthenware dealer, Thursday market
Burton Miss Harriet, Ogleforth
Burton Benjamin, tailor & furniture, &c. broker, High Jubbergate
Bussey and Pearson, dealers in lime, coals, &c. Marygate
Bussey John, draper and tailor, Low Jubbergate
Bussey Thomas, shoemaker, Lord Mayor's walk
Butler Wm. gentleman, Marygate
Butler Edw. miller, Foss bridge
Butler Edward, keeper of the vagrant office, Little Shambles
Butler Ann, cowkeeper, without Walmgate bar
Buttery Geo. tailor & glover, Walmgt.
Bywater Geo. comb mkr. Micklegate
Cable Charles, Racket yd. Petergate
Cade Jas. cowkeeper, Wellington row
Call Thos. woolcomber, Walmgate
Calvert Thos. wholesale confectioner, Spurriergate
Calvert Jas. butcher, Little Shambles
Calvert John, Tanner row
Calvert Francis, shoemkr. Micklegate
Calvert Jonth. shopkpr. Far Water ln.

Calvert J. shoemaker, St. Mary's row
Camidge Jane, gentwmn. Petergate
Camidge John, musical doctor, and assistant organist at the cathedral, Manor house
Camidge Matthew, teacher of music and organist at the cathedral, High Petergate
Camidge Wm. tailor, Tanner row
Camidge Wm. fruiterer, Castlegate
Camidge Len. tailor, Barker lane
Camidge Rd. joiner, Meynell's yard
Canney Wm. bacon, butter & cheese factor, Little Shambles
Cappe Mrs. Mary, St. Saviourgate
Carbutt Francis, gent. Monkgate
Carey John, joiner, Walmgate
Curey John, carpenter, St. George st.
Carey Thos. joiner, St. George st.
Caris Thos. hop bag manufacturer, St. Andrewgate
Cariss Thomas, saddler and harness maker, Walmgate
Cariss John, tailor, Bishop hill
Cariss Mary, calenderer, Fossgate
Cariss James, cooper, Fossgate
Carlton John, cabinet mkr. Pavement
Carr Mattw. conveyancer, Stonegate
Carr Benj. auctioneer, Stonegate
Carr Rhd. shoemaker, Willow street
Carrack Mrs. gentlewoman, Mount
Carrall M. W. printer, bookseller, printing ink manufacturer & engraver on wood, (& circulating library) Walmgate
Carter Miss Ann, Aldwark
Carter G. gentleman's cap maker, College street
Carter Thos. coach driver, Finkle st.
Cartwright John, vict. Wheat Sheaf, Castlegate
Cartwright Wm. gent. Castlegate
Cartwright Eliz. Wellington row
Casson Thos. flax dresser, Walmgate
Castell S. shopkpr. St. Saviourgate
Castell Geo. tailor, St. Saviourgate
Cation John, law stationer, & clerk of the Spiritual Court, Tanner row
Cattley Miss, Marygate
Cattell Geo. trunk mkr. Goodramgate
Cattell Wm. goldsmith & jeweller, Stonegate
Cattell Christopher, dancing master, Barker hill
Cattell Christr. shoemkr. Marygate
Catterall Henry, victualler, White Dog, Beddern
Catterton John, boot and shoe maker, Low Jubbergate
Cattle Robert, coach proprietor, St. Helen's square & Grove house
Cattley Mrs. gentwmn. Marygate
Cattley T. & J. H. timber, iron & slate merchants, North street

Catton, Crosby & Co. tea dealers and tallow chandlers, Micklegate
Cautley Miss J. Blake street
Cautley Mary, chemist and druggist, Low Ousergate
Cave William, engraver and copper plate printer, Stonegate
Cave Henry, artist, Micklegate
Cave Elizabeth, glass, china & earthenware dealer, Micklegate
Cavitt Wm. eating house, Pavement
Cawood Mrs. Sarah, Holgate lane
Cawood Henry, law stationer, Colliergt.
Cawood Thos. vict. Britannia, Walmgt.
Cawthorne Samuel, gent. Swinegate
Chaloner Robert, Esq. M. P. alderman and banker, Castlegate
Champney Geo. surgeon, Colliergate
Champney Wm. bankers' clerk, New st.
Chaplin Wm. ladies boot, shoe & clog maker, Swinegate
Chapman Henry, preserver of birds & quadrupeds, Bootham
Chapman William, bricklayer & plasterer, Bishop hill
Chapman John, farmer, Tanner row
Chapman Anthony, baker and flour dealer, Micklegate
Chapman Wm. millwright, Fetter ln.
Chapman John, cork cutter, Foss bridge
Chapman Geo. joiner, Goodramgate
Charlton George and Co. tailors and earthenware dealers, Peter lane
Charlton John, tailor, Fensegate
Chicken Mrs. Eliz. Castlegate
Chippendale Elizabeth, straw hat maker, Peter lane
Chipstead Thos. vict. Cannon, Lendal
Clapham Miss Ann, Minster yard
Clapham John, vict. Punch Bowl, Thursday market
Clancy Jas. clothes broker, Walmgate
Clark W. S. surgeon, Micklegate
Clark Mrs. Mary, Albion street
Clark Edward, vict. Horse & Jockey, Little Stonegate
Clark J. & J. straw hat mfr. Tanner r.
Clark Mary, straw hat mfr. Tanner row
Clark Wm. shoemaker, Coates' yard, Tanner row
Clark John, gardener, Tanner row
Clark Robert, vict. Admiral Hawke, Walmgate
Clark William, vict. Rose and Crown, without Walmgate bar
Clark Wm. white-smith, &c. College st.
Clark Joseph, joiner, Brunswick place
Clark John, printer, Monkgate
Clark George, coal dealer, without Walmgate bar
Clark Geo. surgeon, St. Helen's sqr.
Clarke Joseph, shoemaker, Ogleforth
Clarkson Thomas, miller, Hungate
Clarkson Wm. grocer, &c. Walmgate

Clarkson Abraham, Wellington row
Clarkson Wm. gardener, &c. Walmgt.
Clarkson Francis, basket maker, Great Shambles
Clarkson Matthew, gardener, Walmgt.
Clayton Robert, solicitor, Stonegate
Clayton Frs. victualler, Robin Hood, Castlegate
Clegg Abrm. whitesmith, Goodramgt.
Clifford John, clerk at the post office, Lendal
Cloak James, straw and chip hat manufacturer, Stonegate
Clough J. W. Esq. banker; house, Oxton hall, near Tadcaster
Clough & Ellis, boot makers, Colliergt.
Clough Ann, pastry cook, Davygate
Coalman S. flax dresser, Walmgate
Coates Amos, surgeon, &c. New Bridge street
Coates William, gent. Gillygate
Coates Mrs. gentlewoman, Micklegt.
Coates Margaret, Pavement
Coates Robert, vict. Sir Sidney Smith, & glove leather dyer, Tanner row
Coates John, boot and shoe maker, (register office for servants) Low Petergate
Coates Wm. joiner, &c. Tanner row
Coates Wm. couch driver, Friar walls
Coates Geo. flax dresser, Walmgt. bar
Cobb John, builder, Ogleforth
Cobb Henry, printer and publisher of the York Courant, Tuesdays; office, Coney street
Cobb Mary, gentlewoman, High Ousegate
Cocker Robert, worsted manufacturer and dyer, 15, New Bridge street
Cockhill Joseph, gunsmith and cutler, Finkle street
Cogbill Richard, gent. Coates yard, Tanner row
Cogling Thomas, broker, Swinegate
Collett Ann, gentwmn. Tanner row
Colley Isaac, vict. Lord Nelson, High Jubbergate
Colley Thomas, joiner, Tanner row
Colley William, joiner, Walmgate
Colley Mrs. widow, Monkgate
Collier L. broker, Micklegate
Collier Michael, whitesmith, Micklegt.
Collier Joseph, printer, Coates' yard, Tanner row
Collier Ambrose, shoemaker, Fossgate
Collier William, baker, Bootham
Collins John, currier, Colliergate
Collins Jane, silk stocking grafter, Colliergate
Collins Wm. flax dresser, Walmgt. bar
Collinson John, shoemaker, Kirby's yard, without Walmgate bar
Collyer Stephen, ladies' boot & shoe maker, Micklegate

Cook Geo. coast waiter, St. Mary's, Bishop hill
Cook Robert, tinner & brazier, Fossgt.
Cook John, butcher, Thursday market
Cook James, brazier, &c. Colliergate
Cook William, sen. flax dresser, without Walmgate bar
Cook William, jun. flax dresser, without Walmgate bar
Cook William, comb cutter, Meynell's yard, Petergate
Cooke Joseph, straw hat manufacturer and furrier, 17, Coney street
Cooper and Beilby, wine and spirit merchants and agents to the Atlas Fire Office, Skeldergate
Cooper Miss Sarah, bdg.school,Gillygt.
Cooper Geo. blacksmith and farrier, High Jubbergate
Cooper Thomas, printer, North street
Cooper Richd. chorister, Patrick pool
Cooper Geo. coach guard, Gillygate
Coopland Rev. Wm. Tanner row
Coopland William, Esq. Tanner row
Cordukes & Holmes, linen & woollen drapers, Haymarket
Coulson John, schoolmaster, Davygt.
Coultas Jeremiah, vict. Coach and Horses, Micklegate
Coultherd John, confectioner, Bootham
Coupland Eliz. gentlewmn. North st.
Coupland John, boot and shoe maker, Goodramgate
Coupland Jas. tailor, &c. Goodramgt.
Coupland Mason, shopkeeper, Petergt.
Court Matthew, gent. St. Martin's ln.
Coverdale John, Goodramgate
Coverdale William, St. Andrewgate
Cowgill William, gardener, Monkgate
Cowling Samuel, solicitor and coroner for the City & Ainsty, Castlegate
Cowling John, solicitor, Lord Mayor's walk
Cowling Misses R.C.A. gentlewomen, Lord Mayor's walk
Cowling Wm. grocer, tea dlr. butter, bacon & ham factor, Goodramgt.
Cowling Mrs. Dorothy, St. Andrewgt.
Cowlman Richard, Far Water lane
Cowper Edward, yeoman, Gillygate
Cowper Wm. shoemkr. High Petergt.
Cox David, broker, Feasegate
Cox Mary, shopkeeper, Far Water ln.
Cox John, baker, &c. Blossom street
Coyney Mrs. Elizabeth, governess of the Convent
Crabtree Eli, plasterer, Lendal
Cracroft Robert, Esq. Bootham
Craggs Mary, hair dresser, Pavement
Craggs Sarah, common carrier; warehouse, Coppergate
Crampton Joseph, shoemaker and dlr. in shoemakers' grindery, Seller's yard, Pavement

Crathorne Wm. St. Andrewgate
Crawford Lady, Blake street
Creaser Thos. watchmaker, Toft green
Creaser Wm. sen. cowkpr. Toft green
Creaser William, jun. cowkeeper and gardener, Micklegate
Creaser Matthew, Bootham square
Creaser Isaiah, cowkeeper, Toft green
Creser James, grocer, tea dealer and fruiterer, Skeldergate
Cressey George, sen. wine and spirit merchant, Fossgate
Cressey Geo. jun. cork mfr. Fossgate
Croce Joshua, barometer and thermometer manufacturer, Grape lane
Croft Miss Grace, Lendal
Croft Mrs. Sarah, gentlewmn. Mount
Croft Mrs. Judith, Aldwark
Croft James, plumber and glazier, Davygate
Croft Edw. shoemaker, Coffee yard
Croft Miss Sarah, Castlegate
Crompton Gilbert, Esq. St. Saviourgt.
Crompton Joshua, Esq. Micklegate
Crosbie Mrs. Mary, Bootham
Crosby Mrs. Susannah, Mount
Crossley Geo. vict. Board, Fossgate
Crowshaw Cornelius, printer & bookseller, (circulating library) Pavement, near Coppergate
Crowther George, Hungate
Crumbie Geo. tobacconist, Fossgate
Crummack William, vict. Wind Mill, (posting house and commercial hotel) Blossom st. Micklegate bar
Cramp Thos. comb maker, Cresser's yard, Micklegate
Cullingworth Wm. gent. Seller's yard
Cummins John, blacksmith. Goodramgt.
Cummins Ann, shopkeeper, Beddern
Cundall M. gent. Mount, Micklegt.bar
Cundall William, cabinet maker and auctioneer, Ogleforth
Cundall Peter, shoemaker, Wellington row
Cundall Richard, shopkpr. Skeldergt.
Cundall John, Red Lion yd. Micklegt.
Cundell Peter, shoemaker, Walmgate
Curtis William, bailiff, Stonegate
Cuthbert Thos. butcher, Skeldergate
Dagget T. W. tailor, College street
Dalby Job. tailor & broker, Jubbergt.
Dalby Richard, vict. Jacob's Well, Trinity lane
Dalby Richd. schoolmaster, North st.
Dalby David, animal painter, without Micklegate bar
Dalby Robt. shopkpr. Little Shambles
Dale Adam, tea mercht.; h. Coney st.
Dale Wm. vict. Unicorn, Tanner row
Dale John, grocer, &c. Fossgate
Dale Emanuel, broker and horses to hire, Feasegate
Dale Mary, straw hat mkr. Micklegt.

Dale Thomas, stone mason, Micklegt.
Dale Sarah, glove finisher, Gillygate
Dale Geo. shoemaker, Ogleforth
Dale Robert, cowkeeper, Blossom st.
Dale Thos. horse hirer, Goodramgate
Dale Geo. painter, Walmgate
Dale Thos. clothes broker, Feasegate
Dale Wm. hair dresser, Low Jubbergt.
Dales & Butterfield, wholesale druggists, Colliergate
Dales John, Esq. alderman, the Cottage, Mount
Dallin Rev. James, Monkgate
Dalton Wm. rope maker, flax dresser and linen mfr. Great Shambles
Dalton Wm. bricklayer, Goodramgate
Dalton Thos. bread baker, Bishop hill
Dalton Geo. butcher, Thursday market
Dalton Thos. yeoman, Bootham row
Dalton Wm. tea dealer, Goodramgate
Danby Samuel, master of the national school, Aldwark
Daniel John, gentleman, without Walmgate bar
Daniel Wm. grocer & tea dlr. Colliergt.
Daniel Simon, bacon dlr. Girdlergate
Darbyshire Robert, linen draper, High Ousegate
Darbyshire Christopher, grocer and tea dealer, Ousegate
Darbyshire George, baker and flour dealer, North street
Darbyshire James, tailor and clothes broker, Peter lane
Darbyshire Christopher, ship owner & coal dealer, Skeldergate
Darbyshire Christopher, coal mercht. Lord Mayor's walk
Darling William, Little Stonegate
Darling John, shoemaker, Marygate
Darling Robt. shopkeeper, Trinity ln.
Davenport John, shopkeeper, Little Shambles
Davies Peter, solicitor, Lendal
Davies Robert, solicitor, Lendal
Davies Mary, coal merchant, Lendal
Davies Samuel, mariner, Bishop hill
Davis William, plumber, glazier and painter, Colliergate
Davis Joseph, woollen draper, military and naval tailor, 21, Coney street
Davis Mrs. pastry cook, Colliergate
Davison Geo. miller, Wellington row
Dawes John, wheelwright, Peaseholm green
Dawson Wm. and Son, hat mfrs. and furriers, Fossgate
Dawson John, clerk of the Spiritual Court, & commissioner for taking special bail, Castlegate
Dawson Joshua, saddler and harness maker, Fossgate
Dawson Thos. baker, Walmgate
Dawson Mary, shopkeeper, North st.

Dawson John, baker, Feasegate
Dawson William, Leopard yard, Pavement
Day James & Edward, linen drapers, High Ousegate
Day James, linen drapers; house, St. Saviourgate
Day Ann, schoolmistress, without Micklegate bar
Deacon Joseph, pipe manufacturer, High Jubbergate
Debnam Frederick, vict. Coffee House and Hotel, Lendal
Deighton Thos. printer, bookseller, binder & stationer, (& circulating library) Pavement
Demier John, bop bag & sacking mfr. Walmgate
Demmey Thos. joiner, Skeldergate
Dempster Anth. watch mkr. Walmgt.
Dempster Anthony, joiner & cabinet maker & undertaker, Mint yard
Denison Thos. rulleymen, Walmgate
Denne Joseph, coach guard, Gillygate
Dennison Rev. W. S. Bootham
Dent Richard, corn miller, Micklegate
Dent Thos. cooper, Stonebow lane
Dent Thos. blacksmith, Walmgate
Dent Christ. shoemkr. Bootham row
Devine John, shopkeeper, Walmgate
Dewse Thos. proctor, College street
Dewse Robert, clerk of the cathedral vestry, Manor house
Dibb Wm. plane maker, North street
Dickens Henry John, Esq. barrister, Ogleforth
Dickinson B. W. thespian circulating library, High Petergate
Dickinson Rt. watchmkr. Goodramgt.
Dickinson Thos. ginger bread baker & fruiterer, North street
Dickinson Wm. horse dlr. Walmgate
Dickinson S. excise officer, Walmgate
Dickinson Wm. cabinet maker, High Jubbergate
Dickinson Wm. joiner, Petergate
Dickson Wm. cowkpr. Walmgate bar
Dickson Robert, joiner, Trinity lane
Diggs Wm. shoemaker, Bootham row
Dinmore Mrs. Cathn, Holgate lane
Dinmore Richd. watch & clock maker, and tea dealer, Coppergate
Dinsdale John, joiner, North street
Dixon Stephen, vict. Unicorn Inn, Monkgate
Dixon James, bookbinder, Colliergate
Dixon Richard, butcher, G. Shambles
Dixon John, vict. Malt Shovel, Walmgt.
Dixon Jane, shopkeeper, Walmgate
Dobson John, tailor, Skeldergate
Dobson Emanuel, grocer and tallow chandler, Low Petergate
Dobson Robert, bookkpr. at the Swan coach office, Copley's ct. Coney st.

Dobson Wm. cooper and butter agent, Trinity lane
Dobson Wm. flax dresser, Walmgt. bar
Dodgson W. F. carver & gilder, dealer in and cleaner of oil paintings, 3, Coney street
Dodgson John, tailor, Goodramgate
Dodsworth Mrs. Ann, Minster yard
Dodsworth Matthew, joiner, Grape ln.
Dodsworth John, College street
Dolby James, brick maker, Hob moor
Donnison Rev. Wm. Bootham
Doughty Mrs. Isabella, book folder & sewer, Peter lane
Doughty John, joiner, St. Andrewgt.
Douglas Miss Mary, ladies' day school, Micklegate
Douglas and Lockwood, whitesmiths, Skeldergate
Douglas Henry, tailor, Aldwark
Douglas Thos. vict. and hair dresser, Bay Horse, Skeldergate
Douglas Wm. hair dresser, Micklegate
Douglas Richard, shoemaker & parish clerk, Bishop hill
Douglas Wm. George Inn tap room, Coney street
Douglas John, tailor, Barker hill
Dove Sarah, gentlewoman, Monkgate
Dove Arthur, cabinet maker, upholsterer, & ironmonger, Pavement
Dove J. hair dresser, High Petergate
Dove Ann, butcher, G. Shambles
Dove Richard, butcher, G. Shambles
Dovenor Mark, vict. Queen Caroline, stone mason & glass cutter, Goodramgate
Dowker Mrs. school, Spurriergate
Dowson Robert, vict. Crown and Cushion, Walmgate
Drake Richard, surgeon, Precentors' ct.
Drake Mrs. Mary, Precentors' ct.
Drew Samuel, carrier, Colliergate
Drewrey Geo. vict. Leopard, Pavement
Drewery John, cowkeeper, Monkgate
Driffield Mary, vict. Bird-in-Hand, Bootham bar
Dring Mrs. Ann, gentlewoman, Lendal
Drinkell John, plumber and glazier, Blue Ball yard, Skeldergate
Druly Mrs. N. Little Blake street
Drummond Joseph, vict. Dog & Gun, Hungate
Drummond Joseph, baker, Hungate
Drury Mrs. St. Andrewgate
Duce Wm. coach painter, Grape lane
Duck Geo. baker, &c. Little Stonegt.
Ducket & Bowes, br cklayers, Walmgt.
Dudley Miss Susan, Little Blake st.
Duffield John, milk dlr. Walmgt. bar
Duffill John, vict. Upholder's Arms, Trinity lane
Duffill Francis, chair maker, Seagrave's court, Micklegate

Duffin Wm. Esq. Micklegate
Dugelby Robt. joiner & cabinet mkr. Davygate ; house, Jubbergate
Duke Michl. schoolmaster, Fossgate
Duke Wm. glover, Fetter lane
Duncan Hy. whitesmith, Dundas st.
Duncanson Geo. bookbinder, High Petergate
Dunn John, tailor, Stonegate
Dunn & Robinson, wholesale tea dealers, High Ousegate
Dunn W. tea dealer, without Micklegate bar
Dunn Rt. shoemaker, Goodramgate
Dunning Mrs. law stationer, High Petergate
Dunning John, vict. Malt Shovel, Walmgate
Dunning John, shoemaker, Fossgate
Dunslay Wm. Esq. Alderman & common brewer, Far Water lane
Dunwell Richard, tailor, Coppergate
Dutton Edward, gent. Bishop hill
Dutton Joseph, yeoman, Gillygate
Dutton Abm. baker, Little Blake st.
Dutton Benj. butcher, Micklegate
Dutton and Chapman, brick makers, Hob moor
Dutton John, miller, Walmgate
Dutton & Co. hosiers & tailors, Fossgate
Dyer John, land surveyor, Castlegate
Dyett Elizabeth, dress maker, without Castlegate postern
Eadon Geo. broker, Peter lane
Eagle Geo. solicitor, Bootham row
Ealand John, gent. St. Andrewgate
Earle Thomas, tailor, &c. Bootham
Earle Wm. tailor and draper, High Petergate
Earle John, gardener and seedsman, Haymarket
Earle Geo. gardener, Aldwark
Earnest Wm. Pump yd. Micklegate
Earnest Chas. Pump yd. Micklegate
Eastburn Mrs. Eliz. Monkgate
Eastgate Robert, linen mfr. Union pl.
Easton John, M. D. Bootham
Eaton Mrs. Sarah, Bootham row
Eaton Robert, gent. Coney street
Eccles Rbt. cowkpr. Walmgate bar
Edeson Wm. butcher, Walmgate
Edson Rt. saddle tree mkr. Walmgt.
Edwards Wm. carver, gilder & looking glass mfr. High Petergate
Edwards M. gardener, Layerthorp
Edwards J. P. High Ousegate
Edward Chs. shoemaker, Newgate
Elgie Mrs. Cicely, Lendal
Elgie & Heseltine, wholesale druggists, Colliergate
Ella Miss Eliz. Ogleforth
Ellerbeck J. sawyer, Petergate
Ellin Geo. Esq Blossom street
Ellin Mrs. Ann, Blossom street

EllingworthCatharine, ladies' boarding school, Minster yard

Ellingworth Richard, private teacher, Minster yard

Ellingworth J. maltster, Tanner row

Elliot Geo. coach guard, Lendal

Elliott John, wholesale & retail confectioner, pastry cook & Italian warehouse (Christmas ornamented game and goose pies sent to any part of the kindom) Spurriergate

Ellis Wm. Esq. alderman, Field house

Ellis Geo. and Co. livery lace weavers & saddler's ironmongers, Castlegt.

Ellis Wm. Joseph, Esq. barrister at law, Castlegate lane

Ellis George, wine & spirit merchant, Mint yard, Little Blake street

Ellis Wilfred, vict. Beverley Arms, Petergate

Ellis Wm. bookkeeper, Tanner row

Ellis Francis, gent. Waterloo place

Ellis Robert, bacon, cheese and ham factor, Spurriergate

Ellis Michl. auctioneer, Swinegate

Ellis Wm. shoemkr. St. Andrewgate

Ellis Robert, butcher, Bootham

Ellison Robert, solicitor & coroner for the City and Ainsty, Davygate

Ellison John, ironmonger and whitesmith, Davygate

Ellison Robert, sacking & wool sheet manufacturer, Hungate

Ellison Robert, bricklayer & builder Grape lane

Ellison Thos. pewterer, L. Shambles

Ellison Thos. shoemkr. Albion street

Ellison Robert, flax dresser, Hungate

Ellison John, plasterer, Lord Mayor's Walk

Ellison Lydia, gentwmn. Gillygate

Ellison Mrs. dress maker, St. Saviour's row

Elston John, gent. Colliergate

Elsworth Henry, gent. Skeldergate

Emmerson John, boot & shoemaker, Spurriergate

Emmerson Ann, dress mkr. Walmgt.

Emmerson John, comb mkr. Walmgt.

Eugland Thomas, ham, cheese, and bacon factor, Spurriergate

English Wm. comb maker, Hungate

English Robt. coffee roaster, Walmgt.

Erskine Mrs. Mary, lodgings, Coney st.

Etherington George, fishmonger, Stonegate

Etherington John, Blossom street

Etridge Thos. vict. Etridge's Royal Hotel, (post chaise) Blake street

Ettles Charles, wood turner, without Walmgate bar

Etty John, wholesale gingerbread baker, Feasegate

Evans Edw. engraver, Newgate

Evers Wm. woollen draper and tailor, Spurriergate

Evers Richard, plane maker, Red Lion yard, Micklegate

Exley Wm. joiner, Newgate

Eyre Charles, Esq. Micklegate

Eyre John L. Esq. Bootham

Eyre Thos. coal merchant, Friar walls

Ezart Wm. tailor, Gillygate

Fall Wm. paper stainer, Hungate

Fall John, cowkeeper, High Petergate

Fall George, confectioner and pastry cook, High Petergate

Farrar Rev. Abraham, Methodist minister, New street

Fawbert Joseph, stay maker, High Petergate

Fawbert Wm. wood turner, toy and cabinet maker, Stonegate

Fawcett Miss, gentwmn. Far Water ln.

Fawcett Mrs. Anne, worsted manufr. and flour dealer, Walmgate

Fawcett Charles, millwright and vict. Wind Mill, Walmgate

Fawcett Charles, jun. coal dealer, Walmgate

Fawcett Robert, cattle dealer & oat sheller, without Walmgate bar

Fawcett Wm. millwright, Walmgate

Fawcett John, coach guard, St. Helen's square

Fawdington John, wheelwright, over Monk bridge

Fearby Henry, miller & flour dealer, Fossgate

Fearby John, whip maker, Dunning's yard, Fossgate

Fearnley Thos. turner, Jubbergate

Fell John, comb maker, Hungate

Fell Geo. dealer in china, Thursday market

Fenton Richard, jun. schoolmaster, Grape lane

Ferraby Geo. flour dealer, Bootham

Ferrand Mrs. Mary, Bishop hill

Ferrand Thos. carver & gilder, Stonegt.

Ferrand Wm. plane mkr. Micklegate

Fether Neville, tailor & glover, Walmgt.

Fettes George, pawn broker, Lady Peckett's yard, Pavement

Field James, shoemaker, Aldwark

Field Wm. miller, North street

Firth J. schoolmaster, Bishop hill

Firth Eliz. shopkeeper, Peter lane

Firth John, butcher, Hungate

Fisher Wm. gent. High Petergate

Fisher Robert, vict. Waggon Inn, without Walmgate bar

Fisher Thomas, vict. Star & Garter, Nessgate

Fisher Joseph, coach mkr. Ogleforth

Fisher Charles, sculptor and mason, Tanner row

Fisher Wm. miller, Skeldergate

Fisher Geo. butcher, Skeldergate
Fisher Joseph, sail maker, Middle Water lane
Fisher Robert, butcher, Walmgate
Fletcher & Scarr, wholesale grocers, flax & tow spinners, linen & thread & sacking manufacturers & flax merchants, North street
Fletcher Benj. basket & brush dealer, 11, New Bridge street
Fletcher Geo. tailor, High Jubbergate
Fletcher Richard, corn miller, Heworth moor, & flour dlr. G. Shambles
Fletcher John, butcher, Thur. market
Fletcher John, Clementhorpe
Flint Geo. hair dresser, Castlegate
Flint Thos. brush maker, Girdlergate
Flower Rev. Wm. sen. High Ousegt.
Flower Rev. Wm. jun. High Ousegt.
Flower Geo. vict. Elephant & Castle, (Commercial Inn) Skeldergate
Flower Elizabeth, fashionable patent stay and corset maker, Stonegate
Forrest Rev. Rd. Precentor's court
Forrington Thos. shoemkr. Walmgate
Forth Mrs. Eliz. Blake street
Forth Mrs. Margaret, Stonegate
Fossett Joseph, brass, iron, ivory, and wood turner, Goodramgate
Foster Robert, tea, coffee, and fruit warehouse, Coney street
Foster Wm. tallow chandler, Fossgate
Foster Leonard, miller, Walmgate
Foster Thomas, tailor, Seller's yard, Pavement
Foster Henry, flax dresser, without Walmgate bar
Foster Jas. currier, Bootham row
Foster Z. & B. milliners, St. Andrewgt.
Foster John, cooper, Micklegate
Foster Robt. cowkeeper, North street
Foster John, cowkeeper, Mount
Foster , bookbinder, North st.
Foster John, Precentor's court
Foster Thos. butcher, Girdlergate
Fountain John, cowkpr. Monkgate
Fountain Thos. cowkpr. Tanner row
Fountain John, comb mkr. Tanner row
Fountain Nathan, shoemkr. Foss bge.
Fowler Thomas, glover, hosier, & furrier, Spurriergate
Fowler John, butcher, Micklegate
Fowler Wm. stone mason, North st.
Fowler Leon. butcher, G. Shambles
Fowler Mrs. Rachael, St. Saviourgate
Fowler Saml. baker, &c. H. Petergate
Fowler Miss Elizabeth, Aldwark
Fowler Matthew, china & glass warehouse, Walmgate
Fowler Wm. proprietor of Selby Providence coach, at Robin Hood, Castlegate
Fox John, joiner, Newgate
Fox John, day school, H. Jubbergate

Fox Thomas tailor, Fossgate
Fox Wm. wood turner, Fetter lane
France Rev. Wm. Methodist min Skeldergate
France Robt. coachman, Stonega
Frankish Richard, joiner, Hungate
Frankish Wm. tailor, Bell's yd. Peta
Frankland James, printer, Cou passage, Coney street
Frank Miss Elizabeth, Mount
Franks Thos. shopkeeper, Skelde
Franks Hannah, shopkeeper, Mi Water lane
Franks Thomas, cowkeeper and s keeper, Skeldergate
Fraser Daniel, gentleman, Davyg
Freeman Henry, hatter, Copperg
Fryer Michael, cabinet maker, Fo
Fryer J. R. proctor, Goodramgate
Fryer Mrs. gentlewoman, Goodra
Fryer Mrs. watchmaker, High Ou
Fryer Richard, vict. King's Arms, Water lane
Fuesdale Isaac, tailor, Little Blake
Furnish Mrs. E. St. Saviourgate
Furnish Wm. linen draper, silk cer, laceman, & importer of linens, (funerals completely nished,) 44, Coney street
Furnish Jane, shopkeeper, Holgat
Furnish John, coach proprietor livery stables, Trinity lane
Furnis Mthw. travelling agt. Moun
Gage Miss Margaret, Micklegate
Gallantry Peter, painter, St. Andre
Gamble Wm. solicitor, Castlegate
Gardener John, stone mason, Nort
Garforth Wm. Esq. Micklegate
Garland Thomas, bricklayer & buil High Jubbergate
Garland Mrs. Elizabeth, Micklega
Garnett John, horse hirer, Wa.mg
Garnett Thos. shopkeeper, Fossga
Garth F. A. and Co. chemists & d gists, Goodramgate
Gatrell Ellen, flour dealer, St. drewgate
Gawthorp Matthew, printer and proprietor of the York Her High Ousegate
Gawthorp Jas. shoemaker, Barker
Geldard F. F. plumber and gla Gillygate
Geldart Thomas, vict. King's Ar Foss bridge
Gell Thos. butcher, Great Shambl
Gell Thos. corn factor; h. Skelde
Gell Robert, butcher, Feasegate
Gentle Robert, saddler, Bookbin lane, Minstergate
Gibbins John, shoemkr. St. Saviou
Gibbins Wm. shoemkr. St. Saviou
Gibson Robert, hop and brandy chant, Petergate

Gibson Elizabeth, straw hat manufacturer, High Petergate

Gibson Thomas, rags dealer, North st.

Gibson Wm. linen draper and haberdasher, Thursday market

Gibson Joseph, ironmonger, iron founder and whitesmith, Pavement

Gibson John, brass founder, Hungate

Gibson Peter, parlour, Walmgate

Gibson Robert, cooper, Trinity lane

Gibson John, coach guard, Petergate

Gilbert John, currier, Gillygate

Giles Mrs. Elizabeth, Hungate

Giles Wm. whitesmith, Coppergate

Gill Henry, gent. Spen lane

Gill Wm. tea dealer & commissioner for taking special bail, for the county & city of York, Colliergt.

Gill Edmund, boot and shoe maker, 15, Coney street

Gill Mary, straw hat maker, Aldwark

Gill Mary, victualler, Mason's Arms, Goodramgate

Gill John, St. Andrew's Church yard

Gill John, tailor and clothes cleaner, Hungate

Gill William, gardener, Walmgate

Gill John, joiner, Walmgate

Gillet Edward, plater, Castlegate

Gilliam Joseph, gent. Skeldergate

Gilliam Thos. wharfinger, Old Wharf, Skeldergate

Gimber William, Esq. Minster yard

Gladden Mary, school, St. Andrewgt.

Gladin John, glover, Middle Water ln.

Glaisby Isabella, gentwmn. Blossom st.

Glaisby Wm. ladies shoemkr. Coney st.

Glaisby John, baker, Davygate

Gleadow William, Esq. Bootham

Gleadow Ambrose, vict. Old George Inn, Foot of Pavement

Gledhill & Edison, milliners and dress makers, St. Helen's square

Glenn Eleazar, house & sign painter, St. Saviourgate

Glover John, cutler and ironmonger, Pavement

Glover Thos. whitesmith, L. Jubbergt.

Glover John, whitesmith, Goodramgt.

Goldie George, M.D. Blake street

Goodricke J. schoolmaster, St. Saviourgate

Gorwood Benj. gent. Little Stonegate

Gorwood & Wiggins, pewterers, tinners and braziers, Spurriergate

Gowland William, gent. Gillygate

Gowland Thomas, vict. Golden Lion, Girdlergate

Gowland Jas. fishmonger, Skeldergt.

Gowland Thos. baker, &c. Coppergt.

Gowland Robert, cowkeeper, Lord Mayor's walk

Graham Rev. John, boarding school, Aldwark

Graham Rev. Geo. master of Archbishop Holgate's school, Ogleforth

Graham Hewley, solicitor; house, Micklegate

Grainger Robert, victualler, White Dog, Stonegate

Grainger Joseph, wheelwright, without Walmgate bar

Grainger Thomas, cooper, Swinegate

Grange Benjamin, coal merchant and vict. Three Cups, Foss bridge

Grange Joseph, victualler, Golden Ball, Fetter lane

Grant Lady, Castlegate

Grant Alexander, painter, Goodramgt.

Graves Benj. shoemaker, Blossom st.

Gray Wm. Esq. distributor of stamps for York and the West Riding, Low Petergate; h. Minster yard

Gray Jonathan, solicitor; h. Ogleforth

Gray John, auctioneer, Nessgate

Gray William, gingerbread baker and fruiterer, Fossgate

Gray Robert, bricklayer, Barker lane

Gray John, rulleyman, North street

Gray Robt. tinner & brazier, Micklegt.

Gray Ambrose, bricklayer, North st.

Gray Geo. grocer, &c. Micklegate

Grayson Rev. Isaac, master of the Royal Grammar School, St. Andrewgate; house, Spen lane

Greaves Eliz. shopkeeper, Micklegate

Green Ralph, steward and secretary to the Lunatic Asylum

Green Robert, tailor, Goodramgate

Green John, shopkeeper, Hungate

Greensides William, vict. Jolly Sailor, Far Water lane

Gregg Christopher, cabinet maker and shopkeeper, Micklegate

Gregory Thos. wholesale tea dealer, High Ousegate

Gregory J. and Co. royal mattin mfrs. carpet & patent floor cloths and brush warehouse, Low Petergate

Gregson Jane, dress mkr. Coffee yard

Greive John, tailor, Goodramgate

Grimwood Hannah, milliner and dress maker, Petergate

Grisswood Mary, dress mkr. Trinity ln.

Groves Chpr. shoemaker, Skeldergate

Groves Geo. joiner, Walmgate

Grunwell Ann, shopkeeper, Blake st.

Guandastague Miss de, teacher of drawing, Petergate

Guy and Arundell, linen draper, Colliergate

Haden William, hat manufacturer and steward of the Assembly Rooms, 8, Coney street

Hague Thos. cabinet maker, Clarkson's passage, Walmgate

Hainsworth Benj. blacksmith, Coffee yard

Halder Robt. joiner, Great Shambles
Hale Wm. Esq. distributor of stamps for the North Riding, New street; house, Acomb
Hall Thos. Esq. collector of the excise; h. Bishop hill; office, Coney st.
Hall Wm. agent to the County Fire Office, and bankers' clerk, High Ousegt.; h. without Walmgt. bar
Hall T. F. glove manufacturer & leather dresser, Ogleforth
Hall David, schoolmaster, Walmgt. bar
Hall Charles, perfumer & hair dresser, 12, Coney street
Hall Wm. shoemaker, High Petergt.
Hall John, shoemaker, Black Horse passage, Fossgate
Hall James, shoemaker, Hungate
Hall John, coach guard, Coney street
Hall Miss, gentlewoman, Blake street
Halliday John, milk dealer, without Walmgate bar
Hamilton Robert, saddler and bridle cutter, Bootham
Hammerton James, Esq. Petergate
Hammerton Wm. gent. Monkgate
Hands Wm. hair dresser & perfumer, Blake street
Hands Richd. bookkeeper, Trinity ln.
Hanley Jas. whitesmith, Walmgate
Hans Richard, gardener and sexton, Smith's yard, Skeldergate
Hansom Richard, joiner & carpenter, Micklegate bar
Hansom Henry, joiner and funeral furnisher, Tanner row
Hanson Mrs. Eliz. gentwmn. Micklegt.
Hanson G. C. chemist and druggist, Low Petergate
Hanthwaite Wm. shoemkr. Gillygate
Harborne Charles, yeoman, Colliergt.
Harborne Mary, dress mkr. Colliergt.
Hardacre Joseph, boot & shoemaker, without Walmgate bar
Hardcastle Thomas, vict. White Swan Inn, (commercial hotel) Pavement
Hardcastle Mary, furniture broker, North street
Hardcastle Ann, baker, Skeldergate
Hardcastle John, flax dresser, Walmgate bar
Hardcastle Saml. joiner, Waterloo pl.
Hardcastle John, shoemkr. Bootham r.
Hardman Edmund, jun. chemist and druggist, 17, New Bridge street
Hardman Edmund, sen. hair dresser and keeper of Bridge toll bar, 12, New Bridge street
Hardman William, musician, 12, New Bridge street
Hardman John, city wait, 12, New Bridge street
Hardy Thos. cowkpr. Parapet buildgs.
Hardy Jas. vict. Lord Nelson, Walmgt.

Hardy Eliz. plane maker, Coates yard, Tanner row
Hardy Thos. house and sign painter, High Petergate
Hardy Thos. breeches mkr. Stonegt.
Hare Matthew, tailor, Meynell's yard, Petergate
Hare John, comb maker, Walmgate
Harger John, vict. Bay Horse, Blossom street
Hargitt Charles, music preceptor, Blake street
Hargitt John, comb mkr. Bootham
Hargitt Richd. comb mkr. Coffee yd.
Hargrave Thos. Middle Water lane,
Hargrave Jas. bricklayer, Racket yd.
Hargreaves John, glazier, Smith's yard, Skeldergate
Hargrove, Gawthorp, and Hargrove, publishers of the York Herald & General Advertiser, (Saturday) Pavement
Hargrove William, joint proprietor and editor of the York Herald; house, 13, Coney street
Hargrave Joseph, joiner, Walmgt. bar
Harker James, agricultural implement maker, Marygate
Harland Lady, Lendal, (country residence Sutton-on-the-Forest)
Harland Jane, (leeches) Court, Coney street
Harle Thomas, attorney, Colliergate
Harmson Wm. shoemkr. Goodramgt.
Harper John, carpenter, Walmgt. bar
Harper Matthew, baker, &c. Walmgt.
Harper Matthew, milk dealer, without Walmgate bar
Harris Ann, calico dyer, Stonegate
Harris Mary, haberdasher, Pavement
Harrison Robert, Esq. Blake street
Harrison John, Esq. Monkgate
Harrison John, wine and spirit merchant, Low Ousegate
Harrison G. E. conveyancer, Coney st.
Harrison Hugh, shoemaker, Elliott's yard, without Walmgate bar
Harrison Thos. cooper, High Petergt.
Harrison Francis, Davygate
Harrison Wm. dealer in British wine, wholesale and retail, Davygate
Harrison Richard, tailor, Skeldergate
Harrison Wm. tea dealer, Jubbergate
Harrison John, ship owner, Skeldergt.
Harrison John, stone mason, Ogleforth
Harrison Jph. brickmaker, Bishop hill
Harrison Wm. calico dyer, Petergate
Harrison Thomas, keeper of the Peter prison, Minster yard
Harrison Rich. butcher, Thursday mkt.
Harrison Nathaniel, master mariner, Gillygate
Harrison James, shoemaker, Gillygt.
Harrison Robert, shopkeeper, Gillygt.

Hart John, vict. Angel, Walmgate
Hart Wm. listing shoemaker, Walmgt.
Hart Thos. mail guard, Gillygate
Hartley Ann, Fossgate
Hartley Amos, comb maker, Micklegate bar walls
Hartley Rt. plumber & glazier, Fossgt.
Hartley Sarah, cowkeeper, Toft green, Micklegate
Hartley Christopher, gardener, without Walmgate bar
Harton Thos. joiner, Walmgate
Harton John, joiner, Walmgate
Harvey Mrs. gentlewoman, Bootham
Harvey J. and M. milliners, &c. Minster yard
Harwood John, chemist and druggist, Petergate
Haslam Wm. shoemaker, & clerk to the Amicable Society, Wakefield Court, Micklegate
Haw Robert, bricklayer, Castlegate
Haw Wm. flour dlr. Peaseholme grn.
Hawkes Thos. farmer, Holgate lane
Hawkeswell Elizabeth, milliner and dress maker, Willow street
Hawkin Wm. gentleman, without Walmgate bar
Hawkins Mrs. H. St. Saviourgate
Hawkins Richd. baker, &c. Nessgate
Haxby Jas. whitesmith, Trinity lane
Haxby Wm. whitesmith, &c. Skeldergt.
Haxby John, whitesmith, &c. Skeldergt.
Haxby Wm. vict. Rose and Crown, Micklegate
Hay J. L. saddler, Micklegate
Hay Eliz. watchmaker, Micklegate
Hayton Mrs. gentlewoman, Micklegt.
Head Wm. vict. Clifford's Tower, Peaseholme green
Headley Hartas, flax merchant, flax & tow spinner, patent coloured and shoe thread manufacturer, Skeldergate
Headley Wm. shoemaker, Aldwark
Headley Geo. shopkpr. Far Water ln.
Healey Geo. Esq. Blossom street
Healey John, gent. without Micklegate bar
Hearon & Dale, wholesale tea dealers, High Ousegate
Hearon Wm. Hutchinson, Esq. alderman, High Ousegate
Hearon John, solicitor, High Ousegt.; house, Coney street
Hebden, Copley & Hebden, wholesale and retail linen drapers and silk mercers, Stonegate
Hebden J. & W. flour dlrs. Willow st.
Hebditch John, shoemaker, bird and animal preserver, Fetter lane
Hebditch Wm. shoemaker, Fetter ln.
Heeles John, patten, last & boot tree maker, Pavement

Helstrip Thomas, joiner, Church yard, North street
Hemsworth Grace, shopkpr. Church yard, North street
Henderson T. shoemkr. Goodramgate
Henderson W. shoemkr. Goodramgt.
Henwood Hy. bankers' clerk, Micklegt.
Heppell James, shoemaker, Beddern
Herbert John, painter, Swinegate
Heselwood Robert, vict. Red Lion, Walmgate
Heselwood Thos. tea dlr. Bootham row
Heslington John, gent. Bootham
Heslington John, grocer and confectioner, without Bootham bar
Heslop Eliz. shopkeeper, Barker hill
Hessay Mrs. widow, Walmgate bar
Hesseltine Jethro, druggist; house, Petergate
Hewdey Wm. bookkeeper, St. Saviour's row
Hewitt Thomas, vict. and shoemaker, Artichoke, Micklegate
Hewson John, linen draper, High Ousegate
Hick Matthew, vict. and whitesmith, Eclipse, Petergate
Hick Matthew, watch & clock maker, and jeweller, &c. Minstergate
Hick Robert, baker, High Petergate
Hick Matthew, butcher, L. Shambles
Hickton William, victualler, Acorn, St. Martin's lane
Hields John, verger and vict. Fox, Low Petergate
Hields John, farmer, Monkgate
Hildred Geo. tailor, Bootham
Hildreth Thos. butcher, G. Shambles
Hildreth Wm. butcher, G. Shambles
Hill Frederick, professor of music, Micklegate
Hill Richard, gent. Holgate lane
Hill William, victualler, Bay Horse, Goodramgate
Hill Sarah, boat builder, Marygate
Hill John, gardener and seedsman, without Walmgate bar
Hill Ann, butcher, Walmgate
Hill Ann, shopkeeper, Jubbergate
Hill John, printer, Skeldergate
Hill Ann, shopkeeper, Newgate
Hill Wm. shipwright, Marygate
Hill Wm. shelling and corn miller, Walmgate
Hillyard Ellen, flour dlr. Micklegate
Hillyard John, miller, flour dealer and baker, Skeldergate
Hinderson Robert, keeper of hack horses, &c. Aldwark
Hindsley Geo. butcher, G. Shambles
Hipworth Susannah, Mount
Hirst Wm. beast jobber, Aldwark
Hirst Francis, tanner, Walmgate
Hirst Sarah, clothes broker, Feasegt.

Hirst John, bricklayer and paviour, Mint yard
Hobson Richard, gent. Stonegate
Hobson Wm. mason, Middle Water ln.
Hodgson John, woollen draper, High Ousegate
Hodgson Joseph, rope maker, linen mfr. & flax dresser, G. Shambles
Hodgson Sarah, milliner and haberdasher, St. Helen's square
Hodgson Thomas, plumber & glazier, and patent lead pipe manufacturer, Stonegate
Hodgson Thos. miller, Clementhorp
Hodgson Elizabeth, miller, Fossgate
Hodgson Seth, miller, Petergate
Hogarth Edward, boot & shoemaker, dealer in hardware, and musical Instruments, College street
Holder Chs. whipmkr. Middlewater ln.
Holdsworth Wm. boot & shoemaker, St. Saviourgate
Holgate Chas. butcher, G. Shambles
Holgate Wm. butcher, G. Shambles
Holland Thomas, linen draper, 5, New Bridge street
Holliday James and Son, painters, Swinegate
Hollins John, woollen draper & tailor, opposite George Inn, Coney st.
Holmes Wm. comb mkr. Trinity lane
Holmes Chas. cowkeeper, Tanner row
Holmes Wm. carver & gilder & porter merchant, Hay market
Holmes Ann, butter, bacon factor, & cheesemonger, Pavement
Holmes Francis, Tanner row
Holmes Joseph, gardener, Tanner row
Holmes Joseph, combmkr. Tanner row
Holmes Chs. Lambert yd. Tanner row
Holmes John, comb maker, 14, New Bridge street
Holmes Hannah, straw hat manufacturer, 14, New Bridge street
Holmes Thomas, livery lace maker, Coffee yard, Stonegate
Holmes Frances, shopkpr. Walmgate
Holtby Wm. brewer, Thursday mkt.
Hood Wells, spirit merchant, New st.
Hooke Arthur, gunmkr. Goodramgate
Hooker and Cariss, hop bag & sacking mfr. St. Andrew's church yard
Hope Wm. surgeon, Castlegate
Hopkinson Geo. flax dresser, Aldwark
Hopps Thomas, corn miller, Castle mills; house, Union place
Hopps Geo. surgeon, Skeldergate
Hopps John, silk dyer, Grape lane
Hopton Geo. staymaker, Stonegate
Hopwood & Harwood, furnishing ironmongers, brass & iron founders, whitesmiths and bellhangers, High Ousegate: house, Hungate
Horn John, mason, Tanner row

Hornby Preston, apothecary, Petergate
Hornby Rd. shoemaker, Stonegate
Hornby Wm. shoemaker, Blake st.
Hornby Wm. joiner, Goodramgate
Horner Mrs. Mary, Manor yard
Hornor & Turner, surgeon dentists, Coney street
Hornor Benjamin, Esq.; house, Fulford road
Hornsey Matthew, vict. Pack Horse, Micklegate
Hornsey Thomas, deputy bailiff for the county, St. Andrewgate
Horsfall Thos. stone mason, Marygate
Horsman Joseph, hair dresser & hatter, foot of the Pavement
Horswell Thos. private brewer, Baker hill
Hotham George, common brewer, Walmgate
Hotham Colonel George, Bishop hill
Hotham Miss Susannah, Goodramgate
Hotham William, Esq. alderman, Blossom street
Hotham E. gentwmn. Goodramgate
Holden Chas. Middle Water lane
Houldgate Thomas, cabinet maker, Petergate
Houldgate Saml. turnkey, Castle
Hoult Joseph, worsted spnr. Walmgate
Housman John, plumber & glazier, & dealer in glass, Peter lane
Howard Geo. shoe mkr. Bootham row
Howard Rd. cooper, St. Martin's lane
Howarth John, Walmgate bar
Howcroft James, victualler, Black Boy, First Water lane
Howlett Henry, solicitor, Lendal
Hoyland John, shoemaker, St. Andrewgate
Hoyland Rd. shoemaker, Hungate
Hubie Wm. joiner, &c. Ogleforth
Hubie John, tailor, Walmgate
Hudson Wm. tailor & umbrella mkr. Davygate
Hudson Miss Ann, Aldwark
Hudson Wm. coal mert. Fryer walls
Hudson Thomas, tailor, Stonegate
Hudson Wm. baker, Stonegate
Hudson Thomas, shoemaker, Racket yard, Petergate
Hudson Wm. proctor, Petergate
Hudson Wm. hair dresser, Walmgate
Hudson John, shoemaker, Aldwark
Hudson Wm. tailor, Feasegate
Hughes Wm. shoemaker, Marygate
Hull John, watchmaker, College st.
Hunt Anna, Colliergate
Hunt Richard, hair dresser, Stonegate
Hunter John, shopkeeper, North st.
Hunter John, vict. Globe, G. Shambles
Hunter Frederick, tailor, Dundas st.
Hunter Mary, shopkeeper Monkgate
Hunter Thomas, joiner, Walmgate

Honston John, shoemkr. Skeldergate
Hupe Caroline, straw hat manufacturer, Low Petergate
Hurst Jas. brassfounder, Aldwark
Hurtley Henry, painter, Aldwark
Hurwood John, gent. Monkgate
Hurworth Thos. stay maker, Micklegate
Hurworth David, tailor, Bootham row
Husband Wm. surgeon, H. Petergate
HustwickGeo. coach guard,Trinity ln.
Hutton Henry, vict. Wheat Sheaf, without Walmgate bar
Hutton Jas. joiner, St. Mary's row
Ibbott Jph. mail guard, L. Stonegate
Ickeringill John, house carpenter, Far Water lane
Imeson Mary, straw hat manufacturer, Minster yard
Ince Philip, painter, St. Mary's square
Ineson John, joiner, Walmgate bar
Ingham Joseph, mfr. of sky & fanlights, Jubbergate
Ingham Jones, wholesale and retail linen draper, hosier, hatter, &c. Spurriergate
Ingham John, clerk of St. Michael le Belfrey church, Bootham row
Inglis James, tailor, Patrick Pool
Ingram Wm. house, sign, furniture, & coach painter, Parsonage house, Coney street
Inman Wm. boot and shoemaker, St. Helen's square
Jackman Wm. solicitor, H. Petergate
Jackson Edward, goldsmith & silver plate mfr. working jeweller, 14, Coney street
Jackson John, spirit merceht.Hay mkt.
Jackson Jas. yeoman, Walmgate bar
Jackson John, jun. plumber & glazier, North street
Jackson Mary Ann, straw hat manfr. Skeldergate
Jackson Geo. grocer, Wellington row
Jackson Geo. shoemaker, Bootham
Jackson Eliz. dress maker, Walmgate
Jackson George, shopkeeper, Walmgate
Jackson Thos. milk dealer, Walmgate
Jackson Eliz. hat box maker, Colliergate
Jackson John, vict. Eagle and Child, Great Shambles
Jackson Robert,victualler,Greyhound, Thursday market
Jackson Edward, gent. Beddern
Jackson Wm. hair dresser, Girdlergt.
Jackson John, plumber, glazier, and shopkeeper, Goodramgate
Jackson J. fruiterer, Goodramgate
Jackson Geo. tailor, Goodramgate
Jackson Mary, straw hat manufacturer, Stonegate

Jackson David, writer, Oglesforth
Jackson Rd. shoemkr. Bishop hill
Jackson John, grocer, Petergate
Jackson John, apparitor and verger of the cathedral, Monkgate
Jakell Joseph, gent. Mount
Jameson Wm. solicitor, College st.
Jameson Geo. shoemaker, Hungate
Jameson Mary, shopkpr. College st.
Jaques John, shoemaker, Jubbergate
Jebson James, millwright, Coppergt.
Jebson Wm. shoemaker, Finkle st.
Jeff John, turnkey at the Castle
Jefferson Geo. joiner, Aldwark
Jefferson T. joiner, Brunswick place
Jefferson John, ship owner, Skeldergt.
Jefferson Robert, merchant and ship owner and grocer, Pavement
Jefferson Thos. ship owner, Skeldergt.
Jefferson John, fellmonger, Walmgt.
Jenkinson Mrs. Bridget,gentlewoman, St. Saviourgate
Jennings Thos. gent. Micklegate
Jennings Geo. linen draper; house, Micklegate
Jennings Robert, linen draper and hosier, opposite the George Inn, Coney street
Jennings Wm. combmkr. Barker lane
Jennings John, shoemkr. Trinity lane
Jewitt Wm. printer, Bootham row
Jewitt Thos. butcher, G. Shambles
Johnson Mrs. A. gentwmn. Bootham
Johnson Robert, Finkle street
Johnson Richd. shoemaker, Feasegate
Johnson John, vict. Saracen's Head, St. Andrewgate
Johnson Joseph, saddler, harness and collar maker, High Petergate
Johnson Ann, victualler, Red Lion, Micklegate
Johnson Ann & Son, grocers, tea dealers & seed dealers, Colliergate
Johnson Joseph, wheelwright, Hungt.
Johnson Robt. racing calender & turf companion printing office, bookseller & stationer, Coney street
Johnson J. vict. Square and Compass, Middle Water lane
Johnson Robert, vict. Three Cranes, Thursday market
Johnson John, cooper, Walmgate
Johnson Joseph, vict. Ship staith
Johnson Richard, saddler, harness and collar maker, Great Shambles and Fulford
Johnson Jas. glass blower, Gillygate
Johnson Jas. cowkeeper, Barker hill
Jolliffe Wm. Esq. Stonegate
Jones John, leather dyer, Layerthorp
Jones Mary, midwife, Walmgate
Jones John, painter, Colliergate
Jordon John, flax dresser, Kirby's yd. without Walmgate bar

Joy Thos. vict. Peach Bowl, Stonegt.
Joy Joseph, vict. Cross Keys, High Jubbergate
Joy Jas. shoemkr. Bell's yd. Petergt.
Joy Wm. tailor, Middle Water lane
Joyce Sarah, vict. Ship, Skeldergate
Joyce Mthw. without Walmgate bar
Judson Wm. trunk mfr. Coney street
Kay John, shoemaker, Bootham row
Kearns Traver, horse breaker, Butcher's yard, Walmgate
Kearsley Mrs. gentlewoman, Castlegt.
Keaseley Miss Mary, ladies' boarding school, Little Blake street
Keighley John, clothier, Swinegate
Kelly Rev. G. D. Minster yard
Kendall John, gent. Skeldergate
Kendall John, gent. Micklegate
Kendall Mrs. gentlewoman, Mintlegt.
Kendall William, vict. Malt Shovel, Little Shambles
Kendrew Jas. bookbinder, Colliergate
Kenmare Robert, traveller, Hungate
Kenrick Rev. John classical tutor to the Manchester Presbyterian College, Monkgate
Kettlewell John, butcher, Haymarket
Kibblewhite James, paper hanging manufacturer, High Petergate
Kidd Wm. joiner, Grape lane
Kidd Joseph, cork cutter, Fettes lane
Kilby John, Esq. alderman, Pease-holme green postern
Kilby John Fryer, ale & porter brewer, Clementhorp
Kilham Thos. cooper, Fettes lane
Kilner and Hick, confectioners, Goodramgate
Kilvington Thomas, vict. Coach and Horses, Low Ousegate
Kilvington Leo. broker, High Jubbergt.
Kilvington Charles, wine worker, Clarkson's passage, Walmgate
Kimber & Bond, grocers, &c. Nessgt.
Kimber Thos. and Son, cut glass mfrs. & porter dealers, St. Helen's sqr.
Kimber Wm. coach inspector, Lendal
King John, governor of the House of Correction, Toft green
King Richd. coal merchant, Walmgt.
King Joseph, grocer, &c. Walmgate
Kirby John, shoemaker, Petergate
Kirby Richard, glover, Fetter lane
Kirby Thomas, horse dealer, without Walmgate bar
Kirby Frs. pill box maker, St. Mary's r.
Kirk Mrs. Mary, Blossom street
Kirk Wm. joiner, St. Mary's row
Kick Wm. tailor, Walmgate
Kitching James, surveyor of taxes, Ogleforth; h. Clifton
Kitchingman Rev. Henry, Bootham
Knapton S. and P. music and musical instrument warehouse, Coney st.

Knapton Philip, professor of music, house, St. Saviourgate
Knerick John, teacher, Ogleforth lane
Knight Wm. gent. Monkgate
Knowles Thos. tea dealer, Coppergt.
Knowles Geo. woollen dpr. H. Ousegt.
Knowles Robert, gent. Mount
Knowles H. gent. Gillygate
Knowles William, register office for servants, Precentor's court
Knowles Robert, hair dresser & shop-keeper, Goodramgate
Knowles Hannah, eating house, Skeldergate
Knowles Geo. shoemkr. Meynell's yd.
Knowlson Richard, gent. Blake st.
Kyle John, rope maker, flax dresser, spinner, sacking and linen manufacturer, Pavement
Lebron William, tobacco and snuff manufacturer, Pavement
Laidlaw Jas. flour and provision dealer, Gillygate
Lakeland Robert, Esq. Micklegate
Lakeland & Poppleton, linen & thread manfrs. flax dressers, and whole-sale drapers, Willow st. top of Walmgate and High Ousegate
Lamb Mrs. Margaret, gentlewoman, Micklegate
Lamb Robt. leather dresser, Bedlern
Lamb Richd. worm doctor, Dundas st.
Lambert Simpson, shoemkr. Swinegt.
Lambert Wm. chorister, Marygate
Lambert Rd. butcher, Great Shambles
Lambert Thos. dealer in old books, & silk stocking grafter, Silver st.
Lambert Thos. vict. Lamb, Tanner row
Lambert John, hair dresser, Coppergt.
Lambert John, shoemaker, Pease-holme green
Land William, comb maker, Blossom street
Land Geo. skinner, Dundas st.
Langdale Nathaniel, grocer, Walmgt.
Latham John, cowkpr. Parapet bldgs.
Law Alex. Judge's Old Lodgings yd.
Law Mary, dress maker, Judge's Old Lodgings yard
Lawn John, vict. (billiards) Theatre Coffee House, Little Blake st.
Lawn Wm. fishmonger, Walmgate
Lawrence Thomas, keeper of Castle-gate postern
Lawrence Mary, shopkeeper, Walmgt.
Lawson John, M. D. Lendal
Lawson Mary, rully owner, Skeldergt.
Lawson W. & F. booksellers, stationers, bookbinders, and engravers, &c. Coney street
Lawson Thos. patten, boot-tree & last maker, Seller's yard, Pavement
Lawson Thos. clog and patten maker, Hungate

Lawson Frabtis, master porter, Little Blake street

Lawson Michael, bricklayer, Hungate

Lawton Harriot, gentlewoman, St. Mary's row

Lawton and Pearson, wine, hop and spirit merchants, Goodramgate

Lawton George, proctor and agent to the Eagle Insurance Company, High Petergate

Lawton Amos, vict. Bay Horse, Gillygt.

Lawton Jonth. vict. Saracen's Head Coffee House, Stonegate

Lawton Saml. whip maker, Walmgt.

Lawton John, breeches mkr. Coffeeyd.

Lawton Mary, gingerbread baker, Little Shambles

Laycock Miss Ann, Micklegate

Laycock John, joiner, Brunswick pl.

Laydock Jacob, plasterer, North st.

Layton Thomas, Micklegate

Lazenby Robert, tobacco pipe manufacturer, Gillygate

Lazenby Geo. shoemaker, Walmgate

Leaf Eliz. gentlewoman, Petergate

Leaf Eliz. dress maker, Petergate

Leaf Joseph, butcher, Smith's yard, Skeldergate

Leake Jeffrey, turner, Walmgate bar

Leatham Wm. ship owner, Skeldergt.

Le Brun Thomas, hair dresser & fishing tackle maker, Wellington row

Ledger Richard, vict. New Bridge, Middle Water lane

Ledger James, sen. butcher, Low Jubbergate

Ledger James, jun. butcher, Low Jubbergate

Lee and Mason, saddlers and harness makers, High Ousegate

Lee John, glass & china dealer, butter and bacon factor, rag merchant, & livery stable kpr. Coppergate

Lee Wm. yeoman, Gillygate

Lee Wm. mustard mfr. Layerthorp

Lee Benj. whitesmith, Goodramgate

Lee Wm. saddler, Thursday market

Lee Thomas, parish clerk & chorister, Marygate

Leeman Mrs. Mary, fruiterer, Stonegt.

Letitall Joseph, vict. Black Horse, Bootham

Lefroy Anthony, captain and barrack master, without Walmgate bar

Letbe Deborah, victualler, Spotted Dog, Walmgate bar

Letbe John, glazier, Walmgate

Letbe Thomas, livery stable keeper, Skeldergate

Lewis Mary, eating house, Skeldergt.

Liddell Charles & Co. white and red lead mills, without Walmgate bar

Lambert Margaret, milliner, L. Petergt.

Linfott Wm butcher, Low Ousegate

Linton Benjamin, gent. Hotham lane

Linton Mary, schoolmistress, Goodramgate

Linton John, joiner, Fetter lane

Lister Christopher, scale beam maker, North street

Lister Major, shoemaker, Ogleforth

Lister Geo. ship owner, Rosemary ln.

Lister Eliz. dress maker, Micklegate

Lister Thos. gardener, Clementhorpe

Lister Thos. coach guard, St. Martin's lane

Little Robert, victualler, Black Boy, North street

Littlewood Solomon, Walmgate

Lloyd Mrs. E. gentwmn. St. Saviourgt.

Lloyd Mrs. Ann, gentwmn. Castlegt.

Lockby Wm. without Walmgate bar

Locke Wm. law stationer, Stonegate

Lockey Wm. cheesemonger & bacon factor, Petergate

Lockey Thomas, grocer and tallow chandler, Great Shambles

Lockey George, joiner and cabinet maker, Fossgate

Lockey John, clothes broker, Feasegt.

Lockey James, shoemaker and coal dealer, Waterloo place

Lockey Wm. coach driver, Jubbergt.

Lockwood Wm. (wholesale) chemist and druggist, Pavement

Lockwood Ann, dealer in grindery, Goodramgate

Lockwood Henry, tailor, Goodramgt.

Lockwood Geo. comb mkr. Tanner row

Lodge Mrs. Jane, Coney street

Lomas Lieut. Ralph, Royal Marines, Holgate lane

Long John, shoemaker, Hungate

Longtoft Geo. mason, Tanner row

Lovegrove Geo. coach guard, Lendal

Lowe John, wheelwright, Gillygate

Loy Samuel, glass blower, without Castlegate postern

Luccock Mrs. gentlewmn. Micklegate

Luckhurst Lieut. Thos. Monkgate

Ludwig Mrs. Eliz. Trinity lane

Lumb Emanuel, tailor, Walmgate

Lund Rev. Thomas, Micklegate

Lund Rev. Wm. Collergate

Lund Richard, gent. St. Saviourgate

Lund Benson, bookkeeper, Hungate

Lund Geo. skinner, Dundas st.

Lund John, victualler, Barrell, Little Blake street

Lund Geo. comb manfr. and porter at the Mansion house, Fetter lane

Lund Wm. wood turner, Albion st.

Lund Wm. farmer, Monkgate

Lupton John, florist, Bootham

Lupton James, gardener, Jubbergate

Lupton John, cabinet maker and upholsterer, and furniture broker, Low Jubbergate

Lutton Geo. gent. Moukgate
Lutton Miss Arabella, Bootham
Lyon Robert, glove manufacturer, Blake street
Lyon Charles, stay maker, Stonegate
Lyth John, grocer, &c. Walmgate
Lyth Robt. cowkeeper, Holgate lane
Machin Henry, baker, Low Jubbergt.
Machin Geo. baker, Far Water lane
Mackerill James, vict. and lamb skin dresser, Bay Horse, North st.
Mackrell James, hair dresser & hatter, Micklegate
M'Carty Peter, Far Water lane
M'Evoy Bernd. hair dresser, Hungt.
M'Gedy M. milliner, &c. Stonegate
M'Lean Mary, ladies' boarding school, Bootham
M'Larum Mrs. gentwmn. Stonegate
M'Lean John, shoemaker, Micklegt.
M'Lean John, shoemaker, Castlegt.
M'Millan John, surgeon, &c. Minstergate, adjoining Stonegate
M'Millan Alexander, tape dealer, Butchers' yard, Walmgate
Maddocks Samuel, inspector of mail coaches, Blossom street
Maddrah Margaret, coal dealer, Skeldergate
Maggi P. French teacher, Stonegate
Making Thos. glove mfr. Gillygate
Malking Wm. tailor, College st.
Mallatrat Frederick, woollen draper, tailor, ladies' habit & pelisse maker, and agent to the Birmingham Fire Office, 46, Coney st.
Maltas John, gardener, Walmgate
Maltby H. D. clock and watch maker, & tea dealer, Pavement
Mangham John, tailor, Aldwark
Mangles John, surgeon, Precentor's ct.
Mann Thos. butcher, Great Shambles
Mann Charles, shopkpr. Tanner row
Margrave Mrs. Hannah, gentlewoman, Monkgate
Marsh Mary, vict. Golden Slipper, Goodramgate
Marsh Joseph, furniture broker, joiner & cabinet maker, Feasegate
Marshall Peter, gent. Barker hill
Marshall G. S. cabinet maker, glass & china warehouse, Goodramgt.
Marshall Martha, fishing tackle, jewellery, cabinet and spinning wheel manufacturer, & toy warehouse, 6, Coney street
Marshall Wm. horse dealer, Gillygate
Marshall Richd. comb mkr. Bishop hill
Marshall John, blacksmith, Walmgate bar
Marshall Geo. joiner, Aldwark
Marshall Francis, shopkeeper, Aldwark
Martin John, coal merchant, Middle Water lane

Martin John, tailor, Skeldergate
Martin Wm. comb maker, Bishop hill
Maskall Robert, gent. St. Saviourgate
Mason & Branton, tea dealers & coffee roasters, Minster yard
Mason John, tea dealer and linen draper, Castlegate
Mason Thomas, gent. White Horse Coffee House yard, Skeldergate
Mason John, jun. tea dealer, Petergt.
Mason Michael, hair dresser, Stonegt.
Mason George, tobacco pipe manufacturer, Lord Mayor's walk
Mason Isaac, joiner, Brunswick place
Mason Jas. joiner & carpenter, Hungt.
Masser Anne, butcher, Ltl. Shambles
Masser John, tailor & habitmkr. Fossgt.
Masser Thomas, shoemaker and vict. Square and Compass, Trinity ln.
Masser Geo. shoemaker, Black Horse passage, Fossgate
Masterman Isaac, gardener, Walmgate bar
Masterman Thomas, Fetter lane
Masterman Geo. coach guard, Davygt.
Matterson Wm. surgeon, Minster yd.
Matthews Wm. cowkpr. Jubbergate
Matthews John, vict. Punch Bowl, High Jubbergate
Maw James, flax dresser, Church yd. North street
Mawson Thos. joiner, Great Shambles
Mawson Jonth. coal dlr. Skeldergate
Mawson John, shoemkr. Wellingtonrow
Mawson Thomas, comb manufacturer & dealer in small wares, Micklegt.
Mawson Jonth. cowkpr. Blossom st.
Mawson John, translator, Hungate
Maxwell Mrs. Jane, Bootham row
May Wm. farrier, First Water lane
Meadley William, vict. Bay Horse, Low Petergate
Meadley Thomas Brown, woollen draper, Great Shambles
Mears John, jeweller, silversmith, hardwareman and toy warehouse, Pavement
Meek James, currier, Goodramgate
Meek John, coal merchant, Gillygate
Meek Richard, wheelwright, Gillygt.
Meek Thos. house painter, Meynell's yard
Meggitt William, gent. Bootham
Meller Samuel, vict. Anchor, First Water lane
Mellon Joseph, First Water lane
Melrose Jas. sen. fellmonger, Walmgt.
Melrose Walter, fellmonger, Walmgate
Melrose Jas. jun. butcher, Foss bridge
Mennell George, gentleman, without Walmgate bar
Mennell Thomas, woollen draper, Coppergate

Mercer Thomas, tailor, Marygate
Mercer Geo. shoemaker, Walmgate
Merrington Robert, vict. Duke of York, Aldwark
Metcalf Mrs. Jane, Monkgate
Metcalfe Mirabella, umbrella and parasol manufacturer, and dealer in lobby cloth, Spurriergate
Metcalfe John, blacking mfr. Skeldergt.
Metcalfe Elizabeth, straw hat manufacturer, Hungate
Metley Chas. dog trainer, Tanner row
Meynell Geo. Esq. barrister, Copley's court, Coney street
Meynell Rt. hair dresser, H. Petergt.
Meyrell John, comb mkr. Blossom st.
Middleton Thos. grocer, Goodramgate
Middleton Mary, shopkpr. Goodramgt.
Middleton Miss Mary, Skeldergate
Middleton John, trunk maker and toy dealer, Nessgate
Middleton John, overlooker, Blue Ball yard, Skeldergate
Middleton Wm. shoemkr. Hungate
Midgley Jonathan, glass, china, and Staffordshire warehs. H. Petergt.
Midgley Francis, gardener, fruiterer, nursery & seedsman, Coney st.
Midgley Geo. butcher, Thursday mkt.
Mills W. & J. R. proctors, L. Petergate ; house Minster yard
Mills Henry & Son, wharfingers, New Wharf, Skeldergate
Mills Mary, fruiterer, &c. 11, New Bridge st.
Mills Philip, coach guard, Church lane, Coney st.
Mills Wm. worsted spnr. Walmgate
Milner Richard, flax dresser, rope, & linen mfr. High Ousegate
Mintoft John, flour dlr. Castlegate
Mitchell Barnabas, builder & slater, Stonegate
Mitchell John, furrier, G. Shambles
Mitchell John, shopkpr. Stonegate
Monkhouse Mrs. gentwn. St. Saviourgt.
Monkman Mrs. poulterer, Peter lane
Monkman James, vict. Old Sand Hill, auctioneer and sheriff's officer, Colliergate
Monkman Wm. hatter, furrier & rag dealer, Coppergate
Monkman Jane, schoolmistress, College street
Monson Hon. George, St. Andrewgt.
Moody Samuel, hat mfr. Pavement
Moody John, currier, Foss bridge
Moon Wm. shopkpr. Skeldergate
Moore Alexander, stone and marble mason, Walmgate
Moore Francis, billiard table keeper, Stonegate
Morgan Mrs. Catherine, without Walmgate bar

Morgan Sarah, milliner & dress maker, 20, Coney street
Morgan Mary, shopkpr. Skeldergate
Morine Mrs. L. gentwmn. Davygate
Morley Mrs. Elizabeth, Blake st.
Morley & Son, coach builders, Little Stonegate
Morley Wm. potter mert. Goodramgt.
Morley John, fishmonger, G. Shmbls.
Morley John, baker, Starcourt lane
Morrell John, shoemkr. Monkgate
Morris Mrs. gentwmn. Minster yard
Morris Thomas, vict. Pack Horse, Skeldergate
Morris Mary, milliner, Walmgate bar
Morris Joseph, gardener, Walmgt. bar
Morritt Wm. toy turner, Feasegate
Morritt Thos. cork cutter, Castlegate
Morritt Wm, tea dealer, Feasegate
Mortimer Joseph, saddler & harness maker, Walmgate
Mortimer Isaac, comb mfr. and toy warehouse, 16, Coney street
Mortimer John, glove maker, Wakefield court, Micklegate
Morton Ann, straw hat manufacturer, Waterloo place
Moses Robert, tailor, Goodramgate
Mosey John, fellmonger, Walmgate
Mosley Benj. cabinet mkr. Tanner row
Moss Francis, posting master & livery stable keeper, Minster yard
Motherby John, comb mkr. Walmgt.
Mottram Chas. mail guard, Gillygate
Mouncer John, currier, North st.
Mountain Mrs. Sarah, L. Blake st.
Mountain Rbt. stone mason, Lendal
Mountjer James cutler, Hungate
Moverley John, rope maker, cooper, & vict. Shoulder of Mutton, Middle Water lane
Moxon John, shopkeeper & printer, St. Saviour's row
Mucklow Thos. gent. Monkgate
Muirhead Mrs. Isabella, Walmgt. bar
Musgrave Christopher, shopkeeper, without Walmgate bar
Mush John, mfr. of paper hangings, & dlr. in carpets, (patterns sent to any part of the kingdom) Monk bar
Musham Frederick, cabinet maker, upholsterer & undertaker, Blakest.
Myers Christr. coach smith, Beddern
Myers John, victualler, Jolly Sailor, Skeldergate
Myers Wm. carpenter & vict. Square & Compass, Willow street, top of Walmgate
Myers Geo. shoemkr. St. Mary's sq.
Nayler M. gent. Coney street
Naylor Wm. huntsman of the Ainsty hounds, Mount
Naylor Geo. coach guard, Monkgate
Naylor Lieut. David, College street

Naylor Rhd. shoemaker, Waterloo pl.
Naylor Richard, shopkeeper, Aldwark
Naylor Matt. Judges' old lodgings yd.
Naylor Miss L. A. & E. dress makers, Judges' old lodgings yard
Nelson George, currier, Petergate
Nelson Robert, farrier & blacksmith, St. Martin's, Coney street
Nelson Mrs. gentlewoman, Bootham
Newcombe Thomas, carrier, Fossgate
Newlove John, clock & watch maker, Pavement
Newmarch T. Wood's yd. Tanner row
Newsam Thos. joiner, Blossom street
Newstead and Sons, sollcitors, Lendal
Newton Robert, tailor, Beddern
Nicholson & Hudson, silk mercers, linen drapers & hosiers, College st.
Nicholson Geo. grocer, Goodramgate
Nicholson and Bell, bricklayers and plasterers, Bootham square
Nicholson Jas. corn merchant, Goodramgate
Nicholson Patience, ladies' boarding & day school, Tanner row
Nicholson James, miller, North street
Nicholson John, tailor and draper, Stonegate
Nicholson Geo. milkman, Barker's hill
Nicholson George, tailor and draper, Goodramgate
Nicholson John, boat builder, Skeldergate postern
Nicholson T. hair dresser, Thu. mkt.
Nicholson Rd. tailor, Girdlergate
Nicholson Charles, leather dresser, Green lane, Hungate
Nicoll S. W. Esq. barrister and city counsellor, and recorder of Doncaster, Blake street and Fulford.
Nightingale John, saddler & harness maker, Fossgate
Nixon Joseph, victualler, Nag's Head, Fossgate
Nixon John, tailor and habit maker, Harker's yard, Micklegate
Noble Jane, shopkeeper, Jubbergate
Noble John, butcher & tailor, Walmgt.
Noble Wm. hair dresser and clothes broker, College street
Noble Geo. machine mkr. Bootham
Noddins Rev. Wm. at Mr. Smith's, Monkgate
Noke Charles, dancing master, High Petergate
Norman Wm. linen draper and tailor, Goodramgate
Norman M. tailor, Goodramgate
Norrison John, coal merchant & common brewer, Tanner row
North George, baker, Gillygate
North Ann, ship owner, Skeldergate
North William Greaves, assay master, Feasegate

Noton Thomas, plumber and glazier, Stonegate
Nutt John, comb mfr. Trinity lane
Nuttbrown Rbt. gardener, Albion st.
Nuttbrown George, city bailiff, St. Mary's row
Ogle Mrs. Martha, St. Andrewgate
Ogram John, shoemkr. Girdlergate
Ohman Andrew, organ builder and violin mfr. Gillygate
Oldfield Wm. post master and wine merchant, Lendal
Oldfield Joshua, gentleman, Parapet buildings, Micklegate bar
Oldfield Richard, gardener & seedsman, Fossgate
Oldfield Wm. coal merchant, First Water lane
Oliver Mary, wine & spirit merchant, Micklegate
Onion Thos. shoemaker, Stonegate
Ord & Pearson, attornies, Ogleforth
Ord John, attorney; h. Micklegate
Osburn Wm. flax dresser, Walmgt. bar
Othick Henry, blacksmith, Monkgate
Othick Henry, coal dlr. First Water ln.
Outhard William, butcher
Outhwaite Wm. shoemkr. Gillygate
Overend Leonard, slate merchant, Skeldergate
Overton Rev. John, A.M. Bootham
Overton James, surgeon, Blake st.
Overton Benj. shopkeeper, Hungate
Overton Charles, joiner, Swinegate
Owen Henry, vict. Globe, Great Shbls.
Owston Thos. merchant, & wholesale linen draper, 7, New Bridge st.
Oxlade Wm. mail guard, Gillygate
Palmer C. S. traveller, Gillygate
Palmer Wm. currier, Church ln. Shbls.
Palmer Alice, pawnbrkr. Patrick pool
Pape Wm. grocer, Micklegate
Pape Mary, grocer, Walmgate
Pape Wm. book-keeper, Lendal
Pardoe James, inspector of nuisances, &c. Blossom street
Pardoe Wm. police officer, Lendal
Parish Saml. shoemkr. Bootham row
Park Wm. hair manufacturer, Great Shambles
Parker Wm. gent. Walmgate bar
Parker Geo. coal merchant, Union pl.
Parker Anthony, florist, gardener, & seedsman, without Walmgate bar
Parker Henry, Walmgate bar
Parker Mark, Cressers yd. Micklegt.
Parker Wm. cowkeeper, Holgate lane
Parker John, joiner, without Castlegate postern
Parker James, bricklayer, Barker hill
Parkin Henry, grocer & tallow chandler, Goodramgate
Parkinson Nathaniel, coach, house, sign & furniture painter, (dealer in

oils, paints, colours, &c.) Stonegt.

Parkinson Sarah, shopkeeper & horses for hire, High Jubbergate

Parr Wm. haberdasher, jean & velvet warehouse, Blake street

Parsons Rev. James, minister of the Calvinist chapel, Lendal; lodgings, Blossom street

Parsons John, perfumery warehouse & ornamental hair mfr. 2, Coney st.

Partridge Wm. shopkeeper, Thu. mkt.

Pattinson Thomas, fishmonger, Little Shambles

Pattison James, whitesmith, Walmgt.

Pavier Wm. blacksmith, Walmgate

Peach Robert, bacon, cheese, and ham dealer, Spurriergate

Peacock Geo. Esq. alderman, Micklegt.

Peacock Thos. & Geo. timber merchants, Skeldergate

Peacock Mrs. Ann, St. Saviourgate

Peacock Mrs. gentlewmn. Skeldergate

Peccock D. J. & G: timber merchants, Skeldergate

Peacock Wm. gold & silversmith, and watch maker, Spurriergate

Peaker Richard, vict. Globe, Great Shambles

Pears Ann, straw hat maker, Hungate

Pears Ellen, shopkeeper, Micklegate

Pears John, comb maker, Bishop hill

Pears Mary, straw hat mkr. Bishop hill

Pearson Matthew, corn factor, Walmgate bar

Pearson Ralph, organ builder, Beddern

Pearson Elizabeth, schoolmistress, Minster gate

Pearson Thos. shoemaker, Albion st.

Pearson Hannah, vict. Red Lion, Goodramgate

Pearson Richd. butcher, Bootham sq.

Pearson Richard, tailor, Walmgate

Pearson Henry, Blossom street

Pearson Wm. attorney & agent to the Sun, &c. fire office, Goodramgate

Peart James, corn miller, maltster, brewer, & seedsman, North st.

Peckett John, schoolmaster, Walmgt.

Peckett Christ. shopkeeper, Petergt.

Peckitt Mrs. Mary, Friar walls

Pellett Geo. tailor, Walmgate

Pemberton John, Esq. barrister, Bootham

Pendleton Wm. shopkpr. Trinity ln.

Pennock George, vict. Barrel, Thursday market

Pennock Eliz. school, Micklegate

Pennistone Thos. bricklayer, Aldwark

Penrose Edw. Excise officer, Palmer ln.

Penrose John, flour dealer, Walmgt.

Penty Robert, vict. Duke of York, Walmgate

Penty William, writer, Lord Mayor's, walk

Perfect Joseph, painter; h. Albion st.

Perry Benj. Middle Water lane

Perry John, shoemaker, Walmgate

Perry Wm. Little Shambles

Peters Thomas, law stationer, Low Petergate; h. Barker hill

Peters Mary, broker, Gillygate

Peters Wm. letter carrier & musician, Gillygate

Petty Christopher, shopkeeper, North street

Pew John, vict. and coal merchant, King's Head, Thursday market

Pew Thos. spice dealer, Walmgate

Pexton Thomas, huntsman of the city harriers, Parapet buildings

Phillips Jonth. architect, Tanner row

Phillips John, cabinet maker and undertaker, Fetter lane

Pick Thomas, bricklayer, Gillygate

Pick Hannah, cowkeeper, Baggergate lane

Pickard Geo. grocer, &c. Nessgate

Pickard Rev. Wm. L. Bootham

Pickering James, shoemaker, Peaseholm green

Pinder John, shoemaker, Stonegate

Pinder Wm. vict. Leopard, Coppergt.

Plowman Ann, Chapter Coffee House, Minster yard

Plows Benj. & Son, stone and marble masons, Foss bridge, Walmgate

Plows Benj. & Wm. glass, china, and earthenware dealers, and stone masons, Coppergate

Plummer Miss Margaret, ladies' boarding school, Goodramgate

Pointer John, grocer, &c. Walmgt. bar

Pole John, comb mfr. Skeldergate

Pollard Catharine, painter, Colliergt.

Pollard Charles, boot and shoemaker, Low Petergate

Pollard John, joiner, cabinet maker, upholsterer & shopkpr. Skeldergt.

Pollard James, Walmgate

Pomfret Wm. glass and china dealer, and glass cutter, Stonegate

Poole John, shoemaker, Skeldergate

Poole John, Goodramgate

Pope Jonathan, shopkeeper, Girdlergt.

Popple M. A. dress mkr. Bootham row

Porritt John, excise officer, Walmgate

Pottage John, dyer, Fossgate

Pottage Rd. gardener, Walmgate bar

Potter Wm. writer, Ogleforth

Potter Thos. currier, Goodramgate

Potter Eliz. baker, Walmgate

Potts Joshua, goldsmith, jeweller, (musical clocks and snuff boxes,) and watch maker, Spurriergate

Powell Rd. bricklayer, Goodramgate

Powell Thos. whip maker, Castlegate

Powell Christopher, cowkeeper, Lambert's yard, Tanner row

Powter Mary, silk stocking grafter, Petergate

Poynton James, shopkeeper, without Walmgate bar

Pratt John, gunsmith, Stonegate

Pratt Thos. tailor, Middle Water lane

Prest Edw. & Sons, wholesale chemists and druggists, Pavement; house, St. Saviourgate

Prest Wm. butcher, Petergate

Prest John, coal merchant, North st.

Prest John, poulterer and bacon dealer, Feasegate

Preston Thos. W. attorney, Stonegt.

Preston Ann, gentlewmn. Gillygate

Preston Jane, gentlewmn. Petergate

Preston Wm. shoemkr. Goodramgate

Preston Thomas, joiner, Goodramgate

Price Thomas, Esq. Clementhorp hall, Skeldergate postern

Price Wm. grocer, Micklegate

Price Aaron, grocer, Great Shambles

Prickett Thos. Esq. St. Saviourgate

Priestley George, grocer and tallow chandler, Goodramgate

Priestley Joseph, furniture, &c. broker, High Jubbergate

Priestman David, tanner, Marygate

Prince and Prest, flint glass manufacturers, Fishergate

Prince John, gent. Fishergate

Prince Wm. clerk at glass house, Prince's court, Coney street

Prince & Gill, dress makers, Stonegate

Prince Matthew, bricklayer & plasterer, Tanner row

Prince Chas. Wood's yd. Tanner row

Prince John, shoemkr. First Water ln.

Prince Wm. tailor, Petergate

Proctor Robt. druggist, Tanner row

Proctor David, Dunning's yard, Fossgate

Pulleyn Mrs. Mary, gentwn. Bootham

Pulleyn Wm. dyer and comb maker, North street

Pulleyn Robert, hatter, hosier, and glover, St. Helen's square

Pulleyn Henry, subscription billiard table, Blake street

Pulleyn Jonathan, bricklyr. Stonegt.

Pullon Thos. London hat warehouse, Spurriergate

Pybus Geo. shoemaker, Tanner row

Quarton Wm. butcher, Barker hill

Radcliffe Charles, saddler and harness maker, Colliergate

Radge Wm. vict. Wheat Sheaf, Silver street

Raiment Rev. Benedict, Blake street

Raine Wm. shoemaker, Stonegate

Raine Mrs. Ann, milliner, Stonegate

Randerson Wm. miller, Bootham row

Randerson Mary, linen draper, Silver street

Randon Miss, gentwmn. Micklegate

Ransley William, agent to the water works, and tea dealer, Lendal

Raper, Swann, Clough, Swann, Bland, and Raper, bankers, Coney street, draw on Sir R. C. Glyn & Co. London

Raper John, Esq. banker; h. Lotherton

Raper J. L. Esq. banker; h. Minster yd

Raper John, joiner, Feasegate

Rathmell Thos. vict. Cross Keys, North street

Rawdon Miss, Micklegate

Rawdon Christr. sen. brush manufacturer, Barker hill

Rawdon Christr. jun. cabinet maker, Barker hill

Rawdon Rd. brush mfr. Micklegate

Rawdon and Deighton, cork cutters, 28, Coney street

Rayner Wm. victualler

Raynerson Joseph, Stonegate

Rayson Thomas, sen. gentleman, Tanner row

Rayson Thos. jun. builder, North st.

Rayson John, joiner, Hungate

Rayson Wm. shoemaker, Bootham

Read James, joiner, Marygate

Reaston Moses, cowkpr. Barker hill

Redforth John, hatter, Dunning's yd. Fossgate

Reed Silvester, vict. Bay Malton, Monk bar

Reed James, tailor, Swinegate

Reed Joseph, butcher, Blossom st.

Reeve Jane, vict. Leopard, Coney st.

Reynolds Wm. flax dresser, Fossgate

Reynolds Wm. plasterer, Gillygate

Reynolds George, vict. Black Horse, Fossgate

Reynolds Mary, earthenware dealer, Fossgate

Reynolds Geo. schoolmaster, Fetter ln.

Reynoldson Thos. gardener, Gillygate

Rhodes Robert, tailor, draper, & clerk of the race course, Blake street

Rhodes John, stuff manufacturer, Barker hill

Rhodes Jas. bricklayer, Walmgate

Richardson Rev. James, Bootham

Richardson James, solicitor, agent to the West of England Fire Office; and coroner for the liberty of St. Peter, Colliergate

Richardson Rev. Thos. classical and commercial academy, Bishop hill

Richardson R. & J. letter press printers, High Ousegate; h. Waterloo place

Richardson John, tailor and clergyman's robe maker, Minster yard

Richardson Mrs. Martha, Ogleforth

Richardson Edward, grocer, Bootham

Richardson William, tanner, thread

manufacturer, and flax spinner, Skeldergate postern
Richardson Jph. shoemkr. Skeldergt.
Richardson & Burrell, tallow chandlers and grocers, Great Shambles
Richardson Harman, sen. cooper, bacon and butter factor, Micklegate
Richardson Eliz. gentwmn. Micklegt.
Richardson Richard, victualler, Blue Bell, Fossgate
Richardson Francis, gentleman, without Walmgate bar
Richardson Francis, coal merchant, Far Water lane
Richardson Wm. joiner, &c. Stonegt.
Richardson Christopher, victualler, Garrick's Head, High Petergate
Richardson John, victualler, Lion and Lamb, Blossom street
Richardson Wm. shoemkr. Jubbergt.
Richardson Wm. vict. Lord Nelson, Little Shambles
Richardson Harman, jun. cooper, St. Martin's lane
Richardson Abm. tailor, Walmgate
Richardson Thos. turnkey, City gaol
Richardson Mrs. Minster yard
Richardson Richd. whip cord & twine spinner, and keeper of the workhouse, Marygate
Richardson Mrs. C. register office for female servants, College street
Richardson Thos. cowkeeper, Skeldergate postern
Richmond J. coach guard, Beddern
Richmond Joseph, clock mkr. Fossgt.
Richmond Sarah, cowkpr. North st.
Richmond Thomas, excise officer, St. Andrewgate
Richmond Joseph, tailor and habit maker, Hungate
Rickards John, broker, Swinegate
Rickell Joseph, victualler, Half Moon, Blake street
Rider Jph. flax dresser, Walmgt. bar
Ridley Cuthbert, stay maker, Lord Mayor's walk
Ridsdale David, plumber & glazier, without Walmgate bar
Ridsdale Robert, gent. Stonegate
Rigg Thos. & Son, wholesale nursery and seedsmen, Fishergate
Rigg Mrs. Ann, Gillygate
Rigsby Robert, cowkpr. Barker hill
Riley John, tailor, Little Stonegate
Riley Thos. conchsmith, Ogleforth
Ripley Alice, Blossom street
Ripley Matthew, shoemkr. North st.
Ripley Jas. bookbinder, College st.
Rippon John, general accountant, schoolmaster and private teacher, Stonegate
Rippon Frances, ladies dress feather maker and cleaner, Stonegate

Rippon G. C. carver, gilder and oil picture cleaner, Stonegate
Roberts Wm. Peaseholme green
Robinson Mrs. E. gentwmn. Bootham
Robinson Lieut. Chas. St. Saviourgt.
Robinson Mrs. Mary, St. Saviourgate
Robinson and Graham, solicitors, Stonegate
Robinson M. A. attorney; house, Barker hill
Robinson Chas. coal dealer, Monk bar
Robinson John, music & musical instrument dealer, Stonegate
Robinson William, hosier & glover, Stonegate
Robinson Wm. flax and tow spinner, Skeldergate postern
Robinson Thomas, joiner, Goodramgt.
Robinson Wm. cowkeeper, Blue Ball yard, Skeldergate
Robinson John, basket mkr. Fossgate
Robinson John, comb mkr. Micklegt.
Robinson John, comb mkr. Fetter ln.
Robinson Mrs. Jesse, Castlegate
Robinson J. auctioneer, Beddern
Robinson Hannah, schoolmistress, St. Andrewgate
Robinson John, stone mason, North st.
Robinson Benjamin, tailor, Black Bull lane, Walmgate
Robinson Rt. tailor, Lord Mayor's walk
Robinson Joseph, gent. Barker hill
Robinson Jas. comb mkr. Grape lane
Robinson Charlotte, straw hat manufacturer, Trinity lane
Robinson Thos. coach guard, Gillygt.
Robinson James, victualler, Rifleman, Grape lane
Robinson Geo. plane mkr. Bishop hill
Robinson Wm. cowkeeper, Monkgate
Robson Hannah; coal dealer, without Walmgate bar
Robson Isaac, carrier, L. Shambles
Rodley Joseph, gent. Walmgate bar
Rodley John, cabinet mkr. Petergate
Rogerson W. R. practitioner of medicine, Goodramgate
Romans John, basket maker, Walmgt.
Rook Mark, corn factor, vict. & wine & spirit dealer, New Bridge st.
Rooke Thomas, silk mercer, haberdasher & dealer in carpets, Minstergate
Roper John & Son, brewers and spirit merchants, Thursday market
Roscoa John, grocer, Coppergate
Rose Miss Elizabeth, gentlewoman, without Micklegate bar
Rotherford Robert, sen. confectioner, Micklegate
Rotherford Bob, jun. tinner & brazier, Micklegate
Rothwell Wm. bookkeeper, Dunning's yard, Fossgate

Rougier Joseph, mfr. of powder flasks, drinking horns, and broad horn shavings for fire places, Tanr. row

Rounding Thomas, earthenware dlr. Trinity lane

Routledge Wm. shoemkr. Goodramgt.

Rowley H. E. milliner, College st.

Rowntree Joseph, grocer, Pavement

Rowntree Robert, watch and clock maker, Coppergate

Rudd John, vict. Labourer, Skeldergt.

Ruddock John, vict. White Swan Inn, Goodramgate

Ruddock Wm. shoemaker, Gillygate

Ruler John, eating house and white-smith, Fossbridge

Rusby James, gent. Hungate

Russell, Thompson & Russell, solicitors, Lendal

Russell Simeon, vict. Barley Corn Inn, Coppergate

Russell Joseph, joiner, Marygate

Russell Mrs. Elizabeth, Petergate

Ruston Miss Mary, Gillygate

Ryan Ellen, gentlewoman, Albion st.

Rylah George, governor of the city gaol, near Bishop hill

Ryland Wm. surgeon, &c. without Micklegate bar

Rymer Peter, coal merchant, &c. St. Saviour's row

Sainton Thomas, stone mason, Pump yard, Micklegate

Salmond Misses Julia and Maria, gentlewomen, Minster yard

Saltmarsh Mrs. gentwmn. Blake st.

Salvin Mrs. Maria, Bootham

Salvin Miss Elizabeth, Mount

Samuel Sarah, pastry cook, Hungate

Sanderson Thomas, furnishing iron-mronger, cutler, crown glass, and iron bar merchant, Low Ousegt.

Sanderson Saml. bricklayer, North st.

Sanderson & Johnson, linen drapers and haberdashers, Pavement

Sanderson John, woollen drpr. Pavemt.

Sanderson Mrs. Anne, gentwn. Gillygt.

Sanderson John, Lord Mayor's officer, Bootham row

Saunders James, Esq. surgeon and alderman, High Ousegate

Savage John, flax dresser, rope & hair cloth mfr. Great Shambles

Saville Wm. cowkeeper, Layerthorp

Saville John, cowkeeper and butcher, Layerthorp

Saville J. B, painter, Beddern

Saville John, butcher, Goodramgate

Saville Richard, butcher, Goodramgt.

Sayer Mrs. Eliz. gentlewoman, Lendal

Scaddlethorp Richard, shoemaker, North street

Scaddlethorp Clement, shoemaker, St. Mary's square

Scadlock John, whip maker, Fossgate

Scaife George, victualler, Black Bull, Thursday market

Scaife Chpr. billiard room, College st.

Scaife Wm. wood turner, Swinegate

Scalling John, shoemaker, Skeldargt.

Scarr & Fletcher, porter merchants, Micklegate

Scarr John, flax and linen merchant, flax and tow spinner, patent coloured and shoe thread manufacturer, Hungate; h. Tanner row

Scawin Wm. chemist, druggist & tea dealer, Low Petergate

Scholefield John, Esq. banker, Castlegt.

Scholfield Wm. vict. Golden Fleece, Pavement

Scott Robert, solicitor, Bootham

Scott John, vict. Fox and Hounds, Blossom street

Scott Wm. blacksmith, Blossom st.

Scott Miss Sarah, Goodramgate

Scott Bartholomew, Walmgate bar

Scott Thomas, cabinet maker, Little Blake street

Scott Elis. milliner, &c. Ltl. Blake st.

Scott Robert, broker, Swinegate

Scott Jonathan, tailor, Beddern

Scott Thomas, joiner, Foss bridge

Scowby Francis, yeoman, without Walmgate bar

Scowby Thos. shoemaker, Feasegate

Scruton Wm. butcher, Gt. Shambles

Scruton Richd. baker, &c. North st.

Seagrave Richd. brazier, &c. Swinegt.

Seagrave Edw. vict. Grapes, Micklegt.

Sedgwick Wm. cabinet mkr. Blake st.

Seller Chas. spirit merchnt. Pavement

Sellers John, vict. Falcon, (commercial inn & posting house) Micklegt.

Sellers Mrs. Mary. gentwmn. Monkgt.

Serry Eliz. dress maker, Bishop hill

Setterington James, linen and woollen draper, Pavement

Settle Isaac, joiner, Ogleforth

Settle Isaac, broker, Feasegate

Settle Edward, tailor, Petergate

Settle George, butcher, Petergate

Settle William, Peaseholm green

Settle Mary, broker, Feasegate

Severs Thomas, gent. Goodramgate

Severs Joseph, grocer, &c. Stonegate

Severs Eliz. dress maker, Petergate

Severs Wm. butcher, Thursday market

Sewell William, gent. Tanner row

Seymour John, attorney and prothonotary, Little Stonegate

Seymour Mrs. Jane, Bootham square

Shackleton Ths. shoemkr. Waterloo pl.

Shackleton Wm. blacksmith, Walmgt.

Shadwell Mirabella, gentwmn. New st.

Shaftoe Sarah, shopkeeper, Walmgt.

Shaftoe Hannah, pipe mkr. Walmgt.

Sharp Thos. butcher, Thursday market

Shaw Arthur, gent. Micklegate
Shaw Ann, vict. Coach and Horses, Swinegate
Shaw Thos. shopkeeper, Micklegt. bar
Shepherd Samuel, rope mkr. North st.
Shepherd Thos. rope maker, Walmgt.
Shepherd John, rope maker, Middle Water lane
Shepherd Joseph, librarian to the Subscription Library, St. Helen's sqr.
Shepherd Robt. shoemaker, Gillygate
Sherwin Mary, straw hat manufacturer, Church yard, North street
Sherwood Eliz. furrier, glover, hatter and hosier, High Ousegate
Sbilletoe Thos. ironmonger, Pavement
Shinton Thomas, boarding academy, St. Saviourgate
Shinton William Edward, writing and drawing master, St. Saviourgate
Shores and Steward, cabinet makers and upholsterers, Micklegate
Shoulksmith Joseph, plumber & glazier, St. Mary's row, Bishop hill
Shout Wm. stone mason, Beddern
Shouter J. R. master porter, Gillygt.
Shuttleworth Mary, broker, Peter ln.
Sibbit Wm. shoemaker, Walmgate
Siddall Emanuel, brewer, Swinegate
Sidwell Geo. shoemaker, Fetter lane
Sigsworth John, grocer and tallow chandler, Castlegate
Silversides Samuel, tailor, Marygate
Silversides Thomas, bacon factor and blacking maker, Middle Water ln.
Silverthorp C. schoolmaster, College st.
Simpson Jas. spirit merchant, Davygate
Simpson Christopher, saddler, &c. Micklegate
Simpson Robert, Esq. Bootham
Simpson Mrs. Bettica, Mount
Simpson Susan, gentwmn. Trinity ln.
Simpson Jas. bookkeeper, Davygate
Simpson L. & J. corn millers, North st.
Simpson J. J. glove mfr. Stonegate
Simpson Wm. vict. York Tavern, (& posting house) St. Helen's square
Simpson Christopher, butcher, Mount
Simpson Jonathan, broker, Peter lane
Simpson T. excise officer, Grape lane
Simpson Joseph, tailor, Walmgate
Simpson John, saddler, Walmgate
Simpson Andrew, gardener, Bishop hill
Simpson John, tanner, Walmgate
Simpson Jas. shopkeeper, Ogleforth
Simpson William, collector's clerk, Spurriergate
Sinclair Robert, Esq. barrister and recorder of the city, 5, Coney st.
Singleton Gregory, cowkpr. Aldwark
Singleton Wm. shoemaker, Aldwark
Skelton Wm. gent. St. Mary's row, Bishop hill

Skelton John, upholsterer, Albion st.
Skelton James, victualler, Wheat Sheaf, Davygate
Skelton Robert, cowkeeper, North st.
Skelton John, shoemaker, St. Mary's row, Bishop hill
Skrimshaw Misses, fancy dress makers, Trinity lane
Slaney Lewis, flax dresser, Walmgate
Slater Mary, fellmonger, Walmgate
Slater Wm. vessel owner, Harker's yard, Micklegate
Slater Thos. gardener, Walmgate
Sledmere Richard, basket maker and toy warehouse, Nessgate
Small John, register office, College st.
Smeaton Mrs. Ann, Bishop hill
Smelt Ralph, Little Shambles
Smelt Elizabeth, broker, Peter lane
Smelt Henry, solicitor, St. Andrewgt.
Smith & Kirlew, merchants & wholesale grocers, Skeldergate
Smith Thos. Esq. alderman, Huntington
Smith Richard, coal and lime dealer, Monkgate
Smith Frances, ladies boarding school, Bootham
Smith Josiah, musical instrument dealer and clerk at post office, St. Saviourgate
Smith John, glass & china warehouse, Colliergate
Smith Wm. cabinet maker, undertaker and auctioneer, Low Petergate
Smith John, gent. Walmgate
Smith Wm. linen draper, flax dresser, and rope maker, Haymarket
Smith Geo. cowkeeper, Walmgt. bar
Smith Geo. shopkeeper, Jubbergate
Smith Thos. shoemaker, Trinity lane
Smith John, gardener and seedsman, florist and fruiterer, Spurriergate; house, Mount
Smith Joseph, whitesmith and hardwareman, Low Petergate
Smith John, vict. Wellington Coffee House, and butcher, Fossgate
Smith Jane, milliner and dress maker, Seagrave court
Smith Henry, tallow chandler, Walmgt.
Smith Miss Elizabeth, Bootham
Smith John, tailor, Wakefield court
Smith Mary, gentlwmn. 19, Coney st.
Smith Daniel, oats and shelling mill, Monkgate
Smith Geo. shoemaker, Stonegate
Smith Thos. gardener, Castlegate ln.
Smith Elizabeth, flour dealer, without Walmgate bar
Smith Mrs. Mary, Blossom street
Smith John, gunsmith, Micklegate
Smith Samuel, gent. Hungate
Smith Robert, vict. Shakespear Tavern, Little Blake street

Smith Benj. gardener, Blossom st.
Smith Rev. Wm. Gillygate
Smith Robt. exciseman, St. Andrewgt.
Smith Wm. hair dresser, Bootham
Smith Geo. milk dealer, Walmgt. bar
Smith Geo. Green lane, Hungate
Smith Thomas, bacon and butter factor, St. Andrewgate
Smith Wm. bookbinder, Lady Peckett's yard, Pavement
Smith Thos. victualler, Red Lion, St. Saviour's row
Smith Wm. mason, College st.
Smith Wm. mail guard, Lendal
Smith Mrs. Mary, Helgate lane
Smith Thos. cowkeeper, Layerthorp
Smith John, printer, Black Horse passage, Fossgate
Smith David, shoemaker, Stonegate
Smith Geo. joiner, Barker hill
Smith Wm. horse dealer, Blake st.
Smith Robert, miller, Walmgate
Smithies Jas. schoolmaster, Friar walls
Smithson Robert, solicitor & agent to the Pelican Life & Phœnix Life offices, Colliergate
Snaith John, blacksmith, Finkle st.
Snary Wm. Gillygate
Snow Geo. butcher, Great Shambles
Snow Peter, bricklayer, Castlegate
Snow Hannah, fruiterer, Skeldergate
Snowball Wm. shoemaker, Swinegate
Snowden Thos. tailor, Beddern
Snowden Wm. whitesmith, Black Bull lane, Walmgate
Snowden Henry, whitesmith, Davygt.
Snowdon and Buckley, stone masons and sculptors, Micklegate
Sollit Jas. mason, High Jubbergate
Sotheran Thos. bookseller, stationer, and binder, 9, Coney street
Southwood Wm. bricklayer, Butcher's yard, Walmgate
Sowerby Mary, vict. White Horse, Coppergate
Sowerby Mary, grocer, Colliergate
Spence James, gent. Walmgate
Spence Robert, gent. Pavement
Spence Wm. butcher & vict. Ham and Firkin, Walmgate
Spencely Thos. wine bottler, Davygt.
Spencer Isaac, Esq. lord mayor, Mansion house, Coney st. & Poppleton
Speheer Francis. broker, Jubbergate
Spencer Isaac and Co. manufacturing chemists, & wholesale druggists, First Water lane
Spencer John, dyer & finisher of patent threads, Tanner row
Spetch Jas. printer, Courant passage, Coney street
Spetch Ann, shopkpr. Thursday mkt.
Spink Jph. whitesmith, Lit. Shambles
Spink James, shoemaker, Ogleforth

Spurr Mrs. Elizabeth, vict. Black Dog, Low Jubbergate
Spurr John, wholesale & retail chemist & druggist, New Bridge st.
Stabler Robt. livery, lace & fringe manufacturer, Monkgate
Stabler Geo. cowkpr. Peaseholme
Stainer Thos. cowkeeper, Walmgate
Stainforth Mrs. Ann, gentwn. Davygt.
Stainforth Captain, Davygate
Stansfield Abraham, linen draper, &c. Micklegate
Stapylton Lady Mary, without Micklegate bar
Staveley Wm. governor of the Castle
Stead Mrs. Mary, Far Water lane
Stead John, solicitor, Tanner row
Stead & Gell, corn dealers, flour and shelling mills, Skeldergate
Stead Henry and Edward, merchants and wholesale grocers, chandlers and hop merchants, Skeldergate
Stead & Son, statuary and stone masons, Skeldergate & North street; house, Micklegate
Stead George, basket maker, near Merchants' hall
Stead Jane, coal dlr. First Water lane
Stead Thos. comb mfr. Castlegate lane
Stears Samuel, tambourine & military drum, &c. manufacturer, & music dealer, Fossgate
Steel Thos. bricklayer, Barker hill
Steel John, shoemaker, Fossgate
Steel Thos. shoemaker, Walmgate
Steel Henry, provision dealer, Davygt.
Stephenson Miss H. Blake street
Stephenson Richard, tallow chandler, Great Shambles
Stephenson Henry coal merchant, Parsonage house, Coney st.
Stephenson Jas. mariner, St. Mary's st.
Steward G. and Sons, combs, lanthorn light and drinking horn manufacturers, Blossom street
Steward Henry, watch & clock maker, Low Ousegate
Steward Wm. flax dresser, Walmgt. bar
Stewart Andrew, box and trunk maker, Walmgate
Stodhart Mrs. Mary, Bootham row
Stodhart Thos. brazier, tin & coppersmith and ironmonger, Coney st.
Stokes Eliz. varnisher, Bootham row
Stones Geo. upholsterer, fancy chair & cabinet maker, Pavement
Stones Thos. newspaper editor, High Petergate
Storry F. W. proctor and agent to the Globe Insurance Co. Low Petergt.
Storry Wm. printer, Low Petergate
Storry John, victualler, Black Horse, Walmgate
Stout John, gardener, Union court

Stowman Thos. tailor, Aldwark
Strafford Thos. tinner Albion street
Straker Wm. baker, Great Shambles
Straker Rachael, baker, &c. Fossgate
Straker Thos. mail guard, Gillygate
Strangeways Captain Thos. Bootham
Strangeways Robt. blacksmith, Bell's yard, Petergate
Streeton Thomas, victualler, Barley Corn, Beddern
Strickland Eustace, Esq. barrister at law, Judges' Old Lodgings, Coney street
Strickland W. & H. woollen drapers, Blake street
Sturdy William, glass and china warehouse, Petergate
Sturdy Christopher, New street
Sturdy William, joiner, Smith's yard, Skeldergate
Saffeld Thos. gardener, Walmgate
Summerwell Matthew, hair dresser, Great Shambles
Sumner James & Oliver, book-binders, Ogleforth
Sumpner John, plumber and glazier, Spurriergate
Sunman Wm. milk dlr. Walmgate bar
Sunter Robt. keeper of the bar watch house, Goodramgate
Sotcliffe John, druggist and professional chemist, 29, Coney st.
Sutcliffe John, shoemaker, North st.
Swails Robt. excise officer, Skeldergt.
Swain William, waiter at Etridge's, Bootham row
Swale John, butcher, 16, New Bridge street
Swales John, flax and tow spinner, Walmgate bar; h. Heslington
Swales Robert, baker, Micklegate
Swales Widow, milk dealer, Hungate
Swan Abel, wine and spirit merchant, and vict. Three Tuns, Coppergt.
Swan M. A schoolmistress, Stonegate
Swan John, butcher, Walmgate
Swan Edward, gardener, without Walmgate bar
Swan Thomas, Esq. banker; house, Blossom street
Swan Robert, Esq. banker; house, Micklegate
Sweeting Michael, linen draper and hosier, High Ousegate
Swift Mrs. Catharine, Skeldergate
Swift Robert, gent. Blossom street
Swift Mrs. Mary, Lord Mayor's walk
Swift Mrs. Sarah, Skeldergate
Swift James, shipowner, Fetter lane
Swift Wm. shopkeeper, Swinegate
Swinbank Henry, bookbinder, Petergt.
Swords Ann, shopkeeper, Walmgate
Tansley Benj. cooper, Davygate; h. Little Shambles

Tate John, grocer and tea dealer High Ousegate
Tate Miss E. A. boarding school (ladies) Manor yard
Tate Mary, book folder and binder, Goodramgate
Tate Wm. bookbinder, Barker hill
Tate John, horses to hire, Silver st.
Tatham Robt. cooper, St. Andrewgt.
Tatham Jas. cooper, Stonegate
Taylor Mrs. Jane, Albion street
Taylor Cook & Co. wholesale druggists, and manufacturing chemists, oil paints, colours, and mustard manufacturers, works, near Ouse bridge; retail warehouse, Spurriergate
Taylor John, cabinet maker, upholsterer, undertaker, and furniture broker, Peter lane
Taylor Jas. tea dealer, New Bridge st.
Taylor Joseph, victualler, Five Lions, Walmgate
Taylor Isaac, grocer, &c. Pavement
Taylor John, bricklayer, Dunning's yd.
Taylor Jas. gardener, Foss bridge
Taylor Jeremh. wheelwright, Walmgt.
Taylor Michael, sculptor, Lendal
Taylor Richd. vict. Blue Bell, Thursday market
Taylor Stephen, gardener, Walmgate
Taylor Eliz. butcher, Thursday mkt.
Taylor Robert, tailor, Bootham row
Teesdale James, shoemaker, Aldwark
Teesdale Christr. dealer in hosiery, worsted and yarn, Aldwark
Telford Isabella, flour dealer, Peaseholme green
Telford John, Esq. Tanner row
Temple Newland, victualler, Boot & Slipper, Beddern
Tennant Eliz. shopkeeper, Walmgt.
Terry Thos. gent. Lord Mayor's walk
Terry Joseph, chemist and druggist, Walmgate
Tesseyman Robert, linen draper and haberdasher, 3, New Bridge st.
Tesseyman Thomas, grocer, 4, New Bridge street
Tesseyman John, clerk at post office, and grocer, Bootham
Thacker John, dyer, Stonegate
Thackeray Robert, butcher, Thursday market
Thackray Joseph, vict. and coal merchant, Jolly Bacchus, Micklegate
Thackray John, butcher, Gillygate
Theakstone Richd. butcher, Petergt.
Theakstone, Robinson & Co, chemists and druggists, Micklegate
Theakstone Peter, butcher, Great Shambles
Thickett John, vict. and spirit dealer, Blacksmith's Arms, Swinegate.

I 3

Thistlethwayte Alex. confectioner, Finkle street

Thomas John, ship owner and coal-merchant, Thomas passage, Skeldergate

Thomas Richard, victualler, Ship, First Water lane

Thomas Mrs. Eleanor, keeper of the Bath, Lendal

Thomas William, register office for servants, Minster yard

Thompson Mrs. Ann, Castlegate

Thompson Miss Grace, Castlegate

Thompson Mrs. gentlewoman, St. Saviourgate

Thompson Wm. solicitor, Lendal

Thompson James, chemist & druggist, corner of Stonegate

Thompson Lewis, house & sign painter, Walmgate

Thompson Miss, dress maker, High Petergate

Thompson John, shoemaker, High Ousegate

Thompson John and Son, joiners and packing box manfrs. Little Stonegate; house, Marygate

Thompson John, cowkeeper, Monkgt.

Thompson Thos. coal merchant, Lord Mayor's walk

Thompson John, joiner, Dunning's yd. Fossgate

Thompson Wm. shoemkr. Bishop hill

Thompson Mrs. Catherine, Bootham

Thompson Robert, glover, Pavement

Thompson John, shoemaker, Peter ln.

Thompson John, shopkeeper, Petergt.

Thompson Geo. shopkeeper, Walmgt.

Thompson Thos. shoemaker, Hungate

Thompson Thos. vict. Crown, Thursday market

Thompson Wm. farmer, Monkgate

Thompson Wm. gardener, Bootham row

Thompson Matthew, milkman, Gillygt.

Thompson Thos. comb maker, Micklegate bar

Thornton and Spink, glovers and leather breeches makers, Spurriergt.

Thornton Philip, vict. Golden Ball, Bishop hill

Thornton Eliz. vict. Flying Horse, Coppergate

Thornton Mary, dress maker, Walmgt.

Thornton Mrs. Anne, broker, Fossegate

Thornton Geo. grocer, &c. Monkgate

Thornton Joseph, broker, Goodramgt.

Thorp Anthony, Esq. Bootham

Thorpe and Gray, solicitors, Low Petergate

Thorpe Edward, boot and shoemaker, and vict. Crispin Arms, Churchlane, North street

Thorpe Wm. shoemaker, Tanner row

Threapland Mrs. St. Andrewgate

Thrush Wm. tailor, College street

Thurgarland Rev. Godfrey, board school, St. Andrewgate

Thurnam Wm. tanner, without Walmgate bar

Tilney John, marble and stone mason, Bootham

Timms Isaac, veterinary surgeon, without Castlegate postern

Tindell John, cowkeeper, Welling row

Tindell John, vessel owner, and coal merchant, Skeldergate

Tireman Mrs. Ann, gentlewoman, Micklegate

Todd John and George, booksellers, stationers & printsellers, Stone

Todd Enoch, corn dealer, Lord Mayor's walk

Todd Thomas, shoemaker, Coppergate

Todd Robert & Son, butchers, Great Shambles

Todd Thomas, shopkeeper, Aldwark

Todd Benj. stocking and worsted manufacturer, Little Shambles

Todd Eliz. straw hat mfr. Goodramgt.

Todd Matthew, Aldwark

Todd Mary, shopkeeper, Monkgate

Toes Wm. currier, Goodramgate

Tomlinson Thomas, preceptor of music, and vender and repairer of musical instruments, &c. Blake st

Tomlinson Jonathan, vict. White Horse Coffee House, Skeldergate

Topham Miss, gentwmn. Minster yd.

Toulson Mrs. J. P. Gillygate

Towler Saml. tailor, Goodramgate

Towler Eliz. shopkeeper, North st.

Townend Richard, solicitor and town clerk, Blake-street

Townend & Bendon, solicitors, Lendal

Townend Mrs. Anne, 18, Coney st.

Townend John, stone mason, Walmgt.

Townson Henry, clerk at the North Riding stamp office, New st.

Triffit Thos. vict. Black Horse, Pavement

Trout Isabella, worsted spinner, Walmgate

Trout and Williamson, boot and shoe makers, Low Ousegate

Tuck Arthur, hairdresser, Goodramgt.

Tuke Wm. sen. house, Castlegate

Tuke Samuel and Co. wholesale tea dealers, Castlegate

Tuke & Ayer, land surveyors, Stonegt.

Tuke Daniel, land agent, Bishop hill

Tuke John, land agent, Bishop hill

Turner John, dentist, h. 4, Coney st.

Turner Jas. linen draper, Petergate

Turner James, Walmgate

Turner John, vict. Cross Keys, Goodramgate

Turner Mary, confectioner, Stonegate
Turner Mary, pastry cook, Leopard yard, Pavement
Turner Oliver, traveller, Walmgate
Turner Thomas, shopkeeper, Hungt.
Turner John, joiner, Bishop hill
Turner James, joiner, Bootham row
Turner Jas, vict. Black Dog, Fossgt.
Turner Rev. Wm. mathematical tutor at the Manchester Presbyterian college, Monkgate
Turner Wm. baker, without Walmgate bar
Turpin Joseph, boat builder, Clementhorp without postern
Turton Isaac, methodist preacher, New street
Tweedy John, Esq. banker, without Castlegate postern
Twentyman Sarah, milliner, High Jubbergate
Underwood Ann, vict. Spotted Dog, St. Saviourgate
Underwood Thomas, joiner, Stonegt.
Underwood Sarah, milliner & repository for fancy work, Gt. Stonegt.
Upton Mrs. Hannah, Blossom street
Vallette Paul, coal dealer, Marygate
Varey Wm. & Son, bacon and butter factors, and coopers, Fetter lane
Varley John, miller, Spittle field, Heworth moor
Varley Mary, wire worker and drawer, Fossgate
Varvill Michael, ironmonger & plane maker, 3, New bridge street
Vaughan Chas. shopkpr. Goodramgt.
Vause Geo. woollen draper and tailor, Pavement
Vause John, vict. Black Dog, Low Jubbergate
Vause Richard, vict. Wind Mill, without Castlegate postern
Veas Wm. shoemaker, Walmgate
Veavers Frances, dressmkr. Walmgt.
Venn John, tin plate worker & brazier, Goodramgate
Venteriss Thos. gardener, Far Wtr. ln.
Verity Thos. shoemaker, Walmgate
Vickers Miss Frances, ladies' boarding seminary, Coney street
Vickers Mrs. Sarah, Monkgate
Vincent Emanuel, blacksmith, Smith's yard, Skeldergate
Viner Thomas, sawyer, Hungate
Viney John, auctioneer and mattress maker, Green lane, Hungate
Vesor Thomas, shopkpr. Grape lane
Vollans Joseph, wine mert. Micklegt.
Waddington Thomas, number agent, Albion street
Wade Mrs. gentlewoman, Marygate
Wade John, woollen draper & tailor, Stonegate

Wade Hannah, victualler, Blue Bell, Micklegate
Wade Wm. bricklayer, Beddern
Wadman Mrs. Eliz. gentlewoman, without Walmgate bar
Wadman John, cowlxpr. Goodramgt.
Waggitt Michael, clock maker, Bull's yard, Petergate
Waind Wm. tailor & dpr. Goodramgt.
Waind Thos. tailor, &c. H. Petergate
Wainwright John, shoemaker, Lord Mayor's walk
Waite John, attorney, Silver street
Waite John, guard of Hull coach, Coppergate
Waite Richard, Lord Mayor's walk
Wake Baldwin, M. D. Little Blake st.
Wake Hannah, dress mkr. Coney st.
Wakefield Mchl. wheelwright, Toft gn.
Wakelin Robt. flax dresser, Walmgt.
Wakeman Mrs. Mary, Blossom st.
Wales John, ship owner, College st.
Wales John, coal mert. Willow st.
Wales Martin, coachsmith, Swinegate
Wales Thomas, shoemaker, Bootham
Wales Elam, sexton of St. Olave's church, Bootham row
Walker Thomas, solicitor, Colliergt.
Walker Wm. gent. Beddern
Walker E. and H. ladies' boarding school, Coney street
Walker Benjamin & Co. earthenware manufacturers, Goodramgate
Walker Thos. & Wm. carvers & gilders, Blake street
Walker Michael, ladies' and gentlemen's glove mfr. 11, Coney st.
Walker John, wholesale confectioner, Low Petergate
Walker Joseph, tailor and draper, Low Petergate
Walker Francis, worsted mfr. North st.
Walker Matthew, plumber & glazier, 10, New Bridge street
Walker Thos. portrait painter, Coneyst.
Walker Thos. joiner and undertaker, Davygate
Walker John, linen & woollen draper, Micklegate
Walker Geo. milk dealer, Walmgate
Walker John, comb maker, Layerthorp postern
Walker Rt. grocer, &c. Goodramgt.
Walker Peter, butcher, L. Jubbergate
Walker John, roper, Silver street
Walker George, joiner, Ogleforth
Walker Peter, master poster, Lord Mayor's walk
Walker Samuel, painter, Grape lane
Walker Sarah, sempstress, Coney st.
Walker Robert, tea dealer, Mount
Wallinger John, gent. Lendal
Wallis John, Esq. Blake street
Wallis Edw. surgeon, High Petergate

Wallis Joseph, baker, &c. Aldwark
Walls Thomas, cabinet maker, undertaker & furniture broker, Peter ln.
Walls Wm. tailor, &c. L. Ousegate
Walls James, coach guard, Coffee yd.
Walsh Thomas, gent. Micklegate
Walton Mr. gent. Tanner row
Walton John, cabinet maker, Cresser's yard, Micklegate
Walton John, vict. Board, Marygate
Walton James, shopkpr. Walmgate
Ward Anthony, victualler, Minster, Marygate
Ward Robt. shoemkr. Peaseholm gn.
Ward Thos. chemist & druggist, Fossgt.
Ward John, common brewer and spirit merchant, Fossgate
Ward John, organ builder, Micklegt.
Ward John, victualler, Turk's Head, Hay market
Ward William, Rosemary lane
Ward Francis, whitesmith and ironmonger, Manor yard
Ward Ralph, shoemaker, Walmgate
Ward Thomas, baker, &c. Walmgate
Ward Peter, tinner, Walmgate
Ward Jas. shoemkr. Peaseholmgreen
Ward John, coachman, Coney street
Ward Arthur, tape dealer, Hungate
Ward Wm. horse dealer, Marygate
Ward Samuel, tailor, Finkle street
Ware Mrs. Eliz. gentlwmn. Gillygate
Ware Christ. saddler, &c. Stonegate
Ware John, yeoman, Gillygate
Warmeth John, dyer, Tanner row
Warmeth Mary, dress mkr. Tanr. row
Warneford John, grocer, butter and bacon factor, Pavement
Warren Eliz. shopkeeper, Stonegate
Warrilow Joseph, fishmonger, Jubbergate
Warvill Thos. yeoman, St. Martin's ln.
Waterhouse John, wheelwright, High Jubbergate
Waterhouse Samuel, vict. Horse and Jockey, Aldwark
Waters Jph. shoemkr. St. George st.
Waterworth John, hatter and furrier, Goodramgate
Waterworth Ellen, St. Mary's square
Waterworth Wm. shoemaker, Wellington row
Waterworth Wm. farmer, Gillygate
Waterworth John, fellmonger, Tanner row
Watkinson Thos. timber, mahogany, & iron merchant, Walmgate; h. St. Saviour's row
Watkinson Elizabeth, gentlewoman, Rosemary lane, Skeldergate
Watson James, musician, Castlegate
Watson & Moyser, corn dlrs. Stonegt.
Watson & Pritchett, architects, Blossom street, Micklegate bar

Watson Christopher, working goldsmith, jeweller, watch maker, &c. in cut glass, teas, &c. L. Ousegt.
Watson Mrs. Eliz. Atkinson's court Micklegate
Watson John, law stationer & agent Copley's court, Coney street
Watson George, grocer and linen draper, Walmgate
Watson Miss Eliza, ladies' boarding school, St. Saviour's row
Watson Sarah, pastry cook, H. Petrgt.
Watson G. turner, Dunning's yard Fossgate
Watson John, Smith's yd. Skeldergt.
Watson Mary, St. Mary's row
Watson Wm. maltster, Skeldergate; house, Stonegate
Watson Geo. auctioneer, Petergate
Watson Thos. comb maker, Coffee yd.
Watson Chs. lace weaver, L. Stonegt.
Watson Rbt. confectioner, Davygate
Watson Wm. hat box manufacturer, Swinegate
Watson Wm. cowkeeper, Gillygate
Watson Wm. druggist, Micklegate
Watterworth Thos. cheese, flour, salt, bacon, butter, & ham factor; and agent for the sale of genuine teas, 7, Coney street
Waud George, bread & biscuit baker, Low Petergate
Waud George, corn miller and flour dealer, Fossgate
Waud Christ. hair cutter, Thu. mkt.
Weagley T. butcher, Bell's yd. Petrgt.
Wear David, solicitor, Castlegate
Weatherill John, gent, Bootham
Weatherill Hy. sen. farmer, Marygate
Weatherill Hy. jun. victualler, Brown Cow, Marygate
Weatherill Thomas, yeoman, without Walmgate bar
Weatherill Wm. hair dresser & grocer, Walmgate
Webb Joseph, vict. Grapes, Feasegt.
Webster Michael & Geo. shoemakers, Hay market
Webster Thomas, brass founder, brazier & tinman, Pavement
Webster Wm. ginger bread baker, North street
Webster Ann, dress mkr. L. Petergt.
Webster Thos. confectioner, Fossgate
Webster Ursula, flour dlr. Walmgate
Webster Thomas, tailor, Walmgate
Webster Michael, Hungate
Webster John, milk dlr. Walmgt. bar
Webster Mrs. St. Andrewgate
Wedgwood John, tailor, Beddern
Weightman Thomas, printer & bookseller, Low Petergate
Welbank William, mercer and draper, High Petergate

Welton Thos. tailor, Walmgate
Wellbeloved Rev. Charles, theological tutor of the Manchester presbyterian College, Monkgate
Weller James, linen mfr. & flour dlr. Walmgate
Wellfoot Rd. brush mfr. Petergate
Wells Thos. brush mfr. Colliergate
Wells George, whitesmith, Leopard, yard, Pavement
Wells Geo. flour dlr. Walmgate
Wells Len. whitesmith, Aldwark
Wells Wm. tailor, Goodramgate
Wemyss Thomas, bookseller, binder, print seller, and depository to the York auxiliary religious tract society, St. Helen's square
Wentworth, Chaloner, Rishworth & Son, bankers, Low Ousegate; draw on Wentworth &Co. London
West William, Walmgate
Westland Joseph, painter, Jubbergate
Whare Wm. gardener, H. Petergate
Wheatley John, shoe horn maker, Fetter lane
Whimp Anthony, cattle dlr. Monkgt.
Whincup Wm. spirit mert. Walmgate
Whip John, baker, Goodramgate
White Geo. shoemaker, Hungate
White Ellen, gentlewmn. Tanner row
White John, horse dlr. St. Andrewgt.
White Thomas, joiner, Walmgate
White John, tailor, Marygate
Whitehead William, linen and woollen draper, Fossgate
Whitehead Mrs. Diana, Ogleforth
Whitehead Lawrence, vessel owner, Blue Ball yard, Skeldergate
Whitehead William, basket maker, Leopard yard, Pavement
Whitehead Mary, (lodgings) Gillygt.
Whitehouse John, shoemkr. Barker hill
Whitehouse Rt. upholsterer, Coffee yd.
Whitehouse Geo. butcher, Feasegate
Whiteley George, tailor, Feasegate
Whiteley John, mason, Albion street
Whitfield & Bewley, bricklayers, St. Andrewgate
Whitley John, stone mason, Albion st.
Whittle Mrs. Ellen, Tanner row
Whittles Miss E. gentlwmn. Petergt.
Whitwell Mrs. Rebecca, Tanner row
Whitwell and Nolton, porter dealers, St. Saviourgate
Whitwell William, grocer, seedsman, and spirit merchant, Pavement
Whitwell John, valuer, &c. Davygate
Whitwell William, Micklegate
Whitwell Richard, baker, Haymarket
Whitwell James, baker, Colliergate
Wickham Misses Ann and Harriet, gentlewomen, Lendal
Wiggins William, gent. Monkgate
Wiggins Wm. baker, &c. Petergate

Wiggins William, brazier & tin plate worker, Monkgate & Spurriergt.
Wikeley Benjamin, joiner, &c. St. Saviourgate
Wilberforce & Cawood, stay makers, Fossgate
Wilberforce Walter, bricklayer & oats shelling mill, Walmgate
Wilberforce John, cowkpr. Blossom st.
Wilkinson John, gent. Walmgate
Wilkinson James, gent. Gillygate
Wilkinson Henry, solicitor, Stonegate
Wilkinson David, cowkeeper, Parapet buildings
Wilkinson John, vict. Shoulder of Mutton, Great Shambles
Wilkinson Rbt. butcher, Gt. Shambles
Wilkinson Ralph, shoemkr. Barker hill
Wilkinson Jas. wholesale spirit merchant, grocer, dealer in genuine teas, opposite the George Inn, Coney street
Wilkinson Thos. shopkpr. Dundas st.
Wilkinson Hannah, schoolmistress, St. Saviourgate
Wilkinson Thos. shopkpr. Monkgate
Wilkinson Hy. vict. Star Inn, Stonegt.
Wilkinson John, sail and rope maker, Middle Water lane
Wilkinson Roht. gardener, Coffee yd.
Wilkinson John, tailor and clothes broker, Feasegate
Wilkinson Harriet, straw hat maker, Goodramgate
Wilkinson Thos. fellmonger, Walmgt.
Wilks John, ironmonger, Bootham
Wilks Paul, blacksmith, North street
Wilks William, blacksmith and farrier, Bootham row
Willey Mrs. gentlewoman, Micklegate
Williams Jonth. painter, Bootham row
Williams Rd. flax dresser, Walmgt. bar
Williamson John, shopkpr. Walmgate
Williamson Richd. tea dlr. Stonegate
Williamson J. & J. shoemkrs. Colliergt.
Williamson Elizabeth, straw hat manufacturer, Walmgate
Williamson Thos. tailor, Ogleforth
Williamson Thomas, shoemaker, Bootham square
Willison John, joiner, St. Andrewgate
Willison Mrs. Margaret, Swinegate
Willmott Joseph, comb maker, Mount
Wilson, Tweedy and Wilson, bankers, High Ousegate, draw on Curtis & Co. London
Wilson and Sons, wholesale booksellers and printers, High Ousegate
Wilson Thomas, Esq. alderman, High Ousegate and Fulford Grove
Wilson Thos. jun.; h. St. Saviourgate
Wilson James, gent. Trinity lane
Wilson Thomas, proctor and notary public, Stonegate

Wilson Mrs. gentlewmn. Holgate ln.
Wilson Thos. vict. BlackBull, Walmgt.
Wilson John, surgeon to the dispensary, St. Andrewgate
Wilson Oliver, shoemaker, Davygate
Wilson Geo. vict. Turf Coffee House, Davygate
Wilson Eliz. confectioner, Stonegate
Wilson Valentine, vict. Waggon and Horses, Gillygate
Wilson Ann, common carrier warehouse, Coppergate
Wilson Wm. blacksmith, Bootham row
Wilson John, butcher, Great Shambles
Wilson Wm. milk dlr. Elliott's yard
Wilson John, butcher, Great Shambles
Wilson John, wheelwright, Ogleforth
Wilson John, vict. Granby, Peter lane
Wilson Mrs. gentlewmn. Goodramgt.
Wilson Hannah, ladies' boarding school, Castlegate
Wilson Jas. vict. Leopard, Coney st.
Wilson Thos. confectioner, L. Petergt.
Wilson Thos. shoemaker, Peter lane
Wilson Robt. hair dresser, Micklegt.
Wilson Samuel, deputy jailor, Castle
Wilson Thos. gardener, Barker hill
Wilson John, whitesmith, Walmgt. bar
Wilson Benj. provision dlr. Grape ln.
Wimbles John, shopkpr. Trinity lane
Wingfield John, comb mkr. Bishop hill
Winn Anne, George Inn, (& posting house), 10, Coney street
Winskill Thos. coach guard, Albion st.
Winter John, tailor, Little Stonegate
Wiseman John, whitesmith, Water ln.
Wisker Mrs. Eliz. optician, Spurriergt.
Wisker Robert, joiner, Coffee yard
Wolstenholme John, bookseller, stationer & printer, Minster gate; & publisher of the Yorkshire Gazette, Saturdays, in the Pavement
Wolstenholme Geo. gent. Palmer ln.
Wolstenholme Joseph, wine & spirit merchant, H. Petergt. & schoolmaster, 16, Coney street
Wolstenholme Fran. carver, Bootham
Wolstenholme Dean, fringe & worsted manufacturer, Bootham
Wolstenholme A. schoolmstr. Bootham
Womack Rd. pastry cook, H. Petergt.
Wood John, solicitor, Fossgate
Wood & Thompson, glovers & leather sellers, Pavement
Wood Mrs. Rachael, Precenter's ct.
Wood Joseph, cutler, gunsmith; and surgeons' instrument manufacturer, Spurriergate
Wood Richard, joiner, Walmgate
Wood Chpr. cowkeeper, Barker hill
Wood James, brazier & tin plate worker, 6, New Bridge street
Wood Geo. coal dealer, Walmgate
Wood Richard, shopkpr. Walmgate

Wood Thos. whitesmith, Bootham sq
Wood Edw. plumber, St. Andrewgt.
Woodall Wm. butcher, Silver st.
Woodburn J. bricklayer, Stonegate
Woodcock Wm. traveller, St. Mary's square
Woodcock Ann, librarian to the Select Subscription Library, Lady Pecket's yard, Pavement
Woodburn Margaret, broker, Peter ln
Woodhall Robt. cowkpr. Holgate ln.
Woods Edward, vict. Nag's Head, Micklegate
Woollons Thomas, furniture broker, Walmgate
Woollons Thomas, vict. Golden Lion, Thursday market
Worfolk John, coal dealer and clerk in the post office, Lendal
Worsley Wm. Esq. Castlegate
Wormald Rhd. solicitor, Blake st.
Wray Mrs. Susannah, Micklegate
Wray John, yeoman, Peaseholm grn.
Wray Thos. mail driver, Mint yard
Wray Thomas, Skeldergate
Wray Wm. shoemkr. Thursday mkt.
Wright Dorothy, gentwn. Skeldergt.
Wright James, gent. Toft green
Wright Frances, gentwn. Castlegate
Wright James, baker, L. Shambles
Wright Isaac, cooper, Friar walls
Wright Wm. shopkpr. Micklegate bar
Wright Geo. vict. Black Horse, Monkgt.
Wright Thomas, tailor, Walmgate
Wright Frances, shopkeeper, without Walmgate bar
Wright Thos. flour dlr. Coppergate
Wright Thos. milk dlr. Walmgate
Wright Ann, straw hat manufacturer, Dundas street
Wright Robert, shoemkr. Coppergate
Wright John, shoemkr. Walmgate
Wright Wm. bailiff, St. Andrew's church yard
Wright John, bookbinder, Dundas st.
Wright Hugh, gardener, Monkgate
Wrightson Thomas, shoemkr. without Walmgate bar
Wrightson Thos. cowkpr. Walmgate
Wrigglesworth Rd. Churchyd. North st.
Wynyard Rev. Mont. Micklegate
Wyrell James, bricklayer, Fetter lane
Wyrell Wm. combmkr. Blossom st.
Wyrell Isaac, shoemaker, Aldwark
Wyvill Mrs. Catharine, Aldwark
Wyville George, tailor, Aldwark
Yates Jas. leather dyer, Layerthorp
Yorke Mrs. gentlewoman, Micklegate
Young Isaac, whitesmith, Coffee yd.
Young James, hair dresser & perfumer, Minster gate
Young John, shoemaker, Petergate
Young Wm. shoemaker, Hungate
Youngstead Ptr. toy turner, College st.

**POST MASTER, WM. OLDFIELD.** Office, in Lendal, near the York Tavern, St. Helen's Square.

| Letters received from | Distance. | Postage. | Arrival. | Departure. |
|---|---|---|---|---|
| 1 London | 196 | 11d. | 8 at night except Monday. | 6 in the morning except Friday. |
| 2 Stamford | 111 | 9 | | |
| 3 Grantham | 90 | 9 | | |
| 4 Newark | 76 | 8 | | |
| 5 Bawtry | 46 | 7 | | |
| 6 Retford | 54 | 8 | | |
| 7 Doncaster | 38 | 7 | | |
| 8 Ferrybridge | 22 | 6 | | |
| 9 Tadcaster | 10 | 4 | ½ past 7 at night. | 12 at night. |
| 10 Leeds | 24 | 5 | | |
| 11 Bradford | 34 | 7 | | |
| 12 Halifax | 42 | 7 | | |
| 13 Rochdale | 58 | 8 | | |
| 14 Manchester | 70 | 8 | | |
| 15 Malton | 18 | 5 | ½ past 7 at night. | 12 at night. |
| 16 Pickering | 26 | 6 | | |
| 17 Whitby | 48 | 7 | | |
| 18 Scarborough | 40 | 7 | | |
| 19 Tadcaster | 10 | 4 | ½ before 8 morning. | ½ before 11 in the morning. |
| 20 Leeds | 24 | 6 | | |
| 21 Bradford | 34 | 7 | | |
| 22 Halifax | 42 | 7 | | |
| 23 Rochdale | 58 | 8 | | |
| 24 Bolton | 72 | 8 | | |
| 25 Manchester | 70 | 8 | | |
| 26 Liverpool | 107 | 9 | | |
| 27 Easingwold | 13 | 4 | 11 at night. | ½ past 8 at night. |
| 28 Thirsk | 23 | 6 | | |
| 29 Stokesley | 42 | 7 | | |

| Letters received from | Distance. | Postage. | Arrival. | Departure. |
|---|---|---|---|---|
| 30 Guisborough | 51 | 8d | 11 at night. | ½ past 8 at night. |
| 31 Yarm | 47 | 7 | | |
| 32 Stockton | 47 | 7 | | |
| 33 Sunderland | 74 | 8 | | |
| 34 South Shields | 81 | 9 | | |
| 35 Northallerton | 32 | 7 | ½ past 11 at night. | ½ past 8 at night. |
| 36 Darlington | 48 | 7 | | |
| 37 Durham | 66 | 8 | | |
| 38 Gateshead | 81 | 9 | | |
| 39 Newcastle | 81 | 9 | | |
| 40 Berwick | 143 | 10 | | |
| 41 Edinburgh | 202 | 11 | | |
| 42 Pocklington | 14 | 4 | ½ past 7 at night. | ½ past 12 at night. |
| 43 Market Weighton | 19 | 5 | | |
| 44 Beverley | 29 | 6 | | |
| 45 Hull | 38 | 7 | | |
| 46 Bedale | 33 | 7 | ½ past 10 at night. | ½ before 8 at night. |
| 47 Boro'bridge | 17 | 5 | | |
| 48 Catterick | 39 | 7 | | |
| 49 Gretabridge | 54 | 8 | | |
| 50 Brough | 75 | 8 | | |
| 51 Appleby | 84 | 9 | | |
| 52 Penrith | 94 | 9 | | |
| 53 Carlisle | 112 | 9 | | |
| 54 Wetherby | 15 | 4 | ½ past 9 at night. | ½ before 8 at night. |
| 55 Skipton | 46 | 7 | | |
| 56 Settle | 62 | 8 | | |
| 57 Helmley | 23 | 6 | 6 at night. | ½ past 12 at night. |
| 58 Kirkbymoorside | 29 | 6 | | |

*Post-Office continued.*

In consequence of recent alterations, the London, Hull, Whitby, Scarbro' and Liverpool Mails arrive here so as to admit of a delivery, at the window, of letters and newspapers (brought by those mails) in the evening, as soon possible after the departure of the mail to the North, which delivery continues until ten o'clock, at which hour the Receiving Box is closed for all parts of the kingdom, but letters are taken in at the window until eleven, by payment of one penny each. It is, however, necessary that all letters intended to be forwarded by the Edinbro' and Shields mails, or the Boroughbridge and Wetherby posts of the same night, should be put into the office before seven o'clock. The office opens every morning at eight o'clock for the delivery of letters, and the letter carriers are dispatched into the city at nine.

LONDON AND PROVINCIAL

# ROYAL MAIL AND POST COACHES.

\*\*\* For route of the Mails, see Post-office Statement for York.

### From the Black Swan and York Tavern, (alternately.)

To LONDON, the Mail at 6 mg. in 25 hrs.
EDINBURGH, by Newcastle, the Mail at ½ p. 8 evg. in 25½ hours.
LIVERPOOL, by Bolton, the Mail at ¼ bf. 11 mg. in 15½ hours.
SCARBOROUGH, the Mail every Mon. Wed. Fri. and Sat. nights at 12, in 6½ hours.
SHIELDS, the Mail every evg. at ½ p. 8, in 10½ hours.
WHITBY, the Mail every Sun. Tu. & Thu. nights at 12, in 7½ hours.

To LONDON, the Wellington at ¼ past 11 at night, in 33 hours.
HULL, the Trafalgar every morning at 7, in 6½ hours.
NEWCASTLE, the Highflyer at 7 mg. in 12½ hours.
NEWCASTLE, the Wellington at ¼ past 9 evening, in 13 hours.
SELBY, the Favourite every mg. at 9 (ex. Sun.) in 2 hours to meet the Steam Packets.

### York Tavern, St. Helen's Square, (regularly.)

#### Departures.
To LIVERPOOL, by Manchester, the Mail at 12 at ngt. in 15½ hours.
HULL, the Mail at 12 at nght. in 5½ hours.
LONDON, the Highflyer at ½ p. 8 mg. in 28½ hours.
LEEDS, the Blucher at ½ p. 1 at noon, (during summer) in 3½ hours.
LIVERPOOL, by Manchester, the Highflyer at 6 mg. in 15 hours.
SCARBROUGH, the Blucher at 1 noon, (during summer) in 7 hours.
SHEFFIELD, the Blucher at ¼ past 1 noon, (during summer) in 9 hours.
WAKEFIELD, the Blucher every Fri. at 6 mg. in 4½ hours.

#### Arrivals.
NEW LIVERPOOL Mail, at 45 min. p. 7 morning.

#### Arrivals continued.
EDINBURGH Mail, at 30 min. past 11 evening.
HULL Mail, at 30 min. past 7 evg.
HULL, Trafalgar, at 8 evening.
LIVERPOOL OLD Mail, at 30 min. p. 7 evening.
LIVERPOOL, Highflyer, at 7 evg.
LONDON Mail, at 8 evening.
LONDON, Wellington, 30 m. p. 7 evg.
LONDON, Highflyer, at 12 noon.
NEWCASTLE, Wellington, 30 min. p. 8 evening.
NEWCASTLE, Highflyer, at 9 evg.
SCARBOROUGH Mail, at 15 min. past 7 evening.
SHEFFIELD, Blucher, at 1 afternoon.
WAKEFIELD, Blucher, at 10 evg.
WHITBY Mail, at 15 min. p. 7 evg.

*From the Black Swan; Coney-street, (regularly.)*

**Departures.**

To CARLISLE, the Express every Mon. Wed. & Fri. at 2 aft. in 16 hours
HARROGATE, the Tally-ho every Tu. Thu. and Sat. at ¼ past 12 noon, in 3¼ hours
HULL, the Rockingham every forenoon at 10, in 7 hours, & the TRAFALGAR, every aft. at 2, in 6 hours
KENDAL, the Union every mg. at a ¼ before 6, in 15¼ hours
LEEDS, the True Blue every aft. at a ¼ before 2, in 3¾ hours
LIVERPOOL, Wellington every mg. at a ¼ before 6, in 15¼ hours
LONDON, Express at 9 morning, in 28 hours
SCARBOROUGH, Old True Blue every day (except Sunday) at 12 at noon, in 7 hours
SHEFFIELD, the Union every aft. (ex. Sunday) at ½ p. 1, in 9 hours
SHEFFIELD and BIRMINGHAM, the Express every morning, at 9, in 9 hours

**Arrivals.**

CARLISLE, Express, at 10 night
EDINBURGH Mail, at 30 min. past 11 night
EDINBURGH, Highflyer, at 9 evg.
HARROGATE, Tally-ho, at 8 evening
HULL, Trafalgar, at 12 morning
HULL, Rockingham, at 4 afternoon
KENDAL, Union, at 7 evening
LEEDS, True Blue, at 11 morning
LEEDS, Wellington, at 7 evening
LIVERPOOL New Mail, at 30 min. p. 7 morning
LONDON Mail, at 8 evening
LONDON, Express, at 30 min. past 11 morning
LONDON, Wellington, at 8 evening
SCARBOROUGH Mail, at 15 min. past 7 evening
SCARBOROUGH, True Blue, at 30 min. past 12 noon
SHEFFIELD and BIRMINGHAM, at 30 min. past 11 morning
SHEFFIELD, Union, at 12 noon
WHITBY Mail, at 15 min. past 7 evg.

## COACHES FROM VARIOUS INNS.

To KNARESBROUGH & HARROGATE, the Union Coach from the Elephant and Castle, Skeldergate, every Mon. Wednesday and Friday, at 2 afternoon, and returns the following morning at ¼ past 11
RIPON & BOROUGHBRIDGE Union Coach from the Elephant and Castle, Skeldergate, every Tuesday & Thursday, at 2 afternoon, returns to York on Wednesday & Friday at ¼ past 11 morning
RIPON, a Coach leaves the Pack Horse, Micklegt. every Monday, Wed. & Fri. at 2 aft. and ret. the following days at 11 o'clock

SELBY, the Providence, from the Robin Hood, Castlegate, at a ¼ before 7 morning, to meet the Steam Packets
YORK and LIVERPOOL Wharfdale Coach, through Wetherby, Otley, Skipton, Clitheroe, Blackburn & Ormskirk, leaves the Elephant & Castle, Skeldergate, York, daily, (except Sundays) at 6 mng. and ret. at 10 evening
The DILIGENCE, to New Malton, from the Red Lion Inn, Monk bar, every Mon. Wed. and Sat. mngs. at ¼ past 7 o'clock, and ret. at 6 in the evening.

## WATER CARRIERS.

*From H. Mills and Sons, New Wharf, York.*

The following York and London New Contract Vessels sail from York every week, and from the Gun & Shot Wharf, London, every Sunday morning:
The York—L. Wilson
— Jubilee—W. Flaxton
— Masham—R. Clark

The Wetherby—J. Temperton
— Ellen—J. Good
— Knaresbro' Castle—J. Shilletoe
— Helmsley—J. Leetham
York, H. Mills & Sons, Skeldergate
London, Emanuel Silva, Gun & Shot Wharf, Tooley street

*The Old Contract Butter Sloops.*
The following Vessels sail from Skeldergate New Wharf, York, to

K

Hull every Sat. evg. & from Hull to York every six days.

The Hopewell—John Stephenson
—— Friends—James Wilkinson
—— Britain—James Swift
—— William & Sarah—Rd. James
—— York Merchant—Wm. North
—— Ploughman—Jas. Stephenson
*York*, Henry Mills and Sons.
*Hull*, G. Darbyshire, Blackfriargt.

†‡† The Masters of the York & Hull vessels, attend at the Black Boy, High street, Hull.

*Steam Packet.*

The Humber Steam Packet, Capt. J. W. Jackson, leaves York for Gainsbro' every Mon. and Thu. at 5 mg. and ret. from Gainsbro' Tu. and Fri. at 9 mg.
*York*, H. Mills and Sons.
*Gainsbro'*, Dean and Beaumont, Bridge street.

*Regular Gainsbro' Traders.*

The Resolution, Thomas Gemmill, & the Brothers, John Wilkinson, sail from York & Gainsbro' every 8 or 9 days, according to freight.

*Market Boats.*

Boroughbridge and Ripon——Vessels, twice per week
Cawood—The Providence, T. Bolton, arr. Sat. mg. ret. the same evg.
Newton—The Victory, G. Thompson, arr. at 9 Sat. mg. ret. at 4 aft.

Selby—The Friendship—John Field, arr. on Fri. and ret. on Sat. evg.

Vessels to Leeds, Wakefield, and Huddersfield, every three or four days, from Thomas Gilliam's, Old Crane, York.

*York Old Contract Vessels to London weekly.*

The Anchor—Thomas Steels, sen.
—— Ebor—James Bevett
—— Meuse—David Leach
—— Ouse—Samuel Davies
—— Spring—Henry Gale
—— Vine—Thomas Steels, jun.
—— York Union—George Hornby.
*Wharfingers*, York, Thomas Gilliam, Old Crane
London, Brome & Co. Stanton's Wharf.

*Old Contract Vessels, from Old Crane, to Hull weekly.*

The Friends, Joseph Best—Success, Thomas Tootle—and The Trial, William Pew.
*Agents*—at York, Thomas Gilliam Hull, G. Mells & Co. High street.

The John & Jane, Wm. Torr, regularly to Newcastle.—*Wharfinger*, James Dalby.

Vessels sail regularly every three days to Gainsbro', Boroughbridge, Ripon, Selby, Cawood, Wakefield, Huddersfield, Manchester and Liverpool, &c.

# LAND CARRIERS.

From *Craggs' General Waggon Warehouse, Coppergate.*

RICHARD PICKERSGILL's old established and only North Waggons, arrive from Easingwold, Thirsk, Northallerton, Darlington, Durham, Newcastle, Penrith, Carlisle, Morpeth, Berwick-on-Tweed, Edinburgh, and Glasgow, and all parts of Scotland, at ½ past 4 on Tuesday & Friday mornings, and ret. at 6 the same morning.

W. & J. PETTIFOR's Waggons arrive from Doncaster, Worksop, Mansfield, Nottingham, Derby, Leicester, Lichfield, Coventry, Birmingham, Wolverhampton, Walsall, &c. every Monday & Thursday evenings at 5, and returns every Tuesday and Friday mornings at 9.

J. HARTLEY's Waggons from Leeds, Bradford, Halifax, Huddersfield, Wakefield, Manchester, and all parts of the West of England, arr. every Wed. at 11 forenoon & ret. the same day at 3 aft.

PEACOCK & MOON's Waggons from Stokesley, Yarm, Stockton, Sedgfield, Hartlepool, Guisbro', Redcarr, Marske, Lofthouse, Staithes, &c. arr. every Wed. and Sat. mgs. at 8, and returns same days at 12 at noon.

J. BLACKBURN's Waggons from Boroughbridge, Ripon, Masham, Bedale, Catterick, Richmond, Middleham, Leyburn, Hawes, Askrigg, Sedbergh, Kendal, Whitehaven, &c. arrive at 8 in the mng. every Tu. and Fri. and ret. same days at 3 in the afternoon.

G. HUDSON's Waggons from Knaresbro' & Harrogate, arr. every Tu. Thu. & Sat. at 8 mg. and ret. at 2 the same afternoon.

SARAH CRAGGS' Waggon from Malton, Snainton, Scarbro', &c. arr. every Tu. and Fn. at 6 mg. ret. 1 at noon. Also a Waggon to Selby every Sat. mg. to Robert Myers' wharf, at 4 and ret. the same evg. at 6. °₀° Goods delivered to Carver and Scott, Manchester, are forwarded by this Caravan to Scarbro' in 4 days. *Goods insured from fire.*

*From Deacon, Harrison and Co's. Warehouse, Swinegate.*

Daily Post Waggons are despatched to London, (in 5 days) every Mon. Wed. and Fri. and goods arrive thence every Tues. Thu. and Sat. Goods and passengers are also conveyed to Leeds, Wakefield, Doncaster, Bawtry, Retford, Newark, Grantham, Stamford, Huntingdon, Cambridge, Oxford, Norwich, Newmarket, and all parts of Norfolk and Suffolk.

*From Newcombe's General Waggon Warehouse, Fossgate.*

JAMES BAYNES arr. from Bridlington, Driffield, Kilham, & Nafferton, every Wed. and Fri. mgs. ret. at noon the same days.

WM. Dawson arrives from Doncaster, Sheffield, Nottingham, Birmingham, Walsall, Derby, Chesterfield, Pontefract, &c. every Tu. and Sat. and returns every Wed. and Sunday mornings.

ROBERT SIMPSON arrives every Mon. & Thu. evgs. from Helmsley, ret. Tu. and Fri. mornings.

JOHN BOLTON's Waggons to Hull, Weighton, Beverley, and North and South Cave, every aft. at 3.

NEWCOMBE & MILLS' Waggons to Knaresbro' and Harrogate every Mon. Thu. & Sat. nights, ret. the following evenings.

WELSH & SONS Waggons to Manchester every mg. ret. every evg.

R. WINGATE's Waggons arrive from Otley, Skipton, Settle & Preston, every Wed. mg. ret. at noon the same day.

J. THOMPSON's Waggons arrive from Pocklington every Thu. and Sat. mornings, and returns at noon the same day.

*From the Waggon Warehouse, White Swan yard, Pavement.*

J. ROBSON, to Sampson's, Wade lane, Leeds, every Tu. Thu. and Sat. whence goods are forwarded to Bradford, Barnsley, Huddersfield, Halifax, Rochdale, Manchester, Chester, Liverpool, and all parts of the West of England.

T. LARKIN leaves York every Tu. & Fri. at 2 aft. for Scarborough and Malton, when goods for Malton are delivered the same night, and for Scarbro' the next morning.

GEO. PEARSON every Wed. at 2 aft. to Malton, Thornton, Pickering, Whitby, Staiths, Lofthouse, and Castleton, &c.

JOHN FISHER every Fri. at 1 at noon for Boroughbridge, Bedale, and Richmond.

G. OUTHWAITE (successor to Tweddle) every Fri. at 3 aft. for Northallerton, Darlington, Durham, Sunderland, North & South Shields, Newcastle, and all parts of the North. *James Allanson, Agent.*

*From Wilson's Waggon Warehouse, Coppergate.*

POCKLEY & Co's. Waggons to Driffield, Bridlington, Kilham, and Nafferton, every Wed. and Fri. mngs. Waggons from the above places arrive in York on the same days at noon.

WM. WARRINGTON's Waggons arr. from Doncaster, Sheffield, Nottingham, Birmingham, Walsall, Derby, Chesterfield, Pontefract, &c. every Tu. and Sat. returns Wed. and Sunday mornings.

ANN WILSON's Waggons arrive from Hull, Market-Weighton, North and South Cave, and Beverley, every Tu. & Fri. ret. every Wed. and Sat. at noon.

JOHN HARTLEY's Waggons arrive from Leeds, Wakefield, Bradford, Halifax, Rochdale, Manchester, Warrington, Liverpool, &c. every mg. (except Sunday) and ret. at 2 aft. J. H.'s waggons arrive from London every forenoon at 11, and dep. at 3 aft.

WIDOW GILES' Waggons arrive from Pocklington, every Wed. & Sat. mgs. ret. at noon the same days.

ANDREW ALLEN arrives from Whitby and Pickering every Wed. mg. ret. same day at noon.

# CARRIERS AND POULTERERS

ATTENDING THE DIFFERENT INNS,

*With the Days of Attendance, and their Hours of Arrival and Departure.*

The Poulterers, who travel a circuit of several miles round their places of abode, are marked thus *.

Abbreviation—Mon. for Monday; Tu. for Tuesday; Wed. for Wednesday; Thu. for Thursday; Fri. for Friday; Sat. for Saturday; a. for Arrival; d. for Departure; the Hours are expressed in Figures.

Aberdeen, see Craggs, Coppergate

Aberford, *Leopard*, Coppergate, John Brown, a Sat. 11 morn. d 5 aft.

Aberford, *Elephant and Castle*, Micklegate, John Seanor, a Sat. 11 morn. d 6 afternoon

*Acaster Malbis, *Elephant and Castle*, Micklegate, Mary Torr, a Sat. 10 morn. d 4 afternoon

*Acaster Selby, *Elephant and Castle*, Micklegate, Margaret Hick, a Sat. 10 morn. d 4 afternoon

Alnwick, see Craggs, Coppergate

*Angram and Askham Bryan, *Pack Horse*, Micklegate, John Todd, a Sat. 10 morn. d 4 afternoon

Appleton Roebuck, *Elephant & Castle*, Skeldergate, Wm. Backhouse, a Sat. 10 morn. d 4 afternoon

Appleton Roebuck, *Elephant & Castle*; Skeldergate; Robt. Shillitoe, a Sat. 10 morn. d 4 afternoon

Askrigg, see Blackburn, at Craggs' warehouse

*Barnby Moor, *King's Arms*, Fossgt. John Wride, a Sat. 8 mg. d 2 aft.

Barnsley, see Robson, White Swan yard, Pavement, and Deacon, Harrison and Co.

Bawtry, see Deacon, Harrison & Co.

Bedale, see Blackburn, at Craggs' warehouse, and Fisher, White Swan yard

Berwick-on-Tweed, see Pickersgill at Craggs' warehouse

Beverley, see Newcombe's, Fossgate, and Wilsons, Coppergate

Bilbrough, see Tadcaster, Rt. Bootland

Bilton, *Jolly Bacchus*, Micklegate, Hannah Jackson, a Sat. 10 morn. d 2 afternoon

Birmingham, see Pettifor, at Craggs' warehouse; Dawson, at Newcombe's Fossgate; W. Warrington, at Wilson's, Coppergate

*Bishop Wilton, *White Horse*, Coppergate, Thomas Pratt, a Sat. 10 morn. d 3 afternoon

Bishop Wilton, *White Swan*, Pavement, A. Rogerson, a Fri. even. d Sat. afternoon

Bishop Wilton, *White Horse*, Coppergate, Thomas Blakey, a Sat. morn. d 3 afternoon

Bishop Wilton, *White Horse*, Coppergate, John Davison, a Sat. 10 mg. d 2

Boro'bridge, see Blackburn, at Craggs' warehouse, and Fisher, at White Swan yard

Boro'bridge, *Elephant and Castle*, Skeldergate, John Richmond, a Tu. & Fri. d same days

Boston, see Thorp Arch carrier at the

Bradford, see Hartley at Craggs' warehouse

Bramham & Leeds, *Pack Horse*, Micklegate, J. E. Ames, a Thurs. morn. d ½ past 1 noon

Bridlington, see Bayes at Newcombe's Fossgate, and Pockley and Co. at Wilson's, Coppergate

*Bubwith, *White Horse*, Coppergate, John Brabbs, a Sat. 10 morn. d 2 afternoon

Bubwith, see Howden

*Bubwith, *Robin Hood*, Castlegate, R. Clegg, a Sat. mg. d evening

*Bugthorpe, *King's Arms*, Fossgate, Peter Armison, a Sat. 8 mg. d 2

*Bugthorpe, *King's Arms*, Fossgate, Geo. Hodgson, a Sat. 8 mg. d 2 aft.

*Bulmer, *White Horse*, Coppergate, John North, a Sat. 10 mg. d 3 aft.

*Bulmer, *White Horse*, Coppergate, Geo. Jeffreys, a Sat. 10 mg. d 3 aft.

Burton-on-Trent, see W. Warrington at Wilson's, Coppergate

Burton, Newcombe's, Fossgate, Wm. Dawson, a Tu. & Sat. d Wed. & Sun.

*Buttercrumb, *White Horse*, Coppergate, John Waud, a Sat. 10 morn. d 2 afternoon

*Buttercrumb, *King's Arms*, Fossgate, Henry Carter, a Sat. 8 mg. d 3 aft.

Cambridge, see Deacon, Harrison & Co.

Carlisle, see Pickersgill, at Craggs' warehouse

Castleton, see Pearson, White Swan yard, and A. Allen, at Wilson's, Coppergate

Catterick, see Blackburn, at Craggs' warehouse

*Catton, Nelson, Walmgate, Henry Rawcliffe, a Sat. 8 mg. d 4 aft.

*Catton, King's Arms, Fossgate, Joseph Gate, a Fri. d Sat.

Cave N. and S. see Bolton at Newcombe's, Fossgate; and Wilson's, Coppergate

Chester, see Robson's, White Swan yard, and Hartley's at Wilson's, Coppergate

Chesterfield, see Dawson, at Newcombe's, Fossgate, and W. Warrington, at Wilson's, Coppergate

Copmanthorp, Pack Horse, Micklegt. William Whincup, a Sat. 8 mg. d 4 afternoon

Coventry, see Pettifor, at Craggs' warehouse

Darlington, White Swan, Pavement, G. Outhwaite, a Fri. 7 mg. d 8 aft.

Darlington, see Pickersgill's, at Craggs' warehouse

Derby, see Pettifor, at Craggs' warehouse; Dawson, at Newcombe's, Fossgate; and W. Warrington, at Wilson's, Coppergate

Dewsbury, see Deacon, Harrison & Co.

Doncaster, see Pettifor, at Craggs' warehouse; Deacon, Harrison & Co.; Dawson, at Newcombe's, Fossgate; and Warrington, at Wilson's, Coppergate

Driffield Great, see Baynes, at Newcombe's, Fossgate; and Pockley & Co. at Wilson's, Coppergate

Durham, see Pickersgill, at Craggs warehouse, and Outhwaite, at White Swan yard

Easingwold, White Swan, Goodramgt. Abm. Dutchburn, a Wed. & Sat. 7 mg. d Wed. & Sat. 3 aft.

*Easingwold, White Horse, Coppergt. Thos. Bilton, a Sat. 10 mg. d 4 afternoon

Easingwold, see Craggs', Coppergate

Easingwold, White Swan, Goodramgt. S. Balmbrough, a Sat. morning, d at noon

East Cottingwith, Five Lions, Walmgt. Geo. Seymour, a Sat. 9 mg. d 4 aft.

East Cottingwith, Five Lions, Walmgt. Geo. Williams, a Sat. 9 mg. d 2 aft.

Edinburgh, see Pickersgill, at Craggs' warehouse

Ellerton, Five Lions, Walmgate, John Haslewood, a Sat. 8 mg. d 3 aft.

Eskcrick, Flying Horse, Coppergate,

Robert Davison, a Wed. & St. mg. d same days, 12, noon

*Everingham, White Horse, Thomas Triffitt, a Fri. 2 aft. d Sat. 1 aft.

Ferrybridge, see Warrington, at Wilson's, Coppergate

Flambrough, see Pockley and Co. at Wilson's Coppergate

Flaxton, White Horse, Coppergt. Jane Deanham, a Fri. evening, d Sat. afternoon

*Flaxton, White Swan, Pavement, John Swan, a Sat. 8 mg. d 3 aft.

Foggathorpe, Robin Hood, Castlegate, Robt. Clegg, a Sat. 8 morning, d 3 afternoon

*Fridaythorpe, Malt Shovel, Walmgt. John Harland, a Sat. 8 mg. d 2 aft.

*Fridaythorpe, White Swan, Pavement, Thos. Pearson, a Sat. 7 mg. d 2 aft.

Glasgow, see Pickersgill, at Craggs' Coppergate

Grantham, see, Deacon, Harrison and Co. Swinegate

Green Hammerton, Pack Horse, Micklegate, Richard Howe, a Thurs. morning, d noon

Green Hammerton, Elephant & Castle, Skeldergate, John Chadwick, a & d Tu. Thu. and Sat.

Guisborough, see Peacock and Moon, at Craggs', Coppergate

Halifax, see Hartley, at Craggs' warehouse; Robson, at White Swan yard, & Deacon, Harrison & Co. Swinegate

Hall, near Easingwold, White Swan, Goodramgate, Thos. Formington, a Sat. 7 morn. d 3 afternoon

Harrogate, Labouring Man, Skeldergt. John Chadwick, a Tu. Thu. and Sat. 10 morning, d same days, 4 afternoon

Harrogate, Blue Bell, Micklegate, Newcombe's, Fossgate, & Newcombe's & Mills, a Tu. Thu. & Sat. mg. d same days 8 evening.

Harrogate, see Hudson, at Craggs' warehouse

Hartlepool, see Peacock & Moon, at Craggs' warehouse

Haughton, White Horse, Coppergate, —— Fowler, a Sat. mg. d aft.

Hawes, see Blackburn, at Craggs' warehouse

Helmsley, see Simpson, at Newcombe's, Fossgate

Helperby, Black Horse, Bootham bar, J. Morrell, a Sat. morn. d noon

Helperby, Black Horse, Bootham bar, M. Riddell, a Sat. morn. d noon

Hovingham, White Horse, Coppergate, Hy. Parnaby, a Sat. 8 mg. d 1 noon

Hovingham, Little Shambles, William

Canby, a Mon. and Thu. morn, d
same days

Hovingham, *Fleece*, Pavement, Geo.
Suffield, a Sat. 5 morn. d 1 noon

*Howden and Bubwith, *Robin Hood*,
Castlegate, Robert Clegg, a Fri.
aft. d Sat. 12 noon

Howden, *Horse Shoe*, Coppergate, F.
Smithson, a Thu. 9 evg. d Sat. 4
morning

Huddersfield, see Hartley, at Craggs'
warehouse; Robson, at White
Swan yard, & Deacon, Harrison
& Co. Swinegate

Hull, see John Bolton, at Newcombe's,
Fossgate; & Wilson's, Coppergt.

Hunmanby, see Pockley & Co. at
Wilson's, Coppergate

Huntingdon, see Deacon, Harrison
and Co.

*Kelfield, *White Swan*, Pavement, ——
Buckle, a Sat. 10 morn. d 4 aft.

Kelfield, *White Horse*, Coppergate,
Jph. Thorns, a Sat. 10 mg. d 8 aft.

Kendal, see Blackburn, at Craggs'
warehouse

Kendal, *Fleece*, Pavement, Henry
Fisher, a Thu. d Sat. 3 aft.

Kilham, see Baynes, at Newcombe's,
Fossgate, & Pockley & Co. at
Wilson's, Coppergate

Kirby Moor Side, *Fleece*, Pavement,
John Wrightson, a Mon. & Thu.
d Tu. & Fri.

Kirk Hammerton, *Elephant and Castle*,
Skeldergate, —— Cooper, a Sat.
10 morn. d 4 afternoon

Knaresbro', *Elephant and Castle*, Skeldergate, Geo. Hudson, a Tu. Thu.
& Sat. 8 mg. d Tu. Thu. & Sat. 4 aft.

Knaresbro', *Blue Bell*, Micklegate, &
Newcombe's, Fossgt. Newcombe
& Mills, a Tu. Thu. & Sat. 7 mg.
d same days, 8 evening

Knaresbro', *Labouring Man*, John
Chadwick, a Tu. Thu. & Sat. 10
morn. d same days, 4 afternoon

Knaresbro', *Blue Bell*, Micklegt. John
Yates, a Tu. Thu. and Sat. d on
same days

Leeds, see Hartley, at Craggs' warehouse, & Deacon, Harrison & Co.

Leeds, *White Swan*, Pavement, and
Newcombe's, Fossgt. Isaac Rob-
shaw, a daily morn. d daily evg.

Leeds, see Bramham

Leicester, see Pettifor, at Craggs'
warehouse

Leven, *Fleece*, Pavement, Leonard
Bogg, a Sat. 8 morn. d 6 evg.

Leyburn, see Blackburn, at Craggs'
warehouse

Lichfield, see Pettifor's, at Craggs'
warehouse

Liverpool, see Robson's, White Sw
yard, Pavement, & Deacon, Ha
rison & Co. Swinegate

Lofthouse, see Peacock & Moon,
Craggs' warehouse, and Pearso
White Swan yd. & Andrew Alle
at Wilson's, Coppergate

London, see Deacon, Harrison & C
& Hartley's, at Wilson's, Co
pergate

Malton, see Craggs' warehouse, Lark
& Pearson, at White Swan yard

Manchester, see Hartley, at Cragg
warehouse; Welsh's, at Nev
combe's, & Deacon, Harrison
Co. Fossgate

Mansfield, see Pettifor, at Cragg
warehouse

Market Weighton, see Newcombe'
Fossgate; Wilson's, Coppergate

Marske, see Peacock and Moon,
Craggs' warehouse

Marston, *Jolly Bacchus*, Micklegat
William Waite, a Tu. & Sat. 1
morn. d Tu. & Sat. 2 aft.

Masham, see Blackburn, at Cragg
warehouse

*Melbourn, *Five Lions*, Walmgt. W
Harrison, a Sat. 9 mg. d 4 aft.

Melbourn, *Five Lions*, Walmgt. W
James, a Sat. 9 morn. d 3 aft.

Middleham, see Blackburn, at Cragg
warehouse

Middleham, *Fleece*, Pavement, Hen
Fisher, a Thu. morn. d evg.

*Millington, *King's Arms*, Fossgat
—— Highton, a Sat. mg. d aft.

*Moor Monkton, *Elephant and Castle*
Skeldergate, Robert Burkhill,
Sat. 10 morn. d 4 aft.

*Moor Monkton, *Elephant and Castle*
Skeldergate, James Fewster,
Sat. 10 morn. d 4 aft.

Morpeth, see Pickersgill, at Cragg
warehouse

Nafferton, see Baynes, at Newcombe'
Fossgate, & Pockley and Co.
Wilson's Coppergate

Newark, see Deacon, Harrison & Co.

Newcastle-on-Tyne, see Pickersgil
at Craggs' warehouse, and Outh
waite, White Swan yard

New Market, see Deacon, Harriso
and Co.

Newton-on-Derwent, Rt. Whitaker
a Sat. 10 morn. d 4 aft.

Northallerton, see Pickersgill, a
Craggs' warehouse, & Outhwaite,
White Swan yard

Northallerton, *White Swan*, Goodan
gate, Geo. Dutchburn, a Wed. &
Fri. d same days

*North Duffield, *Wheat Sheaf*, a Sat.
morn. d aft.

Norwich, see Deacon, Harrison & Co.
Nottingham, see Pettifer, at Cragg's warehouse; Dawson, at Newcombe's, Fossgate; and W. Warrington, at Wilson's, Fossgate
Nun Monkton, *Pack Horse*, Micklegt. Wm. Blenkinsop, a Sat. 10 morn. d 3 afternoon
Nunnington, see Hovingham
Otley, see Wingate, at Newcombe's, Fossgate
Ouseburn Great, *Pack Horse*, Micklegate, Richard Howe, a Thu. 10 morn, d 2 afternoon
*Ouseburn, *White Swan*, Pavement, Thos. Stephenson, a Sat. 7 morn. d 12 noon
Ouseburn, *White Swan*, Pavement, Thos. Hanson, a Thu. mg. d noon
Ouseley, see Green Hammerton, Rd. Howe
Ovingham, see Hovingham
Oxford, see Deacon, Harrison & Co.
Penrith, see Pickersgill, at Cragg' warehouse
Pickering, see Pearson, White Swan yard, and A. Allen, at Wilson's, Coppergate
*Pocklington, *White Horse*, Coppergt. John Thompson, a Thu. and Sat. 10 morn. d same days, 3 aft.
Pocklington, see Newcombe's, Fossgt. and Wilson's, Coppergate
Pontefract, *Fleece*, Pavement, Thomas Dawson, a Tu. and Fri. 1 noon, d Wed. and Sat.
Pontefract, *Fleece*, Pavement, Joseph Dawson, a Tu. Thu. and Sat. d following days
Pontefract, see Newcombe's, Fossgt. William Warrington, at Wilson's, Coppergate
Preston, see Wingate, at Newcombe's, Fossgate
Redcar, see Peacock and Moon, at Cragg' warehouse
Retford, see Deacon, Harrison & Co.
*Riccall, *King's Arms*, Fossgate, —— Tomlinson, a Sat. morn. d aft.
*Riccall, *King's Arms*, Fossgt. Thos. Carr, a Sat. 10 morn. d 2 aft.
*Riccall, *White Horse*, Coppergate, a Sat. 10 morn. d 3 afternoon
*Riccall, *King's Arms*, Fossgate, —— Muschamp, a Fri. evg. d Sat. aft.
Richmond and Ripon, *Elephant and Castle*, Skeldergate, John Richmond, a Tu. and Fri. 10 morn. d Tu. and Fri. 4 afternoon
Richmond, *Fleece*, Pavement, John Fisher, a Thu. aft. d Fri. morn.
Richmond, see Blackburn, at Craggs' warehouse, and Fisher, White Swan yard

Ripon, see Blackburn, at Craggs' warehouse
Ripon, *Fleece*, Pavement, Wm. Heath, a Wed. 8 morn. d 7 evg.
Ripon, see Blackburn, at Cragg's, Coppergate
Rochdale, see Hobson, White Swan yd. and Deacon, Harrison & Co. Swinegate
Rotherham, see W. Dawson, at Newcombe's, Fossgate
Scaithness, see Allen, at Wilson's, Coppergate
Scarborough, *King's Arms*, Fossgate, Thos. Burniston, a Tu. & Fri. 8 morn. d Tu. and Fri. 3 afternoon
Scarborough, *White Swan yard*, Pavement, Thos. Larkin, a Tu. & Fri. mng. d Tu. and Fri. afternoon.
Scarborough, see Cragg's, Coppergate
*Seaton Ross, *King's Arms*, William Craven, a Sat. 8 morn. d 2 aft.
*Seaton Ross, *Fleece*, Pavement, Thos. Batty, a Sat. 8 morn. d 5 aft.
Sedbergh, see Blackburn, at Cragg' warehouse
Sedgfield, see Peacock and Moon, at Cragg' warehouse
Selby, *King's Arms*, Fossgate, a Sat. 10 morn. d 2 afternoon
Selby, *Duke of York*, Aldwark, John Merrington, a Tu. and Fri. d. same days
Selby, see Craggs', Coppergate
Settle, see Wingate, at Newcombe's, Fossgate
Sheffield, *Fleece*, Pavement, Thomas Dawson, a Tu. 1 and Sat. 10, d following days
Sheffield, see Newcombe's, Fossgate, and Warrington, at Wilson's, Coppergate
*Sheriff Hutton, *White Swan*, Goodramgate, Thos. Lockwood, a Sat. 8 morn. d 3 afternoon
*Sheriff Hutton, *Unicorn*, Monk bar, John Lawson, a Wed. and Sat. morning, d same days
Shields N. & S. see Outhwaite, White Swan yard
Skipton in Craven, *King's Arms*, and Newcombe's, Fossgate, Richard Wingate, a Wed. 12 mg. d 6 evg.
Sledmere, see Pockley & Co. at Wilson's, Coppergate
Snainton, see Craggs' warehouse
Snaith, see Warrington, at Wilson's, Coppergate
Snaith, *Duke of York*, Aldwark, R. Merrington, a Wed. and Sat. d same days.
Staithes, see Peacock and Moon, Craggs' warehouse, and Pearson, White Swan yard

Stamford, see Deacon, Harrison & Co.

Stamford Bridge, *White Swan*, Pavement, George Taylor, a Tu. Thu. and Sat. 11 morn. d Tu. Thu. and Sat. 3 afternoon

•Stillington, *White Swan*, Pavement, Wm. Wright, a Sat. 10 morn. d 2 afternoon

Stockton, see Peacock and Moon, at Cragg's, Coppergate

Stokesley, see Peacock and Moon, at Craggs', Coppergate

•Stonegrave, *King's Arms*; — Scaife, a Sat. 8 morn. d 2 afternoon

Stonegrave, see Horingham, William Canny

•Strensall, *White Swan*, Pavement, John Green, a Saturday 8 morning, d 2 afternoon

•Strensall, *White Swan*, Pavement, Wm. Green, a Saturday 8 morning, d 2 afternoon

•Strensall, *White Horse*, Coppergate, —— Hesslewood, Sat. d same day

Sunderland, see Outhwaite, at White Swan yard

Sutton-on-Derwent, *Five Lions*, Walmgate, Thos. Lister, a Sat. 10 mg. d 3 afternoon

Sutton-on-Derwent, *Fleece*, Pavement, John Exelby, a & d daily

•Sutton-on-the-Forest, *White Swan*, Pavement, John Clark, a Sat. 10 morn. d 5 afternoon

Tadcaster, *Elephant and Castle*, Skeldergate, Thos. Shillitoe, a Sat. 10 morn. d 4 afternoon

Tadcaster, *Pack Horse*, Micklegate, Wm. Knowles, a Tu & Sat. mg. d Tu. and Sat. noon

Tadcaster, at Cragg's, Coppergate, J. E. Amos, a Thu. mg. d aft.

Tadcaster, *Pack Horse*, Skeldergate, Joseph Jagger, a Tu. & Sat. mg. d noon same days

Tadcaster, *Elephant and Castle*, Skeldergate, Robt. Bootland, a Sat. 10 morn. d 4 afternoon

Thirsk, *Black Bull*, Thursday market, John Jefferson, a Tu. & Sat. 6 morn. d Tu. & Sat. 11 forenoon

Thirsk, see Pickersgill, at Craggs', Coppergate

Thirsk, *White Swan*, Goodramgate, Geo. Dutchburn, a Wed. and Fri. d same days

Thorganby, Robert Hope and James Thompson, a Sat. 10 mg. d 3 aft.

Thorne, *Duke of York*, Aldwark, R. Merrington, a Wed. and Sat. d same days

Thornton, see A. Allen, at Wilson's, Coppergate, and Pearson, White Swan yard

Thornton, *White Swan*, Pavement, John Hornsey, a Sat. 10 morn. d 2 afternoon

Thorp Arch, *Elephant and Castle*, John Lockhart, a Wednesday 9 morning, d 1 noon

Thorp Arch, *Pack Horse*, Skeldergate, Joseph Jagger, a Tuesday and Saturday 10 morning, d Tuesday and Saturday 1 noon

Thorp Arch, see Pack Horse, Micklegate.

Tickhill, see Pettifor, at Craggs', Coppergate

*Tockwith, *Black Boy*, North street, Wm. Bellerby, a Fri. evg. d Sat. afternoon

•Tollerton, *White Swan*, Goodramgate, T. Fornington, a Fri. evg. d Sat. afternoon

Wakefield, see Hartley, at Craggs' warehouse, and Deacon, Harrison and Co.

Walsall, see Pettifor, at Craggs' warehouse; Dawson, at Newcombe's, Fossgate, W. Warrington, at Wilson's, Coppergate

*Warter, *White Horse*, Coppergate, John Jackson, a Sat. 8 morn. d 1 noon

West Cottingworth, *Three Cups*, Foss bridge, James Thompson, a Sat. 8 morn. d 4 afternoon

Wetherby, *Pack Horse*, Skeldergate, J. Burnley, a Tuesday and Saturday, d noon

Wetherby, *Pack Horse*, Skeldergate, John Cooper, a Tu. and Fri. mg. d Tu. and Fri. 2 afternoon

Wetherby, *Bay Horse*, Skeldergate, Benjamin Gawtress, a Tuesday and Saturday 10 morn. d Tuesday and Sat. 2 afternoon

Wetherby, see Thorp Arch, Lockhart

*Wheldrake, *Nelson*, Walmgate, Edw. Young, a Sat. 8 mg. d 4 aft.

Whitby, see Pearson, White Swan yard, and A. Allen, at Wilson's, Coppergate

Whitehaven, see Blackburn, at Craggs' warehouse

Whitfield, see A. Allen, at Wilson's, Coppergate

Whitwell, *White Horse*, Coppergate, Rd. Wilson, a Wed. and Sat. mg. d same days noon

Whixley, see Green Hammerton, Rd. Howe

Wolverhampton, see Pettifor, at Craggs', Coppergate, & Dawson, at Newcombe's, Fossgate

Worksop, see Pettifor, at Craggs' warehouse

Yarm, see Peacock and Moon, at Craggs' warehouse

# Alphabetical Classification

#### OF THE

## PROFESSIONS AND TRADES

### IN THE CITY OF YORK.

*Academies, Boarding, Day, and Preparatory Schools.*
Allen Geo. (gents. boardg.) Beddern
Bedford David, Blossom street
Birkwood Robert, Walmgate
Bolland Thos. (Catholic) Castlegate
Bolton Mary, Fossgate
Brothertan Geo. without Walmgt. bar
Brown Mary & Wilks Bessey, (ladies' day) Skeldergate
Buckland Mary, Ann & Eliza, (ladies' boarding) Castlegate
Burdon Wm. (com. & mat.) Skeldergt.
Cooper Miss Sarah, (la. bdg.) Gillygt.
Coulson John, Davygate
Coyney Mrs. Eliz. (Catholic ladies' boarding) Convent
Dalby Richard, (day) North street
Danby Saml (nat. boys sch.) Aldwark
Danby Mrs. (ditto girls) Ogleforth
Day Miss Ann, without Micklegate bar
Douglas Mary, Micklegate
Dowker M. Spurriergate
Duke Mrs. Fossgate
Ellingworth Catharine, Minster yard
Ellingworth Richard, (private tutor,) Minster yard
Fenton Richard, jun. Grape lane
Firth John, Bishop hill
Fox John, High Jubbergate
Gladden Mary, St. Andrewgate
Goodrick J. St. Saviourgate
Graham Rev. John, (Holgt. grammar) Ogleforth, & bdg. school, Aldwark
Graham Rev. J. jun. (Holgate, grammar) Ogleforth
Grayson Rev. Isaac, (Royal grammar) St. Andrewgate
Guandastague Miss De, (teacher of drawing) Petergate
Hall David, Walmgate bar
Kearick Rev. John, (classical tutor of Presbyterian college) Monkgate
Keseley Mary, Little Blake street
Linton Mary, Goodramgate
M'Lean Mary, (ladies' bdg.) Bootham
Maggi P. (French tutor) Stonegate
Monkman Jane, College street
Nicholson Patience, (ladies' boarding and day) Tanner row
Pearson Eliz. Minster gate

Pocket John, Walmgate
Plummer Margt.(la. bdg.) Goodramgt.
Peacock Eliz. Micklegate
Reynolds George, Fetter lane
Richardson Rev. Thos. (classical and commercial) Bishop hill
Rippon John, general accountant and private tutor, Stonegate
Robinson Hannah, St. Andrewgate
Shinton Thos. (bdg.) St. Saviourgate
Shinton William Edward, writing and drawing master, St. Saviourgate
Silverthorpe C. F. College street
Smith Frances, (la. bdg.) Bootham
Smithies James, Friar walls
Swan Mary Anne, Stonegate
Tate E. A. (ladies' boardg.) Manor yd.
Thurgoland Rev. Godfrey, (boarding school) St. Andrewgate
Turner Rev. Wm. (mathematical tutor at Presbyterian college) Monkgt.
Vickers Miss Frances, (ladies' boarding) Coney street
Walker E. & H. (la. bdg.) Coney st.
Watson Eliza, (la. bdg.) St. Saviour r,
Wellbeloved Rev. Charles, (theological tutor of the Manchester Presbyterian college,) Monkgate
Wilkinson Hannah, St. Saviourgate
Wilson Hannah, Castlegate
Wolstenholme Joseph, 18, Coney st.
*Accountants Public.*
Bleckley Wm. Low Ousegate
Rippon John, Stonegate
*Architects.*
Atkinson & Sharp, Fetter lane
Phillips Matthew, Tanner row
Watson & Pritchett, Blossom street
*Artificial Flowers maker.*
Ambrose B. Far Water lane
*Attornies, Solicitors, Proctors and Notaries Public.*
Agar Thos. Little Stonegate
Anderson R. H. Stonegate
Askwith Wm. (P. & N.) Gillygate
Blanchard John, 1, New Bridge st.
Brook & Bulmer, New st. Coney st.
Buckle Joseph, (proctor and deputy regist. to the Archbishop's court) Minster yard
Carr Matthew, (conveyancer) Stonegt.

Clayton Robert, Stonegate
Cowling Saml. (& coroner) Castlegt.
Cowling John, Lord Mayor's walk
Davies Peter, Lendal
Dewse Thos. (P. & N.) College st.
Eagle Geo. Bootham row
Ellison Robert, (& coroner) Davygate
Fryer J. R. (P. & N.) Goodramgate
Gamble Wm. Castlegate
Harle Thomas, Colliergate
Harrison G.E.(conveyancer)Coney st.
Hearon John, High Ousegate
Howlet Henry, Lendal
Hudson Wm. (P. & N.) Petergate
Jackman Wm. High Petergate
Lowton Geo. (P. & N.) High Petergt.
Mills W. & J. R. (P.&N.)L.Petergt.
Newstead & Son, (solicitors) Lendal
Newstead Christ. clerk of arraigns on
    northern circuit, Lendal
Newstead C. J. clerk of indictments
    on the northern circuit, Lendal
Ord and Pearson, Ogleforth
Pearson Wm. (solicitor) Goodramgt.
    agent to Sun Fire Office
Preston T. W. Stonegate
Richardson James, (and coroner for
    the liberty of St. Peter's) Colliergt.
Robinson and Graham, Stonegate
Russell, Thompson,& Russell, Lendal
Scott Robert, Bootham
Seymour John, (and Prothonatary)
    Little Stonegate
Smith Henry, St. Andrewgate
Smithson Robert, Colliergate
Stead John, Tanner row
Storry F. W. (P. & N.) Low Petergt.
Thompson Wm. Lendal
Thorp and Gray, Low Petergate
Townend Richard, (town's clerk)
    Blake street
Townend and Baildon, Lendal
Waite John, Silver street
Walker Thomas, Colliergate
Wear David, Castlegate
Wilkinson Henry, Stonegate
Wilson Thos. (P. & N.) Stonegate
Wood John, Fossgate
Wormald Richard, Blake street

*Auctioneers.*

Brown Matthew, Gillygate
Carr Benj. Stonegate
Cundall Wm. Ogleforth
Ellis Michael, Swinegate
Gray John, Nessgate
Monkman James, Colliergate
Robinson J. Beddern
Smith Wm. Low Petergate
Viney John, Green lane, Hungate
Watson George, Petergate

*Bacon and Ham Factors.*

Addinall James, Walmgate
Archbell Robert, Micklegate

Botterill Joseph, Feasegate
Bulmer Francis, sen. Petergate
Bulmer Francis, jun. (butter, cheese,
    ham, & seed mercht.) Tanner row
Canney Wm. Little Shambles
Cowling Wm. Goodramgate
Daniel Simon, Girdlergate
Ellis Robert, Spurriergate
England Thomas, Spurriergate
Holmes Ann, Pavement
Lee John, Coppergate
Lockey William, Petergate
Peach Robert, Spurriergate
Prest John, Feasegate
Richardson Harman, Micklegate
Silversides Thomas, Middle Water ln.
Smith Thomas, St. Andrewgate
Varey Wm. and Son, Fetter lane
Waterworth Thomas, 7, Coney st.

*Bakers, Flour and Provision, &c. Dlrs.*

Agar William, Peter lane
Arthur Thomas, Hungate
Bell Thomas, Walmgate
Bellerby Henry, Stonegate
Bellerby Edward, Peaseholm green
Bingley Thomas, Swinegate
Birbeck James, Walmgate
Bowman Wm. Green lane, Hungate
Bradley Thomas, Walmgate
Brown and Hopps, Great Shambles
Chapman Anthony, Micklegate
Cock John, Blossom street
Collier William, Bootham
Dalton Thomas, Bishop hill
Darbyshire George, North street
Dawson Thomas, Walmgate
Dawson John, Feasegate
Drummond Joseph, Hungate
Duck Geo. Little Stonegate
Dutton Abraham, Little Blake street
Fawcett Mrs. Ann, Walmgate
Fearby Henry, Fossgate
Ferraby Geo. Bootham
Fletcher Richard, Heworth moor and
    Great Shambles
Fowler Samuel, High Petergate
Gatrell Ellen, St. Andrewgate
Glaisby John, Davygate
Gowland Thomas, Coppergate
Hardcastle Ann, Skeldergate
Harper Matthew, Walmgate
Harris Mary, Pavement
Haw William, Peaseholm green
Hawkins Richard, Nessgate
Hebden J. & W. Willow st. Walmgt.
Hick Robert, High Petergate
Hillyard Ellen, Micklegate
Hillyard John, Skeldergate
Hudson William, Stonegate
Laidlow James, Gillygate
Lawton M. (gingerbread) L. Shambles
Machin Henry, Low Jubbergate
Machin George, Far Water lane
Middleton Thomas, Goodramgate

Mintoft John, Castlegate
Morley John, Star Court lane
Musgrave Christ. without Walmgt.bar
North George, Gillygate
Penrose John, Walmgate
Pointer John, Walmgate bar
Potter Elizabeth, Walmgate
Scruton Richard, North street
Shaw Thomas, Micklegate bar
Smith Eliz. without Walmgate bar
Steel Henry, Davygate
Straker Rachael, Fossgate
Swales Robert, Micklegate
Telford Isabella, Peaseholm green
Ward Thomas, Walmgate
Watterworth Thos. 7, Coney street
Wallis Joseph, Aldwark
Waud George, Low Petergate
Webster William, North street
Webster Ursula, Walmgate
Weller James, Walmgate
Wells George, Walmgate
Whip John, Goodramgate
Whitwell James, Colliergate
Whitwell Richard, Haymarket
Wiggins William, Petergate
Wilkinson Thomas, Monkgate
Wilson Benjamin, Grape lane
Wright Thomas, Coppergate
Wright James, Little Shambles

### Banks.

Raper, Swann, Clough, Swann, Bland,
and Raper, Coney st. on Sir R. C.
Glyn and Co. London
Wentworth, Chaloner, Rishworth,
Son and Co. Low Ousegate, on
Wentworth and Co. London
Wilson, Tweedy, & Co. High Ousegt.
on Curtis and Co. London
Savings' Bank, New street, F.Carbutt,
sec. open Tu. from 12 to 1, and
Sat. from 11 to 1

### Barometer and Mirror Makers, Carvers, Gilders, &c.

Croce Joshua, (barom. and thermo-
meter) Grape lane
Dodgson W. F. (dealer in, & cleaner
of oil paintings) 3, Coney st.
Edwards Wm. (carver, gilder, & look-
ing glass mfr.) High Petergate
Ferrand Thos. (carv. & gild.) Stonegt.
Holmes Wm. (carv. & gild.) Haymkt.
Rippon G. C. (carv. & gild.) Stonegt.
Walker Thomas and William, (carvers
and gilders) Blake street
Wisker Mrs. Mary, Spurriergate
Wolstenholme Frs. (carver) Bootham

### Barristers.

Dickens H. J. Ogleforth
Ellis William Joseph, Castlegate lane
Meynell Geo. Copley's ct. Coney st.
Nicoll S. W. (city counsellor and re-
corder of Doncaster) Blake st.

Pemberton John, Bootham
Sinclair Rt.(recorder of York)Coneyst.
Strickland Eustace, Judges' Old lodge.

### Basket Makers and Dealers.

Allen Joseph, Middle Water lane
Clarkson Francis, Great Shambles
Fletcher Benj. (dlr.) New Bridge st.
Robinson John, Fossgate
Romans John, Walmgate
Sledmere Richard, Nessgate
Stead Geo. Merchant's hall, Fossgate
Whitehead Wm.Leopard yd.Pavement

### Billiard Tables.

Benson George, Low Ousegate
Lawn John, Little Blake street
Moore Timothy, Stonegate
Pulleyn Henry, (sub.) Blake street
Scaife Christopher, College street

### Blacking Manufacturers.

Metcalfe John, Skeldergate
Silversides Thos. Middle Water lane

### Blacksmiths, Farriers, &c.

Cooper Geo. High Jubbergate
Cummins John, Goodramgate
Dent Thomas, Walmgate
Hamsworth Benjamin, Coffee yard
May Wm. (farrier) First Water lane
Nelson Robt. St. Martin's, Coney st.
Pavier William, Walmgate
Scott William, Blossom street
Snaith John, Finkle street
Strangeways Robt. Bell's yd. Petergt.
Timms Isaac, (vet. surg.) Fishergate
Vincent Emnl. Smith's yd. Skeldergt.
Wilks Wm. Bootham row
Wilks Paul, North street
Wilson William, Bootham row

### Bookbinders.

Atkinson John, Micklegate
Barker George, Pavement
Brassington Richard, (paper ruler by
machine) Waterloo pl. Spurriergt.
Dixon James, Colliergate
Duncanson George, High Petergate
Ripley James, College street
Sumner J. and O. Ogleforth
Swinbank Henry, Petergate

### Booksellers, Stationers, Binders, &c.

Alexander Wm. and Son, Castlegate
Barclay A. and W. 2, New Bridge st.
Bolland Thomas, Spurriergate
Burdekin Richard, Pavement
Carrall M. W. Walmgate
Crawshaw Cornelius, Pavement
Deighton Thomas, Pavement
Johnson Robert, Coney street
Kendrew James, Colliergate
Lawson Francis, 13, Coney street
Sotheran Thomas, 9, Coney street
Todd John and George, (print sellers)
Stonegate
Weightman Thomas, Low Petergate

Wemyss Thomas, St. Helen's square
Wilson & Sons, (wholsl.) High Ousegt.
Wolstenholme John, Minstergate

*Boot and Shoemakers.*

Those marked thus † are Chamber Masters.

Baines Thomas, Castle mills
Baines Joseph, Goodramgate
Barber Wm. (ladies' shoes) Coney st.
†Barber Thomas, Walmgate
Barmby Samuel, Swinegate
Barmby R. and J. Girdlergate
†Barnard Wm. Petergate
Barnett John, Micklegate
Bell and Rigg, Haymarket
†Bennington James, Fossgate
†Bingley Joseph, Girdlergate
Bramley and Dent, Blake street
Calvert Francis, Micklegate
†Catterton John, Low Jubbergate
†Chaplin William, Swinegate
Clough and Ellis, Colliergate
Coates John, Low Petergate
Collier Ambrose, Fossgate
Collyer Stephen, Micklegate
Coupland John, Goodramgate
Cowper William, High Petergate
Crampton Joseph, (& dir. in grindery)
 Seller's yard, Pavement
Croft Edward and Co. Coffee yard
Douglas Richard, Bishop hill
Dunn Robert, Goodramgate
Dunning John, Fossgate
Emmerson John, Spurriergate
Fortington Thomas, Walmgate
Gill Edmund, 15, Coney street
Glaisby Wm. (ladies) Coney street
Groves Christopher, Skeldergate
Hall William, High Petergate
Hardacre Joseph, without Walmgt. bar
Harrison William, Goodramgate
†Harrison Hugh, Elliott's yd. Walm-
 gate bar
Hart Wm. (listing shoes) Walmgate
Henderson Thomas, Goodramgate
Henderson William, Goodramgate
Hogarth Edward, College street
†Holdsworth Wm. St. Saviourgate
Hornby Richard, Stonegate
Hornby William, Blake street
†Howard Geo. Bootham row
†Hudson Thos. Racket's yd. Petergt.
†Hunton John, Skeldergate
Inman Wm. St. Helen's square
†Jacques John, Jubbergate
Jebson William, Finkle street
Joy James, Bell's yard, Petergate
Kirby John, Petergate
Lazenby Geo. Walmgate
M'Lean John, sen. Castlegate
M'Lean John, jun. Micklegate
Masser Thomas, Trinity lane
Middleton William, Hungate

†Pearson Thomas, Albion street
Perry John, Walmgate
Pinder John, Stonegate
Raine William, Stonegate
†Richardson William, Jubbergate
Scowby Thomas, Feasegate
Sibbit William, Walmgate
Smith Geo. Stonegate
†Snowball William, Swinegate
Steel John, Fossgate
†Sutcliffe John, North street
Thompson John, High Ousegate
Thorp William, Tanner row
Trout & Williamson, Low Ousegate
Ward Robert, Peaseholm green
Ward Ralph, Walmgate
†Waters Joseph, St. George street
†Waterworth Wm. Wellington row
Webster Michael & Geo. Haymarket
Williamson J. and J. Colliergate
Wilson Oliver, Davygate
Wilson Thomas, Peter lane
Wright Robert, Coppergate
Wrightson Thos. without Walmgt. bar

*Boot Tree, Last, and Patten Makers and Dealers in Grindery.*

Heeles John, Pavement
Lawson Thomas, Pavement
Lockwood Anne, (grindery) Good-
 ramgate

*Brass Founders, Braziers, Pewterers Tinplate Workers, Coppersmiths, &c.*

Bollans Robert, Great Shambles
Cook Robert, Fossgate
Cook James, Colliergate
Gray Robert, Micklegate
Rotherford Bob, jun. Micklegate
Seagrave Richard, Swinegate
Stodhart Thomas, Coney street
Venn John, Goodramgate
Webster Thomas, Pavement
Wiggins Wm. Spurriergt. & Monk
Wood James, 6, New Bridge street

*Brewers and Maltsters.*

Those marked thus † are maltsters only

Dunsley Wm. Far Water lane
†Ellingworth Joshua, Tanner row
Hotham Geo. Walmgate
Kilby John Fryer, Clementhorp, with-
 out Skeldergate postern
Norrison John, Tanner row
†Peart James, North street
Roper John, Thursday market
Siddall Emanuel, Swinegate
Ward John, Fossgate
†Watson William, Skeldergate

*Bricklayers and Builders.*

See also Carpenters.

Allen and Nelthorp, Aldwark
Arthur Thomas, Hungate
Bennington James, Walmgate
Bewlay & Whitfield, Heworth moor

Bowes John and Son, Dunning's yard, Fossgate
Bridgewater Christopher, North st.
Chapman William, Bishop hill
†Cobb John, Ogleforth
†Dalton William, Goodramgate
Ducket & Bowes, Walmgate
Ellison Robert, Grape lane
Garland Thomas, High Jubbergate
Gray Robt. Barker lane, Micklegate
Gray Ambrose, North street
Haw Robert, Castlegate
Hirst John, (& paviour) Mint yard
Lawson Michael, Hungate
Mitchell Barnabes, Stonegate
Nicholson & Bell, Bootham square
Pick Thomas, Gillygate
Powell Richard, Goodramgate
Prince Matthew, Tanner row
Rayson Thomas, junr. North street
Rhodes James, Walmgate
Sanderson Samuel, North street
Taylor John, Dunning's yd. Fossgate
Whitfield & Bewley, St. Andrewgate
Wilberforce Walter, Walmgate
Woodburn J. Stonegate
Wyrell James, Fetter lane

### Brickmakers.

Bewley Robert, Heworth moor
Dolby James, Hob moor; residence, Dringhouses
Dutton & Chapman, Hob moor
Pulleyn Robert, Horn fields
Rayson Thomas, North street

### Bridle Cutter.

Hamilton Robert, Bootham

### Brush Makers, and Warehouses.

Fletcher Benj. (dlr.) New Bridge st.
Flint Thomas, Girdlergate
Gregory J. & Co. Petergate
Lawdon Christopher, sen. Barker hill
Lawdon Richard, Micklegate
Wellfoot Richard, Petergate
Wells Thomas, Colliergate

### Butchers.

Anderson William, Walmgate
Armistead Peter, Micklegate
Bardon William, Goodramgate
Bean Richard, Thursday market
Bell Thomas, Thursday market
Bewlay Anne, Great Shambles
Bingley William, High Petergate
Blackburn John, Great Shambles
Bramley John, Great Shambles
Bramley Ambrose, Fossgate
Burrill Hannah, Silver street
Calvert Jas. (tripe dlr.) Ltl. Shambles
Cook John, Thursday market
Cuthbert Thomas, Skeldergate
Dalton George, Thursday market
Dixon Richard, Great Shambles

Dove Anne, Great Shambles
Dove Richard, Great Shambles
Dutton Benjamin, Micklegate
Ellis Robert, Bootham
Fletcher John, Thursday market
Fowler John, Micklegate
Fowler Leonard, Great Shambles
Gell Thomas, Great Shambles
Gell Robert, Feasegate
Harrison Richard, Thursday market
Hick Matthew, Little Shambles
Hildreth Thomas, Great Shambles
Hildreth William, Great Shambles
Hill Mrs. Walmgate
Hindsley George, Great Shambles
Holgate Charles, Great Shambles
Holgate Wm. Great Shambles
Jewitt Thomas, Great Shambles
Kettlewell John, Hay market
Lambert Richard, Great Shambles
Ledger James, sen. Low Jubbergate
Ledger James, jun. Low Jubbergate
Linfott Wm. Low Ousegate
Mann Thomas, Great Shambles
Masser Ann, Little Shambles
Melrose James, jun. Foss bridge
Midgley George, Thursday market
Noble John, Walmgate
Pearson Richard, Bootham square
Prest William, Petergate
Quarton William, Goodramgate
Reed Joseph, Blossom street
Saville John, Goodramgate
Saville Richard, Goodramgate
Scruton William, Great Shambles
Settle George, Petergate
Severs Wm. Thursday market
Sharp Thomas, Thursday market
Simpson Christopher, Moant
Smith John, Fossgate
Snow George, Great Shambles
Spence William, Walmgate
Swale John, 16, New Bridge street
Swan John, Walmgate
Thackeray Robert, Thursday market
Thackray John, Gillygate
Theakstone Richard, Petergate
Theakstone Peter, Great Shambles
Todd Robert & Son, G. Shambles
Walker Peter, Low Jubbergate
Whitehouse Geo. Feasegate
Wilson John, Great Shambles
Wilson John, jun. Great Shambles

### Butter Factors.

See also Bacon and Ham Factors.

Addinall James, Walmgate
Archbell Robert, Micklegate
Bulmer Francis, jun. (ham, cheese & seed merchant) Tanner row
Canney Wm. Little Shambles
Cowling Wm. Goodramgate
Dobson Wm. (agent) Trinity lane
Holmes Ann, Pavement

Lee John, Coppergate
Richardson Harman, Micklegate
Smith Thomas, St. Andrewgate
Varey Wm. & Son, Fetter lane
Warneford John, Pavement
Watterworth Thos. 7, Coney street

*Cabinet Makers.*

Cundall William, Ogleforth
Dickinson Wm. High Jubbergate
Fawbert Wm, Stonegate
Ingham Joseph, (sky and fan lights) Jubbergate
Marshall G. S. Goodramgate
Marshall Martha, (spinning wheels) 6, Coney street
Phillips John, (& undertaker,) Fetter lane
Sedgwick Wm. Blake street
Underwood Thomas, Stonegate
Walls Thos. (& undertaker) Peter ln.

*Cabinet Makers and Upholders.*

Those marked thus * are Upholders only, and those † Undertakers.

†Beal T. & G. Stonegate
Bellerby John (& undertaker) Micklegate
Burniston John, Walmgate
Lupton John, Low Jubbergate
Musham Frederick, (& undertaker,) Blake street
†Shores & Steward, Micklegate
*Skelton John, Albion street
*Smith William, (& undertaker) Low Petergate
Stones Geo. (fancy chairs) Pavement
Taylor John, (& undertaker) Peter ln.
*Whitehouse Rbt. Coffee yd. Stonegt.

*Carpenters—House Builders.*

See also Bricklayers, Builders & Wheelwrights.—Those marked thus † are also Cabinet Makers.

Agar Isaac, Walmgate
Almand Christopher, Walmgate
Bean Samuel, Davygate
†Beedham John, Fetter lane
†Beedham Wm. Skeldergate
†Bell John, Dundas st. Hungate
†Bellerby Thomas, Bishop hill
Benson Thomas, St. Saviourgate
†Bollans Francis, Low Petergate
†Burniston John, Walmgate
Carey John, Walmgate
Carey John, St. George street
Coates William, Tanner row
Demmey Thomas, Skeldergate
†Dempster Anthony, (& undertaker) Mint yard
Dinsdale John, Church yd. North st.
Dodsworth Matthew, Grape lane
Dugelby Robert, Davygate
Frankish Richard, Hungate
Gill John, Walmgate
Groves George, Walmgate

Hansom Richard, Micklegate bar
†Hansom Henry, (and undertaker,) Tanner row
Harper John, Walmgate bar
Hornby William, Goodramgate
†Hubie William, Ogleforth
Ickeringill John, Far Water lane
†Kirk Wm. St. Mary's row, Bishop hill
†Lockey George, Fossgate
†Marsh Joseph, Feasegate
Mason Isaac, Brunswick place
Mason James, Hungate
Myers William, Willow street
†Raper John, Feasegate
Rayson John, Hungate
†Richardson William, Stonegate
Robinson Thomas, Goodramgate
†Thompson John & Son, (packing boxes) Little Stonegate
Walker Thomas, (and undertaker) Davygate
†Wikely Benjamin, St. Saviourgate
†Wisker Robert, Coffee yd. Stonegt
Wood Richard, Walmgate

*Carpet Manufacturers.*

Gregory J. & Co. (patent floor cloth & brush warehouse), L. Petergate
Mush John, (patterns sent to any part of the kingdom) Monk bar
Rooke Thos. (dealer) Minster gate

*Carvers and Gilders.*
See Barometer, &c. Makers.

*Cattle, Sheep & Pig Dealers, Wholesale*
See also Horse Dealers.

Agar Thomas, Peaseholm green
Fawcett Robert, Walmgate bar
Hirst William, Aldwark
Whimp Anthony, Monkgate

*Cheesemongers,*
See also Bacon and Butter Factors.

Alderson Jacob, Fossgate
Bellerby Henry, Stonegate
Bulmer Francis, jun. (butter, ham & seed merchant) Tanner row
Canney William, Little Shambles
Cowling William, Goodramgate
Ellis Robert, Spurriergate
England Thomas, Spurriergate
Holmes Ann, Pavement
Lockey William, Petergate
Peach Robert, Spurriergate
Watterworth Thomas, 7, Coney st.

*Chemists Manufacturing.*

Spencer Isaac & Co. first Water lane
Sutcliffe John, 29, Coney street
Taylor Cook & Co. (wholesale druggists, oil, paint, colours and mustard manufacturers,) near Ouse bridge and Spurriergate

*Chemists and Druggists.*

Allen Oswald, (and apothecary,) Colliergate
Baker J. J. High Ousegate
Bell Richard, Thursday market
Cautley Mary, Low Ousegate
Dales & Butterfield, (wholesale) Colliergate
Elgin & Heseltine, (wholesale) Colliergate
Garth F. A. & Co. Goodramgate
Hanson C. J. Low Petergate
Hardman Edmund, jun. 17, New Bridge street
Harwood John, Petergate
Hornby Preston (apothecary) Petergate
Lockwood William, Pavement
Prest Edward & Sons, (wholesale) Pavement
Scawin William, Low Petergate
Spencer Isaac & Co. first Water lane
Spurr John, (wholesale and retail) New Bridge street
Sutcliffe John, (professional) 29, Coney street
Taylor Cook & Co. Spurriergate
Terry Joseph, Walmgate
Theakstone, Robinson & Co. Micklegate
Thompson Jas. corner of Stonegate
Ward Thomas, Fossgate
Watson William, Micklegate

*Clock and Watch Makers & Repairers.*
See also Jewellers, &c.

Barber & Whitwell, Coney street
Dempster Anthony, Walmgate
Dickinson Robert, Goodramgate
Fryer Mrs. High Ousegate
Hay Elizabeth, Micklegate
Hick Matthew, Minster gate
Hull John, College street
Jackson Edward, 14, Coney street
Maltby H. D. Pavement
Newlove John, Pavement
Peacock William, Spurriergate
Potts Joshua, (musical) Spurriergate
Richmond Jph. (clock mkr.) Fossgate
Rowntree Robert, Coppergate
Steward Henry, Low Ousegate
Watson Christopher, Low Ousegate

*Clog and Patten Makers.*
See also Last and Patten Makers.

Chaplin William, Swinegate
Lawson Thomas, Hungate

*Clothes and Furniture Brokers.*

Those marked thus † are Clothes Brokers.
Thus ‡ Furniture Brokers.
See also Tailors and Woollen Drapers.

‖Bollans Francis, Low Petergate
‖Braithwaite Richard, Swinegate
‖Brown Thomas, High Jubbergate

Burr Francis, Peter lane
Burton Benjamin, High Jubbergate
†Clancy James, Walmgate
‖Cogling Thomas, Swinegate
‖Cox David, Feasegate
Collier L. Micklegate
†Dale Emanuel, Feasegate
†Dalby Joseph, Jubbergate
†Dale Thomas, Feasegate
†Darbyshire James, Peter lane
‖Dugelby Robert, Davygate
†Eadon George, Peter lane
†Hardcastle Mary, North street
Heathley John, (clothier) Swinegt.
†Hirst Sarah, Feasegate
†Kilvington Leonard, H. Jubbergate
†Lockey John, Feasegate
‖Lupton John, Low Jubbergate
†Marsh Joseph, Feasegate
†Noble Wm. College street
†Peters Mary, Gillygate
‖Priestley Joseph, High Jubbergate
‖Rickards John, Swinegate
Scott Robert, Swinegate
Settle Isaac, Feasegate
Settle Mary, Feasegate
Shuttleworth Mary, Peter lane
‖Simpson Jonathan, Palmer lane
†Smelt Elizabeth, Peter lane
‖Spencer Francis, Low Jubbergate
Stephenson John, Feasegate
‖Taylor John, Peter lane
Thornton Joseph, Goodramgate
‖Walls Thomas, Peter lane
‖Woodburn Margaret, Peter lane
‖Woollons Thomas, Walmgate

*Coach builders.*

Bradley Thomas, (& harness maker) High Jubbergate
Breary & Myers, (& harness makers) Little Stonegate & Davygate
Fisher Joseph, Ogleforth
Morley & Son, Little Stonegate

*Coal Merchants.*

Baines George, Blossom street
Bromley James, Fossgate
Buckle Marmaduke, St. Saviour row
Bussey & Pearson, Marygate
Darbyshire Chpr. Lord Mayor's walk
Davies Mary, Lendal
Eyre Thomas, Friar walls
Grange Benjamin, Foss bridge
Hanethick Henry, first Water lane
Hudson William, Friar walls
King Richard, Walmgate
Lockey James, Waterloo place
Maddrah Margaret, Skeldergate
Martin John, Middle Water lane
Mawson Jonathan, Skeldergate
Meek John, Gillygate
Norrison John, Tanner row
Oldfield Wm. First Water lane
Parker George, Union place

Pew John, Thursday market
Prest John, North street
Richardson Francis, Far Water lane
Robinson Charles, Monk bar
Robson Hannah, without Walmgt. bar
Rymer Peter, St. Saviour row
Smith Richard, Monkgate
Stephenson Henry, Coney street
Thackray Joseph, Micklegate
Thomas John, Skeldergate
Thompson Thos. Lord Mayor's walk
Tindell John, Skeldergate
Vallette Paul, Marygate
Wales John, Wilson's street, top of Walmgate
Wood George, Walmgate

*Comb Manufacturers.*

Holmes William, Trinity lane
Lund George, Fetter lane
Mawson Thos. (& small wares dealer) Micklegate
Mortimer Isaac, 16, Coney st.
Nutt John, Trinity lane
Pole John, Skeldergate
Rougier Joseph (powder flasks, drinking horns, & broad horn shavings) Tanner row
Stead Thomas, Castlegate lane
Steward G. & Sons, Blossom street
Walker John, Laythorp postern

*Commissioners for taking Special Bail.*

Dawson John, (city & Ainsty) Castlegate
Gill William, (County & City of York) Colliergate

*Confectioners and Pastry Cooks, &c.*

Arundel Mary, (city cook) Waterloo place
Bell Eliz. (pastry cook) L. Blake st.
Berry Robert, (wholesale)St. Helen's square
Brown William, Coney street
Brown Richard, Coney street
Calvert Thos. (wholesale) Spurriergt.
Coutherd John, Bootham
Elliott John, (wh. & ret.) Spurriergt.
Etty John, (wh. gingerbd.) Feasegate
Fall George, High Petergate
Gray William, Fossgate
Heslington John, without Bootham bar
Kilner and Hick, Goodramgate
Roscoe John, Bootham row
Rotherford Robert, sen. Micklegate
Turner Mary, Stonegate
Walker John, (wholesale) L. Petergt.
Watson Sarah, High Petergate
Wilson Elizabeth, Stonegate
Wilson Thomas, Low Petergate
Womack Richard, (pastry cook) High Petergate

*Coopers.*

Addinell James, Walmgate

Alderson Jacob, Fossgate
Briscomb Robert, Walmgate
Bulmer George, Girdlergate
Dent Thomas, Stonebow lane
Dobson Wm. Trinity lane
Foster John, Micklegate
Harrison Thomas, High Petergate
Kilham Thomas, Fetter lane
Moverley John, Middle Water lane
Richardson Harman, Micklegate
Tansley Benjamin, Davygate
Tatham Robert, St. Andrewgate
Varey Wm. and Son, Fetter lane

*Cork Cutters.*

Chapman John, Foss bridge
Cressey George, jun. Fossgate
Rawdon & Deighton, 28, Coney st.

*Corn Merchants and Millers.*

Those marked thus † are Merchants, those ‡ are Millers—not marked are both

Atkinson & Blenkarn, Walmgate
Bainbridge John, Walmgate
Dent Richard, Micklegate
†Fawcett Robert, Walmgate bar
‡Fearby Henry, Fossgate
Fletcher Richard, Heworth moor and Great Shambles
Hill William, Walmgate
Hillyard John, Skeldergate
Hopps Thomas, Castle mills
Hodgson Thomas, Clementhorp
Hodgson Elizabeth, Fossgate
Hodgson Seth, Petergate
Nicholson John, Goodramgate
Pearson Matthew, Walmgate bar
Peart James, North street
Rook Mark, New bridge street
Simpson L. & J. North street
Smith Daniel, Monkgate
Stead & Gell, Skeldergate
Todd Enoch, Lord Mayor's walk
†Varley John, Spittle field, Heworth moor
Watson and Moyser, Stonegate and Sutton mills
Watson William, Stonegate
Waud George, Fossgate
Wilberforce William, Walmgate

*Curriers and Leather Cutters.*

See also Fellmongers and Tanners.

Agar J. & B. High Ousegate
Bell George, Marygate
Meek James, Goodramgate
Mouncer John, North street
Nelson George, Petergate
Palmer William, Church lane
Potter Thomas, Goodramgate
Toes William, Goodramgate

*Cutlers.*

Bullivant Isaac, Newgate
Cockill Joseph, Pinkle street

Glover John, Pavement
Mountier James, Hungate
Sanderson Thomas, Low Ousegate
Wood Joseph, Spurriergate

*Dancing Masters.*

Cattell Christopher, Barker hill
Noke Charles, High Petergate

*Dentists.*

Horner and Turner, Coney street

*Drysalteries.*

Spencer Isaac, Middle Water lane

*Dyers.*

Batty Eliz. (silk & muslin) Fossgate
Coates Rt. (glove leather) Tanner row
Cocker Robert, 15, New Bridge street
Harris Ann, (calico) Stonegate
Harrison Wm. Petergate
Hopps John, (silk) Grape lane
Pottage John, Fossgate
Pulleyn Wm. North street
Spencer John, (thread) Tanner row
Thacker John, (silk) Stonegate
Warmeth John, Tanner row

*Eating Houses.*

Cavitt Wilham, Pavement
Lewis Mary, Skeldergate
Ruler John, Fossbridge, Walmgate

*Engravers.*

Barber and Whitwell, (on gold & silver) Coney street
Barker John, (copper-plate & printer) Low Ousegate
Carrall M. W. (in wood) Walmgate
Cave Wm. (copper-plate and printer) Stonegate
Evans Edward, (seal and dye sinker) Stonegate
Lawson Wm. & Francis, 13, Coney st.

*Fellmongers, Skinners, &c.*

See also Curriers and Tanners.

Melrose James, sen. Walmgate
Melrose Walter, Walmgate
Mosey John, Walmgate
Slater Mary, Walmgate

*Fire &c. Office Agents.*

Atlas, Cooper & Bielby, Skeldergate
Birmingham, F. Mallatrat, 46, Coney st.
British, Wm. Blanchard, Coney st.
County, Wm. Hall, High Ousegate
Eagle, Geo. Lawton, High Petergate
Globe, F. W. Storry, Low Petergate
Hope, H. Graham, Stonegate
Norwich Union, George Baker, St. Helen's square
Norwich Union Fire Society, Thomas Bolland, Spurriergate
Phoenix and Pelican, Robert Smithson, Colliergate
Provident, Wm. Hall, High Ousegate
Royal Exchange, Rd. Townend, Lendal

Suffolk and General County, William Alexander and Son, Castlegate
Sun, Wm. Pearson, Ogleforth
Union, Newstead and Son, Lendal
West of England, James Richardson, Colliergate
*Engineer*, John Sutcliffe, druggist, 29, Coney street

*Fishing and Fowling Tackle Makers.*

Le Brun Thos. Wellington row
Marshall Martha, 6, Coney street

*Fishmongers.*

Autherson Richard, Great Shambles
Etherington George, Stonegate
Gowland James, Skeldergate
Morley John, Great Shambles
Pattinson Thos. Little Shambles
Warrilow Joseph, Dundas street

*Flax Dressers.*

Bell John, Walmgate
Daltou Wm. Great Shambles
Fletcher & Scarr, (& mercht.) North st.
Hedley Hartas, (lime merchant and spinner) Skeldergate, Albion st.
Hodgson Joseph, Great Shambles
Hyle John, (and spinner) Pavement
Lakeland and Poppleton, Walmgate
Milner Richard, High Ousegate
Richardson Wm. (spinner) without Skeldergate postern
Savage John, Great Shambles
Scarr John, (spinner and merchant) Hungate
Smith Wm. without Walmgate bar
Swales John, (and spinner) Walmgate bar

*Fruiterers.*

See also Gardeners.

Backhouse J. and T. Tanner row
Bellerby Robert, Stonegate
Birkenshaw George, Feasegate
Brown Wm. Coney street
Calvert Thomas, Spurriergate
Camidge William, Castlegate
Cresser James, Skeldergate
Dickinson Thomas, North street
Foster Robert, Coney street
Gray William, Feasegate
Hill John, without Walmgate bar
Jackson John, Goodramgate
Leeman Mary, Stonegate
Midgley Francis, Coney street
Mills Mary, 11, New Bridge street
Pickard George, Nesagate
Smith John, Spurriergate
Wilson Thomas, Barker hill

*Furriers, Dealers in Hatters' Skin.*

See also Hatters.

Cook Joseph, 17, Coney street
Dawson William, Fossgate
Fowler Thomas, Spurriergate

Mitchell John, Great Shambles
Monkman William, Coppergate
Sherwood Eliz. High Ousegate
Waterworth John, Goodramgate

*Gardeners, Nursery, and Seedsmen.*

Anderson Richard, Atkinson's court, Micklegate
Anderson Wm. Walmgate bar
Ardington Wm. Castlegate lane
Backhouse Thos. & Jas. Tanner row
Batty Edw. without Walmgate bar
Bearpark Jas. Benj. & Geo. Bootham
Bearpark Rt. jun. Lord Mayor's walk
Bulmer Francis, jun. (cheese, ham, & butter merchant) Tanner row
Camidge William, Castlegate
Clarkson Wm. Walmgate
Cowgill Wm. Monkgate
Cresser William, Micklegate
Earle John, Haymarket
Hill John, without Walmgate bar
Logan John, (seeds) Fossgate
Lupton John, (florist) Bootham
Lyth John, (seeds) Walmgate
Midgley Francis, Coney street
Nutbrown Robert, Albion street
Oldfield Richard, Fossgate
Parker Anthony, (florist) without Walmgate bar
Peart James, North street
Reynoldson Thomas, Gillygate
Rigg John and Son, (wh.) Fishergate
Smith John, (florist) Spurriergate
Smith Benjamin, Blossom street
Taylor James, Foss bridge
Whare William, High Petergate
Whitwell William, (seeds) Pavement
Wright Hugh, Monkgate

*Glass, China, and Earthenware Dealers.*

Boyes and Fowler, Walmgate
Buckley Joseph, Coppergate
Burrill Mary, Thursday market
Cave Elizabeth, Micklegate
Charlton Geo. and Co. Peter lane
Fell George, Thursday market
Fowler Matthew, Walmgate
Houseman John, (dealer in window glass) Peterlane
Kimber Thos. & Son, St. Helen's sq.
Lee John, Coppergate
Marshall G. S. Goodramgate
Midgley Jonathan, High Petergate
Plows Benjamin, Coppergate
Pomfret William, Stonegate
Reynolds Mary, Fossgate
Rounding Thomas, Trinity lane
Smith John, Colliergate
Sturay William, Petergate
Walker Benjamin, Goodramgate

*Glass Manufacturers.*

Prince and Prest, (bottle) Fishergate

*Glass Cutters.*

Barnett John, (& stainer) College st.
Dovenor Mark, Goodramgate
Pomfret William, Stonegate

*Glass Merchants.*

Sanderson Thos. (crown) L. Ousegate
Watson Christ. (cut) Low Ousegate

*Glove Manufacturers.*

Those marked thus * are Leather Breeches Makers.

Brocklebank Thomas, (leather caps) Micklegate
Buttery George, Walmgate
Carter Geo. (gents. caps) College st.
Fether Neville, Walmgate
Fowler Thomas, Spurriergate
Hall T. F. (&leather dresser)Ogleforth
*Hardy Thomas, Stonegate
Kirby Richard, Fetter lane
Lawton John, (breeches maker) Coffee yard
Lyon Robert, Blake street
Makin Thomas, Gillygate
Pulleyn Robert, St. Helen's square
Robinson William, Stonegate
Sherwood Elizabeth, High Ousegate
Simpson J. J. Stonegate
*Thornton and Spink, Spurriergate
Walker Michael, 11, Coney street
Wood and Thompson, Pavement

*Grocers and Tea Dealers.*

See also Tea Dealers.

Agar Seth and Co. Stonegate
Agar Edward, Micklegate
Allen William, Girdlergate
Anderson Richard, Low Petergate
Armstrong J. H. (agent to London Genuine Tea Co.) Fossbridge
Awmack Joseph, Fossgate
Bell Richard, Thursday market
Bell J. Jubbergate
Bleckley John, Thursday market
Brayshaw Eleanor, High Petergate
Britton and Co. Spurriergate
Brown and Hopps, Great Shambles
Bulmer J. A. Haymarket
Clarkson Wm. Walmgate
Cowling Wm. Goodramgate
Cresser James, Skeldergate
Dale John, Fossgate
Daniel Wm. Colliergate
Darbyshire Christopher, Ousegate
Dinmore Richard, Coppergate
Dobson Emanuel, Low Petergate
Fletcher and Scarr, (wh.) North st.
Gray George, Micklegate
Healington John, without Bootham bar
Jackson John, Petergate
Jefferson Robert, (wh.) Pavement
Johnson Ann and Son, Colliergate
Kimber and Bond, Nessgate
King Joseph, Walmgate

Langdale Nathaniel, Walmgate
Lockey Thos. Great Shambles
Lyth John, Walmgate
Nicholson Geo. Goodramgate
Pape Wm. Micklegate
Parkin Henry, Goodramgate
Pickard Geo. Nessgate
Price Wm. Micklegate
Price Aaron, Great Shambles
Priestley Geo. Goodramgate
Richardson Edw. Bootham
Richardson M. Great Shambles
Roscoe John, Coppergate
Rountree Joseph, Pavement
Severs Joseph, Stonegate
Sigsworth John, Castlegate
Smith & Kirlew, (wh.) Skeldergate
Stead Henry & Edw. (wh.) Skeldergt.
Tate John, High Ousegate
Taylor Isaac, foot of Pavement
Tesseyman Thos. 4, New Bridge st.
Tesseyman John, Bootham
Warneford John, Pavement
Watson Geo. Walmgate
Whitwell Wm. Pavement

*Gun Makers and Smiths.*
Bell David, Walmgate
Brunton Richard, Stonegate
Cockhill Joseph, Finkle street
Hoole Arthur, Goodramgate
Pratt John, Stonegate
Wood Joseph, Spurriergate

*Hair Cloth Manufacturers.*
Park Wm. Great Shambles
Savage John, Great Shambles

*Hardware Dealers.*
See also Jewellers and Ironmongers.
Brookbank John, Coney street
Hogarth Edw. College street
Mears John, Pavement
Smith Joseph, Low Petergate
Whisker John, Spurriergate

*Hat Manufacturers and Warehouses.*
Birks Thos. Low Ousegate
Blanchard Wm. High Ousegate
Dawson Wm. Fossgate
Freeman Henry, Coppergate
Haden Wm. 8, Coney street
Horsman Joseph, foot of Pavement
Mackrell James, Micklegate
Monkman Wm. Coppergate
Moody Samuel, Pavement
Pulleyn Robert, (and laceman) St.
  Helen's square
Pullon Thos. Spurriergate
Sherwood Eliz. High Ousegate
Waterworth John, Goodramgate

*Hat and Pill Box Makers.*
Jackson Eliz. Colliergate
Kirby Francis, (pill boxes) St. Mary's
  row
Stewart Andrew, (boxes) Walmgate

Watson Wm. Swinegate
*Hop Merchants.*
Burnell Geo. Mint yard
Demain John, Walmgate
Gibson Robert, Petergate
Lawton & Pearson, Goodramgate
Stead H. & E. Skeldergate

*Hop Bag & Sacking Manufacturers.*
Cariss Thos. St. Andrewgate
Ellison Rbt. (wool sheets) Green lane
Hooker & Cariss, St. Andrew's Church
  yard
Demier John, Walmgate
Kyle John, Pavement
Lawton & Pearson, Goodramgate

*Horse Dealers.*
Dickinson Wm. Walmgate
Fawcett Rbt. without Walmgate bar
Kirby Thos. without Walmgate bar
Marshall Wm. Gillygate
Smith Wm. Silver street
Ward Wm. Marygate
White John, St. Andrewgate

*Hosiers.*
Blanchard Wm. H. Ousegate
Bott Jonathan, Colliergate
Dutton & Co. Fossgate
Fowler Thos. Spurriergate
Holland Thos. 5, New bridge street
Ingham Jonas, Spurriergate
Jennings Robert, Coney street
Nicholson & Hudson, College street
Pulleyn Robert, St. Helen's square
Robinson Wm. Stonegate
Sherwood Eliz. H. Ousegate
Sweeting Michael, H. Ousegate
Teasedale Christopher, (worsted and
  yarn) Aldwark

*Hotels, Inns and Taverns.*
Acorn, Dan. Smith, St. Martin's lane
Acorn, Wm. Hickton, St. Martin's ln.
Admiral Hawke, Rt. Clarke, Walmgt.
Anchor, Saml. Mellor, first Water ln.
Angel, John Hart, Walmgate
Artichoke, Thos. Hewitt, Micklegate
Artichoke, John Atkinson, Micklegt.
Barleycorn, Sim. Russell, Coppergate
Barleycorn, Thos. Streeton, Beddern
Barrel, John Lund, L. Blake street
Barrel, Geo. Pennack, Tho. market
Barrel, Robert Smith, L. Blake street
Bay Horse, John Blythe, Walmgate
Bay Horse, Thos. Douglas, Skeldergt.
Bay Horse, John Agar, Blossom st.
Bay Horse, Wm. Hill, Goodramgate
Bay Horse, Amos Lowton, Gillygate
Bay Horse, Wm. Meadley, L. Petergt.
Bay Horse, James Mackerill, Tanner
  row
Bay Malton, Silvester Reed, Monk
  bar
Baynes's Hotel, Wm. Baynes, Petergt.

Beverley Arms, John Dunn, High Petergate
Bird-in-Hand, Mary Driffield, Bootham bar
Black Boy, Wm. Bowser, North st.
Black Boy, Robert Little, Lendal
Black Bull, Geo. Scaife, Thurs.market
Black Bull, Thos. Wilson, Walmgate
Black Dog, Eliz. Spurr, L. Jubbergt.
Black Dog, Jas. Turner, Feasegate
Black Dog, John Vause, L. Jubbergt.
Black Horse, Jph. Leetall, Bootham
Black Horse, Geo. Reynolds, Fossgt.
Black Horse, John Storry, Walmgate
Black Horse, Thos. Triffit, Pavement
Black Horse, Geo. Wright, Monkgate
Blacksmith's Arms, John Thickett, Swinegate
Black Swan, (Clarke's Hotel & posting house,) Jas. Barber, Coney st.
Black Swan, Thomas Brabiner, Peaseholme green
Blue Bell, Sarah Bell, Walmgate
Blue Bell, Rhd. Richardson, Fossgt.
Blue Bell, Rhd. Taylor, Thu. market
Blue Bell, Han. Wade, Micklegate
Board, Geo. Cressey, Fossgate
Board, John Walton, Marygate
Board, Richd. Broadmead, Jubbergate
Boot and Slipper, Newland Temple, Beddern
Britannia, Thos. Cawood, Walmgate
Brown Cow, Henry Weatherill, jun. Marygate
Cannon, Thos. Chipstead, Lendal
Canteen, James Bean, Barracks
Chapter Coffee House, Ann Plowman, Minster yard
Clifford's Tower, Wm. Head, Peaseholme green
Coach & Horses, Jeremiah Coultas, Micklegate
Coach & Horses, Thomas Kilvington, Low Ousegate
Coach & Horses, Ann Shaw, Swinegt.
Coffee House, Fdk. Debnam, Lendal
Crispin's Arms, Edw. Thorpe, Church lane, North street
Cross Keys, Joseph Joy, H. Jubbergt.
Cross Keys, Thos. Rathmel, North st.
Cross Keys, John Turner, Goodramgt.
Crown, Thomas Thompson, Thursday market
Crown and Anchor, George Briggs, Low Jubbergate
Crown and Cushion, Robert Dowson, Walmgate
Dog & Gun, Jph. Drummond, Hungt.
Duke of York, Robert Merrington, Aldwark
Duke of York, Rbt. Penty, Walmgate
Eagle & Child, John Jackson, Great Shambles
Eclipse, Matthew Hick, Petergate .

Elephant and Castle, George Flower, (Commercial Inn) Skeldergate
Etridge's Royal Hotel, Thos. Etridge, (posting house) Blake street
Falcon, John Sellers (commercial Inn and posting house) Micklegate
Five Lions, Joseph Taylor, Walmgate
Flying Horse, Eliz. Thornton, Copprgt.
Fox, John Hields, Low Petergate
Garrick's Head, Christopher Richardson, High Petergate
George Inn, Ann Winn, (posting house) 10, Coney street
George and Dragon, Thomas Batty, Pavement
Globe, John Hunter, G. Shambles
Globe, Richard Peaker, G. Shambles
Golden Ball, Joseph Grange, Fetter lane
Golden Ball, Philip Thornton, Bishop hill
Golden Barrel, James Addinall, Walmgate
Golden Fleece, William Scholfield, Pavement
Golden Lion, Thos. Gowland, Girdlergate
Golden Lion, Thos. Woollons, Thursday market
Golden Slipper, Mary Marsh, Goodramgate
Grapes, Edw. Seagraves, Micklegate
Grapes, Joseph Webb, Feasegate
Greyhound, Robt. Jackson, Thursday market
Greyhound, John Duffill, Trinity lane
Greyhound, Abraham Braithwaite, Spurriergate
Half Moon, Joseph Rickell, Blake st.
Ham & Firkin, Wm. Spence, Walmgt.
Horse & Groom, John Buck, Mint yd.
Horse & Jockey, Samuel Waterhouse, Aldwark
Horse and Jockey, Edward Clarke, Little Stonegate
Horse Shoe, Thos. Bell, Coppergate
Jacob's Well, Rd. Dalby, Trinity lane
Jolly Bacchus, Joseph Thackray, Micklegate
Jolly Sailor, William Greensides, Fr Water lane
Jolly Sailor, John Myers, Skeldergat
King's Arms, Richard Fryer, Fim Water lane
King's Arms, Thomas Geldart, Foss bridge
King's Head, John Pew, Thurs. mkt
Labourer, John Rudd, Skeldergate
Lamb, Thos. Lambert, Tanner row
Leopard, Geo. Drewrey, Pavement
Leopard, Wm. Pinder, Coppergate
Leopard, Jane Reeve, Coney street
Lion and Lamb, John Richardson, Blossom street

Lord Nelson, Rd. Agar, Goodramgate
Lord Nelson, Isaac Colley, High Jubbergate
Lord Nelson, James Handy, Walmgt.
Malt Shovel, Sarah Atkinson, Fossgt.
Malt Shovel, John Dixon, Walmgate
Malt Shovel, John Dunning, Walmgt.
Malt Shovel, William Kendall, Little Shambles
Marquis of Granby, John Wilson, Peter lane
Marquis Wellington, John Bell, Goodramgate
Mason's Arms, Mary Gill, Goodramgt.
Minster, Anthony Ward, Marygate
Nag's Head, Joseph Nixon, Fossgate
Nag's Head, Edw. Woods, Micklegt.
New Bridge, Richard Ledger, Middle Water lane
Noah's Ark, Jas. Waterhouse, Silver street
Odd Fellows, John Baines, Hungate
Old George Inn, Ambrose Gledhow, Pavement
Old Sandhill, James Monkman, Colliergate
Pack Horse, Matthew Hornsey, Micklegate
Pack Horse, Thos. Morris, Skeldergt.
Panther, Geo. Drewry, Pavement
Punch Bowl, John Clapham, Thursday market
Punch Bowl, Thos. Joy, Stonegate
Punch Bowl, John Matthews, High Jubbergate
Punch Bowl, John Scott, without Micklegate
Queen Caroline, Mark Dovenor, Goodramgate
Red Lion, Rt. Heselwood, Walmgate
Red Lion, Ann Johnson, Micklegate
Red Lion, Hannah Pearson, Goodramgate
Red Lion, Tho. Smith, St. Saviour row
Rifleman, Jas. Robinson, Grape lane
Robin Hood, Francis Clayton, Castlegt.
Rose & Crown, Wm. Clarke, without Walmgate bar
Rose & Crown, Wm. Haxby, Micklegt.
Royal Oak, Thos. Belt, Goodramgt.
Saracen's Head, John Johnson, St. Andrewgate
Saracen's Head, Jonathan Lawton, Coffee house, Stonegate
Shakespeare's Tavern, Rbt. Smith, Little Blake street
Ship, Sarah Joyce, Skeldergate
Ship, Richd. Thomas, First Water ln.
Ship, Joseph Johnson, Staith
Shoe, Robert Blanchard, Friargate
Shoulder of Mutton, John Moverley, Middle Water lane
Shoulder of Mutton, John Wilkinson, Great Shambles

Sir Sidney Smith, Robert Coates, Tanner row
Slipper, Rt. Blanchard, Far Water ln.
Spotted Dog, Deborah Lethe, Walmgate bar
Spotted Dog, Thomas Tate Underwood, St. Saviourgate
Square & Compass, Thomas Masser, Trinity lane
Square & Compass, William Myers, Willow street
Stanhope Press, Thos. Bartholoman, Swinegate
Star, Henry Wilkinson, Stonegate
Star & Garter, Thos. Fisher, Nessgate
Sun, Thos. Bell, Blossom street
Sycamore Tree, Wm. Black, Minster yard
Theatre Coffee House, John Lawn, Little Blake street
Three Cranes, Robt. Johnson, Thursday market
Three Cups, Benj. Grange, Foss bridge
Three Jolly Butchers, Chpr. Bean, Girdlergate
Three Tuns, Abel Swan, Coppergate
Turf Coffee House, George Wilson, Davygate
Turk's Head, John Bickers, College st.
Turk's Head, John Ward, Haymarket
Unicorn, Wm. Dale, Tanner row
Unicorn, Stephen Dixon, Monkgate
Upholsterers' Arms, John Duffield, Trinity lane
Waggon & Horses, Valentine Wilson, Gillygate
Waggon Inn, Robert Fisher, Walmgate bar without
Wellington Coffee House, Jn. Smith, Fossgate
Wheat Sheaf, John Cartwright, Castlegate
Wheat Sheaf, Henry Hutton, without Walmgate bar
Wheat Sheaf, Jas. Skelton, Davygate
Wheat Sheaf, Wm. Radge, Grape ln.
White Dog, Hy. Catterall, Beddern
White Dog, Rt. Grainger, Stonegate
White Horse, Wm. Bearpark, Bootham
White Horse, Mary Sowerby, Coppergate
White Horse, Jonathan Tomlinson, (Coffee house) Skeldergate
White Horse, John Blyth, Walmgate
White Swan, Commercial Hotel, Thos. Hardcastle, Pavement
White Swan, John Ruddock, Goodramgate
Windmill, Wm. Crummack, (posting house & Commercial Hotel) Blossom street
Windmill, Chas. Fawcett, Walmgate
Windmill, Richard Vause, without Castlegate postern

York Tavern, Wm. Simpson, (posting house) S. Helen's square

*Inkstand Manufacturer.*
Wheatley John, Fetter lane

*Iron Founders.*
Gibson Joseph, Pavement
Hopwood and Harwood, Hungate

*Iron Merchants.*
Cattley Thos. and J. H. North street
Sanderson Thomas, Low Ousegate
Watkinson Thomas, Walmgate

*Ironmongers and Hardware Dealers.*
Baines John, (cut nail mfr.) Hungate
Benson Thos. (saddler's) Green lane, Hungate
Brooksbank John, Coney street
Dove Arthur, Pavement
Ellison John, Davygate
Gibson Joseph, Pavement
Glover John, Pavement
Hopwood & Harwood, High Ousegt.
Mears John, Pavement
Sanderson Thos.(bar iron)Low Ousegt.
Shillitoe Thomas, Pavement
Smith Joseph, Low Petergate
Stodhart Thomas, Coney street
Varvill Michael, 8, New Bridge st.
Ward Francis, Manor yard
Wilks John, (merchant) Bootham

*Jewellers, Gold and Silversmiths.*
Astley Wm. (working) Low Jubbergt.
Barber and Whitwell, (and working) Coney street
Burrell John, (silversmith) Micklegt.
Cattell William, Stonegate
Hick Matthew, Minstergate
Jackson Edw.(working mfr. of mourning rings, &c.) Coney street
Marshall Martha, 6, Coney street
Mears John, Pavement
Peacock Wm.(watch mkr.)Spurriergt.
Potts Joshua, Spurriergate
Watson Chpr.(& working) L. Ousegt.

*Lace and Fringe Manufacturers.*
Brown Robert, Bootham square
Stabler Robert, (livery) Monkgate
Wolstenholme Dean, Bootham

*Land Surveyors, &c.*
Agar John, (& land agent) Castlegate
Bulmer James, (and land agent) Precentor's court
Dyer John, Castlegate
Hare John, Castlegate
Tuke and Ayer, Stonegate

*Law Stationers and Agents.*
Allen John, Bootham
Cation John, (clerk of spiritual court) Tanner row
Cawood Henry, Colliergate
Dawson John, (commissioner for special bail) Castlegate
Dunning Mrs. High Petergate

Locke William, Stonegate
Mason Thos. Skeldergt. & the Castle
Peters Thomas, Low Petergate
Watson John, Copley's ct. Coney st.

*Libraries, Subscription.*
York Subscription Library, St. Helen's square, Joseph Shepherd, librarian
Select Subscription,Lady Peckett's yd.
Pavemnt,Ann Woodcock,librarian

*Libraries, Circulating.*
Carrall M. W. Walmgate
Crawshaw Cornelius, Pavement
Deighton Thomas, Pavement
Dickinson B.W.(thespian) H. Petergt.

*Lime Merchants.*
Bromley James, Fossgate
Bussey and Pearson, Marygate
Smith Richard, Monkgate

*Linen Drapers.*
Marked thus † are also Woollen Drapers.
Bell John, Walmgate
†Blackstone Geo. Low Jubbergate
Bleckley Wm. 3, Low Ousegate
Brewis J. W. Peter lane
Brown & Jennings, (wholsl.)Pavemnt.
†Cordukes and Holmes, Haymarket
Darbyshire Robert, High Ousegate
Day Jas. & Edward, High Ousegate
Furnish William, 44, Coney street
Gibson William, Thursday market
Guy and Arundel, Colliergate
Hebden, Copley & Hebden, Stonegt.
Hewson John, High Ousegate
Holland Thomas, 5, New Bridge st.
Ingham Jonas, Spurriergate
Jennings Robert, Coney street
Lakeland and Poppleton, (wholesale) High Ousegate
Mason John, Castlegate
Nicholson and Hudson, (and silk mercers) College street
Norman William, Goodramgate
Owston Thos. (wh.) 7, New Bridge st.
Parr Wm. (haberdasher, jean & velvet warehouse) Blake street
Randerson Mary, Silver street
Rooke Thomas, (& dealer in carpets) Minstergate
†Sanderson and Johnson, Pavement
Settrington James, Pavement
Smith Wm. without Walmgate bar
Sweeting Michael, High Ousegate
Tesseyman Robt. 3, New Bridge st.
Turner James, Petergate
†Walker John, Micklegate
Watson Geo. Walmgate
Welbank Wm. High Petergate
Whitehead Wm. Fossgate

*Linen Manufacturers.*
Dalton Wm. Great Shambles
Eastgate Robert, Union place
Fletcher & Scarr, North street

Hodgson Joseph, Great Shambles
Kyle John, (and sacking) Pavement
Lakeland & Poppleton, Willow st.
Milner Richard, High Ousegate
Scarr John, (merchant) North street, Hungate
Swales John, Walmgate bar
Weller James, Walmgate
Wolstenholme Dean, (mfr. of fringe) Bootham

*Livery Stable Keepers & Horse Dealers.*

Atkinson Wm. Fossgate
Benson Jeremiah, (& coach proprietor) Little Blake street
Dale Emanuel, Feasegate
Dale Thomas, Goodramgate
Fornish John, Trinity lane
Garnett John, Walmgate
Letbe Thomas, Skeldergate
Moss Francis, (and posting master) Minster yard
Parkinson Sarah, Low Jubbergate
Smith Wm. Blake street
Tate John, Silver street

*Machine Maker.*
Noble Geo. Bootham

*Mattress Makers.*
Hooker & Cariss, St. Andrewgate, Church yard
Viney John, Green lane, Hungate

*Merchants.*
Bulmer Francis, sen. Precentor's ct.
Cattley T. & J. K. (timber, iron and slate) North street
Jefferson Robert, Pavement
Owston Thomas, 7, New Bridge st.
Smith and Kirlew, Skeldergate
Stead H. and K. Skeldergate

*Milliners and Dress Makers.*
See Straw Hat Makers.

Allen Caroline, Micklegate
Armatage Abia, North street
Atkinson Susannah, near Ouse bridge
Bearpark Sally, High Petergate
Bickers and Sowerby, Spurriergate
Bownas & Co. Little Blake street
Brown Jane, Union court, Trinity ln.
Buckle A. Bootham row
Dyott Eliz. without Castlegt. postern
Foster Z. and B. St. Andrewgate
Ellison Mrs. St. Saviour's row
Gledhill & Edison, St. Helen's square
Gregson Jane, Coffee yd. Stonegate
Grimwood Hannah, Petergate
Grisswood Mary, Trinity lane
Harborne Mary, Colliergate
Harris Mary, (haberdasher) Pavement
Harvey J. and M. Minster yard
Hawkswell Eliz. Walmgate bar
Hodgson Sarah, St. Helen's square
Jackson Elizabeth, Walmgate
Law Mary, Judges' old lodgings

Leaf Elizabeth, St. Saviourgate
Limbert Margaret, Low Petergate
Lister Elizabeth, Micklegate
M'Gedy M. Stonegate
Morgan Sarah, 20, Coney street
Morris Mary, Walmgate bar
Naylor Misses A. L. & E. Judges' old lodgings yard
Popple Marianne, Bootham row
Prince and Gill, Stonegate
Raine Anne, Stonegate
Rippon Francis, (& feather maker & cleaner) Stonegate
Rowley H. E. College street
Scott Eliz. Little Blake street
Severs Elizabeth, Petergate
Skrimshaw Misses, Trinity lane
Smith Jane, Micklegate
Thornton Mary, Walmgate
Underwood Sarah, Great Stonegate
Veavers Francis, Walmgate
Wake Hannah, Coney street
Warmeth Mary, Tanner row
Webster Ann, Low Petergate

*Millwrights.*
Chapman William, Fetter lane
Fawcett Charles, Walmgate

*Music Preceptors, Venders, and Instrument Makers.*
Brown Christopher, Micklegate
Camidge Matthew, (organist at the cathedral) High Petergate
Camidge John, M. D. Manor house
Hargett Charles, Blake street
Harman Wm. 12, New Bridge street
Hill Frederick, Micklegate
Hogarth Edward, College street
Knapton S. and P. Coney street
Knapton Philip, (professor) St. Saviourgate
Ohman Andrew, (organs and violins) Gillygate
Robinson John, Stonegate
Smith Josiah, (instrument dealer) St. Saviourgate
Stears Samuel, (tambourines and military drums) Fossgate
Tomlinson Thomas, Blake street
Ward John, (organs) Micklegate

*Mustard Manufacturers & Dealers.*
Bell Michael, (dealer) Monkgate
Lee Wm. (mfr.) Layerthorp
Taylor, Cook & Co. (mfrs.) Spurriergt.

*Newspapers, &c.*
TUESDAY—York Courant, Henry Cobb & Co. Coney street, opposite the end of New street
THURSDAY—York Chronicle, Wm. Blanchard, Coppergate
SATURDAY—York Herald, Hargrove, Gawthorp & Hargrove, Pavement
SATURDAY—Yorkshire Gazette, John Wolstenholme, Pavement

Pick's Racing Calendar, Thomas Sotheran, Coney street
Racing Calendar, R. Johnson, bookseller, Coney street

*Oil and Colour Dealers.*
Hanson C. J. Low Petergate
Parkinson Nathaniel, (and paint)
Stonegate
Spencer Isaac & Co. First Water lane
Taylor Cook & Co. Spurriergate

*Opticians.*
Barnett John, College street
Wisker Widow, (glasses and instru-
ments) Spurriergate

*Painters, Historic, Portrait and Mi-
niature.*
Banks Robert, (min.) Harker's yard,
Micklegate
Brown John, (landscape) Walmgate
Cave Henry, (artist) Micklegate
Dalby David, (animals) without Mick-
legate bar
Walker Thomas, Coney street

*Painters, House and Sign.*
Audaer Robert, (and paper hanger)
St. Andrewgate
Audaer George, St. Andrewgate
Barra James, Low Petergate
Beadle and Perfect, Micklegate
Bean James, Barracks
Bradley Savile, Beddern
Brookbank John, Coney street
Brown John, Walmgate
Brown & Kirlew, (coach) Davygate
Davies William, Colliergate
Glenn Eleazer, St. Saviourgate
Hardy Thomas, High Petergate
Hollidey Jas. Barra, High Petergate
Holliday James and Son, Swinegate
Ingram William, Parsonage house,
Coney street
Jones John, Colliergate
Parkinson Nathaniel, (coach) Stonegt.
Pollard Catharine, Colliergate
Thompson Lewis, Walmgate
Westland John, High Jubbergate

*Paper Hanging Manufacturers.*
Audaer Robert, St. Andrewgate
Baker Geo. St. Helen's square
Kibblewaite James, High Petergate
Mush John, (wholesale) Monk bar

*Pawnbrokers.*
Fettes George, Lady Peckett's yard,
Pavement
Palmer Alice, Patrick pool

*Perfumers.*
Brownridge Robert, Stonegate
Hall Charles, Coney street
Hands William, Blake street
Parsons John, (perfumery warehouse
& ornamental hair mfr.) Coney st.
Young James, Minstergate

*Physicians.*
See also Surgeons and Druggists.
Beckwith Stephen, Coney street
Belcombe William, High Petergate
Easton John, Bootham
Goldie Geo. Blake street
Lawson John, Lendal
Wake Baldwin, Little Blake street

*Plane Makers.*
Bothamley John, Tanner row
Dibb William, North street
Ferrand William, Micklegate
Hardy Eliz. Coates yard, Tanner row
Varvill Michael, 8, New Bridge street

*Plasterers and Slaters.*
Chapman William, Bishop hill
Crabtree Eli, Lendal
Ellison John, Lord Mayor's walk
Laycock Jacob, Church yd. North st.
Nicholson & Bell, Bootham square
Prince Matthew, Tanner row
Reynolds William, Gillygate

*Plumbers and Glaziers.*
Barra Geo. Goodramgate
Barra James, High Petergate
Barra James, Low Petergate
Croft James, Davygate
Davies William, Colliergate
Drinkell John, Blue Ball yd. Skeldergt.
Geldard F. F. Gillygate
Hartley Robert, Fossgate
Hodgson Thomas, Stonegate
Houseman John, Peter lane
Jackson John, jun. North street
Jackson John, Goodramgate
Noton Thomas, Stonegate
Shouksmith Joseph, St. Mary's row,
Bishop hill
Sumpner John, Spurriergate
Walker Matthew, 10, New Bridge st.

*Porter Dealers.*
Harrison John, Low Ousegate
Holmes William, Haymarket
Kimber Thos. & Son, St. Helen's sq.
Morley William, Goodramgate
Scarr and Fletcher, Micklegate
Whitwell & Norton, St. Saviourgate

*Poulterers.*
See also Poulterers among the Country
Carriers.
Baines Hy. without Castlegt. posters
Barker Anne, Little Shambles
Monkman Sarah, Peter lane
Prest John, Feasegate

*Printers, Letter Press.*
Alexander Wm. and Son, Castlegate
Blanchard William, Coppergate
Carrall M. W. (printing ink manufac-
turer) Walmgate
Cobb Henry, Coney street
Crawshaw Cornelius, Pavement
Deighton Thomas, Pavement

Hargrove, Gawthorp, & Hargrove, Pavement
Johnson Robert, Coney street
Kendrew James, Colliergate
Richardson R. & J. High Ousegate
Storry Wm. Low Petergate
Weightman Thos. Low Petergate
Wilson and Sons, (publishers) High Ousegate
Wolstenholme John, Minstergate

### Proctors.
See Attornies.

### Rags—Dealers.
Atkinson Wm. Middle Water lane
Gibson Thomas, North street
Meynell Thomas, Coppergate
Smith Wm. Haymarket
Varey Wm. & Son, Fetter lane
Vause Geo. Pavement

### Register Offices for Servants.
Coates John, High Petergate
Hurworth Thomas, Micklegate
Knowles Wm. Precentors court
Richardson Mrs. C. College st.
Small John, College street
Thomas Wm. Minster yard

### Rope & Twine Manufacturers.
Bell John, Walmgate
Dalton Wm. Great Shambles
Hodgson Joseph, Great Shambles
Kyle John, Pavement
Milner Richard, High Ousegate
Moverley John, Middle Water lane
Savage John, Great Shambles
Shepherd John, Middle Water lane
Shepherd Thomas, Walmgate
Smith Wm. without Walmgate bar
Walker John, Silver street

### Saddlers—Hunting and Military, and Harness Makers.
Barr William, Coney street
Botterill James, Goodramgate
Cariss Thomas, Walmgate
Dawson Joshua, Fossgate
Edson Robert, (saddle tree maker) Walmgate
Gentle Robert, Minster gate
Hamilton Robert, Bootham
Hay John Lepington, Micklegate
Johnson Joseph, High Petergate
Johnson Rhd. Gt. Shmbls. & Fulford
Lee Wm. Thursday market
Lee and Mason, High Ousegate
Mortimer Joseph, Walmgate
Nightingale John, Fossgate
Radcliffe Charles, Colliergate
Simpson Christopher, Micklegate
Simpson John, Walmgate
Ware Christopher, Stonegate

### Sail Makers.
Fisher Joseph, Middle Water lane
Wilkinson John, Middle Water lane

### Salt Merchants.
Watterworth Thos. 7, Coney st.

### Slaters and Slate Merchants.
Cattley and Mitchell, (merchants; North street
Overend Leonard, Skeldergate

### Sloop and Boat Builders.
Birch Thos. without Skeldergate Postern
Hill Sarah, Marygate
Nicholson J. Skeldergate
Turpin Joseph, Clementhorp without Postern

### Spirit and Wine Merchants.
Bean Wm. Stonegate
Benson John, Hungate
Bickers John, College street
Braithwaite Abraham, Spurriergate
Burnell George, Mint yard
Cooper and Bielby, Skeldergate
Cressey Geo. sen. Fossgate
Ellis Geo. (St. Leonard's Vaults) Mint yard
Gibson Robert, Petergate
Harrison John, Low Ousegate
Harrison Wm. (British wine) Davygt.
Jackson John, Hay Market
Lawton and Pearson, Goodramgate
Oldfield Wm. Lendal
Oliver Mary, Micklegate
Rooke Mark, New Bridge street
Roper John and Son, Thursday mkt.
Seller Charles, Pavement
Simpson James, Davygate
Swan Abel, Coppergate
Vollans John, Micklegate
Ward John, Fossgate
Webb Joseph, Feasegate
Whincup Wm. Walmgate
Whitwell Wm. Pavement
Wilkinson James, opposite George Inn, Coney street
Wolstenholme Joseph, High Petergt.

### Stamp Offices.
North Riding, William Hale, Esq. New street
West Riding and York, Wm. Grey, Esq. Low Petergate

### Stay Makers.
Armatage Abia, North street
Brown Thomas, Thursday market
Dunn John, High Petergate
Fawbert Joseph, High Petergate
Flower Elizabeth, Stonegate
Hopton George, Stonegate
Hurworth Thos. Micklegate
Lyon Charles, Stonegate
Ridley Cuthbert, Lord Mayor's walk
Wilberforce and Cawood, Fossgate

### Stocking Manufacturers.
See also Hosiers.
Bott Jonathan, Colliergate

M

Collins Jane, (silk stocking grafter) Colliergate

Todd Benjamin, Little Shambles

*Stone and Marble Masons & Sculptors.*

Bennett & Flintoff, St. Andrewgate
Buckley Joseph, Coppergate
Dovenor Mark, Goodramgate
Fisher Charles, Tanner row
Moore Alexander, Walmgate
Mountain Robert, Lendal
Plows Benj. and Son, Fossbridge, Walmgate
Shout Wm. Beddern
Snowden & Buckley, (and sculptors) Micklegate
Sollitt John, High Jubbergate
Stead Wm. and Son, Skeldergate and North street
Taylor Michael, (sculptor) Lendal
Tilney John, Bootham

*Straw Bonnet and Hat Manufacturers.*

See Milliners.

Aspinall James, Coney street
Banks Catharine, Fossgate
Birks Thos. Colliergate
Borrows Elizabeth, High Petergate
Chippendale Elizabeth, Peter lane
Clark J. J. Tanner row
Clark Mary, Tanner row
Cloak James, Stonegate
Cooke Joseph, 17, Coney street
Dale Mary, Micklegate
Gibson Elizabeth, High Petergate
Gill Mary, Aldwark
Holmes Hannah, 14, New Bridge st.
Hupe Caroline, Low Petergate
Jameson Mary, Minster yard
Jackson Mary, Stonegate
Kidd Wm. Grape lane
Metcalfe Elizabeth, Hungate
Pears Anne, Hungate
Robinson Charlotte, Trinity lane
Todd Elizabeth, Goodramgate
Williamson Harriet, Goodramgate
Wilkinson Elizabeth, Walmgate
Wright Anne, Dundas street

*Surgeons.*

See also Physicians & Chemists & Druggists.

Allen Oswald, (apothecary) Colliergt.
Allen Matthew, (apothecary to the Lunatic Asylum) Bootham
Atkinson James, Lendal
Brown Geo. Castlegate
Champney Geo. Colliergate
Clark W. S. Micklegate
Clarke Geo. Davygate
Coates Amos, New Bridge street
Drake Richard, Precenters court
Hope Wm. Castlegate
Hopps George, Skeldergate
Husband Wm. High Petergate

M'Millan John, Minstergate, near Stonegate
Mangles John, Precenters court
Matterson Wm. Minster yard
Overton James, Blake street
Ryland Wm. without Micklegate bar
Saunders James, High Ousegate
Stubbs Mark, Walmgate
Wallis Edward, High Petergate
Wilson John, (to the dispensary) St. Andrewgate

*Tailors and Habit Makers, &c.*

See also Woollen Drapers.

Blackstone Geo. Low Jubbergate
Brown Geo. Peter lane
Bulmer Richard, Aldwark
Bussey John, Low Jubbergate
Buttrey Geo. Walmgate
Castell Geo. St. Saviourgate
Coupland James, Goodramgate
Dalby Joseph, Jubbergate
Davis Joseph, (naval and military) 21, Coney street
Douglas Henry, Aldwark
Dunn John, Stonegate
Dunn John, High Petergate
Dunwell Richard, Coppergate
Earle Wm. High Petergate
Evers Wm. Spurriergate
Fether Neville, Walmgate
Fletcher Geo. High Jubbergate
Fox Thomas, Fossgate
Hollins John, opposite George Inn, Coney street
Hudson Thomas, Stonegate
Harworth David, Bootham row
Littlewood Solomon, Walmgate
Mallatrat Frederick, 46, Coney st.
Masser John, Fossgate
Nicholson John, Stonegate
Nicholson Geo. Goodramgate
Nixon John, Harker's yd. Micklegate
Norman Wm. Goodramgate
Rhodes Robert, Blake street
Richardson John, Minster yard
Richmond Joseph, Hungate
Stansfield Abraham, Micklegate
Vause Geo. Pavement
Wade John, Stonegate
Waind Wm. Goodramgate
Wairn Thos. High Petergate
Walker Joseph, Low Petergate
Walls Wm. Low Ousegate
Webster Thos. Walmgate
Weldin Thos. Walmgate
Whiteley Geo. Feasegate
Wilkinson John, Feasegate

*Tallow Chandlers.*

Catton, Crosby, and Co. Micklegate
Dobson Emanuel, Low Petergate
Foster Wm. Fossgate
Lockey Thos. Great Shambles

Parkin Henry, Goodramgate
Priestley Geo. Goodramgate
Richardson & Burrell, Gt. Shambles
Sigsworth John, Castlegate
Smith Henry, Walmgate
Stead Henry & Edward, Skeldergate
Stephenson Richard, Great Shambles

*Tanners.*
See also Curriers and Fellmongers.

Hirst Francis, Walmgate
Priestman David, Marygate
Richardson Wm. Skeldergate postern
Thurman Wm. without Walmgt. bar

*Tea Dealers.*
See also Grocers.

Birks Wm. Swinegate
Bleckley Wm. 5, Low Ousegate
Bolland Thomas, (agent to the London Genuine Tea Company, 23, Ludgate hill) Spurriergate
Brown Richard, Coney street
Brownridge Robert, Stonegate
Backle Marmaduke, St. Saviour row
Cutton, Crosby, and Co. Micklegate
Dalton Wm. Goodramgate
Dunn and Robinson, High Ousegate
Foster Robert, Coney street
Gill William, Colliergate
Green John, Feasegate
Gregory Thomas, (wholesale) High Ousegate
Harrison Wm. High Jubbergate
Hearon and Dale, (wholesale) High Ousegate
Heselwood Thomas, Bootham row
Knowles Thomas, Coppergate
Maltby H. D. Pavement
Mason & Branton, (& coffee roasters) Minster yard
Mason John, Castlegate
Mason John, jun. Petergate
Morritt Wm. Feasegate
Ransley Wm. Lendal
Scawin Wm. Low Petergate
Taylor James, 1, New Bridge street
Tuke Samuel and Co. Castlegate
Waller Robert, Micklegate bar
Watson Christopher, Low Ousegate
Watterworth Thomas, (agent for the sale of Genuine Teas) 7, Coney street
Wilkinson James, opposite George Inn, Coney street
Williamson Richard, Stonegate

*Thread Manufacturers.*

Fletcher and Scarr, North street
Hedley Hartas, (patent coloured and shoe thread) Albion street
Lakeland and Poppleton, Willow st.
Richardson Wm. Skeldergate postern

Scarr John, (patent coloured and shoe thread) Hungate

*Timber and Raff Merchants.*
Cattley Thomas and J. H. North st.
Peacock Thomas and Geo. Skeldergt.
Peacock D. J. and G. Skeldergate
Watkinson Thomas, Walmgate

*Tobacco and Snuff Mfrs. and Dealers.*
Aray Reuben, Feasegate
Bell John, Stonegate
Bewlay Thomas, Low Ousegate
Crombie Geo. Fossgate
Labron Wm. Pavement

*Tobacco Pipe Makers.*
Deacon Joseph, High Jubbergate
Lazenby Robert, Gillygate
Mason Geo. Lord Mayor's walk
Shaftoe Hannah, Walmgate

*Toy Manufacturers and Warehouses.*
Adams David, Silver street
Fawbert Wm. Stonegate
Fossett Joseph, Goodramgate
Fox Wm. Peter lane
Marshall Martha, 16, Coney street
Mears John, Pavement
Middleton John, Nessgate
Mortimer Isaac, 6, Coney street
Sledmere Richard, Nessgate

*Trunk Makers.*
Cattell George, Goodramgate
Judson Wm. Coney street
Middleton John, Nessgate
Stewart Andrew, Walmgate

*Turners in Wood, Ivory, &c.*
Adams David, Silver street
Fawbert Wm. Stonegate
Fearnley Thomas, Low Jubbergate
Fossett Joseph, Goodramgate
Fox Wm. Peter lane
Morritt Wm. (toys) Feasegate
Scaife Wm. Swinegate
Stones Geo. Pavement

*Umbrella & Parasol Manufacturers.*
Bean Wm. Stonegate
Metcalfe Mirabella, (& lobby cloths), Spurriergate

*Varnishers.*
Stokes Elisabeth, Bootham row
Taylor Cook, and Co. (varnish mfrs.) Spurriergate

*Watch Makers.*
See Clock and Watch Makers & Repairers.

*Wharfingers.*
Gillian Thos. Old wharf, Skeldergate
Mills Henry and Son, New wharf, Skeldergate

*Wheelwrights.*
See also Carpenters.
Bean John, Patrick pool
Dawes John, Peaseholm green

Johnson Joseph, Hungate
Harker James, (agricultural imple-
  ments) Marygate
Lowe John, Gillygate
Meek Richard, Gillygate
Noble Geo. (thrashing machine mkr.
  and carpenter,) Bootham
Taylor Jeremiah, Walmgate
Waterhouse John, High Jubbergate

*Whip Makers.*

Fearby John, Dunning's yd. Fossgate
Lawton Samuel, Walmgate
Powell Thomas, Castlegate
Scadlock John, Fossgate

*White and Red Lead Manufactory.*

Liddell & Co. without Walmgate bar

*Whitesmiths & Bellhangers, &c.*

Bell David, Walmgate
Briton Wm. Aldwark
Burdsall Wm. Dunning's yd. Fossgate
Clark Wm. College street
Clegg Abraham, Goodramgate
Collier Michael, Micklegate
Douglas & Lockwood, Skeldergate
Duncan Henry, Dundas street
Ellison John, Davygate
Gibson Joseph, Pavement
Giles Wm. Coppergate
Glover Thomas, Low Jubbergate
Glover John, Goodramgate
Haxby John, Skeldergate
Haxby Wm. Skeldergate
Hick Matthew, Petergate
Lee Benjamin, Goodramgate
Lister Christopher, (scale beam mkr.)
  North street
North W. G. Feasegate
Ruler John, Fossbridge, Walmgate
Smith Joseph, Low Petergate
Snowden Wm. Walmgate
Spink Joseph, Little Shambles
Ward Francis, Manor yard
Wells Geo. Leopard yd. Pavement
Wiseman John, First water lane

*Wire Workers.*

Allison H. B. Fossgate
Varley Mary, Fossgate

*Woollen Drapers and Tailors.*
See also Tailors.

Atkinson James, Coppergate
Bainbridge & Woodall, Low Ousegate
Bradley Luke, Fossgate
Brown John, Skeldergate
Cordukes & Holmes, Hay market
Davis Joseph, 21, Coney street
Dunn John, Stonegate
Earle Wm. High Petergate
Evers Wm. Spurriergate
Hodgson John, High Ousegate
Hollins John, (opposite George Inn,)
  Coney street
Hudson Thomas, Stonegate
Knowles George, High Ousegate
Mallatrat Frederick, 46, Coney st.
Meadley T. B. Great Shambles
Meynell Thomas, Coppergate
Nicholson John, Stonegate
Rhodes Robert, (steward of the race
  course) Blake street
Sanderson John, Pavement
Strickland W. & H. Blake street
Vause George, Pavement
Wade John, Stonegate
Waind Wm. Goodramgate
Walker Joseph, Low Petergate
Walls Wm. Low Ousegate
Whitehead Wm. Fossgate

*Woolstaplers.*

Ambler Abraham, Peaseholm green
Buckle Marmaduke, St. Saviour row

*Worsted Manufacturers.*

Cocker Robert, 15, New bridge st.
Fawcett Mrs. Ann, Walmgate
Rhodes John, (stuffs) Barker hill
Todd Benjamin, Little Shambles
Trout Isabella, Walmgate
Walker Francis, North street
Wolstenholme Dean, Bootham

# AINSTY OF YORK.

THE AINSTY OR COUNTY OF THE CITY OF YORK, is a district to the West of York, under the jurisdiction of the Lord Mayor and Magistrates of that city, to which it was annexed in the twenty-seventh of Henry VI. Prior to this time it was a wapentake or hundred of the West-Riding. The *Ainsty* or *Aincity* is supposed by Drake to have been derived from the old northern word ᚨᛁᚾᛖᛁᛏ signifying a hundred contiguous, opposite or near to the city. The whole district or wapentake was anciently a forest, but it was dis-forested by the charters of Richard I. and John. The circuit of the Ainsty is computed at thirty-two miles, according to the following calculation :—

From the confluence of the rivers
Nidd and Ouse, at Nun-Monkton,
  to that of the Wharf and
  Ouse, near Nun-Appleton, 12 miles.
From the junction of the Wharf and
  Ouse to Thorp-Arch, ............ 11
From Thorp-Arch to Wilsthorp, on
  the Nidd, ...................... 6
From Wilsthorp, along the line of
  the Nidd, to its confluence
  with the Ouse, ................. 3
              —— 32

The Ainsty comprises thirty-five towns and villages, of which the following is the enumeration :—

| | |
|---|---|
| Acaster Malbis, | Holgate, |
| Acaster Selby, | Hutton Wansley, |
| Acomb, | Knapton, |
| Angram, | Long Marston, |
| Appleton Roebuck, | Middlethorpe, |
| Askham Bryan, | Moor Monkton, |
| Askham Richard, | Nether Poppleton, |
| Bickerton, | Oxton, |
| Bilbrough, | Rufforth, |
| Bilton, | Steeton, |
| Bishopthorpe, | Tadcaster, to the mid- |
| Bolton Percy, | dle of the bridge, |
| Catterton, | Thorp-Arch, |
| Colton, | Tockwith, |
| Copmanthorpe, | Upper Poppleton, |
| Dringhouses, | Walton, |
| Healaugh, | Wighill, |
| Hessay, | Wilsthorp, |

Exclusive of several hamlets.

In Drake's time the City and Ainsty of York were accounted equal to one-eighth part of the West-Riding, and one-twentieth of the whole county. The extraordinary increase of population and wealth in the West-Riding within the last hundred years has, however, destroyed these proportions, and it appears, from the census of 1821, that the City and Ainsty of York do not now, in point of population, exceed one-twenty-fifth part of the West-Riding, and one thirty-fifth part of the whole county.— In all assessments by act of parliament the City of York is taxed at three-fifths, and the Ainsty at two-fifths. Till the year 1735, a doubt existed whether the freeholders of the Ainsty had a right of suffrage at the election for members of parliament for this county, (on the ground that it formed part and parcel of a separate county) and though their votes were received by the Sheriff, they were always taken with a query prefixed to their names; but after the contest between Sir Miles Stapleton, Bart. and Sir Rowland Winn, Bart. the matter was brought to issue before the House of Commons, when the House, on the 9th of March, 1735, decided, " That the persons whose freeholds lie with- " in that part of the County of the City of " York, which is commonly called the " Ainsty, have a right to vote for Knights " of the Shire of the County of York." The following is a brief description of the places within the Ainsty, taken in alphabetical order with the directory of each place subjoined :

ACASTER MALBIS, (P.) situated on the Ouse; 4 miles S. of York. Here is a good School House, endowed with the products of some lands, under the patronage of certain trustees, who have the appointment of fourteen poor children, as proper objects to receive instruction free of cost. Mr. George Cowper, is the master, and Messrs. William Cundell, John Kettlewell, and John Oates, feoffees. The church is an ancient structure, of which the Rev. Thomas Barker, is perpetual curate. The town derives its name from the family of the Malby's, which flourished here for some centuries after the conquest. Population, 291.

| Farmers & Yeomen, | Pickering Wm. |
|---|---|
| Cundall Wm. | Raines John |
| Darling John | Stokes John |
| Dawson Richard | Thompson Jonth. |
| Elsworth John | *Milliners, &c.* |
| Elsworth Rebecca | Goodall Dorothy |
| Etherington J. | Hatfield Rosamond |
| Harrison John | *Shoemakers,* |
| Kettlewell John | Archer Richard |
| Mawson Charles | Mortimer John |
| Oates John | |

Cooper Geo. schoolmaster
Cooper Wm. parish clerk
Croft John, tailor
Croft Matthew, grocer, &c.
Darling Samuel, tailor and victualler, Fisherman's Arms.
Dawson Richard, constable
Gill Charles, tailor and grocer
Oates Wm. vict. Ship Inn
Preston Philip, gardener
Reader Wm. blacksmith & coal dlr.
Shepherd Wm. gardener
Torr John, impounder

The *Humber Steam Packet,* to Gainsbro', every Monday and Thursday, and to York every Tuesday & Fri.

*Carrier*—John Torr, every Saturday to the Elephant & Castle, Skeldergate, York.

ACASTER SELBY, in the parish of Stillingfleet; 8 miles S. of York. This village is pleasantly situated on the banks of the Ouse, on which river the Steam Packets, and others, pass and repass to Selby, Gainsbro', and Hull, tending considerably to enliven the scene. Here is a Free School, with an endowment of 7l. 7s. per annum, arising out of the fee-farm rents, aided also by voluntary subscriptions of the inhabitants of the township. This place was formerly part of the possession of the Abbot of Selby, and from thence its name is derived. Population, 188.

| Farmers, | Harrap Wm. |
|---|---|
| Cresser J. Hales hill | Middlebrough Geo. |
| Dawson James, | Varley John, Leas- |
| Hales hill | house |
| Fawcett Geo. | Wade Francis |
| Harrap James | Wormald Mary |

Abbey Robert, schoolmaster
Hick Geo. ferryman
Preston John, mole catcher
Stead Catherine, victualler, Blacksmith's Arms
Stead Wm. blacksmith

*Carrier,* Geo. Hick, to York every Sat.

ACOMB, (P.) in the liberty of St. Peter's, 2 miles W. of York. This church is an ancient small structure, and being seated on a dry and elevated situation, a number of families choose it for their place of sepulchre. Here is also a newly-erected Methodist chapel, likewise a school, built by voluntary subscriptions of the inhabitants, and vested in certain trustees, upon Dr. Bell's plan of education. Population, 738.

Anderson Robert, Esq.
Barstow John, Esq.
Barstow Eliz. gentlewoman
Beckley Nathan, gentleman
Britton Thomas, gentleman
Bullivant Thomas, gentleman
Ellis Wm. sen. yeoman
Calvert William, gentleman
Fearby John, yeoman
Fothergill John, gentleman
Gale Conyers, Esq.
Hale William, Esq.
Hill William, yeoman
Jolly John, yeoman, Grange
Kirkby Jonathan, gentleman
Lloyd George, Esq.
Nettleton Edward, gentleman
Peckfield Mary, gentlewoman
Percival Misses
Ramsey Misses M. and S.
Roberts George, gentleman
Torre Kirby, Esq.
Wade C. gentlewoman
Wilkinson William, comedian
Wright Misses

| *Asylum Keepers,* | Benson Wm. |
|---|---|
| Mannering Henry | Benson Geo. |
| Skipwith H. and | Darling Mary |
| lodging house | Harrison Richard |
| Taylor James, sen. | Lamb Richard |
| Villa | Lazenby Wm. |
| *Blacksmiths,* | Machin Thomas |
| Hields Joseph | Pinder Robert |
| Jebson Robert | Richardson Geo. |
| *Bricklayers,* | Robinson Henry |
| Dalton Robert | Skilbeck Joseph |
| Prince Joseph | *Grocers,* |
| *Butchers,* | Coulson John, (& draper) |
| Kirk Richard | Hardy Wm. |
| Syddall George | Hardy Mary |
| *Farmers,* | *Joiners, &c.* |
| Ellis Wm. jun. | Benson Robert |
| Fearne Jane | Hields John |
| Fieldhouse Benj. | Holmes Geo. |
| Forrest Wm. | Hudson Robert |
| Forrest Thos. | Kirk James |
| Fowler Wm. | *Shoemakers,* |
| Heslop John | Briskham Geo. |
| Kirk Richard | Britton John |
| Kirk John | Brownrigg Robert |
| Lakeland Robert | Hields John |
| Prince Wm. | Scruton Wm. |
| Wade David | *Surgeons, &c.* |
| Wright Thos. | Taylor Joseph, jun. |
| *Gardeners,* | Wharton Wm. |
| Askwith Wm. | |

*Tailors,*
Bateman Wm.

Stead Wm.
Swales Sampson

*Hotels, Inns, and Taverns.*
Black Swan, John Benson
Brittannia, John Ward
Grey Horse, William Mason
Grey Hound & Hare, Joseph Prince
Grey Mare, John Wikeley, corn dealer
Coates Robert, baker
Greenbank Geo. pig jobber
Nettleton Thos. schoolmaster
Witterington John, lime & coal mert.

*Carriers* to York & Wetherby every
Tuesday, Thursday, and Saturday.

ANGRAM, in the parish of Long
Marston; 4 miles NNE. of Tadcaster,
and 7 from York. Population, 66.
Carbutt Thos. vict. Board
Todd John, cowkeeper, and carrier to
York every Saturday.

*Farmers,*
Dickinson Benj.
Edeson John
Palfreeman James

Parker Susannah
Rheam John
Rheam Matthew

*Appleton* (Nun), in the parish of
Bolton Percy; 6 miles SE. of Tadcaster;
was formerly a priory, for Nuns of the Cistercian Order, founded in the reign of King
Stephen, by Alice de St. Quintin; and among
the injunctions prescribed to the Nuns of this
house in the year 1489, are the following:—
"That the cloister doors be shut up in winter at seven, and in summer at eight at night,
and the keys delivered to the prioress.—
That the prioress and all the sisters lodge
nightly in the dorter, unless sick or diseased.
That none of the sisters use the ale-house,
or the waterside, where the course of strangers daily resort. That none of the sisters
have their service of meat and drink to their
chambers, but keep the frater and the hall,
unless sick. That no sister bring in any
man, religious or secular, into their chambers, or any secret place, day or night, &c.—
That the prioress license no sister to go a
pilgrimage, or visit their friends, without
great cause, and then to have a companion.
That the convent grant no corodies or
liveries of bread, or ale, or other victual,
to any person, without special licence. That
they take in no perhendinaunceers or sojourners, unless children, or old persons, &c."
On the 5th of December, 1540, this Monastery was surrendered, and afterwards became
a ruin. Thomas Lord Fairfax built a handsome brick house upon the site; which, with
the estate, was subsequently purchased by
Mr. Alderman Milner, a merchant in Leeds;
and is now the seat of his great grandson Sir
W. M. Milner, Bart.

APPLETON ROEBUCK, in the parish of Bolton Percy; 8 miles SW. of York.
Here is a neat brick-built chapel, belonging
to the Methodists of the Old Connexion,
erected about three years ago: likewise a
good National School house, for sixty boys
and fifty girls, built by subscription in 1817,
patronised by the Rev. Archdeacon Markham, and supported by voluntary contributions. The situation is very salubrious, and
there is living here at present an old man, of
the name of John Lamb, aged 94 years.
Population, 585.

Mollett Ann, gentlewoman
Saunders Rev. Wm. curate

*Butchers,*
Jowitt Edward
Stead James
*Coal Merchants,*
Proctor Edward
Wheatley Richard
*Farmers & Yeomen,*
Barker John
Bell Wm.
Carrack John
Hart James
Kilby Henry
Laycock Wm.
Laycock Thos.
Mollett John
Morley Robert
Pickering Matthew
Bat Pudding grn.
Richardson Wm.
Stead Matthias

Vairey Richard
Wheatley Richard
*Gardeners,*
Chambers Nathl.
Stephenson John
Ward Thomas
*Grocers, &c.*
Stephenson John
Wood James
*Joiners, &c.*
Cook John
Richardson Wm.
*Shoemakers,*
Backhouse Wm.
Barnes John
Cartwright John
*Tailors,*
Brown Francis
Shilleto Thomas
Woodhall James

Carrack John, perpetual constable
Carrack Thomas, vict. Crown
Cooper Thos. cattle dealer, &c.
Denton Robert, corn miller
Denton Elizabeth, midwife
Hewson J. master of National school
Pickles David, weaver
Pottage Rd. thrashing machine maker
Richardson William, vict. Shoulder of
    Mutton
Simpson Wm. keeper of ferry
Snare Wm. bricklayer
Stead Thos. blacksmith and farrier
Wheatley Richard, vict. Buck, brewer
    and maltster
*Carriers,* Wm. Bacchus & Thos. Shilletoe, to York every Sat. the latter
    to Tadcaster every Wednesday.

ASKHAM BRYAN, (P.) 4 miles S.
W. of York. The church is an ancient
structure, the living is a vicarage, the
present incumbent Rev. R. S. Thompson; here is also a Methodist chapel,
and an endowed school. Pop. 377.

Champlay Robert, gentleman
Fawcett Misses
Preston D. Esq.

Preston Rev. J. D., A. M.
Wright Rev. Geo. curate and classical
   seminary

| *Blacksmiths,* | Jackson Wm. |
|---|---|
| Allan John | Jackson John |
| Douthwaite John | Knapton Thomas |
| *Butchers,* | Morley Thomas |
| Brown John | Pinder J. Hag farm |
| Dunnington Wm. | Ridsdale Samuel, |
| *Corn Millers,* | Marsh farm |
| Gilson Wm. | Thompson Wm. |
| Leedle Wm. | East farm |
| *Farmers,* | *Grocers, &c.* |

Baker G. Mill farm   Firth John
Brown William, Manstead Luke
  West farm      *Shoemakers,*
Carr John       Beck John.
Dunnington Thos. Stephenson Wm.
Fearby John

Allom John, vict. Red Lion
Cooper Geo. parish clerk
Jackson Wm. schoolmaster
Kilner Wm. joiner and wheelwright
Smooton Sarah, vict. Bay Horse
Vincent Wm. tailor and shopkeeper
Viner Mordecai, gardener

*Carrier*—John Todd, to York and
Angram, every Saturday

ASKHAM RICHARD, (P.); 5 miles
SW. of York. The church here is a
neat ancient structure, there is also a
newly erected Methodist chapel. Population 349.

Chevers Thomas, gentleman
Fearby Jonathan, yeoman
Russell John, gentleman
Swann Robert, Esq. Askham hall

| *Bricklayers,* | Jackson Wm. sen. |
|---|---|
| Buckle Thomas | Jackson Wm. jun. |
| Dalton John | Lightfoot John |
| *Farmers,* | *Shoemakers,* |
| Hick William | Buckle Edward |
| Hudson Thomas | Micklewood Thos. |
| Hudson William | |

Allan Benj. tanner and farmer
Duce Wm. vict. Black Swan
Empson Dealtry, gardener
Gatherbill John, corn miller
Hopwood Miles, vict. Rose & Crown
Kendrick John, blacksmith
Nottage James, butcher and farmer
Schark John, schoolmaster
Spence John, tailor
Webster John, tailor and draper
Westmoreland Geo. mill & wheelwright

*Carrier,*-John Todd to York every Sat.

BICKERTON, in the parish of Bilton; 4 miles NE. of Wetherby. Population 149.

| *Farmers,* | Parker Wm. |
|---|---|
| Clark J. Lincroft | Powell Robert |

Wardle Ann     Webster John
Webster Thomas   Webster Andrew
Webster Anthony
Bellerby Thos. butcher & shopkeeper
Burnley John, joint overseer of the poor
Dixon Robert, toll bar keeper
Hill John, blacksmith and victualler
   Blacksmiths' Arms
Potter Thos. wheelwright
Potter Robert, wheelwright
Potter Wm. tailor and shopkeeper
Webster Anthony, tailor, Mossy carr
Young Wm. vict. Half Moon

BILBROUGH, (P.) 6 miles SW. of
York. In the church here are deposited the remains of Thomas Lord Fa-
fax, first Lord of Denton, and his lady
commemorating the burial place of
this distinguished warrior. Here is a
school endowed with £15 per annum
for teaching 22 poor children the common rudiments of education. Pop. 20

Todd Matthew, Esq.

Thompson Rev. R. vicar of Askham
   Richard, & curate of Askham Bryan
Holdsworth Roger, yeoman
Jackson Mary, gentlewoman
Lambe Ellen, gentlewoman
Lambe Rev. Thomas, curate
Rennison Robert, yeoman
Robson John, yeoman, Normans

| *Farmers,* | Jackson John |
|---|---|
| Colbeck Robert | Wyrill Wm. |
| Dickinson Thos. | *Shoemakers,* |
| Dodgson Henry | Powell Thos. |
| Ingle Thomas | Wilson Charles |

Dickinson John, wheelwright
Dobson Ann, straw hat manufacturer
Jackson John, butcher
Robinson Richard, schoolmaster
Ward Richard, gamekeeper
Waring James, shopkeeper
Wright Robert, vict. Hare
Wright Robert and Sons, blacksmiths
   and farriers

*Carrier*—Robert Bootland, to York
   every Saturday

BILTON, (P.) in the liberty of St.
Peter's; 5 miles ENE. of Wetherby.
The church is a small edifice, of Saxon
architecture, which is dedicated to St.
Helen. Here is a small school, en-
dowed by the late Hall Plumer, Esq.
Population 223.

Kearey Rev. William, vicar
Jessop Rev. Thomas, curate

| *Farmers & Yeomen,* | Fawcett Geo. |
|---|---|
| Acomb Quintin | Greaves Wm |
| Bew John | Lumley Richard |
| Cattley John | Rayson Edward |

Skilbeck Thos.    Wilson Francis,
Stubbs Henry     Wharton lodge
              Wilson John, Sin-
               nithwaite

Bootland John, boot & shoe maker
Fletcher John, schoolmaster
Jackson Hannah, vict. Chequers
Jowitt James, mole and rat catcher
Milner Geo. Bilton park
Parker Geo. tailor

*Carriers* — Hannah Jackson and H.
    Stubbs, to York, every Saturday

BISHOPTHORPE, anciently St.
Andrew's Thorp, (P.); 3 miles S. of York.
The palace of the Archbishop of York, built
by Walter de Grey, in the early part of the
thirteenth century, is situated here. Since
that time the house has undergone several
reparations by the succeeding Archbishops.
The gardens contiguous to the palace were
laid out almost wholly at the expense of
Archbishop Sharp: and the house received
great alterations from Archbishops Dawes
and Gilbert, but the most considerable improvements were made by Archbishop Drummond. Nor did this prelate confine his
munificence to the palace; he took down and
rebuilt the parish church, dedicated to St.
Andrew, in the year 1766, and adorned it
with a curious window, which was brought,
together with the stone used in building the
gateway in front of the palace, from the castle
of Cawood. There is here a National School,
built in 1815, patronised and supported by
the present Archbishop and his family, of
which Mr. Thomas Richardson is master.
Population, 301.

His Grace the Archbishop of York
Vernon Rev. William V. vicar
Campbell John, gentleman
Raison Richard, yeoman
Rawden Mrs. gentlewoman

*Farmers,*    Clemishaw Thos.
Norfolk Thomas, Hewison Richard
  odd house    Stead Thos.
Pickering M.    *Shoemakers,*
Wade Henry    Harrison Jas. sen.
  *Gardeners,*    Harrison Jas. jun.
Challenger Ann    Rawling Benjamin

Barnfather Wm. farmer to His Grace
Challenger Ann, vict. Grey Mare
Davies Mary, coal merchant
Henley John, house steward to His
  Grace
Hodgson Wm. gardener to the vicar
Jackson Wm. gardener to His Grace
Latham William, joiner
Leafy John, parish clerk
March James, tailor
Richardson Thos. schoolmaster
Richmond Mary, blacksmith

Wade James, butcher, farmer, vict. &
  perpetual constable and overseer,
  Brown Cow
Wright William, wheelwright
The *Humber Steam Packet*, to York
  and Gainsbro', weekly
*Carriers*—to York & Appleton, every
  Saturday

BOLTON-PERCY, (P.) 3¾ miles
ESE. of Tadcaster. The church here,
which is one of the neatest in the county,
was built by Thomas Parker, who died in
the year 1423, in the windows are thirty-
three coats of arms, beautifully stained on
glass, and in a good state of preservation,
also in the large window in the choir five
whole length figures. Amongst the testa-
mentary burials in this church are William
Fairfax, 1514; Sir William Fairfax, 1557;
John Vavasour, 1559; Gabriel Fairfax, 1582;
Ferdinando Lord Fairfax, 1648.—Pop. 238.

The Rev. Archdeacon Markham, rector
Clement Mrs. gentwn. Bolton lodge

*Butchers,*    Hodgson Stephen
Green Wm.    Houseman Henry
Wilkinson Thos.    Kilby Thomas
  *Farmers,*    Leedle Thomas
Bean Richard    Stothard John
Beanland John,    Yates John

Appleyard John, shoemaker
Gill George, parish clerk
Head William, blacksmith
Hewson Hannah, schoolmistress
Jeff Thomas, wheelwright
Mollett Thomas, vict. Crown.
  *Carrier.*—T. Shilletoe, to Tadcas-
ter and Appleton every Wednesday.

*Boston,* West-riding, parish of
Bramham, wap. of Barkston Ash.—
See Thorp Arch.

CATTERTON, in the parish of
Tadcaster, 2 miles NNE. of Tadcas-
ter. Pop. 68.
*Farmers,*    Lund Wm.
Cass John    Midlam Thomas
Hasley Benjamin Powell Richard
Jackson John    Powell James

COLTON, in the parish of Bolton
Percy; 4 miles ENE. of Tadcaster.
Here is a small school endowed with
£6 per annum.
Morritt J. B. S. Esq.

*Farmers,*    Ridsell Francis,
Atkin Thomas    Hagg house
Bootland Joseph    Swale Solomon
Copley John    Swale Robert,
Crowder Richard    Brecks house
Dalton Richard    *Flax-dealers,*
Kilby Wm.    Atkin Edward
Marshall John    Marshall John
               Mason Wm.

Arthur George, hardware dealer
Berry John, master of the free school
Dalton J. grocer
Forth James, boot & shoe maker
Jackson Thomas, vict. Star
Morley Robert, butcher
Simpson James, grocer
Spence Thomas, blacksmith
Wheatley John, wheelwright.

*Carriers.*—Dalton and Simpson to York every Saturday.

COPMANTHORPE, in the parish of St. Mary, Bishop-hill the younger, York, and a part in the liberty of St. Peter's; 4 miles SSW. of York. Here is a chapel of ease, and a neat Methodist chapel, also a small school, endowed with £4 per ann. for the teaching of eight poor children. Pop. 281.

| *Butchers,* | Hobson John, jun. |
|---|---|
| Braham Thomas | Greenland |
| Harrison Richard | Lazenby John, |
| *Farmers,* | Davies straits |
| Bateman John | Wade James |
| Bateman T. sen. | Wade Thomas |
| Bond hills | Woodcock Wm. |
| Bateman T. jun. | *Shoemakers,* |
| Dickinson James | Harrison Thos. |
| Hobson Wm. | Hudson Wm. |
| Hobson John, sen. | Webster John |

Benson John, tailor
Dykes David, portable thrashing machine maker and worker
Kilner Thomas, wheelwright
Kirkman John, gardener
Morley John, blacksmith and vict. Royal Oak
Simpson John, bricklayer
Smith John, schoolmaster
Taylor John, game keeper.

*Carrier.*—Wm. Whincup, to York every Saturday.

DRING-HOUSES, in the parishes of St. Mary, Bishop-hill the elder, Holy Trinity and Acomb, liberty of St. Peter's; 1¼ miles SSW. of York. A pleasant village, in which is a chapel of ease, the property of A. S. Barlow, Esq. Pop. 156.

Beal Thomas, Esq. and chief constable for the lower division of the Ainsty
Cooper William, gentleman
Darbyshire George, gentleman
Noddings Rev. Wm.

| *Farmers,* | Calvert Matthew |
|---|---|
| Archer Samuel | Johnson Nath. |
| Ellis Wm. | Leaberry Matthew |
| Hick Robert | Rhodes Ann |
| *Gardeners* | Stead Wm. |
| Bellerby Robert | Wright Sarah |

Bookless David, vict. Cross Keys Inn

Brown Wm. wheelwright
Calvert Wm. tailor
Dalby James, brick and tile maker, surveyor of the York and Tadcaster road
Ellis Robert, butcher
Leafe Benjamin, vict. Fox Inn
Mountain Benjamin, shopkeeper
Stubbs Joshua, herdsman to Knavesmire and Hobmoor stray.

EASDIKE, in the parish of Whixhill; 1¼ mile NW. of Tadcaster.
Thomlinson Matthew, yeoman

HEALAUGH, (P.) 3 miles N. Tadcaster. Here was, in the reign of King John, an hermitage in the wood, which afterwards, in 1218, became a convent of regular black canons, established and dowed by Jordan de St. Maria, and Alice his wife. At the time of the dissolution here were fourteen canons, who had revenues to the value of 72l. 10s. 7d. per annum. This monastery was granted, in 1540, to James Gage, and afterwards came into possession of Sir Arthur Darcy, knight. The church, dedicated to St. John the Evangelist, is a neat modern structure, of which the Rev. E. H. Brooksbank is vicar, pleasantly situated upon an eminence. The village is the property of B. Brooksbank Esq. excepting one tenement and a few acres of land. It is beautifully laid out, with gardens in front of all the houses, and a good carriage road runs through the east, which leads from Wetherby to York. Population 191.

Brooksbank B. Esq. Healaugh hall
Skilbeck Matthew, gentleman

| *Farmers,* | Jepson Richard |
|---|---|
| Darby Edward | Skilbeck Robert |

Blackburn James, tailor
Brown John, vict. Bay Horse
Foster Samuel, wheelwright & grocer
Wright Tobias, shoemaker
*Carriers*—to York and Thorp Arch three days per week.

HESSAY, in the parish of Moor Monkton; 6 miles WNW. of York. This village was given to the Abbey of St. Mary, at York, by Osbern de Archis, and continued in their possession till the dissolution. Pop. 161.

| *Farmers & Yeomen,* | Kirk John |
|---|---|
| Agar Wm. | Nottingham Wm. |
| Agar Richard | Nottingham Ann |
| Birkill John | Powell Wm. |
| Fawcett Wm. sen. | Skilbeck George |
| Fawcett Wm. jun. | Stead Robert |
| Horseley Thos. | Wilson James |

Benson Jonathan, tailor
Birkitt John, shopkeeper

Fowler John, wheelwright
Hey James, blacksmith
Hick Matthew, schoolmaster
Lorryman Wm. vict. Wheat Sheaf
Marston John, linen weaver, &c.
Whitehead Charles, shoemaker

HOLDGATE, in the parish of Acomb, & liberty of St. Peter's; 1 m. SW. of York. In this rural retreat, so well suited to his studying habits, resides the scholar and philanthropist, Mr. Lindley Murray. Pop. 83.

Bownas Mrs. Martha, ladies' boarding school
Hebden Wm. farmer
Hodgson Ralph, gardener
Hoop Joseph, vict. Cross Keys
Jackson John, gentleman
Jenkins Mary, vict. Blue Ball
Sharp R. Hey, architect
Sharp Mary, gentlewoman
Waud George, corn miller

*Hornington*, in the parish of Bolton Percy; 2¾ miles ESE. of Tadcaster.

HUTTON-WANSLEY, in the parish of Long Marston; 6 miles N. of Tadcaster. Pop. 125.
Willoughby Mrs. Eleanor, Hutton hall

| *Farmers,* | Sellers Thomas |
|---|---|
| Acomb Joseph | Smith Elizabeth |
| Allan Benj. | Snowden Arthur, |
| Clark Benjamin, | Marston lodge |
| Grange | Walton Wm. |
| Paver Richard | Wray Wm. |

Adkin Lucy, grocer & vict. Grey Hound
Allan Joseph, tanner
Garland John, bricklayer, &c.

KNAPTON, in the parish of Acomb, & Holy Trinity; 3 miles W. of York. Population 137.
Burton Jonathan, vict. and grocer, Red Lion
Duding Michael, shoemaker

| *Farmers,* | Taylor John, sen. |
|---|---|
| Burton John | Taylor John, jun. |
| Day Ann | Thompson Thos. |
| Goulden Richard | Triffit John |
| Parker Aaron | Wood George |

MARSTON †LONG, (P.) 7 miles W. of York, 6 of Tadcaster, and 7 from Wetherby. Near this village is the field called "Marston Moor:" the tomb of the royalists' hopes, in the contest between Charles I. and the parliament.* The church, which is dedicated to All Saints, is an ancient rectory, and in the year 1400 a commission was granted to the parishioners,

* See Vol. II, p. 32.

because their old church was ruinous and far distant from their habitations, to translate the same from that place to another chapel, in the same parish, and there to build themselves a new parish church, provided that they kept enclosed the cemetry where the old church stood. There is at Marston a free school, endowed with 10l. per annum. Pop. 388.

Crigan Rev. Dr. Alexander, rector
Walton Matthew, yeoman

| *Blacksmiths,* | Mason James |
|---|---|
| Briggs John | Paver Wm. |
| Waite Wm. | Seller Esther |
| *Cattle Dealers,* | Snowden Arthur |
| Coatés Wm. | Wright Robert |
| Ripley Wm. | *Grocers,* |
| *Farmers,* | Gill Charles |
| Acomb Thomas | Jefferson Geo. |
| Acomb Abbey | Vevers Robert |
| Acomb Jane | Wikeley Geo. |
| Bootland Thomas | *Shoemakers,* |
| Clark Benjamin | Bootland Richard |
| Dawson John | Brown Thomas |
| Furniss Wm. | Dickinson Wm. |
| Grainger John | Dickinson Robert |
| Hardcastle Wm. | Wikeley Geo. |
| Hudson Thos. | *Tailors,* |
| Kaye Wm. | Whitehead Wm. |
| Lamb Joseph | Whitehead James |

Briggs Joseph, vict. Three Horse Shoes
Clayton Edward, schoolmaster
Fryer William, whitesmith
Mawson Thomas, saddler
Simpson Mary, vict. Half Moon
Steel John, vict. Board
Styan John, butcher
Wakefield Elizabeth, vict. Board
Wakefield Thos. carpenter, &c.
Waite Wm. carrier to York, Tuesday and Saturday
*Wharfdale Coach,* to Liverpool at 7 mg. to York at 9 evg.

MIDDLETHORPE, in the parish of St. Mary, Bishophill the elder; 2 miles S. of York. Pop. 44.
Breaty Christopher, Esq. Manor house
Stourton Lady Mary, Middlethorpe hall
Hewison Geo. gardener
Smallwood Geo. vict. Board, farmer and cattle dealer

*Moathouse*, in the parish of Wighill; 3 miles NW. of Tadcaster.

MOOR MONKTON, (P.) 8 miles NW. of York, a small village, situated on the banks of the river Nidd, anciently belonging to the family of the Ughtreds, but has for several centuries belonged to that of the Slingsbys. Sir Thomas Slingsby, Bart. is the present lord of this manor. The church is an ancient neat structure, situated about half a mile from the village, on the road leading to Hessay; incumbent the Rev, Thomas Beckwith. Here is a good school-house, founded by Sir Thomas Slingsby, for twelve poor children. *Red House*, built by Sir Henry Slingsby, in the reign of Charles I. is situated in this parish, and from the terrace is a fine view of York, its cathedral, and surrounding country. Population, 269.

*Farmers,*
Cass Wm.
Coates John, Rec-
  tory house
Coupland John
Deighton Eliz.
  Laund house
Hare Joseph
Hopps Richard
Hopps Thos. Red
  house

Kirk John
Kirk Thomas
Morley Sarah
Palfreeman Thos.
Reynolds Thos.
Sampson Samuel,
  Thickpenny nook
Tesseyman Robt.
Walkingham Thos.
Ward Wm.

Coupland John, vict. Board
Hopps Richard, vict. Barley Corn
Hopps Wm. corn miller, Cock hill mill
Kilner Francis, brick maker
May Francis, schoolmaster
Pinder Wm. wheelwright, &c.
Shepherd Thos. black, white and gun smith, manfr. of all kinds of implements of husbandry, thrashing and winnowing machines, &c.
Tesseyman Robert, parish clerk
Tesseyman Chas. shoemkr. & sexton
Tindall Richard, butcher & grocer
Wilson Isaac, tailor & draper
  *Carriers*—James Fewster & Robert Burkill, to York every Saturday.

OXTON, in the parish of Tadcaster; 1¼ mile SE. of Tadcaster. Population, 66.
J. W. Clough, Esq. Oxton hall
Cuttle Lieut. Harman
Fretwell Ann, gentlewoman
Wilkinson Matthew, farmer, Ouston
Varley John, gardener, &c.

POPPLETON (Nether,) (P.); 4 miles NW. of York, is pleasantly situated on the banks of the river Ouse. The church is a neat ancient structure, the living is under the patronage of the Archbishop of York, the present incumbent the Rev. T. Gilpin. Here is a school and house for the master, endowed with 10l. per annum, conducted upon Dr. Bell's plan. Pop. 254.
Gilpin Rev. Thomas, vicar
Gould Thomas, gentleman
Richardson Thomas, gentleman
Spence Isaac, Esq. Poppleton Villa
*Farmers & Yeomen,* Cartwright Benj.
Cartwright Thos.  Poppleton moor

Hawkins J. & W. Whitehouse
  Ruddings  Whitehouse
Prince Wm.  *Shopkeepers,*
Richardson Robt. Fairbourn Robt.
Richardson W. jun. Rider Joseph
Richardson Thos.  *Wheelwrights,*
Sampson Wm. jun. Richardson
Stout John  Richardson J.
Warnford Richard
Atkinson Wm. vict. Fox
Groves John, tailor
Hairsine Thos. schoolmaster
Hodgson Peter, vict. Red Lion
Lupton John, blacksmith & ferry
Richardson Robt. lime & coal
Rider Joseph, shoemaker
Taylor John, vict. Lord Nelson
Tindall Richard, butcher

POPPLETON, (Upper) in the parishes of Lower Poppleton and St. the Younger, York, in the Liberty Peter's; 4 miles NW. of York. There were formerly in the possession Abbot of St. Mary's, at York; Osbern de Arches, to that abbey, its first institution. Sir Thomas Wid-ton writes, that there was a Mayor killed at Poppleton, in the reign Richard II. as he conjectures, in some troversy betwixt the monks and the Here is a small chapel of Ease, with the privilege of christenings and but not marriages, and a Methodist This village is pleasantly situated with mile of the river Ouse. Pop. 346.

Forrest Rev. R. curate
Hall Christopher, gentleman
Harrison Robert, gentleman
Isles Mary, gentlewoman
  *Blacksmiths,*  Nelson Wm.
Cullingworth Jph. Prince John
Lupton Christr.  Richardson
*Farmers & Yeomen,* Richardson
Agar Wm.  Taylor Robt
Buck Wm.  Whitehouse
Carr Robert  Wilkinson J.
Dalton Wm.  *Grocers,*
Duffield Robert  Cundall Jos.
Dutton Thos.  Groves Ann
Fearby John  *Shoemakers,*
Hawkin Geo.  Edon Thos.
Hill John  Whitehouse
Kirk Robert  *Tailors,*
Leadley Thos.  Groves Wm.
Nelson John  Groves Joseph
Nelson Robert
Edon Thos. vict. White Horse, parish clerk
Gray Robert, bricklayer
Hawkes J. gardener
Marston Wm. schoolmaster
Pinder Wm. wheelwright

Preston Edw. vict. Lord Collingwood
Wilkinson Joseph, butcher

RUFFORTH or Rughford, (P.) 5 miles W. of York; a discharged vicarage, of which Mrs. Thompson is the patroness. Population 305.

Rev. Jonas Thompson, vicar
Rev. W. L. Pickard, M. A. perpetual curate
Rev. Robert Swann, B. A. curate

Farmers & Yeomen,
Blackburn Joseph
Brown Jonathan
Clough E. Grange
Dodsworth John
Ellis Elizabeth
Hessell T. Grange
...gate John
...son Wm.
...son Mary
...ly John
...bert James
Mountain Wm.

Siddall John
Theakston Geo.
Thompson Joseph
Ward Wm. Grange
Webster Andrew
Webster Wm.
Schoolmasters,
Cartwright Wm.
Mitchell Wm.
Shoemakers,
Piper Geo.
Scott James

Cammidge Robt. carpenter & grocer
Siddall Thomas, vict. New Inn
Smith Wm. butcher
Thompson Robert, blacksmith and victualler, Buck
Vincent Geo. tailor
Wilstrop Robert, corn miller

Stegglethorpe, in the parish of Moor Monkton; 6 miles NW. of York.

Shurkirk, in the parish of Kirk Hammerton; 7 m. NE. of Wetherby.

SKIPBRIDGE, in the parishes of Moor Monkton and Nun Monkton; 8 miles WNW. of York. A small hamlet on the banks of the river Nidd, over which there is a good stone bridge, of three arches, erected about thirty-four years ago.

Atkinson Richard, farmer & butcher, Gowland
Atkinson Joseph, toll bar keeper
Calver Mary, farmer, Skipbridge lane
Fletcher Wm. vict. & farmer, New Inn

STEETON, in the parish of Bolton Percy, 3 miles ENE. of Tadcaster, for some ages has been the seat of the truly ancient and honourable family of Fairfax, and it is now enjoyed by a younger branch of his family, Thomas Luddington Fairfax, of Newton, Esq. being the present possessor. Population 83.

Mollett Benj. farmer, Steeton hall
Robinson Thomas, farmer and cattle dealer, Bowbridge house
Swindon Geo. farmer, Steeton Low moor
Todd Christr. farmer, Steeton Grange

STREETHOUSES, in the parishes of Bolton Percy and Bilbrough, 3 miles N E. of Tadcaster. This hamlet took its name from its vicinity to the Roman road from York to Tadcaster. All the Roman roads being firmly paved with stone, were called streets, as Watling street, &c. Stratum is the word made use of by the venerable Bede, quite through his work, to denote a Roman road.

Middleton John, farmer & victualler, Wild Man
Ramsison Thomas, farmer

Synnigthwaite, (extra parochial) 4 miles E. of Wetherby. Formerly there was a priory at this place, founded by Bertram Haget, about the year 1160, for nuns of the Cistercian order. Catharine Foster, the fourteenth and last prioress, surrendered the convent in 1534, at which time the annual revenue amounted to £62. 6s. The site was granted in the year 1539, to Sir Thos. Tempest, Knight. The century before the dissolution of this priory, Geoffry, Archbishop of York, took the nuns under his protection, and denounced a malediction against those who should dare to wrong them, and a blessing on their benefactors.

THORP ARCH and BOSTON, (P.) 3 miles SE. of Wetherby. Though situated in different divisions of the county, these two places are so closely connected as to form only one village. The river Wharf runs with a rapid stream through this delightful place, and the cascade seen through the arches of the bridge, with the church and houses embosomed in wood, on the banks of the river, afford a rich and varied landscape that can scarcely be excelled. In the year 1744 John Shires, an inhabitant of the village, while cutting brushwood on the banks of the river, accidentally discovered at this place a mineral spring, which, by its medicinal qualities, has tended to bring Thorp-Arch into considerable repute. This water, when taken fresh from the pump, has a limpid, sparkling appearance, saline taste, and a slight sulphureous smell. It is possessed of purgative and diuretic virtues, and contains a small quantity of inflammable air, generated from iron. The late DR. WALKER, of Leeds, an eminent physician, from whom we quote, submitted this water to a variety of experiments, in the year 1784, the result of which show that it contains inflammable air, fixed air, and muriatic salt, in the proportion of one ounce to a gallon; calcareous earth and selenitical earth, sixteen grains together in a gallon; and a small quantity of iron suspended by fixed air. As the proportion of salt which it contains is considerably less than that in the Harrogate water, it is taken in larger doses. The principles which compose Thorp-Arch water give it a superiority over Harrogate water in general relaxation, bilious disorders, glandular obstructions, and scirrhosities, stomach complaints, and spontaneous vomitings. Harrogate water is to be preferred in cutaneous diseases, the piles, rheumatism, worms, ulcers, and probably in the stone and gravel. In many other cases the medical virtues of the two waters appear to be nearly equal.— The chalybeate water of Thorp-Arch pretty much resembles that of other chalybeate springs; but the air here is of uncommon purity, and many have experienced its good effects who have scarcely tasted the medicinal waters. The accommodations at this fashionable watering place are extremely good; in addition to three capital inns there are a considerable number of lodging houses, suited to the various circumstances and condition of the visitors. Thorp-Arch is supposed to derive the latter part of its name from the family of D'Archis, who came in with the Conqueror, and had large possessions in these parts. The church, which is dedicated to All Saints, was ordained a vicarage by Archbishop Sewall, in 1258, but in the early part of the last century the living was only of the yearly value of £24, till, by the liberality of the Rev. Mr. Robinson, of Leeds, and Lady Elizabeth Hastings, added to a donation from Queen Ann's fund, and a contribution from the Rev. Mr. Wetherherd, vicar, the tythes were purchased as an augmentation to the living. The present church is a beautiful structure, of which the Earl of Huntingdon is the patron, and the Rev. Robert Hemington the incumbent. All the houses in Boston are of modern erection; it is said that the first house built in this division of the village was erected by the late Mr. Joseph Taite, in the year 1753, and that Mr. Samuel Taite, the gentleman who contributed the land upon which the episcopal chapel in that place was erected, seven years ago, was the first person born in Boston.— There is here a charity school, founded by Lady Elizabeth Hastings, and a neat Methodist Chapel. The population, with Clifton included, is 1360, namely, Thorp-Arch 343, Boston 677, and Clifton 340.†

*Post-Office.*—Letters are conveyed to Thorp Arch and Boston from Wetherby every morning. John Smith, the letter carrier, arrives at 10 o'clock, and returns immediately after circulating the letters.

† Erroneously stated in Vol. I. at 1017.

Those marked thus * are residents in Thorp Arch and those without the mark in Boston.

Atkinson Rev. Wm. M. A. Holborn
* Atkinson Miss, gentlewoman
Bainbridge Henry, surgeon, Moor end
*Baker Rev. John, L.L.B. vicar of All Saints
Banks Wm. white and wine cooper, dish turner, and basket maker, Moor end
*Bateson Joseph, dish turner and cooper
*Beverley Charles, butcher
Birdsall Sarah, grocer, Holborn
Boddington Rev. Thos. gentlemen seminary, Holborn
Boothby Mrs. Mary, lodging house, Holborn
Bownas Thos. gent. Clifford street
Broadley Mrs. gentlewoman, Holborn
Brown James, blacksmith, Clifford street
Brownrigg Rev. Thos. perpetual curate of Boston
Burnell John, brazier & tinner, Clifford street
Burnley Jonathan, corn miller, Low Mill, Holborn
Chippendale Abraham, joiner and cabinet maker, chapel street
Clark Thomas, boot & shoe maker
Clark Stephen, gardener, Moor end
Clark John, Esq. Holborn
*Clarkson Thomas, millwright
*Cullingworth Henry, grocer & draper
Dalby Wm. grocer & draper, Holborn
Dalby Eliz. dress maker, Holmes st.
Day Wm. lodging house, Holborn
Day John, stone mason, Holborn
Day Wm. stone mason, Holborn
Dixon Miss Mary, gentlewoman, Holborn
Easterby Mary, lodging house, Clifford street
Ellis Thos. grocer & draper, Holborn
Farra Thos. tailor & draper, Holborn
Farrer John, vict. Red Lion Hotel, Holborn
Farrer John, butcher, Holborn
Foster John, boot & shoe maker, Clifford street
Gatliffe Wm. gent. Holborn
*Gibbon Stephen, farmer
*Gibbon Thomas, farmer
*Gossip Colonel Randal
Gossip Mrs. Joanna, gentwn. Holborn
Green S. ladies' boarding school, Holborn
Hassalwood Wm. joiner, &c. Clifford street
Hawes Richard, tailor, Holmes street
Hawes Mary, baker and confectioner, Holmes street.

Hebden Mrs. Sarah, gentwn. Holborn
*Hornshaw John, farmer
*Huddleston Isaac, corn miller and farmer, Flint Mill
Hutchinson Mrs. Elizabeth, gentlewn. Holborn
Jackson Joseph, excise officer
Johnson Mrs. gentlewoman, Holborn
*King Miss, straw bonnet maker
Lamb Mrs. Betty, lodging house
Marshall Miss, gentlewoman, Holborn
*Mason Thomas, farmer
*Maud Michael, flax spinning mill
M'Kenzie George Smith, gent. Holborn
Mountain Wm. joiner and carpenter, Clifford street
Moverley Wm. fishmonger, Holborn
Nixon Thomas, (gentlemen's boarding school) Holborn
Nottingham John, gent. Holborn
Oldfield Miss Rachael, gentlewoman, Holborn
Paddy Thos. John, gent. Holborn
*Parbery Richard, farmer
Peacup Rev. John, Moor end
Pearson Rosamond, school mistress, Clifford street
Pease T. B. merchant, Briggate
Perfect Grosvenor, Esq. Holborn
Pickards James, tailor and draper, Chapel street
*Poole Mrs. gentlewoman
Powell Thos. vict. Rose and Crown, Holborn
Palfrey Robert, maltster, Holborn
Raynar Thos. tailor, grocer & draper, Holborn
Read Thomas, gent. Holborn
Reed Mrs. (ladies' boarding and day school) Holborn
Richmond Mark, gardener, Moor end
Riddale Ann, dress maker, Spa
Shann Misses, gentlewomen, Holborn
Sharrow Richard, boot & shoe maker, Holborn
Shaw Thos. joint surveyor of Clifford high ways
Shillito Geo. vict. Star, *Bramham*
Skilbeck Mrs. Elizabeth, gentlewmn. *Clifford*
Spink Benj. shoe maker and hair dresser, Briggate
Stourton Hon. Edward Marmaduke, Holborn
Strickland Geo. Esq. Chesnut grove
Taite Wm. gent. Clifford street
Taite Joseph, gent. Briggate
*Thackray John and Horner, corn millers and farmers, Thorp mills
Thomas John, gent. Holborn
*Thurlwell John, stone mason
*Thurlwell Wm. stone mason
*Thurlwell Stephen, stone mason

Tireman Richard, attorney Holborn
Tricket Wm. schoolmaster and parish clerk
Turner John, wheelwright, &c.
Waddington Joseph, yeoman, *Clifford*
Waddington William Lee, yeoman, *Clifford*
Wells John, vict. Admiral Hawke, Holborn
*Wharton Matthew, blacksmith and farrier
*Wharton Elizabeth, grocer & draper
Wharton Joseph, blacksmith & farrier, Clifford street
Wilkinson Samuel, linen draper, hosier, &c. Holborn
Wilkinson Geo. Esq. Holborn
Wilkinson Rev. F. M.A. Holborn
Williamson Nancy, linen draper and dress maker, &c. Chapel street
*Wood and Dunwell, manufacturers of brown, coloured, and glazed paper, millboards, &c. oil millers, (logwood ground, and oil cake crushed)
Wright Mrs. Mary, gentwn. Holborn

*Coaches.*—ALEXANDER *Diligence*, to Leeds, from Mr. John Farrer's, Red Lion, Boston, every Tuesday and Saturday, at 7 morning, returns at 7 in the evening.

*Carriers.*—Joseph Jagger, to York every Tuesday and Saturday, to Leeds every Thursday. & Wetherby daily.— John Lockart, to York every Wednesday, and to Leeds every Saturday.

TOCKWITH, in the parish of Bilton, 7½ miles N. of Tadcaster. At the commencement of the memorable battle of Marston Moor, in the year 1644, the front of the Parliament's army extended from the North end of Marston Moor to this village, a distance of nearly 3 miles.* Here is a small neat Methodist chapel, built in the year 1796, and a Sunday school for 100 children. Population 436.

| *Farmers & Yeomen,* | Wilks S. P. |
|---|---|
| Fowler Joseph | Wilstrop John |
| Hastings Timothy | *Blacksmiths,* |
| Hopwood Joshua | Sharpney John |
| Lazenby Wm. | Wilson Robert |
| Norfolk Thos. | *Brewers & Maltsters* |
| Norfolk James | Abbey Richard |
| Ripley Timothy, | Brogden Robt. |
| Cowthorp moorside | *Butchers,* |
| | Gaunt Richard |
| Spink John, Nether Carr | Thomlinson Benj. |
| | *Earthenware Dlrs,* |
| Tennant Henry, | Gray Wm. |
| Skew Kirk | Ward Thomas |
| Thomlinson Matt. | |

* See page 32.

*Grocers, &c.*
Cartwright Thos.
Lowcock Isabella
Ripley John
Upton Wm.

*Shoemakers,*
Andrews Richard
Bellerby Wm.
Gill John
Nicholson Wm.

*Tailors, &c.*
Bates Joseph
Helmsley Wm.
Thackray Thos.

*Tanners,*
Thomlinson Wm.
Wilks S. P.

*Wheelwrights,*
Chapman Henry
Chapman James, (joiner)

Barrass Thomas, plumber, &c.
Cordukes Richard, surgeon
Fletcher Moses, vict. Bay Horse
Flockton Ann, vict. Blue Bell
Groves J. C. brick and tile maker
Hastings Edw. schoolmaster
Head Wm. tinner and brazier
Sanderson Wm. cooper
Scarbrough Richard, bricklayer
Summerton Edw. vict. Boot & Shoe
Yates John, vict. Spotted Cow

*Carriers*—William Bellerby, to York every Saturday. John Ripley, to Wetherby every Thursday.

WALTON, (P.) 2½ miles E. of Wetherby. This village was long in the possession of the family of Fairfax, but is now the property of G. L. Fox, Esq. Bramham Park, who is lord of the manor. Through this tract of ground runs the great Roman road called Watling street, from the south to the wall now called Redgate. It crossed the Wharf at a place called St. Helen's Ford, near Walton, where formerly stood a chapel, dedicated to St. Helen, the mother of Constantine. The parish church is a very ancient structure. Pop. 247.

Rudd Rev. James, curate

Fisher Charles, gentleman
Goodall Agnes, gentlewoman
Wright Samuel, yeoman

*Farmers,*
Cade James
Farrar Wm.
Farrar Bryan
Hick Wm.
Horner John
Noble Henry
Scott John & Robt.

*Shoemakers,*
Stead Wm.
Tate Bryan

Bentley Michael, wheelwright
Farrar Robert, tailor
Farrar Wm. farmer
Fletcher Jas. swine and cattle dealer
Hick Wm. vict. Black Bull
Pawson Benj. constable
Powell Joseph, vict. Royal Oak, and parish clerk
Smith Samuel, grocer
Whitehead Thomas, blacksmith

WIGHILL, (P.) 3 mls. N. of Tadcaster. The family of Stapleton possessed this estate upwards of 500 years, but it is now the property of Richard Fountayne Wilson, Esq. lord of the manor. The parish church, which is dedicated to All Saints, and of which Mr. Wilson is the patron, and the Rev. T. M. Shann the vicar, is pleasantly situated on a commanding eminence, contiguous to the village. Population 250.

Yorke Richard, Esq. Parkgate
Shann Rev. T. M. vicar
Thompson Samuel, gentleman

*Farmers and Yeomen,*
Dawson John
Milburn Richard
Milburn Marmadk.
Rayson Edward
Stephenson John
Stephenson Jacob
Thomlinson Matt.
Easedike
Thompson John
Warmford Henry,
Lodge
Wood Benj. Park

Easterby Wm. blacksmith and vict. White Swan
Pawson Wm. and Geo. wheelwrights
Prince Francis, boot and shoe maker
Young John, grocer, &c.

*Carriers* to York and Thorp Arch three days per week.

WILSTHORP, (or Wilstrop) in the parish of Kirk Hammerton; 7½ miles WNW. of York. Pop. 95.

*Farmers,*
Easby Richard
Gray Ambler,
Wilsthorpe hall
Richmond Wm.
Royston Henry
Spink Henry
Spink Elizabeth
Wheatley John
Wheatley Eliz.

# EAST RIDING.

*⁎* To render this publication as complete as possible, we have, in each of the parishes of the North and East Ridings, when the information could be had, stated by whom the living is enjoyed, who is the patron, and to what saint the church is dedicated: and similar information relating to the parishes of the West Riding is communicated by a table Appended to this Volume.—See Page 605.

ACKLAM, (P.) in the wap. of Buckrose, and partly in the liberty of St. Peter's; 6½ miles S. of Malton. The parish church, of which the chancellor of York Cathedral is the patron, and the Rev. James Britton the vicar, is dedicated to St. John the Baptist. Here are also a Methodist chapel, and a chapel for the Primitive Methodists. Pop. including Barthorp, 389.

Simpson Rev. John, curate
Gilyard Emanuel, blacksmith
Goodrick William, vict. Half Moon

Carpenters,
Allison Geo,
Heward John

Farmers,
Botterill H. P.
Clarkson Thos.
Coulton R. and T.
Craven Wm.
Dawson Wm.
Ellis James
Gibb Christopher
Hudson Robert
Pape Geo.
Sanderson Robert, (and grocer)

Skelton Robert
Warde John

Shoemakers,
Johnson Edward
Potter William

Stone-masons,
Alderson Jonathan
Foster James
Warde Wm.
Warde John

Tailors,
Fewston Wm.
Herbert Thos.
Theakston Thos.

ADDLETHORPE. See EDDLE-THORPE.

AIKE, part in the parish of Lockington, and part in the parish of St. John of Beverley, wap. of Harthill, division of Bainton Beacon; 5 miles NNW. of Beverley. This village was formerly upon an island, which by draining is now connected with the surrounding country. Pop. 98.

Farmers,
Jackson Wm.
Thursk John

Watson Geo.
Whitaker Wm.

Norris Robert, vict. Board
Plowman John, blacksmith

ALDBROUGH, (P.) in the wap. and liberty of Holderness; 8 miles NE. of Hedon. A flourishing and very lively village pleasantly situated on the declivity of a small eminence, and consists of some elegant and well built houses. The church dedicated to St. Bartholomew, is a large Gothic structure, of which the King is patron, and the Rev. Nicholas Holmes the vicar. In the interior is an ancient circular stone fifteen inches in diameter, commemorating the building of the church, the inscription on which may be translated thus:——ULF COMMANDED THIS CHURCH TO BE ERECTED FOR THE SOULS OF HANUM AND GUNTHARD. Ulf, here mentioned, is supposed to be the same who gave his estate to the church of York, and in this gift was included Aldbrough, where he had a castle, the foundation of which is now entirely levelled. The Roman road from Protorium to Gabrantiessum Sinies, runs through Aldbrough. The following is a copy of an extract from an old history of York, which was lately found here, " York, 1291 1292. Jo. Spear, Mayor." These years the mayoralty was in the king's hands, and Sir John De Malso, or Meaux, was governor of the city, he was a great warrior and tall in stature, as appears from his armour, which is now to be seen in the church of Aldbrough, where he is buried under a stone monument representing him in full length lying, and also the figure of his wife. A Mr. Towry left a quantity of land, the rent arising from which, is distributed to the old and infirm at the discretion of the minister, overseers and churchwardens for the time being, about 20l. of which is appropriated to the education of poor children. Pop. including East and West Newton townships, 996.

Holmes Rev. Nicholas, vicar
Craven Rev. William, curate

N 3

Groves Edward, gentleman
Groves Henry, yeoman
Hall John, Esq.
Moore Peter, yeoman
Stephenson Matthew, yeoman
Stephenson Wm. yeoman
Wilson Mrs. Ann, gentlewoman

*Blacksmiths,*
Cooper Charles
Tarbottom Benj.
(and farrier)
*Bricklayers,*
Anthony John
Foster John
*Butchers,*
Creasser Matthew
Hobson Francis
*Corn Millers,*
King John
Longman John
*Farmers,*
Armstrong Robert
Goldthorp Richd.
Hardy Thos.
Hobson Francis
Hogg Wm.
Longman Robert
Longman Wm.
Smith Geo.
Speck Wm.
Wetherill Charles
Wilson Geo.
Wright Wm.
Wright Francis
Wright Wm. Edw.

*Grocers,*
Johnson Edward
Mainprize John
Robinson Thos.
Scupham Widow
*Schoolmasters,*
Harmery Robert
Stamford Joseph
*Shoemakers,*
Barritt John
Brook John
Dunn Wm.
Jackson John
Marshall Mark
*Surgeons, &c.*
Clark John
Simons James
*Tailors, &c.*
Johnson John
Lamb Robert
Rawson John
Rispin John
*Wheelwrights,*
Brambridge Robt.
Fewster James
Holmes Thomas
Humble Geo.

Harrison Edward, bailiff
Hodgson Thos. riding excise officer
Leak Wm. vict. George Inn
Ockleton Thos. vict. Bricklayer's Arms
Shields Wm. common brewer
Sissons Wm. joiner and auctioneer
Wadsworth John, hair dresser

*Carriers*—Edward Foster, John Mainprize, James Rogerson, David Wright and Edward Harrison, to Hull, every Tuesday and Friday mornings.

ALLERTHORPE, (P.) in the wap. of Harthill, and liberty of St. Peter's; 2 miles SW. of Pocklington. The church is a very small structure. Population with Waplington, 151.

Addison Rev. James, vicar of Thornton-cum-Allerthorpe, & perpetual curate of Barmby and Fangfoss
Burton Robert, gentleman
Hart John, gentleman
Ireland Wm. yeoman and surveyor of taxes and highways
Stephenson Thomas, yeoman

*Farmers,*
Foster Robert

Giles John
Jackson Thomas

Laverack Geo.
Shaw John, (and cattle dealer)
Cook James, shoemaker
Harrison Richard, vict. Plough
Whitaker John, schoolmaster
Winter Edward, wheelwright

Siddall Charles
Simpson Joseph
Theaker William

ANLABY, in the parishes of North Ferriby, Hessle, and Kirk Ella, wap. and liberty of Hullshire; 5 miles W. of Hull, at the western extremity of the marshy plain in which that town is situated. Is a pleasant village, adorned with several elegant seats. This village formerly belonged to the ancient family of the Anlabys, who derived their name from the manor. In the year 1100 the heiress of that house carried it by marriage into the family of Legard, which family resided here from the conquest, till nearly the close of the last century. Pop. 307.

Barkworth John, gentleman
Bodley Mrs. gentlewoman
Broadley John, solicitor, (South Ella)
Fields Daniel, gentleman
Smith Charles, yeoman
Vause William, gentleman

*Farmers,*
Brocklebank Thos.
Cavill Joseph

Clark John
Clark John
Wood Wm.

Appleton Christopher, bricklayer
Bibbins Wm. corn miller
Kemp Richard, shoemaker
Marshall Richard, blacksmith & vict. Red Lion
Petfield Matthew, carpenter

ARGAM, (Extra-parochial) wap. of Dickering; 4 miles SSE. of Hunmanby. Population 35.

*Farmers,*
Bell Richard

Jordon William
Towers Francis

*Arglam,* in the parish of Holme-on-Spalding-Moor, wap. of Harthill; 7 miles SW. of Market-Weighton.

ARNOLD, in the parishes of Long Riston and Swine, wap. and liberty of Holderness; 7 mls. ENE. of Beverley. Population 101.

Fewson Edward, schoolmaster
Palmer Robert, vict. Board

*Farmers,*
Billany David
Billany William
Carr John
Jackson Robert
Riby Robert

Robinson Benj.
Smith George
Smith Thomas
Taylor William
Walker Thomas
Westerby Christ.

*Carrier*—Thomas Allison, to Hull every Tuesday.

ARRAM, in the parish of Atwick, wap. and liberty of Holderness; 4

miles N. of Beverley. Population included with Atwick.

*Farmers,*
Clark Robert
Gray Wm.
Holmes Wm.
Hunsley John
Londsbrough Rd.

Robinson John
Sargeson John
Taylor Wm.
Walker Jane
Wilkinson Susan

Thorley Joseph, shoemaker
Walker Alexander, machine maker

*Carrier.*—Matthew Wallis, to Beverley every Saturday.

ARRAS, in the parish of Market-Weighton, and wap. of Harthill; 2½ miles E. of Market-Weighton. Population included with Market-Weighton.

Stephenson Wm. farmer
Webster Wm. vict. Buck

ASSELBY, in the parish of Howden, and the wap. and liberty of Howdenshire; 2½ miles W. of Howden. Population, 254.
Cook Thomas, farmer & vict. Board
Levett John, blacksmith
Midgley Francis, carpenter
Morritt Wm. corn miller
Singleton Isaac, shopkeeper
Singleton Wm. yeoman
Taylor Geo. tailor
Wood Wm. schoolmaster

*Farmers,*
Birkett Josiah
Bolden Robert
Dalby Elizabeth
Dales John

Greaves John
Humphrey Matth.
*Shoemakers,*
Pease James
Underwood John

ATWICK, (P.) in the wap. and liberty of Holderness; 2 mls. N. of Hornsea. A small, though pleasant village, situated near the sea, from which it suffers greatly by the encroachments of the water, particularly in stormy weather; the greatest part of this village stands at the junction of three roads, in the centre of which stands an old stone cross, which, in the year 1786, was situated at the distance of thirty-three chains and sixty-three links from the sea, from the rudeness of the structure it appears to be of great antiquity; there is round its base a latin inscription, but rendered unintelligible by the dilapidations of time. The church, of which the King is patron, is a plain Gothic structure, dedicated to St. Lawrence. The Rev. James Wilson is the vicar and surrogate, for the dean and chapter; here is also a Methodist chapel, built in 1821; likewise a public school, endowed with about 30l. per annum, paid out of the several charities of this place. Edward Fenwick, in the year 1689, left by deed one Oxgang of land, situated in Bedford, the

annual rent of which is to be applied to apprenticing poor boys and girls of Atwick, at the discretion of the trustees, of which the minister for the time being is one.— Population, 396.

Bainton Thomas, Esq. Arram-hill
Allman Major, tailor
Appleby Richard, wheelwright
Booth Thomas, schoolmaster
Coates Robert, parish clerk
Lawson Wm. corn miller
Pool Patrick, vict. and blacksmith

*Farmers,*
Challand Charles
Dunn Wm.
Foster Ralph
Gofton Smith
Granger John
Hall Joseph
Hogle George

Wilson Wm.
*Grocers,*
Wilson Wm.
Wright Wm.
*Shoemakers,*
Garton John
Tennison Wm.
Ulliet John

*Carrier.*—William Wilson, to Hull on Tuesdays; departs 2 morning, returns 9 evening. To Beverley every Saturday.

AUBURN, in the parish of Fraisthorpe, and wap. of Dickering; 2½ mls. S. of Bridlington. Population included with Fraisthorpe.

Harper Thomas, farmer

AUGHTON, (P.) in the wap. of Harthill; 8 miles NNW. of Howden. A parochial village and vicarage, the present incumbent of which is the Rev. W. Dean, and —— Mosley the patron. This village was the residence of Robert Aske, who in the year 1536, headed the insurrection called the "Pilgrimage of Grace." Aske is represented in history as a man of daring and enthusiastic courage, a gentleman by birth, and of considerable talents. In the latter part of the reign of Charles 1. Sir Richard Aske was master of the crown office, and one of the council of the regicides.— He appears to have been the last of the family that resided at Aughton. There are no remains of the ancient mansion or castle: but the site is marked by ditches or moats one within another, with the interior vallum raised to a great height, which shows it to have been a place of considerable strength. It is situated near the eastern banks of the Derwent. Population, 289.

*Farmers,*
Allan Richard
Brabbs James, yeoman
Buttle Thomas
Cottam George
Gowthorp James
Lambert Edward
Lawson Emanuel

Maltby Wm.
Steel John
Stephen Wm.
Webster John
Wilkinson Robert
Young Wm.
*Shoemakers,*
Morley Richard
Young George

Coney Richard, blacksmith
Dove John, wheelwright
Wilkinson Robert, tailor
Young Matthew, shopkeeper
Young Thomas, vict. Plough

*Carrier.*—Leonard Fowler, to York every Saturday.

*Aughton Ruddings*, in the parish of Aughton, and wap. of Harthill ; 8 miles N. of Howden.

BABTHORPE, in the parish of Heminbrough, wap. of Ouse and Derwent, and liberty of Howdenshire ; 5 miles ESE. of Selby.

Pulleine Robert, yeoman

BAINTON, (P.) in the wap. of Harthill, and liberty of Holderness ; 6 miles SW. of Great Driffield. Here is an ancient parish church, dedicated to St. Andrew.—The living is a rectory, of the value of 1000*l*. per annum, in the patronage of St. John's College, Oxford, and when vacant is bestowed on the oldest B. D. of the college. The present incumbent is the Rev. John Bell, D. D. There are two chapels here, one belonging to the Wesleyan and the other to the Primitive Methodists. In former times a Beacon was erected near this village, for the purpose of alarming the surrounding country on the approach of danger, and this circumstance has given name to that division of Harthill called Bainton Beacon. William le Gross, a Knight of Malta, and Earl of Albemarle, was buried in this church. Population, 300.

*Farmers.*
Angas Caleb
Hardy Robert
Haycroft Wm. & vict. Bainton New Inn
Layburn Wm. & corn miller
Lee Thomas, yeoman
Oxtoby Christopher yeoman
Simpson Robert
Simpson Henry
Topham Wm.
Skinner Wm.
Wright Thomas

Forge Wm. blacksmith
Hardy Robert, shopkeeper
Hudson Edward, tailor and victualler, Speed the Plough
Usber Richard, schoolmaster

*Carriers*—Robert Wallis, to Driffield every Thu. and Beverley every Sat.—Robt. Cole, to Hull, every Fri.

BALKHOLME, in the parish of Howden, wap. and liberty of Howdenshire ; 2½ mls. E. of Howden. Pop. 105.

*Farmers,*
Andrew Wm.
Harrison John
Laverack John
Laverack Joseph
Levett John
Martin Thos.
Overend Robert
Wheldrake John

BARLBY, in the parish or Heminbrough, wap. of Ouse and Derwent, and liberty of Howdenshire ; 1½ mile NE. of Selby. Population, 349.

Bowman Rev. Thos. assistant curate
Aspinall Elizabeth, gentlewoman
Brewer Thomas, yeoman
Huble Thomas, yeoman
Stringer Joseph, Barlby hall
Weddall Mary, gentlewoman
Weddall Robert, land surveyor, Bank house

*Farmers,*
Blanchard Michael
Newham John
Phillips Geo.
Smallwood Wm.
Taylor Mrs.
*Shoemakers,*
Fish John
Woodall Wm.
*Shopkeepers,*
Smith Thos. (and wheelwright)
Wade Wm.

Burkill Thomas, butcher
Davenport Samuel, tailor
Douglas Wm. brick maker
Foster Wm. vict. Bay Horse
Richardson Geo. blacksmith
Smith John, vict. Plough
Thornton John, schoolmaster
Whitehead Matthew, wheelwright

BARMSTON, (P.) in the wap. and liberty of Holderness ; 6 mls. S. of Bridlington. A pleasant village situated at the northern extremity of Holderness ; it is very near to the North Sea, and is much frequented by the people of the neighbouring villages, who come here to purchase gravel to repair their roads with, which is left in abundance on the shores of Barmston by every tide. The church is a very ancient building, dedicated to All Saints, of which the Rev. John Gilby is rector ; in the interior is a marble monument, representing in full figure a Scotch Lord, in armour, with a griffin at his feet. The nobleman whose memory this monument commemorates was the lord of the manor, which was given to him for his valour and essential services rendered to his country. There are here four alms-houses, or hospitals, erected in 1726, by Sir Griffith Boynton, for the comfort of four poor widows of this place, and endowed with the annual sum of £15. to be divided equally amongst them. There is also a school and master's dwelling-house, built by Sir Francis Boynton, Bart. for the accommodation of the place ; he is lord of the manor, and patron of the living. Population, 205.

Day Thos. vict. Bull and Dog
Denis Wm. grocer and blacksmith
Halder Wm. wheelwright
Pickering William, tailor
Sawdon John, schoolmaster
Watson William, parish clerk

*Farmers,*
Anderson Thos.
Boys Geo.
Dalby Charles
Field John
Gofton John

Harland John
Hyde James
Pennock John
Percy Jeremiah
Welburn Samuel

*Coach,* to Bridlington and Hull, three days per week.

BARNBY-ON-THE-MARSH, in the parish of Howden, wap. and liberty of Howdenshire; 4 miles W. of Howden; situated near the Derwent, which here falls into the Ouse. Here are two extraordinary springs of sulphuric and chalybeate water, denominated St. Peter's and St. Helen's Wells, the former of which is represented to possess the rare virtue of curing scorbutic eruptions by external application. The places of worship are a Chapel of Ease, dedicated to St. Helen, of which the Rev. Ralph Spofforth, vicar of Howden, is incumbent and patron; and a small Methodist chapel; there is also a Free Grammar school for ten boys. The inhabitants of this village have the singular privilege of electing their own pastor; all the male adults (with the exception of paupers) have the right of voting. This place is noted for its manufacture of sacking. There are races held here the last Thursday in June, which continue three successive days. Barnby was granted by William the Conqueror, to forty of his soldiers, each of whom received an Oxgang, or (twenty acres) in the whole eight hundred acres of land, and these Oxgangs still bear the names of their original owners. Population, 525.

Atkinson John, gentleman
De La Noy John, yeoman
Fox Robert, gentleman
Fox Thomas, gentleman
Fox William, yeoman
Holmes Henry, gentleman
Noble Robert, yeoman
Poole Rev. Robert, curate
Smith William, gentleman

*Bricklayers,*
Andrew John
Cobb George
*Butchers,*
Douglas Joseph
Wilson Robert
*Corn-millers,*
Howdle Benjamin
Lamb Robert
*Farmers,*
Atkinson Robert
Battle John
Birkitt Thos.
Brooksbank Thos.
Brown John

Fox Wm. jun.
Hall John
Hind Thomas
Spence John
Stiles Thomas
Turton Thomas
*Sacking Mfrs.*
Chapel Wm.
Thompson John
*Ship Owners,*
Gilderdale Geo.
Wright John
*Shoemakers,*
Johnson Thos.
Middlewood Danl.

Pease Thomas
Wood Thomas
*Shopkeepers,*
Atkinson Mary

Johnson Thomas, (and farmer)
Lamb Robert
Thompson John

*Inns.*
Anchor, Robert Robinson
Bull and Butcher, John Swales
Half Moon, James Norton
Sloop, Wm. Potter, Barnby ferry

Bealby William, tailor
Crosley John, blacksmith
Holdsworth Samuel, lock-keeper
Hord Watson, tailor
Noble John, master mariner
Pycock John, joiner
Thompson R.
Watson Thomas, schoolmaster

*Water Carriage*—Two Packets to Selby, every Mon. at 7 mg. for goods and passengers.

*Carrier*—Thos. Hodgson, to Beverley & Howden, every Saturday.

*Barnby-Moor-Inn,* in the parish of Barnby, and wap. of Harthill; 1½ mile W. of Pocklington. This is a large and commodious inn, where travellers are accommodated with post chaises. It has been kept by its present owner and occupier, Mr. Thomas Heard, thirty-six years. The letter bags to, and from Pocklington, are received and delivered here, and the coaches from York to Hull, make it their house of call.

BARNBY-ON-THE-MOOR, (P.) in the wap. of Harthill, and liberty of St. Peter's; 3 miles W. of Pocklington. It is a perpetual curacy, under the patronage of the Dean of York, and the present incumbent is the Rev. James Addison, the church is dedicated to St. Catharine. This is a place of great antiquity; it was formerly a market-town, and has still one market-day annually, on the Thursday preceding St. Peter's day. The annual feast is kept on the day following. The inhabitants enjoy considerable privileges and immunities, on payment of 6s. to the Dean and Chapter of St. Peter's, such as freedom from toll, &c. Pop. 440.

Cooper Tabitha, gentlewoman
Cross John, gentleman
Goldsbrough Richard, gent.
Hornby Thomas, surgeon
Stephenson Edward, gent.
*Farmers & Yeomen,*
Berryman Wm.
Blanchard Francis
Cook John
Dennis Thos.
Gawtry Thos.
Houlden Matthew
Houlden Thos.
Houlden Wm.
Houlden James
Hudson Richard
Jackson John
Kemp Robert
Leadbeater Richd.
Newby James
Ranson John

closely interwoven with the history of Beverley, was born in that place, in the year 640, about the time of the second introduction of christianity into the North of England, by St. Austin and the Roman missionaries. He was descended of a good family. And after a course of religious education, under St. Hilda, the famous abbess of Whitby, and under Theodose, the 5th archbishop of Canterbury, he became himself, in the year 687, the 5th archbishop of York, under the popular name of St. John of Beverley. His fame for sanctity was so great, that the venerable Bede declares *of his own knowledge*, that the holy man performed many miracles. At length, grown aged and infirm, he resigned his bishoprick to Wilfrid II. in 718, and retired to Beverley, where having lived three years in seclusion, he died on the 7th of May, 721, and was buried in the church porch belonging to that college which he had founded.

In 1188, this church was again destroyed by fire, and upon opening a grave, on the 13th September, 1664, a vault was found in which there was a leaden plate, bearing a Latin inscription, which may be thus rendered:—

"In the year of the incarnation of our Lord, 1188, this church was destroyed by fire, in the night following the feast of St. Matthew, the apostle; in the year 1197, on the 6th of the Ides of March, an inquisition was made for the relics of the blessed John, and the bones were found in the Eastern part of the sepulchre, and here reposited; and dust mixed with mortar was in the same place found, and re-interred."

Subsequently, namely in the year 1726, these relics were again taken up, and deposited in an arched vault prepared for their reception. The pious zeal which shone so conspicuously in the 12th century, soon reinstated the Minster in all its former grandeur, and archbishop Kinsius built the great steeple. In the year 1421, Henry V. after the coronation of Catharine of France, made a pilgrimage to Beverley, because, as the Historians of those times say, a strong report prevailed, that the tomb of St. John of Beverley, sweat blood all the day that the famous battle of Agincourt was fought, and it was imputed to the merits of that saint that this great victory was won.

The dissolution of the Collegiate church of St. John, took place on the 20th of March, 1544, in the 37th year of the reign of Henry VIII. The silent and almost imperceptible dilapidations of time, had in five centuries brought the Minster at Beverley, into a state of ruinous decay, and in the year 1710, a considerable sum of money was raised by a general brief, and by individual donations, with which sum it was re-edified and adorned; the choir was paved with marble of various colours; a magnificent arch, curiously engraved was raised over the altar, under which was placed a table of fine white marble; the large East window was decorated with rich painted glass, collected from the other windows, amongst which are the twelve apostles. Since that time, the screen between the choir and the nave has been rebuilt of Roche abbey stone, curiously carved in Gothic work; the floor of the body of the church paved with stone from the same quarry, and the galleries have been re-built, and beautifully finished after the Doric order, resembling those of St. Albans, at Rome. From some cause not explained, the North end of the Minster had shrunk, and hung over the foundation 42 inches; to remedy this dangerous deformity, Mr. Thornton, carpenter, of York, aided by Mr. Burrworth, a stone mason, formed a machine, by which this part of the building, was, in 1739, actually screwed up into its proper place, and restored again to the perpendicular line!

The clergy of the Minster at present consist of a curate, and two assistants, the patronage being in the Mayor, Aldermen and capital burgesses. The certified value of the living is stated in Bacon's *Liber Regis* at £31. 6s. 8d. The curate is the Rev. Joseph Coltman, and the Rev. James Birtwhistle and the Rev. William Hildyard, are the assistant curates. At the South East end sept stands the freed-stool mentioned by Camden, made out of one entire stone, and said to have been removed from Scotland. On which is inscribed

*Hæc sedes Lapidea, Dicitur,* i. e. *Pacis Cathedra, ad quem Reus Fugiendo Perveniens Omnimodam Habet Securitatem.*

In English thus:—" This stone chair is called Freed Stool, i. e. *The chair of Peace*, to which what criminal soever flieth hath full protection."

At the upper end of the body of the church hangs an ancient tablet with the picture of St. John and of King Athelstan, between them this distich,

" Als Free make I The
" As hert may thynke or Egh may see."

Hence the burgesses of Beverley generally pay no toll or custom in any port or town in England, and before they travel, they may, if they choose, receive at the Mayor's office a certificate, setting forth, " That King Athelstan, of famous memory, did grant also, King Henry I. did grant and confirm to the men of the town of Beverley an exemption from all manor of imposts, tolls, pillage, stallage, tunnage, lastage, package, wharfage, and of and from all and every the like exactions, payments and duties, throughout, and in all places whatsoever, by land or sea, within all the dominions of England and Wales; which said grants have been confirmed by all, or most of the succeeding kings and queens of England. And these also to certify, that the bearer, (mentioning his name and trade) is a burgess of the said town of Beverley, and is thereby discharged of, and from all and every the said exactions, payments and duties." Similar privileges extend to the inhabitants of liberty of St. John of Beverley, who also, by application to the deputy steward of the court, obtain a certificate of exemption. This privilege, though of general, is not of universal application; for it appears, that in the year 1803, an act of parliament was obtained in favour of the ... and Driffield navigation, for making an alteration in the bridge, called Hull ..., by which act vessels belonging to burgesses of Beverley have since been subjected to a toll, or tounage. This, however, is the only toll which can be legally ...ed from them, when they are supplied with the requisite certificate. The right of exemption from tolls has been granted, or confirmed by charter and letters patent to burgesses of Beverley, by no fewer than forty-one sovereigns, commencing with king Athelstan, in 925, and ending with James II. in 1688. Another privilege attaching to the free burgesses of Beverley, a much more important one, is the right of pasturage on the fertile and extensive commons belonging to that borough: these are

  *Westwood, containing 504 acres.

  Hurn...................... 110
  *Figham.................... 297
  And Swine moor......... 263
     Total.................——1174

Each freeman is allowed to turn three head of Cattle into Westwood, six into Swinemoor, three into Figham, and one into Hurn. For this privilege only seven shil-

* Westwood is held by a grant from Alexander Neville, Archbishop of York and Figham, by a grant from William Wickham, Archbishop of the same province. There is a tradition, that Westwood was presented to the freemen of Beverley, by two maiden sisters, whose "Virgin tomb" stands in the body of the church, or the pillars of the little South aisle, but this popular error is wholly unsupported by evidence.

lings per head is paid for cattle pastured during the summer upon Westwood, ten shillings and sixpence per head upon Swinemoor, nine shillings upon Figham, and two shillings and sixpence per head upon Hurn, from May-day to the races in the beginning of June; and three shillings and sixpence the remainder of the year.

The church of St. Mary, though greatly inferior to the Minster as a building, is a venerable parish church, of which the King is the patron. In the King's books this living is valued at 14l. 2s. 4½d. In this church there are several monuments, but the most remarkable of them is one dated 1689, which records the fate of two Danish duelists, who are here interred, and whose epitaph runs thus:—

Here two young Danish soldiers lie,
The one in quarrel chanced to die;
The other's head, by their own law,
By sword was severed at one blow.

The places of worship not within the pale of the establishment, are:—the Independent Chapel, Lairgate, the Rev. James Mather, minister; the Methodist Chapel, Walkergate; the Friends' Meeting-House, Wood lane; and the Baptist Chapel, Walkergate, the Rev. John Carlton, minister.

The Hospitals at Beverley consist of MRS. ANNE ROUTH'S HOSPITAL, in Keldgate, for ancient poor widows, in which there are thirty-two inmates, who are each allowed five shillings per week, with a gown and a supply of coals yearly, arising from the rents of estates in different parts of the county. MR. CHARLES WARTON'S HOSPITAL, in Minster moorgate, for poor widows, of whom fourteen are accommodated, and have each allowed four shillings a week, with a gown each, and coals yearly, from an estate called Killingraves, between Beverley and Bishop Burton; the Trustees of which charity also apprentice a number of boys annually, with a premium of four pounds each. SIR MICHAEL WARTON'S HOSPITAL;* in Minster moorgate, for six poor widows, who are each allowed three shillings weekly, with a gown and coals annually. FOX'S HOSPITAL in Minster moorgate, for four poor widows, who have each four shillings a week, a quantity of coals yearly, and a new gown every two years, from a small estate and money in the funds. TEMPERTON'S HOSPITAL, Walkergate, for

* This gentleman contributed during his life time £500 towards the repairs of the Minster; and bequeathed £4000 as a perpetual fund to beautify and keep it in order.

supporting six poor persons, men and women; the funds arising from landed property. There are also twenty-two *Maisons de dieu* and four Bead Houses, which afford accommodation to as many poor families, with some small allowance to each. Exclusive of these benevolent institutions, there are several other charities under the direction of trustees, who make periodical distributions to the poor. Formerly there were in this place a preceptory of Knights Hospitalers of St. John of Jerusalem, and hospitals dedicated to St. Nicholas, St. Giles, and the Trinity; and an hospital without the North Bargate, with a house of black and another of grey friars.

The Free Schools of Beverley are the Grammar School, the National School, and Graves's School. The Grammar School, which is of ancient date, is probably coeval with the Collegiate Society of Saint John, for it does not appear when or by whom it was founded. The patronage of this school is now in the corporation. The old school of brick stood in the Minster yard, on the site of the cloisters and conventual buildings, but in the year 1816 it was taken down to improve the church, and by the liberality of the corporation a new school was built in a commodious and handsome style, in Keldgate, with a large and convenient house attached, for the convenience of the master. The school is open to sons of burgesses indefinitely, on the payment of two pounds per annum for their instruction in the classics, and two guineas for writing and arithmetic. The sons of non-freemen and day scholars pay six guineas for the classics, and three pounds for writing and accounts. The present master is the Rev. J. P. Richards, whose stipend is a hundred pounds a year, being ten pounds from Dr. Metcalf's endowment, twenty pounds as an annual gift from the members of the borough, and seventy pounds as an annual donation from the corporation. There is no church preferment attached to the grammar school, but the parishioners of St. Mary's sometimes give the lectureship of their church to the master. This school has two fellowships, six scholarships, and three exhibitions to St. John's College, Cambridge.— Among the eminent men who have been educated here may be mentioned John Alcock, D.D. Bishop of Ely; John Fisher, D.D. Bishop of Rochester; John Green, D.D. Bishop of Lincoln; Robert Ingham, a worthy divine; and Henry Revel Reynolds, an eminent physician. There is a select library of classical books attached to the school, containing several Aldine editions.— Graves's Free School is situated in the

square adjacent to Tollgavel. This establishment is of modern origin, and owes its institution to the munificence of the Rev. James Graves, late curate of the Minster, who bequeathed a sum of money amounting to about 3000*l.* in the public funds for the education of youth in Beverley. For about two years a temporary school room was used; but in 1814 the trustees purchased the old play house, and having divided it by a partition, fitted it up for schools for boys and girls. Here one hundred boys from the town and neighbourhood receive gratuitous instruction, under the tuition of Mr. William Watson, on the Lancasterian plan; and one hundred girls, on the plan of Dr. Bell, and in the afternoon the girls are taught needle work by Mrs. Watson. At the National School, which is situate in Minster moorgate, about 160 boys are taught by Mr. G. Blyth.

The town of Beverley is airy, well built, and extensive. The market place, in particular, is very spacious, occupying four acres of land; it is ornamented by a cross supported by eight columns, each consisting of a single stone, and was erected at the expense of one of the members of the borough. The market, which is held on Saturday, is well supplied, and the business done here in the corn trade is very considerable. The canal, called Beverley Beck, cut in the year 1727, from this town to the river Hull, affords great facilities to trade, by opening a communication with the Humber, and coals are brought in large quantities to the staiths, for the supply of the interior part of the East-Riding. Here is likewise a trade in malt and leather, and several of the poorer class find employment in the extensive nurseries of Messrs. George and William Tindall, and the mint plantations of Messrs. Walker, Parker, and Hall.

The annual fairs are held on the Thursday before old Valentine's day, on the 5th of July, on the Wednesday before the 25 of September, and on the 6th of November.

During the civil wars this place was alternately the prey of the King's troops and of the troops of Parliament. At the commencement of the quarrel, when Charles the First attempted to make himself master of Hull, and was refused admission by Sir John Hotham, the governor of that garrison, he had his quarters at Beverley, but the place soon fell into the hands of the Parliamentary forces, and Sir John, when he fled from Hull, on account of his treason against that cause which he had originally so much advanced, was taken prisoner in the streets of Beverley, and afterwards executed on Tower Hill.

The population of this town has, within the last ten years, increased nearly 10 per cent. over the population of 1811. In the former return the numbers were 6035; they now are—

St. Martin's Parish..............2937
St. Mary's ditto............ .....3214
St. Nicholas, ditto............ 577
_____
Total....................6728

The government of the Borough is in a Mayor, (who is always coroner for the time being) twelve Aldermen, and thirteen capital Burgesses, under a charter granted by Queen Elizabeth, and renewed by James II. in the year of the revolution. The mayor and capital burgesses are elected annually, on the Monday next before the 29th of September.* By the charter of this corporation the mayor is chosen out of the aldermen by the freemen, and the capital burgesses are nominated by the new mayor, and elected by acclamation (or *shouted in*, as it is called) by the freemen, immediately after the election of the mayor. The power is vested in the King to remove from their respective offices the mayor, recorder, aldermen, capital burgesses, and common clerk, or any of them; and in 1688 this power was exercised, for on the 11th of June, in that year, an order was sent to Beverley, by the King in council, for the removal of the recorder, four aldermen, and three burgesses. So long ago as the reign of Edward I. Beverley returned two members to Parliament, but after the death of that monarch, this borough ceased to make returns till the 5th of Elizabeth, when it was incorporated.— The election is in the free burgesses, resident and non resident, of which there are

* The list of the corporate body for the year 1823 will be found prefixed to this volume, under the head of "Additions and Alterations."

about 2000, and the present members are John Wharton, Esq. of Skelton Castle, and George Lane Fox, Esq. of Bramham Park.

The House of Correction, or gaol of the East-Riding, which was built about the year 1809, on a new site, is situated a little distance without the North bar, and the sessions for the East-Riding are always held in the Court-House within this building.— There is also a court of record held in the Guildhall, called the Provost's Court, in which all causes may be tried arising within the liberties of this borough, except titles to land; and the corporation is said to possess a power of trying capital felonies, but they do not exercise it.

The office for the registration of wills and deeds, established in the 6th year of the reign of Queen Anne, called the Register Office of the East-Riding, gives name to the square in which it is situated. Of this office H. W. Maister, Esq. is registrar, and Mr. C. A. Atkinson is deputy.

The Theatre is a small building situated in Lairgate, and is generally well attended during the race week, which always follows the week of the York spring meeting.

At the Subscription News Room, held at Mr. Thomas Elcock's, in the Market-place, the London daily and some of the provincial papers are regularly received.

The vicinity of Beverley, towards the West, is elevated and pleasant; the common pasture of Westwood commands a beautiful view of the town and Minster, and of the western parts of Holderness. To the East and South the country, to the distance of several miles, is flat and uninviting, but even here the scenery is greatly improved by drainage, inclosure, and cultivation; and this extensive tract of fen land, which fifty years ago was a solitary waste, flooded during the greater part of the year, now presents an aspect of fertility.

POST-MASTER, Mr. John Gardham, *Tollgavel.*

| Places from whence Letter bags are recvd. | Distance. | Postage. | Arrival of Mails. | Departure of Mails. |
|---|---|---|---|---|
| London............ | 225 | 11d. | Daily 5 morning. | 4 evening. |
| Hull .............. | 9 | 4 | ½ past 4 evening. | 4 do. |
| Market Weighton.. | 10 | 4 | 4 do. | 4 do. |
| Pocklington....... | 19 | 5 | 4 do. | 4 do. |
| York ............. | 29 | 6 | 4 do. | 4 do. |

DIRECTORY.

*Academies—Boarding & Day Schools,*
Aldridge Thomas, (day) Butcher row
Armstrong John, (master of blue coat school) Highgate
Dean Joel, (day) Newbeggin

Debraws Miss, (boarding) Wednesday market
Elrington Margaret,(ladies' day) Highgate
Graves's Free School, W. Watson, Register square

Hall Jane,(ladies' seminary) St. John's street

Harrison John, (day) Flemingate

National, G.B. Blythe, Minster moorgt

Prescott Christopher, (day) Flemingate

Renou Mary Ann, (boarding) North bar street without

Richards Rev. G. P. (grammar) Keldgate

Richter Rev. H. W. (boarding) Wednesday market

Robinson Mary, (ladies' boarding) Wednesday market

Simpson Misses, (ladies' boarding) Keldgate

*Agents—particular and general.*

Emery John, (London Genuine Tea Company) North bar st. within

Mosey Mary, (East India Company's teas) Dog and Duck lane

*Architects & Surveyors.*

Cliff John, Wood lane.

Ingle James, Hengate

*Attornies.*

Birt John, (notary public) Keldgate

Bower Wm. Hengate

Dawson Charles, North bar st. without

Duesbery Thomas, Hengate

Hall and Campbell, Lairgate

Iveson Francis, Newbegin

Johnson Anthony, Hengate

Myers John, Tollgavel

Newlove Wm. Butcher row

Shepherd Henry John, Esq. Lairgate

Wilkinson Francis, Walkergate

*Auctioneers and Appraisers.*

Bell Wallis, Walkergate

Cliff John, (appraiser) Wood lane

Jameson Richard, (appraiser) North bar street without

Johnson Henry, Walkergate

Lumley John, Hengate

*Bakers and Flour Dealers, &c.*

Baitson Joseph, Wednesday market

Ellerker Thomas, Market place

Monkman Wm. Tollgavel

Osgerby Edward, Highgate

Pearson Saml. (flour) Minster moorgt.

Routledge Thomas, Laundress-lane

Roxby Wm. Flemingate

Thompson John, sen. North bar street within

Thompson John, jun. Tollgavel

*Banks.*

Bower, Duesbery, Hall, and Thompson, (East-Riding) Lairgate, (on Messrs. Curries, Raikes, and Co. London)

Machell, Pease, and Liddill, North bar street within; on Sir Richard Carr Glyn and Co.

*Blacksmiths.*

Cooper Wm. Beckside

Duncan Peter, Eastgate

Griffin John, sen. Ladygate

Griffin John, jun. Ladygate

Harrison Wm. North bar street within

Harrison Thomas, Dyer lane

Heselhurst Robert, Flemingate

Hustwick Robert, North bar street without

Ralph Wm. Flemingate

*Booksellers, Stationers, and Binders.*

Proctor Thomas, (printer, and circulating library) North bar street within

Ramsden James, Market place

Stoddart Thomas, (binder) Dyer lane

Turner Matthew, (and printer, circulating library) Market place

*Boot and Shoemakers.*

Abbott Wm. Flemingate

Blackstone Christopher, Tollgavel

Botterill Geo. Tollgavel

Cattle Wm. Butcher row

Cook Wm. sen. Tollgavel

Cook Wm. jun. Beckside

Cook John, Market place

Denton Matthew, Eastgate

Flint Wm. Lairgate

Hutton John, Eastgate

Nicholson John, Ladygate

Peacock John, North bar st. within

Reynolds Daniel, Market place

Smelt Stephen, Dog and Duck lane

Sneason Robert, Lairgate

Taylor James, Tollgavel

Tuting Jeremiah, North bar st. within

Tuting John, North bar st. within

Westoby John, Sowhill

Wilcox John, Tollgavel

*Braziers and Tinsmiths.*

Collinson John, Market place

Elcock Thomas, Market place

Oustoby John, Lairgate

Rhodes Thomas, (and glazier) Tollgavel

*Breweries—Ale and Beer.*

Dove John, Market place

Mair Wm. Highgate

Muschamp Christ. Butcher row

Stephenson Robert & Son, Tollgavel

Stephenson George, jun. Wednesday market

*Bricklayers.*

Blacker Robert, North bar st. without

Burton John, Keldgate

Dalton Thomas, Walkergate

Dalton Wm. North bar st. without

Dalton James, Vicar-lane

Duucum Thos. & Christ. Walkergate

Greenhough Thos. Eastgate

Hewson Wm. Eastgate

Hewson Matthew, Flemingate
Horner James, North side Minster
Innis Wm. North bar street without
Robinson James, Keldgate
Taylor Wm. & James, Flemingate

*Butchers.*

Audus Samuel, Wednesday market
Baines John, Lairgate
Barman Edward, Ladygate
Bielby Wm. Tollgavel
Copass Abraham, Tollgavel
Dales Peter, North bar st. within
Ellerington Wm. Lairgate
Hardy Thomas, Friargate lane
Hornigold Christ. Highgate
Kirkman Thomas, Tollgavel
Merritt Daniel, Butcher row
Miller Geo. North bar street within
Oxley Wm. Walkergate
Oxley Robert, Tollgavel
Pearson Harriett, Lairgate
Purdon David, Walkergate
Reed Robert, North bar st. without
Robinson James, Ladygate
Robinson Francis, Flemingate
Shepherd Wm. Flemingate
Spence Robert, Walkergate
Wallis Thomas, Ladygate
Wallis George, Hengate
Wilson Israel Marshall, Ladygate

*Cabinet Makers.*

Bradford John, Fryer lane
Cockerill John, North bar st. without
Lumley John, Hengate
Padget Wm. (& joiner) Highgate
Sever Matthew, Butcher row
Thompson Wm. Flemingate

*Chemists and Druggists.*

Keningham Robert, Market place
Robinson & Stabler, Market place
Tigar Pennock, North bar st. within

*Clock and Watch Makers.*

Baitson Thomas, (and silversmith)
   Market place
Fox Hudson, Sow hill
Mawman George, Market place
Watson Francis, Walkergate

*Clothes Brokers.*

Coupland Elizabeth, Keldgate
Fenteman Samuel, Lairgate

*Coal Merchants.*

Clark Richard, Beckside
Edew Christopher, Beckside
Hodgson John, sen. Beckside
Lee John & Thomas, Beckside
Ouston David, (& lime) Ladygate
Thompson James, Beckside
Webster & Hodgson, Beckside

*Coopers.*

Copass Wm. Silvester lane
Muschamp John, Sow hill

*Corn Factors.*

Dalton Robert, Sow hill
Eden Christopher, Beckside
Lee John & Thomas, Beckside
Muschamp Christopher, Butcher row
Ouston David, Ladygate
Thompson James, Beckside

*Corn Millers.*

Baitson Joseph, Wednesday market
Carlss Thomas, Water mill
Cawkill Wm. Flemingate
Fishwick Robert, Westwood
Lowson Robert Whiting, Westwood
Monkman Wm. Grove hill
Union Mill Society, Westwood
Wilson Edward, Westwood
Wilson John, Grove hill

*Curriers.*

Dawson John Duncan, Tollgavel
Prockter Marmaduke, Dog and Duck
   lane

*Distillers—Mint, Herbs, &c.*

Hall Jane, (still house) Flemingate
Hutchinson Wm. Beckside
Walker John, Eastgate
Parker James, Cherry Orchard

*Fellmongers.*

Clubley R. T. St. John's street
Catterson George, Flemingate
Ingle James, Hengate

*Fire and Life Insurance Offices.*

Atlas, James Ramsden, Market place
County, Francis Wardell, Lairgate
Norwich Union, Anthony Atkinson,
   Market place
Phœnix, John Gardham, Tollgavel
Royal Exchange, Robert Dalton,
   North bar street within

*Fishmongers.*

Cresser Hannah, Ladygate
Proudler Sarah, Dog & Duck lane
Ruddock George, Market place

*Flax Dressers.*

Coaks John, Market place
Robinson M. & L. Market place
Smith George, Market place

*Furniture Brokers.*

Fenteman Samuel, Lairgate
Johnstone Sarah, North bar st. within
Luck Wm. Tollgavel

*Gardeners and Nurserymen.*

Dawson John, Beckside
Downing John, Wood lane
Hodgson Wm. Beckside
Jenkinson John, Norwood
Jennison George, Wilbert lane
Lockey John, England spring
Parker James, Cherry Orchard
Playforth George, Beckside
Ramshaw Thomas, Sow hill
Ramshaw Robert, Eastgate

o 3

Stott Richard, Minster moorgate
Swailes Robert, Wednesday market
Swailes John, Butcher row
Tindall James, Eastgate
Tindall G. & W. (nurserymen) Eastgate, & 25, Market place, Hull
Ward Thomas, Lairgate

*Glass, China & Earthenware Dealers.*
Adamson Wm. Tollgavel
Empson Sarah, Market place
Hobson Edward, Tollgavel
Lee Benjamin, Tollgavel
Watson William, Tollgavel
Watson Wm. Goodlad, Ladygate

*Grocers and Tea Dealers.*
Burkinshaw Matthew, Market place
Brigham Wm. & John, Market place
Brigham Thomas, Market place
Caborn James, Butcher row
Gardham Thomas, Tollgavel
Lundie Thomas, Tollgavel
Oxtoby Robert, Market place
Pinder David, Market place
Raleigh John, Tollgavel
Selley John, North bar st. within
Stephenson Lawrence, Market place
Swann John, (& perfumer) North bar street within
Tigar Pennock, North bar st. within

*Gun Makers and Smiths.*
Forth Wm. (smith) Ladygate
Taylor Wm. (maker) Market place

*Hat Manufacturers and Dealers.*
Cass Robert, Tollgavel
Lockwood Wm. (dlr.) Market place
Suddaby Wm. Flemingate
Wilson James, North bar st. within
Wilson John, Market place

*Hair Dressers and Perfumers.*
Davies Thomas, Hengate
Innis George, Sow hill
Mann Emanuel, Tollgavel
Meadley Thos. North side Minster
Rickell John, Butcher row
Stather W. G. Market place
Stather Robert, North bar st. within
Waite Wm. Tollgavel
Watson Thomas, Tollgavel

*Hosiers, &c.*
Atkinson Wm. North bar st. within
Gothard John, Wednesday market
Jewitt Jonathan, Market place
Moore Thomas, Market place
Shipstone Thos. (& stocking worsted mfr.) Market place
Taylor George, Market place

*Hotels, Inns, and Taverns.*
Admiral Duncan, Stephen Acklam, Hall garth
Anchor, Wm. Gray, Beckside
Angel, Robert Larcum, Butcher row

Beverley Arms, Nathaniel Dalby, (commercial inn & posting house) North bar street within
Black Bull, Rbt. Watson, Lairgate
Blue Boar, Wm. Richardson, (excise office) Tollgavel
Board, Henry Harrison, Grove hill
Boot, Wm. Coombs, North bar street within
Buck, Richard Simpson, Beckside
Carpenters' Arms, James Dutton, Lairgate
Cock & Bottle, John Dove, Beckside
Cross Keys, Wm. Clayton, Lairgate
Dog & Duck, Geo. Sheffield, Ladygt.
Duke of York, Wm. Akester, Keldgt.
George & Dragon, Henry Pickering, Highgate
Globe, Alice Wilson, Ladygate
Golden Ball, Wm. Wadsworth, Tollgavel
Golden Fleece, Sarah Elstob, Beckside
Green Dragon, John Walker, Market place
King's Arms, William Ackrill, North bar street within
King's Head, Robert Witty, Market place
Lion & Lamb, Joseph Turley, Ladygt.
Lord Nelson, Mth. Moore, Flemingt.
Old George and Dragon, John Stockdale, Highgate
Pack Horse, Rbt. Clark, Market pl.
Plough, Samuel Loft, Flemingate
Red Lion, John Atkinson, Tollgavel
Rose and Crown, James Skelton, North bar street without
Ship, Francis Riggall, Sow hill
Sloop, Wm. Lowther, Beckside
Sun, Wm. Stamford, Flemingate
Tiger, Charles Greenwood, (posting house & commercial hotel) North bar street within
Valiant Soldier, John Botterill, Norwood
Wheat Sheaf, Thomas Suggit, North bar street within
White Horse, Wm. Burrell, Hengate
White Swan, James Donaldson, Market place

*Ironmongers.*
Collinson John, Market place
Shepherd John, Market place
Tigar Wm. Market place
Wimble Wm. Wardell, Tollgavel

*Joiners, House Builders, &c.*
Butler Robert, Dog & Duck lane
Cliff & Son, North bar street within
Cliff John, Wood lane
Farrer Wm. jun. Keldgate
Montgomery Samuel, Walkergate
Pashby Thomas, Highgate
Smith George, Beckside

Thwaites Joseph, North bar st. without
Tuton Richard, North bar st. within
Watson John, Flemingate

*Libraries—Subscription & Circulating.*

Elcock Thomas, (subscription)Market
  place
Proctor Thomas, (circulating) North
  bar street within
Ramsden James, (free) Market place
Turner Matthew, (circulating) Market place

*Linen Drapers.*

Amery John, (& agent to the gen. tea
  Co.) North bar street within
Atkinson Wm. North bar st. within
Campbell David, North bar st. within

*Linen Manufacturers.*

Robinson M. & L. (canvas & thread)
  Market place

*Linen and Woollen Drapers.*

Blanchard Stephen, Market place
Burkenshaw Matthew, Market place
Collison Thomas, Market place
Clifton Wm. Market place
Richardson Wm. Lairgate
Robinson M. & L. Market place

*Livery Stable Keepers, &c.*

Brooks John, North bar st. without
Topping James, Tollgavel
Rumshaw Thomas, Sow hill

*Machine Makers.*

Dry Wm. (winnowing, &c.) North
  bar street without
Wilson John, (winnowing) Laundress
  lane

*Maltsters.*

Dargavell Wm. North bar st. without
Green Thomas, St. John street
Hartley Wm. North bar st. without
Mair Wm. Highgate
Muschamp Christopher, Butcher row
Stephenson Robert & Son, Tollgavel
Stephenson Geo. Wednesday market

*Mercers and Haberdashers.*

Amery John, North bar st. within
Blanchard W. S. Market place
Ranson John, Market place
Richardson Wm. Lairgate
Taylor Geo. Calvert, Market place

*Milliners, Dress Makers, &c.*

Bramwell & Parker, Keldgate
Brown Ann, Ladygate
Ellis Ann and Eliz. Market place
Gawan Jane, Flemingate
Maxwell Mary, North bar st. within
Ranson Sarah & Eliz. Market place
Robinson Mary, Tollgavel
Stephenson Caroline, North bar street
  without

Stokell Jane, Highgate
Tattersall Elizabeth, Dog & Duck ln.

*Painters—House, and Sign, &c.*

Fletcher Wm. Walkergate
Hobson Elizabeth, Tollgavel
Issot Joseph, Eastgate
Ridley Wm. Highgate
Townley Wm. Market place
Watson James, Market place

*Pawn Brokers.*

Collinson Robert, Eastgate
Nutchey Eliz. & Ellen Tollgavel

*Physicians.*

Arden John, North bar st. within
Brown James, Norwood
Hull Thomas, Newbiggin
Hutchinson Charles, Market place

*Plumbers and Glaziers.*

Empson & Son, Sow hill
Harrison Henry, Register square
Lundie Geo. Hengate

*Porter Merchants.*

Ross Charles, Register square
Swann John, North bar street
Tigar Pennock, North bar st. within
Wardell James, Ladygate

*Rope and Twine Makers.*

Allison Cooper, Riding fields
Coaks John, Market place
Robinson M. & L. (twine) Market pl.
Webster Robert, Fryer lane

*Saddlers and Collar Makers.*

Clough Thomas, Tollgavel
Edwards Wm. North bar st. within
Empson Hugh, Market place
Fussey Wm. North bar st. within
Porter Edward, (and bridle cutter)
  North bar street within

*Savings' Bank.*

Turner Matthew, Market place

*Seedsmen.*

Brigham Wm. & John, Market place
Gardham Thomas, Tollgavel
Oxtoby Robert, Market place
Pinder David, Market place
Stephenson Laurence, Market place
Tindall Geo. & Wm. Eastgate

*Shopkeepers.*

Arah George, Flemingate
Beal Thomas, Keldgate
Dunn John, Walkergate
Fenteman Elizabeth, Ladygate
Greensides Susannah, Keldgate
Hardwick Mary, Lairgate
Herdsman Henry, Flemingate
Hinley John, North bar st. without
Issott Thomas, Butcher row
Loft Rebecca, Wednesday market
M'Cloud Wm. Flemingate
Mease Isabella, Eastgate
Metcalf Sarah, Tollgavel

Montgomery Samuel, Walkergate
Orr Mary, Tollgavel
Padget Wm. Highgate
Padget Richard, Wednesday market
Pearson Samuel, Lairgate
Sanvidge John, North bar st. without
Shaw Thomas, Eastgate
Sigston Margaret, Keldgate
Smith Eliz. Lairgate
Southwick Thomas, Beckside
Taylor Wm. Flemingate
Taylor James, Flemingate
Thrusk William, Sow hill
Wadsworth John, Keldgate

*Slate and Flag Merchants, and Marble Masons.*
Bennison Appleton, Lairgate
Hayes John, Highgate
Rushworth John, (marble and stone mason) Tollgavel

*Spirit and Wine Merchants & Dealers.*
Arden John Barker, Hengate
Bland Samuel, (spirit) Tollgavel
Dalton Robert, (spirit) North bar st. within
Robinson and Stabler, (dealers) Market place
Ross Charles, (wine, spirit, & porter) Register square
Wardell James, (spirit and porter) Ladygate
Wimble Wm. Wardell, (spirit) Tollgavel

*Stay Makers.*
Adamson Mary, Walkergate
Ellis A. & E. Market place
Johnson Eliz. Lairgate
Tindall John, Tollgavel

*Stocking Worsted Spinners.*
Gothard John, Wednesday market
Jewitt Jonathan, Market place
Shipstone Thomas, Market place

*Straw Hat Manufacturers.*
Booth Margaret, Beckside
Merritt Caroline, Ladygate
Tigar Elizabeth, Tollgavel
Watson Hannah, Market place

*Surgeons.*
Brereton Charles, Wednesday market
Carter Richard, R.N. Market place
Chalmers Matthew, Norwood
Hewitt Marmaduke, Walkergate
Jackson John, Tollgavel
Sandwith Thos. North bar st. within
Williams John, Walkergate

*Tailors and Drapers.*
Blyth Wm. Ladygate
Blyth John, Tollgavel
Brown Matthew, Tollgavel
Cattle John, Butcher row
Clarkson Robert, Beckside

Dosser Rhd. Clark, North bar st. within
Duncum Joseph, Walkergate
Harrison & Robinson, North bar st. without
Harrison John, Lairgate
Harrison Henry, Tollgavel
Holiday Wm. Walkergate
Luck Wm. Tollgavel
Luck Richard, Tollgavel
Mawman Wm. Sow hill
Ransom Samuel, Lairgate
Rennison John, Keldgate
Robinson Samuel, Sow hill
Southwick Thomas, Beckside
Stephenson Thomas, Wood lane
Turner Robert, Lairgate
Walker Peter, Walkergate
Wille John, Walkergate

*Tallow Chandlers.*
Calder Mary, Ladygate
Lareum Thos. North bar st. within
Loft Samuel, Flemingate
Westerby Wm. Martin, Ladygate
Wilkinson John, Tollgavel

*Tanners.*
Beaumont Thos. St. John street
Catterson Geo. Flemingate
Hobson John, Lairgate
Hodgson Wm. Flemingate
Simpson Wm. Keldgate

*Tea Dealers.*
Empson Sarah, Market place
Middleton Eliz. North bar st. within
Stephenson George, sen. Wednesday market

*Timber Merchants.*
Cliff, Milly & Son, Vicar lane; house, Wood lane
Crump Thos. (hard wood) Keldgate
Montgomery Samuel, Walkergate

*Toy and Hardware Dealers.*
Mann Emanuel, Tollgavel
Moore Thos. Market place
Statber W. G. (toy) Market place

*Turners in Wood and Metal.*
Beevers Wm. Ladygate
Cattle John, Dog & Duck lane
Wainman John, Lairgate

*Veterinary Surgeons.*
Lister J. North bar st. without
Lythe J. Butcher row

*Wheelwrights.*
Brownrigg John, Hengate
Davison Wm. Lairgate
Pashley Thomas, Highgate
Ringrose Thomas, Flemingate
Smith George, Beckside
Stamford Wm. Flemingate
Thwaites Joseph, North bar st. without

*Whitesmiths and Bell Hangers.*
Cooper Thomas, Vicar lane

Croskill & Son, Butcher row
Lambert David, Butcher row
Wood John, Wilbert lane
Wynn Joseph, Woodlane

———

Acklam Peter, Esq. North bar street within
Acklam Lieut. Wm. East York Militia, Flemingate
Atkinson A. deputy registrar, Market place
Bethell Misses, Hengate
Boyes Wm. treasurer to the poor, Laundress lane
Charlton Rev. John, Scottish Baptist minister, Laundress lane
Collett C. lamp agent, &c. North bar street within
Coltman Rev. Joseph, North bar st. within
Consitt Mercy, gentlewoman, North bar street within
Dawson Rev. Major, North bar street within
Denton Stephen, gent. Flemingate
Dickenson Joseph, gent. North bar st. without
Duesbery Thos. banker; h. Hengate
Ellison Henry, gent. North bar street within
Eyre Rev. James, assistant curate of the Minster, and lecturer of St. Mary's, Lairgate
Ferryman Rev. Geo. Walkergate
Gillyatt Sumner, gent. Flemingate
Hall Samuel, Esq. North bar street without
Harling Wm. gent. Wednesday mkt.
Hart Nathan, gent. Hengate
Hewitt Marmaduke, Esq. Walkergate
Hewitt James, gent. North bar street within
Hildyard Rev. Wm. Walkergate
Hunter Misses, gentlewoman, North bar street without
Hutton H. W. Esq. Walkergate
Ingram James, surveyor of taxes, North bar street without
James Henry, clerk of the Court of Requests, Walkergate
Kirk Misses, gentlewoman
Lambert G. J. professor of music, Highgate
Lee Mary, gentlewoman
Lockwood John, Esq. clerk of the general meetings for the militia in the East-Riding, and the town and county of Kingston-upon-Hull, and deputy clerk of the peace, Lairgate
Maister Henry Wm. Esq. alderman & registrar for the East-Riding, Register square

Mather Rev. John, Independent minister, Lairgate
Norris Susannah, gentlewoman, North bar street without
Page Edward, land surveyor, Tollgavel
Richardson Hannah, gentlewoman, Tollgavel
Robertson Ebenezer, Esq. Keldgate
Shaw Samuel, gent. North bar street without
Shepherd Henry John, treasurer to the East-Riding, Lairgate
Sherwood Mrs. gentlewoman, Lairgate
Sigston Benj. gent. Flemingate
Smelt Robert, high constable, Wednesday market
Soame S. J. gent. Lairgate
Stephenson John, gent. Wednesday market
Stephenson Wm. gent. North bar st. without
Stewart—Captain of the East-Riding Militia, North bar st. within
Walker James, Esq. Beverley-hall
Weldon Wm. bleacher, Beck side
Wardell Francis, cashier to the East-Riding bank, Lairgate
Willis John, chamber clerk and agent to the Corporation, treasurer and chief constable to the town and liberties, corn inspector, guardian of the poor of St. Mary's, & vestry clerk of the parishes of St. Mary's and St. Nicholas, Register square

———

Baker Isaac, stocking weaver, Keldgate
Brown Thomas, lime burner, Lairgate
Calverley Rachael, midwife, Friargate
Dawson John, waiter at Tiger Inn
Dawson Roger, cartman, Beckside
Day John, game keeper, North bar st. without
Duncan Joseph, parish clerk, Walkergate
Duncan Philip, weaver, Keldgate
Ellis Michael, brush manufacturer, Market place
Fendlater James, cattle dealer, Norwood
Heselhurst Robert, nail maker, Flemingate
Hodgson Richard, gaoler for the town, Register square, Wilbert lane
Jewett Jonathan, dyer, Market place
Johnson W. P. letter press printer, Walkergate
Kitchen John, basket maker, Silvester lane

Lundie Thomas, ham factor and rag merchant, Tollgavel
Monkman Isaac, farmer, Butcher row
Monkman Thos. farmer, Eastgate
Moses William, plasterer, Wednesday market
Newton Pierson, fruiterer, Tollgavel
Nicholls Jonathan, breeches maker, &c. North bar street within
Padgett John, brewer, Silvester lane
Pickering Edw. paviour, Walkergt.
Richardson John, butler at Beverley hall, (Mr. Walker's)
Ruddock Geo. bell-man, Market pl.
Shepherd Samuel, jailor for East Riding
Spenceley Thos. confectioneer, Tollgavel
Stather Wm. umbrella maker, Market place
Tindall John, tobacco pipe maker, Butcher row
Tuting Jermh. sexton to St. Mary's, North bar street within

## COACHES.

*From Robert Clark's, Pack Horse, Market Place.*

The HIGHFLYER on Tuesday, Thursday, Friday, and Sunday, to Hull, at 8 mng. ret. 7 evg.
ACCOMMODATION from Hull on Monday, Wednesday, Thursday, Saturday, and Sunday, at ½ past 10 morn. ret. 5 evg.

*From Nathaniel Dalby's, Beverley Arms, North bar street within.*

BRITISH QUEEN, to Scarborough daily during summer, in Winter three days per week, dep. ½ past 7 morn. ret. at 1 afternoon
ROCKINGHAM, from Hull to York at 11 morn. ret. 3 afternoon
TRAFALGAR, from York to Hull at 11 morn. ret. ½ past 3 aft.

*From Charles Greenwood's, Tiger Inn, North bar street within.*

ROYAL MAIL, from Hull to York, at 4 in the aft. ret. 5 morn.
TRAFALGAR, from Hull daily, at 7 morn. ret. ½ past 6 evg.
WELLINGTON, to Scarbro' daily during summer at 8 morn. ret. at 2 afternoon, in winter three days a week.

## LAND CARRIAGE.

*John Botterill*, Valiant Soldier, Norwood, to the Three Crowns, Market place, Hull, on Tu. and Fri. at 7 morn. ret. 9 evg.
*Samuel Fenteman*, Gardham's yard, to

the Blue Bell, Market place, Hull, daily at 9 morn. ret. at ½ past 8 evening.
*James Swaby*, Walkergate, to Reia Deer, Market place, Hull, daily 9 mg. ret. at ½ past 8 evg.
*Widow Wilson*, from the Green Dragon, to Hull, Mondays & Thursdays; to Market Weighton and York every Wed. and Sat.
*John Cockburn*, to Hull every Mon. & Thur.; to Market-Weighton and Pocklington every Tu. and Fri.
*Thomas Newcombe*, to Hull Mon. and Thur.; to Market-Weighton and York every Tu. and Fri.

## COUNTRY CARRIERS.

*Attending Beverley.*

Arram, Matthew Wallas, *Lion and Lamb*, a 10, d 4 Sat.
Atwick, Wm. Wilson, *Dog and Duck*, a ½ past 10, d 4 Sat.
Baintou, Rbt. Wallis, *Green Dragon*, a 10, d 4 Sat.
Barnby, Thos. Hodgson, *Green Dragon*, a 10, d 4 Sat.
Beeford, Robert Stephenson, *King's Head*, a 10, d 4 Sat.
Beeford, John Witty, *Cross Keys*, a 10, d 4 Sat.
Beswick, John Drew, *Pack Horse*, a 10, d 4 Sat.
Bewholme, Richard Southwick, *Globe*, a 10, d 4 Sat.
Bishop Burton, Christopher Job, *Green Dragon*, a 10, d 4 Sat.
Brandesburton, Wm. Dean, & Thos. Freer, *Valiant Soldier*, a 10, d 4 Sat.
Bridlington, John Ward, *Green Dragon*, arr. Fri. ret. Sat.
Catwick, Thomas Agar, *King's Head*, a 10, d 4 Sat.
Cherry Burton, Robt. Sissons, *King's Head*, a 10, d 4 Sat.
Cherry Burton, Wm. Cook, *Green Dragon*, a 10, d 4 Sat.
Cottingham, Wm. Wride, *King's Head*, a 10, d 4 Sat.
Cottingham, Charles Morrod, *Pack Horse*, a 10, d 4 Sat.
Driffield, see Malton
Etton, Robert Towers, *King's Head*, a 10, d 4 Sat.
Etton, Thos. Whitty, *Cross Keys*, Sat.
Frodingham, Wm. Jefferson, *Pack Horse*, a 10, d 4 Sat.
Ganton, Robert Dawson, *Pack Horse*, at 10, d ½ past 3 Sat.
Goodmanham, William Petch, *Cross Keys*, a 10, d 4 Sat.
Hornsea, W. Wilson, *Globe*, a ½ past 10, d 4 Sat.

Hornsea, David Robinson, *Cross Keys*, a 10, d 4 Sat.

Hull, James Noble, *White Horse*, a 10, d 4 Sat.

Hull, Richard Clapham, *Pack Horse*, a 10, d 4 Sat.

Hull, William Green, *Pack Horse*, a 10, d 4 Sat.

Hull, Thomas Atkinson, *Pack Horse*, a 10, d 4 Sat.

Hull, John Whitaker, *Pack Horse*, a 10, d 4 Sat.

Hull and York, John Boulton, *Green Dragon*, arr. Mon. and Thur. ret. Tu. and Fri.

Hutton Cranswick, John Booth, *Blue Boar*, a 10, d 4 Sat.

Hutton Cranswick, Geo. Summerson, *King's Head*, a 10, d 4 Sat.

Kilham, John Harland, *Green Dragon*, a 10, d 4 Sat.

Kirkburn, Robert Stockdale, *Green Dragon*, a 10, d 4 Sat.

Leven, Richard Roundhill, *Dog and Duck*, a 10, d 4 Sat.

Leven, Robert Adams, *Dog and Duck*, a 10, d 4 Sat.

Leven, Sarah Downs, *Dog and Duck*, a 10, d 4 Sat.

Leven, Thomas Buggs, *Dog and Duck*, a 10, d 4 Sat.

Little Weighton, Marmaduke Constable, *Green Dragon*, arrives at 10, departs 4 Saturday

Lockington, Thomas Walgate, *Pack Horse*, a 10, d 4 Sat.

Lockington, William Brow, *Wheat Sheaf*, a 10, d 4 Sat.

Lund, John Varey, *Blue Boar*, a ¼ past 10, d 4 Sat.

Lund, Wm. Smith, *Wheat Sheaf*

Malton & Driffield, Philemon Ashton, *Green Dragon*, arr. Mon. & Thur. ret. Tu. and Fri.

Market-Weighton, Robert Holmes, *Pack Horse*, a 10, d 4 Sat.

Middleton, George Robson, *Wheat Sheaf*, a 10, d 4 Sat.

Middleton, Robert Bowser, *Green Dragon*, a 10, d 4 Sat.

Newbald North, Joseph Dean, *Pack Horse*, a 10, d 4 Sat.

Newbald North, Robert Smart, *Cross Keys*, a 10, d 4 Sat.

North Dalton, Wm. Jackson, *Wheat Sheaf, North bar*, a 10, d 4 Sat.

North Frodingham, Henry Pickering, *King's Head*, a 10, d 4 Sat.

Riston, John Allmon, *Dog and Duck*, a 10, d 4 Sat.

Riston, Thos. Wardell, *King's Head*, a 10, d 4 Sat.

Riston, William Stockdale, *Globe*, a 10, d 4 Sat.

Routh, Joseph Williamson, *Valiant Soldier*, a 10, d 4 Sat.

Scarbro', Bell and England, *Green Dragon*, arr. Mon. and Thur. ret. Tu. and Fri.

South Dalton, Daniel Battle, *Blue Boar*, a 10, d 4 Sat.

South Dalton, Geo. Biggins, *Beverley Arms*, a 10, d 4 Sat.

South Dalton, Robert Carlin, *Beverley Arms*, a 10, d 4 Sat.

Walkington, Wm. Oliver, *Globe*, a 12, d 4 Sat.

Wetwang, John Holtby, *Green Dragon*, a 10, d 4 Sat.

York, see Hull

*Beverley Park*, see Woodmansea.

**BEWHOLME**, in the parish of Nunkeeling, wap. and liberty of Holderness; 3 miles NW. of Hornsea; pleasantly situated on an eminence, and commanding a most extensive and beautiful view of the surrounding country; the houses are, in general, well built, and chiefly inhabited by farmers. The soil is in a high state of cultivation. Pop. included with Nunkeeling 243.

Hopkinson James, Esq. Billing's hill

| Farmers, | Pickering Wm. |
|---|---|
| Acklam Wm. | Snary Thomas |
| Bainton John | *Shoemakers,* |
| Cornwall Charles | Short Wm. |
| Hornby Robert | Webster John |
| Jordan James | |

Gill George, tailor
Plowman George, wheelwright
Smith Jonathan, blacksmith

*Carrier,*—Robert Southwick, to Beverley every Saturday

**BEWICK**, in the parish of Aldbrough, wap. and liberty of Holderness; 8½ miles NE. of Hedon.

Suddaby Matthew, tanner, Bewick hall

**BILTON**, in the parish of Swine, wap. and liberty of Holderness; 4 miles N. E. of Hull. A small, though pleasant village, healthfully situated on the high road from Hull to Hedon. When most of the towns and villages were built of mud, this place being then the residence of a number of gentry, who erected in it brick buildings, obtained the appellation of Built Town, now contracted to Bilton. The church, dedicated to St. Peter, is extremely ancient, and is thought by most antiquarians to have formerly been parochial, from its having bells in the tower, at the time when none but parochial churches were allowed them. On account of its vicinity to Hull, and being immediately in the public road, land conveyances of every kind pass and re-pass daily. Population 91.

Brigham Richard, Esq.
Calvert George, carpenter, &c.
Watson Rev. Thomas, curate and surrogate

*Farmers,*    Readall Henry
Gibson Jonathan  Reneam George
Matchinson Jeffery

Postman to Hedon four days per week, at 9 mg.; to Hull at 1 at noon

Two coaches to Hull on Tu., and one on Fri. at 9 mg.—To Hedon and Pattrington at 5 evg. same days.

BINNINGTON, in the parish of Willerby, and wap. of Dickering ; 7 miles W. of Hunmanby. Pop. 50.

Coates Thomas, farmer
Walbron Wm. farmer

BIRDSALL, (P.) wap. of Buck-rose; 4 miles SSE. of Malton. There is here a chapel dedicated to St. Mary, of which the Rev. James Green is perpetual curate. Lord Henry Middleton has a seat here, which stands not far from the foot of the Wolds, in a fine sporting country. The mansion is spacious and commodious, and the pleasure grounds adorned with ex-tensive plantations, contribute to render it an agreeable residence. Population 240.

The Hon. Lord Henry Middleton
Jackson William, grocer
Lazenby Isaac, shoemaker
Wood John, tailor

*Farmers,*    Harper Wm.
Callam Isaac    Mortimer Robert,
Carris Robert, Al-   Mount Farran
drow house    Screwton John
Craven Thomas    Smith Wm.
Dale Thomas    Watson Wm.
Dobson Wm.

*Black Dale House,* in the parish of Norton, and wap. of Buckrose ; 2½ miles SSW. of Malton.

BLACKTOFT, (P.) in the wap. and liberty of Howdenshire; 7 miles SE. of Howden, situated on the North bank of the Ouse. Opposite the village sometimes great quantities of vessels anchor, being consi-dered a good road-stead. The steam boats from Selby and Thorne pass daily on their way to and from Hull. A bed of sand, which at low water extends over several acres, serves for the ballasting of small craft. One mile from this place, the Ouse and Trent form a junction, and from this point, (*Trent Falls*) the joint collection of waters are called Humber.—There is

here a chapel, not in charge, to the view of Brantingham. Population 278.

Ward Rev. Edward, curate, Laxton
Cockin Geo. yeoman, Skytom
Jewitt Wm. yeoman, Clementhorpe
Jewitt John, overseer
Lister John, coal dealer and vict. Bay Horse
Lister Thomas, tailor
Poppleton Joseph, constable
Reynolds John, blacksmith
Reynolds Wm. shoemaker
Scott Solomon, parish clerk
Smith John, corn miller, Walling Fen
Taylor William, carpenter

*Farmers,*    Latham John
Jewitt William, Underwood Thos.
Grange    Walling Fen
Lockwood John, and Haldenby Thos. surveyors of highways

*Blanch,* in the parish of North Dalton, wap. of Harthill; 7 miles ENE. of Pocklington.

BOLTON, in the parish of Bishop Wilton, wap. of Harthill, and liberty of St. Peter's ; 3½ miles NW. of Pock-lington. There is here no place of worship except a small Methodist chapel. Pop. 112.

Preston John, Esq. Bolton hall
Leak Richard, yeoman, East Field House
Mosey William, yeoman

*Farmers,*    Ouseley John
Agar Daniel    Watson William
Calton John    Wilson John
Barnes Richard, shoemaker
Herbert Joseph, tailor
Leak John, blacksmith

BONWICK, in the parish of Skip-sea, wap. and liberty of Holderness ; 4 miles NNW. of Hornsea. Pop. 30.

Stork John and Robert, farmers

BOOTH, in the parish of Howden, wap. and liberty of Howdenshire ; 2 miles SW. of Howden. A small ferry on the opposite side of the river to that of Boothferry, is kept by Mr. William Wells, innkeeper

Copley William, vict. Punch Bowl
Ellison Richard, yeoman

*Boreas Hill,* in the parish of Paul; wap. and liberty of Holderness ; 2½ miles S. of Hedon. Its name is very applicable to its situation, which is very much exposed to the winds ; it is very near to the Humber, and the summit of Boreas Hill commands a fine prospect of her wide and expanded ed streams, with the numerous vessels sailing on its bosom.

Borsea, in the parish of Holme-on-Spalding-moor, and wap. of Harthill; 7 miles SW. of Market Weighton.

BOSSHILL, in the parish of Brandesburton, wap. and liberty of Holderness; 8 miles NE. of Beverley.

*Farmers,* Hall Thomas
Burrell John Metcalf Isaac
Duggleby John

BOUASE and BOURNE LEYS, in the parish of Wressle, division of Holme Beacon, and wap. of Harthill; 2½ miles N. of Howden.

*Farmers,* Whitfield Matthew
Clark Wm. Wilson Joseph
Laverock Wm.

BOYNTON, (P.) in the wap. of Dickering; 3 miles W. of Bridlington. The church is dedicated to St. Andrew, and the living is a discharged vicarage, of which Sir William Strickland, Bart. is the patron. On an elevated ridge, to the S. of Boynton hall, is a lofty pavillion, erected by the late Sir George Strickland, Bart. The upper room of this building, which is supported by a circular colonnade, and ascended by steps, commands a very extensive prospect, both by sea and land, particularly of Bridlington bay, and the levels at the Southern foot of the Wolds, as well as of the Northern edge of Holderness. Population, 123.

Strickland Sir Wm. Bart. Boynton hall
Simpson Rev. Thomas, vicar
Davenport Geo. farmer
Gibson Wm. blacksmith
Shepherd Thomas, farmer
Smith Francis, agent

BOYTHORPE, in the parish of Foxholes, and wap. of Dickering; 10 mls. N. of Great Driffield. Population with Foxholes, 160.

Pennock John, farmer
Riby George, farmer

BRACKENDALE, in the parish of Carnaby, and wap. of Dickering; 4½ miles SSW. of Bridlington.
Jordon Francis, farmer

BRACKENS, a township in the parish of Kilnwick, and wap. of Harthill; 7½ miles SSW. of Driffield. This township formerly contained a considerable village and a chapelry, but now consists of only one large farm. The burial ground still remains undisturbed. Population, 30.

Barugh Richard, farmer

BRACKENHOLME, in the parish of Hemingbrough, and wap. of Ouse and Derwent: 7 miles ESE. of Selby; pleasantly situated near the river Derwent. Pop. with Woodhall 90.

Halley Joseph, farmer
Rimmington Henry Wm. yeoman

BRANDESBURTON, (P.) in the wap. and liberty of Holderness; 8½ miles N. E. of Beverley. This extensive and populous village is pleasantly situated on the high road leading from Hull to Scarborough, from which places coaches and other vehicles are passing and re-passing daily, which greatly tends to the benefit of its inhabitants. There are two good inns for the accommodation of travellers. A fortnight fair or market for all sorts of cattle, is held on alternate Wednesdays, which is very fully attended, a sure criterion of its rising prosperity. The church, dedicated to St. Mary, is a very ancient structure, but has suffered much from the corroding hand of time, although it has undergone several repairs; the patronage is in St. John's College, Cambridge. The neighbouring magistrates meet here every Thursday, in a spacious room at the Cross Keys Inn, for the administration of justice. Pop. 562.

Bradshaw Rev. John, rector
Dixon Thomas, yeoman
Duke Wm. farrier
Edmunds Henry, vict. Cross Keys
Pattinson Mary, straw hat mfr.
Poskett George, schoolmaster
Poskett Geo. jun. bricklayer
Russell John, surgeon
Thornton Walter, vict. Black Swan
Todd Wm. painter
Welburn Peter, plumber & glazier
Young Widow, weaver

*Blacksmiths,* *Grocers,*
Griffin Wm. Denby Robert
Wallis James Stephenson Paul
*Butchers,* *Shoemakers,*
Hoult John Hall Robert
Whiting Wm. Hall Marmaduke
*Farmers,* *Tailors,*
Atkinson S. & J. Maxwell John
Bradshaw Wm. Phillips Wm. (&
Clifton John draper)
Grayburn James *Wheelwrights,*
Grayburn John Ashton Thomas
Harrison Richard Cowplin John
Moor John Cowplin Joseph
Ribey Thomas Robinson John
Whiting Wm.

*Carriers,*
William Dean and Thomas Freer, to Beverley every Sat. departs at 8 morn. and ret. 7 night.

P

David Thompson and Thos. Freer, to Hull every Tu. departs at 3 morn. and ret. 9 night.

BRANTINGHAM, (P.) in the wap. of Harthill and Howdenshire; 2 miles SE. of South Cave. The church is dedicated to All Saints, and the Dean and Chapter of Durham are the patrons. The Rev. John Carr, A. M. is the vicar. Pop. 174.

Nelson Captain, Marmaduke
Simpson Rev. James, A. M. curate

*Farmers & Yeomen,* Green William
Atmar George     Richardson John
Beaumont Joseph   Shaw Samuel
Brigham Thos.      Simpson Henry
Emmerson John

Thornton Edward, blacksmith
Thornton Jonathan, shoemaker

BREIGHTON, in the parish of Bubwith, and wap. of Harthill; 5 miles NW. of Howden. Pop. 179.

Bond Alexander, vict. Magpie
Holmes Joseph, gentleman
Howden Matthew, blacksmith

*Farmers,*       Simpson John
Bond John       Steel John
Brown Mary     Wood William
Hoove Thomas

---

### BRIDLINGTON, or *Burlington,*

In the wapentake of Dickering; 8 miles from Hunmanby, 12 from Driffield, 18 from Scarborough, 40 from York, and 201 from London, by way of Lincoln. This town is situated on the Eastern coast, about a mile from the shore, in the recess of the commodious and beautiful bay to which it affords its name. It consists chiefly of one long irregularly framed street, extending along the Southern declivity of a small elevation, and its situation is both pleasant and salubrious. The antiquity of Bridlington it it difficult, perhaps impossible, to ascertain, but it is clearly of Saxon origin. Early in the reign of Henry I. Walter de Gant, the son of Gilbert de Gant, one of the barons of William the conqueror, founded here a priory for the Black Canons of the order of St. Austin, which he dedicated to the blessed Virgin Mary. This priory which stands at the East end of the town, is pleasantly situated, with the command of a fine sea prospect, and was, according to Burton, inclosed with walls and houses, built of stone and lime, in 1388, in order to fortify it from the enemy's ships, which frequently entered the har-

bour. But it was not merely against their enemies, but also against their friends, that the Canons found it necessary to seek protection, for we find them under the pontificate of Pope Innocent III. complaining, "that the archdeacon of Richmond going to one of their churches, had travelled with 97 horses, 21 dogs, and 3 hawks—*tribus avibus venatoriis,* whereby he consumed more of their provisions in one hour than would have maintained their house for a long time;" on which his holiness forbade that ecclesiastics should, for the time to come, travel with a greater retinue than is allowed by the statutes of the council of Lateran, which limits the train of an Archbishop to 50 horses, a Bishop to 30, a Legate to 25, and an archdeacon to 7. This priory continued to flourish, through a succession of ages, but in the time of Henry VIII. it shared the fate of other religious houses, and William Wode, the last prior, was executed for high treason, in the year 1537, on a charge of having engaged in the rebellion in the North and East of Yorkshire, which succeeded the Pilgrimage of Grace, and aimed at the same object. At the period of the dissolution this monastery was endowed with rents, of the value, according to Dugdale, of 547l. 6s. 1d. and according to Speed, of 682l. 13s. 9d. per annum. The church of the priory appears from its remains to have been once a noble structure. The West end yet displays an inconsiderable degree of Gothic magnificence, and the date 1186, preserved on a stone placed conspicuously over the entrance is supposed to mark the year of its foundation; originally it had two towers, but they are now both demolished. The East end and the transepts are also entirely destroyed, and the remaining part is only a small fragment of the ancient building. Of the walls and fortifications which once inclosed the priory, nothing now remains except an arched gate-way, at the distance of about half a furlong from the West end of the church. Above the arch is a large room now used partly as a Town's hall, and partly as a National School,[*] and beneath are some gloomy cells, called the *Kid-cots,* which serve as places of confinement; for petty delinquents. This monastery has been the residence of several persons distinguished in their day and generation: amongst them may be reckoned, Robert the Scribe, who flourished about the year 1180, and who

[*] The average number of boys instructed in this seminary during the last year was 118, and a School for Girls is about to be established on the same system, which is that of Dr. Bell.

possessed not only great dexterity in writing, at a time when that art was a rare accomplishment, but also composed and left several books to posterity; William, of Newburgh, the celebrated Monkish historian, was a native of Bridlington, but having become a Canon of Newburgh; took his surname from that place: John de Bridlington, a native of this town, was distinguished for his abilities, and having at his death, in 1879, left behind him a fame for piety so great, as to obtain for himself a rank amongst the saints, and for his shrine the repute of a place of miracles: Sir George Ripley, a canon of this priory, and a distinguished alchemist, who, after employing about twenty years in the vain endeavour to find out the philosopher's stone, the grand desideratum of an ignorant and credulous age, left behind him at his death, in 1490, twenty-five books, of which the chief was his "Compound of Alchemy, in twelve books, inscribed to Edward IV. and his Aurum Potabile, or the Universal Specific."

On the confiscation of the monastic estates, the manor and rectory of Bridlington became vested in the crown. After several changes, the manor was at length purchased in the year 1633, for 3260l. by Wm. Corbett, and twelve others of the inhabitants, on behalf of themselves, and all the other tenants and freeholders within the manor. This manor does, therefore, in effect, belong to the town, and is held by feoffees on their behalf. On the second day of February, in every year, these feoffees elect one of their number as chief lord of the manor, in whose name the courts are called, and the business of the town transacted. The manor in all its changes was charged with an annual fee-farm rent of 144l. 17s. 5½d, which is still paid to the representatives of the late H. T. Jones, Esq.[*] The lordship contains upwards of 3000 acres.

The Church, or rather the Chapel, dedicated to St. Mary, stands at the East end of the town; and the Archbishop of York is the patron. This venerable Gothic pile indicates its origin to be of the fourteenth century. Not more than one-third of the building is fitted up for religious worship, but that portion of it is calculated to accommodate 1000 persons. The living is a perpetual curacy, of which the Rev. G. Smith is the incumbent, by the nomination of Sir Francis Lindley Wood, Bart. and his Lady, and Catharine Esther Buck, since married to the Rev. Alexander Cooke; these ladies were the

daughters and co-heiress of the late Samuel Buck, Esq. Recorder of Leeds, who inherited the right of nomination from his brother, the Rev. Matthew Buck.

The Quakers, the Baptists, the Independents, and the Wesleyan Methodists, have each their respective places of religious worship here: and the Ranters, or Primitive Methodists, are by their zeal and perseverance swelling their numbers.

The charitable institutions here are neither very numerous nor important; there is, however, in addition to the National School, already mentioned, a Free Grammar School, founded by William Hustler, in the year 1637, and endowed with 40l. wherein twenty boys, the sons of parishioners, receive gratuitous instruction; William Bower, in his life time, founded a school house, and at his death endowed it with 20l. per annum, in which school 12 poor children are now taught to read and knit; and William Cowton, by will, dated April 10, 1696, bequeathed 13l. per annum to the minister of Bridlington, for a sermon to be preached every Wednesday; 6s 8d. weekly, to be distributed in bread to the poor parishioners, and 1s. to the parish clerk for making the distribution, to be paid out of the rental of certain lands demised for the purpose, and the residue distributed amongst the poor of Bridlington, Bridlington Quay, and Hunmanby, for ever, which lands at present let for about 170l. per annum.

The history of Bridlington is not in any material degree mixed up with the general history of the country, but in the time of the civil wars between Charles I. and his parliament, this town served as the point of debarkation for those arms and military stores which the Queen purchased in Holland with the Crown jewels. Her Majesty's debarkation took place on the 20th of February, 1643, and early in the morning of the 24th Admiral Batten, who had been charged with the duty of intercepting her, commenced a heavy cannonade upon that part of the town in which she was known to have landed and placed her ammunition. According to a letter written by the Queen herself to the King, "the balls sung merrily over her head, and a sergeant was killed at a distance of twenty paces from her." After remaining at Bridlington nearly a fortnight, her Majesty departed for York, which city she reached on the 8th of March, with three coaches, and an escort of eight troops of horse, and fifteen companies of foot, conveying the ammunition and arms, which consisted of thirty pieces of brass and two pieces of iron cannon, with

* Thompson's Historical Sketch.

small arms for 10,000 men. Amongst the most zealous and enterprising of Charles's adherents was Richard Boyle, the Earl of Cork, who, for his courage and constancy, received the dignity of an English Earldom, under the title of Earl of Burlington. Contemporary with the last Earl of Burlington was William Kent, a native of Bridlington, born in 1685, whose family name was Cant, the two first letters of which he not very unpardonably changed; and of whom Walpole, in his anecdotes of painting, says—"he was a painter, an architect, and the father of modern gardening. In the first character he was below mediocrity; in the second he was a restorer of the science; and in the last an original, and an inventor of the art that realizes painting and improves nature. Mahomet imagined an Elysium, but Kent created many."

Bridlington, generally so peaceable and obedient to the laws, was roused into a state of insubordination by the passing of the militia act in 1757; on that occasion a very alarming riot took place here, during which the rioters broke open several granaries, and committed other excesses. Several of the ringleaders being apprehended were brought to trial at York, and Robert Coal, an inhabitant of Bridlington, having been convicted, was sentenced to die for the offence, and was afterwards executed.

In the year 1779, when the navy of England was less triumphant than during the revolutionary wars, several engagements took place in the British seas, and the inhabitants of the coast were frequently thrown into a state of alarm by Paul Jones, the intrepid Anglo American Buccaneer.— This man had formerly been in the service of the Earl of Selkirk, whence he was expelled with disgrace; and, having repaired to America, he volunteered to make a descent on the British coast. Being at first entrusted with the command of a privateer, he landed on the coast of Scotland, and in resentment plundered the mansion of his old master; he also burnt several vessels at Whitehaven, and performed a number of other daring exploits. These services insured his promotion, and procured him the command of a small squadron, consisting of the Bon Homme Richard, and the Alliance, each of 40 guns; the Pallas, of 32 guns; and the Vengeance armed brig.— With this force he made many valuable captures, insulted the coast of Ireland, and even threatened the city of Edinburgh.— On Monday, the 20th of September, 1779, an express arrived at Bridlington from the Bailiffs of Scarborough, with intelligence that an enemy was cruising off the coast.

The same night the hostile squadron was descried off Flamborough Head, and it was soon discovered that Paul Jones was the commander. In the night of Tuesday, a large fleet of British coasting vessels sailed into the bay, and the harbour became so completely crowded, that a great number could only find security in being chained to each other on the outside of the pier. Two companies of the Northumberland militia, then quartered in the town, were called to arms by beat of drum, after midnight; and the inhabitants, armed with such weapons as could be most readily procured, prompted to muster at the Quay, while a number of the more opulent were making preparations for sending their families into the interior. Business was now completely at a stand, and the attention of all was directed to the expected invasion. On Thursday a valuable fleet of British merchantmen from the Baltic, under the convoy of the Serapis, Captain Pearson, of forty-four guns; and the Countess of Scarborough, Captain Piercy, of twenty-two guns, hove in sight, and were chased by the enemy. The first care of Captain Pearson was to place himself between the enemy and his convoy, by which manoeuvre he enabled the whole of the merchantmen to escape in safety into the port of Scarborough. Night had now come on, but the moon shone with unusual brightness. About half past seven o'clock the thunder of the cannon announced that the engagement had commenced, and the inhabitants of the coast, on hastening to the cliffs, were presented with the sublime spectacle of a naval engagement by moonlight. The battle raged with unabated fury for two hours, when at length Captain Pearson, who was assailed by the two largest of the enemy's frigates, was compelled to surrender. Captain Piercy made also a long and gallant defence against a superior force, but he was in the end obliged to strike to the Pallas. The enemy purchased his victory at a prodigious price, not less than 300 men being killed or wounded in the Bonne Homme Richard alone, which vessel received so much injury that she sunk the next day, with many of the wounded on board.

The port of Bridlington, though well situated for commerce, has never enjoyed any very extensive trade. Malt and ale were formerly considered its staple commodities, and large quantities of each were, as we learn from Mr. Thompson's historical sketch of that place, annually shipped to London. About half a century ago, the number of malt-kilns here amounted to upwards of sixty, nearly all in full operation;

but this trade has greatly declined, and most of the kilns have been either taken down or applied to other purposes, not more than six remaining, and even those only in partial employment. The market, which is held on Saturday, has existed for upwards of 600 years, and it is plentifully supplied with all the necessaries, and as many of the luxuries of life as the wants of the inhabitants require. The corn market is well attended both by buyers and sellers, and this is one of the few ports from which the data for the average returns of the kingdom are supplied.

There are here two banking concerns: *Messrs. Harding and Holtby*, who draw on Sir J. W. Lubbock, Bart. Foster, Clarke, and Co. London; and *Messrs. Hagues, Strickland, and Co.*, of the North-Riding Bank, who draw upon Barclay, Tritton, Bevan, and Co. London. The post-office is eligibly situated on the North side of the High-street, and the information connected with this establishment will be found under its proper head, subjoined to the directory of the town.

The vicinity of Bridlington is healthful and agreeable. The valley which skirts the town on the South extends many miles to the West, and is adorned by the seats of Sir William Strickland, Bart. of Boynton; and of William Bosville, Esq. of Thorpehall, both which mansions are delightfully situated within a mile of each other, in a pleasant and fertile vale, watered by a romantic rivulet, and sheltered by rising ground on the north and on the south.

BRIDLINGTON QUAY is in the parish of Bridlington, one mile to the SE. of that place. It is a pleasant and healthful sea-bathing place, to which, for the last seventy years, there has been a considerable resort of genteel company in the summer season. The Quay constitutes of itself a small town, and has a brisk and handsome appearance. The houses are in general well built and modern; and the principal street, which opens directly to the harbour, is remarkably spacious. The harbour is formed by two piers which extend a considerable way into the sea, the northernmost of which having a convenient platform, furnishes an agreeable promenade, commanding a delightful view of the lofty promontory of Flamborough Head, and the number of coasting vessels which in time of adverse winds resort to this Bay for safety, frequently impart to the scene a peculiar degree of animation. The port, though small, is clean and secure. It is sheltered on three of its sides, by the coast, the town, and the piers, but the access, owing to the narrowness of the entrance, is somewhat difficult. The harbour is defended against the approach of an enemy by two batteries, one on the North, and the other on the South side of the town, which batteries enfilade the entrance of the port, and form a cross fire at right angles. The first mention of this harbour occurs in a mandate of King Stephen, to the Earl of York, commanding him "to permit the prior of Bridlington to have and to hold, well, and in peace, the harbour of Bridlington, as Walter de Gant, and Gilbert, his ancestor, held the same." The piers were anciently kept in repair by the owners of the manor, but in later times they have been repaired, strengthened, and extended, by certain duties on the imports and exports of the place, imposed under the authority of various acts of parliament. On the expiration of the last act, in 1816, a new act was obtained, further increasing the duties, to continue for twenty-one years, and the commissioners therein appointed were empowered to rebuild the piers with stone, either on the present, or on any other foundations. In compliance with the provisions of this act, the first stone of a new North pier was laid in the summer of 1818, on a plan by Mr. Goodrick, but the work is not yet completed. The harbour, which is dry at low water, has a spring tide flow of about eighteen feet at the entrance, which gradually diminishes as it approaches to the shore.

The harbour presents the striking phenomenon of an ebbing and flowing spring of fine fresh water. This copious fountain was discovered in 1811, by the late Benjamin Milne, Esq. collector of the customs at this port. Mr. Milne, whose public spirit and enterprise were most exemplary, with a view to improve the harbour, bored through the alluvion, which was found to consist of a bed of compact clay, twenty-eight feet thick, and a bed of cretaceous flinty gravel, fifteen feet thick, beneath which was the solid chalk; on the aperture being made, a fine column of fresh water rose with the flow of the tide, and at high water it gushed out in a copious stream; as the tide receded the newly-discovered spring gradually fell, and at low water it disappeared. This discovery, so important to the town and port of Bridlington, was made on the 5th of July, 1811, and in order to keep open the spring, a tinned copper pipe of three inches diameter, was sunk from the surface to the spring, through which the water begins to flow at quarter flood, and stops at three quarters ebb tide; the discharge continuing 4 or 5 hours each flood. At full tide the spring water stands in the perpendicular tube eight feet above the level of the salt water in the harbour, and is so pure and soft, that it is used in the washing of the finest linen, and so copious that it would supply the whole navy of England. A reservoir has since been constructed, into which the waters of this interesting spring is conducted for the use of the town and the shipping.

The most easy and obvious way of accounting for this phenomenon, is to suppose, that the spring has an outlet into the sea, probably beneath low-water mark, which outlet is open at low-water so far as to permit the spring to empty itself into the sea, but is obstructed or choked up by the flood tide, so that the fresh water accumulating in its gravelly receptacle, bursts forth at the opening which has been made for it; and continuing to flow from thence till the falling of the tide permits it to resume its original passage.* This water is of unusual purity; its specific gravity is 1001, distilled water being 1000. In the year 1816, Mr. Hume, of Long Acre, London, an eminent chemist, submitted it to a series of experiments, and the result proves that it contains per gallon about 17

* Young's Geological Survey, page 93.

cubic inches of carbonic acid gas, and the following materials, viz. :—

|  |  |
|---|---|
| Of Carbonate of lime | 9,625 grains |
| Of Muriate of lime | 3,750 |
| Of Silex, and a small portion of Oxide of iron | .125 |
|  | 13,500 |

Mr. Milne, the discoverer of the spring just described, is entitled to rank amongst the principal benefactors of Bridlington. To his public spirit and active mind the town is indebted for its daily post, the public baths, and the erection of the lighthouse at Flamborough. This gentleman was a Yorkshireman by birth, and was born at Brockwell, in Sowerby, near Halifax, on the 15th of October, 1731; in 1784, he was appointed collector of the customs at this port; and on the 23d of February, 1819, he died, to the general regret of all who had witnessed his career of active usefulness. Hitherto his ashes have slept in the north aisle of the church without a monument to do justice to his memory, and to excite others to imitate his example: till that imperious duty is performed by those he so much benefited, the following stanza, written by a gentleman of Bridlington, may contribute to preserve the memory of so much worth :—

" Is MILNE then forgotten?  His works answer, No !
And their voice, like the voice of the loud-sounding deep,
Shall be heard, while its waters continue to flow,
And yon edifice flames from the far-lighted steep.
Like its halo, dispread through the mists of the ocean,
His honours, eclip'd by no envious emotion,
Through the vista of ages shall challenge devotion,
When the spot is unknown, where his ashes shall sleep."

In addition to the ebbing and flowing spring, there is also at Bridlington a chalybeate spring, situated about half a mile to the NW. of the Quay, and issuing out of a pleasant garden near the subscription-mills, the medicinal properties of which resemble the chalybeate springs of Scarborough and Cheltenham, though the water seems to be less purgative.*

Few places present a more inviting beach than that which here descends from the Quay to the sea, and the gentle declivity of the surface is peculiarly favourable to sea-bathing. At low water the promenade is agreeable and extensive, and the compact tension of the elastic sand imparts firmness and buoyancy even to the step of the valetudinarian. Here many elegant and valuable specimens of minerals and fossils are found, which serve to give interest to

* Nicholson's Dictionary of Chemistry.

the shop of the lapidary, and to swell the varieties in the museum of the collector.— Warm and cold baths are provided in rooms replete with conveniences, built beneath the terrace, which supply the invalid or the timid with the advantage of sea-bathing without the necessity of plunging into the open sea.

The sources of amusement here are somewhat circumscribed, but the facilities for aquatic excursions, so inviting to the inhabitants of inland districts, are afforded in every variety; and the news-room and library are at hand, to impart information and amusement in the hours between the intervals of relaxation in the open air.— The neighbourhood abounds with walks and rides, affording extensive prospects of Bessingby, Carnaby, and Boynton, to the west; Sewerby, Marton, and Flamborough, to the north; and Hilderthorpe and Hornton to the south: all possess their several beauties, and claim in succession the attention of the visitors.

The places of public worship at the Quay, are a commodious Methodist meeting-house, and a newly built chapel, appropriately called the *Union Chapel*, which is used alternately for the religious services of the Independents and the Baptists.

Here, as at the parent town, the operations of commerce are very limited. The exports consist chiefly of corn and other agricultural productions shipped to the port of London, and of horses and horned cattle to Germany and Russia. The imports are principally coal from Newcastle, timber from the Baltic and America, and general merchandise from London and Hull.—During the war an extensive ropery was established and flourished at this port, but since the peace it has been greatly reduced, and the ship-yards have also felt the deadening influence of the stagnation in the shipping interest. In a port so situated as Bridlington, a "vessel sacred to humanity" becoming an indispensable requisite, and in the year 1806, a life-boat was purchased by voluntary subscription from Mr. Greathead, at an expense of three hundred pounds, for the use of this port, the beneficial effects of which is experienced every season. The population of Bridlington and the Quay, which in 1811, amounted to 3741, has been swelled during the succeeding ten years to 4272, as appears from the returns made to Parliament up to the 28th of May, 1821. The directory which is subjoined will point out the inns, lodging-houses, &c. in this place, and afford a tolerably complete list of the traders and other inhabitants.

*Bridlington . Office, High street.*

POST-MASTER——Mr. R. CROSS

Mail arrives every morning, at ½ past 7.—Letters delivered at 8 morn. The letter box is closed at 12, and letters dispatched at 20 minutes past 12.

*Quay Post Office, Commercial place,*

Miss E. THOMPSON, Post-Mistress.

Letters are received ½ an hour later and are dispatched ½ an hour sooner than those for the town of Bridlington.

## DIRECTORY.

### Academies.

Beswick Geo. (national) High street
Coates James, Back street, Quay
Hogg James, Spring gardens

Holliday and Jacks Misses, King st. Quay
Hunter James, Queen's place, Quay
Kendall Rev. Wm. Kirkgate
Kidd Wm. High street
Langdale John, High street
Linskill John, (free grammar,) Market place
Marshall Miss, King street, Quay
Pearson Robert, St. John's gate
Pilmore Joseph, Westgate
Stockell Mrs. Kirkgate
Stubbs Ralph, Back street, (French and drawing)
Thompson Mrs. (ladies) High st.

### Attornies.

Dring Henry, (office in Westgate) resides at Quay
Harland Brian Taylor, Market place
Prickett Marmaduke, Westgate
Smith Wm. Westgate
Stockell Wm. (N.P.) High street
Taylor David, High street
Wardell John, New Buildings, Quay

### Auctioneers.

Bullock John, Market place
Forth Thomas, Westgate
Winteringham Wm. Westgate

### Bacon Factors.

Dixon Catharine, High street
Johnson Elizabeth, St. John's gate
Weightman Berry, High street

### Bakers, Flour Dealers, & Shopkeepers.

Baron Geo. New buildings, Quay
Chester Wm. Market place
Cooke Seth, High street
Dixon Catharine, High street
Garbutt John, (fruiterer) High st.
Garbutt Wm. (fruiterer) St. John's gt.
Good Ann, (fruiterer) St. John's gate
Hobson Edward, Baylegate
Holliday John, Market place
Holmes Leonard, St. John's gate
Johnson Elis. St. John's gate
Kidd Wm. High street
Leeson John, Princess street, Quay
Leng Wm. High street
Machen John, Westgate
Mackerill Thos. King street, Quay
Sedman Mercy, New buildings, Quay
Smith Robert, St. John's gate
Snowball Christopher, Market place
Speck John, King street, Quay
Winteringham John, High street
Wise Christopher, Kirkgate

### Bankers.

Harding and Holtby, Market place, draw on Lubbock & Co. London
North Riding, (Hagues, Strickland & Co.) Robert Davison, agent, High street

### Billiard Table Keepers.

Furby Geo. High street

Taylor Allen, Cliffe, Quay

### Blacksmiths.
Bell Peter, Westgate
Coates John, St. John's gate
Dennis Richard, Parrot's Buildings, Quay
Holliday John, (and farrier) Market place
Ireland Wm. High street
Tate Charles, (farrier) High street
Tree Wm. Kirkgate
Turner Geo. Promenade, Quay

### Block and Mast Maker.
Medd Christopher, Queen st. Quay

### Booksellers, &c.
Forth Wm. High street
Furby George, High street

### Boot and Shoemakers.
Barnet Robert, Ship hill, Quay
Beverley John, Market place
Bullock Harland, King st. Quay
Carr John, King street, Quay
Coates John, King street, Quay
Dixon Daniel, High street
Fletcher James, High street
Humphrey John, St. John's gate
Kerry Wm. Baylegate
Kidd Thomas, High street
Lister Mark, Kirkgate
Redpath Robert, Queen st. Quay
Simpson Francis, High street
Watson Robert, Prince street, Quay
Wilkinson Isaac, Prospect row, Quay

### Braziers and Tinmen.
Dale Wm. High street
Forth Benjamin, High street
Sedman George, High street

### Brewers.
Hall Samuel, King street, Quay
Hayes John Johnson, St. John's gate
Holtby & Haggitt, High street
Mather John, High street
Nightingale John & Edw. Kirkgate

### Bricklayers.
Barr Robert, Market place
Bishop Wm. Quay road
Gray Francis, Garrison st. Quay
Gray Geo. Promenade, Quay
Holderness Francis, High street
Holderness Wm. Baylegate
Matson John, (& stone mason) Quay

### Brickmakers.
Horsley Richard and Matthew, Sea Breezes, Quay

### Butchers.
Brambles Thos. King street, Quay
Brown Geo. High street
Cape Geo. High street
Cape James, Market place
Chew John, High street
Coates John, Queen street, Quay

Cook John, Terrace, Quay
Frost Perceval, Prince street, Quay
Frost John, Prince street, Quay
Hardy John, Market place
Harrison Geo. High street
Hodgson Thos. King street, Quay
Moody Richard, Kirkgate
Pool Thos. St. John's gate
Speck Richard, Back street, Quay
Taylor Geo. Queen street, Quay
Watson John, St. John's gate

### Cabinet Makers and Upholsterers.
Bielby Matthew, High street
Bielby Wm. St. John's gate
Forth Thos. Westgate
Seller Wm. Market place
Wardell John, King street, Quay
Winteringham Wm. Westgate

### Cheese and Bacon Factors.
Fletcher Thos. High street
Thompson Benj. St. John's gate
Weightman Berry, High street
Wharton Jane, High street

### Chemists and Druggists.
Cross Ralph, (and post master) High street
Fox John, (& tea dealer) King street, Quay
Parrott James, Market place
Rayner John, High street

### Coal Merchants.
Hall Samuel, King street, Quay
Marshall Stephen, King street, Quay
Simpson John, Prospect row, Quay

### Confectioners.
Leeson John, Prince street, Quay
Pinkney Simon, St. John's gate
Speck John, King street, Quay

### Coopers.
Allison Brown, Market place & Quay
Danby George, High street
Hardy Matthew, Westgate

### Corn Merchants.
Booth Wm. New buildings, Quay
Frankish John, New buildings, Quay
Frost John, sen. Prince street, Quay
Frost Perceval, Prince street, Quay
Gray Jane, Market place
Hall Samuel, King street, Quay
Jewison John, Kirkgate
Lamplugh Thos. King street, Quay
Lawson Richard, Garrison st. Quay
Marshall Stephen, King street, Quay
Sawdon Benjamin, King st. Quay
Simpson John, Prospect row, Quay
Wetwan Geo. Spring Gardens, Quay

### Corn Millers.
Duke Moses, New mill
Hodgson Geo. High street
Parrot Geo. & Paul, Back st. Quay
Wetwan Thomas, Kirkgate

Wetwan Geo. Spring Gardens, Quay
Winteringham Robt. High st.
Winteringham John, High street

*Curriers and Leather Sellers.*
Fletcher Thomas, High street
Gilling Henry, High street

*Dyers.*
Bowland John, (silk) Westgate
Mackley Edward, worsted manufacturer, High street

*Farmers.*
Archer Ralph, St. John's gate
Brambles Thomas, Green Dike
Cape James, Market place
Coverley Francis, Market place
Fox Richard and Geo. High street
Riaby Michael, Kirkgate
Johnson Thos. Green Dike
Morris Thos. High street
Nicholson John, Green Dike
Paul Wm. Westgate
Smith James, Market place
Tasker Timothy, Hundow
Wilsh Wm. Green Dike
Woodcock John, Market place

*Fellmongers.*
Garton Thomas, Westgate
Heseltine Benoner, (and Glover) St. John's gate

*Fire, &c. Offices.*
Atlas, George Furby, High st.
County, Robert Davison, High st.
Eagle, Brown & Son, High st.
Norwich, Joseph Pilmore, Westgate
Phœnix, John Bellard, Promenade, Quay
Sheffield, Robert Harwood, High st.

*Flax Dresser,*
Knowles Gabriel, High street

*Farriers.*
Baron James, High street
Forth Wm. Market place
Forth Abraham, Garrison st. Quay

*Gardeners, Nursery and Seedsmen.*
Bateman Wm. St. John's gate
Brown Geo. (seedsman, &c.) High street
Carr John, St. John's gate
Cowton Wm. Quay Road
Innis James, High street
Mann Hugh, St. John's gate
Nelson Thomas, St. John's gate
Wilson Wm. Church green

*Glass, China, &c. Dealers.*
Chapman Joseph, King st. Quay
Shields Robert, High st.

*Goldsmiths, Jewellers, &c.*
Cowton & Sons, Queen st. Quay
Gardiner Wm. Kennedy, King street, Quay

Lampingh John, High st.
Lyon Craven, High street

*Grocers and Tea Dealers.*
Agars Geo. High street
Baron John & Geo. Baylegate
Bramley Richard, King street, Quay
Chester Wm. Market place
Clarkson Christopher, (tea) St. John's gate
Davison Robert, High street
Dunning Robert, High street, and Queen street, Quay
Fox Richard, High street
John Wm. Market place
Parrott James, Market place
Phillipkirk Geo. Prince st. Quay
Porter Daniel, (and hosier) Market place
Stephenson James, Prince st. Quay
Thompson John, High street
Vickerman John, High street
Weightman Berry, High street
Wise Christopher, Kirkgate

*Hat Manufacturers & Warehouses.*
Baron James, High street
Brown Robert & Son, High street
Forth Wm. Market place
Forth Abraham, Garrison st. Quay

*Horse Dealers.*
Fleck Andrew, Market place
Nicholson Riby, Church green

*Hosiers.*
Brown Robert & Son, High street
Porter Robert, King street, Quay
Vickerman Wm. High street
Wrangham Geo. High street

*Hotels, Inns, &c.*
Admiral Nelson, Thomas Nelson, High street
Admiral Parker, Dorothy Hutchinson, King street, Quay
Anchor, William Stabler, Back street, Quay
Black Bull, Esther Allison, High st.
Black Lion, Ann Harrison, High st.
Britannia Hotel, Robert Carr, (post chaise) Prince street, Quay
Buck, Thomas Collins, High street
Bull & Sun, Thomas Wilson, Church green
Cock & Lion, Fran. Allerston, Prince's street, Quay
Free Mason's Arms, Wm. Bishop, Quay road
General Elliott, Thomas Moody, High street
George & Dragon, Thos. Stephenson, Church green
George Hotel, Robert Edmond, (post chaise) King street, Quay
Globe, Mrs. Cranswick, High street

Green Dragon, Thos. Sawdon, (excise office,) Westgate
Light Horseman, David Whiting, Market place
Nag's Head, Thomas Anlaby, Market place
Newcastle Arms, Geo. Addy, Garrison street, Quay
New Inn, Robert Grange, King st. Quay
Pack Horse, J. Tate, Market place
Scarbro' Castle, Matthew Sinkler, St. John's gate
Ship, Thos. Coates, St. John's gate
Spring Tavern, William Atkinson, Prince's street, Quay
Star, Benj. Collinson, Westgate
Star Rhd. Jefferson, Ship hill, Quay
Stirling Castle, George Chambers, Queen street, Quay
Sunderland Bridge, Thomas Sellers, Garrison st. Quay
Tiger, John Usher, King st. Quay
Tiger, George Dove, Market place
White Swan, William Foster, Market place

*Ironmongers and Hardwaremen.*

Cranswick John, High street
Dale William, High street
Forth Benjamin, High street
Harewood Robert, High street
Sedman George, High street

*Joiners and Builders.*

Baron Robert, King street, Quay
Breckon Wm. (wheelwright) Garrison street, Quay
Jarratt Robert, Promenade, Quay
Speck John, St. John's gate
Wardell John, (& toy) King st. Quay

*Lapidaries.*

Cowton & Sons, High street & Queen street, Quay
Egglestone Francis, King st. Quay
Gardner William Kennedy, King street, Quay
Wilson Walter, Prospect row, Quay

*Libraries—Circulating.*

Forth Wm. High street
Gardner Wm. King street, Quay
Williamson Barbara, Prince st. Quay

*Linen and Woollen Drapers.*

Baron John & Geo. Baylegate
Bramley Richard, King street, Quay
Brown Robert & Son, High street
Chapman Wm. Prince street, Quay
Chapman Joseph, King street, Quay
Davison Robert, Market place
Fox Richard, High street
Greenaway Benjamin, High street
Holdsworth Wm. Commercial place, Quay
Holtby Wm. Market place

Johnson Wm. Market place
Knowles Gabriel, (linen mfr.) High street
Loadman Geo. Queen st. Quay
Porter Daniel, Market place
Porter Robert, Prince street, Quay
Thompson & Fawcett, High street
Vickerman William, (linen manufacturer) High street
Wrangham Geo. High street

*Livery Stable Keepers.*

Atkinson Geo. King street, Quay
Hobson John, Market place

*Lodging Houses at the Quay.*

s. l. Signifies Sea and Land Views, and l. Land Views only.

Arnell Christopher, (s. l.) New buildings
Author Ann, King street
Author F. (s. l.) Prince street
Baron Robert, (l.) King street
Bellard John, (s. l.) Promenade
Booth Thos. (bathing machine) Garrison street
Booth Wm. (l.) New buildings
Brambles Thomas, sen. (s. l.) Promenade
Brambles Thomas, jun. (s. l.) Prince street
Bramley R. (l.) King street
Brandon Mrs. (l.) North Back street
Briggs Mrs. (s. l.) Queen street
Briggs John, King street
Brown Mrs. (s. l.) Promenade
Bullock H. (l.) King street
Calum Mr. (s. l.) Prospect place
Champion Mrs. (s. l.) New buildings
Chapman Joseph, (s. l.) King street
Chapman Wm. (s. l.) Prince street
Clark Saml. (s. l.) Queen street
Coates Thos. (s. l.) King street
Cobb Francis, (s. l.) Queen street
Cook John, (s. l.) Terrace
Coultas R. (s. l.) Queen's place
Cousens Mr. (s. l.) North Back street
Day Geo. (s. l.) Queen street
Doeg Mrs. (s. l.) Terrace
Dring H. (l.) Prospect row
Ellis Henrietta, (s. l.) Prince street
Ellis John, Ship hill
Forth A. (l.) Garrison street
Foxton Mrs. (l.) Prospect row
Frankish John, (s. l.) New buildings
Frankish Mrs. (s. l.) Garrison street
Frost P. (s. l.) Prince street
Frost J. jun. (s. l.) North back street
Gage Geo. (s. l.) King street
Gray G. (s. l.) Promenade
Haddon Mrs. (s. l.) Promenade
Heward Mrs. (s. l.) Queen's place
Holiday Alice, (s. l.) Terrace
Hopper Mrs. (s. l.) Garrison street
Hutton Francis, (s. l.) Queen street

Jarritt Robert, (s. l.) Promenade
Leeson John, (s. l.) Prince street
Locke Mrs. (s. l.) Garrison street
Martin John, (s. l.) Queen's place
Matson J. (l.) Prospect row
Moxley Mrs. (s. L.) New buildings
Owston Mrs. (l.) Spring gardens
Philliskirk G. (s. L.) Prince street
Robinson Edward, (l.) King street
Robinson J. (s. L.) Sea breezes
Rawdon Mrs. (l.) North Back street
Scrivner T. (s. l.) Prince street
Sedman Miss, (s. l.) board & lodging, New buildings
Simpson Mrs. Mary Ann, (s. l.) New buildings
Sinclair R. (s. L.) Queen street
Smith J., (s. l.) King street
Staveley Mrs. (s. l.) King street
Stephenson James, (s. l.) Prince st.
Stephenson James, (l.) Garrison st.
Taylor Mrs. (s. l.) Prospect place
Taylor Allen, (s. l.) Terrace
Taylor G. (s. L.) Queen street
Thompson Mrs. (s. l.) Commercial pl.
Ward Sarah, King street
Wardill J. (l.) King street
Wetwan Geo. (l.) Spring gardens
Wetwan ——, (s. l.) Terrace
Williamson Mrs. (s. l.) Queen street
Williamson Miss, (s. l.) Prince street
Witty Mr. D. (s. l.) Promenade
Witty P. (s. l.) Garrison street
Wright Mrs. (s. l.) Garrison street

### Maltsters.

Baron John and Geo. Baylegate
Fox Richard, High street
Hall Samuel, King street, Quay
Holtby and Haggitt, High street
Nightingale John & Edw. Kirkgate
Simpson Robert, Baylegate

### Mattrass Makers.

Bryan Wm. High street
Pickering Wm. Garrison st. Quay

### Milliners.

Andrew Eliz. Kirkgate
Elliott Charlotte, High street
Furby Mary, High street
Greenaway Eliz. High street
Hall Rhoda, Prospect row, Quay
Redd Ann, Commercial place, Quay
Lafton Milcah, Kirkgate
Thompson and Fawcett, High street

### Perfumers and Hair Dressers.

Allison Joseph, High street
Carter Thomas, High street
Coates John, King street, Quay
Preston Francis, King street, Quay
Preston Wm. Market place

### Physician.

Mayo P. W. Prospect row, Quay

### Plumbers, Glaziers, and Painters.

Allison George, High street
Hopper John, High street
Parrott Thomas, Market place
Sedman Geo. High street
Sedman Wm. Garrison street, Quay
Woodall Richard, King street, Quay

### Printers, Letter Press.

Forth Wm. High street
Furby Geo. High street
Gardener Moses, Westgate
Kemplay Robert, Church green

### Rope and Twine Manufacturers.

Elvidge & Greenaway, Ropery, Quay
Storey Wm. High street

### Saddlers and Harness Makers.

Hall Robert, Market place
Harwood Robert, High street
Pattison John, King street, Quay
Smith Robert, High street

### Sail Makers.

Addy George, Prince street, Quay
Scrivener Thomas, Prince st. Quay

### Ship Builders, &c.

Heward Wm. Nelson, Prince st. Quay
Jarratt Wm. Promenade, Quay
Sedman and Martin, Prince st. Quay

### Ship Owners and Merchants.

Cobb Francis, Queen street, Quay
Davison Ralph, High street
Dixon Thos. Garrison street, Quay
Elvidge Wm. New buildings, Quay
Hall Samuel, King street, Quay
Lamplugh Benj. King st. Quay
Lamplugh Thos. King st. Quay
Marshall Stephen, King st. Quay
Sawdon Thos. Back street, Quay
Simpson John, Prospect row, Quay
Stephenson James, Prince st. Quay
Vickerman John, Ship hill, Quay
Ward Thos. Prince street, Quay
Ward Isaac, Prince street, Quay
Witty David, Promenade, Quay
Witty Peter, Garrison st. Quay

### Spirit and Wine Merchants.

Agars George, High street
Bramley Richard, King street, Quay
Hall Samuel, King street, Quay
Stephenson James, Prince st. Quay
Thompson John, High street

### Stone and Marble Masons.

Gray George, Promenade, Quay
Holderness Wm. Baylegate
Matson John, (and bricklayer) Prospect row, Quay
Radge Thos. St. John's gate

### Straw Hat Manufacturers.

Archer Ruth, Queen street, Quay
Coates Eliz. New buildings, Quay
Draper Mary Ann, Prince street, Quay
Elliott Charlotte, High street

Furby Mary, High street
Hopper Ann, Garrison street, Quay
Nicholson Eliz. Back street, Quay
Thompson and Fawcett, High street
Winteringham S. Westgate

*Surgeons.*
Cordukes Hampton C. High street & Terrace, Quay
Dawson and Son, High street, and King street, Quay
Morris John, Market place
Sandwith Humphrey, High street and King street, Quay
Smith Edmund, Back street, Quay

*Tailors and Drapers.*
Barker Saml. Hopper's yard, High st.
Barnett Smith, Market place
Coates Thomas, High street
Cowling Leonard, St. John's gate
Draper Robert, Baylegate
Dukes Geo. High street
Edmond Christopher, St. John's gate
Garbutt Wm. St. John's gate
Holdsworth Wm. (and draper) Commercial place, Quay
Holmes Leonard, St. John's gate
Hunter Wm. St. John's gate
Kirby Wm. Baylegate
Loadman Geo. (& draper) Queen st. Quay
Pickering Wm. Garrison st. Quay
Porter Robert, Prince street, Quay
Postill Wm. (and draper) Prince st. Quay
Stephenson James, Garrison st. Quay

*Tallow Chandlers.*
Coates Benjamin, Kirkgate
Hopwood and Furness, (and soap boilers) High street
Mather John, High street

*Timber Merchants.*
Brambles Waters, (and tile) Promenade, Quay
Marshall Stephen, King st. Quay

*Watch and Clock Makers.*
Gardner Wm. K. King st. Quay
Hunter John, High street
Lamplugh John, High street
Lyon Craven, High street

*Wheelwrights.*
Breckon Wm. Garrison street, Quay
Clark Samuel, Church green
Ford Thomas, Spring gardens
Furby John, (machine & drill & bone merchant) High street
Heseltine Joseph, Market place
Wardell John, King street, Quay

*Whitesmiths and Bell Hangers.*
Coates Thos. (and anchorsmith) New buildings, Quay
Pool Mark, Kirkgate
Popplewell Benjamin, High street

*Woolstapler.*
Linton Thos. South Back lane

*Miscellany.*
Abbott Thos. E. supervisor, High st.
Agars Mrs. Ann, Market place
Andrew Paul, gent. Westgate
Beauvais Joseph, gent. Kirkgate
Bellard John, harbour master, Promenade, Quay
Blackburn Sleightholme, gent. Queen street, Quay
Booth Miss Ann, Kirkgate
Booth Wm. gent. New buildings, Quay
Boyes Mrs. Frances, High street
Boynton Henry, Esq. New buildings, Quay
Brambles Tho. gent. Promenade, Quay
Brown John, gent. Kirkgate
Brown Mary & Sarah, gentlewomen High street
Burn Stephen, gent. St. John's gate
Clarkson Mrs. Jane, Kirkgate
Clubley Thomas, gent. Westgate
Coverley John, gent. Westgate
Coverley Samuel, gent. High street
Coverley Mrs. High street
Cranswick Matthew, gent. Prospect row, Quay
Davison Edw. gent. Garrison st. Quay
Foxton Mrs. Eliz. Quay
Frankish Mrs. Jane, High street
Frankish Mrs. S. Nungate
Gray Mrs. Alice, Baylegate
Gray James, gent. Market place
Greenaway Miss Mary, Prospect row
Haggitt John, sen. gent. Kirkgate
Harding John, Esq. Field house
Harness Rev. Robert, Baptist minister, Quay road
Hebblethwaite Miss Harriet, West
Hobson Miss Susannah, High street
Hodgson Geo. Esq. High street
Hopkinson John, gent. High street
Jackson Mrs. Ann, Kirkgate
Keith Wm. gent. Baylegate
Kelloway James, gent. Church green
Kendall Rev. Wm. P. curate of Flambro', Kirkgate
Kingston Mrs. Mary, Prospect row, Quay
Landtaff Mrs. Ann, gent. Church green
Lonsdale Mrs. Frances, King st. Quay
Lowish Mrs. Elizabeth, Church green
Lowrey Robert, gent. Spring gardens
Major Mrs. Dorothy, High street
Major Mrs. Mary, High street
Major Francis, gent. High street
Milne Mrs. Ellen, Clough bridge Quay
Moon Mrs. Esther, Westgate
Nicholson Robt. gent. Church green
Ombler Wm. gent. Kirkgate

Owston John, gent. Hill hole Garden
Owston Rich. gent. Applegarth lane
Plumer Christr. gent. High street
Preston Robt. gent. Queen st. Quay
Preston Cowton, gent. Church green
Rickaby Charles, Esq. Prince st. Quay
Savage Wm. and James, gentlemen, Spring gardens, Quay
Smith Rev. Geo. perpetual curate of Bridlington, Kirkgate
Smith Captain Geo. Promenade, Quay
Smith James, gent.
Staveley Mrs. Anne, King st. Quay
Taylor Bryan, Esq. Westgate
Thompson Robt. gent. St. John's gt
Wade Mrs. Jane, gentwn. St. John's gt.
Walmsley Mrs. Elizabeth, Ropery, Quay
Ward Isaac, gent. King st. Quay
White Misses S. and J. High street
Wilson Thomas, gent. Quay road
Yarburgh Henry G. Esq. Fort hall, Quay

*Officers of his Majesty's Customs.*

Hours of attendance from ten to four.

Howard J. B. Esq. collector
Mason John, Surveyor,
Walker John, Searcher
Waters John, Esq. comptroller, Clough bridge

Two Riding officers, two Tide waiters, and two Boatmen.

*Flambro' Preventive Service.*—Chief officer Mr. Wm. Lister and seven boatmen.

*Miscellany of Trades, &c.*

Clarke Samuel, cattle dealer, Queen street, Quay
Craven John, dancing master, Bayle gt.
Dixon John, officer of excise
Dobson Edm. basket maker, High st.
Furby Geo. toyman, High street
Holliday Wm. officer of excise
Kidd Geo. weaver, Kirkgate
Lowrey Wm. breeches maker and glover, high street
Mackley Edward, worsted spinner, High street
Matthews David, engineer, Clough bridge, Quay
Rowley, Newyear, oatmeal sheller, Kirkgate
Simpson Wm. weaver, Kirkgate
Stubbs Ralph, miniature painter, Back street, Quay
Thompson Nicholson, toll collector, High street
Ward John, licensed to let post horses, &c. St. John's gate

*Conveyance of Goods and Passengers by shipping from Bridlington Quay.*

Vessels to London, Leith, Hull, Scarborough, Newcastle, Sunderland, &c. occasionally, according to freight, 1 or 2 Weekly.

## COACHES

*From Bridlington and Quay.*

The WELLINGTON from Scarbro' (daily in summer, and 3 days per week in winter) arrives at the Nelson, Bridlington, and the Britannia Hotel, at the Quay, at 9 morning, and proceeds to Hull, from which latter place it arrives at 12 at noon.

The BRITISH QUEEN from Scarbro', and Hull, arrives at the Globe Inn, Bridlington, and the Stirling Castle, at the Quay, at the same hours as the Wellington.

## CARRIERS.

*Beeford*, Thos. Carr, every Saturday
*Beverley*, John Ward, dep. Fri. ret. Sat.
*Beverley & Hull*, Owston & Sinkler, Tu. & Fri. returns on Wed. and Sat.
*Burton Agnes*, Oliver Stephenson, to the Star, and Geo. Arnett, to the Green Dragon, Sat. arr. 11. dep. 5
*Driffield*, John Leighton and Leonard Denton, Monday and Thursday
*Flambro'*, Thomas Lamplugh, every Wednesday and Saturday
*Flambro'*, General Elliott, Thos. Beal, daily, arr. 2, dep. 12
*Flambro'*, Black Lion, High st. John Lundie, Sat. arr. 12, dep. 4.
*Foston*, Globe Inn, Joseph Hall, Sat. arr. 10, dep. 3
*Grandsmoor*, Black Lion, High street, Saml. Wray, Sat. arr. 12, dep. 4.
*Harpham*, Star Inn, Robt. Storry, Sat. arr. 11. dep. 4
*Hull*, John Ward, dep. Tu. & Fri. ret. Wed. and Sat.
*Hull*, Geo. Bayes, from Admiral Parker, Monday and Thursday
*Hull*, Wm. Jefferson from the Cock & Lion, Monday and Thursday
*Hull*, Thos. Lamplugh, Mon. & Thu.
*Hunmanby, Muston, Filey and Leppington*, Genl. Elliott & Nag's Head John Johnson & John Stephenson, every Tu. & Sat. a 10 mg. d 4 aft.
*Kilham*, Globe Inn, Thos. Hardy. Sat. arr. 9. dep. 3.
*Nafferton*, Star Inn, F. Johnson, Sat. arr. 9, dep. 3.
*North Burton*, Nag's Head, John and Eliz. Dixon, Sat. arr. 9, dep. 3
*Rudston*, Geo. Redhead, to the Pack Horse, & Thomas Taylor, to the Globe, Sat. arr. 8 dep. 3—John Hopper, to the Globe, same days and hours

Q

Scarbro', Robt. Owston, dep. Mon. &
Thu. ret. Tu. & Fri.—John Ward,
Mon. & Thu. ret. same days
Skipsea, Star Inn, Robert Holden, Sa-
turday, arr. 9, dep. 5.
Thornsholme, Star Inn, P. Boynton,
Wed. and Sat. arr. 11, dep. 5
Thwing and Wold Newton, Star Inn,
Mark Hick, Sat. arr. 9, dep. 4
York, Bayes, Pockley & Co. every Tu.
and Thu. ret. on Thu. and Sat.

BRIGHAM, in the parish of Fos-
ton, and wap. of Dickering ; 5 miles
SE. of Driffield. Pop. 103.
Blackstone Geo. vict. Board
Johnson Edmund, vict. Blue Ball,
Frodingham Bridge
Farmers.        Johnson Francis
Bateson Jeremiah Johnson Wm.
Botterill John      Robson Samuel
Hudson James      Walker Francis

BROMPTON POTTER, in the parish
of Ganton, and wap. of Dickering ; 9
miles west of Hunmanby. Population
with Ganton, 278.

Farmers,        Hopper Thos.
Groves Thomas    Robinson Geo.

BROOMFLEET in the parish of
South Cave, wap. of Harthill, and li-
berty of St. Peter ; 4 miles S.W. of
South Cave. Population, 142.

Farmers, &c.    Mainprize Wm.
Bateson John    Purden Joseph
Hopkinson Geo.  Purden John
Coulson Thos. vict. White Lion

BROUGH FERRY, in the parish of
Elloughton, wap. of Harthill, & liberty
of St. Peter's ; 3 miles SSE. of South
Cave. There is a ferry boat kept here
to convey passengers across the Hum-
ber into Lincolnshire, at Ferriby
Sluice, Pop. including Elloughton, 383.
Brown Geo. corn factor
Brown Wm. corn factor & vict. Ship
Holland Mancklin, yeoman
Terry Captain John

BUBWITH, (P.) in the wap. of
Harthill, a part in the liberty of St. Peter's;
6 miles NNW. of Howden : pleasantly situated on the banks of the Derwent, over
which it has a good stone bridge of ten
arches erected in 1793. The livings of this
church are vicarages, in the patronage of
the King and the Dean and Chapter of York.
Here is a Methodist chapel, with a good
Sunday school attached. The ground in this
neighbourhood is remarkably fertilized by
the overflowings of the Derwent, and yields
abundance, not to be surpassed except on the
banks of the Nile. Nicholas de Bubwith,

Bishop of Bath and Wales, resided here, and
he was one of the English prelates, that attended the council of Constance, when J
Huss and Jerome of Prague, were
to the flames. Population, 530.

Chaplain William, gentleman
Eland Thomas, gentleman
Fligg Nathaniel, gentleman
Leng Mary, gentlewoman
Newstead Geo. surgeon
Wilkinson Rev. John, A. B. vicar

Breweries,        Scott Marmaduke
Blanchard George, Smith Thos.
& maltster        Thomas John
Young John,       Tinner Abraham
Butchers,         Whitaker Samuel
Caukill Wm.       Shoemakers,
Clark Edmund      Ask Thomas, (
Cockshaw Mthw.    parish clerk)
Corn-millers,     Sherburn Wm.
Grundon Edw.      Smith Geo.
Howden Wm.        Stubbings Joseph
Hunter Thos.      Shopkeepers,
Farmers,          Gothorp Thos.
Beilby Joseph     Richardson Geo.
Brownbridge Peter  Tailors,
Day John          Bramley Geo.
Hawkin John       Caukill John, (
Hoove Thos.       draper)
Morritt Thos.     Ridsdale Thos.
Newham Richard Scholefield Wm.
Richardson Wm.

Biass Daniel, grocer
Dudding Benj. vict. Anchor
Hepton John, coal mert. & vict.
Holtby Thos. vict. New Inn
Hord Geo. bricklayer
Pratt James, joiner and wheel
Ross Thos. schoolmaster
Ross John, plumber and glazier
Tate Thos. blacksmith
Turner Thos. saddler

Carriers.

Mountain John, packet owner
York to Selby, takes in &
goods at this place once a fortn
Brabbs John, (land) to York every
dep. 3. mng. ret. same day.
Howden, on Tues. dep. 9 mg.
5 evening

BUCKTON, in the parish of B
lington, and wap. of Dickering; 3
miles N. of Bridlington. Pop. 147.

Dowslin John, bricklayer
Robinson Thos. blacksmith
Rounding Samuel, corn miller
Farmers,        Johnson Thos.
Allison Matthew  Oliver Hannah,
Boddy Jane            Buckton hall
Bordass John     Rex. Wm.

BUGTHORP, (P.) in the wap. of Buckrose, and liberty of St. Peter's; 7 miles NNW. of Pocklington. The parish church at this place is a small building, of which the Rev. Christopher Roberts is the vicar and patron. Population, 281.

Banks Wm. schoolmaster and vict.
Dixon Joseph, carpenter
Pexton Joseph, blacksmith

| Bricklayers, | Smith Richard |
| Cooper Thos. | West Wm |
| Cooper Geo. | Wetherill Samuel |
| Farmers, | Whitwell James |
| Bottrill John | Wrigglesworth W. |
| Coverdale James | Wright Robert |
| Flint James | Grocers, |
| Hotham Richard | Flint John |
| Hatchinson Mark | Simpson Thos. |
| Midgley Francis | Shoemakers, |
| Piercy Wm. | Binge Joseph |
| Smith Wm. | Wilkinson Robert |

BURDALE, in the parish of Wharram Percy, and wap. of Buckrose; 10 miles SE. of Malton. Population with Raisthorpe, 47.

Acklam George, farmer

BURLAND, in the parish of Eastrington, wap. and liberty of Howdenshire; 8 miles NE. of Howden.

Bell John, yeoman

BURNBUTTS, in the parish of Watton, and wap. of Harthill; 6 miles SSW. of Driffield.

BURNBY, (P.) in the wap. of Harthill; 2½ miles SE. of Pocklington. The church is dedicated to St. Giles. The Rev. Charles Carr, A.M. of Nunburnholme is the rector, and the Duke of Devonshire is patron. Pop. 95.

Ponsonby Mrs. B. gentlewoman

| Farmers, | Smith Matthew |
| Green Henry | Stubbs Thos. (and |
| Jackson Robert | carpenter) |
| James John | Wilkinson Ann |
| Kirby Robert | Wilkinson Richard |
| Parker James | Williamson Richd. |
| Ringrose Richard | Wright Wm. |

Blyth Wm. parish clerk
Clark Richard, blacksmith
Harrison John, schoolmaster

Bursea, in the parish of Holme, and wap. of Harthill; 5 miles NE. of Howden.

BURSTWICK; for Population, Directory, and other particulars, see SKECKLING.

BURTON, in the parish of Hornsea, wap. and liberty of Holderness; 1½

mile SE. of Hornsea. Population included with Hornsea.

| Farmers, | Lawton Philip |
| Baker Wm. | Watson Wm. |
| Lamplugh Christ. | |

BURTON AGNES, (P.) in the wap. of Dickering; 6 miles SW. of Bridlington. Here is a hospital for four poor widows, founded by the widow of the late William Boynton, Esq. and endowed with 20l. 10s. per annum, and a quarter of a chaldron of coals. The church is dedicated to St. Martin, of which the Rev. Thomas Mills, is the vicar, and Mr. T. A. Mills patron.—Population, 321.

Boynton Sir Francis, Bart. Burton hall

| Farmers, | Wilson Richard |
| Kingston John | Grocers, |
| Kingston Wm. | Owston Francis |
| Major Robert | Topham Phillis |
| Robson James | Tailors, |
| Sawdon John | Bewell Thos. |
| Sawdon James | Day Nickson |

Anderson Francis, gardener
Coupland John, shoemaker
Gibson John, blacksmith
Jefferson Wm. vict. Blue Bell
Lawson Norwood, schoolmaster
Lee Wm. carpenter & wheelwright
Lowson Robert, corn miller

Coaches daily to Beverley, Hull, Bridlington, and Scarbro'.

Carriers—George Arnott, Oliver Stephenson, and Jane Day, to Bridlington, Wed. and Sat.

BURTON BISHOP, (P.) (otherwise South Burton), in the wap. of Harthill; 3 miles W. of Beverley. The church, dedicated to All Saints, is a discharged vicarage, in the patronage of the Dean and Chapter of York. Here is a small Baptist chapel, with a Sunday school, in which one hundred children receive instruction. Hanby's hospital accommodates six poor persons, and there is a small endowed school for ten boys. Population, 534.

*⁺* Letters arrive at ¼ past 4 mg. and at 20 minutes past 4 afternoon.

Berry Rev. Abraham, Baptist minister
Holdsworth Rev. Thos. curate
Watt Francis, Esq.
Watt Richard, Esq.
Wilkinson James, gentleman

| Farmers, | Gregson Thos. |
| Almack Thomas, | Jackson John |
| Burton Lings | Johnson Robert |
| Dunning Robert, | Marr Henry |
| (& corn miller) | Sample Thomas, |
| Escritt John | Burton Grange |

Stephenson Rt.sen.    Watson Wm.
  Mount pleasant    Whiting Thomas,
StephensonRt.jun.    (and butcher)
  Cold harbour    Withell John

Atkinson John, tailor
Cook Mark, schoolmaster & shopkpr.
Dunkin Thomas, agent to R. and F.
  Watt, Esqrs.
Leaf Robert, boot and shoe maker
Linwood John, tailor
Lonsdale Thos. joiner & wheelwright
Merritt William, blacksmith
Nelson Richard, grazier
Nelson Robert, shopkeeper
Reed John, schoolmstr. & parish clerk
Rotherford John, boot & shoe maker
Senior Jane, vict. " Evander"

  *Carrier*, Christopher Ion, to Beverley, every Saturday

  *Burton Cherry*, see Cherry Burton.

BURTON CONSTABLE, in the parish of Swine, wap. and liberty of Holderness; 5 miles N. of Hedon. Near to this hamlet stands the ancient and elegant mansion of Sir Thomas B. Constable, Bart. pleasantly situated in the centre of a large park, well stocked with deer, and fruitful gardens, ornamented with water works.

Clifford George, Esq.
Harrison George, farmer
Hodgson Joseph, farmer
Oman William, corn miller

BURTON FLEMING, (or North Burton) (P.) wap. of Dickering; 3 miles S. of Hunmanby. There is here a church, of which H. Osbaldeston, Esq. is the patron, and the Rev. Thomas Gilbank vicar, and a Methodist chapel. Pop. 386.

Banks Rev. Jabez, curate

| *Carpenters,* | Martin Wm. |
|---|---|
| Agars John | Milner Richard |
| Garton Geo. | Nesfield Thos. and |
| *Farmers,* | William |
| Appleby John | Riby George |
| Artley Robert | Staveley Thomas |
| Coulson Stephen | Wharram Thos. |
| Gray John | *Grocers,* |
| Hall Wm. | Lownsborough W. |
| Major Wm. | Meeke Wm. |

Beswick George, vict. Board
Cape James, schoolmaster
Coulson Stephen, horse dealer
Ezard John, vict. Volunteer
Ireland George, blacksmith
Pudsey Stephen, tailor
Robinson Thomas, shoemaker
Smith Matthew, corn miller

  *Carriers*, John and Betty Dixon, —dlington every Saturday.

BURTON PIDSEA, (P.) in the wap. of Holderness, and liberty of St. Peter's; 4 miles E. of Hedon. A neat and pleasant village, the houses of which are well built, and afford an extensive prospect of the surrounding country. The church is a small building, patrons Dean and Chapter of York, with a lofty tower apparently of great antiquity. The incumbent is the Rev. Jonathan Dixon, vicar; here is likewise a Methodist chapel, built in 18—. Population 378.

Barnes Rev. Joseph Lightfoot, curate
Clapham William, yeoman
Harland William, yeoman
Jones Robert, Lieut. R. N.
Raines Isaac, surgeon, &c.

| *Blacksmiths,* | Salmon Thomas |
|---|---|
| Grasby Thos. | Spencer William |
| Rotsey Walter | Wright John |
| *Farmers,* | *Shoemakers,* |
| Carter John | Brown John |
| Clapham Robert | Carter Wm. |
| Cook Samuel | Hastings Richd. |
| Duke John | *Tailors,* |
| Ford Wm. | Brown Thos. |
| Ford Thomas | Pool Charles |
| Harrison Watson | *Wheelwrights,* |
| Hastings Richard | Stamford John |
| Hopkinson Joseph | Walgate John |

Brown David, plumber, &c.
Brown George, bricklayer
Dibney Wm. parish clerk
Ford Thos. grocer and schoolmaster
Rotsey Walter, vict. Black Bull
Spencer Geo. cabinet maker
Wood James, butcher

  *Carriers*, Peter Drew and David Tavender, to Hull every Tu. dep. 8 mg. ret. 7 evg.

BURYTHORPE, (P.) in the wap. of Buckrose; 5 miles S. of Malton. Here is a Church of the Establishment, of which the Rev. Robert Howard, rector, is the incumbent; and the King is patron; a Methodist chapel with a small Sunday school. In the year 1768, died Francis Consitt, of this place, who had attained the patriarchal age of 150 years. Pop. including Thextonthorpe, 216.

Coates Mark, stone mason
Creyke John, surveyor of East-Riding bridges
Doukes Robert, tailor
Haxby Wm. vict. Bay Horse
Hudson Charles, grocer
Wales C. shoemaker
Ward David, blacksmith

| *Farmers,* | Botterill Geo. |
|---|---|
| Allison Richard | Creykes John |
| Allison & Arnell | Hudson Richard |

Jennings Thos. | Wales Geo.
Preston Wm. | Whitwell Joseph
Taylor Wm. | Wood James

BUTTERWICK, in the parish of Foxholes, wap. of Dickering; 7 miles N. of Driffield. There is a Chapel of Ease, of which the Rev. Wm. Preston is curate, and the rector of Foxholes is patron. Population 98.

Baron Richard, blacksmith
Wood Robert, grocer and tailor

*Farmers,*
Holtby David | Wardell Francis
Spink John | Wilson Matthew

CARLETON, in the parish of Aldbrough, wap. and liberty of Holderness; 8 miles N. of Hedon. Population included with Aldbrough.

Midforth John, farmer
Stephenson Samuel, farmer

CARNABY, (P.) in the wap. of Dickering; 2½ miles SW. of Bridlington. Here is a Church of the Establishment, dedicated to St. John the Baptist, of which the Rev. T. Simpson, vicar, is the incumbent, and Sir G. Strickland, Bart. patron. Pop. 130.

*Farmers,*
Belwood Henry | Robinson Geo.
Jordon John | Seller John
Reastone Wm. | Sharp Thomas
Grange Robert, tailor | Smith Richard
Grime John, grocer
Shaw John, schoolmaster
Wilson Wm. wheelwright
Wright Benjamin, blacksmith

*Carr Houses,* in the parish of Howden, wap. & liberty of Howdenshire; 4 miles ESE. of Howden.

*Castle Hill,* in the parish of Sutton, wap. and liberty of Holderness; 4 miles NE. of Hull. Tradition says that a castle once stood on this hill, of which, however, not a vestige is to be seen at present.

CATFOSS, in the parish of Sigglesthorne, wap. and liberty of Holderness; 9½ miles NE. of Beverley; is a small hamlet situated on an eminence, and affording an extensive prospect of the neighbouring country: this hamlet was formerly the seat of the Bethels, and previously that of the Constables. Tradition says that one of the kings of Mercia resided here. Pop. 49.

*Farmers,*
Hudson Wm. | Salvidge Joseph
Runton James | Stahler James
 | Wheatley Geo.

*Cattle Holmes,* in the parish of Lowthorpe, and wap. of Dickering; 6 miles E. of Driffield.

CATTON (High and Low), in the parish of Low Catton, & wap. of Harthill; 7½ miles ENE. of York. There is a Free Grammar School at High Catton, for teaching a limited number of scholars; here is a Church of the Establishment.

CATTON HIGH, is a village in the parish of Catton Low; 7½ miles S. from York. Population 198.

Hemsell Wm. yeoman
Horsley John, yeoman
Kirby Thomas, yeoman

*Farmers,*
Arnott Thomas | Kirby John
Bell Francis, Catton park | Marshall Thos.
Dales John | Quarton Robert
Johnson John | Quarton Mrs. E.
Kemp John, Catton grange | Skelton Thomas
 | Smith Thomas

Hutchinson Thos. vict. Woodpecker Lass
Lazenby John, tailor
Shepherdson Thos. joiner & carpenter
Shepherdson Wm. wheelwright

*Carriers.*——Henry Rawcliff and Joseph Gate, to York every Sat. dep. at 7 mg. and ret. same day.

CATTON LOW, is a parochial village and a rectory; the Rev. F. H. R. Stanhope, is rector. The church, which is dedicated to All Saints, is in the patronage of the Earl of Egremont. The Rev. Thomas Shield master of the grammar school. Pop. 177.

Bosomworth Richard, yeoman
Caldridge John, steward to Lord Egremont, Catton lodge
Longbotham Rev. Mark, curate

*Farmers,*
Flint Wm. | Kirby Richard
Harbott Wm. | Long William
Hewison George | Marshall Thomas
Horseley Mrs. M. | Marshall Wm.
 | Spence John
Stephenson William, joiner
Vause John, shoemaker

CATWICK, (P.) in the wap. and liberty of Holderness; 7½ miles NE. of Beverley. The church is a small gothic structure, dedicated to St. Michael, of which the King is patron, and the Rev. John Torre is rector.—Population 190.

Gibson George, yeoman
Hood William, yeoman
Park Godfrey, yeoman
Plewress John, corn miller

*Farmers,*
Rainton Henry | Collinson Wm.
Clark James | Dixon Robert
 | Hardy Wm.

*Carrier.*—Thomas Hagar, to Hull every Fri. and Beverley every Sat.

CAVE NORTH, (P.) in the wap. of Harthill, and liberty of St. Peter's; 2 miles NW. of South Cave. The lordships of North and South Cave were given by William the Conqueror, to Jordayne, who after the custom of those times took the surname of Cave. The Methams of Metham, had formerley a seat here which is now pulled down. Here is a church of the establishment, dedicated to All Saints, of which R. C. Burton, Esq. is patron; with a chapel for the Methodists, and another for the Society of Friends. Population, 783.

Clarkson Abraham, yeoman
Foster Charles, gentleman
Foster Elizabeth, gentlewoman
Hilton John, surgeon
Holborn Geo. yeoman
Sissons Edward, yeoman
Todd Rev. Robert, vicar
Torrington Mrs. gentlewoman

| *Butchers,* | *Shoemakers,* |
|---|---|
| Petch Richard | Batty George |
| Stather Edward | Boast Richard |
| *Corn Millers,* | Hicks John |
| Fallowfield Wm. | Stainton John |
| Lee Thomas | *Shopkeepers,* |
| *Farmers,* | Collison John and |
| Blossom Richard | Sons |
| Everingham Saml. | Hewson Wm. |
| Foster Daniel | Murgatroyd John |
| Lee Thomas | Simpson Wm. |
| Moss Wm. | Sutton James |
| Stather Robert | *Tailors,* |
| Walker Thos. | Pieroy Thomas |
| *Fellmongers,* | Ward William |
| Blanchard Geo. | *Wheelwrights,* |
| Brabbs Absalom | Ellison Wm. |
| | Wright John |

Coulson Wm. surveyor of highways
Craggs John, paper maker
Dalton Richard, blacksmith
Dean Thos. vict. Black Swan
Kirby Richard, surveyor of taxes
Marshall Robert, bricklayer
Tindall Matthew, schoolmaster
Walker Thos. vict. White Horse
Watson Robert, gardener and parish clerk
Wilton James, vict. White Horse

*Carrier.*—Wm. Lundy, to Hull every Tu. and Fri.

The RODNEY coach from Hull to London passes here about 8 morn. and ret. about 2 afternoon.

## CAVE SOUTH.

(P.) in the wapentake of Harthill, and liberty of St. Peter's; 7 miles SSE. of Market Weighton; 9 from Beverley; 10 from Hull; & 26 from York; situated in a hollow, from which probably it derives its name; is a small market and post-town in the division of Hunsley Beacon, and at the western foot of the Wolds, in a very pleasant tract of country, about three miles from the river Humber. The parish is very extensive, and comprehends the townships of South Cave, Broomfleet, Faxfleet, and Osmandyke, and is bounded on the south, for a very considerable way, by the Humber. The church is a plain and neat edifice, dedicated to All Saints, the Rev. E. W. Barnard vicar and patron, built, as appears by inscription in the inside, in the year ... There is a National School, Robert Sharp master. The market is held every Monday, at which a great quantity of corn is sold, and sent by the Humber and its branches to Leeds, Wakefield, and the other populous towns of the West-Riding, in vessels, which bring back coals, lime, flags, slate, stone, and various other articles. Near this town is Cave castle, now the seat and principal residence of Henry Barnard, Esq. The mansion-house is a large and noble structure, ornamented with a number of turrets, battlements, buttresses, &c. which give it an air of magnificence. The embellishments of the interior correspond with the grandeur of the exterior. It contains many spacious and elegant apartments, with a very select and valuable collection of pictures, by the best masters; among these is a portrait of the late celebrated General George Washington, the founder of the American Republic, whose great-grandfather, John Washington, lived here and possessed part of this estate; but emigrated from hence to America about the year 1657, and settled at Bridges Creek, in the county of Westmoreland, in Virginia, where the family has ever since remained. Population, 885.

POST-MASTER—BARNARD COOK, *Office at the Fox & Coney, Market pl.*

Letters arrive at 3, and are sent off every afternoon, at 4 o'clock.

### DIRECTORY.

Barnard H. G. Esq. South Cave Castle
Day Francis, surgeon, Market place
King Rev. John, A. M. minister of St. James's church, Leeds.
Leeson Thavill, gent. West end
Levitt James, gent. Market place.

Shackleton Wm. merchant, Market
  place, and at Hull
Senley Eliz. gentwmn. Market pl.

*Academies, &c.*
Jackson Francis, Market place
Sharp Robert, National School
Windross George

*Attornies.*
Robinson John, Market place
Walmsley & Leeson, Market place

*Blacksmiths.*
Levitt Rachael
Morley David, Market place
Pickering Matthew

*Boot and Shoemakers.*
Atkinson Wm. (and leather cutter)
  Market place
Cade Joshua, Market place
Glasby Samuel, Market place
Thompson Robert, West end
Thornham Wm. sen. Westgate
Thornham Wm. jun. Westgate

*Bricklayers.*
Milner James, Westgate
Smith John, Market place

*Butchers.*
Barrett Joseph, Market place
Cade Wm. Market place
Holborn John, Market place
Tindall Valentine, Market place
Wilkinson Wm. Market place

*Farmers.*
Arton Henry, Market place
Ayre Samuel, West end
Barff Abraham, Market place
Bridgeman Giles, Market place
Fisher Thomas, Market place
Fisher Mary, Westgate
Kirby Richard, Cave common
Lancaster Wm. West end
Laverack Wm. Cave common
Marshall Richard, West end
Marshall Robert, West end
Marshall Thomas, (and corn miller)
  Low mill
M'Turk George, West end
Oldfield Samuel, Castle farm
Robinson Matthew, West end
Robson Thomas, Mount airey
Smith George, Cave sands

*Inns and Taverns.*
Bay Horse, Rachel Levett, West end
Bear Inn, Rhd. Newlove, Market pl.
Fox & Coney, Barnard Cook, (excise
  & post office,) Market place
Three Tuns, John Tindall, Market pl.
Windmill, Wm. Cousen, Market pl.

*Shopkeepers,*
Atkinson Wm. Market place
Coates Mary, Market place

Corner Christopher, (& agent for H.
  G. Barnard, Esq.) Market place
Galland Joseph, Market place

*Tailors.*
Moody Matthew, Market place
Wandley John, (& draper) Market pl.

*Wheelwrights.*
Gardam John, Westgate
Nicholson Robert, and David Dennis,
  Market place
Petfield George, Westgate

*Miscellany of Trades.*
Bentley John, weaver, Market pl.
Dunn Timothy, horse dealer, Market
  place
Forge Stephen, auctioneer & appraiser
Goldwell Richard, gardener, Market
  place
Harrison Thos. saddler & collar mkr.
Holborn George, gunsmith
Holborn John, plumber & glazier
Jackson Francis, grocer, druggist,
  linen & woollen draper, & hard-
  ware dealer, Market place
Kemp Robert, tinner & brasier
Oldfield Wm. common brewer
Pinder Thos. grocer & draper, Mar-
  ket place
Stothard Benj. clock & watch mkr.
Tindall John, cooper
Walker Thos. baker, Market place

## COACHES.

*From the Fox and Coney, Market place.*
The RODNEY, from Hull to Thorne,
  at 8 mng. ret. 4 evg.
*Carriers*—Blanchard and Cousens to
  Hull, on Tu. & Fri. dep. 4 morn.
  ret. 9 evg.
Smithson Frank, from Howden to
  Hull, arr. at ½ past 12 on Monday
  noon, and ret. at 3 on Tu. aft.

CAVILLE, in the parish of Eastrington, wap. and liberty of Howdenshire; 3 miles NNE. of Howden. Population included with Portington.

Blanchard Geo. yeoman, Caville hall

CAWKILL, in the parish of Wattos,
and wap. of Harthill; 6½ miles SSW.
of Driffield.

Nicholson Elijah, farmer

CAYTHORPE, (High and Low) in
the parishes of Boynton and Rudstone,
and wap. of Dickering; 3½ miles W. of
Bridlington. Pop. 26.

Milner Major, farmer, Low Caythorp
Daggett Rbt. farmer, High Caythorp

Cheapsides, in the parish of Eastrington, wap. and liberty of Howdenshire: 3 miles from Beverley.

CHERRY BURTON, (P.) (otherwise North Burton,) wap. of Harthill; 3 miles NW. of Beverley. This is a rectory, dedicated to St. Michael, Mr. Robert Moxon and others are patrons, the Rev. R. D. Waddilove, dean of Ripon, rector, and the Rev. H. W. Hunter, B.A. curate. Pop. 417.

Robinson David, Esq. Burton hall

| Farmers, | Stephenson Ralph |
|---|---|
| Almack Thos. | Vickers Robert |
| Burgess. Richard | *Shoe, &c. makers,* |
| Johnson Wm. | Battle John |
| Lee John (& horse | Everingham Benj. |
| dlr.) Gardham | Wilson Thos. |
| Ombler John | *Tailors,* |
| Purdon Robert | Cross Thos. |
| Sissons Wm. (& | Horsfield Thos. |
| shopkeeper) | *Wheelwrights, &c.* |
| Smith Anthony | Archer Thos. |
| Stephenson Buttle | Cook John |
| Stephenson Lawrn. | Watson Stephen |

Arnot John, bricklayer
Bilton John, jun. vict. Bay Horse
Griffin Wm. blacksmith
Johnson Wm. shopkeeper
Midgley Wm. schoolmaster, land surveyor and parish clerk
Watson John, machine maker

*Carriers*—Robert Sissons & Wm. Cook to Beverley every Saturday.

CLIFFE-*cum*-LUND, in the parish of Hemingbrough, and wap. of Ouse and Derwent; 3 miles E. of Selby. The school at Cliffe, has an endowment of about 40l. per annum bequeathed about a century ago by Mrs. Mary Waud, to teach 20 scholars; the salary allowed to the schoolmaster, Joseph Turton, is 30l. per ann. 10l. being reserved for contingencies. Pop. 501.

Burton Wm. gent. Turnham hall
Baxter Jonathan, yeoman
Caukill Thomas, yeoman
Morfitt Wm. yeoman

| Farmers, | Shepherd John, & |
|---|---|
| Appleby Robert | blue slate dlr. |
| Buckle Henry | Shepherd Wm. |
| Bussey Wm. | Barlow ln. end |
| Clarkson Geo. | Templeman Wm. |
| Craven James | White moor |
| Hulton James | Vollans Mary, |
| Longfellow F. | White moor |
| Lelley John, New- | Webster Geo. |
| land's house | Wilson Wm. (and |
| Nappey Mary, | corn miller |
| Goole hall | *Shoemakers,* |
| Philips John, (& | Milner Robert |
| butcher) | Pinder Peter |
| Scarr Thos. | |

Braithwajt Thomas, tailor
Broadbent George, wheelwright
Brown Thos. vict. Plough & Ship
Holmley Wm. shopkeeper
Pratt Wm. blacksmith
Robinson John, vict. Queen's Head
Shaw Henry, shopkeeper
Twiton Joseph, schoolmaster
Walker Wm. corn miller

CLIFFE, (North,) in the parish Sancton, and wap. of Harthill; 3 miles S. of Market Weighton. Pop. 89.

| Farmers, | Geldart Barney |
|---|---|
| Appleton Tim. | Leake Francis |
| Appleton Wm. | Leake Wm. jun. |
| Foster David | |

Appleton Simon, vict. Gate

CLIFFE, (South,) in the parish North Cave, and wap. of Harthill; miles S. of Market Weighton. Population, 131.

| Farmers, | Geldart Wm. |
|---|---|
| Cash James | Knapton Wm. |
| Gardam Robert | Tindale Thos. |
| Geldart Edward | Wild Geo. |

Turner John, shopkeeper

CONISTON, in the parish of Swine wap. and liberty of Holderness; miles NE. of Hull. Pop. 137.

Brook Wm. bricklayer
Hewit Joseph, blacksmith
Lingwood Wm. schoolmaster
Morris Edward, wheelwright
Northgrave Jane, vict. Board
Smith David, tailor

| Farmers, | Tavender Wm. |
|---|---|
| Carrick Thos. | *Shoemakers,* |
| Curtis John | Fairbank Wm. |
| Grave Matthew | Spofford Wm. |
| Hobson Henry | |

CORPS LANDING, in the parish of Hutton Cranswick, and wap. Harthill; 6 miles SE. of Driffield. wharf on the river Hull.

Dalby Nathan, farmer

COTHAM, in the parish of Langtoft, wap. of Dickering, and liberty St. Peter's; 5 miles NNW. of field. Here is a Chapel of Ease Langtoft. Pop. 16.

Brown Rev. Wm. curate
Hornby Thomas, gent. farmer

COTTINGHAM, (P.) in the wap. of Harthill; 4 miles NW. of Hull. This place is of considerable antiquity and ranks amongst the most pleasant, healthful, and populous villages of the East Riding of Yorkshire. Cottingham was known as a manor at the time when Domesday book was compiled; and it is stated by Leland in his *Collectanea*, that William d'Estoteville or Stuteville, being sheriff of Yorkshire, entertained King John at his house in this town, and in 1200, obtained from that monarch a licence to hold a market and fairs* here, and to fortify his castle. This mansion, under the designation of Baynard Castle, remained a monument of feudal magnificence in the successive possession of the Stutevilles, the Bigods and the De Wakes, until the reign of Henry VIII. when it was destroyed by fire,† but the ramparts are still visible, and the fosses with which it was surrounded are seen in the gardens which now occupy the site of the ancient castle and its precincts. The story of the conflagration of Baynard castle is curious, and characteristic of the monarch in whose reign it was destroyed: Henry, who was then at Hull, hearing that Lord Wake of Cottingham, had a very beautiful wife, sent a message to his lordship informing him that it was his intention to dine with him the day following. This intimation the noble baron received with feelings resembling those by which the patriarch was moved when the Princes of Egypt *condescended* to notice him on account of his wife Sarai; to say that Lady Wake, was his sister would have been unavailing, her lord therefore took a still more effectual means of preserving his wife's honour and his own head; for on the very night that the message was received from the king, the steward, by order of his master, set fire to the castle and burned it to the ground: it was of course given out that the fire was accidental, but it appears from certain family manuscripts‡ that it was a sacrifice made by a subject, to avert the consequences apprehended from the contaminating presence of a licentious prince. Henry, in the munificence of his disposition, offered to present his lordship with 2000l. towards the re-building of Baynard castle, but his lordship was in no humour to receive presents from a person whose friendship he so much dreaded, and this once famous edifice has been suffered to sink into utter ruin. On the death of Lord Wake, without male issue, the lordship of Cottingham, with two thousand four hundred and sixty-six acres of land, came into possession of the Duke of Richmond, the Earl of Westmoreland and Lord Powis, who had married his three daughters, since which time the estate has been divided into three manors called Cottingham Richmond,

* The market has long been discontinued, and the only fair now in existence is held on the feast of St. Martin.
† In August, 1541.
‡ Tickell's Hull, page 188.

Cottingham Westmoreland and Cottingham Powis.

In the 15th year of the reign of Edward II. Thomas Lord Wake founded and built a monastery for the canons of the order of St. Austin, or Black Canons at Cottingham; but finding that a perpetual title could not be made to the site, the monastery was removed, in 1324, to a neighbouring hamlet, about a mile to the southward, called Alta-prism, or Haltemprice, in the county of Hull, and dedicated to the nativity of our blessed Saviour, the annunciation of the Virgin Mary, and the exaltation of the Holy Cross. This religious house continued to flourish till the dissolution, when there was a prior and eleven canons, who were endowed, according to Dugdale, with 100l. 0s. 3½d. and according to Speed with 178l. 0s. 10½d. In the 32nd year of Henry VIII. the site was granted to Thomas Culpepper, but the house sunk into ruin, and has now totally disappeared. Haltemprice now belongs to the ancient family of the Ellerkers, is extra-parochial, and pays no parish rates. The parish church of Cottingham is a large and handsome gothic structure, built in the year 1272, and dedicated to St. Mary, the virgin. A stately tower or steeple arises from the centre; the interior is commodious and well lighted, and the walls are adorned with several elegant monuments, especially those of the Burtons of Hotham. In the choir is an old tomb-stone without date, nearly as ancient as the church, erected to the memory of Nicholas de Stuteville the founder. The living is a vicarage, not in charge, of the certified value of 42l. of which the Rev. James Deans, is the incumbent, and the Bishop of Chester, the patron. There are two meeting houses here; the Independent chapel, of which the Rev. Spedding Curwen, is the minister, and the Methodist chapel, supplied with a change of ministers from the annual conference. There is also an endowed school for the education of ten poor children, the revenue of which is 40l. per annum, bequeathed by Mark Kirby, Esq. of Hull, in 1712; and a dole of 10l. a year left by Robert Mills, of Cottingham, and distributed amongst the poor at Christmas.

There are numerous springs of excellent water in and about the town; and in the estate of Thomas Thompson, Esq. adjoining to the ancient road called Keldgate, leading from Cottingham to Eppleworth, are intermitting springs resembling the Vipsies or Gipsies, springs on the wolds. The openings of these springs are numerous and the quantity of water issuing from them is very great. They begin to flow in the spring, and continue for two or three months, when the water totally subsides, and the ground continues perfectly dry for an interval of two, three, or four years. With such intermissions the springs seem sometimes almost forgotten until the re-appearance of the water brings them to the remembrance of the inhabitants, who in their familiar language are accustomed to say, " Keldgate springs have broke out again."

Twenty years ago Cottingham was a favourite place of residence for the more opulent portion of the merchants of Hull, and it still boasts of many handsome country houses, gardens and pleasure-grounds; but they have rather diminished than increased during that period. The parish forms an irregular figure approaching to a square, and is about 4 miles in extent from East to West, and from North to South. The soil is various, and is occupied in a manner suited to its quality. Immediately adjoining the town the land is chiefly cultivated as garden ground, and produces large quantities of fruit and vegetables for the Hull market. In the village of Newland, in the eastern part of the parish, there is a great extent of pasture and meadow land, from which Hull is supplied with milk and butter; and on the edge of the hills to the west are many very considerable farms of arable land, in an improved state of cultivation. Two stage coaches run daily between Cottingham and Hull, and from the facility of communication, the former may be considered in the suburbs of the latter place. The population of the parish of Cottingham, amounts to 2,479.

†*† A foot postman brings letters from Hull every day, except Tuesday.

*Miscellany.*

Deans Rev. James, A.M. vicar
Haworth Benjamin Blayds, Esq. Hull Bank house
Sykes Daniel, Esq. M. P. for Hull, Raywell
Thompson Thos. Esq. Cottingham castle
Askham Martha, gentlewoman
Bilton Wm. gentleman
Carlile Jane, gentlewoman
Carlile George, gentleman
Carlile Robert, gentleman
Champney Thos. Nelson, gent.
Codd Edward, solicitor & town clerk for Hull
Coltish Mary, gentlewoman
Curwen Rev. S. Calvinist minister
Ellis Phineas, gentleman
Habbershaw M. gentleman
Hebblewhite John, gentleman
Holland Manklin, yeoman
Jackson Wm. yeoman

Kay Wm. gentleman
Ker Richard, Esq.
Leek Rebecca, gentlewoman
Melbourn Mary, gentlewoman
Moxon Wm. gentleman
Rennards Mrs. gentlewoman
Ringrose Samuel, gentleman
Ringrose John, yeoman
Ritson Wm. attorney, &c.
Simpson Ann, gentlewoman
Swann Sarah, gentlewoman
Travis John, gentleman
Watson P. W. gentleman
Westoby John, gentleman
White John, gentleman
Wilkinson Wm. Watson, gent.
Witty Wm. gent. (land agent)

*Academies, &c.*
Deans Rev. Jas. A. M. (free gramm
Green Wm. (boys classl. & commen
Jackson Elizabeth, (ladies' day)
Laverack Alice, (ladies' boarding)
Levett John, (gent's. day)
Stather Thos. gent's. boarding)

| *Bakers,* | |
|---|---|
| Gibson Wm. | Briggs Robert |
| Ross Francis | Brigham Wm. |
| *Blacksmiths,* | Bromley Wm. |
| Green John | Buttrick Mark |
| Humble Wm. | Calvert John |
| Martin John | Dalby James |
| Wardle Thos. | Dales Wm. |
| *Brewers,* | Day Robert |
| Curwen Thos. | Deighton Jane |
| Spenceley Wm. | Ellerton Josiah |
| *Bricklayers,* | Ellyard Samuel |
| Coverdale Henry | Everingham Jas |
| Coverdale John | Everingham Tho |
| Hill Wm. | Fisher John |
| Stark Wm. | Green W. E. |
| Stather Samuel | Hall Nicholas |
| *Butchers,* | Hill Wm. |
| Hutty Joseph | Hought John |
| Liversedge Wm. | Hudson John |
| North Geo. | Kirk Geo. |
| Ross John | Longboue James |
| *Cabinetmakers,* | Lund Wm. |
| Carter Joseph | Mantle Geo. |
| Ross Mary | Moore Mrs. E. |
| *Carpenters,* | Prescott Richard |
| Dalby Daniel | Reader Geo. |
| Dickinson Thos. | Ruston Thos. |
| Green Wm. | Smith Robert |
| Scruton Wm. | Smith David |
| *Corn-millers,* | Stainton Thos. |
| Allison & Wright | Stephenson John |
| Burgess Geo. | Thompson John |
| *Farmers,* | Todd Robert |
| Alvin Jonathan | Todd Robert |
| Archbutt Thos. | Tuke Wm. |
| Archbutt Wm. | Turner Robert |
| Atkinson Wm. | Twidle Richard |
| Bailey John | Twidle Wm. |
| Bell Nathaniel | Wallis Wm. |
| | Watson Wm. |

Wilkinson John
Wilkinson Thos.
Wilson Thos.
Wilson Thos.
Witty John
Wride Elizabeth

*Gardeners,*
Archbutt John
Boothby Wm.
Diggs Robert
Burr John
Clark Robert
Cook John
Foster Wm.
Owens Coulson
Ingleby Mthw.
Redhill John
Day Stephen
Mason James
Rick Wm.
Rick Robert
Sherrod John
Smith Geo.
Carson Thos.
Pickering Joseph
Laxton Wm.
Beccam John
Nott Wm.
Siggisson Wm.
Shepherd Matthias
Futher Robert
Stephenson Jonth.
Widle Richard
Wilson Robert
Mason John
Wilson Richard
Night John
*Merchants,*
Biggs R. C.
Featherstone Jas.

Gee Stephen
Hebblethwaite J.
Hentig John Wm.
Horsley John
Kay Wm.
Lee Wm.
Mann Samuel
Rennards Thos.
Smith John
Stephenson Robt.
Stocks Benj.
Tottie Richard
Watson Peter Wm.
Wilkinson Wm.
*Plumbers & Glaziers,*
Agar Thos. jun.
Ellerton Benj.
Noble Geo.
*Shoemakers,*
Butler Martin
Hotham John
Ranson Robert
Whisker Thos.
*Shopkeepers,*
Cook Ann
Dixon Matthew
Gray Stephen
Kellington Joseph
Longbone John
Philipson Sarah
Wallis Geo.
*Surgeons,*
Watson Samuel
Webster Thos.
*Tailors,*
Agar Thomas, sen.
Crosier John
Patterson Robert
Russell Thos.
Wilkinson Thos.

*Inns and Taverns.*

Wilson Thomas, Cross Keys
Atkinson Elizabeth, Angel
Grasby Wm. Waggon and Horses
Hartley Stephen, Tiger
Collinson Wm. Prince of Wales
Rhmill Rhd. Duke of Cumberland
White Thomas, Blue Bell
Witty James, Plough

*Miscellany of Trades.*

Atkinson Thomas, hair dresser
Bolton Samuel, carpet manufacturer
Carhill George, accountant
Barr Wm. H. collector of taxes
Coverdale Henry, organist
Coverdale Wm. sexton
Croft John, linen weaver
Groves Richard, horse dealer
Gunnee Wm. druggist
Martin Abraham, nursery & seedsman
Wallace Elizabeth, cowkeeper
Wilkinson Thomas, parish clerk
Wilkinson William, saddler

*Coaches*—Two Stage Coaches to Hull,
every mg. at 9, and ret. 5 aft.

*Carriers.*
Robert Donkin, Charles Morrod, and
Christopher Todd, to Hull every
Tu. & Fri. dep. 1 mg. ret. evg.
Charles Morrod and Mrs. Wride, to
Beverley every Sat. dep. 8 mg.
and returns in the evening.
Charles Morrod and John Holtham, to
Market Weighton every Wed.

COTTINGWITH (East), in the
parish of Aughton, and wap. of Harthill; 9 miles NE. of Selby. Here is a
Chapel of Ease, of which the Rev. John
Fox is incumbent; likewise a Friends
Meeting-house, and a Methodist chapel. Pop. 306.

Liccup Mrs. Emma, gentlewoman
Nottingham Wm. yeoman
Webster Simeon, gentleman
Wilson Wm. yeoman
Colbert Michael, vict. Ship
Gell John, butcher and vict. Blue Bell
Hall Peter, blacksmith
Hemingway Wm. wheelwright
Seymour Geo. tailor
Tasker John, corn miller
Williamson Geo. bricklayer

| *Cattle dealers,* | *Flax dressers,* |
|---|---|
| Blanchard Geo. | Arnell John |
| Yeoman John | Thomlinson Edw. |
| *Farmers,* | *Shoemakers,* |
| Bailey Thos. | Smith Wm. |
| Bell Wm. | Smith John |
| Cook Richard | *Shopkeepers,* |
| Gell John | Dudding Francis |
| Piercy Wm. | Sherburn John |
| Room James | |

*Carriers.*—George Seymour and
George Williams, to York every Sat.
dep. at 5 morn. ret. 6 evg.

COTTNESS, in the parish of Howden, wap. and liberty of Howdenshire; 5 miles SE. of Howden. A
very small village near the river Ouse.
Population, 29.

Blyth Edward, yeoman
Goundrel David, farmer
Robinson Wm. farmer

COURTGARTH WALK, in the parish
of South Dalton, and wap. of Harthill;
4 miles NE. of Market Weighton.

Richardson John, farmer

COURTHOUSE, in the parish of Yedingham, and wap. of Buckrose; 9
miles NE. of Malton. Population included with Yedingham.

| *Farmers,* | Lovell John |
|---|---|
| Emmerson Rhd. | Smith Samuel |
| Gibson Geo. jun. | Tindale Geo. |

COWDON or COLDON, (Great and Little) both in the parish of Mappleton, and wap. and liberty of Holderness, pleasantly situated near to the sea coast ; 3½ miles S. of Hornsea. A rectory, Rev. J. Wilkinson incumbent, the King is patron. The living still exists, but the church is swallowed by the sea. Population, 146.

| Farmers, | Owston Wm. |
|---|---|
| Ake John | Porter Christ. |
| Broadley Roger | Simpson John, |
| Brown John | Little Cowdon |
| Collinson Wm. | Warcup Wm. |
| Duke Thos. | Whitaker Thos. |
| Gaul Wm. | Little Cowdon |
| Ockleton Benj. | |

COWLAM, (P.) in the wap. of Buckrose ; 6½ miles NW. of Driffield. Here is a Church of the Establishment, of which the present incumbent is the Rev. T. F. Foord, rector. Patron, B. F. Bowes, Esq. Pop. 33.

Lamplagh Wm. farmer, Burrow house
Marshall Jonathan, farmer

CROAM, in the parish of Sledmere, and wap. of Buckrose ; 8½ mls. NW. of Driffield. Population included with Sledmere.

Croxton Rev. Rowland, A. M. vicar, Croam hall
Swales John, farmer

CROWGARTH, in the parish of Beeford, wap. and liberty of Holderness ; 7 miles ESE. of Driffield. Pop. included with Beeford.

Severs John, farmer

DAIRY COATES, in the parish of Ferriby, county of Hullshire, on the banks of the Humber; 2 miles W. of Hull.

Atkinson Anthony, brick and tile mfr. Dairy Coates Lodge
Kidd John, farmer
White John, superintendant of the tile manufactory

DALTON NORTH, (P.) in the wap. of Harthill ; 7½ miles SW. of Driffield. Here is a small episcopal chapel, dedicated to All Saints, patrons J. Micklethwaite and Miss Corthins; also a Methodist chapel. Pop.398.

Blanchard Rev. John, incumbent
Buttle Wm. gentleman
Binning Thomas, yeoman
Lund John, yeoman

| Farmers, | Wilson Wm. |
|---|---|
| Dowker James | Blacksmiths, |
| Hopper Geo. | Ransom John |
| Hudson Thos. | Stephenson John |

| Carpenters, | Shoemakers, |
|---|---|
| Fell Leonard | Fallow John |
| Jackson Ralph | Lyon Henry |
| Corn Millers, | Shopkeepers, |
| Bielby John | Jackson Ralph |
| Imeson John | Stephenson John |

Harper Thos. schoolmaster
Jefferson Isabella, vict. Star
Ruston James, tailor

Carrier.—Wm. Jackson, to Beverley every Sat. dep. 8 morn.

DALTON SOUTH, (P.) in the wap. of Harthill ; 5 miles NW. of Beverley The church is a rectory, dedicated to St. Mary ; patron Sir C. Hotham, Bart. Population, 277.

Best Rev. Francis, M. A. rector

| Farmers, | Ireland Richard |
|---|---|
| Craggs James | Leake Francis |
| Fisher Philip | Malton David |
| Fisher Thomas | Sherwood John |
| Hart John | Turner John |
| Heward John | Wilson Robert |
| Heward Wm. | |

Battle Daniel, shopkeeper
Fenton Edward, vict. Board
Leng Robert, boot and shoe maker
Nelson Wm. weaver and parish clerk
Stephenson Thomas, carpenter and wheelwright
Turner Wm. blacksmith

Carriers.—Daniel Battle, George Biggins, and Robert Carlin, to Beverley every Saturday.

DANES DALE, in the parish and township of Great Driffield, and wap. of Harthill; 3 miles NW. of Driffield. There are within one mile of this place a great number of Tumuli, amounting to about six hundred, which from time immemorial have been called "Danes Graves." History is silent concerning their origin, but it is highly probable that the Danes, who appear to have had a fortified camp near Flamborough, may have issued from thence to ravage the country, and have fallen victims to Saxon valour. Each tumulus is three or four feet high, and from twenty to thirty feet in circumference at the base. Many of these ancient depositaries of the dead have been recently opened, and found to contain each a human skeleton which from the dry calcareous nature of the soil has been kept in excellent preservation upwards of a thousand years.

Turner R. and M. farmers

DANTHORPE, a small hamlet, in the parish of Humbleton, wap. and liberty of Holderness ; 6 miles NE of Hedon. Pop. 52.

Lowson Richard, corn miller

*Farmers,*    Floater George
Collins John    Foster Elizabeth

DEIGHTON, in the parish of Escrick, and wap. of Ouse and Derwent; 5 miles SSE. of York.   Pop. 168.

Beckitt Wm. vict. Swan
Bell Joseph, carpenter
Bland John, shoemaker
Wiley John, bricklayer
Wilkinson Wm. gent.
Wilson James, butcher

*Farmers,*    Raven Wm.
Bentley Thomas    Richardson John
Daniel George    Richardson Thos.
Farrar Wm.    Scholefield Benj.
Graves Robert    Wilson John
Penrose Wm.    Young Francis

*Deighton Hill,* in the parish of Escrick, and wap. of Ouse and Derwent; 4¾ miles SSE. of York.

DEMMING, in the parish of Carnaby, and wap. of Dickering; 4 mls. SSW. of Bridlington.

Prestcod John, farmer

DIMLINGTON, in the parish of Easington, wap. and liberty of Holderness; 6 miles SE. of Patrington.—Pop. included with Easington.

Suddaby Samuel, farmer
Wilson John, farmer

DOWTHORP, in the parish of Swine, wap. and liberty of Holderness; 7 miles NW. of Hull.

Whitaker Thomas, yeoman

DREWTON, in the parish of North Cave, and wap. of Harthill; 1 mile N. of South Cave.   Population, with Everthorpe, 177.

Baron Sarah, gentlewoman

*Farmers,*    Usher Robert
Flint George    Wetherill Robert
Metcalf John    Wood Francis
Usber Edward

---

## DRIFFIELD (Great)

In the wapentake of Harthill, and liberty of St. Peter's; 12 miles from Bridlington, 13 from Beverley, 19 from Malton, 22 from Hull, 23 from Scarbrough, 30 from York, and 192 from London by way of Lincoln. Driffield is a well-built market town, situated at the foot of the Wolds, and is the point at which the river Hull takes its rise, being formed by the confluence of a number of fine trout streams, which run in various courses in the town and neighbourhood. The town consists chiefly of one large and broad street, running nearly from North to South, parallel to which runs (amidst straggling houses) the main stream in the neighbourhood, which at the Southern extremity of the town, is enlarged into a navigable canal, and which, with the other tributary waters, takes the name of the *River Hull,* a little below Frodingham bridge. At Wansford, about three miles to the South of the town, there is a large carpet and linen manufactory, and several large flour mills obtain motion for their machinery from the neighbouring streams. The soil in this neighbourhood yields abundant crops, and is in high cultivation; it is exceeded by scarcely any land in the county. The famous short horned bull *Patriot,* bred by Mr. George Coates, was fed here, and sold for 500 guineas; and Mr. Coates afterwards bred a cow from the same stock, for which he refused, unwisely perhaps, 1000 guineas. The corn trade at Driffield has, during the last half century, greatly increased, and this circumstance is accounted for partly from the central situation of the place, and the prolific nature of the soil; and partly from the facilities which water carriage affords for its transit, both to the London market and the markets of the populous districts of the West Riding. Thursday is the market day here, and the business done in the article of grain is frequently very considerable. The parish Church, which is dedicated to All Saints, is a venerable pile of Gothic and of Saxon architecture; the precentor of York, as prebendary of Driffield, is the patron, and the Hon. and Rev. E. Rice, D.D. is the present Rector. The steeple is of more modern date than the church; and tradition relates, that this light and elegant structure was built by one of the Hotham family, to absolve a vow made during a dangerous illness, to undertake a pilgrimage to the Holy Land; or, as another version of the story has it, as the price of absolution for the sin of incontinence. There are here chapels for the Baptists, the Independents, the Methodists, and the Primitive Methodists. The public institutions are few, but highly beneficial; they consist of a Dispensary, to which Dr. Forge is the physician; a National School, established in 1816, in connexion with the East Riding Society, and supported by voluntary subscription, where upwards of 100 children receive instruction, under the tuition of Mr. Nathaniel Chaplain; and a Book Society, held at Mr. Wm. Turner's, in the Market-place. There is also a Benevolent Society, for the relief of the indigent, a Religious Tract Society, and an auxiliary Bible Society. The neighbourhood of Driffield is healthful, and abounds with gentlemen's seats, of which there are no fewer than six, viz. Sir T.

R

Sykes, Bart. Sledmere; Sir Francis Boynton, Bart. Burton Agnes; W. T. St. Quinton, Esq. Lowthorpe: Horner Reynard, Esq. Sunderlandwick: John Grimston, Esq. Neswick; and Charles Grimston, Esq. Kilnwick. The population of this place is rapidly augmenting: in 1801, it amounted to 1329; in 1811, to 1857; and in 1821, to 2303, making an increase during each 10 years of about five and twenty per cent. and the ratio of mortality, owing to the combined influence of the salubrious situation of the town, and the healthful pursuits of the inhabitants, does not exceed one in sixty per annum.

LITTLE DRIFFIELD is in the parish of Great Driffield, and 1 mile from it to the North West. This is the burial place of Alfred, or Alchfrid, king of Northumberland, who died here in the year 702, and to perpetuate whose memory a tablet, with the following inscription, is placed on the South side of the chancel:—

WITHIN THIS CHANCEL LIES INTERRED

### The Body

OF ALFRED, KING OF NORTHUMBERLAND,
WHO DEPARTED THIS LIFE,
JANUARY 18, A. D. 702,
IN THE 20TH YEAR OF HIS REIGN.
*Statutum est omnibus semel mori.**

It is believed, that there was here at the time of this monarch's death a royal palace, where he died after a long illness. But it is also said that he died of wounds received in battle, at Ebberston, near Scarborough.— That this neighbourhood has, at one time, been the theatre of extensive military operations, is manifest from the numerous tumuli in the neighbourhood, called, "The Danes' Graves;" but we search in vain for any well authenticated historical proof, that the Saxon monarch fell in battle either here or elsewhere; and William, of Malmesbury states distinctly, that he died of a painful disease, which was regarded as a visitation of Providence towards the king, for expelling *Saint* Wilfrid from his dignity and possessions. An idle story, published at the instance of persons whose rank and education out to have taught them better, has been propagated, and found its way into many publications, to the effect—that in the year 1784, the Society of Antiquarians in London, sent a deputation to this place, to search for the body of the king (which king they have converted into Alfred the Great, who died 200 years after the Northumbrian monarch.) The deputation, it is added, began their labours on the 20th of

* It is appointed for all once to die.

September, and terminated them with complete success; for, after digging some within the chancel, they found a coffin, on opening which the entire sk of that prince presented itself, with a part of his steel armour! The *Antiqu* who searched for the remains of Al consisted of a party of gentlemen, Driffield, at the head of whom was a Baronet, but the investigation termin entire disappointment—no stone co steel armour—in fact, no relic what that monarch was found; and the pointed delegation, probably to blu edge of ridicule to which they might been exposed, vamped up this fabri which a regard for the fidelity of h has induced us to explode, on the of the worthy clergyman who at fills the office of perpetual curate. year 1807, when the church of Little field was taken down and rebuilt, the gentleman to whom we have just made another search, but in vain, remains of Alfred. When the found were bared, it was found that the and the chancel had both been contra size, and that if Alfred had really be terred near the North wall, upon which inscription was formerly painted, that mains must now be in the church yard the inscription itself the origin a known; but it is known, that it twice renewed within the memory of and that it has undergone various mo tions. The church of Little Driffie discharged vicarage, with Great Dri dedicated to St. Peter, of which the Richard Allen is the perpetual c There are here four annual fairs, h charter from king Alfred, on Easte day, Whit Monday, the 16th of A and the 19th of September, for h horned cattle, and sheep. Pop. 75.

POSTMASTER, Christopher Laybou
*Office, Middle street.*

Letters from all parts arrive in one bag f
Malton daily, at 7 mg. and are d
patched at 10 minutes past 1 at noo

### DIRECTORY.

Allen Rev. Richard
Barnby Mrs. Jane, Church lane
Beaumont Rev. John, Middle stree
Biass Wm. Esq. Middle street
Borton John, yeoman, Church lane
Boyes Bryan, gent. Beverley road
Broadwick Geo. gent. Middle stree
Brown Mrs. Jane, Middle street
Brown Mrs. Judith, Burlington road
Carter Wm. yeoman, Back street
Conyers Mrs. Ann, Middle street

...ass Wm. gent. Middle street
...es Thos. gent. Middle street
...son Mrs. Eliz. Doctor lane
...krow John, gent. Westgate
...e Francis, M.D. Burlington st.
...win Thos. gent. Bridge street
...y Miss Hannah, Middle street
...rison Christr. Esq. Southorpe lodge
...ing Wm. yeoman, Burlington st.
...itt Rev. Thomas, Middle st.
...ley Ann, gentwn. Middle street
...tson Rev. Thos. Middle street
...ings Tho. Francis, Esq. Whitehall
...ings Rev. Henry, Beverley road
...Lawrence, gent. Burlington st.
...t Mrs. Ann, Market place
...by Mrs. gentwn. Middle street
...rsley Robert, gent. Eastgate
...son Miss Margaret, Bridge st.
...sh Thos. gent. Burlington street
...urne Henry, gent. Burlington st.
...som Mrs. Alice, Mill street
...manton Rev. Jas. Baptist minister
...rison Fras. gent. Burlington st.
...ell John, gent. George street
...son Capt. William, Westgate
...son Robert, gent. Market place
...pson Thomas, gent. George st.
...mer Rev. Wm. Ind. minister

### Academies.
...plin Nathl. (national sch.) Mill st.
...yers Mrs. Eliz. (la.bdg.) Middle st.
...son John, Mill street
...le Rev. John, Bridge street
...and Robert, Doctor lane
...son Thomas, Westgate
...mpson Miss Jane, (ladies' bdg.) Middle street

### Attornies.
...terill John, Middle street
...olton Robert, Middle street
...er John, Burlington road
...ings Richard, Middle street
...chburn Thos. Burlington street

### Auctioneers,
...mplugh John, Bridge street
...assell John, Market place
...oodmansey John, Middle street

### Bakers and Confectioners.
...ank Nutty, Middle street
...eddy James, Market place
...aylor John, Westgate
...ard Matthias, Prospect row
...ard John, Middle street.

### Bankers,
...ast Riding, (branch of) Rbt. Dandy, agent, Middle street
Malton North Riding Bank, (branch of) Hagues, Strickland & Allen, Market pl. draw on Barclay & Co. London, Milburn Allison, agt.

### Blacksmiths and Farriers.
Dickenson Thos. (farrier) North end
Dundas Henry, Middle street
Dunning Geo. (farrier) Bridge st.
Folley Mark, Middle street
Fox Robert, Middle street
Graham Wm. River head
Pool David, Harland lane
Rennison Joseph, George street

### Booksellers, Stationers, and Binders.
Huddlestone George, Market place
Laybourne John, (& printer) Middle st
Turner Wm. (& printer & agent to gen. tea compy.) Market place

### Boot and Shoemakers.
Calam John, Middle street
Cattle Wm. Middle street
Cotton Richard, Middle street
Cotton Thomas, Church lane
Dove Matthew, Westgate
Frankish Robert, Burlington street
Lyon Richard, Middle street
Pinder Jas. (clog & patten) Middle st.
Pool Henry, Harland lane
Ransom Thomas, Middle street
Rayner Wm. Middle street
Robson John, Mill street
Spark Wm. George street
Thompson Thomas, Middle street
Wilkinson John, Doctor lane
Young Wm. North end

### Brewers and Maltsters.
Allison Milburne (maltster only) Doctor lane
Howden Thos. (b. & m.) Middle st.
Pape Wm. (maltster only) Burlington street
Porter Wm. J. (b. & m.) River head
Stephenson George, Westgate
Whitty Wm. (maltster only) Middle st

### Bricklayers and Plasterers.
Atkinson Wm. Middle street
Dandy John, Middle street
Mytom John, Middle street
Pickering Wm. Market place

### Brickmakers.
Pickering Wm. Market place
Waddingham Alex. Burlington street

### Butchers.
Blakeston John, Middle street
Hopper George, Middle street
Hutchinson John, Middle street
Jewison Robert, Market place
Milburn Samuel, George street
Parrot John, Middle street
Parrot Harper, Burlington road
Richardson Robert, Middle street
Stephenson Christopher, Middle st.
Waddingham Thomas, Market place

### Cabinet-makers, &c.
Etherington George, Middle street
Grassam John (broker) Middle stre...

Hall Edward, Mill street
Shepherdson Geo. Middle street
White Geo. Burlington street
Wilson Francis, Middle street

*Carpenters, &c.*
Holtby Wm. Burlington street
Piercy James, River head
Reaston John, (builder) Middle st.
Truslove Geo. (builder) Middle st.
Walker John, (builder) Middle st.
White John, Burlington street
Woodmansey John, Middle street

*Coopers.*
Fletcher John, Market place
Nicholson John, Middle street

*Corn and Coal Merchants.*
Dawson Thomas, Riverhead
Harrison James & Sons, Riverhead
Lamplugh David, Riverhead
Porter Wm. jun. Riverhead

*Corn Millers.*
Dawson Thomas, Riverhead
Dickon Wm. King's mills
Fidler Robert, Bell mills
Parkin Wm. Wind mill
Sever John, Dye Garth mill

*Druggists.*
Sherwood Geo. (tea dlr.) Middle st.
Tigar Pennock, (tea dealer & porter
    merchant) Market place  .

*Farmers.*
Artley John, Wold
Blakestone Matthew, Little Driffield
Botham Henry, Wansford road
Boyes Thomas, Back street
Carter Samuel, Back street
Danby George, Westgate
Drinkrow John, Westgate
Hotham Thomas, Kendale house
Hutchinson James, (grazier) Little
    Driffield
Lamplugh George, Little Driffield
Nipe Wm. Kendale
Odlin James, Little Driffield
Piercy Matthew, Burlington road
Smith Thomas, Scarbro' road
Robson John, Wold
Turner Reed, Danes dale
Whitty Mary, Middle street

*Fire and Life Insurance Offices.*
Hope, Robert Dandy, Market place
Norwich, Wm. Turner, Market place
Phœnix, Wm. Porter, sen. Market pl.

*Flour Dealers.*
Dandy Joseph, Bridge street
Dandy Robert, Market place
Hall George, Middle street
Johnson Samuel, Market place
Keddy James, Market place
Lamplugh David, Middle street
Nicholson John, Riverhead
Porter Wm. jun. Riverhead

Shepherdson George, Middle st.
Stephenson Benjamin, Middle st.
Usbaw Harriott, Middle street
Wilson Francis, Middle street

*Gardeners, Nursery, and Seedsmen.*
Anderson David, Riverhead
Dawson Thos. (seedsman) Riverhead
Farthing Michael, Back street
Harrison James & Sons, (seedsmen)
    Riverhead
Pickering John, Middle street
Pickering Wm. sen. Eastgate
Pickering Wm. jun. Beverley lane

*Glass, China & Earthenware Dealers*
Thompson Jane, Middle street
Woodmansey John, Middle street

*Grocers and Tea Dealers.*
Dandy Robert, Market place
Dandy Joseph, jun. Market place
Hall George, Middle street
Johnson Samuel, Market place
Nicholson John, Riverhead
Otley Wm. Market place
Porter Wm. sen. Market place
Robinson John, Market place
Wilson Francis, Middle street
Wrangham Robert, Market place

*Hatters.*
Lamplugh David, (shoe warehouse)
    Middle street.
Thompson Jane, Middle street
Wrangham Robert, Market place

*Inns and Taverns.*
Black Bull, James Bensell, North st.
Black Swan, M. Walker, Market pl.
Blue Bell, Saml. Witty, Market pl.
Blue Bell, Wm. Scott, Riverhead
Buck, John Snowball, Middle st.
Cross Keys, Mark Gill, Market pl.
Horse and Groom, Wm. Moakson,
    North end
Jolly Sailors. Thos. Pickering, Middle
    street
Nag's Head, Geo. Etherington, Middle
    street
Old Buck, John Walker, Middle st.
Red Lion, Mary Whitty, (excise office
    & post chaise) Middle street
Rose & Crown, Thos. Wardell, Little
    Driffield
Shoulder of Mutton, Christopher
    Stephenson, Middle street
Sloop, Wm. Porter, jun. Riverhead
Star, Geo. Pinder, Burlington street
Waggon & Horses, George Hopper,
    Market place
Wheat Sheaf, John Ashton, Little
    Driffield
White Horse, Wm. Moody, North end

*Ironmongers and Hardware Dealers.*
Atkinson Thomas, Market place
Smelt Thomas, Market place

Ullyott George, Market place

*Land Surveyors.*
Jackson Thomas, Market place
Reaston John, Middle street
Russell John, Middle street

*Linen Manufacturers.*
Barnett John, Chapel lane
Belshaw Thomas, Market place

*Linen and Woollen Drapers.*
Dandy Robert, Market place
Dandy Joseph, jun. (haberdasher,) Market place
Otley Wm. Market place
Porter Wm. sen. Market place
Robinson John, Market place
Wrangham Robert, Market place

*Livery Stable Keepers.*
Brunton Nicholas, Prospect row
Hodgson Elizabeth, Middle street
Kemp John, (horse dlr.) Doctor lane
Luccock George, Middle street

*Machine Makers and Millwrights.*
Booth James, Burlington street
Folley Mark, (portable, thrashing, turnip & corn drill,) Middle st.
Johnson John, Riverhead
Sanderson John, Middle street
Truslove George, Middle street

*Milliners, &c.*
Dandy Hannah, Middle street
Harland Mary & Bessey, Middle st.
Hotham Sarah, Prospect row
Reaston Mary, Bridlington road
Redpath Ann, Market place
Tindale Mary, Market place
Webster Jane, Middle street

*Plumbers, Glaziers and Painters.*
Dry Richard, (pl. & g.) Middle st.
Dry Robert, (pl. & g.) Middle st.
Eggleston Richard, Middle street
Jackson John, Middle street
Winder Andrew, Mill street
Woodmausey John, Middle street

*Rope and Twine Spinners.*
Barclay James, Middle street
Belshaw Thomas, Market place

*Saddlers, and Collar Makers.*
Bellwood Wm. Middle street
Sedman Wm. Middle street
Sherwood John, (collarmkr.) Middle st.
White Mary, Burlington street

*Shopkeepers.*
Humphrey Roger, Middle street
Longcaster Elizabeth, Middle street

*Spirit and Wine Merchants.*
Barnby & Stainton Middle street
Dawson Thomas, Riverhead
Harrison James & Sons, Riverhead
Hodgson Elizabeth, Middle street
Lamplugh David, Middle street

*Stone and Marble Masons.*
Collingwood John, Middle street
Hickson John, Middle street
Hodgson John, (marble) Middle st.

*Straw Hat Manufacturers.*
Dandy Hannah, Market place
Harland Mary & Bessey, Middle st.
Jefferson Isabella, Market place
Sanderson Mercy, Market place
Ullyott Mary, Market place

*Surgeons.*
Clement Joseph, Middle street
Harrison Washington, Middle street
Horwood Joseph, Bridge street
Jackson Francis, Middle street
Watson John, Middle street

*Tailors.*
Baron Matthew, Middle street
Bursell James, North end
Dandy Joseph, jun. Market place
Holmes Robert, Church lane
Houghton John, Bridge street
Johnson John, Burlington street
Meek George, Middle street
Morris Wm. Doctor lane
Oliver James, Middle street
Sellers Wm. Market place
Sproxton Richard, Middle st.
Sproxton Geo. (& dpr.) Middle st.

*Tallow Chandlers.*
Harrison James & Sons, Riverhead
Sherwood John, Burlington st.

*Timber and Raff Merchants.*
Barnby & Stainton, Middle street
Piercy James, Riverhead
Reaston John, Middle street

*Tinners and Braziers.*
Hayes Wm. Market place
Smelt Thomas, Market place

*Watch and Clock Makers.*
Dobson Frank, (fish tackle mfr. and brass founder) Market place
Jefferson John, Market place
Laybourne Christopher, Middle st.

*Wheelwrights.*
Reaston John, Market place
Truslove George, (& wire worker) Middle street
Walker John, Middle street

*Worsted Manufacturer.*
Drury John, Westgate

*Miscellany.*
Carrick Wm. flax spinner, Bell mills
Duxbury Law. paper mkr. Bell mills
Fletcher Jph. excise officer, Westgt.
Fox Wm. tanner, Paradise house
Goodrick Rbt. stay mkr. Middle st.
Hamer John, overlooker of the canal, Riverhead

R 3

Robson Geo. currier and leather seller, Middle street
Huddlestone Geo. hosier and glover, Market place
Jefferson Mary, dress & stay maker, Middle street
Lamplugh John, sheriff's officer, Bridge street
Marsh Wm. exciseman, Middle st.
Mathers James, basket mkr. Mill st.
Pulman Thos. waterman, Middle st.
Randall Wm. vessel owner, Middle st.
Robinson Thomas, hair dresser, &c. Market place
Robson John, letter carrier, Mill st.
Sanderson James, umbrella & parasol maker, Middle street
Sherwood Geo. salt mert. Middle st.
Waddingham Alexander, constable
Walker William, fellmonger, Little Driffield

---

## COACHES.

The WELLINGTON, to Bridlington & Scarbro' every mg. in summer, & 3 days per week in winter, at 10 mg. To Hull ½ bf. 12 mg.

## WATER CARRIAGE.

The *Progress*, Capt. Thomas Randall. The *Hope*, Capt. John Randall, & the *Speedy*, Capt. Chas. Verity, regular traders to Hull every other day for goods.

## LAND CARRIERS.

Bainton, James Wallis, from *Cross Keys*, Thu. a 1 d 5
Beeford, Rt. Stephenson, from *Cross Keys*, Thur. a 11 d 4.
Beverley and Hull, Philemon Ashton, Bell & England, T. Bleukinsop, & James Donkin, Mon. & Thu. at 9 evg.
Bridlington, Leo. Denton, and John Leighton, Mon. Thu. & Sat. a 1 d 5.
Foston, Wm. Hall, *Blue Bell*, Thu. a 1 d 5.
Fridaythorpe, Thos. Pearson, *Cross Keys*, Thu. a 1 d 5.
Frodingham, Robert Jefferson & Hy. Pickering, *Blue Bell*, Thu. a 1 d 5.
Garton, John Foster, *Cross Keys*, Thu. a 2 d 5.
Hull, see Beverley.
Hutton Cranswick, Geo. Summerson, and Dinah Booth, *Black Swan*, Thu. a 1 d 5.
Kilham, John Harland, *for Miss Harlands*, Thu. a 1 d 5.
Kirkburn, Rbt. Stockdale, *Waggon and Horses*, Thu. a 2 d 5.

Langtoft, David Nightingale *Blue Bell*, Mkt. pl. Thu. a 1 d 5.
Malton, Philemon Ashton & Thomas Blenkinsop, every Wed. & Sat.
Middleton, My. Robinson, *Cross Keys* Thu. a 1 d 5,
Middleton, John Shields, *Waggon & Horses*, Thu. a 1 d 5.
Nafferton, Francis Johnson, *Cross Keys*, Thu. a 1 d 5.
Rudston, John Hopper, *Cross Keys* Thu. a 1 d 5.
Scarbro', Bell & England, and James Donkin, every Wed. & Sat.
Wetwang, John Holtby, *Cross Keys* Thu. a 1 d 5.
Whitby, James Donkin, every Wed. and Sat.
York, James Bayes, (& the fish cart) every Tu. & Thu.

DRINGHOW, in the parish Skipsea, wap. and liberty of Holderness; 9 miles E. of Driffield. Population, including Skipsea, Brough, and Upton, 164.

| *Corn millers,* | Halder Emanuel |
|---|---|
| Dawson Wm. | Kendrew James |
| Milner Wm. | Lamplugh Jeremiah |
| *Farmers,* | Lamplugh John |
| Bradshaw Richd. | Runton Geo. |
| Clark John | Shepherd Joseph |
| Dobson John | Wardill Thos. |

*Drypool*, (P.) in the wap. and liberty of Holderness; on the eastern bank the river Hull, and is considered a part Kingston-upon-Hull. Its population amounts to 1409. Near to this place is supposed to have stood the village of Frismeck, swallowed up by the inundations of the Humber. The church is now rebuilding; the windows and arches of the old structure are carefully preserved, and the new ones worked from the same patterns and mouldings, so as to perpetuate the style of the old church, which is about the year 1300. The patron of this parochial curacy is William Wilberforce, Esq. and the church is dedicated to St. Peter.

DUFFIELD (North,) in the parish of Skipwith, wap. of Ouse and Derwent, and liberty of Howdenshire; 6 miles NE. of Selby. Pop. 433.

Millington Wm. yeoman, Duffield hall
Spofforth Samuel, yeoman

| *Butchers,* | Carr Thomas |
|---|---|
| Castle Robert | Daniel John |
| Richardson Wm. | Douglas James |
| *Farmers,* | Duffing J. Blackwood house |
| Addison Thos. | |
| Bell George | Garnett Edw. (& corn miller) |
| Calvert Wm. | |

Gatenby Wm.
Kay James
Kirby Peter
Laverack Thos.
Laverack Thos.
Millington Mthw.
Norwood John
Precious Matthew
Ringrose John
Scott Robert
Thompson Geo.
Todd William

Bellas Thomas, blacksmith and vict.
King's Arms
Daniel Robert, corn factor
Fowler Wm, wheelwright
Gransill Geo. shoemaker
Richardson Ann, vict. Cart & Horses
Sharp John, tailor and shopkeeper
Masons Robert, schoolmaster

DUFFIELD (South), in the parish of Hemingbrough, wap. of Ouse and Derwent, and liberty of Howdenshire; 4 miles ENE. of Selby.  Pop. 181.

Blyth James, yeoman, Northtoft
Maddlesey Wm. yeoman
Robinson John, yeoman
Robinson Joseph, gentleman

*Farmers,*
Atkinson Geo.
  Holmes house
Marshall Philip
Mollitt Thomas
Ripley George,
  Dyson house

Hickinson Geo. blacksmith
Marshall John, shoemaker
Wade James, wheelwright
Weldrake Joseph, vict. Cross Keys

DUGGLEBY, in the parish of Kirby Grindalyth, and wap. of Buckrose; 7 miles SE. of Malton.  Pop. 154.

Spink Francis, yeoman

*Farmers,*
Brown Robert
Hopper John
Spink George
Wray Richard

Bogg Wm. wheelwright
Monkman Robert, blacksmith

*Duncoates,* in the parish of Howden, wap. and liberty of Howdenshire.

DUNNINGTON, in the parish of Beeford, wap. and liberty of Holderness; 7 miles NNW. of Hornsea.  Population, 76.

*Farmers,*
Harrison Francis
Jordan Thos.
Knapton Robert
Moulson Thos.

DUNNINGTON, (P.) in the wap. of Ouse and Derwent, & liberty of St. Peter's; 4 miles E. of York.  The high road here divides the East from the North Riding: the church, of which the Earl of Bridgewater is the patron, and the Rev. Edward Jones the rector, is dedicated to St. Nicholas; here is also a Methodist chapel.  Pop. 551.

Agar John, gentleman
Baines H. M. gent. Eastfield house
Barker Thomas yeoman

Brown Matthew, yeoman
Jones Rev. Edward, rector
Lund William, yeoman
Monckton Wm. gentleman
Prest Wm. gent. Dunnington lodge
Shilitoe Mrs. gentlewoman
Storr Mrs. gentlewoman
Warneford Henry, yeoman

*Blacksmiths,*
Barker John
Creaser Sarah
*Bricklayers,*
Holmes Wm.
Lotherington Wm.
*Butchers,*
Foster Joseph
Foster Wm. & Co.
Smith Thomas
*Butter and Bacon Factors,*
Butler Francis
Butler John
*Carpenters,*
Dales Wm.
Eaden Thos.
Hornshaw Wm.
Wilson Thos.
*Farmers,*
Agar John
Barnard Richard
Bell Robert
Buckle John, sen.
Buckle John, jun.
Buckle Robert
Fletcher Wm.
Gibbon Wm.
Harrison Henry
Hudson John
Palfreeman John
Thompson Ann
Thompson Wm.
Ware Geo.
*Schoolmasters,*
Bell John
Waterworth H.
*Shoemakers,*
Hodgson Robert
Mentoft Wm.
Wilkinson Thos.
*Shopkeepers,*
Mentoft Wm.
Smith Geo.
Thompson Francis,
  (& auctioneer)
*Tailors,*
Consit John
Nelson Wm.

Butterfield James, vict. Cross Keys
Linfoot Sarah, vict. Greyhound
Turner William, corn miller

DUNSWELL, in the parish of Cottingham, & wap. of Harthill; 4½ mls. NNW. of Hull.

Barnby Wm. vict. Waggon & Horses
Bell Wm. vict. Coach and Horses
Plaxton William, gardener

*Farmers,*
Atkinson Wm.
Moore Mrs. Eliz.
Ruston Thos.
Turner Robert
Waslin Robert
Wilkinson John

EASINGTON, (P.) in the wap. and liberty of Holderness; 6 miles SSE. of Patrington.  The Church, dedicated to All Saints, is a very ancient small Gothic structure, of which the Archbishop of York is the patron, and the Rev. George Innan, perpetual curate.  Pop. 488.

Bulson Thomas, butcher
Charlton Michael, schoolmaster and parish clerk
Child John, land surveyor
Curtis Robert, schoolmaster
Cuthbert Robert, corn miller
Fussey Wm. weaver
Johnson Wm. yeoman

Walker Francis, vict. Granby's Head
Wilson William, yeoman

*Blacksmiths,*          *Grocers,*
Douglas Thos.          Mason Wm.
Longman Robert      M'Kee Wm.
*Farmers,*               Richardson Ann
Branton Barthlw.     *Shoemakers,*
Clubley Francis        Charlton Francis
Dalton David           Dunn Daniel
Fewson John           Quinton John
Futty John               *Tailors,*
Hall John                Cockerline Thos.
Lawson John           Cole John
Mason Robert         Johnson Thomas
Milner Sarah           Kemp George
Richardson Peter     *Wheelwrights,*
Tennison Michael     Bridle John
Wilkinson John        Médforth Geo.

*Carriers.*
Thomas Kitson, to Hull Thurs. dep. 10 morning, ret. Sat. 2 afternoon
William Blenkin, to Hull every Mon. evening, ret. Tu. evening

EASTBURN, in the parish of Kirk-burn, and wap. of Harthill; 3 miles SW. of Driffield. Pop. 12.

Boyes Bethuel, yeoman

EASTON, in the parish of Bird-lington, & wap. of Dickering; 1 mile W. of Bridlington. Pop. 21.

Hudson John, farmer
Owston John, farmer

EASTRINGTON, (P.) in the wap. and liberty of Howdenshire; 4 miles ENE. of Howden. Here is an ancient church dedicated to St. Michael, of which the king, is the patron; likewise a Methodist chapel, and a free school, endowed with 30l. per annum. Population, 375.
Battye John, yeoman
Spofforth Rev. Ralph, vicar
*Carpenters,*        Smith Joseph
Thompson Mthw.  Towl Joshua
ThompsonStephen Turner John
*Farmers,*            Watson Thomas
Birks Wm.            *Shopkeepers,*
Goundrell Wm.     Belt William
Horstley Wm.        Holmes John
Norwood John

Brownbridge James, shoemaker
Jackson John, blacksmith
Morritt David, corn miller
Savill Thomas, schoolmaster
Swann Thomas, vict. Bay Horse
Young John, tailor

EASTHORP, in the parish of Londesbrough, and wap. of Harthill, 2 miles N. of Market Weighton. Population included with Londesbrough.

Botterill John, farmer
Botterill Wm. farmer, Middlethorp

*Eastwood,* in the parish of Thornton, and wap. of Harthill; 6 miles SW. of Pocklington.

EDDLETHORP, in the parish of Westow, and wap. of Buckrose; 4 miles S. of Malton. Pop. 62.

Field Joseph, Esq.
Carter Thomas
Cundale Edward, farmer
Otway Frederick, farmer and surveyor of highways

*Eight and Forty House,* in the parish of Eastrington, and wap. of Harthill; 5 miles WSW. of South Cave.

ELLA-KIRK and WEST, in the parish of Kirk-Ella, and wap. of Hullshire; 5 miles WNW. of Hull. From the Domesday book, it appears that at the time of the survey, the village of Kirk-Ella was a part of the possessions of Ralph de Mortimer. At present several branches of the ancient mercantile family of Sykes possess a large property in this parish, and are patrons of the church. Here, as well as at Ferriby and Cottingham, several of the wealthy merchants of Hull have elegant places of residence. In the church at Kirk-Ella dedicated to St. Andrew, which appears to be a very ancient structure, is a handsome monument, erected to the memory of the late Joseph Sykes, Esq. who is supposed to have had more extensive dealings with the nobles and merchants of Sweden, than any other person in England; he was twice mayor of the town of Kingston-upon-Hull; he died in the year 1805. Population, 368.

Bourne Wm. gentleman
Dobson Mrs. gentlewoman
Eggington Joseph, Esq. magistrate
Hammond Peter, gentleman
Huntington Wm. gentleman
Jones Anthony, silversmith
Smith John, gentleman
Sykes Rev. Richard, magistrate, West Ella
Sykes Joseph, Esq.
Sykes Mrs. Ann, gentlewoman
Tiger John, druggist
Wilkinson Rev. Wm. James, A. M.
Wilkinson Mrs. gentlewoman
Williamson Jane, gentlewoman

*Farmers,*            Watson Wm. West
Acey Peter, West       Ella
   Ella                *Shoemakers,*
Brigham John       Hessey Wm.
Foster Peter,          Wilberforce Thos
   West Ella           *Shopkeepers,*
Smith Wm.            Acey Thomas
                          Stather Robert

Crisp John, schoolmaster
Marshall Elizabeth, blacksmith
Ransom Wm. joiner and carpenter, & parish clerk
Thrustle Thos. vict. Anchor
Wilkinson Wm. butcher

*Carriers.*—John Burn and John Whitby, to Hull every Tu. and Fri. to the Bonny Boat, Trinity House ln. dep. 7 evg. ret 7 morn.

ELLERBY, in the parish of Swine, wap. and liberty of Holderness; 6 miles N. of Hedon. Pop. with Dowthorp, Langthorp, & Owbrough, 233.

Barchard Ralph, vict. Board
Batty Wm. blacksmith
Bashell Stephen, shoemaker
Garton John, yeoman
Metcalfe Wm. wheelwright
Whitaker Thos. farmer, Dowthorp

| *Farmers,* | Dunn Peter |
|---|---|
| Biglin Wm. | Spetch Joseph |
| Carlin John | Thompson Wm. |

ELLEAKER, in the parish of Brantingham, wap. of Howdenshire; 1 mile S. of South Cave. Pop. 249.

Arton John, yeoman
Champney Richard, gent.
Hodgson Dennis, yeoman
Leason Thomas, gent.
Levitt John, yeoman
Simpson Rev. James, A. M. curate

| *Farmers,* | Robinson Thos. |
|---|---|
| Boynton Richard | Rudd Charles |
| Pashley Thos. | Thompson Thos. |
| Reed Elizabeth | Coulthwold |
| Risdale Joseph, | |
| Ellerker Sands | |

Bell Thos. corn miller
Dodds Wm. shopkeeper
Haldenby-Richard, tailor
Milson Thos. shoemaker
Wressel Thos. carpenter

*Carrier.*—Thomas Nicholson, to Hull and Wilton every Tu.

ELLERTON, (P.) in the wap. of Harthill; 9 mls. SW. of Pocklington. Here was formerly a Priory of Canons of the Sempringham Order, founded by William Fitz Peter, before the year 1212, which continued to flourish until the 11th of December, 1536; when this priory was surrendered, by John Golding, the prior. Here is a chapel dedicated to St. Mary, of which John Bethell, Esq. is patron; there is also a Methodist chapel. Population, 318.

Brown Robert, gentleman
Wilkinson Rev. John, vicar

| *Farmers,* | Beast Wm. |
|---|---|
| Blanchard James | Brown Robert |

Clark John
Hatfield Peter
Johnson John
Richardson Wm.

Smith Robert
Stephenson Wm.
Wake James
Watson John

Brown John, corn miller
Carr John, tailor
Lee Sarah, shopkeeper
Wilkinson Wm. schoolmaster
Young John, shoemkr. & vict. Board

*Carrier.*—John Haslewood, to York every Sat. dep. at 4 m. ret. at 8 evg.

ELLOUGHTON, (P.) in the wap. of Harthill, a part in the liberty of St. Peter's; 8 miles SE. of South Cave. The church, dedicated to St. Mary, is a very ancient Gothic structure, of which the prebendary of Wetwang, in York Cathedral, is the patron, and the Rev. John Overton, jun. the vicar; here are likewise a Calvinist and a Methodist chapel. Population, with Brough, 383.

Carlill Mrs. Mary, gentlewoman
Carr·Thomas, yeoman
Prescott Wm. yeoman
Thompson Rev. Joseph, curate
Wilkinson James, yeoman

| *Carpenters,* | Jefferson Rbt. |
|---|---|
| Mutch Wm. | Jefferson Wm. |
| Storr Wm. | Ringrose Saml. |
| *Farmers,* | *Tailors,* |
| Brough Francis | Haldenby Rhd. |
| Dixon George | Waddington Rbt. |
| Graves John | |

Beaulah Thomas, blacksmith
Dixon Geo. shoemaker
Fleming James, schoolmaster
Scaife Robert, bricklayer

*Carriers.*—Wm. Carlill, Thomas Easingwood, and Robt. Taylor, to Hull every Tu. and Fri.

ELSTERNWICK, in the parish of Humbleton, wap. and liberty of Holderness; 5 miles NE. of Hedon. In this hamlet there is a small Chapel of Ease, apparently of great antiquity, of which the Rev. John Dixon is incumbent; also a Free School with a small endowment. Pop. 154.

Bell Robert, gentleman
Bell John, gentleman

| *Farmers,* | Warriner Rhd. |
|---|---|
| Close John | Wheldale Thos. |
| Hardbattle John | *Wheelwrights,* |
| Marshall Wm. | Norrison Peter |
| Smith John | Turner Charles |

England Wm. vict. Crown & Anchor
Pool Jane, teacher of the Free School
Turner John, shoemaker
Webster Richard, blacksmith
Whitening Robert, foreman

*Carrier,* Wm. Woodhouse, to Hull every Tuesday.

ELVINGTON, (P.) in the wap. of Ouse and Derwent; 7 miles ESE. of York. The church, dedicated to the Holy Trinity, was built in the year 1801, by the Rev. A. Cheap, L. L. B. rector, and is a neat building, of which the king is the patron. Here are likewise a Methodist chapel and a Subscription school, to the master of which 20*l*. per annum is paid for the instruction of twenty poor boys. Pop. 405.

Cheap Mrs. Mary, gentlewoman
Empson Amaziah, Esq. Manor house
Gillmore Thos. surgeon & apothecary
Green Rev. Wm. curate, (bdg. schl.)
Mather Dr. Alex. Briakworth
Spence John, gentleman
Spence Robert, yeoman

| *Blacksmiths,* | Linfoot Thomas |
| Raney Henry | Morley John |
| Routledge Thos. | Spence Henry |
| (& whitesmith) | Ramsay |
| *Carpenters,* | Tate Wm. |
| Smales Samuel | Walker Wm. |
| Taylor Wm. | Wright Thomas |
| *Farmers,* | *Gardeners,* |
| Barton Matthew | Appleton Anthony |
| Bond George | Routledge Wm. |
| Bowman Mary | *Shopkeepers,* |
| Bowman Wm. | Duckett Wm. |
| Cooper James | Thornton Wm. |
| Emmerson Geo. | *Tailors,* |
| (and brewer) | Holmes Wm. |
| Frear Richard | Johnson Wm. |

Cross John, schoolmaster
Galbress John, butcher
Lorimah Peter, shoemaker and vict. Bay Horse
Lotherington Thomas, bricklayer
Pearson James, shoemaker

EMMOTLAND, in the parish of Frodingham, wap. and liberty of Holderness; 2 miles SE. of Driffield. Pop. included with N. Frodingham.

Harrison Jonathan, farmer
Harrison Richard, farmer

EMSWELL, in the parish of Great Driffield, and wap. of Harthill; 2 mls. W. of Driffield. Pop. with Kelleythorpe, 93.

| *Farmers,* | Lees Wm. Greets |
| Blakestone Math. | Spencer Richard |
| Holtby Richard | |

ENTHORPE, in the parish of Lund, and wap. of Harthill; 4 miles NE. of Market-Weighton.

Wilson John, farmer

EPPLEWITH, in the parish of Skidby, and wap. of Harthill; 4½ miles S. of Beverley.

Holland Manklin, yeoman
Jackson Thomas, farmer

*Ergham,* in the parish of Atwicke, wap. and liberty of Holderness; 3 miles NW. of Hornsea.

ESCRICK, (P.) in the wap. of Ouse and Derwent; 6 miles S. of York. Here is a handsome modern church dedicated to St. Helen, of which Henry Gale, Esq. is the patron, built about forty-five years ago, by the late Beilby Thompson, Esq. (upon the site of the old church). This was anciently the seat of Sir Thomas Knivet, one of the gentlemen of the bed-chamber to King James I. who, on the 5th of November, in the year 1605, was sent, along with some other persons, to search the vaults under the house of Lords, where they discovered 36 barrels of gunpowder, and thereby prevented the perpetration of a deed not to be equalled in the annals of treachery and treason. Population 548.

Thompson Beilby, Esq. Hall
Gale Rev. Henry, rector
Boswell William, steward

| *Blacksmiths,* | Reaston Wm. |
| Hustwick Geo. | Robinson John |
| Nicholson Wm. | Rooke John |
| *Carpenters,* | Rudd Thomas |
| Gell Joseph | Shepherd Wm. |
| I'Anson John | Smith Wm. |
| Lister Michael | Spencer Thomas |
| *Farmers,* | Stephenson Len. |
| Barton George | Strangeway John |
| Blanchard Geo. | Taylor Jonathan |
| Eagle Wm. | Thompson Henry |
| Ellis E. and Son | Walker Josias |
| Elstone John, (& | *Shoemakers,* |
| bricklayer) | Emmerson John. |
| Fairweather Chris. | (& shopkeeper) |
| (& corn dealer) | Haw William |
| Gilbertson Betty | *Tailors,* |
| Gray Wm. | Eagle Thomas |
| Harper Richard | Leake John |
| Hield E. and G. | Pearson Benj. |
| Moody Robert | |

Brown John, butcher & vict. Spotted Bull
Fairweather John, corn miller & baker
Wilkinson Richard, schoolmaster

*Carriers*—Robert Davison to York every Wed. and Sat. dep. 9 mg. and ret. in the evening

*Coaches*—between York & Selby pass daily.

ESKE, in the parish of St. John's, Beverley, wap. and liberty of Holderness; 4 miles NE. of Beverley. Population 18.

Wilson John, farmer

ETHERDWICKE, in the parish of Aldbrough, wap. and liberty of Holderness; 7 miles NE. of Hedon. Pop. included with Aldbrough.

Farmers, Dales Thomas
Adams Wm. Stephenson Thos.

ETTON, (P.) in the wap. of Hart-hill; 4 miles NW. of Beverley. The church, dedicated to St. Mary, of which the Archbishop of York is the patron, and the Rev. W. V. Vernon, the rector, is an ancient structure. Pop. 380.

Creyke Rev. Stephen, M. A.
Grimston Frances, gentlewoman
Legard Lady Jane
Straw William, gentleman
Turner George, gentleman

| Farmers, | Richardson John |
| Carling Wm. | Vickers John |
| Duesberry John | Wardell John |
| Dean Cayley | Whipp John |
| Gray Robert | Whitty Nicholas |

Barran John, carpenter & wheelwright
Cole James, boot and shoe maker
Cooper Thos. vict. Light Dragoon
Goodricke Christopher, schoolmaster and parish clerk
Heward Richard, tailor
Rountree Geo. corn miller
Stainton Elisabeth, shopkeeper
Wardell Robert, shopkeeper

Carriers—Robert Towers & Thos. Whitby, to Beverley every Sat.

EVERINGHAM, (P.) in the wap. of Harthill; 5 miles W. of Market-Weighton. There is here a neat modern built church, dedicated to the Blessed Virgin Mary, the Rev. Wm. Alderson rector and patron; there is also a Roman Catholic chapel. Population 271.

Alderson Rev. Wm. rector
Maxwell Mrs. Constable, Hall

| Farmers, | Rowe Wm. |
| Braithwaite Rhd. | Rudd John |
| Clark Richard | Smith John |
| Dean Thomas | Templeton Edw. |
| Easingwood Thos. | Thomas Henry |
| Kempley Henry | Whipp Wm. (and |
| Kempley Thos. | farrier) |
| Plurit James | |

Atkinson Robert, carpenter
Beetleson Thos. shopkeeper
Gosford Wm. steward for Wm. Constable Maxwell, miner
Johnson John, tailor and vict. Ship
Johnson Wm. schoolmaster
Norwood Francis, shoemaker
Pexton Thos. blacksmith & parish clerk

EVERTHORPE, in the parish of North Cave, and wap. of Harthill; 2 miles WNW. of South Cave. Population, with Drewton, 177.

Farmers, Stather John
Harrison Wm. Thomas George

Lee Thomas, corn miller
Pearson James, vict. Duke of York

FAIRHOLME, in the parish of Swine, wap. and liberty of Holderness; 7 miles NW. of Hedon.

FANGFOSS-WITH-SPITTLE, (P.) in the wap. of Harthill; 4 miles NW. of Pocklington. Here is a chapel, now in charge to the vicar of Barmby-upon-the-Moor, of which the Dean of York is the patron. Pop. 154.

Overend Cholmley, Esq. Fangfoss hall
Addison Rev. James, perpetual curate

| Farmers, &c. | Green Ralph |
| Arnott Wm. | Hodgson John |
| Catton Thomas, Spittle | Leuty Matthew |
| | Norton William |
| Catton Robert | Quarton John |
| Fawcett John | Stephenson John |
| Fawcett Thos. | Stillingfleet John |

Harrison John, schoolmaster
Harrison Wm. shopkeeper, Spittle
Kitchingman Wm. shoemaker
Robinson Thos. carpenter and vict. Carpenter's Arms

FAXFLEET, in the parish of South Cave, wap. of Harthill, and liberty of St. Peter's; 6 miles SW. of South Cave. Pop. 163.

Scholfield John, gent. Hall
Scholfield Wm. farmer, North hall
Bird Wm. brick and tile maker
Hairsine James, farmer
Latham Edward, farmer, Grange
Seaton John, yeoman
Thompson Cornelius, yeoman, Osmerdike

FERRIBY NORTH, (P.) in the wap. of Hullshire; 6 miles SE. of South Cave, is an ancient village, and nearly opposite to South Ferriby, in Lincolnshire.— Here was a priory of the Knights Templars, of the foundation of Lord Eustace Vercy, which survived that order, and was occupied by the Canons of St. Augustine till the suppression, when the site was granted to Thomas Culpepper. This village has, in succession, been the patrimonial possession of the Mortimers, the Poles, and the Bacons. The present church, dedicated to All Saints, and of which the King is the patron, seems only to be a part of a more spacious structure; it contains some handsome monuments of marble, two of which are erected to the memory of the Lillingston family, and one to the memory of the parents of Sir Henry Etherington, Bart.— The village is delightfully situated at the foot of the hills, and not far from the shores of the Humber, to which there is a gentle descent. It is adorned by several elegant mansions. Pop. 347.

Ayres Wilkinson, yeoman
Broadley Henry, Esq.
Egginton Gardiner, gentleman
Hesleden Thomas, gentleman
Schonswar George, Esq.
Scott Rev. John, A. M. vicar
Turner Ralph, gentleman
Wilson Richard, yeoman

*Carpenters,*          *Farmers,*
Andrew Mark, &    Binnington Robert
  shopkeeper          Grey Stephen
Jenkinson Thos.    Kidd John, Dairy
Johnson Samuel .      Cotes

Birks Wm. schoolmaster and parish
  clerk
Brown Thomas, gardener
Carnaley William, tailor
Dunn Thomas, blacksmith
Nicholson John, shoemaker
Stephenson Richard, corn miller
Tapp Mrs. Mary, boarding school
Williams Matthew, vict. Duke of
  Cumberland
*Carriers*—Wm. Coates, to Hull
every Tu. & Fri.—Charles Ellerington,
to Hull every Monday, Wednesday,
Thursday, and Saturday

FILEY, (P.) in the waps. of Pickering Lythe, and Dickering; 7½ miles SE. of Scarborough, situated on the banks of a noble bay, abounding with excellent fish, and famous for its lobsters; the sands are very firm, and are bounded on the north by a remarkable ridge of rocks, extending nearly half a mile into the sea, called Filey Bridge. The parochial chapel, which is dedicated to St. Bartholomew, is in the patronage of the Osbaldeston family; here is likewise a Methodist chapel. A very fine spring adjoins the church yard, and supplies the place with most excellent water. Population 773.

Williams Rev. E. curate
Smith William, yeoman

*Blacksmiths,*      Fenwick Matthew
Chambers James    Parkinson Jackson
Chew Robert        Riley William
*Bricklayers, &c.*    Robinson Ralph
Graise Benjamin      *Fishmongers,*
Johnson Geo.        Bulmer James
*Carpenters, &c.*    Dunn William
Clapham Thos.      Featherstone Geo.
Tindall John        Lorriman Wm.
*Farmers,*          Pashley Wm.
Crawshaw Edw.      Richardson Christ.
Day Matthew

*Grocers & Drapers,*   Mosey James
Clifford Francis    Tindall Peter
Lorriman Richard      *Shoemakers,*
Suggitt Stephen     Collins George
Tindall Peter,      Pickering Rich
  (draper)         Wyvill Wm.
*Mariners,*          *Tailors, &c.*
Williamson Thos.    Cammiss Wm.
Wilson John          Skelton Cr
*Ship-owners,*       Willis Wm.
Jenkinson Wm.

Botran John, hair dresser
Cook Nathaniel, schoolmaster
Goffton George, butcher
Hewson William, corn miller
Newton William, bread baker
Richardson John, vict. Ship
Skelton Crumpton, vict. Pack Ho
Watson Thomas, vict. New Inn
*Carriers*—John Johnson & J
Stephenson, to Bridlington, Hu
by and Muston, every Sat.—F
Mosey, to Scarborough, Mon.
and Saturday.

FIMBER, in the parish of W
wang, wap. of Buckrose, and li
of St. Peter's; 9 miles WNW
Driffield. Here is a Chapel of
of which the rector of Wetw
incumbent curate. Pop. 104.

*Farmers,*          Horsley Thom
Anderson Thos.      Taylor Richard
Cundale Wm.        Welburn Matt
Horsley John        Whitty John
Cooper John, shoemaker
Cooper Richard, tailor
Hopper Askin, grocer

FIRBY, in the parish of We
and wap. of Buckrose; 6 miles
of Malton. Pop. 44.

Harrison Rev. Thomas, Firby hall
Nalton John, farmer
Wilson Martha, farmer

FITLING, a small hamlet, in
parish of Humbleton, wap. and l
of Holderness; 6 miles NE. of H
Pop. 119.

Beacock Thomas, shoemaker
*Farmers,*          Fisher Willia
Atkinson John      Hotham Thom
Brantley Robert    Wright John
Cannon Mrs.        Wright Robert
Dunn John          Wright Robt. j
Dunn James

FLAMBOROUGH, (P.) in the
of Dickering; 4½ miles NE. of Bridl
and 16 SE. of Scarborough. A very
station, formerly of some note, but at p
sent merely a fishing village, situated in th
centre of the promontory. The name of

this place is probably derived from the "Flame," or light, anciently placed on the head to direct mariners in the navigation of the German ocean. The Danes in their hostile attacks upon England, in the early periods of her history, were accustomed to make this one of their principal stations; in later times it was possessed by Harold, Earl of the West Saxons, and afterwards king of England; subsequently, Wm. Le Gross, the founder of Scarborough castle was its lord; it afterwards came into the hands of the Constables, whom some derive from the Lacies Constables of Chester.* This family flourished here for some centuries, and a curious monumental inscription on a brass plate in the chancel of the church, records that Sir Marmaduke Constable, Knt. who fought in France under the banners of Edward IV. and Henry VII. was interred here.

church, an ancient building, dedicated to Oswald, of which the Archbishop of [...], and Sir William Strickland, Bart. have alternately the patronage, is a curacy, and the Rev. William Kendall is the incumbent. Some vestiges yet remain of Danish mansions; an ancient ruin at the West end of the village, is called the Danes Tower, and the entrenchments formed round it, and still visible, have obtained for the place the designation of "Little Denmark."

Flamborough Head is a lofty promontory overlooking the village, and forming one of the most magnificent objects, and greatest natural curiosities in the kingdom. The cliffs, which are of lime-stone rock, white as snow, extend in a range from five to six miles, and rise in many places to the elevation of 300 feet perpendicular from the sea. At the base of this mass of mouldering mountains are several extensive caverns, formed by some mighty convulsions of nature, or worn by the everlasting action of the ocean. The most remarkable of these excavations, are the Dove Cote, the Kirk Hole, and Robin Lyth's Hole; the last of which far surpasses the other in its grandeur and dimensions, and is thus described by the historian of Scarborough:—"It has two openings, one communicating with the land, the other with the sea. The former is low and narrow, giving solemn admission into the cavern, which at the first entrance is surrounded with a tenebrious gloom, but the darkness gradually dispersing, the magnificence becomes unfolded, and excites the admiration of the exploring stranger. The floor is a solid rock, formed into broad steps of an easy descent, and the stones at the sides are curiously variegated. The roof is

* Camden.

finely arched, and nearly fifty feet high at the centre. The many projecting ledges and fragments of suspended rocks, joined to the great elevation, give it an awful, and at the same time, a majestic appearance; and when looking upwards to survey the lofty arch, and reflect upon the superincumbent mass sustained by it, there is a difficulty in suppressing those ideas of danger which intrude upon such an occasion. On approaching the Eastern extremity, a noble vista is formed by its opening to the sea, which appears in its highest grandeur on emerging from the gloom of the cavern." The large masses of insulated rocks formed into columns and pyramids, add to the sublimity of the scene, and when viewed from the sea, seem to form the porticos to a range of lofty temples, which set at defiance all human erections.

In the summer season the ridges of these immensely elevated cliffs, form the rendezvous of myriads of aquatic fowls, which resort to the North side of the promontory, from various regions, to build their nests, and rear their young. In the months of May and June, the rocks seem absolutely animated, being covered with innumerable birds of various plumage, exceeding in number the inhabitants of the largest city, and in varied hue the tints of the rainbow. At the report of a gun, they are in instant motion, more alert than the inmates of a dwelling that has recently burst into a flame, and the eye is as much dazzled with the waving of their innumerable wings, brightened by the rays of the sun, as the ear is stunned with the clamour of a thousand discordant notes all bursting forth at the same moment of time. Hung in air as their nests seem to be, they are still not inaccessible to the depredations of man! boys are let down the rocks by ropes fastened to stakes, and bring away bushels of eggs for the use of the sugar house in Hull, without seeming to diminish their countless number.

For many years the want of a Lighthouse at Flamborough had been felt by the mariners who navigated those seas, and deplored by the merchants whose property was exposed to danger, for want of so essential a monitor. The active mind, and the benevolent disposition of the late Mr. Milne, the collector of the customs at Bridlington, induced him to propose the erection of a light house on the Head, and the proposal was cordially received by the incorporated company of the Elder Brethren, of the Trinity-house, Deptford Strond, London: the site fixed upon was at the distance of nearly a mile and a half Eastward of the town, about 400 yards within the extreme point of the promontory, close to the landing on the South side of Silex bay, and at an elevation of 250 feet; the erection was speedily effected, under the inspection of an able engineer, and on the 1st of December, 1806, the revolving light which has ever since flamed by night from the Head, burst forth for the first time. The utility of this erection cannot be more strikingly illustrated than by the following fact, quoted from the Notes to Coates's Descriptive Poem, on Bridlington Quay—"From June, 1770, to the end of the year 1806, not fewer than 174 ships were wrecked or lost on Flamborough Head and its environs, but since the erection of the lights, to March, 1813, not one vessel had been lost on that station when the lights could be seen." From what has already been said, it will be concluded, that the marine scenery here is grand and imposing, and the milder attractions of Bridlington and the Quay, with the fine country in the rear, unite the beautiful to the sublime. The population of Flamborough amounts to 917, of which number, the fishermen and their families constitute at least one half. In addition to the church of St. Oswald mentioned above, there are here a Methodist chapel, and a chapel for the Primitive Methodists.

*Blacksmiths,*
Spike James
Wiles Wm.
*Butchers,*
Headley Wm.
Hogarth Anthony
*Carpenters, &c.*
Harrington Allison
Tranmer Robert
*Farmers,*
Acklam Geo.
Brambles Thos.
Crowe Thos.
Dawson Mary
Knaggs John
Knaggs Wm.
Lamplugh John
Major John
Morris Wm.
Riley Joseph
Robinson Samuel

Spink James
Stephenson Geo.
Stockdale James
Vickerman Saml.
Walmsley John
*Grocers, &c.*
Lamplugh Thos.
Pockley Sarah
*Light-keepers,*
Moody Christ.
Stratton David
*Shoemakers,*
Edmond Briant
Hewson Wm.
Nicholson Robt.
Robson Wm.
*Tailors, &c.*
Bailey Matthew
Brown Wm.
Maltby Thos.

Castle Thos. stone mason and flour dealer
Johnson James, weaver
Lamplugh Matthew, corn miller
Maw John, schoolmaster
Ogle Mrs. gentlewoman
Pick Milcah, vict. Board
Sawdon James, bacon and flour dlr.
Spike James, vict. Dog and Duck
Woodhouse Samuel, vict. Sloop
Wright Eliz. straw hat manufacturer

*Carriers.*——Pockley and Co. Hall Mon. and Thur. mgs.; to York Tu. and Thur.
Bays and Jefferson, to Hull and York, Mon. and Thur.
John Lundie, to Black Lion, Bridlington, every Sat.
Thos. Short, to Bridlington daily
Thomas Lamplugh, to Bridlington and Hull every Mon. & Thur.

FLINTON, in the parish of Humbleton, wap. and liberty of Holderness; 6 miles NE. of Hedon. Population, 125.

*Farmers,*
Crawforth Mary
Johnson Thos.
Johnson Matthew
Raines John
Walls Hammond
Webster Wm.

FLIXTON, in the parish of Folkton, and wap. of Dickering; 4 m. NW. of Hunmanby. There is here a chapel occupied by the Primitive Methodists. Population, 267.

Appleby Thomas, carpenter
Beswick Wm. vict. New Inn
Green Richard, schoolmaster
Ireland Hopper, blacksmith
Prest Wm. butcher

*Farmers,*
Barnby John, Wold
Glaves Edward
Hudson Robert
Ireland Mary
Ringrose Charles
Spencer Wm.
Stubbs Richard
Walker John
Wood Mary
Woodall Geo.
*Grocers, &c.*
Hogg Christopher

King John
*Shoemakers,*
Champlain Brian
Pratt John
Wharcup Matth.
*Stone-masons,*
Beswick Wm.
Idle John
Newton Wm.
*Tailors,*
Hogg Christopher
Menard Geo.

*Carriers.*
John Blackburn, to Hull, every Tu.
Geo. Mayman and Robt. Watson, Scarborough, every Thur.

FLOTMANBY (East,) in the parish of Folkton, and wap. of Dickering; 1½ mile NNW. of Hunmanby.
Tate Francis, gentleman

FLOTMANBY (West,) in the parish of Folkton, and wap. of Dickering; 2½ miles NW. of Hunmanby.
Wrangham Joseph, gentleman

FOGGATHORPE, in the parish of Bubwith, and wap. of Harthill; 6 miles of Howden. In this township the system of letting out small parcels of land to labourers, for cow-gates, has been attended with great success, and also with a reduction of the poor's rates. Population, 137.

Lewis William, gent.
Musgrave Thomas, gent.

*Farmers,*
Cock George
Bardon John, wheelwright
Clegg Robert, grocer
Gibson Geo. shoemaker
Storey Benj. blacksmith

Harper Thos.
Knapton Charles

*Carrier,* Robert Clegg, to York every Fri.; to Howden every Wed.

FOLKTON, (P.) in the wap. of Dickering; 3 miles NW. of Hunmanby. This is a rectory and vicarage, in patronage of the Osbaldeston family, and of the rector of Folkton, of which the Rev. Robert Phillips is the rector, and the Rev. F. Wrangham the vicar. The church is dedicated to John the Evangelist. Pop. 144.

Brand Catharine, vict. Bell
Mason Rev. Thomas, curate

*Farmers,*
Nesfield Wm.

Rogers Wm.
Simpson Maws.

FORDON, in the parish of Hunmanby, and wap. of Dickering; 4 miles SW. of Hunmanby; a chapelry to the vicarage of Hunmanby.

*Farmers,*
Brigham John

Hutchinson John
Lowish Wm.

FOSHAM, in the parish of Aldbrough, wap. and liberty of Holderness; 6 miles NNE. of Hedon. Pop. included with Aldbrough.

Fox John, farmer
Parkin Thos. farmer, and carrier to Hull every Tuesday.

FOSTON, (P.) in the wap. of Dickering; 6 miles ESE. of Driffield.—There is here a church, dedicated to All Saints, of which the King is patron, and the Rev. Sidney Smith rector; there are also Methodist and Calvinist chapels. Pop. 300.

Bell Robert, boot and shoemaker
Dickinson Thomas, coal dealer
Drinkrow Jane, vict. Cross Keys
Dunn Jonathan, butcher
Garbutt Joseph and Co. corn millers and coal merchants
Stables Robert, tanner
Watson Benjamin, tailor

*Blacksmiths,*
Scott David
Wilson John

Robson Thos.
Seller Thos.
Welburn Wm.
Wright Wm.

*Farmers,*
Allanson John
Danby Matthew
Dickinson Peter
Dickinson Thos.
Johnson John
Mook Richard

*Grocers & Drapers,*
Baker George
Stork Matthew
*Wheelwrights,*
Robinson Matt.
Stork John

*Carriers.*—William Hall, to Hull on Mon.; to Driffield on Thur.; and Bridlington on Sat.—George Mainprize, to Hull & Gemlin every Thur.

FOXHOLES, (P.) in the wap. of Dickering; 6 miles SW. of Hunmanby. The parish church is a rectory, in the patronage of the Sykes' family; there is also a Methodist chapel. Pop. with Boythorp, 169.

Flood Rev. Henry, rector

*Farmers,*
Barker Wm.
Brown Richard
Lawson George
Braithwaite Edward, carpenter and vict. Ship
Myers John, blacksmith

Speck Thos.
*Grocers,*
Foord Thos.
Penrose James

FRAYSTHORPE, in the parish of Carnaby, and wap. of Dickering; 5 miles SSW. of Bridlington.

Simpson Rev. Thomas, curate

*Farmers,*
Jackson Wm.

Jackson Rebecca
Meeke Robert

FRIDAYTHORPE, (P.) in the wap. of Buckrose, and liberty of St. Peter's; 9 miles NE. of Pocklington. The living is a vicarage, in the gift of the Prebendary of Wetwang, of which the Rev. Henry Torre is the incumbent. Here is also a Methodist chapel. Population, 275.

Acklam James, vict. Cross Keys
Blackston James, schoolmaster
Sharp Geo. vict. Hare & Hounds

*Blacksmiths,*
Horsley Wm.
Raney Emlah
*Farmers,*
Coulson Robert
Edmund Richard
Linton John
Marshall Francis
Robinson Wm.
Robson Matt.
Sharp Geo.
Turner Thos.
Turner Wm.
Vickerman Sarah
Wharram Robt.

*Grocers,*
Harland John
Robinson Wm.
*Shoemakers,*
Acklam James
Jackson Thos.
*Tailors,*
Lorriman Thos.
Marshall Wm.
Sharp Mark
*Wheelwrights,*
Harrison Wm.
Sellers John
Wilson Robert

*Carriers.*—Thomas Pearson, to Great Driffield every Thur.; to York every Sat.—John Harland to York every Sat.

FRODINGHAM NORTH, (P.)
In the wap. and liberty of Holderness; 6 miles SE. of Driffield. The market has long been disused, on account of the decreasing population; and the neighbouring town of Drif-

field, which is better situated for trade, having increased so much in wealth and numbers as to cause the charter of Frodingham to be transferred to it about sixty years ago. The church is a very ancient structure, dedicated to St. Elgin, of which the Rev. F. Drake, D. D. is vicar, and Mr. John Atkinson the patron. There are also three chapels of Dissenters, namely, Methodists, Independents, and Ranters, the two latter built in the year 1821. This town is situated within half a mile of the river Hull, which is navigable from Frodingham bridge to Kingston-upon-Hull. Frodingham Grange, (or Great Tythe,) containing 400 acres, belong to Philip Saltmarsh, Esq. and the Vicarage, or Less Tythe, containing 109 acres, to the Rev. F. Drake, D.D. the vicar. Population, including Emmotland, 575.

Grundon Mark, surgeon
Oram Rev. Wm. Independent minister
Stephenson John, yeoman

| *Blacksmiths,* | Nicholson Wm. |
|---|---|
| Huntsman Robert | Noble James |
| Pickering Wm. | Osborne Richard |
| *Bricklayers,* | Pashley Peter |
| Hebb Thomas | Pashley John |
| Hebb Christopher | Robinson Robert |
| *Butchers,* | Wise Miss A. |
| Beckett Thomas | Wise Matthew |
| Dunn Jeremiah | *Grocers,* |
| *Farmers,* | Clark Thomas |
| Beckwith John | Kell David |
| Bickers William | Medforth John |
| Burton Francis | Whitty Wm. (and |
| Cord Richard | draper) |
| Day Peter | *Shoemakers,* |
| Dent John | Dent James |
| Dickinson Felix | Idell Ralph |
| Dickinson Peter | Kilvington Paul |
| Dobson Wm. | *Tailors,* |
| Dunn Richard | Hebb John |
| Harrison Richard | Peck Robert |
| Jarrot William | *Wheelwrights,* |
| Kell David | Fallowdown Peter |
| Milner Richard | Petch Joseph |

Alsop Thomas, vict. Star Inn
Bennet James, vict. Gate
Cook Thomas, weaver
Dinsdale Thos. plumber and glazier
Fenby Wm. rope and twine maker
Fidler John, vict. Red Lion
Lidster John, schoolmaster
Marshall John, bookkeeper
Wilson Amelia, straw hat manfr.

*Carriers*—Henry Pickering & Wm. Jefferson, to Beverley on Sat.; to Driffield every Thu.—Wm. Bellerby, to Hull by water once a fortnight.

FRODINGHAM SOUTH, a small hamlet, in the parish of Owthorne, wap. & liberty of Holderness; 3½ mls.

N. of Patrington. The hall, once a stately mansion, with octagon windows of stained glass, is now in a state of ruin. Population 71.

| *Farmers,* | Smales Wm. |
|---|---|
| Branton Thos. | Wing Mary |
| Hart William | Wright Thomas |

*Carrier,* Christ. Wilson, to Hollym, Ottrington, and Skeffling every Tu. and Fri.

FULFORD GATE, in the parish Fulford Ambo, wap. of Ouse and Derwent, 1½ mile S. of York, a pleasant village containing several good dwelling-houses. chapel is dedicated to St. Oswald; Mr. is the patron, and the Rev. Robert S—— A. B. perpetual curate. There is here slenderly endowed school for 20 boys or so. Population 182.

Bland Henry, Esq. banker
Boyes M. gentleman
Calvert Robert, yeoman
Ellis William, Esq.
Feather John, yeoman
Galbreath Mrs. gentlewoman
Graves Captain
Green Ralph, gentleman
Hamilton John, gentleman
Herbert Samuel, gentleman
Holmes Joseph, gentleman
Horner Benjamin, gentleman
Johnson Wm. chief constable
Lambert Thomas, yeoman
Lawson William, yeoman
Lawson Michael, yeoman
Nicoll S. W. Esq.
Ploughman Paul, gentleman
Richardson Mrs. Eliz. gentlewoman
Robinson Mrs. gentlewoman
Smith J. yeoman
Taylor Cooke, manufacturing chemist
Theakston Francis, druggist
Waite Thomas, gentleman
Waite George, yeoman
Wilson Thomas, Esq. banker
Wodson William, gentleman
Wormald John, gentleman

| *Bankers,* | Handley Wm. |
|---|---|
| Hessel Thomas | Parrott Geo. |
| Hoyle Mary | Wilkinson Geo. |
| Leng John | *Shoemakers,* |
| *Blacksmiths,* | Dixon Thomas |
| Hick Wm. | Thompson Richard |
| Marshall Geo. | *Wheelwrights,* |
| *Farmers,* | Hick Joseph |
| Cartwright John | Hick William |
| Eshelby Ralph | |

Halliday William, vict. Board
Johnson Richard, vict. Saddle
Leaf William, butcher
Ledberry William, tailor
Nicholson Thomas, shopkeeper

Pearson Thomas, schoolmaster
Peckitt James, vict. Light Horseman
Smithson Robert, coal dealer
Strickland William, corn miller
Tomlinson Sarah, vict. Plough
Wilkinson Mrs. vict. Bay Horse

FULFORD WATER, in the parish of Fulford Ambo, wap. of Ouse and Derwent, a part in the liberty of St. Peter's; 2½ miles S. of York. Population 85.

Key Thomas, gent. Hall

*Farmers,*
Daniel Joseph

Elsworth Wm.
Smith Jasper

GALLY GAP, in the parish of Scrayingham, and wap. of Buckrose; 6 mls. NW. of Malton. Pop. included with Howsham.

Thomas Francis, farmer and surveyor of highways

GANSTEAD, in the parish of Swine, wap. and liberty of Holderness; 4½ miles NNW. of Hedon.—Population 61.

Bibb James, corn miller

*Farmers,*
Brown Thomas
Todd William

Turner Thomas
Ulliet Thomas

GANTON, (P.) in the wap. of Dickering; 8 miles W. of Hunmanby. The church is dedicated to St. Nicholas, and the patronage is in the ancient and honourable family of Legard, who have their seat here. Population with Brompton, 278.

Legard Sir Thos. Bart. Ganton hall
Legard Rev. William, vicar
Denton Rev. T. curate

*Farmers,*
Lawson Robert

Monkman John
Warwick Richard

Denison Richard, machine maker
Gill Charles, schoolmaster
Gill John, gardener
Gill John, shoemaker
Lovell William, stone mason
Melton Stephen, vict. and blacksmith
Otterburn Wm. druggist & gun maker
Padsey William, tailor
Ringrose Wm. & Jph. carpenters, &c.

*Carriers*—Robert Dawson, to Beverley every Sat.—John Fowler, to Driffield every Thursday

GANTON DALE INN, in the parish of Ganton, & wap. of Dickering; 10 miles WSW. of Hunmanby.

Groves Robert, vict. Red Lion, (posting house)

GARRABY, in the parish of Kirby Underdale, and wap. of Buckrose; 6

miles N. of Pocklington. Pop. included with Kirby Underdale.

Sir F. L. Wood, Bart.
Weatherill William, farmer
Whitwell John, farmer

GARTON, (P.) in the wap. and liberty of Holderness; 9 miles NE. of Hedon. The church is a neat Gothic structure, dedicated to St. Michael, of which the King is the patron, and the incumbent is the Rev. Jonathan Dixon, vicar. Pop. 160.

Grimston Charles, Esq. Grimston garth
Kipling Anthony, bricklayer
Walker Thos. vict. and blacksmith
Westerdale Henry, carpenter

*Farmers,*
Coates John
Heron Henry
Heron Samuel
Hopper Francis
Hopper Richard, Bracken hall

Marshall Thomas
Rogerson Wm.
Southwick Richd.
Wilson Jeremiah
Wilson John

*Carriers*—Edward Robinson and John Foster to Hull every Tuesday

GARTON-ON-THE-WOLDS, (P.) in the wap. of Dickering, and liberty of St. Peter's; 3 miles WNW. of Driffield. The church, dedicated to St. Michael is a discharged vicarage, of which the King is the patron, and Rev. Thomas Ibbotson the vicar. There are here also a Methodist chapel and a school, the latter of which is partly supported by the proceeds of a share in the Driffield canal, bequeathed by the late Mrs. Jane Cook. Pop. 357.

Dixon Thomas, gentleman
Harper Robert, gentleman
Holliday Robert, gentleman
Sever Michael, gentleman
Wrangham Richard, gentleman

*Butchers,*
Abbey Henry
Robinson Wm.

Lownsborough S.
Robinson Wm.
Watson Wm.

*Farmers,*
Allison James
Crust Joseph
Crust Thos.
Dickinson Geo.
Flintoff George
Foster Richard
Hance Wm.
Hersley John
Leppington Edw.

*Grocers, &c.*
Garton William
Ulliott Geo.

*Tailors, &c.*
Linwood John
Milner Wm.
Ulliott Geo.

*Wheelwrights,*
Robinson Thomas
Wray Thomas

Blowman John, vict. Three Tuns
Dalton John, blacksmith
Gray John, boot and shoe maker
Hillaby Charles W. schoolmaster
Wilson John, vict. Chase Inn

s 3

GEMBLING, in the parish of Foston, and wap. of Dickering; 7 miles E. of Driffield.  Pop. 87.

*Farmers, &c.*
Cook John
Drinkrow Henry
Farden Robert
Howgate John
Lamplugh Edmund
Mainprize John
Peacock Geo.
Simpson Geo.

*Carrier*, John Mainprize, to Hull on Thu. and Foston on Fri.

GILBERDIKE, in the parish of Eastrington, wap. and liberty of Howdenshire; 5¼ miles ENE. of Howden.  Pop. including Hive and Sandholm, 640.

Bell Nathaniel, corn miller
Hutchinson Joseph, vict. Cross Keys
Lawton Wm. overseer
Ramsey John, shoemaker
Robinson Wm. constable, &c.
Sharp Wm. schoolmaster
Turner Wm. churchwarden, &c.

*Blacksmiths,*
Handley John
Wade John
*Farmers,*
Hairsine Isaac
Lee William

*Carpenters,*
Oldfield Thos.
Ward John
Pacy John
Rennison John
Waterhouse John

*Gilridding*, in the parish of St. Dennis, York, and wap. of Ouse and Derwent; 4 miles SSE. of York.

GIVENDALE GREAT, (P.) in the wap. of Harthill, and liberty of St. Peter's; 4 miles N. of Pocklington. The church is a small ancient structure, of which the Dean of York is the patron, and the Rev. Edmund Holmes the vicar.  Pop. 60.

Singleton John, gentleman
*Farmers,*
Cooper William
Ellison John
Wilkinson Matt.

GIVENDALE LITTLE, in the parish of Great Givendale, wap. of Harthill, and liberty of St. Peter's; 2¼ miles NNE. of Pocklington.

Kilby Thomas, farmer

GOODMANHAM, *alias* Godmundia Gaham, is a parish in the wap. of Harthill, partly in the liberty of St. Peter's; one mile and a half NNE. of Market-Weighton, situated on the lowest acclivity of the Wolds. This is a place of great antiquity, and was probably the Delgovitia of the Romans: upon that point Antiquarians are not agreed, some of them assigning this station to Market-Weighton, others to Londesbrough, and others again to Millington; it is, however, agreed on all hands, that Goodmanham was the place on which the primary temple of Pagan worship stood.  This temple was the great Cathedral of Northumbria, laid out in various courts, and inclosed with several walls, containing within it many altars and idols, and attended by the first personages of the priesthood.* The site of this Temple of mystic rites and worship is plainly marked out to this day, by an extensive cluster of artificial hills, now called the Howe Hills.  The venerable Bede in his Ecclesiastical History, chap. xiii. and 2. says, that the place of the idols was standing in his time.  The demolition of these gods took place when Edwin, king of Deira, was converted to Christianity;† and there is reason to suppose, both from the usual practice of the first converts to Christianity, and from the present appearance of some part of the edifice, that the present church, dedicated to All Saints, was built from the ruins of that temple, though not on the same site, as Drake erroneously imagines.  Dr. Stukely, in the Archæ, Vol. I. 44. says, "that the Apostle Paulinus built the parish church of Godmundham, where is the original font, in which he baptised the heathen high priest Coifi."  The font here alluded to is now in the possession of the Rev. J. Stillingfleet, rector of Hotham, who, it is hoped, will restore it to the proper and legitimate situation from which it has doubtless been sacrilegiously abstracted by some Gothic churchwarden.  The church at Goodmanham, of which the Rev. William Blow is the patron and rector, furnishes several fine specimens of Saxon architecture. The exterior arch of the West end of the tower, now intersected by a buttress, the arch of the South entrance, and the internal one, entering into the chancel are Saxon; the upper part of the tower, and the windows on the South side of the body of the church, which has probably been renewed, have the character of modern times.

The process of the introduction of Christianity into this part of the kingdom is curious, and is thus related by the old Chroniclers:—Edwin, the Northumbrian king, under the influence of Ethelburga his queen, and the preaching of Paulinus, convoked a council of his priests and nobles to deliberate on the expediency of embracing the Christian faith.  On the question being propounded by the King, whether he should receive the new faith, and be baptised? Coifi, the chief Pagan bishop, well understanding the bias of Edward's mind, rose first and said, "The religion we have hitherto followed is nothing worth," "for," added he, addressing himself to the King, "there

* See Bede and Camden.
† See Vol. I. page v.

are none of thy people that hath more reverently worshipped our Gods than I have done, and yet there be many that hath received far greater benefits at thy hands: and therefore, if our gods were of any power they would rather help me to high honour and dignity than others. Therefore, if it may be found that this new religion is better and more available than our old, let us with speed embrace the same." A grandee high in power next addressed the assembly, and assigned a much more dignified and disinterested reason than had been given by the high priest, for giving a favourable reception to Christianity : " The religion we possess," he said, " gives us no instruction as the nature of the soul; when it is separated from the body we know not what becomes of it; but the religion of the Christians professes, at least, to open to our view a future state, and is deserving of our unprejudiced consideration." The conclusion was, that Christianity should be embraced; and Coifi, with the zeal of a convert, mounted upon a war horse, repaired to Godmundin Gaham, the place of the idols, and cast his javelin at the principal idol, commanded those around him to burn down the temple and the altars. The new religion was then received by the people, and Edwin himself was baptised by Paulinus at York, in the church of St. Peter's, on Easter Sunday,* in the year 647. Pop. 290.

Bow Rev. Wm. M. A. rector
Clark John, Esq.
Tyson Rev. John, curate

| *Farmers*, | Kirby Nicholas |
|---|---|
| Appleton John | Petch John |
| Appleton Thos. | Reed Thos. |
| Appleton Wm. | Stephenson John |
| Brigham John | Stephenson Rt. |
| Clark Sarah | Stephenson Wm. |
| Foster Wm. | Wade Richard |
| Hewitt Wm. | Wilson John |

Beckett Geo. boot and shoe maker
Bonnard Thos. corn miller
Easingwold Mary, vict. Star
Parkinson Marmaduke, blacksmith & parish clerk
Towse Christopher, wheelwright
Wilson Wm. schoolmaster
Wilson John, shoemaker

*Carrier*, George Petch, to Market Weighton on Thur. and to Beverley on Sat.

GOWTHORPE, in the parish of Bishop Wilton, wap. of Harthill, and liberty of St. Peter's ; 4 miles NW. of

* See Vol. II. page 35.

Pocklington. Population, (included with Youlthorpe) 111.
Blanchard Nicholas, yeoman
Dales Thomas, farmer
Holliday Thomas, farmer

GOWTHORPE, in the parish of Blacktoft, wap. and liberty of Howdenshire ; 8 miles ESE. of Howden.
Haldenby Thomas, farmer

GOXHILL, (P.) in the wap. and liberty of Holderness ; 3 miles SW. of Hornsea. The church, which is of considerable antiquity, is situated on an eminence, and is embosomed in lofty trees, which add much to the solemnity of the scene. Time has impaired the building, but it is at present undergoing a thorough repair. The living is a rectory, dedicated to St. Giles, the patron of which is the Rev. C. Constable ; the Rev. John Courtenay is rector, and the Rev. Christopher Forge, curate. Pop. 70.

| *Farmers*, | Collinson Wm. |
|---|---|
| Alvin Henry | Ellis John |
| Boyes Thomas | Exard Richard |

*Grange House*, in the parish of Humbleton, wap. and liberty of Holderness ; 4 miles from Hedon.

GRANSMOOR, in the parish of Burton Agnes, and wap. of Dickering ; 7 miles ENE. of Driffield. Pop. 85.

| *Farmers*, | Milner Richard |
|---|---|
| Carrick John | Smith William |
| Dalby Richard | Topham John |
| Hyde Botterill | |

*Carrier*—Samuel Wray, to Bridlington every Saturday.

GREEN OAK, in the parish of Eastrington, wap. and liberty of Howdenshire ; 4 miles E. of Howden.
Blyth Robert, yeoman

GREENWICK, in the parish of Bishop Wilton, and wap. of Harthill ; 5 miles NR. of Pocklington.
Askwith Thomas, farmer

GRIBTHORPE, or GRIPTHORPE, in the parish of Bubwith, and wap. of Harthill ; 5 miles N. of Howden. Population, (with Willeytoft) 145.

| *Farmers*, | Laycock Thos. |
|---|---|
| Eland George | Penrose Wm. |
| Eland Leonard | |

GRIMSTONE, in the parish of Dunnington, wap. of Ouse and Derwent, and liberty of St. Peter's ; 3 miles E. of York. Pop. 72.

Summers Robt. vict. Blackwell Ox
| *Farmers*, | Prince Thomas |
|---|---|
| Lofthouse Benj. | Ridsdale Francis |
| Lofthouse Edward | |

GRIMSTONE HANGING, in the parish of Kirkby Underdale, and wap. of Buckrose; 8 mls. N. of Pocklington.

*Farmers,*
Arnell Wm.
Clarkson Leonard,
Baffam
Kirby Wm.
Pearose John
Wass Wm.

GRIMSTONE NORTH, (P.) in the wap. of Buckrose, and liberty of St. Peter's; 4 miles SE. of Malton. The church is a discharged vicarage, dedicated to St. Nicholas, of which the prebendary of Langtoft is the patron, and the Rev. John Buchanan the vicar. Population, 139.

Green Rev. James, curate
Beilby John, blacksmith
Shires Wm. vict. Gelder's Arms

*Farmers,*
Beilby John
Dale James
Marshall Geo.
Wardill John

GRIMTHORPE, in the parish of Great Givendale, wap. of Harthill, and liberty of St. Peter's; 4 miles N. of Pocklington. Pop. 29.

Marshall William, farmer

GRINDALL, in the parish of Bridlington, wap. of Dickering, and liberty of St. Peter's; 4 miles NW. of Bridlington. Pop. 107.

Kendall Rev. William, curate

*Farmers,*
Brown Thomas
Hartley Wm.
Johnson Richard
Jordan James
Shaw Samuel
Smith John

*Grove Hill,* in the parish of St. Nicholas, Beverley, and wap. of Harthill; 1 mile E. of Beverley.

GUNBY, in the parish of Bubwith, and wap. of Harthill; 5 miles NNW. of Howden. This township was given by William the Conqueror to Gilbert Tyson, his standard-bearer, and has been the successive residence of the De Gunnebys, the Knights, the Delmans, and the Vavasours.

Clarkson Michael, gentleman

HAGTHORPE, in the parish of Heminbrough, wap. of Ouse and Derwent; 5½ miles ESE. of Selby.

Jubb William, yeoman

HALSHAM, (P.) in the wap. and liberty of Holderness; 4 miles NW. of Patrington. This village consists chiefly of a number of respectable farm houses, scattered at irregular distances from each other.— The Church is an ancient structure, dedicated to All Saints, of which Lord Montague is the patron, and the Rev. Charles Mace,

the rector. On a small eminence stands a stately Mausoleum, built of the best white free stone, faced with polished marble, and in the centre an elegant monument, in memory of the late Sir William Constable Bart. of Burton Constable, who lies surrounded by the ancestors of that ancient family. The erection of this superb structure cost the sum of £19,000. Sir John Constable, of Kirkby Knowle, in 1594, by will the sum of 20l. per annum, to be paid out of his estate for ever, for the following purposes:—20l. for the education of poor children; 34l. to furnish the other children with satchels, books, &c. and to be distributed amongst eight poor men, and 4l. to two poor old women, the hospital erected for their use. Pop.

Mackereth Rev. John, curate

*Farmers,*
Baxter Edward
Bryan Bedell
Carr Henry
Castle Wm.
Champney Thos.
Collinson Thos.
Dresser Thos.
Fewson James
Garton John
Giles Wm.
Pattinson Geo.
Richardson John
Thorpe Thos.
Whittin John
Wright George
Wright Wm.
*Wheelwrights,*
Hunter James
Richardson Fras.
Robinson Wm.

Ellis Joseph, blacksmith
Fairbank John, schoolmaster
Fairbank Charles, grocer
Harrison Wm. bricklayer
Frost Thomas, yeoman
Smith Francis, vict. Sun.

*Carrier*—Thomas Hutton to Hull every Tuesday.

HALTEMPRICE, (extra P.) in the wap. of Harthill; 4½ miles NW. of Hull. This was formerly a priory, but now a farm house.

Ellyard Samuel, farmer

HARLETHORPE, in the parish of Bubwith, and wap. of Harthill; 4 miles N. of Howden. Pop. 99.

*Farmers,*
Eland T. yeoman
Hessell Gregory
Knapton Wm.
Leverack Thos.
Massey Wm.
Moseley Wm.

Ward James, blacksmith
West Richard, shoemaker

HARPHAM, (P.) in the wap. of Dickering; 6 miles NE. of Driffield; the former residence, and the burial place of the ancient family of the St. Quintins, the founder of which formerly came over to England with William the Conqueror, and received the lordships of Harpham as the price of his military services. Adjoining to

the Church on the Western side, the foundations of the family mansion are yet to be
visited, and certain vestiges of the fish ponds,
but the building has totally disappeared. The
chancel, of which the Rev. Thomas Milnes,
Rector of Barton Agnes, is incumbent, consists of a neat plain stone tower, about 50 feet
high, a nave, repaired and heightened on
the South side with brick, and a chancel.
The arches have been originally all pointed,
and on the North side there has been a small
aisle which is now the cemetery of the family of St. Quintin. The pedigree of the
family from Harbert, in the year 1060, to
Sir Wm. St. Quintin, Bart. who died in
1795, (twenty-eight successions) is represented in stained glass, beautifully executed by
Willett, and placed in the windows of the
vestry, at the expense of the last baronet,
who died about the year 1797, but whose
name is not yet recorded among his ancestors. This pedigree is uninterrupted in
the male line through a period of upwards
of seven centuries! In the same burial
place are two massive plain stone coffins,
which "the grave hath cast up again," but
who were their tenants, or when they were
ejected from their narrow mansion, there is
no record to tell. There are here also a
number of monuments and inscriptions, all
relating to the same family, and several of
them in good preservation; but the principal
is an elegant white marble monument, above
the altar base, exhibiting a full length figure
of grief, with the usual emblems, holding
two profile likenesses, one of the late Sir
William Quintin, Bart. and the other of his
lady. A small tablet contains an inscription
to her memory, and the words—"Also in
memory of"—the blank remaining to be supplied by the hand of the painter, but not by
the hand of fate. Sir William was succeeded by his nephew, who never took the
title, and he dying, left a son, a minor, who
attained his majority in 1818. The village
is wholly agricultural; the farm-home-steads
are good, and the cottages neat and comfortable. On the road side to Hornsea is a fine
clear spring of excellent water, over which is
erected a dome, and on the side of this small
but ancient building, is inscribed "St. John
Well," intended probably as a monumental
tribute to St. John of Beverley, who, according to the tradition of upwards of eleven centuries, was born in this village.* Pop. 251.

Hall John, linen manufacturer
Morris Christopher, wheelwright
Russell Thomas, butcher

* Goodwin is of this opinion: Stubbs
gives Beverley the honour of the Saint's
birth place.

Storry Robert, vict. Anchor
Watson Robert, blacksmith
Webster Wm. tailor

| *Farmers,* | Thompson John |
|---|---|
| Dixon Francis | *Grocers,* |
| Jefferson Robt. | Pearson John |
| Harrison Edw. | Webster Wm. |
| Reaston Wm. | *Shoemakers,* |
| Robson Wm. | Brown Robert |
| Staveley Rhd. | Robson Wm. |
| Taylor John | |

*Carrier.*—Robert Storrs, to Bridlington every Saturday.

HARSWELL, (P.) in the wap. of
Harthill; 4 miles WSW. of Market Weighton. The church is a small ancient structure, dedicated to St. Peter: it is a discharged
rectory, in the patronage of the Slingsby
family, of which the Rev. Henry Mitton is
rector. Population, 76.

Alderson Rev. Wm. A. B. curate
Bean Benjamin, parish clerk

| *Farmers,* | Patchett Timthy. |
|---|---|
| Dunwell John | Swales Abm. |
| Marshall Thos. | Topping Edw. |

*Carrier.*—Thos. Triffit, to Market
Weighton every Wednesday.

HASHOLME, in the parish of
Holme-on-Spalding-moor, and wap.
of Harthill; 7 miles NE. of Howden.

| *Farmers,* | Renard James |
|---|---|
| Holland Elis. | Walkington Wm. |
| Marshall Geo. | |

HATFIELD (Great), in the parish
of Mappleton and Sigglesthorne, wap. and
liberty of Holderness; 4 miles SW. of
Hornsea. This village appears to have been
a place of some importance, from an ancient
stone cross of exquisite workmanship, which
stands in the centre of the place. There is
here a burial place, but no place of worship, the Chapel which formerly stood in it
having been destroyed by fire about a century
ago. The site of the sanctuary is marked
by a large monumental stone, bearing this
inscription:—HERE LIETH THE BODY
OF EXPOPHER CONSTABLE, A.D. 642.
Population, 197.

Fox Rev. T. vicar

| *Farmers,* | Morris Thos. |
|---|---|
| Blenkin James | Rooklidge Jacob |
| Chapman John | Stabler Wm. |
| Jackson Hartley | White Christ. |
| Lowthorp Rbt. | Wright Richard |
| Moor Elizabeth | |

Hastings John, grocer
Robinson Edward, tailor
Stephenson Wm. shoemaker

*Carrier.*—John Hastings, to Hull
every Tuesday.

HATFIELD LITTLE, in the parish of Sigglesthorne, wap. and liberty of Holderness; 4 miles SW. of Hornsea. Population 25.

Tanton Richard, farmer

HAVSTHORP, in the parish of Burton Agnes, & wap. of Dickering; 4 mls. SW. of Bridlington. Pop. 109.

Davison William, jun. butcher
Walker George, shoemaker

*Farmers,*          Piercy James
Charter Thomas      Smith John
Davison Wm.

HAYTON, (P.) in the wap. of Harthill; 2½ miles SSE. of Pocklington. Hayton-cum-Beilby, is a vicarage; present incumbent Rev. Charles Ryves Graham, it is under the patronage of the Dean of St. Peter's, York; the church is dedicated to St. Martin. Population 177.

Crosier William, vict. White Horse
Glazier Thomas, shoemaker
Rowntree Peter, corn miller
Walker William, blacksmith
Wilson Joseph, wheelwright

*Farmers,*          Leak Robert
Binnington John     Ponsonby Wm.
Boys William        Staveley Stephen
Clark William       Winter John
Crain Richard       Withell John
Crain Mrs. Ann      Yeaman Thomas
Holtby William

---

## HEDON, (P.)

In the wap. of Holderness, and liberty of Hedon, and St. Peter's; 8 miles E. of Hull, and 2 miles E. of the Humber. The town consists chiefly of one street, in the middle of which is the Market place; it is well paved, and the road in every direction in good condition. The parish comprises an area of 276 acres, and the population which has been increasing progressively for the last twenty years, now amounts to 902, though, in 1801, the numbers were only 592. The government of the town is in the corporation, which consists of a Mayor, nine Aldermen, two Bailiffs, the latter of whom are Magistrates during their term of office, and an indefinite number of Burgesses: the Mayor is annually chosen from the Aldermen, and the Bailiffs from the Burgesses; the Coroner is one of the Aldermen annually chosen, and usually the person who has served the office of Mayor the preceding year; John Taylor, Esq. is the Mayor, and Charles Gibson and Thomas Jackson, Esqrs. are Bailiffs for 1822-3. The

Aldermen are, William Iveson, Edward Ombler, William Day, James Iveson, John Taylor, Thomas Dring, Henry Harding, Robert Clifford, John Souther, and John Hornby, Esqrs. The Coroner for the year 1822-3, is Henry Harmley, Esq; and James Iveson, is Town Clerk. There is a court of record, that holds plea to an unlimited amount. The court for the wapentake of Holderness, which is held in Hall, takes cognisance of pleas under 40s. and the general quarter sessions for the Borough are held in the same place. Thomas Constable, Baronet, of [...] Constable, is lord paramount of the manor of Holderness, and the corporation of Hedon is bound by charter to provide within the town a hall and prison for the liberty of Holderness. Hedon returns two members to parliament; the present members are Lieut. Colonel John Baillie, of Devonshire place, Cavendish square, London, and Robert Farrand, Esq. of Fenchurch street, London. This Borough first sent members to parliament in the 23d of Edward I. after which no returns were made till the 1st of Edward VI., since which time the returns have been regular. The right of election is in the burgesses, whose privilege is gained either by descent, or by serving seven years to a freeman resident in the Borough, or an honorary gift at the discretion of the chief officers for the time. The number amount to about three hundred. Hedon was anciently a sea port of considerable importance, connected with the river Humber by a navigable creek, but the access from the Humber diminished as the surrounding country became drained and embanked, and was finally choaked up. As Hull increased Hedon declined. In 1774, an act of parliament was obtained for reopening and preserving the haven, and though the work failed of entire success for want of a lock to exclude the tides, the trade has progressively increased, and considerable quantities of grain are shipped here for London, and the West Riding of Yorkshire, for which coal, lime, and general merchandise are received in return. Camden speaks of Hedon as having been "formerly a considerable place by reason of merchants and shipping;" and his commentator adds, that "the remains and marks of two churches, besides the one they now have, argues its former populousness, and by consequence a flourishing trade." This place suffered a severe loss in the year 1656, by a dreadful conflagration, which burnt down great part of the town, and subsequently several houses in the Market-place shared the same fate; but they are now rebuilt, and though individeaths sustained less, the appearance of the town was considerably improved by the disaster. The church of St. Augustine, of which the Archbishop of York is the patron, and the Rev. John Dixon the vicar, is the only church in this place; of the two others, St. Nicholas and St. James, only the traces of the foundations remain. Upon part of seven acres of land, at Newton, near this town, given by Alan, son of Oubernus, was built in the reign of king John, an hospital, dedicated to the holy Sepulchre, for a prior, and seven brethren, or sisters lepers; but it no longer exists. A handsome chapel for Roman Catholic worship was built here, in 1804; and a Calvinist chapel was built in 1801; there is also a Methodist chapel, erected in 1818. The corporation have erected eight houses, appropriated to the maintenance of old burgesses, and three others, appropriated to the widows of burgesses, in which they have a small pension, and an annual supply of coals. There are also two schools, one for boys, and the other for girls, the children of burgesses, supported by the voluntary contributions of the representatives of the borough. The weekly market, which is held on the Saturday, is well supplied with provisions of all sorts. The annual fairs, of which there are four, are held on the second of August, the twenty-second of September, the seventeenth of November, and the sixth of December; and fortnight markets for cattle, established in 1796, are held every alternate Monday throughout the year, with increasing success; the number of sheep penned in 1821, amounted to 13,738. The Holderness Agricultural Society, the operations of which have been highly beneficial to this district, hold their quarterly meetings in this place, and have here their annual show of prize cattle. This society is composed of most of the gentlemen, and principal farmers, and breeders of cattle in this fertile and highly cultivated district, and possesses a valuable and select library of the best books, which have been written on agriculture, and the sciences with which it is connected. There are also several other societies here, amongst the principal of which may be mentioned, the Friendly Union Benefit Society, with 200 members, and a fund of £1300; and the Bible Society, which is extensively patronised. There is a great deal of sociality in this small but interesting town, and the dancing, and card assemblies in the winter, to which all the principal inhabitants of the town and neighbourhood resort, impart to the place a considerable share of gaiety and refinement.

SARAH TODD, *By-post Office.*
Letters arr. from Hull, every Mon. Wed. Thu. and Sat. at ½ past 9 mg. departs at ½ past 12 noon.

### DIRECTORY.

Allen William, gentleman
Burstall Lydia, gentlewoman
Davy Peter, gentleman
Day William, alderman
Dixon Rev. John, vicar
Garforth Edward, gentleman
Howden Mrs. gentlewoman
Iveson William, Esq. attorney and coroner for Holderness
Iveson James, Esq. attorney
Iveson Richard, gentleman
Mitchinson Francis, gentleman
Rank Mary, gentlewoman
Robson Charles, gentleman
Stephenson Rev. Wm. Calv. minister
Swinburn Rev. Joseph, Catholic priest
Thorp Francis, gentleman
Tickell Rev. John
Webster George, gentleman

*Academies.*

Ainsworth Richard, (boys' free school)
Boyce Henry, (classical & commercial)
Dalton Miss, (ladies' boarding)
Mitchinson Jane, (girls' free school)

*Blacksmiths,*
Jackson Thomas
Soutter John, sen.
Soutter John, jun.
*Boot & Shoemakers,*
Easart Francis
Hewson Geo.
Nelthorp Thos.
Ramsay Wm.
Rawson Samuel
Tesseyman John
Turner Wm.
Verser George
Wilson Robert
*Bricklayers,*
Battye Abraham
Burnham Robert
Drew John
Grice David
Leek Samuel
Story Broom
*Butchers,*
Dennison Thos.
Wood Thos.
*Carpenters,*
Battye John
Burn Matthew
Hoe Thomas
Johnson John
Robinson Nicholas
*Drapers,*
Clarkson Joseph
Hassley Henry
Harper George

Story Ann
*Gardeners,*
Clarkson Jph. jun.
Marshall John
Thorp George
*Grocers,*
Baron John
Clarkson Joseph
Harper George
Harper Anne
Marshall John
Pears Alexander
Robinson Nicholas
Wilson Robert
*Hair Dressers,*
Knowles Thos.
Thompson John
*Plumbers and Glaziers,*
Belton John
Broom John
Robinson Wm.
*Saddlers,*
Egglestone Thos.
Hoe Thomas
Rider Robert
*Surgeons and Apothecaries,*
Campbell James
Cautley Henry
Sawyer George
Velvin Daniel
*Tailors,*
Battye George

Hansley Henry        Scarl John
Rawcliffe John       Wright Wm
Rawson Thomas

*Taverns, Hotels, and Inns.*

Dog & Duck, Thomas Dennison
Horse & Jockey, Geo. Whiterwick
King's Head, Jonathan Mitchinson
Old Sun, Mrs. Robinson
Old Sun, Benjamin Bonsell
Saunderson's Arms, Thos. Jackson
Sloop, Geo. Gibson, Haven side
Tiger, Story Broom

*Miscellany of Trades.*

Batty John, parish clerk
Brown Mary, straw hat maker
Butler John, excise officer
Corbrake Francis, farmer
Cowpling James, coal merchant
Darling Robert, huntsman
Ennes Thomas, grazier
Foster John, harbour master, & corn, coal and lime merchant
Gibson Chas. corn miller, Haven mill
Harper Elizabeth, milliner
Hornby John, baker & corn dealer
Hyde Francis, stone mason and marble cutter
Ingleby Wm. tallow chandler
Ingleby Wm. tanner and fellmonger
Jarram John, auctioneer and bailiff
Jekyll Joseph, cooper
Kates Wm. mace bearer
Meckereth Thos. spirit merchant
Potchett Thos. watch & clock maker
Robinson Joseph, farmer & coal dlr.
Simon Edward, sexton
Smith Wm. yeoman
Stewart James, tinner and brasier
Stubbins Robert, common brewer and spirit merchant
Taylor John, merchant
Taylor Wm. merchant
Taylor Thos. mercht. & vessel owner
Taylor Richard, dlr. in earthenware
Wilkinson Charles, printer, bookseller and stationer

### COACHES.

Wm. Thorpe's Coach, (from King's Head) to the Rein Deer, Hull, every Tu. at ¾ past 8 mg. and to Patrington in the evg. at 6.
Wing's Coach, (from King's Head) to Hull, every Tu. and Fri. at 8 mg. returns 6 evening.
Wing's Caravan, (from Hull to Patrington) arr. at Old Sun, at ¾ past 9 mg. every Mon. Wed. and Sat. conveys letters, goods & passengers, dep. same days at 6 evg.

### WATER CARRIAGE.

John Leath's Vessel, to Three Cranes Wharf, London, monthly.

Thomas Taylor's Vessels, to Leeds and Wakefield, once a fortnight, and to London occasionally.

### LAND CARRIAGE.

John Barrett's Waggon, from Patrington to Hull, every Tu. & Fri. returns same days.
Jonathan Mitchinson's and William Rawson's Waggons, (from King Head) to Hull, every Tu. & returns in the evening.

*Carriers* to Hull, Easington, Patrington, Ottringham, Keyingham, Thorngumbald & Paull weekly.

HELPERTHORP, (P.) in the of Buckrose; 9 miles NW. of Driffield. Here is a chapel of the Established church, dedicated to St. Peter, which the Dean and Chapter of York are the patrons; and the Rev. Richard Forrest, the vicar. Pop. 151.

Sandeman William, victualler, Blacksmith's Arms

*Farmers,*        Lovell Wm.
Allinson Wm.            *Shoemaker,*
Barmby Richard     Anderson Thos.
Binning John          Cooper John
Lovell Richard

HEMINGBROUGH, (P.) in the Southern point of the wap. of Ouse & Derwent; 5 miles ESE. of Selby. This place is remarkable for its church, which has a beautiful spire, rising forty-two above the battlements. Dr. Stukeley "that the Romans had a fort in this on each side of the great West tower of present church," and the situation of great wall, which is of a different from the rest of the building, favour supposition, that the church has been upon the site of the Roman fort. The fice, which is dedicated to St. Mary, made collegiate in 1426, for a provost, prebendaries, six vicars choral, and six but these privileges ceased with the tion, and it is now a discharged vicarage, the gift of the King. Population, 500.

*⁎⁎* A Foot-post to Ferrybridge, at the mg. ret. at 2 in the afternoon.

Caile Rev. William, vicar
Robinson Wm. gentleman

Bromitt George, yeoman
Harrison John, yeoman, Grange
Harrison Joseph, yeoman
Middleton Wm. yeoman
Nappy Wm. yeoman

*Bricklayers,*        *Farmers,*
Cobb George        Burton Elizabeth
Cobb Thomas        Burton John
                   Cressey George

Jackson Thomas
Laverack John
Lolley Thomas
Routh Edward
Taylor Esther
*Shoemakers,*
Kay Thomas
Lee Joseph
*Shopkeepers,*
Briggs Thomas

Lambert James
Newham Wm. sen.
Pearson Thomas
*Tailors,*
Abbey Mark
Ward John
*Wheelwrights,*
Pocklington Jph.
Woodill John

Bordman John, saddler
Cressey William, vict. Britannia
Dalby Richard, schoolmaster
Dickinson J. butcher & vict. Half Moon
Emmerson Margaret, schoolmistress
Howdle John, corn miller
Newham William, jun. butcher
Robinson William, constable
Smallwood James, vict. Dog
Stickney Joseph, blacksmith

*Carriers*—Cross and Lambert, to Selby, every Mon. at 8 mg.
*Steam Packet* to Hull at 10 mg.

HEMPHOLME, in the parish of Leven, wap. & liberty of Holderness; 8½ miles SE. of Driffield. Pop. 93.

*Farmers & Yeomen,* Harrison John
Atkinson Wm.
Bilton Ralph
Fallowdown Wm.
Kemp Isaac
Kirk John

Idell Francis, schoolmaster

HESLERTON EAST, in the parish of West Heslerton, and wap. of Buckrose; 10 miles ENE. of Malton. Here is a Chapel of Ease, and a Methodist chapel. Pop. 196.

Judson Richard, yeoman

*Farmers,*
Cross David
Hoofe Thomas
Lamb John
Newlove Mark
Vickerman John
Woodill George
Yates Thomas

Cordiner Matthew, iron master
Cordiner Richard, blacksmith
Knaggs James, carpenter
Speck William, shopkeeper
Woodill James, tailor

HESLERTON WEST, (P.) in the wap. of Buckrose; 9 miles ENE. of Malton. The parish church, dedicated to St. Andrew, is in the patronage of the King. Pop. 273.

Canning Rev. William, M.A. rector
Foulis J. R. Esq. magistrate

*Carpenters,*
Milner George
Smith Thomas
*Farmers,*
Bointon Joseph
Botterill Thos.
Gibson George
Goodill Robert
Hesp John
Marshall Jonathan
Piercy Thomas
Ruston John
Simpson Joseph
Walker Robert
Wilson Francis
*Shoemakers,*
Boy Thomas
Stephenson Wm.

Blanchard Charles Dale, tailor
Lovel John, churchwarden
Petch William, grocer
Robinson John, schoolmaster
Wilson Francis, vict.

*Carrier*—J. Boyes, to Malton daily.

HESLINGTON, (P.) in the wap. of Ouse and Derwent; 2 miles SE. of York—The chapel is dedicated to St. Peter and St. Paul, and the prebendary of Ampleforth in York cathedral is the patron, the Rev. Francis Metcalf is the incumbent. Here is a hospital for 8 poor men, and 1 poor woman, with a rental from the Castle Mills, at York, which let for 50*l.* per ann. and also 5*l.* per ann. from a rectory in Cleveland. Pop. 513.

Coates General James
Hodgson Martha, gentlewoman
Porter Captain Henry
Reynolds Ann, gentlewoman
Richardson Rev. James, curate
Yarburgh Henry, Esq. Hall
Yarburgh Major Nicholas

*Corn-millers,*
Hodgson Seth
Holborn John
*Farmers & Yeomen,*
Ayer John
Carr Francis
Carr William
Cooper William
Dickson George
Dickson John & Rd.
Dover John
Feather Wm.
Hick William
Lambert John
Lazenby Thos.

Lockwood Robert
Nicholson John
Ponty Robert
Pool Thomas
Robinson Thos.
Seller Thomas
Sigsworth Geo.
Turner Robert
Umpleby Wm.
Ware William
Wilberforce Thos.
Wright George
*Shoemakers,*
Brayshaw Wm.
Smith Richard

Beckett Thomas, vict. Robin Hood
Boardman William, bleacher
Dale John, vict. Ship
Foster Thomas, tailor
Lambert Robert, bricklayer
Pool John, carpenter
Skelton John, day school & parish clerk
Swales John, linen manufacturer
Ware Robert, blacksmith

HESSLE, (P.) in the wap. of Hull-shire; 5 miles WSW. of Hull. This is an ancient parish and manor, the date of which may be traced to the conquest. The manor of Hessle was formerly a possession of the Stutevilles, and Joan Stuteville carried the estates to Hugh de Wake. This lady was the first to introduce the custom of females riding sideways on horseback, and the device on her seal exhibits a lady in that posture, holding the bridle in her right hand. The proximity of this village to the Humber rendered it an advantageous situation for

T

building, which until lately was carried on to a considerable extent. A little to the westward of Hessle, is Hesslewood house, a handsome mansion belonging to Joseph Robinson Pease, Esq. an eminent banker, at Hull. This house commands a fine view of the Humber, but less extensive than from the house of Mr. Cooper, and others on the top of the hill. The church is dedicated to All Saints; it is a vicarage, in the gift of the crown, and the Rev. Edmund Garwood, A.M. vicar, is the incumbent. The Rev. Timothy Raikes, an ancestor of the present family of Raikes, of Hull, London, and Gloucester, was vicar of Hessle in the commencement of the last century. There are here a small hospital and school, slenderly endowed, and several doles to the poor, under the direction of the vicar and the churchwardens. The late Mr. Raikes, of Gloucester, the founder of those valuable institutions, the Sunday Schools, was a member of this family. Population 1021.

Garwood Rev. Edmund, A.M. vicar
Locke T. B. Esq. banker
Mawhood Rev. Richard, A.M. curate
Pease J. R. Esq. Hesslewood house
Roe Chas. Esq. comptroller of customs
Wilson Isaac, printer

*Gentry,*
Bailey Curtis
Barkworth Eliz.
Bean Mercy
Burstall Samuel
Cooper Samuel
Dickinson Samuel
Earnshaw L. B.
Earnshaw Robert
Hall Francis, sen.
Hall Francis, jun.
Newmarch John
Railey Richard
Riplingham Joel
Spicer John
Stovin Cornelius
Todd John
Watson J. K.
Wood Thomas
*Blacksmiths,*
Rudston William
Wainman Joseph
*Bricklayers,*
Brocklebank Wm.
Storey John
*Butchers,*
Carlill John
Michael Jacob
*Corn millers,*
Marshall Wm.
Thompson Leond.
*Farmers,*
Briggs John
Carlill Thomas
Escrett Thomas
Gooddy John
Leighton Thomas
Lotherington Tho.
Thompson John
Thrustle Aaron
*Grocers,*
Campbell John
Collinson James
*Joiners,*
Booth William
Wasencroft Chas.
Waudley Philip
*Paris White Mfs.*
Pease, Trigg & Co.
Pinning, Ward & Co.
*Plough makers,*
Bilton John
Saunders John
*Shoemakers,*
Bellard Samuel
Extoby Robert
Sissons Wm.
*Surgeons,*
Anderson F. B.
Hodgson William
*Yeomen,*
Brough Robert
Green William
Green Thomas
Levitt Robert
Robinson Daniel

Appleton Simon, maltster
Gibson John, gardener
Green Mark, vict. Marquis of Granby
Harrison Wm. tailor and draper
Houghton W. L. book binder
Sellars John, vict. Three Crowns, Cliff
Smith Christopher, vict. Adm. Hawke
Thirkell Joseph, officer of excise
Webb Benj. schoolmaster & clerk
Wright Thos. vict. Ship, Ferry

The *Hessle Market Coach* to Hull, every Tu. & Fri. dep at 8 in the morn. and ret. at 6 evening—*Carriers,* Speck & Wallis, to Hull, every Tu. & Fri.

HILDERTHORPE, in the parish of Bridlington, and wap. of Dickering; 1½ mile S. of Bridlington. Pop. 51.
Bordass John & Lundy Wm. farmers

HILSTON, (P.) in the wap. and liberty of Holderness; 9 miles ENE. of Hedon. The church is dedicated to St. Margaret. The Rev. Christopher Sykes, of Rooss, is the incumbent and patron.—Population 39.

*Farmers,*        Hutchinson Brian
Foster Joseph     Hutchinson Thos.
Foster James

HIVE, in the parish of Eastrington, wap. and liberty of Howdenshire; 4 miles ENE. of Howden.

*Farmers,*        Lawton Wm.
Craven Thomas     Prince Richard
Hall Thomas       Westoby John
Gibson Robert

HOLLYM, (P.) in the wap. and liberty of Holderness; 2 miles NE. of Patrington. This village is pleasantly situated on a small eminence. The present church was built in the year 1814, by the vicar, the Rev. Charles Barker, M. A. and is dedicated to St. Nicholas. Pop. 260.

Barker Rev. Charles, M.A. vicar
Bassindale Hugh, corn miller
Dickinson Thos. schoolmaster
Wales Mary, vict. Plough

*Farmers,*        Hilton John & Jas.
Ballany Jonth.    Hunton George
Bilton Thomas     Hutchinson Robert
Carr John         Major Robert
Charlton Benj.    Marshall Wm.
Croft Wm.         Marshall John
Futty Francis     Preston Richard
Gell Thomas       Simpson Seth
Greensides John   Stephenson Wm.

*Carrier,* Wm. Greensides to Hull Tu.

HOLME - ON - SPALDING - MOOR, (P.) in the wap. of Harthill; 5 miles SW of Market Weighton, and well known by the name of Hemp Holme, from the quantity of hemp formerly cultivated here.—The hill or mount on which stands the ancient church, is a very fine object, particularly on the high road to York from Market Weighton. From this elevated situation a delightful survey may be had of the surrounding country, in which Howden church and York Cathedral are prominent objects. Upon this mount stands a beacon, from which that division of this extensive wapentake of Harthill, called Holme Beacon, is said to take its name. Here is a bed of gypsum, in which are also found ammonite, or snake stones. A practice has been adopted in this parish, by some of the principal landholders, of allotting a certain quantity of land, as a cowgate, to their labourers, which has materially tended to the comfort of their families, and to the ease of the parish. A shock of an earthquake was felt in this neighbourhood on the 18th of January, 1822, at 10 o'clock at night. The church is dedicated to All Saints, and is in the patronage of St. John's College, Cambridge, who let out the rectory to the vicar, by lease, for his life, at a pepper corn yearly rent. There are here two chapels, one for the Roman Catholics and the other for the Methodists. Pop. 1318. A tradition exists that in times long since passed, when a great part of this region was a trackless morass, a cell was founded, either by the Vavasours or the Constables, at Welham bridge, on the edge of Spalding moor, for two monks, one of whom was employed in guiding travellers over the dreary wastes, and the other in imploring the protection of heaven for those who were exposed to the dangers of the road; and there are persons yet living who can remember the time when, in foggy weather, it was considered a dangerous attempt to cross the common without a guide.

Clarkson B. J. banker, Holme House
Crosskill J. steward to Lady Stourton
Holmes Mrs. Mary, gentlewoman
Lambert Thos. gentleman
Langdale Hon. Charles, Hall
Thompson H. surgeon
Turner Rev. John

*Farmers & Yeomen,*
Atkinson Geo.
Atkinson Robert
Bilbrough John
Bramley Thos.
Brown Geo.
Burton Eliz.
Buttle John
Coates Thomas
Dickinson John
Holmes Wm.
Jewitson Thos.
King John
Kirby Peter
Loftus Robert
Mackley John
Quarton Sarah
Rider George
Simpson William
Taylor Robert
Thackray John
Vaux Robert

Wardell John
Wild John
*Blacksmiths,*
Hudson John
Mason Mark
Pexton Thomas
*Coal merchants,*
Hutchinson John
Loftus Wm.
*Corn millers,*
Charter John
Maltby Wm.

*Shoemakers,*
Bramley Charles
Massey George
Sturdy Marm.
*Shopkeepers,*
Breadley Francis
Cade Ann
Hill Robert
Smith Geo.
*Wheelwrights,*
Cade John
Gill Benjamin

Brooksbank John, gents. bdg. school
Buck James, ornamental plasterer
Cook John, tailor
Fish Thomas, butcher
Hudson John, vict. Blacksmiths' Arms
Hutchinson Matthew, vict. Sun
Johnson Wm. joiner
Simpson Robert, bricklayer
Stainton Wm. parish clerk
Stewardson John, vict. New Inn
Whitehead Wm. vict. Hare & Hounds

*Carrier,* J. Smith, to Market Weighton Weds.; and to Howden Sats.

**HOLME-ON-THE-WOLDS, (P.)** in the wap. of Harthill; 6 miles NW. of Beverley. Pop. 138.

*Farmers,*
Harland Wm.
Suddaby Dorsey
Suddaby John
Suddaby Samuel
Swift John

Horsfield John, boot and shoe maker
Kay Robert, shopkeeper
Teall Wm. blacksmith

**HOLMPTON, (P.)** in the wap. and liberty of Holderness; 4 miles E. of Patrington. A village near the sea, which is extremely healthy; the church is a small structure, of which the King is the patron, and the Rev. Charles Cornelius Chambers, M.A. the rector. Pop. 256.

Lacey Richard, gent.
Paris Rev. Samuel, M.A. curate

*Farmers,*
Bashill Wm.
Dennison Fred.
Fewster John
Green Wm.
Mann Richard
Richardson John
Sowerby Thos.
Stephenson Wm.
*Tailors,*
Hastings Wm.
Wilkinson Geo.
*Wheelwrights,*
Graham Joseph
Harmon William

Bilton Richard, blacksmith
Cockerline Thos. vict. Board
Cockerline Wm. shoemaker
Hildyard Nathan, schoolmaster
Pearson Francis, shopkeeper
Richardson Mary, milliner

*Carriers,* Wilson & Greensides, to Hull, every Tu. and Fri.

## HORNSEA, (P.)

In the wap. and liberty of Holderness; 12 miles from Beverley, 15 from Hedon, and 16 from Hull. There was formerly a market here weekly, but it has long been disused.—The church is a large gothic structure, dedicated to St. Nicholas, of which the King is the patron, and the Rev. Robert Croft, vicar, the incumbent; there are likewise Calvinist and Methodist chapels, and a church school. Hornsea is much frequented, in the bathing season. Within three quarters of a mile to the NE. of the town run the mighty streams of the German Ocean, and immediately to the SW. is a lake covering upwards of four hundred acres of land, and full of most excellent and highly flavoured fish. There is in this place, as in many of the other watering places of Yorkshire, a fine chalybeate spring. Races are held here on a variable day, between the 17th and 24th of July. Pop. with Burton 790.

William Burn, foot post-man to Leven, on Mon. Wed. Thur. and Fri. dep. at 9 morn. ret. at 1 noon.

Corey Rev. Charles, curate
Forge Rev. Chpr. curate of Mappleton
Layburn Captain John
Sykes Rev. James, Calvinist minister

*Gentry,*
Bedell Benjamin
Day Rebecca
Eagle Mrs.
Gibson Mrs.
Green Geo.
Hudson John
Runton John
Smith Dorothy
Wilson C. B.
*Blacksmiths,*
Smith Thos.
Wadforth John
*Boot & Shoemakers,*
Acklam Thos.
Grantham Wm. & parish clerk
Greensides Wm.
Harrison John
Lawson Robert
Welburn Robert
*Bricklayers,*
Gale John
Grantham Rhd.
Russell Wm.
Russell John
Taylor Wm.
*Butchers,*
Bennet John
Bulson John
Bulson Wm. and tallow chandler

Linskin Stephen
*Farmers & Yeomen,*
Bennet Geo.
Burn Thos.
Davison Wm.
Fisher Samuel
Foster Ralph
Frost Samuel
Galloway John
Harrison Thos.
Heron Robert
Jackson Richard
Merrit Francis
Noble James
Simpson Joseph
Stork Wm.
Warcup Isaac
Whiten Wm.
*Grocers & Drapers,*
Cooper Richard
Henderson Wm.
& druggist
Hillaby John
Leesom William, baker & gardener
Loundsbrough W.
Walter Robert
Woodhouse Wm.
*Schoolmasters,*
Brown Geo.
Nicholson John

*Surgeons,*
Ballantine James
Harrison Charles
*Tailors, &c.*
Pool John
Southwick Matt.
*Wheelwrights,*
Dawson John
Southwick Wm.
Wallis Thomas
Amers Wm. vict. & miller, Pr. of Wales
Bald S. chief constable of N. Holderness
Barnard John, excise officer
Byass Robert, rope and twine maker
Capes & Son, plumbers and glaziers
Heslop John, vict. Old Hotel
Marsh Thos. saddler
Milnes Wm. painter
Pool Joseph, clock and watch maker
Stafe John, weaver
Straker Martin, vict. Hare & Hounds
Tate Wm. vict. New Hotel
Wallis John, mole catcher
Ward Mary, hosier
Waters Geo. lapidary
Wells Wm. gardener
West Benj. hair dresser

*Coaches,* to Hull daily except Fri.
*Carriers,* D. Robinson, J. Noble, M. Harwood, & W. Wilson, to Hull Tu. & Fri.; to Beverley every Sat.

## HOTHAM, (P.)

in the wap. of Harthill; 3 miles NW. of South Cave.—The church is dedicated to St. Oswald; the Rev. James Stillingfleet, A. M. is the rector, and the King is the patron. Hotham was the property of the ancient family of the Hothams, now of South Dalton. A Roman road passes near this village, in a direction to North and South Newbald. Pop. 293.

Gee Mrs. Hannah, gentlewoman
Stillingfleet Rev. James

*Farmers & Yeomen,*
Butteriok John
Hopkinson John
Ingram Thos.
Jackson Robert
Reader Geo. Carr
Rhodes Wm.
Stather John
Stather Wm.
Watson Ann
Butterick Charles, shopkeeper
Dean Joel, shoemaker
Denton John, bricklayer
Eccles Thomas, blacksmith
Hembrough Robert, corn miller
Postill Geo, shopkeeper
Sargeson Geo. carpenter
Wilson John, tailor
Withill Thos. clock mkr. & day school

*Carrier,* Robert Smart to Hull & Weighton, every Tu. and Fri.

## HOWDEN, (P.)

In the wap. and liberty of Howdenshire; 9 miles from Snaith, 10 from Selby, and 21 from York. Here is a very good market on Saturday. This town is of considerable antiquity, but it contains nothing remark ble except its church, formerly collegiate, and the remains of the ancient palace of the bishops of Durham. The jurisdiction, called Howdenshire, is a peculiar, under the Dean and Chapter of Durham, and comprises Howden, Laxton Chapel, Barmby Chapel, Eastrington, Hemingbrough, Barlby Chapel Holtby, Brantingham, Skipwith, Elleker Chapel, Blacktoft, Welton, and Walkington. The collegiate church of Howden was dissolved in the first year of Edward VI. and the temporalities thereby became vested in the crown. The revenues for supporting the choir being disposed of into private hands, the choir fell gradually into decay, and at length becoming totally unsafe, the parishioners, in the years 1634, and 1636, fitted up the nave for the celebration of divine worship. In the year 1696, the groined-roof of the chancel fell in, and from that time the East-end of the church has exhibited the appearance of a magnificent and venerable ruin. The church is built in the form of a cross with an elegant square tower of forty-five yards in height, rising from the centre upon pointed arches, supported by clustered pillars. Over the communion table is a painting of the Lord's supper, by Mr. Bell, of Selby, which fills the bows of the closed central arch between the nave and the choir. The most curious, and once the most elegant part of this sacred edifice, is the Chapter-house, built about the middle of the fourteenth century. Its form is octagonal, resembling the chapter-house at York; but its dimensions are greatly inferior, its width being only eight paces. The style of architecture, however is superb; it contains thirty canopied seats, separated by clustered pillars of various members, very small, and extremely delicate, having foliated capitals of pierced work, from which rises rich tabernacle work, ornamenting Gothic arches. The whole is constructed of a fine durable free stone, and had a beautiful octagonal stone spire, which fell in on St. Stephen's day, 1750. The tower of the church is a plain but well proportioned and stately structure, built of a durable kind of stone. Its erection has by all writers been ascribed to Walter Skirlaw, bishop of Durham; but most probably it was only heightened by that prelate, as the following homely couplet asserts :—

" Bishop Skirlaw indeed was good to his
" people,
" He built them a school-house and
" heightened the steeple."

The present church appears to have been erected from the materials of a previous structure. And it is probable, that as the Gothic style of building was recently come into fashion, when the prebends were endowed in 1267, the church was finished about that period, excepting the steeple and chapter-house, which were built by Walter Skirlaw, in the fourteenth century. This prelate died at Howden, and his bowels were buried in the church. The living of Howden is a vicarage, not in charge, of which the king is the patron, and the Rev. Ralph Spofforth, M.A. the incumbent. [The church is dedicated to St. Peter. There is an ancient palace here, which the bishops of Durham formerly made their summer residence : the palace is supposed to have been erected by Walter Skirlaw, whose arms are yet seen in some parts of the ruins. His successor, bishop Langley, also made several additions to the edifice ; the brick arch, through which lies a passage to the orchards, ponds, &c. appears to have been of his erection, as his arms yet remain on a stone placed in the corner of the arch. The venerable ruins of this ancient palace, being patched up with modern building, are now converted into a farm house. It is situated almost close to the church-yard, and nearly opposite to the South side of the choir, which presents to the eye a majestic ruin. On the south side of the palace was a park extending to the banks of the Ouse. Howden is situated about a mile from the Ouse, where it has a small harbour for boats, and a ferry over the river In the Market palace there is a large building, called the Moot-hall, in which the courts for the jurisdiction are held. There are here two meeting houses, one for the Methodists, and another for the Independents ; and a Free School, of which the Rev. Thomas Grey is the master.— The population amounts to 2080.

POST-MASTER—W. A. JUSTICE,
*Office, Bridgegate.*
Letters arrive at 9 morning, and are despatched at 1 noon, daily.

### DIRECTORY.

*Academies, Boarding and Day.*
Free School, Rev. Thomas Grey Northolmby street
James Mrs. D. (la. bdg.) Northolmby st.
Lee J. & S. (ladies' bdg.) Church yd.
Walker John, (day) Hailgate

*Attornies.*
Earnshaw George Rawdon, Bridgegte
Harrison Hugh, Bridgegate
Robinson John, Pinfold street
Spofforth, jun. Peirsons and Dyson, Bridgegate

*Auctioneers and Appraisers.*
Buckle John, Hailgate
Shepherd John, (appr. only) Bridgegt.

Walmsley Robert, Town end

*Bacon and Ham Factors,*
Banks Robert, Market place
Ullathorne F. (& cheese) Church yd.

*Bakers and Flour Dealers.*
Fish Thomas, High Bridge street
Fitch Mrs. Church yard
Maw Holiday, Market place

*Bank.*
Schofield, Coates & Co. High Bridge st.
(on Spooner, Attwood & Co. London)
*Savings' Bank,* W.A. Justice, Bridge st.

*Blacksmiths.*
Jackson Thomas, Bridgegate
Little E. and T. Bridgegate
Norman Robert, (farrier only) Flatgt.
Peart John, Bridgegate
Wood William, Hailgate

*Bookseller, Stationer, Printer, &c.*
Justice W. A. (circulating library,
patent medicines, paper hangings,
&c. and post office) Bridgegate

*Boot and Shoemakers.*
Arnold George, Hailgate
Clark Christopher, Market place
Cooper Garbut, Bridgegate
Croft Richard, Bridgegate
Goulden William, Church yard
Grasby Wm. High Bridge street
Green Robert, Hailgate
Maskell George, Market place
Pease John, Bridgegate
Storey David, Bridgegate
Vollans Edward, Hailgate
Wilson Thomas, Pinfold street
Young George, Bridgegate

*Braziers and Tinsmiths.*
Hutchinson Joseph, Market place
Matthewman Wm. Market place

*Brewers—Ale and Beer.*
Carter John, Hailgate
Crow William, Hailgate
Hutton Francis, Hailgate

*Bricklayers.*
Foster Joseph, Hailgate
Goodworth John, Hailgate
Johnson Wm. Hailgate

*Butchers.*
Broom Benjamin, Hailgate
Favell John, Bridgegate
Hawcroft John, Market place
Mason John, Market place
Rushworth Wm. Bridgegate
Wilson Joseph, Hailgate

*Chemists and Druggists.*
Cooper G. A. Bridgegate
Goodall Thomas, Market place

*Clock and Watch Makers.*
Richardson John, Market place
Walker John, Market place

*Confectioners.*
Leaper Jane, Vicar lane
Rushworth Mary, Bridgegate

*Coopers.*
Dunn John, Market place
Pears Thomas, Hailgate

*Corn Millers.*
Harper Thomas, Flat Field mill
Leighton Thomas, Flat Field mill
Smith George, Hale mill

*Curriers.*
Dixon Henry, Applegate
Fewster Robert, Hailgate
Ostler Thomas, High Bridge street

*Fire and Life Insurance Offices.*
County, W. A. Justice, Bridgegate
Phœnix, Robert Banks, Market place
Royal Exg. G. R. Earnshaw, Bridge

*Flax Dressers.*
Chambers William, Market place
Fearn Wm. Pinfold street
Sugden John, Pinfold street

*Gardeners.*
Bentley William, High bridge
Mann Wm. Corn market hill
Taylor George, Bridgegate
Taylor William, High Bridge street

*Grocers and Tea Dealers.*
Banks Robert, Market place
Brooks Withers, Bridgegate
Cocker Robert, Bridgegate
Cook Ellis, Market place
Favill Hannah, Bridgegate
Gray Mary, Corn market hill
Leaper Jane, (agent to Ludgate
Tea Company) Vicar lane
Thompson Susannah, Pinfold stre
Ullathorne Francis, Church yard
Wetherell Joseph & John, Market
Wilkinson Joshu, (tea dlr.) Brid

*Hair Dressers.*
Batty Thomas, Bridgegate
Farrar Wm. Market place
Nutbrown Mary, Bridgegate
Raby Robert, Market place

*Hat Manufacturers and Dealers.*
Featon John, Market place
Raby Robert, (dealer) Market pla
Wetherell J. & J. (dlrs.) Market

*Hosiers.*
Carr Mary, Market place
Peirson E. and G. Bridgegate

*Hotels, Inns, and Taverns.*
Angel, James Hewson, Bridge stre
Black Bull, Moses Jewitt, Bridge
Black Horse, Thos. Jackson, Bridg
Blacksmith's Arms, J. Voase, Bridge
Black Swan and Cross Keys, Jo
Waterworth, Corn market hill
Blue Boar, John Padgett, Bridge

rapes, Joseph Ducker, Bridgegate
Half Moon, Robt. Foster, (commercial
   inn & posting house) Market pl.
King's Head, Robt. Crow, Bridgegt.
Lincoln Tavern, J. Townsend, Mkt. pl.
Red Lion, Thomas Nothard, Hailgate
Rose & Crown, Geo. Auty, Church yd.
Seven Stars, Thos. Iveson, Market pl.
Wellington, Wm. Bowman, Bridgegt.
Wheat Sheaf, Joseph Taylor, Hailgt.
White Horse, John Buttle, (& sheriff's
   officer) Market place

*Ironmongers.*
Day Geo. (& dlr. in paint) Market pl.
Hutchinson Joseph, Market place
Matthewman William, Market place

*Joiners and Cabinet Makers.*
Archer John, Bridgegate
Goulden John, Bridgegate
Matt John, Hailgate
Anderson Geo. (joiner) Pinfold street
Shepherd John, Bridgegate
Watson Geo. Hailgate
Windle Thomas, Bridgegate

*Linen Drapers.*
Carr Mary, Market place
Coates Joseph, Market place
Harrison Sarah, Market place
Peirson E. & G. (tea dlrs.) Bridgegate

*Linen and Woollen Drapers.*
Brewster T. W. (& agent to the Tea
   Company) Market place
Ullathorne Francis, Church yard
Wetherell J. and J. Market place

*Maltsters*
Carter John, Hailgate
Crow William, Hailgate
Hutton Francis, Hailgate

*Milliners and Dress Makers.*
Hadley Mary, Market place
Liscomb Ann, Northolmby street
Pearson Mary, Church yard
Peirsons E. and G. Bridgegate
Renardson Elizabeth, Applegate
Scott Ann, Vicar lane
Waudby Elizabeth, Hailgate
Zacchary Mary, Flatgate

*Plumbers and Glaziers.*
Meggitt Robt. (& painter) Market pl.
Sugden John, Bridgegate

*Porter Dealers.*
Carter Thomas, Market place
Sanderson John, Market place
Voase James, Bridgegate

*Rope and Twine Manufacturers.*
Newton Samuel, Bridgegate
Richmond Richard, Hailgate

*Saddlers and Collar Makers.*
Johnson Abraham, St. Helen's square
Sanderson George, Bridgegate

*Seedsmen.*
Banks Robert, Market place

Carter Thomas, Market place

*Shopkeepers.*
Chambers William, Market place
Empson Charles, Bridgegate
Favell John, Bridgegate
Holdsworth Sarah, Market place
Killingbeck Elizabeth, Hailgate
Leighton Thomas, Hailgate

*Spirit & Wine Merchants & Dealers.*
Carter Thomas, Hailgate
Hutton Francis, Hailgate
Tyas Thomas, Hailgate
Voase James, Bridgegate

*Stay Makers.*
Rennison S. (& clothes bkr.) Bridgegt.
Tindle Joseph, Rose and Crown yard

*Straw Hat Manufacturers.*
Archer and Wager, Bridgegate
Dunn Ann, Market place
Johnson Hannah, Bridgegate
Keyworth Elizabeth, Market place

*Surgeons.*
Elletson John, Hailgate
Jones Thomas, Bridgegate
Pass Joseph, Hailgate
Turton Thomas, Bridgegate

*Tailors.*
Dinsdale Rhd. (& draper) Church yd.
Fleming Wm. (& draper) Bridgegate
Hutchinson William, Hailgate
Jackson Wm. Market place
Leaf Edw. (& draper) Market place
Thompson Jas. (& draper) Pinfold st.
Walker John, Hailgate
Watson Peter, Vicar lane

*Tallow Chandlers.*
Banks Robert, Market place
Cook Ellis, Market place

*Turners in Wood and Metal.*
Fletcher John, Bridgegate
Goulden John, Bridgegate
Shepherd John, Bridgegate

*Wheelwrights.*
Little E. and T. Bridgegate
Seaton Joseph, Bridgegate

*Miscellany.*
Arden James, physician, Bridgegate
Campbell James, gent. Pinfold street
Cornwall Madam Ann, Pinfold street
Daniel Robert, gent. Bridgegate
Dunn Robt. agent of the Lord Bishop
   of Durham, Market place
Holliday John, corn factor, Hailgate
Robinson James, gent. Hailgate
Schofield Wm. Esq. Sands hall
Schofield and Co. timber merchants,
   High bridge
Spofforth Rev. R. M. A. vicar, Bridgegt.
Spofforth Robert, gent. Bridgegate
Spofforth Robert, jun. coroner for
   Howdenshire, Bridgegate
Watson John, gent. Church yard

Webb John, stamp office, Hailgate
Whitaker Mrs. Ellen, Hailgate
Whitaker Mrs. Eliz. Hailgate
Wilkinson Rev. Joshua, Bridgegate
Worsop R. A. gent. Flatgate
Wright John, tanner, St. John street
Aldridge Wm. nail mfr. Hailgate
Bilbrough John, basket mkr. Applegt.
Bowman John, farrier, livery stable
keeper, gigs to let, &c. Bridgegt.
Cocker Robert, rag merchant, Hailgt.
Day Stephen, music preceptor, Mkt. pl.
Dunn John, glass dlr. &c. Market pl.
Goodworth John, plasterer, Hailgate
Hawcroft John, shopkpr. Market pl.
Holdsworth Eliz. shopkpr. Market pl.
Meggitt Ann. dlr. in paint, Market pl.
Palmer Edw. sexton, Church yard
Staveley Wm. whitesmith, Bridgegate
Tyas John, parish clerk, Hailgate
Walker John, toy & hardware dealer,
·Market place
Ward John, millwright, brass founder
and machine maker, Flatgate
Wikeley and Peirson, linen, sail cloth,
sacking and nail bagging manu-
facturers, Pinfold street
Willoughby Wm. stone mason, Hailgt.
Witham John, swine dealer, Hailgate

COACH.

RODNEY—from the *Angel Inn*, to
Sheffield, at ¼ past 9 mg. and to
Hull, at ¾ past 1 afternoon

WATER CARRIAGE.

Wm. Otley, to Swinefleet, every Tu.
Taylor Joseph, Packet to Hull, Tu. &
Fri. nearest the full and change

LAND CARRIAGE.

Francis Smithson, to Hull, on Mon.;
to York, on Thu.
George Young, post-man to Whitgift,
Mon. Wed. and Fri.

COUNTRY CARRIERS.

Barmby, *Black Swan*, T. Hodgson, Sat.
Bubwith, *White Horse*, John Brabbs, Tu.
Foggathorp, *White Horse*, Robt. Clegg,
Wed. arr. at 12, dep. at 2
Holme, *Angel Inn*, John Smith, Sat.
arr. at 12, dep. at 4
Rawcliffe, *Half Moon*, T. Ramskill, Sat.
Selby, *Angel Inn*, William Howcroft,
Sat. arr. at 12, dep. at 3
Snaith, *White Horse*, J. Kilham, Sat.

HOWDEN DYKE, in the parish of
Howden, wap. and liberty of Howdenshire; 1 mile S. of Howden.

Eccles Richard, ferryman
Savage John, ferryman
Singleton Charles, vict. Steam Packe
Singleton David, farmer

The steam packets from Selby t
Hull pass this Ferry, and land passe
gers for Howden; the earliest time t
o'clock morning to 12 noon, and r
turns from Hull according to the tide
generally about three hours after flo
at Hull.

*Howden Price*, in the parish
Cottingham, and wap. of Harthill;
miles WNW. of Hull.

HOWSHAM, in the parish of Scra
ingham, & wap. of Buckrose; 8 m
SSW. of Malton. Pop. 225.

Cholmley Geo. Esq. Howsham hall
Wilson William, steward to Ditto,

| *Farmers*, | Hudson Robert |
|---|---|
| Gibb Robert | Leefe Robert |
| Horsley Wm. | Paver Richard |

Hudson W. chief constable of Buckr
Gascoign N. blacksmith and vict.
Kilvington James, shoemaker
Lumley John, grocer and shoemake
Wade Thomas, tailor

HUGGATE, (P.) in the wap.
Harthill; 7½ miles NE. of Pocklington
The church, of which the King is the
tron, is well built, with a good spire; th
is also a Methodist chapel. There is in
village a well, 116 yards deep, which sup
the inhabitants of this village with w
Here are races held in the latter end of J
Population 413.

Elliott Rev. Robert, A. M. rector
Rankin Rev. Thomas, curate
Cautley Rev. William, A. B. vicar
Warter

| *Farmers & Yeomen*, | Holliday Robert |
|---|---|
| Appleton Wm. | Holtby Thomas |
| Boast Wm. | Hotham John |
| Brigham Robert | King George |
| Buttle John | Pape Edward |
| Cook Francis | Turner John |
| Cross Thomas | Wilson Amos, (& |
| Hodgson James | butcher) |

Allison William, carpenter
Bagley Miss E. shopkeeper
Haggard Wm. shopkeeper
Ireland John, blacksmith, gunsmith,
and vict. Chaise Inn
Ruston John, tailor
Ward Richard, shoemaker

*Carriers*,
John Metcalf & John Ward, to Pock
lington every Saturday

# HISTORY OF KINGSTON-UPON-HULL.

## CONTENTS.

# HISTORY OF

# KINGSTON-UPON-HULL.

HULL, one of the principal seaports of the United Kingdom of Great Britain, 39 miles from York, and 170 from London, in 53 deg. 45 min. N. latitude, and 0 deg. 16 min. W. longitude, is situated at the point where the river Hull discharges its waters into the estuary of the Humber—the common receptacle of all the eastern rivers of England, from the Swale to the Trent. Hull, like the rival port on the opposite side of the island, has no claim to high antiquity, but its rise is of a date at least three centuries before that of Liverpool; the habitations of the shepherds and cowherds of Hull having given place to the wharfs and warehouses of the merchant in the reign of Edward I. while the tents of the fishermen of Liverpool retained their station until the time of James I. When the Domesday survey was taken, Myton appears to have been the principal place in this neighbourhood, but so diminutive were its buildings, that it would scarcely at this day have ranked amongst our villages. In the reign of Stephen, William le Gros, Earl of Albemarle and Lord of Holderness, to commute a vow he had made to visit Jerusalem, founded a monastery at Meaux, seven miles north of Hull, and endowed it with possessions sufficiently ample to maintain the establishment. Some ages after, the Lords of Wake inhabited a mansion at Cottingham, called Baynard Castle, and Edward I. on his return from the battle of Dunbar, where the Scottish King, John Baliol, lost his crown to the conqueror, honoured this lordship with a royal visit. During his stay at this place, while he was engaged in the pleasures of the chase, he came to the hamlets of Myton and Wyke, where Hull now stands, and was so much impressed with the advantages of the situation for a fortified town and commercial port, that he sent for the Abbot of Meaux, who was lord of the soil, and negotiated with him an exchange for other lands of a much higher nominal value. Edward's next care was to issue a proclamation, offering privileges and immunities to all those who should fix their habitations in this place; at the same time he

built a manor house, which he considered as a royal residence, and honoured the town, which soon sprang up around him, with the appellation of Kingston, or *King's town*, adding the terms *upon-Hull* to distinguish it from Kingston-upon-Thames. In the 27th year of his reign the harbour was finished, and the town, by a royal charter, dated in 1299, was constituted a free borough. The advantages enjoyed by Hull gave it a decided preponderance over all the ports in the neighbourhood; and Ravenspurn, Hedou, and Grimsby, were drained by degrees of the greatest part of their trade and commerce. Since that time Ravenspurn has been washed away by the incursions of the sea, and not a vestige of the town or its suburbs remains to indicate their existence, or to fix the date of their overthrow. It appears that in the time of Edward I. Ravenspurn sent members to Parliament, though it is probable that within a century from that time the Borough ceased to exist. In the year 1350, the bones of the dead were removed from the chapel of Ravenspurn to the church-yard of Easington; but so tenacious were some of the edifices of their station that, not more than fifty years ago, the remains of the engulphed wall were visible to the fishermen at low water.[*] The stately structure of the Holy Trinity was begun about the close of the 13th century, and Edward II. contributed liberally towards its erection. The necessary consequence of the prosperity of Hull was, the establishment of a ferry across the Humber, and in the year 1316 vessels were established between Barton and Hull, for the conveyance of passengers and cattle, which have been continued through successive ages to the present day. Ten years afterwards, the town was fortified with a ditch and wall, and so rapid was its progress that, in about sixty years from its foundation, Hull was called upon to furnish Edward III. with 16 ships and 466 men,

[*] Mr. Thompson, in his *Ocellum Promontorium*, fixes the site of Ravenspurn near the south-western extremity of the Holderness Promontory, about a mile within the *Spurn Head*,

U

towards an armament, to which the quota of the city of London amounted only to 25 ships and 662 men. In 1331, Gilfred de Hotham, a devout Knight, founded a priory for black monks, in the street ever since called Blackfriargate. Of this religious house a square tower, and a pile of buildings used as an inn, remained, when Tickell wrote, behind the old Guild-hall, at the top of the Market place. These were removed when the House of Correction was built; and when, subsequently, the hall itself was pulled down, and the present range of buildings erected for shambles in 1806, some groined arches of brick were discovered under the hall, with which perished the last remains of this ancient structure. It was built chiefly of brick, as was the east end of Trinity church, previously,—and there can be no doubt that the art of brick-making, disused from the time of the Romans, was then revived here, though Bishop Littleton, who visited Hull, deceived by the covering of plaster on the church, fixes the date of the revival in the reign of Richard II.

Edward III. on attaining his majority, visited Hull, on his way to fight the Scots, and was entertained by William de la Pole, a wealthy merchant, born at Ravenspurn, and then the mayor of this borough.— Edward, after four campaigns against the Scotch, resolved to attack France, with the intention of wresting the crown from Philip de Valois, which Edward claimed in right of his mother. With this view, he sailed to Antwerp, where he was obliged to remain inactive, from the want of " the sinews of war." Sir William de la Pole, who was then at Antwerp, pursuing his mercantile adventures, lent Edward a large sum of money, and mortgaged his ample estates for the use of his sovereign. This act of loyal devotion the King rewarded by conferring upon him the honour of Knight-Banneret, in the field. On the return of Edward from the contest, he made Sir William de la Pole gentleman of his bed-chamber, and lord of the Seigniory of Holderness; advancing him from time to time to places of profit and trust, and at length made him baron of the exchequer. In every stage of his progress Sir William remained the constant benefactor of Kingston-upon-Hull, and the De la Poles became to this place what the Cliffords were to Skipton, and the Talbots to Sheffield.— Before his death, which happened in 1356, he founded a monastery and hospital here, to the glory of God and the benefit of the poor; but he was summoned from this world before the house was complete, and his son, Sir Michael de la Pole, his successor, completed the work, and endowed it

for thirteen poor men and as many poor women. Sir Michael was no less the favourite of Richard II. than his father had been of Edward III. and in the ninth year of this sovereign's reign, he was made Lord Chancellor, and afterwards created Earl of Suffolk. The Earl began to erect the stately and superb palace called Suffolk palace, which stood opposite to the west end of St. Mary's church, in a place at this time called Market gate. Before the great bay window was a delightful and spacious flower garden, and other grounds, on which are now erected warehouses, sheds, &c. and the other parts are occupied as yards for different artificers. The Earl, like most other court favourites, became obnoxious to the people, by whom he was stigmatized as a flagrant public peculator, and he was ultimately removed from his office, and died in voluntary exile in 1388. The history of the De la Poles is intimately connected with that of Hull. Few towns can boast of having given rise to so celebrated a family, thus advancing from obscurity to eminence, flourishing in such splendour, and experiencing all vicissitudes of fortune. Michael, the second Earl of Suffolk, accompanied Henry V. in his expedition into France, and in displaying signal proofs of courage and capacity, fell a victim to the malignant temper which then ravaged the English army. Michael, the third Earl, was also a soldier, and was slain at the memorable battle of Agincourt, fighting by the side of his Sovereign. William de la Pole, the fourth Earl, was distinguished alike in the field and in the cabinet. This Earl served twenty-four campaigns in France, and was seventeen years on the Continent without ever returning to his native country. On the death of the Earl of Salisbury, who, at the seige of Orleans, in 1428, the chief command of the besieging army devolved upon the Earl of Suffolk, but the laurels which the army had gathered began to wither in his keeping; the heroic heroine, that military and political prodigy, the Maid of Orleans, turned the fortune of the war and ultimately expelled the invaders from the French territory. On the return of the Earl of Suffolk to England, the duty of negotiating a peace with France was confided to his hands, and this affair being settled, he proposed the marriage of the King, Henry VI. with Margaret of Anjou, daughter of René, King of Sicily, and niece of Mary of Anjou, the Queen of France. The negotiation of this marriage was also confided to the Earl, on which he was advanced a step in the peerage, and appointed by the King, when the preliminaries were settled, to espouse the princess Margaret in his name.— This espousal was ominous, and if the court rumours of those days were to be relied upon, Margaret so far forgot her marriage vows as sometimes to confound the proxy with the principal. The Queen soon perceived the weakness of her consort, and ruled him with absolute sway. By this means the Marquis of Suffolk, the Cardinal of Winchester, and the Archbishop of York, saw their power more firmly established.— A strict union was formed between them and the Queen; and the Duke of Gloucester, who had opposed the King's marriage, and whom they regarded as the common enemy, was thrown into prison, and found dead in his bed before the time for his trial arrived. The people considered Suffolk as the principal author of Gloucester's death; and in proportion as he sunk in public estimation he rose in favour at court, and on the second of June, 1448, he was, through the influence of his royal mistress, created Duke of Suffolk. The loss of Normandy, which followed, was attributed to Suffolk, who was publicly accused of having delivered Maine, the key of that province, to the French; it was further charged upon him that he had murdered the Duke of Gloucester, and that he had removed from the King's presence all virtuous counsellors, and filled their place with his own creatures. The Duke, when these charges were brought before Parliament, gave them a flat denial; but the court, alarmed at his situation, and desirous to withdraw him from the impending storm, undertook, without awaiting the slow formality of a trial, to banish him for five years. The Duke embraced upon his exile without reluctance, but while he was on his passage to France he was met by an English vessel, called the Nicholas, belonging to the Duke of Exeter, constable of the tower, the Captain of which seized the Duke, and struck off his head. Thus fell William de la Pole, Duke of Suffolk, who, during the space of four and twenty years had distinguished himself at the head of the English armies in France, who had ruled the cabinet of London, and had been the most powerful man in the kingdom. The mutilated body of the Duke was left upon the sands at Dover, and, according to Stow, it was brought to Hull, and interred in the Charter house there. From this nobleman was descended John de la Pole, Duke of Suffolk, who married Elizabeth Plantagenet, sister of Edward IV. and by her had issue John de la Pole, Earl of Lincoln. This Earl aspired to the throne; and Richard III. after the death of his only son, declared the Earl of

Lincoln presumptive heir to the Crown.— The battle of Bosworth Field destroyed these aspiring hopes, by elevating the Earl of Richmond to the throne. Lincoln submitted to his disappointment with an ill grace, and having joined in the rebellion of Lambert Simmel, a baker's son, who personated the late Duke of Clarence, he landed near Lancaster, with an army consisting of 8000 Irish and German troops, whence he marched, to encounter the King, through Yorkshire, to the village of Stoke, in Nottinghamshire. Here an obstinate battle was fought on the 6th of June, 1487, in which the rebels were routed, and the Earl of Lincoln, with the greatest part of his army, was left dead upon the field. The brother of this brave but unfortunate nobleman was Edmund de la Pole, Earl of Suffolk, the last of that family who bore this title.— The jealous temper of Henry VII. led him to cast Edmund into prison, on a charge of conspiring against the state, and, after languishing for seven years in confinement, he was put to death by Henry VIII. without the formality of a trial. By the attainder of the last Earl of Suffolk, all the revenues and manors of that nobleman were confiscated to the King's use, amongst which was the Manor Hall, with the buildings and gardens adjoining, and the family became extinct in the male line by the death of the younger brother, William, who fled to Italy, and was killed at the battle of Pavia in 1525. It has been seen, that at the time when William de la Pole resided here as a merchant, Hull had attained a considerable rank in the list of maritime towns, and in the year 1369 the fraternity called the Guild of the Holy Trinity, was founded at this place, for the relief of distressed seamen and their widows.

The inhabitants of Hull had, ever since the foundation of the town, laboured under great inconvenience for want of fresh water, and the neighbouring villages of Hessle, Anlaby, Cottingham, and others, unmoved by their distress, combined together, so early as the year 1376, to withhold from them a supply of this necessary of life. Long, and, in some instances, fatal contests, existed between the town and the villages upon this subject for some years, till at length the Sovereign Pontiff of Rome found it necessary to interpose the authority of the Vatican, and to issue an extraordinary writing, dated at Rome the 20th of July, 1413, reminding these, "who, at the instigation of Satan, had endeavoured to ruin the inhabitants of a large and flourishing town, by depriving them of water, that they must give an account of their deeds at the day of judgment; and by exhorting and praying every one of them, by the bowels of charity, to contribute freely to the maintenance of the water courses, by which means they would, in some measure, atone for their past offences;" and all who should be instrumental in promoting this public work, by contributing thereto, were promised "the release of one hundred days in any penance that was already or might hereafter be enjoined them." The good effects of this instrument were astonishing; all attempts to corrupt or poison the water, or to fill up the canals, ceased, and the town, from that time, has been plentifully supplied with the pure beverage of nature. During the reign of Richard II. when the Scots were making their inroads into England, and menacing the country from the Tweed to the Humber, the fortifications of Hull were repaired, the ditches cleansed, and a strong castle was built at the east side of the river Hull, for the better defence of the town and haven. The original charter, granted by Edward I. was renewed and enlarged by subsequent charters granted by Richard II. Henry IV. and Henry V. but it was not till the 18th year of Henry VI. that the corporation of Hull received that form which it still preserves. The municipal government was then placed in the hands of a mayor, recorder, sheriff, and twelve aldermen, who were to be justices of the peace; and at the same time the King constituted the town, with its precincts, a county of itself, comprising the towns and parishes of Hessle, North Ferriby, Swanland, West-Ella, Kirk-Ella, Tranby, Willerby, Woolferton, Anlaby, and all the site of the priory of Haltemprise. That monarch also, by another charter, bearing date the second of July, in the same year, granted, that the Mayors of Hull should, for the future, have the sword carried erect before them, and that the mayor and aldermen should have a cap of maintenance. In the year 1443, the town was divided into six wards, each of them governed by two aldermen, and the mayor presiding as head of the whole.— In the month of September, 1448, Henry VI. on his return to London, from the north, visited Hull, and was received with every demonstration of loyal affection by all classes of the people. At this period the famous William de la Pole, fourth Earl of Suffolk, had the chief share of the administration of the government of the country, and whatever might be his errors as a minister of state, he was to Hull a distinguished benefactor, and this town received, through his influence, numerous marks of

royal favour. The inhabitants were not unmindful of the obligations they owed to their Sovereign; and when those intestine contests, between the houses of York and Lancaster, which shook the country to its centre, raged so fatally, this town continued to the last firm and unshaken in its fidelity to Henry. In the battle of Wakefield,[*] fought on the 24th of December, 1460, Richard Hanson, Esq. the brave mayor of Hull, having greatly distinguished himself by his valour and intrepidity, fell covered with wounds, in the moment of victory, in the presence of his Queen. At Towton[†] too the blood of the people of Hull, who had volunteered in Henry's cause, flowed freely and the public coffers of the borough were so much drained by the expenses of the war, that the corporation were obliged to take down a stately market cross, which had been erected about thirty years before in order to raise money from the sale of the materials of which it was constructed. On the elevation of Edward IV. to the throne, the town of Hull reluctantly acknowledged him as their sovereign; but no sooner had Henry VI. again resumed his royal seat, by the support of Warwick the king-maker, than they again professed their cordial allegiance to the restored monarch; and when Edward IV. landed at Ravenspurn, in Holderness, with 2000 men, on the 14th of March, 1471, he marched by the way of Beverley to York, without venturing to attack Hull. The sequel is known to every reader of English history. Warwick was slain in the decisive battle of Barnet. Prince Edward, the son of Henry, was murdered in cold blood by the Dukes of Clarence and Gloucester, aided by Lord Hastings and Sir Thomas Gray; Henry and his Queen were thrown into the tower, where the former expired in a few days, for " short is the distance between the prison and the grave of princes;" and Margaret was suffered afterwards to retire to Anjou, where she closed her eventful life in the year 1482.

In 1472 Hull was visited by the plague which swept off a great number of the inhabitants, and among the rest John Whitfield, Esq. its chief magistrate. For four years the disorder seemed to have ceased, but in 1476 it broke out again with increased fury, and John Richards, Esq. the Mayor, was of the number of its victims. Two years afterwards it raged so violently that 1500 persons died in a short time, and Thomas Alcock, Esq. the mayor, his wife, and all his children, died of the fatal distemper. The sweating sickness, that singular and fatal

[*] See Vol. I. p. 422.   [†] Vol. I. p. 411.

malady, which seemed to be peculiarly English, and which, if historians may be credited, followed the people of this nation into foreign countries, making them its peculiar victims, broke out in Hull in the year 1551, and committed dreadful ravages. In 1576 the plague was again brought into this town by some seamen, from neglect of quarantine. This fatal disorder was, however, confined to Blackfriargate, which was so deeply infected that it was judged necessary to wall up all the avenues leading to that street, leaving open only two doors, where watchmen were placed to take in provision and medicine, and to see that none of the infected made their escape. These wise, though rigorous precautions, had the desired effect, the epidemic soon subsided, and not more than one hundred of the inhabitants became its victims.

The affairs of Hull glided smoothly on amidst a successful and continually extending commerce, till the suppression of the religious houses in the reign of Henry VIII. excited a general spirit of discontent here and elsewhere. The lesser monasteries, those with a revenue under 200*l.* a year being so denominated, were first suppressed, and all those of Hull fell under that description. These were the White Friary, in Whitefriargate; St. Austin's Friary, commonly called the Black Friars; and the Carthusian Monastery, founded by Michael de la Pole, and dedicated to St. Michael. At the time of the insurrection, called the Pilgrimage of Grace, in 1537, while one division took Pontefract, and another entered York, a third, conducted by a person named Hallam, took Hull by surprise, and repossessed the ejected Monks and Friars of their houses. The triumph of the insurgents was, however, of short duration; their main body, under Aske, who had advanced into the neighbourhood of Doncaster, being dispersed, the magistrates and other inhabitants of Hull seized Hallam, and the other ringleaders, who were soon after tried, by a special commission, at this place, and the charge of rebellion being clearly established against them, they were convicted and executed. The measures taken by Henry to reform the established religion, accompanied as they were by the dissolution of the monasteries and the seizure of their property, were extremely unpopular in Yorkshire, and this year another insurrection broke out in the neighbourhood of Scarborough and Malton, from whence the insurgents made a hasty march towards Hull, with the intention of taking the town by surprise: being disappointed in this expectation, they besieged the place;

but finding themselves unable to carry the town by force, Sir Robert Constable, and some others of the leaders, projected the stratagem of introducing themselves into the fortress disguised as market people, in which way they made themselves masters of the place. Sir Robert then assumed the title of governor, but having received intelligence that his partizans in the country were all either killed or taken prisoners, he fell into a state of despondency, and after keeping possession of the garrison for about thirty days, surrendered it into the hands of the mayor, with only a faint resistance. These deluded people being afterwards tried and convicted of high treason, under a commission, sitting here, of which the Duke of Norfolk was the head, numbers of them were hanged and quartered, and Sir Robert Constable, their leader, was hanged in chains over Beverley gate.

These rebellions having subsided, Henry made a visit into the north, in the year 1541, and in the month of August arrived in Hull, accompanied by his Queen, Catharine Howard, and attended by a train of courtiers. After partaking of the hospitalities of the Corporation, and condescending to receive at their hands a present of one hundred pounds, the royal personages proceeded to York; from thence his Majesty returned to Hull on the 30th of September, and after taking an accurate view of the town, gave orders for erecting a castle and two strong block houses, with additional fortifications, to environ the town. He also ordered that a new ditch should be cut from Newland to Hull, and that the stately manor house, formerly called Suffolk's palace, should undergo a thorough repair.— The King, after remaining five days in Hull, crossed the Humber, and returned to London through Lincolnshire. In the 26th year of this King's reign, an act passed for the appointment of twenty-six Suffragan Bishops, whose duty it was, in the absence of the bishops, to supply their place in all matters of order, though not of jurisdiction. Of the twenty-six towns appointed for Suffragan Sees, Hull was one, and the prelate had a magnificent palace, in High street, principally built of freestone, adorned with painted windows, like those of churches, and with spacious gateways and lofty towers.* Their office was nearly the same with the Chorepiscopi, or bishops of the country, in the primitive church; but this office had been discontinued for nine centuries, till it was now again revived in England. The institution was, however, of short du-

* Tickell's Hull, page 156.

ration, not exceeding, at most, sixty years, and Robert Pursglove, consecrated Suffragan of Hull, in the year 1552, seems to have been the last of that order in this place.

Edward VI. on ascending the throne, endeavoured to allay the popular discontent occasioned by the indiscriminate suppression of charitable institutions, which had marked the conduct of his father, and among the first acts of his reign he reformed the Hospital of the Charter House and the Trinity House in this town. In the same reign, John Harrison, Esq. an alderman of Hull, built and endowed a hospital in Chapel lane, near the church of St. Mary's, which still bears the name of this learned magistrate and valuable citizen. The reformed religion was now making considerable advances: by a royal ordinance, it was directed that all images and pictures should be removed out of the churches of this kingdom, and those which had hitherto been displayed in the church of the Holy Trinity at Hull were committed publicly to the flames. In the same reign the King granted to the burgesses of Hull the entire manor of the town, and conferred upon them the custody of the castle and block-houses, erected in the former reign at an expense of 23,755*l*.

The gloomy reign of Philip and Mary passed over without making any important additions to the records of this place, and the rapid and repeated changes in religion under Edward, Mary, and Elizabeth, seem to have excited here no very material sensation.

Though great pains had been taken about the middle of the fourteenth century, by elevating the roads and repairing the banks, to guard against the unusual swell of the tides, which prevailed for some years in the Humber, yet in the year 1527 the tide rose to such a height as to overthrow the banks, and to do incredible damage both to the town and the adjacent country. All the low lands, for many miles round, were laid under water; the farmers, deprived of their crops, were reduced to indigence and want ; and the merchandize, furniture, and other effects in the town, that were lodged in low rooms, were either destroyed or greatly damaged. In 1549 a similar visitation befel this place; the waters rose higher than the highest point to which they had ever before attained, and the injury sustained, both in the town and in the country, was immense. The trade of Hull still continued to increase, and the wealth of her ships tempted the cupidity of the pirates by which the seas were then infested; till at length the Lord High Admiral of England required the town to fit up two ships of war, to protect

their own coast. These ships being well equipped and manned, sailed in quest of the maritime robbers, and they had soon the good fortune to capture several of them, and to bring them into Hull. A special commission, at which the Earl of Huntingdon presided, attended by the mayor and aldermen, as judges, was soon assembled here, when six of the pirates were found guilty, and, in virtue of their sentence, were executed and hung in chains on the adjacent coasts. As late as the year 1583, a court of jail delivery was held here, at which three persons were convicted of felony, and suffered the punishment of death ; and a poor old woman, being tried and convicted of witchcraft, was sentenced to stand in the pillory on four separate market days, and to suffer a year's imprisonment. Nor did the players experience much more lenient treatment than the witches; the theatrical corps resorting to this town were, in a proclamation issued by the mayor, in 1598, styled "idle, lewd persons," "players or setters out of plays," and seeing that these persons, from their vagabond habits, could not be conveniently restrained, it was ordered and agreed that every inhabitant, man or woman, resorting to their theatre, should forfeit and pay 2s. 6d. to the mayor and burgesses. This very extraordinary attack upon the theatre, and upon the entertainments of the inhabitants, did not, it should appear, arise from any humble or puritanical disposition, which at that time possessed the leading inhabitants of the place, particularly the fair sex; for, in the same year, it was found necessary, in order to allay the heats and animosities which had arisen amongst the alderwomen and others, about precedency at church, to institute an ecclesiastical commission for regulating these important affairs, in which it was directed by the Archbishop " that the commissioners should place every of the said gentlewomen in their places according to their respective callings or dignities." The men, it is said, were easily governed, and content to sit and place themselves where they were ordered, according to the new arrangement of the pews in the church, which had recently taken place; but the women, like the Pharisees of old, sought the uppermost places in the synagogue, and, whatever might be the fervour they displayed in securing for themselves good places in heaven, they were not less sollicitous about those they occupied on earth. The fears of the censures of the church were sufficiently powerful to allay the high-blooded feuds of these aspiring dames, and when the magistrates mentioned in the commission had, for some time discharged the duties of masters of the ceremonies in the sanctuary, the religious services were allowed to proceed without further interruption.

The reign of James I. is almost a blank in the history of Hull. It is only mentioned that this Monarch granted, or rather sold, the corporation a charter to choose an assistant preacher in the church of the Holy Trinity, which charter cost them 690*l.* and which was the precise sum that the town had lent to Queen Elizabeth, to repel the menaced attack of the Spanish Armada. In this reign, the merchants erected an exchange in the High street, at an expense of 500*l.* which is now disused; and those works were commenced, and completed, by which the town has ever since been abundantly supplied with pure and wholesome water.

The disastrous reign of Charles I. will, through all time, occupy a distinguished place in the annals of England. Every part of the kingdom was agitated by that mighty collision which arose between the monarchial and the democratical branches of the legislature, but in the county of York, and in the town of Kingston-upon-Hull, the shock was felt with greater violence than in any other county or town in Great Britain. It is not within the province of this history to investigate the causes of the unhappy differences which arose between the King and the popular branch of the legislature, nor to decide whether privilege or prerogative was in the wrong, such inquiries, and decisions appertain rather to general history than to topography, and our present duty will be discharged by a faithful, though brief relation, of those local occurrences and military operations which arose in the town and neighbourhood of Hull. When Charles ascended the throne, in 1625, England was menaced by a war with France, and the three ships required of Hull, as the contribution of this port, for the prosecution of the contest, were very cheerfully granted, and well manned and victualled.— This spirit of loyal acquiescence was the next year carried still further, for while the metropolis, and other places, resisted the tax on all ships and goods, called *tonnage and poundage,* because it was levied by the King, without the consent of Parliament, the merchants of Hull paid the impost without murmur or complaint.

While the storm was gathering by which the whole kingdom was so speedily to be convulsed, the plague, which, for some time past, had raged in some of the ports of the continent, made its appearance in this town, and such was the terror it created, that numbers of the inhabitants left their houses,

and fled into the country; the gates were kept continually shut, except when provisions were brought in; all assemblies or meetings, as well for religious as for secular purposes, were forbidden; and the whole town exhibited a scene of horror, silence, and despair. As Lent approached, the Mayor and Aldermen thought it necessary to petition the protestant Archbishop of York, to give licence, and toleration to the convalescents to dress, and eat flesh the ensuing Lent, for their nourishment and more speedy recovery! To which his Grace replied, " that the ministers, upon certificate from the physicians, might give permission to particular persons to eat flesh during that holy season!"[*] This indulgence, great as it was, did not stem the overwhelming torrent of disease, the pestilence continued to rage for three years, and 2730 persons fell victims to it in the town, exclusive of those who fled into the country, and died there, which, according to one authority, almost doubled the number, making a sum total probably equal to one half the population of Hull at that period. As this dreadful contagion disappeared, commerce began to revive, and the town, though so recently threatened with ruin, attained in a few years its former prosperity.

In the year 1639, the King levied an army, to impose the Scotch the episcopal form of church government, to which they had invincible objections, and to resist which, they entered into their celebrated League and Covenant. The war which ensued, led to the accumulation of vast quantities of arms, and military stores in the port of Hull; and in the same year, the King, in his progress towards Scotland, paid a visit to Hull, where he was received with great pomp and ceremony, and assured by Mr. Recorder Thorpe, as the organ of the corporation, in one of those hyperbolical and adulatory addresses which bodies corporate are so prone to address to majesty, that it was more difficult to address him, than to address the King of Kings, and that they would " adhere to him against all his enemies, with the utmost of their lives and fortunes." How this unmeaning pledge was redeemed the sequel will show. The next morning, being the 29th of March, his Majesty viewed the town, and carefully

* By the statute of the 5th of Elizabeth, chap. v. sec. 15, it is provided, that any person eating flesh on a fish day shall be liable to a penalty of £3. or suffer three months imprisonment—but by the 2nd and 3rd Edward VI. cap. 19. sec. 5. a dispensing power is given to the Archbishop of Canterbury, which power was probably afterwards extended to him of York.

inspected the fortifications, after which he proceeded to Beverley, and the day following arrived in York. A treaty was soon after concluded between Charles and the Scots, and the kingdom was flattered with illusive prospects of peace; but the Scots still kept up their army, and the dissatisfaction felt by the people of England, at the proceedings of the King and his ministers, threatened an immediate explosion. At this juncture, Charles finding all his supplies dried up, was obliged to assemble that memorable parliament,* which was speedily to contend with him for the sovereign authority. After long and fruitless altercations, both parties prepared to decide the contest by arms. In this situation of affairs, the possession of Hull, a place rendered strong both by nature and art, became an object of the first importance, and the immense magazine of arms and ammunition collected in the garrison served greatly to enhance its value. The King, in order to secure the town, sent the Earl of Northumberland here, to take possession in his Majesty's name, but the Mayor, Aldermen, and Burgesses, unmindful of their recent declaration, "that they would adhere to his Majesty against all his enemies, with the utmost of their lives and fortunes," declined to receive the king's general, and after some hesitation and delay admitted Sir John Hotham, as governor, by order of parliament. The king had now fixed his residence at York, and it was not difficult to forsee, that he would endeavour to obtain possession of the vast magazines at Hull, which at that time far exceeded the collection of warlike stores in the tower of London. The policy of the parliament was to have these stores removed to London, and the two houses sent petitions to the king for that purpose, but his majesty refused his consent, and the stores remained at Hull undisturbed.

On the 23d of April, 1642, a memorable period in the history of Hull, and in the history of the kingdom, his majesty, attended by his son, afterwards Charles II. and by a train of from two to three hundred of his servants, with many gentlemen of the county, set out early in the morning from York for Hull, and when he was within about four miles of this place, he sent forward an officer to inform the governor, that he intended that day to dine with him.†

* The Long Parliament assembled November 3, 1640.

† It is remarkable, that the Duke of York, (afterwards James II.) was in Hull at this time, and actually dining at the Trinity House, when Sir John Hotham was parleying with his father at the gate.

This unexpected honour Sir John Hotham was not disposed to accept, and he dispatched a message to the King, humbly beseeching him " to decline his intended visit, seeing that the governor could not, without betraying the trust committed to him, open the gates to so great a train as his majesty was attended with." The king, however, continued to advance, and Sir John ordered the bridges to be drawn up, the gates to be shut, and the soldiers to stand to their arms round the walls. The king having arrived at Beverley-gate demanded entrance, at least for himself, and twenty of his attendants, but the governor continued to plead the trust reposed in him by parliament, protesting, at the same time, upon his knees, that he wished " God might bring confusion upon him and his, if he was not a faithful and loyal subject to his Majesty." The threats and the entreaties of the king were, however, alike unavailing, and in the evening he retired to Beverley, where he lodged that night. The next morning he sent a herald to Sir John, summoning him once more to open the gates on pain of being proclaimed a traitor, in case of refusal, and with a promise of forgiveness for the past, if he consented. The herald, like his royal master, proved unsuccessful, and the king, grievously disappointed, returned to York.

This was the first act of hostility between the king and the parliamentarian party, and proved the commencement of that civil war, which, for the space of four years, desolated England, and brought her monarch to the block. On his arrival in York, the king sent a message to the two houses of parliament, demanding justice against the governor of Hull, for his treasonable refusal to obey the royal commands; but, instead of punishing Sir John Hotham, parliament bestowed upon him and his supporters a vote of thanks. The king having mustered about 3800 troops, of which 3000 were foot, and 800 horse, and procured a supply of arms from Holland, by the sale of the crown jewels, and by the seal of his royal consort, resolved to commence the war by an attack upon Hull, the fortress of which he hoped to carry, rather by the defection of the governor, than by the force of his own arms. On his arrival at Beverley, Sir John Hotham called a council of war, by which it was determined, that the surrounding country should be laid under water, in order to render all access to the town impracticable to the king's army. This resolution was immediately carried into effect; the sluices were pulled up, and the banks both of the Humber and the Hull were out, so that the next morning, by the aid of the spring tides, the meadows and pastures, to the extent of two miles on every side of Hull, were inundated with water. The next care of the governor was to put the town in the best possible state of defence; for this purpose, the Charter-house, Hospital, and several houses in Myton-lane, were demolished; the walls and the fort at the South-end were fortified with cannon; batteries were erected at the Myton, Beverley, and the North gates; draw bridges were thrown over the town ditch, which was there both broad and deep: and the country being under water, the royalists could make no near approaches, either to plant their batteries, or to practise any other species of annoyance. While the garrison of Hull was thus making every preparation for defence, the king was not inactive at Beverley: Two hundred men were employed in cutting trenches, to divert the current of fresh water which supplied the town of Hull; posts were placed at the Humber side, in Lincolnshire, to prevent succours being introduced from that quarter, and two forts were erected, one at Paul, five miles below Hull, and the other at Hessle Cliff, about the same distance above it, to prevent supplies from being conveyed by the river. The siege of Hull having now commenced, Sir John Meldrum, a Scotch officer, was sent down by parliament to assist the governor, and greatly distinguished himself in the defence of the town. Notwithstanding the inundation, the king had brought his cannon to play on the town with some effect, and he was answered with equal spirit by guns planted on the walls, though no material slaughter was made on either side. Reports were raised in the town, that the king contemplated measures of the greatest cruelty against the inhabitants, and that should he succeed in carrying the place, as he intended by storm, every person, without respect to age, sex, or condition, was to be put indiscriminately to the sword. By these arts the troops in the garrison were violently inflamed against the royal cause, and about the end of July, 500 of them, under the command of Sir John Meldrum, made a desperate sally from that fortress, and attacked the king's forces with so much spirit, that they were obliged to retire to Beverley with considerable loss. After repeated similar repulses, the king called a council of war, and by their advice he resolved to raise the siege, and draw off his forces. This attempt on Hull having thus entirely failed, the king's army retired to Beverley, where the train-bands, a species of militia, were dismissed, and his majesty, with his

court, and the rest of his army, returned to York.

It was matter of great surprise to all who were not in the secret, that the king, with such inadequate means, should have attempted the siege of Hull, which was one of the strongest fortresses in the whole kingdom; but his majesty's reason for undertaking this enterprise was founded on other and surer grounds, than the precarious success of arms. This attack was in pursuance of a plan formed between Sir John Hotham, the governor, and Lord Digby, the son of the Earl of Bristol. This young nobleman, in whom the king placed unbounded confidence, had, it appears, been taken prisoner by one of the parliament's ships, and carried into Hull. Under the disguise of a Frenchman he remained for some time unknown, but at length he introduced himself to the governor, and had the romantic hardihood to propose to him the surrender of the town to the king. The manner in which Sir John received the overture, encouraged him to press the negotiation; and, it was at length agreed between them, that the king should advance from York, at the head of his small army, and that Sir John should deliver up the place at the firing of the first shot. This was the true cause which prevailed with his majesty to besiege that town; but either through the pusillanimity, the inconstancy, or the inability of the governor, the whole project proved abortive, and its failure served only to damp the spirits of the adherents of this ill-advised and ill-fated monarch. The town of Hull and the adjacent country, notwithstanding the success of the garrison, were in a deplorable condition. In the town the spirit of party ran high, and those who were suspected of favouring the royal cause were imprisoned, and their property confiscated. In the villages the inhabitants had sustained great loss by the inundation of their land; and the detachments sent out of the garrison almost daily, to distress the royalists, committed terrible devastations, both in Yorkshire and Lincolnshire, so that a vast many families were plunged into utter ruin. The treachery of Sir John Hotham, which already began to be suspected by parliament, induced them to watch his movements, and the appointment of Lord Fairfax to the office of general of the army of the North, gave deadly umbrage to the baronet, who aspired to that honour, and induced him to seek opportunities to deliver up Hull to the royalists. Into this conspiracy, his son, Captain Hotham, very readily entered, and became the medium of negotiation for the accomplishment of this treacherous purpose. The mayor of Hull, Thos. Raikes, Esq. having learnt that the plot for delivering up the town was now ripe for execution, held a consultation with the chiefs of the parliamentary party, and it was resolved to defeat the project by seizing the governor and his son. On the 29th of June, 1643, Captain Moyer, who commanded the ship Hercules, stationed by parliament in the Humber, landed a hundred men from his ship, and seized the Castle and block-houses almost without resistance. About the same time, 1500 of the soldiers and inhabitants, who had been waiting in the town for the word of command from the mayor, seized the main-guard, near the magazine, and next took possession of all the artillery on the walls. These measures having so far succeeded, Captain Hotham was then secured, and a guard was placed at the door of the governor's house; all this was effected in the space of about an hour, and without the shedding of a drop of blood. Sir John Hotham having in the mean time obtained information of what was transacting, found means to escape, but being secured by Captain Boynton, in Beverley, the governor was conveyed under a strong guard to Hull, where he was put on board the Hercules, together with his son, Captain Hotham, and conveyed to London. The catastrophe is universally known: after a long and strict confinement, Sir John Hotham was brought before a court-martial, at Guildhall, in London, on the 30th of November, charged with "traitorously betraying the trust reposed in him by parliament," which charge being clearly substantiated, the court, on the 7th of December, pronounced sentence, that he should suffer death, by having his head severed from his body. Two days after the conviction of his father, Captain Hotham was arraigned before the court martial, charged with "having betrayed the trust reposed in him by the parliament, and with perfidiously adhering to the enemy." This charge was supported by satisfactory evidence, and the son was condemned to die in the same way as his father. On the first of January, Captain Hotham was brought to the scaffold, on Tower-hill, and underwent the sentence of the law; and on the day following, Sir John suffered decapitation upon the scaffold at the same place—the victim of his own inconstancy and want of resolution. The fate of Sir John Hotham and of his son, called to the mind of the king, the imprecation of—"May God bring confusion on me and mine, if I be not a faithful and loyal subject to your majesty!" This profane denunciation, it will be remembered, was uttered at the time when Sir John re-

fused to admit the king into Hull, and Charles considered the execution of the governor as a visitation of Providence for his disloyalty, for which his subsequent repentance was not sufficient to atone; but this case, considered in connexion with Charles's own fate, may serve to show the danger of writing the judgments of heaven upon the sufferings of our adversaries, for the question naturally arises, if the execution of Sir John Hotham, by parliament, in 1644, was a judgment of heaven, what name must be given to the execution of the king, in 1648, under the sanction of the same authority!

After the seizure of the governor, as already related, the custody of the town was entrusted to the care of a committee of eleven, approved by the parliament, and at the head of which was the mayor. Soon afterwards Lord Fairfax arrived in Hull, and on the 22d of July, 1643, was constituted the governor of this place. The Marquis of Newcastle, the commander of the king's forces, having made himself master of Gainsborough and Lincoln, and driven Sir Thomas Fairfax out of Beverley with great slaughter, appeared with his whole force before Hull, on the 2d of September, and immediately began his operations against the town, from which he cut off its supplies of fresh water, and of provisions as far as depended on the adjoining parts of Yorkshire. The siege and defence were conducted with all the military skill of that age, and with all the determination of deep-rooted hostility, which generally distinguishes intestine wars. The besiegers erected several batteries, which opened on the town, and were answered by an incessant fire from the walls. After extreme labour, and at the expense of many lives, the royalists, though exposed to heavy and constant fire from the walls, at length succeeded in erecting a fort about half a mile from the town, which was called the king's fort. On this was placed several pieces of heavy ordnance, and a furnace was constructed for heating balls. The firing of red hot balls into the town threw the inhabitants into great consternation, but the prudent precautions of the governor prevented them from doing any material injury, and by adding two large culverins to the Charter-house battery, and the erection of another fort, which flanked the royalists, he demolished the king's fort, and deprived the Marquis of Newcastle of the means of firing hot balls into the town. On the 14th of September, Lord Fairfax ordered the banks of the Humber and the Hull to be cut, and the country being thus once more laid under water, the royalists were obliged to abandon all their works, except those erected on the banks of the river. On the 20th the royalists made their approaches to the town on the West, and erected batteries, on which they placed heavy artillery; and on the 27th, they repaired the fort at Paul, and erected another at Whitgift, near the confluence of the Ouse and the Trent, in order to prevent Hull from receiving supplies of water. But the ships of war which the parliament had stationed in the Humber soon demolished these forts, and kept open the way for ample supplies to the town and to the garrison. The siege still continued to be prosecuted with the greatest vigour, and almost every day was marked by some active operation. On the 9th of October, a combined attack was made by a strong party of royalists under Captain Strickland, on the fort at the foot of the West Jetty, while another body of forces attacked the Charterhouse battery on the other side of the town; but both these enterprises failed, and the assailants were nearly annihilated. The last operation of importance which took place during this siege, was a grand sortie made from the town, on the 11th of October. At seven o'clock in the morning the whole garrison was under arms; and at 9 o'clock, 1500 men, consisting of inhabitants, soldiers, and seamen, with four troops of horse, sallied out of the West side of the town, with the determination to compel the royalists to raise the siege. This attack was made with so much vigour, that the besiegers, after an obstinate contest, were driven from their works. The timely arrival of a strong reinforcement enabled them to recover their cannon, which had fallen into the hands of the assailants, who were obliged to retreat under the cover of their batteries. Here Lord Fairfax and Sir John Meldrum used every endeavour to inspire their men with fresh courage, and the attack was renewed with such desperate impetuosity, that the Marquis of Newcastle was at length obliged to abandon both his forts and batteries, after experiencing a dreadful loss from his own cannon, which were turned against him. The siege, which had continued nearly six weeks, was now drawing to a close, and the Marquis of Newcastle perceiving that all his efforts to carry the town must be unavailing, called a council of war, on the 11th of October; the deliberations of which resulted in a determination immediately to raise the siege. This resolution was carried into effect the same night, and the Marquis, who retreated with the greater part of his army to York, in order to prevent a pursuit, cut open the canals, destroyed the bridges, and broke up the roads in the line of his retreat. On the

following morning, when it was perceived that the enemy was gone, Lord Fairfax commanded that the day should be observed as a day of public thanksgiving, and the anniversary was celebrated here in the same manner till the restoration.

The following year, 1644, almost every part of Yorkshire became, in its turn, a theatre of hostilities, and the battle of Marston Moor, fought on the second of July, in that year, decided the fate of the war. But amidst all the miseries with which it was surrounded, this town remained tranquil. Next year, the liturgy of the Church of England being abolished, the soldiers quartered in Hull entered the churches, took out the common prayer books, and with drums beating and trumpets sounding, carried them to the Market place, where they consigned them to a fire already provided for the purpose, amidst the acclamations of the spectators. In little more than three years afterwards Charles I. terminated his life on the scaffold. The Protector of the Commonwealth was accepted with the usual demonstrations of affectionate regard towards the head of the government, and the corporation, in their address to Cromwell, "humbly acknowledged their thankfulness to God, in whose guidings are the hearts of princes, that he had made him the ruler over us." On the death of Cromwell, his son, Richard, was proclaimed the "rightful Protector of the Commonwealth," and adulatory addresses were presented to him from this and the generality of the boroughs of England.[*]—In this protectorate, Andrew Marvel, the incorrupt senator, of whom more hereafter, was first elected member for this borough. Hull followed the current of the rest of the kingdom, and united in the expression of general joy on the restoration of Charles II. to the throne of his ancestors.

In the year 1661, Trinity Church, in Hull, which had hitherto been only a chapel, dependent on Hessle, was constituted a parish church; and in the same year the King not only conferred upon the town its former charter, but added several other privileges to those it formerly enjoyed.—In 1680 a new citadel of great strength was added to the garrison, at an expense of one hundred thousand pounds. "About this time," says Tickell in his history of Hull, "a suit took place between this corporation and the town of Leeds, which is in the honour of Pontefract and the Duchy of Lancaster. The cause of this suit was on account of some goods belonging to Leeds, which

* Tickell's Hull, p. 507.

the water bailiff of Hull had distrained for port fees. To establish their exemption from this claim it was urged by Leeds that the Duchy of Lancaster was invested with large privileges, that the inhabitants thereof were free of all pannage, passage, lastage, stallage, tollage, carriage, &c. through all England, and that all these privileges were confirmed by act of parliament until Henry IVth's days, and were always enjoyed by the tenants of Leeds, both in Hull and in all other towns in England." " The result of the contest," adds Tickell, " was, that the corporation of Hull, finding their cause untenable, thought proper to make some compromise for the goods distrained by the water bailiff," and the exemption of Leeds from these imposts was of course established. Towards the close of this reign, the King intimidated the different corporations of the realm into a surrender of their charters, partly for the purpose of obtaining money for their renewal. Hull, which had paid tonnage and poundage, and ship-money, in the reign of Charles I. without reluctance, was one of the first considerable corporations that made the surrender of its charter to Charles II. and the King, on the payment of the required consideration, renewed the charter to the entire satisfaction of the burgesses. The arbitrary conduct of the Second Charles excited general discontent in the country towards the latter part of his reign, and the nation was again threatened with a repetition of those horrors from which it had so recently escaped, when a stroke of apoplexy sent the Monarch to his last audit, and saved his country from the degradation of being sold to France, to administer to the profligacy and profusion of a royal voluptuary. James, Duke of York, for whose exclusion so many efforts had been made, on account of his known attachment to the Catholic faith, ascended the throne without opposition.— James soon discovered his intention to complete the fabric of despotism begun by his predecessor, and the nation, at length taking the alarm, called in the Prince of Orange.— As soon as it was known that the fleet equipping in Holland was intended for England, James formed the design of securing the important fortress of Hull, and Lord Langdale was sent down in haste for that purpose.— The Prince of Orange sailed on the first of November, 1688, and the new governor fully expecting that he would enter the Humber, caused great quantities of warlike stores and

provisions to be brought into Hull, for the purpose of sustaining a siege. The inhabitants, in the meantime, having in the last age experienced the horrors of war within their own borders, were thrown into the utmost consternation; but on receiving intelligence that William had landed in Torbay on the 4th of November, their apprehensions were removed. The town and garrison of Hull remained in possession of the Catholic party till the 3d of December, and an apprehension was entertained that a plot was formed by the governor and his adherents, to secure all the Protestant officers. Under this impression Fort Major Barrat and Captain Copley, being themselves protestants, sent for all the officers of that persuasion, and consulted with the magistrates what was to be done in this emergency.— At that meeting it was resolved to call privately to arms such of the soldiers as were attached to the Protestant cause, and to secure the Governor, and the principal persons of his party. These measures were concerted with so much prudence and secrecy, that the Governor, Lord Langdale, knew nothing of the business until he was seized in his quarters. Nearly at the same moment Lord Montgomery was secured by Captain Fitzherbert, and Major Mahony by the Fort Major. The inferior officers of that party were also secured, and the next morning Captain Copley, with one hundred men, marched out to relieve the guard, who were still ignorant of what had been transacted in the night, and, without difficulty, seized the Catholic officers and soldiers whom he found there. The town, fort, and citadel were now easily secured; and the anniversary of this event is still celebrated at Hull by the name of " *The town taking day.*" The glorious revolution being now completed, and the members of the misguided and ill-fated house of Stuart cashiered for misrule by the national will, the House of Nassau was raised to the distinguished elevation from which their predecessors had fallen; and William and Mary took possession of the throne. In the following year an act was passed, imposing upon the country a species of property tax, of one shilling in the pound, for one year, and the following duplicate of assessment, under the operations of this law, will serve to show the amount of landed and personal property in the town and county of Kingston-upon-Hull at the end of the seventeenth century :—

An extract of the assessments for the town and county of Kingston-upon-Hull.

| | Personal Estates. | Offices | Rents. |
|---|---|---|---|
| | £. s. | £. | £. s. |
| Town ............ | 49400 0 | 1146 | 6538 15 |
| County ........ | 300 | 0 | 2865 16 |
| Total sum ... | 49700 0 | 1146 | 9404 11 |

The Centenary of the Revolution of 1688 was celebrated in every part of the kingdom, and in none with more striking demonstrations of joy, than in the town of Kingston-upon-Hull. The 5th of November, 1788, was ushered in by the ringing of bells, as a signal for the opening Jubilee. The concourse of persons who flocked into the place from all parts of the surrounding country was immense, and the visitors, as well as the inhabitants, were splendidly decorated with orange ribands. In the course of the day the different corporations, headed by the mayor, and honoured with the presence of the representatives of the Borough, S. Thornton and W. S. Stanhope, Esqrs. formed splendid processions through the town: divine service was performed on the occasion by the Rev. Thos. Clarke, D. D. the vicar of the Holy Trinity; and elegant and sumptuous entertainments were provided at the Guildhall, and at the principal Inns. In the evening the festive scene was heightened by a brilliant illumination, and a triumphal arch erected over the statue of King William, shone forth with peculiar effulgence. That the ladies might participate in the celebration of this illustrious event, a ball was given at the Assembly Rooms on the following night, at which nearly three hundred of the principal inhabitants of the town and neighbourhood were present. This revolutionary jubilee is even yet remembered in Hull with great pleasure; and the lapse of four and thirty winters has chastened without obliterating the vivid impressions of that festival, which was meant to celebrate one of the most impressive lessons ever read in the history of the world by subjects to their sovereigns.

When George III. attained the 50th year of his reign the nation held a general Jubilee; and at Hull, as in other places, the demonstrations of an affectionate loyalty were strikingly manifested on the 25th Oct. 1809. The processions were numerous and splendid, and the festivities little less so. Public thanks were returned to the Almighty for the mercies with which he had crowned us. The hungry were fed and the naked clothed. Several valuable public institutions were formed in different parts of the country, and the Hull Auxiliary Bible Society dates its origin from this day.

At the end of "the campaign of the liberties of Europe," by which name the military operations on the continent in the year 1813, were dignified, Great Britain rung with the voice of joy and gratulation. Every town in the kingdom had its rejoicings, and at Hull the public feeling was exhibited by the strongest demonstrations. Wednesday, the fifteenth of December, was the day specially set apart for this purpose. At 11 o'clock in the forenoon, a splendid procession, consisting of all the public bodies in the town, attended by music and flags, was formed, and proceeded to the church of the Holy Trinity, where an excellent sermon was preached by the vicar: but the most interesting feature of this day's proceedings consisted in the presence, by special invitation, of the Dutch captains in the port whose country had just been liberated from the thraldom of France, and who were provided with a superb orange flag, on which was inscribed in their own characters "ORANGE BOVEN." At three o'clock the park of artillery in the citadel paraded through the town, and at four 150 of the principal inhabitants sat down to a sumptuous dinner. The festive scene was kept up here and in other parts of the town till nine o'clock in the evening, at which hour the company separated to witness a grand display of fire-works, which for an hour & a half delighted at least 20,000 spectators. These festivities were concluded on Friday, by a splendid and numerously attended ball given to the ladies.

It has ever been the practice in Hull to celebrate the coronation of each of our successive sovereigns by some mark of loyal regard, and at the festival of the coronation of George IV. on the 19th of July, 1821, all the children in the town belonging to the Church of England Sunday School Association, and to the Dissenters' Sunday School Union, marched in procession to the church of the Holy Trinity, where an appropriate sermon was preached to them by the Rev. J. Scott. The number of children amounted to 4000. The constituted authorities, and the Masonic societies, also attended divine service; and the scene is described as highly interesting and impressive.

The public buildings in Hull do not display any great degree of magnificence, nor many traces of antiquity. They may be arranged under three heads:—places of religious worship—charitable foundations—and commercial edifices.

The *Church of the Holy Trinity,* coming within the first class, is a stately and beautiful structure, consisting of a nave, chancel, and transepts, at the intersection of which rises an extremely fine tower, upon four lofty arches. The period of its foundation is not recorded; it is, however, certain, that it was existing in the reign of Edward I. a licence for a cemetery to it being granted by Archbishop Corbridge, in 1301, to the Prior of Gysburn, patron of the mother church of Hessle, in which parish the rising town was principally situate. The present chancel and transepts exhibit the style of that period, and being built partly of brick, may fairly claim to be the most ancient known specimen of brick building in England, since the time of the Romans. The east window is a particularly fine example of the tracery of that time, and was, externally, at least, restored to view some years ago, on the removal of the old shambles, whilst internally it is chiefly filled up with plaster, on which is indifferently painted the last supper, by Parmentier. The nave and tower are probably of the early part of the 15th century; the west front has been very fine, but is hidden by a row of houses, built about fifty years ago; and the whole appearance of this noble structure is grievously injured by the loss of all the pinnacles which crowned the buttresses on the north and south sides, which now present to the eye a naked line of flat coping, utterly at variance with the genius of the pointed arch. On the south side of the chancel have been several splendid chantries, now almost wholly destroyed, and converted into vestries and burial vaults, in repairing which, were lately discovered a recumbent female figure, and an arch charged with figures and armorial bearings. Internally, the view of this church is striking to the beholder, the pillars of the chancel are uncommonly light and elegant, and the arches lofty. It contains many memorials of the dead, not a few of whose names and families have become wholly extinct. The most remarkable monuments are that of the Rev. Joseph Milner, M.A. by Bacon; and one, erroneously attributed to the De la Poles, representing a merchant and his wife in the costume of the 14th century. Divine service is performed, contrary to usual custom, in the nave, the chancel being entirely open. This church, as before stated, was originally only a Chapel of Ease to Hessle, from which it was separated by act of parliament, and made a vicarage, in 1661, under the patronage of the Corporation. It is the largest parochial church, not collegiate, in the kingdom, and occupies an area of not less than 20,056 square feet.— The clergy attached to the Holy Trinity are the Rev. John Healey Bromby, M.A. vicar;

the Rev. John Scott, M.A. lecturer; and the Rev. G. J. Davies, M.A. curate. The service commences in the Summer at half past 10 in the morning, and at three o'clock in the afternoon; and in Winter half an hour earlier in the afternoon. There is also divine service at ten o'clock on Wednesday mornings.

The *Church of St. Mary* was built before the year 1333, a licence to perform divine offices, &c. therein, being then granted, by Archbishop Melton, to the prior and brethren of Ferriby, for the convenience of that part of the town of Hull which was in their parish. It was formerly more magnificent than it is at present, the greater part of it being demolished by Henry VIII. because it obstructed the prospect from his manor house, when nothing was left standing but the chancel. Part of the materials of the nave and the steeple were employed to enlarge and repair the manor house, and the rest in constructing the block houses which Henry caused to be erected on the eastern bank of the river Hull. In this state of comparative ruin the church remained till about the year 1570, when a considerable addition was made to the east end of the chancel, by the parishioners, but for more than a century it stood without a steeple; in 1696 the present steeple was begun, and in the following year it was completed. St. Mary's was to Ferriby, what the Holy Trinity was to Hessle, but it is now a parochial chapelry, of which Samuel Thornton, Esq. is the patron; the Rev. John Scott, M.A. the incumbent; and the Rev. William Wilson the curate. Divine service commences, both in summer and winter, at the same hour as at Trinity church; there is also service in the evening, which commences at half-past six o'clock.

*St. John's Church*, in Trinity parish, is a modern erection, built in the year 1791, and opened for divine service on the 13th of May, 1792. It is a brick building, neat and simple without, and elegant and commodious within. A tower has been added to the original structure, and the organ has been introduced since the church was built. The Rev. Thomas Dikes, LL.B. is the present incumbent, and though but at the sole expence of that gentleman, the future presentation is vested in the vicar. The Rev. William Knight, B.A. is curate of St. John's. Morning service commences on Sunday at half past ten, and afternoon service at three: there is also an evening lecture on Tuesday at 7 o'clock.

The churches of Sculcoates and Drypool are described under their proper heads.

At the Pottery licensed Chapel, which is situated in the western suburb, the Rev.

Thomas Dikes is minister, and divine service is performed here on Sunday and Thursday evenings at 7 o'clock, without any stipend whatever.

There are in Hull eighteen chapels, or meeting-houses, which afford accommodation to three Baptist, three Calvinist, six Methodist, two Unitarian, one Roman Catholic, one Swedenborgian, & one Quaker congregation: there are also two synagogues for the Jews. The following synopsis will show the situation of each chapel, the name of the minister who officiates, and the hours of divine service:—

| Denomination and Ministers Names. | Situation of Chapel. | Hours of Divine Service. |
| --- | --- | --- |
| Baptists' (General) Rev. Thomas Thonger | George street | Sunday—Prayers at 7 mg. Lecture at ½ past 10 mg. at ½ p. aft. and 7 evening. |
| Baptists' (Particular) Rev. James M'Pherson | Salthouse lane | Sunday—at ½ p. 10 mg. ½ p. 2 aft. and ½ p. 6 evg. Prayers at 7 Monday evening, and Lecture at 7 on Wednesday. |
| Baptists' (Jehovah Jireh) Rev. William Arbou, | Mason street | Sunday—Prayers 7 mg. Lect. ½ p. 10, Pr. ½ p. 2 aft. and ½ p. 6 evg. Prayers Monday at 7 evg. Lecture Thursday at 7. |
| Calvinist (Baptist) Rev. E. Thompson, | Roper's row | Sunday—½ p. 10 mg. ½ p. aft. and 6 in the evening. |
| Calvinist (Ebenezer) Lady Huntingdon's Rev. Saml. Lane, V.D.M. | New Dock street | Sunday—at 10 mg. Prayers at 3 aft. and Lecture 6 evg. Monday Prayers 7 evg. and Lecture at 7 Wednesday evening. |
| Calvinist (Providence) Rev. J. Morley, | Hope street | Sunday—at ½ p. 10 mg. Prayers ½ p. 2 aft. Lecture 6 evg. Monday Prayers 7 evg. Lecture Wed. and Thurs. evg. at 7 |
| Catholic Rev. John Smith, | North street Prospect street | Sunday—½ p. 10 mg. 3 aft. in summer, and ½ p. 2 aft in winter. |
| Friends Meeting House | Lowgate | Sunday meeting at 10 morning, 3 afternoon in summer and 2 in winter, on Thursday at 10 morning. |
| Independent Calvinist Rev. Joseph Gilbert and Rev. Spedding Curwen | Fish street | Sunday—at ½ p. 10 mg. ½ p. 2 aft. 6 evg. Monday Prayers 7 evening, Wednesday Lecture 7 evening. |
| Methodist (Old Connexion) | Drypool | Sunday—½ p. 10 mg. 3 aft. & 6 evening. Tuesday evening at 7, |
| Ditto | George yard | Sunday—Prayers ½ p. 7 mg. 10 mg. and 6 evg. Thursday 7 evening. |
| Ditto | Pottery | Sunday evening at 6 & Friday evening at 7 |
| Ditto | Scott street | Sunday morning ½ p. 10, and 6 evening. Wednesday evening at 7. |
| Ditto | Waltham street | Sunday—at ½ p. 10 mg. 3 aft. and 6 evg. Monday at 7 evening. |
| Methodist (Bethel) (New Connexion) | North street Charlotte street | Sunday—Prayers 7 mg. ½ p. 10 mg. 3 aft. and 6 evg. Lecture Mon. & Thu. 7 evg. |
| Methodists Primitive | Mill street | Sunday—Pr. 6 mg. ½ p. 9 mg. Lect. ½ p. 10 mg. 3 aft. and 6 evg. Pr. 8 evg. Mon. Lect. 7 and Pr. 8 evg. Tu. Pr. 7 evg. Fri. Lect. 7 evg. Sat. Prayer 7 evening. |
| Swedenborgh (New Jerusalem) Rev. J. Proud | Prince street Dagger lane | Sunday—at ½ p. 10 mg. and ½ p. 2 aft. at 2 in Winter. |
| Synagogue (Jewish) Rabbi Samuel Symons | Parade row | Saturday—at 8 mg. 2 aft. and 5 evg. in winter; at 9 evg. in summer; Mon. and Thursday at 7 morning. |
| Synagogue (Jewish) Service performed by the persons present | Posterngate | Friday evg. at 5, and Sat. morn. at 8. |
| Unitarian Rev. William Worsley, | Bowlalley lane | Sunday—½ p. 10 morning & 3 afternoon |
| Unitarian (Baptist) Rev. ——— Jordan, | New Dock street | Sunday—11 morning, ½ p. 6 evening, and Wed. at 7 evening. |

The Missionary monthly prayer meeting is held alternately at Fish street, Hope street, George street, and Salthouse lane chapels, on the first Monday evening of the month.

In addition to the other places of religious worship, there is in Hull a floating chapel supported by voluntary contributions, and which does honour to the town. This chapel is formed of the hull of an old merchant ship; of four hundred tons burthen, and which is safely moored at the west end of the old dock. The object is to accommodate seamen with a place of worship suited to their peculiar habits of life, and it will contain from six to seven hundred persons, and seat five hundred comfortably. The service is performed gratuitously, by ministers of the Church of England, by the Calvinistic Dissenters, and by the Methodist ministers. Instead of bells to announce the time of public worship, a flag is hoisted at the mast head; two sermons are preached every Sunday, and a prayer meeting is held every Tuesday night in summer. In the winter season this buoyant sanctuary is well attended by a nautical congregation, whose appearance is clean and decent, and their conduct orderly and exemplary. The service on Sunday commences at half-past ten in the morning, and at half-past two in the afternoon.

The charities in Hull are numerous, and amongst the most ancient and important of them may be ranked the Trinity House and Hospital. It has already been seen that the fraternity, or brotherhood, of masters and pilots, seamen of the Trinity House in Hull, was first instituted in the year 1369, for the relief of decayed seamen and their widows; and in order to provide a fund for the purpose, the members engaged to pay 2s. each, annually, which sum was then equal in value to about two pounds of our present money. Since that time the funds have been considerably increased by legacies and benefactions, and they are continually replenished by a contribution of sixpence per month from every seaman sailing from this port. The corporation of the Trinity House, is composed of twelve elder brethren, six assistants, and an unlimited number of younger brethren. Out of the elder brethren are chosen annually, on the first Wednesday in September, two wardens, who are at the head of the corporation during their period of office; and at the same time are elected two stewards from among the younger brethren; these offices for the year 1822-3, are

Mr. William Collinson, sen. }
Mr. William Busney......... } Wardens.

Mr. Isaiah Pearson.......... }
Mr. Robert Gill. ...,........ } Stewards.

The first royal charter conferred upon this community was granted by Henry VI. in the year 1442, and this grant has been confirmed and extended by seven subsequent charters, from the time of Henry VIII. to Charles II. the privileges of the guild consist principally in the right to levy and receive primage for the support of poor mariners, and their wives and widows in alms houses, by weekly and quarterly pensions; in affording relief to shipwrecked mariners; in licensing and appointing pilots; in placing buoys and beacons for the safety of navigation in the river Humber; in settling differences between masters of ships and their men; and in various other powers relating to maritime affairs.

The Trinity House, where the business of the corporation is transacted, was originally founded in 1457, and was re-built in 1753. The building consists of four sides surrounding a spacious area or court. The north, the south, and the east sides consist of single apartments for thirty-four pensioners. The front is a handsome brick structure, in the Tuscan order of architecture, with a pediment of free stone, ornamented by the King's Arms, with the figure of Neptune on one side, and Britannia on the other, respectably executed by the late Mr. Jeremiah Hargrave of this place. On the side towards the west are the hall and housekeepers' rooms, with kitchens and other offices. Over these offices are two elegant council chambers for transacting the business of the house. The various apartments of this building contain several curiosities brought from foreign countries, and are ornamented with a number of paintings calculated to gratify the traveller and the man of taste. Adjoining the front of the Trinity House is a handsome chapel, built in 1772, and fitted up in an elegant manner for the purpose of divine worship, wherein service is performed three times a week, and a sermon preached monthly by the Rev. George John Davies, M. A. the present chaplain. In the same year that the chapel was built, a Marine School was founded by the Trinity House, in which institution thirty-six boys receive the advantage of a nautical education, each member of this corporation appointing two. The children remain in this seminary three years, during which period they are annually provided with a neat uniform and every other article of dress.

The other alms houses belonging to the Trinity House, are Robinson's Hospital, given to this corporation in the year 1682, by William Robinson, Esq. then sheriff of

Hull; and in 1769, re-built and enlarged for the reception of decayed younger brethren and their wives; six rooms in the hospital, for the reception of as many widows of seamen, erected by Dr. Thomas Watson, Bishop of St. David's, about the year 1687: the Merchant Seamen's Hospital, in Whitefriargate, built by this corporation in 1781, for the reception of poor worn-out seamen and their widows; and a Hospital for decayed seamen and their wives adjoining the Trinity House Chapel, established in 1787. In addition to these charitable foundations, the corporation of the Trinity House have just completed on part of their property, situated near the site of the town's walls, another large and handsome pile called Ferris's Hospital, in memory of Alderman Ferris, their benefactor, which will afford accommodation to from twenty to thirty inmates. Extensive benefits do of course result to the seamen of the port of Hull from this munificent foundation, the revenues of which, appropriated to charitable purposes alone amount to five thousand pounds a year.

The Charter House, another of the ancient Hospitals of Hull, was founded in the year 1384, by Michael de la Pole, the first Earl of Suffolk, of that name, adjoining to his other foundation of the monastery of St. Michael. In the rage for sweeping away religious and charitable foundations, this establishment was seized by Henry VIII. but afterwards re-founded, as has been already seen, by his son and successor Edward VI. In the year 1642, when Hull was besieged by Charles I. the governor, Sir John Hotham, totally demolished the buildings of the Charter House, to prevent the royalists from obtaining a lodgment here. At the end of the civil wars, this hospital was re-built, and the sum of 278l. 18s. 3d. was paid out of the public purse, by the then governor, Lord Fairfax, towards the expenses of the new erection. This building stood till the year 1780, when it was taken down, and the present spacious and handsome structure erected in its stead. The building forming the Charter House as it at present stands, has two projecting wings, and is in a style of architecture suited to the humble purpose to which it is applied. On the top of the portico before the front door, supported by six handsome stone pillars, are the following inscriptions:—*Deo et pauperibus Michael de la Pole has Œdes posuit, A. D. 1384. Renovatas iterum auctiusque instauratas piæ fundatoris memoriæ, D. D. Johannes Bourne, rector, A. D. 1780.* In the principal body of the building is a handsome chapel, which not only serves for the use of the house, but also as a substitute for Sculcoates church

during the winter months: the Rev. Kingsman Beckett, M. A. is the master and chaplain. The apartments in the hospital for the brothers and sisters amount to fifty-seven, of which twenty-nine are for women, and twenty-eight for men; they are well fitted up and exceedingly convenient, and each individual is allowed three shillings and sixpence a week besides fuel, with some few occasional payments. The revenues of this foundation which arise from rents of lands and a share in the Hull Dock Co.'s concerns, now amount to from 800l. to 1890l. a year, though in 1600, the annual rents only produced 54l.

There are in Hull several other hospitals: these are Lister's Hospital, founded by Sir John Lister, alderman and member of parliament for Hull, in 1641, for the reception of twelve poor persons, who each receive two shillings and sixpence per week, there is also allowed 2l. per annum, and suitable apartments for a lecturer: Gregg's Hospital, of the date of 1416, for twelve poor old women, who receive one shilling and sixpence per week: Crowle's Hospital, erected and endowed by George Crowle, alderman and merchant, in 1661, where twelve poor women, the youngest of the age of fifty years, receive an allowance of fourteen pence per week, eighteenpence of that sum being derived from funds left by the founder, and sixpence received from the parish: Watson's Hospital, founded in the year 1687, by Dr. Thomas Watson, Bishop of St. David's, where fourteen poor persons receive a stipend of one shilling and sixpence per week, (exclusive of the six pensioners belonging to the Trinity House:) Goe's Hospital, built about the year 1600, affords an asylum to ten poor aged women, and one shilling and twopence per week towards their support: Harrison's Hospital, built in 1548, yields one shilling and twopence per week to ten poor women: and a foundation of this nature situated in Dagger lane, bequeathed by a person of the name of Ratcliff, a weaver, endowed by Mr. Buttery, and augmented by the corporation, yields one shilling and sixpence a week to six poor men and women, with an annual supply of fuel which is common to all these minor hospitals.

The *Lying-in Charity,* established in the year 1802, extends its benefits to between three and four hundred poor married women annually, and from the time of its institution to the beginning of the year 1822, six thousand four hundred and twenty-two patients have been admitted, and given birth to six thousand four hundred and forty-one children. Mrs. Forbes, of Robinson row, is the matron of this excellent institution, and to her recommendations are sent,

The *Female Penitentiary*, situated in Portland place, established in 1811, has for its object to receive and employ, and ultimately to restore to society such women as, having followed vicious courses, are desirous of obtaining the means of reformation. From the opening of the Penitentiary to the beginning of the year 1822, 151 patients have been received into the house, of whom it is reported that ten left without leave, twenty-seven by permission, sixteen were dismissed, forty-one went to service, thirty-two were restored to their friends, seven were sent to the Infirmary, one died, four were married, and thirteen remained in the house. Mr. J. B. Briggs is the treasurer and honorary secretary; Miss Thorp is the matron, and Miss C. Thorp her assistant.

The *General Infirmary* may rank amongst the most important monuments raised to benevolence in the town of Hull. The want of a public hospital for the recovery of the sick and lame poor had for some years been apparent in this place, when a few charitable individuals assembled in the month of October, in the year 1781, and opened a subscription for erecting and supporting a house of mercy, where the skill of the ablest practitioners might be united to the advantages of pure air, and proper food and medicine in effecting the recovery of the objects of their bounty. A proposal so laudable could not fail to meet with supporters, and a sufficient fund was soon raised to furnish a house for a temporary infirmary till a suitable and more permanent building could be prepared. This temporary establishment was opened on the 26th of September, 1782. In the mean time a field of two acres, situated within a short distance from the town on the Beverley road, at the end of the street, now called Prospect street, was purchased at a cost of 550l. and buildings erected upon it which swelled the amount to 4,126l. The accommodation thus afforded allowed of the reception of seventy in-patients. In the construction of the building great attention was paid to the interior arrangement, and no hospital in the kingdom has a freer circulation of air or more complete provision in every respect, for the objects of its care. The principles of the establishment are the most liberal and humane: not only are all the distinctions of sect and party disregarded, but locality itself gives no peculiar privileges, and the recommendation of a governor, at all times easily obtained by a proper object, form a passport into the house, and a claim upon all its healing benefits, as well to the sick natives of the Ganges or the Nile, as to him who drew his first breath upon the Humber, and to none of them is

any recommendation whatever necessary, when the case does not admit of delay.— The average expenditure of this Infirmary is about 1400l. per annum, and the number of in-patients yearly 300, and the out-patients 800, exclusive of the vaccine cases. Since the first opening of the house, in 1782, to the first of January, 1822, no fewer than 22,656 patients have been admitted, of whom 17,279 have been cured, and 2,696 greatly relieved; and the total number of persons vaccinated here to the beginning of 1822 was 11,240. Three physicians and three surgeons give their attendance *gratis*. The Right Hon. Earl Fitzwilliam is the president; and Mr. J. Higson, the house surgeon, apothecary and secretary.

The *Dispensary*, for Hull and Sculcoates, situated in High street, near Scale-lane staith, was established on the 1st of September, in 1814, at an annual expense of 350l. and is supported by subscriptions, and other voluntary donations. Some estimate may be formed of the benefits of this institution when it is stated, that it now affords relief to about 2000 patients a year, and that, from the first opening of the establishment to the 5th of April in the present year, 14,540 patients have been admitted. Six surgeons are in attendance in turns, daily, *gratis*, and two physicians whenever their advice is required. The treasurer is J. C. Parker, Esq. and secretary W. Laverack.

There is at Sculcoates a Refuge for the Insane, established in the year 1814, by Dr. Alderson and Mr. Ellis, surgeon. It is now conducted by the former and Mr. Casson.— It is capable of containing from 80 to 90 patients; its present number from 50 to 60. The magistrates of the East Riding of this county direct all pauper lunatics to be placed here, having previously inspected the establishment and expressed their approbation of it, by which this part of the county was saved the expense of erecting a pauper lunatic asylum. A considerable portion of the place is set apart for the reception of private patients. It is surrounded by large gardens and apparently very convenient for the purposes intended.

A Dispensary for diseases of the eye and ear was instituted in 1822, at No. 55, Myton-gate, where patients, properly recommended, are admitted, from 10 to 12 o'clock every Tuesday and Friday. The surgeon of this institution is T. Buchanan, C. M.

The *Charity Hall* is a spacious and convenient structure, in Whitefriargate, for the reception of the poor of the parishes of the Holy Trinity and St. Mary's, in Hull. In the 9th and 10th of William III. an act of Parliament was obtained for erecting workhouses and houses of correction in Hull, for the better maintenance and employment of the poor; and under the authority of this act, the premises called the Charity-hall, formerly used as a cloth-hall, were purchased and appropriated to the purpose of a workhouse. The provisions of the original act were confirmed and extended by an act of the 9th of Anne, and by another act of the 15th and 28th of George II. by which the mayor, recorder, and aldermen for the time being, and twenty-four other persons, to be selected by the six wards, were constituted a corporation, to continue for ever within the said town, by the name of the governor, deputy-governor, assistants, and guardians of the poor, to have the care of them and to provide for their maintenance. The parochial expenditure of Hull has been subject to great fluctuations: from 1801 to 1806 it averaged ten thousand pounds per ann.; in 1813, it amounted to 17,680*l.*; in 1817 to 31,200*l.*: and from the second of February, 1821, to the second of February, 1822, to 16,279*l.* which sum includes the county rate of 1,197*l.* The average number of paupers in the house during the past year was 365, and the average cost of their support exclusive of clothing, about 3s. per head weekly. Sculcoates workhouse, situated in Wilson's row, Wincolmlee, is under the direction of a visitor and four guardians.

The *House of Correction*, which is a small plain building, situated in Fetter-lane, near the Market-place, receives criminals for misdemeanours, and debtors from the Court of Requests. The keeper is Henry Lee. The gaol, situated in Myton-place, is kept by Francis Coates, where prisoners are confined previously to their removal to the County gaol for trial. This prison was erected, pursuant to an act of parliament, obtained in 1783.

In Hull, as in most of the other towns of England, there are Free Schools, as well for the higher as for the more humble branches of learning. Amongst these the Free Grammar School, founded in the reign of Richard III. in the year 1486, by the Right Rev. John Alcock, a native of Beverley, and successively Lord Bishop of Rochester, Worcester, and Ely, takes its precedency. In 1579, the old structure being at that time in a ruinous state, William Gee, Esq. an alderman of Hull, opened a subscription for erecting a new school house, himself subscribing twenty thousand *bricks*, and eighty pounds in money for that purpose.— The erections were soon completed, and the school room, which is large and commo-

dious, is said to be one of the best in England. This school is open to all sons of burgesses, on the payment originally of 14s. then of 20s. and now of 40s. per annum, for classical instruction only—of which description of scholars there are none at present. Writing and arithmetic were introduced into this school by the present master, and are now taught at a charge of four guineas per annum, for free boys, and eight guineas for the sons of non-freemen. The number of scholars are, at present, only 10 free boys, and 14 other scholars. They are admitted at any age, and there is no prescribed time of superannuation. This school has one exhibition of 40*l.* per ann. to any college in Cambridge, founded by a person of the name of Barry, or Berry, and a scholarship, founded by Alexander Metcalf, of 12s. 9d. per week, and rooms at Clare hall. The present master is the Rev. George John Davies, A.M. and his emoluments are

| | £. | s. | d. |
|---|---|---|---|
| Salary paid by the Corporation out of trust land, | 63 | 0 | 0 |
| Paid by the King's receiver, | 13 | 2 | 2½ |
| Rent of a tenement adjoining the school, | 6 | 0 | 0 |
| Total, | £82 | 2 | 2½ |

The lectureship of the Holy Trinity has usually been enjoyed by the master of the Free School, though that is not the case at present. The masters of this school who have been distinguished are:—the Rev. Andrew Marvel, M.A. father of the renowned patriot of that name; John Catlyn, originally a bricklayer, but who, by the force of his genius and application, became a great proficient in the learned languages; Rev. John Clarke, M.A. the translator of Suetonius and Sallust, and the Rev. Joseph Milner, M.A. author of the History of the Church. Amongst the eminent men educated here, may be mentioned Andrew Marvel, M.P. for Hull; Thomas Watson, D.D. Bishop of St. David's; the Rev. William Mason, M.A. the poet; Isaac Milner, D. D. F. R. S. Dean of Carlisle; William Wilberforce, Esq. M. P.; the Rev. Francis Wrangham, M. A. F. R. S.; and the eloquent Archdeacon of Cleveland.

The *Vicar's School*, situated in Vicar Lane, was founded by the Rev. William Mason, father of the poet, in the year 1737, (in commemoration of the blessings of the revolution,) and it affords education to 54 boys, appointed by the vicar of Trinity Church for the time being; but the present vicar, with his usual liberality, rarely admits any, except such as are recommended by respectable inhabitants of the town, and whose parents are needy and industrious; in which way the school becomes in reality, more the property of the public, than it would have been had the right of nomination been vested in a committee. In addition to gratuitous instruction in reading, writing, and arithmetic, the scholars are provided with books, pens, and paper: and annual rewards are given to the meritorious. Mr. Stephen Gardham is the present master. The funds for the support of the school are supplied, partly by a collection made after a sermon preached at the parish church, on the first Sunday in December, and partly by the Corporation, who make up the deficiency.

The *Marine School*, in the Trinity house, instituted in the year 1786, where 36 boys are taught writing, arithmetic, and navigation, and are completely clothed every year, has already been mentioned. Of this school Mr. Michael Fulham is the present master.

*Cogan's Charity School*, situated on the south side of Salthouse lane, was founded by William Cogan, Esq. alderman, on the 2nd of July, 1753, for clothing and instructing 20 poor girls, who are allowed to remain in the school three years each. This school is placed under the direction of three trustees, being aldermen, who have the power to increase the number of scholars according to the increase in the funds, and so well have the affairs of this institution been administered, that on Whit-Monday, in the year 1822, the number of scholars was augmented from twenty to forty. The trustees at present are Joseph Egginton, Nicholas Sykes, and Christopher Bolton, Esqrs.— Mrs. Chapman is the schoolmistress.

Mr. Alderman Cogan bequeathed also a sum of money in the public funds, for the purpose of placing out poor boys as apprentices to mariners, handicrafts-men, and artizans, preference to be given to the sons of the freemen of Hull. The management of this excellent institution is in twelve trustees, who, in addition to the expenses of binding each apprentice, pay to his master 20s. a year for clothing, and at the expiration of the term, present the master with two pounds, and the apprentice with four pounds towards his outfit in life. The treasurers are Messrs. Smiths and Thompson, and the Secretary Mr. Marmaduke Thomas Pricket. This charity was founded in the year 1787.

The *Subscription Schools* in Hull, erected in 1806, at an expense of 3000l. are situated in Perrott street, Salthouse lane, and afford instruction to about 300 boys, and 170 girls, on the system of mutual instruction, at a cost of about 270l. per annum, which fund is supplied, partly by voluntary subscriptions, which amount to 110l. a year, partly by a payment of 1s. a quarter, made by the parents of the children, and the residue by the rent of vaults under the school room. Upwards of 5000 children have already received instruction in these schools, at an average expense of not quite 12s. a year. The schools are open to all denominations, every child being allowed to attend his particular place of worship, on a proper certificate being produced to the committee, which is open to all subscribers of one guinea per annum. The chairman is J. N. Crosse, Esq. and Avison Terry, Esq. is the treasurer. Mr. George Wilkinson, land surveyor, is the master of the boys' school, and Mrs. Sarah Pantry, the mistress of the girls' school.

The *Sunday Schools* of Hull are upon a large and liberal scale, and form themselves into two grand divisions, under the designation of " *The Church of England Sunday School Association;*" and " *The Sunday School Union,*" both formed in 1819. In the former of these it appears, from the report published in June, 1822, that 987 boys, and 991 girls, forming a total of 1978 scholars, receive instruction from 242 teachers; and in the union, which consists of the Sunday school scholars in fourteen Methodist and Dissenting congregations, 430 teachers give instruction to 1375 boys, and 1212 girls; the Union has also associated with it 35 Sunday schools in the circumjacent towns and villages, which swell their whole number of scholars to 5596, and the teachers to 1142. There are, besides in Hull, several other Sunday schools which are not in the Union.

The Societies here for the diffusion of religious knowledge are, the Bible Society; the Missionary Societies; the Religious Tract Society; and the Evangelical Society.

The *Auxiliary Bible Society* of Hull, was established in the year 1809, on the 25th of October, the day on which his late Majesty George III. entered the 50th year of his reign. The president of this institution is Earl Fitzwilliam, and the treasurer Avison Terry, Esq. The sum raised by the society and its associates is from 900l. to a 1000l. a year. Since the commencement of the Society, the sum of 9926l. has been remitted to the parent institution, and the remainder of the money collected applied in the dissemination of the holy scriptures within the circle of the society's own operations.

The *Missionary Societies* are, " *The Hull, Beverley, and East-Riding Church Missionary Association,*" established in 1814, of which Simon Horner, jun. Esq. is the treasurer, and the Rev. Thomas Dikes, and the Rev. John Scott the secretaries. The sum raised by this society is about 600*l.* per annum; and it has raised in all £5,500.—" *The Hull and East-Riding Auxiliary Missionary Society*," (in connection with the London Missionary Society,) established in 1815, of which Mr. William Briggs is treasurer, and the Rev. Joseph Gilbert and Mr. James Bowden the secretaries. " *The Methodist Missionary Society*," of Hull, Howden, Bridlington, Barton, Gainsbro', Grimsby, Driffield, Patrington, Snaith, and Brigg, established 1814, of which Thomas Thompson, Esq. is the treasurer; and the superintendant preacher, Mr. John North, Mr. Robert Garbutt, and Mr. Francis Reynalds, secretaries.—The sum raised by this society is nearly 500*l.* per annum. And the " *Baptist Auxiliary Missionary Society*," established in 1822, of which J. Thornton, Esq. is treasurer, and the Rev. T. Thonger, secretary. These societies raise, collectively, upwards of 2000*l.* a year for missionary purposes, from collections, donations, and annual subscriptions.

On the 28th September, 1819, an *Auxiliary Religious Tract Society* was established in this place, of whose publications Mr. George Turner, No. 65, Market-place, is the depository. The object of this society is to promote the distribution of tracts in the town and neighbourhood of Hull, and to advance the general purpose of the Religious Tract Society in London.

Allied to these institutions, is the *Hull Evangelical Society*, for promoting the gospel in Holderness, and in other neighbouring places. Of this institution, Mr. A. R. Rutherford is the treasurer; and the Rev. Joseph Gilbert, Mr. William Briggs, and Mr. W. F. Towers, the secretaries.

Another class of charitable institutions, seeking humbler objects, but well deserving of public support, is formed by the Educational Clothing Society, the Poor &Strangers' Friend Society, and the Humane Society.

The *Educational Clothing Society*, established in 1820, by the teachers and managers of the Sabbath School, connected with Fish-street chapel, has for its object to furnish the children of extremely poor parents with decent clothing, to enable them to attend Sunday schools; and we learn, from the report, that the society, though on a very limited scale, has already produced many beneficial effects.

The *Poor and Strangers' Friend Society*, established in the year 1795, seeks out and relieves those who have no other earthly helper. With the moderate funds of 220*l.*

per annum, six hundred poor families, in the very extremity of their distress, found relief; and as none are relieved till their situation is accurately ascertained, it is scarcely possible to imagine how the same sum of money could be applied in effecting a larger sum of good. The treasurers to this institution, which knows no distinction of nation, sect, or party, are Messrs. Smiths and Thompson; the stewards are Mr. Henry Green, and Mr. James Henwood; and the secretary Mr. Robert Bellby.

The *Humane Society* of Hull was established in the year 1800, and has for its president the Right Worshipful the Mayor, and for its patrons the principal authorities of the town; B. Crosley, M.B. is the physician; Mr. John Young the secretary and registrar. Mr. Young also fills the office of surgeon to the institution, which receives the gratuitous assistance of all the other surgeons in the town, when it is required.— Various sets of instruments, provided by the society, are placed in different situations in the town, the most contiguous to places where accidents are likely to occur. Rewards are given by the society to persons who contribute to restore animation, and no fewer than 334 cases claiming rewards, have already arisen, out of which one in six, or nearly in that proportion, has been unsuccessful. The directions given by the Royal Humane Society for restoring the apparently dead, will be found in the 56th page of this volume.

Akin to the Humane Society, is the establishment formed at Spurn, by the Trinity House of Hull, for the accommodation of the crew of a life boat, with which buoyant vehicle they are furnished, and the duty of the crew is to afford every assistance in their power to those ships and vessels in distress, which may stand in need of their aid. Mr. Robert Richardson, the present master of the life-boat, is invested with the full command of the boats' crew, which consists of eleven men, exclusive of the captain, and who all participate in the benefits, rewards, and emoluments, arising from the services of the boat.

The *Annuitant Society* of Hull, for the benefit of widows, orphans, and aged members, though not a charitable institution, is one of those provident associations, which, like benefit societies, of which there are here a considerable number, claim the public countenance. This society was first established by the Methodists of the New Connexion, for the members of their body, on the 1st of April, 1802, but it now admits persons of all religious denominations, under the restrictions and limitations prescribed by the rules.   Mr. Thomas Cassons is the president; Mr. Benjamin Clarkson, the treasurer; and Mr. S. Trumble, the steward.

The *Savings Bank* is held in Exchange buildings, Bowlalley lane, and was established in 1818.   This institution is proceeding prosperously, as the following statement, made up to the 30th of September, 1822, will serve to show :—

|  | £. | s. | d. |
|---|---|---|---|
| Amount of deposits to this date | 143,385 | 13 | 8 |
| Interest on deposits | 7,436 | 1 | 6 |
|  | 150,821 | 15 | 2 |
| Withdrawn | 65,527 | 3 | 7 |

Due to 2,122 depositors, £85,294 11 7 The patron of this institution is Thomas Thompson, Esq.; the mayor is the president; and Joseph Robinson Pease, George Liddell, James Kiero Watson, and Thomas Raikes, Esqrs- are the trustees: the secretary is Mr. George Carlill.

The commerce of Hull, that rich mine of wealth from which all her public institutions draw their main support, comes next under consideration.   So early as the time of Camden, we are told that Hull was famous for its trade and shipping, and it still holds the rank of one of the first commercial towns in the kingdom.   The commerce of this port divides itself into three leading branches: The coasting trade, of which it enjoys a greater share than any other port in England, London alone excepted;—the Baltic and Eastland trade, for which Hull is peculiarly well situated; and the Greenland fishery, which owes its revival half a century ago, and its subsequent, and now somewhat diminished consequence, to the mercantile enterprize of Hull.   Owing to the facility of communication with the great manufacturing districts of Yorkshire, Lancashire and Nottinghamshire, by means of the Aire and the Calder, the Ouse and the Trent, and by the canals communicating with them, the quantity of goods poured into this port from the interior is immense, and it is admitted that from the West Riding alone the manufactured goods, coal, stone, &c. yearly introduced into Hull, amount in value to at least five millions of pounds sterling.   The Baltic trade received a shock during the revolutionary wars from the anti-commercial decrees, and the hostile occupation of the ports of that sea which it has never completely recovered, but it is still very considerable, and will it is hoped, in time, recover its former importance.

Hull sent, until the present year, nearly three times as many ships to the whale fisheries of Greenland and Davis's Straits as London, and exclusive of the latter port,

more than all Great Britain besides.   The merchants of Hull were, originally in 1598, the first in England who fitted out ships for the whale fishery, but that trade had declined until the year 1765, when it was almost wholly monopolised by the Dutch, and was at that period reduced to such a languid condition that not more than twenty ships were employed in it from all England, of which ten were sent from London.   In the following year the active and enterprising spirit of Mr. Standidge, a merchant of Hull, induced him to equip and send out to the Greenland seas a ship on his own account—an adventure which was thought extremely hazardous, and of which individual speculation did not at that time afford an example in all Europe. This ship returned with one whale and four hundred seals.   Prior to this time the skins of seals were generally thrown overboard, not being considered of the intrinsic value of more than threepence each; but Mr. Standidge had them tanned into leather, and, in this way advanced their price to five shillings per skin.   Stimulated by his success he twice after visited Greenland himself, and prosecuted his commercial concerns with distinguished spirit both at home and abroad. The notion of exploring the regions of the North Pole was then, as now, very prevalent, and Mr. Standidge equipped a ship, and meant himself to embark in it upon that expedition, when he found that a legal impediment, arising out of his filling the office of sheriff of Hull, disabled him from leaving the country.   This disappointment, however, did not check the ardour of his commercial enterprise; he subsequently fitted out three ships for the Greenland sea, and his example diffused a spirit of emulation throughout the trading part of the community, so that vessels began to be fitted out yearly, not only from Hull, but also from Whitby, Newcastle, Liverpool and London, as well as from the principal ports of Scotland.

The following table, exhibiting the number of ships fitted out from this port during the last seven years, for Greenland and Davis' Straits, with the average product of whale oil per ship, will serve to show the state of the Fisheries :—

|  |  | Ships |  | Tons |
|---|---|---|---|---|
| 1816, | Greenland | 32 | average | 76 |
|  | Straits | 23 | | 110 |
| 1817, | Greenland | 29 | | 64 |
|  | Straits | 28 | | 82 |
| 1818, | Greenland | 31 | | 108 |
|  | Straits | 32 | | 90 |
| 1819, | Greenland | 35 | | 74 |
|  | Straits | 27 | | 91 |
| 1820, | Greenland | 37 | | 109 |
|  | Straits | 23 | | 163 |

1821 { Greenland......31..............86½
     { Straits.........22..............109
1822 { Greenland.....24.......... ...71½
     { Straits. ......16.................55½

The total number of vessels sent out to the Fisheries from the ports of England and Scotland, during the like period, with their total produce in oil and bone, is as follows:

|  | Oil Tons. | Bone Tons. |
|---|---|---|
| In 1816, 142 ships...... | 13,590 | 631 |
| 1817, 145............. | 10,871 | 539 |
| 1818, 155 ............ | 14,196.: | 666 |
| 1819, 147........... | 11,514 | 520 |
| 1820, 156............. | 18,725 | 902 |
| 1821, 145............. | 16,892 | 851 |
| 1822, 120............. | 8,000 | 350 |

Owing to the large quantity of fish oil produced, and the introduction of coal gas lights, oil of this description has, within the last few years, fallen from 46l. to 19l. per ton, a price far from remunerating the expenses.—It is the opinion of well-informed men that the Greenland Fishery has been greatly overdone, and has been productive of injury to the general trade of this port, by absorbing in undue proportion of capital from other branches of commerce. The Mediterranean and Leghorn trade, from the want of due cultivation, have here dwindled away into insignificance, and the American trade, that rich source of wealth to Liverpool, is in Hull of very limited extent. The West India trade has been attempted several times, but never established; and two or three vessels have sailed hence to the East Indies, without as yet producing any profitable returns.

The following is the gross amount of the customs at this port for the last 10 years:
In 1812...176,568l. In 1817...391,364l.
   1813 ..326,022l.    1818 ..512,996l.
   1814...405,598l.    1819 . 381,822l.
   1815...391,884l.    1820...401,401l.
   1816...340 967l.    1821 . 457,084l.
And the following the number of ships (British and Foreign) that entered inwards and cleared outwards from and to foreign parts, also of coasting vessels, for the last 7 years:

| Years. | Cargoes | | Ballast. | | Coasters. | |
|---|---|---|---|---|---|---|
|  | Inw. | Out. | Inw. | Out. | Inw. | Out. |
| 1815 .. | 719 | 270 | 29 | 214 | 2411 | 2335 |
| 1816 .. | 475 | 379 | 109 | 154 | 1994 | 2061 |
| 1817 .. | 824 | 409 | 41 | 302 | 2274 | 2628 |
| 1818 .. | 1425 | 413 | 18 | 697 | 2482 | 2306 |
| 1819 .. | 948 | 409 | 63 | 407 | 2470 | 2676 |
| 1820 .. | 744 | 352 | 74 | 306 | 2567 | 2692 |
| 1821 .. | 684 | 318 | 40 | 265 | 2828 | 2896 |

About 80,000 tons of shipping belong to the port of Hull, exclusive of many hundreds of small craft employed on the river Humber. Within the last ten years the export of cotton twist and of manufactured cottons, from this port, has prodigiously increased: in 1814, 7,330,000 pounds of cotton twist and 9,240,000 yards were exported from hence; this amount has been yearly augmented, and in 1820, 12,000,000 pounds of twist, and 50,600,000 yards of cotton, chiefly to Hamburgh, appear upon the list of exports in the custom-house books. In 1821 it was rather less, but this year it is more than any former one.

The Custom House is a very large and handsome edifice, in Whitefriargate, and nearly in the centre of the town. It was originally built by the Corporation of the Trinity House, for an inn, with a room for public entertainments, 52 feet long by 24 feet wide, and 22 feet high. This is now the long room for the transaction of the general official business of the custom house. The building also affords spacious and appropriate offices in every department, with extensive King's warehouses. The Collector for the port is Charles Lutwidge, Esq. and the established clerks in his office amount to eight. The Comptroller is Charles Roe, Esq. No. 12, Dock street. Attached to these departments are coast waiters, guagers, timber measurers, King's coopers, tide surveyors, a superintendant of quarantine, and a number of mariners; and dependent upon the custom house establishment are coast officers at Selby, Gainsbro', Stockwith, York, and Goole.

The Pilot Office, which is under the direction of commissioners, appointed by, and acting under, the Humber Pilot act, is well conducted, and the principal members of the corporation, a selection from the wardens of the Trinity house, and a respectable body of merchants, form the list of commissioners. The pilots attend the observatory by turns, from six in the morning to nine in the evening, from the vernal to the autumnal equinoxes, and the remainder of the year from nine in the morning to six in the evening. Mr. Francis Clifford is commodore of the pilots, and Mr. G. D. Thompson his clerk. The office consists of a modern lofty brick building, opposite the Ferry boat dock.

Nothing has more essentially contributed to the extension of commerce in Hull than the handsome and capacious docks with which this port is provided. For some years previous to the opening of the wet dock, which took place, Sept. 22, 1778, the average annual revenue derived to the state from the customs in this port, amounted to about 70,000l. it is now, as has just been seen, swelled to 437,684*l.* and though part of the increase is doubtless owing to the increased rate of duties imposed during the late war, yet, previously to that period, the augmentatin was in the proportion of more than two to one, as will appear from the following returns :—

Average of revenue derived annually from the customs of the port of Hull

From 1753 to 1763....*l.*£70,000
     1763 to 1773...... 80,000
     1773 to 1783...... 91,000
     1783 to 1793......149,000

The next ten years swell the average to about 250,000*l.* and the succeeding decennial period to about 300,000*l.* The last ten years has yielded an annual average of 376,572*l.*

The docks for shipping having thus tended so largely to the advantage of the port, constitute a prominent and interesting feature in the history of Hull. In the year 1774, a subscription was entered into at this place for making the wet dock on the north side of the town, now called the old dock, and an act of parliament was applied for and obtained for carrying the work into execution, by which act the share-holders were incorporated under the name of " The Dock Company of Kingston-upon-Hull;" by this act the military works surrounding the town were appropriated to the purpose of the intended dock, and a further aid of 15,000*l.* was voted by parliament towards its completion. The company proceeded with great spirit and alacrity in the work assigned to them; the first stone was laid on the 19th of October, 1775, and the whole undertaking was completed in the course of four years, though seven years was the time allowed by act of parliament. And on the 22d of Sept. 1778, the first ship, called the Manchester, a Greenland trader, sailed into the dock, which, when opened, was the largest in the kingdom, and is now exceeded only by those of London and by some of the recently formed docks of Liverpool. It extends in length about 600 yards, in width 85 yards, and is 23 feet deep, and nearly ten acres of land are occupied by the excavation. Originally the number of shares was 120, but the trade of the port requiring further accommodation, two other acts of parliament were obtained, the former in 1802 and the latter in 1805, by which the company was empowered to increase the number to 180; the money arising from the sixty additional shares amounted to 82,390*l.* which sum was appropriated towards making a new dock, called, " The Humber Dock," the first stone of which was laid on the 13th of April, 1807, and being completed at an expense of

220,000*l.* was opened on the 30th of June, 1809. The Humber Dock opens into the river from which it takes its name, by a lock, of excellent workmanship, large enough to admit a fifty gun ship, crossed by an iron bridge, in two parts, of very ingenious mechanism. This dock is 300 yards in length, 114 yards wide, and 29 feet deep.— The admeasurement of both the docks stands thus :—

| | | |
|---|---|---|
| Old Dock............9a. 3r. 29r. | | |
| Humber Dock......7a. 0a. 10r. | | |
| Total............16a. 3a. 39r. | | |

And they will contain six hundred sail of vessels. At present the two docks do not communicate, and although this object was always contemplated by extending the Humber dock northward to the extremity of Whitefriargate, which, when effected, would insulate the whole of the old town, and for which purpose the ground was given by the Crown ; yet every plan, for carrying into execution a junction of the present docks, so essential to the interests of the trade of the port, has hitherto proved abortive ; and the ground, appropriated for a middle dock, has recently been covered with buildings of a very inferior description, the income arising from which, if suffered to accumulate, would in time form a fund for effecting the proposed communication. The revenue of the Dock Company arises from certain duties on all ships entering the port. The present average value of each share is about 1000*l.* and the profits for the year ending the 2d of February, 1822, were 38*l.* 16s. yielding rather more than 3 per cent. interest upon the capital, which is somewhat below the usual annual average.

The following are the Dock Rates and Duties on Shipping :—

On every ship or vessel coming to and going from Hull, to any port to the northward of Yarmouth, or southward of the Holy Island, per ton...............2*d.*
From ditto to any port between the North Foreland and Shetland, east side of England, except as above, per ton, 3*d.*
From ditto to any port in Great Britain, not before described, per ton...............4*d.*
From ditto to any port in the Baltic and all ports above the Sound, per ton.....12*d.*
From ditto to any port in Denmark, Sweden, or Norway, below Elsinore, or any port in Germany, Holland, Flanders, France, to the eastward of Ushant, Ireland, the islands of Guernsey and Jersey, per ton..........................10*d.*
From ditto to any port westward of Ushant, without the Straits of Gibraltar, per ton ..................................15*d.*

From ditto to any port in the West Indies, North or South America, Greenland, any port eastward of North Cape and southward of Cape St. Vincent, per ton 21d.

For every Foreign ship or vessel coming to, or going with merchandise from any of the above named ports or places, double the rates of tonnage, or duties abovementioned, unless the said ships belong to British owners.

For every ship or vessel sailing coastwise or otherwise, and coming into the said haven in ballast, to be laid up (coasting duty included) per ton............6d.

*,* The hours of attendance at the Dock-office, from ten until three o'clock.

The office of Clerk to the Dock Company has been for many years filled by Mr. John Levett, and Mr. Peter Bennett is the dock master of the Old Dock, and Mr. John Dewear the master of the Humber Dock.

Besides these Wet Docks, there are here several dry docks for the convenience of repairing vessels, constructed with flood gates, to admit or exclude the water, as may best suit the convenience of the works carried on within them.

The *Excise Office* is situated in that part of Hull which has the voluminous name of The Land of Green Ginger; the offices are tolerably commodious, and this important branch of the public service is under the direction of William Cramp, Esq. the collector; Mr. Simpson Miller, of No. 6, Spencer street, is his first clerk. The office hours are from 9 o'clock in the morning to 3 o'clock in the afternoon.

Closely connected with the commercial interests are the Banking concerns, of which there are four in Hull; which, taken in alphabetical arrangement, stand thus—Harrison, Watson, and Locke, Whitefriargate, who draw upon Marryat, Kay, Price, and Coleman, 1, Mansion House Street, London; Pease and Liddell, No. 18, High street, who draw upon Pole, Thornton, Free, Down, and Scott, 1, Bartholomew lane, London; Raikes and Co. 19, Scalelane, who draw upon Curries, Raikes, and Co, No. 29, Cornhill, London; and Smiths and Thompson, 25, High street, who draw upon Smith, Payne, and Smiths, Mansion-House place, London.

The *Exchange* holds a respectable rank amongst the institutions of Hull.— Till the year 1794, the town was destitute of this important requisite for a commercial place; the building in the High street, erected by the merchants in 1619, as an Exchange and Custom house, and used by them for many years, having been neglected, and subsequently used wholly by the customs. The merchants of Hull are therefore under obligations to Mr. William Bell, by whose enterprise and public spirit this gratifying and beneficial medium of general intercourse and free communication was afforded. Over the Exchange is a News room. During the present year this establishment, which is supported by subscription,[a] has been greatly improved and ornamented, the Exchange Room is handsomely coloured in imitation of stone, and the News Room is supported by two fine Doric pillars, dividing the Exchange into two walks, which are entered by a handsome portico erected in front.

The manufactures of Hull are not so extensive and numerous as those in many of our inland towns; they are, however, by no means contemptible; amongst the principal of them is the expressing and refining of oil from linseed, and preparing the residue for feeding cattle; the process is chiefly effected by mills worked by wind, and the largest and finest mills in the kingdom of this kind, both for the above purpose and for grinding corn, are found in great numbers near this town. The mode of refining rape oil was brought to perfection by Dr. Daniel Bridges of Hull, who also invented the improved system of purifying spermaceti oil now practised here with great success. There is also a sugar house, (Messrs. Thornton, Watson, and Co.'s) on a large scale; an extensive soft and hard soap manufactory, (Messrs. Crosse and Co.'s) several white lead manufactories; numerous ship-builders' yards; turpentine and sail-cloth manufactories; and some large rope walks, which have, however, suffered considerably from the introduction of the chain cables; some large breweries claim a place in the list of manufactures, of which those enumerated above form but a small part.

Under the head of the trade of Hull may be arranged the Post-office and Stamp-office departments; the carriers and coaches; the markets and fairs; and the corn exchange and the shambles.

The *Post-Office* is situated in Bishop-lane, and Thomas Rodmell, Esq. is the post-master. The business of this branch of the public service, with its foreign and inland dependencies, is exhibited in detail at page 347-8 of this volume, so fully as to supersede the necessity of any further information on the subject here.

The *Stamp-Office* for the town and county of Hull and the East-Riding is at

[a] The annual subscription to the News Room is £1 11s. 6d. and to the Exchange, 15s. 6d.; gentlemen residing more than seven miles from Hull are admitted without charge for a month, on the introduction of a subscriber.

No. 2, Bowlalley-lane, and Robert Osborne, Esq. is the distributor; Mr. Wm. Dryden, attorney, is his deputy, and attendance is given at the office from 9 o'clock in the morning to 4 o'clock in the afternoon.

The conveyances to and from the different parts of the kingdom, both by waggon and coach, are detailed at considerable length at pages 349 and 354. The particulars of the vessels in the coasting trade will be found at pages 350-1, and copious information relating to the steam packets and the sailing packets is contained at pages 352-3, with the requisite details concerning the market-boats.

The chartered market days here are on Tuesday and Friday; and the annual fair on the 11th October.* There is also a market for vegetables and butchers' meat, held on the Saturday.

The *Corn Exchange* is situated in the Market place, on the north side of the Holy Trinity Church. The grain is sold by sample, and the corn market, which is well attended, is held on Tuesday; business commencing at one o'clock. Mr. John French is clerk of the market, and his residence is No. 12, Whitefriargate.

In the year 1806, the Guildhall, situated in the Market place, which had fallen into a state of dilapidation, was removed, and commodious and well ventilated shambles were erected on the site. The new erections are only partially occupied, partly because the accommodation they afford is more than the town at present requires, and partly because the rents are considered high. About 5600 beasts, 1100 calves, and 25,000 sheep and lambs are annually slaughtered here.

The *Waterworks* of Hull are situated at the east end of Waterhouse lane, and afford that great *desideratum* sought with so much earnestness and perseverance by our ancestors—an ample supply of fresh water. Prior to the year 1773, the works, which were established in 1616, were wrought by horses, but the water is now forced by means of a powerful steam-engine into the reservoir, and thence conveyed through pipes to the dwellings of the inhabitants in all the principal streets of the town. Mr. Anthony Atkinson, of No. 23, Albion street, is clerk of the works, and Mr. T. O. Atkinson, of No. 3, Portland place, the collector. One important advantage of the waterworks in a large commercial town arises from the facility they afford in case of accidental fires, and the authorities in this place, with a provident care for the lives and property of the inhabitants, have pro-

* Erroneously stated in the distance table accompanying the 1st vol. as on the 10th.

vided no fewer than a dozen fire-engines, one or more of which may be found in the engine-houses at the following stations:—

At the end of the Shambles in Blackfriargate

At Sculcoates hall, Jarratt street

In Church street, Sculcoates

At the Dock Office, entrance of Old Dock

At the Garrison

At the Custom House, Whitefriargate

At the Trinity house

At the Coach Manufactory, Carr lane

At the Sugar house, Lime st. North bridge

And at the Millwrights, Sykes street.

In a place giving and receiving so much support to and from the fisheries as Hull, it was to be supposed that every exertion would be made to introduce the practice of generating gas from oil instead of coal.— This experiment has been made under the authority of an act of parliament, passed in the year 1821, by which a gas company was instituted, and the result has hitherto proved satisfactory to the share-holders and to the consumers. The gas works are situated in Broadley street, and the consumers are supplied by the company with a meter, suited to their consumption, at a small annual charge. The street lamps are supplied with gas from the works, and a great number of the shopkeepers and other inhabitants avail themselves of this brilliant and economical light, which, reckoning the quantity of light evolved, it is calculated costs about one-third the price of candles.— a hundred cubic feet of gas, valued at from five to six shillings, yielding as much light as eighteen pounds of tallow candles. The company have just completed an Ionic pillar of cast iron, for the purpose of lighting the ships into the harbour. This pillar rises twenty feet from the ground to the top of the capital, and is surmounted with a smaller pillar, three feet six inches high, on the top of which is placed an hexagonal lantern, with an argand light and reflector six feet in height. It is to be hoped that a small annual contribution from each ship will be voluntarily made for the support of this useful beacon, which otherwise must be discontinued. Samuel Cooper, Esq. is the chairman of the committee, and Mr. Richard Witty, clerk of the works.

The government of Hull is vested in the body corporate, which consists of the Mayor, the Recorder, twelve Aldermen, the Sheriff, two Chamberlains, a Town Clerk, a Water Bailiff, and other officers, under a High Steward, who must be a nobleman of the Privy Council. The mayor is Admiral of the Humber, and is possessed of the power of life and death over convicts within his jurisdiction. The Right Honourable

Earl Fitzwilliam is the High Steward, and the following is a list of the Corporation for the years 1822-3.

### HULL CORPORATION.

Christopher Bolton, Esq. *Mayor.*

*Recorder*—Daniel Sykes, Esq. M. P.

*Aldermen*—William Osbourne, Wm. Watson Bolton, Joseph Eggington, William Jarratt, Edward Foster Coulson, Richard William Moxon, Nicholas Sykes, George Schonswar, Wm. Hall, John Carrick, Henry Thompson, and Charles Whitaker, Esqrs.

*Sheriff*—John Barkworth, Esq.

*Under Sheriff*—Mr. Robert Sandwith, 29, Bishop lane.

*Chamberlains*—Mr. Thomas Firbank, and Mr. William Bolton.

*Water Bailiff*—Charles Roe, Esq. 12, Dock street.

*Agent to the Corporation*—P. W. Price, Esq.

*Town Clerk*—Edward Codd, Esq. 6, Parliament street.

*Deputy*—Mr. George Bramwell, 48, Osborne street.

*Town's Husband*—Mr. William Bolton, 22, High street.

*Sword Bearer*—Mr. Samuel Doyle, 18, Waterhouse lane.

*Mace Bearer*—Mr. Robert Bamford, 6, Broadley square.

*White Mace Bearer*—Mr. Philip Ward, Holderness road.

*Serjeant at Mace*—Mr. Francis Stamp, 4, Broadley street.

No place in the kingdom perhaps is able to produce more testimonies of royal regard than the town of Hull. Since its first charter, in the 27th year of the reign of Edward I. its privileges and immunities have been granted, confirmed, or enlarged by no fewer than nineteen different charters, extending over a period of nearly four hundred years.

Myton lordship is under the direction of commissioners established by an act passed in 1810, who regulate coal-porters, street drainage, &c. and Sculcoates has a local act of a similar nature, passed in 1801.

The parliamentary history of the borough of Hull is singular and interesting:—formerly the burgesses chose their representatives out of their own order, and allowed them, while engaged in the performance of their public duties, a sum which was at that time thought sufficient to support the state of a gentleman. Matters however in the lapse of a few ages, greatly altered, for instead of receiving three or four shillings a day, by way of support, from their constituents, members sometimes give large

sums to their constituents for the honour of representing them. In the year 1818, the number of free burgesses polled amounted to 2143, and a large proportion of the voters expect (though of course they do not receive, as such a proceeding would be in violation of the laws against bribery and corruption) two guineas each for a split vote, or four guineas for a plumper. The right of election is derived either from being born the son of a burgess, from having served seven years apprenticeship to a burgess, from purchase, or from donation for public service, of which honour the corporation have been very sparing, although the conferring of it upon individuals of public spirit and character has been proposed, and would be beneficial to the town. But a very small portion of inhabitants in the upper, or even in the middle classes of society, enjoy the elective franchise in this borough, though wealth, which will always confer influence, is not without its effect on the elections. The present representatives for Hull are, John Mitchell, Esq. of 35, Wimpole street, London; and Daniel Sykes, Esq. of Raywell, near Hull, the present Recorder.

The courts of law in Hull are, the Court of Requests, originally established in 1761, for the recovery of small debts, not amounting to forty shillings, but by an act in 1808, extended to five pounds, of which Mr. John Alderson is the clerk; the Sheriff's Court, held twice a year, within a month after Easter, and a month after Michaelmas, but its proceedings have become almost obsolete; and the County Court, for holding pleas of *replegiarum*. The Court of *Venire*, for determining civil causes, has a jurisdiction extending to the town and county of Hull, and sums can be recovered exceeding forty shillings: this court is held before the mayor, the Recorder, and the Sheriff, and the rules and practice of the court resemble those of the Court of King's Bench. Mr. Edw. Codd is the Prothonotary.

Formerly the assizes for the town and county of Hull were held in this place, sometimes septennially, and at other times triennially, or annually, when capital punishments were inflicted; but the infrequency of these gaol deliveries became an evil of so great a magnitude, that an arrangement was made for the more speedy administration of justice; and civil suits, capital offences, and misdemeanours are now removable to the assizes at York, on the application of either of the parties, which application always takes place. The last assize held in Hull was on the 31st of July, 1794, and the last public execution in the summer of 1778. The Quarter Sessions of the peace are held at the regular periods in the Guild Hall, where the business of the other courts is also transacted.

The places of public amusement in Hull are the Theatre Royal and the Olympic Circus, both in Humber street. The theatre is quite a new building, having been only completed as recently as 1809; it is decidedly one of the handsomest, and since the improvements made by Mr. Mansel, in 1821, one of the most convenient provincial theatres in the kingdom. It is erected upon what was formerly designated the Fore-shore, over which the tide washed twice in twenty-four hours; the industry and skill of man having rescued a large portion of this ground from the visitation of the river Humber. The house is calculated to accommodate an audience to the amount of nearly three hundred pounds, at the usual rate of admission: namely, boxes, 4s.; pit, 2s.; first gallery, 1s. 6d.; upper gallery, 1s. The Assembly Rooms, in Dagger lane, having been disused for three or four years, a house has been purchased in North street, by a party of gentlemen, who intend converting it into an assembly room, with apartments attached for billiards, a club room, &c.

The inhabitants of Hull enjoy the inestimable advantage of a good public Subscription Library, which was first instituted on the 6th of Dec. 1775, but the foundation stone of the present building, in Parliament street, was not laid till the 21st of June, 1800. The library possesses a spacious reading room, which is open to the subscribers, amounting to four hundred and seventy-five in number, every day; and the collection of books, which comprises above fifteen thousand volumes, is said to be the most extensive between the Humber and the Tweed. Great facilities have been afforded to the consultation of books in this library, by an excellently classified catalogue recently published. The subscription is 25s. per annum, yielding a gross revenue, with other contingencies, of about 700l. a year. The concerns of the institution are managed by a committee of twenty-one, chosen yearly, and John Broadley, Esq. F. S. A. is the president; John Crosse, Esq. F. S. A. the treasurer; and Mr. Thomas English, the librarian. There is also a Subscription Library, at No. 5, in the Market place, established in 1807, on a similar plan to the above, consisting of nearly 200 members, whose annual subscription is 12s. 6d. each; of this library Mr. James Henwood is the president; Mr. Wm. Baron the treasurer; and Mr. George Turner the librarian. The most ancient library in Hull is that held in a room on the south side of the choir of the Holy Trinity church, which was formerly used as a chapel, but has since the year 1669 being appropriated to its present purpose; and which, in addition to many ancient theological works, contains a number of modern publications in divinity.

A Literary and Philosophical Society is in the course of formation, with a museum attached to it, for which several articles have already been collected together.

There are three weekly newspapers here: the Hull Packet, established June 5, 1787, printed by Mr. Richard Allanson, 36, Scale lane, and published on Monday in the afternoon; the Hull Advertiser, established July 5, 1794, printed by Mr. Isaac Wilson, 49, Lowgate, and published on Friday in the afternoon; and the Hull Rockingham, established January, 2, 1808, printed and published by Mr. Wm. Ross, 9, Bowlalley lane, on Saturday in the afternoon. The two former of these publications support the Tory, and the latter the Whig principles of government.

The first state of civilised society is indicated by an attention to agriculture, the second to horticulture, and the last to botany. The two former are decidedly the most important, and the last is the more refined and scientific. A few, and only a few, of the cities and towns of England, can boast of their botanic garden, and Hull is one of that number. This elegant institution was commenced in July 1811, and opened to the subscribers on the 3d of June following. The garden is situated about a mile from the centre of the town, on the Anlaby road, at the bottom of an intended new street, appropriately named Linnæus street, and comprehends about five statute acres of land. At the entrance are two lodges—one for the dwelling of the curator, and the other, (in which a Botanic library is forming,) for the use of the committee. The ground is laid out with great skill, and ample room has been left for one specimen at least of every tree, shrub, and hardy plant in the kingdom, as well as for a vast number of exotics. There is here a bog compartment in the highest perfection, another for alpine plants, and an aquarium thirty yards in length. The garden is the property of three hundred subscribers, holders of five hundred and fifty transferable five guinea shares, bearing interest, and subject to a subscription of a guinea and a half per annum. The merit of originating this establishment, and of bringing it to its present state of advancement, is, in a considerable degree, due to Dr. John Alderson, the president, and to the other officers of the institution. The garden has, from its commencement, been under the superintendence of Mr. William Donn, who still discharges the duties of curator much to the satisfaction of its patrons and friends.

Freemasonry, like Botanic science, thrives amazingly in Hull, but all that it is permitted us to say of the former is that there are here two numerous lodges, the Minerva and the Phœnix. The Rodney Lodge, which possessed an elegant and commodious room, has been dissolved; and concerts and other public meetings are held in the present, till an assembly room is provided.

The *Hull Medical and Chirurgical Society*, is a recent establishment instituted on the 1st of February, 1821, of which John Alderson, M.D. is president; Alexander Turnbull, M.D. vice-president; and Thomas Beckwith, C.M. secretary and treasurer.—This society consists of about thirty members, and meets regularly every fortnight on Thursday at 8 o'clock in this evening, to read essays and discuss medical news. Their library already contains nearly one hundred preparations, and is kept in the Hall No. 53, High street.

The *Public Baths* here are kept by Mr. Peter Remsley, at the Bath Tavern, on the Humber bank; and by Mr. George Malcolm, also on the Humber bank. By an improved mode of filtration the water is raised without dilution from the bed of the river, and visitors are accommodated with the use of the water in either a hot, cold or tepid state.—There are also vapour and shower baths.

Mendicity has been considerably checked in almost all the great towns in the kingdom, and imposition and crime diminished, by the institution of Vagrant Offices. The Vagrant Office of Hull was established by a meeting of the inhabitants, held at the Guildhall, on the 1st of February, 1819, this office is situated at No. 9, Quay street, and Mr. Andrew Daniel is the officer under whose superintendence it is placed.

Having thus sketched with a rapid, but it is hoped with a faithful hand, the History of Hull from its earliest foundation to the present time; having enumerated and detailed its public edifices and multitudinous institutions; having dwelt without prolixity, but not without precision, upon its trade, its commerce, and its manufactures, we come in conclusion to describe the town as it was in times past, and as it exists at the present day. The vicissitudes to which this town and port have been subjected have been already pretty fully detailed. For many ages, indeed for several centuries, the town of Hull was confined between the Humber to the south, the Hull to the east, and the town's wall to the north and west. Beyond these limits all is new; and so late as the year 1640, the number of streets in this place amounted only to from thirty to forty. What is their present number will be seen

from the list subjoined to this history, which by way of contrast is introduced by an enumeration of those which existed at the period just referred to. In the ancient buildings in the town little regard appears to have been paid to elegance or regularity; convenience alone was the object of the proprietors, and to that point principally the skill of the architect was directed. A flourishing and extended commerce, with gradually increasing wealth, at length introduced a taste, if not for magnificence, at least for elegance and public accommodation. The town as it now stands is well built, principally of brick, most of the streets are well paved, and in the new parts, to the north and to the west, they are spacious and commodious. From the year 1322, when it was first surrounded with fortifications, the town of Kingston-upon-Hull, and from its strength and situation established as an impregnable fortress; and the wide ditches with the frowning walls and embattled towers overlooking the adjacent country presented a formidable aspect, emitting ideas of hostility and danger. These symbols of war have happily disappeared within the last forty years. Towards the close of the last century the ditches were filled up; and the ramparts and walls which had long been useless and ruinous, were finally levelled to promote the convenience of the inhabitants. Hull therefore is now an open town, and instead of those formidable bulwarks which displayed the menacing apparatus of war, it presents, on every side, docks filled with merchant ships, the vehicles of commerce and the emblems of peace. From an accurate admeasurement taken before the military works were demolished, it appears that the walls of Hull were two thousand six hundred and ten yards in circuit, being thirty yards less than a mile and a half. Of the whole of these works of defence two of the three fortresses built by Henry VIII. alone remain. They are guarded by several batteries and modern erections, on the east bank of the river, intended for the defence of the town and harbour, and form magazines capable of containing twenty thousand stand of arms, and ordnance stores for twelve or fifteen sail of the line, defended by a regular garrison. The post of governor of this town is generally bestowed on some officer of high rank, and Lord Hill, the present governor, succeeded the Duke of Richmond.

The intervention of the docks which occupy the greater part of the space where the walls formerly stood, separates Hull into three principal divisions, and nearly insulates the old town, which forms the first division. On the north side of the old dock is the parish of Sculcoates; all its buildings having been erected within the last thirty years, and they now constitute several spacious and handsome streets; a neat hall has been built here for the administration of justice and other public purposes, this part of the town being in the county of York, and not under the jurisdiction of the magistrates of Hull. The third and last division has arisen still more recently, and lies to the west of the Humber dock, occupying the situation of the ancient hamlet of Myton, by which name it is now distinguished, and is included in the county of the town of Hull. A suburb has also lately sprung up on the Holderness side of the river, in the parishes of Drypool and Sutton, encompassing the garrison, and connected with the town by a bridge of four arches, with a draw bridge in the centre wide enough to admit the largest vessel that has to pass through it.

The population of Hull has increased at the rate of about 15 per cent. during the last twenty years. In 1801, the aggregate number of inhabitants was 27,502, in 1811, that number was swelled to 32,944; and by the last returns to 39,073.

The following is the Population return of 1821, including the suburbs:—

POPULATION OF HULL IN 1821.

|  | Males. | Females. | Total. |
|---|---|---|---|
| North | 1585 | 1445 | 3030 |
| First Trinity | 691 | 791 | 1482 |
| Second Trinity | 436 | 582 | 1018 |
| Austin | 1440 | 1528 | 2968 |
| Humber | 1577 | 1854 | 3431 |
| St. Mary's | 1412 | 1884 | 3296 |
| Whitefriar | 1100 | 1393 | 2493 |
| N. Myton | 2153 | 2731 | 4884 |
| S. Myton | 2700 | 3322 | 6022 |
| Sculcoates | 4502 | 5947 | 10449 |
| Making the total for Hull | 17595 | 21477 | 39073 |
| Drypool | 650 | 745 | 1395 |
| Sutton & Stoneferry | 423 | 461 | 884 |
| Witham & Groves | 1309 | 1465 | 2774 |
| Southcoates | 366 | 432 | 798 |
| Total | 20344 | 24580 | 44924 |

The mortality of the place is rather below than above the usual average, which may be taken at one in thirty. Here the average is one in thirty-three, while in London it is one in twenty.

The eminent men born in, or closely connected with Hull, are quite as numerous as in most other places. Passing over the De la Poles and coming nearer to our own times, we find Admiral Sir John Lawson, who fought and died for his country on the 2d of June 1665, and to whom Hull and Scar-

borough make joint pretensions. Andrew Marvel, the friend and colleague of Milton; at the time of his birth his father was the rector of Winestead near Patrington in the East Riding, and the baptism of his son is entered in the parish register of that place, on the last day of March 1621, in his father's hand writing.* Having received the rudiments of his classical education in the Free Grammar School at Hull, of which his father was then master, he was sent to Cambridge, and pursued his studies at Trinity College. He afterwards made the tour of Europe, and was secretary to the embassy at Constantinople in the time of the Commonwealth. His first appearance in public business at home was to assist John Milton, Latin secretary to the Protector. In 1658, two years before the Restoration, he was elected member for Hull, and during the twenty years that he represented this borough in parliament, he maintained the character of an honest man, a true patriot, and an incorruptible senator. He is recorded as the last member of parliament who received the wages anciently paid to members by their constituents. His integrity rendered him obnoxious to a corrupt court, which spared no pains to seduce him from his fidelity and to obtain the powerful influence of his name and character for their measures. Many instances are adduced of his heroic firmness in resisting the alluring offers made to win him over to the court party, one of which may suffice as an example: The King, Charles II. sought by the fascination of his own company to attach to him the patriot, and one morning after having on the preceding evening given Marvel an entertainment, he dispatched the Lord Treasurer, Danby, to his lodgings which were on a second floor in a court in the Strand. The courtier owing to the narrowness of the stairs fell into the room where he found the patriot at his desk. After apologizing for the abruptness of his entry, his lordship said that he came on a message from the King, who wished to do Mr. Marvel some signal service to testify his high opinion of his merits.

Mr. Marvel expressed himself highly sensible of this mark of his sovereign's affection, but declined to accept any place in his Majesty's service; alleging, that if after having done so he should vote against the wishes of his ministers, he might be deemed guilty of ingratitude, and if he voted with them, he might do injustice to his country and to his conscience; he therefore begged that his Majesty would allow him to enjoy a state of liberty, and to esteem him his

* It has been generally but erroneously supposed that Mr. Marvel was born at Hull.

faithful and dutiful subject. The Royal offer of a place under the government having proved vain, Lord Danby begged to assure Mr. Marvel that the King had ordered him a thousand guineas, which he hoped he would be pleased to receive, till he could bring his mind to accept something better and more durable. At this Mr. Marvel, with his usual smile, said that his means were equal to his wants. His apartments he said were sufficiently commodious, and as for his living it was plentiful and wholesome; as he would prove to his lordship, then calling to his servant, he said—Pray what had I to dinner yesterday?—"A shoulder of mutton, Sir," was the reply "And what do you allow me to-day," continued the master?—"The remainder hashed," replied the servant, and withdrew. "And to-morrow, my Lord," said Mr. Marvel, "I shall have the blade bone broiled; and when your lordship makes honourable mention of my cook and diet, I am sure his Majesty will be too wise in future to attempt to bribe a man with golden apples, who lives so well on the viands of his native country!" Many other instances might be adduced of his heroic firmness, which would have done honour to Fabricius or Cincinnatus. Mr. Marvel was eminent as a poet as well as a senator; and his satires against the vices of the age, which did not spare majesty itself, and which lashed Dr. Parker, the Bishop of Oxford, into phrensy, are very well known. The general tendency of his works was against popery and arbitrary power, which were then too closely allied; and his memorable assertions, which the records of history have since abundantly established, that the Dutch war, entered into by Charles II. was owing to the corruption of the court, and that the French were the leaders of our councils, establish his claim to political sagacity, as well as to undaunted firmness. The death of this distinguished patriot, which took place on the 16th August, 1678, was sudden and unexpected; nearly up to the hour of his dissolution he was in full health and vigour, and there is but too much reason to believe that he died by poison, administered by some murderous hand, but by whom and for what reason will now probably remain for ever unexplained. The corporation of Hull, in gratitude for his services, voted the sum of 50l. to defray the expenses of his funeral, and contributed a sum of money to erect a monument over his remains in the Church of St. Giles in the Fields, London, where he was interred, but the minister of that church forbad the monument to be erected,

and the inscription was never placed there which recorded that "he was a man so endowed by nature, so improved by education, study, and travel, so consummate by experience, that joining the most peculiar grace of wit and learning, with a singular penetration and strength of judgment, and exercising all these with unalterable steadiness in the ways of virtue, he became the ornament and the example of his age;—beloved by good men, feared by bad, and admired by all; though imitated, alas! by few, and scarcely paralleled by any."

Thomas Watson, D. D. the unfortunate Bishop of St. David's, was born at North Ferriby, near Hull, in the year 1637. He founded the hospital at Hull, which is still called by his name, and entertained the intention of liberally endowing it, but his misfortunes overtook him before that intention could be fulfilled, and he fell, partly the victim of his own violence, and partly of the violence of the times in which he lived.

Hull has also given birth to several other persons of distinction, amongst these may be mentioned Dr. Thomas Johnson, the physician, &c.; the Rev. Wm. Mason, the poet, precentor of York, who was born at the vicarage; William Wilberforce, Esq. the senator and philanthropist; and William Porden, Esq. the architect. We may also mention several living gentlemen of literary talent: Charles Frost, Esq. F.S.A. author of some tracts on legal subjects; John Crosse, Esq. F.S.A. and John Broadley, Esq. F.S.A. the unostentatious but efficient promoters of every object of literature and science connected with their native town and county; and A. H. Haworth, Esq. F.L.S. author of Lepidoptera Britannica, &c. Wm Spence, Esq. F.L.S. author of tracts on Political Economy, and an introduction to Entomology; Thomas Thompson. Esq. F.S.A. author of tracts on the Poor Laws, and on the antiquities of this district; and P. W. Watson, Esq. the author of Dendrologia Britannica, are all natives of the neighbourhood and residents in Hull. Nor ought the venerable name of the late vicar, the Rev. Joseph Milner, M. A. the author of "The History of the Church," to be passed over in an account of that town with which his memory is so nearly associated.

Hull does not at present give title to any noble family. Robert de Pierrepont, who was created by Charles I. Baron Pierrepont and Viscount Newark, was made Earl of Kingston-upon-Hull in 1628; and Evelyn, 4th Earl, was advanced to be Duke of Kingston, in 1715; on the death of whose grandson, William, the second Duke, in 1772, all the titles became extinct.

# List of Streets, &c. in Hull.

## IN 1640.

| | | | | |
|---|---|---|---|---|
| Beverley gate | Corn market | Hornsey stairs | Old ferry | The Lowgate |
| Bishop stairs | Dagger lane | Horse stairs | Postern gate st. | The Ropery |
| Blackfriargate | Denton lane | Hutchinson lane | Salter lane | Vicar lane |
| Blanket row | Finkell street | King's stairs | Salter stairs | Whitefriar gate |
| Brewer lane | Fruit market | Myton gate | Sebole lane | Whitefriar lane |
| Chapel lane | Herring stairs | Myton gate st. | Schole lane st. | White meat markt |
| Chapel stairs | High street | North gate | | |

## IN 1822.

Adelphi court, George yard, 17, Lowgate
Air street, Church street, Sculcoates
Albany court, 17, Finkle street
Albion place, Naylor's row, Witham
Albion street, Bond street
Albion street, Mews, Bond street
Aldbro' street, 5, Katharine street
Alfred street, Humber bank
Atlass alley, 22, Trippet
Atlass gallery, 20, Trippet
Altofts yard, 50, Scott's street
Anlaby road, N. W. from Carr lane
Ann street, 3, Robert street
Ann street, Newton street
Ann's court, 20, Spencer street
Apollo court, Marvel street, Drypool
Appleton's court, Charlotte street
Atkinson's court, 50, Blanket row
Back square, Humber street
Back walls, St. John street
Baines' court, 13, Ordovas place
Baker's entry, 12, Mill street
Baker street, 1, New Brook street
Bambrough court, 31, West street
Bank's court, 37, Blackfriargate
Bank's court, Dagger lane
Bank's place, 13, Sykes street
Barker's court, 40, Blanket row
Barker's court, 1, Spencer street
Barker's entry, 116, High street
Barnaid's square, 13, Sykes street
Bartlett's buildings, 31, Church lane
Bean's court, 30, Blanket row
Bean's gallery, Wincolmlee
Beast market, New John street
Bellamy's square, 32, Mill street
Belshaw's yard, 48, West street
Belt's place, 5, Blanket row
Berridge court, 9, Aldbro' street
Beverley road, 46, Prospect street
Beverley street, Prospect street
Bielby's square, 11, North street
Bilton's court, 3, Machell street
Bishop lane, 29, Lowgate
Blackfriargate, 10, Queen street
Blackfriargate alleys, 27, Blackfriargate
Blanket row, 9, Queen street
Blanket row court, 37, Blanket row
Blaydes' staith, 8, High street
Bloomsbury square, 47, Dock street
Blue Bell entry, 107, High street
Blue Bell entry, 17, Waterworks street
Boalk's yard, Green lane, Drypool
Bond street, George street
Bores' entry, 1, Trippet street
Botelar street, 4, Cannon street

Boulton's square, Whitefriargate
Bourne street, 9, North street
Bowlalley lane, 16, Lowgate
Bowlby's place, 2, Aldbro' street
Bowling green court, 5, Mill street
Brazil gardens, Patrick ground lane
Bricklebank's square, Hodgson's street
Bridge street, N. E. end of Old Dock
Broad entry, 36, Scale lane
Broadley's entry, 39, Humber street
Broadley's square, 8, Manor alley
Broadley street, Manor alley
Brook street, 19, Prospect street
Brook street square, 27, Brook street
Brown's square, 27, Scott street
Bryant's entry, High street
Builder's court, 28, Scale lane
Burden street, 77, West street
Burke's entry, Market place
Burnham's yard, 33, West street
Burton's street, 18, Great Passage street
Caley's court, 6, Trippet street
Cannon place, Gibson street
Cannon place, 1, Cannon street
Cannon street, 3, Foundry
Capes lane, Great Union street
Carr lane, 39, Waterhouse lane
Carr street, 44, Scott street
Cartwright place, 1, Spring bank
Castle row, 2, Myton place
Castle street, New Dock bridge
Carlisle street, 19, Chariot street
Caroline street, Worship street
Catherine square, Mason street
Catterson's entry, 34, Lowgate
Cent per cent street, Pottery
Chafer's alley, Witham
Chapel court, 79, West street
Chapel court, George yard
Chapel court, 15, Salthouse lane
Chapel lane, 36, Blanket row
Chapel lane, 25, Lowgate
Chapel lane, Castle street
Chapel place, 21, Scott street
Chapel street, 1, Paragon street
Chariot street, 10, Waterworks street
Charles court, 15, Wincolmlee
Charles square, 1, Mason street
Charles street, 14, Jarratt street
Charlotte street, North side Old Dock
Charlotte street, Mews, back of Charlotte
  street
Charter house lane, 29, Trippet
Church lane, 17, Market place
Church street, 36, Wincolmlee
Heighley's court, 3, Prospect street

Church street, Drypool
Clappison's square, 23, Sykes street
Clarence court, 2, Princess street
Clark's square, 22, Sykes street
Clark's yard, 7, Carr lane
Clarkson's square, 24, Silver street
Clean Alley, Witham
Cleveland street, Lime street
Cliff's square, Hodgson street
Cockpit yard, 7, Castle street
Colley's entry, 14, Mytongate
Colton's square, 24, New George street
Commerce lane, Edgar street
Commercial buildings, 29, 30, High st.
Commercial court, 195, High street
Conduit street, Worship street
Constable's buildings, 11, English street
Cook's buildings, 16, Bowlalley lane
Corn market, North side Trinity church
Cottage row, Anlaby road
Cross street, 59, West street
Cross's yard, Myton place
Crown court, 4, Dock street
Cumberland street, 18, Church street
Cutsworth's entry, 4, Dock street
Dagger lane, 48, Mytongate
Daltry's entry, 30, Mytongate
Daltry's square, Mytongate
Damaris square, Garden street
Dawson lane or Mill lane, end of Witham
Darley's court, 9, New George street
Darley's square, 15, New George street
Dawson's court, 16, Wincolmlee
Deighton's entry, 185, High street
De la Pole court, 6, Manor street
Dent's row, English street
Derby court, 23, Scott street
Dibb's yard, 30, North street
Dickin's entry, 6, Grimsby lane
Dickson's entry, Mytongate
Discount court, 6, Cent per cent street
Dixon's court, Blue Bell entry, 107, High street
Dixon's entry, 14, Lowgate
Dixon's square, Fetter lane
Dock office row, 40, Bridge street
Dock street, 27, Bridge street
Dennor's entry, 2, Blanket row
Drewer's entry, 129, High street
Drewer's entry, 129, High street
Dryden's entry, 49, Salthouse lane
Drypool, over the North bridge
Drypool green, Drypool
Drypool square, Great Union street
Ducket's yard, 136, High street
Duke street, 1, South side Old Dock
Duke street, Hanover square
Duncan's court, Silver street
Duncan's place, 13, Manor street
Duncan street, Jennings street
Dunn's court, Witham
Dyer's place, 4, Wells street
East street, Church street, Drypool
Eaton street, Lowgate
Edgar street, Cent per cent street
Edward's place, Love lane
Elephant & Castle entry, 37, Mytongate
Elizabeth's square, Great Union street
Elliott's gallery, 10, Milk street
Engine street, 36, Waterworks street
English street, Pottery
Etherington place, 7, Prospect street
Etherington square, 37, High street

Exchange alley, 19, Bowlalley lane, and 49, Lowgate
Exchange buildings, Exchange alley
Exmouth buildings, 52, Humber street
Farrow's entry, Whitefriargate
Fawcett's court, 18, Fawcett street
Fawcett street, 10, Great Passage street
Featherston's entry, 178, High street
Fetter lane, 35, Market place
Finkle place, 18, Finkle street
Finkle street, 16, Mytongate
Fish shamble alley, Blackfriargate alley
Fish street, 67, Mytongate
Fish street court, 14, Fish street
Fishwick's yard, 11, Waterworks street
Foster's square, 6, Wilson's row, Wincolmlee
Foster's yard, Whitefriargate
Foundry row, Cannon street
Fountain's square, Hodgson street
Fox street, 25, Bond street
Foy's square, Grimsby lane
Free Masons' Lodge yard, 34, Mytongate
Friends' burial ground, Hodgson street
Gallows lane, Anlaby road
Garden Cottage row, Great Passage st.
Garden passage, Castle row
Garden place, Hodgson street
Garden place, 24, Sykes street
Garden place, Church street, Drypool
Garden place, Raikes street
Garden square, 9, Princess street
Garden street, 21, Brook street
Garrison side, North bridge
Gell's court, 11, Middle street
George's place, 14, Mytongate
George's place, 14, Dock street
George's place, 12, Lower Union street
George street, 27, Savile street
George yard, 17, Lowgate
Gibson's square, 18, Brook street
Gibson's square, 22, English street
Gibson street, 2, Botelar street, Foundry
Gibson's yard, 43, Carr lane
Gibson's yard, Lime street
Globe entry, 182, High street
Goodwin's square, 39, West street
Graham's row, St. Quintin's place
Granby square, Pig alley
Grantham's entry, Dagger lane
Great passage street, 2, Myton place
Great Union street, Drypool
Green lane, 3, Church st. Wincolmlee
Green lane, end of Church st. Drypool
Green's court, 10, Machell street
Grimsby lane, 27, Market place
Grimsby lane alley, 9, Grimsby lane
Grimsby lane court, 27, Grimsby lane
Grimston court, 20, Savile street
Grimston street, 25, Dock street
Grotto square, 10, Mason street
Groves, Lime street
Hackman's square, Katharine street
Hale's entry, 12, Market place
Hanover square, 66, Lowgate
Harcourt street, Great Union street
Hardy's court, 15, Posterngate
Hardman's entry, 18, Chapel lane
Hardy's yard, 4, North street
Harewood place, 21, English street
Hatters' alley, New Dock walls
Hatters' square, 13, Queen street
Hawthorn court, 4, Fawcett street

Mellard's yard, Green lane, Drypool
Henry's square, 33, Lower Union street
Herdsman's place, 14, English street
Hewett's entry, 44, Whitefriargate
Hewett's yard, 46, Whitefriargate
Hickson's yard, Castle street
High street, West side river Hull
Higson's court, 39, Blanket row
Hill's court, 17, Princess street
Hill's court, 8, Machell street
Hipponas court, 12, Spencer street
Hitching's court, English street
Hodgson's square, 16, Sykes street
Hodgson street, Lime street
Holderness road, Witham
Holdsworth's entry, 54, Salthouse lane
Holland's yard, 65, Church street, Wincolmlee
Holland's yard, 25, Mill street
Holmes' court, 12, Blackfriargate
Hood street, Jennings street
Hope street, 8, Chariot street
Horner's square, 23, Humber street
Hospital entry, Whitefriargate
Hospital yard, 12, Chapel lane
Hudson's entry, 53, Mytongate
Humber bank, West side of New Dock
Humber street, Queen street
Humble's school entry, 159, High street
Hutchinson's court, 12, Ordovas place
Hyperion street, Great Union street
Irish court, 38, Scott street
Irvin's court, 12, Roper's row
Jackson's court, 3, Posterngate
Jackson street, Neptune street
James' court, 18, Waterhouse lane
James' place, 2, Mason street
Jarratt street, Grimston street
Jarvis square, 29, Bridge street
Jarvis street, Jennings street
Jefferson's passage, 31, Waterhouse lane
Jennings street, Lime street
John street, Church street, Drypool
John street, Neptune street
John's court, Osborne street
John's place, 18, Osborne street
Johnson's court, 156, High street
Johnson's court, 14, Princess street
Johnson's square, 7, New George street
Johnson's yard, 1, New George street
Johnson's yard, 31, North street
Joiners' court, 3, Mill street
Joseph's court, 13, Lower Union street
Katharine square, 4, Mason street
Katharine street, 19, Machell street
Keeling's entry, 84, Mytongate
Kelsey's court, 20, West street
Kelsor's entry, Dock street
Kidd's entry, 16, Chariot street
King's court, 126, High street
King's place, 19, Dock street
King street, 14, North side Trinity church
Kingston court, 19, Blanket row
Kingston court, 19, Church street
Kingston square, Jarratt street
Kingston street, 13, Church street, Wincolmlee
Kirkus's buildings, 65, Lowgate
Knowles' square, 30, Spencer street
Lady's passage, 23, Scott street
Lamp black alley, Witham
Land of green ginger, 17, Silver street
Lawson's court, 19, Wincolmlee

Leadenhall square, 62, Lowgate
Leadmill entry, Whitefriargate
Leak's court, 19, Garden street
Leek's buildings, 2, Mill street
Leek's square, 12, Trippet street
Lee's entry, 193, High street
Lee's entry, 3, Lower Union street
Lee's gallery, Waltham street
Lee's row, 24, Milk street
Lee's square, 2, Great Passage street
Lever's place, West street
Levitt's court, 19, Ordovas place
Levitt's square, Hodgson street
Lewis square, Upper Union street
Lime street, over the North bridge, 6
Lincoln street, Wapping
Lingard's court, 5, South side Old Dock
Linnæus street, Anlaby road
Little lane, 10, Blackfriargate
Little Passage street, 6, Providence
Locke's court, 21, Humber street
Lock's entry, Humber street
Long entry, 48, Salthouse lane
Love lane, 1, Great Passage street
Low church alleys, 26, Lowgate
Lower Union street, Great Passage st
Lowgate, 17, North end of Market pl
Lowther's square, 45, West street
Mabb's entry, 165, High street
Machell square, 23, Machell street
Machell street, 21, Wincolmlee
Malt kiln entry, 8, Trinity house lane
Manor alley, Lowgate
Manor square, Manor alley
Manor street, 12, Bowlalleylane
Marine row, 29, Great Passage street
Mariner's square, 13, Sykes street
Market place, Queen street to Lowgate
Marvel court, Marvel street
Marvel place, 17, Mason street
Marvel square, 30, English street
Marvel square, Marvel street
Marvel street, Raikes street
Mary's square, 19, Lower Union street
Mary's square, 56, West street
Mary's square, 30, New George street
Mason place, 1, Mason street
Mason street, 4, Bourne street
Mechanic lane, 27, Edgar street
Medley's entry, 5, Machell street
Medley's square, Great Union street
Mews street, Bond street
Middle street, 4, Cross street
Milk street, 1, Mews street
Mill court, Prospect street
Mill court, 17, Princess street
Mill court, 21, Machell street
Mill court, 36, New George street
Mill hill, 1, Prospect street
Mill lane, Garden cottage row
Mill square, 9, Beverley road
Mill street, 4, Burdon street
Milton's square, 24, Bourne street
Mitchell's court, 35, Aldbro' street
Moira buildings, 58, Prospect street
Mulgrave street, 17, Aldbro' street
Myton court, 17, Chariot street
Mytongate, 33, Market place
Myton place, Castle street
Myton square, Passage street
Myton street, 19, Castle street
Naylor's row, Holderness road
Nelson square, 6, New George street

Slater's court, 42, West street
Sleight's court, 6, Salthouse lane
Smith's court, 52, West street
Snell's entry, 123, High street
Snuff Mill entry, 1, Machell street
Somerstown, Holderness road
Southcoates, Holderness road
South end, 46, Humber street
South end Battery, 51, Humber street
South side Trinity church, Market place
South street, Carr lane
Southern's court, 154, High street
Spencer street, 39, Prospect street
Spread Eagle entry, Market place
Spring bank, end of Prospect street
Spring garden, South end of Gallows lane
Spring row, Prospect street
Spring street, 4, Spring bank
Stable yard, 52, Salthouse lane
Staniforth place, Patrick ground lane
Steeple's entry, 125, High street
Stephenson's gallery, 8, Chariot street
Stephneson's yard, 5, Chariot street
Stepney place, Beverley road
Stewart's yard, 152, High street
St. John's square, Chapel street
St. John's street, 3, Whitefriargate
St. John's street, Church street, Drypool
St. Mark's square, English street
St. Peter's street, Alcot street
St. Quintin's place, Church street, Drypool
Storey street, 59, Prospect street
Strawberry garden, Church st. Drypool
Stubbin street, Church street, Drypool
Stubb's court, 16, West street
Stubbs' square, West street
Summergangs, Holderness road
Sydney square, 19, Bourne st. Trippet
Sykes street, 9, Charter house lane
Temple's court, 5, Love lane
Temple's entry, 139, High street
Temple's yard, High street
Terrington's entry, 6, Blanket row
Theatre court, 21, Finkle street
Thompson's court, Hodgson street
Thornham's square, Blanket row
Thornton's square, 25, Posterngate
Thornton street, Great Union street
Thring's entry, 26, Wincolmlee
Todd's entry, 21, Silver street
Todd's entry, 6, Salthouse lane
Trafalgar square, 34, Wincolmlee
Trinity house lane, 14, Silver street
Trippet, Bridge street
Trippet street, 27, Bridge street
Tripp's court, 3, Paradise row
Trundle street, 17, Waterhouse lane
Tuke's court, 17, Roper's row
Turner's court, 4, Aldbro' st, Sculcoates
Turner's square, 37, West street
Union court, 15, Roper's row
Union square, 59, West street
Union square, 18, Milk street
Union square, 42, Spencer street
Union square, 14, New George street
Union street, 32, Albion street
Upper Harcourt street, St. Peter's street

Upper Union ct. top of Great Passage st.
Upper Union street, 1, Great Passage st.
Valentine court, 6, Robinson row
Vicar lane, 88, Mytongate
Vine court, 166, High street
Vine court, end of Botelar st. Foundry
Walker's court, 9, Waltham street
Walker's entry, Whitefriargate
Walker's entry, 8, Bond street
Walker's entry, Posterngate
Walker's square, 19, Sykes street
Waltham's entry, 32, Mytongate
Waltham street, 27, Chariot street
Walton's court, 4, Scott street
Walton's court, 28, Wincolmlee
Walton's row, Hodgson street
Want's square, 3, New George street
Wapping, 4, North end of Wincolmlee
Wardman's entry, 18, Chapel lane
Ward's court, 37, Whitefriargate
Ward's entry, 51, Mytongate
Waterhouse lane, 3, Engine street
Waterworks street, 1, St. John's street
Watson's entry, Alfred street
Webster's entry, 156, High street
Webster's yard, 5, New George street
Wellington place, Beverley road
Wellington street, Queen street
Wells street, 25, Waterworks street
Wentworth street, Church st. Drypool
Westerdale's entry, 45, Salthouse lane
West parade, Anlaby road
West's court, Silver street
West street, 9, Carlisle street
West street court, 41, West street
Whitefriargate, 14, Silver street
White Hart entry, 25, Silver street
White Horse yard, Market place
Whitham's yard, 10, Market place
Whiting's square, 38, Garden street
Williams' court, 3, Paradise row
Williams' square, New George street
Williams' square, 6, Mason street
Williams' square, 6, Upper Union street
Wilmington, Cleveland street, Groves
Wilson street, Church street, Drypool
Wilson's court, 40, Dock street
Wilson's row, Church street, Wincolmlee
Wilson's square, Wilson's row
Wincolmlee, 29, North end of Trippet
Winter's alley, 8, Land of green ginger
Witham, over North bridge
Witherwick's yard, 29, North street, Prospect street
Witty's square, 6, Trippet street
Woodle's entry, 17, Carr lane
Wood street, 23, Jennings street
Wood's court, 41, Dock street
Wood's entry, 18, Carr lane
Wood's entry, High street
Wood's square, South street
Woolf's entry, 4, Lowgate
Woolpack entry, 35, Mytongate
Worship street, Grimston street
Wright street, 58, Prospect street
York parade, Beverley road
York street, 3, Albion street
Yucatan place, 9, Osborne street

In order to introduce as great a body of information as possible into each page, Contractions are sometimes used; but they are such as, it is hoped, will be perfectly intelligible.

Abbey Geo. bricklayer, 12, Page's square, Dagger lane

Abbey Thos. shoemaker, 12, Silver st.

Abbey Wm. whitesmith, 85, Bridge st.

Abbey John, lighterman, 1, Stable yard, 52, Salthouse lane

Abbott Charles, victualler, Horse and Jockey, 3, Garden street

Abbott Wm. cooper, 12, Machell st.

Abbott Geo. 16, Blanket row

Abraham Edw. gent. 17, Fish street

Abraham Phineas, silversmith, jeweller, &c. 22, Paradise place

Abraham John, baker, 17, Fish street

Acrid Robert, vict. Crown & Anchor, 28, Humber street

Acrid Thos. rope maker, 86, High st.

Acton Ann, shopkpr. 39, Humber st.

Adam Edw. grocer, 2, Waterworks st.

Adam Peter, vict. Neptune, 161, High st.

Adams Elizabeth, gentlewoman, 8, Clarence court, Princess street

Adams Thos. farmer, 13, English st.

Adamson Wm. tailor, 26, Bridge st.

Adamson John, builder, 16, Aldbro' st.

Adamson Ann, lodging house, 4, Upper Union street

Adamson Margaret, 16, Newton's court, Machell street

Addock John, whip maker, 10, St. Mark's square, English street

Adland Christ. baker, 21, Dagger ln.

Agar Thomas, schoolmaster, Bore's entry; house, 1, Broadley street

Agar John, hair dresser, 19, Church ln.

Ainley Wm. shopkeeper, Jensing's st.

Ainsworth John, shoemkr. 4, Church ln.

Airey Wm. pipe maker, Myton court, 17, Chariot street

Aire Robt. shoemaker, 15, Worship st.

Aislabie and Jackson, grocers and tea dealers, 12, Market place

Ake and Witty, joiners and builders, 18, Trippet street

Ake William, joiner, &c. 11, Regent's square, Sykes street

Akid Wm. mariner, 1, Park place

Akister Robt. ship carpenter, 14, Winter's alley, Land of Green ginger

Alcock Geo. joiner & builder, Parade row; house, 4, Myton place

Alcock John, shopkpr. 6, Prospect st.

Alcock Wm. joiner, Myton street

Alders and Hansell, merchants, corn factors and cheesemongers, 66, High street

Alders Geo. sen. corn factor; house, 12, Prospect street

Alders Geo. jun. corn merchant; h. 6, Dock street

Alderson John, M. D. 4, Charlotte st.

Alderson John, solicitor, 36, Salthouse lane; house, 4, Charlotte street

Alderson Ralph Carr, Lieut. Royal Engineers, South end battery

Alderson John, vict. Butcher's Arms, 6, Shambles square

Alexander George, dealer in watches, plate and jewellery, 6, Vicar lane

Alexander Francis, straw platter, 12, Wincolmlee

Allanson Richard, printer & publisher of the Hull Packet, (Monday) & patent medicine warehouse, 36, Scale lane

Allen W. S. bookseller, stationer, binder, and circulating library, 24, St. John street

Allen John, gent. 21, Mill street

Allen Thos. shoemaker, 19, George yd.

Allen and Hunton, sail makers, Broadley street

Allen Charles, shopkpr. 28, Saville st.

Allen John, mariner, Horner square, 23, Humber street

Allen John, mariner, Thornton street

Allen Robert, pilot, Wellington street

Allen John, mariner, New row, Anlaby road

Alley Thomas, painter, 23, Bourne street; house, 14, Trippet street

Allinson Mark, porter merchant, 16, Dock side

Allinson Joseph, vict. Shakespeare Tavern, (steam packet house) 68, Humber street

Allinson Wm. wire worker & drawer, flour machine mkr. &c. 5, Low gt.

Z

Allison Francis, mariner; 5, Princess row, Dock street

Alsop James, woollen draper, &c. 48, Market place

Amery Wm. victualler, Fleece Inn, 197, High street

Amos Mrs. Maria, 58, Carr lane

Amott George, surveyor of customs ; house, *Sutton*

Anderson John, attorney, 27, Bishop lane ; house, 25, Charlotte street

Anderson James, ship owner, 23, Story street

Anderson Mrs. Lucy, 11, Portland pl.

Anderson John, mariner, 22, West st.

Anderson John, mariner, 17, Osborne st.

Anderson Geo. custom house locker, 21, Bridge street

Anderson James, custom house officer, 1, Carr lane

Anderson Jas. banker's clerk, Story st.

Andrew Wm. linen draper, &c. 17, Whitefriargate

Andrew Mrs. Elizabeth, 9, Mason st.

Andrew Mrs. Elizabeth, 31, Albion st.

Andrew Eliz. flour seller, Manor alley

Andrew Richard, hair dresser and perfumer, 28, Scale lane

Andrew Jas. shoemkr. 3, Trundle st.

Anfield Wm. gent. 1, George yard

Anfield Wm. butcher, Market place ; house, 8, Prince street

Anfield Christopher, butcher, Great Union street

Anfield John, baker, 20, Waterworks street

Anfield Thomas, custom house boatman, Great Union street

Angel James, block maker, North side old dock ; house, 1, Mason street

Angus Jas. mariner, New George st.

Annison Wm. day school, Trippet

Ansdell Jas. mariner, 18, Hanover sq.

Ansdell Jas. pawnbroker, 18, Scott st.

Appleby John, whitesmith and bellhanger, 16, King street

Appleby William, whitesmith & bellhanger, 136, High street

Appleby Rd. shopkpr. Great Union st.

Appleton John, pawnbroker, 169, High street

Appleton and Vickerman, plumbers, glaziers, & wholesale & retail dlrs. in glass & lead, 38, Savile street

Appleton Wm. hat mfr. 28, Savile st.

Appleton Wm. baker, 19, North st.

Appleyard William, pawnbroker, New John street

Appleyard Mary, pawnbroker, and clothes broker, 21, Mytongate

Appleyard Geo. draper & slop seller, 38, Mytongate

Appleyard Frank, bricklayer & brick maker, 2, Manor street

Appleyard John, joiner & builder, Waterhouse lane ; h. 17, Robinson row

Archibald Ann, 16, Scale lane

Armatage Jonathan, butcher, 24, Great Passage street

Armit Wm. wheelwright, 32, Savile st.

Armistead Miss Catherine, Wellington lodge, Beverley road

Armitage Jane, milliner, &c. 17, Scott st.

Armstrong Wm. druggist, apothecary, & tallow chandler, 29 & 43, Lowgate

Armstrong Thos. tailor, 12, George's place, Lower Union street

Arnett John, baker, 9, Gt. Passage st.

Arnett John, baker, 2, Prospect street

Arnett Wm. baker, 145, High street

Arnold Benj. gent. Raikes street

Arthur Thos. butcher, 31, Salthouse ln.

Arton Mary, schoolmistress, 21, Fawcett street

Arundel Geo. shopkpr. 25, Scale lane

Ash John, coal merchant, 9, Princess court, Princess street

Ash Robert, mariner, 28, West street

Ashley George, tailor, Parade row

Ashton John, butcher, 1, Shambles ; house, 5, Myton street

Ashton William, vict. Black Horse, 42, Blackfriargate

Ashton Frances, milliner and dress maker, 1, Edgar street

Ashton Thomas, 1, Edgar street

Askew, Johnson, & Todd, fishmongers, 13, Queen street

Askwith Joshua, pipe maker, 96, Blanket row

Astrop Henry and John, rag, rope, & paper merchants, 68, High street

Astrop John, paper merchant ; house, 27, Salthouse lane

Astrop Henry, paper merchant. ; house, Myton cottage, Patrick ground ln.

Astrough Christ. corn miller, Mill ln.

Astrough Thos. corn miller, Mill ln.

Atkin John, mast block & pump mkr. 84, North side Old Dock ; house, 27, Charlotte street

Atkin Thomas, sail maker, 31, High street ; house, Upper Union st.

Atkin Jas. currier, &c. 24, Mytongate

Atkin James, mariner, 11, William's square, Mason street

Atkin Peter, gent. 12, Charles street

Atkin Mary, midwife, 1, William's court, Paradise row

Atkin William, gentleman, 20, North street, Prospect street

Atkin Ann, stocking grafter, 82, Mytongate

Atkinson Anthony, merchant, brick & tile mfr. & manager of the waterworks, Dairy coates ; house, 22, Albion street

Atkinson T. O. agent to the Norwich Union Fire office, Waterworks st. house, 3, Portland place

Atkinson James, gent. 7, South street

Atkinson Susannah, gentlewoman, Patrick ground lane

Atkinson Wm. butcher, 8, Alfred st.

Atkinson Wm. furniture broker, 4, New Dock street

Atkinson William, music seller, 42, Whitefriargate

Atkinson William, landing waiter, 3, Spring bank

Atkinson Ralph, shipwright, 12, Great Union street

Atkinson Thomas, pork butcher, 4, New Dock street

Atkinson Jas. coal mercht. Duncan st.

Atkinson Mrs. Eliz. 1, Bourne street

Atkinson Mrs. Mary, lodging house, 4, Waltham street

Atkinson John, 53, Mill street

Atkinson Thos. farmer, White house, Anlaby road

Atkinson Emma, shopkpr. 107, High st.

Atkinson Benj. mariner, 16, Savile row

Atkinson John, trunk maker, 5, North court, North street

Atkinson Thomas, trunk maker, 4, Hodgson's square, Sykes street

Atkinson Thos. dyer, Duncan place

Attridge James, broker, Grimsby lane court

Audus John, vict. Old Dock Tavern, 6, North side Old Dock

Ayre Joseph, M. D. 25, George street

Backhouse Rd. auctioneer & general agent; house, 10, Waltham st.

Backhouse Jane, shopkpr. Jennings st.

Backwell Joseph, brass founder, 12, Upper Union street

Bagley John, shoemkr. 42, Savile st.

Bailes Jonathan, tide waiter, 3, Catherine street

Bailey Francis, vict. Nelson Tavern, Great Union street

Bailey Wm. shopkpr. 36, Lower Union street

Bailey Eliz. tea dlr. 18, Prospect st.

Bailey John, exporter of horses, 8, Wright street

Bailey Thos. pawnbroker, 8, Scott's square, Blanket row

Bailey Geo. wheelwright, Witham

Bailey Wm. baker, 15, Cook's court, Broadley street

Bailey John, merchant's clerk, Edward's place, Love lane

Bailey Marmaduke, hackney sawyer, North side Old Dock

Bailey John, cowkeeper, Witham

Bailey Wm. traveller, 13, Charter hs. ln.

Baines Robert Raines, patent log mfr. and baker, Wincolmlee

Baines David, timber mercht. Humber st.; house, 98, High st.

Baines Mary, gentlewoman, 1, Hutchinson's court, Ordovas place

Baines Richd. butcher, 21, English st.

Baker Susannah, gentlewoman, 18, Savile street

Baker Eliz. grocer, &c. Witham

Baldwin Christ. mariner, 34, Charlot st.

Balk John, shopkeeper, 2, Trippet st.

Ball William, stocking weaver, 27, Wincolmlee

Bambrough Robert, bricklayer, 9, Castle row

Bamford Robt. mace bearer, collector of taxes and billet master, 6, Broadley square

Bancroft Miss Eliz. 24, George street

Banks John, vict. Bull & Sun Inn, 1, Mytongate

Banks William, coach maker, Parade row; house 35, St. John st.

Banks Matthew Colliford, brazier and tin plate worker, 11, North walls

Banks W. C. cooper, Jarvis street

Banks Wm. H. gent. 24, Prospect st.

Banks Geo. mariner, 10, Page's sq. Dagger lane

Bardhard Mrs. Ann, 16, New George st.

Barclay Wm. cooper, 114, High st.

Barker Hannah and Sons, bricklayers, 26, Savile street

Barker James, builder, 2, Engine st.

Barker Rd. currier, &c. 32, Lowgate

Barker John, victualler, Nag's Head, *Summergangs*

Barker Robert, baker & confectioner, 49, Mytongate

Barker James, bricklayer, 10, New John street

Barker James, painter, 10, Trippet

Barker Geo. flax dresser, 140, High st.

Barker Geo. cooper, Witham, 16 and 22, Trippet; house, Sculcoates

Barker Mrs. Ann, 7, North street

Barker Geo. baker and confectioner, 42, Bridge street

Barker Marmaduke, baker, 22, Blackfriargate

Barker Mrs. Mary, 72, Lowgate

Barker Wm. baker, 15, Church street, Drypool

Barker John, millwright, Graham's row, St. Quintin's place

Barker Wm. butcher, 20, Nile street

Barker Mark, shoemkr. 41, Church ln.

Barker Wm. shoemaker, Lime st.

Barker Wm. cooper, 114, High st.

Barkworth and Spaldin, timber merchants, Dock street

Barley John, fishmonger, Queen st.

Barmby Thos. corn factor, 42, Bridge street; house, *Sutton*

Barnard John, gent. 13, Sykes st.

Barnard Sarah, clothes broker, 131, High street
Barnard Jas. gardener, 65, Prospect st.
Barnby Robert, black beer brewer, 8, Grimston street
Barnby Jas. shoemkr. Summergangs.
Barnby Bishop, jeweller, 7, Paradise place
Barnby Jonathan, boot & shoemaker, 14, Scule lane
Barnby William, merchant's clerk, Edward's place, Love lane
Barnes Wm. ship builder, 52, Church street, Sculcoates
Barnes Wm. vict. King's Head, 94, Mytongate
Barnes Thos. shopkeeper, 7, Scott st.
Barnett Thos. grocer, 4, Trippet
Barnett Joseph, tin plate worker, 16, Mill street
Barnett John, gent. 13, Sykes street
Baron Cornwall, merchant's clerk, Cent per cent street
Baron Edward, clerk of customs, 48, Spencer street
Baron Thos. mariner, 3, Finkle place, 18, Finkle street
Barrett John, smith and boiler maker, Humber bank ; h. Roper's row
Barrett Wm. Smith, gent's day school, Great Union street ; h. Hodgson street
Barrett John, schoolmaster, Hanover square
Barrick Wm. basket maker, 6, Blackfriargate
Barrow Robert, cowkeeper, Drypool square
Barrowby Sarah, milliner, 3, North court, 19, North street
Barry Wm. printer, 16, New Dock side
Bartle John, miller & ship biscuit baker, 49, Whitefriargate
Bartlett Robert, cork mfr. 12, Church lane
Bartlett Wm. cooper, 137, High st.
Barthorp Wm. gent. 4, Cannon st.
Barton Mrs. Ann, 28, Salthouse lane
Baskett Rev. Kingsman, M.A. 6, Charter house lane
Baskett John, baker, &c. 8, Mytongt.
Bassingdale John, vict. Founder's Arms, Drain bank
Bastow Wm. S. chemist & druggist, 2, Carlisle street
Bateman John A. searcher of customs, 1, Spring street
Bateman Robert, gent. 2, Winters alley, Land of Green ginger
Bates John, whitesmith, Parade row
Battle Robert Grey, writing ink and blacking mfr. 16, Paradise place
Batty Isaac, cornfactor, Lime st. ; h. Witham

Baxter John and Son, corn merchants, 5, Wright street
Baxter John, vict. Durham Ox, 4, Blanket row
Beach Mrs. Jane, 18, Nile street
Beach Jeconiah, hat mfr. 9, Winter's alley, Land of Green Ginger
Beach Robert, painter, 51, Salthouse lane
Beadle John and Co. general merchts. and ship owners, 8, Dock walls
Beadle John, underwriter and ship owner ; house, 14, Albion st.
Beadle James, grocer, &c. 25, Waterworks street
Beadling Wm. mariner, 12, Sykes st.
Beaman John, brazier and tin plate worker, 50, Blackfriargate
Beaumont Robert, tide waiter, 3, John's street
Bean Robert, merchant's clerk, 42, Humber street
Beatie Jesse, gentlewoman, Mill ln.
Beck John, vict. Blue Ball, 12, Blackfriargate alley
Beck Wm. baker, 3, Cannon st.
Beckett Wm. bone merchant, 160, High st. ; h. Holderness road
Beckett Robert, flour dealer, 35, Spencer street
Beckwith Margaret, straw hat mfr. 20, Chariot street
Bedell Edward Watson, attorney, 19, George street
Bedell Benj. landing surveyor, Charles street
Bedell Percival, landing waiter, 19, George street
Bedell Peter, watch and clock maker, North bridge
Bedingfield Miss, 1, Cent per cent st.
Bedford Colley, tailor, Crown court, Dock street
Beecroft Thos. tailor, 41, Spencer st.
Beecroft John, cowkeeper, Alfred st.
Beecroft Samuel, farmer, Pesthouse ln.
Beedle John, gent. Witham
Beeforth Ann, shopkeeper, 1, Bourne street
Beet Matthew, joiner, Queen st.
Beetson Robert, painter, 51, Salthouse lane
Beetson John, tailor, 3, Dryden's entry, 49, Salthouse lane
Beever John, barrack master, Strawberry gardens, Drypool
Bee Joseph, timber measurer, Humber bank
Beharrel Robert, livery stable keeper, 7, Princess st. Princess st
Bell Robert, surgeon, 3, Saville st.
Bell Thomas, wax & sperm chandler, & oil merchant, 58, Wincolmlee
Bell Wm. gent; house, 1, English st.

Bell John, merchant, 6, High st.; h. 12, Albion street

Bell Thomas, general and commercial agent, Commercial buildings, 29, High st.

Bell George, cork manufacturer, 40, Scale lane

Bell John and Robert, coopers, 172 & 173, High st.

Bell Michael, tin plate worker, 58, Whitefriargate

Bell Robert, whitesmith, bellhanger, and wire worker, Myton st.

Bell Wm. bookseller and periodical agent, 5, Queen street

Bell John Francis, ship owner, 28, Mason st.

Bell John, landing waiter, 30, North street

Bell Mrs. Ann, 12, Albion st.

Bell Wm. gent. 32, Dock st.

Bell Mrs. Rachel, gentlewoman, 37, Church st.

Bell Mrs. Elizabeth, 6, Engine st.

Bell Mrs. Margaret, 8, Savile st.

Bell Robert, gent. 19, Charlotte st.

Bell Jeremiah, tide waiter, Church st. Drypool

Bell Abraham, tailor, 10, New John st.

Bell Wm. lumper, 3, Page's sq. Dagger lane

Bell Robert, custom house officer, Locke's court, 21, Humber st.

Bell Robert, shoemaker, 13, Ordovas place

Bellamy John, vict. Ship, 3, Church lane

Bellard Robert, tailor and woollen draper, 3, Dock office row

Bellard John, shoemaker, Charles ct. 15, Wincolmlee

Bellas A. B. brazier, 9, Blackfriargate

Bellerby Godfrey, tailor, 19, Chariot st.

Bellshaw John, bacon factor, &c. 30, West st.

Bellshaw W. bacon factor, &c. 14, Wincolmlee

Bellwood Mrs. Jane, ship owner, 7, York parade, Beverley road

Bellwood Henry, foreman, New Dock sheds, 70, West st.

Belt Robert, tailor and draper, 12, Grimsby lane

Bennett Thos. excise port surveyor, 14, Princess st.

Bennet Thos. clothes broker, 4, Wincolmlee

Bennett Peter, old dock and harbour master, 19, West st.

Bennett John, mariner, 3, Jarratt st.

Bennison Appleton, architect and builder, 2, Baker st.

Bennison Wm. vict. Windmill, 14, Trinity house lane

Benson John, vict. Board, 5, Stewart's yd. High st.

Benson John, shoemaker, 15, Dryden's entry, 49, Saltbouse lane

Bentley Thos. baker, 157, High st.

Berridge Edward, bread and ship biscuit baker, 11, Mytongate

Berridge Samuel, shopkeeper, 17, New George st.

Berriman Wm. blacksmith, 2, Vine court, Botelar st.

Berry John, day school, 15, New Dock st.

Berwick Samuel, gardener, Barrack garden, near New George st.

Best Wm. hair dresser, 7, Prospect st.

Bettison Samuel, brewer, 5, Humber street

Bettison Wm. brewer, 6, Humber st.

Betts Mary, ladies' day school, Parade row

Betts John, bricklayer, 1, Fish st.

Betty Wm. S. surgeon, 34, George st.

Beverley Tristram, shopkeeper, 8, Grotto sq. Mason st.

Bewell Wm. tailor and habit maker, 1, King st.

Bielby Geo. gent. 1, Paragon place, Sykes st.

Bielby W. T. clerk at the Trinity house, Trinity house lane

Bielby Walter, clerk at custom house, 19, Albion st.

Bielby Wm. T. bookkeeper, 4, English street

Bielby Wm. clerk in the Trinity house, 4, Humber bank

Bier Thomas, vict. Duke of Clarence, 49, South end

Biglin Wm. woollen draper, 29, Market place

Bilby Thos. shoemaker, 147, High st.

Billaney Wm. corn dealer, 21, Carr lane

Bilton Robert, banker's clerk, 12, Parliament st.

Bilton Walter, mariner, 8, Paragon place

Bingham E. W. linen draper, 17, Dock street

Binks Richard, merchant, ship & insurance broker, 12, High street; h. 12, Story street

Binks Wm. painter; house, 6, Commercial court

Binning Geo. mariner, Mill court, New George street

Binnington Edw. plumber & glazier, 14, Chapel lane

Binnington Christopher, schoolmaster, Church street, Drypool; house, Raikes street

Binnington Richard, cabinet maker, Newton st.; h. Leadenhall sq.

Binnington Richard, agent to Newcomb and Co. York and Hull carriers, 2, Castle st.
Binnington Thos. butcher, Witham
Binnington Eliz. bonnet foundation maker, 2, Castle st.
Birch Peter, hair seating & curled hair mfr. Fawcett st.; h. 16, English st.
Bird Robert, gentleman, 6, Trinity house lane
Bird John, shoemaker, 121, High st.
Birkett Thos. bricklayer, 63, Mill st.
Birtwistle Samuel, gent. 18, North st. Prospect st.
Bishop Joseph, victualler, Neptune, Neptune st.
Bishop Thos. bricklayer, 26, Mill st.
Blackburn Thos. agent to the London Cheese Co. 16, Paradise place
Blackston Samuel, vict. Black Horse, Witham
Blaine and Green, haberdashers, hosiers, lacemen and glovers, 64, Market place
Blaine Benj. mercer, &c.; house, 12, Nile street
Blakey Mary, vict. Duke of York, 11, Blackfriargate
Blakey Wm. flax dresser, Blackfriargt.
Blanch Thos. pilot, 16, Manor street
Blanchard William, clock and watch maker, 11, Silver street
Blanchard James, baker, 34, Scale ln.
Blenkin Geo. wholesale grocer & tea dlr. importer of fruit, seedsman, &c. 67, High st.; h. 4, Savile st.
Blenkin Wm. wholesale grocer and tea dealer, and seedsman, 67, High st.; house, 32, Posterngate
Blenkin Wm. cowkpr. *Summergangs*
Benkinsop Jph. mariner, 18, Bourne street
Blezard Rev. John, gent's. academy, Chapel st. Porter's gardens; h. 10, Prospect st.
Blossom John, joiner, 57, Scott st.
Blumfield Samuel, musical repository, 52, Whitefriargate
Blundell Henry, paint and colour mfr. Beverley road; h. 49, Spencer st.
Blundell Joseph, gentleman, 7, Portland place
Blyth Robert and Co. merchants, ship & insurance brokers, 33, High st.
Blyth Robert, mert.; h. 10, Jarratt st.
Blyth Eliz. pipe maker, 16, Chariot st.; h. 10, Chariot st.
Blyth Wm. mariner, Holderness road
Blyth Wm. merchant's clerk, 15, Saville row
Boalk Richd. gent. Green ln. Drypool
Boddy Wm. gent. 16, Prince st.
Bodley Wm. Hulme, M.D. 12, Charlotte street

Bolton William and Christopher, merchants, brokers and ship owners, 21, High street
Bolton Wm. Watson, mercht.; h. 11, Charlotte st.
Bolton Benj. furniture broker, New Dock street
Bolton Wm. jun. town's husband, 22, High street
Bolton Robert, grocer, &c. Church st. Sculcoates
Bolton Mrs. B. 1, Worship street
Bolton John, agent to Widow Wilson, York and London, &c. carrier, Whitefriargate
Boomer Eliz. vict. White Swan, South street
Boocock John, 27, Chapel lane
Boocock Hannah, stay and corset maker, 27, Chapel lane
Booth Wm. gent. 42, Spencer street
Booth Wm. shopkeeper, 123, High st.
Booth John, tailor, 15, Salthouse lane
Boothman John, whitesmith, Witham
Boothroyd Wm. bricklayer and plasterer, 6, Paragon place, Sykes st.
Boraman Zechariah, toyman, New John street
Boraman Sarah, dress maker, New John street
Boraman Wm. tailor, 17, Trippet
Borden John, cowkpr. 11, Providence row
Bores John, baker, 1, Trippet street
Bosomworth Ann, shopkpr. 31, Church lane
Boss Elizabeth, basket maker, 31, Humber street
Boss Thos. Staffordshire warehouse, 47, Blanket row
Botham Richard, surgeon, 2, South st.
Botham Wm. surgeon, 4, Engine st.
Bott John, glass, china, &c. dealer, Vicar lane
Botta Joseph, baker, &c. 22, Dock st.
Botterill Matt. vict. King's Coffee House, 41, High street
Bouch Wm. John, mariner, 7, Garden street, Princess street
Boulby John, gent. Great Union st.
Boulby John, lighterman, John street
Boulter Benj. clothes broker, 7, Mytongate
Boumer Thos. whitesmith and bellhanger, Red Lion entry, High st.
Bourne Wm. underwriter, 5, Quay st.
Bowden Jas. mert.; h. 55, Prospect st.
Bowden Wm. mercht. West parade, Anlaby road
Bowden Mrs. M. West prd. Anlaby rd.
Bowden James, biscuit, &c. baker, 5, Duke street
Bower Henry, shopkpr. Great Union street

Bowes Thomas, timber merchant, 2, Foundry row

Bowes Richard, vict. Ship Tavern, 25, Posterngate

Bowes Thomas, timber measurer, 82, Grimsby lane

Bowman John, merchant's clerk, 2, Clark's sq. Sykes st.

Bowman Sarah, boot and shoemaker, 34, Market place

Bowser Wm. butcher, 165, High st.

Bowser Wm. shopkpr. 8, Chariot st.

Boxtead John, vict. Board, 16, Charterhouse lane

Boyd Geo. and Wm. millwrights and millstone mfrs. Witham

Boyes and Constable, ironmongers, 43, Market place

Boyes Bethel, merchant and deputy Hanoverian consul, 8, Castle st.

Boyes Anthony, mariner, Church st. Drypool

Boyes Joseph, mariner, 12, Clark's sq. Sykes st.

Boyle Richard, ship chandler, North side of Dock; h. 4, George's st.

Boyle William, auctioneer, appraiser and ship surveyor, 9, Page's sq. Dagger lane

Boyle and Thorney, shipsmiths, 2, Dock street

Boyle Richard, shipsmith; h. Geo. st.

Boynton Thos. corn dealer, Alfred st.

Brabiner Wm. shopkeeper, &c. 11, Manor st.

Brace Anthony, hackney cartman, 46, Carr lane

Bradbury John, parish clerk of St. Mary's, Sculcoates, 35, New Geo. st.

Bradley John, whalebone cutter and whip mfr. 5, St. Mark's sq.

Bradley Ann, straw hat mfr. 18, New Dock st.

Brady Cornelius, mariner, 14, Paragon place

Bramwell Geo. solicitor, 8, Osborne st.

Brändström J. S. merchant; house, 4, George st.

Brayshaw Misses Alice and Ann, 69, West street

Bregazzi Domenico, drawing master, & teacher of the Italian language, 4, Waltham st.

Brewins John, shoemkr. 21, North st.

Brewis Wm. mariner, 4, St. Quintin's place, Church st.

Brewster Thos. shoemkr. 6, Myton st.

Briggs John & Wm. merchants, 21, High street

Briggs Mary, gentlwmn. 9, Jarratt st.

Briggs Wm. mercht.; h. 9, Jarratt st.

Briggs Christopher & Son, insurance brokers & general agents, 7, Bowl-alley lane; h. 15, Albion st.

Briggs John B. & Co. woollen drapers, silk mercers & ship owners, 39, Market place

Briggs J. B. mercht.; h. 13, Albion st.

Briggs Henry, grocer, &c. 38, Market place

Briggs Robert, chemist & druggist, 33, Whitefriargate

Briggs John, painter & colour manfr. 42, Salthouse lane

Briggs Misses E. J. & S. ladies' seminary, 25, Finkle st.

Briggs Thos. joiner, 36, Scott st.

Briggs Thos. vict. Board, Trippet

Briggs Thos. joiner, 36, Scott st.

Briggs Richard, merchant's clerk, Discount ct. Cent per cent st.

Briggs Wm. tide waiter, Raike's st.

Briggs John, shopkeeper, &c. 99, High street

Briggs James, dealer in galoon, 17, Aldbro' street

Briggs Wm. dealer in old books, 2, Queen street

Brigham Wm. mariner, 16, Charles st.

Bright William, custom house locker, Wentworth st. Church st.

Bristow Chas. grocer, &c. 14, Queen st.

Britain James, grocer, tea dealer and seedsman, 61, High street, & 48, Market place

Britain Wm. baker, &c. 32, Chariot st.

Broadbent Wm. jun. ship insurance broker, and general commission agent, Commercial buildings, 29, High st.; house, *Somerstown*

Broadley Henry, gent. 2, Mason st.

Broadwell Robert, shopkeeper, 30, Aldbro' st.

Brocklebank Mrs. Hannah, 21, Prospect place, Drypool

Brocklebank Mary, furniture broker, 9, New Dock st.

Brocklebank Rachel, shopkpr. Witham

Brocklebank James, tide waiter, 9, New Dock st.

Brodrick John, mert. ship owner and underwriter, 21, High st.; house, *Summergangs*

Bromby and Clark, merchants, insurance brokers, wharfingers, and agents for Leeds-Union Company, 26, High street

Bromby Rev. J. H. vicar of Trinity church, 4, South side Trinity ch.

Bromby Mrs. J. 5, York parade, Beverley road

Bromby Thos. ship breaker, Hodgson street

Bromfield Thos. clothes broker, 58, Carr lane

Brooks Thos. carver, gilder, tea dlr plate glass & comb warehouse, 16, Whitefriargate

Brooks Ann, gentlewoman, 2, Savile row

Brooks Wm. sea biscuit and public baker, yard, 7, Lowgate

Brooks S. & J. hair dressers and perfumers, 32, Whitefriargate

Brooks Benj. hair dresser, perfumer & comb warehouse, 20, Whitefriargt.

Brooks John, shopkpr. 12, Alfred st.

Brooks Lydia, vict. Queen Caroline, 34, Salthouse lane

Brothill John, grocer, &c. 179, High st.

Broughton Wm. gent. 10, Providence row, Beverley road

Broughton James, miller, Lincoln st. Wincolmlee

Brown Jonas, Esq. magistrate, 38, George street

Brown Jonas and Co. merchants and navy agents, 40, George st.

Brown Thos. timber merchant & ship owner, Old Dock side; h. West parade, Anlaby road

Brown Henry, hatter, hosier, glover, (and music preceptor, &c.) 29, Lowgate

Brown Mrs. Anne, 25, Albion street

Brown Mrs. Elizabeth, 5, Osborne st.

Brown Daniel, mariner, 17, Prospect place, Drypool

Brown Geo. tailor, 6, Crown court, Dock street

Brown John, grocer, &c. 1, Myton pl.

Brown Jonathan, gent. Beverley road

Brown Thos. gent. 15, Trundle st.

Brown Harry, gent. Wellington place, Beverley road

Brown Luke, vict. Duke of Cumberland, 22, Sewer lane

Brown Matthew. vict. Full Measure, 80, Mytongate

Brown John, butcher, 37, Chariot st.

Brown Robert and John, joiners and builders, West end of the Dock

Brown Robert, joiner; h. 30, Mill st.

Brown John, house and ship joiner; h. 27, Scott street

Brown John, joiner, Bond st. Mews; h. 15, Hodgson's ct. Sykes st.

Brown Robert, thrashing machine maker, Witham

Brown John, tanner, 7, Providence row, Beverley road

Brown Thos. tailor, 54, Scott street

Brown Joseph, tailor, 52, Mytongate

Brown Thomas, merchant's clerk, 3, Robson's place, Mason street

Brown Leonard, mariner, New row, Anlaby road

Brown John, fishmonger, Queen st.

Brown Mary, straw hat mfr. 30, Great passage street

Brown Thomas, 48, Carr lane

Brown Thomas, 12, Church street

Brown Thomas, solicitor, 5, Parment street

Brownrigg John, shoemaker, Builders' court, Scale lane

Bruce Geo. mariner, 2, Grimston st.

Brumby Wm. tide surveyor, 8, Paradise place

Bryan Robert, vict. Recruiting Serjeant, Chariot street

Bryant Mrs. Elizabeth, Cottage row Anlaby road

Buchanan Thos. master of surgery Lycentiate of the Royal Colle of Glasgow, secretary to the H medical and chirurgical societ and surgeon to the dispensary f diseases of the eye and the ear 55, Mytongate

Buck Christopher, gent. 5, English st

Buck Francis, house and ship painter 150, High street

Buck John, vict. Crown, 29, Bri street

Buck Hy. warehouseman, Broadley s

Buckland Mrs. Mary, 31, Prospect st

Buckle Wm. joiner, 8, Aldbro' st.

Buckton Geo. general mert. shipp' agent and wharfinger, 56, Hi st.; house, 6, Bourne st.

Buckton Thos. vict. Juno Tavern, 33 Church lane

Buckton Edw. clerk of customs, 7 Spencer street

Buckton Thos. J. banker's clerk, 26 George's street

Buckton F. S. and M. C. Newcombe professors of dancing and m 26, George street

Bugg Wm. lath render, 39, Church l

Bull Robert, coachman, 8, Parliame street

Bulmer Wm. bricklayer, Trundle st

Bulmer John, 5, Providence row, verley road

Bunney Wm. ship owner, 19, Whit friargate

Bunney Wm. jun. solicitor, Parliame st.; house, 19, Whitefriargate

Burge John, schoolmaster & accou ant, 7, Providence ct. 19, Brook st

Burgess Wm. butcher, 39, Shambles house, Finkle street

Burgess John, butcher, 42, Shambles house, Scott's sq. Blanket row

Burks Maria, silk dyer, 7, Waltham st

Burman Richard, merchant's clerk, 2 Clark's sq. Sykes street

Burnett Margaret, milliner, North st.

Burnett Benj. gent. 43, Prospect st.

Burnett Ann, ladies' day school, 29 Paradise place

Burnett Miss J. Court, 29, North st.

Burnham Watson, cowkeeper, 34, West street

Burnhill David, 2, Carr lane
Bursell David, pawnbroker, 15, Grims-
  by lane
Burstall John & Saml. merchants &
  ship owners, 39, High st.
Burstall John, mercht. & underwriter;
  house, 15, Charlotte st.
Burstall Samuel, merchant; h. *Hessle*
Burton Cornelius, gent. 4, Jarratt st.
Burton John, gent. Church st. Drypl.
Burton John, chemist and druggist,
  40, Lowgate
Burton Matthew, dealer in marine
  stores & rigger, 20, Wincolmlee
Burton Jph. lighterman, 24, Geo. yd.
Burton Thos. landing waiter, 5, Brook
  street
Burton Wm. traveller, 5, Park place
Burton Thos. landing waiter, 14, Wor-
  ship street
Butler Holden, butcher, Bilton's ct.
  8, Machel street
Butler John, tailor & clothes broker,
  15, North walls
Butter John F. butcher,81, Shambles;
  house, 45, Blanket row
Butter Thos. 20, Cook's buildings,
  Bradley street
Butter Rhd. shopkpr. 81, West st.
Butterworth Mrs. Eliz. 10, St. Mark's
  square
Butterworth Geo. twine spinner, 26,
  Wincolmlee
Buttery Mrs. Elisabeth, Cottage row,
  Anlaby road
Buttery Jph. mariner, 8, Spencer st.
Buttery Thos. tide waiter, Hedgson st.
Buttle Rhd. shoemkr. 20, Prospect st.
Byass John, cowkpr. 11, Spencer st.
Byron Mrs. Eliz. 17, Story street
Bywater Rhd. bricklayer, 20, Scott st.
Bywater John, upholsterer, 6, Wal-
  tham street
Cable Thos. H. M. ship carpenter, 10,
  Church street
Cade Geo. pawnbroker, 17, Bridge st.
Cade James, vict. Sculcoates Tavern,
  81, Wincolmlee
Cade Martin, vict. Crown, 17, Silver st.
Cairns John, bookbinder, 11, Bishop
  lane
Calam Matthew, shoemaker, 47, Dock
  street
Calbert James, butcher, 36, Market
  place; house, Blanket row
Caley James, grocer, &c. 25, Trippet
Caley Wm. grocer, &c. 48, Bridge st.
Caley John, vict. Blue Bell, Witham
Calvert Ann, dress mkr. Myton st.
Calvert John, pilot, Edward's place,
  Love lane
Cammel Geo. mariner, 31, English st.
Campbell Duncan, merchant & iron
  founder; house, 1, Cannon st.

Campbell Geo. merchant's clerk, 1,
  Crown ct. 4, Dock street
Campbell James, shoemaker, 19, North
  street, Prospect street
Campleman Wm. harbour master, 27,
  George yard, Lowgate
Campleman Mrs. Ann, Porter's court,
  Carr lane
Cankrien John, C. mert. & Nether-
  land Consul, 18, Whitefriargate;
  house, 4, Albion street
Capes Benj. iron dealer, rag & rope
  merchant, Great Union st.
Capes Mary & Sons, plumbers and
  glaziers, 2, Lime street
Capes Robert, vict. Golden Ball, 10,
  Pickering's entry, High street
Carlill & Co. merchants, commercial
  agents, & agents to Eagle Insu-
  rance Company, 33, High st.
Carlill Briggs, merchant; house, 22,
  Prospect street
Carlill John, merchant's clerk, 6,
  Hope street
Carlill Thos. cabinet maker & uphol-
  sterer, 45, Whitefriargate
Carlill George, accountant, agent to
  the Hope fire office, and secretary
  to Savings' bank, 5, Quay street;
  house, *Cottingham*
Carlin Christopher, boot and shoe
  maker, Lime street
Carnagie Wm. straw hat manufactu-
  rer, 33, Lowgate
Carnley John and Co. brandy mer-
  chants, 3, King street
Carnley John, medicine vender, Nel-
  son street
Carnochan John, linen draper, 11,
  Spring row
Carr Wm. schoolmaster, 14, Harden's
  court, Posterngate
Carr Christopher, cooper, Chariot st.
  house, Waterworks st.
Carr James, gardener and seedsman,
  Drypool square
Carr Henry, hair dresser, 12, St. John
  street
Carr Jas. hair dresser, 175, High st.
Carr Thos. tailor, 164, High street
Carr Mary, straw hat maker, Church
  street, Wincolmlee
Carr Ellen, straw hat manufr. 2, New
  George street
Carrall Mary, grocer, 26, Sykes st.
Carrall Roger, hair dresser and per-
  fumer, 26, Queen street
Carrick John & Co. tobacco & snuff
  manufacturers, 9, Grimsby lane
Carrick John, tobacco manfr. h. 16,
  Albion street
Carrick Wm. miller, Summergangs
Carrick Wm. gent. 33, Posterngate
Carrick Mrs. Ann, 18, King street

Carrott Eliz. milliner, 53, Dock st.
Cart John, stocking and sewing cotton manfr. 18, Lowgate
Carter Mrs. Ann, 4, Osborne st.
Carter John, saddler and harness maker, 4, Chariot street
Carter John, saddler, 6, Carr lane
Carter Wm. bone setter, 42, Prospect st.
Carter Geo. 103, High street
Cartwright John, gent. 29, Brook st.
Cass John, painter, 8, Waterhouse ln.
Cass Thos. schoolmaster, 1, Knowles square, Spencer street
Cass Wm. millstone mfr. Witham
Casson Richard, surgeon, 1, North st.
Casson Benj. tanner, Providence row, Beverley road
Casson John, ship bread baker, North court, house, 45, Dock street
Casson and Penrose, corn millers, 20, Machel street
Cassons Henry, plumber and glazier, Hatter's square, Queen st.
Catterson John, currier, 28, Bishop ln.
Cattley Rich. merchant, 45, High st.
Cawkwell Wm. joiner, 3, Pothouse yard, Wincolmlee
Cawood Frances, milliner, Posterngt.
Chafer Robert, farmer, Drypool
Chamberlain Lyddell, gent. 20, Blanket row
Chambers Anthony, merchant, 10, Sewer lane
Chambers John, mariner, 1, Garden's square, Princess street
Champney John, butcher, 3, Waterworks street
Chandler Geo. gent. 4, Story street
Chaplin Maria, ladies' day school, 7, Story street
Chapman Edward, druggist, &c. 3, Queen street
Chapman & Parkin, joiners, Princess street
Chapman Edward, joiner; h. 18, Princess street
Chapman John, schoolmaster, 3, King's court, High street
Chapman Joseph, shoemaker, 7, Ordovas place, Chariot street
Chapman Hannah, shopkeeper, 19, Carr lane
Chapman John, shoemaker, 2, Salthouse lane
Chapman Wm. officer of excise, 5, Broadley square
Chapman Robert, eating house, 16, Chariot street
Chapman Joseph, whitesmith, 2, Vicar lane
Chapman Richard, wheelwright, New George street
Chappel Samuel, hackney cartman, 6, Albion place

Charlton John, house, ship, and sign painter, 36, Savile st.
Charlton Thomas, ladies' shoemaker, 16, Silver street
Charlton John, cabinet maker, Lovett's square, Hodgson st.
Chatterton Robert, merchant & ship owner, Stewart's yard, 152, High street; house, Summergangs
Cheetham Geo. grocer & tea dealer, 2, Carlisle st.
Cherry Edward, vict. & spirit dealer, Mermaid, 5, Silver st.
Cherry John, flour dlr. 2, North walls
Cherry Daniel, mariner, 26, Bridge st.
Cherry Samuel, custom house officer, 51, Scott street
Chew Richard, mariner, 1, Wood's court, South street
Chidson John, lodging house, 5, Castle row
Chilton Thos. vict. White Hart, 7, Cross street
Chimley Thos. corn and flour dealer, 77, High street
Christie David, vict. Grapes, 6, Waterhouse lane
Christie David, baker, &c. 58, Lowgt.
Christie John, vict. Societies Tavern (billiard room) 6, Dagger lane
Christopher Matthew, tide surveyor, 95, High street
Clappison Thos. mariner, 8, Osborne st.
Clappison Mary, gentlewoman, Clappison's sq. Sykes st.
Clark Peter, wharfinger, 37, High st. house 12, Paragon place
Clark James, bone merchant, & bell button maker, Church st. house, 13, New George st.
Clark Geo. druggist, &c. Myton place
Clark Wm. coal, hop, and seed merchant, Castle street; house, 11, Bond street
Clark Wm. grocer, &c. 33, Mytongt.
Clark Wm. joiner, 2, Crown court, 4, Dock street
Clark Wm. vict. Ship, Anlaby road
Clark James, painter, 62, Prospect st.
Clark Thos. plasterer, agent, & worker of P. Hamelin's cement, 5, Spring Bank
Clark Mrs. Mary, matron to the Lying-in-charity, 9, Robinson row
Clark Mrs. Elizabeth, 11, Bond st.
Clark John, gent. 18, English st.
Clark Joseph, gent. 6, Marine row
Clark Peter, gent. 19, Trippet
Clark Ralph, sawyer & timber dealer, 19, English st.: h. Parade row
Clark Thos. corn miller, Summergangs
Clark John, butcher, 3, Trippet
Clark Wm. butcher, Nichols' court, 6, Fawcett street

Clark George, baker, 16, Brook st.
Clark John, bricklayer, 19, Castle st.
Clark Wm. basket maker, 148, High st. and 36, Grimsby lane
Clark Wm. shopkeeper, 33, Mytongt.
Clark Thos. eating house, Mytongate
Clark Gowland, mariner, 19, Paradise place
Clark R. S. mariner, 15, Clark's sq. Sykes st.
Clark Geo. mariner, 15, Katharine st.
Clark John, mariner, 4, James court, 18, Waterhouse lane
Clark Thomas, shopkeeper, &c. 38, Blackfriargate
Clark Thomas, pilot, 9, Scott square, Humber street
Clark Wm. pilot, Bank's court, Dagger lane
Clarkson Thomas, ship chandler, 154, High st.; h. 2, Southern's ct.
Clarkson Benj. house and ship joiner, Parade row
Clarkson Thos. glover, 28, Silver st.
Clarkson John, silk dyer, 8, Robinson row
Clay and Squire, merchants, North side Old Dock
Clay John, merchant, Swedish and Norwegian consul; house, 30, Posterngate
Clay Joseph, gent. Marvel street
Clay Samuel, furniture broker, 5, Bowlalley lane
Clay George, mariner, Marvel st.
Claydon Mary, vict. Lord Nelson, Marvel street
Clayton Geo. cowkeeper, Short st.
Clement R. W. grocer, &c. 5, Spencer street
Clervas Wm. vict. Golden Barrel, & wine and spirit dealer, 24, Sewer lane
Clifford Wm. cornfactor, Moira buildings, 51, Prospect st.
Clifford Mark, corn, general commission, and ship insurance agent, 17, High st.; house, 3, Spencer st.
Clifford Mrs. Mary, 9, Charles st.
Clifford Francis, commodore of the pilots, Queen street
Clifton J. C. shopkeeper, 4, North st.
Clough John, tea dealer, &c. 30, St. John street
Cloughton John, lodging house, 24, Dock street
Clutterbuck Jasper, dealer in marine stores, 8, Clappison's sq. Sykes st.
Coates Henry, gent. 23, George st.
Coates T. C. 10, West street
Coates Francis, gaoler, Myton place
Coates George, tide walter, Ordnance place, Drypool
Coates Jas. traveller, 31, North st.

Coates Wm. marine painter, 2, North street
Coates Jas. tide waiter, 11, Albion st.
Cobb Geo. grocer, 59, Salthouse lane
Cobb Thomas, joiner and builder, 21, George yard, 170, High st.
Cobb John, superintendent of the Exchange and News room; house, Exchange alley
Cobb Wm. malt dealer, 3, Salthouse lane
Cobb Wm. wharfinger, 21, High st.
Cockerill W. S. baker, Trundle st.
Codd Edward and George, solicitors, 6, Parliament st.
Codlin Wm. cabinet maker, 11, Bond st. Mews
Coldwell Wm. shoemaker, St. John street
Collender John, gent. Cottage row, Anlaby road
Collender Thos. shopkpr. 15, Chapel ln.
Colley Wm. wine cooper, 152, & h. 44, High street
Colley Joseph, vict. Prince of Wales, Bourne street
Colley Isabel. shopkpr. 17, Wincolmlee.
Colley Robt. mariner, 22, Mason st.
Collier John, shopkpr. 2, Blanket row
Collier John, hackney cartman, 39, Chariot street
Collier George, Burnand's yard, 33, West street
Collings Mrs. Eliz. 3, Waltham st.
Collings John, trunk maker, 17, Waterhouse lane
Collins Joel, gardener, Pothouse yard, Wincolmlee
Collinson Wm. and Son, merchants, Garrison side Wharf
Collinson Wm. merchant; h. Wyton
Collinson John, merchant; house, Summergangs
Collinson and Maude, wharfingers, Garrison side
Collinson Moses, joiner, &c. Jarvis st.
Collinson Robert, sail maker; h. 60, High street
Collinson Samuel, joiner, &c. 11, Manor alley
Collinson Wm. mariner, 4, Princess st.
Collinson Samuel, merchant's clerk, 31, Trippet
Collinson Thos. merchant's clerk, 7, Paragon place
Coltish Wm. merchant, Summergangs
Coltman Mrs. Eliz. 44, Dock street
Colton Samuel, grocer, &c. 6, New George street
Colton Thos. 27, George yd. Lowgate
Columbani Barbara, teacher of the French language, 37, Aldbro' st.
Colquhoun Rev. James, Church st. Drypool

Colquhoun James, mariner, 8, New George street

Comingworth Wm. furniture broker, New Dock street

Conkerton Richard, bread and ship biscuit baker, 8 Chapel lane

Cotsitt and Goodwill, engravers and copperplate printers, 4, Bowl-alley lane

Consitt Richd. mustard manufacturer, 53, Market place

Consitt Richd. gent. 9, Paragon place, Sykes street

Constable John, ironmonger; house, 14, Salthouse lane

Constable Joseph, grocer, &c. 30, English street

Cook & Frankish, wholesale & retail grocers and tea dealers, opposite KING WILLIAM, 34, Market pl.

Cook Simon, timber mercht. Witham

Cook Samuel, butcher, 15, West st.

Cook Mrs. Mary, 2, Hatter's square, 13, Queen st.

Cook John, vict. Sir John Falstaff, 17, Humber street

Cook Joseph, vict. Jolly Bacchus, 19, Dagger lane

Cook Rt. livery stables, 13, Carr lane

Cook Thomas, schoolmaster, 1, New Dock st. : h. 12, Katharine st.

Cook Joseph, shoemaker, 31, New George street

Cook Robert, merchant's clerk, 20, Prospect place, Drypool

Cook Robt. merchant's clerk, 9, Beverley road

Cook Thos. mariner, 2, Nile place, Love lane

Cooke Isabella, straw hat manufacturer, Prospect place, Drypool

Cookman Geo. currier, leather cutter, & tallow chandler, 42, Market pl.; h. Cottage row, Anlaby road

Cookman Samuel, shoemaker, 34, Garden street

Cooper John, wine and spirit dealer, Great Union st.

Cooper Thos. vict. Newcastle Tavern, 39, Whitefriargate

Cooper Wm. house and ship painter, 8, and house 54, Salthouse lane

Cooper Matthew, stocking manfr. 10, Waterhouse lane

Cooper W. S. merchant ; house, 13, Charlotte street

Cooper Saml. ship owner ; h. Tranby

Cooper John, vict. Black Swan, 5, Mytongate

Cooper Richard, vict. Wellington, Witham ; and joiner, 12, Trippet

Cooper Richard, coal dlr. Jarvis st.

Cooper John, baker, 190, High st.; h. 11, Carlisle st.

Cooper Thos. butcher, 3, Carlisle st.

Cooper Wm. hair dresser, 15, Trip..

Cooper Mrs. Mary, 46, Dock st.

Cooper Miss Eliz. 1, Saville row

Cooper Mrs. M. 18, Charlotte st.

Cooper Wm. 10, Spencer st.

Coopland Francis, shoemkr. 22, Low

Coopland Esther, shopkeeper, Waterhouse lane

Copass Wm. cooper, 2, Constable buildings, English st.

Copeland Wm. mariner, 6, Featherstone's entry, High st.

Copley Wm. gent. 23, Gibson street

Corbett John, mariner, 7, Catharine square, Mason st.

Corden Enoch, tailor, 51, Humber st.

Cordingley Wm. mariner, 10, Robinson row

Corlass Robert, wine & spirit mercht. 70, Lowgate

Cornell Edw. smith & farrier, 3, Parade row

Cornish Wm. hair dresser, 26, Garden

Cortis Richard, mariner, 6, Crescent street

Cotsworth John, solicitor, 28, Whitefriargate ; house, 3, Engine st.

Cotterill Mrs. Jane, 24, Paradise pl.

Coulson Edw. and Geo. general merchants & underwriters, Old Dockside, Lowgate end

Coulson Edw. Foster, Esq. 9, Charlotte street

Coulson George, merchant ; house, Charlotte street

Coulson Wm. surgeon, 11, Newton court, Macbell st.

Coulson Mrs. Sarah, lodging house, Quay street

Coulson Wm. butcher, 5, Market pl. house, 6, Prince street

Coultas Dorothy, vict. Bull and Dog, Witham

Coulton Mrs. 5, Duncan's place, Manor street

Coupland John, coach & sign painter, 1, Waterhouse lane

Coupland Geo. mariner, 1, Engine st.

Coupland John, bacon factor, New John street

Coupland Wm. mariner, 6, Featherstone's entry, 178, High st.

Courts Philip, flour seller, 31, Whitcolmlee

Courser Wm. sail mkr. 11, Nile st.

Coverdale John, landing waiter, 14, Robinson row

Cowen John, grocer, and sheriff officer, 2, Whitcolmlee

Cowie & Brandström, merts. & gen. commission agts. 7, Castle st.

Cowl George, joiner & builder, Carlisle street

Cowley Wm. cut glass mfr. wholesale & retail, dlr. in china, glass, and Staffordshire ware, opposite the church, Lowgate

Cowley John, shoemkr. 26, North st.

Cox Edward Thos. mert. 43, High st.; house, George street

Cox Samuel, schoolmaster, Hale's entry, Market place

Cox Wm. mariner, 5, West street

Coxford Rd. baker, 12, Manor st.

Coxon John, shoemkr. 11, Church st.

Crabtree Thos. shoemkr. 4, Lowgate

Crackles and Horncastle, whalebone manfrs. 35, Wincolmlee

Crackles John, brush mfr. house, 27, Brook street

Crackles Samuel, vict. Labour in Vain, South end

Crackles Richard, cabinet maker, 28, Charlot street

Crackles Samuel, clock and watch cleaner, 55, Humber street

Craggs John, bookseller, binder, stationer, & music seller, 9, Silver st. paper manfr. *South Cave*

Craggs Mary, vict. Fox and Grapes, 21, Humber street

Craggs John, shopkr. 10, Low Union st.

Crake Robt. vict. Blue Bell, & maltster, 57, Market place

Cramp William, collector of excise, 2, York parade

Crampton Keziah, gentlewoman, 15, Fawcett street

Craven Alice & Co. wine and brandy merchants, 19, Bowlalley lane

Craven Mrs. Esther, 39, Paradise pl.

Craven James, Jordan & Co. grocers and tea dealers, 8, Queen st.

Craven Martin Robert and Son, surgeons, 9. Blanket row

Craven Reuben, surgeon, 21, Charlotte street

Craven John, gent. 19, Nile street

Craven Geo. sexton, Trinity church, Scott street

Crawford James, brazier, 11, New Dock street

Craygill Geo. extra locker, 3, Cross st.

Creaser Thos. cowkeeper, Green lane

Creighton James, mariner, North st.

Creighton Mary, schoolmistress, 29, Scott street

Cressey Robert, gent. 4, West st.

Cripling John R. painter and dealer in oils and colours, Witham

Croft Wm. merchant, 20, High street; house, 1, Nile street

Croft Jonas, linen dpr. 14, Queen st.

Croft Daniel, shoemkr. 11, Scott st.

Crompton Mrs. Martha, 44, Mill st.

Crosby Richard, joiner, Grimston st. ; h. 2, Walker's sqr. Sykes street

Crosby John, saddler, &c. Witham

Crosby Elizabeth, dress maker, Church street, Wincolmlee

Crosby Wm. mariner, 45, Salthouse la.

Crosley Benj. M.B. 16, Mytongate

Crosley Ellen, gentwma. 6, Nile pl.

Crosley Mrs. Sarah, *Wilmington*

Cross and Glen, auctioneers and appraisers, Sale room, Silver st.

Cross Geo. & Sons, sail cloth & sacking manufacturers, Castle street ; house, 4, Marine row

Cross Robert, gent. 4, Bond street

Cross Thos. ship owner, Wood's court, 41, Dock street

Cross John, schoolmaster, 68, Mytongt.

Cross Robert, joiner, Milk street

Cross Lucy, spirit dlr. 9, Queen st.

Cross Jas. whitesmith, 41, Scale lane

Cross Eliz. lodging house, 2, Paragon place, Sykes street

Crosse & Co. soft and hard soap mfrs. & Russian merchants, Lime st.

Crosse John, jun. mert. ; h. Lime st.

Crosskill Mary, baker, 5, Little lane, Blackfriargate

Croskill John, whitesmith and bellhanger, North walls

Crowder William, cabinet maker and broker, 10, New Dock street

Crowley Thomas, baker, 24, Trippet

Croyle Jas. hardware dlr. 6, Church ln.

Crozer William, bookbinder, 1, New Dock side

Crozer J. H. day school, Mews street

Cundell D. R. surgeon, (army,) 1, Charles street

Cunningham Alexander, grocer & tea dealer, 31, Mytongate

Cunningworth Robert, joiner, King's place, 19, Dock street

Curtis Geo. butcher, 13, Wincolmlee

Cussons Thomas, merchant's clerk, 18, Savile row

Cuthbert John, vict. Spread Eagle, Lime street

Cutsforth Thomas, cabinet maker and upholsterer, 57, Whitefriargate

Cuttle Thos. tailor, 16, Cook's buildings, Broadley street

Cyprian Caminada, artificial flower maker, 36, Mill street

Daggitt Robt. letter carrier to Hedon, Mytongate

Dails John, ship and insurance broker, & general commission agent, 23, Parliament street

Dails Wm. mariner, 23, Brook street

Dale Thos. insurance broker and ship owner, 20, High street

Dale Geo. fishmonger, 4, Trundle st.

Dale Francis, bricklayer, Witham

Dale Wm. miller, Danson lane

Dalrymple Mary, milliner, 44, Carr ln.

Dalton Henry, timber merchant ; h. 18, Mason street
Dalton Benj. broker, New Dock st.
Daltry Thomas, vict. Golden Cup, 23, Mytongate
Danby Bethel, schoolmaster, 19, Osborne street
Danby Matthew, livery stables, 4, Bourne street
Daniels Thos. auctioneer & sheriff's officer, 2, Savile street
Daniels Andrew, master of the vagrant office, 9, Quay street
Daniels Geo. mustard mfr. 120, High st.
Dannatt Edw. mariner, 18, Osborne st.
Dannatt Peter, mariner, 6, Brook st.
Darbyshire Geo. broker to the York & Hull traders, & agent to Messrs. Mills, wharfingers, York, 12, Blackfriargate
Darcy Jas. vict. New Dock Tavern, and bookbinder, 5, Sewer lane
Darling Wm. cabinet maker, Kirkus' buildings, Lowgate
Dauber Wm. timber & slate mercht. Yard, west end of the Dock ; h. 14, Bond street
Davey John, butcher, 5, Silver street
Davies Rev. Geo. John, A.M. master of the grammar school, 6, South side of the Trinity church
Davies Thomas, pawnbroker, 4, Great Passage street
Davies Mary, straw hat manufacturer, 18, Hodgson square, Sykes st.
Davies Thomas, merchant's clerk, 12, Savile row
Davison Thos. tailor, 2, King street
Davison Mary, tailor, 24, Grimsby ln.
Davison Mary, shopkpr. 48, Blanket row
Dawson Wm. bookseller, stationer, bookbinder, dlr. in genuine tea, & patent medicines, &c. 47, Lowgt.
Dawson Benjamin, cabinet maker, 8, Dibb's yard, Scott street
Dawson Thos. brewer, 5, Robert st.
Dawson Joseph, miller, Summergangs
Dawson John, boot & shoemaker, 44, Blackfriargate
Dawson Rd. shoemkr. 18, Chariot st.
Dawson Jph. excise officer, Hodgson st.
Dawson Robt. joiner, 12, Carr ln. ; h. Freemason's yd. 34, Mytongate
Dawson Thos. shopkpr. 77, High st.
Day John, attorney, 26, Waterhs. ln.
Day Mrs. Ann, Cobourg pl. Anlaby road
Deain John, hatter, Stable yard, 52, Saltbouse lane
Dean Joseph, auctioneer and cabinet maker, 45, Market place
Dean John, victualler, Dog and Duck Tavern, 12, Scale lane
Dean Geo. stone mason, Witham
Dean Daniel, mariner, 4, Love lane

Dean Mary, straw hat mfr. Alfred st.
Deans Alexander, bricklayer, St. Quintin's place, Drypool
Dearman John, mariner, 10, Prospect place, Drypool
Deighton Richard, silk, cotton and woollen dyer, 35, Brook street
Deloitte John Oliver, teacher of the French language, 15, Robinson row
Denham Wm. tailor, 7, King's place, 19, Dock street
Dennis Wm. vict. Golden Pot, and spirit & wine mert. 13, Lowgt.
Dennis John, wine & spirit merchant, &c. and vict. Board, 13, Chapel ln.
Dennison John, brandy mert. & black beer brewer, 20, Parliament st.
Dent Thos. shoemkr. 10, Church lane
Denton Mark, gent. Joseph's court, 15, Lower Union street
Denton Henry, gent. 10, Marine row
Denton Hy. jun. gent. 10, Osborne st.
Denton Joseph, gent. 1, Savile street
Denton Jas. shopkpr. 22, Chariot st.
Denton Samuel, butcher, 13, Waterworks street
Depledge & Prissick, merchants, Old custom house, High street
Depledge Wm. merchant ; house, 24, Finkle street
Des Forges Joseph, grocer & rag and paper merchant, 65, High street
Dewear & Harrison, commercial agts. and spirit & porter merchants, 22, Parliament street
Dewear John, Humber dock master, 3, Castle row
Dewick John, cabinet maker & wood turner, Old Dock end
Deyes John, shoemkr. New Dock side
Dibb Emanuel and Joseph, common brewers, 43, Mill street
Dibb Joseph, gent. 20, Gibson st.
Dibb Samuel, last and pattern maker, 3, Mytongate
Dibb Wm. foreman at the lead works, 2, Hewitt's yard, Whitefriargate
Dible Wm. mariner, 2, Edgar street
Dick John, cooper, 20, George yard ; house, 5, Hanover square
Dick Benj. vict. George and Dragon, 20, George yd. 170, High street
Dickinson Stephen, solicitor, 10, Dock street
Dickinson Mrs. Dorothy, 4, Brook st.
Dickinson Francis, tailor, 8, Castle st.
Dickinson Wm. collector of taxes for Humber and Austin ward, 24, Queen street
Dickinson Wm. cowkpr. Southcoates
Dickon John, cabinet maker & upholsterer, 19, St. John street
Dickon Edward, cabinet maker, 60, Mytongate

Dikes Rev. Thos. L.L.B. 8, Pryme st.
Dikes & Gibson, ship & boat builders, Lime street
Dikes William Hey, ship builder; h. Lime street
Dinmore Hny. butcher, N. bridge foot
Dinsdale Joseph, fishmonger, 9, St. John street
Dinsdill Geo. stay maker, 2, George yard, Lowgate
Dix J. B. classical & commercial academy, 22, Parliament st.
Dix J. B. gent. 4, Dock street
Dixey J. A. dress maker, Mill hill
Dixon Wm. grocer & flour dealer, 2, Whitefriargate
Dixon Anthony, confectioner, baker & fruiterer, 55, Humber street, and 19, Queen street
Dixon Geo. butcher, 34, Mytongate
Dixon George, tailor, 5, Scott's square, Humber street
Dixon John, silk dyer, 10, Waterworks street
Dixon John, clothes broker, 16, Waterhouse lane
Dobson John, furniture broker, 1, New Dock street
Dobson Robert, jun. basket maker, 122 & 142, High st.
Dobson Robert, cabinet maker and broker, 5, New Dock st.
Dodds John, merchant's clerk, 206, High street
Dodsworth Wm. vict. Nag's Head, 132, High street
Doakin Geo. principal clerk at the post office, 27, Bishop lane
Dunkinson Rt. shopkpr. 2, Ordovas pl.
Dunn Wm. curator to the botanic garden, Linnæus st. Anlaby road
Dennison Henry, sacking mfr. Kidd's entry, 16, Chariot st.
Dennison Robert, gent. Beverley road
Dorrington Thos. Esq. 11, North st.
Dorsey Robert, earthenware dealer, 14, St. John's street
Dorsey Rbt. constable, Queen's alley, South end
Dossor James, brewer and maltster, 10, Chapel lane
Douglass Thos. vict. Commercial Tavern, 7, Fish street
Deagle Wm. mariner, Prince George entry, High street
Dove John, clothes broker, 38, Chariot street
Dove George, vict. Hare & Hounds, Spencer street
Downes Richard, gent. 2, St. Quintin's place, Drypool
Dowsland Robert, joiner, Carr lane; house, Mytongate
Doyle Saml. gent. 18, Waterhouse ln.

Doyle Saml. sword bearer to the corporation, 18, Waterhouse lane
Draine Wm. gent. Beverley road
Drant George, gent. Providence row, Beverley road
Drant John, hair dresser, 77, Mytongt.
Drescher John, German clock maker, 66, Mytongate
Drewry Geo. & Co. ship breakers, Hodgson street and Witham
Drewry John, vict. Spread Eagle, 1, Castle st. & timber merchant, Queen street
Drewry Joseph, tailor, Hodgson st.
Driffield Joseph & Co. lath renders, Old Dock end
Driffield Joseph, lath render; house, 17, Savile row
Driffield Thos. lath render, 16, Wells st.
Driffield Ann, perfumer, 25, Savile st.
Driffield Wm. Lincoln yeast warehouse, 3, Mytongate
Driffield Rhd. flour dlr. 2, Hope st.
Dring & Thackray, sailmakers, North side Old dock
Dring Henry, insurance broker, 12, Mason street
Dring Mrs. Anne, 16, Charles st.
Dring Robert, mariner, 1, Nile place
Drinkall John, vict. Board, St. Quintin's place
Driver Wm. shoemkr. 1, Manor st.
Drummond Wm. tea dealer, 20, Princess street
Drury Elizabeth, ship owner, 21, New Dock walls
Drury John, mariner, 12, Myton st.
Drury Wm. mariner, 6, Blue Bell entry, High street
Drury John, constable, George place, Mytongate
Dry John, tailor, 6, Keeling's entry, Mytongate
Dryden Wm. solicitor & distributor of stamps, 3, Bowlalley lane
Dryden James, mariner, 24, Prospect place, Southcoates
Duck Geo. shopkpr. & clothes broker, 13, Trippet
Ducker Thos. baker, 40, Church ln.
Duckett R. K. druggist, 11, Myton pl.
Duckett Mrs. Ann, 1, Waltham st.
Duckett Mary, 4, Regent's place, Sykes street
Duckles Wm. mariner, 3, Pr. George entry, 184, High street
Dudding Mrs. Elizabeth, 2, West st.
Duffee Robt. shopkpr. 29, Dock st.
Duffield George, cooper, Witham
Duffill George, grocer, butter & bacon factor, 154, High street
Dukes Geo. confectnr. 23, St. John st.
Dumleton Wm. cooper, Nelson's sq. New George street

Duncan David, brandy merchant, 19, Bowlalley lane

Duncan John, gent. 7, Prospect place, Drypool

Duncum Sarah, victualler, Board, 2, Trundle st.

Duncum Saml. gent. 5, Neptune st.

Dunderdale Mary, shopkr. Hodgson st.

Dunhill Jane, shopkpr. 5, Shambles sq.

Dunley Edw. wood turner, Parade row

Dunn Wm. paper, rope, and rag warehouse, 58, Salthouse lane

Dunn Ann, vict. Ship, Beverley road

Dunn Catherine, vict. American Tavern, 16, Dock street

Dunn Geo. vict. Anchor, 33, Waterhouse lane

Dunn John, watch mkr. 33, Finkle st.

Dunn David, shoemkr. 28, Scott st.

Dunn M. A. ladies' day school, 5, King st.

Dunn Robert, preserver of. birds, Waterhouse lane

Dunn Thos. shopkpr. 40, Mytongate

Dunning James, vict. Four Alls, 19, Lower Union st.

Dunning Thos. hair dresser, 4, Silver st.

Dunwell Wm. wheelwright, Witham; house, Holderness road

Dutchman John, gent. 6, English st.

Dutchman John, sail maker, 144, High st.; house, 7, Cent per cent st.

Du Vivier John, mert. 4, Worship st.

Dwyer Thos. mariner, 24, Mason st.

Dykes & Gartans, tar, turpentine, & paint mfrs. oil & seed merchants & importers of wines & spirits, 19, Salthouse lane

Dykes Thos. oil and seed merchant; house, Pryme st.

Earle Geo. sen. 14, Osborne st.

Earle Geo. & Thomas, merchants, cement manfrs. ship & insurance brokers, 43, High st.

Earle Geo. jun. mert. 83, Osborne st.

Earle Thos. mert.; 11, Osborne st.

Earle John, architect, builder, &c. 30, Whitefriargate; h. 12, Osborne st.

Earle John, stone mason, 5, St. John's square

Easten Wm. grocer, 5, Blanket row, & lath render, Old Dock side

Easten Thos. principal labourer and constable, Old Dock side

Easton John, sawyer, Hodgson st.

Eastwood Anthony, linen & woollen - draper, 37, Market place

Eastwood Anth. pawnbkr. 1, Mews st.

Eastwood Paul, cloth dealer, Snell's entry, 123, High st.

Eastwood Joseph, worsted manfr. 17, Brook st.

Eaton Thos. stone mason, Cross st.

Eden James, shoemaker, 6, Cross st.

Edgebury Fred. grocer, 23, Scott st.

Edgecomb Jas. cowkeeper, Boalk's yard, Green lane

Edgin Wm. joiner, 6, Ordovas place

Edmonds Mrs. Eliz. 26, Dock st.

Edwards Rt. butcher, 40, Bridge st.

Edwards Wm. flax dresser, 13, Queen street

Edwards Edward, blacking mfr. 56, Edgar st.

Egginton G. & J. oil & general merchants, ship owners, & seed crushers, 8, North walls

Egginton Gardiner, merchant; house, 10, Charlotte st.

Egginton Jph. mert.; h. 31, George st.

Eggleston Harriot, gentlewoman, 4, Humber st.

Eggleston Edw. bookkpr. 5, Union st.

Eglin Mrs. Sarah, 24, Albion st.

Eglin Joseph, gent. 24, Albion st.

Elderton John, last & patten maker, 8a, Mytongate

Ellerby Bartholomew, sen. cabinet maker, 21, New Dock st.

Ellerby Bartholomew, jun. cabinet maker, 2, New John st.

Ellaby John, mert's. clerk, 4, Spring bank

Ellerker John, gent. Marvel st.

Ellerker Mrs. Mary, 41, Spencer st.

Ellerton Benj. gent. 10, Katherine st.

Elliott John, stone mason, Elliott's gallery, Milk st.

Elliott Robt. bone setter, John st.

Elliott Edmund, tailor, 74, West st.

Elliott Eliz. milliner, 17, Garden st.

Ellis Wm. vict. Yorkshire Sloop, coast & river broker, 87, Salthouse lane

Ellis Winfred, baker, 27, Waterwks. st.

Ellis Mrs. Isabella, 3, Nile place

Ellis Richard, clerk of the workhouse, 15, Charles st.

Ellis W. S. mariner, 1, Dyer's place, Waterworks st.

Ellison Thos. nail cutter and patten maker, 9, Dock office row

Ellison Wm. shopkeeper, Raikes st.

Ellison John, butcher, Fawcett street, Great passage st.

Ellison Joseph, excise officer, 21, Bourne st.

Ellison John, cowkpr. Jenning's st.

Ellors Thos. vict. Bee Hive, spirit mert. & ship owner, 4 & 5, Prince st. and Posterngate

Else Joseph, governor of the refuge, Cannon place

Elsey Henry, grocer, &c. 6, South st.

Emerson Agnes, dress maker, Church st. Wincolmlee

Emmett Ann & Sons, mfr. chemists, Botelar st.; h. 6, York parade

Emmett Wm. shoemkr. 29, Chapel ln.

Empson James, corn miller & baker, Strawberry gardens; h. Witham

England & Shackles, attornies, 7, Land of Green ginger

England Thos. jun. cabinet maker, undertaker and furniture broker, Witham; Great Union st.

England Wm. sail mkr. 43, Blackfrgt.

England Elis. gentlwmn. 12, Charter house lane

England Thos. vict. Carpenter's Arms, Great Union st.

England Geo. tin plate worker, Witham

England Francis, butcher, 8, Carlisle st.

England Rbt. butcher, 26, Mytongate

English Thos. & Sons, wharfingers & coal merchants, 3, Humber bank, h. 8, Parliament st.

English Joseph, cowkeeper, Graham's row, St. Quintin's place

Ennis Henry, cornfactor, 33, Mason st.

Ennis Jas. fishmonger, 26, Chariot st.

Esart Thos. mariner, 11, Gibson st.

Escreet Thos. sen. gent. 12, Brook st.

Escreet Michael, tailor, 166, High st.

Escreet Henry, merchant's clerk, 6, Castle row

Etherington Thos. gent. Harcourt st.

Etherington Wm. custom house officer, 2, Scott's square, Blanket row

Etherington Richard, tailor, 24, Great Passage street

Etty Thos. wholesale confectioner, 17, Church lane

Evans Jane, straw hat mfr. 40, Saville street

Evans Richard, harbour master, 12, Charterhouse lane

Evans James, mariner, Ordnance pl. Drypool

Everingham Wm. upholsterer, 24, Saville row

Everington G. B. linen draper, 61, Whitefriargate

Evison Mary, day school, 2, North st. Prospect st.

Exley John, excise post gauger, 4, Spence st.

Eyre Wm. gent. 12, Castle row

Eyre, Marriott and Co. bone crushers, Church st. Wincolmlee

Eyre John mariner, 2, New John st.

Fairbank Geo. saddler, 27, Silver st.

Fairbank Henry, shoemkr. 23, Edgar st.

Fairclough Richard, excise officer, 20, Aldbro' st.

Fairfield Mrs. Eliz. 2, Thornton st.

Falkner Wm. hackney cartman, 7, Alfred st.

Fallas Chs. shopkpr. 23, N. D. walls

Fallowfield Rt. house & ship joiner, 17, Great Passage st.

Farahill Elizabeth, register office, 27, Bridge st.

Farquharson Thos. sawyer, 17, Ordovas place

Farrar Mrs. Ann, Grotto sq. Mason st.

Farrar Isaac, furniture broker, 13, New Dock st.

Farrar Wm. vict. Grapes, Jennings st.

Farrar Rd. cabinet maker, Green lane

Farrar John, rope maker, Lime st.

Farrow Edw. vict. " Town and Trade of Hull," 25, Blanket row

Farrow Edw. straw plat and hat mfr. 9, Dock office row

Farrow Benj. furniture broker, 14, Bowlalley lane

Farthing Wm. commercial agent and broker, Commercial bldgs. 30, High st.; house, 13, Paragon place

Faulding Joseph, M.D. 9, Marine row

Faulding Saml. surgeon, 20, Trinity house lane

Faulding Wm. grocer, Naylor's row, Witham

Faulding Saml. shoemkr. 15, Church st.

Faulkner Jeremiah, shopkeeper, 6, Chapel lane

Fawcett Henry, slater, Old Dock side, 59, Prospect st.

Fawcett John, tailor & drpr. 1, Queen st.

Fawcett Thos. bacon factor, &c. 36, Waterworks st.

Fawcett John, bricklayer, 3, Duncan's place, Manor st.

Fea and Haggerston, oil merchants, Commercial buildings, 29, High st.

Fea Magnus, mert.; h. 4, Prospect st.

Fea John, commercial agent & auctioneer, 33, High st.; house, 11, Church st. Drypool

Fea Peter, mariner, 27, Dock st.

Fean Jas. vict. Bridge Inn, North bdg.

Fearn John, commercial agt. 6, High st.; house, 9, Prospect place

Fearn John, linen draper & importer of Irish linens, 8, Market place

Fearn Thos. grocer, cheese and butter factor, 17, Lowgate

Featherstone James & Co. distillers of turpentine & tar, & mfrs. of rosin, pitch, varnishes, &c. Russia court, 14, High st.

Featherstone John, merchant; house, 20, Bowlalley lane

Featherstone R. brazier, &c. 56, High st.

Feetam Thos. cabinet mkr. & undertaker, 62, Mytongate

Fell John, mariner, 10, Fish st.

Fenwick Rt. shopkpr. 33, Wincolmlee

Fenwick Stephen, tide waiter, Regent's sq. 7, Upper Union st.

Ferraby John, printer, bookseller, and Lottery agent, 44, Market place

Ferrier Thornton, clock and watch maker, Queen st.

Fewson Peter, grocer, &c. 36, Lowgt.

Fewster James, lath render, West end of Dock; house, 12, Crown court, 4, Dock st.

Fewster Thos. tailor, Witherwick's yard, Spencer st.

Field Thos. gent. 12, Bishop lane

Field Wm. ship owner, 2, Jarratt st.

Fielding Geo. surgeon, 3, Albion st.

Fillingham Thos.joiner,Wentworth st.

Fillingham Wm. carpenter, Raikes st.

Findlay James, gent. 10,Cook's buildings, Broadley st.

Findlay Wm. gent, 6, Prospect place, Drypool

Findlay John, cooper, 6, Quay st.

Findlay John, custom house officer, 17, Winter's alley

Findlay Wm. mariner, 5, Catherine sq. Mason st.

Findlyson Wm. pilot, 93, High st.

Finningley Edmund, bread & biscuit baker, 13, High st.

Finningley Edward, bread and biscuit baker, 26, Blanket row

Finningley Wm. butcher, 2,Shambles; house, 11, Myton st.

Firbank Thos. merchant and Russian consul, Lime st.

Firbank George, hair dresser, 22, Broadley st.

Firby Mthw. shopkpr. 32, Middle st.

Fisher John, corn factor, 1, Hatter's square, 13, Queen st.

Fisher Mrs. Eliz. 18, West. st.

Fisher Robt. vict. Crooked Billet,wine, spirit & porter dlr. 36, Trippet

Fisher John, vict. Old Andrew Marvel, 37, Whitefriargate

Fisher John, stay mkr. 3, Paradise row

Fishwick Maria, lodging house, 12, Worship st.

Fitchett Josiah, gent. 16, Savile st.

Fleming John, master of the workhs. Wilson's row, Sculcoates

Fleming Hannah, matron Sculcoates workhouse, 2, Wilson's row, Wincolmlee

Fleming E. B. house & ship painter, 6, Finkle st.

Fletcher Rounceval, carver & gilder, and clerk of Trinity church, 65, Mytongate

Fletcher John, carver & gilder, 18, Dagger lane

Fletcher John, cabinet maker and broker, New Dock st.

Fletcher Richd. milkman, Church st.

Flower Robert, coal dealer, 21, New George st.

Flower and Burton, dealers in marine stores, &c. Wincolmlee

Foord J. T. timber merchant; house, 12, George st.

Forbes Alex. surgeon, 18, Charlotte st.

Forbes Mrs. Eleanor, midwife, Norman's entry, 11, George st.

Ford John, gent. Church st. Drypool

Ford James, cabinet maker & uphol sterer, 4, New Dock st.

Forrest Wm. cooper, 26, Warehouse

Forrester Patrick, goldsmith; h 7, King st.

Forsey Thos. tide waiter, 8, Carr

Forsey Wm. shoemkr. 29, Chariot

Forster Charles, linen draper (Glasgow House) 40,White

Foster A. C. mercht.; h. 10, Ge

Foster R. tallow chandler, 16,P gate, & soap boiler, Trundle

Foster John, coach master and stable kpr. 8,Land of Green

Foster Ann,gentlewoman,5,Mason

FosterMrs.F. lodging hs. 13,Charles

Foster Mrs. R. tea dealer, 7,Brooke

Foster Geo. wire worker, Porter's yd 5, Waterhouse lane

Foster Geo. vict. Barrel, Edgar st.

Foster William, merchant's clerk, 27 Prospect st.

Foster Rd. dancing master, 12, Fish

Foster Wm. grocer, &c. 23, Salths.

Foster Thomas, draper and tailor, 43 Whitefriargate

Foster Thos. joiner, 12, Machell st.

Foster Wm. shoemkr. 12, Machell st.

Foster Jph. sexton, Air st.

Foster Wm. cabinet mkr. 32, Wes

Foster Wm. perfumer, 7, Cross st.

Foster Wm. mariner, 42, Humber

Foster Wm. mariner, 16, Pros place, Drypool

Foster Timothy, mariner, 42, H ber st.

Foster Christopher, Carr lane

Fothergill Miles, slater, W.end,O.

Fountain John, potatoe pealer, Hale entry, Market place

Fowler Chrpr. shopkpr. 185, High st.

Fowler John, vict. Wheat Sheaf, 61 Prospect st.

Fowler Wm. ship owner, 2, Baker s

Fowler Joseph, 8, Wood's sq.South s

Fox Geo.Lieut.RoyalNavy,2,Story st

Fox Pearson, principal constable and collector of taxes for Sculcoates, 15, Jarratt st.

Fox Thos. confectioner, 35, Savile st.

Fox John, builder&joiner,28,Mason st.

Fox John, builder, Bourne st.

Fox John, butcher, 8, Machell st.

Fox Ambrose, baker, 35, Blanket row

Fox James, butcher, Market place

Fox J. C. mariner, Parade row

Foxton Thomas, merchant, 37, High st.; house, 18, Prospect place

Foy Wm. broker and cabinet maker, Cockpit yard, 6, Castle st.; h. 2, New Dock st.

Francis Elix. day school, 15, Harcourt st.

Frank John, shopkpr. Waterhouse ln.

Frank Mrs. Margaret, 15, Savile st.

Frankish Joseph, vict. Jolly Bacchus, and spirit dealer, 86, Mytongate

Frankish Samuel Cook, grocer, &c. 33, Market place

Frankland John, shoemkr. 14, Manor st.

Free Thomas, chest and trunk maker, 12, Queen street

Freeman Saml. brass founder, 8, New Dock street

Freeman Robert, grocer and tallow chandler, 57, Salthouse lane

Freeman Edw. butcher, 1, Church ln.

Freeman Wm. shopkpr. 30, Salths. ln.

French John, corn inspector & school-master, 21, Bond street

French Sarah, day school, 21, Bond st.

French W. dancing master, 21, Bond st.

French Rountree, shoemaker, Church street, Sculcoates

Frith & Vause, plumbers & glaziers, 24, Silver street

Frost Thos. & Charles, solicitors and notaries public, 37, Scale lane

Frost Chas. solicitor; h. 9, Albion st.

Frost Robt. merchant; h. 6, Albion st.

Frost John & Co. rope makers, Win-colmlee

Frost John, rope mkr.; h.56, Prospect st.

Frost John, gent. 56, Moira buildings, Prospect street

Frost Saml. mariner, 17, Portland pl.

Fullam Michael, teacher of Marine school, 17, Trinity house lane

Fullan J. M. surgeon, 17, Trinity hs. ln.

Fulshar Captain Robert, 60, Carr lane

Furnace Wm. shoemkr. &c. Newton st.

Fussey Thos. sail cloth mfr. Roper's row, 20, Waterhouse lane

Fussey Thomas, coal merchant, 4, Dyer's place, Well street

Grace Nathaniel, cabinet maker, 12, Blue Bell entry, Wells street

Grace Ann, mantua maker, 12, Blue Bell entry, Well street

Gadsden James, sugar refiner; house, West parade

Galbraith John Murray, music & mu-sical instrument dealer, 55, White-friargate

Gale George, gent. 17, Mytongate

Gale Robert, last, patten & clog mkr. 96, High street; h. 100, High st.

Gale Frederick, butcher, 13, Shambles; house, Blanket row

Ganderton John, British wine dlr. 17, Parliament st.; h. 18, Middle st.

Garbutt Robt. mercht. ship insurance broker, underwriter & Lloyds agt. 1, Exchange alley; h. 36, Dock st.

Garbutt Joseph, vict. Dock Arms, 5, Dock office row

Garbutt Richard, joiner, 16, Myton st.

Garbutt Geo. shoemaker, 86, Bond st.

Garbutt John, shoemkr. 41, Wincolmlee

Garbutt Jonathan, tailor, 1, Todd's entry, Manor alley

Garbutt Samuel, custom house officer, 3, Knowles' square, Spencer st.

Gardham Stephen, day school, Vicar ln.

Gardham Robt. tailor, 3, Lee's entry, Waterhouse lane

Gardham John, shopkpr. 50, Scott st.

Gardiner Ann, brazier, &c. 16, Queen st.

Gardiner John, shopkeeper, Church street, Wincolmlee

Gardiner John, mariner, 5, Regent's place, Sykes street

Gardner George, gent. 9, Worship st.

Gardner Wm. watch & clock mkr. 5, Whitefriargate; h. Posterngate

Gardner Jonth. mariner, Dennis sq.

Garforth Joseph, solicitor, 3, Exchange alley; h. 36, Prospect street

Garland Rd. solicitor, Bowlalley ln.; house, Baker street, Sculcoates

Garlick Lionel, mariner, 5, Queen's place, Blackfriargate

Garnett Ann, gentlewoman, 3, Nay-lor's row, Witham

Garniss Richd. cattle dlr. 14, Castle st.

Garton and Hopper, tobacco and snuff manufacturers, 58, Market place

Garton John, tobacco manufacturer; house, 16, Story street

Garton Geo. tar & turpentine distiller, &c.; house, 18, Salthouse lane

Garton Rd. brandy mert. 59, Market pl.

Garton Marmaduke, butcher, Water-house lane

Garton John, manure mercht. Cottage garden, Nile place

Gatecliffe John, mariner, 3, Portland pl.

Gaunt Geo. shoemaker, 23, Lowgate

Gawin Allanson, confectioner and fruiterer, 38, Bridge street

Gawthorp Jane, shopkpr. 112, High st.

Gawthorp John, mariner, 2, Naylor's row, Witham

Gawthorp James, mariner, 4, Clappi-son's square, Sykes street

Gay Thos. cutler & surgeons' instru-ment maker, 13, Queen street; house, Broadley square

Gedney Wm. corn factor, 35, Bond st.

Gedney Joseph, tailor, 8, Dagger lane

Gedney Robt. tailor, Great Union st.

Gee, Loft, and Co. Hamburgh mer-chants, Nelson street

Gee Stephen, underwriter, 7, North end, High street

Gee Joseph, hosier, 18, Lowgate

Geeve Edw. bone mert. 24, Bourne st.

Gell John, vict. Tiger, 1, Waterworks st.

Gell Richd. furniture painter, 8, New Dock street

Gell John, mariner, 10, Regent's pl. Sykes street
Gelson Thos. grocer, 27, George st.
Gelson Mary, gentwman. 12, Manor alley
Gibb Thos. baker, 1, Charlot street
Gibbons Richard, gent. Alfred street
Gibbs John, shoemaker, Garden place, Raikes street
Gibson Wm. ship builder; h. Bridge st.
Gibson Edward, ship builder & owner, Great Union street
Gibson Robert, mert. & ship owner, 149, High st.; house, 6, Clark's square, Sykes street
Gibson Wm. sail mkr. 2, Wellington st.
Gibson John, haberdasher & silk mercer, 31, Silver street
Gibson John, spirit mert. 19, High st.
Gibson Wm. and Sons, grocers & tea dealers, cheesemongers & butter factors, 38, Salthouse lane
Gibson Wm. grocer and bacon factor, 90, Mytongate
Gibson Eliz. gentlewoman, Patrick ground lane
Gibson John, merchant's clerk, 4, Paragon place, Sykes street
Gibson John, butcher, 18, Shambles; house, 1, Dagger lane
Gibson Mary Ann, haberdasher, silk mercer & straw hat manufacturer, 54, Market place
Gibson Sarah, confectnr. 11, Humber st.
Gibson Wm. shopkpr. 80, Finkle st.
Gibson Geo. tailor & draper, Duncan's place, Manor street
Gibson John, foreman at the foundry, 5, Spring row
Gibson Samuel, tide waiter, Irving's court, 12, Waterhouse lane
Gibson John, cowkeeper, *Wilmington*
Gibson Thomas, cowkeeper, 44, Gibson's yard, Carr lane
Gibson Mark, merchant's clerk, Walker's square, Sykes street
Gilbank Wm. gent. 5, Clark's square, Sykes street
Gilbert Rev. Joseph, 8, Nile street
Gildart and Jackson, wine & brandy merchants, 43, High street
Gildart Mrs. Ann, 11, Albion street
Gilder Wm. tobacco and snuff mfr.; house, 19, Saville street
Gilder John, merchant's clerk, 17, Lower Union street
Gilderdale Tho. ship carpenter, Carr ln.
Gilaspy John, shoekr. Church st. Dry pl.
Giles Edw. hair cutter, 3, Charlot st.
Gill Geo. oil and Russia broker, &c. Stewart's yd. 152, High st.; house, 8, Parliament street
Gill John, sail maker, 15, Hanover sq.
Gill M. B. F. midwife, Pease's entry, 42, Salthouse lane

Gill Robert, ship owner, 3, Bond st.
Gill Luke, shoemaker, Raikes st.
Gill Robert, baker, 137, High st.
Gibson Eliz. milliner, &c. 33, Saville st.
Gilyard Benj. bricklayer, 20, Scott st.
Gillyard Wm. vict. Lime Kiln House, 18, Humber bank
Gillyatt Wm. vict. Hope and Anchor, 7, Bishop lane
Gillyott Wm. mariner, Mill lane
Gleadow & Scutter, wholesale & retail ironmongers, 24, Market pl.
Gleadow Robt. ship builder & owner, South end, and common brewer, Dagger lane; h. 15, Humber st.
Gleadow James, captain of the Bee Cutter, Nelson street
Gleadow Robert Ward, merchant, 15, Parliament street
Gleadow Susannah, vict. Seven Stars, 19, Fish street
Gleadow William, landing waiter, 13, Castle row
Gleadow Mary, milliner, &c. 13, Humber street
Glen Geo. auctioneer, &c.; house, 14, Hodgson sq. Sykes st.
Glenton Thomas, vict. Bird-in-Hand, Cook's court, Broadley street
Glenton Wm. shoemkr. 8, Middle st.
Glenton Jas. mate of the Bee Cutter, 21, English street
Glenton Mary Ann, milliner and dress maker, 3, New George street
Glew James, bricklayer, 27, Trippet
Goddard & Thornhill, coach makers, &c. 9, Chariot street
Goddard Jas. coach mkr.; h. 9, Hope st.
Goddard Jonathan, engineer, Blanket court, 37, Blanket row
Godmond Joseph, mert. ship owner & underwriter, George st.; house, Moira buildings, 58, Prospect st.
Godmond Saml. Hall, gent. 6, Saville st.
Godmond Eliz. (lodgings) 21, Trinity house lane
Goforth Mrs. Diana, 1, Jarratt st.
Guldfinch Thos. ostrich feather mfr. & furrier, 25, St. John street
Golding Robert, tailor, draper, and clothes broker, 9, Lowgate
Golding Robert, tailor & draper, 164, High street
Goldsmith Wm. shopkpr. 26, Bridge st.
Goldsmith Ann, green grocer, 26, Bridge street
Good Joseph, bankers' clerk, 35, Prospect street
Good Wm. master of Barton Packet, 5, Blue Bell entry, High street
Good James, custom house boatman, 8, English street
Goodill Wm. hair dresser, &c. 30, Waterworks street

Goodlad John, shoemkr. 4, Wells st.
Goodlass Rt. eating h. 58, Humber st.
Goodman C. S. horse dealer, 15, Leadenhall sq. Lowgate
Goodrick Edm. shopkpr. 51, West st.
Goodwin John, gent. Goodwin's sq. West street
Goodwin Wm. glass, china, &c. dlr. 21, North walls
Goodwin Geo. merchant & ship owner, North walls ; house, Bond st.
Goodwin Elizabeth, milliner, &c. 81, St. John street
Goody Rd. corn dealer, Trippet ; h. Holderness road
Goody Thos. gent. 7, Grimston st.
Gorwood Wm. hackney cartman, Witham
Gould Thos. shoemaker, Hospital yd. Chapel lane
Goulden Jerm. tailor, 130, High st.
Gouthwaite Elis. gentlwn. 4, Edgar st.
Gowland & Tindall, joiners, Lime st.
Gowland Geo. joiner ; h. Jenning's st.
Graham Rbt. shoemkr. Parade row
Graham John, rigger, 3, Cayley's ct. 6, Trippet street
Graham Geo. shopkpr. 38, High st.
Graham John, shoemkr. 37, Chariot st.
Grant Wm. vict. Unicorn & Blue Ball, & shipwright, 49, Salthouse ln.
Grant Thomas, ship carpenter, Westerdale's entry, Salthouse lane
Grant John, umbrella manufacturer, 24, Bridge street
Grantham Wm. gardener, Post house yard, Wincolmlee
Grassby Rhd. carpenter, 3, Brook st. square
Grassby John, shoemkr. 2, Burton st.
Grassby Thos. cowkpr. English st.
Graves Francis, tailor and broker, New Dock side
Gray Robert, gent. Beverley road
Gray Robert, corn and flour dealer & baker, 4, Waterworks st.
Gray Mrs. Susannah, 14, Savile st.
Gray John, bricklayer, 42, Spencer st.
Gray Adolphus, vict. Wellington Hotel, 42, Mytongate
Gray Wm. currier, 3, New Dock st.
Gray Geo. tailor, 1, Fish st.
Gray Susannah, straw hat mfr. 23, Bridge street
Gray Thos. mert's. clerk, 17, Paradise pl.
Gray Catherine, milliner, George yd. 170, High street
Grayburn John, sail maker, and ship owner, 83, High st. ; h. 10, York parade
Grayburn Thomas, shopkpr. agent to Garbutt & Co. Foston mills, warehouse, Barnby's staith, N. bridge, and Thornton street

Grayburn John, mariner, G. Union st.
Grayburn T. flour dlr. 6, Wincolmlee
Greaves Mrs. Frances, 7, Nile st.
Greaves Mrs. Sarah, 16, Sykes st.
Greaves Thos. saddle tree maker, 5, Paradise place
Green & Binks, painters, 195, High st.
Green John, painter ; h. High st.
Green Mrs. Sarah, 16, Charlotte st.
Green Mrs. Judith, 2, Marine row
Green Miss H. 10, Prospect pl. Drypool
Green Mrs. Martha, 3, York st.
Green Joseph, gent. 2, Albion st.
Green Henry, ship owner, 10, Nile st.
Green T. R. gent. 3, Cent per cent st.
Green Wm. haberdasher, &c. 5, Marine row
Green James, brickmkr. *Wilmington*
Green Thos. oatmeal warehouse, 26, Church lane
Green Abednigo, cowkeeper, 4, St. John's square
Green Julia, confectioner, 4, Keeling's entry, 24, Mytongate
Green Wm. turner, 14, Bond st. Mews
Green John, stay and umbrella maker, 36, Savile street
Green Wm. shoemkr. 9, Machell st.
Green Rd. flour dlr. 22, Machell st.
Green Wm. poulterer, 27, Church ln.
Greenwood George, insurance broker, and agent to the commercial life office, Commercial buildings, 29 and 30, High st. ; house, 5, Nile street
Greenwood Geo. shoemkr. 18, Trippet
Gregson and Keighley, merts. & ship owners, Old Custom hs. High st.
Gregson Wm. linen draper, &c. 37, Lowgate
Gresham John, tailor & dealer in plate, clothes, watches, jewellery, &c. 16, Queen street
Gresham Wm. steward of Kingston packet, & shopkpr. 21, Queen st.
Grey Eliz. glass & china dealer, 20, Silver street
Grey Paul, day school, Charlotte st.
Grey Thos. brush mfr. 5, Todd's entry, Silver street
Grieve David, Scotch linen warehouse, 37, St. John st. ; h. 9, Portland pl.
Griffin Thos. painter, 12, North walls
Griffith Wm. excise officer, Blue Bell entry, High st.
Griggs John, vict. Ship Molly, 82, Dock street
Grimston Elizabeth, vict. Black Horse, 77, West street
Grimston Mtthw. sawyer, 3, Duke st.
Grindall Oliver, coast waiter, Church street, Drypool
Griswood Ann, gentlewoman, Carlisle street

Grocock Ann, furniture broker, 57, Mytongate
Groves Geo. gent. Great passage st.
Groves Mary Ann, register office, 22, Parliament st.
Grubb Wm. cowkpr. 11, Spencer st.
Gruby Robert, mariner, Harcourt st.
Gunnee Saml. druggist, 35, Chariot st.
Gunnell Benj. gent. 1, York parade
Guppy Joseph, porter merchant, 168, High street
Guy Thos. rope maker and furniture broker, 10, New Dock st.
Guy Wm. solicitor's clerk, 4, Schonswar's sq. Dagger lane
Guy Thos. landing waiter, Stepney place, Beverley road
Hackney Anthy. butcher, 4, Bishop ln.
Haddon Geo. chair mkr. 40, Carr lane
Haddon James, town's beadle, 40, Carr lane
Haggerston Edw. oil merchant; house, 16, Portland place
Haggott Samuel, excise officer, 9, Garden square
Hague Wm. shopkpr. 3, Machell st.
Haigh Geo. haberdasher, hosier, laceman and glover, 14, Silver street
Haigh Thos. fruiterer, 25, Church lane
Haigh Abm. mariner, 6, Union square
Haigh John, perfumer, 91, High street
Haire Galen, solicitor, 1, Trinity house lane; h. Patrick ground lane
Haire Geo. shopkpr. 41, Blanket row
Haire Mrs. Eliz. 28, Prospect street
Halden Wm. brush mkr. 27, Scale ln.
Hall & Gilder, tobacco & snuff mfrs. 2, Posterngate
Hall Robert, tobacco mfr.; house, 43, Blanket row
Hall Robert, jun. tobacconist, 11, Marine row
Hall Thos. West of England woollen warehouse, 17, Parliament st.; h. 9, York parade
Halls, Todd and Hassell, merchants and general agents, Blayd's staith, 8, High street
Hall Thos. & Sons, ship owners, merchants, ship insurance brokers & commission agents, 5, North walls
Hall John, mercht. 5, North walls; h. 24, Mason street
Hall Wm. Esq. alderman, 2, Geo. st.
Hall Wm. mercht.; h. Humber bank
Hall Frincis, merchant; h. 22, Whitefriargate
Hall Francis, jun. mercht.; h. Hessle
Hall John and Co. patent rope mkrs. 199, High street
Hall Wm. mercht.; h. Humber bank
Hall Francis, sail maker, 5, North walls; h. 1, Bourne street
Hall Mrs. Milcah, 9, York parade

Hall John, corn factor & general agt. 20, High st.; h. 8, Wood's court, Dock street
Hall Mrs. L. 5, North walls
Hall Miss Ann, 10, Portland place
Hall Geo. ship owner, 54, Moira buildings, Prospect street
Hall Bridget, gentlewoman, 5, Land of Green ginger
Hall Joseph, whitesmith, &c. Patrick ground lane
Hall Ed. shoemkr. 21, Grotto square, Mason street
Hall Samuel Miller, subscription mill, Danson lane
Hall Wm. butcher, 47, Shambles; h. 6, Burton street
Hall Thos. vict. and gardener, Crooked Billet, Strawberry gardens, Drypool
Hall Wm. vict. Robin Hood & Little John, 18, Myton place
Hall William, vict. Crooked Billet, 6, Love lane
Hall Robt. gardener, Hide's entry, 11, Market place
Hall Robert, shoemaker, North end, Number dock
Hall Ed. shoemkr. Broad entry, Scale ln.
Hall Wm. 10, Leadenhall square
Hall John D. merchant's clerk, 17, Parliament street
Hall Henry, clerk of customs, 9, York parade
Hall Henry, guard of Trafalgar coach, 9, Trinity house lane
Hallam Mary, stay mkr. 26, Water works street
Hallam Thomas, merchant's clerk, 11, Bourne street
Haller Thos. shoemkr. 5, St. John st.
Halley Edmd. coach mkr. 23, Bond st.
Hallin W. S. mariner, 13, Crown ct. 4, Dock street
Hambleton Edw. butcher, 4, Saltho. ld.
Hambrough Robert, umbrella repairer, 24, Lower Union street
Hamilton John, grocer, &c. 1, Thornton street
Hammond Mrs. Ann, 26, Charlotte st.
Hammond Charles, druggist, Withrd
Hammond Geo. gent. 2, North street
Hammond Geo. corn factor, 7, Myton place
Hammond John, gent. 3, Bewlalley ln.
Hanby Thos. smith & farrier, Water house lane; h. 3, Dyer's place
Hancock Robert, gent. 24, George yd. Lowgate
Haunah John, spirit mert. 1, King st.
Hannen Harriet, dancing, needlework, &c. seminary, 41, Saville st.
Hansell William, merchant; house, 4, Jarratt street

Ansley Wm. ironmonger, 16, Market place

Hanson Charles, hosier, glover and laceman, 14, Queen street

Hanson J. tailor, &c. 32, Blanket row

Happy Mary, shopkpr. 2, Grimsby ln.

Hardenstle Henry, linen draper, 17, Prospect street

Hardisty Wm. bread & biscuit baker, 15, Sykes street

Hardy and Astrop, paper hanging mfr. 3, St. John street

Hardy Thos. paper stainer; house, 4, Prospect street

Hardy Robert, plane mkr. 33, Waterworks street

Hardy James, baker, 37, Church lane

Hardy James, mariner, 97, Dock st.

Hardy Henry, shopkpr. 35, Mytongate

Hardy Wm. cowkpr. 4, North street, Prospect street

Hare John, wax and tallow chandler, South side Trinity church; house, 5, Myton place

Hare Marmaduke, landing waiter, 11, Sykes street

Harford Geo. shopkpr. 9, Broadley st.

Hargrave Eliz. dress mkr. 5, Engine st.

Hargrave John, fashionable straw hat maker, 28, Lowgate

Hargrave Robert, tailor and draper, 6, Lowgate

Harker John, butcher, 11, Savile st.

Harker Edw. butcher, 39, Bridge st.

Harker M. J. butcher, 45, Shambles; house, 11, Paradise place

Harker Robert, vict. Anchor, 31, Waterworks street

Harker Mrs. Ann, schoolmistress, Want's sq. New George street

Harland Thos. landing waiter, New row, Anlaby road

Harley John, mariner, 31, West st.

Harper John, joiner, 6, Queen's place

Harper Richard, baker, 75, West st.

Harper John, tailor, 5, Thornton's sq. Posterngate

Harper James, tailor, Green lane, Drypool

Harper Richard, joiner, Castle street

Harris Jas. mariner, 8, West street

Harrison, Watson & Locke, bankers, Whitefriargate; (on Marriett and Co. London)

Harrison John, mert.; h. 49, Geo. st.

Harrison Rd. underwriter, Garrison side

Harrison Richard & John, ship owners & timber merts. 49, Garrison side

Harrison Biolby, woollen draper, 40, Market place; h. 1, Portland pl.

Harrison John, spirit merchant, 7, North side Trinity church

Harrison Wm. spirit merchant, 3, Paragon place, Sykes street

Harrison Wm. ship owner, 7, Pryme st.

Harrison Rev. John, 5, Paragon place, Sykes street

Harrison Robert, vict. Indian Chief, 10, Blackfriargate

Harrison Thos. vict. Crown, Summergangs

Harrison Wm. schoolmaster, Great Union st.; h. John st. Church st.

Harrison Samuel, baker & shoemkr. 117, High street

Harrison John, tailor, 22, Gt. passage st.

Harrison Robert, tailor, 3, Featherstone's entry, 178, High st.

Harrison Wm. tailor, 8, Featherstone's entry, 178, High st.

Harrison John, millwright, 12, New Drain bank, Wincolmlee

Harrison Rachael, ladies' school, Postern place, Posterngate

Harrison Richd. keeper of the Lunatic Asylum, 8, Charterhouse lane

Harrison Richard, twine spinner, 14, Carr lane

Harrison James, mariner, 6, West st.

Harrison Richd. mariner, 3, Mason st.

Harrison Henry, bellhanger, English st.

Harrop Thomas, clerk of St. John's church, 3, Dyer's pl. Waterwks. st.

Harrow Mary, dress mkr. 18, West st.

Hansley John, pawnbroker, 14, King st.

Hart Jacob, silversmith and jeweller, 25, Humber street

Hartley Christr. vict. Sir John Falstaff, Church street

Hartley James, vict. Humber Dock Coffee House, 8, New Dock side

Hartley Edw. turner, Parade row

Harvey Richard, cabinet maker and broker, 18, Posterngate

Harwood James, vict. Grapes, 12, Waterhouse lane

Harwood Richard, butter and bacon factor, 41, Whitefriargate

Hassell Samuel T. merchant; h. 22, Whitefriargate

Hasslewood John, mariner, Chapel ct. George yard

Hasslewood Mary, gentwn. 4, Nile st.

Hastings Jas. farmer, 5, Albion place

Hastings John, constable, Pottery

Haswell Jane, milliner, 17, Aldbro' st.

Hatfield James, tailor, 18, New Dock street

Hattersley John, mariner, 7, Clappison's sq. Sykes street

Havelock Geo. cooper, 19, New Dock walls

Havelock Rt. cooper, W. end Old dock

Havitson James, oil merchant & ship owner, 7, Bourne street

Hawden John, butcher, 88, Mytongt.

Hawes J. H. hosier, glover, &c. 45, Lowgate

Hawkes Wm. gun maker and dentist, 27, Scale lane

Hawkins Edw. oil and colourman, 58, High street

Hawkins Phœbe, stay mkr. 20, Bridge street

Hawkins Thos. mariner, 3, Princess st.

Hawley Geo. vict. General Abercrombie, 39, High street

Haworth Francis, insurance broker, agent and lighter owner, 2, North walls; h. Jennings street

Haworth Joshua, gent. 201, High st.

Haworth Mrs. Mary, 23, Humber st.

Haye Henry, mariner, 19, New Geo. street

Hayes Chas. surgeon, 8, Dock street

Hayes H. B. surgeon, 8, Dock street

Hays J. B. ship and insurance broker, and general agent, Commercial buildings, 29, High street; h. 15, George street

Haythorn Joseph, vict. and gardener, Pine Apple, Spring row

Haythorn James, excise officer, 14, Regent's place, Sykes street

Hayton Thos. tailor, 56, Scott street

Hayward Wm. shoemaker, 7, Blackfriargate

Haywood James, Albion place

Head Thos. shoemaker, 36, Blackfriargate

Headley Geo. whitesmith, 36, Chariot street

Headley James, rope maker, &c.; h. 15, Osborne street

Healey Geo. druggist, 12, Queen st.

Heaton Thos. grocer, &c. 13, Mill st.

Heaton Wm. bricklayer, 16, Savile row

Heawood and Jebson, house, ship and sign painters, North side Old dock

Heawood Joseph, painter; house, 17, Gibson street

Hebblewhite John and Benj. woollen drapers and hatters, 20, Market place

Hebblewhite John, woollen draper; house, *Cottingham*

Hebblewhite Benj. woollen draper; house, 4, Cent per Cent street

Hebblewhite Francis, tailor, 193, High street

Heckenberry Henry, baker, Alfred st.

Heighley William, vict. Blue Bell, 8, Prospect street

Heighley Ann, milliner, 30, Wincolmlse

Hellard John, farmer, Green lane

Hembrough Francis, druggist, 10, Bond street

Henderson Wm. hair dresser, 1, Queen street

Hendry Thos. gentleman, 13, Worship street

Hendry and Hyde, auctioneers and appraisers, Exchange Sale Room, Exchange alley

Hendry Martin, general commission agent and broker, Stewart's yd. 152, High st.; h. 21, Prospect st.

Hendry Wm. auctioneer, & agent to the European Life Office, &c.; house, 49, Prospect street

Henekey Wm. excise officer, 25, Mytongate

Hentig John, Wm. & Co. merchants and ship owners, 24, High st.

Hentig John Wm. Prussian Consul; house, *Cottingham*

Hentig Henry Wm. merchant; b. 18, Albion street

Henwood and Robinson, linen and woollen drapers, haberdashers, & silk mercers, 21, St. John st.

Henwood James, banker's clerk, *Somerstown*

Henwood Thos. banker's clerk, *Somerstown*

Hepper John, shoemkr. 141, High st.

Hepple Robert, butcher, Market place; house, Robinson row

Herbert Wm. gent. 76, High st.

Herratt John, vict. Sloop Chance, 52, High street

Herring James, pork butcher, 60, West street

Herrington Mary Ann, day school, 36, Grimsby lane

Heseltine Benj. mert. 14, Savile row

Heseltine Jph. druggist, 70, Mytongt.

Heseltine Wm. mariner, 4, West st.

Heseltine Thos. (lodgings) 44, Geo. st.

Heseltine Charles, locker at the Custom house, and miniature painter, 16, Grotto square, Mason street

Heselton Thos. gent. 20, Great Passage street

Hessey Wm. cowkpr. 28, North st.

Hesslewood Lieut. John, R.N. George yard, Lowgate

Hesslewood Francis, merchant's clerk, 2, Chapel street

Hesslewood Samuel, cowkpr. Church street, Drypool

Heward John & Robert, hosiers and silk stocking mfrs. 18, St. John st.

Heward Wm. shoemkr. 7, Blackfriargt.

Heward Joseph, bread & ship biscuit baker, 15, Bishop lane

Hewetson James and John and Co. oil merchants & ship owners, 16, Wincolmlee; h. 7, Bourne street, country houses, *Stone Ferry*

Hewetson Joseph, merchant's clerk, 10, Charles street

Hewitt Thomas, jun. and Co. general agents, ship & insurance brokers, Stewart's yard, 152, High street

Hewitt Thos. jun. agent, &c.; house, 8, York parade
Hewitt John, shoemaker, 22, St. John street
Hewitt Mary, tea dlr. 22, Silver st.
Hewitt Thos. merchant's clerk, 9, Savile st.
Hick Geo. clerk of customs, 8, Page's square, Dagger lane
Hick John, gent. 12, Clark's square, Sykes street
Hick John, merchant's clerk, 8, Page's square, Dagger lane
Hick John, custom house officer, Edward's place, Love lane
Hicks John, cabinet maker & broker, 30, Blackfriargate
Hicks Joseph, cabinet & chair maker, 10, Wells st.
Hides Christ. bricklayer, 4, Mytongt.
Higson John, secretary & house surgeon, Infirmary, and 21, Lowgate
Hildyard Richd. gent. 12, Marine row
Hilkin Henry, vict. Billy Boy, 19, North walls
Hill Henry, lieut. in the Royal Navy, Stubbin st.
Hill John, wine and spirit merchant, and agent to the Phœnix Fire Office, and the Pelican Life Assurance Co. 18, Parliament st.
Hill Robert, gent. Love lane
Hill Mrs. Mary, 12, Finkle st.
Hill Eliz. pawnbroker, 22, Bishop ln.
Hill Paul, vict. Original Andrew Marvel, 35, Whitefriargate
Hill James, shopkpr. 4, Bourne st.
Hill Wm. butcher, Hood st. Jennings street
Hill Robert, shoemkr. 1, Wincolmlee
Hill Joseph, shopkpr. 37, Scott st.
Hindle Joseph, canvasser, 9, Hodgson square, Sykes st.
Hinsley John, cabinet mkr Parade row
Hinsley John, shopkpr. 10, New Dock street
Hipsley John, mustard mfr. and agent to the Suffolk Amicable and General Country Fire Office, 8, Finkle st.; house, *Bell Field*
Hird Wm. lighterman, 36, Humber st.
Hirst Jonathan, ironmonger, 41, Market place
Hirst Abraham, worsted mfr. 35, Wincolmlee; house, Witham
Hirst Jas. ship owner, 9, Dock st.
Hirst Joseph, furniture broker, 5, Lowgate
Hirst Marmaduke, schoolmaster, Jackson st. Neptune st.; house, New John street
Hitchen Wm. grocer,&c. 23,Chariot st.
Hitchen Wm. tin plate worker, 28, Garden st.

Hizard Mary, dress mkr. Church st.
Hobson W. E. gent. Stubbin st.
Hobson Michael, vict. Bay Horse, 1, West st.
Hobson Francis, grocer, Witham
Hobson Michl. butcher, New John st.
Hodge Wm. and Co. sail makers, 52, Humber st.
Hodgson Jas. currier, &c. Witham
Hodgson Geo. shoemkr. 4, Mytongt.
Hodgson Francis, baker, 174, High st.
Hodgson Ralph,grocer, 1, Salthouse ln.
Hodgson John, shoemkr.1, Prospect st.
Hodgson Wm. baker, 11, North st. Prospect st.
Hodgson Jas. shopkeeper, 46, Edgar street
Hodgson John, corn factor, 1, Princess street
Hodgson Thos.mariner,6,Thornton st.
Hodson John, vict. Shepherdess, Myton st. and cabinet maker, Trundle street
Hogg Thos. joiner; h. Salthouse lane
Hogg Wm. custom house officer, 28, Aldbro' street
Hoggard John, shopkpr. 11, Waterhouse lane
Holden Geo. Son and Co. shipping agents, wharfingers & insurance brokers, 52 and 181 High st.
Holden Geo. merchant; h. 6, Providence row
Holden Geo. merchant; house, 59, Prospect st.
Holden Thomas, solicitor, 7, Land of Green ginger
Holden Wm. cabinet maker, Upper Union street
Holder Wm. druggist, 24, Wincolmlee
Holderness Thos. ship, &c. broker; house, 2, Portland place
Holderness Francis, joiner, St. Quintin's place, Drypool
Holderness Sarah, lodging house, 6, Castle row
Holdstock and Wright, house & ship painters, 171, High st.
Holdstock Henry, painter; house, 15, George yard
Holdstock Mark, bread & ship biscuit baker, 15, George yard
Holdsworth Wm. book, print, and music seller, stationer, and circulating library, 69, Lowgate
Holdsworth John, mert.; h. 7, Albion street
Holdsworth David, boot & shoe mkr. 62, Lowgate
Holdsworth Mrs. J. 71, West st.
Holdsworth Thos. horse dealer and livery stable keeper, 3, Fox st.
Holdsworth John, shopkeeper, 1, Beverley road

Holland Wm. ship owner, 2, Charles street

Holland Benj. ship owner, 20, High st.; house, 22, Albion st.

Holland Mrs. Charlotte, 58, Mill st.

Hollingworth and Holderness, ship and insurance brokers, Exchange buildings

Hollingworth Thos. mariner, Hodgson street

Holmes Joseph, mahogany merchant, opposite Exmouth buildings, Queen street

Holmes Richard Henry, clock maker, 6, Bishop lane

Holmes Wm. vict. Golden Cup, Steam Packet house, and Subscription News room, Humber st.

Holmes David, plumber and glazier, 26, Bond st.

Holmes John, tanner, Church street, Sculcoates

Holmes Charles, furniture broker, 15, Blackfriargate

Holmes Joseph, furniture broker, 32, Blackfriargate

Holmes Stephen, whitesmith, 49, Blackfriargate

Holmes Wm. tide waiter, 12, Waterhouse lane

Holmes Thos. tailor, 2, Neptune pl. 15, Trippet

Holmes Samuel, tailor, 17, Sewer ln.

Holroyd Thomas, grocer, 23, Blanket row

Holroyd Timothy, mariner, 14, Humber street

Holt John, eating house, 15, Scale ln.

Hooper J. R. silk dyer, 22, Waterhouse lane

Hope John, butcher, 14, Fish st.

Hopkin Wm. comb mfr. & toy dealer, 4, Market place

Hopkins James, shopkeeper, Church st. Drypool

Hopp Thos. hair dresser, 4, Scott st.

Hopp John, hair dresser, 45, Bridge st.

Hopper Wm. tobacco mfr.; house, 18, George st.

Hopper Eliz. (lodgings) 14, Robinson row

Hopper Wm. furniture broker, 5, New Dock st.

Hopper Wm. furniture broker, 58, Carr lane

Hopwood Wm. wine and spirit mert. underwriter, ship owner and insurance broker, 33, High st.; h. 23, Dock st.

Hopwood Wm. & Co. common brewers, 1, West st.

Hordon John, schoolmaster, 47, Geo. street

Hornby Mrs. Jane, 18, Finkle st.

Horncastle Thos. bone merchant; h. 2, Bourne st.

Horncastle Wm. ship owner, 18, Osborne st.

Horner John and Simon, merchants, 28, High st.

Horner Simon, gent.; h. 34, Prospect street

Horner James, vict. Three Tuns, Leadenhall square

Horner John, plumber and glazier, Witham

Hornor Jane, grocer, &c. 19, Lowgt.

Hornsby Jas. shoemaker, Queen st.

Hornsby Jas. fruiterer, 3, Blanket row

Horsley John, ship owner and underwriter, 12, Scale lane

Horsley Eliz. confectioner, &c. 18, New Dock walls

Horsley Stephen, tobacconist, snuff and tea dealer, 30, Silver st.

Horst Joseph, shopkpr. 5, Lowgate

Horwood D. G. bankers' clerk, Wilson st. Drypool

Hotham Thos. butcher, 8, Lowgate

Houlder Wm. wheelwright, 9, Cook's buildings, Broadley st.

Howard Mrs. Ann, 47, Spencer st.

Howard J. Saml. M.D. 47, Mytongt.

Howard Jph. butcher, 18, St. John st.

Howden Geo. vict. Ship Diana, 18, Church lane

Howe Geo. vict. Sam's Coffee House, South side Trinity church

Howe John, printer, bookseller, binder and stationer, 3, Scale lane

Howe John, coachman, Posterngate

Howlett Robert, tailor, 8, Trippet

Howlett Thos. tailor, 2, Church lane

Hoyland Samuel and Co. cutlers and elastic steel truss makers, 10, Queen st.

Hoyland Saml. cutler; h. 32, Finkle street

Hudson Francis, gent. 23, Prospect pl. Drypool

Hudson John & Son, linen & woollen drapers, 47, Market place

Hudson John, linen draper; house, 14, Nile st.

Hudson John, chemist and druggist, and importer of leeches, 22, Waterworks st.

Hudson W. C. joiner, Grantham's entry, Dagger lane

Hudson Geo. baker, 1, Machell st.

Hudson Rt. whitesmith, 36, Blanket row

Hudson Thos. toll collector, 11, St. John street

Hudson Thos. hair cutter, 5, Waterworks st.

Hudson Wm. overlooker, 5, Prince George entry, 184, High st.

Hudson Wm. Waterhouse lane

Hugall Thomas, solicitor, and clerk of Court of Requests, 17, Bowlalley lane; h. 3, Charlotte street

Hulley Christopher, patten maker & cutler, 63, Prospect street

Humberston Mark Edward, spirit merchant and insurance broker, 5, Blackfriargate

Humberston Edward, gent. Staniforth place, Patrick ground lane

Humble Richard, wine and brandy merchant, 31, High street

Humble Thomas, schoolmaster, 159, High street

Humphrey Wm. vict. Golden Measure, 88, Mytongate

Humphrey Thomas, auctioneer, ship surveyor, ship smith, and agent to underwriters, 50, Dock street; house, 3, North street

Humphrey Rd. mariner, 21, Waterhouse lane

Hunsley Peter, vict. Bath Tavern, Humber bank

Hunt Mrs. Ann, ladies' seminary, 19, Grimston street

Hunt Jane, brewer, George yard, 170, High street

Hunt Robert, vict. Anchor, 63, Whitefriargate

Hunt Etty, vict. White Swan, 77, High street

Hunter Wm. sail maker, Broadley street

Hunter Francis, vict. George and Dragon, 102, High street

Hunter Joseph, whalebone cutter, 19, Machell street

Hunter Mrs. Mary, 17, Charles st.

Hunter James, mariner, John's place

Hunter Francis, mariner, 7, Sykes st.

Hunter Wm. mariner, 22, Prospect place, Drypool

Huntington Charles, wine, &c. merchant; house, Anlaby road

Huntington Mrs. Olive, 17, George st.

Huntington Christopher, gent. 4, Regent's place, Sykes street

Huntington Miss M. A. 12, Bond st.

Huntley Richard, saddler, Witham

Hurst John, timber merchant and ship owner, Old Dock side; house, 24, Humber street

Hurst Jas. ship owner, 9, Dock street

Hurst Wm. mariner, 6, North street

Husband Charles, merchant's clerk, *Summergangs*

Hussard John, livery stable keeper, 52, Salthouse lane

Hustwick Robt. coach manufacturer; house, 11, Osborne street

Hutchcroft Rt. vict. Ship, Hodgson st.,

Hutchcroft William Benson, schoolmaster, 1, Mason street

Hutchinson Jas. joiner, 2, St. John st.

Hutchinson John, grocer and tea dlr. 9, Whitefriargate

Hutchinson John, printer, 29, Silver st.

Hutchinson Js. whitesmith, 8, Castle st.

Hutchinson Rd. pawnbroker, 3, West st.

Hutchinson Wm. joiner and builder, 4, George yard, Lowgate

Hutchinson Mary, milliner, 50, W friargt.

Hutchinson Isabella, dress maker, 9, Prospect street

Hutton Geo. butcher, Lime street

Hutton Sarah, shopkpr. Hodgson st.

Hutton Mary, shopkpr. 14, Garden st.

Hutty Wm. (lodgings) 9, George st.

Hyde Robt. landing waiter, 6, King st.

Hyde W. W. auctioneer; h. Land of Green ginger

Ingmire William, butcher, 37 and 38, Shambles; house, Blanket row

Innes David, printer, 11, Manor st.

Inness Thos. surgeon, 27, Blanket row

Irving and Edwards, flax dressers, 13, Queen st.; house, Pier street

Irving Wm. flax dresser; h. Nelson st.

Irving Geo. shoemaker, 16, Castle st.

Irving John, bricklayer, 2, Duke st.

Irving Edw. bricklayer, Ann st.

Irving John, mariner, 4, Garden sq. Princess st.

Jackson John, mert. 16, Bowlalley ln.

Jackson Thos. mert. 17, Charlotte st.

Jackson and Smith, confectioners, 89, Mytongate

Jackson Jno. & Son, grocers, &c. Witham

Jackson Richard, grocer, Witham

Jackson Ralph, grocer, &c. Queen st.

Jackson William, wine and brandy merchant, 49, High st.

Jackson Edw. pawnbroker, 6, Fish st.

Jackson Robt. commercial agent, 149, High street; h. 4, Hanover sq.

Jackson John, ironmonger, 2, St. John st.

Jackson John, tallow chandler, 5, Grimsby lane court

Jackson Geo. butcher, 3, Shambles; house, 21, Great passage st.

Jackson Wm. joiner, 12, Quay st.

Jackson Geo. bricklayer & brick mkr. 7, Prince st.

Jackson Wm. Lincoln yeast warehouse, New John st.

Jackson Jane, straw hat mfr. 9, King st.

Jackson Wm. fellmonger, Cliff's sq. Hodgson st.

Jackson Jas. fruiterer, 1, St. John st.

Jackson Mrs. Ann, 2, Brook st. square

Jackson Mary, gentwmn. 2, English st.

Jackson John, gent. 36, Brook st.

Jackson John, gent. 4, Beverley road

Jackson Richd. ship owner, 8, Cent per cent. st.

Jackson Thomas, tallow chandler & soap boiler, 36, Church lane

Jackson Richd. yeoman, 1, Walker's court, 9, Waltham st.
Jackson Wm. ladies' shoemaker, 5, Fishwick's yd. 11, Waterworks st.
Jackson Wm. gent. *Summergangs*
Jackson Joseph, baker, 64, High st.
Jackson Robt. tailor, 39, West st.
Jackson Wm. hair dresser, 1, Bowl-alley lane
Jackson Matthew, merchant's clerk, 2, Catherine sq. Mason st.
Jackson H. I. mariner, 27, Grimsby ln.
Jackson Joseph, clerk of customs, Holderness road
Jackson William, mariner, New row, Anlaby road
Jackson Robt. pilot, 21, Harcourt st.
Jackson James, painter, New Dock side; house, 2, English st.
Jackson Peter, hatter, 15, Queen st.
Jackson Matthew, mariner, Wilson st. Drypool
Jacobs Israel, jeweller & silversmith, 19, Silver st.
Jacobs Thos. vict. Grapes, Fawcett st.
Jagger Richd. butcher, 7, L. Union st.
Jagger Aaron, hair dresser, dealer in hats, &c. Dock office row
Jakeman John, cabinet mkr. Church st. Drypool
Jakeman Joseph, miller and flour dealer, Marvel st.
Jalland William Empson, solicitor, 13, Bishop lane
James Richd. broker and commercial agent, Commercial buildings, High st.; house, *Hessle*
James Lieut. T. E. 2nd West York, 17, English st.
James John, shopkpr. 19, Garden st.
Jameson Robt. joiner, 13, Fish st.
Jameson Peter, mariner, Back walls, St. John st.
Jaques James, gent. East st. Church st. Drypool
Jaques Thos. painter, 16, St. John st.
Jaques Edmund, plumber & glazier, 31, Mill st.
Jaques John, shoemkr. 13, Myton st.
Jaques John, chair maker and ship joiner, Parade row
Jaques Geo. earthenware dealer, 9 Wincolmlee
Jardin John, vict. Gallon Measure, 5, Great Passage st.
Jarratt Mrs. Ann, 3, Pryme st.
Jarratt Mary, shopkpr. 39, Wincolmlee
Jarvis Timothy, bricklayer and plasterer, 10, Machell st.
Jarvis Hannah, shopkpr. 73, West. st.
Jarvis Wm. gent. Linnæus st. Anlaby rd.
Jarvis Rt. tide waiter, 42, Providence pl.
Jay Palmer, mariner, North parade, Beverley road

Jebson Joseph, painter; h. 8, Bond st.
Jeff Geo. tailor, 27, George st.
Jeffells J. & E. milliners, &c. 65, W. fringt.
Jefferson Christopher, cowkeeper, 33, Waterhouse lane
Jefferson Henry, joiner, 18, Chapel ln.
Jeffery James, furniture broker, 14, New Dock st.
Jefferey John, tailor, 111, High st.
Jeffery William, clerk in the tax office, Webster's yd. New George st.
Jenkins Richd. surgeon, 6, Carlisle st.
Jenkinson & Richmond, glass, china & Staffordshire warehs. 39, Lowgt.
Jenkinson David, schoolmaster, 6, Foundry row
Jenkinson Robt. grocer, 11, Postemgt.
Jenkinson Wm. shoemkr. 40, Edgar st.
Jenkinson Geo. mariner, Walker's sq. Sykes st.
Jenkinson William, baker, Mill street; house, New George st.
Jennison Matthew, vict. Golden Ball, 22, Salthouse lane
Jepson Joseph, painter; h. 8, Bond st.
Jerom Wm. shopkeeper, 15, Finkle st.
Jervis Mary, sempstress, 4, Love lane
Jessop Wm. traveller, 3, York parade, Beverley road
Jewell Ann, house and ship painter, West end of the Dock
Jewett Simon, commission cornfactor, Walker's sq. Sykes st.
Jewett John, vict. and spirit dealer, Full Measure, 59, Mill st.
Jewett Mrs. S. 1, Spencer st.
Jewson Mrs. Ann, 9, Bourne st.
Jewson John, merchant's clerk, St. Quintin's place, Drypool
Johns Wm. umbrella mfr. 27, Lowgt.
Johnson B. L. attorney, 7, Mason st.
Johnson Wm. gent. 6, Paradise place
Johnson Richard, gentleman, 9, Commerce lane, Edgar st.
Johnson Joseph, spirit mercht. James's place, 2, Mason st.
Johnson Edw. linen draper, haberdasher & silk mercer, 5, Market place
Johnson Thos. haberdasher, hardware & toy dealer, 18, Mytongate
Johnson Wm. grocer, &c. 9 and 10, Waterworks st.
Johnson James, commercial agent, 23, North st.
Johnson Thos. shoemaker, 11, Trippet
Johnson Mrs. Ann, 39, Prospect st.
Johnson Edw. gent. 6, Beverley road
Johnson John, gent. 13, Dock st.
Johnson John, gent. 4, Scott's square, 11, Blanket row
Johnson Mrs. Mary, 7, Mason st.
Johnson Rd. tinner, 14, Charterhs. ln.
Johnson Abm. pawnbroker, 13, Trippet
Johnson Aaron, tinner, 13, Vicar lane

Johnson Ann, hosier and glover, 20, Scale lane

Johnson Deborah, ladies' boarding school, 4, Bourne street

Johnson Geo. tailor, 1, Sykes st.

Johnson John, vict & gardener, Blue Bell, Green lane, Drypool

Johnson Wm. vict. "Jack on a Cruise," North st. Prospect st.

Johnson Ann, fishmonger; b. Posterngt.

Johnson Joseph, travelling draper, 21, Garden st.

Johnson & Parrot, lath renders, Old Dock end

Johnson Jas. poulterer, 11, Grimsby ln.

Johnson Jas. farmer, Johnson's yard, North st. Prospect st.

Johnson Harriet, shopkpr. 4, Myton st.

Johnson Geo. shopkpr, 48, Mytongate

Johnson Jph. baker, 6, Dock office row

Johnson Lawrence, shopkeeper & confectioner, 11, Dock office row

Johnson Rd. engraver, 30, Scale lane

Johnson Richd. livery stable keeper, 12, Carr lane

Johnson John, mariner, 1, Clark's sq. Sykes st.

Johnson Henry, cowkeeper, Air st.

Johnson Wm. cowkpr. 3, Chapel st.

Johnson John, mariner, 2, Castle row

Johnson Richd. mariner, Posterngate

Johnson Robt. horse dlr. 5, Chapel st.

Johnson John, green grocer, 2, Blue Bell entry, High st.

Johnson John, baker, 38, Mill st.

Johnson Timothy, shopkeeper, 33, Chariot st.

Johnston Maria, book and toy seller, 7, Market place

Jones and Forrester, goldsmiths, jewellers & watch mkrs. 17, Market pl.

Jones Anthony, goldsmith; h. Kirkella

Jones & Kirk, linen & woollen drapers & haberdashers, 66, Market place, and 1 & 2, Silver st.

Jones Wm. cutler & surgeon's instrument maker, 35, St. John st.

Jones Thos. shoemkr. 32, Bridge st.

Jones Thos. G. ship owner, 31, Mason st.

Jones Thos. shoemkr, 5, Prospect st.

Jones Isaac, hair dresser & tea dealer, 64, Whitefriargate

Jones Hannah, day school, 6, Osborne st.

Jones Daniel, shopkpr. 7, Burton st.

Jopling Jas. gardener, 6, Wincolmlee

Jordan Michael, mariner, 8, West st.

Jowitt Robt. poulterer, 17, Scale lane

Jowitt Sam. straw hat mfr. New John st.

Jubb Wm. vict. Sun, Garrison

Jubb Ann, day school, 3, Neptune pl.

Kay & Liddle, wine merchants, Commercial buildings, 29, High st.

Kay John, gent. Discount court, Cent per cent. st.

Kay Cornelius, glass and china dealer, Shambles, & lime burner, Humber bank

Kay Geo. plumber and glazier, 50, Blanket row

Kay Ralph, shoemaker, Summergangs

Keddey Robt. merchant, ship owner & Spanish consul, 6, Blanket row

Keddey Ralph, vict. Vittoria Tavern, 28, Queen st. Waterside

Keel Thos. blacksmith, 24, Machell st.

Keen Wm. joiner, trunk mkr. & furniture broker, 20, New Dock st.

Keeton Mary, shopkpr. 110, High st.

Keighley Rt. mert. & ship owner, Old Custom hs. High st.; h 5, Worship st.

Keighley Hannah, saddler, 12, Silver st.

Kelah Robert, mariner, 23, Waterhouse lane

Kelly Thomas, shopkeeper, 23, Low Union st.

Kelsey Thos. vict. Blue Ball, Air st.

Kelsey John, joiner & cabinet maker, Walker's sq. Paragon place

Kelsey James, furniture broker, &c. 13, Blackfriargate

Kelsey John, shopkeeper, 7, Grotto sq. Mason st.

Kemp William, gent. Discount court, Cent per cent st.

Kemp Mary, straw hat mfr. 44, Savile st.

Kemplay William, clerk of customs, 28, Brook st.

Kennedy Jas. Esq. barrister, 11, Geo. st.

Kennedy Wm. millwright & machine maker, Summergangs

Kennington Adam, blacksmith and clerk of the parish of Drypool, Church st.

Kent Robt. day school, 5, Wincolmlee

Kent Robt. cabinet mkr. Drypool sq.

Ker Edw. gentleman, 1, Albion st.

Kerman Wm. cowkpr. Summergangs

Kerman Jph. cowkpr. Summergangs

Kerman Nathaniel, cowkeeper, Holderness road

Kerry Richard, merchant's clerk, 8, Clarke's square, Sykes st.

Kershaw John, grocer, &c. 48, Lowgt.

Kershaw Edw. eating house, 52, South end

Kidd John G. linen draper, &c. 52, Market place

Kidd Anthony, classical school, 30, Brook st.

Kidd Dan. bricklayer, 12, Castle st.

Kidd John, clerk of customs, 14, Upper Union st.

Killingbeck John, brazier, 3, Water house lane

Killin Peter, vict. Blue Bell, 17, Waterworks st.

King Rev. John, M.A. 9, Pryme st.

King Robert, merchant, 3, Baker st.

King, Turuer & Co. iron merts. iron-mongers & plane manufacturers, 59, Market place

King Robert, attorney, 24, Chapel ln. house, Neptune st.

King & Pinn, linen & woollen drapers, 8, Whitefriargate, and 4, North bridge

King John, linen draper; house, 4, York parade

King Thos. bricklayer, 4, New Geo. st.

King John, cabinet maker, 14, New Dock st.

King Chas. worsted mfr. 5, Finkle st.

King John, land wtr. 16, Osborne st.

King Ann, baker, 48, Blackfriargate

Kipling John, river broker; h. 12, New George st.

Kirby Mary, vict. Bowling green Tavern, 13, Waltham st.

Kirby Wm. bricklayer, 6, Waterworks st.

Kirby Thos. mariner, Dock st.

Kirby Thos. mariner, 2, Princess st.

Kirby Mark, mariner, 17, Harcourt st.

Kirkling James, gent. 15, Mason st.

Kirkman John, gent. 13, Blanket row

Kirkus & Backhouse, auctioneers & appraisers, auction mart, 66, Lowgate

Kirkus & Bromby, common brewers, Julian spring brewery, Waterhouse lane

Kirkus Robert, painter, 27, Trippet

Kirkus John, mariner, 2, Robson's place, 3, Mason st.

Kirkus Jeremiah, ship owner; house, Waterworks st.

Kirk Rt. draper; h. 18, Trinity hs. ln.

Kirk Wm. vict. Yarmouth Arms, 168, High st.

Kirk Thos. pawnbroker, 29, Grimsby ln.

Kirkham Joseph, pawnbroker, 45, Mill st.

Kirkwood Stephen, vict. "Opening New Dock," 30, Blanket row, & timber Merchant, Queen st.

Kirkwood Stephen, surveyor of roads, 1, Naylor's row, Witham

Kirlew Rd. Morley, collector of taxes, Hodgson st.

Kirlew Hannah, shopkpr. 17, Chapel ln.

Kirlew Mary, shopkeeper, 18, Great Passage st.

Kitchingman Charles, mariner, 14, New George st.

Kitching Geo. grocer, tallow chandler, & cheesemonger, 11, Market pl.

Kitching Geo. hatter, and straw hat mfr. 26, Whitefriargate

Kitching Thos. tailor and hatter, 10 and 11, Queen st.

Kitching Nainby, mfr. of sail cloth, sacking, shoe thread, &c. Witham

Kittle Albine, druggist, &c. 55, Market place

Kneal Thos. gardener, Humber bank

Knight John, clothes broker, 30, Great Passage st.

Knight John, clerk of St. Mary's, Cent per cent. st.

Knill Thos. mariner, 4, Grimston st.

Knott Francis, mariner, Nile place, Cottage gardens

Knowles Anthony, shopkeeper, 4, Waterhouse lane

Knowsley, Swann & Co. wine merts. & insurance brokers, 5, Commercial buildings, High st.

Knowsley Edw. mert.; h. 15, Geo. st.

Labon Wm. mattrass mkr. 51, Edgar st.

Lacup Henry, number carrier, 6, Horner's square

Laidlaw Alexander, tanner, 37, High st.; house, 7, English st.

Lake Mrs. Sarah, John's court, 18, Osborne st.

Lalouel Henry, corn and flax broker, 20, High st.

Lamb George, grocer and draper, 12, Grimston st.

Lamb Jane, vict. Globe, 182, High st.

Lamb Wm. painter, Globe entry, 182, High st.

Lamb Edward, lighterman, Old Penitentiary, Church st.

Lambert Saml. tailor, 4, Chapel lane

Lambert Wm. grocer and tea dealer, 56, Market place

Lambert C. linen drpr. 27, W. friargate

Lambert Mrs. Eliz. 5, Fish st.

Lambert Mrs. M. 11, Castle st.

Lambert George, music preceptor, 33, Finkle st.

Lambert Joseph Cassimir, teacher of the French lang. 19, Savile row

Lambert John B. wine mert. underwriter, & ship owner, 8, Quay st.; house, 12, North st.

Lambert Joseph, gent. 20, Osborne st.

Lambert Joseph, coal inspector, (and agent for Brightmore and Co. Gainsbro',) 49, South end; house, 81, Brook st.

Lambert Wm. whitesmith & wire cut fender maker, 11, New Dock st.

Lambert Sarah, flour dlr. 9, Trippet

La Marche John Bernard, ship and insurance broker, and agent to the Royal Exchange Assurance Company, 200, High st.

Lancaster Jane, gentwn. Hodgson st.

Lane Rev. Saml. 29, West st.

Langdale J. R. turner, Dock st.

Langley Jas. eating house, 1, Seale ls.

Langley Thos. vict. Dog and Duck, 86, High st.

Langrick Wm. shoemaker, 18, Mill st.

Langrick Thos. mariner, 2, Park place, Witham

Langrigg Elizabeth, day school, 7, Church st. Wincolmlee

Lapish Joseph, earthenware manfr. Church st. Sculcoates ; house, 57, Scott street

Lapish James, jun. earthenware mfr. 18, Church st. Sculcoates

Larard Thos. clock and watch maker, 32, Market pl. ; h. 29, English st.

Large Rd. bellman, 8, New Dock st.

Lascelles James, oil refiner, 1, Church street, Sculcoates

Lascelles Ralph, tailor, 45, Savile st.

Lascelles Thos. shoemkr. 17, Bond st.

Lascelles James, broker & merchant, Commercial buildings, 29, High st. ; house, Wincolmlee

Lathangue Robert, apothecary to the Sculcoates dispensary, 51, High st.

Laverack Wm. ship & insurance broker, wharfinger, and general commission agent, 70, High st.

Laverack & Co. cornfactors & wharfingers, 3, High st.

Laverack Martin, cornfactor ; house, Naylor's row, Witham

Law James, spinning master to the Workhouse, 5, Humber bank

Lawer Peter, joiner, 42, Wincolmlee

Lawrence John, brush mfr. 9, New Dock st. ; h. 16, Blanket row

Lawson Mrs. Mary, 36, Albion st.

Lawson Geo. mariner, Edward's place, Love lane

Lawson William, tide waiter, 54, Carr lane

Lawton John, joiner, Old Dock end

Lawton Mrs. Ann, 16, Castle row

Laybourn Robt. druggist, 36, Aldbro' street

Laycock Thos. mariner, 9, Yucatan place, 9, Osborne st.

Laycock Wm. mariner, 4, Holme's court, Blackfriargate

Lazarus Samuel, silk hat manufacturer, 34, Blackfriargate

Leach Wm. shopkpr. 26, Church ln.

Leadbethorp John, paper stainer, Beverley road

Leake Geo. gardener, Halfpenny hatch, Caroline st.

Leake Wm. mariner, 7, West st.

Leake John, butcher, 43, Shambles ; house, 11, Waltham st.

Leake John, victualler, Windmill, 59, Whitefriargate

Leake Wm. plumber and glazier, 59, Whitefriargate

Leake John, shopkpr. 48, W. Friargt.

Leake John, vict. Three Tuns, 16, Great Passage st.

Leake Robert, poultry dlr. Bond st.

Leaper Jph. cork cutter, 127, High st.

Leavens John, gent. 2, Up. Union st.

Leavens Rt. turner, W. end of Dock

Ledell Ann, butcher, 6, Raikes st.

Ledell Geo. day schl. 23, Gt. pasg. st.

Lee Rev. Geo. teacher of classics, 5, Posterngate

Lee Hill, general commission agent, ship and insurance broker, and agent to the Birmingham Fire office, 19, Bowlalley lane ; house, *Summergangs*

Lee & Tall, tar and turpentine distillers, general commission agents, ship & insurance brokers, Church st. Sculcoates

Lee Newmarch, ship chandler, 166, High st.

Lee Beilby, tallow chandler & bacon factor, 16, Bridge st.

Lee Thos. general agent, accountant, & insurance broker, 159, High st ; house, 29, George st.

Lee Mrs. Elizabeth, 21, Nile st.

Lee Wm. gent. 2, Great Passage st.

Lee Mary Ann, 5, Baker street

Lee John, butcher and bacon factor, 51, Market place

Lee Geo. butcher, 39, High st.

Lee Henry, governor of the house of correction, Fetter lane

Lee Titus, shoemkr. Church st. Drypl.

Lee John, pilot, Kelsey's entry, Blackfriargate

Lee Thos. mariner, 40, Wilson's court, Dock street

Lee Wm. green grocer, 48, B. Friargt.

Leek Wm. grocer, &c. 20, North st.

Leggott James, bricklayer & plasterer, Parade row

Leggott John, bricklayer, plasterer, & brick maker, 1, Bourne st.

Leggott Eliz. shopkpr. 113, High st.

Leigh Mrs. Elizabeth, 21, Nile st.

Leighton John, shopkpr. 17, Mill st.

Leith John, adjutant, Church street, Drypool

Leng Adam, baker, 14, Waterhouse ln.

Leng Geo. day school, White Horse yard, Market place

Leng Joseph, day school, Mason st.

Leonard Wm. Watts, butcher, 49, Shambles ; house, 16, Lowgate

Leonard John, butcher, 31, Market pl. house, 9, West st.

Leonard John, butcher, 7, Chariot st. h. 16, Lower Union st.

Leonard Thos. butcher, 72, West st.

Leonard Abm. butcher, 72, West st.

Leonard Hanh. lodgings, 19, Sykes st.

Leslie Sarah, schoolmistress, 7, Clarence court, Princess st.

Letbe Wm. bookbinder & stationer, 43, High st. ; h. Nelson st.

Leuted Jas. whitesmith, &c. 17, Blanket row

Levett, Roberts, & Co. seed crushers, oil merchants, &c. 2, North walls

Levett Henry, oil merchant; house, 2, South side of the dock

Levett John, merchant & ship owner, agent to the Atlas Fire, &c. office, 2, South side old dock

Levett Quarton, merchant, commercial buildings, 29, High st.; h. *Newland*

Levett Wm. & Sons, grocers, tea dealers, seedsmen, and importers of fruit, 30, Market pl. & 71, High st.

Levett Wm. grocer, &c. house, 21, Whitefriargate

Levett Wm. jun. grocer; h. Posterngt.

Levett Thos. gent. 10, North side of Trinity church

Levett Sarah, bacon factor, 4, Shambls.

Levett John, grocer; h. 30, Market pl.

Levett Wm. gent. 10, Princess st.

Levett Thos. shopkpr. 3, Roper's row

Levett Math. cabinet mkr. 62, Edgar st.

Levett Richard, tailor, 47, Mill st.

Levett John, clerk to the Dock Co. 2, South side old dock

Levett Henry, oil merchant; house, 2, South side old dock

Levett John, tailor and broker, 14, Waterworks st.

Levi Joseph, quill and pencil merchant, New dock street

Levin James, travelling hawker, 25, Humber street

Lewis & Jackson, house, ship, & sign painters, 18, New Dock walls

Lewis Wm. painter; house, Cobourg place, Anlaby road

Lewis Wm. vict. Humber Tavern, 28, Humber street

Lewis Hugh, supervisor, 3, Clappison's square, Sykes street

Lewis Benj. mariner, 13, Savile row

Lewis Wm. 17, West street

Lewsley Joseph, shopkpr. Hodgson st.

Lickis Wm. glass, &c. dealer, 44, Blanket row

Lickis Henry, shoemaker, 25, Grimsby lane

Lickis Robert, shoemkr. Cleveland st. Groves

Liddell Geo. banker; h. *Hessle Wood*

Liddell Wm. wine merchant, Commercial buildings, 29, High st.

Liddell Geo. gent. 12, Irving's court, Waterhouse lane

Lightfoot Robert, vict. Old Elsinore, and eating house, Witham

Lightley Eliz. vict. Bridlington Tavern, 17, Manor street

Lilley John & Edwin, mahogany and hard wood merts. N. S. Old Dock

Lilley John, timber merchant; house, 6, Wright street

Lilley Edwin, timber merchant; h. 20, Bourne street

Lincoln John, cowkeeper, 5, North st. Prospect st.

Lind Major Geo. 6, Story st.

Linforth Mrs. Eliz. 9, Osbourne st.

Linskill Mrs. Mary, Beverley road

Linsley Wm. cabinet mkr. 55, Mill st.

Linton & Lloyd, woollen drapers, 19, Market place

Linton Mary, woollen draper; house, 12, Robinson row

Linton Mrs. Margaret, 4, Fish st.

Linton Geo. gent. 7, Neptune st.

Linton Wm. shopkpr. 4, Myton st.

Linwood Joseph, plumber & glazier, 136, High street

Linwood Rbt. butcher, 37, Bond st.

Linwood Eliz. staymkr. 27, Bond st.

Lison Edward, vict. Hull Packet, 105, High street

Lison Thomas, bookbinder, White Horse yard, Market place

Lison Thos. hair dresser, Mytongate

Lison Wm. shopkpr. 5, Church lane

Lister Ann, shopkpr. 14, Sykes st.

Lister Jph. excise port gauger, Nile st.

Lister Geo. mariner, 10, Paragon pl. Sykes street

Lister Wm. grocer, 8, Bond st.

Little Thos. merchant's clerk, Lime st.

Littlewood James, schoolmaster, Barker's court, Blanket row

Littlewood Thomas, flax dresser, 12, Waterworks street

Livingston Catharine, house and ship smith, Perrott st. Salthouse lane

Livingston James, whitesmith, 6, Waterhouse lane

Livingston Wm. whitesmith, 8, Spring bank

Lloyd Wm. mariner, 10, Hodgson sq. Sykes street

Lobley James, coal dealer, Saddle tree passage, 6, Myton st.

Lobley Isabella, day school, 27, Great Passage street

Locke T. B. Esq. banker; h. *Hessle*

Locke Thos. gent. 22, Humber st.

Lockhart Walter, botanical surgeon, 1 Brook street

Locking Geo. merchant, ship owner, underwriter, & insurance broker, 12, High st.; h. 11, Story st.

Locking Misses, ladies' boarding schl. 21, Story street

Lockwood Thomas, flax broker, 32, Humber street

Lockwood John, gardener, Green lane, Wincolmlee

Lodge & Metcalf, milliners, 10, South side Trinity church

..d, Thos. mert. ; h. 39, George st.

..oft Benj. brush maker, 139, High st.

..oft Mrs. Mary, gentlewn. Sleight's court, 4, Salthouse lane

..ofthouse John, bookbinder, 49, Market place

..omas Wm. shoemkr. 55, Salths. lane

..ongfield Joseph, mariner, 2, Hardy's court, Posterngate

..ongford Wm. lighterman, 13, Posterngate

..otherington Richard, shopkeeper &c. 12, Vicar lane

..ovitt Richard, butcher, 41, Shambles; house, 17, Finkle street

..ow John, day school, Walker's sq. Sykes street

..owe Susannah, vict. Blucher, 29, Finkle street

..owson Rd. schoolmaster, 9, North st.

..outh Dorothy, gentlewoman, 30, Bridge street

..owther Phineas, portrait painter, & artists repository, 5, Savile st.

..owther Frederick, house, ship, and sign painter, 31, Savile st.

..owther Joseph, gent. 2, Hope st.

..owther John, wharfinger, 8, Blackfriargate

..owther John, bricklayer, 6, Clarence court, Princess street

..owther Wm. gent. 5, Cross street

..owther James, cowkeeper, Air st.

..ucas Joseph, hair dresser, 34, Blanket row

..ucas Samuel, mariner, 13, Queen's place, Sykes street

..umley, Jameson, & Co. sail cloth & sacking mfrs. 46, Carr lane

..umley John, painter, 20, Carr lane

..undie Robert, ship owner and wine merchant, 1, Union street, 30 & 31, George st. : h. Albion st.

..undie Henry, vict. Sculcoates Arms, 43, Scott street

..undie T. J. tide surveyor, 11, Fish st.

..unn Wm. surgeon, 24, Charlotte st.

..upton Heneage, gent. 7, William's square, Mason street

..upton Heneage, clerk at the Trinity house, 34, Posterngate

..upton Mrs. Harriet, 71, West st.

..upton Richard, wholesale wine merchant, 20, Sykes street

..upton Eliz. register office, 2, Catharine square, Sykes street

..utwidge Charles, Esq. collector of customs, Whitefriargate

..yell Ann, shopkpr. New Dock side

..yon Matthew, vict. White Horse, Carr lane

Lyon Mrs. Rose, 11, Prospect st.

Mabb Wm. clerk to Dock Company, Anlaby road

Mackereth Rev. Geo. 13, Princess st. French's gardens

Maddison Rockliff, whitesmith, 4, Mews street

Maddison Josiah, mariner, 12, William square, Mason street

Mair Wm. day school, Waterwork st.

Maisters and Archbell, timber & oil merts. & seed crushers, Trippet

Major Robert, butcher, Mytongate

Makem Ann, confectioner, 39, Saville st.

Makin Michael, mariner, John street

Malcolm George & Sons, wharfingers and general commission agents, Union Wharf, where Scotch vessels load, & 63, High street, and Three Cranes Wharf, London

Malcolm G. public baths, Humber bnk.

Mallery Geo. mariner, 14, Paradise place

Malleys Simeon, timber merchant and general commission agent, North side Dock; house, 46, George st.

Malkinson William, druggist, 4, Prospect street

Malton William, shoemaker, 4, Featherstone's entry, 178, High st.

Manby Mary, baker, Mill bill

Mandeville Thos. vict. Gainsbro' Coffee House, 82, High street

Manger William, mariner, 16, Regent's place, Sykes street

Mann Mrs. Sarah, 2, Osborne street

Mapplebeck William, joiner, builder, and umbrella mfr. 34, Lowgate

Mapplebeck Elizabeth, day school, 4, Sewer lane

Margerison Richard, shopkeeper, Bradley's entry, 39, Humber street

Margeson Moses, broker for Leeds, Gainsbro', Knaresbro', and Tadcaster contract vessels, 174, High street; house, 3, Charles st.

Marginson Smith, corn dealer, Boalk's yard, Green lane

Markham Joseph, cowkeeper, Holderness road

Marley Mrs. Ann, 5, Bond street

Marley Hannah, shopkpr. 15, Mill st.

Marris Charles, watch maker, 47, Blackfriargate

Marris Henry, merchant, 154, High st. house, 22, Savile row

Marsh Samuel, auctioneer, Discount court, Cent per cent street

Marsh Joseph, guardian's clerk for the Sculcoates poor, 9, New Geo. st.

Marshall Thos. salt and bottle merchant, 75, High street: house, 5, Robinson row

Marshall John, oil merchant and ship owner, 32, Mason street

Marshall Thomas, ship owner, 8, Jarratt street

Marshall Matthew, bookbinder, 29, Lowgate
Marshall Edw. vict. and spirit dealer, Bottle, 10, Grimsby lane
Marshall Thos. rope maker, Dock st.; house, 16, Trippet st.
Marshall Mrs. Elizabeth, 35, Dock st.
Marshall John, butcher, 58, Whitefriargate; house, 10, Princess st.
Marshall John, cabinet maker, &c. New John street
Marshall Rd. shipowner, 22, Mason st.
Marshall Geo. whitesmith, &c. 58, Scott street
Marshall Wm. shoemkr. 15, Mytongt.
Marshall Mrs. Margaret, 27, Sykes st.
Marshall Wm. shoemaker, 12, Trinity House lane
Marshall Thomas, upholsterer, 14, Trundle street
Marshall John, corn miller, 18, New George street
Marshall Wm. miller, *Summergangs*
Marshall Christopher, tailor, 19, East street, Drypool
Marshall Thomas, shopkeeper, *Summergangs*
Marshall Wm. joiner, 43, Savile st.
Martin & Keddey, shipping agents & insurance brokers, and agents to the West of England Life & Fire, &c. Office, 49, High street
Martin Robert, joiner & builder, Hyperion st. Great Union st.
Martin Francis, gent. Neptune st.
Martin and Hogg, house and ship joiners, Dock street
Martin Samuel, gent. 17, Albion st.
Martin Peter, billiard table keeper, Corn Exchange, Market place; h. Southern's court, 154, High st.
Martin Thomas, butcher, 40, Shambles; house, 2, Myton place
Martin John, cooper, 24, Church st. Sculcoates
Martin William, mariner, 4, Knowles square, Spencer street
Martin Wm. pig jobber, Gt. Union st.
Marwood Samuel, baker, 39, Blackfriargate
Mason Thos. boat builder, Lime st.
Mason Christopher, tailor, 14, Mytongate
Mason Henry, shoemkr. 68, Lowgate
Mason Mrs. Sarah, 13, Mytongate
Mason John, mariner, 18, Sykes st.
Mason Samuel, mariner, 25, Great Passage street
Mason Wm. shopkpr. 26, Posterngate
Mason Wm. tailor, 8, Vicar lane
Mason John, shopkpr, 9, Finkle st.
Masterman John, tea and coffee dealer, 37, Market place
Masterman John, gent. 15, Story st.

Matchan Edward, merchant's clerk, 10, Princess street
Matson Thomas, gent. 12, Hodgson's square, Sykes street
Matteson Thomas, landing waiter, 4, Charles street
Matthew George, furniture broker, 12, New Dock street
Matthewman Esther, milliner, 2, Great Passage street
Matthews & Bingham, linen drapers, 29, Whitefriargate
Mattinson Jph. shoemkr. 109, High st.
Mattocks John, linen weaver, Sewer la.
Maude William M. merchant, shipowner, and underwriter, Garrison side; house, 8, Charlotte st.
Maulson John, mariner, 5, William's square
Maw John, cowkeeper, &c. Church street, Drypool
Mawhood Thos. gent. 3, Cobourg pl.
Maxwell Mrs. Elizabeth, (lodgings,) 42, George street
May Charles, confectioner, fruiterer and Italian warehouse, (and billiard table,) 29, Silver st.
May Elizabeth, (lodgings) 2, Page's square, Dagger lane
Mayfield Wm. shoemaker, Alfred st.
Mayfield John, earthenware dealer, 14, Scott street
Mayfield Joseph, potter, Beverley rd.
M'Allum Mary, hatter, glover, &c. 17, Silver street
M'Bride Peter, cordage agent & porter dealer, 20, High street; house, 9, Sykes street
M'Cann Daniel, shoemaker, Drypool square
M'Clean John, shoemaker, 56, Whitefriargate
M'Cleod Benj. shopkr. 1, Burton st.
M'Coll Maria, dress mkr. Stubbin st.
M'Colvin Colin, smith and nail mkr. 5, Trippet street
M'Donald Angus, vict. Sloop Clothier, 2, Bishop lane
M'Dougal Andw. tailor, Providence row
M'Gregor John, traveller, 40, Dock st.
M'Gregor Charles, mariner, 7, William's square, Mason st.
M'Guire Dennis, practitioner in physic, 61, Carr lane
M'Intire John, chair spindle maker, Waterhouse lane
M'Intosh James, mariner, 5, Paradise place
M'Kay Jas. gardener, 3, Providence row
M'Kenzie John, confectioner, 2, New Dock st.
M'Kennedy Sarah, shopkeeper, 4, North street

M'Turk Thomas, woollen draper, 2, Market place
M'Yawn Alex. vict. Hand & Glass, Little lane, Blackfriargate
Meadley Rd. excise officer, 7, Hope st.
Mearns James, vict. Edinbro' Packet, 163, High st.
Meats Elizabeth, gentlewoman, John street, Church street
Medd John, gent. 26, English st.
Medley Thos. vict. Gate, 21, Trippet
Medley John, ship and boat builder, Church st. Sculcoates; house, 9, English st.
Mee John, gent. mert. 20, Paradise pl.
Meggitt Mary, ladies' boarding school, 8, George st.
Meggitt Thomas, sen. gentleman, 6, Adelphi court, Lowgate
Meggitt Thomas, jun. house and ship painter, 10, George yd. Lowgate
Meggitt Wm. joiner, 1, Paragon pl.
Meggitt John, mariner, Barker's ct. 46, Blanket row
Megson John, cabinet mkr. 23, Carr ln.
Mellor Joseph, shopkpr. 11, Wells st.
Mells & Kipling, riverbrokers&agents 1, Commercial ct. 195, High st.
Mells Geo. broker; h. 5, Commercial court, 195, High st.
Melson Ambrose, vict. Ship Tavern, 73, Lowgate
Mennell Joseph, shoemaker, 5, Waterhouse lane
Mennell John, bricklayer and maker, 2, Chapel ct. 15, Salthouse ln.
Mennell Francis, brushmaker, 5, Waterhouse lane
Mennell Jemh. shoemkr. 5, Waterhouse lane
Mercer Wm. druggist, 60, Market pl.
Mercer John, straw hat manufacturer, Belts place, Blackfriargate
Mercer Ann, day school, 13, Trippet
Mercer Matt. mariner, 3, Savile row
Merrikin G. mariner, 1, Clarkson's square, Silver st.
Merrikin Wm. plumber and glazier, St. Quintin's place, Drypool
Metcalf David, boat builder, Church street, Sculcoates
Metcalf David, gent. 46, Scott st.
Metcalf William, traveller, Edward's place, Love lane
Metcalf Geo. joiner, 7, Machell st.
Metcalf Jas. shoemkr. 12, Blanket row
Metcalfe H. & S. general repository, 18, Whitefriargate
Mews James, vict. Coach and Horses, 9, Mytongate
Meynell Christopher, druggist, 52, Whitefriargate
Meynell Thomas, druggist, 1, Lowgate; h. 6, George yard

Middlemiss Robert, watch, &c. maker, 34, St. John st.
Middleton Thomas, grocer, &c. 196, High st.
Middleton Geo. stone mason; h. 11, Riddell's entry, Savile row
Middleton Jas. shoemaker, 27, Posterngate
Middleton James, vict. Ship, 20,Church st. Sculcoates
Middleton Geo. bread & biscuit baker, 33, Grimsby lane
Middleton Miss Ann, gentlewoman, Anlaby road
Milan Michl. earthenware dlr. Witham
Millburn Andrew, lath render, 4, Princess st.
Miles Thomas, whitesmith, Mason st.
Miller Benj. bricklayer and plasterer, 19, Brook st.
Miller Josiah, vict. Golden Cup, West street
Miller Geo. surveyor to the Dock Co. 26, Paradise place
Miller John, professor of music, 46, Savile st.
Miller Simpson, first clerk in the excise office, 6, Spencer st.
Miller John, sawyer, Wilson's court, 40, Dock st.
Millfield John, smith and farrier, 13, Trinity house lane
Mills Alex. painter, 56, Mytongate
Mills John, butcher, 1, Paradise row
Milne David, joiner, 22, Bridge st.
Milner Johanna, gentwmn. 7, Savile r.
Milner John & Ann, grocers, Witham
Milner Geo. saddler, 3, Market place
Milner Wm. vict. Marrow Bone and Cleaver, Fetter ln. 85, Market pl.
Milner Josiah, wood turner, Turner's square, West st.
Milner Harriet, milliner, 5, Constable's buildings, English st.
Milnes, Heywood, and Holdsworth, merchants, 33, High st.
Milson Ann, vict. Providence Inn, Groves
Mings John, tailor, 8, Broadley st.
Minitt Thos. mariner, 5, Prospect pl.
Mintoft Robert, pilot, 93, High st.
Mitchell Rt. shoemkr. 25, Chariot st.
Mitchell Wm. dyer and glazier, 23, North st.
Mitchell Rd. hair dresser, 18, Silver st.
Mitchell Eliz. china, &c.dlr. Carlisle st.
Mitchell Thos. mariner, 1, Union sq. Spencer st.
Mitchinson W. and C. straw hat mfrs. 17, St. John st.
Monday Wm. timber merchant, North Side Old dock; h. 6, Jarratt st.
Monday John, clerk, 8, Savile row
Monday Wm. clerk, 38, Scott st.

Monk Mary, straw hat manufr. 33, Spencer street

Monkman Thos. export officer, 11, Worship street

Montgomery John, vict. & bookbinder, Plough, 21, Robinson row

Moon Geo. ship owner, King's cooper, and General merchant, Dock side, 4, Quay st. and Manor st.

Moor Chpr currier, &c. 30, Lowgate

Moor Wm. ironmonger, and agent to the British Fire and Westminster Life offices, 35, Lowgate

Moor Peter, gent. 16, Harcourt st.

Moor Thos. vict. Bull, Beverley road

Moor Francis, sawyer, 21, Gibson st.

Moore Launcelot Charles, attorney, 4, Whitefriargate

Moore Hannah, shoemkr. 19, Myton st.

Moore John, gent. 2, Garden sq. Princess street

Moore Jonathan, excise officer, 24, Garden street

Moore Eliz. cork mfr. 6, Grimsby lane

Moore Mary, straw hat manufactr. 30, Spencer street

Morehead John, engraver and printer, 10, Scale lane

Morehead Thos. joiner, Up. Union st.

Morehouse and Brown, brokers and general commercial agents, 124, High street

Morey Elihu, music master, 10, Clark's square, Sykes street

Morley Thomas B. ship owner, corn & Baltic agent, and auctioneer, 25, Lowgate

Morley Geo. vict. Fleece Inn, 43, Market place

Morley Robert, joiner and builder, 16, Bond street

Morley Rev. John, Anlaby road

Morley John, shoemkr. 54, Humber st.

Morrell John, shoemaker, 8, Warehouse lane

Morris W. B. general broker, Stewart's yard, 152, High st.; h. 9, Savile row

Morris Charlotte, gentlewoman, 1, Myton street

Morris Prince Rupert, vict. Board, corner of Chariot st.

Morris Thos. grocer and flour dealer, 1, North end Humber dock

Morris John, coach proprietor, 32, Market place

Morris Francis, straw hat manufactr. 29, Mytongate

Morris Wm. straw hat mfr. 7, Queen st.

Morrison John, clothes broker, 72, High street

Morrod John, brush mfr. 29, Mytongt.

Mortier Joannas, mariner, 11, Featherstone's entry, High st.

Mortimer Geo. excise officer, 3, ___gon street

Morton R. T. retail spirit dealer, Lowgate

Morton John, hat mfr. 120, High and 40, Grimsby lane

Morton Thos. staymkr. 22, Scale ___

Morse John, baker, Raikes street

Moss Mttw. shopkpr. 12, Salthouse

Mountain Charles, architect, 59, ___pect street

Mowatt Clara, bookseller & circul___ library, 57, Market place

Moxon Geo. & John, general c___ mercial agents, and agents to Norwich Union Fire office, High street

Moxon Geo. agent; h. 24, Mason

Moxon John, agent; h. 18, Bour___

Moxon Benjamin, druggist and salter, oil and colour dealer, Market place

Moxon R. W. merchant & ship ow 1, Trinity hs. ln.; h. 12, Jarr___

Munn Meshach, shopkr. 19, Prospec___

Munroe M. mariner, 5, Grimston ___

Munton Edw. surgeon, 66, Myto___

Murdock Jas. tea dlr. 19, Waterh___

Murgatroyd Wm. grocer and tea 7, Waterworks street

Murphy Richd. vict. American C___ House, 1, Duke street

Murray John, gent. 2, Clappison'___ Sykes street

Murray Mary, hatter, 34, Church

Murray Jas. mariner, 16, Mason ___

Murton Joseph, mariner, 9, St. M___ square

Musgrave Ralph, vict. Full Meas___ 56, Lowgate

Musgrave Samuel, shoemaker, ___ Whitefriargate

Musgrave Wm. butcher, 59, Lowg___

Musgrave David, Turner's square, ___ Mason street

Musgrave Rd. mariner, 4, Castle row

Myers Frederick, schoolmaster, 8, Ordovas place

Myers Geo. whitesmith, Chariot st.

Nainby Thos. clerk, Hanover square

Naylor George, vict. Grapes, 14, Harcourt street

Naylor John, victualler, King's Arms, Witham

Neach Ann, straw hat mfr. 32, Bond st.

Neal Thos. traveller, Humber bank

Neavis John, hair dresser, 28, Dock st.

Neesom Mark. cowkeeper, Scott st.

Neesom Charles, cowkpr. Spencer st.

Nelson Jas. butcher, 30, Shambles; house, Terrington's entry, Blanket row

Nelson John, whitesmith, 3, Blackfriargate alley

Nelson Thomas, whitesmith, Reed's buildings, 14, Waterhouse lane
Neria J. E. hatter, 9, Mytongate
Neris Robert, builder and surveyor, 9, Mytongate
Newbald Charles, seedsman & cheese-factor, 79, High st.
Newham Nathaniel, mariner, 6, Catharine sq. Mason st.
Newmarch John & Sons, timber merchants, Thornton st.
Newmarch John timber merchant; house 2, Charlotte st.
Newmarch Ann, umbrella mfr. 32, St. John st.
Newmarch & Hunt, joiners, &c. Savile st.
Newrick Hodgson,grocer & tea dealer, 2, Salthouse lane
Newsam Wm. saddler, 24, Whitefriargate
Newsom Thomas, furniture broker, 7, New dock st.
Newton Isaac, mast, block, and pump maker, North side old dock; h. 2, Clarence court, Princess st.
Newton Christopher, weigher at the custom house, Great Union st.
Newton Thos. corn & coal merchant, North bridge foot
Newton Saml. baker, 21, Chariot st.
Newton Geo. cooper, *Wilmington*
Newton Rbt. shopkpr. 19, Bond st.
Nichols Wm. pawnbroker, English st.
Nicholson & Wood, brokers & commission agts. Old custom hs. High st.
Nicholson John, vict. Ship and Shears, 25, Bridge st.
Nicholson Geo. vict. Gate, 12, Lower Union st.
Nicholson Thos. gent. 5, Garden st.
Nicholson Launcelot, milkman, 4, Pothouse yd. Wincolmlee
Nicol John, Scotch linen warehouse, 19, Silver st.
Nield James, colour maker, Mill sq. Beverley road
Nightingale Henry, grocer & tea dlr. 8, North st. Prospect st.
Nisbet James, bread & biscuit baker, 48, Salthouse lane
Nisbett Wm. mariner, 12, William's sq. Mason st.
Nixon John, gent. 27, Garden st.
Nixon John, tailor, &c. Witham
Nixon John,hairdresser,28,Wincolmlee
Nixon Geo. lighterman, 9, Queen's pl. Sykes st.
Noble Joseph, wholesale & retail bookseller & stationer, 23, Market pl.; house, 20, English st.
Noble William, vict. White Swan, 16, North walls

Norman W. V. general commission agent & merct. Garrison side; h. North parade, Beverley road
Norman & Smithson, millwrights and millstone mfrs. Sykes st.
Norman J.millwright; h. 7, Worship st.
Norris Thos. glover, &c. 19, Scale ln.
Norris John, confectioner, 52, Scott st.
Norris Jonth. shoemaker, 3, South st.
North Wm. merchant, 25, Bishop lane
North John, merchant's clerk, St. Quintin's place, Drypool
North Geo.vict.Black Boy, 151,Highst.
Northen Rbd. watch mkr. & optician, 46, Lowgate; h. Nelson st.
Northgraves Denton, clock & watch maker & jeweller, 32, Silver st.
Norton Wm. livery stables, Posterngt.
Nundy Christopher, joiner & draper, 13, Church lane
Nutchey John, mariner, New Geo. st.
Nuttel James, gent. 4, Broadley sq.
Oates Bartholomew, cabinet mkr. & furniture broker, 17, Blackfriargt.
Oates John, mariner, Medley's sq. Great Union st.
Oates Ann, shopkpr. 15, North walls
Ockerby Wm. tailor, &c. 14, High st.
O'Conner Mrs. Jemima, 1, N. Brook st.
O'Conner Michl. mariner,19,Princes st.
Odlin John, tailor, Broad entry, 26, Scale lane
Officer Wm. glue mfr. *Wilmington*
Officer Joseph, shopkpr. 5, Spencer st.
Ogden Jas.blacksmith,6 & 28,Finkle st.
Oglesby Mrs. Mary, 25, Charlotte st.
Oglesby Thos. shopkpr. 180, High st.
Ogram Wm. shoemaker, 26, Edgar st.
Oldfield R. S. merchant & cork mfr. 78 and 119, High st.
Oldham Wm. millwright, 10, Trippet; house, 7, Waterworks st.
Oliver Thos. tallow chandler & soap boiler, 11, Dagger lane
Oliver Richard, vict. Royal Oak, 21, Posterngate
Oliver Thos. shopkpr. 50, Salths. ln.
Oliver Mary, shopkeeper, English st.
Oliver T. shopkr. Grotto sq. Mason st.
Onion Thos. shoemaker, 21, Savile st.
Orrey J. pilot, 7, Scott's sq.Humber st.
Orton Thos. mariner, 24, Waterhs. ln.
Orton Thomas, permit writer, 22, Robinson row
Osbourne Wm. timber merchant; h. 22, Story st.
Osbourne Nicholas, tide surveyor, 11, Dock st.
Osbourne Mary, straw hat manfactr. Scott's entry, 9, Mill st.
Osgerby Edw. baker, 22, New Geo. st.
Ostler Rt. confectnr. 60, Whitefriargt.
Oswald Etherington, ship carpenter, Church st. Wincolmlee

Ouston Joseph, grocer, 42, Prospect st.
Outhwaite Wm. shopkpr. 11, Carr ln.
Overton & Smith, engineers, steam engine mkrs. & ironfounders, Scott st.
Overton James, engineer; house, 10, New George st.
Overton Thomas, mariner, 8, James' court, Waterhouse lane
Owen Jas. mariner, 28, Waterhs. lane
Oxley Margt. grocer, &c. 6, Saltbs. ln.
Oxley John, port guager, 4, Spencer st.
Oxtoby Danl. vict. Unicorn, 9, Carr ln.
Oxtoby Geo. shopkpr. 45, Garden st.
Oxtoby Wm. butcher, 16, Prospect st.
Oxtoby Isaac, cowkpr. *Summergangs*
Pacey Wm. tobacco pipe mfr. Trafalgar sq. 23, Wincolmlee
Packett Joseph, mariner, New row, Anlaby road
Palmer T. W. wine merch. Broadley st.; house, 13, Charles st.
Palmer Robert, vict. Barrel, 20, New George st.
Palmer P. J. whitesmith, 38, Chariot st.
Palmer Martha, shopkpr. 7, Chariot st.
Pannill Thomas, shoemaker, Walker's entry, Posterngate
Pape John, cattle dlr. Castle street; house, 4, Nile place
Pape Mthw. day school, Wincolmlee
Pape M. A. dress maker, Wincolmlee
Parish Thomas, schoolmaster, 29, Church st. Sculcoates
Park Godfrey & Richd. merchts. ship owners and insurance brokers, 183, High st.
Park Godfrey, merchant; h. *Cottwick*
Park Richd. merchant & underwriter, 183, High st.; h. 82, Dock st.
Parke Wm. London carriers & Lincoln yeast warehouse, 17, Queen st.
Parker John Cowham, wine & spirit mert. 62, High st; h. 1, Charlotte st.
Parker John, copper, brass & tinplate warehouse, 19, Blackfriargate
Parker John, paper hanging & colour mfr. North st.; h. 31, Bond st.
Parker Jane, gentlwmn. 7, Charles st.
Parker Mordue, tailor and woollen draper, 22, Queen st.
Parker Wm. linen draper, 31, Whitefriargate
Parker Wm. fishmonger, 81, Chariot st.
Parkes Edw. hair dresser, Witham
Parkin Edw. dealer in marine stores, rope & sail maker, 11, Quay st.
Parkin Wm. maker & dealer in burrs, and other millstones, Stewart's yd. 152, High st.; h. 13, Princess st.
Parkin Geo. joiner, Gibson st.
Parkin Jas. joiner; house, Sykes st.
Parkin Thos. ship & insurance broker, and agent, 38, Grimsby lane
Parkinson John, shopkpr. 78, Mytongt.

Parks Geo. common bakehouse, 17, Hale's entry, 113, High st.
Parrott Geo. grocer, &c. 15, Princess st.
Patrick Wm. vict. Sir John Falstaff, South end
Patrick Charles, vict. Red Lion, 44, Whitefriargate
Patrick Mary, shopkpr. 4, Cross st.
Patrick Theodosia, milliner, 9, Trippet
Patrick Pouley, tanner, Burton st.
Pattinson Robt. ship owner, ship and insurance broker, tar & turpentine mercht. & commission agent, 37, High st.; h. 59, Church st. Sculcts.
Pattinson Ann, gentlewoman, Holderness road
Paty Charlotte, milliner & dress maker, 1, Albion st. Mews
Pauling Robert, baker, Witham
Pawson Thos. gent. 22, English st.
Payler Thornton, joiner & cabinet mkr. 13, Dryden's entry, 14, Salths. ln.
Peacock Dennis, John & Geo. timber merchants, Dock st. & North side Old Dock
Peacock Dennis, timber merchant; h. Great Union st.
Peacock Jabez, hosier & linen drapes, 16, Trippet
Peacock Ann, baker, 6, Clappison's sq. Sykes st.
Peacock Ann, milliner, 3, Robinson's court, Princess st.
Peacock John, cowkeeper, Green la. Drypool
Peacock John, exciseofficer, 10, Newton's court, 14, Machell st.
Pearce Wm. auctioneer & appraiser, 21, St. John st.
Pears Thos. vict. 3 Tuns, 21, Grimsby ln.
Pearson James, merchant, High st.; house, *Summergangs*
Pearson Zechariah, mert. 80, High st.
Pearson Wm. surgeon, 14, Dock st.; house, 37, George st.
Pearson Elizabeth, gentlewoman, 2, Albion place, Witham
Pearson Robt. ship chandler, North side Old Dock
Pearson Sarah, gentlewoman, 10 Vine court, Bolelar st.
Pearson John, bacon factor, 24, Waterworks st.
Pearson John, vict. coal meter and shipping cook, Royal George, 14, North walls
Pearson Wm. vict. Lion and Key, 47, High st.
Pearson Sarah, (lodgings) 11, Geo. st.
Pearson John, baker, 25, Blackfriargt.
Pearson Jonathan, worsted mfr. Walker's entry, Posterngate
Pearson John, baker, 23, Grimsby ln.
Pearson Sarah, (lodgings) 10, Geo. st.

Pearson Sarah, straw hat mfr. 10, Beverley road

Pearson Isaiah, mariner, 22, Scott st.

Pearson Ann, cowkpr. 28, Blanket row

Pearson Wm. custom house officer, 5, Scott st.

Peart Robt. translator, 17, Chariot st.

Peart Joseph, itinerant preacher, Chapel court, 79, West st.

Pease & Liddell, bankers, 18, High st. (draw on Sir Peter Pole & Co. London)

Pease, Trigg & Co. seed crushers and oil merchants, 18, High st.

Pease Clifford, mert.; h. *Willerby*

Peasegood & Sanderson, wholesale & retail tea & coffee dlrs. 8, Lowgt.

Peat Joseph, bricklayer, Hodgson st.

Peck Mrs. Tomasin, 2, Wright st.

Peck Thos. cabinet mkr. & upholsterer, 33, Blackfriargt. & 12, Queen st.

Peckett Robt. baker, Henry's court, Lower Union st.

Peckett Joseph, mariner, Anlaby road

Peel Thos. ship and insurance broker, 10; Bishop lane

Pegg John, shipsmith; h. Hanover sq.

Peter Nancy, milliner, 20, English st.

Penn Wm. C. engraver & copperplate printer, near North end, High st.

Pennock John, shopkeeper, 7, Trippet

Penny Saml. shoemkr. 16, North walls

Penrose Charles, shopkpr. 125, High st.

Penrose John, bookbinder, 26, Savile st.

Penrose Wm. miller, *Summergangs*

Pentith John, baker, 72, Mytongate

Pepper Rd. painter, 3, New John st.

Perkins John, managing clerk for the proprietors of the Rockingham newspaper, mfr. of writing and copying ink, & agent for country newspapers, 10, Bowlalley lane

Perritt Mrs. Susannah, 4, Robinson row

Petch Thomas, butcher, 47, Scott st.

Petchell Robt. wine, spirit & porter mert. 62, High st.; h. 10, Mason st.

Peter Thos. cowkpr. *Summergangs*

Peters Wm. hosier, 24, Lowgate

Peterson Mark, cowkpr. *Summergangs*

Pettingell Edmund, boot & shoemkr. and dealer in cabinet oil paintings, 15 & 86, Mytongate

Pettinger Wm. turner, 21, New Dock st.

Pettinger Wm. shoemaker, 1, Todd's entry, 6, Salthouse lane

Petty Geo. butcher, 35, Shambles; h. Blue Bell entry, High st.

Petty John, fishmonger, 4, Dennis' row, English st.

Pexton Wm. linen draper, 12, Dock office row

Pexton James, tailor, Shewood's sq. Marvel st.

Pexton Wm. tailor, Raikes st.

Philips C. H. solicitor, 7, Bowlalley ln.

Phillpson Henry, nursery & seedsman, Jackson st. Neptune st.

Philipson Michael, hair dresser, 91, Mytongate

Picard & Son, white lead mfrs. North side Old Dock

Picard I. K. lead mfr.; h. Anlaby road

Pickard Anthony, grocer, 27, Blriargt.

Pickard Matthew, vict. Baltic Tavern, English st.

Pickard Thos. shoemkr. 34, Grimsby ln.

Pickard John, schoolmaster, 3, Norris' yd. Wells st.

Pickard Wm. vict. Sir John Moore, 47, Salthouse lane

Pickering Wm. & Son, maltsters and brewers, Pickering's entry, 10, High st.; h. 3, Manor alley

Pickering Danl. tailor, 10, Salths. ln.

Pickering William, shipsmith, &c. 14, Trippet st.

Pickering John, wheelwright, 2, Wincolmlee

Pickering Andrew, cowkpr. Old Glue house, Beverley road

Pickersgill Geo. mariner, Salthouse court, Salthouse lane

Pickhover Thos. wheelwright, Roper's row, 20, Waterhouse lane

Pickwell Francis, cowkpr. Short st.

Piercy and Thomas, ship chandlers, 9, High st.

Piercy Mrs. Ann, Church st. Sculcoates

Pierson Jas. mercht. & general agent, 162, High st.; h. Holderness road

Pinchon Mary, shopkpr. 90, High st.

Pinder Wm. dealer in marine stores, Old Dock side; h. 30, Bond st.

Pinder Charles, boot and shoemaker, 57, Lowgate

Pinder Wm. shopkeeper, 39, Scott st.

Pinder Thos. tailor, &c. Dixon's sq. Fetter lane

Pinkney Jas. shoemkr. 128, High st.

Pinn John, linen draper, North bridge; house, 12, Trippet

Pinn Wm. clerk, 7, Robinson row

Pinshin Robt. flour warehouse, Shambles, Blackfriargate

Piotti Jas. optician, carver, gilder, and looking glass mfr. 2, Queen st.

Piper Thomas, vict. Spread Eagle, Market place

Piper Mrs. Mary, gentlewoman, 8, Hanover sq.

Pitch Wm. gent. 7, Neptune st.

Pitts Wm. Lieut. R. N. John's st.

Pitts Benj. builder & undertaker, 1, Hewett's yd. Whitefriargate

Pitts Elizabeth, gentlewoman, 1, Charter house lane

Place Thomas, gent. Mill lane

Platford John, gent. 11, York parade, Beverley road
Plaxton Mrs. Martha, 17, Nile st.
Plaxton Jas. mariner, 9, Charterhouse ln.
Plummer W. B. ironmonger, 6, Market place
Plummer Mrs. Harriot, 57, Prospect st.
Poling Robt. baker, Witham
Pollock James, clerk of the customs, 7, Spencer st.
Poole Robt. trunk and portmanteau maker, Queen st.; h. 6, Silver st.
Poole Wm. vict. Ship, 20, Finkle st.
Popple Geo. gent. 9, Pryme st.
Popplewell Henry, gent. Crown ct.
Popplewell John, vict. Full Measure, 8, High st.
Pordon Francis, cooper, 6, Finkle st. house, 5, Middle st.
Porrill Mary, shopkeeper, 11, Great Passage st.
Portass Sarah, vict. Blue Ball, 12, Trippet st.
Porter Peter, commercial traveller, 1, Milton's sq. 24, Bourne st.
Porter Wm. shopkeeper, 15, Vine court, 8, Botelar st.
Porter Geo. fellmonger, 14, Burton st.
Porter, Raines & Co. Greenland yard, Sculcoates
Postell Andrew, bedstead maker, L. Passage st.
Potcherd Wm. straw hat manufactr. 3, Trippet st.
Potchett John, day school, New George st.
Potts Joseph, sail cloth and sacking manfr. Queen st.; h. Spring row
Potts M. & B. gentlewomen, 22, George st.
Poulton Robt. musical instrument repairer, Chapel lane
Pounsbury John, pilot, 27, Humber st.
Powell Ann, dress mkr. 20, Edgar st.
Power Wm. traveller, 18, Osborne st.
Power Wm. nail agent, 20, High st.
Poynter Geo. painter, 28, Bridge st. house, 16, North st.
Preston Henry, hatter, woollen draper, & silk mercer, 26, Market pl.
Preston Abm. shoemkr. 5, Trippet st.
Preston James, grocer and whip mfr. 21, Osborne st.
Preston John, shopkpr. 35, Savile st.
Preston Edw. coal dealer, 5, Keeling's entry
Prickett and Robinson, solicitors, 9, Scale lane
Pricket Marmaduke Thos. solicitor; house, 13, North st.
Prickett Arthur, gent. 5, Worship st.
Prickett Josiah, gent. 20, Charlotte st.
Priddon Wm. gent. 13, Alfred st.
Priest Mrs. Ann, 2, Love lane

Priest Wm. ship owner, 13, Nile st.
Priest Geo. porter, 16, Humber st.
Priest Robt. mariner, 2, Love lane
Priestley Eliz. day school, Posterngt.
Priestman David, wine & porter merchant, 62, Mytongate; house, 8, Castle row
Priestman Thos. currier, house, East Mount, near Sutton
Prince John, shoemaker, 6, Duke st.
Pringle Mary, vict. Hammer & Hand, 187, High st.
Prissick Thomas, merchant and ship owner; house, 7, Marine row
Prissick Wm. cabinet maker, 16, Worship st.
Procter Ezekiel, butcher, 21, Brook st.
Procter Mrs. Ann, 21, Brook st.
Procter Thos. grocer, 23, Wincolmlee
Proctor Francis, plumber & glazier, 14, Bridge st.
Proctor Wm. gent. 11, Whitefriargate
Profit John, brazier, 36, Blanket row
Proom John, plumber and glazier, 26, Bond st.
Proudley Thos. shopkpr. 133, High st.
Proudlove John, mariner, 1, Grimston street
Proudlove Mary, dress maker, 1, Grimston street
Prudhoe Mrs. Hannah, (lodgings,) 41, George st.
Prust John, shopkeeper, Carr lane
Pudsey William, tailor, 8, George yd. Lowgate
Pullan Benjamin and Son, anchor smiths, 2, Dock office row
Pullan Thomas, anchor smith, Dock office row
Purdon John, brazier and tin plate worker, 25, Lowgate
Purdon William, brazier and tin plate worker, 68, Whitefriargate
Purdy Henry, common baker, Preston entry, 22, Posterngate
Pybus Wm. law stationer & commissioner for taking special bail, IV Bowlalley lane; h. 29, Bridge st.
Pybus John, pawnbroker, 3, West st.
Quarton John, miller, Humber bank and 2, North end, Humber Dock
Quickfall John, cattle dealer, Witham
Quickfall Wm. butcher, Church street, Drypool
Quipp Wm. hair dresser, 50, Wincolmlee
Race Harriet, milliner, 27, Charlotte st.
Radford John, Southern & Co. merchants, ship & insurance brokers, 154, High st.
Radford John S. mert.; h. 8, Castle st.
Radford Thomas Edward, commercial agent, insurance broker, & agent to the London Union Assurance Company, 24, Parliament st.

aikes & Co. bankers, 12, Scale lane, on Currier, Raikes & Co. London

aikes Thomas, Esq. banker; h. 7, Charlotte st.

aines Thos. butcher, 4, Shambles; house, Waterworks st.

aines Mrs. Sarah, 31, Bridge st.

aines Mary, brazier and tin plate worker, 3, Waterworks st.

ainford Thos. butcher, 42, Lowgate; house, 3, Trinity house lane

aisbeck Edw. surveyor of customs, 14, Prospect place, Drypool

aisbeck William, mariner, 7, Waterhouse lane

aisbeck Chas. tide waiter, 3, Scott st.

aleigh Mrs. Catharine, 3, Bourne st.

amsay Ann, glass, china, &c. dealer, 7, Whitefriargate

amsey Richard, butcher, 50, Shambles; h. 10, Myton st.

amsey Mrs. Ann, 6, George st.

amlaf Edw. notary public & conveyancer, North st. Prospect st.

andale Wm. flour seller, 36, Bridge st.

anderson Thos. tailor, South side Trinity church

anson John, mariner, 8, Regent's place, 10, Sykes st.

anson John, shopkeeper, Stubbin st. Drypool

awing William, potter, Church st. Sculcoates

ay Sarah, dress maker, 4, Blanket row

aylor and Co. lime merchants and plaster manfrs. Humber bank

aylor G. J. lime mert. h. Princess st.

ayner Saml. grocer, 186, High st.

aynerJohn, calico glazer, 7, Sewer ln.

ayner Samuel, mariner, 23, Savile row

ayner Geo. roper, 16 & 189, High st.

ayner Sarah, milliner, 1, Story st.

ayner Thos. calico glazer, 5, Chapel lane

ayner John, landing waiter, 3, Myton place

ayner Richard, lighterman, 3, High st.

ayner John, shopkpr. 1, New John st.

aa Jas. vict. White Hart, Silver st.

eed Thos. stocking maker, 11, Blanket row

easton Mrs. A. 6, Posterngate

edfearn Geo. shopkpr. 24, Milk st.

eed John, ship broker, 159, High st.

eed E. & M. dress makers, 3, Quay st.

eed John, vict. Ship tavern, 73, Dock st.

eed Joseph, painter, 15, Wincolmlee

eed Chpr. lighterman, 4, O. Dock side

eeder Geo. cooper, Charlotte st. Mews

eeder Wm. shopkpr. 29, Wincolmlee

eeves Timothy, gent. Neptune st.

eeves Timothy, jun. solicitor, 2, Exchange alley

Renardson Geo. pipe mkr. 6, Castle st·

Rennards Mrs. Ann, 25, Dock st.

Rennards Richard, merchant, ship insurance broker, & general agent, North side Old dock; h.33, Geo. st.

Rennards David, tailor, Chariot st.

Renney Wm. pilot, 18, Blanket row

Rennison George, vict. Mason's Arms, 21, Chapel lane

Retalic George, teacher of music, 14, Bishop lane

Revell Aaron, schoolmaster, 5, Milton's square, 24, Bourne st.

Revell Rt. engineer, New John's st.

Reynalds Francis, mariner, 2, Stubbin street

Reynard Thos. shoemkr. Wincolmlee

Reynolds John, gent. 3, Gt. Passage st.

Reynolds John, painter, Cockpit yard, 6, Castle st.

Reynolds John, mariner, 3, Great Passage st.

Reynolds Thomas, livery stable keeper, 3, Hope st.

Rheam and Priestman, curriers and leather cutters, 14, Blanket row

Rheam E. currier, &c.; house, *Salts House*, near *Sutton*

Rhodes & Rutherford, linen drapers, & lacemen, 61, Market place

Rhodes Francis, furniture broker and cabinet maker, 92, Mytongate

Rhodes Benj. brass founder, Red Lion entry, High st.; h. *Cottingham*

Rhodes Thos. baker, 2, Mytongate

Rhodes Thomas, mariner, 12, Garden street

Rhodes Francis mariner, 92, Mytongt.

Rhodes Eliz. bakehouse, 21, Finkle st.

Riby William, tailor, Turner's square, West st.

Ribey Robert, shopkeeper, 28, New Dock walls

Richards Thos. gent. 19, Parliament st.

Richards John, day school, 16, Aldbro' street

Richards Simeon, furniture broker, 5, Grotto square, Mason st.

Richardson John Cressey, solicitor, 18, Bowlalley lane; house, 7, Old Dock side

Richardson John and Robert, wine & brandy merchants, 31, High st.; house, 12, Savile st.

Richardson Thomas, merchant and ship owner, 14, Quay side; house, 26, Dock st.

Richardson William, wine and brandy merchant, 10, Story st.

Richardson John, cornfactor, 42, Dock street

Richardson Mrs. Mary, 30, Albion st.

Richardson Eliz. gentlewoman 34, Mytongate

Richardson Mrs. Mary, 7, Old Dock side
Richardson Edward, builder & brick-layer, Patrick ground lane
Richardson Nathaniel, gent. Carr lane
Richardson Wm. gent. Carr lane
Richardson Francis, vict. Black Swan, 1, Princess street
Richardson Edmond, smith & farrier, 1, Fishwick's yd. Waterworks st.
Richardson Thomas, cabinet maker, 6, Cockpit yard, Castle street
Richardson William, plumber & glazier, 17, Brook street
Richardson H. A. M. and H. milliners, Lime street
Richardson Thos. rag, rope, & paper dealer, 20, Charlot street
Richardson Mary Ann, straw hat mfr. 75, Mytongate
Richardson Wm. bricklayer, 47, Carr lane
Richardson John, shoemkr. Church ln.
Richardson Rt. blacksmith, Witham
Richardson Ann, blacksmith, Witham
Richardson William, gardener, 3, Worship street
Richardson William, lighterman, 9, Bishop lane
Richardson John, cowkeeper, 18, Brook street
Richmond Richard, merchant, Old Custom house, High street
Richmond Mrs. Mary, 46, Spencer st.
Richmond Geo. twine spinner, 50, Carr lane
Richmond Hannah, shopkeeper, Great Union street
Richmond Geo. painter, 11, High st.
Rickatson Wm. confectioner, 75, Mytongate
Rickatson Mary Ann, straw hat mfr. 75, Mytongate
Rickinson Thomas, butcher & bacon factor, 60, Market place ; house, 8, Paradise place
Riddell Mrs. Jane, Portland house, Prospect street
Ridgway John, hair cutter, 3, Lowgt.
Ridley Eliz. clothes broker, Queen st.
Ridsdale Mrs. Jane, 9, Spencer st.
Ridsdale Jas. tailor, 6, Kirkus bldgs.
Ridsdale Wm. vict. John Bull, *Wilmington*
Ridsdale Stephen, corn & flour dealer, New Dock street
Riley Robt. shopkpr. 26, N. D. walls
Rimington Thomas, clothes broker, 18, Charlot street
Ringrose W. & C. L. merts. 42, High st.
Ringrose Wm. mert. ; h. 1, Geo. st.
Ringrose Wm. vict. Joiners' Arms, 6, Trippet street
Ripley Francis, vict. Ship Brunswick, 20, Dock street

Rispin Richard, tailor and broker, 19, New Dock street
Ritchie Mrs. Jane, 5, Princess st.
Ritson & Dryden, solicitors, 3, Bowlalley lane
Rivis John, maltster & brewer, 65, Church st. Sculcoates
Roberts James, oil merchant ; house, 4, Mason street
Roberts Thos. black beer brewer, 3, North walls ; bone mert. Union mills, Wincolmlee, & 3, High st. ; house, 3, North walls
Roberts Thos. London paper hanging & carpet warehouse, 36, Lowgate
Roberts Mrs. Betsey, (lodgings) 15, Dock street
Roberts Thos. spectacle maker, 28, Middle street
Roberts Jane, shopkr. 22, Robinson row
Roberts Jane, dress maker, 19, Geo. place, 14, Mytongate
Roberts James, mariner, Jennings ct.
Roberts Wm. miller and flour dealer, 16, Garden street
Robinson Charles, timber & raff mert. 15, North st. ; h. 56, Prospect st.
Robinson, Foord, & Smith, timber deal, and stave merchants, North side Old Dock
Robinson James, solicitor, 9, Scale ln.
Robinson Michael & Sons, hosiers, & stocking mfrs. 15, Queen st.
Robinson John, shipowner, 9, Wright st.
Robinson and Parkes, herb distillers, Hale's entry, 133, High st.
Robinson Edw. gent. 12, Portland pl.
Robinson Mrs. Eliz. 9, Wright st.
Robinson Mrs. Hannah, 40, Savile st.
Robinson Aaron, joiner, Stephenson's yd. Charlot st. ; h. 17, Carr lane
Robinson Thos. gent. 2, Upper Union st. 12, Great Passage st.
Robinson Isaac, hatter, 11, Lowgate
Robinson Wm. grocer, 32, Blanket row
Robinson John, grocer and tailor Trundle street
Robinson James, joiner, 4, Machell st
Robinson Thomas, grocer and draper 12, Scott street
Robinson Geo. bricklayer, 5, Dyer's pl
Robinson James, vict. Greenland Fishery, Church st. Sculcoates
Robinson Jane, vict. Jolly Banker Witham
Robinson John, vict. Prince George 183, High street
Robinson Edw. broker, 11, N. D. st.
Robinson Hanh. dress mkr. 14, Geo. street
Robinson M. A. straw hat mfr. West street
Robinson J. & M. straw hat mfrs. Church st. Wincolmlee

Robinson John, pawnbroker and hat warehouse, 52, Lowgate

Robinson Rd. basket mkr. 118, High st.

Robinson John, whitesmith, yard 2, New George st.

Robinson John, shopkr. 6, Marvel st.

Robinson Elizabeth, day school, 4, St. Mark square

Robinson Michael, pilot, 7, Little ln.

Robinson Wm. shopkeeper, 15, Church st. Wincolmlee

Robinson John, tailor, 5, Scale lane

Robinson John, hair dresser & dealer in herbs, 124, High st.

Robinson Thomas, tide waiter, 1, Elephant & Castle entry,37,Mytongt.

Robinson Wm. cowkpr. Up. Union st.

Robinson Saml. clerk, 43, Geo. st.

Robinson Wm. shopkpr. Finkle st.

Robinson Wm. flour dlr. 26, High st.

Robinson John, mariner, 9, George yd. Lowgate

Robinson John, tailor,&c. Trundle st.

Robinson Richard, tailor, 8, North side Trinity church

Redford John, bookseller, stationer, binder, & agent to the London genuine Tea Co. opposite St. Mary's, 52, Lowgate

Rodgers John, gent. 1, Vine court, Boteler st.

Rodmell Thos. Esq. postmaster, and comptrolling surveyor of customs, 3, Wright st.

Roe W. S. gent. 22, Charlotte st.

Roe Wm. gent. Anlaby road

Roe Charles, Esq. comptroller of customs, 12, Dock st.

Rogers Hy. tobacconist, 31, Dock st.

Rollitt John, shopkpr. 19, N. Dock st.

Rooth George, gent. 8, Story st.

Rooth Joseph, wine & brandy merchant, 36, High st.

Rooth Wm. tanner, 15, Burton st.

Roper Jackson, vict. Paragon Inn, Chariot st.

Rose Mrs. Mary, 2, Bourne st.

Rose Charles, clerk, 19, Wright st.

Rosindale Thos. shoemaker, 7, Commercial ct. 195, High st.

Rosindale Geo.mariner,5,Waltham st.

Ross & Burton, druggists, 40, Lowgt.

Ross Saml. druggist; h. 13, Savile st.

Ross Benj. wharfinger, & commercial agent, 6, High st.; h. Sutton road

Ross James, tailor, 1, New John st.

Ross Henry, commission agent, 17, Bowlalley ln.; h.5,Cent per cent st.

Ross Wm. printer and publisher of the Rockingham newspaper, (Saturday) 9, Bowlalley lane

Ross Wm. butcher, 25, Sykes st.

Rotsey Richard, vict. & hackneyman, Black Horse, 21, Carr lane

Rounding John, shoemaker, 40, St. John st.

Roundtree French, shoemaker, 24, Sykes street

Rounthwaite Sarah, tailor, 4, King st.

Rowbotham Richard, king's pilot, 5, James ct. Waterhouse lane

Rowlett Thos. day school, 25, Great Passage st.

Rountree Wm. grocer, 15, Wincolmlee

Rountree & Colton, sawyers, Parade row

Rowson John, slater, 12, William's sq. Mason st.

Roxby H. W. botanist, 66, West st.

Ruddiforth Hy. shoemkr. Aldbro' st.

Rudston and Preston, wholesale & retail woollen drapers, silk mercers, & hatters, 26 & 27, Market place

Rudston G. woollen dpr.; h. Newland

Rudston Francis,mariner,Beverley rd.

Runton Wm. timber merchant, and joiner, Great Union st. Witham

Rushton Mrs. Eliz. 6, Wincolmlee

Rushworth Edw. solicitor and public notary, 9, Parliament st.

Rusling Joseph, sail maker, Dock office row; house, 20, Dock st.

Rusling Sarah, linen draper, Blackfriargate

Russell John, livery stable kpr. and dealer in hay & straw, Dagger ln.

Russell Jane, vict. Schooner, 170, High st.

Russell Thomas, coach guard, 3, Herner's sq. Humber st.

Russell Robert, tailor, Todd's entry, Silver st.

Russell Wm. tailor, 41, Garden st.

Russell Geo. mariner, Blanket row

Rust & Shipham, watchmakers, gold & silversmiths, & jewellers, opposite the church, 21, Market pl.

Rust Wm. silversmith; house, 16, Nile street

Rust Wm. farmer, Mill lane

Ruston Francis, gent. North Parade

Rutherford Andrew, linen draper, &c. house, 42, Blanket row

Rutherford Jeremiah, butcher, 32, Wincolmlee

Rutherford John, shopkr. 52, Mill st.

Ryding John, excise officer, 2, James court, Waterhouse lane

Rylar Robert Dawson, gent. 30, Prospect place

Ryley Samuel, organ builder & piano forte maker, 27, Waterhouse lane

Rymer T. shopkpr. 20, N. Dock walls

Sacker Isaac, mariner, 11, Clark's sq.

Sadler John, woollen draper, 22, Market place

Sadler Thomas, oyster shop, 40, New Dock street

Sage Robert, custom house officer, 19, Macbell st.

Sagg J. B. gent. 11, Upper Union st.

Sainter Wm. worsted mfr. Roper's row, Waterhouse lane

Salmond George, hair dresser, 12, Blackfriargate

Salter John, vict. & broker, Queen's Head, 155, High st.

Sampson J. H. shipping agent; house, 7, Dock st.

Sampson Thomas, eating house, 7, Trundle street

Sanderson Joseph, woollen draper & silk mercer, 16, Market place

Sanderson Wm. druggist; house, 3, Nile st.

Sanderson John, corn merchant, Lime st.; house, Great Union st.

Sanderson Mrs Elizabeth, 18, Osborne street

Sanderson Thomas, shoemaker, 6, Marine ct. Sykes st.

Sanderson Sarah, stay and corset maker, 11, Queen st.

Sanderson Richard, shopkeeper, 162, High st.

Sanderson Henry, joiner, Stubb's ct. West st.

Sanderson Ann, shopkpr. 56, Mill st.

Sandwith Robert, solicitor & notary public, 23, Bishop lane; house, 21, Albion st.

Saner & Sleight, surgeons, 68, Lowgt.

Saner Hannah, tailor and draper, 18, Humber st.

Saner Wm. mariner, Higson's court, Blanket row

Sansby Richard, carver and gilder, 23, Savile st.

Sansby John, hair cutter & toy seller, Queen street

Sargeant Thos. farmer, 1, Up. Union street

Saul John, grocer, tea dealer, and tallow chandler, 37, Humber st.

Saunderson & Grassby, house & ship joiners, Parade row

Saunderson Thos. wine and brandy merchant, 53, Whitefriargate; h. Patrick ground lane

Savage Geo. gent. Posterngate

Savage Joseph, tallow chandler, 9, Queen st.

Sawden John, mariner, 11, Paragon pl.

Sawney Rt. cowkpr. Humber bank

Sawyer Charles, mariner, Cottage gardens, 8, Nile place

Sayer Charles, mariner, Wellington st.

Sayer Edward, pipemaker, Clark's yd. Carr lane

Sayes James, tailor, 15, Ordovas pl.

Sraddlethorp John, paper stainer, 11, Beverley road

Scafe & Newsom, rag merchants, and dealer in marine stores, Waterhouse lane

Scafe Matthew, shopkr. 9, Bond st.

Scaling Thomas, clerk, 25, Harcourt st. Drypool

Scatchard Wm. fishmonger, Queen st.

Scaum Wm. turnkey, Mytongate

Scaum Geo. shoemkr. 60, Prospect st.

Scholefield Daniel, gent. Anlaby road

Scholefield Mrs. Ann, Wellington pl. Beverley road

Scholefield Samuel, attorney, Land of Green ginger; h. 12, Bowlalley la.

Scholes John, mariner, 1, Regent's pl.

Schonswar Geo. & Henry, merchants and ship owners, 31, George st. house, *Ferriby*

Scultz J. P. mariner, New John st.

Scoffin Thos. black beer merchant, 2, Waltham st.

Scoresby Wm. ship owner, 50, Geo. st.

Scott Rev. John, M.A. 23, Prospect st.

Scott Peter, tailor, Scott's ct. Broadley st.

Scott Jph. pipe maker, 36, Dagger la.

Scott Ann, milliner, 17, St. Mark's sq.

Scott Ann, day school, 46, West st.

Screwton Wm. common brewer, 38, Church lane

Scurrfield John, joiner, 43, Salthouse la.

Searby Charles, vict. Duke of Cumberland, Church st. Sculcoates

Seaton Herbert, gent. 9, English st.

Seaton John M. currier, 8, King st.

Sedgwick and Gervas, silk mercers, haberdashers & lacemen, 7, Silver st.

Seipkworth Sarah, 6, Princess st.

Sellers Michl. mariner, 6, Duncan's place

Senior William, vict. London Tavern, (passengers and goods booked for the London and Antwerp, &c. Steam Packets) 20, Queen street

Setterington John, plumber & glazier, 22, Waterworks st.

Settle Thos. gent. Stubbin st.

Shackels L. G. attorney; h. 3, Story st.

Shackles Wm. linen draper and ship owner, 49, Market place; h. 5, Castle st.

Shackles Thos. cabinet maker upholsterer, and ship owner, Eaton st. Lowgate; house, 2, Pryme st.

Shackleton James, merchant, 72, High st. house, *Summergangs*

Shapman John, tailor, 2, Scale lane

Sharp Joseph, gent. 2, Parade row

Sharp Thos. vict. Lincoln Arms, 60, High st.

Sharp Jph. worsted mfr. 90, Blackfriargate

Sharp Wm. ship owner, 34, Brook st.
Sharrah Richd. waterproof hat coverer, 9, Dock office row
Shaw Wm. mahogany merchant, Old dock side; house, 6, South st.
Shaw Ann, spirit dealer, 54, Mill st.
Shaw Jas. vict. Greenland Fishery, 44, Bridge street
Shaw Wm. shoemaker, Witham
Shaw Nathanl. overlooker, 54, High st.
Shaw John, whitesmith, Robert st.
Shaw Philip, shoemaker, 7, Carr lane
Shaw Richd. shopkpr. 11, Middle st.
Shaw Thos. farmer, 5, Machell st.
Shemmels Edw. mariner, 1, James' court, Waterhouse lane
Shepherd Wm. tailor, 9, Mytongate
Shepherd Thos. vict. Duncan's Arms, 13, Manor st.
Shepherdson Thos. vict. Blade Bone, 6, Scale lane
Sheppard Alex. clerk, 23, North st.
Sherboon Geo. bricklayer, 18, Wells st.
Sherlock John, mariner, 5, Portland pl.
Sherwin H.C. surgeon, 16, Charlotte st.
Sherwood Thos. gent. 17, Princess st.
Sherwood Geo. joiner, 27, Bond st.
Sherwood Joseph, comb maker, Marvel street
Sherwood Henry, excise officer, 4, Union square
Shields Robert & Son, house and ship painters, 49, Blanket row
Shields Henry, tailor, 7, Cook's court
Shields Rt. clerk, 10, Charterhouse ln.
Shillito Jas. vict. American Tavern, 37, Mytongate
Shillito Thos. mariner, 24, Blanket r.
Shiner Joseph, glass and china dealer, 7, Church lane
Shipham David, joiner, New John st.
Shipham John, watchmaker, &c. 21, Market place
Shipman John, ship and insurance broker, Broadley st.; h. 4, Portland st.
Shores Wm. bookseller, stationer and circulating library, 16, Lowgate
Shores John & Co. druggists, 72, Lowgt.
Short Wm. mariner, 5, South street
Shotlin Eliz. vict. Old Harbour, 116, High street
Shwerer Joseph, German clock mkr. 10, Lowgate
Shwerer Matthew, German clock maker, 27 and 34, Mytongate
Shwerer Joseph, German clock mkr. 2, Manor square
Siddle Wm. mariner, Prior st. Church st.
Silbou Wm. bedstead manufactr. 8, Providence st. Myton st.
Silbon Hannah, furniture broker, 8, New Dock st.
Silverwood Thos. millstone manufr. 24, New George st.

Simison Ann, gentlewoman, 1, Chapel court, Salthouse lane
Simon Wm. grocer, Jennings street
Simpson John, gent. Staniforth place
Simpson Mrs. Ann, 34, North street
Simpson Richd. timber merchant; h. 11, Charles st.
Simpson James, vict. Spaw Bone, 8, Church st. Wincolmlee
Simpson Thos. shopkeeper, yeast and whiting warehouse, &c. Witham
Simpson John, oil, colour, paint, whiting and bone dust manufacturer, *Wilmington*
Simpson Thos. bacon dlr. 180, High st.
Simpson Wm. shoemaker, 98, Mytongate
Simpson Geo. joiner, 4, North st.
Simpson Wm. horse provender dealer, Grimston st.
Simpson Geo. hair dresser, 52, Dock st.
Simpson Sarah, (lodgings) 2, Providence row
Sissison Wm. currier & leather cutter, 19, Waterwork st.; h. West st.
Sissons, Weddle & Co. oil and colourmen, manfrs. of mustard, blue, French and pearl barley, Lime st. Groves
Sissons Thos. paint, &c. manufr.; h. 4, Wright st.
Sissons Richd. grocer, tea dealer, and ham factor, Queen st.
Sissons Jonathan, clothes broker, 7, Dock office row
Sissons Hannah, bakehouse, 98, Mytongate
Sivers Joseph, vict. Mariner's Tavern, 6, New Dock st.
Skelton Thos. vict. Blue Ball, Church st. Sculcoates
Skelton Lucy, vict. Blue Ball, Dixon's entry, Lowgate
Skelton Wm. tailor, 15, Prospect pl. Drypool
Skelton Thos. cowkpr. Air street
Skinner Edward, joiner, Waterhouse lane
Skinner Edward, hair cutter, 4, Scale lane
Skirrow Mrs. Tabitha, Prospect place, Drypool
Slater Thos. commercial broker and general agent, 43, High st.; h. 30, Prospect street
Slater Thomas, gent. West st.
Slater Thomas, ship chandler, 35, North st. Prospect st.
Sleight R. P. surgeon, 9, Salthouse ln.
Sleight Geo. ship & boat builder, 45, Scott street
Sleight John, shipwright, 16, Church st. Wincolmlee
Slide Wm. tailor, Church st. Drypool

Slingsby John, pawnbroker, 15, Posterngate
Slingsby Wm. tailor and broker, 8, Mytongate
Smart Geo. shopkpr. 62, Lowgate
Smeeton Edw. druggist, 20, Lowgate
Smith John & Co. merchants, oil merchants & ship owners, 21, High st.
Smith John, underwriter, 21, High st.; h. *Kirk Ella*
Smith & Headley, ship owners, rope mfrs. Lime st. N. side Old Dock
Smith and Richardson, cabinet mkrs. 19, Chapel lane
Smith John T. silk mercer and haberdasher, 12, Silver street
Smith Rev. John, Catholic pastor, 32, North st.
Smith Mrs. Marian, 9, Story st.
Smith Mrs. S. 13, Castle street
Smith Simon, gent. 19, English st.
Smith and Colley, worsted mfrs. 44, Blanket row
Smith Joseph, butcher, Castle st.
Smith Thos. butcher, 44, Shambles; house, 13, Robinson row
Smith Thos. grocer, 26, Lowgate
Smith Saml. trunk mkr. 7, Scale lane
Smith Wm. cabinet mkr. New John st.
Smith Thos. plumber and glazier, 22, Bridge street
Smith Isaac, bricklayer and plasterer, 26, Lowgate
Smith Joseph, vict. Prince of Wales, Raikes street
Smith Samuel, vict. Lord Collingwood, 42, Lowgate
Smith Samuel, vict. Jack's Return, 32, Grimsby lane
Smith Wm. vict. Crown, Wincolmlee
Smith Wm. vict. Bay Horse, 22, Wincolmlee
Smith Viner, earthenware dealer, Castle street
Smith Tobias, shopkeeper, Witham
Smith Wm. cabinet mkr. 6, Castle st.
Smith Saml. trunk maker, Scale lane
Smith Francis, furniture broker, 33, Trippet
Smith John, pork butcher, 11, Scale ln.
Smith Noah, basket mkr.3,Grimsby ln.
Smith John, butcher, Castle street
Smith Mary, straw hat manfctr. 20, Great passage street
Smith Edw. shopkpr. 14, English st.
Smith Joseph, shoemaker, 2, Grotto square, Mason street
Smith Robert, shoemkr. New Geo. st.
Smith Wm. engineer, 11,New Geo. st.
Smith Wm. baker, Spring bank
Smith Wm. shoemaker, 15, Brook st.
Smith Robt. ship carpenter, Raikes st.
Smith John, banker's clerk, Owen's place, New George street

Smith Thos. mariner, 12, New George street
Smith John, cowkeeper, Summergang
Smith Geo. hackney cartman, Scott st.
Smith Chas. merchant's clerk, Lime st.
Smith Richard,shopkeeper, 16, George yard, 170, High street
Smith Thos. shoemaker, 176, High st.
Smith Moses, custom house boatman, 18, Roper's row
Smith John,tide waiter,18,Roper's row
Smith John, constable, Charterhs. ln.
Smiths and Thompson, bankers, 25, High st. (on Smiths, Payne, and Smiths, London)
Smithson Wm. grocer, 44, Scott st.
Smithson Robert, paper maker, Bereas mill, Beverley road
Smithson John, wharfinger, 11, Page's square, Dagger lane
Smithson Thos. mariner, 7, Regent's place, Sykes street
Smithson Geo. landing waiter, 32, Prospect street
Snell Wm. turner, 7, Queen's passage, Blackfriargate
Snell Wm. flax dresser, rope maker, and sacking mfr. Witham
Snell Thos. baker, 101, High street
Snell John, shopkeeper, 49, Dock st.
Snow John, vict. Cross Keys Inn, and posting house, opposite King William, 32, Market place
Snow John, merchant's clerk, 18, Osborne street
Snowden Mary, gentlewoman, 19, Blanket row
Snowden Ann, furniture broker, 4, Page's square, Dagger lane
Snowden Benj. mercantile academy, 10, Blanket row
Snowden John,shopkpr.15,St.John st.
Somerscales Anthony, merchant, underwriter, and agent to the Globe Fire office, 11, Parliament street
Somerscales Joseph, linen draper, 10, Market place
Somerscales Mrs. Ann, 60, Prospect st.
Somerscales John, tailor, 5, Vicar la.
Somerscales Charles, coast waiter, 60, Prospect street
Soppit John, clerk, Anlaby road
Soulby William, vict. and wine and spirit merchant, Corn Exchange, 49, Corn market
South Jonathan, spirit & porter mert. ship & insurance broker,& general agt. 123, High st.; h. 1, Charles st.
Southerland Robert, vict. Ordnance Arms, Great Union street
Soutter Wm. wholesale & retail ironmonger, 24, Market place
Soutter James, muslin, &c. dealer, 2, Church street, Wincolmlee

Soutter Gabriel, eating house, 11, Waterhouse lane

Sowby William, wine & brandy merchant, 64, Lowgate

Spain Henry, ship carpenter, 11, Pell mell court, Broadley street

Spaldin William, timber merchant; house, 5, Charles street

Sparkes Mrs. Eliz. 25, George street

Spence Edw. Russia merchant, 167, High st.; house, 40, Prospect st.

Spence, Watson and Co. brewers and maltsters, Prospect street

Speuce Wm. mercht.; h. 40, Dock st.

Speace T.W. linen weaver,9,Alfred st.

Spencer and Barker, boot and shoe makers, 14, St. Mark's square

Spencer Samuel, coal merchant, 18, Grotto square, Mason street

Spencer Charles, bricklayer, 8, Hodgson's square, Sykes street

Spencer Ann, dealer in earthenware, Grotto square

Spencer George, mariner, 4, Prince George entry, 184, High street

Spencer Thos. mariner, 3,Charterhs.ln.

Spencer Wm. cowkpr. Danson lane

Spendlove Mrs. Mary, 1, Chapel st.

Spink John, vict. White Swan, 19, Wincolmlee

Spink Edw. plumber and glazier, 22, Wincolmlee

Spink John, baker, 3, Salthouse lane

Spraggon Rt. horse breaker,59,Carr ln.

Spyvee & Cooper, oil merchants, ship owners and ropers, 61, High st. and Lime street

Spyvee W.C. roper; h. 13,Charlotte st.

Spyvee Robert, shopkeeper, 1, Grotto square, Mason street

Squire Edw. mercht.; h. 14, Dock st.

Squires Henry, furrier, White Horse yard, Market place

Stainbank Edw. merchant's clerk, 6, Portland place

Stainton M. milliner, 32, George st.

Stainton Thos. bookkpr.32, George st.

Stamp Francis, sheriff's officer and auctioneer, 4, Broadley street

Stanford Joshua, fruiterer, Market pl.; h. 6, North side Trinity church

Staniforth S. C. milliner and dress maker, 10, Waterhouse lane

Staniland and Garbutt, haberdashers and silk mercers, 8, Silver street

Staniland Thos. broker & auctioneer, North Dock side; h. 51, George st.

Staniland Susannah, linen draper, 21, Bridge street

Staniland Mrs. Mary, 5, Story street

Stanley Jas. locker at custom house, 4, Mulgrave street

Stannard Joseph, butcher, 11, St. John's square

Stannard Germain, artist, 6, Wtriargt.

Stanton Robt. store keeper, Ordnance place, Drypool

Stark Jermb.pawnbroker,Broadley st.

Stark Ann, schoolmistress, 2, Featherstone's entry, 178, High street

Stathers John, shoemaker, 2, Schonswar's square, Dagger lane

Stathers Robert, joiner, 12, Pycock's gallery, 21, Sewer lane

Stathers Thos. shoemkr. 13,Dagger la.

Statters Robt. vict. King, 20, Bond st.

Staveley W.clothes broker,22, West st.

Stead Mrs. Ann, 12, Paradise place

Stead John, banker's clerk,Paradise pl.

Stead Richard, shopkpr. 14, Manor st.

Steele Maria, ladies' boarding school, 2, Prince street

Steele Wm. hat mfr. 12, Queen street

Steemson Mrs. Susannah, 20, Story st.

Steeple W. and S. plumbers, glaziers and painters, 31, Scale lane

Steer Richard, shoemkr. 41, West st.

Stephens Wm. gent. 13, Silver street

Stephenson Robert, gent. Church st.

Stephenson Thomas, linen draper, 22, Waterworks street

Stephenson Robert, linen draper, &c. 46, Market place

Stephenson Rt. spirit mert. 62, High st.

Stephenson Peter, vict. Golden Cup, 22, Blanket row

Stephenson W. vict. Windmill, Witham

Stephenson Richd. gent. 3, Mason st.

Stephenson J. tallow chandler, 58, Lowgate

Stephenson M. H. clerk of customs, 24, Brook street

Stephenson William, whitesmith and wheelwright, Chariot street

Stephenson Richard, wood turner, 2, Drewer's entry, 129, High street

Stephenson Joanna, straw hat mkr. 4, Sir John's row, Wincolmlee

Stephenson Mary, dress maker and repository, 21, George's street

Stephenson John, baker,5,L.Union st.

Stephenson Thos. shopkpr.49,West st.

Stephenson Hy.shopkpr.37,Spencer st.

Stephenson Tabitha, (lodgings) 6, Savile row

Stephenson John, shopkpr. Marvel st.

Stephenson John, cowkpr.Beverley rd.

Steward John, baker, 15, Bishop lane

Steward John,mariner,17,Waterhs.ln.

Stewart Charles, wine & spirit mert. 1, Stewart's yd. 152, High street

Stickney Mthw. currier, 36, St.John st.

Stickney Abraham, patten maker and fruiterer, 33, Bridge street

Stickney Mary, ladies' boarding academy, 19, Trinity house lane

Stockburn Ann, vict. Dock Coffee House, 10, Quay street

Stockdale Jane, ladies' boarding school, 5, Albion street
Stockdale Wm. furniture broker, 17, New Dock street
Stocks Benj. mercht. ship owner and agent to the Imperial Fire, &c. office, 18, High st.; h. Cottingham
Stockton John, shopkeeper, Queen st.
Stokes Cornelius, varnisher, 1, Grimston court, Savile street
Stone John, sail maker, ship & insurance broker, & dealer in paint, tar and varnish, 83, High street
Stone Saml. sail mkr. &c.; h. Dagger ln.
Stone Sarah, vict. Whale, 83, High st.
Stone David, watch mkr. 7, St.John st.
Storey Mrs. Eliz. 4, Trinity house lane
Storey William, gent. 14, North side Trinity church
Storey Wm. grocer, 36, Whitefriargate
Storey Rev. John, 15, Princess street
Storey Eliz. straw hat mfr. 17, Grotto sq.
Storey William, furniture broker, New John street
Storey Geo. matting mfr. 14, Lowgt.
Storey Thos. shopkeeper, 14, Lowgt.
Storey John, mariner, Church st. Drypl.
Storm John, gent. 2, Parliament st.
Storr Jane, eating house, 38, Scale ln.
Stothard Jas. painter, 23, Trippet st.
Stothard John, shoemkr. 70, Mytongt.
Strafford John, pilot, 5, Belt's place, Blackfriargate
Stratton Wm. lighterman, 1, Upper Union street
Strawson Richard, plumber & glazier, 11, Waterworks street
Stray Miles, tailor & broker, 21, Lowgt.
Street Wm. truck master, 29, Bishop ln.
Stretton Mrs. Mary, 14, Crown court
Stringer Matthew, cooper, 29, Aldbro' street
Strother John, corn agent & factor, 30, High st.; house, Summergangs
Stubbs Mark, surgeon, 27, Queen st.
Stubbs Wm. hair cutter, 15, Charlot st.
Stubbs John, bricklayer, Naylor's row, Witham
Stubbs Wm. number carrier, 6, Vine court, High street
Suddaby John, cowkpr. 6, Cannon st.
Sugden John, gent. 8, Sewer lane
Suggitt Jefferson, grocer & tea dealer, 44, Lowgate
Summers Joseph, tailor, 2, Fish street
Sumpner John, corn factor, 149, High st.; h. 25, Prospect pl. Drypool
Sutcliffe Wm. flour dlr. 46, High st.
Sutherland Peter, bookbinder, 30, Grimsby lane
Sutton Thos. gent. 10, Paradise place
Sutton Thos. joiner, 49, Market place
Swainston Robert, shopkeeper and bacon-factor, 67, Lowgate

Swann and Ayre, solicitor, 7, Parliament street
Swann J. W. solicitor; house, West parade, Anlaby road
Swann A. & M. milliners, &c. 7, Geo. st.
Swavy Eliz. dress mkr. 34, Bond st.
Swift Robt. ordnance officer, Garrison
Swinbank John, gent. 33, Brook st.
Sykes Daniel, Esq. M. P. barrister & recorder of Hull, 16, Bowlalley lane; house, Raywell
Sykes Thos. merchant, 2, Exchange alley; house, 7, Paradise place
Sykes Joseph, Son and Co. iron merchants, 20, Bowlalley lane
Sykes James and Co. woollen cloth mfrs. 1, Vicar lane
Symons Moses, jeweller & bullion dlr. 6, Queen st.; house, 1, Kingston court, 19, Blanket row
Symons Samuel, dealer in spectacles, 2, New Dock side
Tacey Wm. baker, 26, Bond street
Tadman Francis; solicitor, 3, Clark's square, Sykes street
Tadman Hannah, vict. Unicorn Tavern, 192, High street
Tadman Francis, bricklayer, Posterngt.
Tadman William, bird cage maker, New Dock street
Tadman John, paviour, 4, Catherine st.
Tadman Benj. bricklayer, 29, Blanket row
Tankersley Rt. day school, Waterhse.
Tarbotton John, shoemkr. 1, Carlisle
Tarbotton Wm. currier and leather cutter, 4, North side Trinity church
Tarn Joseph, ordnance clerk, St. Quintin's place
Tate Benj. printer, 49, Market place
Tate Wm. hair dresser, 86, Mytonga.
Tate Ann, shopkpr. 22, Bourne st.
Tather John, gent. 7, Carlisle street
Tather Thos. brewer, 1, Fox street
Taylor & Clifford, general agents and corn factors, 160, High street
Taylor John, corn factor; h. 1, Chas. st.
Taylor Misses A. E. & M. 35, Dock st.
Taylor John, gent. 18, Dock street
Taylor Edw. bone merchant & button mfr. Church street, Scalcoates
Taylor James, bone mercht. & button mould mfr. Waterworks street
Taylor G. C. whitesmith, 9, Chapel st.
Taylor Jane, vict. Bonny Boat, 10, Trinity house lane
Taylor Samuel, vict. Sawyers' Arms, Lime street
Taylor John, rope maker, Raikes st.
Taylor John, gent. 18, Dock street
Taylor Sam. straw hat mfr. 12, Whitefr.
Taylor Wm. hair dresser, 37, Bridge
Taylor William, mariner, 9, New Dock side

Taylor Wm. foreman at Messrs. Bolton's, Greenland yd. *Willington*
Taylor Thomas, mariner, 6, Regent's place, Sykes st.
Taylor Thos. mariner, 9, Grimston st.
Taylor Dnl. shopr.& joiner,11,West st.
Taylor Anthony, shoemkr. 2, Trippet
Taylor Jph. mariner, 8, Grimston st.
Taylor Robert, mariner, Aldbro' st.
Tealby, Dalton & Co. timber merchts. and ship owners, Garrison side
Tealby Eliz. timber merchant; house, Thornton st.
Tealby Mrs. Mary 70, West st.
Teale Mrs. Jane, 11, Brook st.
Teale Geo. cowkeeper, Dibbs' yard, 30, North st.
Teale John, poulterer, 58, Scott st.
Teanby Thos. corn agent, 9, Vine ct. Botelar st.
Tedd John, house & ship smith, bellhanger & edge tool maker, Pease's entry, 45, Salthouse lane
Teesdale T. bookseller, 6, New dock st.
Temperton Eleanor, stay and corset maker, 13, Bond st.
Tempest John, vict. & worsted manfr. Hope, 8, Little passage st.
Temple Mrs. Isabella, lodging house, 25, Savile row
Temple Thos. brewer and maltster, 13, Marine row
Templeman John, cowkeeper, Air st.
Terrington T.A. gent. 41, Prospect st.
Terry Mrs. Ann, Humber bank
Terry Richd. & Sons, merchts. ship owners, &underwriters, & agents for Henry Ewbank, 39, High st.
Terry John, mert. ; h. Humber bank
Terry R.G. merchant; house, 9, Cent per cent st.
Terry Wm. auctioneer, 10, Savile row
Terry Wm. watch and clock maker, 61, Lowgate
Tessyman Francis, currier and leather cutter, 3, New Dock st.; house, Anlaby road
Tesseyman Wm.currier,&c.9, Fish st.
Tesseyman Joseph, shoemaker, 15, Prospect st.
Thackray John, sail maker and ship owner, Dock side ; h. 20, Albion st.
Thackray Wm. shoemkr. 57, Carr ln.
Thistleton Jas. hair dresser, 84, High st.
Thistleton Wm. vict. Britannia, Trippet
Thom Rhoda, earthenware dealer; 6, St. John st.
Thomas & Piercy, merchants, brush & paint mfrs. oil & colourmen, (late new sugar house) Wincolmlee
Thomas John, currier, 23, Scale lane
Thomas Richd. gent. 10, Parliament st.
Thomas John, hairdresr: 1,Prospect st.
Thomas Jph. mariner, 47, Prospect st.

Thomas Peter, cowkpr. *Summe*
Thomas John, cattle doctor, C alley, Witham
Thompson Caius and Co. mer ship insurance brokers, a owners, 2, Trinity house la
Thompson Caius, underwriter for the County Fire, &c. o Trinity house lane
Thompson Thos. Esq. banker ; High st. and *Cottingham C*
Thompson Edw. and Johs, a agents, wharfingers, ship c & coal merts. 15, Parliame
Thompson Edw.mert. , h. 7, Jar
Thompson Henry, timber mei 9, George st.
Thompson Thomas, solicitor,8,' house lane ; house, 5, Pryn
Thompson John, gent. 32, Albi
Thompson Rev. Joseph, aca Charles st.; house, 5, North
Thompson Thos. mert. 9, Hum
Thompson Misses Ann & Mary, ( bdg. school) 14, Blanket ro
Thompson Mrs. Eliz. 21, Charl
Thompson Miss Mary, 15, Portl
Thompson Sarah, gentlewom Newton's court, Manhell st
Thompson John, saw maker an monger, 6, North walls
Thompson Abrm. currier, Winc
Thompson G. D. clerk to the office, Queen st.
Thompson Geo. miller & corn Holderness road
Thompson Geo. commission de horses, Porter's ct. Carr lan
Thompson James, glazier, Kir st. Wincolmlee
Thompson Jph. miller, Scotch & barley, &c. Steam mill; Scul
Thompson Isaac, piano forte 19, Grotto sq. Mason st.
Thompson Mrs. Sarah, lodging 8, Brooke st.
Thompson Archibald, lumper, 62, I
Thompson Francis, house & ship ter, 13, New Dock st.
Thompson William, vict. Glou Coffee House, 2, High st.
Thompson Matthew, cooper & man, *Somerstown*
Thompson John, broker, 19. N.D
Thompson Wm. leather cap m Posterngate
Thompson Wm. baker, 1, Hano
Thompson Lydia, shoemkr 25, Sal
Thompson John, comptrolling se of customs, 18, Story st.
Thompson Edw. mariner, 13, C sq. Sykes st.
Thompson John, tide waiter, D square

DD

Thompson Samuel, merchant's clerk, 4, Mason street

Thompson Wm. cowkpr. Southcoates

Thonger Rev. Thomas, West parade, Anlaby road

Thorney Dent, shipsmith, 2, Dock st.

Thorney Ann, spirit dealer and vict. 4, Queen st.

Thorney Timothy, timber merchant, broker & general agent, North side Old Dock; house, 10, Worship st

Thorney Dnl. tide waiter, 9, Grotto sq.

Thornham and Todd, veneer sawyers and bone crushers, Wincolmlee

Thornham Geo. watch & clock maker, 10, Queen st.

Thornham John, jun. gent. Church st. Drypool

Thornham John, whalebone mfr. 24, Albion st.

Thornhill John, coach maker; house, 9, Chariot st.

Thornton, Watson and Co. sugar refiners, &c. Lime st.

Thornton John, gent. 28, Albion st.

Thornton Wm. gent. 10, Humber st.

Thorp S. and D. builders and joiners, Waltham st.

Thorp Samuel, joiner; h. Wincolmlee

Thorp David, joiner; h. 18, Carlisle st.

Thorp Charlotte and Emma, superintendants of the penitentiary, 1, North st.

Thorp John, gent. 19, Harcourt st.

Thorp William, surveyor and builder, 26, Mason st.

Thorp Jonathan, saddler, 33, Waterworks st.

Thorp Wm. tailor, 18, Osborne st.

Thorp Stephen, mariner, 5, Love lane

Thring Margaret, gentlewoman, 6, Thring's entry, 26, Wincolmlee

Thundercliff John, grocer, 58, Wfriargt.

Thundercliff Anthony, hair dresser, 31, Waterhouse lane

Thurgarland Thomas, cheesemonger, 12, North side Trinity church

Thurlow John, fishmonger, Queen st.

Thwaites Frederick, schoolmaster, Porter's yard, Waterhouse lane

Thwaites Geo. shipwright, 2, Horner's sq. Humber st.

Thwaites Mary, shopr. 1, Garden st.

Tibb Mary, gentlewoman, 4, Princess row, 23, Dock st.

Tigar John, druggist, 30, Silver st.

Tiffin Peter, vict. Blue Bell, Waterworks st.

Tindale Robert, 6, James' court, 18, Waterhouse lane

Tindale Thos. ship owner, West st.

Tindall G. & W. nursery & seedsmen, 25, Market place, and at *Beverley*

Tindall Mrs. Isabella, 5, Brook st.

Tindall Geo. shipowner, 14, Mason st.

Tindall Rt. joiner, North side Old Dock

Tindell and Gowland, house and ship joiners, Lime st.

Tindell Thos. joiner; h. Hodgson st.

Tingate John, shopkeeper, Church st.

Tingate John, corn miller, Drypool

Tinkler Wm. hat maker and furrier, 55, Lowgate

Tiplady William, whalebone mfr. 2, Osborne st.

Todd & Campbell, iron & brass founders, millstone dealers, &c. Foundry row, Sculcoates

Todd Jno. iron founder; h. 1, Wright st.

Todd John, mercht.; h. 10, Savile st.

Todd Mrs. Jane, 11, Jarratt st.

Todd Wm. gent. 15, Whitefriargate

Todd Richd. gent. 9, Catherine sq.

Todd Wm. gent. 6, Hanover sq.

Todd T. H. bone mert. 13, Mason st.

Todd Eliz. toy seller, 13, Market pl.

Todd Wm. wharfinger, 5, Garden sq. Princess st.

Todd Thos. copying machine, pump & engine maker, 156, High st.; h. Broadley st.

Todd S. plumber, &c. Blanket row ct.

Todd Joseph, clock & watch mkr. 13, Market pl.; h. 30, Whitefriargate

Todd Wm. gent. 11, Robinson row

Todd Sarah, dress mkr. 30, Wfriargate

Todd Thos. mariner, 5, Spencer st.

Todd Samuel, fishmonger; h. Lowgt.

Toft Wm. gent. 38, Prospect st.

Tomalin Joseph & Saml. ironmongers, cutlery, and button warehouse, 18, Queen st.

Tomalin Samuel, ironmonger; house, 5, Castle row

Tomlinson James, wine & spirit merchant, 80, High st.

Tomlinson Richard, vict. Ge Elliott, 87, High st.

Tomlinson John, joiner & ironmonger Hyperion st.; house, Witham

Tonge Robt. gent. 6, Garden square Princess st.

Toothill John, day school, Jennings

Topham Richard, shoemaker, 3, Silver street

Topping Thos. letter press printer, 47 Lowgate; house, 39, Dock st.

Topping Joseph, vict. Stewart's Patrick ground lane

Torry John, shoemkr. 6, Marvel sq.

Tottie Richd. mert. & American con sul, 33, High st.; h. *Spring head*

Tottie Launcelot, vict. Lugger, 92 High st.

Towers Wm. Frank, haberdas hosier & glover; 1, Whitef

Townsend James, clothes broker, South end, Humber st.

Trant Geo. gent. Wellington place, Beverley road
Travis Mrs. Frances, 196, High st.
Travis Samuel, hatter, Queen st.
Trees Jas. shopkpr. 20, Roper's row
Tressidor John, notary public, conveyancer & accountant, 6, High st. ; house, 27, English st.
Trevor Charles, gent. 36, Wincolmlee
Trigg M. T. mustard mfr. Cockpit yd. Castle st. ; h. 27, Albion st.
Tripp Thos. gent. 19, Bridge st.
Trower Mrs. Sarah, 17, Savile st.
Truefit Mrs. Ann, 29, George st.
Truefit James, marble & stone mason, 39, Savile st.
Trumble S. hair dresser, 153, High st.
Tucker Thos. mariner, 2, New Geo. st.
Tummon & Smithson, general wharfingers and shipping agents, 60, High st.
Tummon Wm. wharfinger; house, 4, Thornton st.
Tummon Jph. vict. Angel, Chapel ln.
Tummon Joseph, river broker & agt. 8, Commercial ct. 195, High st.
Tummon Geo. hair dresser,60,High st.
Turnbell Robt. shoemkr. 66, West st.
Turnbull Alexdr. D. M. 30, George st.
Turnbull Ann, agent for Newcastle Fire office, 43, Dock st.
Turnbull Andrew, mariner, 1, Hill's court, Princess st.
Turner Geo. bookseller & stationer, (subscription library) and agent to Carroll's Lottery office,65,Mkt.pl.
Turner Isaac, general merchant & insurance broker, 44, High st. ; h. 9, Brook st.
Turner Jonth. druggist, 24, Bridge st.
Turner Rt. joiner & shopkpr. Milk st.
Turner S. corn miller, Holderness rd.
Turner John, joiner, Parade row
Turner John, ironmonger; h.14,Fish st.
Turner John, butcher, 24, Bond st.
Turner Thomas, joiner, Waterhouse lane ; h. 18, Fawcett st.
Turner John, joiner, &c. New John st.
Turner Stephen, whiting manufacturer, *Sutton bank*
Turner Thomas, clerk, 32, Dock st.
Turner Rt. shoemkr. 10, Waterhs. ln.
Turner Robt. poulterer, 6, Grimsby ln.
Turner Wm. mariner, 11, Katherine st.
Turner Thos. (lodgings) 16, Geo. st.
Turner John, mariner, 31, Grimsby ln.
Turpin Wm. shopr. 28, New Geo. st.
Turpin Edw. tide waiter, 8, Nile pl.
Tutill Mercy, shopkeeper, Finkle st.
Tweed Richd. shopr. 28, L. Union st.
Twist Jph. rope mkr. N. bridge foot
Tyson Eliz. day school, 2, Engine st.
Underwood & Hawkins, haberdashers, 14, Market place

Unthank John, mariner, 2, Sykes st.
Uppleby Rev. Wm. 14, English st.
Usher Wm. gent. 7, Beverley road
Usher John, coach master, 2, Fox st.
Valentine James, butcher, 46, Shambles ; house, 6, Robinson row
Valentine Smith,butcher,2,Chariot st.
Vallance John, shoemaker, 29,Lowgt.
Vanderkiste Tilden, exciseman, New John st.
Varley John, fishmonger, Queen st.
Vause John, wine dealer & maltster, 2, Myton place
Vause John, maltster,28, Paradise pl.
Vause Richd. plumber & glasier, 24, Silver st. ; house, Anlaby road
Vause John, tailor, 26, Humber st.
Vessey Eliz. straw hat maker, Dibb's yard, 30, North st.
Vickerman David, house & ship painter, 13, Waterworks st.
Vickerman T.D. painter,15,Well's st.
Vincent Eliz. vict. Old England, 106, High st.
Vincent Henry, pawn broker, 28, Blackfriargate
Vincent Eliz. shopkeeper, Humber st.
Voase John & Son, wine and spirit merchts. & ship owners, 23, High st. ; house, Anlaby road
Vollans Gervis, gent. 68, West st.
Von Roy Frederick, merchant, 8, Scale lane
Waddingham John, miller, Holderness road
Waddingham Nathaniel, gent. 32, Brook st.
Waddington John, shopr. 29, Savile st.
Wade Richard & Sons, timber and mahogany merchts. Garrison side
Wade Abraham, timber merchant; h. 28, Harcourt st.
Wade John, timber mert.; h. *Summergangs*
Wade William, clerk to the Dock Co. Patrick ground lane
Wade Alice, baker, Alfred st.
Wadland John, butcher, 26, Trippet
Waite&Collinson,sail mkrs.60,High st.
Waite Richard, sail maker; house, 5, North side Trinity church
Wake James, sen. glue mfr. oil merchant, ship owner & shipping agt. *Wilmington* ; h. 21, Dock st.
Wake James, jun. grocer, North st.
Wales Wm.confectioner,39,Garden st.
Wales T. bricklayer, 32, New Geo. st.
Wales John, barrister's clerk, 11, George st.
Wales John, vict. Angel, 23, Clappison's sq. Sykes st.
Wales Wm. vict. Bridge Coffee House, 40, Bridge st.
Walker Mrs. Susannah,1,Wellington st.

Walker Wm. & Jonth. wholesale, retail & furnishing ironmongers, tinners & braziers, register & other stoves, fenders & fire irons, cutlery, locks, joints & nails, lamp, sperm and other oils, steam kitchens and kitchen furniture, Britannia metal & japan goods, &c. &c. 50, Lowgt.

Walker Thomas & Co. lath renders, Old Dock end

Walker Lieut. Wm. 66th regt. of foot, Park pl. Albion pl. Witham

Walker Wm. turner and basket mfr. 23, Market place

Walker Geo. watch mkr. 22, Lowgate

Walker Ann, vict. Ship Artois, 64, Mytongate

Walker Robert, tinplate worker, 1, Hope street

Walker George, vict. Blue Ball, Leadenhall sq.

Walker Wm. joiner, 10, Spencer st.

Walker Wm. shoemaker, 9, Broadley square

Walker John, sail maker, Ordnance place, Drypool

Walker John, joiner, Bond st. mews; house, Spencer st.

Walker John, surveyor of taxes, 9, Mason st.

Walker John, cabinet maker, upholsterer, paper hanger & agt. to the Sheffield Fire office, 32, Savile st.

Walker Matthew, meter, 5, Vine court, High st.

Walker Matthew, commercial traveller, 15, Queen's pl. Sykes st.

Walker Thos. shopkr. 8, Bishop lane

Walker Thos. cowkeeper, 3, Waterhouse lane

Walker John, tailor, 7, Quay st.

Walker John, cabinet maker, &c. 24, Blackfriargate

Walker Hy. mariner, 24, Harcourt st.

Walker Richard, excise officer, 20, Robinson row

Walker Samuel, landing waiter, 50, Lowgate

Walker Thos. mariner, Somerstown

Walgate Wm. woollen draper, 9, Market place

Walkington Robert, 7, Humber st.

Walkington Isabella, gentlewoman, John st. Drypool

Waller Henry, gent. 3, Princess row, 23, Dock st.

Wallis Ann, grocer, 11, Grimston st.

Wallis Edward, whalebone manufr. Lincoln st. Wincolmlee

Wallis Rd. butcher, 68, Lowgate

Wallis Samuel, cabinet maker, Katharine sq.

Wallis George, gun maker, 19, Mytongate

Wallis Henry, 19, Mytongate

Wallis Hannah, dyer, Green ln. Dryp.

Wallis John, gent. 8, Witty's sq.

Walsam Stephen, shopkpr. Witham

Walmsley David, grocer, tea, hop, seed dealer, and cheesemong. 35, Market place

Walmsley Wm. gent. 17, English st.

Walmsley Wm. jun. solicitor, 4, Parliament st. and South Cave

Walsham John, gent. 2, Wood's ct. South st.

Walsham R. corn miller, Summergan.

Walsham & Fewson, corn miller, Holderness road

Walter Moses, quill dealer and pen cutter, 10, Lee's entry, 198, High

Waltham Saml. gent. 3, Worship st.

Walton Thos. gent. 2, Foundry row

Walton Thos. gent. Lime st.

Walton Thos. shoemaker, Church st.

Ward Miss Ann, 57, Humber st.

Ward Thos. merchant, ship owner, ship and insurance broker, 1, Parliament st.

Ward Michael, brandy merchant, 8, Chapel court, George yard

Ward Thomas, carver and gilder, 36, Waterworks st.

Ward Rhd. vict. Grapes, 22, Sykes st.

Ward Thomas, vict. Volunteer, Waterworks st.

Ward John, tobacco and snuff mfr. 34, Bridge st.; h. 20, Mason st.

Ward Benj. cabinet maker and upholsterer, 28, Chariot st.; house, Sykes st.

Ward Ann, slater, Dock st.

Ward Burnell, druggist, 189, High st.

Ward Hy. ship chandler, 16, High st.

Ward Jas. shoemaker, 45, Mytongate

Ward Wm. sail maker, 13, Pell Mell

Ward Sarah, confectnr. 1, Humber st.

Ward Wm. shopkpr. 31, Bishop lane

Ward John, hair dresser, 36, Bond st.

Ward John, hair dresser, 19, Great Passage st.

Ward Philip, white lead bound?, Holderness road

Ward John, tailor, 70, Mytongate

Ward Thos. clerk, 13, Princess st.

Ward Abm. mariner, Neptune st.

Ward Rhd. mariner, 12, Waltham st.

Ward Philip, 2, King's ct. 126, High st.

Ward Thos. mariner, 2, Chapel court, George yard

Wardale Mary, (lodgings) 4, Sykes st.

Wardale Rbt. shopkpr. 2, Finkle st.

Wardell J. carver & gilder, 5, Lowgt.

Wardell John, grocer and tea dealer, 194, High st.

Wardle Wm. mariner, 8, Paradise row

Ware Francis, sail maker, Temple entry, 198, High st.; h. N. John's st.

Ware Francis, shopkpr. 138, High st.
Ware John, fishmonger, 36, Mkt. pl.
Ware Joseph, mariner, 6, Myton pl.
Warham Rd. mariner, 17, Sykes st.
Waring Mrs. S. Staniforth place
Warney M. & S. dress makers, 15, Mason st.
Wass Ann, shopkpr. 13, L. Union st.
Waterhouse Vincent, shopkeeper, 25, Chapel lane
Waterland George, shopkeeper, 14, Blackfriargate
Waterland John, gent. 27, Paradise pl.
Waterlow Saml. shopkr. 17, Carr ln.
Waters John, tobacconist, 46, Whitefriargate
Waters Gavin, gardener, 23, Bond st.
Waters Mary, clothes broker, 15, New Dock st.
Waters J. D. tobacconist, 2, Commerce lane
Waterson & May, bacon factors, 35, Church lane
Watkin Mrs. Ann, 43, Spencer st.
Watkinson Rd.comb mkr.27, Savile st.
Watkinson John, hatter, Johnson's ct.
Watson J. K. Esq. banker, 8, Albion st. and *Hessle Mount*
Watson Thomas, brewer ; house, 12, Prospect st.
Watson Geo. builder, 10, Carlisle st.
Watson Geo. cabinetmkr.7, Castle row
Watson Wm. grocer, 22, Bridge st.
Watson Geo. joiner and broker, 16, Blackfriargate
Watson Jas. shoemkr. Blue Bell yard, Wells st.
Watson Henry, plumber & glazier, 3, New Dock st.
Watson John, shoemkr. 29, St.John st.
Watson John, vict. and bricklayer, Golden Ball, 9, Dagger lane
Watson John, vict. Union Coffee House, 16, Bishop lane
Watson John, vict. White Hart, 11, Salthouse lane
Watson Mary, vict. 3 Crowns, Lime st.
Watson Wm. fruiterer, Mytongate
Watson Thos. shopkpr. 64, Prospect st.
Watson Amelia, (lodgings) 18, Charles street
Watson John, tailor, 15, Bridge st.
Watson John, tailor, 18, Robinson row
Watson John, mariner, Charles st.
Watson G. B. mariner, Cottage gardens, 8, Nile place
Watson Henry, mariner, 5, Carlisle st.
Watson Ralph, mariner, 1, Catharine square, Mason st.
Watson John, mariner, Higson's ct.
Watson Jas. wheelwright, Queen st.
Watmuff James, worsted maker, 28, Chariot st.
Watters Rbt. shoemaker, Parade row

Watts John, cabinet maker, 4, St. Mark's sq.
Waud Mary, gentwn. 5, Nile place
Waudby John, cowkeeper, Short st.
Waudby Wm. painter, Dock side
Waudby Wm. shopkpr. 53, Salths. ln.
Waugh James, vict. & cooper, Malt Shovel, 10, N. side Trinity church
Waugh James, sexton of St. Mary's church, 20, Chapel lane
Waugh J. & Co. cabinet makers and upholsterers, 8, Trinity house ln.
Waugh John, hair dresser, 91, High st.
Wayre Wm. hatter & furrier, 28, St. John st.
Weatherhill John, vict. Royal Oak, 47, Spencer st.
Weatherhill Esther, milliner, 52, Market place
Weatherhill Miss Mary, 2, Springbank
Weatherhill Joseph, glass, china, earthenware, and joiners' tools dealer, 44, Mytongate
Webster Mrs. Eliz. 2, Worship st.
Webster E. & W. surgeons & druggists, 3, Whitefriargate
Webster Rbt. builder; h. 30, Scott st.
Webster Wm. cooper, Webster's entry 156, High st.
Webster James, cabinet maker, &c. 37, St. John st.
Webster Michael, stone mason, Waterworks st.
Webster Jane, confectr. 52, Carr ln.
Webster Michael, bricklayer, Norris yard, Well st.
Webster Stephen, shopkpr. 9, Mill st.
Webster & Ward, millers, Southcoates
Webster Jane, fruiterer, Chariot st.
Webster John, mariner, Robinson row
Weddle and Brownlow, commission agents, ship & insurance brokers, agents for theLondonsteam packet Co. and the regular contract of sailing vessels between Hull and London, Beal's wharf, London, and 62, High st. Hull
Weddle Thomas, wharfinger; house, 10, Prince st.
Welbury John, whitesmith & chain maker, 159, High st.
Wellburn Geo. hair cutter, 32, Salthouse lane
Wellburn Matthew, mariner,7, Clark's square, Sykes st.
Wellburn John, hair drsr. 14, Geo. st.
Wellburn John, gardener, Greenlane, Wincolmlee
Welch Wm. Outwith, Russia merchant, 36, High st.; h. 2, Prince st.
Welch Charles, day school, Webster's court 156, High st.
Wells & Morley, timber merchants & insurance brokers, N. S. old dock

Wells Wm. timber mert.; h. 1, York st.
Wells Peter, mert.; h. 71, Lowgate
Wells Mrs. Bellamy, 4, Robson's pl. Sykes st.
Wells Joseph, gent. 24, Bourne st.
Wells Richard, draper, tailor, & spirit dealer, 4, Blackfriargate
Wells Robert, gent. Neptune st.
Wells John, Lieut. R. N. Walker's square, Sykes st.
Wells Mary, shopkpr. 47, South end
Wells George, chair maker and wood turner, 4, Queen st.
Wells John, tailor, 6, New Dock st.
Wells Thos. hair dresser, 46, Mytongt.
Wells John, clerk, 20, Charles st.
Welptun Geo. shopkpr. 30, North st.
West John, gent. 10, Mytongate
West Geo. gent. 20, New Geo. st.
West Edw. tanner, 12, Providence row
West Leonard, grocer, and British wine dealer, 13, Silver st.
West Jas. pawnbroker, 22, Brook st.
West Wm. coal mert. 28, Trippet
West Thomas, hosier, 4, Carlisle st.
West Wm. baker, 6, Trippet
West Wm jun. baker, 5, Trippet
West Wm. bricklayer and maker, 2, Mason st.
West Thomas, collector of market tolls, New road, Anlaby road
West Joseph, fishmonger, 5, St. John street
West John, mariner, 3, Neptune pl.
Westerdale Wm. mast, block & pump mkr. 1, Pier st. & Old Dock side
Westerdale Mary, pipe maker, 24, Finkle st.
Westerdale Wm. traveller, 8, North st.
Westerdale Samuel, merchant's clerk, Lime st.
Westoby Edward, paper hanging warehouse, 1, North st.
Westoby John, vict. and bricklayer, Sl op, 2, Great Passage st.
Westoby Mary, shopkeeper, 12, West street
Westoby Samuel, clerk, Lime st.
Wetwand Wm. vict. Three Jolly Sailors, 191, High street, and 1, Salthouse lane
Whaplate Wm. timber merchant; h. 14, Portland place
Wharton Thomas, merchant and commercial agent, Exchange alley; h. 4, Pryme st.
Wharton Chpr. joiner, Parade row
Wharton John, vict. Ship, Witham
Wharton Geo. clerk, 8, Beverley road
Wharton Wm. mariner, 9, Prospect st.
Wheat James, clerk, Hodgson st.
Wheatley Mary, shopkpr. 8, Trippet
Whinham Robert, hat maker and turner, 98, Waterhouse lane

Whip Matthew, butcher, 20, Brook st
Whitaker Charles, Esq. 10, North st. and Sutton
Whitaker Mrs. Sarah, 8, Paradise pl.
Whitaker John, sail cloth and sail manufacturer, Scott st. & Dock office row; h. 55, Wincolmlee
Whitaker John, shopkpr. Jennings st.
White Mrs. Mary, 2, Nile st.
White Robert, M.D. 32, Mason st.
White Thomas, grocer, tea dealer, & coffee roaster, 62, Market place; house, 9, Prince st.
White John, butcher, 24, Chariot st.
White Samuel, grocer, 33, Church st. Sculcoates
White Ann, shopkpr. 20, Church st.
White Jonas, shopkeeper, 13, Church st. Sculcoates
White William, joiner and builder, 17, Hanover square
Whitehead John, vict. Painters' Arms, 7, Finkle st.
Whitehead Lawrence, mariner, 8, Dryden's entry, 19, Salthouse lane
Whitehead William, eating house, 22, Church st.
Whitehouse John, manufacturer of shoe trimmings, 57, West st.
Whiteley James, tailor, 18, Mill st.
Whitfield David, shoemaker, Hodgson street
Whiting William, clerk, Whiting st. Garden st.
Whitton John, general agent, Commercial Buildings, 29, High st.; house, 11, Mason st.
Whitworth and Co. linen and woollen drapers, 4, Whitefriargate
Wier Matt. shopkpr. 10, Wincolmlee
Wigglesworth Benjamin, tanner Wilmington
Wilbe Wm. grocer, Lime st.
Wilbe Richard, tailor, 3, Fish st.
Wilbe Richard, tailor, 33, Bishop la.
Wilberforce Walter, hair dresser, 21, Scale lane
Wilberforce William, patten maker, 2, Lowgate
Wilby and Pegg, ship smiths, Robert street
Wilcockson Mrs. Margaret, 8, Prospect street
Wilcockson William, mariner, 3, Osborne street
Wiles Wm. shopkpr. 10, Trippet st.
Williford James, joiner, 2, Union st. Spencer street
Wilkins Chas. bookbinder, 19, Bishop lane
Wilkinson, Whitaker, and Co. iron merchants, 47, High st.
Wilkinson Anthony, merchant; house, ...

Wilkinson Ralph, general merchant, 10, Dock office row ; h. Wincolmlee
Wilkinson Geo. master of National School, Perrott street ; and land surveyor, 4, Clark's sq. Sykes st.
Wilkinson John, chemist and druggist, 10, Dock office row
Wilkinson John, druggist, &c. 25, Brook street
Wilkinson Wm. fruiterer, &c. 6, John street
Wilkinson Eliz. whiting manfr. 32, Wincolmlee
Wilkinson James Whitworth, linen draper, 13, Whitefriargate
Wilkinson John, bricklayer, 26, Brook street
Wilkinson John, vict. King's Arms, 90, North walls
Wilkinson Robert, vict. Blue Ball and Anchor, 158, High street
Wilkinson Wm. land surveyor, Witham
Wilkinson Wm. tax collector, New George street
Wilkinson Daniel, shoemaker, 4, St. John street
Wilkinson Mrs. Dorothy, 15, Grotto sq.
Wilkinson Mrs. Ann, 11, English st.
Wilkinson Percival, gent. Park place, Witham
Wilkinson Edward, baker, Great Union street
Wilkinson Thomas, brush manufacturer, 4, Providence row
Wilkinson Richard, baker, New John street
Wilkinson Thomas, cabinet maker, Stubbs court
Wilkinson Thos. nail maker, Witham
Wilkinson Thomas, cork cutter, 14, Church lane
Wilkinson Faith, poulterer, 24, Scale lane
Wilkinson Wm. flour dlr. Hospital yd.
Wilkinson John, shopkpr. 4, Lowgate
Wilkinson Wm. joiner, 18, Charlotte street
Wilkinson John, eating house, 21, Waterworks street
Wilkinson Geo. tailor, Whiting's sq. Brook street
Wilkinson Charles, clerk, 13, Paradise place
Wilkinson Chas. clerk, 20, Bourne st.
Wilkinson M. book-keeper, William's square, New George street
Wilkinson John, mariner, 16, Sykes st.
Wilkinson Thos. mariner, 17, Sykes st.
Wilkinson William, warehouse keeper to the Dock Company, South side Old Dock
Williams Robert, mariner, 7, King's place, Dock street

Williams Thomas and Co., woollen drapers, 1, Market place
Williamson Thos. brewer, Lime st.
Williamson Robert, gun maker, 29, Silver street
Williamson Benjamin, gent. 4, Clarence court, Prince street
Williamson Barker, joiner, Parade row
Williamson Jas. hatter, 21, Bishop ln.
Williamson John, gent. 4, Albion pl.
Willis Thos. landscape, sign, & ornamental painter, Humber st.
Willis Wm. shopkeeper, 10, Trippet
Willis Geo. vict. Three Tuns Tavern, Humber bank
Willis Wm. blacksmith, Fawcett st.
Willoughby Geo. shoemkr. 23, Queen st.
Willoughby Elizabeth, lodging house, 16, George st.
Willoughby John, painter, Carr lane
Willows John, mariner, Scott's sq.
Wilmore Jas. vict. Portsmouth Town, 29, Church lane
Wilson Isaac, bookseller, stationer, printer and publisher of the Hull Advertiser, (Friday) 49, Lowgate ; house, 2, York st.
Wilson, Wilkinson, & Co. merchants, 47, High st.
Wilson Rev. Wm. assistant at St. Mary's, 8, Worship st.
Wilson Rev. J. K. ladies' seminary, 23, Market place
Wilson John, chemist & druggist, soda water mfr. & importer of leeches, 15, Market place
Wilson Wm. attorney, 13, Bowlalley ln.
Wilson Eliz. gentwn. 11, Bowlalley ln.
Wilson Mrs. Abigail, 33, Dock st.
Wilson Mrs. Ann, 2, Hodgson's sq.
Wilson Mrs. Susannah, 56, Carr lane
Wilson Mrs. Sarah, 6, Boulton's sq. Manor alley
Wilson William, gent. 1, Dock st.
Wilson John, circulating library and teacher of mathematics, 6, Sewerln.
Wilson Thomas, vict. Rein Deer, 62, Market place
Wilson Sarah, vict. Gate, Lime st.
Wilson Wm. vict. Gate, 13, Alfred st.
Wilson Mary, vict. Red Lion, 2, Manor alley
Wilson Richard, vict. Golden Ball, 27, Middle st.
Wilson Robt. vict. Ship, 14, Scale ln.
Wilson Thos. vict. 3 Crowns, 45, Mkt. pl.
Wilson John, glover, 6, Queen's pl. Blackfriargate
Wilson Joseph, coal merchant, 5, Clarence court, Princess st.
Wilson Thos. linen & woollen draper, 42, Market place
Wilson Thos. grocer, &c. 5, Scale ln.
Wilson John, stay maker, Mytongate

Wilson John, shoemkr. 40, Spencer st.
Wilson Thomas F. portrait & animal painter, 29, Bond st.
Wilson Christopher, cabinet maker & undertaker, 5, Hope st.
Wilson Matth. joiner and cabinet maker, Johnson's ct. ; 156, High st.
Wilson Wm. corn mert. 13, Bourne st.
Wilson William, cowkeeper, 9, Nile place, Cottage gardens
Wilson Wm. nail maker, Witham
Wilson Amiah, day school, 11, Grotto sq.
Wilson John, gardener, 9, North side Trinity church
Wilson Saml. gardener, 1, Boulton's sq.
Wilson William, bacon factor, 17, Shambles ; h. Drypool
Wilson Chas. mariner, 46, George st.
Wilson Jas. bookpr. 7, James' ct.
Wilson Thos. clerk, Anlaby road
Wilson Wm. mariner, 10, Sykes st.
Wilson Mark, mariner, 44, Dock st.
Wimble, Preston, & Co. ironmongers and iron merchants, 50, Market place, and 61, High st.
Wimble Jas. iron mert, 11, High st.
Wincup John, lath merchant, North side Old Dock
Wing John, Hull & Patrington carrier, 3, North bridge
Winship Jas. shoemkr. Bartlett's bldgs.
Winship Wm. shopkeeper, Church st.
Winter, Simpson, & Whaplate, timber merchts. North side Old Dock
Winter T. W. raff mert. ; h. 19, Mason st.
Winter Francis, fishmonger, Queen st.
Winter Rd. tide waiter, 2, Knowles sq.
Wise Featherstone, watch and clock maker, 8, New Dock st.
Wise John, wharfinger, 10, George yd.
Wise Wm. mariner, 4, Wm. sq. Mason st.
Wise Wm. extra locker, 25, Scott st.
Wiseman Caroline, confectioner, 30, Savile st.
Wiseman Dnl. wheelwright, 35, Scott st.
Wiseman Wm. portgauger, 13, Portland place
Witherwick John, cowkpr. 29, North st.
Witherwick John, farmer & cowkpr. Naylor's row, Witham
Witting Jas. shoemkr. 1, Queen's passg.
Witty Richard, clerk to the Gas Company ; h. Bond st.
Witty Rt. builder & joiner, 18, Trippet
Witty Joseph, baker, 58, West st.
Wood Mrs. Eliz. 9, Waltham st.
Wood Mrs. Jane, Staniforth place
Wood Mrs. Mary, 30, Bridge st.
Wood Mrs. Frances, Bridge st.
Wood Wm. gent. 8, Princess st.
Wood Mrs. Betty, 6, Wood's ct. South st.
Wood Matthew, gent. 6, Grimston st.
Wood Thomas, general agent, &c. h. 11, Albion st.

Wood and Bell, general commission agents, ship & insurance brokers, 43, High st.
Wood Samuel, vict. Whittington and his Cat, 15, Castle row
Wood Wm. vict. Blue Bell, High st.
Wood Wm. butcher, 33, St. John st.
Wood Thos. broker, 10, Albion st.
Wood Thomas, cabinet maker, Woolpack entry, 35, Mytongate
Wood Abraham, lath render, Nelson's sq. New George st.
Wood Richard, gardener, Queen st.
Wood Robert, tailor, 13, Manor alley
Wood Edm. weigher, 10, Catharine sq.
Wood Joseph, banker's clerk, 35, Prospect st.
Wood Ann, shopkpr. Great Union st.
Wood Jonth. farmer, Hood st. Drypool
Wood Jonth. tide waiter, Raikes st.
Wood William, merchant's clerk, 2, Regent's place, Sykes st.
Wood Wm. mariner, 26, Harcourt st.
Wood Thos. cork cutter, Raikes st.
Woodcock Ann, shopr. 19, Broadley st.
Woodhead Samuel, vict. Neptune Inn, Chariot st.
Woodhouse Jph. cloth dlr. 5, Sykes st.
Woodhouse Joshua, woollen mfr. 34, Scale lane
Woodmancy Ann, gentlewoman, 4, Naylor's row, Witham
Woodmancy Thos. corn & coal dealer, Witham
Woodmancy Geo. shoemkr. N. John st.
Woodmancy John, livery stable keeper, Great Union st.
Woodmancy John, shopr. 8, Humber st.
Wooffinden John, blacksmith, 23, Chariot st.
Woolf John, ship owner, 29, Albion st.
Woolf John, collector of taxes, Providence row
Woolhouse Richard, furniture broker, New Dock st.
Woolley John, vict. George Inn, (general coach office, 66, W. friargt.
Woolley Wm. attorney, 10, King st.
Woolley Edw. shoemkr. 23, Silver st.
Worrill John, foreman to the Old Dock labourers, Dock side
Worsley Rev. William, 4, Nile st.
Wray Wm. gent. 7, Savile st.
Wray William, gent. Moira buildings, 50, Prospect st.
Wray Richard, vict. Hope & Anchor, 35, High st.
Wray Chas. linen draper, Queen st.
Wray Susannah, clothes club keeper, 18, Wincolmlee
Wray John, joiner and cabinet maker, 1, Gibson's yd. Carr lane
Wride Shadrack, timber merchant, 11, Charter house lane

Wrigglesworth Thomas, butcher, 10, New Dock walls
Wrigglesworth Thomas, bookkeeper, Great Union st.
Wright Mrs. Betty, 4, Princess st.
Wright Robert, gent. 2, Scott's sq. Blanket row
Wright, Bowden, & Co. Russia merchants, 18, High st.
Wright Wm. stationer & bookbinder, 4, Lowgate
Wright John, boat builder, Garrison side; house, Marvel st.
Wright Thomas Dails, wharfinger, 18, Prospect place, Drypool
Wright Robert, cabinet maker & upholsterer, 38 and 39, Bond st.
Wright Francis, painter; house, New George st.
Wright Thomas, wheelwright, Wellington st.
Wright Michael, earthenware dealer, &c. Witham
Wright Hannah, shopkr. 6, Machell st.

Wright Elias, (lodgings) 15, Bond st.
Wright John, farmer, Marvel st.
Wright Eliz. clothes bkr. 39, Chariot st.
Wright Geo. clothes cleaner and silk dyer, 5, Carr lane
Wright Geo. cowkpr. *Summergangs*
Wroot Jane, register office, 11, Norman's entry, George st.
Wrottesley Mrs. Ann, 7, Wright street
Yeale Chas. mert. 10, Mason street
Yelverton Richard, leather dresser, 29, Trippet
York John, bricklayer, 11, New Dock street
Youle John, Henry, & Edward, timber merts. North side Old Dock
Youle John, mert; h. 3, George st.
Young R. C. merchant and general agent, Commercial buildings, 29, High st.; house, *Summergangs*
Young John, surgeon, 2, Bond st.
Young Nancy, day school, Lower Union street
Young Andrew, joiner, Ann street

---

# ALPHABETICAL CLASSIFICATION

### OF THE

## Professions and Trades of Hull.

### *Academies, Schools, &c.*
Agar Thos. Bores' entry, 1, Trippet st.
Annison Wm. 7, Trippet street
Barrett W. S. (gent.'s) Great Union st.
Barrett John, Hanover square
Berry John, 16, New Dock street
Bianington Christ. Church st. Drypool
Blezard Rev. John, Chapel st. Porter's gardens
Breggazzi Dominico, 4, Waltham st.
Briggs Eliz. Jane & Sarah, 25, Finkle st.
Buckton & Newcombe, (dancing and music) 26, George st.
Burge John, 7, Providence court, 19, Brook street
Burnett Jane, 23, Paradise place
Carr Wm. 14, Hardy's ct. 15, Posterngt.
Cass Thos. 1, Knowles' sq. Spencer st.
Chaplin Maria, (ladies' day) 7, Story st.
Chapman John, King's ct. High st.
Columbani Miss Barbara, (French teacher) 37, Aldbro' st.
Cook Thos. 1, New Dock st.
Cox Saml. Hale's entry, Market pl.

Cross John, 68, Mytongate
Crozier J. H. 8, Mews street
Danby Bethel, (writing master) 19, Osborne street
Davies Rev. Geo. John, A. M. (grammar school) 6, S. side Trinity ch.
Deloitte John Oliver, (French) 15, Robinson row
Dix J. B. 22, Parliament street
Dunn Mary Ann, 5, King street
Evison Mary, 2, North st. Prospect st.
Foster Richd. (dancing) 12, Fish st.
Francis Eliz. 15, Harcourt street
French John, 21, Bond street
French Sarah, 21, Bond street
French Wm. (dancing) 21, Bond st.
Fullam Michl. 17, Trinity house lane
Gardham Stephen, Vicar lane
Godmond Eliz. 21, Trinity house lane
Grey Paul, Charlotte street
Hannen Harriot, 41, Savile street
Harrison Wm. Great Union st,
Hirst Margd. Jackson st. Neptune st.
Humbles Thos. 150, High street

Hunt Anne, 10, Grimston street
Hutchcroft Wm. 1, Mason street
Jenkinson David, 6, Foundry row
Johnson Deborah, (la. bdg.) 4, Bourne street
Kent Robert, 5, Wincolmlee
Kidd Anthony, 30, Brook street
Lambert Joseph Casimir, (French) 19, Savile row
Lee Rev. Geo. (gent.'s) 1, Posterngt.
Leedel Geo. 23, Great passage street
Leng Geo. White Horse yd. Market pl.
Leng Joseph, Mason street
Littlewood J. Barker's ct.Blanket row
Locking Misses, (la. bdg.) 21, Story st.
Low John, Walker's sq. Sykes street
Lowson Richard, 9, North street
Mair Wm. Waterworks street
Meggitt Mary, (la. bdg.) 8, George st.
Mercer Ann, 13, Trippet street
Pantry Sarah,(girls' natnl.) Perrott st.
Pape Matthew, Wincolmlee
Pickard John, Well's street
Potchet John, New George street
Revell Aaron, 5, Milton sq. Bourne st.
Richards John, 16, Aldbro' street
Rowlett Thos. 25, Great passage st.
Snowden Benj. (commercial & gent.'s boarding) 10, Blanket row
Steel Maria, (ladies' bdg.) 2, Prince st.
Stickney Mary, 19, Trinity house lane
Tankersley Robert, Carr lane
Thompson Rev. Joseph, Charles st.
Thompson A. & M. 14, Blanket row
Thwaites Frederick, Waterhouse lane
Toothill John, Jennings street
Tyson Eliz. 2, Engine street
Welch Charles, Webster's entry, 156, High street
Wilkinson Geo. (national) Perrott st.
Wilson Rev. J. K. (ladies' seminary) 23, Market place
Wilson John, 6, Sewer lane

*Accountants.*

Burge John, 7, Providence court, 19, Brook street
Carlill George, (and secretary to the Savings' Bank) 5, Quay street
Lee Thos. 150, High street
Tressidor John, 6, High street

*Agents, &c.*
See also Merchants and Ship Owners.
Those marked 1 are General Agents; 2 Commercial Agents; 3 Shipping Agents; 4 Brokers; 5 Ship & Insurance Brokers; and 6 Wharfingers.

1 Bell Thos.Commercial buildings, 29, High street
5 Binks Richard, 12, High street
1 Blackburn Thos. (to the Cheesemongers Co. London) 56, High st.
5 Blyth Robert & Co. 33, High st.
4 Bolton Wm. & Christ. 21, High st.

5 Briggs Christopher & Sons, 7, Bowlalley lane
5 Broadbent Wm. commercial buildings, 29, High street
3 4 6 Bromby & Clark, (to the Leeds Union Co.) 26, High street
3 5 6 Buckton Geo. 56, High street
2 Carlill and Co. 33, High street
6 Clark Peter, 37, High street
1 Clifford Mark, 37, High street
6 Cobb Wm. 21, High street
6 Collinson & Maude, Garrison side
1 Cowie & Brändström, 7, Castle st.
Croft Wm. (wool) 20, High street
1 5 Dails John, 23, Parliament
5 Dales Thos. 20, High street
3 Darbyshire Geo. (to Mills, finger, York) 12, Blackfi
2 Dewear & Harrison, 21, P street
5 Dring Henry, 12, Mason street
5 Earle Geo. and Thos. 43, High s
4 Ellis Wm. (coast and river) Salthouse lane
6 English T. & Son, 3, Humber bank
4 Farthing Wm. 30, High street
2 Fea John, 33, High street
2 Fearn John, 6, High street
Garbutt Robert, (Lloyd's) 1, change alley
4 Gill Geo. (oil and Russia) art's yard, 152, High street
1 Greenwood Geo. Commercial ings, 30, High street
1 Hall John, 20, High street
5 Hall Thos. & Sons, 5, North walls
1 Halls, Todd & Hassell, 8, High st.
2 Hayworth Francis, jun. 2, N.
1 5 Hayes John B. Commercial buildings, 29, High street
1 4 Hendry Martin, Stewart's 152, High street
5 Hewitt Thos. jun. & Co. yard, 152, High street
3 5 6 Holden George, Son & Co. 181, High st. and wharf, 52, High st.
5 Hollingworth Widow & Holderness, Exchange buildings
5 Hopwood Wm. 33, High street
5 Humberston M. E. 5, Blackfriargt.
Humphreys Thos. (to underwriters) 3, North street
2 Jackson Robert, 149, High street
2 4 James Richd. Commercial buildings, 30, High street
Jewitt Simon, (corn) Walker's square, Sykes street
2 Johnson James, 22, North street
5 Knowsley, Swann & Co. 30, High st.
4 Lalouel Henry, (corn and flax) 20, High street
5 La Marche J. B. 200, High street
Lambert Joseph, (coal) 49, South end

Lascelles James, Commercial buildings, 29, High street
3 5 6 Laverack Wm. 70, High st.
averack and Co. (corn) 4 and 5, High street
5 Lee & Tall, Church st. Sculcoates
5 Lee Hill, 18, High street
Lee Thomas, 150, High street
Locking George, 12, High street
Lockwood Thos. (flax) 32, Humber street
Lowther John, 8, Blackfriargate
3 6 Malcolm G. & Sons, 63, High st.
Malleys Simeon, Old Dock side
Margeson Moses, 174, High street
3 6 Martin & Keddey, 49, High st.
'Bride Peter, (cordage) 20, High st.
Medley John, Church st. Sculcoates
4 Mells and Kipling, 1, Commercial court, 195, High street
4 Morehouse & Brown, 184, High st.
Morley Thos. B. (and Baltic) 25, Lowgate
Morris Wm. B. Stewart's yard, 152, High street
Moxon Geo. & John, 160, High st.
4 Nicholson & Wood, Old Custom house, High street
Norman W. V. Garrison side
Park Godfrey & Richd. 183, High st.
Parkin Thos. 38, Grimsby lane
Pattinson Robert, 37, High street
Peel Thos. 10, Bishop lane
erkins John, (for country newspapers) 11, Bowlalley lane
Pierson James, 162, High street
ower Wm. (nails) 21, High street
Radford Thos. Edw. 24, Parliament st.
Radford John Southern and Co. 154, High street
Reed John, 159, High street
Rennard Rd. North side Old Dock
6 Ross Benj. 6, High street
Salter John, 155, High street
Shipman John, Broadley street
Slater Thos. 43, High street
5 South Jonathan, 183, High street
Staniland Thos. North side Old Dock
5 Stone John, 83, High street
Brother John, (corn) 30, High street
Taylor and Clifford, 160, High st.
Teanby Thos. (corn) 9, Vine court, 8, Botelar street
3 6 Thompson Edward & John, 15, Parliament street
Thompson Caius and Co. 2, Trinity house lane
Thorney Timothy, North side Old Dock
Todd Wm. 5, Garden sq. Princess st.
4 6 Tummon and Smithson, 60, High street
Tummon Joseph, 8, Commercial court, 195, High street

5 Turner Isaac, 44, High street
5 Ward Thos. 15, Parliament street
3 4 6 Weddle and Brownlow, (to the Hull, London & Antwerp Steam Packet Co.) 62, High street
5 Wells & Morley, North side O. Dock
2 Wharton Thos. 1, Exchange alley
1 Whitton John, 29, High street
1 Wood and Bell, 43, High street
6 Wright T. D. 18, Prospect place, Drypool
1 Young R. C. Commercial buildings, 29, High street

*Anchor Smiths.*

Pullan Benj. & Son, Dock office row
Thorney J. D. and Co. 2, Dock street

*Architects.*

Bennison Appleton, (and builder) 17, Albion street
Earle John, (and sculptor) 30, Whitefriargate
Mountain Charles, 59, Prospect street

*Artificial Flower Maker.*

Cyprian Caminada, 36, Mill street

*Attornies.*

Alderson John, 36, Salthouse lane
Anderson John, 27, Bishop lane
Bedell W. E. 19, George street
Bramwell Geo. 8, Osborne street
Brown Thos. 5, Parliament street
Bunney Wm. jun. Parliament street
Codd Edward and Geo. 6, Parliament street
Cotsworth John, 28, Whitefriargate
Day John, 26, Waterhouse lane
Dickinson Stephen, 16, Dock street
England and Shackles, 7, Land of Green ginger
Frost Thos. & Charles, 37, Scale lane
Garforth Joseph, 3, Exchange alley
Garland Richard, 6, Bowlalley lane
Grimston Matth. 3, Duke street
Haire Galen, 1, Trinity house lane
Holden Thos. 7, Land of Green ginger
Hugall Thos. 17, Bowlalley lane
Johnson B. L. 7, Mason street
Jolland Wm. Empson, 13, Bishop lane
King Robert, 24, Chapel lane
Moore L. C. 4, Whitefriargate
Phillips Charles Henry, 7, Bowlalley ln.
Prickett and Robinson, 9, Scale lane
Reeves Timothy, jun. 2, Exchange alley
Richardson J. C. 18, Bowlalley lane
Ritson and Dryden, 3, Bowlalley lane
Rushworth Edw. 9, Parliament street
Sandwith Robert, 23, Bishop lane
Scholefield Samuel, Land of Green ginger
Swann & Ayre, 7, Parliament street
Tadman Francis, 3, Clark's square, Sykes street
Thompson Thos. 8, Trinity house ln.

Tressidor John, (and conveyancer) 6, High street
Walmsley W. jun. 4, Parliament st. and at *South Cave*
Wilson Wm. 13, Bowlalley lane
Woolley Wm. 10, King street
Pybus Wm. law stationer, and commissioner for taking special bail, 17, Bowlalley lane

*Auctioneers and Appraisers.*

Boyle Wm. 9, Pages square, Dagger lane
Cross and Glenn, Silver street
Daniels Thos. 2, Savile street
Dean Joseph, 45, Market place
Fea John, 156, High street
Hendry & Hyde, Exchange sale room
Humphreys Thos. (and ship surveyor) 3, North street
Kirkus and Backhouse, 66, Lowgate
Marsh Saml. Discount court, Cent per cent street
Morley Thos. B. 25, Lowgate
Pearce Wm. 21, St. John street
Stamp Francis, 4, Broadley street
Staniland Thos. Old Dock side
Terry Wm. 10, Savile street

*Bacon and Ham Factors.*

Those marked thus * are Butter Factors, thus † are Cheese Factors.

Bellshaw John, 30, West street
Bellshaw Wm. 14, Wincolmlee
Coupland John, New John street
*Duffield Geo. 115, High street
Fawcett Thos. 36, Waterworks street
*†Fearne Thos. 17, Lowgate
*†Gibson Wm. 91, Mytongate
*Harwood Richard, 41, Whitefriargate
*†Kitchen Geo. 11, Market place
Lee Bielby, North street
Lee John, 51, Market place
Levett Sarah, 4, Shambles
Pearson John, 24, Waterworks street
Rickinson Thos. 60, Market place
Savage Joseph, 17, Queen street
Simpson Thos. 130, High street
Sissons Richard, 18, Queen street
Swainston Robert, 67, Lowgate
†Walmsley David, 35, Market place
Waterson and May, 35, Church lane
Wilson Wm. 17, Shambles

*Bakers, Bread and Ship Biscuits, &c.*

Abraham John, 17, Fish street
Adlard Christopher, 21, Dagger lane
Anfield John, 20, Waterworks street
Appleton Wm. 19, North street
Appleyard Robert, 49, Mytongate
Arnett Wm. 145, High street
Arnett John, 2, Prospect street
Arnett John, 9, Great passage street
Bailey Wm. 15, Cook's ct. Broadley street

Baines Robert Raines, Wincolmlee
Barker Geo. 44, Bridge street
Barker Robert, 49, Mytongate
Barker Wm. Church st. Drypool
Barker Marmaduke, 22, Blackfriargate
Bartle John, (ship biscuit) 49, Whitefriargate
Basket John, 8, Myton place
Beck Wm. 3, Cannon street
Bentley Thos. 157, High street
Berridge Edw. 11, Mytongate
Blanchard James, 34, Scale lane
Bores John, 1, Trippet street
Botta Joseph, 22, Dock street
Bowden James, 8, Duke street
Britain Wm. 32, Chariot street
Brooks Wm. yard, 7, Lowgate
Casson John, North ct. 19, North st.
Christie David, 58, Lowgate
Clark Geo. 16, Brook street
Cockrill W. S. Trundle st. Watch house lane
Conkerton Richard, 8, Chapel lane
Cooper John, 190, High street
Coxford Richard, 12, Manor street
Crosskill Mary, 5, Little lane
Crowley Thos. 34, Trippet
Dixon Anthony, 55, Humber st. and 19, Queen street
Ducker Thos. 40, Church lane
Ellis Wilfred, 27, Waterworks street
Empson James, Witham
Finningley Edmund, 13, High street
Finningley Edward, 26, Blanket row
Fox Ambrose, 35, Blanket row
Gibb Thos. 1, Chariot street
Gill Robert, 137, High street
Gray Robert, 4, Waterworks street
Hardisty Wm. 15, Sykes street
Hardy James, 37, Church lane
Harper Richard, 75, West street
Harrison Samuel, 117, High street
Heckenbery Henry, Alfred street
Heward Joseph, 15, Bishop lane
Hodgson Wm. 11, North street
Hodgson Francis, 174, High street
Holdstock Mark, 15, George yd. 138, High street
Hudson Geo. 1, Machell street
Jackson Joseph, 54, High street
Jenkinson Wm. Mill street
Johnson Joseph, 6, Dock office row
Johnson John, 36, Mill street
King Ann, 47, Blackfriargate
Leng Adam, 14, Waterhouse lane
Manby Mary, Mill street
Marwood Samuel, 89, Blackfriargate
Middleton Geo. 33, Grimsby lane
Morse John, Raikes street
Newton Samuel, 21, Chariot street
Nisbet James, 48, Salthouse lane
Osgerby Edw. 22, New George st.
Parks George, 17, Hale's entry, 19, High street

Panling Robert, Witham
Peacock Ann, 6, Clappison's square, Sykes street
Pearson John, 26, Blackfriargate
Peckitt Robt. Henry's ct. L. Union st.
Pentith John, 72, Mytongate
Purdy Henry, 22, Posterngate
Rhodes Elizabeth, 21, Finkle street
Rhodes Thomas, 2, Mytongate
Smith Wm. Spring bank
Snell Thos. 101, High street
Spink John, 3, Salthouse lane
Stephenson John, 5, Lower Union st.
Steward John, 15, Bishop lane
Tacey Wm. 26, Bond street
Thompson Wm. 1, Hanover square
Wade Alice, Alfred street
West Wm. 6, Trippet
Wilkinson Edw. Great Union street
Wilkinson Richard, New John street
Witty Joseph, 58, West street

*Banks.*

Harrison, Watson and Locke, Whitefriargate, (on Marryatt and Co. London)
Pease & Liddell, 18, High st. (on Sir P. Pole, Thornton & Co. London)
Raikes and Co. 12, Scale lane, (on Curries, Raikes and Co. London)
Smiths & Thompson, 25, High street, (on Smiths, Payne and Smiths, London)
SAVINGS' BANK, Exchange alley, attendance Tues. from 11 to 1 noon, & Saturday from 6 to 8 evening. George Carlill, secretary.

*Barristers.*

Kennedy James, Esq. 11, George st.
Osborne Robert, Esq. (stamp office) 2, Bowlalley lane
Sykes Daniel, Esq. M. P. (recorder) 16, Bowlalley lane

*Basket Makers.*

Barrick Wm. 6, Blackfriargate
Boss Elizabeth, 31, Humber street
Clark Wm. 148, High street, and 36, Grimsby lane
Dobson Robt. jun. 122 & 143, High st.
Robinson Richard, 118, High street & 4 and 5, Grimsby lane
Smith Noah, 3, Grimsby lane court
Walker Wm. 28, Market place

*Blacksmiths and Farriers.*
See also Whitesmiths.

Berriman Wm. 2, Vine ct. Botelar st.
Cornell Edward, 3, Parade row
Hanby Thomas, Waterhouse lane
Kell Thomas, 24, Machell street
Kenningham Adam, Church st. Drypl.
Millfield John, 13, Trinity house lane
Ogden James, 6, Finkle street

Richardson Robert, Witham
Richardson Ann, Witham
Richardson Edmund, 1, Fishwick's yard, Waterworks street
Willis Wm. Fawcett street
Woofinden John, 22, Carr lane

*Blacking Manufacturers.*
Battle Robert Gray, 18, Paradise pl.
Edwards Edward, 56, Edgar street

*Bone Merchants.*
Beckett Wm. 10, Trippet
Clark James, 13, New George street
Eyre, Marriot and Co. 13, Church st. Sculcoates
Horncastle Thos. 2, Bourne street
Roberts Thos. Union mill, Wincolmlee
Simpson John, *Wilmington*
Taylor James, 15, Norris' yd. Well st.
Taylor Edw. Church st. Sculcoates
Thornham & Todd, Wincolmlee

*Bookbinders.*
Cairns John, 11, Bishop lane
Darcy James, New Dock walls
Letbe Wm. (& stationer) 43, High st.
Lison Thomas, White Horse yard, Market place
Lofthouse John, 49, Market place
Marshall Matthew, 29, Lowgate
Montgomery John, 21, Robinson row
Penrose John, 26, Savile street
Sutherland Peter, 30, Grimsby lane
Wilkins Charles, 13, Bishop lane

*Booksellers and Stationers.*
Allen W. S. 24, St. John street
Bell Wm. 5, Queen street
Craggs John, 9, Silver street
Dawson Wm. 47, Lowgate
Ferraby John, 44, Market place
Holdsworth Wm. 69, Lowgate
Howe John, 3, Scale lane
Johnston Maria, 7, Market place
Mowatt Clara, 57, Market place
Noble Joseph, 23, Market place
Rodford John, 52, Lowgate
Shores Wm. 16, Lowgate
Teesdale Thomas, (old books) 6, New Dock street
Turner Geo. 65, Market place
Wilson Isaac, 49, Lowgate
Wright William, (and print seller) 4, Lowgate

*Boot and Shoemakers.*
Abbey Thomas, 10, Silver street
Ainsworth John, 4, Church lane
Aire Robert, 15, Worship street
Allen Thos. 19, Geo. yd. 170, High st.
Andrews James, 3, Trundle street
Barker Wm. Lime street
Barnby Jonathan, 14, Scale lane
Bilby Thos. 147, High street
Bird John, 121, High street
Bowman Sarah, 34, Market place
Brewins John, 21, North street

Brewster Thos. 6, Myton st.
Buttle Richard, 20, Prospect st.
Campbell James, 19, North st.
Carlin Christopher, Lime st.
Chapman John, 2, Salthouse lane
Charlton Thos. (ladies') 16, Silver st.
Coldwell Wm. St. John st.
Cook Joseph, 31, New George st.
Cookman Samuel, 34, Garden st.
Coopland Francis, 22, Lowgate
Cowley John, 26, North st.
Coxon John, 11, Church st. Sculcoates
Crabtree Thomas, 4, Lowgate
Croft Daniel, 11, Scott st.
Dawson Richard, 18, Chariot st.
Dawson John, 44, Blackfriargate
Dent Thos. 10, Church lane
Deyes John, 8, New Dock side
Driver Wm. 1, Manor st.
Dunn David, 26, Scott st.
Eden James, 6, Cross st.
Emmott Wm. 29, Chapel lane
Forsey Wm. 29, Chariot st.
Foster Wm. 12, Machell st.
Garbutt Geo. 36, Bond st.
Garbutt John, 41, Wincolmlee
Gaunt Geo. 23, Lowgate
Grasby John, 2, Burton st.
Greenwood Geo. 18, Trippet
Hall Robt. 3, N. end of Humber dock
Haller Thos. 5, St. John st.
Harrison Samuel, 117, High st.
Head Thos. 36, Blackfriargate
Hepper John, 141, High st.
Heward Wm. 7, Blackfriargate
Hewitt John, 22, St. John st.
Hill Robert, 1, Wincolmlee
Hodgson John, 1, Prospect st.
Hodgson Geo. 4, Mytongate
Holdsworth David, 62, Lowgate
Hornsby James, Queen st.
Irving Geo. 16, Castle st.
Jaques John, 13, Myton st.
Johnson Thos. 11, Trippet
Jones Thos. 32, Bridge st.
Jones Thos. 5, Prospect st.
Lascelles Thos. 17, Bond st.
Lomas Wm. 55, Salthouse lane
Marshall Wm. 15, Mytongate
Mason Henry, 63, Lowgate
Mattinson Joseph, 109, High st.
M'Cleman Alex. 47, Carr lane
Mennell Jeremiah, 5, Waterhouse ln.
Mennell Joseph, 5, Waterhouse lane
Metcalf James, 12, Blanket row
Mitchell Robert, 25, Chariot st.
M'Lean John, 56, Whitefriargate
Moore Hannah, 19, Myton st.
Morley John, 54, Humber st.
Morrell John, 8, Waterhouse lane
Musgrave Saml. 67, Whitefriargate
Penny Samuel, 16, North walls
Pettingell Edmund, 85, Mytongate
Pinder Charles, 57, Lowgate

Pinkney James, 128, High st.
Prestyn Abraham, 5, Trippet st.
Richardson John, Church lane
Rounding John, 10, St. John st.
Roundtree F. 24, Sykes st.
Scaum Geo. 60, Prospect st.
Simpson Wm. 93, Mytongate
Smith Wm. 15, Brooke st.
Smith Thos. 176, High st.
Smith Robert, New George st.
Spencer & Barker, 14, St. Mark's st.
Steer Richard, 41, West st.
Stothard John, 70, Mytongate
Tarbotton John, 1, Carlisle st.
Taylor Anthony, 2, Trippet
Tesseyman Joseph, 15, Prospect st.
Thompson Lydia, 25, Salthouse lane
Topham Richard, 3, Silver street
Turnbell Robert, 66, West st.
Turner Robert, 10, Waterhouse lane
Vallance John, 29, Lowgate
Varley Samuel, 62, Carr lane
Wales John, (agent) 11, George st.
Walton Thos. Church st. Sculcoates
Ward James, 45, Mytongate
Watson John, 29, St. John st.
Wilkinson Daniel, 4, St. John st.
Willoughby Geo. 23, Queen st.
Woodworth Geo. 1, New John st.
Woolley Edward, 23, Silver st.

*Brass Founders.*

See also Iron Founders, Tin-plate Workers
and Braziers.

Blackwell Joseph, 12, U. Union st.
Freeman Samuel, New Dock st.
Rhodes Benjamin, Red Lion entry
141, High st.
Todd and Campbell, Foundry row
Sculcoates

*Brewers and Maltsters.*

Those marked thus * are Ale Brewers
† Porter; ‡ Black Beer: § Maltsters.

§Allison Mark, Wilson's court, 44,
Dock st.
‡Barnby Robert, 8, Grimston st.
*Bettison Samuel, 5, Humber st.
*Bettison Wm. 6, Humber st.
§Crake Robert, 57, Market place
*Dawson Thos. 5, Robert st.
‡Dennison John, 20, Parliament st.
*Dibb E. & J. 43, Mill st.
*§Dossor James, 10, Chapel lane
*Gleadow Robert, Dagger lane
*Hopwood Wm. & Co. 1, West st.
*Hunt Jane, 22, Geo. yd. 170, High st.
*Kirkus and Bromby, (Julian Spring)
Waterhouse lane
*†Liddell John, 29, Waterworks st.
*§Pickering Wm. & Son, 10, High st.
*§Rivis John, 65, Church st.
‡Roberts Thos. 3, North walls
‡Scoffin Thos. 2, Waltham st.

Screwton Wm. 38, Church lane
Spence, Watson & Co. Prospect st.
Father Thos. 1, Fox st.
Temple Thos. 13, Marine row
Vause John, 7, Trinity house lane
Williamson Thos. Lime st.

*Brick Makers.*

Appleyard Frank, 2, Manor st.
Atkinson Anthony, (& tile) 23, Albion street
Breen James, *Wilmington*
Jackson Geo. 7, Prince st.
Leggott John, 3, Bourne st.
Lennell John, 2, Chapel court, 15, Salthouse lane
Tadman Francis, Patrick ground lane
West Wm. 2, Mason st.

*Bricklayers and Builders.*

Abbey Geo. 12, Page's sq. Dagger ln.
Adamson John, 16, Aldbro' st.
Appleyard Frank, 2, Manor st.
Appleyard John, 17, Robinson row
Bambrough Robt. 9, Castle row
Barker Hanh. & Sons, 26, Savile row
Barker James, 2, Engine st.
Barker James, 10, New John st.
Betts John, 1, Fish st.
Birkett Thos. 63, Mill st.
Bishop Thos. 26, Mill st.
Botheroyd W. 6, Paragon pl. Sykes st.
Palmer Wm. Trundle st.
Bywater Richard, 20, Scott st.
Clarke John, 19, Castle st.
Deans Alex. St. Quintin's pl. Drypool
Fawcett John, Duncan's place
Fox John, 5, Bourne st.
Hyard Benj. 26, Scott st.
How James, 27, Trippet
Iray John, 42, Spencer st.
Jeaton Wm. 16, Savile row
Ides Christopher, 4, Mytongate
Irving John, 2, Duke street
Irving Edward, Ann street
Jackson Geo. 7, Prince street
Jarvis Timothy, 10, Machel street
Kidd Daniel, 12, Castle street
King Thos. 4, New George st.
Kirby Wm. 6, Waterworks st.
Leggott James, Parade row
Leggott John, 1, Bourne st.
Lowther John, 6, Clarence court, Princess st.
Mennel John, 2, Chapel court, 15, Salthouse lane
Miller Benj. 19, Brook st.
Nevis Robert, 9, Mytongate
Peat Joseph, Hodgson st.
Richardson Wm. 47, Carr lane
Richardson Edw. Patrick ground lane
Robinson George, 5, Dyer's place, Waterworks st.
Sherbon Geo. 13, Wells st.
Smith Isaac, 26, Lowgate

Spencer Charles, 8, Hodgson's square Sykes st.
Stubbs John, Naylor's row, Witham
Tadman Francis, Posterngate
Tadman Benj. 29, Blanket row
Wales Thos. 32, New George st.
Watson John, 9, Dagger lane
Webster Michael, 4, Norris yard, Wells st.
West Wm. 2, Mason st.
Westoby John, 2, Upper Union court, 12, Great Passage st.
Wilkinson John, 26, Brook st.
York John, 41, New Dock st.

*British Wine Merchants & Dealers.*

Ganderton John, 17, Parliament st.
West Leonard, 13, Silver st.

*Brokers.—See Agents.*

*Brush Makers.*

Burgess Wm. 39, Shambles
Burgess John, 42, Shambles
Grey Thomas, 5, Todd's entry, Silver street
Halden Wm. 24, Scale lane
Lawrence John, 9, New Dock st.
Loft Benj. 130, High st.
Mennell Francis, Waterhouse lane
Morrod John, 2, Daltry's entry, 39, Mytongate
Thomas and Piercy, Church st. Wincolmlee

*Bullion Dealers.—See Watchmakers, &c.*

Jones & Forrester, 17, Market place
Rust and Shipham, 21, Market place
Symons Moses, 7, Queen st.

*Butchers.*

Anfield Wm. Market place
Anfield Christopher, Great Union st.
Armitage Jonathan, 24, Great Passage street
Arthur Thos. 31, Salthouse lane
Ashton John, 1, Shambles
Atkinson Wm. 8, Alfred st.
Baines Richard, 21, English st.
Barker Wm. 20, Nile st.
Binnington Thos. Witham
Bowser Wm. 165, High st.
Brown John, 37, Chariot street
Burgess John, 42, Shambles
Burgess Wm. 39, Shambles
Butler Holden, Bilton's ct. 8, Machell street
Butter John Farrar, 31, Shambles
Calbert James, 36, Shambles
Champney John, 8, Waterworks st.
Clark Wm. Nichols' ct. 6, Fawcett st.
Clark John, 3, Trippet
Cook Samuel, 15, West st.
Cooper Thos. 3, Carlisle st.
Coulson Wm. 5, Market place
Curtis Geo. 13, Wincolmlee

Davy John, 5, Silver street
Denton Samuel, 18, Waterworks st.
Dinmore Henry, North Bridge foot
Dixon Geo. 34, Mytongate
Edwards Robert, 40, Bridge street
Ellison John, Fawcett street
England Francis, 8, Carlisle street
England Robert, 28, Mytongate
Finningley Wm. 2, Shambles
Fox James, Market place
Fox John, 8, Machell street
Freeman Edward, 8, Church lane
Gale Frederick, 13, Shambles
Garton Marmaduke, Waterhouse lane
Gibson John, 48, Shambles
Hackney Anthony, 4, Bishop lane
Hall Wm. 47, Shambles
Hambleton Edw. 4, Salthouse lane
Harker Edw. 39, Bridge street
Harker John, 11, Savile street
Harker Matth. Johnson, 45, Shambles
Hawden John, 88, Mytongate
Hepple Robert, Market place
Hill Wm. Hood street, Jenning's st.
Hobson Michael, New John street
Hope John, 14, Fish street
Hotham Thos. 7, Lowgate
Howard Joseph, 13, St. John street
Hutton Geo. Lime street
Ingmire Wm. 37 and 38, Shambles
Jackson Geo. 3, Shambles
Jagger Richard, 7, Lower Union st.
Leake John, 43, Shambles
Ledell Ann, 6, Raikes street
Lee Geo. 39, High street
Lee John, 51, Market place
Leonard Wm. Watts, 49, Shambles
Leonard John, 7, Chariot street
Leonard John, 31, Market place
Leonard Abraham, 72, West street
Leonard Thos. 72, West street
Linwood Robert, 37, Bond street
Lovitt Richard, 41, Shambles
Major Robert, Mytongate
Marshall John, 58, Whitefriargate
Martin Thos. 40, Shambles
Mills John, 1, Paradise row
Musgrave Wm. 59, Lowgate
Nelson James, 80, Shambles
Oxtoby Wm. 16, Prospect street
Petch Thomas, 47, Scott street
Petty Geo. 35, Shambles
Procter Ezekiel, 21, Brook street
Quickfall Wm. Church st. Drypool
Raines Thos. 4, Shambles
Rainford Thos. 41, Lowgate
Ramsey Richard, 50, Shambles
Rickinson Thos. 69, Market place
Ross Wm. 25, Sykes street
Rutherford Jeremiah, 32, Wincolmlee
Smith John, Castle street
Smith Joseph, Castle street
Smith Thomas, 44, Shambles
Stannard Joseph, 11, St. John's square

Turner John, 24, Bond street
Valentine Smith, 2, Chariot street
Valentine James, 46, Shambles
Wadland John, 26, Trippet
Wallis Richard, 68, Lowgate
Whip Matthew, 20, Brook street
White John, 24, Chariot street
Wood Wm. 33, St. John street
Wrigglesworth Thos.10,New Dock side

*Cabinet Makers and Upholsterers.*

Those with a * are Cabinet Makers only.
See also Furniture Brokers.

Binnington Richard, Newton street
*Carlill Thos. 45, Whitefriargate
Charlton John, Levett's sq. Hodgson
Cobb Thos. 21, Geo. yd. 170, High
Codlin Wm. 11, Bond street, Mews
Crackles Richard, 28, Chariot street
Cutsforth Thos. 57, Whitefriargate
Darling Wm. Kirkus' buildings, Lowgate
Dawson Benj. 8, Dibb's yd. Scott
Dean Joseph, 45, Market place
Dewick John, Old Dock end
Dickon Edward, 81, Mytongate
Dickon John, 19, St. John street
Ellerby Bartholomew, senr. 31, New Dock street
Ellerby Bartholomew, junr. 2, New John street
England Thos. junr. Witham
Farrar Richd. Hellard's yd. Green la
*Feetham Thos. 62, Mytongate
*Ford James, 4, Dock street
Gace Nathaniel, 12, Blue Bell yd. Waterworks street
Hicks Joseph, 10, Wells street
Hinsley John, Parade row
Hodson John, Trundle street
Holden Wm. Upper Union street
Jakeman John, Church st. Drypool
Kent Robert, Drypool square, Great Union street
Levett Matthew, 62, Edgar street
Linsley Wm. 55, Mill street
*Marshall John, New John street
Megson John, 28, Carr lane
*Peck Thos. 23, Blackfriargate
Prissick Wm. 16, Worship street
Richardson Thomas, Cockpit yard, Castle street
Shackles Thos. Eaton st. Lowgate
Shepherd John, 10, Roper's row
Silbon Wm. 3, Providence street
Smith and Richardson, 19, Chapel la.
Smith Wm. New John street
Smith Wm. Cockpit yd. 6, Castle st.
Walker John, 32, Savile street
*Walker John, 25, Blackfriargate
Wallis Samuel, Katherine street
Ward Benj. 28, Chariot street
*Watson Geo. 7, Castle row
Watts John, 4, St. Mark's square

Waugh J. & Co. 8, Trinity house ln.
Webster James, 38, St. John street
Wilkinson Thomas, Stubbs' court, 12, West street
Wilkinson Wm. 18, Charlotte street
Wilson Christopher, 5, Hope street
Wilson Matthew, 156, High street
Wood Thomas, Woolpack entry, 35, Mytongate
Wright Robert, 38 and 39, Bond st.

Carpenters, Ship.—*See Ship Builders.*

### Carvers and Gilders.
Brooks Thos. 16, Whitefriargate
Fletcher John, 18, Dagger lane
Letcher Rounceval, 65, Mytongate
Petti James, 2, Queen street
Rasby Richard, 23, Savile street
Ward Thos. 30, Waterworks street
Wardell John, 5, Lowgate

### Cattle Dealers.
Harniss Richard, 14, Castle street
Hope John, 4, Nile place
Quickfall John, Quickfall's ct. Witham

### Chair Makers.
Haddon Geo. 40, Carr lane
Haques John, Parade row
Smith Wm. New John street
Wells Geo. 4, Queen street

### Cheesemongers.
See also Bacon and Ham Factors.
Elders and Hansell, 66, High street
Hewbald Chas. (wholesale) 79, High st.
Hurgarland Thomas, 12, North side Trinity church

### Chemists, Manufacturing.
Emmett Ann and Sons, Botelar st.
Wilson John, 15, Market place

Clothes Brokers.—*See Tailors.*

### Coach Builders.
Banks Wm. 35, St. John street
Goddard & Thornhill, 28, Chariot st.
Halley Edmund, 23, Bourne street
Austwick Robert, 11, Osborne st.

### Coal Merchants and Dealers.
Clark Wm. 12, Castle street
English Thos. & Son, 3, Humber bank
Gibson Robt. 6, Clark's sq. Sykes st.
Newton Thos. North bridge
Thompson E. and J. Trippet wharf
West Wm. 28, Trippet

### Comb Makers and Dealers.
Brooks Benj. 20, Whitefriargate
Brooks Thos. 16, Whitefriargate
Hopkin Wm. 4, Market place
Sherwood Joseph, Marvel street
Watkinson Richard, 27, Savile st.

### Confectioners.
Barker Robert, 49, Mytongate
Barker Geo. 42, Bridge street
Dixon Anthony, 19, Queen street

Dukes Geo. 23, St. John street
Etty Thos. 17, Church lane
Fox Thos. 35, Savile street
Gawin Allanson, 38, Bridge street
Gibson Sarah, 11, Humber street
Green Julia, 4, Keeling's entry, 24, Mytongate
Hornor Jane, 19, Lowgate
Horsley Eliz. 18, New Dock side
Jackson and Smith, 89, Mytongate
Johnson Lawrence, 11, Dock Office row
M'Kenzie John, 2, New Dock street
Makem Ann, 39, Savile street
May Charles, 29, Silver street
Norris John, 52, Scott street
Ostler Robert, 60, Whitefriargate
Rickatson Wm. 15, Mytongate
Wales Wm. 39, Garden street
Ward Sarah, 1, Humber street
Webster Jane, 52, Carr lane
Wilkinson Wm. 6, St. John street
Wilkinson Wm. 31, Chariot street
Wiseman Caroline, 30, Savile street

### Consuls.
*American,* Richard Tottle, 23, High st.
*Hanoverian,* (Deputy) Bethuel Boyes, 8, Castle street
*Netherlands,* John C. Cankrien, 18, Whitefriargate
*Prussian,* John William Hentig, 24, High street
*Russian,* Thomas Firbank, Lime st.
*Spanish,* Robt. Keddey, 6, Blanket row
*Swedish and Norwegian,* John Clay, 30, Posterngate

### Coopers.
Abbott Wm. 12, Machell street
Atkinson James, Duncan st. Lime st.
Banks W. C. Jarvis street
Barclay Wm. 114, High street
Barker Geo. Witham, 16 & 22, Trippet
Barker Wm. 114, High street
Bartlett Wm. 137, High street
Bell John & Robt. 172 & 173, High st.
Carr Christopher, Chariot street
Colley Wm. (wine) 152, High street
Copass Wm. 2, Constable's buildings, English street
Dick John, 20, Geo. yd. 170, High st.
Duffield Geo. Witham
Dumleton William, Nelson's square, New George street
Findlay John, 6, Quay street
Finningley John, 6, Quay street
Forrest Wm. 26, Waterhouse lane
Havelock Robt. West end Old Dock
Havelock Geo. 19, New Dock walls
Martin John, 24, Church st. Sculcoates
Moon George, *King's wine cooper,* 4, Quay street
Newton Geo. *Wilmington*
Pordon James, 6, Finkle street
Reeder Geo. Charlotte street, Mews

Stringer Matthew, 29, Aldbro' street
Thompson Matthew, *Somerstown*
Webster Wm. Webster's entry, 156, High street

*Copper, Brass and Tin Warehouse.*

Parker John, 19, Blackfriargate

*Cork Cutters.*

Bartlett Robert, 12, Church lane
Bell Geo. 40, Scale lane
Leaper Joseph, 127, High street
Moor Elizabeth, 6, Grimsby lane
Oldfield R. S. 73 and 119, High st.
Wilkinson Thomas, 14, Church lane
Wood Thomas, Raikes street

*Corn Factors.*

Alders and Hansell, 65, High street
Barmby Thomas, 42, Bridge street
Batty Isaac, Witham
Baxter John and Son, 5, Wright st.
Billaney Wm. 21, Carr lane
Boynton Thomas, Alfred street
Chimley Thos. (and flour) 77, High st.
Clifford Wm. High street
Clifford Mark, 37, High street
Ennis Henry, 23, Mason street
Fisher John, 1, Hatter's square, 13, Queen street
Geduey Wm. 35, Bond street
Goody Richard, 35, Trippet
Hall John, 20, High street
Hammond Geo. 7, Myton place
Hodgson John, 1, Princess street
Laverack and Co. 4 and 5, High st.
Marginson Smith, Boalk's yard, Green lane
Newton Thomas, North bridge
Richardson John, 42, Dock street
Sanderson John, Lime street
Strother John, 30, High street
Sumpner John, 149, High street
Taylor and Clifford, 160, High st.
Thompson Geo. Holderness road
Wilson Wm. 13, Bourne street
Woodmancy Thomas, Witham

*Corn Millers.*

Astrough Christopher, Mill lane
Astrough Thomas, Mill lane
Bartle John, 49, Whitefriargate
Broughton James, Lincoln street, Wincolmlee
Carrick Wm. *Summergangs*
Casson & Penrose, 20, Machell st.
Clark Thomas, *Summergangs*
Dales Wm. Danson lane
Dawson Joseph, *Summergangs*
Simpson James, Strawberry gardens, Drypool
Hall Samuel, Danson lane
Jakeman Joseph, Marvel street
Marshall Wm. *Summergangs*
Marshall John, 18, New George st.

Penrose Wm. *Summergangs*
Quarton John, 2, North end of Humber Dock
Roberts Wm. 15, Garden street
Thompson Jph. Steam mill, Sculcoates
Thompson Geo. Holderness road
Tingate John, Drypool
Turner Stephen, Holderness road
Waddingham John, Holderness road
Walsham & Fewson, Holderness rd.
Walsham Robert, *Summergangs*
Webster and Ward, Southcotes

*Cotton Thread Manufacturer.*

Cart John, (sewing) 18, Lowgate

*Curriers and Leather Sellers.*

Atkin James, 24, Mytongate
Barker Richard, 82, Lowgate
Cookman Geo. 42, Market place
Gray Wm. 2, New Dock street
Hodgson James, Witham
Moor Christopher, 30, Lowgate
Rheam & Priestman, 14, Blanket row
Seaton John M. 8, King street
Sissison Wm. 19, Waterworks street
Stickney Matthew, 36, St. John st.
Tarbotton Wm. 4, North side of Trinity church
Tesseyman Francis, 3, New Dock
Tesseyman Wm. 9, Fish street
Thomas John, 23, Scale lane
Thompson Abraham, (and Morocco Spanish leather drsr.) Wincolmlee

*Cutlers.*

Gay Thos. (and surgeons' instrument maker) 13, Queen street
Hoyland Samuel and Co. (and truss manufacturer) 10, Queen street
Hulley Christopher, 83, Prospect st.
Jones Wm. (& surgeons' instrument maker) 35, St. John street
Walker W. & J. 50, Lowgate

*Dentist.*

Hawkes Wm. 39, Scale lane

*Distillers.*

Robinson and Parks, (herb) 19, High street

*Druggists.*

Armstrong Wm. (apothecary & man wife) 43, Lowgate
Barker J. B. corner of New John and Waterhouse lane
Bastow W. S. 9, Carlisle street
Briggs Robert, 33, Whitefriargate
Chapman Edward, 3, Queen street
Clark George, 9, Myton place
Duckett Robert Kay, 11, Myton place
Gunnee Samuel, 35, Chariot street
Hammond Charles, Witham
Healey George, 12, Queen street
Hembrough Francis, 10, Bond street
Heseltine Joseph, 70, Mytongate
Holden William, 24, Wincolmlee

dson John, 28, Waterworks st.
ttle Albine, 55, Market place
yburn Robert, 38, Aldbro' street
llinson Wm. 4, Prospect st.
nner Wm. 60, Market place
eynell Christ. 62, Whitefriargate
eynell Thomas, 1, Lowgate
ixon Benj. 22, Market place
es and Burton, 40, Lowgate
derson Wm. 48, High street
ores John & Co. 73, Lowgate
eeton Edward, 20, Lowgate
gar John, 30, Silver street
rner Jonathan, 24, Bridge st.
ard Burnell, 103, High st.
ebster E. & W. 3, Whitefriargate
ilkinson John, 10, Dock office row
ilkinson John, 25, Brook st.
ilson John, (and importer of leeches)
   15, Market place

*Drysalter.*
oxon Benj. 32, Market place
*The Druggists of Hull are for the most part also Dealers in Drysaltery Articles.*

*Dyers.*
kinson Thomas, Duncan place
rks Maria, (silk) 7, Waltham st.
arkson John, (silk) 8, Robinson row
ighton Richd. (silk) 35, Brook st.
Dixon John, (silk) 10, Waterworks st.
ooper J. R. (silk) 22, Waterhouse ln.
tchell Wm. 23, North st.
allis Hannah, (silk) Green lane,
   Drypool
right Geo. (silk) 5, Carr lane

*Earthenware Manufacturers.*
Lapish Joseph, 57, Scott street
Lapish Joseph, Church st. Sculcoates
apish James, jun. 18, Church street,
   Wincolmlee

*Eating Houses.*
Clark Thos. 78, Mytongate
Dickinson Wm. 24, Queen st.
Goodlass Robert, 53, Humber st.
enekey Wm. 25, Mytongate
ides Christ. 4, Mytongate
Holt John, 15, Scale lane
Kershaw Edward, 52, South end
ightfoot Robert, Witham
Soutter Gabriel, 11, Waterhouse lane
torr Jane, 38, Scale lane
Walker John, 24, Blackfriargate
Whitehead Wm. 32, Church lane
Wilkinson John, 21, Waterworks st.

*Engravers and Copperplate Printers.*
Consitt & Goodwill, 4, Bowlalley ln.
Johnson Richard, 30, Scale lane
Morehead John, 10, Scale lane
Penn Wm. C. High st.

*Fellmongers.*
Jackson Wm. Cliff's sq. Hodgson st.
Porter Geo. 14, Burton street

*Fire and Life Insurance Offices.*
Albion, John Hudson, 47, Market pl.
Atlas, John Levett, 2, South side Old
   Dock
Birmingham, Hill Lee, 18, Bowlalley
   lane
British Fire and Westminster Life,
   Wm. Moor, 35, Lowgate
Commercial Life, Geo. Greenwood,
   Commercial buildings, High st.
County, Caius Thompson, 2, Trinity
   house lane
Eagle, Briggs Carlill, 34, High st.
European Life, Wm. Hendry, Ex-
   change buildings
Globe, Anthony N. Somerscales, 11,
   Parliament street
Guardian, John Holdsworth, 32, High
   street
Hope, John Carlill, 15, Bowlalley ln.
Imperial, Benjamin Stocks, 18, High
   street
London Union, T. E. Radford, 24,
   Parliament street
Newcastle, Ann Turnbull, 48, Dock
   street
Norwich, G. and J. Moxon, 160, High
   street
Norwich Union, T. O. Atkinson, 4,
   Waterworks street
Phœnix and Pelican, John Hill, 18,
   Parliament street
Royal Exchange, J. B. La Marche,
   200, High street
Sheffield, John Walker, 32, Savile
   street
Suffolk, Amicable & General Coun-
   ty, John Hipsley, 8, Finkle st.
Sun, Christ. Boulton, 18, High st.
West of England, Martin & Keddy,
   49, High street

*Fishmongers.*
Askew, Johnson, & Todd, 13, Queen
   street
Bailey John, Queen street
Brown John, Queen street
Dale Geo. 4, Trundle street
Dinsdale Joseph, 9, St. John street
Ennis James, 26, Chariot street
Parker Wm. 31, Chariot street
Petty John, 4, Dennis' row, English
   street
Scatcherd Wm. Queen street
Thurlow John, Queen street
Varley John, Queen street
Ware John, 36, Market place
West Joseph, 5, St. John street
Winter Francis, Queen street

*Flax Dressers.*
Barker Geo. 140, High street
Blakey Wm. 33, Blackfriargate
Irving and Edwards, 13, Queen st.

Littlewood Thos. 12, Waterworks st.
Snell Wm. Witham

*Fruiterers.*

Blenkin Geo. 67, High street
Clough John, 30, St. John street
Dixon Anthony, 19, Queen st.
Gawin Allanson, 38, Bridge st.
Haigh Thos. 25, Church lane
Horsley Eliz. 18, New Dock side
Hornsby James, 3, Blanket row
Jackson James, 1, St. John street
Levett Wm. and Sons, 30, Market place and 71, High st.
May Charles, 29, Silver street
Neal Thomas, Humber bank
Rymer Thos. 20, New Dock walls
Stanford Joshua, 6, North side Trinity church
Stickney Abraham, 33, Bridge st.
Watson Wm. Mytongate
Webster Jane, Chariot street
Wilkinson Wm. 6, St. John street

*Furniture Brokers.*

See also Cabinet Makers and Joiners.
Those marked thus * are Cabinet Makers & Furniture Brokers; thus † are Joiners and Brokers.

Atkinson Wm. 4, New Dock st.
Bolton Benj. New Dock street
Brocklebank Mary, 9, New Dock st.
Clay Samuel, 5, Bowlalley lane
Conningworth Wm. New Dock st.
†Cowl Geo. Carlisle street
*Crowder Wm. 10, New Dock st.
Dalton Benj. New Dock street
Dobson John, 1, New Dock st.
†Dobson Robert, 5, New Dock st.
England Thos. jun. Witham
Farrar Isaac, 13, New Dock street
Farrow Benj. 14, Bowlalley lane
*Fletcher John, 1, New Dock street
*Foy Wm. 2, New Dock st.
Grocock Ann, 57, Mytongate
Guy Thos. 10, New Dock st.
*Harvey Richard, 18, Posterngate
*Hicks John, 30, Blackfriargate
Hirst Joseph, 5, Lowgate
Holmes Charles, 16, Blackfriargate
*Holmes Joseph, 32, Blackfriargate
Hopper Wm. 58, Carr lane
†Hopper Wm. 5, New Dock st.
†Jeffreys James, 14, New Dock st.
*Keen Wm. 20, New Dock st.
*Kelsey James, 13, Blackfriargate
*King John, 14, New Dock street
Matthews Geo. 12, New Dock st.
Newsom Thos. 7, New Dock st.
*Oates Bartholomew, 17, Blackfriargt.
*Rhodes Francis, 92, Mytongate
Richards S. 5, Grotto sq. Mason st.
Robinson Edw. 11, New Dock st.
Silbon Hannah, 3, New Dock st.
Smith Francis, 33, Trippet

Snowden Ann, 4, Page's square, Dagger lane
Stockdale Wm. 17, New Dock st.
Story Wm. New John street
Thompson John, 10, New Dock st.
Watson Wm. Mytongate
*Watson Geo. 16, Blackfriargate

*Furriers.*

Goldfinch Thos. (and ostrich feather mfr.) 25, St. John street
Squire Henry, White Horse yard, Market place
Tinkler Wm. 55, Lowgate
Wayre Wm. 28, St. John st.
Winham Robert, 38, Waterhouse lane

*Gardeners Nursery, and Seedsmen.*

Barnard James, 65, Prospect st.
Barrell Robert, Hodgson st.
Berwick Samuel, New George st.
Carr James, Drypool square
Clark Thos. 38, Blackfriargate
Clark Wm. Anlaby road
Collins Joel, Pothouse yd. Sculcoates
Donn Wm. (curator to the Botanic Garden,) Linnæus street
Grantham John, Pothouse yd. Sculcoates
Hall Robert, Hale's entry, 11, Market place
Haythorne Joseph, 6, Spring bank
Hindle Wm. 9, Hodgson's square, Sykes street
Jopling James, 6, Wincolmlee
Johnson John, Green lane, Drypool
Kneal Thos. Humber bank
Leaf Geo. Halfpenny hatch, Caroline street
Lockwood John, Green lane, Wincolmlee
Mackay James, 3, Providence row, Beverley road
Philipson Henry, Jackson st. Neptune street
Richardson Wm. 3, Worship street
Tindall G. and W. 25, Market place, and at *Beverley*
Waters Gavine, 23, Bond st.
Welburn John, Green lane, Wincolmlee
Wilson John, 9. North side Trinity ch.
Wilson Samuel, 4, Boulton's sq.
Wood Richard, Queen street

*Ginger Beer Manufacturers.*

Rymer Thos. 20, New Dock walls
Saunderson Thos. 53, Whitefriargate

*Glass Bottle Dealer.*

Marshall Thos. 75, High street

*Glass Cutters and Manufacturers.*

Cowley William, (mfr.) opposite the Church, Lowgate
Shiner Jph. (engraver) 7, Church lane

*Glass, China & Earthenware Dealers.*
These marked thus • are Earthenware Dlrs.

Bott John, Vicar lane
Cowley Wm. opposite Church, Lowgt.
Dorsey Robert, 14, St. John street
Goodwin Wm. 21, North walls
Grey Eliz. 20, Silver street
•Hodgson James, Witham
•Jaques Geo. 9, Wincolmlee
Jenkinson and Richmond, 39, Lowgt.
Kay Cornelius, Queen street
Lickis Wm. 44, Blanket row
•Mayfield John, 14, Scott st.
•Milan Michael, Witham
•Mitchell Eliz. Carlisle street
Ramsay Ann, 7, Whitefriargate
Shiner Joseph, 7, Church lane
•Smith Viner, Castle street
•Spencer Ann, Grotto square
•Thorn Rhoda, 8, St. John street
Weatherill Joseph, 44, Mytongate
•Wright Michael, Witham

*Glove and Breeches Makers.*

Clarkson Thos. 23, Silver street
Norris Thos. 13, Scale lane
Wilson John, (glover) 6, Queen's passage, Blackfriargate

*Glue Manufacturers.*

Officer Wm. *Wilmington*
Porter, Raines, and Co. Sculcoates
Wake James, *Wilmington*

*Grocers and Tea, &c. Dealers.*

Adam Edward, 2, Waterworks st.
Aislabie and Jackson, 12, Market pl.
Baker Elizabeth, Witham
Barnett Thos. 4, Trippet
Beal James, 25, Waterworks st.
Blenkin Geo. (wholesale) 67, High st.
Blenkin Wm. (wholesale) 67, High st.
Briggs Henry, 39, Market place
Bristow Charles, 14, Queen st.
Britain James, 61, High street and 48, Market place
Brothill John, 179, High street
Brown John, 1, Myton place
Caley James, 25, Trippet
Caley Wm. 43, Bridge st.
Carrall Mary, 26, Sykes street
Cheetham Geo. 2, Carlisle st.
Clement R. W. 5, Spencer st.
Cobb Geo. 59, Salthouse lane
Colton Samuel, 6, New George st.
Constable Joseph, 30, English st.
Cook and Frankish, 84, Market place
Cowen John, 2, Church st. Wincolmlee
Craven Jas. Jordan & Co. 8, Queen st.
Crowley Thos. 24, Trippet
Cunningham Alexander, 31, Mytongt.
Des Forges Joseph, 85, High st.
Dixon Wm. 2, Whitefriargate
Duffield Geo. 115, High st.
Easten Wm. 5, Blanket row

Elsey Henry, 6, South street
Faulding Wm. Naylor's row, Witham
Fearne Thos. 17, Lowgate
Fewson Peter, 36, Lowgate
Foster Wm. 23, Salthouse lane
Freeman Robert, 57, Salthouse lane
Gelson Thos. 27, George st.
Gibson Wm. 90, Mytongate
Gibson Wm. & Sons, 33, Salthouse ln.
Goldsmith Wm. 26, Bridge street
Hamilton John, 1, Thornton st.
Heaton Thos. 13, Mill street
Hitchin Wm. 23, Chariot st.
Hobson Francis, Witham
Holroyd Thos. 23, Blanket row
Horner Jane, 19, Lowgate
Hutchinson Jonathan, 9, Whitefriargt.
Jackson Ralph, Queen street
Jackson John and Son, Witham
Jenkinson Robert, 11, Posterngate
Johnson Wm. 9 & 10, Waterworks st.
Kershaw John, 48, Lowgate
Kitching Geo. 11, Market place
Lamb Geo. 12, Grimston st.
Lambert Wm. 56, Market place
Leek Wm. 20, North street
Levett William and Sons, 30, Market place, and 71, High street
Lister Wm. 8, Bond street
Middleton Thos. 198, High street
Milner John and Ann, Witham
Morris Thos. 1, North end of Humber dock
Murgatroyd Wm. 4, Waterworks st.
Newrick Hodgson, 2, Salthouse lane
Nightingale Henry, 8, North st.
Ouston Joseph, 42, Prospect st.
Oxley Margaret, 6, Salthouse lane
Parrott Geo. 15, Princess st.
Pickard Anthony, 27, Blackfriargate
Preston James, 21, Osborne street
Proctor Thos. 23, Wincolmlee
Rayner Samuel, 186, High street
Robinson Wm. 82, Blanket row
Robinson Thos. 12, Scott st.
Rowntree Wm. 15, Wincolmlee
Saul John, 37, Humber street
Simon Wm. Jennings street
Sissons Richard, 18, Queen street
Smith Thos. 26, Lowgate
Smithson Wm. 44, Scott street
Storey Wm. 36, Whitefriargate
Suggitt Jefferson, 44, Lowgate
Thundercliff John, 58, Whitefriargate
Wake James, North street
Wallis Ann, 11, Grimston street
Walmsley David, 35, Market place
Wardell John, 194, High street
Watson Wm. 22, Bridge street
West Leonard, 18, Silver street
White Thos. 62, Market place
White Saml. 33, Church st. Sculcoates
Wilby Wm. Lime street
Wilson Thos. 5, Scale lane

*Gun, &c. Makers.*

Hawkes Wm. 39, Scale lane
Wallis George, 19, Mytongate
Williamson Robert, 26, Silver st.

*Haberdashers.*

See Linen and Woollen Drapers.

*Hair Seating and Curled Hair Manufacturer.*

Birch Peter, 4, Fawcett street

*Hat Manufacturers, Dealers and Warehouses.*

Appleton Wm. 28, Savile street
Beach Jeconiah, 9, Winter's alley, Land of Green ginger
Deain John, 52, Salthouse lane
Hebblewhite John and Benjamin, 20, Market place
Jackson Peter, 15, Queen street
Jagger Aaron, Dock office row
Kitchen Thos. 9, Queen street
Kitching Geo. 26, Whitefriargate
Lazarus Saml. (silk) 34, Blackfriargt.
M'Allum Mary, (and glover) 15, Silver st.
Morton John, 40, Grimsby lane, and 120, High st.
Murray Mary, 34, Church lane
Nevis J. S. 9, Mytongate
Robinson Jph. (late Binks) Bishop ln.
Robinson Isaac, 11, Lowgate
Rudston and Preston, 26 and 27, Market place
Steele Wm. 12, Queen street
Tinkler Wm. 55, Lowgate
Travis Samuel, 25, Queen street
Watkinson John, Johnson's court, 156, High st.
Wayre Wm. 23, St. John street
Whinham Robert, 38, Waterhouse lane
Williamson James, 21, Bishop lane

*Hatter and Hosier.*

Brown Henry, (& glover) 29, Lowgt.

*Hop Merchants and Dealers.*

See also Grocers.

Clark Wm. 12, Castle street
Walmsley David, 35, Market place

*Horn Button Manufacturer.*

Clark James, 13, New George st.

*Horse Dealers.*

Bailey John, (exporter) 8, Wright street
Cook Robert, 13, Carr lane
Goodman C. S. 15, Leadenhall sq.
Holdsworth Thos. 3, Fox street
Johnson Robert, 5, Chapel street
Thompson George, Porter's court, 15, Carr lane

*Hosiers.*

See Linen and Woollen Drapers.

*Hotels, Inns and Taverns.*

American Coffee House, Richard Murphy, 1, Duke street
American Tavern, Catharine Dunn, 16, Dock street
American Tavern, James Shillito, 37, Mytongate
Anchor, Rbt. Hunt, 63, Whitefriargt.
Anchor, Geo. Dunn, 33, Waterhs. ln.
Anchor, Robert Harker, 31, Waterworks street
Angel, Jph. Tummon, 20, Chapel ln.
Angel, John Wales, 23, Clappison's square, Sykes street
Baltic Tavern, Matthew Pickard, English street
Barrel, George Foster, Edgar st.
Barrel, Rt. Palmer, 20, New Geo. st.
Barrel, Robert Morton, 12, Lowgate
Bath Tavern, Peter Hunsley, Humber Bank
Bay Horse, Michl. Hobson, 1, West st.
Bay Horse, Wm. Smith, 22, Wincolmlee
Bee Hive, Thos. Ellors, 4 & 5, Prince street
Billy Boy, Hy. Hilkin, 19, North walls
Bird in Hand, Thos. Glenton, Cook's buildings, Broadley street
Black Boy, Geo. North, 151, High st.
Black Horse, Wm. Ashton, 42, Blackfriargate
Black Horse, Rich. Rotsey, 21, Carr ln.
Black Horse, Elizabeth Grimston, 77, West street
Black Horse, Sam. Blackston, Witham
Black Swan, Francis Richardson, 1, Princess street
Black Swan, John Cooper, 5, Mytongt.
Blade Bone, Thomas Shepherdson, 6, Scale lane
Blucher, Susah. Lowe, 29, Finkle st.
Blue Ball, John Beck, 12, Blackfriargate alley
Blue Ball, Sarah Portass, 12, Trippet st.
Blue Ball, Thos. Kelsey, Air street, Sculcoates
Blue Ball, Thomas Skelton, Church street, Wincolmlee
Blue Ball, Lucy Skelton, Dixon's entry, Lowgate
Blue Ball, George Walker, Leadenhall square
Blue Ball & Anchor, Robert Wilkinson, 158, High st.
Blue Bell, John Wilkinson, 26, Brook street
Blue Bell, John Johnson, Green lane
Blue Bell, Wm. Heighley, 6, Prospect street
Blue Bell, John Caley, Witham
Blue Bell, Rbt. Crake, 57, Market pl.
Blue Bell, Wm. Wood, Blue Bell entry, High street

Blue Bell, Peter Tillin, 17, Water-works street

Board, John Benson, 5, Stewart's yd. High street

Board, John Drinkall, 3, St. Quintin's place, Drypool

Board, Sarah Duncum, 2, Trundle st.

Board, John Boxtead, 16, Charter-house lane

Board, Ann Thorney, 4, Queen st.

Board, Prince Rupert Morris, corner of Chariot street

Board, Thomas Briggs, Trippet

Bonsy Boatsman, Jane Taylor, 10, Trinity house lane

Bottle, Edw. Marshall, 10, Grimsby lane

Bowling Green Tavern, Mary Kirby, 13, Waltham st.

Bridge Inn, James Fean, North bridge

Bridge Coffee House, Wm. Wales, 40, Bridge street

Bridlington Tavern, Eliz. Lightley, 17, Manor street

Britannia Inn, Wm. Thistleton, 34, Trippet

Bull, Thos. Moor, Beverley road

Bull & Dog, Dorothy Coultas, Witham

Bull & Sun, John Banks, 1, Mytongt.

Butchers' Arms, John Alderson, 6, Shambles square

Carpenters' Arms, Thos. England, Great Union street

Coach and Horses, James Mews, 9, Mytoogate

Commercial Tavern, Thos. Douglass, 7, Fish street

Corn Exchange, Wm. Soulby, 49, Corn market

Crooked Billet, Robert Fisher, 36, Trippet

Crooked Billet, Wm. Hall, 6, Love ln.

Crooked Billet, Thos. Hall, Straw-berry gardens, Drypool

Cross Keys, John Snow, (posting hs.) opposite King William, 33, Market place

Crown, Wm. Smith, Wincolmlee

Crown, Martin Cade, 17, Silver st.

Crown, John Buck, 29, Bridge st.

Crown, Thos. Harrison, Summergangs

Crown and Anchor, Robert Acrid, 38, Humber street

Dock Arms, Joseph Garbutt, 5, Dock office row

Dock Coffee House, Ann Stockburn, 10, Quay street

Dog & Duck, John Dean, 12, Scale ln.

Dog & Duck, Thomas Langley, 86, High street

Duke of Clarence, Thomas Bier, 49, South end

Duke of Cumberland, Luke Brown, 22, Sewer lane

Duke of Cumberland, Charles Searby, Church st. Wincolmlee

Duke of York, Mary Blakey, 11, Blackfriargate

Duncan's Arms, Thomas Shepherd, 13, Manor street

Durham Ox, John Baxter, 1, Blanket row

Edinbro' Packet, James Mearns, 163, High street

Fleece, Geo. Morley, 43, Market pl.

Fleece Inn, Wm. Amery, 197, High street

Founders' Arms, John Bassingdale, Drain bank

Four Alls, James Dunning, 19, Lower Union street

Fox and Grapes, Mary Craggs, 21, English street

Free Masons' Tavern, Geo. Rennison, 21, Chapel lane

Full Measure, Ralph Musgrave, 56 Lowgate

Full Measure, John Popplewell, 8, High street

Full Measure, John Jewett, 52, Mill street

Full Measure, Matthew Brown, 90, Mytongate

Gainsborough Coffee House, Thomas Mandeville, 82, High st.

Gallon Measure, John Jardin, 5, Great Passage st.

Gate, Thomas Medley, 21, Trippet

Gate, George Nicholson, 12, Lower Union street

Gate, Sarah Wilson, Lime street

Gate, Wm. Wilson, 13, Alfred st.

General Abercrombie, Geo. Hawley, 39, High street

General Elliott, Richmond Tomlinson, 87, High street

George Inn, John Woolley, 23, Silver street

George and Dragon, Francis Hunter, 102, High street

George and Dragon, Benjamin Dick, 20, George yard, 170, High st.

Globe, Jane Lamb, 182, High st.

Gloucester Coffee House, Wm. Thompson, 2, High street

Golden Ball, Rbt. Capes, Pickering's entry, 10, High street

Golden Ball, Matthew Jennison, 22, Salthouse lane

Golden Ball, Richard Wilson, 27, Middle street

Golden Ball, John Watson, 9, Dagger lane

Golden Barrel, Wm. Clervas, 24, Sewer lane

Golden Cup, Wm. Holmes, Humber st.

Golden Cup, Peter Stephenson, 22, Blanket row

Golden Cup, Thomas Daltry, 22, Mytongate

Golden Cup, Josiah Miller, West st.

Golden Measure, Wm. Humphrey, 88, Mytongate

Golden Pot, Wm. Dennis, 13, Lowgt.

Grapes, David Christie, 6, Waterhouse lane

Grapes, Geo. Naylor, 14, Harcourt st.

Grapes, James Harwood, 12, Waterhouse lane

Grapes, Benj. Miller, 19, Brook st.

Grapes, Thomas Jacobs, Fawcett st.

Grapes, Wm. Farrar, Jennings st.

Grapes, Richard Ward, 22, Sykes st

Grapes, Thos. Ward, 30, Waterworks st.

Greenland Fishery, James Shaw, 44, Bridge street

Greenland Fishery, James Robinson, 27, Church st. Wincolmlee

Hammer and Hand, Mary Pringle, 187, High street

Hand and Glass, Alexander M'Yawn, Blackfriargate

Hare and Hounds, George Dove, 36, Spencer street

Hope, John Tempest, L. Passage st.

Hope and Anchor, Richard Wray, 85, High street

Hope and Anchor, Wm. Gillyatt, 7, Bishop lane

Horse and Jockey, Charles Abbott, 3, Garden street

Hull Packet, Edw. Lison, 105, High st.

Humber Dock Coffee House, James Hartley, 8, New Dock side

Humber Tavern, William Lewis, 28, Humber street

Indian Chief, Robert Harrison, 10, Blackfriargate

Jack on a Cruise, Wm. Johnson, 7, North street

Jack's Return, Samuel Smith, 32, Grimsby lane

John Bull, Wm. Ridsdale, *Wilmington*

Joiners' Arms, William Ringrose, 6, Trippet street

Jolly Bacchus, Joseph Frankish, 87, Mytongate

Jolly Bacchus, Joseph Cook, 19, Dagger lane

Jolly Bankers, Jane Robinson, Witham

Jolly Sailor, Wm. Cunningworth, 37, Blanket row

Jug, John Boxtead, Wincolmlee

Juno Tavern, Thomas Buckton, 38, Church lane

King, Robert Statters, 20, Bond st.

King's Arms, John Wilkinson, 20, North walls

King's Arms, John Naylor, Witham

King's Coffee House, Matthew Botterill, 41, High street

King's Head, Wm. Barnes, 94, Mytongt.

Labour in Vain, Samuel Crackles, South end

Limekiln House, Wm. Gilyard, 10, Humber bank

Lincoln Arms, Thos. Sharp, 50, High st

Lion and Key, William Pearson, 48, High street

London Tavern, Wm. Senior, Queen street

Lord Collingwood, Samuel Smith, Lowgate

Lord Nelson, Mary Claydon, Mason street

Lugger, Launcelot Tottle, 92, High

Malt Shovel, James Waugh, 10, North side Trinity Church

Mariner's Tavern, Joseph Siven, New Dock street

Marrow Bone and Cleaver, Wm. Miner, Fetter lane

Masons' Arms, Geo. Rennison, Chapel lane

Mermaid, Edw. Cherry, 5, Silver st.

Nag's Head, Wm. Dodsworth, 132, High street

Nag's Head, John Barker, Summergate

Nelson Tavern, Francis Bailey, Green Union street

Neptune Inn, Samuel Woodhead, Chariot street

Neptune, Peter Adams, 161, High st

Neptune, Joseph Bishop, Neptune st

Newcastle Tavern, Thomas Cooper, 39, Whitefriargate

New Dock Tavern, James Darcy, Sewer lane

Old Andrew Marvel, John Fisher, Whitefriargate

Old Dock Tavern, John Audus, Old dock side

Old Elsinore, Rbt. Lightfoot, Witham

Old England, Eliz. Vincent, 166, High

Old Harbour, Elizabeth Shotling, 13, High street

Opening New Dock, Stephen Kirkwood, 50, Blanket row

Ordnance Arms, Robert Southerland, Great Union street

Original Andrew Marvel, Paul Hill, 35, Whitefriargate

Painters' Arms, John Whitehead, Finkle street

Paragon Inn, Jackson Roper, Charles street

Pine Apple, Joseph Haythorn, Spring bank

Plough, John Montgomery, 21, Robinson row

Portsmouth Town, James Wilson, 29, Church lane

Prince George, John Robinson, 104, High street

Prince of Wales, Joseph Colley, 36, Bond street

Prince of Wales, Jph.Smith, Raikes st.
Providence Inn, Ann Millson, Groves
Queen Caroline, Lydia Brooks, 34, Salthouse lane
Queen's Head,John Salter,155,High st.
Recruiting Serjeant, Robert Bryan, Chariot street
Red Lion, Chas. Patrick, 44, Wfriargt.
Red Lion, Mary Wilson, 2,Manor alley
Regent's Inn, Jas. Allison, 2, High st.
Rein Deer, T. Wilson, 63, Market pl.
Robin Hood, Wm. Hall, 12, Myton pl.
Royal George, J. Pearson, 14, N. walls
Royal Oak, Rd. Oliver, 21, Posterngt.
Royal Oak, John Weatherhill, 47, Spencer street
Sun's Coffee House, George Howe, South side Trinity church
Sawyers' Arms, Saml.Taylor, Lime st.
Schooner, Jane Russell, 170, High st.
Sculcoates Arms, Henry Lundie, 42, Scott street
Sculcoates Tavern, James Cade, 31, Wincolmlee
Seven Stars,Susan Gleadow,16,Fish st.
Shakespeare Tavern, Joseph Allison, 56, Humber street
Shepherdess, John Hodson, Myton st.
Ship, John Bellamy, 3, Church lane
Ship, Wm. Poole, 20, Finkle street
Ship, Wm. Clark, Anlaby road
Ship, Robert Wilson, 15, Scale lane
Ship, John Wharton, Witham
Ship, Robert Hutchcroft, Hodgson st.
Ship, Ann Dunn, Beverley road
Ship, J.Middleton, 20, Church st. Scul.
Ship Artois, Ann Walker,64, Mytongt.
Ship&Shears,J.Nicholson,25,Bridge st.
Ship Brunswick, F. Ripley,20,Dock st.
Ship Diana,Geo.Howden,18,Church ln.
Ship Molly, John Griggs, 82, Dock st.
Ship Tavern, John Reed, 3, Dock st.
Ship Tavern, A. Mellson, 78, Lowgt.
Ship Tavern, Rd.Bowes,25,Posterngt.
Sir John Falstaff, Christopher Hartley, 1, Church street, Wincolmlee
Sir John Falstaff,J.Cook,17,Humber st.
Sir John Falstaff, W.Patrick,South end
Sir John Moore, Wm. Pickard, 47, Salthouse lane
Sloop, John Westoby, 16,Up.Union st.
Sloop Chance,John Herratt,53,High st.
Sloop Clothier, Angus M'Donald, 2, Bishop lane
Societies' Tavern, John Christie, 6, Dagger lane
Spaw Bone, Jas. Simpson, Church st.
Spread Eagle, Thos. Piper, Market pl.
Spread Eagle, J. Drewry, 1, Castle st.
Spread Eagle,John Cuthbert, Lime st.
Stewart's Inn, Joseph Topping, Patrick ground lane
Ship, William Jubb, Garrison
Three Crowns,T.Wilson,45,Market pl.

Three Crowns, Mary Watson, Lime st.
Three Jolly Sailors, Wm. Westwood, 191, High st. & 1, Salthouse lane
Three Tuns, Geo.Willis,Humber bank
Three Tuns, J. Horner, Leadenhall sq.
Three Tuns, T. Pears, 21, Grimsby ln.
Three Tuns, J.Leake, 16,G.Passage st.
Tiger, John Gell, 1, Waterhouse st.
Town and Trade of Hull, Edward Farrow, 25, Blanket row
Turk's Head, Jph.Jarvis, 39, Mytongt.
Unicorn, Daniel Oxtoby, 9, Carr lane
Unicorn & Blue Bell, William Grant, 49, Salthouse lane
Unicorn Tavern, Hannah Tadman, 192, High street
Union Coffee House, John Watson, 16, Bishop lane
Vittoria Tavern, Ralph Keddey, 28, Queen street
Volunteer, Tho.Ward,Waterworks st.
Wellington, Richard Cooper, Witham
Wellington Hotel, Adolphus Gray, 42, Mytongt. & 29, New Dock walls
Whale, Sarah Stone, 82, High street
Wheat Sheaf, John Fowler, 61, Prospect street
White Hart, James Rea, Silver street
White Hart, Thos.Chilton, 7, Cross st.
White Hart,John Watson,11,Salths.ln.
White Horse, Mw. Lyon, 45, Carr ln.
White Swan, J.Spink, 19, Wincolmlee
White Swan, Etty Hunt, 77, High st.
White Swan, W. Noble, 16,North walls
White Swan, Eliz. Boomer, South st.
Whittington & his Cat, Saml. Wood, 15, Castle row
Windmill, Wm. Stephenson, Holderness road
Windmill, Wm. Bennison, 14, Trinity house lane
Windmill, John Leake, 59, Wfriargt.
Yarmouth Arms,W.Kirk,168,High st.
Yorkshire Sloop, William Ellis, 37 Salthouse lane

*Ink (Writing) Manufacturers.*
Battle Robert Gray, 18, Paradise pl.
Perkins John, 10, Bowlalley lane

*Iron Founders, &c.*
See also Brass Founders.
Barrett J. (boiler mkr.) Humber bank
Overton & Smith, (steam engine makers) Scott street
Todd & Campbell, Foundry row,Scul.

*Iron Merchants.*
Cowie & Brändström, 7, Castle st.
King, Turner and Co. 54, High street
Sykes Joseph, Sons and Co. 20, Bowlalley lane
Wilkinson,Whitaker& Co.47,High st.
Wimble, Preston & Co. 61, High st.

*Ironmongers.*
Boyes and Constable, 42, Market pl.

F F

Croyle Jas. (hardware) 6, Church ln.
Gleadow and Soutter, 24, Market pl.
Hansley William, 18, Market place
Hirst Jonathan, 41, Market place
Jackson John, 2, St. John street
King, Turner and Co. 59, Market pl.
Moor William, 35, Lowgate
Plummer W. B. 6, Market place
Thompson John, (and saw maker) 6,
    North walls
Thompson John, Witham
Tomalin Joseph & Saml. 10, Queen st.
Tomlinson John, Hyperion street
Walker Wm. and John, 50, Lowgate
Wimble, Preston & Co. 50, Market pl.

*Joiners, House Builders, &c.*
See also Cabinet Makers.

Ake and Witty, 18, Trippet street
Alcock George, Parade row
Alcock William, Myton street
Appleyard John, 17, Robinson row
Beet Matthew, Queen street
Blossom John, 57, Scott street
Briggs Thomas, 36, Scott street
Brown John, 27, Scott street
Brown Robert & John, Old Dock side
Brown John, Bond street, Mews
Buckle Wm. 8, Aldbro' street
Cawkwell William, 3, Pothouse yard,
    Church street, Wincolmlee
Chapman Edward, 6, Sykes street
Clark Wm. 2, Crown ct. 4, Dock st.
Clarkson Benjamin, Parade row
Collinson Samuel, 11, Manor alley
Collinson Moses, Jarvis street
Cooper Richard, 12, Trippet
Crosby Richard, Grimston street
Cross Robert, Milk street
Dawson Robert, Freemasons' yard,
    34; Mytongate
Dowsland Robert, Carr lane
Edgin Wm. 6, Ordovas pl. Chariot st.
Fallowfield Rt. 17, Great passage st.
Fillingham Thos. Wentworth street
Foster Thomas, 12, Machell street
Fox John, 28, Mason street
Fox John, 5, Bourne street
Garbutt Richard, 15, Myton street
Gowland and Tindell, Lime street
Grassby Richard, 3, Brook st. square
Harper Richard, Castle street
Holderness Frs.Graham's row,Drypool
Hudson W. C. Grantham's entry, Dag-
    ger lane
Hutchinson Wm. 4, George yd. Lowgt.
Hutchinson Jas. 2, St. John sq. Lowgt.
Jackson Wm. 12, Quay street
Jameson Robert, 13, Fish street
Jaques John, Parade row
Jefferson Henry, 18, Chapel lane
Kelsey John, Walker's sq. Paragon pl.
Lawer Peter, 42, Wincolmlee
Lawton John, Old Dock end
Levens Robert, Old Dock end

Mapplebeck William, 34, Lowgate
Martin Robert, Hyperion street
Martin and Hogg, Dock street
Metcalf George, 7, Machell street
Milne David, 22, Bridge street
Morehead Thos. 12, Upper Union st.
Morley Robert, 16, Bond street
Newmarch and Hunt, 1, Savile street
Nundy Christopher, 13, Church lane
Parkin George, Gibson street
Payler Thornton, 49, Salthouse
Pitts Benj. 1, Hewett's yd. W
Raven Enos, Old Post Office e
Robinson James, 4, Machell
Robinson Aaron, Stephenson's
    Chariot street
Runton William, Witham
Sanderson Hy. Stubb's ct. 16, W
Saunderson & Grassby, Parade
Scurrfield John, 43, Salthouse lane
Sherwood George, 27, Bond street
Shipham David, New John street
Simpson George, 4, North street
Skinner Edward, Waterhouse lane
Stathers Robert, 12, Pycock's
    21, Sewer lane
Sutton Thomas, 49, Market pl
Taylor Daniel, 11, West street
Thorp Samuel & David, W
Thorp William, 26, Mason street
Tindale Robert, 6, James' court,
    Waterhouse lane
Tindell Thomas, Hodgson street
Tomlinson John, Witham
Tomlinson John, Hyperion street
Turner Robert, Milk street
Turner John, Parade row
Turner Thomas, Waterhouse lane
Walker John, Bond street, Mews
Walker William, 10, Spencer
Watson Geo. 10, Carlisle street
Webster Robert, 30, Scott str
Wharton Christopher, Parade
White William, 17, Hanover
Wilkinson William, 18, Ch
Willford Jas. 2, Union sq. Spencer
Williamson Barker, Parade row
Young Andrew, Ann st. Broadley

*Land Surveyors.*

Wilkinson Geo. 4, Clark's sq. Syke
Wilkinson William, Witham

*Last and Boot Tree Makers.*
Dibb Samuel, 2, Mytongate
Elderton John, 83, Mytongate
Gale Robert, 96, High street

*Lath Renders.*
Bugg William, 39, Church lane
Driffill Joseph and Co. Old Dock
Easton William, Old Dock side
Fewster James, Old Dock side
Johnson and Parrott, Old Dock
Milburn Andrew, West end Old
Walker Thos. & Co. Old Dock

incup John, North side Old Dock  
Food Abraham, Nelson's square, New George street

*Lead Merchants and Manufacturers.*  
icard I. K. & Son, (white lead) Old Dock side

*Leather Dresser and Seller.*  
elverton Richard, (bookbinder's) 20, Trippet

*Libraries, Subscription & Circulating.*  
llen W.S.(circulating) 24, St. John st.  
aggs J. (circulating) Silver street  
oldsworth Wm. (circ.) 69, Lowgate  
owe J. (circulating) 3, Scale lane  
ull Subscription Library, (Thomas English, librarian) Parliament st.  
ull New Subscription Library, (G. Turner, librarian) 65, Market pl.  
owatt Clara, (circ.) 57, Market pl.  
ores Wm. (circulating) Lowgate  
ilson John, (circulating) 6, Sewer ln.

*Lightermen.*  
bbey John, 1, Stable yd. Salthouse ln.  
olton James, Witham  
ocock John, 27, Chapel lane  
ilby John, John street, Drypool  
arton Joseph, 24, George yd. Lowgt.  
ilton Thos. 27, George yd. Lowgate  
uke John, 2, Vine court, High st.  
aworth Francis, 2, North walls  
ird Wm. 36, Humber street  
ackson Rt. St. Quintin's pl. Drypool  
amb Edward, Church st. Drypool  
ongford Wm. 13, Posterngate  
ilner Peire, 2, Sleights court  
ixon Geo. 9, Queen's pl. Sykes st.  
ickard Jph. 9, Featherstone's entry  
ayner Richard, 3, High street  
edhead Thomas, 6, Todd's entry, 6, Salthouse lane  
eed Christopher, 4, Old Dock side  
ichardson Wm. 9, Bishop lane  
eaton John, 18, Chariot street  
atton Wm. 1, Upper Union street  
ard Saml. 9, Clappison's sq. Sykes st.

*Lime Burners and Dealers.*  
Lay Cornelius, Humber bank  
ayler and Co. 17, Humber bank

*Linen and Woollen Drapers, &c.*  
Those marked 1 are Linen Drapers; 2 Woollen Drapers; 3 Haberdashers; 4 Silk Mercers; and 5 Hosiers.  
See also Tailors and Drapers.  
1 Alsop James, 48, Market place  
1 5 Andrew Wm. 17, Whitefriargate  
2 Biglin Wm. 29, Market place  
1 Bingham E. W. 17, Dock street  
1 5 Blaine and Green, (lacemen and glovers) 64, Market place  
2 4 Briggs John B. & Co. 39, Market pl.

1 Carnochan John, 11, Spring row  
5 Cart John, 18, Lowgate  
1 Croft Jonas, 14, Queen street  
1 2 Eastwood Anthony, 37, Market pl.  
1 Everington G. B. 61, Whitefriargt.  
1 Fearne John, 8, Market place  
1 Forster Charles, (Glasgow House) 40, Whitefriargate  
5 Gee Joseph, 15, Lowgate  
3 4 Gibson Mary Ann, 54, Market pl.  
3 4 Gibson John, 31, Silver street  
1 3 4 5 Gregson Wm. 37, Lowgate  
1 Grieve David, (Scotch) 37, St. John st.  
3 5 Hague George, 14, Silver street  
2 Hall Thomas, (West of England cloths) 17, Parliament street  
1 Hardcastle Henry, 17, Prospect st.  
2 Harrison Beilby, 40, Market place  
5 Hawes J. H. 45, Lowgate  
2 Hebblewhite J. & B. 20, Market pl.  
1 2 3 4 Henwood and Robinson, 26, St. John street  
5 Heward J. and R. 18, St. John st.  
1 2 Hudson John & Son, 47, Market pl.  
2 Johnson Thos. 18, Mytongate  
1 3 4 Johnson Edward, 5, Market pl.  
5 Johnson Ann, (& glover) 20, Scale ln.  
1 2 3 Jones & Kirk, 66, Market place, and 1 and 2, Silver street  
1 3 5 Kidd John G. 52, Market place  
1 King & Pinn, 8, Whitefriargate, & 4, North bridge  
2 5 Kitching Thos. 9 & 10, Queen st.  
1 Lamb Geo. 12, Grimston street  
1 Lambert C. 27, Whitefriargate  
2 Linton & Lloyd, 19, Market place  
1 Matthews & Bingham, 29, Wfriargt.  
2 M'Turk Thomas, 2, Market place  
1 Nichol John, 19, Silver street  
1 Nundy Christopher, 13, Church lane  
1 Parker Wm. 31, Whitefriargate  
1 5 Peacock Jabez, 16, Trippet  
5 Peters Wm. 24, Lowgate  
1 Pexton Wm. 12, Dock Office row  
1 3 5 Rhodes and Rutherford, (lacemen & glovers) 61, Market place  
5 Robinson Michael and Sons, 15, Queen street  
1 Robinson Thomas, 12, Scott street  
2 4 Rudston and Preston, 26, and 27, Market place  
1 Rusling Sarah, Blackfriargate  
2 Sadler John, 22, Market place  
2 4 Sanderson Joseph, 16, Market pl.  
1 3 Sedgwick & Gervas, 7, Silver st.  
1 Shackles Wm. 49, Market place  
3 4 Smith John T. 12, Silver street  
1 Sumerscales Joseph, 10, Market pl.  
1 2 4 Staniland & Garbutt, 8, Silver st.  
1 Staniland Susannah, 21, Bridge st.  
1 Stephenson Robert, 46, Market pl.  
1 Stephenson Thos. 23, Waterworks st.  
3 5 Towers W. F. (glover) Wfriargt.  
3 Underwood & Hawkins, 14, Mkt. pl.

2 Walmgate Wm. 9, Market place
2 Wells Richard, 4, Blackfriargate
5 West Thomas, 4, Carlisle st.
1 2 Whitworth & Co. 4, Whitefriargt.
1 Wilkinson J. W. 13, Whitefriargate
2 Williams Thos. & Co. 1, Market pl.
1 2 Wilson Thos. 42, Market place
Wray Charles, Queen street

*Livery Stable Keepers.*
Beharrell Rt. Princess st. French's gdns.
Cook Robert, 13, Carr lane
Danby Matthew, 4, Bourne st.
Foster John, Whitefriargate
Holdsworth Thos. 3, Fox st.
Hussard John, 6, Stable yard
Johnson Richard, 12, Carr lane
Norton Wm. 1, Posterngate
Reynolds Thos. 8, Hope street
Russell John, Dagger lane
Woodmancy John, Great Union st.

*Log Manufacturer, (Patent.)*
Baines Robert Baines, Wincolmlee

*Looking Glass Manufacturers.*
See also Carvers and Gilders.
Brooks Thomas, 16, Whitefriargate
Piotti James, 2, Queen street

*Machine Makers.*
Brown Robert, (thrashing) Witham
Kennedy Wm. *Summergangs*
Todd Thos. (copying, pump, and engine) Webster's entry, 156, High st.

*Maltsters.*
See Brewers and Maltsters.

*Marine Stores, Dealers.*
Flower and Burton, Wincolmlee
Kirkus Jeremiah, Waterworks st.
Knowles Anthony, 4, Waterhouse ln.
Parkin Edward, 11, Quay street
Pinder Wm. Old Dock side
Rayner Geo. 16 & 189, High st.

*Mast, Block, and Pump Makers.*
Angel Thos. North side Old Dock
Atkin John, West end Old Dock
Newton Isaac, Old Dock side
Westerdale Wm. 1, Pier st. and Old Dock side

*Measurers (Sworn) of Timber.*
Bowes Thomas, 22, Grimsby lane
Bower Thomas, 3, Foundry row

*Merchants.*
See also Agents, &c.
Alders and Hansell, 65, High st.
Atkinson Anthony, 23, Albion st.
Beadle John & Co. 8, Dock walls
Beckett Wm. 100, High st.
Bell John, 6, High street
Binks Richard, 12, High street
Blyth Robert & Co. 83, High st.
Bolton Wm. & Christ. 21, High st.
Bowden James, 18, High st.
Bowden Wm. West Parade

Boyes Bethuel, 8, Castle street
Briggs John & Wm. 21, High st.
Briggs Christ. & Sons, 7, Bowlalley la.
Brodrick John, 21, High st.
Bromby and Clark, 26, High st.
Brown Jonas & Co. 40, George st.
Buckton Geo. 56, High st.
Burstall John & Saml. 39, High st.
Cankrien John C. 18, Whitefriargate
Carlill Briggs, & Co. 33, High street
Cattley Richard, 45, High street
Chambers Anthony, 10, Sewer lane
Chatterton Robert, Stewart's yard, 152, High st.
Clay and Squire, North side Old Dock
Collinson Wm. & Son, Garrison side
Coltish Wm. *Summergangs*
Cooper W. S. Lime street
Coulson Edw. and Geo. Old Dock side, Lowgate
Cowie & Brandström, 7, Castle st.
Cox Edward Thomas, 43, High st.
Croft Wm. (wool) High street
Crosse & Co. (Russian) Lime st.
Depledge and Prissick, Old Custom house, High street
Du Vivier John, 4, Worship st.
Earle Geo. & Thos. 43, High street
Eggington G. & J. 8, North walls
Featherstone John, 20, Bowlalley la.
Firbank Thos. Lime street
Foster A. C. 14, Russia ct. High st.
Foxton Thomas, 37, High street
Garbutt Robert, 1, Exchange alley
Gee, Loft, & Co. Nelson street
Gibson Robert, 149, High street
Gleadow Rt. Ward, 15, Parliament st.
Godmond Joseph, George street
Godwin George, 11, George st.
Greenwood Geo. Commercial buildings, 30, High street
Hall Thos. & Sons, 5, North walls
Halls, Todd, & Hassell, 8, High st.
Hentig John Wm. & Co, 24, High st.
Heseltine Benj. 14, Savile row
Hewetson J. J. & Co. 16, Wincolmlee
Horner J. and S. 28, High street
Jackson John, 16, Bowlalley lane
Jackson Thos. (Russian) 11, Charlotte street
Keighley Robert, Old Custom ho. High street
King Robert, 3, Baker street
La Marche J. B. 200, High street
Lascelles James, 29, High street
Levitt Quarton, Commercial buildings 29, High street
Locking George, 12, High st.
Marris Henry, 154, High street
Maude Wm. Millthorp, Garrison si.
Mee John, 20, Paradise place
Milnes, Heywood, and Holdsworth 33, High street
Moon George, 3, Old Dock side

Ioxon R. W. 1, Trinity house lane
Iorman W. V. Garrison side
Iorth Wm. 25, Bishop lane
Idfield R. S. 73 and 119, High st.
Iark G. and R. 183, High street
Iearson James, 80, High street
Iearson Zechariah, 80, High street
Ierson James, 162, High st.
Iadford J. S. and Co. 154, High st.
Iennards Richard, North side O.Dock
Iichardson Thos. 14, Quay street
Iichmond R.O.Custom house, High st.
Iingrose Wm. & C. L. 42, High st.
Ioss Henry, 17, Bowlalley lane
Ichonswar Geo. & Henry, 31, Geo. st.
Iackleton James, 72, High st.
Iipman John, 4, Portland place
Imith John and Co. 21, High st.
Iomerscales A. N. 11, Parliament st.
Ipence Edw. (Russian) 167, High st.
Ipence Wm. 16, High street
Itocks Benjamin, 18, High street
Iykes Thos. 2, Change alley
Ierry Richard and Sons, 39, High st.
Ihomas and Piercy, Church st. Wincolmlee
Ihompson Caius and Co. 2, Trinity house lane
Ihompson Thos. 9, Humber st.
Iodd John & Co. 10, Savile st.
Iodd and Campbell, Foundry row, Sculcoates
Iottle Richard, 33, High st.
Iurner Isaac, 44, High street
Ion Roy Frederick, 8, Scale lane
Vard R. G. 15, Parliament street
Vard Thos. 15, Parliament st.
Velch W. O. (Russian) 36, High st'
Vells Peter, High street
Vharton Thomas, Exchange alley
Vhitton John, 22, High st.
Vilkinson Ralph, 10, Dock office row
Vright, Bowden, & Co. (Russian) 18, High street
Ieale Charles, 10, Mason st.
Ieung R. C. Commercial buildings, 29, High street

*Milliners and Dress Makers.*
Irmitage Jane, 17, Scott street
Iahton Frances, 1, Edgar street
Iarrowby S. 3, North ct. 19, North st.
Ioraman Sarah, New John st.
Iurnett Margaret, North street
Ialvert Ann, Paradise lodge, Mytonst.
Iarrott Eliz. 53, Dock st.
Iawood Frances, Posterngate
Irosby Eliz. Church st. Sculcoates
Dalrymple Mary, 44, Carr lane
Dixey Jane Agnes, 63, Mill hill
Iibson Elizabeth, 38, Savile st.
Ioodwin Eliz. 31, St. John st.
Hargrave Eliz. 5, Engine st.
Iarrow Mary, 13, West st.
Ilizard Mary, Church st. Sculcoates

Hutchinson Isabella, 9, Prospect st.
Hutchinson Mary, 50, Whitefriargate
Jeffells J. & E. 63, Whitefriargate
Lodge & Metcalfe, 10, S.S. Trinity ch.
Milner Harriot,5,Constable's buildings, 21, English street
Peker Nancy, 20, English st.
Proudlove Mary, 1, Grimston st.
Race Harriot, 27, Charlotte st.
Raines Sarah, 31, Bridge st.
Ray Sarah, 4, Blanket row
Rayner Sarah, 1, Story street
Reed E. & M. 3, Quay street
Richard-on Misses, H. A. M. and H. Lime street
Roberts Jane, 19, George's place, 14, Mytongate
Robinson Hannah, 11, George st.
Stainton M. 32, George st.
Staniforth Sarah, 19, Waterhouse lane
Stephenson Mary, 21, George st.
Swaby Eliz. 34, Bond street
Swann Ann and Mary, 7, George st.
Swift Eliz. 18, Bond street
Todd Sarah, 30, Whitefriargate
Wasney Mary & Sarah, 15, Mason st.
Weatherill Esther, 53, Market place

*Millstone Makers.*
Boyd Geo. an1 Wm. Witham
Cass Wm. Witham
Norman and Smithson, Sykes st.
Parkin Wm. Stewart's yd. 152,High st.
Silverwood Thos. 22, New George st.
Todd & Campbell, (dealers) Foundry row, Sculcoates

*Millwrights.*
Barker John, Graham's row, Drypool
Boyd George & Wm. Witham
Harrison John, 2, New Drain bank
Kenedy Wm. *Summergangs*
Kennedy Wm. Holderness road
Norman & Smithson, Sykes st.
Oldham Wm. 10, Trippet

*Music Preceptors & Instrument Dealers.*
Atkinson Wm. 42, Whitefriargate
Blumfield Samuel, 52, Whitefriargate
Brown Henry, 29, Lowgate
Galbraith J. M. 55, Whitefriargate
Holdsworth Wm. 69, Lowgate
Lambert Geo. 33, Finkle st.
Miller John, 46, Savile st.
Morey Elihu, 10, Clark's sq. Sykes st.
Retalic Geo. 14, Bishop lane
Ryley Samuel, (piano forte and organ builder) New John street
Thompson Isaac,(piano forte tuner) 19, Grotto square, Mason street

*Mustard Manufacturers.*
Carrick John and Co. Grimsby lane
Consitt Richard, 52½, Market place
Daniels Geo. 120, High street
Hipsley John, 8, Finkle st.

Sissons, Weddle, and Co. Groves
Trigg M. T. Cockpit yard, 6, Castle st.

### Nail Makers.

Ellison Thos. (cut) 9, Dock office row
M'Colvin Colin, 23, Trippet st.
Wilkinson Thomas, Witham
Wilson Wm. Witham

### Navy Agents.

Brown Jonas & Co. 40, George st.

### Newspaper Offices.

ADVERTISER, Isaac Wilson, (Friday afternoon) 49, Lowgate
PACKET, Richard Allanson, (Monday afternoon) 36, Scale lane
ROCKINGHAM, Wm. Ross, (Saturday afternoon) 9, Bowlalley lane

### Notaries, Public.

Frost Thos. & Chas. 37, Scale lane
Randal Edward, 29, North st.
Rushworth Edw. 9, Parliament st.
Sandwith Robt. 23, Bishop lane
Tressidor John, 6, High st.

### Oil and Colourmen.

Cripling John, Witham
Hawkins Edw. 58, High st.
Moxon Benj. 22, Market place
Simpson John, *Wilmington*
Sissons, Weddle, & Co. Groves
Thomas & Piercy, Church st. Wincolmlee

### Oil Merchants and Dealers.

Bell Thomas, 58, Wincolmlee
Briggs J. & W. 39, Market place
Dykes & Garton, 19, Salthouse lane
Eggington G. & J, 8, North walls
Fea & Haggerston, Commercial buildings, 29, High st.
Gibson Edw. Great Union street
Hewetson Jas. & Co. 16, Wincolmlee
Lascelles James, (refiner) 7, Church street, Wincolmlee
Lee Wm. and Son; *Cottingham*
Levett, Roberts, & Co. 2, North walls
Maisters and Archbell, Trippet
Marshall John, 32, Mason street
Pease, Trigg, & Co. 18, High st.
Smith John & Co. 21, High st.
Spyvee & Cooper, Lime street
Wake James, *Wilmington*
Walker W. & J. 50, Lowgate

### Opticians.

Northen Richard, 46, Lowgate
Piotti James, 2, Queen street
Roberts Thos. (spectacles) 23, Middle st.

### Painters—Historic, and Portrait.

Coates Wm. (marine views) 2, North st.
Heseltine Chas. 15, Grotto sq. Mason st.
Lowther Phineas, (portrait) 5, Savile st.
Stannard Germain, (miniature) 6, Whitefriargate

Willis Thomas, Humber street
Wilson T. F. 29, Bond street

### Painters—House Decorators, and Sign Board Writers, &c.

Alley Thomas, 23, Bourne street
Barker James, 10, Trippet
Beach Robt. 51, Salthouse lane
Beetson Robt. 51, Salthouse lane
Briggs John, (and colour manfr.) 42, Salthouse lane
Buck Francis, 150, High st.
Cass John, 8, Waterhouse lane
Charlton John, 36, Savile st.
Clark James, 62, Prospect st.
Cooper Wm. 8, Salthouse lane
Coupland John, 1, Waterhouse lane
Cripling John R. Witham
Fleming E. B. 6, Finkle st.
Gell Richard, 8, New Dock street
Green & Binks, 195, High st.
Griffin Thomas, 12, North walls
Heawood & Jebson, N. side O. Dock
Holdstock & Wright, 171, High st.
Jackson James, New Dock side
Jaques Thomas, 16, St. John st.
Jewell Ann, West end Old Dock
Kirkus Robt. 37, Trippet st.
Lamb Wm. 182, High st.
Lewis & Jackson, 18, New Dock walls
Lowther Frederick, 31, Savile st.
Lumley John, 20, Carr lane
Meggitt Thos. jun. 10, George yard
Mills Alexander, 56, Mytongate
Pepper Richard, 3, New John st.
Poynter Geo. 16, North st.
Reed Joseph, 15, Wincolmlee
Reynolds John, Cock pit yard, 6, Castle street
Richmond Geo. 11, High street
Shields Robert & Son, 49, Blanket row
Steeple Widow & Son, 31, Scale lane
Stothard James, 23, Trippet st.
Thompson Francis, 13, New Dock st.
Vickerman David, 13, Waterworks st.
Vickerman T. D. 15, Wells street
Waudby Wm. Dock street
Willis Thos. (fancy) Humber st.
Willoughby John, 64, Carr lane

### Paint and Colour Manufacturers.

Blundell Henry, Beverley road
Dykes and Garton, 19, Salthouse lane
Simpson John, *Wilmington*
Sissons, Weddle, & Co. Groves
Stone John, (dealer) 33, High st.
Thomas & Piercy, Church st. Sculcoates

### Paper Hanging Manufacturers.

Hardy and Astrop, 3, St. John st.
Parker John, 31, Bond street
Roberts Thomas, 38, Lowgate
Westoby Edward, 1, North st.

### Paper Makers.

Craggs John, 9, Silver st. & South Cave
Smithson R. Boreas mill, Beverley rd.

*Paper Merchants.*

Cattrop Henry & John, 68, Hight st.
New Forges Joseph, 85, High street
Mann William, 58, Salthouse lane
Richardson Thos. 20, Chariot street

*Patten Makers.*

Cobb Samuel, 2, Mytongate
Elderton John, 82, Mytongate
Mason Thos. 9, Dock Office row
Dale Robert, (& clog) 96, High st.
Lulley Christopher, 63, Prospect st.
Sickney Abraham, 33, Bridge st.
Wilberforce Wm. 2, Lowgate

*Pawnbrokers.*

Mudell James, 13, Scott street
Appleton John, 169, High street
Appleyard Mary, 21, Mytongate
Appleyard Wm. New John street
Bailey Thomas, 8, Scott's square,
    Blanket row
Barsell David, 16, Grimsby lane
Cade George, 17, Bridge street
Davies Thomas, 4, Great Passage st.
Eastwood Anthony, 1, Mews street
Harsley John, 14, King street
Hill Elizabeth, 22, Bishop lane
Hutchinson Richard, 3, West street
Jackson Edward, 6, Fish street
Mason Abraham, 13, Trippet
Kirk Thomas, 29, Grimsby lane
Kirkham Joseph, 45, Mill street
Nichols Wm. English street
Nybus John, 3, West street
Robinson Jph. (late Binks) Bishop ln.
Ringsby John, 16, Posterngate
Mark Jeremiah, 13, Broadley st.
Vincent Henry, 28, Blackfriargate
West James, 22, Brook street

*Perfumers, Hair Dressers, &c.*

Andrew Richard, 26, Scale lane
Best Wm. 7, Prospect street
Brooks Benj. 20, Whitefriargate
Brooks S. & J. 32, Whitefriargate
Carrall Roger, 26, Queen street
Grant John, 77, Mytongate
Driffield Ann, 25, Savile street
Jackson Wm. 1, Bowlalley lane
Jones Isaac, 64, Whitefriargate
Pastor George, 6, Whitefriargate
Ridgway John, 3, Lowgate
Ransby John, Queen street
Skinner Edward, 4, Scale lane
Thomas John, 1, Prospect street
Ward John, 36, Bond street
Welburn John, 14, George street
Wilberforce Walter, 21, Scale lane

*Periodical Agents.*

Bell Wm. 5, Queen street
Jacup Henry, (for Kelly, London) 6,
    Horner's square, Humber st.
Stubbs Wm. 6, Vine court, High st.

*Physicians.*

Alderson John, 4, Charlotte street
Ayre Joseph, 85, George street
Bodley Wm. Hulme, 12, Charlotte st.
Crosley Benj. M. B. 16, Mytongate
Faulding Joseph, 9, Marine row
Howard Joseph Samuel, 47, Lowgate
Turnbull Alexander, 30, Geo. st.
White Robert, 32, Mason street

*Piano Makers.*

Hardy Robert, 33, Waterworks st.
King, Turner & Co. 59, Market place

*Plasterers, Stucco & Cement Workers,*

Boothroyd Wm. 6, Paragon place
Clark Thomas, Spring bank
Leggott James, Parade row
Leggott John, 1, Bourne street
Smith Isaac, 26, Lowgate

*Plumbers and Glaziers.*

Appleton & Vickerman, 38, Savile st.
Binnington Edward, 14, Chapel lane
Capes Mary & Sons, 2, Lime street
Cassons Henry, Hatter's sq. Queen st.
Frith & Vause, 24, Silver street
Holmes David, 26, Bond street
Horner John, Witham
Jaques Edmund, 31, Mill street
Kay George, 50, Blanket row
Leake Wm. 59, Whitefriargate
Linwood Joseph, 186, High street
Proctor Francis, 14, Bridge street
Proom John, 22, Bond street
Richardson Wm. 17, Brook street
Roebuck Ann, 44, Wincolmlee
Settrington John, 22, Waterworks st.
Smith Thomas, 22, Bridge street
Spink Edward, 22, Wincolmlee
Steeple Widow & Son, 31, Scale lane
Strawson Richd. 11, Waterworks st.
Thompson Jas. (glazier) Kingston st.
Todd Samuel, 37, Blanket row
Watson Henry, 3, New Dock street

*Pork Butchers.*

Atkinson Thos. 4, New Dock street
Herring James, 60, West street
Smith John, 11, Scale lane

*Porter Merchants, Dealers, &c.*

Allinson Mark, 16, New Dock side
Dewear & Harrison, 21, Parliament st
Ganderton John, 17, Parliament st.
Fisher Robert, 36, Trippet
Guppy Joseph, 183, High street
M'Bride Peter, 20, High street
Petchell Robert, 62, High street
Priestman David, 62, Mytongate
South Jonathan, 183, High street

*Poulterers.*

Green Wm. 27, Church lane
Johnson James, 11, Grimsby lane
Jowitt Robert, 17, Scale lane
Leake Robert, 9, Bond street
Teale John, 53, Scott street

Turner Robt. 6, Grimsby lane
Wilkinson Faith, 24, Scale lane

*Provision, Flour, &c. Dealers.*

Acton Ann, 39, Humber st.
Alcock John, 6, Prospect st.
Allen Charles, 38, Savile st.
Appleby Richard, Great Union st.
Arundel Geo. 25, Scale lane
Atkinson Emma, 107, High st.
Bailey Wm. 86, Lower Union st.
Barnes Thos. 7, Scott st.
Beckett Robert, 35, Spencer st.
Beeforth Anne, 1, Bourne st.
Bellshaw John, 30, West st.
Bellshaw Wm. 14, Wincolmlee
Berridge Samuel, 17, New George st.
Bolton Robt. Church st. Sculcoates
Booth Wm. 123, High st.
Bosomworth Ann, 31, Church lane
Bower Henry, Great Union st.
Bowser Wm. 8, Charlot st.
Briggs John, 99, High st.
Broadwell Robert, 30, Aldbro' st.
Butler Richard, 81, West st.
Cherry John, 2, North walls
Clark Thos. 38, Blackfriargate
Clark Wm. 33, Mytongate
Clifton J. C. 4, North court, North st.
Collender Thos. 11, Chapel lane
Collier John, 2, Blanket row
Coopland Esther, 30, Waterhouse lane
Courts Philip, 34, Wincolmlee
Craggs John, 10, Lower Union st.
Dawson Thos. 77, High st.
Dawson Mary, 48, Blanket row
Denton James, 22, Charlot st.
Driffill Richard, (flour) 2, Hope st.
Duck Geo. 13, Trippet
Duffee Robert, 29, Dock st.
Dunhill Jane, 5, Shambles
Dunn Thos. 40, Mytongate
Edgeburn Frederick, 33, Scott st.
Fallas Charles, 23, New Dock walls
Faulkner Jeremiah, 6, Chapel lane
Fawcett Thos. 36 Waterworks st.
Fenwick Robt. 33, Wincolmlee
Fowler Christopher, 185, High st.
Franks John, Waterhouse lane
Freeman Wm. 30, Salthouse lane
Gardham John, 50, Scott st.
Gardner John, Church st. Wincolmlee
Gawthorp Jane, 112, High st.
Gibson Wm. 33, Finkle st.
Goodrick Edmund, 51, West st.
Graham Geo. 38, High st.
Graham John, 27, Charlot st.
Gray Robert, 4, Waterworks st.
Grayburn Thos. 6, Wincolmlee
Green Thos. 28, Church lane
Gresham Wm. 21, Queen st.
Haire Geo. 41, Blanket row
Hardy Henry, 36, Mytongate
Harford Geo. 9, Broadley st.
Hill Jas. 4, Bourne st.

Hill Joseph, 37, Scott st.
Hinsley John, 10, New Dock st.
Hoggard John, 11, Waterhouse lane
Holdsworth John, Beverley road
Jakeman Joseph, Marvel st.
James John, 19, Garden st.
Jerom Wm. 15, Finkle st.
Johnson Geo. 48, Mytongate
Johnson Timothy, 33, Charlot st.
Johnson Lawrence, 11, Dock office
Kelly Thos. 23, Lower Union st.
Leake John, 48, Whitefriargate
Levett Thos. 3, Roper's row, 20, Waterhouse lane
Lison Wm. 5, Church lane
Lotherington Richd. 12, Vicar lane
Marshall John, New John st.
Marshall Thos. *Summergangs*
Marshall Geo. 58, Scott st.
Mason Wm. 26, Posterngate
Mason John, 9, Finkle st.
Maw John, Church st. Drypool
M'Cleod Benj. 1, Burton st.
Moss Matthew, 12, Salthouse lane
Munn Meshach, 19, Prospect st.
Newton Robert, 19, Bond st.
Oates Ann, 15, New Dock side
Officer Joseph, 40, Spencer st.
Oglesby Thos. 180, High st.
Oliver Thos. 14, Grotto sq. Mason st.
Oliver Thos. 50, Salthouse lane
Outhwaite Wm. 11, Carr lane
Oxtoby Geo. 45, Garden st.
Parkinson John, 73, Mytongate
Pennock John, 7, Trippet
Penrose Charles, 125, High st.
Pinder Wm. 39, Scott st.
Pinshin Robert, Blackfriargate
Preston John, 33, Savile st.
Proudley Thos. 133, High st.
Randall Wm. 86, Bridge st.
Rayner John, 1, New John st.
Reeder Wm. 29, Wincolmlee
Ridsdale Stephen, New Dock st.
Riley Robt. 28, New Dock walls
Roberts Jane, 22, Robinson row
Roberts Wm. 15, Garden st.
Robinson John, 6, Marvel st.
Robinson Wm. Finkle street
Robinson Wm. 24, High st.
Robinson Wm. 15, Church st. Sculcoates
Rollitt John, 10, New Dock st.
Sanderson Richard, 162, High st.
Scafe Matthew, 9, Bond st.
Shaw Richard, 11, Middle st.
Simpson Thos. Witham
Smart Geo. 62, Lowgate
Smith Tobias, Witham
Smith Edward, 14, English st.
Snell John, 49, Dock st.
Snowden John, 15, St. John st.
Spivey Robt. 1, Grotto sq. Mason st.
Stephenson Henry, 37, Spencer st.
Stephenson John, Marvel st.

Stephenson Thomas, 49, West st.
Stockton John, Queen street
Storey Thomas, 14, Lowgate
Sutcliffe Wm. 49, High street
Swainston Robert, 67, Lowgate
Tate Ann, 22, Bourne street
Taylor Daniel, 11, West street
Tindell Thomas, Hodgson street
Tingate John, Church st. Drypool
Trees James, 20, Waterhouse lane
Turner John, New John street
Turner Robert, Milk street
Turpin Wm. 28, New George street
Tweed Richard, 28, Lower Union st.
Waddington John, 29, Savile st.
Wallsam Stephen, Witham
Ward Wm. 31, Bishop lane
Ward Sarah, 1, Humber street
Wardale Robert, 2, Finkle street
Ware Francis, 138, High street
Waterland Geo. 14, Blackfriargate
Waterhouse Vincent, 25, Chapel lane
Watson Thomas, 64, Prospect st.
Waudby Wm. 53, Salthouse lane
Webster Stephen, 9, Mill street
Wells Mary, South end
Welptun George, 30, North street
Whitaker John, Jennings street
White Jonas, 13, Church st. Sculcoates
Wiles Wm. 10, Trippet street
Winship Wm. Church st. Drypool
Woodcock John, 9, Broadley street
Woodmancy John, 8, Humber st.
Wright Michael, Witham

### Printers, Letter Press.

Allanson Richard, 36, Scale lane
Ferraby John, 44, Market place
Howe John, 3, Scale lane
Hutchinson John, 29, Silver street
Innes David, 11, Manor street
Ross Wm. Bowlalley lane
Tate Benj. 49, Market place
Topping Thos. 47, Lowgate
Wilson Isaac, 49, Lowgate

### Quill Dressers and Feather Merchants.

Levi Joseph, New Dock street
Walter Moses, (and pen cutter) 10, Lee's entry, 193, High st.

### Rag Merchants.

Astrop Henry & John, 68, High st.
Capes Benj. Great Union street
Des Forges Joseph, 85, High st.
Dunn Wm. 178, High street
Richardson Thos. 20, Chariot street
Scafe & Newsom, Waterhouse lane

### Registry Offices.

Farnill Eliz. 27, Bridge street
Grove M. A. 22, Parliament street
Lupton Eliz. 3, Catharine sq. Mason st.
Wroot J.Norman's entry,11,George st.

### Repositories.

Brookes Thos. (artists') 16, W.friargate

Lowther Punneas (artists') 5, Savile st.
Metcalfe's H. & S. 18, Whitefriargt.
Stephenson Mary, 21, George street

### Riggers.

Burton Matthew, 20, Wincolmlee
Graham John, 3, Cayley's court, 6, Trippet street

### Rope Merchants and Manufacturers of Rope and Twine.

Those marked thus * are Merchants.

Acrid Thos. 86, High street
*Astrop Henry & John, 68, High st.
*Capes Benj. Great Union street
Dunn Wm. 178, High street
Farrar John, Lime street
Frost J. & Co. Church st. Wincolmlee
Guy Thos. 10, New Dock street
Hall John & Co. 199, High street
Harrison Richard, 14, Carr lane
Marshall Thomas, Dock street
Parkin Edward, 11, Quay street
Rayner Geo. 16 & 189, High street
*Richardson Thos. 20, Chariot street
Smith & Headley, North side Old dock
Snell Wm. Witham
*Spyvee & Cooper, 61,High st.Lime st.
*Taylor John, Raikes street
Twist Joseph, North Bridge foot

### Sacking Manufacturers.

Cross Geo. and Sons, Castle street
Donnison Henry, 16, Chariot street
Kitching Nainby, Witham
Lumley, Jameson & Co. 46, Carr ln.
Potts Joseph, 30, Queen street
Snell William, Witham

### Saddlers, Harness & Collar Makers.

Carter John, 4, Chariot street
Carter John, 6, Carr lane
Crosby John, Witham
Fairbank George, 27, Silver street
Huntley Richard, Witham
Keighley Hannah, 12, Silver street
Milner Geo. 3, Market place
Newsam Wm. 21, Whitefriargate
Thorp Jonathan, 33, Waterworks st.

### Saddle Tree Maker.

Greaves Thos. 6, Paradise square

### Sail Cloth Manufacturers.

Cross George & Sons, Castle street
Kitching Nainby, Witham
Lumley, Jameson & Co. 46, Carr lane
Potts Joseph, 30, Queen street
Whitaker John, Dock office row

### Sail Makers.

Allen and Hunton, Broadley street
Atkin Thos. 31, High street
Courser Wm. 11, Nile street
Dring & Thackray, N. S. old Dock
Dutchman John, 144, High street
England Wm. 43, Blackfriargate
Fussey Thos. 20, Waterhouse lane
Gibson Wm. 2, Wellington street

Gill John, 15, Hanover square
Grayburn John, 83, High street
Hall Francis, 5, North walls
Hodge Wm. & Co. Humber street
Hunter Wm. Broadley street
Parkin Edward, 11, Quay street
Potts Joseph, 30, Queen street
Rusling Joseph, Dock office row
Stone John, 83, High street
Waite & Collinson, 60, High street
Walker John, Ordnance place
Ware Frs. Temple's entry, 139, High st.
Whitaker John, Dock office row

*Salt Merchant.*
Marshall Thomas, 75, High street

*Seed Crushers.*
Eggington G. & J. 8, North walls
Levett, Roberts, and Co. Church st. Sculcoates
Maisters & Archbell, Trippet
Pease, Trigg, & Co. 18, High st.

*Seedsmen.*
See also Gardeners, Nurserymen, &c.
Blenkin Wm. 67, High street
Blenkin Geo. 67, High street
Britain James, 61, High street
Clark Wm. 12, Castle st. & 48, Market pl.
Dykes & Garton, 19, Salthouse lane
Levett Wm. and Sons, 30, Market place, and 71, High street
Newbald Charles, 79, High street
Thompson Matthew, Somerstown
Walmsley David, 35, Market place

*Ship and Boat Builders.*
Barnes Wm. 52, Church st. Sculcoates
Dikes & Gibson, Lime street
Gibson Edw. Great Union street
Gibson Wm. Bridge street
Gleadow Robert, South end
Mason Thos. (boat) Lime street and Garrison side
Medley John, Church st. Sculcoates
Metcalf David, (boat) Church street, Sculcoates
Sleight Geo. (boat) 45, Scott street
Wright John, (boat) Garrison side

*Ship Chandlers.*
Boyle Rhd. North side of Old Dock
Clarkson Thos. 154, High street
Lee Newmarch, 166, High street
Pearson Rbt. North side Old dock
Piercy & Thomas, 9, High street
Pinder Wm. 30, Bond street
Slater Thos. 35, North st. Prospect st.
Stone John, 83, High street
Ward Henry, 16, High street

*Ship Owners.*
Beadle John & Co. 8, Dock walls
Bell J. F. 28, Mason street
Bellwood Mrs. Jane, 7, York parade
Bolton Wm. & Christr. 21, High st.
Briggs John B. & Co. 39, Market pl.

Brodrick John, 21, High street
Brown Thomas, Old Dock side
Bunney Wm. 19, Whitefriargate
Burstall John & Saml. 39, High st.
Chatterton R. Stewart's yd. 152, High st.
Collinson Wm. Garrison side
Cross Thos. Wood's ct. 41, Dock st.
Dales Thomas, 20, High street
Drury Eliz. 21, New Dock walls
Eggington G. & J. 8, North walls
Ellors Thomas, 4, Prince street
Field Wm. 2, Jarratt street
Fowler Wm. 2, Baker street
Gibson Robert, 149, High street
Gibson Edw. Great Union street
Gill Robert, 3, Bond street
Gleadow Robt. 15, Humber street
Godmond Joseph, Moira buildings
Goodwin George, North walls
Grayburn John, 83, High street
Green Henry, 10, Nile street
Gregson and Keighley, Old Custom House buildings
Hall Thomas & Son, 5, North walls
Hall Francis, 22, Whitefriargate
Hall George, Moira buildings
Hardy James Thorp, 37, Dock st.
Harrison Wm. 7, Pryme street
Harrison Richd. & John, Garrison side
Hentig John, Wm. & Co. 24, High st.
Hewetson J. J. & Co. 16, Wincolmlee
Holland Benj. 20, High street
Holland Wm. 2, Charles street
Hopwood Wm. 23, Dock street
Horncastle Wm. 13, Osborne street
Horsley John, Scale lane
Hurst James, 9, Dock street
Hurst John, Old Dock side
Jackson Richd. 3, Cent per cent st.
Jones Thomas G. 31, Mason street
Keddey Robert, 6, Blanket row
Kirkus Jeremiah, Waterworks st.
Lambert John B. 8, Quay street
Levett John, South side Old Dock
Locking George, 12, High street
Lundie Robert, 30, George street
Marshall Richard, 32, Mason street
Marshall John, 32, Mason street
Marshall Thomas, 8, Jarratt street
Maude Wm. M. Garrison side
Moon George, Old Dock side
Morley Thomas B. 25, Lowgate
Moxon R. W. 1, Trinity house lane
Park Godfrey & Richd. 183, High st.
Pattinson Robert, 37, High street
Priest Wm. 13, Nile street
Prissick Thomas, 7, Marine row
Richardson Thomas, 14, Quay street
Robinson John, 9, Wright street
Schonswar G. & H. 31, George st.
Scoresby Wm. 50, George street
Shackles Thomas, Lowgate
Shackles Wm. Market place
Sharp Wm. 34, Brook street

Smith John & Co. 21, High st.
Smith & Headley, Lime st.
Spyvee & Cooper, Lime st.
Stocks Benj. 18, High st.
Tealby, Dalton & Co. Garrison side
Terry Richard & Sons, 39, High st.
Thackray John, Old Dock side
Thompson Caius, 1, Trinity house lane
Thompson E. & J. 15, Parliament st.
Tindall Geo. 14, Mason st.
Toase John & Son, 23, High st.
Vake James, 21, Dock st.
Ward Thos. 15, Parliament st.
Woolf John, 29, Albion st.

*Silk Mercers.*
See Linen and Wollen Drapers.

*Silversmiths.—See Watchmakers.*

*Slate, &c. Merchants.*
Dauber Wm. N. side Old dock
Dauber Wm. West end of Old dock
Fawcett Henry, Old Dock side
Fothergill Miles, West end Old Dock
Lowson John, 12, William's square, Mason st.
Ward Ann, Old Dock side

*Soap Manufacturers.*
Crosse & Co. (soft & hard) Lime st.

*Soda Manufacturer.*
Wilson John, 15, Market place

*Spirit Dealers (Retail).*
See also Wine and Spirit Merchants.
Cooper John, Great Union st.
Cross Lucy & Co. 9, Queen st.
Hewitt John, 59, Mill st.
Marshall Edw. 10, Grimsby lane

*Stamp Office, 2, Bowlalley lane.*
Open daily from 9 morning to 4 afternoon.
Distributor, Robert Osborne, Esq.
Deputy, Wm. Dryden

*Stay Makers.*
Boocock Hannah, 27, Chapel lane
Medill Geo. 2, Geo. yard, Lowgate
Fisher John, 3, Paradise row
Green John, 36, Savile st.
Hallan Mary, 26, Waterworks st.
Hawkins Phoebe, 20, Bridge st.
Inwood Eliz. 37, Bond st.
Norton Thos. 32, Scale lane
Sanderson Sarah, 11, Queen st.
Temperton Eleanor, 13, Bond st.
Wilson John, Myton st.

*Stocking Manufacturers.*
Ball Wm. 27, Wincolmlee
Cooper Matthew, 10, Waterhouse ln.
Heward Jonathan & Robert, (silk) 18, St. John st.
Read Thos. 11, Blanket row
Robinson Michael & Sons, 15, Queen st.
Tailor John, 7, Kingston court, 19, Blanket row
Taylor John, 1, Sewer lane

*Stone & Marble Masons & Statuaries.*
Those marked thus * are Stone Masons; thus † Marble.
Dean Geo. Witham
Eaton Thos. Cross st.
†Earle John, 30, Whitefriargate
Elliott John, Elliott's gal. Milk st.
Middleton Geo. Parade row
*†Truefit James, 39, Savile st.
Webster Michael, Waterworks st.

*Straw Hat Manufacturers.*
Beckwith Margaret, 12, Charlot st.
Boyle Francis, Trippet
Bradley Ann, 18, New Dock st.
Brown Mary, 80, Great Passage st.
Carnegie Wm. 32, Lowgate
Carr Ellen, 2, New George st.
Evans Jane, 40, Savile st.
Farrow Edw. 9, Dock office row
Gibson Mary Ann, 54, Market place
Gray Susannah, 23, Bridge st.
Hargrave John, 28, Lowgate
Jackson Jane, 9, King st.
Jowitt Samuel, New John street
Kemp Mary, 44, Savile st.
Kitching Geo. 25, Whitefriargate
Mercer John, Belt's place, Black friargate
Mitchinson W. & C. 17, St. John's st.
Moore Mary, 30, Spencer st.
Morris Wm. 52, Salthouse lane
Mortis Francis, 22, Mytongate
Morris Wm. 7, Queen st.
Neach Ann, 32, Bond st.
Pearson Sarah, 10, Beverley road
Potcherd Wm. 3, Trippet street
Rickatson Mary Ann, 75, Mytongate
Robinson J. & M. 14, Church street, Sculcoates
Smith Mary, 20, Great Passage st.
Taylor Samuel, 12, Whitefriargate

*Sugar Refiners.*
Thornton, Watson & Co. Lime st.

*Surgeons.*
Bell Robt. 3, Savile st.
Betty Wm. Snow, 34, George st.
Botham Wm. 4, Engine st.
Botham Richd. 2, South st.
Buchanan Thos. 55, Mytongate
Casson Richd. 1, North st.
Coulson Wm. 11, Newton's court, Machell st.
Craven M. R. & Son, 9, Blanket row
Craven Reuben, 21, Charlotte st.
Cundell D. R. (army) 1, Charles st.
Faulding Saml. 20, Trinity house lane
Fielding Geo. 3, Albion st.
Forbes Alexander, 18, Charlotte st.
Fullan J. M. 17, Trinity house lane
Hayes Charles, 8, Dock st.
Hayes H. B. 8, Dock st.
Higson John, (infirmary) & 21, Lowgt.
Innes Thos. 27, Blanket row

Jenkins Richard, 6, Carlisle st.
Lunn Wm. 24, Charlotte st.
Munton Edw. 66, Mytongate
Pearson Wm. 37,Geo.st.&14, Dock st.
Saner & Sleight, 68, Lowgate
Sherwin Henry Chas. 16, Charlotte st.
Stubbs Mark, 27, Queen st.
Webster E. & W. 3, Whitefriargate
Young John, 2, Bond st.

*Tailors and Clothes Brokers, &c.*

Those marked thus 1 are Tailors; thus 2
are Clothes Brokers; thus 3 are both;
thus 4 are Tailors and Drapers.

2 Appleyard Mary, 21, Mytongate
2 Appleyard Geo. 36, Mytongate
2 Barnard Sarah, 131, High street
1 Bell Abraham, New John street
4 Bellarby Geo. 19, Chariot street
4 Bellard Robert, 3, Dock Office row
4 Belt Robert, 12, Grimsby lane
2 Bennett Thomas, 4, Wincolmlee
1 Bewell Wm. 1, King street
1 Booth John, 15, Salthouse lane
1 Boraman Wm. 17, Trippet
2 Boulter Benj. 7, Mytongate
2 Bromfield Thos. 53, Carr lane
1 Brown Thos. 54, Scott street
1 Brown Joseph, 52, Mytongate
3 Butler John, 15, North walls
1 Carr Thos. 164, High street
4 Corden Enoch, 51, Humber street
1 Davison Thos. 2, King street
1 Davison Mary, 24, Grimsby lane
2 Dixon John, 15, Waterhouse lane
1 Dixon George, 6, Scott's square, Humber st.
2 Dove John, 38, Chariot st.
2 Duck Geo. 13, Trippet
1 Elliott Edmund, 74, West st.
1 Etherington Rhd. 24, Gt. Passage st.
1 Fawcett John, 1, Queen st.
1 Foster Thos. 43, Whitefriargate
4 Gibson Geo. Duncan's pl. Manor st.
3 Goulden Jeremiah, 55, High st.
4 Golding Robert, 9, Lowgate
3 Graves Francis, 12, New Dock st.
1 Gray Geo. 11, George st.
3 Gresham John, 16 Queen st.
3 Hanson Joshua, 32, Blanket row
4 Hargrave Robert, 6, Lowgate
1 Harrison John, 22, Great Passage st.
1 Hatfield James, 18, New Dock st.
1 Hayton Thos. 56, Scott st.
4 Howlett Robert, 8, Trippet
1 Jackson Robert, 39, West st.
4 Jeff Geo. 27, George st.
1 Johnson Geo. 1, Sykes st.
3 4 Kitching Thos. 9 & 10, Queen st.
2 Knight John, 30, Great Passage st.
1 Lascelles Ralph, 45, Savile st.
3 Levitt John, 14, Waterworks st.
1 Mason Christopher, 14, Mytongate
1 Mings John, 3, Broadley st.

2 Morrison John, 72, High street
4 Ockerby Wm. 14, Manor alley
4 Parker Mordue, 22, Queen street
1 Pexton Wm. Raikes street
1 Pudsey Wm. 3, George yd. Lowgt.
1 Randerson Thos. S. side Trinity ch
1 Rennard David, Chariot street
2 Ridley Eliz. Queen street
2 Rimmington Thos. 13, Chariot st.
3 Rispin Richard, 19, New Dock st.
1 Robinson John, 5, Scale lane
1 Robinson Rd. 8, N. side Trinity ch.
3 Ross James, 1, New John street
4 Rounthwaite Sarah, 4, King st.
4 Saner Hannah, 18, Humber street
1 Shapman John, 2, Scale lane
2 Sissons Jonth. 1, Dock Office row
1 Skelton Wm. 15, Prospect pl. Drypl.
3 Slingsby Wm. 8, Mytongate
1 Somerscales John, 5, Vicar lane
2 Staveley Wm. 23, West street
3 Stray Miles, 21, Lowgate
4 Summers Joseph, 2, Fish street
1 Thorp Wm. 18, Osborne street
2 Townsend James, 52, South end
1 Vause John, 26, Humber street
1 Walker John, 7, Queen street
1 Ward John, 70, Humber street
2 Waters Mary, 15, New Dock st.
1 Watson John, 18, Robinson row
1 Wells John, 6, New Dock street
4 Wells Richard, 4, Blackfriargate
1 Wilbe Richard, 38, Bishop lane
1 Wilbe Richard, 3, Fish street
1 Worrall Thos. 63, Carr lane
2 Wright Eliz. 39, Chariot street

*Tallow Chandlers and Soap Boilers.*
See also Soap Manufacturers.

Armstrong Wm. 29, Lowgate
Bell Thomas, (wax and sperm) 58, Wincolmlee
Cookman Geo. 42, Market place
Foster Robert, 16, Posterngate
Freeman Robert, 57, Salthouse lane
Hare John, (and wax) South side of Trinity church
Jackson Thos. 36, Church lane
Kitching Geo. 11, Market place
Lee Beilby, 16, Bridge street
Oliver Thos. 11, Dagger lane
Saul John, 37, Humber street
Savage Joseph, 9, Queen street
Stephenson John P. 58, Lowgate

*Tanners.*

Casson Benjamin, 13, Providence row, Beverley road
Holmes John, 1, Church st. Sculcoates.
Laidlaw Alexander, 7, English street;
Rooth Wm. 15, Burton street
West Edward, 12, Providence row, Beverley road
Wigglesworth Benj. *Wilmington*

*Tar and Turpentine Distillers, &c.*

ykes & Garton, 19, Salthouse lane
Featherstone Jas. & Co. (& mfrs. of rosin, pitch, varnishes, &c.) 14, High st.
re and Tall, Church st. Sculcoates
attinson Robt. 37, High street

*Tea Dealers.*

lley Eliz. 18, Prospect street
ooks Thos. 16, Whitefriargate
ough John, 30, St. John street
wson Wm. 4, Lowgate
ammond Wm. 20, Princess street
ster Rebecca, 7, Brook street
witt Mary, 22, Silver street
nsley Stephen, 30, Silver street
nes Isaac, 46, Whitefriargate
ardock Jas. 19, Waterhouse lane
asegood & Sanderson, (and coffee,
   wholesale) 8, Lowgate
sterman John, (& coffee) 37, Mktpl.
dford John, 52, Lowgate

*Timber and Raff Merchants.*

ines David, 96, High street
rkworth and Spaldin, Dock st.
pwn Thos. Old Dock side
ark Ralph, 19, English street
ok Simon, Witham
mber Wm. West end of Old Dock
ewry John, Queen street
uning John, (mahogany) O. Dock sd.
urison Richd. & John, Garrison side
dmes Joseph, (mahogany) Queen st.
nt John, Old Dock side
rkwood Stephen, Queen street
ley J. & E. North side Old Dock
sters and Archbell, Trippet
alleys Simeon, Old Dock side
nday Wm. North side Old Dock
wmarch John & Sons, Thornton st.
bourne Wm. 5, Trippet
acock D. J. & G. N. side Old Dock
binson, Ford & Smith, North side
   Old Dock
nton Wm. Whitham
aw Wm. Old Dock side
alby, Dalton & Co. Thornton st.
ompson Henry, 9, George st.
orney Timothy, N. side Old Dock
ade Abraham, 28, Harcourt street
ade Richard & Sons, Garrison side
ells & Morley, North side Old Dock
inter, Simpson & Whaplate, North
   side Old Dock
ride Shadrack, 11, Charter house ln.
ode J. H. & E. North side Old Dock

*Tinplate Workers and Braziers.*

see also Copper, Brass, and Tin Warehouses

anks M. C. 11, North walls
arnet Joseph, 16, Mill street
eaman John, 50, Blackfriargate
ell Michael, 38, Whitefriargate
ellas A. B. 9, Blackfriargate
rawford Jas. 11, New Dock street

England Geo. Witham
Featherstone Robt. 56, High street
Gardiner Ann, 16, Queen street
Johnson Aaron, 13, Vicar lane
Johnson Robt. 14, Charter-house lane
Killingbeck John, 3, Waterhouse lane
Profitt John, 36, Blanket row
Purdon John, 25, Lowgate
Purdon Wm. 68, Whitefriargate
Raines Mary, 3, Waterworks street
Walker Robt. 1, Hope street
Walker Wm. & Jonth. 50, Lowgate

*Tobacco and Snuff Manufacturers.*

Carrick John & Co. 9, Grimsby lane
Garton and Hopper, 68, Market place
Hall and Gilder, 2, Posterngate
Horsley Stephen, 30, Silver street
Rogers Henry, 31, Dock street
Ward John, 34, Bridge street
Waters John, (dealer) 46, W. friargate

*Tobacco Pipe Makers.*

Airey Wm. 17, Chariot street
Askwith Joshua, 36, Blanket row
Blyth Eliz. 16, Chariot street
Pacey Wm. court, 33, Wincolmlee
Renardson Geo. Cockpit yd. 6, Castle st
Sayer Edw. Clark's yd. 2, Carr lane
Scott Joseph, 30, Dagger lane
Westerdale Mary, 24, Finkle street

*Toy Warehouses.*

Boraman Zechariah, New John street
Hopkin Wm. 4, Market place
Johnson Thos. 13, Mytongate
Johnston Maria, 7, Market place
Sansby John, Queen street
Todd Eliz. 13, Market place
Walker Wm. (mfr.) 28, Market pl.

*Trunk Makers.*

Collings John, 17, Waterhouse lane
Free Thos. 12, Queen street
Keen Wm. 20, New Dock street
Poole Robt. 6, Silver street
Smith Saml. 7, Scale lane

*Turners in Wood, &c.*

Dewick John, Old Dock end
Dunley Edw. Parade row
Green Wm. 14, Bond st. Mews
Hartley Edw. Parade row
Langdale John Robinson, Dock st.
Leavens Robt. West end of Old Dock
Milner Josiah, Turner's sq. West st.
Pettinger Wm. 21, New Dock street
Snell Wm. 7, Queen's passage
Stephenson Richd. court, 129, High st.
Walker Wm. 28, Market place
Wells Geo. 4, Queen street

*Umbrella Makers.*

Grant John, 24, Bridge street
Green John, 36, Savile street
Johns Wm. 27, Lowgate
Mapplebeck W. (late Grant) 34, Lowgt
Newmarch Ann, 32, St. John street

## Undertakers.

See also Cabinet Makers.

Carlill Thos. 45, Whitefriargate
England Thos. jun. Witham
Feetam Thos. 62, Mytongate
Webster Jas. 38, St. John street
Wilson Christopher, 5, Hope street
Wright Robt. 38 and 39, Bond st.

## Underwriters.

Bedale John, 14, Albion street
Bourne Wm. 5, Quay street
Brodrick John, 21, High street
Burstall John, 39, High street
Coulson E. & G. Dock end, Lowgate
Garbutt Robt. 1, Exchange alley
Gee Stephen, 7, North end, High st.
Godmond Joseph, George street
Harrison Richard, Garrison side
Hopwood Wm. 33, High street
Lambert John B. 8, Quay street
Locking Geo. 12, High street
Maude Wm. M. Garrison side
Park Richd. 183, High street
Smith John, 21, High street
Somerscales A. N. 11, Parliament st.
Terry Avison, (& for Henry Ewbank)
    40, High street
Thompson Caius, 2, Trinity house ln.

## Upholsterers—Working.

Bywater John, 6, Waltham street
Everingham Wm. 24, Savile row
Marshall Thos. 14, Trundle street

## Watch and Clock Makers.

Those * are also Gold and Silversmiths, and
Jewellers.

*Abrahams Phineas, 22, Paradise pl.
*Alexander Geo. 6, Vicar lane
Bedell Peter, North bridge
Blanchard Wm. 11, Silver street
Drescher John, 68, Mytongate
Dunn John, 33, Finkle street
Ferrier Thornton, Queen street
Gardner Wm. 5, Whitefriargate
*Hart Jacob, 25, Humber street
Holmes Richard Henry, 6, Bishop ln.
*Jacobs J. 19, Story street
*Jones & Forrester, 17, Market place
Larard Thos. 32, Market place
Marris Charles, 47, Blackfriargate
Middlemiss Robt. 34, St. John street
Northen Richd. 46, Lowgate
*Northgraves Denton, 32, Silver st.
*Rust & Shipham, 21, Market place
Shwerer Joseph, 2, Manor square
Shwerer Joseph, 10, Lowgate
Shwerer Matthew, 84, Mytongate
Stone David, 7, St. John street
*Symons Moses, 6, Queen street
Terry Wm. 61, Lowgate
Thornham Geo. 10, Queen street
Todd Joseph, 13, Market place
Walker Geo. 22, Lowgate
Wise Featherstone, 8, New Dock st.

## Whalebone Cutter.

Bradley John, 5, St. Mark's square

## Whalebone Manufacturers.

Crackles & Horncastle, 35, Wincolmlee
Thornham John, 24, Machell street
Tiplady Wm. 2, Osborne street
Wallis Edw. Lincoln st. Wincolmlee

## Wheelwrights.

Armit Wm. 32, Savile street
Bailey Geo. Witham
Dunwell Wm. Whitham
Chapman Richd. New George street
Houlder Wm. 9, Cook's buildings
Pickering John, 2, Wincolmlee
Pickhover Thomas, Roper's row
Stephenson Wm. 4, Chariot street
Watson Jas. Queen street
Wiseman Daniel, 35, Scott street
Wright Thos. Wellington street

## Whip Makers.

Addock John, 10, St. Mark's square
Bradley John, 5, St. Mark's square
Preston Jas. 21, Osborne street

## Whitesmiths, &c.

Those marked thus * are Bell Hangers;
thus † Shipsmiths.

Abbey Wm. 35, Bridge street
*Appleby Wm. 136, High street
*Appleby John, 16, King street
Bates John, Parade row
*Bell Robt. Myton street
Bootham John, Witham
*Boumer Thos. court, 141, High st.
†Boyle & Thorney, 2, Dock street
Chapman Joseph, 2, Vicar lane
Cross Jas. 41, Scale lane
Crosskill John, North walls
Hall Joseph, Patrick ground lane
Headley Geo. 36, Chariot street
Holmes Stephen, 49, Blackfriargate
Hudson Robt. 36, Blanket row
†Humphrey Thos. 3, New Dock st.
Hutchinson Jas. 6, Castle street
Lambert Wm. 11, New Dock street
*Leuted Jas. 17, Blanket row
†Livingston Catharine, Perrott street
Livingston Wm. 8, Spring bank
Livingston Jas. 6, Waterhouse lane
Maddison Rockliff, 4, Mews street
Marshall Geo. 58, Scott street
Miles Thos. Mason street
M'Colvin Colin, 23, Trippet street
Myers Geo. Chariot street
Nelson John, 3. Blackfriargate alleys
Nelson Thomas, 14, Waterhouse lane
Palmer P. J. 38, Carr lane
†Pickering Wm. 14, Trippet
Robinson John, court, 2, New Geo. st.
Shaw John, 1 Robert street
Stephenson Wm. 4, Chariot street
Taylor G. C. 9, Chapel lane
†*Tedd John, Pease's entry, 45, Salt-
    house lane

†Welberry John, 152, High street
Wilby and Pegg, Ann street

*Whiting Manufacturers.*

Simpson Thomas, Witham
Simpson John, *Wilmington*
Turner Stephen, Sutton bank
Wilkinson Elizabeth, 32, Wincolmlee

*Wine and Spirit Merchants.*

Those marked thus * are Wine and Spirit Merchants, the others are Spirit Merchants only.

*Carnley John and Co. (brandy) 3, King street
*Clervas Wm. (dlr.) 24, Sewer lane
Cook Joseph, 19, Dagger lane
*Cooper John, Great Union street
*Corlass Robert, 70, Lowgate
*Craven and Co. 19, Bowlalley lane
Denison Joseph, North Bridge foot
Denison John, (brandy) Parliament st.
*Dennis Wm. (and retail) 13, Lowgt.
*Dennis John, (& retail) Chapel lane
Dewear & Harrison, 23, Parliament st.
*Dykes and Garton, (importers) 19, Salthouse lane
Ellors Thos. 4, Prince st. King st.
Fisher Robert, 36, Trippet
Frankish Joseph, 17, Mytongate
Ganderton John, (British wines) 17, Parliament street
Garton Richd. (brandy) 59, Market pl.
Gibson John, 19, High street
Gildart and Jackson, 49, High street
*Hannah John, 1, King street
Harrison John, 7, North side Trinity church
*Hill John, (brandy) 18, Parliament st.
*Hopwood Wm. 33, High street
Humberston M. E. 5, Blackfriargate
*Humble Richard, 3, High street
*Jackson Wm. 49, High street
Johnson Joseph, James's place, 2, Mason street
*Knowsley, Swann, & Co. 30, High st.
*Lambert John, B. 8, Quay street

*Liddell Wm. Commercial buildings, 29, High street
*Lundie Robert, 1, Union street, Albion street
*Lupton Richard, 20, Sykes street
Morton Robert Tinkler, (& retail) 12, Lowgate
*Palmer T. W. Broadley street
*Parker John Cowham, 62, High st.
*Petchell Robert, 62, High street
*Priestman David, 62, Mytongate
*Richardson John and Robert, 31, High street
*Richardson Wm. 10, Story street
*Rooth Joseph, 36, High street
*Sanderson Thos. 53, Whitefriargate
Shaw Ann, 51, Mill street
*Soulby Wm. Corn Exchange
South Jonathan, 183, High street
*Sowby Wm. 64, Lowgate
Stephenson Robert, 62, High street
*Stewart Charles, (& retail) 1, Stewart's yard, 152, High street
Tomlinson James, 80, High street
*Vause John, 7, Trinity house lane
*Voase John and Son, 23, High st.
Ward Michael, 2, Chapel ct. Geo. yd.
Wells Richard, 4, Blackfriargate

*Wire Drawers and Workers.*

Allinson Wm. 54, Lowgate
Foster Geo. 5, Waterhouse lane

*Woollen Cloth Manufacturers.*

Sykes James and Co. 1, Vicar lane
Woodhouse Joshua, 34, Scale lane

*Worsted Manufacturers.*

Eastwood Joseph, 17, Brook street
Hirst Abraham, 35, Wincolmlee
King Charles, 5, Finkle street
Pearson Jonathan, Walkers's entry, Posterngate
Sainter William, Roper's row, Waterhouse lane
Sharp Joseph, 20, Blackfriargate
Smith and Colley, 44, Blanket row
Tempest John, 8, Little Passage st.

# THE POST-OFFICE

Is situated at 27, Bishop-lane, Lowgate,

POST-MASTER—THOMAS RODMELL, ESQ.

*Principal Clerk and Office Keeper*—MR. GEORGE DONKIN.

The office opens at a quarter before 8 in the morning.

*General Arrival.*

Letters from the principal towns of the United Kingdom, and all Foreign letters arrive with the mail from York, at 10 minutes past 6 morning, and are ready for delivery at a quarter before eight morning. The letters belonging to merchants are called for at the office. Those for the public gene-rally are sent out by the letter carriers at the time of opening the office.

*General Departure*

The Mail, with letters for York, London, Leeds, Manchester, Liverpool, and for Ireland, Scotland, Wales, and the British Islands, and all other places not specified hereafter in the Riding, or Water postage, departs at 3 o'clock every afternoon; the letter box is closed at 40 min. past 2 aft. Letters however continue to be received with 1d. each, until 5 min. before 3, when the bags are closed and the mail despatched.

Foreign Mails are despatched from Hull in the following order: The letters being previously sent to the office at the same time as for the general departure:

Baltic—every Monday and Thursday, to meet the Glasgow mail.

France—Every M. Tu. Wed. & Thur.

Lisbon—By cross post to Falmouth every Sunday.

Gibraltar, Malta, Corfu, Madeira, and Brasils—On the Sunday before the first Tuesday in every month.

America and Jamaica—On the first Monday in every month.

Leeward Islands and Demerara—On the first and third Mondays monthly.

Letters to any of the before named Foreign places or parts, except the West India Colonies and British America, cannot be forwarded unless the Inland and Foreign postage, (the rates of which are stated below) be first paid.

The inland postage from Hull to London is 1s. and to Falmouth 1s. 2d. which sum will have to be added to the following rates:—

### Foreign Postage from London to

| | s. d. | | s. d. |
|---|---|---|---|
| America | 2 2 | Netherlands | 1 4 |
| Brasils | 3 6 | Norway | 1 8 |
| Corfu | 3 2 | Portugal | 2 6 |
| Denmark | 1 8 | Prussia | 1 8 |
| France | 1 2 | Russia | 1 8 |
| Germany | 1 8 | Spain | 2 2 |
| Gibraltar | 2 10 | Sweden | 1 8 |
| Holland | 1 4 | Switzerland | 1 8 |
| Italy | 1 11 | Turkey | 1 11 |
| Madeira | 2 7 | West Ind. Islands | 2 2 |
| Malta & Medtnn. | 3 2 | | |

### Foreign Postage from Falmouth to

| | s. d. | | s. d. |
|---|---|---|---|
| America | 1 3 | Madeira | 1 8 |
| Brasils | 2 7 | Malta & Medtnn. | 2 3 |
| Corfu | 2 3 | Portugal | 1 7 |
| Gibraltar | 1 11 | West Ind. Islands | 1 3 |

Seamen and Soldiers within any part of his Majesty's dominions, to and from which there are regular mails, can send and receive single letters, on their own private concerns only, while they are employed in his Majesty's service, for one penny: the penny must be paid at the time the letter is put into the office.

### SHIP LETTER OFFICE,

*No. 4, Abchurch-lane, London.*

The postage for letters forwarded through this office to the Cape of Good Hope, Isle of France, Bombay, Ceylon, Madras, Ben-

gal, Bencoolen, and Prince of Wales's Island is the full inland rate of postage to the port where the ship may be, and 2d. sea-postage in addition for every letter not exceeding 3 ounces, and 1s. per oz. for every oz. above.

Newspapers and Price Currents, that have paid the stamp duty, are forwarded to India, if made up open at the ends, at one penny per ounce; but to the Coast of Africa, St. Helena, Batavia, New South Wales, Surinam, Havannah, Hayti, Honduras, and all places where there are no packets, one-half the packet rates are charged.

All letters from abroad, except the Cape of Good Hope, Isle of France, Bombay, Ceylon, Madras, Bengal, Bencoolen, and Prince of Wales's Island, are liable to a sea-postage of 8d. single and 1s. 4d. double, and so on over and above all inland rates whatever; but those from the Cape of Good Hope, Isle of France, Bombay, Ceylon, Madras, Bengal, Bencoolen, and Prince of Wales's Island, are liable to the full inland rate, and a sea-postage of 8d. for every letter under the weight of three ounces, and 1s. per ounce for every ounce exceeding that weight.

†† All letters to be forwarded through the Ship letter office must be paid for at the time they are put into the office.

### WATER POSTAGE,

*From Hull Post Office.*

Thomas Serneton, Hickson's court, Blanket row, conveys the letters to Barton, Brigg and Lincoln, every morning at seven o'clock, by the Waterloo steam hoy, from Keddey's, the Vittoria Tavern, Queen st. and returns to Hull at 2 past 8 evening.

Robert Fenn, of Grimsby, conveys the letters to and from Hull and Grimsby, by the Moor Park sailing packet, from Senior's, the London Tavern, Queen street, daily, according to tide, for account of which see daily shipping list, printed by Allanson, at the packet-office, 36, Scale lane.

### RIDING POST-MEN.

To Hedon, Robert Daggitt, of Mytongate, every Mon. Wed. Thu. and Sat. dep. from Hull at ½ before 9 morning, returns at 2 afternoon.

To Pattrington, John Wing, foot of North bridge, Witham, every Mon. Wed. and Sat. dep. at 8 mg. ret. at ½ p. 8 evg.

*Letter Carriers for Hull and the immediate vicinity.*

Coverdale Thos. Hickson's st. Blanket row
Jarvis Joseph, Turk's Head, Mytongate
Mossey Richard, Grimsby lane.

*Letter and Parcel Carriers, not in the pay of the Post Office.*

Anlaby, Kirk and West Ella, Swanland

nd Willerby, Allen Salmon, Hall's entry, Whitefriargate, daily, except Tuesday.

To Cottingham and Newland, John 'atterson, arr. from Cottingham every mg. t 8, and returns an hour after.

To Ferriby, Hessle, Melton & Welton, Charles Ellerington, at the Rein Deer, every ay except Tu. and Fri. arr. at 12 dep. at 2.

To Roughton, Skirlaugh, Sutton and wine, letters are conveyed by the respec- ve carriers to these places, on Tuesdays nd Fridays.

### MAILS & POST COACHES, &c.

*From John Morris's Coach Office, 32, Market-place.*

he Mail to York, through Beverley and Market Weighton, dep. at 3 aft. daily ; ret. from York at 6 morning.

'rafalgar, to York at 6 mg. ret. at 8 evg.

'rafalgar, to York, dep. at ½ p. 2 aft. ret. at ½ p. 12 the following day.

he Rockingham, to York, at 10 morn. ret. at 4 aft.

Wellington, to Scarbro', through Beverley, Driffield, and Bridlington, in Summer daily, in Winter Tu. Thur. and Sat. at ½ past 6 mg. ret. at ½ p. 3 aft.

*From John Banks and Co.'s, the Bull and Sun, 1, Mytongate.*

he British Queen Post Coach, to Scarbro', through Beverley, Brandsburton, and Bridlington, the same days and hours as the Wellington.

Coach from Patrington, arr. every Tu. morn. at 10, and ret. at 4 aft.

*From G. Foster's, Land of Green ginger.*

aach to Beverley every morn. except Tu. and Fri. at 9 and ret. at 6 evg.

aach to Cottingham every morn. at 8, and at 5 evg.

aach to Hornsea every Sun. Mon. Wed. and Thur. at a ½ bf. 7 morn. and Sat. at a ½ bf. 1, noon, ret. same evg.

aach to Sutton, every Tu. and Friday, at a ½ bf. 8 morn. ret. same evening.

*orge Inn and Hotel, Whitefriargate.* General Coach Office.

e York Coaches call here four times per day. †‡† Passengers and parcels book- ed to all parts of the kingdom.

*'rom the Dog and Duck, Scale-lane, and Neptune Inn, Chariot-street.*

he Rodney Post Coach, to Doncaster, Sheffield, and London, by way of Booth Ferry, every mg. at 6, ret. 6 evg.

*rom William Heighley's, Blue Bell, Prospect street.*

Coach to Beverley every mg. at 9, ret. at ½ p. 6 evg.

A Coach to Hornsea, every Sun. Mon. Wed. and Thur. at 7 mg. and on Sat. at 2 aft. during summer.

*Coaches from Barton Waterside.*

The Royal Mail, to London every morn. at 9 o'clock, in 22 hours, ret. to Barton Waterside every evg. at 6, in time for the Waterloo steam-packet to Hull.

The Express Post Coach, to London every evening, except Sunday, at 6, ret. the next evening in time for the Packet to Hull.

†‡† Passengers and Parcels for the above coaches booked by Mr. Keddey, at the Vittoria Tavern, Queen street, Hull.

*From the Rein Deer, Market-place.*

A Coach arrives from Beverley every Sun. Tu. Thur. and Fri. ret. at 5 evg.

*From the Neptune Inn, Chariot street.*

A Coach arr. from Cottingham every morn- ing at ½ before 10, ret. at 5 evg.—Wm. Allinson, proprietor.

*From John Wing's, 3, North Bridge.*

A Coach to Hedon and Patrington every Mon. Wed. and Sat. at 8 morn. ret. ½ p. 8 evg.

A Coach, belonging to Mr. Wing, arr. from Hedon (only) every Tu. and Fri. at 9 mg. ret. at ½ past 4 aft.

*From the Black Horse, Carr-lane.*

Mark Green's Coach, from Hessle, arr. every Tu. and Fri. at 10 mg. ret. at 5. evg.

*Hackney Coach Stands.*

Fox street, Bond street, at Mr. John Usher's

Land of Green ginger, at Mr. George Foster's.

Prospect street, at Mr. William Heighley's the Blue Bell.

### SHIPPING AT THE PORT OF HULL.
#### HULL TIDE TABLE.

| Moon's Age. | | | Time of High water. |
|---|---|---|---|
| Days. | Days. | | Minutes. |
| 1 | 16 | ...High-water... | 41 past 6 |
| 2 | 17 | .................. | 36 .... 7 |
| 3 | 18 | .................. | 24 .... 8 |
| 4 | 19 | .................. | 12 .... 9 |
| 5 | 20 | .................. | .... 10 |
| 6 | 21 | .................. | 48 .... 10 |
| 7 | 22 | .................. | 36 .... 11 |
| 8 | 23 | .................. | 24 .... 12 |
| 9 | 24 | .................. | 12 .... 1 |
| 10 | 25 | .................. | .... 2 |
| 11 | 26 | .................. | 48 .... 2 |
| 12 | 27 | .................. | 36 .... 3 |
| 13 | 28 | .................. | 24 .... 4 |
| 14 | 29 | .................. | 12 .... 5 |
| 15 | 30 | .................. | .... 6 |

*Coasting and River Traders.*

BROMBY & CLARK, (at their general shipping wharf and counting-house, 26, High-street) are agents for vessels which convey goods regularly to the following places:—Aberdeen, Blakeney, Colchester, Dundee, Fife, Gainsbro', Ipswich, Leeds, Leith, Norwich, Perth, Wells, and Yarmouth.

Aberdeen and Hull Regular Traders—one sails every 8 days:—Fox, Alexander Allan; Bromby, C. Middleton; Wellington, J. Gilbertson.
*Agent*, James Smith, Hull Shipping Co.'s office, Quay, Aberdeen.

Blakeney and Hull Regular Trader—sails every 14 days:—Hull Packet, Robert Seeker.
*Agents*, M. Temple & Son, Blakeney.

Colchester, Hull, and Gainsbro' Regular Traders—one sails every 10 days:—St. Petersburg Packet, Jos. Morden; Bess, Wm. Harvey; Adventure, Wm. Payne.
*Agents*, Robert Taber, Hythe, near Colchester; and Dean and Beaumont, Gainsbro'.

Dundee, Perth, and Hull Regular Traders—one sails every 14 days:—Fife Packet, James Clark; Fame, William Wann.
*Agents*, Robert Christie, Dundee; and Thos. Matthew, Perth.

Gainsbro', Hull, and Ipswich Regular Traders, one sails every 10 days:—Enterprise, John Norman; Halcyon, Joseph Barker; Providence, John Cutting.
*Agents*, F. F. Seekamp, Ipswich—Dean and Beaumont, Grainsbro'.

Hull and Leith Regular Traders, one sails from each port every 8 days:—Montague, John Story; John Watson, John Tyrie; Fife, William Sword; Leith, Thomas Calder; Friendsbury, Adam Smith.
A. B. Mabon, manager, Hull and Leith Shipping Co.'s office, Leith.

Leeds and Hull regular Contract Sloops, one leaves each place every 6 days.
*Agent*, Richard Clark, Bridge wharf, Leeds.

Yarmouth, Norwich, and Hull regular Traders, one sails every week:—Swallow, John Carridge; Vigilant, Wm. Ives; Norwich Merchant, John Lark; Windham, William Elgate.
*Agents*, Wm. Saunders, Yarmouth; James Boardman, Duke's palace wharf, Norwich.

Wells and Hull regular Trader, sails every 14 days:—Hopewell, Matthew Cusson.
*Agents*, J. Bloom and Son, Wells.

Geo. BUCKTON, wharf and counting house, 56, High street,) agent for vessels which sail weekly for Bridlington, Newcastle, Scarbro', Stockton, Sunderland, and Whitby;—Newcastle old established regular Contract Vessels, The Lively, Wm. Innis; The George, Wm. Bouch; The Rockliffe, John Tayler; The Friends, Wm. Copeland; Hull Packet, John Gardner.
Stockton and Sunderland vessels,—Tees, Thos. Mellanby; Cynthia, John Mellanby; Veracity, Joseph Richardson.
Bridlington Trader, Leaflower, John Eaton.
Scarborough—The Ribston, Philip Wand, once a fortnight.
Whitby—The Alert, J. Mowatt, once a fortnight.
*Agents* at Newcastle, Nichol, Ladlow and Co. and John Robson.
*Agents* at Stockton, J. Wilkinson & Co. and Christopher Martin.
*Agent* at Sunderland, Tho. Robinson.

G. DARBYSHIRE, 12, Blackfriargate, agent to the York old Contract Butter Sloops, which sail for York every 6 days.
H. Mills and Son, York, owners.
†§† The masters attend at the Black Boy, High street, Hull.

GEORGE HOLDEN, SON AND CO. (counting house, 181, High street) shipping agents for the following regular trading vessels:—
London a set of smacks sail to and from Upper Iron Gate wharf, every Saturday.
Leith—The Hull and Leith Shipping Company's vessels sail every 8 days.
Lynn—Six vessels are employed, and sail every six days.
Blakeney and Clay—The Hull Packet sails every week.
Whitby—The smacks Smeaton and Ruby sail weekly.
Leeds, Skipton, Liverpool, &c—The Aire and Calder sloops sail every two or three days.
Sheffield, Rotherham, Doncaster, Burnley, &c. sloops sail twice a week regularly.
Goods forwarded to Wells, Yarmouth, and all ports upon the coast of England and Scotland, with despatch.

WM. LAVERACK, (wharf and counting house, 70, High street,) agent for the London and Hull Union Contract; and for vessels to the following places:—Halifax, Huddersfield, Leeds, Manchester, Rochdale, Stockport, Todmorden, Wakefield, and York. Goods despatched every three or four days.

*Agents,* at Manchester, J. and L. Marsden, wharf, Store st. ; at Rochdale, Isaac Marsden.

London—One of the following vessels from Griffin's wharf, to Hull every Saturday :—The Yorkshire, William Laycock ; Huddersfield, R. Massum ; Rochdale, William Foreman; Planter, George Banks; Search, John Saddler; Nottingham, Thomas Maw ; Friends, William Tonge.

*Agents* at London, Mr. J. Eccles, Griffin's wharf, Tooley st. Borough.

LEITH & HULL Shipping Company's Regular Traders, sail from the Union wharf, 21, High street, Hull.

For account of vessels and names of masters, see Bromby and Clark's list.

*Agents* at Hull, Bromby and Clark, Geo. Holden, Son, and Co., Martin and Keddey, and Geo. Malcolm and Sons ; Manager at Leith, A. B. Mahon, Esq.

GEO. MALCOLM & SONS, (counting-houses 63, High st. and at the Union Wharf, 21, High st.) agents for vessels which sail every eight or ten days to Aberdeen, Dundee, and Leith.

MARTIN & KEDDEY, (wharf and counting-house, 49, High street,) agents for the London cheese-mongers ships, and for the Aire and Calder Co.'s river traders, which convey goods to Leeds & Wakefield, &c. daily ; and for the Hull and Leith Co.'s fast-sailing smacks, and for vessels to the following places :— Alnmouth, Berwick, Boroughbridge, Halifax, Huddersfield, Inverness, Leith, Manchester, Newcastle, Ripon, Rye, Wakefield, Wells, &c.

Cheesemongers ships to London :—The Ocean, Wm. Foster ; Briton, Joseph Ware ; Swift, T. B. Foster ; and Neptune, John Mason.

Cheese and Butter *agent* at Hull, Thos. Blackburn, 56, High st.

The London traders, which load at Chamberlain's wharf, Tooley street, sail to and from Hull every eight days.

Vessels sail for Boroughbridge and Ripon weekly, and to Ipswich and Colchester every three weeks.

To Norwich and Yarmouth, the Norwich Packet, Wm. Hudson ; the Dove, Francis Ducker ; and the Diligence, Thos. Relph—a vessel weekly.

To Newcastle, the Jane, Joseph Hume ; the Ann, B. Lattimey ; and the Amos, Joseph Parke—a vessel weekly.

SELLS & KIPLING, (counting-house, 1, Commercial court, 195, High st.) agents for the Leeds Original Contract, and for vessels to the following places, in which goods are forwarded by the Union Company to Blackburn, Burnley, Keighley, Lancaster, Leeds, Liverpool, Preston, Skipton. &c.

One or more of the following Original Contract vessels sail every three days for Leeds :—the Mary Ann, Rd. Maddrah ; Zebulon, John Drury ; Mells, Robert Hopwood ; Huddersfield, Christopher Harrison ; Bowling, Geo. Connill ; Henrietta, Edmund Marshall ; Elizabeth, Thomas Dawson ; Hope, James King ; Anne and Betsey, Amos Crawshaw ; and Two Sisters, Joseph Jewitt.

A regular set of vessels to York, Wakefield, and Halifax. *Agent* at York, Thomas Gilliam.

THOS. PARKIN, (counting-house, 38, Grimsby lane,) agent for the Boston, Spalding, and Wisbeach traders, which sail weekly.

BENJAMIN ROSS, (counting-house, 6, High street,) agent for the following vessels, one of which sails weekly, from Hull to Harrison's wharf, St. Catherine's, London, and vice versa :—Search, John Saddler ; Diana, John White; Resurrection, John Scuth ; & Syren, P. Whitty.

GEORGE SPENCER, 4, Prince George entry, 104, High st.—The Fancy, to Driffield weekly.

E. & J. THOMPSON, (counting-house, 15, Parliament street,) proprietors of the Liverpool, Manchester, and Rochdale canal Regular Traders.

Two, three, or four of the following vessels sail to and from Manchester and Hull every week :—Atlas, Wm. Tunningley ; Brothers, Thomas Wetherill ; Chase, John Tunningley ; Diligence, John Sheard ; Four Brothers, William Oates ; Friendship, Samuel Oates ; Friendship, Wm. Clay ; Good Intent, Thomas Scarby ; Guard, John Oates ; Hull Packett, John Naylor ; Harriet, Joseph Peckett ; Jubilee, Benjamin Wood ; Maria, Marmaduke Barker ; Mary, John Copley ; Perseverance, Wm. Welton ; Providence Goodwill, Samuel Moore ; Reward, John Woodall ; Single Sister, Jeremiah Oxley ; Trial, Francis Buckley ; Three Sisters, James Webster ; and Two Brothers, James Hanshaw.

Warehouse in Manchester at the Upper end of Piccadilly.

TUNNON & SMITHSON, (counting-house, 60, High street) vessels regularly to Gainsbro', Louth, and Sunderland.

*Agents* at Sunderland, Edw. Wynn ; at Gainsbro', Geo. Thorp.

WEDDLE&BROWNLOW,(counting-house,62, High st. agents for London & Hull regular weekly traders, to and from Beal's Wharf, Tooley st. London, & Church lane wharf, 62, High st. Hull.

Humber, M. Jackson; Jubilee, W. Howarth; Kingston, T. Sailes; Manchester, R. Cusworth; Nancy, W. Turner; and Surrey, W. Taylor.

*Agent*, Simon Smithson, Beal's Wharf, London.

\*₊\* Weddle and Brownlow are also agents for the Kingston and Yorkshireman London and Hull steam packets.

WELLS & MORLEY, (counting-house, North side Old Dock,) agents for vessels which sail twice per week to Barnsley, Doncaster, Rotherham, Sheffield, Wath and places adjacent.

## STEAM SHIPS & PACKETS, &c.
### LONDON.

*The Kingston* Steam Ship, Charles Grayburn commander, leaves the Humber Dock Basin, Hull, every Sat. morn. at 6 o'clock, and proceeds with passengers, packages, and parcels direct for London; returns from the Tower Wharf, London, to Hull every Tuesday morning at 7 o'clock.

*The Yorkshireman* New Steam Ship, (400 tons measurement) John Eyre commander, leaves the Humber Dock Basin, Hull, every Wednesday morning, at 6 o'clock, and proceeds with passengers, packages, and parcels direct for London; returns from the Tower Wharf, London, to Hull every Saturday morning at 7 o'clock.

*Agents* at Hull, for booking passengers and goods to go by the Kingston and Yorkshireman, William Senior, London Tavern, Queen street; and Messrs. Weddle and Brownlow, Church lane wharf, 62, High street.

*Agent* Robert Pearson, Stainton's wharf, Tooley street, London.

*Fares to and from London.*

Best cabin, 1*l*. 11*s*. 6*d*.—Fore cabin, 1*l*. 1*s*. Provisions furnished on board at a reasonable rate.

| *Freights.* | *s.* | *d.* |
|---|---|---|
| Bales and Cases, linens, per cwt. ... | 2 | 6 |
| Ditto woollen, per foot... | 0 | 6 |
| Hardware, and heavy goods generally, per cwt. ..................... | 2 | 6 |
| Furniture, and light goods generally, per foot, .................... | 0 | 6 |
| Glass, pictures, or goods requiring special care, per foot, ... ......... | 0 | 9 |
| Parcels, and packages of heavy goods, not exceeding 28lbs. ....... | 1 | 6 |
| Ditto, above 28lbs. and not exceeding 112lbs. ..... ..... | 3 | 0 |
| Light goods, under 6 feet measurement, per foot, ........... | 0 | 9 |
| No single package less than ...... | 1 | 0 |

### GAINSBOROUGH.

The following Steam Packets leave on the days specified, according to tide.

*The Albion* Steam Packet, John Cook, master, to Gainsbro', with passengers and goods every Mon. Wed. & Fri. returning to Hull on the following days.— The Albion communicates on her passage with the towns of Burton Stather, Flixbro' Stather, Keadby, Burringham, Butterwick Ferry, and Stockwith.

*Agent* at Hull, Wm. Senior, London Tavern, Queen street.

*Agents* at Gainsbro', Henry Smith, wharf, Lord street, and John Watkinson, Marquis of Granby, Beast market.

*The British Queen* Steam Packet, William Waterland master, to Gainsbro' every Tu. Thu. and Sat. and returns to Hull the following days (Sundays excepted). The British Queen calls at the same towns, and has the same agents as the Albion.

*The Nottingham* Steam Tug, James Bell master, to Gainsbro' Tu. Thu. & Sat. with goods and passengers.

*Agents* at Hull, Martin and Keddey, 49, High street, and Robert Acrid, Crown and Anchor, 30, South end, Humber street.

*Agents* at Gainsbro', Flower & Sons, Lord street.

*The Maria* Steam Tug, James Hawksley master, plies occasionally with goods to Gainsbro'. Inquire at Wm. Senior's, London Tavern, Queen street, Hull, and at Henry Smith's wharf, Gainsbro'.

### SELBY.

*The Favourite* Steam Packet, Frank Potter master, and *The Leeds* Steam Packet, John Popplewell master, with passengers and goods daily, in rotation to Selby, communicating on the passage With Witton, (Line.) Blacktoft, Whitgift, Swinefleet, Howden Dyke, Booth Ferry, and Long Drax.

*Agents* at Hull, Wm. Close, 9, Dock wall, and at Mr. Wm. Senior's, London Tavern, Queen street.

*Agents* at Selby, Mr. Thos. Adams, Market place, and at Hawden's, the George Hotel.

On the arrival of the Packets at Selby, coaches leave for the following destinations, viz. 3 to Leeds; 1 to Wakefield; 2 to York; and 1 to Harrogate, by Knaresbro'.

The *Caledonia* Steam Packet, John Thompson, master, and the *Aire*, Benjamin Matthewman, master; daily in rotation, to Selby, communicating with the same places as the Favourite and Leeds.

*Agents* at Hull, Martin and Keddey, and at Joseph Allinson's, Shakespeare Tavern, Humber street

*Agents* at Selby, Mr. John Adams, at the Black-a-moor's Head, and R. Precious, Finkle street.

### THORNE.

The *Rockingham* Steam Packet, John Jackling master, and the *John Bull* Steam Packet, Wm. Colbridge master, convey passengers and goods to Thorne, daily, in rotation, and communicating with Witton, Blacktoft, Whitgift, Swinefleet, Goole Bridge, Rawcliffe Bridge, and New Bridge.

*Agent* at Thorne, John Grayburn; at Hull, inquire at the London Tavern, Queen street, and the Humber Tavern, South end.

On the arrival of the Packets at Thorne, a coach proceeds with the passengers for Doncaster, Rotherham, and Sheffield.

### BARTON.

The *Waterloo* Steam Hoy, Wm. Good, master, proceeds from the New ferry boat Dock, end of Queen street, every morning at 7 o'clock, and every afternoon at 4, with the Mail, passengers & goods for Barton, Brigg, & Lincoln. Returns to Hull at 11 mg. and at ½ past 7 evg.

Inquire at Mr. Ralph Keddey's, the Vittoria Tavern, Queen st. Hull, and at Mr. Wood's, Water side, Barton.

\*\*\* The contractors for Barton Ferry are Messrs. Boyes, Chapman, & Co. Grace church street, London.

### SAILING PACKETS.

#### GRIMSBY.

The *Britannia* Packet, Valentine Morvinson, master, sails for Grimsby, daily, at high tide.

Inquire at Mr. William Lewis's, the Humber Tavern, South end, Hull, and at Mr. Wise's, Yarborough Tavern, Grimsby.

The *Moor Park*, Mail Packet, Clayton Croft, master, sails every day for Grimsby, at high water.

Inquire at Mr. William Senior's, the London Tavern, Queen street, and at the Shakespeare Tavern, Humber st. and in Grimsby, at Mr. Brown's, the Steam Packet Tavern.

*Luggage Boat*, John Blow, master, arrives from Grimsby, every Tu. an hour before high water, and returns Thursday, half an hour after high water.

Inquire at Gen. Elliott, 87, High st.

The *Barton Horse Boat* Sailing Packet, conveying passengers and cattle from the New Ferry Dock, end of Queen street, Hull, sails once or twice per day to Barton Waterside, leaving Hull about 2½ hours before high water, and returns about an hour afterwards.

Inquire at Mr. Keddey's, the Vittoria Tavern, Queen street.

### MARKET BOATS.

The *Market Boats* (which attend Hull markets once per fortnight) generally come with goods and passengers on that market day (Tu. or Fri.) which falls nearest the full or new moon, being the periods of spring tides, the markets on such days are thence called *full boat days*.

#### *From the General Elliott.*

The following Market Boatmen attend the General Elliot, 87, High street:—

*Brigg Packet*, William Cotton, sails 2 hours after flood.

*Burton Stather Packet*, Thomas Holt, once a fortnight.

*Ferriby Sluice Packets*, Wm. Speight, sails 3 market days in a fortnight, 2 hours after flood, and John Howell, sails 4 hours before high water, 3 market days in a fortnight.

*Garthorpe Packet*, Wm. Burkpill, sails once a fortnight, first of flood.

*Howden Packet*, Joseph Taylor, sails once a fortnight, first of flood.

*Swinefleet Packet*, Geo. Taylor, sails once a fortnight, first of flood.

*Weighton Lock Packet*, Thomas Dudding, sails once a fortnight, first of flood.

*Whitgift Packet*, Thomas Parrott, sails once a fortnight, first of flood.

*Whitton Packet*, John Dinsdale, sails once a fortnight, 4 hours before high water.

*Wintringham Packet*, Wm. Sarjeant, sails 4 hours before high water 3 days in a fortnight.

#### *From the Humber Tavern, South End.*

*Barrow Packet*, Thomas Bell, sails every Tuesday, 2½ hours before high water.

*Stallingbrough Packet*, Robert Franks, sails once a fortnight, at high water.

#### *From various Inns.*

From the George and Dragon, 102. High st. *Brough Packet* Wm. Chadwick, once a fortnight.

From the Falstaff, Humber street, the *Goxhill Packet*, William Dent, every Tu. and Friday, 3 hours before high water, (wind permitting.)

From the Dog and Duck, 85, High street, *Paul Packet*, Wm. Starkey, every Tu. and Sat. an hour after high water.

From Samuel Crackles, the Labour in Vain, South End, *Skitter Packet*, William Etherington, sails every Tuesday and Friday, at tide time.

## LAND CARRIAGE.

*Newcombe's Waggons*, 2, Castle street, opposite New Dock, Richard Binnington, agent, conveys goods to Beverley, Market-Weighton, York, Manchester, and Liverpool, &c. every Tuesday and Friday at 12 o'clock; arr. from the above places every Monday and Thursday at 12 at noon.

*From Parke, Wilson, and Co.'s* Warehouse, 17, Queen street, goods are conveyed every Thursday and Saturday, by waggon, (from Barton Waterside,) thro' Lincoln to London, where they arrive in five days. Goods by this conveyance arrive in Hull every Tues. and Thu.

Waggons from the same warehouse, with goods for Lincoln, Nottingham, Leicester, Birmingham, Barton, Brigg, Derby, Coventry, Bristol, Bath, and London, leave Hull every Tu. and Thu. and ret. every Thu. and Sat.

*Widow Wilson's Waggons*, convey goods with regularity and despatch to York every Mon. and Thu. and thence to all parts of the kingdom. Agent, John Bolton, office, Foster's yard, Whitefriargate; waggon warehouse, Dagger lane

### Carriers from the Inns.

See also Market Boats, page 333.

Aldbrough, Blue Bell, Market place, James Rogerson, Tu. and Fri. a 10, d 1

Aldbrough, Rein Deer, Market place, Edw. Foster, Tu. and Fri. a 10, d 1

Aldbrough, Spread Eagle, Market place, David Wright and Edw. Harrison, Tu. and Fri. a 7, d 2

Aldbrough, Bonny Boat, Trinity house lane, John Mainprize, Tu. and Sat. a 10, d 2

Alford, Hull Packet, High street, John Rayner, arr. every Wed. and ret. Fri.

Arnold, Blue Bell, Market place, Thomas Allison, Tu. a 10, d 1

Atwick, Blue Bell, Market place, William Wilson, Tu. a 8, d 1

Bainton, Three Crowns, Market place, Robert Cole, Fri. a 9, d 1

Barton, see Parke's, 17, Queen street

Bath, see Parke's, 17, Queen street

Beeford, Coach and Horses, Mytongate, Thomas Jordan, Tu. a 6, d 3

Beswick, Three Crowns, Market place, John Drew, Fri. a 8, d 1

Beverley, Three Crowns, Market pl. John Botterill, Tu. and Fri. a 10, d 4

Beverley, Blue Bell, Market place, Samuel Fenteman, Mon. Tu. Thu. and Fri. a 8, d 4

Beverley, Rein Deer, Market place, James Swaby, Mon. Tu. Thu. & Sat. a 8, d 4

Beverley, see Newcombe's, 2, Castle street

Beverley, Richard Chapman, New George st. dep. 6 morn. ret. 6 evg.

Birmingham, see Parke's, 17, Queen street

Bonby, Dog and Duck, High street, John Walker, two market days in a fortnight

Boston, London Tavern, Queen street, J. Allen, arr. Wed. and ret. Thu. weekly

Brandsburton, Coach and Horses, Mytongate, Thomas Frear, Tu. a 5, d 1

Brandsburton, Full Measure Tavern, Mytongate, David Thompson, Tu. a 5, d 2

Bridlington, Black Swan, Mytongate, Wm. Jefferson, Tu. and Fri. tide time

Bridlington, King's Head, Mytongate, Geo. Bayes, Tu. and Fri. a 6, d 1

Bridlington, see Flambro'.

Brigg, see Parke's, 17, Queen street

Bristol, see Parke's, 17, Queen street

Burstwick-cum-Skeckling, Bonny Boat, Trinity house lane, James Fewster, Tu. and Fri. a 10, d 2

Burton Pidsea, Coach & Horses, Mytongate, David Tavender, Tu. a 9, d 2

Burton Pidsea, Spread Eagle, Market place, Peter Drew, Tu. a 7, d 1

Caistor, London Tavern, Queen street, J. Jubb, Tu. & Fri. at tide time, dep. do

Caister, see Louth

Catwick, Wheat Sheaf, Mytongate, Thomas Agar, Tu. a 8, d 1

Cottingham, Rein Deer, Market pl. Charles Morrod, Tu. and Fri. a 10, d 3

Cottingham, Mermaid, Silver street, Christ. Todd and Robert Donkin, Tu. and Fri. a 11, d 3

Coventry and Derby, see Parke, Wilson and Co. 17, Queen street

Driffield and Malton, Black Swan, Mytongate, Philemon Ashton, Tu. and Fri. a ½ past 6, d 1

Driffield, see Scarborough

Easington, Coach and Horses, Mytongate, William Blenkin, arr. Mon. 6 evg. ret. Tu. at 12

Easington, Coach and Horses, Mytongate, Thomas Kitson, Tu. a 9, d 2

Ellerker, see Welton

Elloughton, Thorp Brantingham, & Welton, Black Swan, Mytongate, Ellen Taylor, Tu. and Fri. a ½ past 6, d 1

Elloughton, Three Crowns, Market pl. Wm. Carlill, Tu. a 9, d 2

Elloughton, Bonny Boat, Trinity house lane, Thos. Easingwood, Tu. & Fri. a 10, d 2

Elsternwick, Three Crowns, Market place, Wm. Woodhouse, Tu. a 10, d 1

Etton, Bull and Sun, Mytongate, Thomas Witty, Tu. a 6, d 12

Etton, Coach & Horses, Mytongate, Robert Towers, Tu. a 9, d 1

Ferriby, Fleece Inn, Market place, Wm. Coates, Tu. and Fri. a 10 d 2

Ferriby, Rein Deer, Market place, Charles Ellerington, Tu. and Fri. a 9, d 3

Flambro' and Bridlington, Bull and Sun, Mytongate, Thomas Lamplugh, Tu. and Fri. a 6, d 12

Fixton, Blue Bell, Market place, John Blackburn, Tu. a 10, d 1

Fosham and West Newton, Blue Bell, Market place, Thos. Parkin, Tu. a 10, d 1

Foston, Bull and Sun, Mytongate. Wm. Hall, Tu. a 6, d 12

Foston and Gemlin, Rein Deer, Market place, Geo. Mainprize, ar. Thu. 7 evg. dep Fri. at 1

Frodingham South, Hollym, Ottringham, Skeffling, and Sunk Island, King's Head, Mytongate, Christopher Wilson, Tu. and Fri. a 7, de 1

Garton, King's Head, Mytongate, John Foster, Tu. a 7, d 1

Garton, Bonny Boat, Trinity house lane, Edw. Robinson, Tu. a 10, d 2

Gemlin, see Foston

Halsham, Bull and Sun, Mytongate, Thos. Hutton, Tu. a 6, d 12

Hatfield, Bull and Sun, Mytongate, John Hastings, Tu. a 6, d 12

Hedon, King's Head, Mytongate, Wm. Rawson, and Jonathan Mitchinson, Tu. & Fri. a 11, d 1

Hedon, see Pattrington

Heale, King's Head, Mytungate, Robert Speck, Tu. and Fri. a 11, d 3

Heale, Fleece Inn, Market place, Robert Wallace, Tu. and Fri. a 11, d 3

Hollym, Blue Bell, Market place, Wm. Greensides, Tu. a 6, d 12

Hollym, see Frodingham

Horncastle, London Tavern, Queen street, Wm. Allen, arr. Wed. at tide time, and dep. Thu. at do.

Hornsea, Full Measure Tavern, Mytongate, David Robinson, Tu. a 8, d 12

Hornsea, Three Crowns, Market place, James Noble, Tu. & Fri. a 8, d 1

Hornsea, Blue Bell, Market place, Wm. Wilson, Tu. a 9, d 1

Hornsea and Mappleton, Rein Deer, Market place, Mary Harwood, Tues. and Fri. a 8, d 2

Otham, Newbald, Sancton, & Weighton, King's Head, Mytongate, Rt. Smart, & Joseph Dean, Tu. & Fri. a 7, d 12

Owden, and York, King's Head, Myton-

gate, Francis Smithson, at 6 Mon. mg. d 9 Tu. mg.

Humbleton, Rein Deer, Market pl Francis Charlton, Tu. and Sat. a 10, d 2

Humbleton, Blue Bell, Market place, John Blackburn, Tu. and Fri. a 10, d 1

Hutton Cranswick, Three Crowns, Market place, John Booth, and Geo. Summerston, Tu. a 9, d 1

Keyingham, Black Swan, Mytongate, John Capes and Robert Buckland, Tu. and Fri. a 6, d 1

Keyingham, King's Head, Mytongate, Rhd. Burrell, Tu. a 7, d 1

Kilham, Rein Deer, Market place, John Harland, Tu. a 6, d 12

Kirk Ella, Bonny Boat, Trinity house lane, John Burn, Tu. and Fri. a 10, d 2

Kirk Ella, White Horse, Carr lane, John Whitty, Tu. and Fri. a 9, d 3

Kirton, Fleece, Market place, Alice Hall ar. tide time Mon. dep. tide time Tu.

Leeds, see Newcombe's, 2, Castle street

Leicester, see Parke's, 17, Queen street

Lelsy, Three Crowns, Market place, Alex. Peters, Tu. a 8, d 1

Leven, Blue Bell, Market place, Sarah Downs, Tu. a 9, d 1

Leven, Rein Deer, Market place, Widow Bugg, Tu. a 9, d 12

Leven, Wheat Sheaf, Mytongate, Robert Adams, Tu. a 7, d 1

Limber, see Louth

Lincoln, London Tavern, Queen st. Joseph Whaltham, ar. Wed. at tide time, dep. at tide time Thursday

Lincoln, see Parke's, 17, Queen street

Little Weighton, Fleece Inn, Market place, Marmaduke Constable, Tu. a 10 d 2

Liverpool, see Newcombe's, 2, Castle street

Lockington, Coach and Horses, Mytongate, Thomas Wallgate, and Wm. Brown, a 9, d 2

London, see Parke's, 17, Queen street

Louth, London Tavern, Queen st. Joseph Hines, ar. on Mon. at tide time, dep. Tu. at tide time

Louth, Limber, and Caistor, Vittoria Tavern, Queen street, John Nettlam, ar. Fri. at tide time, d at ditto

Malton, Black Swan, Mytongate, Thomas Blenkinson, Tu. a 8, d 1

Malton, see Driffield

Manchester, see Newcombe's, 2, Castle st.

Mappleton, Spread Eagle, Market place, Thomas Shaw, Tu. a 7, d 1

Mappleton, see Hornsea

Market Weighton, and Pocklington, Coach and Horses, Mytongate, John Cockburn, Tu. and Fri. a 6, d 1

Market Weighton, see Newcombe's, 2, Castle street

Marton, Coach and Horses, Mytongate, Wm.
  Wright, Tu. a 9, d 1
Newark, see Parke's, 17, Queen street
Newbald, Black Swan, Mytongate, Wm.
  Gardham, Tu. and Fri. a 6, d 1
Newbald, see Hotham
North Cave, Black Swan, Mytongate, Wm.
  Lundy, Tu. and Fri. a 10, d 1
Nottingham, see Parke's, 17, Queen street
Ottringham, King's Head, Mytongate, John
  Willingham, Tu. & Fri. a 7, d 1
Ottringham, see Frodingham
Oustwick, Blue Bell, Market place, William
  Ford, Tu. a 8, d 1
Patrington and Hedon, Rein Deer, Market
  place, Wm. Barrett, Tu. & Fri. a 7, d 1
Patrington, (carrier and post man), No. 3,
  Witham, John Wing, Mon. Wed. &
  Sat. at 8 mg. ret. ½ an hour after
Paul, Coach and Horses, Mytongate, Geo.
  Wright, Tu. and Sat. a 10, d 1
Pocklington, Coach and Horses, Mytongate,
  Robt. Manners, Tu. & Fri. a 7, d 1
Pocklington, see Market Weighton
Preston, Coach & Horses, Mytongate, Thos.
  Dalton and Robt. Brown, Tu. and Fri.
  a 10, d 2
Rimswell, Blue Bell, Market place,———
  Moatson, Tu. a 7, d 12
Rimswell, Fleece, Market pl. John Batty,
  Tu. a 7, d 1
Riston, Blue Bell, Market place, Thomas
  Allison, Tu. a 10, d 1
Riston, Rein Deer, Market place, Thomas
  Wardell, Tu. a 9, d 3
Roos and Tunstall, Coach & Horses, My-
  tongate, Stephen Ganton, Tu. a 9, d 1
Roos, Blue Bell, Market place, Benjamin
  Cockman, and Thomas Dunn, Tu.
  a 7, d 1
Roughton & Skirlaugh, Bonny Boat, Trinity
  house lane, John Dales, Fri. a 10, d 2
Ryehill, Spread Eagle, Market pl. Jonathan
  Drew, Tu. a 7, d 1
Saltfleet, Dog & Duck, High street, Henry
  Rathby, every Monday, and returns
  same day.
Sancton, Coach & Horses, Wm. Blyth, Tu.
  and Fri. a 7, d 1
Sancton, see Hotham
Scarbro', Driffield, & Whitby, Full Measure
  Tavern, Mytongate, James Donkin,
  Tu. and Sat. a 7, d 1
Scarbro', see Whitby
Seaton, Blue Bell, Market place, John
  Miller, Tu. a 8, d 1
Skeckling, see Burstwick
Skeffling, see Frodingham
Skidby, King's Head, Jane Jefferson, Tu.
  and Fri. a 11, d 2
Skidby, Bull and Sun, Mytongate, George
  Hall, Tu. a 6, d 12

Skipsea, Full Measure Tavern, Mytongate,
  Thomas Agar and John Jennison, Tu.
  a 8, d 12
Skipsea, Bull and Sun, Mytongate, John
  Carter, Tu. and Fri. a 6, d 1
Skipsea, Coach and Horses, Mytongate, Rht.
  Holder, Tu. a 5, d 12
Skirlaugh, Blue Bell, Market place, Thos.
  Gibson, Tu. a 9, d 1
Skirlaugh, Spread Eagle, Market pl. Wm.
  Pexton, Tu. a 8, d 1
Skirlaugh, see Roughton
Skirlaugh, Blue Bell, Market place,
  Braithwaite, Fri. a 9 d 1
South Cave, Bull and Sun, Mytongate,
  Blanchard, Tu. & Fri. a 6, d 12
South Cave, Coach and Horse, M
  Wm. Cussons, Tu and Fri. a 10,
Sproatley, Three Crowns, Market
  Thos. Hodgson, Tu. a 10, d 1
Sproatley, Fleece, Market - place,
  Longhorne, Tu. and Fri. a 10, d 1
Sunk Island, see Frodingham South
Swanland, Windmill, Trinity house la
  Robert Hodsman, Tu. and Fri. a
  d 3
Thorngumbald, Blue Bell, Market pl. John
  Green, Tu. a 9, d 1
Thorpe Brantingham, see Elloughton
Tunstall, see Roos
Walkington, Fleece, Market place,
  Oliver, Tu. a 10, d 1
Weighton, see Hotham
Welton, Full Measure Tavern, John
  Tu. and Fri. a 10, d 3
Welton and Ellerker, Three Crowns,
  ket place, Thomas Nicholson, 7
  9 d 2
Welton, Bonny Boat, Trinity house
  Thos. Cade, Tu. and Fri. a 10, d 1
Whitby and Scarbro', Black Swan, M
  gate, Bell & England, Tu. & Fri. a 6,
Whitby, see Scarbro'
Willerby, Crown, Silver street, Matth
  Andrew, Tu. and Fri. a 10, d 2
Winterton and Brigg, Geo. & Dragon,
  st. T. Teanby, Tu. & Fri. at tide
Winterton and Brigg, Dog & Duck, High st.
  Geo. Hewson, Tu. and Fri. at tide time
Winterton, Gen. Elliot, 78, High st. George
  Gildin, Tu. and Fri. at tide time
Withernwick, Blue Bell, Market place,
  David Hewson, Tu. and Fri. a 9, d 2
Withernwick, Coach and Horses, Mytongate,
  Wm. Wray, Tu. and Fri. a 10, d 1
Withernwick, Blue Bell, Market pl. Thos.
  King, Tu. and Fri. a 9, d 1
Wotten, Durham Ox, Blanket row, Tu. and
  Fri. arr. and ret. at tide time
York, see Howden; Newcombe's, 2, Castle
  st. and Widow Wilson's, Foster's yard,
  Whitefriargate

*Humber* (Little), in the parish of Paul, wap. and liberty of Holderness; 3 miles S. of Hedon.

HUMBLETON, (P.) in the wap. and liberty of Holderness; 5 miles NE. of Hedon. The parish church is dedicated to t. Peter, and the living is in the gift of the King. There is here a public school, endowed by Francis Heron, for the education f the poor children of the parish, the present salary allowed for teaching them is 21*l.* annually. This parish is known as the birthplace of the late Admiral John Storr.—Population 136.

Bell Robert, gentleman
Nixon Rev. Jonathan, vicar

*Farmers,*
Bennington Henry     Harrison Francis
                     Witherill Richard
Blackburn Joseph, shoemaker
Boltman Francis, carpenter
Nibnah James, blacksmith
Nightingale Henry, tailor

*Carrier,* Francis Charlton, to Hull every Tuesday and Friday.

---

HUNMANBY, (P.)

in the wap. of Dickering, 8 miles from Bridlington, 39 from York, and 207 from London, about midway between Scarbro' and Bridlington, is well built, and pleasantly seated, being surrounded by 6,000 acres of fertile land, and adorned by a considerable quantity of ornamented wood, chiefly growing on an elevated site, called the Castle Hill, where are still to be traced the foundations of an ancient fortress. Hunmanby had formerly a market, which was held on Tuesday, but it has long been discontinued. The manorial rights, anciently tripartite, under the names of Ross, Lennox, and Rossmore, are now united together, with the property more than two-thirds of the township, in the hands of Humphrey Osbaldeston, Esq. The mansion-house is an ancient structure, adorned with modern embellishments; the gardens are spacious, and the plantations flourishing. A splendid monument, on the North side of the chancel in the parish church, commemorates those of the Osbaldeston family who died within the last century, from William Osbaldeston, Esq. (who died A.D. 1707, and whose name was inserted in the list of the intended Knights of the Royal Oak,) down to Fountayne Wentworth Osbaldeston, Esq. M. P. for Scarborough, who died June 10, 1770. The church is dedicated to All Saints, and the living is a vicarage, in the gift of the Osbaldestons, of which the Rev. Francis Wrangham is the in-cumbent. The other places of worship are a Methodist chapel and a Baptist chapel. There is here a *Lending* Library, on Dr. Bray's plan, for the use of the neighbouring clergy; and a Parochial Library has been established nearly twenty years, for the benefit of the poor. A Lancasterian school was established in this place, by H. Osbaldeston, Esq. in 1810, under Mr. Thomas Duggleby, who enjoys a salary of about 60*l.* per annum for his services. The population amounts to 1012.

POST MASTER--WM. VICKERMAN.

\*\*\* A Riding Postman to Bridlington, Mon. Thu. and Sat. dep. 10 morning, ret. at 2 afternoon, extra charge 1d.

Osbaldeston Humphrey, Esq. Hunmanby hall
Wrangham Rev. Francis, M.A. F.R.S. archdeacon of Cleveland and vicar of Hunmanby

Clarkson John, gentleman
Dunn Richard, gentleman
Hagyard Thomas, surgeon
Hithersay Rev. John, Baptist minister
Hutchinson Ann, gentlewoman
Mallory Ellen, gentlewoman
Nesfield Ann, gentlewoman
Wilson William, yeoman

*Bakers,*
Brewers Mary
Plewes Thomas
*Blacksmiths,*
Cowling Thomas
Dickman Wm.
Scrivener Michael
*Bricklayers,*
Dowsling Geo.
Mallory John
Mallory Geo.
Mallory James
*Butchers,*
Cowton Francis
Smith William
Vickerman Wm.
*Carpenters,*
Dewell John
Dunn Robert
Harper Thomas
Taylor Geo.
*Farmers,*
Baker Robert
Brown Leonard
Brown Francis
Clarke Richard
Clarke Thomas
Clarkson John
Cowton Francis
Cowton Benj.
Cowton Christpbr.
Crosier Francis
Crosier Wm.
Dodson James

Ellis Charles
Fisher John
Gray Wm.
Harper Thos.
Hutchinson Francis
Jordan Samuel
Kirby Thos.
Lowson Richard
Mercer John
Nessary John
Raper Geo.
Raper Thos.
Simpson John
Smith Robert
Smith Wm.
Smith Wharton
Thompson John
Walker Wm.
Waters Luke
Watson John
Watson Robert
Witty Robert
*Grocers, &c.*
Bayes Elizabeth
Bird Elizabeth
Harper John
Harrington James
Haxby Wm.
*Hair Dressers,*
Frankish Geo.
Scott Matthew
*Linen Drapers,*
Edmond Wm.
Lawty Wm.

H H

*Rope & Twine Spinrs.* Hart Edward
Bird Robert          Jackson Thos.
Braithwaite John     Scott Matthew
  *Shoemakers,*         *Tailors,*
Adamson Thos.        Cooper Peter
Dove Geo.            Harper John
Elliott Wm.          Speck Matthew
Flinton John         Speck Francis

Chandler William, gardener
Clarke Christopher, cattle dealer
Cross Thomas, vict. White Swan
Denison Christphr. plumber & glazier
Dickinson Geo. fishmonger
Dobson Thomas, bacon factor
Duggleby Thomas, schoolmaster
Grindel Christopher, gamekeeper
Grindel Ellen, mistress of the workhs.
Haxby Geo. farmer and maltster
Lawty Christopher, hatter
Lowson John, corn miller
Mayner William, farrier
Moor Thomas, flour dealer
Pratt Thomas, vict. Buck
Richardson William, bailiff to H.
  Osbaldeston, Esq.
Scrivener Michael, vict. Black Horse
Waite John, saddler & collar maker

### COACHES.

The *Wellington* and *British Queen,* to
  Hull, Tu. Thu. and Sat. at ½ past
  8 mg. to Scarbro', at 2 aft.

### CARRIERS.

*Pockley and Co.* to York, Thu. & Sat.
*John Johnson,* from the General Elliott,
  & *John Stephenson,* from the Globe,
  to Bridlington, on Tu. and Sat.;
  and to Scarbro' on Thursday.

HUNSLEY (High and Low), in the
parish of Rowley, & wap. of Harthill;
4 mls. NE. of South Cave. Formerly
this was a place of some consequence,
and the foundations of ancient buildings are sometimes dug up here.

Brough Francis, farmer
Fawsitt Mrs. Anne, gentlewoman
Fawsitt James, corn factor
Fawsitt John, yeoman
Stephenson James, farmer

HUTTON CRANSWICK, (P.) in the
wap. of Harthill; 3½ miles S. of Driffield. The church is dedicated to St.
Peter; and the living which is a vicarage in the patronage of Lord Hotham,
is at present enjoyed by the Rev.
Joseph Rigby. Here is also a Methodist
chapel, and a Sunday school. Pop. 917.

  *Blacksmiths,*        *Farmers,*
Bowers William     Boulby George
Norris John        Calton John
                   Cole Thomas

Danby Matthew      Forth Wm. Board
Denton Thomas      Goodlass William,
Dowson William       Board
Fletcher John        *Schoolmasters,*
Goodlass Wm.       Richardson Robt
Goodlass Geo.      Vaukes Rd. (na
Granger Robert       *Shoemakers,*
Granger Joseph     Brown George
Jameson John       Hessey Christphr.
Nicholson Richard  Parker Anthony
Pinder David         *Shopkeepers,*
Simpson John       Dove Robert
Wilkinson James    Jennison Francis
Williamson Andw.   Richardson Robt
  *Joiners,*       Stephenson Marg
Newlove Thos.        *Tailors,*
Sommerson Frs.     Sanderson John
  *Public Houses,* Sanderson Geo.
Barnby Thomas,     Todd Mark
  Pack Horse         *Wheelwrights,*
Bilton William,    Anderson Wm.
  Decoy Inn        Wilson John

Best William, rope maker
Caseley Edward, butcher
Dawson Thomas, corn miller

  *Carriers.*
John Booth and Geo. Summerston, to
  Hull Tu., to Beverley Sat. and
  Driffield Thursday.

*Hythe,* in the parish of Eastrington, wap. & liberty of Howdenshire;
5 miles ENE. of Howden.

KYINGHAM, or Keyingham, (
in the wap. & liberty of Holderness; 5
NW. of Patrington. This village is delightfully situated on an eminence, affording a
fine prospect of the Humber and its various
shores; the church dedicated to St. Nicholas,
and in the patronage of the Archbishop
York, is a small but ancient structure, and
has undergone many repairs. In the year
1802, Edward Ombler, Esq. left 200*l.* to be
invested in the funds; the interest to be appropriated to the education of poor children
belonging to the parish of Kayingham, and
under the direction of the clergyman and
churchwardens for the time being. Pop. 629.

Smyth Rev. Joshua, perpetual curate

Lowton Jane, vict. Gate
Ross John, bricklayer & parish clerk
Smith John, schoolmaster
Steenr Wm. vict. Blue Bell
Tindall John, corn miller

  *Blacksmiths,*    Clark John
Willingham Geo.    Hutchinson John
Wright John        Scott Edward
  *Farmers,*       Scott John
Booth William        *Grocers,*
Buckland Robert    Bowers Stephen
Champney Thos.     Burn Thomas
Champney Robt.     Burrel Peter

Wright John
Shoemakers,
Coldman John
Ellotson Job
Illotson John
Hancock Wm.
Harrison Edward
Willingham John

Tailors,
Londsbrough John
Wreathall Mathw.
(and draper)
Wheelwrights,
Norton Robert
Wright John

Carriers to Hull, John Capes every Tu. & Fri. Richard Burrell every Tu.

KELFIELD, in the parish of Stillingfleet, wap. of Ouse and Derwent; miles N. of Selby. Here is a public school for the benefit of the poor children of this township, endowed with a annual income of 21l. 6s. per ann. Population 286.

uy Robert, yeoman
ague Barnard, Esq. Hall
Johnson Matthew, yeoman
Mitchell Thomas, yeoman

Carpenters,
Buckle Geo. (& gunsmith)
Buckle Robert, (& shopkeeper)
Farmers,
Kam Philip
Hanshard Wm.

Dixon Robert
Dunn Jonathan
Fox Thomas
Reader John
Reader Joseph
Tindall John
Wells Joseph, sen.

ester John, shoemaker & victualler, Boot and Shoe
ewton John, tailor
aff James, schoolmaster
ells Joseph, jun. butcher

KELK (Great), in the parish of Foston, and wap. of Dickering; 6¾ miles E. of Driffield. Pop. 158.

Farmers,
alton David
iddlow John
ambler Richard
owersby Wm.

Thompson John
Ulliott John
Ulliott William
Woodhouse Wm.

ixon George, gardener
owgate Joseph, shoemaker
atson Robert, vict. Board

KELK LITTLE, (Extra-parochial) the wap. of Dickering; 6 mls. ENE. Driffield. Population 51.

alton John, farmer
ovel Philip, farmer

KELLEYTHORPE, in the parish of reat Driffield, and wap. of Harthill; miles SSW. of Driffield.

ee William, farmer

Kendal House, in the parish and township of Great Driffield, and wap. of Harthill; 2 miles N. of Driffield.

Kennythorp, in the parish of Langton, and wap. of Buckrose; 3½ miles of Malton. Population 83.

KEXBY, in the parish of Low Catton, and wap. of Ouse and Derwent; 6 miles E. of York. Pop. 149.
Sherwood Wm. vict. Coach & Horses

Farmers,
Dresser Mrs. Mary,
Greyleys
Horsley Wm.
Lambert Thos.
Meggison Richard

Meggison Robert
Ricksdale Thomas
Robinson Edward
Robinson George
Usher William
Walker William

## KILHAM, (P.)

In the wap. of Dickering, and liberty of St. Peter's; 6 miles NNE. of Driffield, had once a market on Thursday, but it has long declined, and is now wholly disused. The town is situated in a pleasant vale amidst the Weld hills, and the soil is fertile in corn.— The town is nearly a mile and a quarter long, running from East to West. The church, dedicated to All Saints, and in the patronage of the Dean of York, is large and lofty, and seems to have been designed for containing a more numerous congregation than the present population of the parish can supply.— The free grammar school in this town was founded by John Lord D'Arcy, of Aston, in this county, in the ninth year of the reign of Charles I. with appointments for a master and usher, 20l. per annum being allowed the former, and 10l. the latter. In this parish there is a mineral spring, near the road leading to Rudston, said to be efficacious in curing various disorders; and the Vipsey or Gipsey, after a wet autumn, breaks out at a place called Hempit Hole, near the road to Langtoft, the violence of this spring or spout, when it first issues out of the ground, is said to be so great, that a man on horseback may ride under its arched stream. The Methodists and Baptists have each a chapel here. The population amounts to 971.

Letters are delivered at 8 morning, and are sent off at 12 at noon.

Anderson Christopher, master, Royal Navy
Anderson Richd. master, Royal Navy
Baines Rev. Alexander, vicar
Berriman Elizabeth, gentlewoman
Dawson Richard, gentleman
Dickenson Michael, gentleman
Eggleton William, gentleman
Leadlow Robert Lieut. Royal Navy
Lowish Mary, gentlewoman
Otterburn Rev. Ralph, curate
Outram Thomas, Esq.
Rouse Rev. M. Baptist minister
Sharp John, yeoman
Stephenson John, gentleman

*Blacksmiths,*
Belt William
Ireland Thos. sen.
Ireland Thos. jun.
Towse Robert
　*Bricklayers, &c.*
Bastiman Thos.
Mallory Gibson
Mallory William
Mallory John
　*Butchers,*
Cook William
Hodgson Peter
　*Carpenters, &c.*
Sunley John
Wardell Peter
　*Farmers,*
Anderson John
Berriman John
Berriman Peter
Berriman Wm.
Blenkin James
Cranswick Wm.
Dickinson John
Hardy Geo.
Hopper Richard
Hutchinson Ralph
Jackson Charles
Knaggs Richard
Lamplugh Rt. sen.
Lamplugh Rt. jun.
Lamplugh Mathw.
Lamplugh Samuel
Lamplugh Wm.
　*Middledale*
Marson John
Milner Richard

Milner John, Middledale
Stevenson John
Taylor Christopher
　*Glove Makers,*
Bell Thomas
Spavin Hannah
　*Grocers,*
Lamplugh Thos.
　(and draper)
Lamplugh Thos.
Robson Michael
Sowerby Thos. (&
　draper)
Towse Richard, (&
　draper)
　*Joiners,*
Maltby Wm.
Robson Michael
Wardell Peter
　*Shoemakers,*
Carr John
Clarke Crispin
Johnson Thomas
Marshall John
Pinder Robert
Reed John
Thompson Francis
　*Surgeons,*
Atkinson Thomas
Dobson Francis
　*Tailors,*
Bailey John
Bailey Thomas
Maltby Matthew
Maltby Michael

Dickinson John, brick and tile maker
Elvidge Christ. linen & woollen draper
Fisher John, vict. Black Bull
Gibb Robert, gardener & seedsman
Hardy Thomas, bacon factor
Harland Richard, vict. Star
Lamplugh Matthew, schoolmaster
Major Thomas, fellmonger
Mead Wm. saddler and bridle cutter
Rawson Thos. plumber and glazier
Vasey Wm. bookseller
Vokes John, vict. Royal Oak
Wardell Peter, vict. Plough
Williams John, corn miller

*Carriers.*
John Harland, to Driffield, Beverley,
　and Hull, every Thursday.
Wm. Hardy, to Bridlington every Sat.

KILLINGWOLD GRAVES, or
GROVES, in the parish of Bishop Burton,
and wap. of Harthill; 2 mls. W. of Beverley.
There are many marks of antiquity about
this place, and it appears, from Tanner's
Not. Mon. that there was here an old hospital, dedicated to St. Mary Magdalene,
chiefly for women, before the year 1169.—

Human skeletons are frequently dug up
here, and about thirty-five years ago a
tomb-stone was found with the rem
three bodies beneath it. Near the
on the road leading to Beverley, is
cross, called *Stump Cross,* bearing
inscription, which may be thus
" Pray for the soul of William de 
The only inhabitant in the villag
the rank of a labourer is Mr. John J
farmer.

*Kilnsea,* (P.) in the wap.
berty of Holderness; 8 mls. SE. of
ton. The church, dedicated to St
is now in a state of dilapidation, and
a dangerous situation, being near
cliff, that the inhabitants think it
bestow on it any further repairs,
from the annual encroachments of t
that it will, in a short time, be shall
the abyss which has already swept aw
of the burial ground. The Rev. Geo.
A.M. vicar, resides at Skeffling, the patr
the living is L. Thompson, Esq. Pop.

KILNWICK PERCY, (P.) in
wap. of Harthill; 1½ mile ENE
Pocklington. This is a vicarage,
which the Rev. Charles Wolf Byn
the incumbent, and the Dean of Y
the patron. Population 42.

Dennison Robert, Esq.

KILNWICK-ON-THE-WOLDS,
in the wap. of Harthill; 7½ mls. SS
of Driffield. Incumbent, the 
Francis Lundy; curate, the Rev. W
Legard; patron, Charles G
Esq. Population 230.

Grimston Charles, Esq.

　*Farmers,*　　　Jordan Wm.
Coxworth John　　Linwood Wm.
Hornby John　　Staveley James
Horseley John　　Staveley Robert
Huddleston John　Todd Robert
Johnson Francis

Coxworth John, vict. Bay Horse
Dalton Richard, joiner
Dawton John, blacksmith
Newton John, tailor
Newton Wm. shoemaker
Yates John, carpenter

KILPIN, in the parish of Howden,
wap. and liberty of Howdenshire; 2
miles SE. of Howden. Pop. 318.

Phearson Thomas, yeoman

　*Farmers,*　　　Swales John
Bason Peter　　Taylor John
Dowson John

KILPIN PIKE, in the parish of
Howden, wap. & liberty of Howdenshire; 1 mile S. of Howden.

Issit Wm. vict. Blue Bell
Booth John, butcher
Rayton Thos. vict. Admiral Nelson
Suttle Richard, shopkeeper
Hewitt Thos. shopkeeper
Savage Wm. gentleman
Ward Richard, coal merchant

KINGSFIELD NORTH, in the parish of Carnaby, & wap. of Dickering, miles S.S.W. of Bridlington.

Jefferson John, farmer
Spanding Thomas, farmer

KIPLING COATES HOUSE, in the parish of Middleton-on the-Wolds, & wap. of Harthill, 4 miles NNE. of Market Weighton. Races are held here on the third Thursday in March annually, and tradition says, that these are the oldest races in England.

Barrett John, Farmer

*Kirby Grindalyth*, (P.) in the wap. of Buckrose, 8 miles ESE. of Malton ; vicarage, in the patronage of Miss Allingtone, incumbent, Rev. Rowland Croxton. Population. 178.

KIRBY GUDERDALE, (P.) in the wap. of Buckrose, 7 miles N. of Pocklington. The church is dedicated to All Saints, and the living is in the patronage of the King. Pop. 385.

Lidley Rev. Henry D.D. rector

*Farmers,*    Newlove John
Harper Marmdk. Wrigglesworth Rd.
   (& butcher)
Collinson Richard, carpenter
Laycock Wm. grocer
Leake Wm. blacksmith

KIRKHAM, (P.) in the wap. of Harthill, 4 miles W. of Driffield. The church is dedicated to St Mary, and the living which is a vicarage, in the patronage of the King, and enjoyed by the Rev. William Cautley, B.A. This village forms part of the ample property of Sir T. Sykes, Bart.— Population. 119.

Harrison W. J. vict. Hare & Hounds
Piercy George, farmer
Shepherdson Thos. wheelwright
Turner John, blacksmith

*Carrier,* Robert Stockdale, to Beverley, every Saturday ; to Driffield every Thursday.

*Kirkham,* (extra-parochial) in the wap. of Buckrose ; 6 miles SW. of Malton. Formerly a priory of canons of the order of St. Austin, founded in the year 1121, by Sir Walter L'Espee, Knight, and Adelina his wife, and dedicated to the Holy Trinity, stood here, and some vestiges of it still remain. The priory is situated in a delightful vale, watered by the Derwent, and the scattered ruins of this venerable structure sufficiently evince its ancient magnificence. A noble Gothic tower, beautifully covered with ivy, stood till the year 1784, when it was blown down by a high wind. The northern part of the gate is the principal vestige now remaining of the monastery. To the south end the cellars are yet to be seen, but in a ruinous state ; and a small part of the wall of this chancel has withstood the ravages of time. The property belongs to Henry Leatham, Esq. of Barton. The chapel of Kirkham is dedicated to the Holy Trinity. Pop. 7.

KNAPTON, in the parish of Winteringham, and wap. of Buckrose, 7 miles NE. of Malton. The river Derwent at this place is navigable for small vessels. Population, 200.

Tindall James, Esq. Knapton-house
Tindall Wm. Esq. Knapton-house
Harburn Matthew, surveyor of taxes
   *Farmers,*    Holtby John
Batty Geo.    Spanton John
Dale Christopher    Tindall Mary
Freer John    Tindall John
Holtby Wm.

Lovel Francis, mason.
Spink Joshua, gardener.

KNEDLINGTON, in the parish of Howden, wap. and liberty of Howdenshire, 1 mile W. of Howden. At the west end of the village stands the ancient hall built in the reign of Queen Elizabeth. Population, 118.

Campbell James, yeoman, chief constable, and agent to the Guardian Assurance Company, London
Backhouse Samuel, farmer
Clark Thomas, gentleman
Maw Francis, horse dealer
Waterhouse E. farmer & vict. Anchor
Wadsworth James, yeoman

*Langthorpe,* in the parish of Swine, wap. and liberty of Holderness, 9 mls. N. of Hedon.

LANGTOFT, (P.) in the wap. of Dickering, and liberty of St. Peter's, 6 miles N. of Driffield. The church is dedicated to St. Peter, and the living, which is a vicarage, in the patronage of the Prebendary of Langtoft, is enjoyed by the Rev. Jones Thompson. Pop. 416.

   *Butchers,*    Crosby Richard
Robinson John    Gray Richard
Wherram Wm.    Grace Christopher
   *Farmers*    Harnell Wm.
Brunton James    Lamplugh Robert

Lamplugh James
Lamplugh Wm.
Outhwaite Geo.
Sowerby Thomas
Wardell John
Waters Wm.
Wilson John
*Grocers,*
Nightingale David

Woodmancy Wm.
*Shoemakers,*
Hill Thomas
Johnson Samuel
Lawty Francis
*Tailors,*
Beilby Robert.
Wood Thomas

Leading Wm. blacksmith
Linskill Thos. corn miller
Medd Richard, vict. George & Dragon
Sawden James, stone mason
Wilson Wm. vict. Nelson

*Carrier,* David Nightingale, to Driffield every Thursday

LANGTON, (P.) in the wap. of Buckrose; 3½ miles S. of Malton.—The church is dedicated to St. Andrew, and the living; which is a rectory, in the patronage of the King, is enjoyed by the Rev. Francis Drake.—Population, 280.
Norcliffe Mrs. Ann, Langton hall
Norcliffe Norcliffe Major, Langton hall

*Farmers,*
Eity William
Calam Isaac
Marshall Wm.
Nalton Francis
Harrison David, tailor and draper
Rawling Jonathan, schoolmaster
Strangeway James, vict. & blacksmith, Horse Shoes
Walton Robert, butcher
Wilson Geo. shoemaker
Witton Robert, constable

West John
*Grocers,*
Hardy Wm.
Nelson John

*Langwith,* in the parish of Wheldrake, wap. of Ouse and Derwent; 3 miles SE. York. Pop. 39.

LAXTON, in the parish of Howden, wap. and liberty of Howdenshire; 4 miles of SE. of Howden. Pop. 268.
Saltmarshe Philip, Esq. *Saltmarshe*
Ward Rev. Edward, curate
*Farmers,*
Andrew Wm.
Ealand Geo.
Fentiman Joshua
Kay Thomas

Popple John
Wadsworth Geo.
Windas William
*Bishop soil*

Cottom Geo. schoolmaster
Driffield W. blksmith & vict. Cross keys
Dyson John, carpenter
Ealand John, corn-miller
Freeman Taylor, bricklayer and vict. Mason's Arms
Hatfield B. tailor
Hatfield Wm. shopkeeper
Wade Geo. shoemaker
Watson Geo. carpenter
Underwood Jewitt, vict. White Horse
   *Bishop soil*

LAYTHAM. in the parish of Aughton, and wap, of Harthill; 9 miles N. of Howden. Pop. 225.
Nottingham R. F. gentleman

*Farmers,*
Brables James
Gell John
Gowry Charles

Hatfield Thomas
Relph Thomas
Thompson John
Vause John

LEAVEN, (P.) in the wap. and liberty of Holderness; 6½ miles W. of Hornsea. Sir W. O. Pennyman, Bart. is the patron of the church, which is a rectory. Pop. 658.
Sampson Rev. G. rector
Jackson and Co. merchants
Medford John, gentleman
Robinson Geo. yeoman
Spruce William, yeoman
Spruce Richard, yeoman

*Blacksmiths,*
Coates Ralph
Turner Wm.
*Butchers,*
Naylor Edward
Whiting Thomas
*Corn millers,*
Cook Wm. & Geo.
Foster John
Richardson John
*Farmers,*
Cammorin Alex.
Elvidge Thomas
Glenton Wm.
Lamplugh Jonth.
North Wm.
Smith Wm. yeoman

Smith Jonathan.
Wise John
*Grocers, &c.*
Hobson J. & dpr.
Richardson John
*Maltsters,*
Kemp Jeneson
Whiting G. and R.
*Shoemakers,*
Hustings Edw.
Rounding Rd.
Ruddiford John
Vickerman A.
Winn John
*Wheelwrights,*
Caitall Thomas
Tomlinson Wm.

Fewson John, vict. Minerva
Foster Samuel, parish clerk
Heble Creaser, bricklayer
Herdsman Robert, vict. Blue Bell
Stevenson John, schoolmaster

*Carriers,*

William Burn, foot-post to Hornsea; every Mon. Wed. Thu. and Friarr. at 11 morn. ret. immediately.
Adams, Robert, to Hull, Tu. dep. 2 morn. ret. 7 evg.
Buggs Thomas, to Beverley on Sat. and to Hull on Tu.
Downs Sarah, to Beverley Sat. Hull Tu.
Roundhill Richard, to Beverley on Sat. dep. 8 mg. ret. 7 evg.
Thompson Robert, by water to Hull every Tuesday.

LEAVENING, in the parish of Acklam, wap. of Buckrose, and liberty of St. Peter's; 5½ miles S. of Malton. Pop. 294.

*Carpenters,*
Binge Thomas
Binge Samuel
*Farmers,*
Addison Peter
Boulton Henry
Colby John
Craven Joshua
Creaser John
Jenning Thos.
Mitchell Samuel
Robinson Thos.
Seller Geo.
Seller Thos.
Seller Wm.

Weatherill Wm.
Wilkinson John
*Grocers,*
Hartis Richard
Layton Francis
*Nurserymen,*
Bean Wm.
Bean Eliz.
Seller Richard
Waters Joshua
*Shoemakers,*
Kibby Thos.
Lyon John
Richardson Harm.

Garbutt James, linen manufacturer
Layton Francis, blacksmith
Raper Matthew, corn miller
Rooks Francis, vict. Hare & Hounds
Tinsley Roger, schoolmaster
Waite James and Son, butcher
Whitwell Francis, tailor

LECKONFIELD, (P.) in the wap. of Harthill; 3 miles NNW. of Beverley. There is here a church, which is a vicarage, of which the Earl of Egremont is the lay patron, and the Rev. Robert Rigby, of Beverley, incumbent. This is a place of considerable antiquity, and was formerly the lordship of Peter de Brus. Pop. 302.

Langdale John, yeoman

*Farmers,*
Almack John
Brandham John
Clark Thomas
Fisher John
Hornby John

Lee Wm.
Moss Thos. & vict.
Roebuck
Sugden John
Seymour Hugh
Witty George

Arnot Richard, bricklayer
Atkinson Wm. shopkeeper
Giles Richard, carpenter
Sellers Mary, vict. Bay Horse
Sellers Thomas, blacksmith
Sugden Robert, butcher

*Lelley,* in the parish of Preston, wap. and liberty of Holderness; 4 miles NE. of Hedon. Pop. 119.

*Carrier,* Alexander Peters, to Hull every Tuesday.

LEPPINGTON, in the parish of Scrayingham, aud wap. of Buckrose; 8 miles S. of Malton. Pop. 129. The Grange House is occupied by William Atkinson, Esq.

*Lincoln Flatts,* in the parish of Seaton Ross, and wap. of Harthill; 7 miles from Market Weighton.

*Lingeroft,* in the parish of St. Dennis, York, and wap. of Ouse and Derwent; 3 miles S. of York.

*Linton,* in the parish of Winteringham, and wap. of Buckrose; 10 miles E. of Malton.

LINTON, (East and West) in the parish of Howden, wap. and liberty of Howdenshire; 3 mls. E. of Howden.

Goundrell Thos. farmer, E. Linton
Goundrell Wm. farmer, W. Linton

*Linton Grange,* in the parish of Winteringham, and wap. of Buckrose; 11 miles E. of Malton.

*Lissett,* in the parish of Beeford, wap. and liberty of Holderness; 6 miles SWW. of Bridlington. Here is a small Chapel of Ease; incumbent, the Rev. John Mason, curate of Beeford. Pop. 95.

LITTLE WEIGHTON, in the parish of Rowley, and wap. of Harthill; 5 miles SSW. of Beverley.

*Farmers & Yeomen,* Hudson Carlill
Bailey John       Stephenson Ralph
Green Thomas      Watson Joseph
Hopper James

Boynton Benjamin, shoemaker
Cash Luke, blacksmith
Constable Marmaduke, shopkeeper
Hill Wm. vict. and carpenter, Black Horse
Lyon John, tailor.

*Carrier,* Marmaduke Constable, to Beverley every Sat. and Hull every Tu. dep. 6 morn. and ret. in the evg.

LOCKINGTON, in the parishes of Lockington and Kilnwick, and wap. of Harthill; 6½ miles NNW. of Beverley. Here is a church, dedicated to St. Mary, and a National School. The living is a rectory, in the patronage of the rector, the Rev. Francis Lundy.—Population, 491.

Waudby John, gentleman

*Farmers,*
Cherry Francis
Dalby Wm.
Fox Robert
Hotham John
Jefferson John
Nornabb Antby.
Nornabb Wm.
Richardson Eliz.
Robinson John

Robinson Robert
Rountree Robert
Smith Thomas
Wilson Thomas
*Carpenters,*
Hants John
Levett Robert
*Shoemakers,*
Acklam Wm.
Burgess Wm.

Binnington Henry, tailor
Brealey Mary, vict. Buck
Hudson John, parish clerk
Ireland Geo. blacksmith
Lamplough Robert, schoolmaster
Rountree Thos. corn miller

Walgate Thos. grocer
Welbourne Robert, bricklayer

*Carriers*—Thomas Walgate and Wm. Brown, to Hull every Tu. to Beverley every Sat.

LOFTSOME, in the parish of Wressle, wap. of Harthill; 3 miles NW. of Howden, situated near the Derwent, over which it has a wooden bridge, constructed, so as to admit the passage of vessels.

Brown William, farmer
Foster Geo. farmer, maltster, coal mert. & vict. Loftsome Bridge Inn
Webster Launcelot, shoemaker

LONDESBROUGH, (P.) in the wap. of Harthill; 9¾ miles N. of Market Weighton; one of the places claiming to be the ancient Delgovitia. The Roman road from Brough is continued in a direct line to Londesbrough Park, and, without mentioning the Roman coins, a great many repositories of the dead have been discovered in digging in different parts of the village, the park, and the gardens. Londesbrough was for several centuries one of the seats of the ancient family of the Clifford's. The only daughter and heiress of Henry, the fifth and last Earl of Cumberland, was married to the Earl of Cork, from whom his Grace, the present Duke of Devonshire, who possesses this estate, is descended. The mansion of Londesbrough, which was very pleasantly situated, being surrounded with a variety of charming landscapes, & commanding beautiful prospects, has lately been taken down. The church is dedicated to All Saints, and the living is in the gift of the Duke of Devonshire. His Grace has also the patronage of a hospital in this place for six old bachelors or widowers, and six widows. Population, 244.

Dickinson Robert, Esq. agent to the Duke of Devonshire
Ewbank Rev. Andrew, M.A. rector
Fenton Charles, schoolmaster and parish clerk
Hagyard Robert, maltster and vict. Devonshire Arms
Hampshire Wm. clerk
Martin James, blacksmith

*Longbrough Lane House*, in the parish of Humbleton, wap. and liberty of Holderness; 8 miles from Hedon.

LOWTHORP, (P.) in the wap. of Dickering; 5 miles NE. of Driffield. The church, dedicated to St. Martin, is in the gift of the St. Quintin family, and the Rev. Thomas Ibbotson is the perpetual curate. Pop. 149.

St. Quintin William Thomas, Esq. Lowthorp hall
Smith John, gentleman
Smith Thomas, corn miller

*Farmers,*
Agar Robert
Baker John
Barnard Wm.
Barnett Wm.

Catton Thomas
Catton Wm.
Jackson John
Jefferson Robert
Milner Mary

Hillaby Wm. linen manufacturer
Nicholson James, rope maker, &c.

LUND, (P.) in the wap. of Harthill; 8 miles NW. of Beverley. The church is dedicated to All Saints, and living, which is a vicarage, is in the age of T. Grimston, Esq. In the place are the remains of a cross, which place goods are exposed for sale Thursday in Lent. Here is also an old of Jarratt family, now occupied by a farmer. There is in this place a public school, for an unlimited number of children, erected by the parishioners. Pop. 357.

Legard Rev. Wm. A.B. vicar

*Farmers,*
Broadley John
Chapman Wm.
Foster Thomas
Fox George
Harland John
Hornby Ann
Horsley John
King Stephen
Lowson Wm.
Orrah Ann
Spence Thomas
Stephenson Isaac

Walgate Eliz.
Walgate Geo.
Wilkinson Wm.
*Shoemakers,*
Biggins Geo.
Robson Wm.
Varey James
*Shopkeepers,*
Cobb Benjamin
Walgate Isaac
*Tailors,*
Gray George
Hardbattle John

Cobb Benjamin, jun. vict. Lord Wellington
Holdsworth Thos. parish clerk
Orrah Robert, constable
Robinson John, bricklayer
Robinson John, schoolmaster
Sherwood Ann, governess of workhouse
Smith Matthew, carpenter and wheelwright
Smith Wm. vict. Plough
Waddington John, blacksmith
Walker Geo. saddler
Wilson Richard, butcher

*Carriers,* George Biggins, John Varey, and Wm. Smith, to Beverley every Sat. to Market Weighton every Wednesday.

Lund, (see Cliff-cum-Lund.)

LUTTON, (East) in the parish of Weaverthorpe, wap. of Buckrose, and liberty of St. Peter's; 11 miles E. of Malton.

Brand William, farmer
Cattle John, corn miller
Harrison James, tailor
Kirby Christopher, shoemaker
Kirby William, farmer
Park Charles, grocer and draper
Megginson John, farmer
Williamson Francis, farmer

LUTTON, (West) in the parish of Weaverthorpe, wap. of Buckrose, and liberty of St. Peter's 10 miles E. of Malton. Population, including East Lutton, 311.

Addison Thos. wheelwright
Booth Thomas, shoemaker
Brown George, farmer
Dickinson Wm. blacksmith
Miller Thos. shoemaker
Rice John, sen. farmer and grocer
Rice John, jun. wheelwright and farmer
Harper John, tailor
Roe James, farmer
Kirk Wm. wheelwright
Lawden Wm. farmer
Train Richard, farmer
Train Richard, vict. Board
Wood Robert, tailor

MAPPLETON, (P.) in the wap. of Holderness, and liberty of St. Peter's; miles SSE. of Hornsea. The church a plain Gothic structure, dedicated to All Saints, and the living, which is a vicarage, in the patronage of the Arch-deacon of the East-Riding, is enjoyed by the Rev. Christopher Forge.—There is here a small public school, erected in 1820 by voluntary subscrip-ion, and conducted on Dr. Bell's plan. Pop. with Rowlston, 187.

Ike William, farmer
Bastard Robert, carpenter
Bray Robert, farmer
Hill Mary, farmer
Jackson Charles, farmer
Gillerby Geo. corn miller
Forster Michael, farmer
Tennison Lawrence, farmer
Reed Thomas, schoolmaster & parish clerk

Carriers, Thomas Shaw and M. Harwood, to Hull every Tuesday and Friday.

MARFLEET, (P.) in the wap. and liberty of Holderness; 3½ miles E. of Hull, a small village situated near the Northern bank of the Humber. The church is a small brick building, erect-ed on the site of the old one in the year 1793, and the incumbent is the

Rev. Thos. Watson, curate of Bilton. Population, 127.

Carrick Robert, farmer
Conyers Thomas, vict. Humber bank
Gibson John, farmer
Holt John, farmer
Jackson Edward, farmer
Leonard Benjamin, farmer
Longman William, farmer
Petty Benjamin, farmer
Ramsey George, farmer
Ramsey Robert, farmer
Rodmell William, farmer
Saunderson John, shoemaker
Swift John, farmer
Vickerman Robert, farmer
Vickerman David, farmer
Wiles Thomas, farmer

## MARKET-WEIGHTON, (P.)

In the wap. of Harthill, and liberty of St. Peter's; 7 miles from Pocklington, 8 from South Cave, 10 from Beverley, 12 from Howden, 21 from from Selby, 19 from York, and from London 188—This is a small brisk market town, situated at the western foot of the wolds, and on the high road from York to Beverley. The market, which is held on Wednesday, is ex-tremely well attended. There is also a great corn market, where some thousands of quar-ters are weekly disposed of by sample. The trade of this town and neighbourhood is considerably increased by means of a navi-gable canal to the Humber. The patronage of the church is in the Prebend of Weigh-ton.—This ancient edifice had formerly a wooden spire, which has been taken down, and a more permanent one substituted for it; and the church, which has been beauti-fied within, is now furnished with an addi-tional gallery, and a number of commodi-ous pews. There are here also chapels for the Methodists, the Independents, and the Primitive Methodists. There is here a place called ARRAS, and a tradition prevails, which is, however, supported by no authen-tic documents, that a great battle was fought on this spot, with bows and arrows, from which it is supposed to derive its name, and a considerable number of instruments of war have, unquestionably, been dug up out of the earth here. There is in Market-Weighton a free grammar school, of which the Rev. T. Mitchell is the master, William Bradley, the Yorkshire giant, was born here, whose height was seven feet eight inches; he died in 1820. Pop. 1734.

POST MASTER—JAMES HOLMES, *Office, Market place.*

| Places from whence Letter bags are recvd. | Distance. | Postage. | Arrival of Mails. | Departure of Mails. |
|---|---|---|---|---|
| Beverley.......... | 10 | 4*d.* | 4 min. past 5 evg. | ¼ past 3 morning |
| Everthorp........ | 6 | 4 | ¾ past 3 morning | 6 morning |
| Hotham.......... | 5 | 4 | 5 evening | Ditto. |
| Hull.............. | 19 | 5 | 4 min. past 5 evg. | ¼ past 3 morning |
| London.......... | 188 | 11 | ¾ past 3 morning | 15 min. past 5 evg. |
| Newbold ........ | 4 | 4 | 5 evening | 6 morning |
| North Cave ...... | 7 | 4 | Ditto. | Ditto. |
| South Cave ...... | 8 | 4 | Ditto. | Ditto. |

### DIRECTORY.

Blowe William, gent. Market place
Bradley John, gent. Hungate
Button Misses Sarah & Ellen, Bridge
Dickins Thomas, gent. Southgate
Donkin John, gent. Hungate
Flockton Rev. George, Independent minister, Hungate
Leighton Robert, Esq. Market place
Swales Abraham, gent. Hungate
Turner John, gent. Southgate
Tyson Rev. John, Southgate
Whitaker Thomas, gent. Hungate
Wilson William, gent. Southgate
Winpenny Rev. Rd. M.A. vicar, Back st.

*Academies.*
Barrow John, (day) Back street
Flocker Rev. Geo. (day) Northgate
Hall Edward, (day) Southgate
Midgley Eliz. (girls day) Northgate
Mosey Joseph, (day) Market place
Plummer Charlotte, (la. bg.) Northgt.
Richardson Luke, (gent. bdg.) Northgt.

*Auctioneers.*
Eagle Thomas, Northgate
Oxtoby Peter, Northgate

*Blacksmiths and Farriers.*
Johnson William, Chapel yard
Kent James, Northgate
Lewis John, (and farrier) Market pl.
Patrick Thomas, Market place
Routledge John, Southgate
Weatherill Peter, Northgate

*Booksellers, Stationers, &c.*
Crabtree John, (binder) Market place
Mosey Joseph, Market place

*Boot and Shoemakers.*
Hembrough Robert, Southgate
Hewson Nicholas, near the Church
Wilson Matthew, Market place

*Braziers and Tinsmiths.*
Brown George, Northgate
Sapcoate Abraham, Market place

*Breweries.*
Jewison Thomas, near the Church
Kirby Thomas, Southgate

*Bricklayers.*
Berry James, Northgate

Hewson Robert, Southgate
Hopwood James, Chapel yard
Wilkinson John, Market place

*Butchers.*
Barker Marshall, Northgate
Bradley Robert, Market hill
Edwards John, near the Bridge
Fish William, Market place
Foster Richard and Wm. Market pl.
Pottage William, Northgate

*Clock and Watch Makers.*
Cade George, Market place
Thorp Richard, Market place

*Coal Merchants.*
Clark John, Southgate
Dickins Thomas
Haire Thomas
Scott George, Market place

*Corn Millers and Factors.*
Cade William, Market place
Dawson John and Robert, Hungate
Peart James, St. Helen's square
Vause William, Cave road
Scott George, Market place

*Farmers.*
Blackburn Robert, Back street
Consitt Thomas, Northgate
Craven William, Weighton wold
Craven John, Southgate
Edwards Henry, Back street
Flint George, Hungate
Foster Thomas, Southgate
Gell James, Southgate
Gill Robert, Southgate
Hatfield James, Back street
Hembrough John, Cliff road
Kelsey Robert, Holm road
Leeming Robert, Market hill
Marshall John, Gallows hill
Plaxton Benjamin, River head
Robinson Leonard, Hungate
Suggitt Robert, Weighton common
Wake John, Cliff road
Windlass John, Southgate

*Fire and Life Insurance Offices.*
*Atlas*, James Holmes, Market place
*County*, Peter Oxtoby, Northgate

*Gardeners.*

Iall John, Northgate
Iolmes Thomas, Northgate
Iohnson John, Chapel yard
Ihompson Charles, Market place
Foule Thomas, Southgate

*Grocers and Tea Dealers.*

Iarron Robert, Market place
Iandham John, Market place
Ieast Ralph, Market place
Iade Wm. Market place
Iembrough Robert, Southgate
Iewison Vickerman, Northgate
Iyon John, Market place
Oxtoby James, Market place
Smith Joseph, Market place
Iavin Ann, Market place
Iephenson Geo. Bridge
Iephenson Christopher, Southgate
Iwainson Thomas, Southgate
Iate Robert, Southgate
Iilkinson Wm. Market place

*Hair Dressers.*

Iaitson Thomas, Market place
Iybourn Wm. Market place

*Horse dealers.*

Iamsdale Robert, Market place
Iamsdale Thomas, Market place
Iotsey Thomas, Market place

*Hotels, Inns, and Taverns.*

Iagel, Richard Hodgson, Market pl.
Iay Horse, Nicholas Hewson, Market place
Iack Horse, Geo. Sturdy, Market pl.
Iack Swan, Thomas Eagle, Northgate
Iard, John Ramsdale, Bridge
Ioss Keys, John Wilkinson, Market place
Ievonshire Arms, John Simpson, (posting house) Market place
Iffin, Robert Marshall, Market pl.
If Moon, Wm. Wardle, Market pl.
I King's Arms, Robert Ramsdale, (excise office) Market place
I Pretender, Thos. Rotsey, Market place
It Boy, Peter Weatherill, Hungate
Iiite Swan, Wm. Hall, Market place

*Joiners—House builders.*

Ihose with a * are also wheelwrights.

Iooksbank Thomas, Bridge
Iibby John, Holm road
Ickley Wm. Northgate
Iottage Thomas, Northgate
Itmer Robert, Maltkiln yard
Itmer James, Foster's yard
Isons John, Northgate
Iung George, Southgate

*Linen and Woollen Drapers.*

Int Ralph, Market place
Ie Wm. (linen) Market place

Mosey Joseph, (woollen & hatter) Market place
Smith Joseph, Market place
Oxtoby James, Market place
Wilkinson Wm. (linen) Market place

*Maltsters.*

Jewison Thos. near the Church
Key Mark, Market place
Kirby Thos. Southgate

*Milliners and Dress Makers.*

Bradley E. and J. Northgate
Burton Sarah, Southgate
Ellah Mary Ann, Back street
Whiteley Eliz. Southgate

*Rope and Twine Makers.*

Gardam Peter, Market hill
Holmes Henry, Southgate
Lyon John, Market place
Richmond Wm. Northgate
Shaw John, Southgate

*Saddlers and Collar Makers.*

Wallis Wm. A. Market place
Wregit Christopher, Bridge

*Seedsmen.*

Gardham Peter, Market hill
Richmond Wm. Hungate
Scott George, Market place

*Spirit Merchants.*

Jewison Thomas, near the Church
Ramsdale John, (dealer) Gt. Bridge

*Straw Hat Manufacturers.*

Brigham Foster, Market place
Hyde Wm. Market place
Lofthouse Ann, Market place
Stephenson Geo. Bridge.

*Surgeons.*

Dove John, Northgate
Loman John, Market place

*Tailors.*

Holmes Abraham, Market place
Kelsey John, Market place
Moor John, sen. Northgate
Moor Robert, Northgate
Moor Michael, Northgate
Moor John, jun. Northgate
Oxtoby James, Market place
Skinn Joseph, (and draper) Bridge
Steel Thomas, Hungate

*Miscellany.*

Crabtree John, agent to the London Genuine Tea Co. Market place
Creaser Thomas, druggist, Market pl.
Giles John, swine dealer, Southgate
Kirby Thos. tallow chandler, Southgt.
Lyon Peter, baker and flour dealer, Market place
Ombler Wm. plumber and glazier, ironmonger, and earthernware dealer, Market place
Oxtoby Peter, Sheriff's officer, Hungate

Pottage Mattw. surveyor, Northgate
Prust Thos. excise officer, Bridge
Snowden J. currier, Hungate
Stephenson Geo. silk dyer, Bridge
Tate James, basket maker, Market
place
Thorp Robert, cooper, Market place
Wilson Robert, tanner, Bridge

## COACHES.

*From the Old King's Arms, Market pl,*

ROYAL MAIL, daily at 3 in the morn.
to Hull, ret. 5 evg.
TRAFALGAR, to Hull at 10 morn.
ret. 5 evg.
ROCKINGHAM COACHES, meet at
1 from York and Hull, each ret.
half an hour afterwards.
TRAFALGAR, to York 9 morn. to
Hull 5 evening.

## CARRIERS.

Barnby, (Half Moon, Market place,)
Wm. Smith, arr. 3, dep. 6.
Barnby, (Cross Keys, Market place,)
John Wride, arr. at 2, dep. at 6.
Beverley, Widow Wilson, on Mon. &
Thu. at 7 o'clock morn. ret. Tu.
and Fri. at 9 evg.
Beverley, Robert Holmes, on Sat.
dep. 7 morn. ret. 5 evg.
Cottingham, (Half Moon, Market pl.)
Chas. Morrod and John Hotham,
arr. 2, dep. 6.
Harswell, (Black Horse, Market pl.)
Thomas Trippet, arr. 2, dep. 6.
Holme, (Black Horse, Market place,)
John Smith, arr. 2, dep. 6.
Hull, Widow Wilson, on Mon. and
Thu. at 7 o'clock morn. ret. Tu.
and Fri. at 9 evg.
Hull, John Cockburn, on Mon. evg.
at 9 o'clock, and on Thu. morn.
at 9. o'clock, ret. Tu. and Fri. at
12 night.
Hull, Thomas Newcombe, on Mon.
and Thu. at 7 o'clock morn. ret.
on Tu. and Fri. at 9 evg.
Lund, (Old Pretender, Market place,)
Geo. Biggins, arr. 2, dep. 6.
Lund, (Griffin, Market place,) Wm.
Smith, arr. 2, dep. 6.
Pocklington, John Cockburn, on Wed.
& Sat. dep. 9 morn. ret. 9 evg.
Pocklington, (Angel, Market place,)
Mary Hodgson, arr. 2, dep. 6.
Sancton, (Half Moon, Market place,)
Wm. Blith, arr. 2, dep. 6.
Seaton Ross, (Cross Keys, Market
pl.) Thos. Batty, arr. 2, dep. 6.
York, Widow Wilson, every Tu. and
Fri. at 7 o'clock morn. ret. on
Wed. and Sat. at noon.

York, Thomas Newcombe, on Tu. &
Fri. at 7 o'clock morn. ret. on
Wed. and Sat. noon.

MARTON, in the parish of Bridlington, and wap. of Dickering; 2 miles N.
of Bridlington.   One of the most remarkable
remains of former ages that is to be seen in
this neighbourhood is a ditch, or ravine, of
immense width and depth, nearly at the base
of the triangle which forms the promontory
of Flamborough Head.   This ditch, which
is called "Danes Dike," is apparently the
effect of art, and contains two lines of
fence, one above the other, with its
works. It extends above a mile and a quarter
from the South shore, where its bottom
on a level with the beach, and becomes gradually shallower, till it entirely disappears.
History affords no account of this stupendous
work; but tradition ascribes it with great
probability to the Danes.   Pop. 317.

Creyke Ralph, Esq. Marton hall
Simpson George, farmer
Smith John, farmer

MARTON, in the parish of Swine,
wap. and liberty of Holderness;
miles N. of Hedon.   There is no place
of worship here except a Catholic
chapel.  Population, 129.

Hodgson Rev. Thos. Catholic minister

| Farmers, | |
|---|---|
| Beal George | Hatch John |
| Bird Mary | Hepple Robert |
| Denton Isaac | Savage George |
| Grasby Robert | Savage Wm. |
| | Swales Barthw. |

Naisby Thomas, shoemaker
Wright Wm. vict. and carrier to Hull
every Tuesday and Friday.

MEAUX, in the parish of Waghen
or Wawn, wap. and liberty of Holderness;
miles N. of Hull.   This lordship was given
by William the Conqueror, to one of his officers named Gamel, born at Meaux, in Normandy, who made it his seat, and peopled it
with his townsmen, from whom it obtained
the name of Meaux.   A monastery of the
Cistercian order was founded here in the
year 1136, by William le Gros, Earl of
Albemarle.   From the small remains of
curious Mosaic pavement of brick, the foundations of buildings are yet to be traced, with
the extensive moats, or ditches, by which it
was surrounded, and which are yet discover-
able, it is evident that this famous monastery
once displayed considerable magnificence.
Population, 74.

*Farmers & Yeomen,* Smith William
Acaster James       Storey Thomas
Clappison Francis  Wise Robert

MELBOURNE, in the parish of Thornton, and wap. of Harthill; 5 miles SSW. of Pocklington. There is here a chapel for the Wesleyan Methodists, and another for the Primitive Methodists. Pop. 437.

Wharton James Lieut. General, one of his Majesty's Justices of the Peace, & Commissioner of Taxes for the East and North Ridings, Rosehill cottage
Lowell Samuel, Esq. Melbourne hall
Bottam Geo. yeoman, Melbourne cotg.
Hodgson George, gentleman

*Blacksmiths,*
Lamer Wm.
Bowdles Mark
*Farmers,*
Bickett Rd. (and vict.) Cross Keys
Boddil Thos.
Brabbs Thos.
Gibson Robert
Goodrick Wm.
Clayton Wm.
Holmes Wm.
Widd James
More Francis
Richardson G. & J.
Smith John, sen.
Smith John, jun.
Thompson J. & J.
Williamson Wm.
*Joiners,*
Gibson Wm.
Nichols George, (wheelwright & machine maker)
*Shoemakers,*
Bell Thos.
Corner Richard

Bant James, bricklayer
Hodgson George, cattle dealer
Ames William, shopkeeper
Gale Henry, brick and tile maker

*Carrier.*
Wm. Harrison, to York every Sat.

MELTON, in the parish of Welton, wap. and liberty of Howdenshire; 4 ms. SSE. of South Cave. A pleasant and handsome village, and although seated without the limits of the county of Kingston-upon-Hull, is the favourite residence of some of the gentlemen of that opulent town. Population including Melton-hill, 107.

Rough Robert, farmer
Ring Samuel, iron merchant
Stephenson Thomas, farmer
Dikes Henry, Esq.
Wilson Mrs. gentlewoman

MELTONBY, in the parish of Pocklington, and wap. of Harthill; 2½ mls. NW. of Pocklington. Pop. 78.

*Farmers & Yeomen,*
Lofthouse Charles
Ates John
Watson John
Voss Wilson
Wright Wm.
Green James

MENNYTHORPE, in the parish of Weston, and wap. of Buckrose; 3 les S. of Malton. Pop. 131.

*Farmers,*
Owlbeck John
Hetherington Rd.
Revis John
Sollitt John
Wilson George

Nixon Geo. surveyor of highways
West William, schoolmaster

MENTHORPE-cum-BOWTHORPE, in the parish of Hemingbrough, wap. of Ouse and Derwent; 5 miles ENE. of Selby. Pop. 49.

Chaplin John, gentleman
Waterworth Richard, gentleman
Fligg Thomas, farmer
Maw Ralph, farmer
Shaw Robert, vict. Board

METHAM, in the parish of Howden, and wap. of Howdenshire; 6 miles SE. of Howden. This village was once the seat of the ancient family of Metham. Sir Thomas Metham, Knight, was slain at the battle of Marston Moor; being then captain of the Yorkshire gentlemen, who served as volunteers, on the part of Charles I. in that battle. Upon a moor in the neighbourhood, a Roman pottery has been discovered, where a great quantity of cinders, pieces of broken urns, and other vessels are found: it is about a mile distant from the Roman military high-way. Pop. 45.

Schofield Philip, gent. Metham hall
Ealand John, yeoman
Empson Richard, gentleman
Holmes D. farmer
Jepson Richard, yeoman, *Bishopsoil*

MIDDLETON-ON-THE-WOLDS, (P.) in the wap. of Harthill; 8½ miles NW. of Beverley. There is in the church at this place a Saxon font, church dedicated to St. Andrew, Rev. John Blanchard, rector; Abraham Hoskins, Esq. patron. Pop. 441.

Blanchard Rev. John, rector & magistrate, Middleton hall
Wood John, surgeon

*Blacksmiths,*
Dove Wm.
Morris James
*Farmers,*
Anderson John
Bell Richard
Burnell John
Constable John
Edmund Richard
Garnett Isaac
Grubb Geo.
Jackson Wm.
Knaggs Matthew
Lofthouse Edw.
Martin Henry
Moat John
Piercy Thos.
Railton John
Railton Robert
Railton Wm.
Robinson Samuel
Tranmer Wm.
Whitehead Wm.
Wilson John
Witty Mary
*Innkeepers,*
Kirby Matthew, vict. Board
Petch John, vict. Robin Hood
*Shoemakers,*
Etherington Thos.
Oxtoby Wm.
Robinson David
*Shopkeepers,*
Burkinshaw Mthw.
Welch Wm.
Witty Wm.

Coventry James, gardener
Imeson Philip, parish clerk

Lamplough Matthew, schoolmaster
Newlove George, butcher
Rountree Robert, corn miller
Sterriker Wm. carpenter & wheelwright

*Carriers.*
Robert Bowser, Philip Imeson, Geo. Robson and John Shields, to Beverley on Sat. & Driffield on Thu. dep. mgs. ret. same evgs.

*Mill Houses,* in the parish of Kirby-Underdale, and wap. of Buckrose; 9 miles from Pocklington.

MILLINGTON, (P.) in the wap. of Harthill, and liberty of St. Peter's; 3 miles NE. of Pocklington. The living is a discharged curacy, of which the Dean of York is patron. Pop. 282.

Holmes Rev. Edmund, vicar
Wilkinson William, gentleman

*Farmers,*    Brigham William
Brigham Richard    Kirkley James
Crosby John, wheelwright
Dales James, vict. Gate
Gospel William, corn miller
Harrison Richard, schoolmaster
Morritt J. A. blacksmith
Randerson William, wheelwright
Slightam James, shopkeeper

MOLESCROFT, in the parish of St. John of Beverley, wap. of Harthill, and liberty of Beverley; 1 mile NW. of Beverley. Pop. 111.

Ashley Edward, gentleman
Bell Mark, gentleman
Thompson Miss Jane

*Farmers,*    Jackson John
Clark James    Ward Mountain
Jackson H. W.

Johnson Francis, vict. Wellington

MOORBY, in the parish of Stillingfleet, wap. of Ouse and Derwent; 5¼ miles S. of York. The lordship of John Lord Gray, of Rotherfield, which was with his other estates seised by the king in the 6th of Edward III., for his quarrelling with Lord Zouch, and drawing his dagger in the king's presence, but upon his submission he was afterwards restored to favour, and soon after employed in the wars with Scotland. Pop. included with Stillingfleet.

Preston Thomas, Esq. magistrate, Moorby hall
Kettlewell William, farmer
Ryder Henry, farmer

*Moor House,* in the parish of Humbleton, wap. & liberty of Holderness; 5 miles from Hedon.

*Moor Town,* a small hamlet, in the parish of Brandesburton, wap. and

liberty of Holderness; 7 miles WNW. of Hornsea. Pop. 29.

MOUNT ABBEY, in the parish of South Cave, liberty of St. Peter, and wap. of Harthill; ¼ mile E. of South Cave.

Robinson Thomas, farmer

*Mount Farran,* in the parish of Birdsall, and wap. of Buckrose; 4 miles S. of Malton.

MOWTHORPE, in the parish of Kirby-Grindalyth, and wap. of Buckrose; 8 miles SE. of Malton.

Kirby Richard, farmer
Topham John, farmer

MUSTON, (P.) in the wap. of Dickering; 2 miles N. of Hunmanby. The church is dedicated to All-Saints and the living is a discharged vicarage in the patronage of H. Osbaldeston, Esq., of which the Rev. Francis Wrangham, M.A. F.R.S. archdeacon of Cleveland is vicar. There is also a Calvinist chapel, built by Mrs. Hannah Tate. Population 350.

Beswick George, gentleman
Russell Christopher, gent. Muston lodge

*Butchers,*    Hutchinson Wm.
Hamcoat Wm.    Hutchinson Chpha.
Welburn Allinson    Hutchinson John
*Carpenters,*    Major John
Brunton William    Prince Wm.
Dunn William    Swales Wm.
*Farmers,*    Welborn John
Abraham Thos.    Welburn John
Davison Andrew    *Grocers, &c.*
Dixon Ann    Pool Francis
Dobson G. Grange    Walker Isaac
Foster William    Ward Johnson
Gardener Geo.

Atkinson Thomas, schoolmaster
Barnby John, tanner
Burnett William, bricklayer
Collins William, corn miller
Dixon William, vict. Boat
Greenlay William, shoemaker
Maltby Elizabeth, vict. Cross Keys
Pool John, earthenware dealer
Pool John, tailor
Wilson Richard, blacksmith

*Coaches* to Hull & Scarborough, daily

*Carriers,* John Johnson & James Stephenson, to Bridlington, Hunmanby and Filey, every Wed. and Sat.

NABURN, in the parishes of Acaster Malbis, and St. George, York, wap. of Ouse and Derwent; 4 miles S. of York. Here is a Chapel of Ease of the Established Church, and likewise a Methodist chapel. The town is situate near to the bank of the river Ouse

There is here also an endowed school of 10*l.* per annum, for ten boys; 5*l.* of which was left by Lady Hewley, and 5*l.* by Mr. Edward Loftus. Pop. 366.

Baines H. J. Esq. Bell hall
Gray Rev. John, curate
Palmes George, Esq. Naburn hall
Tuite Captain, Crockey hill
Walmsley T. G. Esq. Ling croft

| *Farmers & Yeomen,* | Leaf John |
|---|---|
| Allan Thomas | Leaf Richard |
| Bell Joseph, (& butcher) | Tasker Margaret |
| | Throssell Thos. |
| Burton Geo. | Wharram Matthias |
| Burton Wm. | Wigglesworth Wm. |
| Croft Joseph, (& butcher) | Yeoman Joseph |
| | *Shoemakers,* |
| Dickinson Thos. | Bell John, sen. |
| Hardgrave Joseph | Brown Christopher |
| ... John | |

Cooper Thomas, wheelwright
... Thomas, shopkeeper
Holliday John, schoolmaster
Hadley Joseph, blacksmith and vict. Horse Shoe
Hardon Amelia, lock keeper
Whitwell John, corn miller
Young William, tailor

*Carrier*—Wm. Leaf, to York, every Saturday at 9 morning, returns at 7 evening.

NAFFERTON, (P.) in the wap. of Dickering; 2 miles NE. of Driffield. The church is dedicated to All-Saints, and the living is a vicarage, of which the Rev. John Ubank, is the incumbent, and the Archbishop of York the patron. Here are chapels of the Methodists and Independents, also a well endowed school. Pop. 917.

Allen Rev. George, curate
Aybourn Jacob, gentleman
Lovell Richard, gentleman
Larkin William, corn miller, coal and lime merchant

| *Blacksmiths,* | *Farmers & Yeomen,* |
|---|---|
| Morris William | Crumpton R. |
| Walker Francis | England Richard |
| *Bricklayers,* | Forge William |
| Johnson William | Forge George |
| Longbottom Chas. | Forge Thomas |
| Watson William | Forge Robert |
| Watson Robert | Forge John |
| *Butchers,* | Helme William |
| Fears Thomas | Jefferson Paul |
| Matteson Leonard | Keld Thomas |
| Fenton John | Kirby Robert |
| Dickerman Wm. | Lovel Wm. |
| *Carpenters,* | North J. and W. |
| Morris Robert | Robson George |
| Gray John | Severs J. and P. |
| | Smallwood Wm. |

*Grocers, &c.*
Barker Samuel
Danby John
Sherwood Thos.
Sherwood Robert
Ward Robert
*Linen & Woollen Drapers,*
Barker Samuel
Sherwood Thos.
*Schoolmasters,*
Johnson Robert

Smith Thomas
*Shoemakers,*
Barker Valentine
Byram Wm.
Hillaby John
Ireland Francis
Walker Wm.
*Tailors,*
Barchard John
Kirby Thomas
Spanton Wm.

Barker John, vict. Bell
Cawood Thomas, brick maker
Fairbotham James, vict. Cross Keys
Gill Thomas, earthenware dealer
Grindell Christopher, vict. King's Head
Hardington Paul, gardener
Johnson John, plumber and glazier
Medforth Robert, horse dealer
Park David, last shoe maker
Preston Francis, cabinet maker
Spanton Richard, linen manufacturer
Storry William, vict. White Horse
Winter John, rope and twine mfr.

The *Wellington Coach,* from Hull to Scarborough, every day during the bathing season

*Carrier,* Thos. Johnson, to Bridlington every Saturday, and to Driffield every Thursday.

NESWICK, in the parish of North Dalton, and wap. of Harthill; 8 miles SW. of Driffield. Here is a National school for girls, supported by the munificence of Mrs. Grimstone. Population 55.

Grimstone John, Esq.
Thorold Henry, Esq.
Wheatley Timothy, bailiff to Digby Legard, Esq.

*Neville Grange,* in the parish of Leaven, wap. and liberty of Holderness; 5 miles NE. of Beverley.

NEWBALD NORTH, (P.) in the wap. of Harthill, and liberty of St. Peter's; 3½ mls. N. of South Cave. The church is an ancient structure, dedicated to St. Nicholas, with a tower in the centre, it has four fine arches at the entrance of the south door, which are in the Norman style of architecture. The figure over the south entrance is supposed to be that of one of the Priors. The patronage is in the Prebendary of N. Newbald. A sum of money left by an inhabitant of the name of Gill, was laid out in the purchase of land, the rental of which is distributed every New Year's Day to 20 resident parishioners, who have never received parochial relief; in the present year the dividend to each amounted to 5*l.* 3*s.* Pop. 543.

*Blacksmiths,* | Shipton Thomas
Kirby Wm.
Langdale Wm.
*Bricklayers,*
Hornsey Thomas
Hornsey William
*Farmers,*
Coates John
Danby Robert
Holt William
Hopper Christphr.
Johnson John
Smith John
*Shoemakers,*
Norman Robert
Tindale Jeremiah
*Shopkeepers,*
Kirby Mary

*Yeomen,*
Barker John
Bowers Anthony
Braithwaite M.
Burgess Richard
Carbutt George
Coates Thomas
Galland Thomas
King William
Kirby Frank
Pears Abraham
Towle Thomas
Turner Richard
Turner William
Turner John,
Bushy hill

Medd William, tailor
Scott John, corn miller & vict. Rose and Crown
Tindale Rt. butcher & vict. New Inn
Wilkinson William, vict. Tiger
Wilson William, schoolmaster and collector of taxes

Carriers, Joseph Dean, Robert Smart, & Wm. Gardham, to Hull every Tu. and Fri., to Beverley every Sat., and to Market-Weighton every Wednesday.

NEWBALD SOUTH, in the parish of North Newbald, wap. of Harthill, and liberty of St. Peter's; 3 miles N. of South Cave. Pop. 179.

Atkinson Rev. Thos. vicar of North Newbald
Clough G. W. Esq. banker
*Farmers & Yeomen,* Waltham John
Burnell William  Waltham Jonathan
Jewitson Wm. sen.  *Corn-millers,*
Jewitson Wm. jun.  Atkinson Richard
Marshall John  and William
Stephenson Wm.  Blackburn Thomas
Hutchinson Thomas, overseer

*New Fields,* in the parish of Howden, wap. and liberty of Howdenshire; 1 mile from Howden.

*New Land,* in the parishes of Howden and Eastrington, wap. and liberty of Howdenshire; 8 miles E. of Howden.

NEWLAND, in the parish of Cottingham, and wap. of Harthill; 2 miles NNW. of Hull. Here is a Methodist chapel, and a school with a small endowment.

Haworth B. B. Esq. (Hull bank)
Holder John, yeoman
Reynolds Mrs. gentlewoman
Rudstone George, merchant
Terry Avison, merchant

*Farmers,*
Bullock John
Bullock Thomas
Chambers John
Dugelby John
Dugelby Matt.
Gardham John
Jackson Robert

Pearson Richard
Pearson Thomas
Pearson William
Preston William
Smith Robert
Twidale Richard
Wilkinson Thomas
Wilson Thomas

Breeding John, vict. Blue Bell, Newland Clough
Chandler George, corn miller
Clark Thomas, schoolmaster
Gibson Thomas, grocer
Machon Thomas, shoemaker
Pearson William, tailor
Popple Joseph, blacksmith
Thompson Saml. vict. Duke of York

NEW PORT or NEW VILLAGE, partly in the parish of Eastrington, (& part extra-parochial) wap. and liberty of Howdenshire, and wap. of Harthill; 5 miles W. of South Cave. A pleasant thriving village situated on the high road from Howden to Hull, and on the Market-Weighton canal, celebrated for its manufacture of tiles, bricks, and coarse earthenware; there being 1,700,000 tiles and 2,000,000 of bricks made annually. This now considerable village was fifty years ago, a wild uncultivated morass, called "Walling Fen." There is here a bed of clay, superior to any in the country, which is got to the depth of thirty feet below the surface. This land which lately was a barren waste, is now sold for the purposes of the above manufacture for 20l. per acre. There is a neat brick chapel here belonging to the Wesleyan Methodists, erected in 1814, and a Sunday school belonging to that society for the instruction of two hundred poor children of this and the neighbouring villages. Pop. 339.

Those marked thus * are in New Village, thus + in West Side, and those without out marks in Newport.

*Blacksmiths,*  *Coal-merchants,*
Thornton John  Dudding James
*Woodall Wm.  Grasby Richard
*Brick & Tile Mfrs.  *Corn-millers,*
Armatage Geo.  Clarkson John
Brittain Joseph  Robinson William
Brown Thomas  Smith John
Brown John  *Drapers,*
Brown William  Bennington John
Garnett James  Hornsby Thomas
Moss Thomas  Kemp Robert
*Butchers,*  Scott William, (& druggist)
Cryer William  Scott Anthony
Kirk William
*Carpenters,*  *Farmers,*
Brown Thomas  Armatage George
*Mouncey Arthur  Barker Thomas

Clarkson John
Cock George
Cryer Wm.
Hudson Wm.
*Kirk James
*Naylor Thomas
Robinson Wm.
*Grocers.*
Bennington John
Kemp Robert
Scott Wm.
*Master mariners.*
Armatage Thos.
Joyes Joseph
Craven John
Craven Benjamin
Dudding Tho. sen.

Dudding Thomas, jun.
Holmes Peter
Mouncey James
*Saddlers.*
Brown John
Prince John
*Shoemakers.*
Barff Peter
Ramsby Edward
*Tailors.*
Coulson James
Hewson George
Hornsby Thos.
Scott Richard
Scott Anthony

Armatage Thos. vict. Turk's Head
Baines Charles, gentleman
Brittain Geo. bricklayer
Button Amelia, hair dresser
Dudding Wm. sacking weaver, and basket maker
Dudding John, shopkeeper
Rich George, baker
Foster James, vict. King's Arms Inn
Willie George, earthenware mfr.
Bell John, gardener
Thompson Thos. shopkeeper
Turner Geo. vict. Crown & Anchor
Wardell Wm. schoolmaster

Goods are conveyed to and from Hull by Tuesday nearest the full and change the moon, by Thomas Dudding's packet, which also conveys passengers.

Frank Smithson conveys goods and passengers, by land, to Hull, every Monday 10 morning; to Howden every Tuesday morning at 6.

The Redney Post-coach to Doncaster, every mg. at 9, to Hull at 4 aft.

NEWSHOLME with BAIND, in the parish of Wressle, wap. of Harthill, and liberty of Howdenshire; 3 miles W. of Howden. Pop. 177.
Clark John, gent. Prickett hill
Hand James, gent. Rowland hall

*Newton,* in the parish of Eastring-, wap. and liberty of Howdenshire, miles E. of Howden.

NEWTON, in the parish of Winter-ham, wap. of Buckrose; 8 mls. E. of ton. Here is the residence of Geo. Ackland, Esq. of Newton House.

NEWTON, (East) in the parish of Brough, wap. and liberty of Hol-nese; 8 miles SSE. of Hornsea.—ulation, 38.
*Farmers.*
Althorp Samuel
son William

Shepherdson Wm.
Wells Thomas

NEWTON (Out), in the parish of Easington, wap. and liberty of Holderness; 4 miles ESE. of Patrington. Population, 69.

*Farmers & Yeomen.*
Bennington Robt.
Cross John
Hall John
Turner Robert
Wallis Richard
Winteringham T.

NEWTON-UPON-DERWENT, in the parish of Wilberfoss, wap. of Hart-hill, and liberty of St Peter's; 6 miles W. of Pocklington. Pop. 205. Robert Harrison, music preceptor, who resides here, is a blind man, and famous for his mechanical ingenuity.

*Farmers & yeomen.*
Bradley Thos.
Brown Wm.
Brown Thos.
Chapman Thos.
Collings Mary
Cook Wm.
Easingwood John
Fowler H. N.
Gilbert Charles
Gray John
Harrison Thos.
Jackson John
Machin Thomas
*Newton Grange.*
Patchett Thos.
Penrose Wm.
Pierson Thomas
Young George
*Shoemakers.*
Brown Edward
Harrison Wm.
Taylor John
*Shopkeepers.*
Purdon Sarah
Whitaker Wm.

Cook Edward, wheelwright
Easingwold John, constable
Purdon John, tailor
Young Thomas, butcher

*Carrier,* Robert Whitaker, to York every Sat.

NEWTON (West), in the parish of Aldbrough, wap. and liberty of Holderness; 5 mls. N. of Hedou. Pop. 158.
Camplins Ann, vict. Gate
Evan Thomas, smith and farrier
Walton John, plumber and glasier
*Farmers.*
Caley William
Godolphin James
Johnson Charles
Masterman Robt.
Sumpney Thos.
Walker Edward
Wray George

*Newton-on-the-Wolds,* see Wold-Newton.

NORTON, (P.) in the wap. of Buckrose; ½ mile SE. of Malton. The church is a perpetual curacy, in the patronage of Mr. Ewbank, of which the Rev. John Richardson is the incumbent. At the foot of the bridge, between this place and Malton, was, pretty early in the time of Henry II. a hospital, dedicated to St. Nicholas, founded by Roger de Flamvill, and placed under the government of the canons of Malton. Population, 1017.

*Gentry, &c.*
Bower Robt. Esq.
Coverdill John
Ellis Charles
Greenwood Rev. William

Hall George
Hill James
Ingleby John
Monkman Thos.
Nalton James
Owston Elizabeth
Preston Elizabeth
Priestman David
Rawlin James
Sellers Bridget
Watson Thos.
  *Blacksmiths.*
Beckett Ann
Chilton Robert
  *Butchers.*
Holliday Francis
Judson Wm.
Witfield Geo.
Wrapp Wm. jun.
  *Farmers.*
Adamson Wm.
Dale Lawrence
Ellis Wm. & lime burner
Wardle Richard
Wise Robert

*Grocers.*
Bell Wm.
Robinson Thos.
Smith Richard
Smith Ann
Wilson James
Wrapp Wm. sen.
  *Horse Jockies.*
Garbutt James
Gray John
  *Raff Merchant.*
Corps Edward
Elmer Thos.
Setchfield Edw.
  *Schoolmasters.*
Warters John
Wood John
  *Shoemakers.*
Crawford John
Monkman Wm.
Ruston Thos.
Stamper Richard
Waters John
  *Tailors.*
Crawford Wm.
Foster Anthony
Sanderson Robt.

Barraclough Francis, corn miller
Clark Thos. saddler
Collier Thos. assistant overseer
Dickenson Wm. vict. Oak Tree
Fawcett Wm. stone mason
Ingilby Richard, linen draper
Lucas Thos. pipe maker
Sellers James, cabinet maker
Shepherd John, sen. horse trainer
Shepherd John, jun. surgeon
Stelling Richard, fellmonger
Stonehouse John, gardener
Waddy Thomas, boarding school, Norton grange
White Phillip, vict. Bay Horse
Wilson Wm. wheelwright
Wray Robert, roper

NUNBURNHOLME, (P.) in the wap. of Harthill; 3½ miles ESE. of Pocklington. The church is dedicated to St. James, and the living is a rectory, in the patronage of the Archbishop of York.— There was formerly here a small Benedictine nunnery, founded by the ancestors of Roger de Morley. The villagers show a mound, a little above the village, at the bottom of a wood, in a most romantic situation, as the site on which the nunnery stood. Pop. 203.

Carr Rev. Charles, M. A. rector of Burnby
Dyson Rev. Charles, M. A. rector of Nunburnholme

*Farmers & Yeomen.*   Brigham Richard
Adamson Robert    Freer Thos.
Brigham Thos.    Leak Wm.

Pape Thos.    Wilkinson Wm.
Pipes John    Yates Robert
Simpson Robert

Buttle Saml. shoemaker & shopkeeper
Overend John, schoolmaster
Vause Francis, wheelwright

NUNKEELING, (P.) in the wap. and liberty of Holderness; 6 miles NW. of Hornsea. Agnes de Arches, in the reign of King Stephen, built a priory here for Benedictine Nuns. Nunkeeling is a perpetual curacy, in the patronage of R. R. Dixon, Esq. and of Harrington Hudson, Esq. lord of the manor. Pop. with Bewholme, 245.

Beal John, (private Asylum,) Moor cottage

*Farmers.*    Johnson Wm.
Dixon Thos.    Robson George
Holland Wm.

OCTON, in the parish of and wap. of Dickering, 8 miles W. Bridlington.

*Farmers.*    Lowson John
Brigham Mary    Webster Thos.
Stephenson John, gamekeeper

OCTON GRANGE, in the parish Thwing, and wap. of Dickering, miles WNW. of Bridlington.

Brigham John, farmer
Marshall Robert, farmer

OSGODBY, in the parish of Hemingbrough, wap. of Ouse and Derwent, and liberty of Howdenshire, 2 miles NE. of Selby. Population, 185.

*Farmers.*    Lakeland James
Bussey Benj.    Morritt George
Calvert John    Quarton Thos.
Calvert George    Tennant Richard
Dibb Thos.    Tindall Geo.
Hobson Robert,    Tindall Wm.
  Osgodby hall    Wood Wm.

Brown Michael, corn miller
Douglas Eliz. vict. Half Moon
Wales Thos. shopkeeper

OTTRINGHAM, (P.) in the wap. and liberty of Holderness, 6 miles SE. of Hedon. The church is an ancient structure, dedicated to St. Winifred, in the gift of the Chancellor of the college of Oxford, and the Rev. John Mackereth is the perpetual curate.— There is also a neat Methodist chapel built in 1815, and a small free school for 20 children. Population, 637.

Letters are received every Mon. Wed. and Sat. by Wing's caravan, arrives at noon, departs 5 evening.

Dunn R. Christopher, gentleman
Dunn Robert, schoolmaster

ggleston Wm. horse dealer
'igg Benj. vict. White Horse
Yebster Robert, corn miller

| Blacksmiths. | Webster Richard |
| ngram Wm. | Grocers. |
| Wellingham Geo. | Morris Richard |
| Wright Hugh | Smith John |
| 'armers & yeomen. | Wright Hugh |
| Henkin Wm. | Shoemakers. |
| Henkin Christr. | Boynton Wm. |
| Henkin Eliz. | Boothby James |
| arlin Wm. | Holderness John |
| Junn Isaac | Robinson Robert |
| ggleston Wm. | Tailors. |
| Hibson John | Bridling James |
| Hibson Jonathan | Jackson Wm. |
| lefferson Wm. | Wheelwrights. |
| azenby Mary | Johnson Edward |
| ider James | Morris Richard |
| Ichofield Isaac | |

Carriers— Christopher Wilson &
John Wellingham to Hull, South Frod-
ngham, Holmpton, and Skeckling,
every Tu. and Fri.

*Owbrough*, in the parish of Swine,
wap. and liberty of Holderness, 6 mls.
NNW. of Hedon.

*Owsthorpe*, in the parish of Pock-
ington, and wap. of Harthill, 2½ mls.
NNE. of Pocklington. Pop. 9.

*Owstrop*, in the parish of Eastring-
on, wap. and liberty of Howdenshire,
N miles ENE. of Howden.

OWSTWICK, in the parishes of
Garton and Rooss, wap. and liberty
of Holderness, 8 mls. ENE. of Hedon.
Population 139.

| Farmers. | Ford John |
| Baxter Wm. | Smith Joseph |
| Coates John | |

· *Carrier*—Wm. Ford to Hull every
Tuesday.

OWTHORN, (P.) in the wap. and
liberty of Holderness; 5 mls. NE. of Pa-
rington. This village, situated on the shore
of the German Ocean, has suffered much
from the encroachments of the sea, which
are averaged at from 1 to 2½ yards annually
along the coast. The church, dedicated to
St. Peter, which was erected here by one of
the benevolent Sisters, (so well known in the
annals of history) on the night of February
16th, 1816, fell with a most tremendous crash
into the bosom of the ocean. The living is
a vicarage, of which the King is the patron,
and the Rev. James Robson the incumbent.
Population, 143.

| Farmers. | Ingram John |
| Atkinson Peter | Wing Daniel |
| Biglin Thomas | Wheelwrights. |
| Cookman Francis | Westerdale J. sen. |
| Dibb Wm, | Westerdale J. jun. |

Drew Newark, boatman
Hussey Phineas, grocer
Lamb John, blacksmith
Smith David, tailor
Tiplady Wm. schoolmaster
Turner Wm. corn miller

*Oxmardyke*, in the parish of Blacktoft, wap. and liberty of Howdenshire,
6 miles E. of Howden.

PAINTHORPE, in the parish of
Kirby Underdale, and wap. of Buck-
rose, 7 miles N. of Pocklington.
Machell Robert, Esq.

| Farmers, | Kirby John |
| Beal Richard | White John |
| Clarkson Wm. | Wilson Timothy |
| Jennings Geo. | Wright Philip |

*Park - House*, in the parish of
Thornton, and wap. of Harthill; 7
miles SW. of Pocklington.

## PATRINGTON, (P.)

in the wap. and liberty of Holderness; 10
miles from Hedon, 18 from Hull, 25 from
Hornsea, 57 from York, and 188 from London. The church, which is a beautiful
Gothic structure, in the form of a cross, is
dedicated to St. Patrick, from which Saint
the town is said to derive its name. The
patronage of the living is in Clare Hall,
Cambridge, and the Rev. John Mansfield is
the rector. Here is a Methodist Meeting
House, and an Independent chapel. The
market is on Saturday. Several small vessels trade from hence to Hull and London
with corn chiefly, and many vessels are employed in the lime and coal trade from the
West Riding. A navigable creek of the
Humber, called Patrington Haven, comes
within about a mile of this place. Patrington is supposed by Camden to have been the
Prætorium of Ptolemy, and about sixty
years ago a stone was dug up here, which has
evidently formed part of a Roman altar,—
Population, 1244.

*Post-master*—W. JEFFERSON.

Letters arrive every Mon. Wed. and Sat. by
John Wing's Accommodation coach, at
12 o'clock, and are dispatched at 4 in
the afternoon of the same days.

Fewson David, gentleman
Metcalfe Rev. Robert, curate, Rec-
tory house
Pearson John, gentleman
Sawyer John, gentleman
Wreghit Margaret, gentlewoman

| Blacksmiths. | Edson Robt. sen. |
| Carter Edward | Edson Robt. jun. |

*Boot & Shoemakers.*
Bell John
Carter John
Carter Wm.
Cartwright Geo.
Conniston Samuel
Cousins John
Dring Robert
Gibson John
Lazenby John
Wallis John
Watson North

*Bricklayers.*
Drew Wm.
Moore Thomas

*Butchers.*
Newcombe John
Pearson Robert
Pearson Widow

*Corn-millers.*
Hopper Wm.
Hopper Thos.
Kirk Porter

*Farmers.*
Chesman William
Eastfield house
Chesman John
Dunn James
Fenwick Thos.
Fewson John
Giles John
Hall Matthew
Johnson Eliz.
Little Wm.
Marshall George
Munby Joseph
Pearson Robert
Sayles Robert
Thorp John
Thorp Wm.
Towse Richard

*Gardeners.*
Wood Christr.

*Inns and Taverns.*
Board, William Holmes
Board, Richd. Burrell, (& corn mert.) Haven side
Sloop, Thomas Jackson, Haven side
Three Tuns, Wm. Jefferson, (& common brewer)
Three Tuns, John Escreet
Andrew Wm. cooper
Arnet Rev. Wm. (Methodist)
Barron Wm. coal dealer
Blenkarn Thos. joiner
Coates Edw. principal waiter
Conniston Jas. governor of poor-house
Foster Robert, veterinary surgeon
Foster John, castrator
Hill Thomas, excise officer
Holmes Wm. common brewer
Kirkwood Matthew, coal dealer
Kemp Rev. Wm. (Methodist)
Langthorp Thomas, parish clerk

Wright John
*Grocers & Drapers.*
Aisthorpe Wm.
Barrow Jane
Chapman Jane
Dunn Robert
Harper Isaac
Lazenby John
Thompson Jane
Wallis Richard

*Mole Catchers.*
Penrose Richard
Penrose George

*Plumbers & Glaziers*
Blenkarn John
Blenkarn Thos.
Johnson Christr.
Langthorne Thos.

*Saddlers.*
Harrison John
Wright George

*Schoolmasters.*
Clapham John
Hobson Edmund
Smith Henry

*Straw Hat Mfrs.*
Blenkarn Eliz.
Webster Mary Ann

*Surgeons.*
Bromley James
Clifford Robert
Kirkby N. W.

*Tailors.*
Firth Robert
Hilton John
Medforth Robert
Newcombe John
Norton Robert
Ramsey Thos.

*Wheelwrights.*
Andrew Aaron
Harrison James

Mortson John, fruiterer
Overton Edward, painter
Penrose Mary Ann, millnr & dress mkr.
Pinder Wm. toll bar keeper
Pratman James, hawker
Rider Thomas, brick and tile maker
Robinson Joseph, hawker
Smiles David, coal and lime merchant, Haven side
Sutcliffe Wm. vessel owner, Havenside
Wreghit John, clock and watchmaker

*Carriers.*
John Barrett to Hull every Tuesday & Friday, dep. 1 mg. ret. 9 night.
John Wing, (caravan) to Hull every Mon. Wed. & Sat. at 4 afternoon.
*Water Carrier*—W. Sharp to Wakefield
COACH—William Thorp, to the Rein Deer, Hull, every Tuesday, dep. 6 morn. ret. 9 at night.

PAUL or PAGHILL, (P.) in the wap. and liberty of Holderness; 3 miles SW. of Hedon, pleasantly situated on the East side of the Humber. This village, during the late war, was in great fame for its dock-yard, where ships of the line of as high a rate as seventy-fours were built. The church, dedicated to St. Andrew and St. Mary, is a very ancient building, and is generally supposed to have been erected before the Conquest. The living is a vicarage, in the patronage of the Archbishop of York. Here is also a Methodist chapel, with a Sunday school attached to it.   Pop. 486.

Rev. Lamplugh Hird, vicar
Bowman Rev. John, curate

*Farmers.*      Roundhill Widow
Champney George  Tomlin Alfred D.
Hall Thos.          Willingham Rich.
Harrison & Empson  *Shoemakers.*
Iveson Wm.          Eastwood Wm.
Leonard Abraham  Lee George
Malthouse Wm.    *Tailors.*
Richardson John   Rider Thomas
Richardson Thos.  Walker Robert
Aucock John, vict. Royal Oak
Craddock Geo. vict. Humber Tavern
Iveson Robert, land surveyor
Liddle Wm. assessor
Sanderson James, grocer
Stovin Susanna, Boreas hill
*Carriers by Land*—George Wright, to Hull, Tu. & Sat. dep. at 6 morn. ret. 7 evening.
*Carriers by Water*—John Aucock and Wm. Starker, every Tuesday and Saturday to Hull.

*Peasthorpe*, in the parish of Welwick, wap. and liberty of Holderness; 1 mile SSE. of Patrington.
*Ploughlang*, in the parish of Welwick, wap. and liberty of Holderness; 1 mile SSE. of Patrington.

*Pluckham*, in the parish of Wharram Percy, and wap. of Buckrose ; 8 miles NE. of Pocklington.

## POCKLINGTON, (P.)

In the wap. of Harthill, and liberty of St. Peter's ; 7 miles from Market-Weighton, 17 from Driffield, 17 from Malton, 13 from York, and 195 from London. The places of worship in Pocklington are the parish church, a very plain homely structure, dedicated to All-Saints, of which the Rev. Charles Wolf Eyre, B.D. is vicar, and the Dean of York, the patron. An Independent chapel, of which the Rev. Thomas Hutton is minister ; a Methodist chapel, a small Roman Catholic chapel, and a chapel belonging to the Primitive Methodists. Here is a nobly endowed Free School, for teaching the dead languages to an unlimited number of scholars, belonging to the town and neighbourhood of Pocklington, with a revenue from lands of from twelve to fourteen hundred pounds per annum, Rev. Thos. Shield, B.D. master, Rev. Thomas Brown, sub-master, who is entitled to one-third of the profits, & Rev. David Jones, usher. There is also a National School, erected at the sole expense of Robert Dennison, Esq. of Kilnwick Percy, and very liberally supported by the gentry in the town. Average number of scholars, 75 boys and 60 girls. In 1814, an act of parliament was passed for making a navigable canal from East Cottingwith to Street Bridge, (about a mile from Pocklington) which has been completed and considerable business is now carried on in bringing to the place coal, lime, manure, and merchandise, and taking away corn, flour, timber, and other articles. The market day is on Saturday, and the races on the second of May in every year. In a gravel pit in Barnsley field, near this town, were dug up in 1763, four human skeletons ; three were without coffins, the fourth was enclosed in a coffin with an urn at the head, on the outside of which were engraved several ancient characters. Population, 1962.

## POST-MASTER—Matthew Jackson, *Office, New Pavement.*

| Places from whence Letter bags are recvd. | Distance. | Postage | Arrival of Mails. | Departure of Mails. |
| --- | --- | --- | --- | --- |
| York, .......... | 13 | 4d. | 8 morning, winter. | 4 evening summer and winter. |
| Hull, .......... | 27 | 6 | 7 morning, summer | |
| Beverley, ........ | 18 | 5 | ditto. | ditto. |
| Market-Weighton, | 7 | 3 | ditto. | ditto. |
| Driffield, ....... | 17 | 7 | ditto. | ditto. |

### DIRECTORY.

Armitage Rev. John, Chapmangate
Bagley Geo. high constable of Wilton Beacon, Hungate
Beal Thomas, yeoman, Hungate
Bland Anthony, yeoman, Hungate
Brown Rev. Thos. curate, Chapmangt.
Clarkson Geo. gent. Chapmangate
Clarkson Geo. yeoman, Chapmangate
Cook Wm. gent. West green
Craggs Wm. gent. Smithy hill
Dewsbury Mrs. Mary, gentlewoman, Union street
Elliott Samuel, gent. Brass castle hill
Hagyard Thos. yeoman, Chapmangt.
Harrison Jonathan, gent. Chapmangt.
Holmes Sarah, gentwmn. Chapmangt.
Howden Matthew, yeoman, Hungate
Hudson Mrs. Ann, gentlewmn. Hungt.
Hutton Rev. Thomas, Independent minister, George street
Johnson Thomas, gent. Hungate
Jones Rev. David
La Plain John, gent. Market place
Lofthouse John, gent. Hungate
Lofthouse Thos. gent. Hungate
Lofthouse Geo. yeoman, Hungate
Richardson Thos. gent. Hall garth
Richardson Mrs. Ann, Swine market
Scaife Christr. gent. Brass castle hill
Seymour W. P. gent. Chapmangate
Spurr Mrs. Jane, Chapmangate
Stalliard John, gent. Yellow house
Staveley Mrs. Susannah, Brasscastle hill
Thompson Richd. gent. Chapmangate
Walker Wm. gent. Chapmangate
Wedell John, gent. Chapmangate
Wilkinson Mrs. Ruth, George street
Wolton Mrs. Eliz. Chapmangate

*Academies, Boarding and Day.*
Jackson Robert, (day) Chapmangate
National, John Banks, West green
Newsom Daniel, (day) George street
Pocklington School, Rev. Thomas Shield, B. D. West green
Wilkinson John, (day) Chapmangate
Wright Miss Ann, (ladies' boarding) Chapmangate
Wrightson Miss Ann, (ladies' boarding) Yellow house

*Attornies and Solicitors.*
Holmes Nathaniel, Chapmangate
Powell James, George street

*Auctioneers and Appraisers.*
Lowe John Nathan, George street
Scaife Thomas, Chapmangate

*Bacon and Butter Factors.*
Hudson Henry, Market place
Pape Henry, (& corn dlr.) Swine mkt.

*Bakers.*
Fife Thomas, Market place
Think James, Hungate
Whitwell Ann, Market place

*Blacksmiths.*
Easton John, Church lane
James Wm. George street
Myers Emanuel, Hungate
Richardson Thomas, Hungate
Richardson Thomas, Chapmangate
Richardson John, Back lane

*Booksellers and Stationers.*
Abbey Thomas, Market place
Easton John, (& printer) Market pl.
Jackson Robert, Market place

*Boot and Shoemakers.*
Donn Robert, Smithy hill
Easton John, (and inspector of raw hides) Market place
Lund Wm. May, Swine market
Marshall Thos. (& tea dlr.) Union st.
Pexton Geo. Market place
Richardson Wm. Market place
Richardson Robert, Smithy hill
Rispin William, Market place
Todd Robert, Chapmangate
Wright William, (and patten maker) Chapmangate

*Braziers and Tinners.*
Barnby Richard, Market place
Graves Thomas, Market place

*Breweries.*
Collison Elisha, Chapmangate
Stables Seth, Chapmangate
Staveley Mrs. Ann, Chapmangate

*Bricklayers and Builders.*
Dove William, Chapmangate
Grant Thomas, Chapmangate
Ireland John, George street
Richardson Wm. Chapmangate
Richardson Thos. Market place
Ward Stephen, Market place

*Butchers.*
Brown Henry, Market place
Catton Thomas, New pavement
Cook Thomas, West green
Harland Thomas, Chapmangate
Silborn James, Swine market
Staveley Thomas, George street
Terry Thomas, Market place
Thomas John, Market place
Todd John, Hungate

Wilson James, Chapmangate

*Chemists and Druggists.*
Botterill William, Market place
Hornby Thomas, Market place
Kittle Albine, Market place

*Clock and Watch Makers.*
Fryer John, (& silversmith) Waterloo buildings
Milner Reuben, West green

*Coopers.*
Nicholson John, Waterloo buildings
Stockton Robert, Market place
Tindale James, (and winnowing chine maker) Market place
Tindale William, Smithy hill

*Corn Millers.*
Dunn Richard, London street
English Richard, Market place
Overend Timothy, Devonshire mills
Peart James, Low mill
Smith Ellen, Clock mill

*Currier and Leather Seller.*
Rispin George, Union street

*Farmers.*
Beal James, Clay field
Beal Thomas, Hungate
Catton Thomas, New pavement
Cook Wm. West green
Fallowfield Francis, Market place
Giles John, Toft house
Ibbotson Hugh, Chapmangate
Kettlewell Thos. sen. Chapmangate
Moor Wm. Pocklington common
Robinson Richard, Woodhouse
Smith William, North field
Staveley Thomas, Chapmangate
Vause John, Pocklington common
Walker John, Hungate
Wragg Thomas, Chapmangate

*Farriers.*
Catton Thomas, Hungate
Prest Jas. (& cow doctor) Market pl.

*Fellmongers.*
Blanchard John, Chapmangate
Blanchard George, Union street

*Flour and Provision Dealers.*
Allison Ann, Market place
Bellerby William, Hungate
Biass Daniel, Market place
Martindale Thomas, Hungate
Rispin James, Market place
Skelton John, opposite Smithy hill
Smith George, Market place
Smith John, Hungate
Stathers William, Market place
Stathers James, Chapmangate
Swann Thomas, New pavement

*Gardeners and Seedsmen.*
Evans John, Union street
Foster John, Union street

Goodyear Wm. Chapmangate
Murgatroyd John, Union street

*Glovers.*

Blanchard John, Chapmangate
Blanchard Geo. Union street
Hall Wm. Market place
Hall John, Market place

*Grocers and Drapers.*

Baldwin Mary, Market place
Bellerby Wm. Hungate
Biass Daniel, Market place
Catton John, Market place
Clark John, Market place
Davison Sawden, Market place
Hagyard Wm. Market place
Hagyard Thomas, Market place
Martindale Thomas, Chapmangate
Powell Wm. (& tailor) Market pl.
Rocks Charles, (and agent to the
  Phœnix Fire office) Market place
Wright Thos. (& tailor) New pavement

*Hair Dressers.*

Hodgson Henry, Swine market
Kispin James, Market place

*Hat Dealers, &c.*

Barnby Richard, Market place
Catton John, Market place
Hagyard Thomas, Market place
Jackson Thomas, Market place
Alister Thos. (mfr.) Chapmangate
Powell Wm. Market place
Wright Thomas, New Pavement

*Inns and Taverns.*

Bay Horse, Ralph Johnson, Market pl.
Black Bull, Thos. Terry, Market pl.
Black Swan, Dnl. Harland, Market pl.
Buck, Thos. Richardson, Market pl.
Canal Inn, Robt. Marfitt, Canal head
Cross Keys, Wm. Johnson, Smithy hill
Dog & Duck, Rt. Hay, New pavement
Feathers Inn, Francis Fallowfield,
  Waterloo buildings
Horse Shoes, Thos. Wilson, Market pl.
New Inn, John Geo. Overend, Canal hd.
Red Lion, Thos. Staveley, George st.
Star, Ann Walker, Market place
Wellington Inn, Ann Mary Davill,
  Canal side
White Swan, Francis Bell, New
  pavement
Windmill, Thos. Grant, Chapmangt.

*Ironmongers and Dealers in Hardware.*

Abbey Thomas, Market place
Barnby Richard, Market place
Cook James, Market place
Jackson Robert, Market place

*Joiners, Builders, and Cabinet Makers.*

Branswick Francis, George street
Hall Richard, Back lane
Harrison John, Chapmangate
Hodge Thos. Swine market
Ilson Robert, George street

Richardson Wm. (cabinet maker and
  upholsterer) New pavement

*Milliners and Dress Makers.*

Dove Ann, Smithy hill
Hudson Eliza, Hungate
Judson Miss Mary, George street
Swan Ann, New pavement

*Painters.*

Scaife William, Church lane
Suarr William, New pavement

*Plumbers and Glaziers.*

Gash John, Swine market
Johnson John, Market place
Scaife Thomas, Hungate

*Saddlers.*

Gilbertson Thomas, Market place
Linwood John, Market place

*Shopkeepers.*

Allison Ann, Market place
Bishop Ann, Union street
Cook Thomas, Market place

*Spirit Merchants.*

English Richard, Union square
Gardham William and John, (and
  seedsmen) Union street
Johnson Ralph, Market place

*Straw Hat Makers.*

Cook James, Market place
Cook Mary, Market place
Ware Elizabeth, Market place

*Surgeons.*

Bell John, Market place
Bell Richard, (& coroner for the East
  Riding) Chapmangate
Danson Edward, Chapmangate
Hornby Thomas, Market place
Kettlewell Thomas, Chapmangate
Marshall Wm. Market place
Raeburn J. D. White house, near
  George street

*Tailors and Drapers.*

Brigham George, Chapmangate
Butler Thomas, Chapmangate
Cook William, Hungate
Craggs Thomas, Chapmangate
Scaife James, Market place
Stubbs Wm. Church lane
Ward Robert, Chapmangate
Watt Bannister, Swine market

*Tallow Chandlers.*

Jackson Matthew, New pavement
Jackson John, Hungate

*Tanner.*

Wilson Thos. Knowlton, Union st.

*Wheelwrights.*

Bradley Joseph, Market place
Stubbs Richard, Chapmangate
Stubbs Henry, Chapmangate
Winter Wm. Hungate

*Miscellany.*

Armitage Wm. cattle dlr. London st.
Askham James, woolstapler & dealer in worsted & yarn, Chapmangate
Briggs Wm. dealer in hosiery yarn, Chapmangate
Gardham Thos. rope mkr. Union St.
Gash John, earthenware dealer, Swine market .
Hodgson John, dyer, Hungate
Kirtland Wm. whip-maker, Union st.
Richardson William, stone mason, George street.
Sanderson Robert, constable.
Scalfe Jas. sub-distributor of stamps, (for Robert Osborne, Esq. Stamp Office, Hull)
Stables Seth, maltster, Chapmangate
Stonehouse F. excise officer, Chapmangate .
Swan Clifford, wood turner and fancy chair maker, New pavement
Swan Mark, lock keeper, Canal head
Wilson Geo. glass, &c. dlr. Market pl.
Witty John, corn factor,

### CARRIERS BY LAND.

Mary Giles, to Coppergate warehouse, York, on Wed. and Sat. departs 3 morning, returns 9 evening
John Metcalf & John Ward to Huggate, every Saturday
Robert Manners, to the King's Arms, Fossbridge, York, on Thu. and Sat. dep. 3. mg. ret. same day.—
To Hull, every Mon. dep. 7. evg. and ret. at 3 on Wed. (stops at Coach & Horses, Mytongt. Hull)
Mary Hodgson, to Market-Weighton, every Wednesday
Jas. Thompson, to York, Thu. & Sat. dep. 3 mg. ret. same day
John Cockburn, to Hull, Mon. & Thu.

### CARRIERS BY WATER.

The *Union Packet*, sails alternately from Pocklington Canal head to Tummon and Smithson's wharf, High st. Hull, and from thence to Pocklington Canal hd. every week

POCKTHORPE, in the parish of Nafferton, and wap. of Dickering ; 4 miles NNE. of Driffield.

Hall Wm. Esq. Pockthorpe hall
Milner John, farmer

PORTINGTON, in the parish of Eastrington, wap. and liberty of Howdenshire ; 4 miles NE. of Howden. Population with Cavil, 98.

*Farmers.*
Bell John
Bell Elizabeth
Bell Henry, Grange

PRESTON, (P.) in the wap. of Holderness, and liberties of St. Peter and Holderness; 1 mile N. of Hedon. The church, of which the Rev. John Dixon is vicar, and the Sub-dean of York patron, is dedicated to All Saints. Here is a public school, erected in October, 1718, and endowed with the moiety of the rent of 39 acres of land, which is annually let to the best bidder, in pursuance of the will of Thomas Holme, the other moiety is given for the benefit of the poor of the township, at the discretion of the minister and churchwardens. Here are chapels for the Methodists and Primitive Methodists. Pop. 828.

Harrison Sarah, gentlewoman
Mackereth George, surgeon

*Blacksmiths,*
Ireland David
Sharp William

*Bricklayers,*
Pickering Wm.
Stephenson Richd.
Sunderland Adam.

*Butchers,*
Allinson John
Campion John
Drew Edward

*Corn Millers,*
Simpson John
Watson Robert S.

*Farmers & Yeomen,*
Asey J. F.
Biglin John
Branton Francis
Branton John
Brocklebank Geo.
Burn John
Burn Edward
Burnham Edward
Burnham Wm.
Dixon Richard
Dodds Thomas
Garnett Wm.
Johnson John
Johnson Wm.
Luck William
Machill John
Pallister John
Park Godfrey
Reed Thomas
Robinson Martin

Shillito Wm.
Simpson Joseph
Smith William
Storey Robert
Trowill John
Walker John
Ward Michael
Watson John
Wellington John
Wilson Thomas
Winteringham G.

*Gardeners,*
Fisher John
Hockney John
Hockney Wm.

*Grocers,*
Fewster David
Mackereth John
Mason Catharine
Milner James
Webster Francis

*Shoemakers,*
Harrison Richd.
Harrison Wm.
Jackson Peter
Jackson George
Pearson Wm.
Pearson John
Penrose Thomas
Stow John

*Tailors,*
Parker John
Pearson Thomas
Robinson John

Avison Thomas, horse breaker
Champney Mary, spirit merchant
Duke Isaac, weaver
Dunn Joseph, parish clerk
Fewster David, wheelwright
Hanson John, governor of poor house
Leaf James, vict. Queen's Head
Luck Mark, schoolmaster
Milner James, beast jobber
Pickard Wm. vict. King's Head
Robinson Martin, overseer

Thompson Jane, vict. Cock & Bell

West John, schoolmaster

*Carriers*—Robert Brown and Thomas Dalton, to Hull, Tuesday and Friday, depart 8 at morning, return 9 at night.

*Wing's Coach*, to Patrington & Hull, every Tuesday and Friday.

*Pricket Hill*, in the parish of Wresle, and wap. of Harthill; 2 miles NW. of Howden.

*Province* or *Provost's Fee*, in the parish of South Cave, liberty of St. Peter, and wap. of Harthill; 3 miles SW. of South Cave. Pop. 209.

RAISTHORPE, in the parish of Wharram Percy, and wap. of Buckrose; 8 miles SE. of Malton. Pop. with Birdsall, 47.

Jewitson John, farmer

*Raywell*, see Gentlemen's Seats.

REIGHTON, (P.) in the wap. of Dickering; 2½ mls. SE. of Hunmanby. The living is a discharged vicarage, of which the Rev. John Strickland is the incumbent, and Sir Wm. Strickland, Bart. the patron. Pop. 217.

Strickland Arthur, Esq. Reighton hall

| *Blacksmiths,* | Johnson Thomas |
|---|---|
| Hutchinson Ralph | Myers John |
| Scrivener John | Whitty Robert |
| *Farmers,* | Wood John |
| Cross Richard | *Grocers, &c.* |
| Fowler Thos. | Waller Christphr. |
| Garton Thos. | Welbourn Thos. |

Holtby Richard, carpenter

Omand Thos. vict. Dotterill Inn

RICCALL, (P.) in the wap. of Ouse and Derwent, liberties of Howdenshire and St. Peter's; 10 miles S. of York. The church is dedicated to St. Mary, and the living, which is a discharged vicarage, is in the gift of the prebendary of Riccall. There is at this place an endowed school, for teaching twelve poor children to read. The village of Riccall is situated near the river Ouse, and is memorable as the landing place of Harfager, king of Norway, in 1066.* Here are two manors in this parish, one of them belonging to the Prebendary, and the other to the Bishop of Durham. On the west of the village, and impending on the banks of the river are the magnificent remains of the episcopal manor-house of *La. Wel. Hall;* and the mansion is surrounded by three broad moats, the river being the

* See vol. ii. page 21.

western boundary. About fifty years ago, when the land in this village first came into cultivation, several entire skulls were dug up in good preservation, and a rough flag, four feet square, with a cross barbarously sculptured, was found here, and at present forms part of the pavement of the parish church. The population of this village now amounts to 599.

Hare John, gentleman

Hayland Thos. surgeon & apothecary

Kendall Rev. Frederick, A.B. vicar

Parker Rev. Wm. vicar of Skipwith, (magistrate)

Richardson Toft, Esq. Riccall hall

| *Blacksmiths,* | Romans Ann, |
|---|---|
| Douthwaite Jonth. | Wheel hall |
| Hare Geo. | Romans John |
| *Bricklayers,* | Ruff Robert |
| Davis James | Silversides Mark |
| Wood Charles | Silversides Rbt. |
| *Carpenters,* | Smith W. J. |
| Pratt T. sen. | Thompson Wm. |
| Pratt T. jun. | (& butcher) |
| *Corn millers,* | Tomlinson Geo. |
| Camplejohn Rd. | (& shopkpr.) |
| Spink John | Walker Joseph |
| *Farmers & Yeomen,* | Wardle James |
| Ayres Job | Wardle Ann |
| Blanshard Jas. | Wilson Richard |
| Boswell W. & J. | Wormley Thos. |
| Bulmer Wm. and | *Shoemakers,* |
| coal merchant | Camplejohn Wm. |
| Burland Wm. | Patrick Richard |
| Daniel Thos. | Silversides Guy |
| Fentiman John | *Shopkeepers,* |
| Longfellow Wm. | Carr Thomas |
| Moody Geo. | Davison Wm. |
| Myers Geo. | Jefferson Wm. |

Newsham Richard, parish clerk

Pratt Richard, cabinet maker

Silversides Guy, vict. Grey Hound

Smith W. J. vict. Drovers Inn

Stokes James, tailor

Swinbank Isaac, vict. Hare & Hounds

Thompson Elizabeth, vict. Shoulder of Mutton

Wilson Robert, schoolmaster

*Carriers.*

John Carr, Sarah Carr, and Thomas Muschamp, to York, every Sat. and to Selby, every Mon. dep. 7 mg. and ret. in the evg.

Two Coaches pass through this place from York at ¼ past 8 mg. to meet the Steam Packets at Selby, and return according to tide.

RILLINGTON, (P.) in the wap. of Buckrose; 5 miles NE. of Malton. Situated on the banks of the Derwent, which is navigable from hence to the Humber, for small vessels. The church is dedicated to St. Andrew; and the living which is in the gift of the king, is enjoyed by the Rev. James Carter Green. In addition to the parish church, there is here a chapel for the Independents, and another for the Methodists. A court-baron is held here annually for the recovery of debts under 40s. Pop. 683.

Allanson Thomas, surgeon
Ruston Nicholas, sen. gentleman
Ruston Thos. jun. gentleman
Sykes Rev. Geo. Independent minister

*Blacksmiths,*
Simpkin Robert, (& farrier)
Simpkin Joseph, (& farrier)
*Farmers & Yeomen,*
Adamson James
Banks Robert
Dale Jonathan
Harper Robert
Harrison John
Lamb Thos. sen.
Lamb Thos. jun.
Ouston Charles
Pickering Saml.
Preston Thos. sen.
Ruston Nicholas, jun.
Ruston Thos. jun.
Stephenson John, sen.
Stephenson John, jun.
Young Wm.
*Farmers at Rillington Moor,*
Bower Mark
Calam John
Edwards Matthew

Harrison Wm.
Hill John
Hopper John
Kay John
Stephenson Thos.
Ward Geo.
Wilkinson Wm.
*Grocers,*
Dennison John
Hazlewood John, sen.
Simpkin John, sen.
Simpkin John, jun.
Turner Ann
*Shoemakers,*
Collinson Wm. sen.
Collinson Wm. jun.
Collinson Robert
Harrison Thos.
Severs Wm.
*Tailors,*
Fetherstone John
Spink David
*Wheelwrights,*
Hazlewood John, sen.
Hazlewood John, jun.

Beilby John, gardener
Cook Joseph, butcher
Croser William, flour dealer
Dixon James, brick maker
Mason Francis, stay maker
Owston Francis, bricklayer
Piercy Robert, schoolmaster
Postdill Christopher, plough maker
Preston Thomas, jun. vict.
Shaw John, shopkeeper
Simpkin John, sen. watch maker
Spanton Matthew, brewer
Stephenson Anthony, vict.

RIMSWELL, in the parish of Owthorn, wap. and liberty of Holderness; 6 miles N. of Patrington. The church is a modern structure, built in 1800, and the manor belongs to Geo. Liddle, Esq. banker, Hull. Pop. 129.

*Farmers & Yeomen,* Cuthbert John
Biglin David    Harper Wm.
Burnham Robert    Harrison John

Rank James    Tennison Ann
Shields Marmaduke    Wright John
Tennison John

Batty John, grocer, &c.
Castle Henry, vict. Dog & Duck
John Batty, carrier to Hull every Tu.

*Ringbrough,* in the parish of Aldbrough, wap. and liberty of Holderness; 8 miles SE. of Hornsea.

RIPLINGHAM, in the parish of Rowley, and wap. of Harthill; 2½ miles E. of South Cave.

Thompson Rev. Joseph, curate Rowley.

*Risby,* in the parish of and wap. of Harthill; 4 miles of Beverley.

RISE, (P.) in the wap. and ty of Holderness; 6½ miles SW Hornsea. The church is a small pidated ancient structure, in chantry of which are several monuments, erected to the of the opulent family of Bethell, living is in the gift of the King the Rev. Nicholas Torre is the Population, 221.

Bethell Richard, Esq.
Holmes Rev. Nicholas, vicar of brough

*Farmers,*    Hudson Thos.
Carr Hugh    Jackson Francis
Dawson Francis    Knaggs John
Faulding John    Tanton Sarah
Faulding Charles

Cooper Robert, blacksmith
Evens Henry, shoemaker
Hall Thomas, carpenter
Hodgson Michael, parish clerk

RISTON LONG, (P.) in the and liberty of Holderness; 6½ ENE. of Beverley. The church dicated to St. Margaret, appears of great antiquity, and the which is a rectory in the patron the crown, is enjoyed by the James Torre. Pop. 361.

Jackson Peter, Esq. Riston grange
*Blacksmiths,*    *Grocers,*
Allman John    Allman John
Peck John    Harland Thos.
*Farmers,*    Wardill Thos.
Ball Wm.    *Shoemakers,*
Dales Peter    Coulson Dennis
Dales Thos.    Woodward Wm.
Green Wm.    *Tailors,*
Hornby John    Hall Robert
Jackson Thos.    Matthews James
Lowson Wm.    *Wheelwrights,*
Wise Wm.    Hall Wm.
Marshall Thos.

Green Wm. vict. Traveller
Matthews Edward, butcher
Peck Wm. bricklayer
Peck Simon, hawker
Walker Matthew, parish clerk

*Carriers.*—Thomas Wardell and Thomas Allison, to Hull every Tu. to Beverley every Sat.
John Allmon and Wm. Stockdale, to Beverley every Sat.

**Rooss**, (P.) in the wap. and liberty of Holderness; 8 miles E. of **Hedon**. The church, dedicated to All Saints, is a fine specimen of Gothic architecture, and the patron and rector is the Rev. Christopher Sykes.— The family vault of the Sykes's of **Sledmere**, is in this church. Population, 442.

Bilton Wm. gent.
Lorrimer Eliz. gentlewoman
Sykes Rev. Christopher, rector
Swann Rev. Charles, curate

| *Butchers,* | Wright John |
|---|---|
| Hoggit James | *Grocers,* |
| Johnson John | Thompson Robert |
| *Farmers,* | Wilkinson Jonth. |
| Atkinson J. | *Schoolmasters,* |
| Brown Wm. | Hodgson John |
| Clapinson Francis | Wallis Edward |
| Clapinson Thos. | *Shoemakers,* |
| Crissey Wm. | Dixon Wm. |
| Dent Thos. | Ellaby Geo. |
| Dickinson Wm. | Hayson John |
| Foster James | Marshall John |
| Ogram Thos. | Thompson Robt. |
| Pearson Richard | *Tailors,* |
| Smales James | Cook Thos. |
| Spoffard Thos. | Norrison Richard |
| Tindall Richard | (& draper) |
| Wallis John | *Wheelwrights,* |
| Wilkinson Marm. | Ion David |
| Wilkinson Robt. | Wilkinson Jonth. |

Atkinson Richard, bricklayer
Dunn Thomas, vict. Board
Ellaby J. & J. corn millers
Johnson John, brick mfr.
Patrick Matthew, blacksmith
Pattinson John, weaver

*Carriers*—Benjamin Cookman, Thomas Dunn, and Stephen Ganton, to Hull every Tuesday, depart at 1 in the morning, and return at 8 at night.

*Rotsea*, in the parish of Hutton Cranswick, and wap. of Harthill; 6 miles SE. of Driffield. Pop. 23.

**Routh**, (P.) in the wap. & liberty of Holderness; 4½ miles NE. of Beverley. The church, dedicated to All Saints, is a very ancient structure, and the living, which is a rectory, in the patronage of the Misses Ellerkers, is enjoyed by the Rev. John L. Hutchinson. Pop. 124.

Mitchin Richard, vict. Nag's Head
Newlove Thos. wheelwright

| *Farmers,* | Rayner Richard |
|---|---|
| Foster John | Stephenson Wm. |
| Hutty Rebecca | Whitty George |
| Jackson John | Wrigglesworth R. |
| Leonard Wm. | |

*Carrier*—Joseph Williamson, to Beverley every Sat.

*Rowton*, in the parish of Swine, wap. and liberty of Holderness; 7½ miles E. of Beverley.

*Rowley*, (P.) in the wap. of Harthill; 8½ miles ENE. of South Cave. The church, dedicated to St. Peter, is a small neat building, and the living, which is a vicarage, in the gift of the Hildyard family, is enjoyed by the Rev. Robert Croft. Population, 425.

*Rowlston*, in the parish of Mappleton, wap. and liberty of Holderness; 2 miles SSE. of Hornsea. The hall at this place is occupied by Miss Theresa Arneman. Pop. 54.

*Ruddings*, see Aughton Ruddings.

**Rudston**, (P.) in the wap. of Dickering; 5 miles W. of Bridlington. In Domesday book it is called Rodestane, and is probably so named from an Obelisk which stands in the church yard. The obelisk is one entire natural stone of the coarse rag, or mill stone grit, of the same kind and shape as the celebrated stones near Boroughbridge, which Camden, Leland, and Drake suppose to be Roman trophies, erected in commemoration of some victory. This obelisk is twenty nine feet four inches in height, and its length within ground has been traced to the depth of more than twelve feet, without reaching its bottom.— The church is dedicated to All Saints, and the living, of which the Rev. R. Metcalf, is vicar, is in the patronage of the Archbishop of York. Pop. 417.

Bosville Hon. Godfrey, Thorp hall
Metcalfe Rev. Francis, curate

| *Farmers,* | Moody Thos. |
|---|---|
| Dixon Thos. | Raywood James |
| Harris John | Robson James |
| Hopkinson Jph. | Shepherd Thos. |
| Hopper Martha | Sutterington Wm. |
| Moody John | |

*Grocers, &c.,*
Harrison Richard
Taylor Wm.
*Shoemakers,*
Goforth Wm.
Laycock James

*Tailors, &c.*
Howgate John
Preston Simon
Richardson Geo.
*Wheelwrights,*
Brown Wm.
Thomlinson Chas.

Bell John, blacksmith
Harrison Richard, schoolmaster
Major Ann, vict. Red Lion
Sutterington Wm. butcher

*Carriers,* George Redhead and Thomas Taylor, to Bridlington Wed. and Saturday.
Thomas Taylor and John Hopper go also to Driffield every Thur.

RUSTON, (Parva) in the parish of Lowthorpe, and wap. of Dickering; 4 miles NE. of Driffield. Pop. 140.

*Farmers,*
Baker George
Dixon Aaron

Lamplugh Jerm.
Ombler Richard
Welburn Geo.

Laycock James, shoemaker
Lowson Stephen, corn miller
Mallory Gibson, lime burner
Mallory Wm. bricklayer
Marshall John, vict. Gate
Oliver Thomas, gentleman

RYHILL, in the parish of Burstwick-cum-Skeckling, wap. and liberty of Holderness; 3 miles SE. of Hedon. Pop. 315.

Dunn Abraham, solicitor
Dunn Elizabeth, gentlewoman
Robinson John, land surveyor
Stickney Rebecca, gentlewoman

*Farmers,*
Brigham Richard
Dixon Wm.
Gibson Marm.

Goundrell David
Ingleby Wm.
Johnson Timothy
Rhodes Benjamin

Calvert Thomas, wheelwright
Heron Aaron, shoemaker
Hutchinson Robert, corn miller
Jackson Francis, tailor
Pickering John, blacksmith
Robinson James, tailor and grocer
*Carrier,* Jonathan Drew, to Hull every Tuesday.

*Rytham Gate,* in the parish of Seaton Ross, and wap. of Harthill; 5 miles S. of Pocklington.

*Saltagh,* in the parish of Ottringham, wap. and liberty of Holderness; 5 miles W. of Patrington.

SALTMARSHE, in the parish of Howden, wap. and liberty of Howdenshire; 4 miles SE. of Howden.—Population, 179.

Saltmarshe Philip, Esq. Hall.

*Farmers,*
Burton John, sen.
Burton John, jun.
Freeman T. Carr House
Barker Thomas, vict. Punch Bowl
Carlisle Wm. corn miller

Sissons Jonathan,
Walling Fen
Thompson John
Walker Wm. Saltmarshe Grange

SANCTON, (P.) in the wap. of Harthill; 2½ miles SE. of Market-Weighton. The church is dedicated to All Saints, and the living, which is in the gift of J. Broadley, Esq. is enjoyed by the Rev. Thomas Atkinson, vicar. There is a public charity school at this place for the education of the boys and girls, and endowed by Lady Vavasour with £20 per ann. There is a Catholic chapel in the East wing of Houghton hall for public worship of which the Rev. James Wrennall minister. Pop. with Houghton, 320.

Carr Wm. gentleman
Marshall James, gentleman
Nottingham John, gentleman
Selby Catharine, gentwmn. Houghton hall

*Blacksmiths,*
Kirby William
Lyon James
*Carpenters, &c.*
Atkinson Thomas
Hallam John
Kemplay Mark
*Farmers,*
Allison Thomas
Campbell John
Carr Wm.
Dickinson Thos.
Donkins John
Ella John
Hudson Thomas

Jewitt Robert
Leake John
Marshall Wm.
Stephenson Wm.
Swann Wm.
Todd Wm.
Turner George
Turner John
*Shoemakers,*
Berry John
Hudson John
Hutton John
*Shopkeepers,*
Atkinson Thomas
Turner Robert

Carter William, parish clerk
Hopper Mary, vict. Star
Swan Wm. schoolmaster

*Carriers*—Wm. Blythe, to Hull Tu. and Fri.; to Market-Weighton on Wed.
Robert Smart, to Hull Tu. & Fri.

*Sandholme,* in the parish of Eastrington, wap. and liberty of Howdenshire; 4½ miles ENE. of Howden.

*Sandholme,* see Storkill.

SCAGGLETHORPE, in the parish of Settrington, and wap. of Buckrose; 3½ miles ENE. of Malton. There is no place of divine worship here, except a chapel for the Primitive Methodists, who have also a Sunday school. Population, 222.

Day Rev. Edmund

*Butchers,*
Aveson Thomas
Thompson Mark
*Farmers & yeomen,*
Beal William
Brand Thomas
Candell Thomas

Doukes John
Harper Richard
Holmes Geo.
Lownsborough E.
Nichols James
Stockdale Nicholas
Taylor Thomas

Hutchinson Thomas, toll bar keeper
law Newyear, tailor
Joon John, shopkeeper
aylor Robert, vict. Ham & Cheese

*Scalby*, in the parish of Blacktoft, ap. and liberty of Howdenshire; 5½ iles WSW. of South Cave. Pop. 179.

SCAMPSTON, in the parish of Rillington, and wap. of Buckrose; 6 miles E. of Malton. The family of St. Quintin has a seat here; the mansion has a handsome appearance, and the grounds are graced with numerous plantations: an grat stone bridge crosses a fine stream of ar which runs through the park, where mous herds of deer give animation to prospect. Pop. 200.

Hckhobs Rev. Frederick
urrow Rev. John
arow Rev. Thomas
ood C. T. Esq. Mansion House

*Farmers,*
rdy John
dgson John
vell Wm.
see Wm.

Tindell Robert
Tindell Ann
*Wheelwrights,*
Holtby Thomas
Youngson Thos.

lner Samuel, gardener
ungson John, butcher

*Scaff* or *Sceaf,* in the parish of lme-on-Spalding-Moor, and wap. Harthill; 5½ miles SSW. of Market-ighton.

SCORBROUGH, (P.) in the wap. of thill; 5 miles N. of Beverley. Here is urch, dedicated to St. Leonard; the ng is a rectory, patron the Earl of Egre-t, and incumbent the Rev. Penistone La ir. There is also a seat of Lord Hotham, he cottage style, (occupied by John Hall, ) on the spot where stood the ancient sion of the Hothams, Baronets, which three times destroyed by fire. Pop. 86.

ll John, Esq.
ll Rev. Charles, curate

*Farmers,*
rk John
ferson John
Decoy
llace Ann, vict. Board

Milner Robert
Moore John
Moore William

SCORBBY, in the parish of Low ton, and wap. of Ouse & Derwent, illes ENE. of York.

Cooper Geo. yeoman, Grange

*Farmers,*
Craddock E.
Hallliey Robert
Johnson John
Johnson Richard

Newsum John
Robinson John
Rookes Thomas
Shaw John

SCRAYINGHAM, (P.) in the wap. of Buckrose; 10 miles NE. of York. The parish church is a small structure, dedicated to St. Peter, and the living, which is a rectory, in the gift of the King, is enjoyed by the Rev. Stuart Corby. Pop. 157.

Kirkby Henry, yeoman
Smyth Rev. J. R. B.A. curate

*Farmers,*
Bolton Richard
Dale William
Horsley Marm.
Horsley Wm.
Slater Joseph
Slater John

Thomas Francis
Todd Richard
Todd James
*Tailors,*
Driffield Wm.
Harbutt James

Bainbridge Robert, vict. Horse and Jockey
Fentiman John, schoolmaster
Foster John, cooper

SCULCOATES, (P.) in the wap. of Harthill, an ancient village, 1½ mile N. of Hull, on the west bank of the river Hull; and contained, not a century ago, only 100 inhabitants, but at present contains 10,449. The southern part of the parish, adjoining the town of Hull, is now formed into extensive streets, since the formation of the dock in 1774, and cannot be distinguished by a stranger from the town of Hull, properly so called; it is, however, in the county of York, and the petty sessions are held in a hall erected a few years ago. Jonas Brown, Esq. is the only resident magistrate, but some of the East-Riding magistrates attend weekly. The church is in the old village, and was rebuilt in 1760; it is dedicated to St. Mary, the King is the patron, and the Rev. William Preston, vicar. Near the Sessions-hall, and in the populous part of the parish, has this year been erected a new church, called Christ church, for which an act of parliament was obtained in 1814, vesting the presentation in the then subscribers of £100, and their survivors, when reduced to eight in number, who, with the vicar of Sculcoates, are the patrons.—It is a very handsome structure, with a square tower of white brick and Roche Abbey stone, in the pointed style of the time of Henry IV. æra 1400.—It will contain 1300 persons, 500 of whom are provided with free sittings. The whole cost was about £7000, part of which is not yet subscribed. The incumbent is the Rev. John King, M. A. who liberally advanced the sum necessary to complete the building, taking the chance of the sale of seats in return. On the 26th of September, 1822, this church received consecration from the Archbishop of York. Sculcoates can boast of a higher antiquity than Hull, being mentioned in Domesday book as one of the lordships of Ralph de Mortimer, who was one of the fortunate adventurers that accompanied the Conqueror from Normandy, and was lord of several manors hereabouts.

(Directory included with Hull.)

SEATON, in the parish of Sigglesthorne, wap. and liberty of Holderness; 3 miles WSW. of Hornsea.—The only place of public worship is a Methodist chapel, built in 1810, by subscription. Pop. 301.

*Farmers & yeomen,* Smith John
Garbert John
Granger John
Hall Wm.
Hardy John

*Shoemakers,*
Hall John
Harmon Wm.

Hardy Peter, vict. Barrel
Leak John, joiner
Miller John, grocer & draper
Paul Esther, widow, Seaton Grange
Pinder Geo. wheelwright
Smith David, blacksmith

*Carrier,* John Miller, to Hull on Tu. dep. 3. morn. ret. 9 evg.

SEATON ROSS, (P.) in the wap. of Harthill; 6 miles SSW. of Pocklington. The church, dedicated to St. Edmund, is a neat modern structure, of which the Rev. Thomas Brown is vicar, and the University of Cambridge the patron. Here is also a Methodist chapel. A smart shock of an earthquake was felt at this and several of the neighbouring villages, on the 18th of January, 1822. Pop. 477.

Alderson Rev. Wm. A. B. curate
Holmes John, yeoman

*Farmers,*
Chapham Robert
Cook Geo.
Dales James
Douthwaite Rt.
Hunter John, Rythamgate
Johnson Geo. Lincoln Flats
Kempley James

Robinson Richard
Seaton hall
Spite Hannah
Stubbins Thomas,
(& parish clerk)
Sykes John
Varvle Robert
Ward Matthew
Watson John, sen.
Watson John, jun.

Cook James, shoemaker
Cook Matthew, corn miller
Grant Nathaniel, tailor

Ibbotson Robert, carpenter & shopkeeper
Pexton William, blacksmith and vict. Blacksmiths' Arms
Rook Robert, corn miller
Train Wm. butcher
Watson William, collector of taxes, Seaton Lodge

*Carriers,* Thomas Batty, to the Fleece, Pavement, York; and Wm. Craven, to the King's Arms, Fossgate, York, every Sat. dep. 2 morn. ret. in the evening.
Thomas Wickliffe and Thomas Batty, to Market - Weighton every Wednesday.

SETTRINGTON, (P.) in the wap. of Buckrose; 4 miles ESE. of Malton—Sir Mark Masterman Sykes, Bart. has a seat here; it formerly belonged to the honourable family of the Mastermans, and by marriage with the heiress, came into possession of the present proprietor. The church is dedicated to St. Michael, and the Earl of Bridgewater is the patron. Pop. 535.

Todd Rev. Henry, F.S.A. rector, and chaplain in ordinary to his Majesty.
Mewers Wm. steward to Sir M. M. Sykes, Bart.

*Farmers,*
Atkinson John
Atkinson Robert
Bogg John
Brittain Joseph
Carr John
Carr Francis
Dunn John
Ford Jeremiah
Ford John
Haw Thos. and miller
Haw John, and miller

Harrison Francis
Hesp John
Kettlewood Matt.
Mawman John
Perren John
Potts John
Settrington Anth.
Smith John
Spink Francis
Stelling Richard
Taylor Tobias
Thomson John
Thomson Robert
Welbourn Wm.

Brown Leonard, joiner, painter, and victualler
Blackwell John, tailor
Chapman John, schoolmaster
Dixon Wm. grocer, draper, &c.
Dunn John, gamekeeper to Sir M. M. Sykes, Bart.
Edmandson John, wheelwright
Habkirk John, gardener to Sir M. M. Sykes, Bart.
Kettlewood John, blacksmith
Kirby John, shoemaker
Mawman John, horse dealer
Nelson John, joiner and appraiser
Wardell Thomas, butcher

SEWERBY, in the parish of Bridlington, and wap. of Dickering; it mile NE. of Bridlington. Population, including Marton, 317.

Greame. John, Esq. Sewerby hall

*Farmers & Yeomen,*
Clarkson Wm.
Jeweson Robert
Kirby Richard
Mason Richard
Rex Thomas
Sawdon Wm.
Smith Richard

Caisley Robert, vict. Bottle & Glass
Hodgson Francis, blacksmith
Pickering Christopher, shoemaker
Robson John, wheelwright
Rounding Wm. corn miller

SHERBURN, (P.) in the wap. of Buckrose; 12 miles ENE. of Malton. The church, dedicated to St. Hilda, is in the patronage of the Stricklands, and the Rev. Wm. Legard, A. B. is the vicar. Pop. 496.

Denton Rev. Charles Jones, B. A.
Raeburn T. D. surgeon

*Carpenters,*
Forge Wm.
Knaggs John
*Farmers & Yeomen,*
Barker Robert
Calverley Wm.
Clifford James
Colley Christr.
Dickinson Wm.
Ellis Wm.
Fox Robert
Fox Richard
Knaggs John
Morris John
Revis George
Steel Thomas
White John
Wilson Charles

*Grocers, &c.*
Fox Robert
Marston James
Smith Wm.
*Millers, (Corn)*
Owston Peter
Revis Theophilus
Revis John
*Shoemakers,*
Billingham Wm.
Boreman Wm.
Thompson John
Welburn Francis
*Tailors,*
Knaggs James
Lightfoot John
Watson George

Bell Wm. blacksmith
Johnson Robert, weaver
Marshall John, butcher
Revis George, vict. . and brewer, Pidgeon Pie
Whitehead John, schoolmaster

*Carrier,* Henry Clarkson, to Scarborough on Thu. and to Malton on Wed. and Sat.

SHIPTON, in the parish of Market Weighton wap. of Harthill, & liberty of St. Peter's; 2 miles NW. of Market-Weighton. There is a charity school here for the education of ten poor boys. The present trustees are Mr. John Smith and the Rev. R. C. Winpenny. Pop. 369.

Rev. R. C. Winpenny, B. A. curate & vicar of Market-Weighton.

*Butchers,*
Brigham Robert
Jackson Thomas
*Farmers,*
Brigham James
Dean Philip

Dickens Wm.
Martin Eliz.
Myers John
Smith John
Smith Robert
Stephenson Wm.
Thomas Henry
Walker John
Wilson John

*Shoemakers,*
Ogram Henry
Webster John
Wharton Robert
*Shopkeepers,*
Hagyard Robert
Thistlewaite Jas.
Thomas Wm.

Beal Peter, carpenter & wheelwright
Braithwaite John, blacksmith
Harrison Thomas, schoolmaster and land surveyor
Jackson Thomas, vict. Ship
Sherwood Wm. weaver

SIGGLESTHORNE, (P.)in the wap. and liberty of Holderness; 5 miles SW. of Hornsea. The church is a large Gothic structure, dedicated to St. Lawrence, of which the Rev. Wm. H. E. Bentick, A. M. is rector, and the King the patron. Here is a good national school, built by subscription, in 1813, and endowed with a donation of 400l. left by Sir Marmaduke Constable, Bart. late of Burton Constable. There is also a Girls' National School, erected in 1818, at the cost of Mrs. Bentick, and supported by her benevolence. Pop. 163.

Gibson ——, Esq. Sigglesthorne hall

*Farmers,*
AtkinChristopher
GrangerAlexander
Pexton John
Taylor Wm.
*Shoemakers,*
Harrison Geo.
Wilkinson John

Day John, schoolmaster
Fenwick John, blacksmith
Harrison Francis, shopkeeper
Harrison Wm. tailor and draper
Pinder James, carpenter

SKECKLING, or Burstwick-cum-Skeckling, (P.) in the wap. and liberty of Holderness; 3 miles SE. of Hedon. The church is an ancient structure, dedicated to All Saints, of which the Rev. Wm. Clarke, M. A. is vicar, and the executors of the Earl of Cardigan the patrons. There is in the chancel an elegant painting, representing the Sacrament of the Lord's supper. Population, 436.

Harrison John. gent.
Walker Margaret, gentlewoman

*Farmers,*
Alder David
Alvin Bartholomew
Binnington John, North Park
Champney Jas. Nut hill
Craggs Elizabeth
Crawforth Jane
Fisher George, Hall Field
Gibson William
Dairy Houses
Goundrill David
Grice Wm.
Harrison Wm. Kelsey Hill
Harrison Edmund
Kemp John

Kemp Simon
Kemp Wm.
Marritt John
Nicholson Mary
Robinson John,
  South Park
Stickney William,
  Ridgemout
Todd William,
  Nuttles
Vickerman John,
  Dairy Houses
Ward Edward

Wray Jas. Burst-
  wick hall
  *Grocers,*
Birks Thomas
Fewster James
  *Shoemakers,*
Kemp Wilfred
Marritt Thomas
  *Tailors,*
Birks Thomas
Ellerby Wm.
  *Wheelwrights,*
Crosby John
Jackson John

Alvin Robert, vict. Nag's Head
Drew John, schoolmaster
Rennardson Mark, blacksmith
Vickerman Wm. vict. Hare & Hounds

*Carriers.*—James Fewster, to Hull
  Tu. and Fri.
Christopher Wilson, to Hull, South
  Frodingham, Holmpton, and Ot-
  trington every Tu. and Fri.

SKEFFLING, (P.) in the wap. and
liberty of Holderness; 4 miles SE. of Pat-
trington. The church, dedicated to St
Helen, is a small but neat building, in the
patronage of the rector of Rise, and the
Rev. George Inman, A. M. is the perpetual
curate. Pop. 201.
  *Farmers,*          Grindall John
Atkinson Abraham   Jefferson Christr.
Baron Thomas       Stark John
Buck John          Wilson John
Catton Wm.

Buck Wm. vict. Sun
Coxworth Joseph, blacksmith
Crawforth John, shoemaker
Dunn Thomas, tailor
Harland John, shopkeeper
Marshall John, wheelwright
Pears Edward, schoolmaster

SKELTON, in the parish of Howden, wap. and liberty of Howdenshire;
2 miles SSE. of Howden. This village lies close to the river Ouse, and
near the Howden Dyke Ferry, where
passengers are landed from the steam
packets from Selby to Hull about
noon. Pop. 221.

Brown William, gent
Scholefield Wm. gent. Sand hall
Spofforth Samuel, yeoman, Newfield
  *Farmers,*          Long John, Grange
Jewitt Edward       Scruton John
Leighton Thos.      Ward William

Chester Thomas, carpenter
Hall Mary, vict. Lamb

SKERNE, (P.) in the wap. of Hart-
hill; 2½ miles SSE. of Driffield. The
church living here is a perpetual cura-
cy, in the patronage of R. Ark-
wright, Esq. and the Rev. Thomas
Ibbotson is the incumbent. Pop. 251,
  *Farmers,*          Peacock Duke
Dickson Geo.        Peacock John
Dickson Wm.         Taylor Michael
Goodlass Robert     Taylor Wm.
Goodlass John       Taylor Francis
Jennison Robert     Teale Ralph

Carrick Wm. flax dresser & corn miller
Eskrick David, tailor
Layburu Charles, vict. Board

SKIDBY, (P.) in the wap. of
Harthill; 4 miles SW. of Beverley.
The chapel, dedicated to St. Michael,
is subject to the vicar of Cottingham.
Population, 813.

Andrew Robert, gent,
Deans Rev. James, A. M. vicar
Jackson Wm. yeoman
  *Farmers,*          Thompson Barbara
Andrew Richard      Wilkinson John
Brankley Robert     Woflin Robert
Harrison John         *Grocers,*
Lyon Wm.            Hall George
Stephenson John     Jefferson John

Barton John, carpenter
Dickinson Robert, blacksmith
Hessey Wm. schoolmaster
Marshall Wm. tailor
Patrick Robert, shoemaker
Train Christr. vict. Half Moon
Watson Wm. corn miller

*Carriers*—George Hall and Jane Jefferson, to Hull every Tu. and Fri.

SKIPSEA, (P.) in the wap. and liberty of Holderness; 9 miles S. of Bridlington. The first lord of the whole of
Holderness resided here, in a stately castle;
the lofty mountain on which it proudly
stood is at Skipsea Brough, about half a
mile from Skipsea. The church is dedicated to All Saints; the Rev. Joseph Lowe
is vicar, and the Archbishop of York is the
patron. A ghost, of very ancient date, the
wife of Drugo de Brueres, murdered by her
husband, in the reign of William the Conqueror, is said to haunt the villa to this day.
Population, 29.

Foster William, gent.
North Thomas, gent.
Robinson Thomas, gent.
  *Butchers,*          Crook Thomas
Chadwick Richard    Cross Peter
Dunn George         Day Thomas
  *Bricklayers,*       Foster Jonathan
Cammidge Thos.      Foster Wm.
Coley Wm.           Garton Leonard
  *Farmers,*          Hornby William
Baron Robert        Lamplugh Thos.

Pape Mrs.
Porter George
Simpson Wm.
Southwick Thos.
Stork Ray
Suddaby Wm.
Tennison Geo.
Walker Ralph

*Shoemakers,*
Braimbridge John
Fletcher John
Hill Godfrey & Son
Maimprize Samuel
*Tailors,*
Allman Thos.
Gowforth Thos.

*Grocers,*
Gowforth Thos.
Smith Wm.

*Wheelwrights,*
Coates John
Harrison Wm.

Baron Robert, vict. Board
Burrell Ralph, parish clerk
Day Peter, corn miller
Hall Wm. blacksmith
Harland James, schoolmaster

*Carriers,* John Carter, Robert Holder, Thomas Agar, and John Jennison, to Hull every Tu. and Fri. to Bridlington every Sat.

SKIPSEA BROUGH, in the parish of Skipsea, wap. and liberty of Holderness; 9 miles S. of Bridlington.—Pop. included with Dringhoe & Upton.

Lamplugh Jeremiah, gent.

*Farmers,*
Denby John

Hall Thomas
Holder Emanuel

Blenkin James, vict. and blacksmith

SKIPWITH, (P.) in the wap. of Ouse and Derwent, and liberty of Howdenshire; 5½ miles NNE. of Selby. The church is an ancient structure, dedicated to St. Helen, of which the King is the patron. A donation to the school was left by Mrs. Dorothy Wilson, of York, spinster, in the year 1714; the property now is worth 20*l.* per annum. The Rev. Joseph Nelson, vicar of Skipwith, also left 400*l.* in the 3 per cent. consolidated annuities. Pop. 315.

Atkinson Miles, Esq.

*Farmers,*
Bellas George
Brown John
Carlton Wm.
Jackson Geo.
Moat John

Simpson Thos.
Swales Anthony
Wilson Thomas
*Shoemakers,*
Sherburn Robert
Townsley John

Burton Thos. vict. Hare & Hounds
Copley Wm. shopkpr. & wheelwright
Hailstone George, tailor
Lister Thomas, parish clerk
Newsham Wm. schoolmaster
Savage Wm. shopkeeper & blacksmith

SKIRLAUGH (North), in the parish of Swine, wap. and liberty of Holderness; 7½ miles SW. of Hornsea. The chapel of Ease at this place, said to have been built by Walter Skirlaw, Bishop of Durham, a native of this place, is the finest specimen of Gothic architecture in Holderness. Population, including Rowton, 260.

Wilson Benj. Neasham, Esq.

*Farmers,*
Clapham John
Clapham Thos.
Jackson Benj.
Johnson John
Mair Robert

*Shoemakers,*
Brown Robert
Lundy Robert
*Weavers,*
Shepherd James
Todd Thos.

Batty Jacob, bricklayer

SKIRLAUGH (South), in the parish of Swine, wap. and liberty of Holderness: 9 miles NE. of Hull. Marmaduke Langdale, Esq. left by will to the townships of South and North Skirlaugh 32 acres and a few perches of land, the rental to be appropriated to the following purposes, viz.—one half to be applied to the repairs of the church, &c. the other half to be applied to the education of ten poor children, and the overplus given to the poor on their marriage. According to the testator's will, the schoolmaster was to teach scholars on the work-days, and to preach on the Sundays; he was also to be an unmarried man, "For I," says the testator, "hold it unnecessary for a man living in so barren a place as Skirlaugh is, to have the use of a woman." The population of this place amounts to 211.

Barker Thomas, schoolmaster
Braithwaite John, grocer
Burn Timothy, wheelwright
Gray Samuel, blacksmith
Jamieson Rich. surgeon & apothecary
Stabler John, vict. Duke of York
Stabler Robert, vict. Sun
Staveley John, shoemaker
Todd Reuben, tailor
Waldby Robert, miller

*Farmers,*
Foster Wm.
Foster Mark
Garton Wm.
Gibson Thos.

Johnson Geo.
Johnson Geo. jun.
Sturdy Thos.
WilliamsonCuthbt.

*Carriers,* Thos. Gibson, John Dales, & Wm. Pexton, to Hull Tu. & Fri.

SKIRLINGTON HILL, in the parish of Atwicke, wap. & liberty of Holderness; 4 miles NNW. of Hornsea.

Brown Francis, farmer
Etherington George, yeoman

SKIRPENBECK, (P.) in the wap. of Buckrose, and liberty of St. Peter's; 6 miles NW. of Pocklington. There is no place of worship here except the parish church, which is a rectory, in the gift of the King, of which the Rev. William Dealtry is incumbent. Population, 263.

Ware Wm. steward to H. Darley, Esq.

*Farmers,*
Beal Thomas
Beal Richard

Burton Wm.
Clement Hick
Kirby Nathaniel

Midgley Alice
Milner James
Richardson Wm.
Ware George

Wharram Thomas
*Shoemakers,*
Ianson John
Wells Christopher

Cottom John, shopkeeper
Dickons Wm. blacksmith and vict.
Oxtoby Richard, farmer and miller
Ware Wm. winnowing machine mkr.
Wyrill John, schoolmaster

SLEDMERE, (P.) in the wap. of Buckrose; 8 miles NW. of Driffield. It is situated in a spacious vale in the centre of the Yorkshire Wolds, and may be considered as the ornament of that bleak and hilly country. The parish church here is dedicated to St. Mary, patron Sir M. M. Sykes, Bart. The seat of the worthy Baronet at this place is spacious and superb. The library contains many rare and most valuable books in all languages, and is esteemed one of the most extensive collections in the kingdom; there are also in it an exceeding fine collection of old portraits, &c. by the earliest masters. Population including the hamlet of Croam, 425.

POST-MASTER—ROBERT KING.
A Horse post arrives from Malton ½ past 5 every morning, going to Bridlington, &c. and returns at 40 minutes past 2 o'clock in the afternoon.

Sykes Sir M. M. Bart. (Hall)
Evans John, Esq. Sledmere castle
Torre Rev. Henry, B. A. perp. curate

*Farmers,*
Bainton Thomas
Bradley James
Clark Richard
Hicks Jonathan
Horsley Widow
Huggin John

Leak John
Pickering Wm.
Severs John
*Tailors,*
Bogg David
Hesp John

Coates John, shoemaker
Pickering Wm. vict. Triton Inn
Pickering Abraham, bricklayer
Row John, baker
Truelove John, carpenter & shopkpr.

*Carriers,* Blenkin & Ashton, from Hull to Malton, Tu. and Fri.

*Smithy Brigg,* in the parish of Swine, wap. & liberty of Holderness; 7 miles NNE. of Hedon.

SOUTHBURN, in the parish of Kirkburn, and wap. of Harthill; 4 miles WSW. of Driffield. Pop. 103.

*Farmers,*
Botterill Wm.
Foster Richard

Harrison John
Jefferson Francis

SOUTHCOATES, in the parish of Drypool, wap. and liberty of Holderness; 2 mls. NE. of Hull. Pop. 798.

Harrison Robert, vict. Crown

Hart John, gardener, &c.
Mattinley Richard, merchant

*Corn-millers,*
Dawson Joseph
Fewson David
*Farmers,*
Clark James
Dales James
Foster John
Gibson Geo. sen.
Gibson Geo. jun.
Gray Miles
Johnson Joseph

Landal Alexander
Loundsbrough M.
Robson Wm.
Roe Thomas
Roe Joseph
Stickney John
Taylor Roger
Weatherill Henry
Wilson Wm.
Wood Thomas

SPALDINGTON, in the parish of Bubwith, and wap. of Harthill; 4 miles N. of Howden. The hall at this place was formerly the seat of the ancient and honourable family of Vavasour, but now the property of Lord Howden, it exhibits a fine specimen of architecture of the time of Queen Elizabeth. Pop. 361.

*Farmers,*
Barker John
Bell Henry Wade
Blanchard John
Hance John
Johnson S.
Leaper John

Simpson John,
Grange
Stogdale George
Stogdale Robert,
Ivy House
Thomlinson John
Thompson Wm.

Dove James, carpenter & vict. Board
Holderness James, corn miller
Howden Thomas, blacksmith
Lazenby John, tailor
Sanderson John, shopkeeper

*Spaldington Outside,* in the parish of Bubwith, and wap. of Harthill; 4 miles NNE. of Howden.

SPEETON, in the parish of Bridlington, and wap. of Dickering; 4 miles SE. of Hunmanby. One Chapel of Ease. Population 116.

Plowes George, corn miller

*Farmers,*
Crow Robert
Jordon John

Jordon William
Vickerman Edw.

*Spittal,* in the parish of Fangfoss, wap. of Harthill, and liberty of St. Peter's; 3½ mls. NW. of Pocklington. Pop. with Fangfoss, 154.

*Spittal House,* in the parish of Willerby, and wap. of Dickering; 5 miles S. of Scarborough.

*Spring Head,* in the parish of Cottingham, and wap. of Harthill; 3 miles WNW. of Hull. There is here an excellent spring of water, from which the town of Hull is supplied.

SPROATLEY, (P.) in the wap. and liberty of Holderness; 5 miles N. of Hedon. There is here a handsome new church, built in 1819, of white brick, and dedicated to

All-Saints, it is built upon the site of the old edifice, which was dedicated to St. Swithin. The rector is the Rev. Charles Wapshaw, and the patron the Earl of Cardigan. Here is likewise a Charity school for ten poor boys and ten girls, built in the year 1739, and endowed by Mrs. Bridget Briggs, with 100*l.* per annum out of the rents of land near Sheffield. In digging the foundation for the new church, in 1819, some very ancient tomb-stones were found, one of which had an inscription on the side of a crosier, in Saxon characters. Pop. 357.

Daunt R. G. gentleman
Hatfield Rev. Joseph, curate
Cott Joseph, gentleman
Naudby Elizabeth, gentlewoman

*Blacksmiths,*
Orkwell John
Hudson John
*Corn-millers,*
Dawson John
Williamson John
*Farmers,*
Dashill Henry
Dickenson Thos.
Dobson John
Milner Ann
Robinson Henry
Uvidge George
*Grocers,*
Dobson John

Williamson John
*Shoemakers,*
Fairbank Henry
Fairbank James
Hodgson James
*Tailors,*
Newton Henry
Pickering Hardy
Pickering David
Turner James
*Wheelwrights,*
Hickson Francis
Ringrose John
Simpson Thomas
Winter Richard

Braithwaite Peter, rope maker
Gibson John, schoolmaster
Atkinson John, butcher
Hall William, vict. Blue Bell
Ingrose Susannah, straw bonnet mkr.
Snell George, bricklayer
Bead Joseph, saddler
*Carriers* to Hull, Thos. Hodgson Tu. & Mary Longhorne Tu. & Fri.

SPURNHEAD; the Ocellum Pro-montorium of Ptolemy, in the parish of Holderness, wap. and liberty of Holderness; 12 miles SSE. of Patrington. This is the utmost part of Yorkshire, extended by a narrow neck of land into the Humber, at its junction with the German Ocean, and may fairly be called an island, as the overflow of the tides frequently render it impassable from Spurnhead to the main land. There are here two light-houses, and a few small sea, inhabited by a number of old seamen, who are pensioned by the Trinity House of Hull, for the purpose of managing the boats and life boats, which are kept here, for the purpose of rendering assistance to distressed sailors, Spurnhead being too frequently the scene of maritime misery.—included with Kilnsea.

on James, vict. Tiger
Richardson Robt. vict. Mason's Arms

Watson Mary, keeper of the low light
Wonnocot Jph. keeper of the high light

*Staddlethorpe,* in the parish of Howden, wap. & liberty of Howdenshire; 7 miles ESE. of Howden.

STAMFORD BRIDGE, in the parishes of Low Catton and Gate Helmsley, waps. of Ouse and Derwent and Harthill, a part in the liberty of St. Peter's; 7½ miles ENE. of York. The river Derwent divides the village into two parts, called the East and West, and the high road from York to Bridlington passes through it. Here is a small Methodist chapel, and also a school, free to a few poor children, endowed with 30*l.* per annum. The memorable battle, in the year 1066, between Harold and Tosti, was fought here.* Population E. and W. including Scoreby, 449.

Hardwick George, gentleman
Longbotham Rev. Mark, master of the free school
Quarton Robert, gentleman
Wright John, surgeon
*Farmers,*
Cook John
Kirby Matthew
Kirk Charles
Matterson Thos.
Parker Francis
Shaw John, (West)
*Shoemakers,*
Gawtry Thomas
Holdsworth John
Wales George

Burden Francis, wheelwright
Danby Thomas, brewer, (West)
Duce William, blacksmith
Flint George, vict. Bay Horse
Gawtry Francis, bread baker
Gray Thos. & Sons, brick & tile mkrs.
Hood Richard & Co. grocers & seedsmen, importers of and dealers in Foreign & British spirits, butter, bacon, cheese, and corn factors
Jackson Wm. lock-keeper, (West)
Ormond James, toll bar keeper
Pearson Francis, butcher
Rotherford John, corn miller & dealer
Seamour Robert, vict. Three Tuns
Seamour John, shopkeeper
Spence William, butcher
Walker George, tailor and draper
Wallis John, saddler
Wigglesworth ———, excise officer

*Stanningholme,* in the parish of Watton, and wap. of Harthill; 8 miles SSE. of Driffield.

STAXTON, in the parish of Willerby, and wap. of Dickering; 5 miles WNW. of Hunmanby. Pop. 213.

Jacques Rev. Arthur, vicar of Willerby

STEPNEY, in the parish of Sculcoates, and wap. of Harthill; 1 mile N. of Hull.

* See Vol. II. page 21.

Birch Eliz. gentlewoman, Stepney pl.
Clark Wm. gent. Stepney lodge
Donaldson Robert, gent. Stepney pl.
Heath Robert, gent. Stepney place
Norman William, gentleman

*Corn-millers,*  *Cowkeepers,*
Cuss William       Beilby George
Hargrave Edward, Storey Thomas
  (and factor)     Waudby Thomas

Barker Francis, brush board cutter
Camplen John, coal merchant
Fletcher Jane, schoolmistress
Mayfield Joseph, earthenware mfr.
Moore Thomas, vict. Spotted Bull
Rhodes George, tailor
Smith James, warehouse keeper, Custom house
Smithson Robert, paper maker

STILLINGFLEET WITH MORKBY, (P.) in the wap. of Ouse & Derwent, a part in the liberty of St. Peter's ; 7 miles S. of York. The church is dedicated to St. Helen, the Dean & Chapter of York are patrons. Pop. 404.

Ingham James, Esq. (hall)
Eyre Rev. Anthony Wm. M. A. vicar
Eglin Ann, gentlewoman
Foster Miss Frances, gentlewoman

*Farmers,*      Sledge Francis
Atley Thomas    Spencer Wm.
Brockelby John  Thompson John
Jackson Thos.   Triffitt Robert
Mallory Wm.     Triffitt Wm.
Moody John      Waddington Thos.
Pinder T. J.    *Shoemakers,*
Ryder Wm.       Creaser Robert
Silversides John Robinson Francis

Buckle Thos. carpenter
Chambers John, vict. White Swan
Hornshaw Thomas, blacksmith
Lazenby John, tailor
Leedle Robert, corn miller
Mountain Thomas, schoolmaster
Plummer Thos. parish clerk
Turner John, shopkeeper

STONE FERRY, in the parish of Sutton, wap. and liberty of Holderness ; 2 miles N. of Hull. Here is a small Methodist chapel, built in 1821, also an almshouse for the comfort of seven poor widows, or old maids, with the annual allowance of 13*l.* each, established in pursuance of the will (dated 1720) of Ann Waters, late of this place, who also bequeathed 5*l.* annually for the instruction of ten poor girls in reading, writing, and needlework, which is performed by one of the old women in the almshouse, who receives the benefit. Population included with Sutton.

*Farmers,*      Blenkin James
Agus Robert     Brown Wm.

Foster Thomas      Runton George
Foster Charles     Thomas Charles
Harp Wm.           Thompson Geo.
Hudson Samuel      Tindall Thomas
Kay Thomas         Tran John
Marsh George       Tran James
Matthew Robert     Worrill Henry
Robinson Martin

Cooper Wm. schoolmaster
Grayson Peter, dealer in hair
Hewetson James and John, whiting, oil, and paint manufacturers
Jackson Philip, vict. Sloop
Peacock John, grocer and gardener
Robson David, shoemaker
Walker Thos. vict. Ferryhouse, wood turner

*Stork Hill with Sandholme,* in parish of St. John's Beverley, wap. Harthill, and liberty of Beverley ; miles NE. of Beverley.   Pop. 48.

STORWOOD, in the parish Thornton, and wap. of Harthill ; miles SW. of Pocklington. Pop. l

Gray John, yeoman
Jennings Thomas, gentleman
Jennings Robert, gentleman
Webster Mrs. Ann, gentlewoman

*Farmers.*       Gardam John
Abbot William    Parker William
Chatterton Charles
Ouston Peter, shopkeeper

SUNDERLANDWICK, in the of Hutton Cranswick, and wap. of H 2 miles SSW. of Driffield on the road.   This was anciently a village. It now contains only a few houses. The township and manor property of Horner Reynard, Esq. landwick lodge.   Pop. 60.

SUNK ISLAND, (Extra-p in the wap. and liberty of Holderness ; 8 SE. of Hedon.   This island was formed part of the river Humber, and about a tury ago contained only about 800 acre land, but from the perpetual warping of tides since that period, it now contains 5000 acres, in a state of high culti There is also a fine tract of land at t end of the island, which has been since the last embankment in 1800, is expected will be saved in a few yea the overflowing of the tides.   The preserved from the encroachments Humber, by strong banks being around it, except on the north side, is separated from the main land by a drain extending from Stone Creek to Winmore Clough, at which two places the tides are confined by the junction banks from the main land to Sunk Island.   This land be

ngs to the crown. That part which was
rst embanked, was originally about two
iles from the shore, and many persons are
ving, who recollect vessels passing between
and the main land, to which it is now
sited by a bridge across a narrow channel,
hich serves as a drain to the adjacent coun-
y. There is here a small chapel of the
hurch of England, at present unconsecrat-
, under the patronage of the Archbishop
York. The Rev. Robert Metcalfe, curate.
pulation 218.

| Farmers, | Lambert John |
|---|---|
| ayen Widow | Rhodes John |
| land Wm. | Richardson Wm. |
| awkins Wm. | Richardson Widow |
| pkins James | Suddaby Matthew |
| nson Wm. | Vicarman M. |

lbert James, wheelwright
ckinson John, shoemaker
atson John, vict. Board
rrier, C. Wilson, to Hull Tu. & Fri.

SUTTON, (P.) in the wap. and
rty of Holderness; 3 miles NNE. of
ll, is a very pleasant village, and one of
country retreats of the merchants and
try of Hull. The church, dedicated to St.
nes, is an ancient structure, of which H.
adley, Esq. is the patron, and the Rev.
G. Davies is the incumbent curate.
ar the centre of the village is an hospital
ed in pursuance of the will of Mr.
ard Chamberlain, late of this place, for
comfort of eight poor widows, and two
owers, who have each the benefit of a
d house and garden, and 3s. per week;
hospital was re-built in 1800, by the
tees of the charity. Near to the above-
tioned alms-house, also stands another
chiefly of stone, for the reception of
poor widows and daughters of deceased
rymen, built in 1819, by the trustees of
Watson, late of this place. In the time
dward I. a house of White Friars stood
Pop. with Stone Ferry, 3658.

| Gentry, | Corn-millers, |
|---|---|
| r Geo. | Keilington Joseph |
| n James | Sergent Henry |
| aby Thos. | Farmers, |
| Thos. | Anfield James |
| and Benj. | Blashill Robert |
| lell Geo. | Calvert Thos. |
| stman Thos. | Casson Henry |
| ter Nichols | Cook Joseph |
| tinson Auth. | Cundell John |
| llacksmiths, | Eyre Andrew |
| n Wm. | Hewson Geo. |
| nson Daniel | Kirkhouse Anthony |
| bricklayers, | Leaper Thos. |
| Ambrose | North Thos. |
| erell Jonth. | Rheam Edward |

Richardson Thos.
Ross Thos.
Sissons Thos.
Storey John
Thompson Geo.
Vause Geo.

| Gardeners, | Shoemakers, |
|---|---|
| Hart John | Carrick James |
| Smith Richard | Clappinson Jonah |
| Grocers, | Crook John |
| Harrison Geo. | Gibson Robert |
| Holmes Geo. | Sanderson John |
| | Tailors, |
| | Sharp Geo. |
| | Simpson Richard |
| | Wheelwrights, |
| | Cowl John |
| | Hunter Wm. |

Dibb Thomas, schoolmaster
Frost Thomas, solicitor
Habbershaw David, vict. Ship
Hipsley John, merchant
Westerby Dinah, vict. Duke of York

Carriers.—R. Clappinson and T.
Rodman, to Hull Tu. and Fri. dep. 9
morning, ret. 6 evening.

SUTTON, in the parish of Norton,
and wap. of Buckrose ; 1 mile E. of
Malton. Pop. 87.

Parker George, Esq. Sutton house

Farmers.
Rutter Ralph, Cheese Cake house
Wise William, High field

Trainers.
Ackroyd Joseph, White wall house
Marson Job, Sutton cottage
Noble Mark, jockey, White wall
Sykes Thomas, High field

SUTTON FULL, (P.) in the wap. of
Harthill, a part in the liberty of St. Peter's;
5½ miles NW. of Pocklington. Here is
a small parish church, of which the Rev.
James Rudd, D. D. is incumbent rector,
and J. Simpson, Esq. the patron. Pop. 125.

Coulton William, yeoman
Johnson Edward, yeoman

SUTTON-ON-DERWENT, (P.) in
the wap. of Harthill; 7 miles ESE. of York.
The church dedicated to St. Michael, Sir
T. Charges, Bart. is the patron. There is
also a Methodist chapel. This village is
beautifully situated on the banks of the
Derwent, over which there is a good stone
bridge, where is a spring strongly impreg-
nated with ferruginous matter. Pop. 400.

Wheeler Rev. Wm. A. M. rector
Howard Charles, gent. Sutton farm

| Farmers, | Watson Walker |
|---|---|
| Barn Thos. | Yeoman Thos. |
| Dixon John | Shopkeepers, |
| Moyser Jph. jun. | Hutchinson Alice |
| Newton Thos. | Voce Thos. |
| Newton John | Timber-merchant, |
| Preston John | Massey Wm. |

Bonnard Thomas, shoemaker
Gray John, schoolmaster

L L

Horsley J. vict. & maltster, Cross Keys
Lister John, vict. Ram's Head
Midgley Samuel, tailor
Moyser Joseph, corn miller & dealer, and lime and coal merchant
Waterworth John, butcher

*Carriers*—J. Exelby & T. Lister, to York, Mon. Wed. and Sat. dep. 8 mg. ret. at 7 evg.

SWANLAND, in the parish of North Ferriby, wap. and liberty of Hullshire; 7 miles W. of Hull. The landscapes seen from this village are greatly admired by strangers for their beauty, variety, and grandeur. An elevated spot near Swanland mill commands a view of the Trent and the country adjacent, the whole course of the Humber down to the Spurn Lights, the Lincolnshire and Yorkshire coasts of that river, and the low country of Holderness, as far as the eye can reach, where the distant prospect is bounded by the horizon. Pop. 418.

Osborne Robert, Esq. Braffords hall
Sykes Nicholas, Esq. hall
Prickett Josiah, solicitor
Williams Rev. David, Dissenting minister

| *Farmers & Yeomen,* | *Shoemakers,* |
|---|---|
| Bateman John | Drew Gabriel |
| Binnington John | Skinn Robert |
| Everingham John | *Shopkeepers,* |
| Garland Samuel | Clark Robert |
| Ringrose John | Kemp James |
| Shaw Nathaniel | *Tailors,* |
| Todd John | Hoggard Christr. |
| Westerdale Thos. | Poole Francis |

Beilby Thomas, corn miller
Cherry William, schoolmaster
Crowther James, butcher
Habershaw William, carpenter
Kirby Richard, bricklayer
Reed Thomas, corn factor
Westerdale George, blacksmith

*Carrier,*—R. Hodsman, to Hull Tu. and Fri.

SWINE, (P.) in the wap. and liberty of Holderness; 7 miles NW. of Hedon. A religious house consisting of a Prioress and fourteen or fifteen Nuns of the Cistercian order, was founded here by Robert de Verli, before the end of the reign of king Stephen, but there are now no remains of the building to be traced; a farm house stands on the site, near which, were lately dug up several silver and copper coins, amongst which was one of Constantius, with the head of Flavius. The church, which is a Gothic structure, dedicated to St. Mary, claims to be of the age of Prince Offa; the patron is Mrs. Bramley, and the Rev. Matthew Williamson is the vicar. Population 239.

| *Farmers,* | Jackson John |
|---|---|
| Acklam Francis | Medson Jane |
| Dibb John | More John |
| Foster Samuel | Ross Wm. |
| Graves John | Shepherd Ann |
| Grayburn Wm. | Walgate W. & R. |

Courtney John, wheelwright
Dowthwaite Robert, cow doctor
Garton John, shoemaker
Heselton Mark, schoolmaster
Sharp William, grocer
Shaw John, tailor
Smith Thomas, blacksmith
Wright James, vict. White Lion

*Swinkell,* in the parish of Watton, and wap. of Harthill; 5 miles from Driffield.

*Tanston,* in the parish of Aldbrough, wap. and liberty of Holderness; 7 miles NE. of Hedon. Pop. included with Aldbrough.

THEARNE, in the parish of St. John's, Beverley, wap. of Harthill, & liberty of Beverley; 3 miles SE. of Beverley. Pop. 90.

Ramsay John, gentleman

*Thirkleby,* in the parish of K Grindalyth, and wap. of Buckro miles E. of Malton. Pop. 44.

*Thirkleby,* in the parish of S and wap. and liberty of Hold 7 miles NE. of Hull. Pop. 61.

*Thixendale,* in the parish of ram Percy, and wap. of Buckros miles N. of Pocklington. Pop. 1

THORGANBY-*cum*-COTTINGW in the parish of Thorganby, and of Ouse and Derwent; 10 miles of York. The church is a small neat structure, dedicated to St. He Rev. Joseph Mitchinson is incum and Mrs. Baldwin the patroness. Population 381.

Jefferson J. D. Esq. Thorganby hall
Mitchinson Rev. Joseph, incumbent
Abbey Richard, Grange

| *Farmers & Yeomen,* | Rickell John |
|---|---|
| Barton Thos. | Simpson John |
| Belwood John | Smith Thos. |
| Blacker Robert | Stabler Christ. |
| Blacker John | Stephenson M. |
| Brown James | Stephenson M. |
| Buttle Geo. | Thompson |
| Dunnington Jph. | *Shoemakers,* |
| Fowler Robert | Taylor James |
| Gamble Thos. | Underwood Wm. |
| Hall Robert | *Shopkeepers,* |
| Halley Benj. | Hope Robert |
| Richmond Geo. | Thompson James |

Allison Robert, wheelwright
Gill Richard, parish clerk

Matthews Wm. blacksmith and vict.
Mountier Wm. schoolmaster
Forth John, vict. Ferryboat
Forth John, cabinet maker
Vollans Samuel, butcher and farmer
Young Robert, tailor and draper

*Carriers*—Robert Hope & James Thompson, to York every Sat.

THORNGUMBALD, in the parish
[ Paul, wap. and liberty of Holderness; 2
mls SSE. of Hedon. Here is a small
chapel of Ease, of which the Rev. John
Cowman is curate; likewise a small Independent chapel, built in 1801. This village
is formerly called Thorn-cum-Paul, on
account of its being in the parish of Paul,
and is now corrupted to Thorngumbald.
Population 259.

Richardson John, lieutenant
Seldon Edward, Esq.
Stephenson Rev. W. (academy)

*Farmers,*
Renshaw Thos.
Hardy Phillip
Marshall James
Rock George
Watt Samuel
Rhodes Thomas
*Shoemakers,*
Ritson James
Richardson John

Slater Samuel S.
Smith Wm.
Stother Robert
Straker Thos.
Whitelock Geo.
Wilson Wm.
*Wheelwrights,*
Garton John
Island Wm.

Brar James, gardener
Dixon Wm. tailor
per Wm. vict. Cross Keys
Wood Geo. horse dealer
Wright Robert, blacksmith

THORNHOLME, in the parish of
Burton Agnes, and wap. of Dicker-
ing; 5 miles SW. of Bridlington.—
Population 94.

*Farmers,* Mosey G. and F.
Hadley Wm. Ouston Michael

*Carrier,* Philip Boynton, to Bridlington Wed. and Sat.

THORNTHORP, in the parish of
Scrayingham, and wap. of Buckrose;
miles S. of Malton. Population included with Burythorp.

*Farmers,* Taylor John
Hilton J. Taylor Wm.

*Thornton,* (P.) in the wap. of
Ouse & Derwent; 4 miles SW. of Pocklington.
Living is a vicarage, the Rev.
James Addison is incumbent, and the
Dean of York the patron. Pop. 198.

*Thorpe,* in the parish of Howden,
and liberty of Howdenshire; 1
N. of Howden. Pop. 53.

THORPE BASSETT, (P.) in the
of Buckrose; 5 miles E. of

Walton. Here is a Church of the Establishment, dedicated to All Saints,
of which the Rev. Basil Wood is rector, and the Archbishop of York, by
lapse, the patron. Pop. 156.

Dale William, gentleman
Darling William Wilbert
Lovell Thomas, yeoman

*Farmers & Yeomen,* Lovell Thos.
Allinson John        Owston Christ.
Atkinson John        Owston Thos.
Banks Wm.            Puckrin John
Calvert David        Taylor John
Chapman Thos.        Wilkinson Wm.
Gypson Wm.           Wilson Walter
Atkinson John, vict. Blue Bell
Young Geo. schoolmaster

THORPE BRANTINGHAM, in the
parish of Brantingham, & wap. of Harthill; 2 mls. SE. of South Cave. Pop.174.

Barnard Rev. Edward Wm. A. M.
vicar of South Cave

Haigh Thomas, gentleman
Pinder Robert, farmer
Storr Robert, carpenter
Wray John, yeoman

*Carrier,* R. Taylor, to Hull Tu. & Fri.

*Thorpe-le-Street,* in the parish of
Nunburnholme, & wap. of Harthill;
3 miles NW. of Market-Weighton.
Population 37.

THWING, (P.) in the wap. of
Dickering; 8 mls. WNW. of Bridlington. The church is dedicated to All
Saints, and the living, which is a rectory in medieties, in the gift of the
crown, is enjoyed by the Rev. John
Kirk. There is also a Methodist
chapel. Pop. 314.

Bennison Mary, gentlewoman
Moorsom Rev. Richard, curate

*Farmers,* Vickerman Sarah
Bennison John        Vickerman Richd.
Bordass Isaiah       Vickerman Wm.
Gibson Geo.

Braithwaite Wm. carpenter
Cape Wm. grocer, &c.
Chambers Wm. schoolmaster
Coultus Vickerman, butcher
Johnson Robert, shoemaker
Jordon James, vict. Bottle and Glass
Lownsbrough Francis, tailor

*Carrier,* Mark Hick, to Bridlington and Wold Newton on Sat.

*Tibthorpe,* in the parish of Kirkburn, and wap. of Harthill; 6½ miles
SW. of Driffield. Pop. 221.

TICKTON, in the parish of St.
John's, Beverley, wap. of Holderness, and

liberty of Beverley; 2½ miles NE. of Beverley. The river Hull is navigable to this place. Pop. 110.

Marshall Saml. maltster, Hull bridge
West Wm. Esq. Mount Pleasant
Woodmancey Thos. yeoman
Charlton Thos. vict. Crown & Anchor, Hull bridge

*Towthorpe*, in the parish of Wharram Percy, and wap. of Buckrose; 10 miles SE. of Malton. Pop. 61.

*Tresswick*, in the parish of Hayton, and wap. of Harthill; 3½ miles NW. of Market-Weighton.

TRANBY, in the parish of Hessle, county of Hullshire; 6 mls. W. of Hull.
Barkworth Eliz. gentlewoman
Cooper Samuel, merchant
Todd John, merchant
Watson John Kiero, banker

TUNSTALL, (P.) in the wap. of Holderness, and liberty of St. Peter's; 8 miles ENE. of Hedon. This village is situated near to that part of the sea coast known by the name of Sand le Mar, and is much frequented by the inhabitants of the neighbouring villages, for the purpose of procuring pebbles and gravel to repair the roads. The church is an ancient structure, dedicated to All Saints, the Rev. Jonathan Dixon is vicar, and the patron the Dean and Chapter of York. Pop. 169.

Snaith Thos. gentleman
Swan Rev. Charles, curate

*Farmers,*
Atkinson James
Baron Henry
Brainton Geo.
Close Thos.
Dent John

Lorimer Edw.
Snaith Henry
Snaith John
*Shopkeepers,*
Cross Jane
Mainprize Christ.

Baron Robert, cornfactor
Cross Robert, tailor
Dalton Wm. parish clerk
Robinson Jane, vict. Cock
*Carrier,* S. Ganton, to Hull every Tu.

*Turner Hall,* in the parish of Swine, wap. and liberty of Holderness; 4 miles from Hedon.

ULROME, in the parish of Skipsea, and wap. and liberty of Holderness; 6½ miles NNW. of Hornsea. Here is a Chapel of Ease, of a very ancient structure, and the incumbent is the Rev. John Gilby, rector of Barmston. Population, 170.

*Farmers,*
Bevill Christ.
Danby Thos.
Dobson Thos.
Foster Wm.
Garton Mrs.

North Wm.
Pape Thos.
Sharp John
Sharp John, jun.
Smith John
Smith Thos.

Etherington Geo. shoemaker
Woodhead Wm. wheelwright

UNCLEBY, in the parish of Kirby Underdale, and wap. of Buckrose; 7 miles N. of Pocklington.

Clarkson Abraham, farmer
Pudsey Seth, yeoman
Pudsey Geo. farmer
Webster John, schoolmaster
White Ann, gentlewoman

UPTON, in the parish of Skipsea, wap. and liberty of Holderness; 11 miles SSW. of Bridlington. Pop. included with Skipsea Brough.

Severs John, Crowgarth

WAGHEN or WAWN, (P.) in the wap. of Holderness, and liberty of St. Peter's; 6 miles N. of Hull. The church, dedicated to St. Peter, is a small ancient edifice, the seats of which have never been renewed, and are much corroded by time. The vicar is the Rev. Jeremiah Burn, and the patron the Chancellor of the Church of York. Pop. 251.

*Farmers,*
Ewbank Peter
Hopkinson Thos.
Jackson John
Leake Matm.
Munby & Son

Nicholson Christ.
Ransom Wm.
Whiting Wm.
*Wheelwrights,*
Calvert Richard
Calvert Thos.

Allison James, shoemaker
Breedin Wm. vict. Anchor
Johnson Wm. day schl. & parish clerk

WALDBY, in the parish of Elloughton, and wap. of Harthill; 4 miles E. of South Cave.

Watson Thomas, farmer

WALKINGTON, (P.) in the wap. of Harthill and Howdenshire; 2½ mls. SW. of Beverley. The church is dedicated to All Hallows; and W. Thompson, Esq. is the patron. Population, 324.

Brownlow Geo. sen. gent.
Ferguson Rev. Daniel, B.A. rector
Hague Francis, gent.

*Blacksmiths,*
Hutty Wm.
Nicholson Daniel
*Carpenters,*
Bennison Ralph
Robinson Jas.
*Farmers,*
Atkinson Isaac
Barley Thos.
Bennison John
Brigham Geo.
Brownlow G. jun.
Brownlow Wm.
Clarkson John

Crawthorne Wm.
Dales John
Harper Wm.
Hodgson R. & T.
Hood Wm.
Jackson Wm.
Jefferson Thos.
Johnson Robert
Oliver Timothy
Spence Robert
Stephenson John
Watson Wm.
Webster Wm.

Wilkinson M.
*Schoolmasters,*
Carling Wm.
Northend Wm.
(& parish clerk)
*Shoemakers,*
Ramsay Thos.
Richardson Fras.

Speck Thos.
Watson Joseph
*Shopkeepers,*
Loft John
Shaw Samuel
*Tailors, &c.*
Cole Samuel
Heward Ambrose

Joynton John, nurseryman, &c.
Carter Robert, bone setter
Jutty Wm. vict. Black Horse
ankinson John, coal merchant
oft Timothy, corn miller
Jonkman Francis, butcher
adgett Wm. vict. Duke of York
age Richard, land surveyor

*Carrier,* Wm. Oliver to Hull every
'u. to Beverley every Sat.

*Wallingfen,* see New Village and
lewport.

WANSFORD, in the parish of Naf-
rton, and wap. of Dickering; 3
les E. of Driffield. Here is a con-
derable cotton and carpet manufac-
ry, the only establishment of the
d in this part of the country,
anding on the navigable river Hull.
pulation, 344.

oyes John, jun. carpet manufr.
arkson Jonas, overlooker
rby Thos. vict. Valiant Soldier
nowsley Geo. corn miller
mplugh John, vict. Trout
urgatroyd Christ. schoolmaster

*Farmers,*
mby Michael
ster Geo.
mplugh Geo.
ompson Saml.

Watson Wm.
*Grocers, &c.*
Clough John
Watson James

WAPPLINGTON, in the parish of
erthorpe, & wap. of Harthill; 2¾
. SSW. of Pocklington. Pop. 19.

*Farmers,*
sby W. & T.

Hord James
Hotham Wm.

WARTER, (P.) in the wap. of
rthill; 4 miles ENE. of Pockling-
. The church, dedicated to St.
es, is a vicarage, of which Lord
ncaster is the patron, and the Rev.
. Courtley, the incumbent. There
so a small Methodist chapel. Po-
tion, 428.

nington Mrs. Jane, Warter house
er Thos. steward

*Blacksmiths,*
th Wm.
on Nathaniel
rpenters, &c.
on Benj.
on Robert
*Farmers,*

Alderson Richard
Alderson Rd. jun.
Dosser Wm.
Dosser Thos.
Harrison M.
King John
Kirton Thos.

Oxtoby Chas.
Richardson Geo.
Richardson Wm.
Reckell Wm.
Smith Thos.

Tasker John
Wilson Thos.
*Shoemakers,*
England John
Levitt Thos.

Cook Thomas, schoolmaster
Gray Robert, tailor
James Robert, shopkeeper
Tasker Richard, corn miller
Wilson Thomas, tallow chandler and
vict. Creeping Jane

*Carrier,* J. Jackson, to York on Sat.

WASSAND, in the parish of Sigglesthorne, wap. and liberty of Holderness;
2 miles SW. of Hornsea; a small village
pleasantly situated on the declivity of a
small eminence, where stands the mansion
of a branch of the Constable family; an
elegant structure, built of white brick,
commanding a full prospect of that extensive lake, called Hornsea Mere.

Constable Rev. Chas. Wassand hall
Blenkin Robert, farmer

WATTON, (P.) in the wap. of
Harthill; 6 miles S. of Driffield, situated
on the high road leading from that place to
Beverley; it is called the ancient Vetadun,
a place which, at an early period, was consecrated to religion. It appears from Bede's
Ecclesiastical History, that here was a
nunnery, about A.D. 686, but by whom
founded, or how demolished, does not appear. About the year 1150, Eustace Fitz
John, founded here a priory of Gilbertine
nuns, of the Order of Sempringham, and
thirteen canons; the number of nuns was
fifty-three. Like all other religious houses,
this monastery has suffered great dilapidations; but the worthy family of the Bethel's
have preserved what remains of the buildings, since it came into their possession;
and the venerable relics of this ancient structure still merit the attention of the antiquary. The church here, like the ancient
monastery, is dedicated to St. Mary; George
Bethell, Esq. is the patron, and the Rev.
George Ferreman the incumbent. Pop. 307.

Legard Digby, Esq. Watton abbey
Scruton Thos. corn miller
Scruton John, bleacher

*Wauldby,* in the parish of Rowley, and wap. of Harthill; 4 miles E.
of South Cave. Pop. 44.

WAXHOLME, in the parish of
Owthorn, wap. and liberty of Holderness; 5¼ mls. N. of Patrington. Pop. 72.

*Farmers,*
Atkinson James
Atkinson Geo.
Grandell Francis

Harrison Wm.
Giles Stephen
Stearn Thos.
Tate John

*Woodland*, in the parish of Brandesburton, wap. and liberty of Holderness; 5 miles SE. of Driffield.

WEAVERTHORPE, (P.) in the wap. of Buckrose; 12 miles E. of Malton. The living of the parish church is in the gift of the Dean and Chapter of York, and the Rev. Rd. Forrest is the vicar. Pop. 334.

Ashworth Rev. Abraham curate

*Carpenters,*
Johnson Wm.
Milner John
*Farmers,*
Anderson Thos.
Dickenson Vasey
Grice Matthew
Langhorn Thos.
Marshall Wm.

Smith Wm.
Wallgate Thos.
*Grocers,*
Ashwell Thos.
Cooper Leonard
Pattison Edw.
*Tailors,*
Jeffrey John
Kirby Benj.

Cnilby John, shoemaker
Hodgson John, butcher
Postill Richard, vict. Blue Bell
Robson John, smith & farrier

*Weedley*, in the parish of South Cave, and wap. of Harthill; 2¼ miles E. of South Cave.
Lamplugh George, farmer

*West*, a small hamlet in the parish of St. John's, Beverley, wap. and liberty of Holderness; 1 mile E. of Beverley. Pop. 101.

*Weeton*, in the parish of Welwick, wap. and liberty of Holderness; 3 miles SE. of Patrington; a small hamlet, chiefly inhabited by farmers. Pop. included with Welwick.

*Welham Bridge*, in the parish of Holme-on-Spalding-Moor, and wap. of Harthill; 5 miles NNE. of Howden.

WELTON, (P.) in the wap. of Howdenshire; 4 miles SE. of South Cave, and 10 miles S. of Beverley. There is here an ancient church, with a tower in the centre, dedicated to St. Helen, of which the king is the patron, & the Rev. H. W. Champney the vicar. There is also a Methodist chapel. The church contains an effigy of a Knight Templar, which carries its antiquity beyond 1327, when that order was dissolved, and it is supposed to have been built by Wm. Rufus, who succeeded Wm. the Conqueror, in 1088. Pop. 576.

Popple Rev. Miles, A.M. curate

*Gentry,*
Collins Mrs. Marg
Gallond Mrs. Mary
Johnson John
Johnson John, jun.
Lowthorp James
Lowthorp Wm.
Maude Miss

Raikes Robert
Richardson Mrs.
Salisbury Mrs.
Whitaker Charles
*Academies,*
Osbourne Misses,
(ladies' bdg.)
Smith John

*Bakers,*
Brittain Henry
Nicholson Thos.
*Bricklayers,*
Andrew Wm.
Penrose John
Wilkinson Rhd.
*Carpenters,*
Dodsworth Geo.
Dorsey Peter
Ingmire John
*Farmers & Yeomen,*
Beilby John
Brough Wm.
Clapham Geo.

Stickney Watson
*Grocers,*
Hudson John
Hunter Wm
*Shoemakers,*
Deighton Richard
Rogers John
Williamson Thos.
*Surgeons,*
Gledston Wm.
Jackson Richard
*Tailors,*
Farrow Wm.
Hessey Mark
Kidd Samuel

Bartram John, butcher
Dixon Geo. shopkeeper
Fenwick John, plumber & glazier
Hargraves James, saddler
Hopper Francis, yeoman
Johnson Jane, linen draper, &c.
Nelson Wm. blacksmith
Ogilvie Edw. Johnson, cabinet makr.
Stephenson Thos. corn miller
Wright Eleanor, vict. Green Dragon

*Carriers,* T. Nicholson, T. Cade, & J. Ianson, to Hull every Tu. & Fri.

The RODNEY COACH, from Hull, passes through about half past 7 mg. and ret. about 4 afternoon.

WELWICK, (P.) in the wap. and liberty of Holderness; 2 miles SE. of Patrington, is a small village, pleasantly situated on the high road from Patrington to Spurn Head. The church is a very ancient Gothic structure, dedicated to St. Mary, of which the King is the patron, and the Rev. C. C. Chambers the vicar. This church contains the ruins of an antique monument, supposed to have been removed from Burstall Abbey, and though it is now in a state of dilapidation, it has a grand and imposing appearance to the searching eye of the antiquarian: it is supposed by some to have been erected in memory of John de Fortibus, by others, William le Gros, Earl of Albemarle; but time has obliterated any positive conclusion on this point. There is a small Friends' Meeting house, also a Methodist chapel. Pop. including Thorpe Plewland and Weeton, 416.

*Blacksmiths,*
Dibnah James
Warrener Wm.
*Farmers,*
Baron Thos.
Burnham Robert
Clubley John
Coy James
Fewson Wm.
Jefferson Wm.
Marshall John

Roberts Joseph
Simms Thos.
Ward Henry
Wright Thos.
*Schoolmasters,*
Hunton Robert
Wilson John
*Shoemakers,*
Green Wm.
Hessle Wm.
Hilton John

Wheelwrights, Ombler Wm.
Mempos Thos. Stamford Robert
Cockrane Catharine, vict. Wheat Sheaf
Eddson Eliz. grocer and draper
Greenhead Wm. corn miller
Kemp Martin, butcher
Wright Edward, tailor

*Welwickthorpe*, in the parish of Welwick, wap. and liberty of Holderness; 1 mile SE. of Patrington.

*Westall*, in the parish of Aldbrough, wap. and liberty of Holderness; 9 mls. from Hedon.

WESTOW, (P.) in the wap. of Buckrose; 6 miles S. of Malton. The parish church is in the patronage of the Archbishop of York, and the Rev. Robert Affleck is the incar. There is here also a Methodist chapel, and a school, in which the interest of £. left by Mrs. Sagars, serves to educate some children. Population, 423.

...field Joseph, Esq.
...ykes Tatton, Esq. Westow hall

| Carpenters, | Walker Richard |
| Eliott Thos. | Ward Mercy |
| ...hnson Wm. | Wilson John |
| ...ooly Thos. | Shoemakers, |
| Farmers, | Massey Wm. |
| ...arkson Peter | Wakes Mark |
| ...ypson John | Shopkeepers, |
| ...rwood Tindale | Bullivar Mary |
| ...kson Thos. S. | Hill John |
| ...herington Wm. | Stone Masons, |
| ...rritt John | Holmes John |
| ...tter John | Smith Joseph |
| ...tter Ann | Wilson John |
| ...ade John | Tailors, |
| ...ilker Geo. | Barker Geo. |
| ...ilker Wm. | Holmes Thos. |

...ton John, butcher and jobber
...useley Thomas, schoolmaster
...odwill Mary, blacksmith
...hardson Isaac, vict. Fox

WETWANG, (P.) in the wap. of Buckrose, & liberty of St. Peter's; 7 mls. W. Driffield. Exclusive of the parish church, dedicated to St. Michael, of which the Rev. ...land Croxton is the vicar, and the Prebendary of Wetwang the patron; there is ...apel for the Methodists. This village, ...hich Thomas Wilberfoss, Esq. resides, ...rincipally occupied by farmers and their ...urers. Population, 422.

*Wharram Grange*, in the parish of Wharram-le-street, and wap. of Buckrose; 7 miles SE. of Malton.

*Wharram-le-Street*, (P.) in the wap. of Buckrose; 6 miles SE. of Malton. The parish church is a small ancient structure, of which the Rev.

James Green is the vicar, and Lord Middleton the patron. Pop. 137.

*Wharram Percy*, (P.) in the wap. of Buckrose; 6 miles SSE. of Malton. The Rev. Richard Allen is the vicar of this parish, and the living is in the gift of Miss Isted and Miss Englefield. Pop. 44.

WHELDRAKE, (P.) in the wap. of Ouse and Derwent; 8 miles SE. of York. The church, which was re-built in the year 1789, is dedicated to St. Helen; the Hon. Robert Elliott is the rector, and the Archbishop of York the patron. There is here a well endowed school, for the education of 19 boys and girls, of which Mr. William Dawson is the master, and a manor court for the recovery of small debts, of which George Fearn is the Bailiff; there are also two Methodist chapels, one of the Old and the other of the New Connexion. Pop. 638.

Viccars Rev. John, curate
Dodsworth Geo. gentleman
Savage Richard Raines, gentleman

| Farmers & Yeomen, | Lacy Joseph |
| Acomb Quintin | Lamplugh Wm. |
| Acomb Joseph | Myers John |
| Appleyard James | Mosey Francis |
| Barker Emanuel | Parker John |
| Bolton Richard | Petch Wm. |
| Bradley Wm. | Raines Robert |
| Broadbelt Edw. | Rotsey George |
| Camidge Amos | Reston Thos. |
| Collins Wm. | Reston David |
| Coulson Thos. | Robinson Richard |
| Cowper Robt. | Silvester Walker |
| Etherington Wm. | Slater T. |
| Etty Thomas | Tate John |
| Fearn George | Turton Richard |
| Fletcher John | Shoemakers, |
| Fowler Mary | Bolton John |
| Gray Thos. | Holmes Geo. |
| Harrison Richard | Hopps Christopher |
| Hebnon E. | Tailors, |
| Herbert Wm. | Pottage Matthew |
| Herbert Sarah | Watson Christr. |
| Hughes John | |

Biscomb Robert, cooper
Davison Wm. schoolmaster
Myers Wm. wheelwright
Myers John, vict. Red Lion
Nicholson Christopher, corn miller
Pottage Richard, blacksmith
Pottage Thos. vict. Blacksmith's Arms
Wood Tabitha, shopkeeper
Young Wm. vict. County Hospital
Carrier—E. Young, to York every Sat.

*Wholsea*, in the parish of Holme-on-Spalding-Moor, and wap. of Harthill; 6 mls. SSW. of Market Weighton.

WILBERFOSS, (P.) in the wap. of Harthill; 5 miles WNW. of Pocklington.—

The parish church is dedicated to St. John the Baptist. The ancient and respectable family of Wilberfoss, of which William Wilberforce, Esq. is a descendant, resided here from the conquest till the year 1710, when the family estate and the mansion were sold, but the patronage of the living is still in the Wilberforce family. Elias de Cotton founded a priory of Benedictine nuns here, in the reign of Henry II. which was valued at the suppression at 26*l*. 10*s*. 8*d*. per annum.—Population, 335.

Willis Rev. James, perpetual curate
Wright Robert, gentleman

| *Blacksmiths,* | Lister Richard |
|---|---|
| Linfoot John | Newbald Thomas |
| Wood Thomas | Nicholson Richd. |
| *Farmers & Yeomen,* | Owst Robert |
| Bell John | Saltmarsh Thos. |
| Calam Richard | Silversides John |
| Cook Thomas | *Shopkeepers,* |
| Elliott Thomas | Bell John |
| Gillah John | Nalton John |
| Harrison Matthew | Seamour Richard |
| Hotham John | *Wheelwrights,* |
| Jepson Thomas | Gilbank Thos. |
| Leng Wm. | Shepherdson Geo. |

Batty Wm. vict. Horse Shoes
Bell Francis, wholesale brewer
Brown Jabez, tailor
Catton Wm. vict. True Briton
Craven John, baker
Kidd John, schoolmaster
Lotherington Geo. bricklayer
Pearson Samuel, butcher
Rowntree Thos. corn miller
Wood John, vict. Waggon & Horses

*Wilfeholme,* in the parish of Kilnwick, and township of Beswick, and wap. of Harthill; 9 mls. S. of Driffield.

*Willerby,* (P.) in the wap. of Dickering; 6 miles W. of Hunmanby. The church, of which the Rev. Arthur Jaques is the vicar, is dedicated to St. Peter, and the King is the patron of the living. Pop. 34.

WILLERBY, in the parishes of Cottingham and Kirk Ella, and waps. of Harthill and Hullshire; 6 miles W NW. of Hull.

Pease Clifford, merchant
Pease Rev. George
Smith Mrs. gentlewoman
Thomas Wm. ship chandler

| *Farmers,* | Pickering R. & R. |
|---|---|
| Bursell H. | Thompson John |
| Kirk John | |

Carrier—M. Andrew to Hull Tu.& Fri.

*Willytoft,* in the parish of Bubwith, and wap. of Harthill; 5½ miles NW. of Howden. Population with Gribthorpe, 145.

WILSTHORPE, in the parish of Bridlington, and wap. of Dickering; 2½ miles S. of Bridlington. Pop. 16.

Woodcock John, farmer

WILTON BISHOP, (P.) in the wap. of Harthill, and liberty of St. Peter; 4 miles N. of Pocklington. The church is an ancient structure, dedicated to St. Michael, the Rev. William Metcalfe is the vicar, & Sir Mark Masterman Sykes, lord of the manor, the patron. Bishop Neville had founded a palace here, which was mostly round, and from which it is supposed the village derived its name. Pop. 570.

Richardson George, gentleman

| *Farmers & Yeomen,* | Wilson Geo. jun. |
|---|---|
| Bunks John | *Shoemakers,* |
| Butterfield Thos. | Failess Thos. |
| Hotham Francis | Ogram James |
| Layton R. & W. | *Surgeons,* |
| Matthew John | Meggison Robert |
| Myers Geo. | Seymour Francis |
| Rogerson Abm. | *Tailors,* |
| Stillborn John | Cross Wm. |
| Todd John | Seller Robert |
| Wilson Geo. sen. | |

Anderson Thos. vict. Garraby Inn
Duggleby Wm. shopkeeper
Gowland Wm. blacksmith
Richardson Wm. vict. Cross Keys
Scaife John, corn miller
Shepherd Thos. schoolmaster
Tenneson John, carpenter
Wells Joseph, vict. Buck
Wilkinson Robert, bricklayer

Carriers—Thos. Blakey and John Davison, to York every Sat.

*Winbry Hill,* in the parish of Wilberfoss, and wap. of Harthill; 6 miles WNW. of Pocklington.

WINESTEAD, (P.) in the wap. and liberty of Holderness; 1½ mile NW. of Patrington; a small pleasant village surrounded by a variety of beautiful picturesque scenery. There are two elegant halls, which may rank, for pleasantness and neatness of structure, with many of the noble villas in England. The church is a low Gothic structure, surrounded by lofty trees, that give it an air of deep solemnity; there is in the interior a stone monument, representing the late Sir Robert Hildyard, laying in armour; the monument stands in an unusual part of the church, being placed immediately before the pulpit. This edifice is dedicated to St. Germain; Thomas Thornton Hildyard, Esq. is the patron. The famous Andrew Marvel, M.P. for Hull, son of the rector of this place, was born here on the 31st of March, 1621, as appears from the parish register. The manor of Winestead came into the possession of the Hildyard family about the reign of Richard II. Sir Robert D'Arcy Hildyard, the last baronet, dying in Nov. 1814, without issue, bequeathed his estate to his niece, Anne Catharine Whyte, who married in 1815, Thomas Thornton of Flintham house, in the county of Nottingham, who, in compliance with Sir Robert's will, assumed the name and arms of Hildyard. Pop. 129.

Hildyard Colonel, Winestead hall
Hildyard Rev. Wm. rector
Maister Colonel Arthur
Moyser Robert, Esq.
Raines William, chief constable of the South Division of Holderness, & steward to Thos. Hildyard, Esq.

| *Farmers,* | Linsdell John and |
| Dawson Edmund | Robert |
| Ford —— | Medforth Wm. |
| Giles Stephen | Wright Thos. |

*Winkton*, in the parish of Barmston, wap. and liberty of Holderness; 5 miles S. of Bridlington.

WINTRINGHAM, (P.) in the wap. of Buckrose; 7 miles ENE. of Malton. The church is dedicated to St. Peter; the Rev. L. Grainger, Dean, is the curate, and the patronage is in the Strickland family. Pop. including Newton and Linton, 826.

| *Farmers,* | Jackson Wm. |
| Coultas Thomas | Puckrin John |
| Creaser Francis | Robinson Wm. |
| Dale Wm. | Spink Wm. |
| Hollingworth John | |

Creaser Thomas, wheelwright
Leckenby John, schoolmaster
Spauton John, blacksmith

WITHERNSEA, in the parish of Hollym, wap. and liberty of Holderness; 4 miles NE. of Patrington. A small village situated near the sea; the church has long been a ruin; formerly it was a magnificent building, and is supposed to have been suffered to decay, as the village from its decrease in wealth and population, was unable to support so large and costly a structure. This is one of the sister churches, and is dedicated to St. Nicholas. In the records of the reign of king John, it is mentioned that there was a priory here subordinate to the abbey of Albemarle, in France. Pop. 106.

| *Farmers,* | Newsome Wm. |
| Coates Mary | Osmond Henry |
| Cross John | Sharp Walter |
| Fenby Richard | Watson Henry |
| Hutchinson Henry | *Shoemakers,* |
| Lamb Thomas | Drew William |
| Mager Wm. | Mawer William |

WITHERNWICK, (P.) in the wap. of Holderness, and liberty of St. Peter's; 8 miles N. of Hedon, 6 from Hornsea. The church, of which the Prebendary of Abp. Holm, in York cathedral, is the patron, is a low ancient structure, dedicated to St. Alban; the Rev. George Kelly, is the vicar, and the Rev. Wm. Craven, the curate. Pop. 370.

Denton Samuel, surgeon

| *Butchers,* | Riby J. & G. |
| Dunn John | Robinson Michael |
| Gardham John | Simpson Joseph |
| *Farmers & Yeomen,* | Taylor Robert |
| Acklam Thomas | Taylor John |
| Croft Mrs. | Watson Wm. |
| Ennis Robert | *Grocers, &c.* |
| Fisher John | Hewson David |
| Hardy Thomas | Pickering Robert |
| Hewson Wm. | *Wheelwrights,* |
| Hobson Henry | Bainbridge James |
| Jenkinson John | Todd Thomas |
| Leaper John | |

Allman John, corn miller
Couthard John, blacksmith
Fenby George, shoemaker
Godolphin Joseph, tailor
Palmer Thomas, schoolmaster
Robinson Wm. vict. & bricklayer, Gate
Wilson Thomas, bricklayer

*Carriers*—Thos. King and Wm. Wray to Hull, Tu. and Fri.

*Wold Cottage*, in the parish of Thwing, and wap. of Dickering; 8 mls. W NW. of Bridlington. A very extraordinary phenomenon was observed here on the 13th of December, 1795; in order to commemorate which, Mr. Topham has erected an obelisk, with this inscription :—" Here on this spot, December 13th, 1795, fell from the atmosphere AN EXTRAORDINARY STONE, in breadth 28 inches, in length 36 inches, and whose weight was 56 pounds: this column, in memory of it, was erected by Edward Topham, 1799." The stone, while it resembles in composition those which have fallen in various parts of the world, has no counterpart or resemblance in the natural stones of the country. In its fall, which was witnessed by two persons, it excavated a place to the depth of 12 inches in the earth, and 7 inches into the chalk rock, making in all a depth of 19 inches from the surface. This stone was subsequently deposited in the museum of Mr. Sowerby.

WOLD NEWTON, (P.) in the wap. of Dickering; 9 miles WNW. of Bridlington. The patron of the living is in the Langley family. Pop. 177.
Preston Rev. Wm. vicar

| *Carpenters,* | Summers John |
| Knaggs George | |

*Farmers,*
Gibson Thomas
Greice Peter
Lowson John

Simpson Wm.
Wade William
Watson James

Bell Thomas, blacksmith
Southwick John, corn miller
Summers John, vict. Plough
Watson James, grocer
Watson Thomas, shoemaker

*Carrier*—Matthew Hick, to Thwing & Bridlington every Saturday

WOODHALL, in the parish of Heminbrough, wap. of Ouse and Derwent; 6 miles E. of Selby. Pop. with Brackenholme, 90.

Reeves Charles, sen. gent. Old hall
Reeves Charles, jun. Woodal hall
Farr James, farmer
Lake William, gardener

*Woodhouse,* in the parish of Sutton-on-Derwent, and wap. of Harthill; 5 miles WSW. of Pocklington.

*Woodley,* in the parish of Kirby-Underdale, and wap. of Buckrose; 9 miles from Malton.

WOODMANSEA - *cum*- BEVERLEY PARK, in the parish of St. John's, Beverley, wap. of Harthill, and liberty of Beverley; 1½ mile SE. of Beverley. Population, 276.

Carus Thomas, corn miller
Cooke Thomas, bleacher
Stephenson, John, gardener
Wilkinson John, vict. Altisidora

WRESSELL, (P.) in the wap. of Harthill; 4 miles NW. of Howden. The church, dedicated to St. John, of Beverley, is a very ancient building, in the patronage of the Earl of Egremont. Wressell castle was founded by Thomas Percy, Earl of Worcester, who was taken prisoner at the battle of Shrewsbury, and beheaded there in the year 1403. This castle became afterwards a seat of the Northumberland family, continuing in its splendour till the civil wars in the reign of Charles I. when it shared the fate of many other castles, being dismantled by an order of parliament. Little more than the shell of this once princely mansion now remains. The inhabitants of Wressell have a current tradition, that all the men capable of bearing arms in that parish were with the Earl of Northumberland at the battle of Chevy Chase, where most of them were slain; Dr. Percy says that the first Earl of Northumberland fought the battle of Chevy Chase; but the well known song of that name has been embellished with several circumstances relating to the battle of Otterburn. Pop. including Loftsome, 183.

Stanhope Rev. Fitzroy, H. R. vicar
Guy Rev. Thomas, curate
Waterworth Richard, gent. Castle

*Farmers,*
Calvert John

Keighley Robt.
Neville John

Hutchinson Miles, corn, &c. merchant
Markham John, blacksmith
Revell Thomas, corn miller
Williamson George, carpenter

WYTON, in the parish of Swine, wap. & liberty of Holderness; 4 miles N. of Hedon. A delightfully situated village. Population, 95.

Collinson William, gentleman
Green Captain J. Wyton house
Harrison Richard, Esq. Wyton hall

*Farmers,*
Fenwick Robert
Myers Thomas
Simpson William

Simpson Joseph
Wilson George
Withernwick Geo.

YAPHAM, in the parish of Pocklington, and wap. of Harthill; 2 miles NW. of Pocklington. Here is a Chapel of Ease under the vicarage of Pocklington; curate, Rev. Charles Brown. Population, 114.

Biass Thomas, corn miller
Leak William, yeoman
Pickering John, yeoman, Smilet hall

YEDDINGHAM, (P.) in the wap. of Buckrose; 9 miles NE. of Malton. Situated on the banks of the Derwent, which is navigable from hence to the Humber for small craft. The parish church is a small structure, dedicated to St. John the Baptist. Earl Fitzwilliam is the patron of the living. Robert de Clere, before the year 1163, founded near this place a small monastery for 9 nuns of the Benedictine order, which at the dissolution had a revenue of 26l. 6s. 9d. Population, 127.

Ellis Rev. John, curate

YOKEFLEET, in the parish of Howden, wap. and liberty of Howdenshire; 6 miles SE. of Howden. This village is situated near to the river Ouse, and the windmill serves as a mark for the sailors to navigate the river. Population, 199.

Empson John, gentleman
Blanchard Robert, yeoman
Blanchard Thomas, corn miller
Blanchard William, cattle dealer

*Foulthorpe,* in the parish of Bishop Wilton, wap. of Harthill, and liberty of St. Peter's; 5 miles NNW. of Pocklington. Population, including Gowthorpe, 111.

# NORTH RIDING.

ABBOTSIDE, (High and Low) in parish of Aysgarth, wap. of Hang West, liberty of Richmondshire; 1 mile NW. Hawes, pleasantly situated on the North e of the river Ure, and extending west-rd from Askrigg to the borders of West-reland. Population, 181.

| Farmers, | Scarr Thos. |
| ll Mark | Scarr George |
| ll Robert | Scarr James |
| ll Matthew | Scarr George |
| ades Francis | Thistlethwaite A. |
| aydes Cornelius | Thompson Matt. |
| rter Richard | Thompson Alex. |
| ttlewell Anth. | Tunstal George |
| & hosier | Weatherit James |
| etcalf Joseph | Webster James |
| obinson Thos. | Willis John |

ACKLAM, in the wap. and liberty Langbargh; 7 miles N.E. of Yarm.— e church, lately rebuilt, is a perpetual acy, in the patronage of the Archbishop York, incumbent the Rev. J. Walstall. klam hall, in this village, is the residence Thos. Hustler, Esq. Population, 105.

Acre Ings, in the parish of Lythe, p. and liberty of Langbergh; 8 les WNW. of Whitby.

AGGLETHORPE, in the parish of verham, wap. of Hang West, and liberty Richmondshire; 3 miles WSW. of Mid-ham, a small hamlet, pleasantly situated Coverdale. Agglethorpe Hall is the resi-ace of Matthew Chaytor, Esq. Pop. 131.

Aikber, in the parish of Fingall, p. of Hang West, and liberty of chmondshire; 5¼ miles ENE. of yburn. Population, 43.

Ainderby Myers, in the parish of ornby, wap. of Hang East, & liberty Richmondshire; 4 mls. N. of Bedale. pulation, including Holtby, 79.

AINDERBY QUERNHOW, in the rish of Pickhill, wap. of Halikeld, d liberty of Richmondshire; 6 miles SW. of Thirsk. Pop. 99.

llerby John, vict. Crabtree House anger Ralph, vict. Board een David, cattle dealer ghmoor Mrs. Nancy ckersgill Francis, common carrier, Leeming lane

Pickersgill & Co. have daily post wag-gons from London, Manchester, Leeds, Sheffield, &c. to Durham and Newcastle-upon-Tyne, viz.— From London to Durham & New-castle-upon-Tyne, in 7 days; from Leeds in 2 days; from Man-chester in 5 days; from Sheffield in 4 days. Goods for Sunderland, Houghton--le--Spring, Fatfield, Chester - le - Street, Sedge-field, Wolsingham, &c. &c. are prompt-ly forwarded by the respective carriers.

AINDERBY STEEPLE, (P.) in the wap. of Gilling East, and liberty of Rich-mondshire; 3 miles WSW. of Northaller-ton. A parochial village, the church of which is dedicated to St. Helen. The living is a vicarage, in the patronage of the King; incumbent the Rev. James Robson, A.M. Population, 266.

Bearpark Richard, gentleman
Pattison Mrs. gentlewoman
Wormald John, Esq. Ainderby hall

| Farmers, | Shoemakers, |
| Appleton James | Barnett Cuthbert |
| Bailey Wm. | White Thomas |
| Dodsworth Geo. | Shopkeepers, |
| Miller Ralph | Milburn John |
| Todd Joseph | Watson Eliz. |

Alton Christ. vict. Farmer's Delight
Christon Wm. schoolmaster
Grundy John, vict. and butcher, Wel-lington
Haw Francis, churchwarden
King Leonard, churchwarden
Mitchell and Carps, carpenters, &c.
Ragg John, tailor and draper
Robson Benj. blacksmith
White Thos. parish clerk
Woodhouse John, churchwarden

AINTHORPE, in the parish of Dan-by, wap. and liberty of Langbargh; 9 miles SE. of Guisbrough, a small ham-let, situated at the eastern extremity of Danby Dale. There is here a small Methodist chapel, built about 12 years ago, and a stone bridge, remarkable for its antiquity, crossing the river Esk.

Duck Rev. Daniel, curate of Danby

*Butchers,*
Bennison Wm.
Proud Richard
Smith John
*Drapers & Grocers,*
Hugill Jacob
Watson Thos.
*Farmers & yeomen,*
Dale James

Coward Thos. vict. and blacksmith, Fox and Hounds
Galloway Thos. corn miller
Robinson John, vict. and cartwright, Lord Wellington
Raddock Wm. day school & parish clerk
Sanderson Joseph, shopkeeper
Thornton and Petch, coal proprietors, Clitherbecks
Wilks Wm. joiner

*Carrier*—Joseph Bailiffe, to Whitby, every Sat. dep. 1 mg. ret. 8 evg.

*Airsholme*, in the parish of Acklam, wap. and liberty of Langbargh; 6 mls. NE. of Yarm.

AIRYHOLME, in the parish of Hovingham, and wap. of Rydale; 8 miles W. of Malton
Morrell Wm. farmer

AISENBY, in the parish of Topcliffe, wap. of Halikeld, and liberty of Allertonshire; 5 miles N. of Boroughbridge. Pop. 230.

*Farmers & yeomen,*
Anderson Wm.
Barker John
Dresser Joseph
Fall Thos.
Faudington Jane
Groves Ralph
Rocliffe John

Johnson Thomas, butcher and vict. Shoulder of Mutton
Poulter William, shoemaker
Robinson Wm. tailor
Walker Thomas, saddler, &c.
Yeates William, blacksmith and vict. Three Horse Shoes

AISKEW, in the parish of Bedale, wap. of Hang East, and liberty of Richmondshire; ½ mile NE. of Bedale. This village is separated from the town of Bedale by a rivulet, called Bedale Brook. Here are two Anabaptist chapels, (ministers non-resident) and a Roman Catholic chapel, Monsieur Francis Herman, minister. Pop. 690.

Arden Mrs. Anna Maria, Leases
Dinsdale Wm. Esq. coroner for the county
Dryden George, gentleman
Foss James, gentleman
Fothergill Mrs. Hannah, gentlewoman
Gilden Mrs. Ann, Leases
Hebden William, gentleman

Harding Richard
Harrison Robert
Hugill Thomas
Nellis Joseph
*Nellis George*
Predom Thos.
Rudsdale Thos.
Scarth Thos.
Smith Geo.

*Carpet, Damask, Diaper & Linen Manufacturers,*
Lodge Francis
Webster & Son
*Coopers,*
Corbett Wm.
Fisher John
*Farmers,*
Chapman Simon
Duck William
Dunn John
Ellerton Geo.
Elwood Thomas
Fothergill Charles
Kendall Edward
Lonsdale John
Simpson Richard

Sturges Thos.
Strangeways Edw.
*Gardeners,*
Caven John, (nursery & seedsman)
Mickles Adam, (landscape)
*Shoemakers,*
Pearson Richard
Webster James
Wood James
*Shopkeepers,*
Copeland Geo.
Johnson Mary
Weatherhill John
*Wheelwrights,*
Bateman Michael
Merryweather Rd.

Arnett John, saddler
Britch George, blacksmith
Fryer Wm. violin maker & gunsmith
Fryer Joseph, vict. Waggon
Harrison Thos. supervisor
Humphreys Geo. vict. Malt Shovel
Langborn Richard, dyer
Prudah John, corn miller
Steed John, vict. Anchor, Leeming bar
Walmsley James, bread baker
Whitton Geo. butcher
Wilson John, tailor and draper

AISLABY, in the parish of Middleton, wap. & liberty of Pickering Lythe; 1½ m. W. of Pickering. Pop. 147.

Hayes Mrs. Mary
*Farmers,*
Brewster Thos.
Golding Stockton
Monkman Robt.
Trueman Richard
Wardell Francis
Watson Richard

Frank Thomas, joiner, &c.
Kilvington Wm. vict. and blacksmith

*Aislaby,* in the parish of Whitby, wap. and liberty of Langbargh; 3 miles W SW. of Whitby. Here is a Chapel of Ease to the parish church, of which the Rev. Joseph Robertson is incumbent, and the Rev. Timothy Castley, officiating curate.—Population, 253.

ALDBROUGH, in the parish of St. John Stanwick, wap. of Gilling West, and liberty of Richmondshire; 7 miles N. of Richmond. Here is a handsome free school, erected at the expense of S. M. Barrett, Esq. M.P. for Richmond, and now conducted on the Lancasterian system, and supported by voluntary contributions. Population, 544.

A Foot Post to Richmond Mon. Wed. & Sat.

Glover Michael, surgeon
Hutchinson Ingledew, steward to S. M. Barrett, Esq.

*Blacksmiths,*
Hogg Charles
Malthouse Mary
Robinson Robert
   *Farmers,*
Clark John
Dawson Wm.
Dobbin Richard
Elliot Percival
Gent Wm.
Greenwood Wm.
Ingledew Geo.
Milburn Wm.
Shipton Matthew

Spencely Mary
Stephenson Martin
Stockell Robert
   *Shoemakers,*
Chambers Thos.
Miles Newton
   *Shopkeepers,*
Bland Matthew, (& tailor)
Hildrew Wm. (& draper)
   *Stone-masons,*
Pattinson John
Watson Robert

Allinson Eliz. brewer
Arnett M. vict. Half Moon
Bland Wm. miller
Cowle George, joiner, &c.
Dobbinson Thos. schoolmaster
Hutchinson James, spirit merchant
Hutchinson Henry, vict. Fleece
Kyle Robert, weaver
Story George, farrier
Wake John, tailor

*Aldburgh*, in the parish of Masham, wap. of Hang East; 2 miles SSE. of Masham. A place of great antiquity; the castle and lordship belonged to William le Gros, Earl of Albemarle, who, in the year 1138, was created Earl of York, in consequence of his gaining " the battle of the Standard," fought at Northallerton. Aldbrough Hall is the residence of James Henry D'Arcy Hutton, Esq.

*Aldwark*, in the parish of Alne, and wap. of Bulmer, a part in the liberty of St. Peter's; 5 miles ESE. of Boroughbridge. This village is situated on the eastern bank of the Ure, which is here navigable. Pop. 163.

ALLERSTON, (P.) in the wap. and liberty of Pickering Lythe; 5 miles E. of Pickering. There is here an ancient church, dedicated to St. Mary. The living is a perpetual curacy, of which the Rev. Thomas Simpson, vicar of Ebberston, is the incumbent. Pop. 401.

   *Farmers,*
Anderson Christr.
Dale Wm.
Dale Lawrence
Hardwick Ralph, (and grazier)
Jackson Geo.
Linton Francis
Myers Robert

Taylor Samuel
Wilkinson Geo.
   *Shopkeepers,*
Goodill Robert
Stephenson Mary
   *Weavers,*
Fowler Geo.
Watson Wm.

Greenley Richard, vict. Heart
Hansell John, bleacher and fuller
Hardy John, blacksmith
Hartsey James, joiner
Lockwood Mark, shoemaker

Pickup John, warrener
Ruston Timothy, corn miller

*Allerthorp*, in the parish of Pickhill, wap. of Halikeld, and liberty of Allertonshire; 5 mls. ESE. of Bedale.

ALNE, (P.) in the wap. of Bulmer, a part in the liberty of St. Peter's; 3½ miles SW. of Easingwold. The church is a handsome edifice, dedicated to St. Mary. The living is a vicarage, and in the patronage of W. J. Bethel, Esq. of which the Rev. Henry Chaloner, A. M. is the incumbent. This village takes its name from the Latin word Alnus, (the alder tree) it being situated in a low swampy country, which formerly abounded with alders, and thence was called the Forest of Alders. Pop. 386.

Brooksbank Stamp, Esq.
Burgess Mrs.
Matterson Mrs. Ann
Wilkinson Rev. John, vicar of Ellerton

   *Corn-millers,*
Mitchell John
Stanhope J.
   *Farmers & Yeomen,*
Allison Thos.
Brown Richard
Coulson Christr.
Coulson Michael
Cundall John
Dinnington Jon.
Dodd Elizabeth
Driffield John
Eagle John
Ellis Wm.
Flawith Robert
Flawith John
Harrison Christr.
Moon John
Penrose Geo. sen.
Robinson Robert

Shepherd Robert
Wedell Wm.
   *Shoemakers,*
Atkinson John, (& vict. Board)
May Wm.
Penrose Geo. jun.
   *Shopkeepers,*
Douthwaite John, (& day school)
Hall Thos.
Hopwood John
White Geo.
   *Tailors,*
Robinson Robert
Whitwell Thos.
   *Wheelwrights, &c.*
Dunnington John
Hall Thos.
Smithson Richard

Bell John, blacksmith
Burgess Thos. linen manufacturer
Carr Wm. vict. Fox
Dunnington Wm. sen. vict. Blue Bell
Dunnington Wm. jun. butcher
Foster Joseph, bricklayer

*Carrier*—Thomas Fordington to York, dep. Sat. 4 morning, ret. the same day.

*Amotherby*, in the parish of Appleton-le-Street, and wap. of Rydale; 2½ miles NW. of Malton. Here is a grammar school, endowed with twenty acres of land, present rent 22l. per annum. And a Chapel of Ease to the parish church, of which the Rev. Wm. Sutcliffe is curate. Pop. 340.

AMPLEFORTH, in the parishes of Ampleforth and Oswaldkirk, waps. of Rydale and Birdforth, a part in the liberty of St. Peter's; 4 miles SSW. of Helmsley. T

M M

church is dedicated to St. Hilda. The living is a vicarage, in the patronage of the Prebendary of York cathedral, incumbent the Rev. Anthony Germaine. Population in the parish of Ampleforth, wap. of Birdforth, 192; in the wap. of Rydale, 214;—total, 406.

Smith George, attorney

| Blacksmiths, | Wood Robert |
| Furby Thos. | Joiners, |
| Scott John | Boynton Barth. |
| Farmers & Yeomen, | Fox Jeremiah |
| Bellwood Wm. | Mason Thos. |
| Harding Thos. | Shopkeepers, |
| Linfoot Wm. | Pybus Matthew |
| Little Wm. | Trenholm John |
| Medd Thos. | Wiley Mary |
| Nawton John | Stone-masons, |
| Pollard Wm. | Cooper John |
| Sotheran Geo. | Preston Richard |
| Waller Eliz. | Spence John |
| White Geo. | Thompson Robert |

Barker William, tailor
Cariss Robert, shoemaker
Harrison Wm. vict. White Swan
Heselgrave Wm. vict. White Horse
Rushton John, butcher

ANGRAM, in the parish of Grinton, wap. of Gilling West, and liberty of Richmondshire; 7 miles NW. of Askrigg.

Alderson Edward, yeoman
Alderson William, yeoman
Clark James, coal agent

*Angram Grange*, in the parish of Coxwold, wap. of Birdforth, & liberty of Ripon; 4 miles N. of Easingwold. Population 29.

APPERSET, in the parish of Aysgarth, and wap. of Hang West; 1½ mile W. of Hawes. A small hamlet on the south side of the river Ure, near the western extremity of Wensley Dale.

*Farmers & Yeomen*, Metcalf Christphr.
Branton Thos.    Metcalf Thos.
Hunter Simon    Willan James
Jackson James

*Applegarth*, see Marske.

*Appleton*, (East and West), in the parish of Catterick, wap. of Hang East, and liberty of Richmondshire; 4½ miles NNW. of Bedale.  Pop. 87.

*Appleton-le-Moor*, in the parish of Lastingham, and wap. of Rydale; 4 miles NE. of Kirkby-Moor-Side.—Population 276.

APPLETON-LE-STREET, (P.) in the wap. of Rydale; 4 miles WNW. of Malton.  The church, dedicated to All Saints, is an ancient structure; the living is

a vicarage, of which the Rev. James Jarvis Cleaver, is the incumbent, and the Rev. Wm. Sutcliffe, the curate; is in the patronage of Trinity College, Cambridge.  Pop. 173.

Hebdin James, gentleman
*Farmers*,      Dobson Thos.
Cooper Wm. sen. Harrison Geo.
Cooper Wm. jun. Snary John
Brown Richard, carpenter
Hobbs Thomas, shoemaker
Oliver George, blacksmith

APPLETON-UPON-WISK, (P.) in the wap. and liberty of Langbargh; 7 miles SSW. of Yarm. Here is a small church, the living is a perpetual curacy, of which the Rev. James Hewgill, rector of Great Smeaton, is the incumbent.  Here is also a Methodist chapel. This village is in the district called Cleveland, and takes its name from the Wisk, a small rivulet which runs through the township.  The linen manufacture is carried on here to a considerable extent.  Pop. 492.

Alderson Robert, gentleman
Kingston George, gentleman
Morton Edward, gentleman
Williams Cuthbert, surgeon

| Blacksmiths, | Ward Stephen |
| Russell Michael | Wilson John |
| Russell Benj. | Joiners, &c. |
| Bricklayers, &c. | Errington Ralph |
| Bell John | Peacock Robert |
| Story William & | Watson Peter |
| Thomas | Shoemakers, |
| Butchers, | Brekin Thompson |
| Mawer John | Chipchase Wm. |
| Mawer Wm. | Chipchase Joseph |
| Peacock Robert | Green Thos. |
| Coopers, | Richardson Richd. |
| Martin Richard | Shopkeepers, |
| Suggitt John | Holmes Mary |
| Farmers, | Mankin Christphr. |
| Alderson Wm. | Story Thos. jun. |
| Davison John | Wilkinson Henry |
| Herring Thos. | Tailors, |
| Mawer Geo. | Ianson Christphr. |
| Ord Robert | Smith James, sen. |
| Swainton Harrison | Smith James, jun. |

Rhymer John, schoolmaster
Rhymer John, vict. Lord Nelson
Rountree Thos. corn miller
Routledge Wm. & Sons, linen mfrs.
Watson Peter, vict. Queen's Head
Wilkinson Wm. fishmonger

ARDEN, in the parish of Hawnby, and wap. of Birdforth; 7½ miles NE. of Thirsk.  Darcey Tancred, Esq. resides at the hall.  Population, with Arden-Side, 139.

*Arden-Side*, in the parish of Hawnby, and wap. of Birdforth; 8 miles NE. of Thirsk.

ARKENGARTHDALE, (P.) in the wap. of Gilling West, and liberty of Richmondshire. The Dale is about 7 or 8 miles in length, commencing at Dale Head, running in a SE. direction, and terminating in the town of Reeth. There is a small but neat stone church, (lately erected, the old one being in ruins) situated near the most populous part of the Dale, consecrated in 1820, and dedicated to St. Mary. The living is a perpetual curacy, in the patronage of Lord Viscount Lowther; there is likewise a Methodist chapel built by subscription, and a free school built and endowed by the late George Brown, Esq. of Stockton, lord of the manor; the school and books are free for all children residing in the Dale; the endowment is 60£. per annum, paid out of the rents of the manor; the master has also a house and a piece of land. The inhabitants of Arkengarthdale are principally miners, and Arkengarthdale possesses one of the most productive fields of lead ore worked at the present day, and a smelting mill the most complete and extensive in the country. Pop. 1812. The Dale of Arkengarth contains the following villages and hamlets :—

ASKLE ; 3 miles NW. of Reeth.
Bradwell Esther, vict. C. B.

DALE HEAD ; 7 miles NW. of Reeth.
Hird Thomas, yeoman
Wilkinson Rev. Wm. perpetual curate

ESKELITH ; 4 mls. NW. of Reeth.
Alderson Thomas, yeoman

LANGTHWAITE ; 3½ miles NW. of Reeth.
Hall Nathaniel, yeoman
Tilburn Charles, agent
Barningham John, vict. Red Lion
Barningham Thomas, clogger
Calder George, flour dealer
Christie William, shoemaker
Harker James, grocer and draper
Heslop John, vict. Bull
Weesham William, vict. C. B.
Raine John, flour dealer
Lender Anthony, schoolmaster

SEAL HOUSES ; 5 miles NW. of Reeth.
Alderson Joseph, mining agent
Brown Christopher, yeoman
Calder Matthew, mining agent
Marsden John, yeoman
Peacock Wm. yeoman

WHAGH ; 5 miles NW. of Reeth.
Brown Ralph, yeoman, Faggergill
Langstaff John, yeoman, Plantation
Lyddel John, yeoman, Faggergill

Alderson George, vict. Board
Winter John, mining agent

*Arncliffe*, see Ingleby Arncliffe.

*Arrathorns*, in the parish of Patrick Brompton, and wap. of Hang East; 5 miles SSE. of Richmond. Pop. 64.

ASHGILL, in the parish of Coverham, and wap. of Hang East ; 2 miles W. of Middleham.

Oates George, horse trainer

ASKE, in the parish of Easby, wap. of Gilling West, and liberty of Richmondshire ; 1½ mile N. of Richmond. This small township consists of a few straggling houses occupied by the tenants of Lord Dundas, who is lord of the manor, and has a very beautiful seat here. Pop. 109.

Mitchell Gabriel, agt. to Lord Dundas
Temple Wm. Heslop, bailiff to Lord Dundas

| Farmers, | |
|---|---|
| Allinson John, Aske moor | Emmerson Wm. |
| | Firby Geo. |
| | Fletcher John |
| Ayre Geo. Bent Hagg | Silvers Leonard |
| | Walton Wm. |

## ASKRIGG,

In the parish of Aysgarth, wap. of Hang West, and liberty of Richmondshire ; 5 mls. ENE. of Hawes. Askrigg is a place of great antiquity, and is situated in the centre of Wensley Dale, near the northern bank of the Ure, in a district abounding with romantic and beautiful scenery. The church, which is dedicated to St. Oswald, is a very ancient structure; there is an ash tree growing out of the roof of the vestry. The living is a curacy in the patronage of the vicar of Aysgarth. There are in the township six alms-houses for the comfort of six poor widows, with an allowance of 4s. per week to each. These houses are situated about one mile from Askrigg, and were erected in pursuance of the will of Christopher Alderson, late of Hommerton, in Middlesex. The market day is on Thursday. About half a mile from Askrigg is a water-fall, called Milgill Force, which makes one grand vertical fall of about twenty or thirty yards, and then rushes down the rocky bed of the ravine. One mile further is Whitfield's Force, a spectacle highly gratifying to the lover of picturesque scenery ; and about five miles up the Dale from the town is Hardow Force, a cascade where the water falls in one vast sheet, from a ledge of rocks 99 feet in perpendicular height.— The ravine or chasm which extends below the fall is bounded on each side by huge masses of rock, and is about three hundred yards in length. Behind the fall is a deep recess, whence a good view of it may be obtained with safety. During the hard frost, in the year 1740-41, a prodigious icicle is recorded to have been formed here, of the whole height of the fall, and nearly equal in circumference. Population, 765.

### PENNY POST.

Post Master—*William Terry.*

*.* A Letter Bag arr. from Bedale, (Post-Town) every Mon. Wed. Thu. & Sat. at 10 each mg. and dispatched at 12 noon.

### DIRECTORY.

Balderston Richard, solicitor
Brougham Rev. Samuel Lindsey, officiating curate
Hastwell Mrs. gentlewoman
Jackson Ann, gentlewoman
Lodge John, gentleman
Metcalfe Jane, gentlewoman
Metcalfe Rev. John
Parke Miles R. yeoman
Tiplady Alice, gentlewoman
Wood Rev. Richard, perpetual curate

*Blacksmiths,*
Lee Christopher
Sager James
*Boot & Shoemakers,*
Caygill James
Clarkson Thos.
Graham John
Graham John, jun.
Storey Anthony
*Brewers,*
Lodge Joseph, (& spirit merchant)
Thompson John, (and maltster)
*Butchers,*
Bleakinson James
Lambert Thos.
*Clock and Watch makers,*
Pratt J. & Wm.
Standcliffe John
*Farmers,*
Caygill Christphr.
Cloughton Robert
Thompson Leond.
Woodward John
*Grocers & Drapers,*
Dinsdale James
Holmes Roger, (& dlr. in hardware)
Sykes Samuel
Terry John, (and auctioneer)

Terry Wm. (and auctioneer)
*Flour dealers,*
Caygill Ellen
Dinsdale James
Hodgson Edmund
Hunt James
Robinson Wm.
Tiplady Edmund
*Joiners, &c.*
Bell George
Bell Clement
Thompson Edw.
Thompson Francis
*Knit Hose Mfrs.*
Pratt Thomas
Wood Jeffery
*Stonemasons,*
Heseltine Leonard
Metcalfe John
Metcalfe James
*Surgeons,*
Bowman John,
Moor
Metcalfe James
*Tailors,*
Dinsdale Jeffery
Dinsdale Jeffery, jun.
Dinsdale John
Thompson James

Addison Robert, dyer
Addison Ralph, corn miller & gamekpr.
Atkinson Richard, saddler

Birkett James, officer of excise
Cay Charles, schoolmaster
Clarkson John, wool comber
Crowther Benj. plumber & glazier
Dinsdale James, vict. New Inn
Halton Elizabeth, vict. Bay Horse
Hodgson Jane, straw hat maker
Metcalfe John, bread baker
Prestman Stephen, weaver
Robinson Joseph, painter and gilder
Siddall Joseph, flax mfr. Water mill
Thompson Mthw. vict. Geo. & Dragon
Thwaites John, vict. (slater) Red Lion
Tiplady Metcalfe, parish clerk
Tiplady Edmund, beast jobber
Whitton John, vict. (excise office)
    King's Arms
Wiggan Nicholas, cooper.

*Carriers,*

Edw. Hunter to Hawes, every Tu. & Fri. dep. 9 mg. ret. 7 evg.

J. Blackburn weekly from York to Kendal and Whitehaven.

AYSDALE or AISDALE, in the parish of Guisborough, wap. & liberty of Langbargh; 3 miles ESE. of Guisborough.

*Farmers,*
Dunn Richard
Handersides Jph.
Miller Michael
Seaton Jonathan
Thompson Joseph
Thompson Wm.

AYSGARTH, (P.) in the wap. of Hang West, and liberty of Richmondshire; 4 miles ESE. of Askrigg. This parish is very extensive, and contains three market-towns, viz. Hawes, Askrigg, and Burton in Bishop's Dale, and is famous for its romantic situation on the banks of the river Ure. The church, dedicated to St. Andrew, is a handsome edifice, and the living, which is a discharged vicarage, in the patronage of Trinity College, Cambridge, is enjoyed by the Rev. John Brasse; the Rev. John Winn is the curate. There is here a curious bridge, called Yore, which rises thirty-two feet, and spans seventy-one; the concave of which is embellished with pendent petrifactions, and its airy battlements beautifully festooned with spreading ivy. The cataracts near this place also claim the attention of every traveller; so much so, that the learned Dr. Pocock, whose search after the sublime and marvellous brought him to Aysgarth, is said to have owned, with exultation, that these cataracts exceeded those so celebrated on the Nile. In addition to the parish church there are two meeting-houses, one for the Society of Friends, and another for the Methodists. Population, 293.

Hammond John, gentleman

*Blacksmiths.*
Pickering John
Wray Thomas
Wray John
  *Corn millers,*
Hunter Matthew
Thompson James
Watson Jeremiah
*Farmers & Yeomen,*
Hades Charles
Brown Cornelius
Canfield George
Tomlinson Wm.
Tunstall Francis
Tunstall Thomas
Wilson Mary
Winnington Francis
Winnington John
Winnington Anth.

*Flour dealers, &c.*
Hogg William
Mason Christopher
Metcalfe James
Routh Wm.
Scott David
Simpson John
Terry Ellen
Thomlinson John
Thompson Thos.
Wilson Humphrey
  *Shoemakers,*
Harper John
Thompson Francis
Tunstall Francis
  *Wheelwrights,*
Hammond Marmd
Summer Wm.

Drummond John, sen. parish clerk
Drummond John, jun. F. R. S. classical and commercial academy
Garth John, clogger
Holmes Timothy, vict. Geo. & Dragon
Sayer Francis, victualler and butcher, Miners' Arms
Staveley Geo. millwright
Tomlinson Christopher, druggist
Tomlinson John, cattle dealer

AYTON GREAT, (P.) in the wap. and liberty of Langbargh; 3 miles NE. of Stokesley, at the foot of Roseberry Topping. In the centre of Great Ayton stands a small school house, in which humble seminary the immortal Captain Cook received his school education, at the expense of Thomas Scottowe, Esq. under whom his father acted as hind, at his farm at Airyholme, in this parish. In the church is a monument of elegant workmanship, to the memory of William Wilson, Esq. formerly commodore and commander-in-chief of the marine force of the English East India Company, in which situation " he displayed one continued series of acts of disinterested patriotism and distinguished services." The church, dedicated to All Saints, is a neat plain ancient edifice, and the living is a perpetual curacy, in the patronage of the Rev. G. Marwood. Here are also chapels for the Society of Friends, Independents, Methodists, and Primitive Methodists.— The river Leven may be said to take its rise from Ayton beck, a small rivulet which runs through this village.—Population, 1023.

Letters arrive daily at 7 morn. and are dispatched at 4 aft.

Cookson Colonel
Davison James, gent.

Deason Rev. Wm. M.A. curate
Garbut Mary, gentlewoman
Graham Thomas, Esq.
Jackson Geo. gent.
Jackson Ralph, gent.
Keasley John, gent.
Martin Isaac, gent.
Richardson John, gent.
Richardson Wm. gent.
Richardson Robert, gent.
Sanders J. W. gent.
Slinger Eliz. gentlewoman
Thompson Rev. John
Wilson Thomas, gent.

  *Blacksmiths,*
Gowland Wm.
Snowden James
  *Butchers,*
Easby John
Hebden Wm.
Hodgson Wm.
Napper Thomas
*Farmers & Yeomen,*
Alderson John
Armstrong Thos.
Barker Mark
Barker Wm.
Barr John
Benton Ralph
Biggin Thos.
Chapman Wm.
Clayton Wm.
Conning John
Donaldson James
Fletcher Wm.
Gibson Ann
Hackle John
Hill Wm.
Hunter John
Jackson John
Jackson Joseph
King Thomas
Lamb Richard
Newton Robert
Pearson Roger
Shepherd Daniel
Simpson Barthw.
Tweedale John
Weatherill Wm.
White Isaac
Wilson Thomas
  *Grocers,*
Easby John
Galloway Wm.

Ingram John
Potter Ralph
White E. & W.
  (& drapers)
Wilson Joseph
  *Linen Mfrs.*
Hesleton P. and
  Son
Lamb Richard
Nattriss Thos.
  *Oil Millers,*
Heseltine Philip
Richardson and
  Bowron
  *Schoolmasters,*
Flockton John
Maston John
Sanderson H.
  *Shoemakers,*
Sanderson Francis
Simeson John
  *Stone masons,*
Bulmer Jeffrey
Fawcitt Thos.
Rickaby Thos.
  *Surgeons,*
Ley Thos. M.D.
Pannell F. M.D.
  *Tanners,*
Martin Wm.
Wilson Wm.
  *Tailors,*
King and Shaw,
  (& drapers)
Shaw Wm.
  *Wheelwrights,*
Hebron John, (& joiner)
Humphrey Thos.
Wright Thos.

Ayre Joseph, corn miller
Brown Wm. cowkeeper
Carlin Joseph, brewer & maltster
Charlton Jasper, nail mfr.
Hawkswell John, vict. Red Lion
Hawkswell John, millwright
Kilvington Robert, saddler
Peacock Wm. book-keeper
Notton Francis, tallow chandler

Theakston John, baker
Watson Joseph, cooper
Watson Joseph, vict. Buck
Wilson Joseph, vict. Royal Oak
West Wm. vict. Old Crown

*Carrier*, James Sherwood, to Stokesley every Sat.

AYTON LITTLE, in the parish of Great Ayton, wap. and liberty of Langbargh; 8 miles NE. of Stokesley. Pop. 68.

| *Farmers*, | Rigg Thos. |
|---|---|
| Atkinson Robert | Sherwood John |
| Eagleson Geo. | White Hannah |
| Lund John | White Isaac |
| Masterman John | |

AYTON, (East and West), in the parishes of Seamer and Hutton Bushel, wap. and liberty of Pickering Lythe; 5 miles SW. of Scarborough, each pleasantly situated on the opposite banks of the river Derwent, over which is a bridge of four arches, which, after winding in a confined current through the valley of Hackness, here displays a broader stream. In West Ayton stand the ruins of an ancient building, once the fortified residence of the family of the Ewers, or Evers, who possessed large demesnes in this place. The village of East Ayton is celebrated for its charming valley. The lofty hills which embosom this valley rise almost perpendicular, clothed with pendent woods, under which the river Derwent meanders through the vale. These villages comprise the lordship of Gilbert, who from them assumed the name of Ayton, in the reign of Henry I. The heir of this family, in the reign of Edward II. inherited, in right of his mother, the estates of William Lord Vesci, who died without issue. From this family, it came by marriage with the heiress into the possession of Henry de Bromflete; and, by the same mode of inheritance, it became the property of the martial family of the Cliffords, of Skipton castle. Pop. 562.

AYTON EAST.
Wilson Robt. steward to Mr. Dennison
Taylor Barnham, land surveyor

| *Coopers*, | *Schools*, |
|---|---|
| Flinton Thos. | Linskell Ann |
| Ward Geo. | Robinson John |
| *Farmers*. | *Shopkeepers*, |
| Gibson Wm. | Robinson John |
| Greaves John | Stephenson John |
| Greaves Wm. | *Tailors*, |
| Meggison John | Green John |
| Newton Francis | Linskell John |
| Pexton John | *Weavers*, |
| Taylor Peter | Baines John |
| ...on James | Hayes Wm. |

| *Wheelwrights*, | Lightfoot John |
|---|---|
| Jefferson Geo. | |

Gibson Francis, butcher
Hodgson Wm. gamekeeper
Huddleston Francis, blacksmith
Monkman Wm. shoemaker
Newton Thomas, vict. Shoulder of Mutton
Robinson Stephen, corn miller
Stewardson Ann, vict. Black Bull

AYTON WEST.
Campbell Captain W. M.
Candler Thos. Esq. Low Hall
Cooke Lieut. W. Y.
Thistlethwaite Thos. gent.

| *Farmers*, | *Stone masons*, |
|---|---|
| Coverley John | Houson John |
| Darrell John | Johnson Thos. |
| Prince Francis | Wilson Thos. |
| Robinson John | *Wheelwrights*, |
| Robinson Geo. | Cordukes Matth. |
| Thompson Geo. | Greenley Joseph |
| | Jefferson John |

Atkinson Geo. maltster
Cooke Mrs. schoolmistress
Etherington Geo. shopkeeper
Pickup Henry, under steward
Robinson Richard, miller
Robinson Phatuel, tailor
Winteringham Francis, vict. Board

BAGBY, in the parish of Kirby Knowle, and wap. of Birdforth; 3 miles SE. of Thirsk. Here are two chapels, a Methodist chapel and a Chapel of Ease, of which the rector of Kirby Knowle is curate. Pop. 242.

Farra Richard, yeoman
Robinson Wm. yeoman

| *Farmers*, | Miller Geo. |
|---|---|
| Carver Wm. | Nelson Widow |
| Chapman Thos. | Oastler John |
| Coates Wm. | Robinson Geo. & |
| Coates Thos. | John |
| Farrar John | Smithson Christ. |
| Gates Christopher | Thompson Wm. |
| and William | *Tailors*, |
| Greenhill Henry | Shepherd John |
| Holling Wm. | Wright Geo. |

Anderson Richard, shoemaker
Dennis Robert, wheelwright, &c.
Pinkner Francis, vict. Griffin
Thompson Richard, blacksmith
Thompson James, vict. Roebuck
Wood Jane, shopkeeper

BAINBRIDGE, in the parish of Aysgarth, wap. of Hang West, and liberty of Richmondshire; 1 mile SW. of Askrigg; situated upon the river Ure, over which is a good stone bridge of three arches. This was anciently a Roman garrison, of which some remains are still visible: several muniments of Roman antiquity have been found amongst these ruins, and a statue of Aurelius Commodus, with an inscription, was also found here, which was preserved by Mr. Metcalf, of Nappa. By the antique corn mill at Cappagh, near Bainbridge, a pair of ancient mill stones were discovered in 1817; they were covered with the remains of a strong leather hide, and measured in circumference nine feet six inches, and twenty-four inches in depth; being put in motion by Mr. Wm. Paxton, they ran in the form of a dish, one within the other, and worked in a very superior manner. Here are a Methodist chapel and a Friends' Meeting House. Bainbridge has a Free Grammar school, erected and endowed in the 43d year of Queen Elizabeth, by Anthony Besson, Esq. a native of Askrigg, and the Rev. Anthony Wharton is the present master.— An ancient custom prevails here of blowing a horn in winter, as a guide to travellers, said to have originated when the country was an open forest. Pop. 872.

Latimer Wm. surgeon
Scarr Mrs. Sarah, gentlewoman
Scarr Patience, gentlewoman
Terry Geo. yeoman
Wharton Rev. Anthony, master of the free grammar school

*Blacksmiths,*
Fawcett Geo.
Metcalf John
Stockdale Geo.
Knowles John
Lawson Richard
Scarr Geo.
Sidgwick John
Sunter Robert
Whitton Jane

*Butchers,*
Metcalf James
Metcalf John
Metcalf Charles

*Corn Millers,*
Chapman Alex.
Cockburn John

*Farmers,*
Baines Wm.
Baines Thos.
Calvert John
Chapman Christ.
Chapman Wm.
Coulthard James
Kilburn Geo.
Kilburn Alex.

*Grocers,*
Alderson Richard
Metcalfe Geo.
Tiplady Alex.

*Hosiers,*
Coates Geo.
Preston Wilfred

*Shoemakers,*
Mart Francis
Routh Wm.

*Tailors,*
Horner John
Horner Henry

Banks James, vict. Rose & Crown
Kilburn Thos. joiner & tea dealer
Mason Jas. governor of the poor house
Milner George, stone mason
Sidgwick Margaret, schoolmistress
Stockdale Ann, vict. White Lion
Aislethwaite James, clogger

*Baldersby,* in the parish of Topcliffe, wap. of Halikeld, and liberty of Richmond; 6 miles SW. of Thirsk. Population, 241.

*Balks,* in the parish of Kirby Knowle, wap. of Birdforth; 3½ miles ESE. of Thirsk. Pop. 125.

*Barden* and *Barden Dykes,* in the parish of East Hawkswell, wap. of Hang West, and liberty of Richmondshire; 3 miles NE. of Leyburn; a small straggling township, chiefly inhabited by farmers. Pop. 106.

*Barf End,* see Melbecks.

BARFORTH, in the parish of Forcett, wap. of Gilling West, and liberty of Richmondshire; 12 miles N. of Richmond; a small township situated on the banks of the Tees. This township, which is the property of the Earl of Harewood, comprises Old Richmond, but nothing now remains except the ruins of an old chapel, and a few irregularities in the neighbouring fields, which, together with the stones and other relics that are occasionally dug up, prove it to have been a place of considerable extent. Pop. 141.

*Farmers,*
Brown Thos.
Clark Robert,
  Barforth Hall
Clement Joseph
Dobbinson John
Elgie John
Hodgson John

*Barnaby House,* in the parish of Guisborough, wap. and liberty of Langbargh; 3½ miles WNW. of Guisborough.

*Barnby,* see Bossall

*Barnby,* (East and West) in the parish of Lythe, wap. and liberty of Langbargh; 5½ miles WNW. of Whitby. Population, 270.

BARNINGHAM, (P.) in the wap. of Gilling West, and liberty of Richmondshire; 9 miles NW. of Richmond. The church is an ancient structure, dedicated to St. Michael, and the living is a rectory, in the patronage of the King. Here is also a school, conducted on the National plan, endowed with 25l. per annum, and which was re-built in 1820. Pop. 364.

Collin Rev. Thos. B. D. rector
Milbank Mark, Esq. M. P. Barningham hall
Todd John, Esq.

Horn Catharine, gentlewoman
Hutchinson Ann, gentlewoman
Monkhouse Rev. Edward, B. A.
Newby Mark, boarding academy
Newby Wm. boarding academy

*Blacksmiths,*
Etherington Jph.
Hind Wm.
*Farmers & Yeomen,*
Barker John
Dunn Wm.
Hardy Matthew
Heslop Ralph
Hutchinson Anth.
Lee Thomas

Marley John
Marley Geo.
Mecca James
Middleton John
Newby Thos.
Todd Wm.
Todd Anthony

Wilkinson Thos.
*Shopkeepers,*
Atkinson Thos.
Carter Thos.
*Wheelwrights,*
Atkinson Richard
Sayer Matthew

Bowman Eliz. vict. Royal Oak
Bowman Andrew, parish clerk
Ewbank Thomas, mason
M'Donald Alex. vict. Black Horse
Westmoreland Thos. butcher

BARTON ST. MARY'S, (P.) in the wap. of Gilling East, & liberty of Richmondshire; 7 miles NE. of Richmond. There are in this township two churches, one of them dedicated to St. Mary, and the other to St. Cuthbert. The living of St. Mary is a pepetual curacy, in the patronage of the vicar of Gilling; incumbent, the Rev. John Atkinson. Here is also a Free School, with an endowment of 8*l.* per annum; and an excellent lime stone quarry, for the purposes of agriculture, containing, by a late analysis, a greater proportion of pure lime than any other stone in the neighbourhood. A water fall bridge was erected here in 1821. Population, 436.

Stelling George, gent.

*Blacksmiths,*
Coates James
Malthouse Thos.
*Farmers & Yeomen,*
Benson Edward
Charge Thos.
Heslop Robert
Hutchinson Francis
Lax George
*Shoemakers,*
Hepson John
Parkin Charles

*Shopkeepers,*
Bales Matthew
Ewbank Ann
*Tailors.*
Hobson John
Scaife Christ. (and parish clerk)
*Wheelwrights,*
Colling Stephen
Marshall John
Thompson Wm.

Gibson Jph. vict. Shoulder of Mutton
Guy Wm. vict. Volunteer
White James, schoolmaster

BARTON-SUR-LE-STREET, (P.) in the wap. of Rydale; 5 miles WNW. of Malton. The church, dedicated to St. Michael, is antique, and was built from the ruins of St. Mary's Abbey, York; it contains a great deal of curious sculpture; the living is a rectory, and in the gift of the Marchioness of Hertford; incumbent, the Rev. Thomas Lund, A.M. Pop. 176.

Leatham H. C. Esq. deputy lieutenant
*Farmers & Yeomen,*
Brewer Marm.
Frost Wm.
Hardisty Thomas
Leigh George
Marshall Thos.
Moon Wm.

Craven John, shoemaker
Thompson James, carpenter

Thompson John, shoemaker
Whitehead John, blacksmith and vict. Light Horseman

*Barton-le-Willows,* in the parish of Crambe, and wap. of Bulmer; 8 miles SW. of Malton. Here is a Methodist chapel. Pop. 188.

*Barugh,* (Great and Little) in the parish of Kirby Misperton, wap. and liberty of Pickering Lythe; 5 miles SW. of Pickering. Pop. 241.

*Battersby,* in the parish of Ingleby Greenhow, wap. and liberty of Langbargh; 5 miles E. of Stokesley. Population, 87.

*Baxter House,* in the parish of Hovingham, and wap. of Rydale; 8 miles WNW. of Kirby-Moor-Side.

BAYESDALE, in the parish of Stokesley, wap. and liberty of Langbargh; 7 miles S. of Guisborough. Here was a small Cistercian nunnery, founded and endowed by the benefactions of Ralf de Nevill and Guido de Bovingcourt, dedicated to the Blessed Virgin. This house had a prioress and nine or ten nuns, whose income at the dissolution was valued at 90*l.* 1s. 4d. The scite of the priory, with the lands, were granted to Ralph Bulmer and John Thynde, to be held of the King in capite.—After divers grants and alienations, it became, by purchase, the property of the Piersons; but Matthew Russell, Esq. of Brancepeth Castle, in the county of Durham, is the present proprietor.

BEADLAM, in the parish of Kirkdale, and wap. of Rydale; 3 miles WSW. of Kirby-Moor-Side. Population, 143.

*Farmers,*
Barker John
Fisher Robert
Hodgson John
Seaton Daniel, & land agt. Grange
Smales John
Stockton John, & vict. Board
Tate John
Thompson John

Barker Robert, vict. White Horse
Yeward Geo. shoemaker

## BEDALE, (P.)

In the wap. of Hang East, and liberty of Richmondshire; 6 miles from Masham, 8 from Northallerton, 9 from Middleham, 14 from Ripon, and 224 from London. The town is tolerably well built, and contains, according to the census taken in 1821, a population of 1137. The church, dedicated to St. Gregory, is a spacious structure, in the

Gothic style of architecture, and has a good tower or steeple. The Market is on Tuesday, and is well supplied with all kinds of butcher's meat, poultry, butter, and vegetables. Bedale is situated in a rich valley, about two miles to the west of Leeming-lane; the surrounding country is extremely fertile, and the crops, both of corn and grass, are abundant. From a monument in the church it appears there was a castle here, built by Brian Fitz Allen, Earl of Arundel, in the reign of Edward I. but not any remains of it are now to be seen. The church living is a rectory, in the gift of Henry Pierce, Esq. M.P. and of Miles Stapleton, alternately. Here is also a Methodist chapel, built A. D. 1821. The poor of Bedale enjoy the benefit of many munificent charitable bequests, and here is a hospital for six poor men of the parish, founded and endowed by Peter Samwaies, D. D. and rector, A. D. 1698. Also, a hospital for three poor widows, founded by Richard and Thomas Young. There is also a free grammar school, endowed with the annual sum of 7l. 11s. 4d. by the Crown, and 13l. 6s. 8d. by a Countess Dowager of Warwick, which is now converted into a National School.

*Post-Mistress*—FRANCES MAPHAM.

Letters from London, York, Wetherby, Boroughbridge, and Thirsk arrive daily at 50 minutes past 4 in the morning, (delivery of Letters at 8 in the morning.) A Riding post departs at 50 minutes past 5 in the morning, taking bags for Middleham, Spennythorne, Leyburn, Askrigg, and Hawes, all Penny-post towns, and returns at 4 in the afternoon, departs immediately with letters for Thirsk, York, London, &c.
N.B. A Penny-post to Masham at 6 in the morning.

### DIRECTORY.

Pierce Henry, Esq. M.P.
Monson Hon. & Rev. Thos. M. A.
Monson Rev. J. J. T. M. A.
Barker Wm. gentleman
Cookson Mrs. A.
Marshall John, gentleman
Williamson Mrs. Elizabeth

*Agent.*

Burton John, County Fire and Provident Life office

*Attornies & Solicitors* Braithwaite John
Glaister H. R.    Elwood John
Janson W. R.    Hird Robert
Peacock T. D.    Hodgson Wm.
  *Blacksmiths,*    Johnson Wm.
Brown Timothy    Slater Wm.
Clough Joseph    Smith John
*Boot & Shoemakers,* Stapleton John
Barnett Simon    Walton Wm.

  *Butchers,*
Backhouse Wm.
Banks Joseph
Hewson Wm.
Nicholson Henry
Nicholson Henry
Whitton Thomas, Firby Grange
  *Cabinet Makers,*
Gill Wm.
Peacock Wm.
Place Mary
Webster Christr.
*Chemists & Drugsts.*
Place Mary
Slater John
*Curriers & Leather Sellers,*
Prest Henry
Wright Thomas
  *Farmers,*
Barker Wm.
Braithwaite Sarah
Chapman George
Hardy James
Kendrew Henry
Jameson Christr.
Mason Wm.
Stonehouse Jas.
Walburn Wm.
  *Fellmongers,*
Hird Wm.
Hird Davies
*Flour and Provision Dealers,*
Barker Wm.
Deighton Christr.
Santon Vincent
  *Gardeners,*
Deighton Christr.
Robinson Wm.
  *Grocers,*
Burton John
Harker Wm.
Kirby Wm.
Kirtlan George
Porter John
  *Hair Dressers,*
Bridgewater John
Fawcett John
  *Hatters,*
Hewson Josh. mfr.
Shepherd Edw.
Sweeting Wm.
Wright Thos. jun.
  *Hosiers,*
Pratt Matth. mfr.
Shepherd Edw.
Sweeting Wm.
Thorns Matt. mfr.
*Joiners & Carpenters,*
Gill William
Johnson James
Peacock Wm.

Webster Christr.
*Linen and Woollen Drapers,*
Sherwood Wm.
Shepherd Edw. (& haberdasher)
Sweeting Wm. (& haberdasher)
  *Milliners, &c.*
Carver Hannah
Robinson Ann
Smith Mary
  *Painters,*
Bucktrout Wm.
Cooper Francis
*Plumbers & Glaziers*
Barrass George
Bucktrout Robt.
Chapman Joseph, (dealer in glass)
*Printers, Bookbinders, and Stationers,*
Taylor Richard
Todd James
  *Rope Makers,*
Court Henry
Webster Wm.
  *Saddlers,*
Kay George
Motley Thos.
Nicholson Francis
*Schoolmasters, &c.*
Bailey Ann
Brownbridge Thos.
Brownbridge Elis.
Naitby David
*Straw Hat Mkrs.*
Bussey Eleanor
Fawcett Jane
Naitby Eliz.
Simpson Elis.
  *Stone Masons,*
Horner Abraham
Johnson Robert
Pearson Jas. (bricklayer & plasterer)
Pearson Robert, (& architect)
  *Surgeons,*
Campbell Archibald
Spence Wm.
Theakstone Wm.
  *Tailors,*
Atkinson Mark, (& draper)
Carter John
Ellick James
Ellick Wm.
Gale Thomas
Pearson John
Smith Geo. (and draper)
Sweeting Wm. (& draper)

*Tea Dealers,*
Dennison Frances
Horn Ann
*Tinners & Braziers,*
Fryer Wm. and
ironmonger
Harrison John,
(& ironmonger)
Thompson Thos.
(dir. in hardware
& jewellery)
*Watch and Clock Makers,*
Dunn Thos.

Pearson Henry
Raper Thos.
*Wheelwrights,*
Clarkson Thos.
Johnson James
*Whitesmiths,*
Pearson W. & J.
*Wine and Spirit Merchants,*
Atkinson Henry
Burton John
Kirby Wm.
Smith Wm. jun.

Bailey Wm. wood turner
Bedford Richard, vict. Black Swan
Blenkhorn Simeon, vict. Black Bull
Clapham Robert, bread baker
Cooper Jane, confectioner
Dobby Thos. sheriff's officer for the county
Dobby Christr. vict. Golden Lion
Gale Robert, wool comber
Hellier John, vict. Mason's Arms
Hopper George, vict. Cross Keys
Hunsley George, linen weaver
Johnson Robert, basket maker
Nicholson Henry, vict. King's Head
Pearson James, vict. White Bear
Plews Hy. common brewer & maltster
Saddler Edward, vict. Green Dragon
Skurrah John, cooper
Slater Wm. auctioneer
Slater Wm. vict. Old Anchor
Smith Wm. vict. Royal Oak
Storrow George, cattle dealer
Swan Thomas, horse dealer
Thompson Benj. vict. Waggon & Horses
Walker Margaret, vict. Blue Boar

A COACH arrives here from Redcar (by way of Northallerton) at ¼ past 12 at noon, every Mon. Wed. and Sat. during the bathing season, and ret. each of the said days at two o'clock.

*Carriers,*

Wm. Hird, to Thirsk, every Mon. dep. at 8 morn. and ret. the same day. To Richmond on Sat. at 3 morn. and ret. the same day.
Christopher Horner, to Boroughbridge twice a week, days uncertain.— To Leyburn generally once a week. To Richmond once in 2 or three weeks.

BELLERBY, in the parish of Spennythorpe, wap. of Hang West, and liberty of Richmondshire; 1 mile N. of Leyburn. The Chapel of Ease is a small neat structure, rebuilt in 1801, patron J. C. Chaytor, Esq. incumbent the Rev. Francis Blackburn, rector of Croscombe, Somersetshire. The

village consists of one open street of irregular buildings, along the whole length of which runs a never-failing rivulet of clear spring water. Pop. 407.

Kirkbank Rev. Wm. officiating curate
Metcalfe Miss Ann, gentlewoman

*Blacksmiths,*
Metcalf Thos.
Simpson Joseph
*Farmers & Yeomen,*
Armstrong Wm.
Favill Henry
Favill Edward
Fryer Wm.
Hanson Geo.
Hodgson Wm.
Horn John
Lonsdale Charles
Lonsdale Francis
Metcalf Mary
Outhwaite John
Rider John

Robinson Geo.
Robinson Thos.
Snaith James
Walker John
White James
Wishby James
*Shoemakers,*
Caygill Matthew
Collinson Wm.
*Stone Masons,*
Coates Thos.
Holdsworth Wm.
Jones Francis
Raw James
Raw John

Auton Leonard, schoolmaster
Outhwaite James, corn miller
Plant Edward, cartwright
Rider John, vict. White Swan
Thistlethwaite John, vict. Cross Keys
Wray John, common brewer, Red bank

*Beningbrough,* in the parish of Newton-upon-Ouse, and wap. of Bulmer; 8 miles NW. of York. Here is the seat of Mrs. Margaret Earle, of the ancient family of the Bouchiers, who came into England with William the Conqueror. Pop. 99.

*Berwick,* see Ingleby Berwick.

*Bilsdale East Side* or *Mid Cable,* in the parish of Helmsley, & wap. of Rydale; 7 miles NNW. of Hemsley. Here is a church under Helmsley, incumbent the Rev. John Dixon, in the gift of the vicar of Helmsley, likewise a meeting-house for the Society of Friends. Population, including Bilsdale Kirkham, 780.

*Bilsdale West Side,* in the parish of Hawnby, wap. of Birdforth; 8 mls. NNW. of Helmsley. Pop. 127.

*Bincoe,* in the parish of West Tanfield, and wap. of Halikeld; 2 miles ESE. of Masham.

*Birch,* see Newton.

*Birdforth,* (which gives name to the wapentake,) in the parish of Coxwold, and wap. of Birdforth; 5½ miles SE. of Thirsk. Here is a Chapel of Ease, of which the Rev. John Overton, B. A. is curate.— Population, 42.

BIRKBY or BRETBY, (P.) in the wap. and liberty of Allertonshire; 6 miles N. of Northallerton. The church is dedicated to St. Peter; the living is a rectory, in the patronage of the Bishop of Durham. Population, 90.

Parrington Rev. Matthew, rector
Wilkinson Ralph, gentleman

BIRKDALE, in the parish of Grinton, wap. of Gilling West, and liberty of Richmondshire; 7 miles NW. of Muker.

*Farmers & Yeomen,* Alderson John
AldersonChas.sen. Alderson Christ.
AldersonChas.jun. Peacock Christr.
Alderson Geo.

*Birk Riggs,* in the parish of Aysgarth, wap. of Hang West, and liberty of Richmondshire; 3 miles WNW. of Hawes.

BIRKS, in the parish of East Witton, and wap. of Hang West; 5 miles W. of Masham. A small hamlet pleasantly situated in Colsterdale. Pop. included with East Witton.

Robinson John, vict. Board
Wintersgill Wm. coal agent

BISHOP'S DALE, in the parish of Aysgarth, and wap. of Hang West; 6 miles SE. of Askrigg. A township consisting of farm houses, scattered at irregular distances from each other; in this picturesque and fertile dale there are several cascades of prodigious height, and vast rocky sides, intermixed with a variety of foilage, rich and beautiful. Population, 95.

Hesletine James, gentleman
Hopper Miss Ann
Lodge Ralph, chief constable
*Farmers & Yeomen,* Metcalf James
Bushby Wm.　　　Metcalf Thos.
Dixon Edmund　　Mudd James
Dixon John　　　Preston Ralph
Hopper Joseph　　SerjeantsonFrancis
Lambert Thos.　　Skinner John
Lodge Robert　　 Slinger John

BLACKRAKE, in the parish of Coverham, and wap. of Hang West; 8 miles SSW. of Middleham. A small hamlet in Coverdale.

Wilson Benjamin, gentleman

*Farmers & Yeomen,* Swales James
Dixon George　　　Tennant Richard
Lofthouse Ralph　 Utley John
Stubbs John　　　 Yeoman Joseph

*Blades,* see Melbecks.

*Blakehow House,* in the parish of Lastingham, and wap. of Rydale; 9 miles N. of Kirkby-Moor-Side.

*Blakehow Topping,* in the parish of Allerton, wap. and liberty of Pickering Lythe; 9 mls. NE. of Pickering.

*Bleas,* (High & Low) in the parish of Aysgarth, and wap. of Hang West: 4 miles S. of Askrigg. A small hamlet situated in Raydale

BOLDRON, in the parish of Startforth, wap. of Gilling West, & liberty of Richmondshire; 2 miles SSW. of Barnard Castle. Pop. 168.

*Farmers,*　　　　Metcalf Christ.
Benson Geo.　　　Newton John
Dent John　　　　Shaw Geo.
Lockey Wm.

Dawson Richard, wheelwright
Hurworth John, vict. Board

BOLTBY, in the parish of Feliskirk, and wap. of Birdforth; 6 miles NE. of Thirsk. Here is a Chapel of Ease, of which the Rev. T. Kilby is curate. Pop 403.

*Blacksmiths,*　　Beilby Mark
Bell Abraham　　 Severs Richard
Jarvis Joseph　　 Sturdy Robert
*Farmers,*　　　　Sturdy Thomas
Beilby Roger　　　Tate Peter

Body Christopher, schoolmaster
Bransby M. shoemaker
Hornby —— corn miller
Kerry Wm. linen manufacturer
Scurr Francis, vict. Board
Shepherd Roger, tailor

BOLTON CASTLE, in the parish of Wensley, wap. of Hang West, and liberty of Richmondshire; 5 miles WNW. of Leyburn. The church here is a Chapel of Ease to the parish church, of which the Rev. Jacob Costobadie, rector of Wensley, is incumbent, and was built by Richard Lord Scroope,chancellor of England in the reign of Richard II. The tower, on the south-west angle, where the unfortunate Mary, Queen of Scots, was confined, in the year 1568, is now occupied by a farmer. During the civil wars, this castle was for a long time gallantly defended for the king, by Colonel Scroope and a party of the Richmondshire militia, against the parliamentary forces; but at length, Nov. 5, 1645, surrendered on honourable conditions. Emanuel Lord Scroope, Earl of Sunderland, who died without male issue, in the reign of Charles I. was the last of that ancient family that inhabited this castle. From neglect, and the damage it received during the siege, the tower on the north-east angle became so much injured, that on the 19th of November, 1761, it fell to the ground. But though the east and north sides are mostly in ruins, the west front is in good repair. Pop. 278.

*Farmers,*　　　 Robinson Ralph
Fawcett John　　Stainley W. W.
Heslop John, Low　West Bolton
Mason Roger

*Stone Masons,* Storey James
Fawcett Wm.    Storey Henry
Mason Robert, carpenter
Plewes Christopher, tailor

**BOLTON-UPON-SWALE,** in the parish of Catterick, wap. of Gilling East, and liberty of Richmondshire; 6 miles ESE. of Richmond. Here is a very ancient church, which is a Chapel of Ease to the parish church of Catterick, of which the Rev. Thomas Wilson Morley is curate. A monument is erected here to the memory of Henry Jenkins. (see Ellerton.) Pop. 100.

*Farmers,*    *Wheelwrights,*
Milburn Wm.    Jaques Francis (&
Outhwaite Thos.      parish clerk)
Weight Richard    Newton John
Wilkinson James

Bennison Richard, shopkeeper
Lumley Thos. vict. Henry Jenkins

**Boose,** in the parish of Arkengarthdale, wap. of Gilling West, and liberty of Richmondshire; 3 miles N.W. of Reeth.

**Bornesess,** in the parish of Croft, and wap. of Gilling East; 7 miles NE. of Richmond.

**Borrowby,** in the parish of Lythe, wap. and liberty of Langbargh; 9 mls. N.W. of Whitby. Pop. 64.

**BORROWBY,** in the parish of Leake, waps. of Allertonshire & Birdforth; 5½ miles SE. of Northallerton. Here is a Methodist chapel. Pop. 267.

Warrington Rev. William, A.M. vicar of Leake
Addison John, gentleman
Hammond Thomas, gentleman
Hiley Michael, gentleman
*Blacksmiths,*    Weldon Jonah
Cussan Wm.    Windross Wm.
Oliver Thos.    Wright Thos.
*Coopers,*    *Grocers,*
Dresser Cuthbert   Eshelby John
Souter Wm.    Shaw Ann
*Farmers & Yeomen,* Wright Joseph
Almack John    *Joiners, &c.*
Almack James    Eshelby John
Atkinson Michael   Sadler Thos.
Britton John    *Shoemakers,*
Coupland John    Britton Thos.
Hamilton Thos.    Lee Thos.
Harrison John    Marshall Wm.
Harrison Mark    Shepherd John
Highly Sarah    *Tailors,*
Hurworth John    Kendrew Daniel
Johnson Simeon    Wright Joseph

Britton & Hunton, linen mfrs.
Charnley Francis, vict. Grey Horse
Cheeseman Robert, wheelwright
Drummond Jas. surveyor of highways

Foster George, schoolmaster
Highley Amos, butcher
Johnson Beatrice, vict. Wheat Sheaf
Kirk Cuthbert, stone mason
Lyon Wm. bricklayer
Moon Geo. & John, corn millers
Pearson Miles, tanner
Wright John, bacon & butter factor

**BOSSALL,** (P.) in the wap. of Bulmer; 9 miles NE. of York. Here is a very handsome church dedicated to St. Botolph, and built in the form of a cross; the living is a vicarage, in the patronage of the Dean and Chapter of Durham, of which the Rev. James Britton, D. D. is the incumbent. This place, which now consists of three houses, was once a considerable village. Foundations of many houses have from time to time been discovered in an adjoining field, which on that account is called, "Old Bossall." Robert Belt, Esq. resides at the hall. Population, 31.

**BOULBY,** in the parish of Easington, wap. and liberty of Langbargh: 11 NW. of Whitby. Noted for its alum works, situated on the verge of a stupendous cliff where, on entering the vast cavern formed by human labour in the centre of the rock, the spectator is astonished to behold the different strata arranged with symmetry and exactness, as declare the workmanship of the Omnipotent. The alum works here were established about the year 1615; they extend eastward and westward from Whitby, and this is the most part of England where that commodity is produced. In Catholic times the production of alum was a manufacture of the Popes, and any infringement of the monopoly subjected the offender to excommunication: The present state of this manufacture at its principal seats will be seen by the following table, exhibiting the gross produce on an average of 12 years:—

*Situation of works.*    *Proprietors.*
Peake & Stoupe
Brow............. Messrs. Cooke...
Eskdale Side H. W. Yeoman, Esq.
Sandsend............Earl Mulgrave...
Kettleness.........Earl Mulgrave...
Boulby.........Baker & Jackson...
Lofthouse .........Lord Dundas...

Total annual average...............

Baker & Jackson, alum min.
Dodds Geo. agent to the alum
Marley Robert, farmer, Red [    ]
Trousdale Michael, farmer, [    ]
Westgarth Geo. clerk, (alum [    ]

**Bowbank,** in the parish of [    ] kirk, wap. of Gilling West, and [    ] of Richmondshire ; 9 miles NW. of Barnard Castle.

*Bow-Bridge Hall,* in the parish of Aysgarth, wap. of Hang West, and liberty of Richmondshire ; 1 mile W. of Askrigg.

BOWES, (P.) in the wap. of Giling West, and liberty of Richmondshire ; 4 miles SW. of Barnard Castle. Here was a castle said to have been built by Alan, Earl of Richmond, soon after the conquest. The situation is near the Roman road, which led to Getaractonium : and which Camden supposes to be the ancient Lavatra. The present walls are fifty-three feet in height, forming a square of equal sides of fifty-three feet each. Bowes is situated on the edge of Stanemore, near the north point of the county, on the banks of the river Greta, and consists principally of one street, nearly three quarters of a mile long from east to west. Though now an inconsiderable place this was anciently a Roman station. About two miles from Bowes is a singular curiosity, called God-bridge, being a natural bridge of limestone rock, where, through a rude arch, sixteen feet in the span, the river Greta precipitates its waters; the way formed on the crown of the rock is about twenty feet wide, and is occasionally the carriage road over the river. After the Greta has passed this bridge, at a little distance it gains a subterraneous passage near half a mile; and in a lineal direction, breaks out again through the cavities of the rock. The church is dedicated to St. Giles; the living is a perpetual curacy, in the patronage of C. Harrison, Esq. and the Rev. Richard Wilson, is the incumbent. There is here a Methodist chapel, also a Free School, endowed by William Hutchinson, Esq. of Clement's Inn, London, with 90*l.* per annum, out of which the master is paid 70*l.* and the mistress 20*l.* In addition to the above endowment, the Rev. Charles Hope, left a scholarship at Cambridge for its benefit. Pop. 1,095.

Dale John, gentleman
Robinson George, gentleman
Scott Jane, gentlewoman

*Academies,* Hobson Wm.
Braithwaite Mar- Langstaff John
garet, (bdg.) Lockey Wm.
Robinson G. (bdg.) *Joiners and Wheel-*
John *wrights,*
Raisbeck Miss Cow John
Raw Wm. (bdg.) Denham James
*Farmers & Yeomen,* Sayer Michael
Bowron Richard *Shopkeepers,*
Hunter Wm. Addison Rachael
Peterson Matth. Addison Francis
Whitmore John

Bowron John, tailor
Campbell John, shoemaker
M'Kay Charles, classical tutor
Raisbeck Henry, superintendant
Rudd Robert, vict. Union Inn
Sayer James, vict. Rose & Crown
Sayer Wm. parish clerk
Smith J. blacksmith
Walton Wm. maltster & brewer
Walton John, miller

*Bowforth,* in the parish of Kirkdale, and wap. of Rydale ; 2 miles S. of Kirkby-Moor-Side.

BRACKENBROUGH, in the parish of Kirby Wiske, wap. of Birdforth ; 4 miles W. of Thirsk. A village anciently belonging to the family of Lascelles ; of which Roger de Lascelles was summoned to parliament, amongst the barons, in the 22nd of Edward I. and the following year. Pop. including Newsham, 173.

Armitage John Leathley, Esq.
*Farmers,* Huson John
Bailey Richard Kirk Thos.
Bullock Robert
Lunn Geo. butler to J.L.Armitage,Esq.
Morley John, gardener to ditto

*Bradley,* in the parish of Coverham, wap. of Hang West, and liberty of Richmondshire ; 7 miles SW. of Middleham. A small hamlet, situated at the SW. extremity of Coverdale.

BRAFFERTON, (P.) in the waps. of Bulmer and Halikeld, and liberty of St. Peter's ; 5 miles W. of Easingwold. This village has a parish church dedicated to St. Peter; the living is a vicarage, in the patronage of the Crown. Here is a National School for children of both sexes, supported by subscription. Brafferton and Helperby are apparently but one village, occupying opposite sides of the same street. The village takes its name from a ford across the Swale, it being originally Broad-Ford-Town, and now by a natural contraction Brafferton. Population 178.

Gray Rev. William, A. M.
Jackson William, surgeon
*Bricklayers,* Brown John
Almgill John Leng Wm.
Canby Wm. Pickard Christphr.
*Farmers,* Potter James
Banks Christopher
Bannister Sarah, vict. Fox
Bannister John, saddler
Coates Richard, shoemaker
Franklin John, wheelwright
Simpson James, blacksmith

BRANSBY, (P.) in the wap. of Bulmer ; 6 mls. ENE. of Easingwold

Here is a very neat little church dedicated to All Saints, the living is a rectory, in the patronage of Francis Cholmeley, Esq. Population including Stearsby, 277.

Cholmeley Francis, Esq. Bransby hall
Smith Rev. William, rector

*Farmers,*
Appleby Geo.
Appleby Francis

Maskell Robert
Wiley Samuel
Wood Wm.

Armstrong John, agent to F. Cholmeley, Esq.
Dobson Thomas, corn miller
Hall Thomas, carpenter
Parvin George, schoolmaster
Rowntree John, blacksmith
Thompson Wm. butler at Bransby hall

BRANSDALE EAST & WEST SIDE, in the parishes of Kirkby-Moor-Side, and Kirkdale, and wap. of Rydale; 7 miles NW. of Kirkby-Moor-Side. Here is a Chapel of Ease, of which the Rev. Henry King, is curate. Population of East, 455; of West, 286;—total, 741.

*Farmers,*
Hawnby Wm.
Scarf Isaac
Scarf John

Sigsworth Geo.
Simpson Henry
Wean John

*Bransby,* in the parish of Salton, wap. of Rydale, and liberty of St. Peter's; 5 miles SSE. of Kirkby-Moor-Side. Pop. 188.

BRIGNALL, (P.) in the wap. of Gilling West, and liberty of Richmondshire; 4 miles SE. of Barnard Castle. The church, which is an ancient structure, is dedicated to St. Mary; the living is a vicarage, in the patronage of the King, incumbent the Rev. O. W. Kilvington. Here is a school erected in 1817, and allowed 15*l.* per annum, by J. B. S. Morritt, Esq. Pop. 216.

*Farmers,*
Barker Geo.
Bellwood Ralph
Middleton Wm.

Pratt John
Todd Joseph
Turner John
Wilkinson Wm.

Brown Anthony, blacksmith
Green Wm. quarry owner
Middleton Wm. shopkeeper
Sanderson Henry, schoolmaster and parish clerk
Spenceley Simon, miller

*Briscoe,* (East and West) in the parish of Romaldkirk, wap. of Gilling West, and liberty of Richmondshire; 7 miles WNW. of Barnard Castle. A small hamlet in the township of Cotherston.

*Broakes Gill,* in the parish of Catterick, wap. of Hang East, and liberty of Richmondshire; 3 miles SW. of

Richmond. A small hamlet in the township of Hudswell.

*Broates,* in the parish of Middleton, wap. and liberty of Pickering Lythe; 2 miles NNW. of Pickering.

BROMPTON, in the parish of Northallerton, wap. and liberty of Allertonshire; 1½ mile NNE. of Northallerton. The living is a perpetual curacy, incumbent the Rev. R. G. Bouyer. Besides the church here are two chapels belonging to the Wesleyan and Primitive Methodists. In the year 1694, a farm was left by the Rev. John Kettlewell, the rent of which was at that time 44*l.* the proceeds of which were to be expended in instructing and apprenticing poor children in this township and that of Northallerton, which, in consequence of the increased value of land is now a very considerable charity. The memorable battle of the Standard was fought in this township in the year 1138. Here is a considerable manufactory of linen cloth, in which there are upwards of three hundred weavers employed. Pop. 1,223.

Bowes Wm. Harker, gentleman
Gibson Rev. Edward
Harrison Mrs. Ann
Stainthorp Thomas

*Blacksmiths,*
Lowther John
Stainforth Wm.
Thompson Thos.

Stainthorp Geo.
Stanger Robert
Stockdale Ralph
Swinburn Wm.

*Bricklayers,*
Fawcett G. & T.
Johnson Thos.

Trewhitt Barthw.
Wilson Robert
Wright Thos.

*Butchers,*
Cowell Wm.
Smith John
Spence John
Stokell Mark

*Grocers, &c.*
Ayton Geo.
Byers Jane
Day Ellen
Fawcett Henry

*Farmers & Yeomen,*
Appleton Wm.
Appleton Matthew
Aungill John
Cornforth Jonth.
Herdman Edward
Hodgson Joseph
Kidson Robert
Marwood Wm.
Miller Thos.
Mustard Geo.
Newsome Thos.
Plews John
Reynard John
Robinson Henry
Robson John
Sanderson James
Sanderson Jackson
Smith James
Smith John
Snowden Wm.

Leng Smith
Robinson Ann
Thompson Jane
Wilford John

*Joiners, &c.*
Byerley Henry
Coates Geo.
Lunn John
Metcalf Thos.
M'Lane Wm.

*Linen Mfrs.*
Joblin Wm.
Parnaby Christphr.
Pattison John
Ramshaw Thos.
Richardson Isaac
Tireman John
Wilford John
Wilson Geo.

*Shoemakers,*
Foster Robert

Garget Geo.
Metcalf John
Mitchinson Wm.
Suggitt Geo.
*Straw Hat Mfrs.*
Foster Eliz.

Richardson Ann
*Tailors,*
Mirfield Edw.
Swales Geo.
Wright Geo.

Atkinson Samuel, slay & geer maker
Dickson Geo. excise officer
Dodsworth James, vict. Crown ·
Elgie Wm. corn miller
Garnett Benj. brick maker
Jackson Sanderson, vict. Ship
Langdale Roger, tallow chandler
Lowther John, victualler, Three Horse Shoes
Meesome Mark, hair dresser
Pattinson Geo. earthenware dealer
Pearson William, victualler, Durham Ox
Scarlett John, gardener & seedsman
Wilson George, victualler, Weaver's Arms

*Carrier,* Robert Pearson to Stockton, Mon. Wed. and Fri., to Masham, Wed., to Bedale, Tu. & Fri., to Northallerton, Tues. Wed. Thur. and Saturday.

BROMPTON, (P.) in the wap. and liberty of Pickering Lythe; 8 miles SW. of Scarborough. Is said to have once been a residence of the Northumbrian Kings. The foundations of an ancient building are still visible on an eminence, called Castle Hill, now surrounded by venerable pines, planted by the late Sir George Cayley, Bart. The estate has been in the ancient and honourable family of Caley for upwards of two centuries. Brompton is usually considered as the birth-place of John de Brompton, the English historian, whose chronicle commencing with the arrival of Austin in 558, and ending with the death of Richard I. is published among the X Scriptores. Brompton has one of the most beautiful, elegant, and capacious village churches in Yorkshire; it is dedicated to All Saints; the living is a vicarage, and the patron Sir G. Caley, Bart. Pop. 516.

Caley Dowager Lady, Green
Caley Sir George, Bart. Hall
Caley Rev. John, Low hall
Caley John, Esq. Low hall
Caley Edward, Esq. Low hall
Proud Rebecca, gentlewoman

*Farmers,*
Barker Robert
Botterill Thos.
Carr Wm.
Craven Thos.
Crossby Thos.
Dickinson Saml.
Dousling Francis

Hall Robert
Pexton Thos.
Williamson Wm.
*Schoolmasters,*
Bell Alexander
Gibson Peter
Rymer Tinsley

*Shoemakers,*
Adamson Matthias
Brown Thos.
Hardwick John
Sterriker Bethel
*Shopkeepers,*
Cass Elizabeth
Eccles Samuel

*Tailors,*
Geldart Love
Hopper Robert
Nelson James
*Wheelwrights,*
Hopper Wm.
Stephenson John

Cordiner John, blacksmith & farrier
Crossby Wm. agent to Lady Caley
Hamer Simon, brick, tile & pot maker
Hawkswell Thos. clock, &c. maker
Kendal W. L. vict. Grapes
Warrington Wm. skinner
Watson Matthew, common bakehouse
Woodall Wm. butcher

BROMPTON-UPON-SWALE, in the parish of Easby, wap. of Gilling East, and liberty of Richmondshire; 3 miles E. of Richmond. Pop. 388.

\*\*\* The post from Catterick to Richmond, passes through here daily, at 6 mg. and returns at ½ past 4 afternoon.

*Blacksmiths,*
Layfield Henry
Ward James
*Farmers,*
Arrowsmith Wm.
Arrowsmith Joseph
Barrass John
Corner Wm.
Dixon James
Fletcher James
Hutchinson Thos.

Meynell Geo.
Pattison Timothy
Priest Geo.
Proctor Joseph
Simpson James
*Shoemakers,*
Clayton John
Orton Solomon
*Wheelwrights,*
Carter Robert
Robinson Timothy

Duck Joseph, schoolmaster
Haw Christopher, vict. Buck
Huntingdon Geo. victualler, Farmers' Arms
Leadley Thomas, vict. Crown
Pratt Matthew, bricklayer
Stevenson Thomas, butcher
Thompson Robert, currier
Thompson John, vict. Bay Horse
Todd Thomas, shopkeeper
Wellock Francis, corn miller

BROTTON, (P.) in the wap. and liberty of Langbargh; 6 miles NE. of Guisborough. The village is inhabited chiefly by farmers; it is pleasantly situated on an eminence, commanding an extensive view of the surrounding country. The chapel is a plain, modern structure, built in 1741, and the living is a perpetual curacy, in the patronage of the Archbishop of York, of which the Rev. William Close, is the incumbent. Population 332.

Carlen John, gentleman
Stephenson Robert, Esq.

*Blacksmiths,*
Beadnall John
Jackson Joseph

*Farmers & Yeomen,*
Adamson Geo.
Breckon Francis

Breckon Richard
Brittain Wm.
Chapman John
Child William
Gatenby John
Longstaffe Geo.
Marley Christr.
Mills Lawrence
Wood John

*Farriers,*
Child William
Child Richard

*Shoemakers.*
Brown John
Thompson Thos.

*Tailors,*
Readman John, (&
   grocer & draper)
Watson Thomas

Beadnall George, stone mason
Gledston James, vict. Ship
Robinson James, jun. schoolmaster
Robinson James, wheelwright
Sayer George, butcher
Webster Richard, vict. Green Tree

BROUGH, in the parish of Catterick, wap. of Hang East, and liberty of Richmondshire; 5 miles SE. of Richmond. There is here a Catholic chapel, of which the Rev. Mr. Lauriston is minister. This township is rendered highly picturesque and beautiful by the venerable woods, verdant lawns, and smooth lakes, which surround the stately mansion of Sir H. Lawson. Population, 90.

Lawson Sir Henry, Bart. Brough
   Hall
Douthwaite Geo. agent. Ash house

*Broughton,* in the parish of Appleton-le-Street, and wap. of Rydale; 1½ mile NW. of Malton. Population, 94.

BROUGHTON, (Great and Little) in the parish of Kirkby, wap. and liberty of Langbargh; 9 miles SE. of Stokesley. On the summit of a mountain that overlooks this village and Kirkby, there is a singular monument, called by the neighbouring people the wain stones, which, according to the most probable etymology of the word, may denote the stones of lamentation, and are probably Danish, erected in memory of some Danish chieftain slain here. It consists of a rude collection of stones, some of them of an immense size, and all of them apparently in their natural position, except one, which stands erect, and appears to have formed a part of some ancient Cromlech.—Population, 517.

Moor Lieutenant R. N.

*Farmers & Yeomen,*
Dixon Garbutt
Fawcett John
Hebron Joseph
Hodgson Thos.
Hodgson Barwick
Holliday Wm.
Hutchinson Jph.
Metcalf Thos.
Moor Robert
Norman James
Reed Robert
Taylor Robert
Weatherell Wm.
Winn John

Carter Wm. wheelwright
Coverdale Geo. linen manufacturer
Greame Geo. cattle dealer
Hind George, vict. and blacksmith,
   Black Horse
Hugill Thomas, schoolmaster
Hunt John, stone mason
Layton James, butcher
Skilbeck John, horse dealer
Waugh Wm. blacksmith
Webster E. shoemaker
Wilson Nicholas, vict. Bay Horse

(BROUGHTON LITTLE.)
Greensides Miss, gentlewoman
Nelson Dorothy, gentlewoman

*Farmers,*
Batters John
Bolton Wm.
Garbut John
Hart James
Robinson Thos.
Tate Joseph
Winn David

Grice John, corn miller

*Brox,* in the parish of Hackness, wap. and liberty of Whitby Strand; 8½ miles NW. of Scarborough. Population, 61.

*Bullamoor Houses,* in the parish of Northallerton, wap. and liberty of Allertonshire; 1½ mile ENE. of Northallerton.

BULMER, (P.) (which gives name to the wap.) 7 miles SW. of Malton. Here is a church, dedicated to St. Martin. The living is a rectory, in the patronage of Earl Fitzwilliam, incumbent the Rev. William Preston. Population, 839.

*Farmers,*
Blanchard Thos.
Clark Mary
Coverdale Richard
Foster Tristram
Hogard Henry
Hough John
Jones John
Kirby Robert
Linsley John
Louderington Wm.
Peacock Matth.
Saltmer John
Styring Robert
*Shoemakers,*
Sedgefield Wm.
Spence Robert
Suggitt Richard
*Stone Masons,*
Bradley Robert
Bradley Simon
*Tailors,*
Marshall John
Peacock John

Atkinson Wm. schoolmaster
Howgate David, blacksmith
Murray Andrew, vict. White Swan
Nicholas Francis, carpenter
Watson Charles, joiner
Webster Wm. butcher

BURNISTON, (P.) in the wap. of Hallkeld, and liberty of Richmondshire; 3½ miles SSE. of Bedale. The church is a large and ancient edifice, and the living is a vicarage, in the patronage of G. Elsley, Esq. incumbent the Rev. Henry Elsley. Here is a small Methodist chapel; also a Free Gram mar school, founded by one of the ancestors of the present Lord Rokeby, in 1680, together with a hospital for five poor parishioners, aged sixty years before their admission; the endowment is upwards of sixty pounds per annum. Pop. 288.

Wright Joseph, master of the free grammar school, and clerk of subdivision meetings in the wap. of Halikeld.

*Farmers & Yeomen,* Thomas Wm.
Barf Thomas        Townend James
Harrison Robert        *Shoemakers,*
Metcalf Geo.        Blakeborough John
Philipson John        Turbutt Peter
Thackray Timothy Walker Christ.

Coldwell Richard, vict. Royal Oak, and posting-house, Leeming-lane
Glave Wm. schoolmaster and parish clerk
Kitching David, mason and vict. Black Swan
Metcalf Richard, butcher
Metcalf Wilks, blocksmith and vict. Four Alls
Pearson Wm. machine maker
Pratt Richard, joiner
Whitling John, vict. Old Oak, Leeming lane
Wood Edward, wheelwright

BURNISTON, in the parish of Scalby, wap. and liberty of Pickering Lythe; 4 mls. NNW. of Scarborough. There is here a small Methodist chapel. Population, 347.

*Blacksmiths,*        Harland Isaac
Anderson John        *Shopkeepers,*
Middleton John        Anderson John
*Butchers,*        Harrison Wm.
Calvert Adam        *Wheelwrights,*
Sedman John        Haxby Geo.
*Schoolmasters,*        Robinson S.
Hanson Wm.

Calvert Adam, vict. Black Bull
Robinson Sleightholm

BURRILL WITH COWLING, in the parish of Bedale, wap. of Hang East, and liberty of Richmondshire; 2 miles SW. of Bedale. Pop. 113.

Blackburn John, farmer
Dixon Thomas, shoemaker
Gill James, schoolmaster
Mason Charles, farmer
Plews Ralph, blacksmith

*Burtersett,* in the parish of Aysgarth, and township of Hawes, wap. of Hang West, and liberty of Richmondshire; 1 mile E. of Hawes; pleasantly situated on an eminence, on the south side of the river Ure.

BURTON - cum - WALDEN, (in Bishopdale,) in the parish of Aysgarth, wap. of Hang West, and liberty of Richmendshire; 6 miles ESE. of Askrigg. The town consists chiefly of one open street of irregular buildings. At the northern extremity stands a good stone building, erected in the year 1749, for a free school, by John Saddler, late of this place, who endowed it with the annual sum of 60*l.* to be paid out of a certain estate, but, unfortunately, the charitable intention of that benevolent gentleman is now frustrated, the tenant of the estate having refused to pay the rent, on some legal quibble, and the school house having been appropriated by an inhabitant to his own use, and now claimed as his property. The only manufactory here is the combing of wool, and the only place of worship is a Methodist chapel, built about ten years ago. The town is surrounded by picturesque scenery, and the river abounds with Salmon and other fish. Population, 478.

*Post-town, Bedale; John Ibbotson, post-man.*

Letters arrive every Mon. Wed. Thur. and Sat at 12 a'clock noon, and despatched at 2 aft.

Heseltine Mrs. gentlewoman
Irwin John, surgeon
Purchase Wm. Esq. Hall
Purchase Wm. jun. gentleman
Tennant Miss, gentlewoman
*Blacksmiths,*        Metcalf Thos.
Swainston Robert        *Shoemakers,*
Whitehead Matth. Hutchinson Thos.
*Coopers,*        Peacock James
Elmsley Wm.        Spence Geo.
Elmsley Geo.        *Stone Masons,*
*Farmers,*        Hammond John
Cleasby John        Heseltine Thos.
Graham Wm.        Ibbotson Christr.
Hepple Wm.        Lawson Thomas
Humphrey James Lawson John
Morody James        *Tailors,*
Pearson Edward        Matson Thomas
Purchase Thos.        Matson J. and J.
Rider Francis        Metcalf Leonard
Robinson Wm.        *Wool Combers,*
Tennant Christr.        Beverley John
Webster John        Richardson John
*Grocers,*        Richardson Ralph
Barns Simon
Lawson Thomas, linen draper
Peacock Thomas, joiner
Richardson James, vict. Black Bull
Tennant Christopher, schoolmaster
Tennant Edward, corn miller
Tunstall Thomas, butcher
Webster James, shopkeeper
Wellock John, vict. Fox & Hounds

BURTON CONSTABLE, in the parish of Fingall, wap. of Hang West, and liberty of Richmondshire; 4 mls. ENE. of Leyburn. Pop. 201.

Cockhill John, gent.
Wyvill Marmaduke, Esq. M.P. Hall

| Farmers, | Robson Thomas |
|---|---|
| Busby John | Thornton Thos. |
| Gill Wm. | Wilson John |
| Heslop Nathan | Wilson George |
| Robinson John | |

Bearpark John, blacksmith
Harker George, land steward
Nelson John, corn miller
Robinson Ellen, vict. Board
Scott Richard, shoemaker

BURTON-UPON-URE, in the parish of Masham, wap. of Hang East, and liberty of Richmondshire; 1 mile N. of Masham. This township consists of a number of detached farm-houses, at a considerable distance from each other, and includes Aldborough, a place of great antiquity, where formerly stood the castle of Wm. le Gros, Earl of Albemarle, who, in the year 1138, was created Earl of York, in consequence of his gaining the battle of the standard, near Northallerton, in that year. High Burton is a farm-house, formerly the seat of the Wyvil's, a family of great distinction.— Population, 170.

| Farmers, | Harrison Henry |
|---|---|
| Appleton Thos. | Head Jane |
| Appleton John | Hewbank John |
| Burton John | Newby Mark |
| Clark Thos. | Wilkinson Ann |

Prest Thos. flax spinner, Burton house

BUSBY, (Great and Little) in the parish of Stokesley, wap. and liberty of Langbargh; 2 miles S. of Stokesley. Pop. 117.

Marwood Rev. Geo. Bushby hall

| Farmers, | Hymers Percival |
|---|---|
| Appleton James | Medd Thomas |
| Bailiffe John | Nightingale John |
| Carter John | Shepherd Benj. |
| Dobson Robert | Shepherd Christ. |
| Hammond John | Weatherill Thos. |
| Hudson Henry | |

Weatherill Michael, blacksmith

Bushby Stoop, in the parish of Topcliffe, wap. of Birdforth; 4 miles SW. of Thirsk.

Busco, in the parish of Lythe, wap. and liberty of Langbargh; 6 miles W. of Whitby.

Buttercrambe, in the parish of Bossall, wap. of Bulmer; 9 miles NE. of York. This village is most delightfully situated on the western bank of the navigable river Derwent, over which it has a good stone bridge. On an eminence, close to the village, stands the noble mansion of Henry Darley, Esq. Here is a Chapel of Ease under Bossall; the Rev. James Britton, D.D. vicar, officiates at both places. Population, 235.

Butterwick, in the parish of Barton-in-the-Street, wap. of Rydale; 7 miles NW. of Malton. Pop. 50.

Byland and Byland Abbey, in the parish of Coxwold, and wap. of Birdforth; 5 miles SW. of Helmsley. Gerald, the Abbot, with twelve Monks from Furness, in Lancashire, having been disturbed by the incursions of the Scots, fled to York, and afterwards was entertained some time at the castle of Thirsk, by Roger de Mowbray, who gave him the church and town of Byland, near which the Abbot and the Monks founded a monastery, and a noble cathedral, about the year 1177, which flourished till the general dissolution. It was surrendered in the year 1540, by the last Abbot and twenty-four monks, when its yearly revenues amounted to 238l. 9s. 4d. This Abbey was situated near the foot of Combe Hill, in a place well suited to devotional retirement, and was a large and magnificent structure; the site is in the possession of the Stapleton family. In the summer of 1818, Martin Stapylton, Esq. of Myton Hall, by whose family the property is now possessed, caused a quantity of rubbish to be removed from the South side of the ruin, when a stone coffin, with the bones entire was discovered here, and conveyed to Myton; and tradition says they are the remains of Roger de Mowbray; there also was discovered some beautiful Roman pavement, in high preservation. Population, 372.

BYLAND OLD, (P.) in the wap. of Birdforth; 4½ mls. WNW. of Helmsley. The church is an ancient dilapidated structure; the living is donative, in the patronage of the Earl of Falconberg; incumbent, the Rev. Michael Mackereth; the Rev. William Dowker curate. Pop. 133.

| Farmers, | Freer Thomas |
|---|---|
| Barker John | Hornby Martin |
| Bradley Thos. | Hunter Thos. |
| Chapman Thos. | Smith Thos. |
| Cole John | |

Brass William, gamekeeper
Harrison Thomas, shoemaker
Peacock John, vict. Board

Caldbridge or Caldberg, in the parish of Coverham, wap. of Hang West; 4 miles SW. of Middleham. Pop. 109.

CALDWELL, in the parish of St. John Stanwick, wap. of Gilling West;

) miles N. of Richmond. Anciently a
place of considerable extent, but now
a mere farming village. Pop. 188.

| *Farmers,* | Lennie John |
| Allison Wm. | Newhouse James |
| Davison Geo. | Wheatley G. sen. |
| Dent John | Wheatley G. jun. |
| Sells Henry | |
| Dent Joseph, spirit merchant | |
| Hall Geo. blacksmith | |
| Sutton Francis, vict. Bell | |

*Calvert House,* in the parish of
Grinton, township of Muker, wap. of
Gilling West, and liberty of Rich-
mondshire; 8 miles W. of Reeth.

CAMS HOUSES, in the parish of
Aysgarth, wap. of Hang West, and liberty of Richmondshire; 2½ miles W.
of Askrigg. Said to have derived its
name from Cam Hill, whose rugged
side appears immediately to the south
of this place.

Lodge John, gent. Cam house

| *Farmers.* | Lambert David |
| Hudson Mrs. | Brown paddock |
| Johnson Wm. | Metcalf Margaret |

*Corkin,* in the parish of Forcett,
wap. of Gilling West, and liberty of
Richmondshire; 7 miles N. of Richmond. Pop. 24.

CARLETON & HIGH DALE, in
the parish of Coverham, wap. of Hang
West, and liberty of Richmondshire;
6 miles SW. of Middleham. Pop.
Carleton 280, and High Dale 398—
Total 678.

Backle Anthony, Esq.
Constantine Henry, gent.
Law Rev. Jas. curate of Coverham

| *Blacksmiths,* | Metcalf Chpr. |
| Metcalf Thos. | Walker Joseph |
| Thompson John | Ward Robert |
| *Carpenters,* | *Grocers,* |
| Cobley John | Hammond John |
| Wright James | Rider Ralph |
| *Farmers,* | Runder Richard, |
| Iddart James | (& tailor) |
| Harrison Thos. | *Shoemakers,* |
| Harrison T. jun. | Pickard Francis |
| Hutchinson John | Prest Edward |

Bennett George, lead agent
Law Christopher, plumber & glazier
Metcalf Thomas, vict. XYZ
Ramshaw John, slater
Pennant Thos. vict. & butcher
Walls Wm. vict. Hare & Hounds
Watson Wm. schoolmaster

CARLETON, (P.) in the wap. and
liberty of Langbargh; 3 miles S. of Stokes-
ly. The church is a small modern built
structure, and the living is a perpetual curacy,

in the gift of Joseph Reeve, Esq. of which
the Rev. John Starkey, is the incumbent.
Here is also a Methodist chapel. A little to
the south of the village there is an extensive
mountainous waste, abounding with alum
rock; for the extraction and dissolving of
which there was formerly an extensive
establishment, but on the discovery of this
mineral, more contiguous to the sea, the
works at Carleton were discontinued.—
Pop. 260.

Brown Rev. Thos. officiating curate
Medd Scarth, gent.

| *Butchers,* | *Schoolmasters,* |
| Gibson Charles | Close Ralph |
| Leng John | Scotson Geo. |
| *Farmers,* | *Shoemakers,* |
| Atkinson Joseph | Fisher Wm. |
| Calvert John | Robinson John |
| Hall Geo. | Smurfitt John |
| Hunter Wm. | *Stonemasons,* |
| Kitchen Saml. | Eeles Thos. |
| Oswald John | Waller Henry |
| Potts Geo. | *Tailors,* |
| Thompson Thos. | Clark John |
| Wrightson Thos. | Johnson Robert |

Douglas Richard, grocer
Gill Richard & Thos. blacksmiths
Leng James, carpenter
Smith Benj. vict. Fox & Hounds
Wake Matthew, vict. Blackwell Ox

*Carleton,* in the parish of Helmsley, wap. of Rydale; 2 miles N. of
Helmsley.

CARLETON HUSTHWAITE, in
the parish of Husthwaite, wap. of
Birdforth, and liberty of St. Peter's; 6
miles NW. of Easingwold. Here is a
Chapel of Ease, the Rev. J. Winter,
curate. Pop. 169.

Kitchingham Valentine, Esq.
Ward John, gent.
Welbank John, Esq.

| *Farmers,* | Lancaster Edw. |
| Coates James | Metrick Wm. |
| Ezard John | Pallister Joseph |
| Foster Wm. | Robinson Wm. |

Busomworth John, carpenter
Coates John, cooper
Fewster Thos. shoemaker and vict.
    Yorkshire Jenny
Lawn Thos. blacksmith
Till Wm. tailor

*Carleton, Islebeck,* or *Miniott,* in
the parish of Thirsk, wap. of Birdforth,
and liberty of St. Peter's; 2 miles S
W. of Thirsk. Pop. 221.

CARPERBY, in the parish of Ays-
garth, wap. of Hang West, and liberty of
Richmondshire; 4 miles E. of Askrigg.
Pleasantly situated on the high road from

Leyburn to Sedbergh; this village suffered much in 1810, by a dreadful fire that destroyed upwards of 12 houses, some of the ruins of which are still standing as a memorial of the catastrophe. Pop. 283.

| Blacksmiths, | Terry Wm. |
|---|---|
| Naylor John | Taylor Geo. |
| Nicholson Thos. | Thistlethwate Rd. |
| *Farmers,* | Thompson Geo. |
| Baynes Oswald | Watson Wm. |
| Carter James | Webster Matthew |
| Harland John | Willis Charles |
| Holmes John | Willis Thos. |
| Holmes Brian | Willis Rbt. sen. |
| Metcalfe Brian | *Shopkeepers,* |
| Raw Wm. | Sunter Brian |
| Raw Robert | Webster Eliz. |
| Spenceley Ralph | Willis Rbt. jun. |

Plewes Joshua, shoemaker
Raw Joseph, joiner
Thompson Robert, vict. Board
Tomlinson Wm. schoolmaster

*Carr Bridge,* in the parish of West Rounton, wap. and liberty of Allertonshire; 7 miles S. of Yarm.

CARTHORPE, in the parish of Burneston, wap. of Halikeld, and liberty of Richmondshire; 4½ miles SE. of Bedale. Here is a small Methodist chapel. Camphill, the elegant seat of Col. Sergeantson, is in this township, about which are many vestiges of an ancient encampment. Pop. 301.

Beckett Rev. Wm. A. B. curate of Burneston
Sergeantson W. R. L. Esq. Camp hill

| *Farmers,* | Gill Wm. |
|---|---|
| Fall Dorothy | Hunton Wm. |
| Gatenby Wm. | Hutchinson R. |
| Gill Christopher | Sledhill Richard |

Anderson Wm. vict. New Inn
Clark Geo. shoemaker
Horner Christopher, wool comber, stapler and grocer
Kirby Richard, blacksmith
Richardson Henry, wheelwright
Robinson Chpr. butcher & shopkpr.
Sadler Thomas, vict. Unicorn
Tunstall Edward, butcher
Umpleby Thomas, tailor

*Casey Green,* in the parish of Kirkby Ravensworth, wap. of Gilling West, and liberty of Richmondshire; 6 miles NE. of Reeth.

CASTLETON, in the parish of Danby, wap. and liberty of Langbargh; 9 miles SE. of Guisbro'. Situated on a small eminence rising from Danby dale, and surrounded by the Cleveland moors; the places of worship are, a Methodist chapel, built in 1813, and a Friends' Meeting house, erected

about 40 years ago. The only manufactory is linen thread, for the spinning of which there is a neat and commodious stone building, erected a few years ago, the machinery of which is put in motion by the power of water. The lord of the manor is Lord Downes. The river Eske passes on the N. side in its way to Whitby.

*Post-town, Guisbro'.*—From whence letters are sent by the carriers, and despatched in the same manner.

Weatherill Wm. gent.

| *Blacksmiths,* | *Shoemakers,* |
|---|---|
| Frankland John | Braithwaite Thos. |
| Hansell Robt. | Johnson John |
| Humphrey Thos. | Tindale Jerm. |
| *Farmers,* | *Surgeons,* |
| Hansell Eliz. | Moore John |
| Langbourn Wm. | Stoddy Christpr. |
| Langbourn John | *Tailors,* |
| Leng Geo. | Balfour John |
| Lewis Wm. | Saunderson Wm. |
| Plewes John | Scarth John |
| Seaton John | Scarth Wm. |
| *Grocers & Drapers,* | Shaw Benj. (& |
| Baker Wm. (& | draper) |
| druggist) | *Weavers,* |
| Hall John | Appleton Rd. |
| *Joiners,* | Carter Wm. |
| Featherstone Wm. | *Wheelwrights,* |
| M' Bean John | Featherstone Wm. |
| *Milliners,* | Jackson John |
| Duck Jane | Langbourn Nath. |
| Shaw Sarah | |

Batty Amariah, dyer
Chapman Robert, butcher
Coulson George, vict. Robin Hood
Harcourt Richard, governor of the poor house
Hartley Wm. vict. Buck
Hawkswell Thos. millwright
Redman George, master mariner
Shepherd Richard, flax dresser
Taylor Thomas, saddler
Watson Thos. linen thread spinner
Webster John, plumber & glazier
Wilson Wm. corn miller

*Carriers*—To Guisbro', James Barker & John Norman, every Tu. dep. 6 mg. ret. 6 evg. To Whitby, Joseph Agar, and John Jeffells, every Fri. ret. Sat.

CATTERICK, (P.) in the wap. of Hang East, and liberty of Richmondshire; 5 miles ESE. of Richmond, and about one mile from the Southern banks of the Swale. Here was the Cataractonium of the Romans, once a great city, but finally destroyed by the Danes, about the year 769. Here is a large and ancient parish church, dedicated to St. Ann; the living is a vicarage in he gift of the Crown, and the Rev. Alexander John Scott, D. D. chaplain to His Majesty, is the incumbent. This Rev. gentleman was chaplain to the lamented Hero of Trafalgar, who expired in his arms. In Catterick is a free grammar school, founded by the Rev. Michael Siddall, vicar of this parish, in 1645, and very liberally endowed. Here is also a hospital for six poor widows belonging to the parish. The modern Catterick is only a village, containing 561 inhabitants.

*Post Master*—JAMES YOUNG.

Letters arrive here from the North at ½ past 5 evg. from the South at ½ past 11 at night; letters from this place are sent off at the same time. A horse post to Richmond at ½ past 5 mng. and ret. at 5 evening.

Burke Edmund, gent.
Carter John, gent.
Hodgson Ralph, Esq.
Kay Richard, gent.
Lofthouse Henry Booth, gent
Powels Harrison, Esq.
Outhwaite John, gent.
Walker Jonathan, Esq. *Oram.*

| *Academies, &c.* | Ryder J. & draper |
|---|---|
| Bradley Rev. Jas. | Wheatley Mary |
| Bradley John | White Wm. |
| Caton Miss Mary, | Young James |
| (ladies' bdg.) | *Joiners and Cabinet* |
| James Abraham | *makers,* |
| Singleton Joseph | Barwick Benj. |
| *Attornies,* | Binks Thos, |
| Bradley James | Smith Wm. |
| Caton Richard | *Milliners and Dress* |
| Ferguson James | *makers,* |
| *Butchers,* | Sott Margaret |
| Dunn G. & Co. | Sedding Eliz. |
| Dunn Joseph | *Shoemakers,* |
| Spedding Geo. | Boddy Richard |
| *Farmers,* | Carter Thos. |
| Britain James | Clarkson Thos. |
| Outhwaite John | Place Wm. |
| Todd Joseph | White Wm. |
| Wilson John | *Tailors,* |
| *Grocers,* | Coates Thos. |
| Rowntree Wm. & | Taylor James |
| tallow chandler | Walker Mthw. |

Bradley Robert, vict. Bay Horse
DeatG.commission wine & spiritmert.
Foster Geo. governor of the workhs.
Greathead Robert, vict. Angel
Healey Wm. corn miller
Heslop John, vict. Golden Lion
Mason Charles, stone mason
Peacock Thos. plumber & glazier
Ridsdale Thos. painter
Smith John, saddler
TaylorGeo.bricklayer,mason&builder
Temple Thos. vict. Royal Oak
Walton Thos. blacksmith

Young James, druggist, draper, hosier and hatter

CATTERICK BRIDGE INN, in the parish of Catterick, wap. of Hang East, and liberty of Richmondshire: 4 miles E. of Richmond. The amateurs of the turf enjoy an annual treat on the beautiful race ground, opposite this Inn; the races are on the Wednesday & Thursday in Easter week.

Ferguson Thomas, George & Dragon Inn, & posting house, Catterick Bridge
Thompson John, blacksmith

*The following Coaches stop at this Inn,*

The Royal Glasgow MAIL, Southward at a ¼ before 5 in the afternoon, Northward at midnight.
The EXPRESS, from Carlisle to York and London, at 5 in the afternoon, Northward at 8 in the evening.
The TELEGRAPH, from Leeds to Newcastle, at 10 in the morning, from the North and South at the same time.

*Catto,* in the parish of Leek, wap. and liberty of Allertonshire; 4 miles E. of Northallerton. Pop. with Landmoth, 59.

*Catton,* in the parish of Topcliffe, and wap. of Birdforth; 5 miles SW. of Thirsk. Pop. 99.

*Cawthorne,* in the parish of Middleton, wap. and liberty of Pickering Lythe; 4 miles NNW. of Pickering. Pop. 22.

*Cawton,* in the parish of Gilling, and wap. of Rydale; 6 miles SSE. of Helmsley. Pop. 105.

CAYTON, (P.) in the wap. and liberty of Pickering Lythe; 4 miles S. of Scarbro'. Here is an ancient church, dedicated to St. Leonard, also a small neat Methodist and Primitive Methodist chapel, and a school with an endowment of 15l. per ann. Population, with Deepdale & Killerby, 447.

Howson Wm. gentleman
Raylor Thos. gentleman
Whaley Mrs. Ann

| *Blacksmiths,* | Johnson Geo. |
|---|---|
| Elliott John | Lancaster James |
| Hardy David | Marfiltt Robert |
| *Farmers,* | Nesfield Guy |
| Bradford John | Robinson Geo. |
| Denton Richard | Stephenson Thos. |
| Dowson Francis | Whitfield Wm. |
| Emmerson Thos. | *Schoolmasters,* |
| Glaves Cornelius | Hudson Robert |
| Jackson John | Smailes Richard |
| Johnson John | |

| *Shoemakers,* | Lilley Ann |
|---|---|
| Dagget John | *Wheelwrights,* |
| Flinton Wm. | Smith Wm. |
| Robinson Stphn. | Tindall Thos. |

*Shopkeepers,*
Flinton Wm.

Coulson Thomas, tailor
Elliott John, vict. Horse Shoe
Hardy David, vict. Nag's Head
Shaw Thomas, butcher

*Cittadilla,* in the parish of Easby, wap. of Gilling East, and liberty of Richmondshire, 4 mls. E. of Richmond.

*Claxton,* in the parish of Bossall, and wap. of Bulmer; 8 miles NE. of York on the Malton road. The Rev. Dr. Britton, vicar of Bossall, is resident here. The Lobster House Inn, kept by Mr. G. Taylor, is in this township. Population, 135.

CLEASBY, (P.) in the wap. of Gilling East; 3 miles W. of Darlington. The church is a very ancient structure, and the living is a perpetual curacy, in the patronage of the Dean and Chapter of Ripon: incumbent, the Rev. Wm. Downill Waddilove. Here is a free school for six poor boys, endowed by Bishop Robinson, formerly Bishop of London, and a native of this place, with the rents arising from 16 acres of land, the Rev. Richard Waistell master, and officiating curate. Pop. 147.

Hird David, gentleman

| *Farmers,* | *Blacksmiths;* |
|---|---|
| Todd John | Fowell John |
| Waistell Charles | Johnson Joseph |
| Wray Geo. | *Butchers,* |
| Wright Miss | Dixon John |
| | Sokehill Robert |

CLEVELAND PORT, in the parish of Ormesby, wap. and liberty of Langbargh; 9 miles N. of Stokesley.

Eldon George, clerk to the Port
Heseltine Philip, wharfinger
Nixon Geo. vict. Board
Tindall Wm. miller

*Cliffe,* in the parish of Manfield, wap. of Gilling West, and liberty of Richmondshire; 6 miles WNW. of Darlington. Here is no place of worship, except a Catholic chapel; the Rev. William Hogarth, minister, Cliffe hall. Pop. 53.

CLIFTON, in the parishes of St. Michael le Belfrey and St. Olave, York, wap. of Bulmer, and liberty of St. Peter; 1 mile NW. of York, situated on the road to Easingwold. Pop. 469.

Bebb Margaret, gentlewoman
Briggs Wm. gentleman

Craycroft Robert, gentleman
Dyson John, gentleman
Harrison Robert, gentleman
Kitching James, surveyor of taxes
Kitchinman Rev. Henry
Kitchinman Rev. R. H.
Maude Mary, gentlewoman
Overton Rev. John
Palmer Jane, gentlewoman
Poole David, gentleman
Robson Hannah, gentlewoman
Russell David, attorney
Siddall George, gentleman
Staveley John, gentleman

| *Corn millers,* | *Gardeners,* |
|---|---|
| Darby John | Bearpark John |
| Scurr John | Brittain James |
| *Farmers,* | Hodgson John |
| Cattle Robert | Norton Richard |
| Cuthbert John | *Grocers,* |
| Ellison Geo. | Darby Wm. |
| Ellison Wm. | Hodgson John |
| Elston Joseph | *Shoemakers,* |
| Gibson George | Catton Robt. |
| Giles John | Gray Edward |
| Greaves Robert | Jackson George |
| Holgate Wm. | *Tailors,* |
| Holgate Thos. | Pratt Thos. |
| Holgate Christr. | Wood Benj. |
| Kay John | *Wheelwrights,* |
| Lund Richard | Bellerby Wm. (and |
| Moss James | carpenter) |
| Scruton John | Bilbrough Wm. |
| Shepherd John | |

Clarkson Isabella, matron to Dr. Belcombe's private lunatic asylum
Cowl Thos. vict. Plough Inn
Cuthbert Geo. saddler
Hainsworth David, blacksmith
Marchant John, vict. Marque Gardens
Rhodes Abm. coal merchant
Richardson Martin, vict. Board
Shepherd Ann, vict. Grey Horse

CLIFTON-UPON-URE, in the parish of Thornton Watlass, wap. of Hang East, and liberty of Richmondshire; 2 mls. N. of Masham. Pop. 50.

Hutton Timothy, Esq. Clifton Castle
Chaytor John Clerveaux, Esq. Clifton house

CLOUGHTON, in the parish of Scalby, wap. and liberty of Pickering Lythe; 5 miles NNW. of Scarborough. Here is a Chapel of Ease, at which the Rev. Wm. Smelt Grundon, vicar of Scalby, officiates. A large free stone quarry, from which (it is supposed) the stone was got to build Scarborough Castle, is situated in this township. Population, 366.

| *Farmers,* | Ellery John |
|---|---|
| Burnett Philip | Gibson Jane |
| Cooper Thos. | Harrison Wm. sen. |

Harrison Wm. jun.
(and grazier)
Hodgson Jane
Hodgson John
Langdale Christr.
(& grazier)
Leadley Thos.

Leadley John
Stonehouse H.
Tindall Rob.
Wharton Wm. (&
grazier)
Willis Thos.

Atkinson John, shoemaker
Craven Geo. butcher
Hodgson Thos. corn miller
Hovington Wm. stone mason
Jackson John, wheelwright
Jackson Geo. blacksmith
Nicholson John, miner
Pickering Thos. vict. Red Lion
Pierson Wm. vict. Blacksmith's Arms
Rawling Thos. tailor
Shaw Jane, shopkeeper

COATHAM EAST and WEST, in the parish of Kirkleatham, wap. and liberty of Langbargh; 6 miles NNW. of Guisbo-ough. The delightful scenery, and exten-ive prospects, with which this place is sur-ounded, conspire to attract the admiration of all who visit and contemplate its beauties. The air is remarkably salubrious, the sands extensive and peculiarly fine. There is here a small free school, conducted on the Ma-dras system, for the education of 50 poor children; twelve of the number have annu-ally given them a suit of clothes each.

Ferry Miss Jane, gentlewoman
Fisher John, gentleman

*Farmers,*
Agar Robt.
Boden Wm. West
Coatham
Buckton Jackson
Hudson Thos.
Thompson Robt.

Wilkinson John
*Grocers,*
Potts John
Prudom Wm.
*Schools,*
Wrighton P. boys'
Wrighton M. girls'

Bradley John, blacksmith
Coverdale Wm. farrier
Hardy Thos. shoemaker
Henderson Henry, pilot
Robinson Geo. tailor
Sedgwick Thos. fishmonger
Shaw Ralph, joiner
White Thos. vict. Lobster Inn, (two bathing machines)

*Carriers*—John Atkinson and George Gowton, to Stockton Wed. & Sat. dep. 4 morn. ret. 9 night.

COLBURN, in the parish of Cat-terick, wap. of Hang East, and liberty of Richmondshire; 2½ miles SE. of Richmond. Population, 133.

Plews John, chief constable of Hang East, Cockfield house
Thwaites Abraham, vict. Lord Nelson

Cold Cam, in the parish of Scaw-ton, and wap. of Rydale; 6 miles W SW. of Helmsley.

Common Dale, in the parishes of Guisbrough and Danby, wap. and li-berty of Lanbargh; 8 miles SE. of Guisborough. A narrow dale begin-ing near Castleton, and winding itself in a westerly direction to Kildale. Population, 86.

Coneysthorpe, in the parish of Bar-ton-le-Street, and wap. of Bulmer; 5 miles W. of Malton. A very plea-sant little village, close to the park wall of Castle Howard. Pop. 160.

Cornbrough, in the parish of She-riff Hutton, and wap. of Bulmer; 7 miles E. of Easingwold. Pop. 68.

Cotcliffe, (Extra-parochial) in the wap. and liberty of Allertonshire; 4½ miles ESE. of Northallerton. The property of the Bishop of Durham.

COTHERSTONE, in the parish of Romaldkirk, wap. of Gilling West, and li-berty of Richmondshire; 4 miles NW. of Barnard Castle. Pleasantly situated upon the banks of the Tees, near which is the re-mains of a castle, once the property of the Fitzhugh family, now in the possession of Mr. Hutchinson, of Hall Garth hill. Here are three chapels for divine worship, one of each belonging to the Independents, Me-thodists, and Society of Friends; likewise two boarding schools, chiefly occupied by boarders from London. Also a free school for twenty-five poor children, supported by Mr. Charles Waistell, a gentleman of Lon-don. Population, 706.

Allison Jacob, stuff manufacturer
Bourne Elizabeth, gentlewoman
Carnson Rev. Andrew, Indep. minister
Whicher Christopher, surgeon
Wilson Ann, gentlewoman
Wilson Miss Sarah

*Butchers,*
Bourne George
Dixon Thos. (and grazier)
*Farmers,*
Allison John
Bainbridge John
Bowron Margaret
Bowron John
Brown John
Butson Thos.
Chapman Eliz.
Colling John
Elliot Philip
Helmer William
Hutchinson John

Kipling Alice
Kipling Francis
Lanstaff Thos.
Parkin John
*Schoolmasters,*
Chapman M.
Raine Jonathan
Smith John
*Shoemakers,*
Hutchinson John
Lamb Henry
Raine Thomas
*Shopkeepers,*
Raine Christopher
Scrafton James

Chapelow John, dying mill

Dent Christopher, tailor
Gargett John
Heslop Joseph, vict. Red Lion
Hutchinson Wm. vict. Fox & Hounds
Smith John, blacksmith
Walton Edward, wheelwright
Wilson Caleb, chandler

*Cotterdale*, (in High Abbot Side,) and parish of Aysgarth, wap. of Hang West, and liberty of Richmondshire; 4 miles NNW. of Hawes. In this small and fertile vale there is a beautiful cataract, much frequented and admired; near to which the lofty hill (commonly called Cotter Hill) rears its ponderous head, whose rugged sides render the scene as beautiful as it is various. Population, 105.

*Coulton*, in the parish of Hovingham, and wap. of Rydale; 7 miles S. of Helmsley. Population, 113.

COUNTERSIDE, in the parish of Aysgarth, wap. of Hang West, and liberty of Richmondshire; 3 miles SSW. of Askrigg, a small village pleasantly situated in Raydale, at the NW. extremity of Simmer Water. The only place of worship is a Friends' Meeting House, erected a few years since by subscription.

Alderson Christopher, yeoman
Blakey Richard, yeoman, Wood end
Fothergill Wm. gent. Carr end
Middlebrook Wm. yeoman

*Cover Bridge*, in the parish of Coverham, and township of East Wilton, wap. of Hang West; 4 miles SE. of Leyburn.

COVERHAM, (P.) in the wap. of Hang West, and liberty of Richmondshire; 1½ mile SW. of Middleham. Here was a priory, of the order of the *Præmonstratenses*, founded by Ralph, son of Robert Lord of Middleham, about the 14th year of King John. The ruins of the Abbey are scattered about in Coverdale, so called from the river which runs through it. The Church, dedicated to the Holy Trinity, is a neat structure, the living a curacy; patron, the Rev. S. Hardcastle; incumbent, the Rev. Wm. Otter; officiating curate, the Rev. James Law. It is worthy of remark, that, though the church yard contains little more than an acre of ground, yet, from a sudden descent along the SE. side of it, a person stationed in this part of the burial ground can neither see the church nor hear the bells; the sudden rise of the church-yard entirely obstructing the view of the church, and the noise of a waterfall drowning the sound of the bells. Population, with Agglethorpe, 131.

Lister Mrs. gentlewoman, Coverham Abbey
Buck Stephen, corn miller
Clapham John, horse trainer
Johnson Robert, jockey
Lonsdale John, horse trainer
Otter Rev. Wm. incumbent
Oates Geo. horse trainer
Raw David, parish clerk
Robinson Wm. vict. Coverham lane
Smith Benjamin, horse trainer
Thompson Thomas, farmer

COWLING, in the parish of Bedale, wap. of Hang East, and liberty of Richmondshire; 2 miles W. of Bedale. Pop. with Burrill, 113.
Croft Sir John, Bart. Cowling hall
Dodsworth Mrs. F. Cowling hall

*Farmers,*
Blackburn Wm.    Cannon Sarah
Cannon Wm.    Tindale John

*Cowsby*, (P.) in the wap. of Birdforth; 7 miles NNE. of Thirsk. The church is an ancient edifice, the living is a rectory, in the patronage of Thos. Alston, Esq.; incumbent, the Rev. Vere John Alston. Pop. 91.

COWTON EAST OR LONG, (P.) in the wap. of Gilling East, and liberty of Richmondshire; 8 miles NNW. of Northallerton. The parish church at this place is dedicated to St. James; the living is a vicarage, in the patronage of St. John's hospital, in Kirkby Ravensworth; incumbent, the Rev. Thomas Jackson. Here is a free school, allowed 27l. per annum by the Kirby Hill free school. Pop. 332.

*Blacksmiths,*    Edgar Matthew
Carter Wm. and    Hall Anthony
  parish clerk    Kelsey A. T.
Dixon Edward, &   Neesham Wm.
  grocer    Pearson Geo.
*Farmers,*    Plews John
Alcock Nicholas    Robinson Thos.
Alcock Ralph    Walker Ralph
Atkinson John    White John
Best James    *Tailors and Drapers,*
Booth John    Palmer John
Dawson Robert    Watson Wm.
Dixon John
Cansfield Philip, vict. Bay Horse
Didsdale Wm. butcher
Hall Wm. wheelwright
Maise Wm. schoolmaster
Peverley George, vict. Shoulder of Mutton
Walker James, vict. Turk's Head
*Carrier*, Philip Cansfield, to Northallerton every Wed.

COWTON, (North) in the parish

d Gilling, wap. of Gilling East, and liberty of Richmondshire; 7½ miles W. of Northallerton. Pop. 370.

| Bricklayers, | Parkinson Thos. |
| Bell John | Plews John, (and |
| Brown Wm. | common brewer) |
| Carter John | Robinson Thos. |
| *Farmers & Yeomen,* | Simpson Wm. |
| Barker Ann | *Shopkeepers,* |
| Loyd John | Craggs Matthew |
| Oldman Mary | Robinson Christ. |
| Hodgson John | *Wheelwrights,* |
| Johnson Wm. | Best Wm. |
| Jordison John | Layfield Wm. |
| Page Thomas | Tate John |

Davison Richard, vict. Blacksmith's Arms
Day Lascelles, parish clerk
Glover Michael, vict. Dainty Davy
Metcalf Joseph, blacksmith
Tweedale Milton, vict. Board
Walker Wm. shoemaker

COWTON (South) a chapelry in the parish of Gilling, wap. of Gilling East, and liberty of Richmondshire? 6 miles E. of Richmond. Here is a Chapel of Ease under Gilling; the living is a perpetual curacy, in the patronage of the Dean and Chapter of Ripon; incumbent, Rev. William Darley Waddilove; curate, the Rev. John Atkinson. Population, 148.

Arden John, Esq. Pepper hall

COXWOLD, (P.) in the wap. of Birdforth; 9 miles SE. of Thirsk. A pleasant village situate on an eminence; at the entrance into the town from the West stands Shandy Hall, where Sterne resided seven years, and in which he wrote Tristram Shandy and other works. The church is an elegant structure, dedicated to St. Michael and of a very ancient date, supposed to have been built about the year 700. The tower is octagonal, and the chancel was rebuilt in the year 1777, by Henry Earl of Fauconberg. The living is a perpetual curacy, in the patronage of the Earl of Fauconberg. Here is a Free School, which was endowed by Sir John Hart, Knight, alderman, citizen, and grocer, of the city of London, wherein he provided competent maintenance and a stipend for one school-master and one usher, dated 1600, salary 32l. Here is an hospital for ten poor men. In the church are several monuments for the noble family of Belayse, the most elegant of which is that for the Right Honourable Thomas Belayse, Earl of Fauconberg, (in beautiful statuary) who died the 31st of December, 1710, aged 72; the most ancient, is

one for Sir William Belayse, dated 14th of April, 1603, and at the bottom is wrote

" Thomas Browne did carve this tome
Himself alone of Hesselwood stone."

Population, 342.

Newton Rev. Thos. A.M. magistrate
Winter Rev. John, curate

| Blacksmiths, | Shoemakers, |
| Asquith Christphr. | Bowser John |
| Featherstone Tho. | Cooper John |
| *Farmers,* | Roberts Wm. |
| Allison Robert | *Stone mason,* |
| Bleakin James | Cooper Joseph |
| Earnshaw Wm. | Fox Thos. |
| Harrison Richard | *Surgeons,* |
| Robinson Robert | Skaif Robert |
| Sunlay George | Spencelay George |

Abbey William, saddler
Abbey Thos. schoolmaster
Barker William, tallow chandler
Barwick Wm. vict. Belayse Arms
Battye James, butcher
Beverley George, painter
Brown Isaac, grocer and draper
Burnett Christopher, tailor
Burton Alexander, exciseman
Hallyburton Wm. exciseman
Roberts Francis, sexton
Rymer Peter, carpenter
Salmon William, cooper
Smith John, joiner, carpenter, and vict. Black Eagle

J. Dutchburn, carrier, arrives from Easingwold, every Fri. and ret. same days.

*Crackpot,* in the parish of Grinton, wap. of Gilling West, and liberty of Richmondshire; 5 miles WSW. of Reeth. Situated on the south side of the river Swale in Swaledale. At the source of a brook that runs past it in its road to the river, is a curious cavern, the entrance of which is extremely narrow. A few yards from the entrance is a spacious cavern; proceeding a few paces further, it descends rather abruptly; at the bottom cavern is a deep water issuing out of the rock below, near which there is a curious pillar of solid stone. The narrow passages beyond it is not safe to traverse.

CRAIKE & CRAIKE CASTLE, (P.) in the Bishopric of Durham, though locally situated in the wap. of Bulmer; 2 miles E. of Easingwold. Craike, with the land three miles round it, was given by Egfrid, King of Northumberland, to St. Cuthbert, in the year 685, by whom it came to the church of Durham; about which time the said St. Cuthbert founded a monastery here. This village is delightfully situated on the south ern declivity of a lofty detached hill or mount, on the summit of which stands the ruins of Craike Castle, which is supposed to have been a Roman fortress, and which, in the time of the Saxons, was a royal palace. From hence is a most extensive and delightful prospect of the forest of Galtres, and the beautiful and picturesque vale of Mowbray; so called from its ancient owner, Roger de Mowbray, who was bowman to William Rufus, and possessed one hundred and forty manors in England, and twenty in Normandy. He was founder of the monasteries of Newborough and Byland. Near the ruins of the castle (which is now occupied as a farmhouse) stands the church, a handsome antique edifice, inclosed within lofty trees, and which is dedicated to St. Cuthbert. The living is a rectory, in the patronage of the Bishop of Durham. In addition to the parish church, here is a Catholic chapel, of which the Rev. Thos. Coupe is minister; likewise a Methodist chapel. The freeholders in this place vote for knights for the county of Durham; pleas of land are held in the county of Durham, and the jurisdiction of the palatine extends thereto; but in the militia service the legislature thought it expedient to embody the inhabitants with the men of Yorkshire. Population, 538

Coupe Rev. Thos. Catholic pastor
Dixon Rev. Wm.
Guise Rev. P. C. A. M. rector and magistrate
Harper John, surgeon
Shepherd James, Esq.

*Blacksmiths,*
Dennison Wm.
Dennison Wm. jun.
*Carpenters,*
Blakey John
Bosomworth John
Clark William
Coward Thos.
Hogg Charles
*Farmers & yeomen,*
Abbey Francis
Abbey Philip
Atkinson James
Bland William
Bowland Henry
Brayshaw John
Britton Thos.
Burnett William
Coates Samuel
Coates William
Dale Thomas
Dobson Thomas
Dunning Jonathan
Foster James
Jarum William
Johnson Geo.
Johnson Thos.
Johnson Samuel
Johnson John
Judson Wm.
Leaf John
Linton William
Luty Samuel, (and corn miller)
Meek Silvester
Meek Thomas
Morton Thomas
Norton Thomas
Pape Richard
Parkinson John
Peckett John
Stillingfleet John
Wiley Edward
*Shoemakers,*
Barnett Wm.
Fountain Wm.
Severs Henry
Stabler Thos.
*Shopkeepers,*
Hall Ralph

Rymer George
*Tailors,*
Cariss Sample
Snowball John
Tose William

Bland Wm. common brewer & maltster
Dennison Sarah, vict. Hare & Hounds
Gibson Henry, butcher
Humble John, tanner
Jackson John, linen manufacturer
Rymes Geo. schoolmaster and parish clerk
Steward Francis, cooper
Thompson Wm. cattle dealer and vict. Durham Ox
Wheatley Wm. stone mason

*Carrier*—John Knowles to York, every Sat. dep. 4 mg. ret. same day.

*Crakehall,* in the parish of Topcliffe, and wap. of Birdforth; 6 miles S. of Thirsk. Pop. with Elmer, 78.

CRAKEHALL, (Great and Little), in the parish of Bedale, wap. of Hang East, and liberty of Richmondshire; 2 miles W. NW. of Bedale. A most delightful village, forming a square on the sides of an extensive green, finely ornamented with lofty trees. On one side is the mansion of Colonel H. P. Pulleine, and on another that of James Robson, Esq. Here is a Methodist and an Anabaptist chapel. Pop. 550.

Pulleine Colonel Henry Percy
Robson James, Esq.
Robson Mrs. Ann, gentlewoman

*Cornmillers,*
Bateson Tobias
Musgrave Mthw.
*Farmers & yeomen,*
Braithwaite Mary
Carter Nicholas
Caslin Wm.
Caslin John
Dunn Thos.
Fishburn John
Hodgson Henry
Hunton John
Linskill Mark
Linskill Elizabeth
Lonsdale Wm.
Moses Joseph
Plews William
Simpson John
Wray Margaret
*Shoemakers,*
Johnson Wm.
Saddler Thos.

Allen James, linen weaver
Boddy George, schoolmaster
Cannon Thomas, butcher
Graham Wm. joiner & cabinet maker
Hall Wm. blacksmith
Johnson Thos. vict. Octavian
Marshall Thos. vict. Revellers
Remmer John, grocer and draper
Saddler George, tallow chandler
Stapylton Thomas, tailor

CRAMBE, (P.) in the wap. of Bulmer; 6 mls. SW. of Malton. Here is a church dedicated to St. Michael; the living is a vicarage, of which the Archbishop of York is the patron, and the Rev. John Cleaver, D. D. incumbent. Population, 152.

Dales Rev. George, curate

CRATHORNE, (P.) in the wap. and liberty of Langbargh; 4 miles SSE. of Yarm. The church, which is dedicated to All Saints, is an ancient plain structure; in the chancel is an effigy of a knight cumbent in armour cross-legged, with the arms of Crathorne on his shield. This, it is conjectured, is the monument of Sir William Crathorne, Knight, who lived A.D. 1322, near which is a mural monument, to the memory of Ralph Crathorne, Lord of Crathorne. The living is a rectory, in the patronage of Lord Viscount Cullen. Here is likewise a Catholic chapel, and a place of worship for the Primitive Methodists. A mineral spring has been discovered about half a mile from this place. The village consists of about sixty-six houses, pleasantly situated on the banks of the river Leven. Pop. 330.

Corless Rev. Geo. Catholic minister
Greensides Rev. Ralph, A.M. rector
Stringer John, gentleman

| *Blacksmiths,* | Robinson John |
|---|---|
| Goldie John | Storey S. D. |
| Goldie Wm. | Stringer Wm. |
| *Farmers,* | *Grocers,* |
| Appleton John | Goldie John |
| Humble Richard | Meynell Joseph |
| Meynell Joseph | *Joiners and Wheel-* |
| Middlemas Edw. | *wrights,* |
| Newton Wm. | Fawcett John |
| Pickering Wm. | Goldie Wm. |
| Robinson Thos. | Meynell John |

Chapman Thos. butcher
Hall William, tailor
Humble John, vict. Punch Bowl
Kilburn William, schoolmaster
Metcalf Thos. bricklayer
Nevill Joseph, linen manufacturer, bleacher, and corn miller
Rountree Richard, parish clerk
Tattersall John S. bailiff
Walton George, round timber merchant
Welford Robert, shoemaker

CROFT, (P.) in the wap. of Gilling East, and liberty of Richmondshire; 4 miles S. of Darlington. The church, which is dedicated to St. Peter, is a very ancient structure, and the living is a rectory, in the patronage of the king, of which the Rev. James Dalton is the incumbent. Here is also a school, supported by voluntary contributions. A remarkable ceremony is performed on the bridge, at the coming of every new Bishop of Durham, by which a certain family hold their lands. The chief of that family presents an old sword to the prelate, pronouncing the following words :—" My lord, this is the falchion that slew the Worm

Dragon, which spared neither man, woman, nor child." The bishop takes the sword and returns it immediately. This is one of those singular tenures, the origin of which cannot now be accounted for. Here is a very ancient mill, which was granted to one of the Clarvaux family of that place, by Allan Earl of Richmond, in the time of William the Conqueror. This place is much noted for its sulphureous spa waters, which resemble both in smell and medicinal properties the Harrogate sulphur spa. It is used both for drinking and bathing. About seven years ago a suite of baths with dressing rooms and a bath keeper's house were erected here, and fitted up in a commodious and complete manner, by Wm. Chayter, Esq. Pop. 368.

Chayter William, Esq. Croft hall
Colling Charles, Esq. Monk end
Newby Mrs. M. gentlewoman

*Lodging Houses.*

Batenby El. 4, Terrace
Benison Henry
Carr Richard, 1, Terrace
Cundall Michael, (and blacksmith)
Radon James, and gardener
Gouldsbrough Widow
Hall John, (and farmer)
Hobson Ralph, sen. & wheelwright
Holborn Catharine, 2, Terrace
Munby Mary, and keeper of the bath
Outhwaite Ann, 3, Terrace
Williamson John, jun. Spa

Chapman Wm. schoolmaster
Coates John, parish clerk
Fletcher Michael, yeoman
Flintoff Francis, yeoman
Gouldsbrough Anthony, wheelwright
Hobson Ralph, jun. shoemaker
Johnson John, miller
Munby Joseph, vict. Spa Hotel
Peacock Wm. vict. Bay Horse

CROPTON, in the parish of Middleton, wap. and liberty of Pickering Lythe; 4 miles NW. of Pickering. At this village is a large circular mount, called Cropton Castle, near which are the remains of a Roman camp, with a number of tumuli, of several sizes, in its vicinity. The situation is on an eminence, at the foot of which are the remains of a Roman road, twelve feet broad, paved with flint pebbles, in great perfection, which may be traced from thence, over the moors, near 16 miles, to Dunsley. Population, 321.

Clapham William, gentleman
Smith John, gentleman

| *Blacksmiths,* | *Farmers,* |
|---|---|
| Shepherd Wm. | Atkinson George |
| Underwood John | Barker John |

Barnes Jane
Berriman Robert
Boyes Wm.
Bulmer Tabitha
Ellis Francis
Gibb Martin
Green James
Green Wm.
Humphrey John
King Thomas
Lownsbrough Rbt.
Marwood Roger

Morley Moses
Otterburn Abm.
Pierson James
Smithies Geo.
ThompsonPennock
Thorp Geo.
Wellburn Richard
Wood Thos.
Wood Joseph
Wood John
*Shopkeepers,*
Barker James
Carr Benj.

Berriman Joshua, vict. Board
Dodgson Matthew, wheelwright
Ellis Francis, shoemaker
Fletcher John, tailor
Harker Wm. schoolmaster
Mackley Wm. wheelwright
Morley Geo. corn miller
Pennock Rachel, vict. Sun

CROSBY, in the parish of Leak, wap. and liberty of Allertonshire; 4 miles SE. of Northallerton. Pop. 39.

Hudson Christopher, farmer & Chief Constable of Allertonshire

*Crossel,* in the parish of Helmsley, and wap. of Rydale; 8 miles NNW. of Helmsley.

Cross Butts, in the parish of Whitby, wap. & liberty of Whitby Strand; 2 miles WSW. of Whitby.

*Crosswick,* (see Holwick.)

*Cubeck,* in the parish of Aysgarth, wap. of Hang West, and liberty of Richmondshire; 2 miles SSE. of Askrigg.

*Cundall,* (P.) in the wap. of Hallikeld, and liberty of Richmondshire; 5 miles NNE. of Boroughbridge. Here is a church, dedicated to St. Mary; the living is a vicarage, in the patronage of the Cholmondley family, the incumbent of which is the Rev. William Gregg. Pop. including Leckby 170.

*Dalby,* (P.) in the wap. of Bulmer, 7 miles ENE. of Easingwold. Here is a church, dedicated to St. Mary; the living is a rectory, in the gift of Mrs. Leybourne, of which the Rev. Benjamin Lumley is incumbent. Mrs. Leybourne resides here.—Pop, including Skewsby, 169.

*Dalby,* in the parish of Thornton, wap. and liberty of Pickering Lythe; 5 miles NE. of Pickering.

Dale Head, (see Arkengarthdale.)

*Dale Town,* in the parish of Hawnby, and wap. of Birdforth; 6 miles NW. of Helmsley. Here is a cliff, called Peak Scarr. Pop. 68.

DALTON, in the parish of Topcliffe, and wap. of Birdforth; 5 miles S. of Thirsk. Here is a Methodist chapel, old connexion. Pop. 235.

*Farmers & Yeomen,* Raper Wm.
Barker Wm.          Smithson Stephen
Dale Thos.                    *Shoemakers,*
Gott John             Buckle Wm.
Hatton Thos.        Poulter Andrew
Kendrew Wm.      Swales John
Lascelles John               *Shopkeepers,*
Meek Edward      Hogg Mary
Meek Andrew      Poulter James

Bell Wm. vict. Bay Horse
Burton Thos. vict. Black Swan
Dale C. butcher
Hatton Joseph, gardener
Poulter Jane, milliner
Poulter James, tailor
Smith George, schoolmaster
Walbran John, carpenter
Whitolk Joseph, blacksmith

*Dalton,* in the parish of Kirkby Ravensworth, wap. of Gilling West, and liberty of Richmondshire; 7 miles NW. of Richmond. Here is a Free School, which the Methodists are permitted to use occasionally as a chapel. A Foot-post from hence to Richmond every Wednesday, Thursday and Saturday. Pop. 265.

DALTON-UPON-TEES, in the parish of Croft, wap. of Gilling East, and liberty of St. Peter; 10 miles NE. of Richmond. Pop. 167.

*Farmers,*           Thomas Robert
Coates Wm.        Todd Wm.
Hutchinson Wm.   Weal Wm.

Cutter Robert, vict. Crown
Heavysides James, blacksmith
Plews J. vict. Board
Squire Christopher, wheelwright

DANBY, in the parish of Thornton Steward, wap. of Hang West; 2 miles E. of Middleham. Danby hall is an extensive stone building apparently of great antiquity.

Scroope Simeon Thomas, Esq. Danby hall

Buck Peter, corn miller
Dowthwaite Thomas, land agent
Pool Wm. farmer

*Danby,* (P.) in the wap. and liberty of Langbargh; 8 miles SE. of Guisbro'. The church is an ancient edifice, and the living is a perpetual curacy, of which Lord Viscount Downe is patron, and the Rev. Daniel Duck the incumbent. The Castle of which there are still some considerable remains, stands on the brow of a naked hill, of no great elevation, at a little distance to the South from the banks of the.

river Esk. It was probably built soon after the conquest, by Robert de Brus; and was afterwards the occasional residence of the Lords of Danby. Pop. 1373.

DANBY on WISKE, (P.) in the wap. of Gilling East, and liberty of Richmondshire; 4 mls. N.W. of Northallerton. The living is a rectory, in the patronage of the incumbent Rev. Wm. Cust. Pop. 323.

*Farmers & Yeomen,* Pinkner Henry
Bulmer Wm.     Ward Edmund
Crooks Richard     *Wheelwrights,*
Ingleden Joseph     Butterwick Geo.
Lodge Wm.     Peacock Abraham
Peacock Geo.

Chipchase R. vict. & parish clerk, Swan
Harrison Luke, vict. Ox
Wilkinson Thomas, blacksmith

*Deepdale,* in the parish of Romaldkirk, wap. of Gilling West, and liberty of Richmondshire; 1 mile W  W. of Barnard Castle.

*Deepdale,* see Cayton.

*Deighton,* in the parish of Northallerton, wap. and liberty of Allertonshire; 5¼ miles N. of Northallerton. Here is a Chapel of Ease, under the vicarage of Northallerton, the Rev. Edward Gibson, of Brompton, curate. This village is chiefly the property of Sir Robert Preston, Bart. Pop. 154.

DINSDALE-OVER, in the parish of Sockburn, which is partly in the county of Durham, wap. and liberty of Allertonshire; 5¼ miles SW. of Yarm, situated on the banks of the Tees. Pop. 66.
Mewburn Henry, gent.
Ward Miss Ann, gentwn. hall

DISHFORTH, in the parish of Topcliffe, wap. of Halikeld, and liberty of Richmondshire; 4 miles N. of Boroughbridge. Here is a Chapel of Ease, under Topcliffe, incumbent the Dean of Ripon, and the Rev, Thos. Allanson, curate. Here is also an Anabaptist chapel, the ministers are supplied from the academy at Bradford. This neighbourhood is famous for the growth of Barley. Pop. 340.

*Farmers & Yeomen,* Prince Frs. sen.
Anderson Francis    Prince Frs. jun.
Appleton Geo.    Smith John
Appleton Thos.    *Shoemakers,*
Barrowby Fras.    Appleton John
Deighton Thos.    Holiday Richard
Grove James    Morris Christphr.
Hustwaite John    *Shopkeepers,*
Jordan John    Horngill Ann
Mason John    Morris Christ.
Morley John

Brockhill Wm. butcher
Burnett Robert, schoolmaster
Clark Wm. surveyor of Leeming lane
Dent John & Wm. carpenters
Horner Wm. vict. Crown & Cushion
Hustwaite Thos. vict. Windsor Castle, Leeming lane
Parker Francis, vict. Black Swan
Smith George, blacksmith
Thornton Ralph, tailor

*Docwe Holme,* (P.) in the wap. of Hang West, and liberty of Richmondshire; 4 miles E. of Reeth. The church is an ancient Gothic structure, the living is a perpetual curacy, in the patronage of John Hutton, Esq. of which the Rev. James Tate, A. M. is the incumbent. Pop. 113.

DROMANBY, (Great and Little) in the parish of Kirkby, wap. and liberty of Langbargh; 3 miles SSE. of Stokesley.

*Yeomen,*    Farrer Robert
Cook John    Harrison Robert
Dobson Christphr.   Scooley Wm.
Emerson James

*Dunbogs,* in the parish of Lythe, wap. and liberty of Langbargh; 6 miles W. of Whitby.

*Dunsley,* in the parish of Whitby, wap. and liberty of Whitby Strand; 3¼ miles WNW. of Whitby. A small village, situate upon the bay, called by Ptolomy, Dunus Sinus. That this was a landing place used by the Romans, is evident from an inscription on a stone, dug up here in the year 1774; by which it appears, that the Emperor Justinian built a maritime fort, or castle here, from which is a Roman road extending for many miles over the moors to York, called Wade's Causeway. The Danes, in the year 867, landed at this place with a numerous army, and spread desolation and misery over all the country. Population with Newholme, 259.

*Earswick,* in the parishes of Huntington and Strensall, wap. of Bulmer, a part in the liberty of St. Peter; 3¼ miles NNE. of York. Pop. 116.

*Easby,* (P.) in the wap. of Gilling West, and liberty of Richmondshire; 1 mile E. of Richmond, pleasantly situated on the banks of the Swale. The parish church here is dedicated to St. Agatha. The living is a vicarage, in the patronage of the King, of which the Rev. Caleb Readshaw, M.A. is incumbent. Here are the remains of an abbey of Premonstratentian Canons, dedicated to St. Agatha, founded by Roaldus, constable of Richmond, about the year 1151. There is here likewise a hospital for four poor persons. The principal inhabitants of the village are Robert Jaques, Esq. Abbey house, and Capt. James Jackson. Pop. 106.

EASBY, is the parish of Stokesley, wap. and liberty of Langbargh; 3½ miles E. of Stokesley. The village, which consists chiefly of a few farm houses, stands in a pleasing wooded vale, watered by a branch of the Leven; on the eastern bank of which stands Easby Hall, formerly a seat of the Lords Eures, but now used as a farm house, and falling into decay. The principal inhabitant in this village is Mrs. Eliz. Adamson. Population, 124.

EASINGTON, (P.) in the wap. and liberty of Langbargh; 10 miles ENE. of Guisborough, gives name to a parish of considerable extent, stretching from North to South upwards of six miles, and about two miles broad, it comprehends the several manors of Easington, Boulby, and Liverton, all of which, according to Domesday survey, were anciently within the soke of the manor of Lofthouse, held in the Conqueror's time by Hugh, Earl of Chester, and was then uncultivated, except Easington, in which there was one villain, with one plough, a church without a minister, and a wood, with a pasturage for cattle one mile long and half a mile broad. The church is dedicated to All Saints, the living a rectory, in the gift of the King, incumbent the Rev. Matthew Mappletoft, D. D. the Rev. James Metcalf, curate. Pop. 507.

| Farmers, | Hall Thos. |
|---|---|
| Adamson Wm. | Jennings Richard |
| Andrew Isaac | Mailey Robert |
| Brittain Henry | Pennick Mary |
| Clark James | Pennick Wm. |
| Craggs Geo. | Webster Richard |
| Dawson Wm. | |

Abrahams Hill, joiner
Craggs Wm. vict. Board
Whelbury Thos. blacksmith

---

### EASINGWOLD, (P.)

In the wap. of Bulmer, and liberty of Pickering Lythe; 10 miles from Thirsk, 10 from Boroughbridge, and 13 from York, is a small market town, and, from its inland situation, without any navigable communication, has no great trade, except in bacon, and butter, of which considerable quantities are sent to York, and forwarded by water to London. The weekly market is on Friday. The church, which is dedicated to St. John, is pleasantly situated on an eminence above the town, commands a most extensive and delightful prospect over the ancient forest of

Galtres, and the vale of Mowbray, with the venerable and stately cathedral of York in full view. The living is a vicarage, in the patronage of the Archbishop of York. (In this turn.) In the church is deposited a large coffin, made of oak, and secured at the joints with plates of iron, which, (it is said) was used by the inhabitants in carrying dead bodies to the grave, previous to the introduction of coffins for interment, and on their arrival at the place of burial, the corpse was carefully taken out of this common coffin, and laid in the grave, with no other covering than the shroud. Here is likewise a chapel for the Methodists, another for the Calvinists, and one for the Primitive Methodists. The poor of this town enjoy the benefit of several excellent charities, the principal of which is a free school, endowed by Mrs. Wealthman, a native of Easingwold, who, by her will, bearing date 1781, bequeathed the sum of 2500l. 4 per cent. bank annuities, for establishing a charity school in Easingwold, in which school are to be taught to thirty boys Latin, the English grammar, reading, writing, arithmetic, and book-keeping; and thirty girls reading, writing, and arithmetic; also another school, with a small endowment, free for ten boys of the township, and two Sunday schools, belonging to the Methodists. Here are several chalybeate springs, the principal of which supplies the reservoir of a neat little bathing house. Pop. 1912.

POST-MASTER—LEONARD SMITH, Office, Long street,

Letters are received from York, Thirsk, Northallerton and Darlington every evening at 10 o'clock, and are also dispatched at the same time.

John Burrill, Postman.

DIRECTORY.

Blinks J. R. gentleman
Carver John, yeoman
Chaloner Rev. Henry, A. M.
Coverdale Richard
Crawford Thomas, gentleman
Dixon Thomas, yeoman
Driffield Thomas, yeoman
Driffield Henry, gentleman
Driffield Mrs. Ann, gentlewoman
Gill Wm. gentleman
Harrison Misses A. & M. gentlewomen
Holgate John, gentleman
Horner George, gentleman
Jackson Misses A. J. & D. gentlewomen
Jackson Thomas, gentleman
Jackson Wm. gentleman
James Mrs. Mary, gentlewoman
Oliver James, yeoman
Paley Rev. Edmund, A. M. vicar
Peacock John, yeoman
Petch Richard, yeoman

Raper John, gentleman
Robinse William Lodge, M. D.
Sigsworth George, yeoman
Singer Rev. Thomas, Dissenting minister
Smith Mrs. Sarah, gentlewoman
Smith John, gentleman
Smith W. E. M. gentleman
Stables Mrs. Ann, gentlewoman
Sweeting Ann
Thornton Mrs. Alice, gentlewoman
Waring Mrs. Eliz. gentlewoman
Wark James, gentleman
Whytehead Mrs. Margaret
Williams William, gentleman
Wilson John, yeoman

*Academies and Day Schools,*
Arnett M. A.
Barton Rev. R.
Bates M. A.
Jackson Thos.
Bowling Frs. Easingwold academy
Scott Ann
Stephenson G. W.

*Attornies and Solicitors,*
Foster Jonathan
Lockwood Wm.

*Bakers,*
Holmes James
Johnson Mary
Nelson Christphr.
Windross Joseph

*Blacksmiths,*
Bean John
Elmer John
Farrow Robert
Holgate Wm.

*Boot & Shoemakers,*
Bell John
Bosomworth Geo.
Cowling John
Craike Wm.
Dale Thos.
Mountain Wm.
Rookledge Francis
Skaife Thos,
Skaife John
Skaife Wm.
Smith Martin
Todd Geo.
Todd Jonathan

*Bricklayers and Builders,*
Dixon & Sowray
Littlewood Robt.
Preston Wm.
Preston John
Ray Wm.

*Brick-makers,*
Petch Richard
Pulleine & Raper

*Butchers,*
Cariss Jethro
Gatenby Robert
Middlemiss John
Peacock Wm.
Shepherd Geo.
Sturdy John

*Clock and Watch Makers,*
Barker Joseph
Richardson Ann

*Corn-millers,*
Bedom Wm.
Dale Christopher

*Cowkeepers,*
Burrill John
Hall John
Horsman Richard

*Curriers & Leather Cutters,*
Barnborough Wm.
Hutchinson Thos.

*Dress Makers,*
Lund Dorothy
Smith Mary Ann

*Druggists,*
Bainbridge C. T.
Seavers Wm.

*Farmers,*
Bellwood Jonth.
Coverdale John
Coverdale Richard
Craike Wm.
Dobson John
Eatson Leonard
Gibson Wm.
Gibson James
Gill Christopher
Gill Wm.
Hobson Joseph
Hobson John
Jackson Geo.
Jefferson John
Kendrew Thos.
Layton Wm.
Leek Thomas
Leng Wm.
Lund John

Matson Wm.
Nicholson John
Noton Francis
Pickard James
Plumber Francis
Ridsdale Wm.
Sigsworth John
Sigsworth Wm.
Smithson Wm.
Stead Wm.
Sturdy John
Tranmer Robert
Wales Edward
Ward Wm.
Watson Wm.
Welburn Thos.
Whitwell James
Whorley Thos.
Williamson Wm.
Wilson Thos.
Wright Benj.

*Fire and Life, &c. Offices,*
Bainbridge C. T.
Eagle
Foster Jonathan,
Globe

*Flax Dressers,*
Ball Geo.
Clark Richard
Clough T. & F.
Dunning John
Smith Leonard

*Grocers & Tea Dlrs.*
Bainbridge C. T.
Bilton Thos.
Galtry Geo.
Seavers Wm.
Sigsworth David
Smith Wm.

*Hair Dressers,*
Arnett John
Wood John

*Hardware Dealers,*
Barker Joseph
Farrow Hannah
*Hat Dlrs. & Mfrs.*
Burrows Wm, (& furrier)
Johnson Charles
Ridley John
Sigsworth David
Smith John

*Joiners, &c.*
Preston Thos.
Reacher Wm.
Reacher Edw.
Rookledge Frs.
White Wm.
White Wm.

*Linen Mfrs.*
Clough T. & F.
Dunning John
*Linen and Woollen Drapers,*
Ashton John
Dunning John
Johnson Charles
Smith John
Stephenson Geo.
*Nursery & Seedsmen,*
Ezard Emanuel
Harrison Thos.
Lambert Francis
*Plumbers and Glaziers, &c.*
Smith Wm.
Smith John
*Printers Letter press*
Dalton Thos.
Todd James
*Rope, &c. Mfrs.*
Miller John
Smith Leonard
*Saddlers,*
Barker David
Earnshaw Thos.
Gatenby Henry
*Shopkeepers,*
Atkinson M. & M.
Atkinson Thos.
Bickerdike James
Britton Robert
Hall John
*Spirit Merchants,*
Bainbridge C. T.
Garbutt Robt. (& porter dealer)
*Straw Hat Makers,*
Atkinson Ann
Fisher Mary
*Surgeons,*
Cock Geo.
Scott John
*Tailors & Drapers,*
Bland John
Bland Thos.
Bland Wm.
Hodgson Robert
Hornby John
*Tallow Chandlers,*
Windross John, (& woolstapler)
Wood John
*Turners, &c,*
Banks John
Brown Wm.
*Wheelwrights,*
Reacher Wm.
Rookledge Richard

*Hotels, Inns, and Taverns.*
Angel, Wm. Calway, (& auctioneer)
Bay Horse, John Harrison
Blue Bell, John Lyon

George Inn, Wm. Preston
Green Tree, Wm. Harrison
Horse Shoe, John Bean
Jolly Farmer, James Furbank
Malt Shovel, Edward Reacher
New Inn, Thos. Hawkes, (posting hs.)
New Rose and Crown, Benj. Lacy, (posting house)
Old Rose & Crown, John Britton
Punch Bowl, Isaac Colley
Red Lion, Robert Driffield
Sun & Punch Bowl, Samuel Hutton
Unicorn, Wm. Boulton
Unicorn, Richard Silversides
Waggon & Horses, Wm. Gray
White House, John Appleby

Bainbridge Matthew, supervisor
Barker Wm. steel maker
Barker Geo. ironmonger, whitesmith, and gunsmith
Bland George, cooper
Cattle Christ. clerk at the brewery
Clemishaw Thomas, gunsmith
Fairbourn Henry, painter & gilder
Hirst John, fishmonger
Hobson John, tanner
Moor Thomas, earthenware dealer
Mountain Edward, furniture broker
Outhwaite John, excise officer
Rocliffe John & Co. common brewers
Stephenson Geo. vestry clerk
Sunley Thos. collector of the tolls
Turton Richard, cattle dealer
Walker John, breeches maker, &c.

### COACHES.

*From the Old Rose and Crown.*
The ROYAL MAIL, from York to Edinbro', and from Edinbro' to York, at 10 evg.
*From the New Rose and Crown.*
The SUNDERLAND MAIL, to & from York at 10 evg.
The WELLINGTON, from York to Newcastle, at ¼ past 11 evng. southward at 7 evg.
The HIGHFLYER, from York to Newcastle, at a ¼ before 9 mg. stops breakfast 20 minutes; southward at 8 evening.

### CARRIERS BY LAND.

Mary Jefferson, to Thirsk Mon. and Thu. dep. at 6 mg. ret. same day, to White Swan Inn
To York Tu. Thu. & Sat. dep. at 2 mg. ret. same day, to Black Bull, Thursday market
Abraham Ditchburn, to York, Wed. and Sat. dep. at 2 mg. ret. same day; to White Swan Inn, Goodramgate

*Easterside,* in the parish of Hawnby, wap. of Birdforth; 7 miles NW. of Helmsley.

*East Moors,* in the parish of Helmsley, and wap. of Rydale; 4 miles N. of Helmsley.

EAST ROW, in the parish of Whitby, wap. & liberty of Whitby Strand; 2½ miles NW. of Whitby.

Greathead Francis, exciseman
Lair Christopher, vict. Red Hart
Linton John, common brewer

EBBERSTON, (P.) in the wap. and liberty of Pickering Lythe; 6½ miles E. of Pickering, is adorned with a small but elegant country seat, constructed on the plan of a Roman villa, by one of the Hotham family, but now occupied by George Osbaldeston, Esq. It is situated about a mile to the North of the York road, at the foot of a fine eminence, decorated with an amphitheatre of plantations, and a small sheet of water rushing down the declivity and falling in cascades behind the house, round which is is conveyed by an aqueduct. On the hill, above the house, is a small cave in a rock, called by the country people, "Ilfred's hole," a corrupt name for Alfred's Cave.— The church is dedicated to St. Mary. The living is a vicarage, in the patronage of the Dean of York. Incumbent, the Rev. Thos, Simpson. Here is a very neat Methodist chapel. Pop. 505.

Hayes Rev. Thomas, curate
Osbaldeston George, Esq. Lodge
Watson Richard, gentleman

*Farmers,*
Allanson Wm.
Barker Richard
Craven Richard
Holliday Thos.
Mawman Matth.
Pearson Wm.
Stubbs Francis
Vazey Thos.
Yeoman Joseph
Yeoman James
*Shoemakers,*
Slater John
Stubbs Wm.

Clifford W. schoolmaster & bookbinder
Herbert Moses, warrener, Scambridge
Metcalfe Robert, stone mason
Riby John, vict. Black Legs
Robinson and Newton, brewers and maltsters
Rodgers Christopher, corn miller
Rodgers Richard, blacksmith
Saunderson John, grocer
Spink Joseph, tailor
Temple John, wheelwright
Thompson James, linen weaver
Thorp Frs. vict. joiner & glazier, Board
Yeoman John, fellmonger

EDSTONE GREAT, (P.) in the wap. of Rydale; 2 miles SSE. of Kirby-Moor-Side. The living is a vicarage, in the patronage of the Marquis of Salisbury; incumbent, the Rev. Christopher Roberts. Pop. 156.

*Farmers,*
Boys George
Fenwick Brian
Goodwill Wm.
Hood Stephen
Smith John

Clark Richard, shoemaker & shopkpr.
Clayton Geo. vict. White Horse
Ventriss Wm. blacksmith

*Edstone,* (Little) in the parish of Sinnington, and wap. of Rydale; 3 miles SE. of Kirby-Moor-Side. Population, 16.

EGGLESTON ABBEY, in the parish of Rokeby, wap. of Gilling West, and liberty of Richmondshire; 2 miles SW. of Barnard Castle. There are here the remains of an Abbey, said to be founded by Ralph de Multon, about the year 1189, parts of which are now converted into cottages, and the walls on the inside of the ruins are covered with fruit trees; it is situated on the banks of the Tees, and greatly adds to the many beauties of Teesdale.

Cook Henry, paper manufacturer
Harker Joseph, farmer
Layton Sarah, farmer
Miller Jonathan, farmer

EGTON, (P.) in the wap. and liberty of Langbargh; 7 miles SW. of Whitby, pleasantly situated on the edge of the moors bearing that name. It has a charter for a market and four annual fairs, granted by William the Third to Henry Viscount Longvilliers, in the 12th year of his reign. The markets were formerly considerable for corn and cattle, but now only held from the Tuesday before Palm Sunday to Midsummer, weekly, and on the Tuesday before Old Michaelmas for cattle. The places of public worship are, the church, an ancient Gothic structure, dedicated to St. Hilda, and consecrated by the Bishop of Damascus, June 12th, 1349, situated about half a mile from the town; the living is a perpetual curacy, in the patronage of the Archbishop of York, of which the Rev. Benjamin Richardson is incumbent.——Here is also a Catholic chapel, the Rev. John Woodcock minister; also a Sunday school, supported by voluntary subscription. There is here a fine spring of water, called Cold Keld Well, much resorted to for strengthening weakly children. Egton parish consists of the following hamlets :——Egton Banks, Newbegin, Egton Grange, Delves, Hazlehead, Dawson Garth, Lace Rigg, Hollins, Limber hills, and Shorpitt. Pop. 1037.

*Blacksmiths,*
Pringles Geo.
Roe Francis

*Farmers,*
Elders Wm.
Elders Henry
Frankland J. jun.
Frankland J. sen.
Helm John
Helm Ellen
Hodgson Francis
Pearson Francis
Peckitt John
Roe George
Smith Robert

Wood Ralph
*Shoemakers,*
Roe William
Roe John
White Thomas
*Weavers,*
Roe William
Roe Matthew
*Wheelwrights,*
Foster John
Sanderson Wm.

Frankland Wm. vict. Fox & Hounds
Hutchinson Francis, schoolmaster
Jackson Robert, shopkeeper
Peckitt John, wood agent
Roe John, cooper
Roe Francis, vict. Barley Mow
Smallwood John, vict. Plough
White Joseph, vict. Wheat Sheaf
Wilson Joseph, vict. Horse Shoe

EGTON BRIDGE.
Smith Richard, Esq.
Woodcock Rev. John, Catholic pastor

*Farmers,*
Duck William
Frankland Wm.

*Tailors,*
Barker Joseph
Barker George
White George

Garbutt John, miller
Nagg Charles, shoemaker
Rea Leonard, vict. and butcher
Underwood James, blacksmith
Underwood Wm. vict. Board

*Ellerbeck,* in the parish of Osmotherley, wap. and liberty of Allertonshire; 5 miles NE. of Northallerton. Pop. 81.

*Ellerburn,* (P.) in the wap. and liberty of Pickering Lythe; 3 miles ENE. of Pickering. The parish church is dedicated to Saint Hilda. The living is a vicarage, in the patronage of the Dean of York; incumbent, the Rev. Michael Mackreth. This parish has no township of its name. See Farmanby.

*Ellerby,* a small village in the parish of Lythe, wap. and liberty of Langbargh; 7 miles NW. of Whitby. Population, 80.

*Ellerton,* in the parish of Downholme, wap. of Hang West, and liberty of Richmondshire; 3 miles SE. of Reeth. Pop. 47.

ELLERTON-UPON-SWALE, in the parish of Catterick, wap. of Gilling East, and liberty of Richmondshire; 5 miles ESE. of Richmond. This place is remarkable for having been the birth-place of Henry Jenkins, who lived to the amazing age of 169 years, being sixteen years older than the famous old Parr; he died December 9th,

1670, at this place.* A monument was erected to his memory in the church of Bolton-upon-Swale, in 1743, and the following epitaph, composed by Dr. Thomas Chapman, placed upon the Tablet :—

" Blush not marble
To rescue from oblivion the memory of
HENRY JENKINS,
A person obscure in birth,
But of a life truly memorable ;
For he was enriched with the goods of nature
If not of fortune;
And happy in the duration, if not the variety
of his enjoyments ;
And though the partial world despised and
disregarded
His low and humble state,
The equal eye of providence beheld and
blessed it
With a patriarch's health and length of days ;
To teach mistaken man
These blessings are entailed on temperance,
A life of labour, and a mind at ease."

Population, 140.

*Ellingstring*, in the parish of Masham, wap. of Hang East, and liberty of St. Peter's ; 4 mls. WNW. of Masham. Here is a small Methodist chapel. Pop. 204.

ELLINGTHORP, in the parish of Aldborough, wap. of Halikeld ; 1 mile E. of Boroughbridge.
Clark Thomas, Esq. Ellingthorp hall
Clark H. gent. Ellingthorp lodge
Clark Edwin, gent.

*Ellington*, (High) in the parish of Masham, and wap. of Hang East ; 3 miles NW. of Masham.  Pop. 152.

*Ellington*, (Low) in the parish of Masham, wap. of Hang East, a part in the liberty of St. Peter's ; 3 miles NW. of Masham.

*Elmyre*, in the parish of Topcliffe, and wap. of Birdforth ; 5 miles S. of Thirsk.  Pop. with Crakeball, 78.

*Enter Common*, in the parish of Great Smeaton, and wap. of Gilling East ; 8 miles N. of Northallerton.

*Eppleby*, in the parish of Gilling, wap. of Gilling West, and liberty of Richmondshire ; 9 miles N. of Richmond.  Pop. 157.

*Eryholme*, a chapelry in the parish of Gilling, wap. of Gilling East, and liberty of Richmondshire ; 4½ miles SE. of Darlington. Here is a chapel, under Gilling; the living is a perpetual curacy, in the patronage of the Rev. Wm. Wharton, vicar

* See page 33 of this Vol.

of Gilling, of which the Rev. Caleb Readshaw is incumbent, and the Rev. J. Jackson, curate.  Pop. 177.

*Eskdaleside*, in the parish of Whitby, wap. & liberty of Whitby Strand ; 5 miles WSW. of Whitby. Here was a small priory, founded in the reign of king John, which continued until the general dissolution. There are also the remains of a Chapel, which formerly belonged to Whitby Abbey, where an hermit was slain by some hunters, whilst chasing a wild boar, for which offence a penance of cutting down a quantity of stakes with a penny knife, and carrying them to Whitby, once in the year on ascension day, was enjoined upon them, and made the tenure by which they and their descendants should hold their lands.  Pop. 305.

*Esklith*, see Arkengarthdale.

ESTON, in the parish of Ormesby, wap. and liberty of Langbargh ; 6 miles NW. of Guisbro'. There is here a very ancient chapel, subject to the parish church. The village of Eston is small, and irregularly built, and stands on the skirts of a detached hill of considerable elevation, called Barnaby, or Eston Moor ; the summit of which runs out into a bold point or promontory, called Easton Nab, where a telegraphic beacon, or watch house, has been lately erected, commanding a rich and varied prospect of vast extent. On the summit of this promontory, which spreads out to the southward into an extensive plain ; there is an ancient encampment, conjectured to be of Saxon origin, also of the date of 492, and coeval with the battle of Badon hill, fought in this neighbourhood.  Pop. 272.

Thompson Rev. Jas. perpetual curate

| Farmers, | Shoemakers, |
|---|---|
| Hall M. & J. | Dale John |
| Hart George | Johnson John |
| Hugill Wm. | *Wheelwrights,* |
| Jackson Ralph | Allcroft James |
|  | Heart Thos. |

Appleton George, butcher
Chisman Thos. vict. King's Head
Dale Luke, tailor
Neasham Thos. vict. Ship
Snowden Geo. vict. Stapylton's Arms

*Everley*, in the parish of Hackness ; wap. and liberty of Whitby Strand ; 4½ miles W. of Scarbro'.

*Eure*, or *Wether Cote*, in the parish of Kirkdale, and wap. of Ryedale ; 4 miles NW. of Kirby-Moor-Side.

EXELBY, in the parish of Burneston, wap. of Halikeld, and liberty of Richmondshire ; 2 miles ESE. of Bedale.  Pop. including Leeming and Newton, 562.

affield Richard, gent.

*Farmers & Yeomen,* Metcalf Robert
arrett Wm.  Nixon Thomas
ell John  Penrith John
bates Thos.  Saddler Wm.
assett Launclt.  Spence Wm.
ettlewell Wm.

lgin Wm. butcher
Hutchinson John, blacksmith
Jirtlam James, joiner

ayer John, tailor
Falburn Francis, butcher
Walker Matthew, vict. Board
Wilkinson Leonard, vict. Pig

*Carrier*—Christopher Pickersgill, Exelby grange, to Leeds every Wed.
dep. at 2 mg. and arr. at Leeds on
Thu. mg. at 10, ret. at 6 evg. and
arr. at Exelby on Fri. night. To
Bedale on Tu. and ret. the same
day. To Richmond on Sat. at 8
mg. and ret. the same day.

*Faceby,* in the parish of Whorlton,
wap. and liberty of Langbargh ; 4 mls.
W. of Stokesley. Jas. Favell, Esq.
resides at the lodge here. Pop. 178.

*Fadmoor,* in the parish of Kirkby-
Moor-Side, and wap. of Rydale ; 2
miles NNW. of Kirkby-Moor-Side.
Pop. 162.

*Fagger Gill,* in the parish of Arkengarthdale, wap. of Gilling West,
and liberty of Richmondshire ; 6 miles
W. of Reeth.

*Falling Foss,* in the parish of
Whitby, wap. and liberty of Whitby
Strand ; 5 miles SSW. of Whitby.

*Fareholme,* in the parish of Ainderby Steeple, wap. of Gilling East,
and liberty of Richmondshire ; 5 miles
from Northallerton.

*Farlington,* a chapelry, in the parish of Sheriff Hutton, wap. of Bulmer; 6 miles ESE. of Easingwold.—
Here is a chapel, the living is a curacy
in the patronage of the Archbishop of
York, the Rev. Major Dawson is the
incumbent, and the Rev. Richard Baron, officiating curate. Pop. 170.

FARMANBY, in the parishes of
Ellerburn and Thornton, wap. and
liberty of Pickering Lythe ; 2 miles
ESE. of Pickering. Pop. 403.

Champion Robert, gent.
Mackereth Rev. Michael, vicar

*Farmers,*  Smailes Rhd.
Baker Benj.  Smailes Robt.
Benson Robert  Smailes Wm.
Gamble Geo.  *Tailors,*
Pickering Geo.  Crossby Stephen

King Thomas  Walker Thomas
Skelton Thomas
Cass and Saddler, lime burners
Hodgson John, shoemaker
Hickey Wm. draper and hatter
Nattriss John, woollen draper and
spirit merchant
Nattriss E. vict. Pack Horse
Park John, general shopkeeper
Robson James, exciseman

*Farndale,* (High & Low Quarter)
in the parishes of Lastingham and
Kirkby-Moor-Side, & wap. of Rydale ;
4 mls. N. of Kirkby-Moor-Side. There
is here a Chapel of Ease, of which the
Rev. H. Kendall is curate. Pop. 499.

*Farndale,* (East Side) in the parish of Lastingham, and wap. of Rydale ; 4 miles N. of Kirkby-Moor-Side.
Pop. 455.

*Fawdington,* in the parish of Cundall, and wap. of Birdforth ; 5 miles
NNE. of Boroughbridge. Pop. 39.

*Fearby,* in the parish of Masham,
wap. of Hang East, and liberty of
Richmondshire ; 2½ miles W. of Masham. Pop. 214.

Blackburn Robert, yeoman
Dawson Robert, yeoman
Hutchinson Rev. Henry, curate of
Kirby-Malzeard

*Farmers,*  London James
Beck James  Rider Thos.
Edon Wm.  Simurthwaite T.
Hutchinson Jph.  Spence Matthew
Imeson Thomas

Ascough George, blacksmith
Clark Wm. vict. Golden Lion
Horner John, vict. Black Swan
Jackson Thos. vict. New Inn

*Feetham,* see Melbecks.

*Feldom,* in the parish of Marske,
wap. of Gilling West, and liberty of
Richmondshire ; 6 miles NW. of
Richmond.

*Feliskirk,* or *Felixkirk,* (P.) in
the wap. of Birdforth; 3 mls. NE. of Thirsk.
The church is an ancient structure, dedicated to St. Felix ; the living is a vicarage, in
the patronage of the Archbishop of York ;
the Rev. W. S. Dennison is the incumbent,
and the Rev. Thomas Kilby the resident
curate. Pop. 113.

*Fencote,* (Great and Little) in the
parish of Kirkby-Fleatham, wap. of
Hang East, and liberty of Richmondshire ; 4½ miles NNE. of Bedale.

*Filey,* see East-Riding.

FINGALL, (P.) in the wap. of
Hang West, and liberty of Richmondshire;

5 miles E. of Leyburn. A small village, pleasantly situated on an eminence; the church is an ancient structure; the living is a rectory, in the diocese of Chester, and in the gift of the incumbent. Pop. 126.

Wyvill Rev. Edward, rector

| *Blacksmiths,* | Jaques Wm. |
| Rutter Jonathan | Jaques Joseph |
| Wilkinson Stphn. | Robinson Thos. |
| *Farmers & Yeomen,* | Stelling Chpr. |
| Darnbrough Chpr. | Thompson Chpr. |
| Dodsworth John | |

Clarkson James, wheelwright
Kilburn Stephen, vict. Board
Lumley Thomas, tailor

*Firby,* in the parish of Bedale, wap. of Hang East, and liberty of Richmondshire; 1 mile S. of Bedale. Pop. 76.

*Flawith,* in the parish of Alne, wap. of Bulmer, and liberty of St. Peter's; 5 miles E. of Boroughbridge. Pop. 94.

FLAXTON, in the parishes of Bossall and Foston, wap. of Bulmer, a part in the liberty of St. Peter's; 8 miles NE. of York. In the autumn of 1807, a lead box was turned up by the plough in a field near this place, which contained about 300 small Saxon silver coins, in high preservation, some silver rings, and several pieces of spurs. Pop. 299.

Ash Richard, gent
Bowman Thomas, gent
Dodsworth Mary, gentlewoman
Smithson Thomas, gent.
Smithson Wm. gent.

| *Blacksmiths,* | Lund Wm. |
| Cummins John | Smith Wm. |
| Leake John | Tate John |
| *Farmers & Yeomen,* | Whitwell Thos. |
| Arnett Robert | Wilson Thos. |
| Ash Robert | *Shoemakers,* |
| Ash Richard | Calvert Thos. |
| Chapman David | Cresser John |
| Dobson Thos. | *Tailors,* |
| Gill John | Alney Wm. |
| Lazenby Thos. & | Wood Francis |
| cattle dealer | |

Linfoot Thos. bricklayer
Oates Wm. butcher
Wilson Jane, vict. Blacksmith's Arms
Wright John, carpenter

*Fleetham,* see Kirkby Fleetham.

*Foulrice,* in the parishes of Bransby and Whenby, and wap. of Bulmer; 7 miles E. of Easingwold.

FORCETT, (P.) in the wap. of Gilling West, and liberty of Richmondshire; 6 miles N. of Richmond. The church is dedicated to St. Cuthbert; the living is a perpetual curacy, in the patronage of the vicar of Gilling. Here are the remains of a Roman entrenchment, extending East and West of the village to Gatarby moor.—Pop. 86.

Heslop Rev. Wm. perpetual curate
Mitchell Charles, Esq. Forcett hall
Brown John, vict. Brown Cow
Collinson Gibson, farmer
Keet Wm. farmer
Race Benjamin, miller

FOSTON, (P.) in the wap. of Bulmer; 7½ miles SW. of Malton. The church is dedicated to All Saints, the living is a rectory, in the gift of the Crown; incumbent, the Rev. Sidney Smith. Pop. 91.

Simpson Rev. Francis, Hall

| *Farmers,* | Wetherill Wm. |
| Duck Francis | Wright Leonard |
| Tuke Robert | |

*Fosgill,* in the parish of Arncliffe, wap. and liberty of Langbargh; 6 miles from Stokesley.

*Foxton,* in the parish of Sigston, wap. and liberty of Allertonshire; 5 miles ENE. of Northallerton.

FREMINGTON, in the parish of Grinton, wap. of Gilling West and liberty of Richmondshire; 1 mile E. of Reeth.—Here is a Free School, founded and endowed in 1634, by James Hutchinson, formerly of All Hallows parish, York, merchant and alderman, a native of this place. His relict, Mary Hutchinson, left an estate, situate at Gate Fulford, near York, the rents to be divided between this school and the poor croppers of Wakefield.

Atkinson George, surveyor of bridges, North-Riding, Hagg cottage
Davis John, gent.
Deacon John, miller
Littlefair James, agent to Sir G. & W. Alderson
Ward Wm. master of the free school
Wilson Thomas, lead carrier

*Frith,* in the parish of Grinton, wap. of Gilling West, and liberty of Richmondshire; 9 miles NNW. of Askrigg.

FRYUP, (Great and Little) in the parish of Danby, wap. and liberty of Langbargh; 11 mls. SE. of Guisbro'.

| *Farmers,* | Chapman John |
| Agar John | Cornforth Geo. |
| Agar Matth. | Coverdale Thos. |
| Allen Joseph | Frank John |
| Breckon Wm. | Frank Robert |
| Camplin George | Franklin Joseph |

Ling Wm.
Ling Jonathan
Milbourn Robert
Pearson Robert
Robinson Richd.
Rose John

Venes John
Venes Thomas
Webster Thomas
Yeurt John
Young Wm.

Dale William, blacksmith
Summerson John, shopkeeper
Wilson John, schoolmaster

FRYUP-LITTLE.

*Farmers,*
Camplin Peter
Camplin John
Easton Wm.
Macwood John
Middleton John
Nellist Wm.

Pearson J. sen.
Pearson J. jun.
Pearson Thomas
Raw John
Robinson Richard
Watson Geo.
Wright Robert

*Fryton*, in the parish of Hovingham, and wap. of Rydale; 6½ miles WNW. of Malton. Pop. 62.

*Fylingdales*, (P.) in the wap. and liberty of Whitby Strand; 4 miles SE. of Whitby; consists of the seven following hamlets, viz.—Hawsker Bottoms, Bay Ness, Row, Thorpe, Stoupe Brow, Park Gate, and Robin Hood's Town; the church is situated between Thorpe and Robin Hood's bay, the living is a perpetual curacy, in the patronage of the Archbishop of York; incumbent, the Rev. James Harrison. Pop. 1702.

*Gallow Green*, in the parish of Smeaton, wap. and liberty of Whitby Strand; 2 miles SW. of Whitby.

*Galtres*, in the wap. of Bulmer, anciently a large forest, extending from the walls of York to those of Isurium, now Aldbrough, near twenty miles to the north west. A toll was anciently taken at Bootham bar, for the payment of guides, who conducted men and cattle through the forest, and protected them from wild beasts and robbers.

*Gammersgill*, in the parish of Coverham, wap. of Haag West, and liberty of Richmondshire; 6 miles SW. of Middleham. A small hamlet situated in Coverdale.

*Ganthorpe*, in the parish of Terrington, wap. of Bulmer; 6 miles WSW. of Malton. Here is a school endowed by the Earl of Carlisle with about 20l. per annum. The Rev. Robert Frear is the resident clergyman, and Mr. Richard Spruce the schoolmaster. Pop. 106.

*Garrick*, a small hamlet in the parish of Skelton, and wap. of Langbargh; 7 miles NNE. of Guisborough.

*Garriston*, in the parish of East Hawkswell, wap. of Hang West, and liberty of Richmondshire; 3 miles NE. of Leyburn. Pop. 52.

*Gatenby*, in the parish of Barneston, wap. of Halikeld, and liberty of Richmondshire; 4 miles E. of Bedale. Population 88.

*Gaterley*, (High and Low) in the parish of Catterick, wap. of Gilling East; 5 miles ENE. of Richmond.

GAYLE, in the parish of Aysgarth, wap. of Hang West; ½ mile S. of Hawes. There are vestiges of an encampment, supposed to have been Roman, a few hundred yards to the east of this village. There is here no place of worship except a chapel for the Sandemanians, of which Mr. Edward Allen is minister. This village is noted for its manufactures of coarse flannels, worsted yarn, and hosiery, which give employment to a great number of the inhabitants. Pop. included with Hawes.

Alderson William, gentleman
Allen Leonard, gentleman
Allen Leonard, yeoman
Metcalfe Richard, attorney
Routh Thomas, yeoman
Routh Oswald and Christopher, manufacturers of hosiery, &c.
Whaley Rev. John, perpetual curate of Hawes
Whaley Christopher, yeoman

*Butchers,*
Iveson Jas. & John
Iveson John & Edw.
Spencer Jeffrey

Whaley W.
Whaley Thos.
Whaley James
*Shopkeepers,*

*Cattle Dealers,*
Routh J.

Constantine John
Dinsdale John

Buck Wm. clock and watch cleaner
Dinsdale Wilfred, hat manufacturer
Hick John, boot and shoe maker

GAYLES, in the parish of Kirkby-Ravensworth, wap. of Gilling West, and liberty of Richmondshire; 5 miles NW. of Richmond. Mr. Thomas Wickliffe, the last male branch of the reformer Wickliffe's family, was born at Gayles hall, which is now the property of Lord Prudhoe, and occupied as a farm-house. Pop. 218.

*\*† A foot-post to Richmond every Mon. Thu. and Sat.*

Brumskill Mrs. Isabella
Head John, gentleman

*Farmers,*
Coates Isaac
Dawson Geo.
Etherington Wm.
Kay Wm.
Softley Samuel

*Maltsters and Brewers,*
Hind John
Sampson Geo.
*Shoemakers,*
Belwood Charles
Heslop Joshua

Angles John, vict. Board
Fenwick John, excise officer
Harrison Thomas, butcher

Hind Joseph, vict. Bay Horse
Liddell John, wheelwright
Marwood Robert, blacksmith

*Geldable*, in the parish of Leak, and wap. of Birdforth; 4 miles N. of Thirsk. Pop. 128.

*Giles St.* in the parish of Catterick, wap. of Hang East, and liberty of Richmondshire; 3 miles ESE. of Richmond.

*Gillamoor*, in the parish of Kirkby-Moor-Side, wap. of Rydale; 2½ miles N. of Kirkby-Moor-Side. Here is a Chapel of Ease, of which the Rev. Henry King is curate. Pop. 195.

GILLING, (P.) in the wap. of Gilling West, and liberty of Richmondshire: 3 miles N. of Richmond. Is a place of great antiquity, and once of sufficient consequence to give name to two wapentakes, Gilling East and Gilling West. The castle was built by Alan, Earl of Richmond, soon after the conquest, Richmond being then only a fort in subordination to it, and built afterwards to defend the lord and his tenants against the attempts of the Saxons and Danes, who, being deprived of their estates, made frequent attacks upon their invaders, to recover their rights. About half a mile from Gilling is Gilling Wood hall, now a farmhouse, but formerly the residence of a branch of the Duke of Wharton's family, it was burnt down about eighty years ago, and is now the property of John Wharton, Esq. of Skelton Castle, in Cleveland, M. P. for Beverley, who is lord of the manor, and has a large estate here, with the patronage of the living. The present vicar, his brother, has lately erected a noble vicarage, and improved the village very considerably. In addition to the parish church, which is dedicated to St. Agatha, there are here a Methodist chapel and a National school, the latter of which affords instruction to 75 poor children. The free stone quarry of this place is of the finest quality, said to be one of the best in Yorkshire, and of which nearly all the bridges in the North Riding are built. Pop. including Hartforth and Stedbury. 921.

\*†\* There is a foot-post to Richmond every Monday at 10 o'clock.

Atkinson Rev. R. M. M. A. curate of Stanwick
Coulson Thomas, gentleman
Ingledew Mrs. gentlewoman
Mason Mrs. gentlewoman
Sayer Mrs. gentlewoman
Porritt George, yeoman
Topham John, yeoman
Waterworth Eliz. gentlewoman

Wharton Rev. Wm. M. A. vicar
Wilson Jane, gentlewoman, Gilling lodge

| Blacksmiths, | Gardeners, |
|---|---|
| Curry David | M'Dougall Geo. |
| Curry Joseph | Rumley Wm. |
| Johnson James | *Shoemakers,* |
| *Butchers,* | Ellis Ralph, (& |
| Canswick Stephen | parish clerk) |
| Chisman Wm. | Raine Wm. |
| Heslop Thos. | Raine John |
| Spedding S. jun. | *Shopkeepers,* |
| *Farmers,* | Christian John |
| Belwood Charles | Ellis Ralph |
| Collier Anthony | Gill Austin |
| Elgy Ralph | *Tailors,* |
| Greathead John | Merrington John |
| Hall Ralph | Spence Ralph |
| Husband Wm. | *Wheelwrights,* |
| Peacock Philip | Shaw Lawrence |
| Todd John | Stainmore Wm. |
| Walton Wm. | |

Brown John, saddler
Brown Robert, vict. and joiner, Swan Inn
Brown Robert, jun. joiner
Palmer Robert, spirit merchant
Spedding Samuel, chief constable
Spedding Francis, maltster & brewer
Spicer Samuel, vict. Angel
Waller Fanny, vict. Shoulder of Mutton
Walton John, vict. Bay Horse
Watson Thomas, schoolmaster

GILLING, (P.) in the wap. of Rydale; 5 miles S. of Helmsley, formerly the principal town in this part of the North Riding. The church is dedicated to the Holy Cross; the living is a rectory, in the patronage of the Archbishop of York, by lapse. In the church is a family vault of the Fairfax's. Here is a public school, endowed with 20l. a year, by the Hon. Ann Fairfax. Population 168.

Fairfax Charles Gregory, Esq. Castle
Young Rev. Thomas, rector

| Farmers, | Hildrith John |
|---|---|
| Abbey Francis | Hunter John |
| Coates Hezekiah | Pearson Geo. |
| Heseltine Wm. | Simpson Richard |

Cooper John, blacksmith
Fox Wm. vict. and joiner, Board
Kilton Robert, tailor

*Gilmonby*, in the parish of Bowes, wap. of Gilling West, and liberty of Richmondshire; 5 miles SW. of Barnard Castle. A small but rural village, built round a neat green, at the head of which stands Gilmonby hall, now occupied as a boarding school, by Mr. M. Horn. Pop. 175.

*Girsby*, in the parish of Sockburn, part in the county of Durham, wap.

and liberty of Allertonshire; 5 miles SW. of Yarm. It is bounded on the north by the river Tees, which the inhabitants have to cross in boats to their parish church. Population 96.

GLAISEDALE, a chapelry, in the parish of Danby, wap. and liberty of Langbargh; 9 miles WSW. of Whitby.—A new chapel was erected here in 1793, upon the site of the old one, which was consecrated in the year 1388; the living is a perpetual curacy, in the patronage of the Archbishop of York. Here is likewise a new Wesleyan Methodist chapel, erected by subscription in 1821. The population returns is 1043 for the whole of the township of Glaisedale, comprising the following villages and hamlets, viz.—Fryup, Lealholm, Lealholm Bridge, Hawisike, and Green Houses. The Dale is remarkably fertile, surrounded on every side with barren hills, which, when contrasted give that imposing appearance which never fails to produce the most delightful sensations.

Hodgson Benjamin, surgeon
Richardson Rev. B. perpetual curate

*Farmers & Yeomen,*          Miller Wm.
Addison Francis          Oxley Thos.
Blackburn Thos.          Pearson Benj.
Breckon Francis          Pearson John
Breckon Thos.          Pennock Thos.
Campion Wm.          Shaw Wm.
Camplin Geo.          Stockton Isaac
Cockeraine H.          Thompson Wm.
Cook John          Thompson Joseph
Cook Wm.          Thompson Peter
Cooper Wm.          Watson James
Dale Joseph          Watson John
Ellerby James          White Thos.
Featherstone Peter          Wilson Joseph
Frank John          Wilson Yeoman
Frank Robert          Wood Wm.
Frankland Philip          Woodark Geo.
Harding John, (&          Woodark Wm. sen.
    miller)          Woodark Wm. jun.
Harding Wm.          Woodhouse Matt.
Harrison Wm.          Youart John
Harrison Joseph          *Schoolmasters,*
Hart Thos.          Dines Geo.
Headlam Wm.          Watson Geo.
Hogarth Thos.          *Stone-masons,*
Lacey Wm.          Edland Wm.
Lester John          Watson John
Ling Eliz.          *Wheelwrights,*
Lister Wm. Allan          Ackritt John
Mead Richard          Dawson Timothy
Mead John          Fenwick Stephen

Fenwick John, butcher
Hogarth Joseph, shoemaker & shopkeeper

Macridge John, fuller and bleacher
Wood William, vict. Board
Wood George, joiner

*Goathland,* in the parish of Pickering, wap. and liberty of Pickering Lythe; 9 miles SW. of Whitby. In the Dale of Goathland, within the liberties of Pickering forest, the farmers were obliged, by the ancient tenures of their land, to attend to the breed of hawks, which annually built their nests in a cliff or scar, called Killing Nab Scar, in Newton Dale, in order to secure them for the King's use.—These hawks are of a large size, and still continue to frequent their ancient place of resort; and it is singular, that there is every year one breed, and very seldom more. There is here a neat new Chapel of Ease, built in 1821, of which the Rev. Benjamin Richardson is curate. Pop. 335.

GOLDSBROUGH, in the parish of Lythe, wap. & liberty of Langbargh; 6 miles WNW. of Whitby.

*Farmers,*          Laverick Richard
Bean John, Over-          Newton Wm.
    dale          Stanghow John
Jackson Robert

*Gowton,* in the parish of Whorlton, wap. and liberty of Langbargh; 4 miles SW. of Stokesley.

*Grange,* in the parish of Aysgarth, wap. of Hang West, and liberty of Richmondshire; 1 mile SW, of Askrigg.

*Grange,* in the parish of Oswaldkirk, and wap. of Rydale; 2½ miles S. of Helmsley.

*Graystones,* in the parish of St. John Stanwick, wap. of Gilling West, & liberty of Richmondshire; 10 miles from Richmond.

*Greenhow,* in the parish of Ingilby Greenhow, wap. and liberty of Langbargh; 5 miles SE. of Stokesley.—Population 102.

GRETA BRIDGE, in the townships and parishes of Brignall and Rokeby, wap. of Gilling West, and liberty of Richmondshire; 4 miles SE. of Barnard Castle. Is a small village, taking its name from a bridge of one arch, over the river Greta, which river soon after runs into the Tees. The place is of modern erection, consisting of two handsome inns, one on each side of the bridge. Here are the remains of a Roman camp, where a number of coins and an altar were dug up some years ago.

*Post-Master*—RALPH CHAMBERS.

| Places from whence Letter Bags are recd. | Distance. | Postage. |
|---|---|---|
| Appleton, ........ | 27 | 6d. |
| Barnard Castle, .. | 4 | 4 |
| Boroughbridge, .. | 37 | 7 |
| Brough, .......... | 19 | 5 |
| Carlisle,.......... | 59 | 8 |
| Catterick, ........ | 15 | 4 |
| London,.......... | 240 | 1s. 0d. |
| Penrith, .......... | 41 | 7 |
| Thirsk, .......... | 60 | 7 |
| Wetherby, ...... | 49 | 8 |
| York,............ | 54 | 8 |

Bags from the South at 20 minutes past two o'clock A. M. by the Glasgow Mail, which takes letters to the offices North of this place. Bags from the North by the same Mail, at there o'clock P. M. when letters are forwarded to the South.
There is a Riding-Post to Barnard Castle, at 6 o'clock A. M. which returns 40 minutes past two o'clock P. M.

Chambers Ralph, George Inn & Post Office
Martin George, Morritt's Arms, where the Magistrates meet the first Tuesday in every month.

*Grimestone*, in the parish of Gilling, and wap. of Rydale ; 6 miles S. of Helmsley. Pop. 56.

GRINTON, (P.) in the wap. of Hang West, and liberty of Richmondshire ; 1 mile SE. of Reeth. The church, dedicated to St. Andrew, is a very ancient structure, and has lately undergone many repairs; the windows, which are much corroded by time, are beautifully ornamented with stained glass. The living is a vicarage, in the patronage of the King. There were fairs formerly held here, but owing to its decreasing population they were transferred to Reeth, a market town in this parish. This parish is divided into four townships, each of which maintains its own poor, namely, Grinton, S. of the Swale; Reeth, on the N.; Melbecks, W. of Reeth; and Muker, on both banks of the Swale, which extends to the Dalehead. Population, 689.

Edmundson Rev. Thos. vicar
Whitelock Matthew, Esq. Cogden hall

| *Carpenters,* | Hird Robert |
|---|---|
| Wilkinson Wm. | Hird John |
| Wood Wm. | Holmes Richard |
| *Corn Millers,* | Hunts Thomas |
| Buxton Christr. | Hutchinson Christ. |
| Penwick Richard | Kendell Mark |
| *Farmers,* | Kendell Paul |
| Cover George | Miller James |
| Dunn Leonard | Spence Mary |
| Harker James | Spenceley Jas. sen. |

Spenceley David   Raw Thomas
Spenceley Jas. jun.Spenceley Thos.
Tomlin Cuddy    *Stone Masons,*
White Joseph    Allen Simon
   *Shopkeepers,*    Siddall George
Musgrave Francis
Atkinson Mark, parish clerk
Bowes Geo. blacksmith
Cooper James, vict. and shoemaker, Board

GRISTHORPE, in the parish of Filey, wap. and liberty of Pickering Lythe ; 7 miles SE. of Scarborough. Population, 212.

Beswick Colonel George, Lodge
Beswick William, Esq.

## GUISBOROUGH, (P.)

In the wap. and liberty of Langbargh; 9 miles from Stokesley, and 49 from York.— In the year 1129, Robert de Brus founded the priory here for canons of the order of St. Austin. Some idea may be formed of the extent of this establishment, when the priory was in the plenitude of its prosperity, from a manuscript in the Cottonian Library, in which it is said—" That the prior kept a most pompous house, insomuch that the towns, consistings of 500 householders, had no lands, but lived all in the abbey." At the dissolution, the annual revenue was to the amount of 698l. 3s. 4d. and the site was granted to Francis Chaloner, Esq. in 1688. Camden says of this place, that it is really beautiful, and adds, that it resembles Puteoli, in Italy, but exceeds it in healthiness." Guisborough is pleasantly situated in a narrow but fertile vale, and consists chiefly of one main street, running nearly East and West. The street is very broad, and many of the houses being built in a modern style, the town has a neat and pleasant appearance. A handsome town-hall, of free-stone, was built in the year 1821, upon the site of the ancient toll-booth, in the Market place, erected upon projecting pillars and arches, with four cast iron pillars in the centre, the lower part or area serves as a shambles, &c. for the market people, and the Magistrates hold their meetings on alternate Tuesdays, in the upper story. The markets are well attended, and are held on Tuesday. Early in the month of May, 1822, a mineral spring was discovered, at about a mile SE. of Guisborough, to which a great number of people daily resort, and who generally obtain relief in rheumatic, scorbutic, and bilious complaints; this water, which is a good diuretic, has been analysed by Mr. William

Faraday, of London, and the result shows that the specific gravity is 1000,7.—A pint contains three grains, nearly, of dry salts, the salts are Muriatic of Soda, Carbonate of Soda, Carbonate of Lime, Carbonate of Magnesia, Carbonic Acid; Sulphats the smallest quantity. An hotel is about to be erected for the accommodation of visitors who may come to Guisborough for the benefit of the waters, by Robert Chaloner, Esq. M. P. the lord of the manor, at a convenient distance from the spring. The church of Guisborough is a neat structure, partly rebuilt in the year 1791, dedicated to St. Nicholas; the living is a perpetual curacy, in the patronage of the Archbishop of York, and the Rev. T. P. Williamson, A. M. is the incumbent. There are here also three chapels or meeting-houses, one for the Methodists, a second for the Independents, and the other for the Quakers. Mr. George

Venables, of London, a native of this place, left by will a fund for founding a school here, which was opened in 1790, for the education of 50 poor boys and 40 poor girls, and called Providence School, in allusion to the blessings of God upon the founder's labours. Till the year 1821, the children were taught by the old system, but at that time two new school rooms were built by subscription, and 100 boys and 100 girls are now taught on the system of Dr. bell, the funds left by the benevolent Mr. Venables being applied to defray the charges of the establishment. Mr. Ralph Medd is the master, and Mrs. Isabella Peacock the mistress. The population of Guisborough amounts to 1912. It is worthy of remark, that the first alum works in this kingdom were erected here in the reign of Queen Elisabeth, and it was against the proprietor that the Pope fulminated his anathemas.

**MRS. MARY PULMAN, Post-Mistress, *Market-place.***

| Places from whence Letter bags are recvd. | Distance. | Postage | Arrival of Mails. | Departure of Mails. |
|---|---|---|---|---|
| London, ........ | 248 | 12*d.* | 8 morning | 3 P. M. |
| York, .......... | 49 | 8 | ditto. | ditto. |
| Thirsk, .......... | 28 | 6 | ditto. | ditto. |
| Stokesley,........ | 8 | 4 | ditto. | ditto. |

### DIRECTORY.

Agar Mrs. gentlewoman, Church st.
Barker John, gent. Westgate
Bulmer Thos. gent. Westgate
Chaloner Robert, Esq. M. P.
Coming Ann, gentlwmn. Westgate
Corney Samuel, gent. Westgate
Danby Eliz. gentlwmn. Market pl.
Harrison John, Esq.
Hickson Joseph, chief constable for the E. Division of Langbargh
Lincoln David, gent. Church st.
Mason George, gent. Westgate
Napper Thos. yeoman, Waterfalls
Pearson Richard, yeoman, Woodhouse
Pulman Thos. gent. Westgate
Ricaby Thos. gent. Bellmangate
Sanders Thos. gent. Westgate
Starth Richard, yeoman, Northcote
Small Thos. gent. Church street
Weatherill Thos. gent. Westgate
Williamson Rev. T. P. perpetual curate

*Academies—Boarding & Day Schools.*
Best Ann, (ladies' day) Westgate
Chipchase Wm. (day) Church st.
Endowed Grammar, Rev. James Willock, master
National, R. Medd & Isaac Peacock

Sunley Geo. (coml. day) Market pl.
West Mary, (ladies' day) Westgate
York Joseph, (commercial day)

*Agents—Particular and General.*
Child Rd. (Phoenix Fire) Westgate
Clark Henry, (Atlas Fire) Westgate
Dale M. H. (newspapers) Market pl.
Marshall Thos. (Newcastle and Durham newspapers) Market place

*Attornies.*
Clark Henry, Town's hall
Hodgson Barwick, Market place
Irvene John, Westgate
Stephenson Thos. Westgate

*Auctioneers and Appraisers.*
Dale M. H. Market place
Watson & Marshall, Market place
*Bank.*
Skinner and Co. Westgate, draw on Barclay, Tritton and Co.

*Billiard Rooms.*
Dale M. H. Market place
Watson John, Market place
*Blacksmiths.*
Culley Robert, Church street
Hewitt John, Westgate
Pulman Ralph, near Market place
Pulman Alex. (& farrier) Westgate
Rawling Thomas; Bow street

Rutter Wm. Patten lane

*Booksellers, &c.*
Dale M. H. Market place
Hodgson Ralph, Westgate
Marshall Thos. (& printer) Mkt. pl.
Pearson Wm. Westgate

*Boot and Shoe Makers.*
Carter Matthew, Bow street
Garbutt Thos. Westgate
Johnson Wm. North-out-gate
Mills George, Bow street
Pattison Wm. Bellmangate
Porritt Thomas, Westgate
Robinson Thomas, Church street
Rymer Richard, Westgate
Wharton Robert, Church street

*Bread Bakers.*
Pollard Christopher, Westgate
Shepherd Roger, Westgate
Williamson Wm. Westgate
Williamson John, Patten lane

*Bricklayers, &c.*
Moore Wm. (plasterer) Church st.
Knaggs John, Westgate
Williamson Robert, Church street
Winter Thomas, Church street

*Butchers.*
Corney Samuel, Westgate
Darton Wm. Westgate
Mascall Wm. Westgate
Sanders Wm. Westgate
Walker Robert, sen. Church st.
Wright Wm. Market place

*Clock and Watch Makers.*
Belt Thos. (watch) Market place
Unthank George, Westgate
Wilson Thomas, Market place

*Coopers.*
Walker Wm. Bellmangate
Wright Thomas, Market place

*Corn Millers.*
Askew John, Holbeck
Pollard Christopher, Westgate

*Curriers and Leather Cutters.*
Ord Richard, Westgate
Small John, (cutter) Church street
Thompson John, Patten street
Walker Robert, jun. Church street

*Druggists.*
Robinson Thomas, Westgate
Smith John, Market place

*Farmers.*
Askew Robert, Parkhouse
Atkinson Thomas, Cass bank
Barker Thomas, Holbeck
Boys Wm. Barnaby
Corney Harland
Dale George, Westgate
Dale John
Garbutt Wm. Seagdale
Gofton Wm. Waterfalls

Harding Thomas, Bellmangate
Johnson Robert, Westgate
Mallam Wm. Church street
Moon James, Apple orchard
Pearson John, Westgate
Pollard Wm. Bellmangate
Potter Thomas, Bellmangate
Potter Wm. Bellmangate
Rowland Thomas, Cross Keys
Wardle Wm. Barnaby grange

*Flax Dressers.*
Corney John, Market place
Hindson Joseph, North-out-gate
Smith Wm. Westgate

*Gardeners.*
Cooper Wm. Bellmangate
English John, Bellmangate

*Grocers and Tea Dealers.*
Baker Hannah, Church street
Campion John, Westgate
Child Richard, Westgate
Corney John, Market place
Davison Ralph, Church street
Dixon Thomas, Westgate
Edwards Elizabeth, Church street
Hodgson Ralph, Westgate
Hutchinson John, Market place
King Matthew, Westgate
Lacey E. and T. Market place
Robinson Thos. Westgate
Small John, (tea dealer) Church st.
Smith John, Market place
Unthank John, Westgate

*Hair Dressers.*
Pulnam Robert, Westgate
Sanders Thos. North-out-gate

*Hat Manufacturers and Furriers.*
Laing James, Westgate
Wainwright Thos. Market place

*Inns and Taverns.*
Anchor, Wm. Page, Bellmangate
Black Swan, John Husband, Westgate
Buck, John Watson, Market place
Cock, T. Marsh, commercial inn and posting-house
Fox, John Holdforth, Bow street
George and Dragon, John Scaife, Market place
Golden Lion, William Pulman, Market place
Highland Laddie, R. Greathead, Church street
King's Head, Ed. Williamson, Westgate
Lord Nelson, Alice Jowsey, Church street
Mermaid, John Peart, Westgate
Red Lion, Thomas Nattby, Church street
Seven Stars, Thos. Medd, Bow st.
Ship, James Walker, Westgate
Sloop, Mary Hewitt, North-out-gate

Jun, M. H. Dale, Market place
Three Fiddles, S. Boys, Westgate

*Ironmongers and Hardwaremen.*
Dale John, Market place
Dennis Francis, (and jeweller) North-out-gate
Moore Edw. (& jeweller) Bellmangt.
Skelton Wm. Westgate
Wiley James, Market place
Wilson Thomas, Market place

*Joiners and Cabinet Makers.*
Davison Thomas, Church street
Harpley William, jun.
Johnson Thomas, Church street
Small Thomas, jun. (and upholsterer) Church street
Taylor Benj. Westgate

*Libraries.*
Bulmer Thos. (subscription) Westgt.
Dale M. H. (circulating) Market pl.
Hodgson Rd. (circulating) Westgate
Marshall Thomas, (circulating) Market place

*Linen Manufacturers.*
Hindson John, North-out-gate
Smith Wm. Westgate

*Linen and Woollen Drapers.*
Baker Hannah, Church street
Campion John, Westgate
Child Richard, Westgate
Dillifield Philip, Bow street
Dixon Thomas, Westgate
Hutchinson John, Market place
King Matthew, Westgate
Lacy R. T. Market place
Smith John, Market place

*Maltsters and Brewers.*
Morritt Wm. North-out-gate
Peart John, (brewer) Westgate

*Milliners and Dress Makers.*
Campion Isabella, Westgate
Child Eliza, Westgate
Eston Ann, Westgate
Pulman Elizabeth, Westgate
Unthank Hannah, Westgate

*Painters, &c.*
Bulmer John, Bow street
Hicks Rt. (colourman) Westgate
Sanders Francis, Westgate
Wright Robert, Market place

*Plumbers and Glaziers.*
Bulmer Thomas, Bow street
Campion Zechariah, Westgate
Wright Robert, Westgate

*Porter Merchants and Dealers.*
Dale M. H. Market place
Dixon Thomas, Market place
Shepherd Roger, Westgate

*Rope Makers.*
Corney John, Market place

Hindson Joseph, North-out-gate
Lincoln John, Church street
Smith Wm. Westgate
Walker James, Westgate

*Saddlers and Collar Makers.*
Cole John, (& tawer) Bow street
Dale John, Market place
Husband John, Westgate
Morley George, Market place

*Saddle Horses and Gigs to Let.*
Butement Mrs. Market place
Dillifield and Johnson
Medd Thomas, Bow street
Nedby Thomas, Church street

*Seedsmen.*
Askew Wm. Westgate
Corney Wm. Market place
Small John, Church street

*Shopkeepers.*
Easton Thomas, Westgate
Watson Elizabeth, Market place
Wray Joseph, Bow street

*Skinners.*
Askew Wm. Westgate
Bird James, Westgate

*Spirit and Wine Merchants and Dealers*
Baker Hannah, (British wines) Westgate
Corney Wm. Market place
Dale M. H. Market place
Dixon Thos. (British wines) Westgate

*Stone Masons.*
Pretty William, Patten lane
Pretty Richard, Church street
Stockton John, Westgate
Williamson Edward, Westgate

*Straw Bonnet Makers.*
Cornforth Sarah, Bow street
Moore Hannah, Church street
Walker Elizabeth, Westgate
West Elizabeth, Westgate
York Hannah, Westgate

*Surgeons, &c.*
Makereath Michael, Westgate
Wilson Wm. & Son, Bow-street

*Tailors, &c.*
Burn Wm. North-out-gate
Dillifield P. (& draper) Bow street
Havelock Thomas, Bow street
Hodgson Thos. and Son, Westgate
Williamson Richard, Bellmangate

*Tallow Chandlers.*
Askew William, Westgate
Bird James, Westgate
Corney Wm. Market place

*Tinners and Braziers.*
Bulmer Thomas, Bow street
Skelton William, Westgate

Wiley James, Market place

*Wheelwrights.*

Davison Thomas, Church street
Harpley Wm. jun. Market place
Nedby James, Church street
Orton Michl. (& plough mkr.) Westgt.

*Miscellany.*

Aisleby Anthony, cattle dealer
Askew George, attorney's clerk
Lacey E. and T. sub-distributors of stamps, Market-place
Page Wm. wood turner and line wheel maker, Bellmangate
Pulman Robert, Bailiff for the manor, Westgate
Robson Benjamin, whitesmith, Church street
Scaife John, slater, Market place
Shepherd Roger, distiller of herbs, Westgate
Symmonds Chas. confectioner, Church street
Watson John, bailiff for the liberty of Langbargh
Wright William, agent for Genuine Tea Company

---

COACHES.

*From the Cock Inn, T. Marsh's, Market-place.*

The CLEVELAND, from Redcar to Bedale, during the season, on Mon. Wed. & Sat. arr. at 8 mg. ret. 7 evg.
The UNION, from Whitby to Sunderland, on Tu. and Sat. arr. at 11 mg. and ret. at ½ past 1 aft.

LAND CARRIAGE.

Baker William, from Castleton on Tu. arr. at 10, ret. 3.
Barker James, from Castleton on Tu. and Fri. arr. 10, ret. 3
Johnson John, to Stockton on Mon. Wed. Fri. and Sat. ret. same evg.
Johnson Robert, to Stockton on Mon. Wed. and Sat. ret. same evg.
Johnson Thomas, to Whitby on Mon. and Thur. ret. on Tu. and Fri. ; and to Stockton and Stokesley on Sat. ret. same evg.
Kitchen Peter, to Redcar, Marsk, and Kirkleatham, on Monday, Thursday, and Saturday.

*Gunnersides,* see Melbecks.

HABTON, (Great and Little,) in the parish of Kirby-Misperton, wap. and liberty of Pickering Lythe ; 4 ml⁻. NW. of Malton. Pop. 186.

Pickering Thomas, Esq. lord of the manor
Snowden William, gentleman

HACKFORTH, in the parish of Hornby, wap. of Hang East, and liberties of St. Peter's and Richmondshire; 4 miles NNW. of Bedale. Pop. 184.

| *Farmers,* | Outhwaite Richd. |
| Davison Robert | Smith Joseph |
| Mitchell Gabriel, | *Joiners,* |
| agent to Lord | Grasham Thos. |
| Dundas | Metcalf Abraham |
| Mitchell John | |

Brown Jonathan, linen weaver
Cartwright John, shoemaker
Hall Ralph, vict. Cow
Plews Matthew, blacksmith
Thornton John, corn miller
Walker Anthony, schoolmaster
White John, tailor

HACKNESS, (P.) in the wap. and liberty of Whitby Strand; 8½ miles NW. of Scarborough, is a small village in a most romantic situation, in a delightful vale, from which several others run in various directions of the country. The principal road thither from Scarborough, lies over Haybrow, a lofty eminence, from the summit of which is a noble view of the castle, the coast, and the ocean. The subjacent country, and the village of Scalby, also form a picturesque landscape. In the descent from this hill to the vale of Hackness, the road lies along the precipitous edge of a glen, of which the sides are adorned with lofty trees. This deep and picturesque ravine, which lies to the left of the road, meeting at length with another from the right, which is equally romantic, their junction forms the commencement of the valley of Hackness. In proceeding a little way farther are two other glens, of which the declivities to the bottom are covered with a profusion of wood. At the western extremity, the valley divides itself into two branches; one of these, in which the present village of Hackness is seated, runs into the moors: through the other the Derwent pursues its course towards the village of Ayton. The hills which surround the vale of Hackness are from one hundred to one hundred and twenty yards in perpendicular height, and their steep declivities are profusely adorned with lofty trees, of the richest foliage. The hand of nature, indeed, has here been lavish of her embellishments, and has moulded these sylvan scenes into such different forms and projections, as render them at once sublime and beautiful. Springs of water bursting from the sides of the hills in natural cascades, or falling with gentle murmurs, contribute to enliven the scenery; and the Derwent, which has its source in the mountainous country in the north, glides with a gentle stream past the village, to the westward of which the bleak and barren moors form a striking contrast to the luxuriant scenes of Hackness. There is a small ham here called the Johnstone Arms, kept by Mrs. Hannah Waites. The church, dedicated to St. Mary, is a very ancient structure; the living is a perpetual curacy, in the patronage of the Marquis of Annandale, and the Rev. Thomas Irvin is the incumbent. Here was formerly a cell, belonging to Whitby Abbey, which, at the dissolution, contained four monks of the order of Benedictines. The very elegant mansion at this place, was built by the late Sir Richard Vanden Bempde Johnstone, Bart. Pop. 143.

Johnstone Sir John Vanden Bempde Johnstone George, Esq.

*Hagg*, in the parish of Kirkdale, and wap. of Rydale; 2½ miles WNW. of Kirkby-Moor-Side.

*Hagg*, in the parish of Whitby, wap. and liberty of Whitby Strand; 3 miles S. of Whitby.

*Hagworth Hall*, in the parish of Romaldkirk, wap. of Gilling West, & liberty of Richmondshire; 8 miles W. of Bernard Castle.

*Halikeld*, in the parish of Sigston, wap. and liberty of Allertonshire; 2½ miles NE. of Northallerton.

*HALL GATE*, in the parish of Kirkby-Ravensworth, wap. of Gilling West, and liberty of Richmondshire; 5 miles NE. of Reeth. The residence of Leonard Spenceley, yeoman

*HALNABY*, in the parish of Croft, wap. of Gilling East, and liberty of Richmondshire; 7 miles NE. of Richmond. The residence of John Peniston Milbanke, Esq. of Halnaby hall.

*Handall*, in the parish of Lofthouse, wap. and liberty of Langbargh; 8 miles ENE. of Guisborough. William, son of Richard de Percy, in the year 1133, founded at this place a small priory for Benedictine nuns. There is here a shooting box of Edmund Turton, Esq.

*HARDRAW*, in the parish of Aysgarth, wap. of Hang West, and liberty of Richmondshire; 1½ mile NW. of Hawes. Here is a small Chapel of Ease, built about fifty years ago, of which the Rev. Edmund Fawcett is incumbent; the living is a perpetual curacy, in the gift of J. A. Stuart Wortley, Esq. M. P. who is lord of the manor, and who has recently endowed a small school here with 10*l.* 10*s.* per annum. There is here a magnificent water-fall, commonly called Hardraw Scarr; the chasm ex-

tends above three hundreds yards in length, with huge rocks impending on every side. At the northern extremity is a cascade which pours forth in one perpendicular fall a vast quantity of water into a deep bason below. In the year 1740, when fairs were held on the Thames, this cascade was frozen, and constituted a prodigious icicle of a conic form, thirty-two yards and three quarters high, and the same dimensions in circumference.

Johnson Wm. vict. Green Dragon

| Farmers, | Parker John |
|---|---|
| Hunter John | Parker Francis |

*HARLESEY EAST*, (P.) in the wap. of Birdforth; 7 miles NE. of Northallerton. The church is a perpetual curacy, in the patronage of W. Bennett, Esq. Pop. 420.

Maynard Chas. John, Esq. Harlesey hall
Steel Rev. Jonathan Walton, curate & bdg. school for young gentlemen

| Butchers, | Newsom Simon |
|---|---|
| Raper Stockell | Oxendale Christr. |
| Wright Thos. | & cattle dealer |
| Farmers, | Russell George |
| Ayre Thos. | Smith Benj. |
| Bamlet Robert | Turnbull Robert |
| Clark Ann | Weighell Wm. |
| Clough Thos. sen. | Wilkinson John |
| Clough Thos. jun. | Shoemakers, |
| Eden Thos. | Boston John |
| Hugill Thos. | Robinson Geo. |
| Metcalfe James | Tailors, |
| Mitchell Christphr. | How William |
| Myles Thos. | Ragg William |

Bainbridge John, common brewer
Cowell Wm. smith, farrier and vict. Cat and Bagpipes
Nevison Wm. vict. Black Swan

*Harlesey West*, in the parish of Osmotherby, wap. and liberty of Allertonshire; 5 miles NE. of Northallerton. Population, 51.

*HARMBY*, in the parish of Spennithorne, wap. of Hang West, & liberty of Richmondshire; 1 mile E. of Leyburn. Population, 194.

| Farmers, | Shoemakers, |
|---|---|
| Bulmer Christphr. | Cloughton Henry |
| Butterfield John | Dodsworth John |
| Whitelock Peter | Stone masons, |
| Winsby Ann and | Brotherton Francis |
| Mary | Constantine John |

Bennett Geo. vict. Royal Oak
Craggs George, wheelwright
Dennison Wm. lime burner
Harker John, blacksmith
Hudson Wm. vict. Bolton Inn

Raper James, cabinet maker
Sedgwick James, weaver

HARTFORTH, in the parish of Gilling, wap. of Gilling West, and liberty of
Richmondshire; 4 miles N. of Richmond.
Here is a free grammar school, founded and
endowed by Sir Thomas Wharton, K.B. in
the year 1678, for thirty poor scholars selected
from the following places, Hartforth, 14;
Gilling, 8; Skeeby, 2; Aske, 2; Melsonby,
2; Layton and Carken, 2; to be elected by
the overseers of the poor, and chief inhabitants, and approved by the trustees. The
endowment is the school-house and buildings
with a freehold farm, situate at West Rounton, containing one hundred and eighteen
acres, the Rev. John Atkinson is the master,
and the perpetual curate of Barton and South
Cawton. Pop. included with Gilling.

Craddock Sheldon, Esq. M. P. Col. of
   North York militia, Hartforth hall

*Farmers*,        Hunt George
Greathead Richd.  Jackson Charles
Fairbairn Adam, miller

*Hartoft*, in the parish of Middle-
ton, wap. and liberty of Pickering
Lythe; 7 miles NNW. of Pickering.
Population, 134.

*Harton*, in the parish of Bossall,
and wap. of Bulmer; 9 miles NE. of
York. Population, 190.

*Harum*, in the parish of Helmsley,
and wap. of Rydale; 2½ miles ESE. of
Helmsley. Here is a Chapel of Ease,
of which the Rev. George Dixon is
curate; also a Methodist chapel.—
Population, 461.

*Harwood Dale*, in the parish of
Hackness, wap. and liberty of Whitby
Strand; 8 miles NW. of Scarborough.
Population, 235.

*Harriottier* or *Harriot Air*, in the
parish of Helmsley, & wap. of Rydale;
2½ miles WNW. of Helmsley.

## HAWES,

In the parish of Aysgarth, wap. of Hang
West, and liberty of Richmondshire; 5½
miles from Askrigg, 17 from Sedbergh, and
17 from Leyburn, with a market on Tuesday. A considerable quantity of stockings
are knitted in this neighbourhood, which
give employment to a great number of the
inhabitants. The Chapel of Ease is a low
plain structure; the living is a perpetual
curacy, in the gift of the land owners, and
the incumbent is the Rev. John Whaley. The
dissenting places of worship are a Sandems-
nian chapel, and a Friends' Meeting house:
here is a public school, with a small endowment of 10l. per annum. The markets and
fairs of Hawes are in a thriving state. There
are two extensive manufactories of knit hose.
The town is pleasantly situated near the east
bank of the Ure, and commands an extensive
view of the mountainous country by which
it is surrounded. From these mountains are
extracted large supplies of coal, lead and
lime. Much to the honour of the town,
there is here an extensive subscription
library, stocked with well selected books of
the best authors. A great number of the
inhabitants are freeholders of the County of
York. Pop. 1408.

POST MASTER—CHRISTOPHER
   CLARKE, *Office, White Hart Inn.*

*** Letters arrive from Bedale, &c. every
   Mon. Wed. Thu. &c. at 11 mg. and are
   dispatched same days at ½ past 11 mg.
   to all parts.

### DIRECTORY.

Allen Oswald, yeoman, Scarr head
Burton Miss, gentlewoman
Capstack Isabella, gentlewoman
Coulton Capt. Jeremiah, land agent
Dinsdale Miss Ann
Harrison Ann, sen. gentlewoman
Harrison Ann, jun. gentlewoman
Metcalfe Rev. J. W. *Askes*
Metcalfe Christopher, chapel warden
Routh Christopher, gentleman
Tennant Elizabeth, gentlewoman
Whaley Alexander, chapel warden
Whaley Mrs. gentlewoman

| *Attornies*, | Scarr Clement |
| Metcalf Richard; | *Grocers, &c.* |
| house, Gayle | Frankland John, |
| Whaley Alex. | & parish clerk |
| *Blacksmiths*, | Kidd Rodger, and |
| Brenkley James | druggist, stamp |
| Dinsdale Alex. | office |
| Hodgson John | Scarr John, and |
| *Boot and Shoemkrs.* | draper |
| Constantine John | Storey John, and |
| Harrison Matthew | tallow chandler |
| Routh Thos. | Willan J. & M. |
| Stockdale Thos. | *Joiners and Cabinet* |
| *Butchers*, | *Makers*, |
| Iveson Christ. | Mason Wm. |
| Iveson Wm. | Metcalf Warren |
| *Cloggers*, | Taylor John |
| Blythe Richard | *Knit Hose, Caps,* |
| Granger Richard | *Shirts, &c. Mfrs.* |
| *Farmers*, | Blythe John |
| Allen John H. | Routh O. and C. |
| Metcalf Thos. | Gayles mill |
| Moor Christopher | Thompson Wm. |
| Morland Leonard | *Schoolmasters, &c.* |
| Pratt John | Hogg Sarah |
| Pratt Edward | Lambert Oswald |
| Routh Oswald | Whaley Francis |

Wilson Elizabeth    Chapman Thos.
  *Shopkeepers,*    Harker James
Harker Francis, &    Scarr John
  wool comber    *Tea Dealers,*
Metcalfe Nathan    Metcalfe John
Morland Matthew    Metcalfe Ann
Moss John    White Ann
  *Stone masons,*    *Tinsmiths, &c.*
Moor John    Bowe George, &
Scarr George    plumber & glazier
  *Surgeons,*    Fawcett James
Balderston Wm.;    *Wine and Spirit*
  house, *Sedbusk,*    *Merchants,*
Rudd Launcelot    Metcalfe John
  *Tailors,*    Willan J. & M.
Blades Richard

  *Innkeepers,*
Black Bull, Wm. Lister
Fountain, Wm. Dixon
King's Arms, William Ridding, (and
  hat manufacturer)
King's Head, Wm. Mallison
Masons' Arms, John Moor
White Hart, Christopher Clarke, (ex-
  cise office and posting house)

Bell Thomas, corn miller
Buck Thomas, weaver
Bywell George, cooper
Dowes James, cattle dealer
Frankland Richard, hair dresser
Lister B. milliner and dress maker
Metcalfe Ann, draper & ironmonger
Metcalfe Ann, subscription library
Wade John, saddler

## CARRIERS.

Wm. Banks to Lancaster, every Thu.
  at 6 mg. ret. 9 night.—To Richmond, every Mon. at 6 morning,
  returns Tu. 8 morning.
John Benson, (to the White Hart,)
  from Sedbergh & Kendall, every
  Tu. and Fri. at 10 morning, ret.
  2 afternoon, same days.
Thos. Blackburn (to the White Hart,)
  from York, every Tu. at 10 mg.
  ret. 2 afternoon, same days.
Edward Hunter (to the White Hart,)
  from Askrigg & Richmond, every
  Tu. & Fri. at 10 morning.
Wm. Marsden (to the King's Head,)
  from Settle, every Tu. at 9 mg.
  ret. 2 afternoon, same days.
John Moss to Kirby Stephen, every
  Mon. dep. at 4 mg. ret. 7 evg.
William Smithson from Manchester,
  every Tu. at ½ past 9 mg. ret. 2
  afternoon, same days.

HAWKSWELL EAST, (P.) in the
wap. of Hang West, and liberty of
Richmondshire; 5 miles NE. of Leyburn. The church is an ancient structure, and the living is a rectory, in the
gift of Mr. and Mrs. Gayle, incumbent
the Rev. Henry Gayle; officiating curate the Rev. Joseph Abbot. Mrs.
Orton is the principal inhabitant. Pop.
with West Hawkswell, 176.

HAWKSWELL WEST, in the parish of East Hawkswell, wap. of Hang
West, and liberty of Richmondshire;
1½ miles NE. of Leyburn.

Coore Col. Fletcher Lechmere, hall
Abbot Rev. J. curate & schoolmaster
Fawell Leonard, farmer
Mangle George, farmer

HAWNBY, (P.) in the wap. of
Birdforth; 6 miles NW. of Helmsley.
The church is dedicated to All Saints,
the living is a rectory, in the patronage
of the Cavendish family; and the Rev.
Godfrey Wolley, is the incumbent.
Population, 286.

Dowker Rev. Wm. curate
Dowson John, corn miller

*Hawsker,* (High and Low) in the
parish of Whitby, wap. and liberty of
Whitby Strand; 3 mls SSE. of Whitby.
Here is a House of Industry for the
poor. Population, including Stain-
siker, 634.

HAXBY, (P.) in the wap. of Bulmer, and liberty of St. Peter's; 4
miles N. of York. Here is a church,
the living is a curacy, incumbent the
Rev. John Ellis, vicar of Strensall.
There is also a Methodist chapel.—
Population, 417.

Arnitt Robert, gentleman
Bilton Wm. gentleman
Darley John, gentleman
Edmondson John, gentleman
Heslop Rev. John, classical & mathe-
  matical academy, Haxby hall
Hudson Joshua, gentleman
Plowman John, clerk to the Magis-
  trates, High Constable of the
  wap. of Bulmer, and Coroner for
  the liberty of St. Peter's.

| *Blacksmiths,* | Braithwaite Marm. |
| Reynolds John | Burrill Wm. |
| Silversides John | Daniel Thos. |
| *Bricklayers,* | Ellis Wm. |
| Arnitt John | Foster Hannah |
| Linfoot Wm. | Hugill John |
| *Carpenters,* | Leadley Robert |
| Bell Thos. | Linfoot Thos. |
| Pearson John | Mazeen Thos. |
| Wright Thos. | Pearson Wm. |
| *Farmers & Yeomen,* | Riby David |
| Arminson Thos. | Richmond Wm. |
| Batty Eden | Shepherd Martha |
| Benn Andrew | Skelton Thos. |

Snowden Wm.
Wilkinson Geo.
*Gardeners,*
Beal Richard
Hopps John
*Linen Weavers,*
Entwistle Wm.
Herring John

*Shoemakers,*
Clark Geo.
Hardisty Benj.
*Shopkeepers,*
Hardisty Thos.
Healop Wm.
*Tailors,*
Lorriman John
Stablers Matthew

Batters Richard, vict. Red Lion
Millington Matthias, schoolmaster
Teal John, bacon and butter factor
Thompson Thos. bacon factor
Whitwell James, butcher

HEALAUGH, in the parish of Grinton, wap. of Gilling West, and liberty of Richmondshire; 1½ mile SW. of Reeth.— This village is situated in Swaledale, between two hills, Harkes to the South, and Calver to the North. The land in the valley is particularly fertile, and divided into small lots for the accommodation of miners.

Barker Samuel, gentleman

*Farmers,*
Arundale Geo.
& flour dlr.
Harper Simon
Lonsdale James

Peacock Ralph
Pedley John
*Mining Agents,*
Gill Francis
Waugh Geo.

Gallaway Francis, blacksmith
Swalwell Geo. vict. Black Bull
Wetherald John, butcher & grasier

HEALEY-WITH-SUTTON, in the parish of Masham, waps. of Hang East and West, and liberty of Richmondshire; 3 miles W. of Masham. A school was erected here in 1820, by William Danby, Esq. of Swinton Park, and endowed with 11 acres, 2 roods, and 18 perches of land, a donation of 450l. having been given by Mr. Wm. Heslington, of Masham. Pop. 413.

*Farmers,*
Barker Ephraim
Barker John
Briden Thos.
Carter John
Carter Peter
Glew John, and
  butcher
Hutchinson Mat.

Hutchinson Thos.
Lightfoot Wm.
Rider Thos.
Rider Wm.
Smorthit Dorothy
Smorthit John
Suttill James
Wilson John
Wintersgill Thos.

Barnes Robert, shopkeeper
Close George, schoolmaster
Johnson Geo. carpenter
Pratt Peter, blacksmith & vict. Blacksmith's Arms
Robinson Peter, shoemaker
Rudd Edw. tailor & vict. Black Horse
Suttill Geo. stone mason
Walker Thos. tailor
Wintersgill Matthew, corn miller

Holbeck Lunds in High Abbotside, in the parish of Aysgarth, wap. of Hang West, and liberty of Richmondshire; 6 miles NW. of Hawes. Population, 92.

## HELMSLEY UPON THE BLACK MOOR, (P.)

In the wap. of Rydale, 6 miles from Kirby-Moor-Side, 16 from Malton, and 23 from York; formerly a place noted for stately Elms, in the midst of which the Druids on the hill, still bearing their name, performed their mystic rites. The town is situated on the declivity of a small eminence, gently sloping towards the banks of the Rye, from whence the wapentake derives its name. The houses are mostly built of stone, and the inhabitants, according to the population returns of 1821, amount to 1526. The market day is on Saturday. The parish of Helmsley may rank amongst the most extensive parishes in the kingdom. It is more than 16 miles from N. to S. and comprises 6 distinct villages with the valley of Bilsdale, which stretches out to the hills in Cleveland. The adjacent country is exceedingly fertile, and is interspersed with extensive woods and rich valleys. A rivulet running through the town of Helmsley, still retains the old Saxon name of Boro' Beck, and Camden remarks of it, that in his time the water disappeared, at about a mile from the town, and rose again at Harum, a few miles below, which phenomenon still takes place. Formerly the manufacture of lines from yarn, spun on the hand wheel from the distaff, was carried on here to a considerable extent, but the introduction of machinery has destroyed this domestic system, and introduced in its stead a process of manufactures more conducive to national wealth, but less conducive to public morals. This change has deprived Helmsley of its manufacture, and rendered the inhabitants almost exclusively dependent upon agriculture. There is here a court for the recovery of debts under 40s. and a charity school on the national plan, supported by C. Duncombe, Esq. of Duncombe Park, where 80 children receive gratuitous instruction. The parish church is an antique office, dedicated to All Saints; and the living is a vicarage, of which C. Duncombe, Esq. is the patron, and the Rev. G. Dixon the incumbent. The other places of worship, are a Friends' Meeting house, and a Methodist chapel. Helmsley was the favourite scene of the sports and revelries of George Villiers, Duke of Buckingham, after he had retired m the court and cabinet of Charles II. and neighbouring town of Kirkby-Moor-Side s the scene of his humiliation, after pro- jacy had wasted his fortune, and dissipa- n ruined his health. Here, in the worst t's worst room, he breathed his last.

Alas! how changed from him,
sat life of pleasure and that soul of whim.

what part of the burial ground this fallen mpanion of princes was interred, is not town, but in the parish register of Kirkby is recorded, that on the 17th of April, 1687, George Villars lord dooke of bookingham," is buried here. Helmsley castle, built by a noble family of Ross, is near to the town, it is distinguished for having been the an- ust baronial residence of its lords, and for wing stood a siege in 1644, in favour of the ing against the Parliamentary forces, un- t Lord Fairfax, and surrendered on the 4th of November. Soon after, in common ith the other castles of Yorkshire, this cas- t was dismantled by order of Parliament. t the western side the remains of a range f apartments, constituting the mansion- suse and offices, still exist, and sufficient of he ruins of the Keep remain to indicate s former strength. The surrounding sce- try is beautiful and picturesque in the ex- tme, and the scattered masses of building, sen through the rich foliage of the stately tes, and the still more stately double gate- ay, have long formed a favourite subject t the painter's pencil.

Duncombe Park, the seat of Charles Juncombe, Esq. is situated in this parish, ad within one mile of the town. The tansion house, which was designed by Van- ragh, but executed by Wakefield, and com- leted in 1718, is in the Doric order of rehitecture, and the front in particular is seemed a happy specimen of architectural skill and combination. The hall is a mag- ficent room, sixty feet long and forty wide, surrounded by fourteen lofty Corinthian llars and ornamented with a number of sts of the Greek and Latin poets, with age medallions of the twelve Cæsars. The on is eighty-eight feet by twenty-four, is formed into three divisions by Ionic rs, and elegantly adorned with antique es, and family pictures. Communi- g with the saloon to the north is a sdsome dining room, and to the south an ast suite of apartments, all appropriately nished; but the most interesting part of furniture is derived from the pencils of minent painters, and consists in the valuable tures which ornament the interior of this erb dwelling. The grounds are laid out h an elegance of taste equal to that which

has been displayed in the selection of the paintings. The garden adjoining to the house has a terrace which affords many delightful prospects. From hence is seen an Ionic Temple, which itself commands a variety of landscapes; a beautiful valley winds at the base of a noble amphitheatre of hanging wood, and the opposite plantations, which spread over a fine extent of hill, fringe the shore of the Rye, which runs through the valley, and forms almost in its centre a charming cascade. Nothing can be more truly beautiful than the assemblage of objects seen in a bird's eye view from this spot. This view is beheld with delightful variation in walking along the terrace to the Tuscan Temple, as fresh scenery breaks upon the eye almost at every step. The temple, situ- ated at the point of a bold promontory, orna- mented with stately plantations, and pro- jected into a winding valley, commands the most sublime and beautiful scenes. The valley, the river, and the cascade, are seen beneath; and in the front the prospect ex- tends and becomes beautifully variegated. The castle, Helmsley church, and the tower, appear in the midst; and the valley here forming into a rich sequestered lawn, is well contrasted with the rougher visage of the' hilly moors which are seen in the distance. Such is the picturesque description which Young and Hinderwell give of the paradi- saical scenes of Duncombe park. The beautiful monastic ruin of Rivalx Abbey, only two miles distant, adds to the interest of the vicinity; and four miles to the SW. at the entrance to the vale of York, stands the companion ruin of Byland Abbey.

POST-MASTER, *Tho. Pape, Castlegate.*

Letters from York arrive at 5 morning, and are sent off to York at 2 aft.
Letters from Kirkby arrive at 1 noon, and and are sent off to Kirkby at 7 mng.

### DIRECTORY.

Dixon Rev. G. vicarage, Bondgate
Duncombe Charles, Esq. Duncombe Park
Sandwith Major Wm. Market place

*Academies, (Bdg. and Day.)*
Simpson Rev. Geo. Market place
Ward John, (National) Church st.

*Bank.*
Hutchinson S. agent to the North- Riding bank, Market place

*Blacksmiths.*
Clark John, sen. Market place
Clark John, jun. Market place
Cooper John, Castlegate
Mason John, (and hardware dealer) Bondgate

Q Q

*Boot and Shoemakers.*
Jones Hugh, Church street
Moorhouse Jonah, Pottergate
Sunlay Wm. Market place
Thompson Thomas, Bondgate
Tutin Wm. & Son, Market place

*Butchers.*
Newby Wm. Pottergate
Pape Richard, Market place
Richardson Thomas, Church street
Simpson Benjamin, Church street
Sunlay John, Pottergate

*Corn Factors.*
Comins Robert, Church street
Winn Thomas, Church street

*Druggist.*
Myers Richard, Market place

*Farmers.*
Bentley John, Market place
Shaw Joseph, Church street
Sigsworth Wm. Bondgate

*Gardeners.*
Cummings Matthew, Pottergate
Smith George, Ryegate
Watson George, Ryegate

*Grocers, Tea Dealers, Linen and Woollen Drapers, &c.*
Barker Thomas & John, (and bacon & butter factors) Market place
Bentley W. W. Market place
Hutchinson Simeon, (and agent to the Norwich Union Fire, &c. Office,) Market place
Snowden L. Church street
Trueman David, Church street

*Hatters and Furriers.*
Burrows James, Boroughgate
Canniel David, Castlegate

*Inns and Taverns.*
Black Swan, Matthew Agar, (& excise office) Market place
Board, B. Simpson, Church street
Crown, John Cowen, Market place
Golden Lion, S. Caterson, Market pl.
New Inn, Tate and Coates, (& posting house) Boroughgate
Royal Oak, Ann Pape, Market place

*Ironmongers, &c.*
Pape Thos. (& glover) Castlegate
Spark John, Market place

*Joiners and Cabinet Makers.*
Frank Wm. Castlegate
Milner Michael, Ryegate
Spark John, Market place
Wean George, Bondgate

*Provision Dealers.*
Barker Thomas, Church street
Moorhouse Ralph, Boroughgate
Shepherd John, (& bacon) Church st.
Shout Charles, Bondgate

*Perfumers.*
Rountree Wm. (and sub-distributor of stamps, & last mkr. Market pl.
Tyreman Abraham, Boroughgate

*Plumbers and Glaziers.*
Dawson Robert, Bondgate
Jackson John, Church street

*Rope Manufacturers.*
Buck John, Church street
Wilson Thomas, Pottergate

*Saddlers.*
Barrick Thomas, Market place
Ward Wm. Market place

*Spirit Dealers.*
Sigsworth Sarah, (& maltster) Church street
Simpson Benjamin, Church street

*Surgeons.*
Harris Robert, Market place
Ness Job, Market place
Sandwith John, Market place

*Tailors.*
Betts Charles, Pottergate
Betts James, Pottergate
Cooper Thomas, Bondgate
Johnson Robert, Castlegate
Webster John, Church street

*Tallow Chandlers.*
Cowen John, Market place
Shout Charles, Bondgate
Smith Wm. Church street

*Watch and Clock Makers.*
Stewart Robert, Bondgate
Ward Wm. Market place

*Wheelwrights.*
Warrener Thomas, Bondgate
Warrener Richard, Pottergate

*Miscellany.*
Craggs Jane, milliner, Church st.
Dawson John, exciseman, Castlegate
Fenwick John, corn miller, Church st.
Harrison John, Church street
Harrison Thomas, Church street
Hutchinson John, accountant, Boroughgate
Jackson Wm. turner in wood, Church street
Milner John, house and sign painter, bottom of Castlegate
Munford Thos. stay maker, Church st.
Park John, tanner, Boroughgate
Rook Thos. brazier, &c. Castlegt.
Sigsworth Sarah, maltster, Church st.
Tate John, Boroughgate
Thompson John, Boroughgate
Ward Geo. gunsmith, Church st.
Ward John, Market place
Windress James, currier, Boroughgt.

*Carriers.*
William Simpson, to York Mon. and

Thur. ret. Tu. and Fri. dep. 1 mg. ret. 6 evg.

William Howe, to Malton Tu. and Thur. dep. 3 mg. ret. 6 evg.

William Wood, to Thirsk Mon. dep. 8 mg. ret. same day; and to Kirkby on Tu. dep. 1 aft. ret. same day.

John Pearson, (to the Black Swan) from Scarbro', arr. Fri. at 7 night, ret. Sat. at 2 aft. by way of Kirkby and Pickering.

HELMSLEY GATE, (P.) in the wap. of Bulmer, and liberty of St. Peter's; 6 miles ENE. of York. Here is a church, dedicated to St. Mary; the living is a vicarage, of which the prebend of Osbalderick is the patron. This village is one mile from Stamford bridge, where there is a great annual fair for cattle, cloth, &c. which was formerly held here. Pop. 209.

Dawson Matthew, gent.
Holmes Rev. Thomas, curate of Skirpenbeck
Horseley Marmaduke, gent.
Ridley Mrs. Jane, gentlewoman
Wilkinson Rev. John, vicar

| *Blacksmiths,* | *Farmers,* |
|---|---|
| Dickens Thos. | Beal Robert |
| Waite Thos. | Hall John |
| *Butchers,* | Slater John |
| Horseley John | Tanfield John |
| Whitwell Benj. | Twinum John |
| Whitwell Leonard | |

Cooper Wm. vict. Three Cups, Stamford bridge West
Cooper Thos. joiner & cabinet mkr.
Fewster Thomas, cooper
Izard Richard, wheelwright
Marshall Wm. shoemaker
Martin James, keeper of the lunatic asylum
Pashley John, tailor
Rather James, vict. Black Horse

*Helmsley Over* or *Upper,* (P.) in the wap. of Bulmer; 7 miles NE. of York. Here is a church, dedicated to St. Peter; the living is a rectory, in the patronage of the King, and the Rev. Francis Wm. Dealtry is the incumbent.

HELPERBY, in the parish of Brafferton, wap. of Bulmer, and liberty of St. Peter's; 4 miles NE. of Boroughbridge. Pop. 611.

| *Blacksmiths,* | Kirk Edward |
|---|---|
| Darby Wm. | Lund John |
| Knowlson John | *Carpenters, &c.* |
| *Butchers,* | Frankland John |
| Ellis Robert | Hodgson Wm. (& |
| Gatenby Geo. | parish clerk |

| | *Gardeners, &c.* |
|---|---|
| Leadley Mark | Metcalfe Thos. |
| Wheatley G. sen. | Moiser Robert |
| Wheatley G. jun. | *Grocers & Drapers,* |
| Wilson Ralph | Coates Christ. |
| *Farmers,* | Gilbert Thos. |
| Allanson John | Parker Meek |
| Buttery Roger | Wetherill Thos. |
| Coates Jonathan | *Shoemakers,* |
| Coates James | Clifford Wm. |
| Fawcett Matth. | Hildreth Richard |
| Jackson Wm. | Mills Wm. |
| Kettlewell Wm. | Skaife John |
| Kirk Robert | Stead Emanuel |
| Lawson Geo. | Yarker John |
| Marwood Geo. | *Tailors,* |
| Neeson John | Hodgson Edward |
| Nicholson Andw. | Holmes Wm. |
| Parker John | Spence Thos. sen. |
| Ryder Robert | Spence Thos. jun. |
| Smithson John | |
| Smithson Thos. | |

Bean John, cooper
Belt George, stone mason
Bosomworth John, hair dresser
Broader Thos. national schoolmaster
Buttery Thomas, maltster
Cavendish Joseph, tinner & brazier
Darley Thomas, vict. Oak Tree
Easterby Thomas, baker
Ellis Joseph, vict. Golden Lion
Gatenby Wm. vict. Dog
Haw John, bricklayer
Lambert Wm. brewer & maltster
Watson Thos. earthenware dealer
Wheatley Geo. vict. Crown

HELWITH, in the parish of Kirkby-Ravensworth, wap. of Gilling West, and liberty of Richmondshire; 4 miles NE. of Reeth.

Hutchinson Simon, yeoman

*Hemlington,* in the parish of Stainton, wap. and liberty of Langbargh; 4 miles N. of Stokesley.—Population, 72.

HENDERSKELFE, in the parish & wap. of Bulmer; 7 miles WSW. of Malton, containing a population of 159 souls.

Castle Howard, the seat of the most noble Frederick Earl of Carlisle, is situated in this township. This magnificent mansion was built between the years 1722 and 1731, from a design of Sir John Vanbrugh, in the same style as Blenheim House, in Oxfordshire, by the Right Hon. Charles Howard, the third Earl of Carlisle, on the site of the old castle of Henderskelfe, which was destroyed by an accidental fire. Castle Howard has a longer line of front than Blenheim House, and its exterior is extremely magnificent; the state apartments are particularly distinguished for grandeur of appearance;

and the princely collection of paintings, statues, busts, &c. with which this mansion is enriched afford a high gratification to the admirers of the fine arts, whilst the liberality of the noble proprietor, in admitting the public to view this elegant repository, entitles him to grateful applause. The hall is 35 feet square, and 60 feet high, terminating at the top in a spacious dome, 100 feet high, and adorned with columns of the Corinthian and Composite order. The walls are painted by Peligrini with the history of Phaeton, and the room is ornamented with several antique statues and busts. To describe all the different rooms in this princely mansion, together with the superb paintings, statues, &c. which it contains, would fill a volume. The museum, 24 feet square, and the antique gallery, 160 feet by 30, contain a vast assemblage of curiosities. In the south-west corner of the museum is a cylindrical altar, about four feet and a half high, which anciently stood in the temple of Delphi, brought from Italy, and was presented to the Lord of Castle Howard by the immortal Nelson. The taste displayed in the pleasure grounds corresponds with the magnificence of the house. The park is beautiful and extensive; and the present Earl of Carlisle has greatly improved the scenery by the addition of a fine sheet of water, at an appropriate distance from the south front. A beautiful intermixture of wood and lawn delights the eye; and the prospects are every where rich and full of pleasing variety. The ornamental buildings in the park are in a style of grandeur. At the entrance on the south, is an elegant inn, for the accommodation of strangers. In the centre of beautiful avenues, bordered on each side with lofty trees, and crossed at right angles, stands a stately quadrangular obelisk, 100 feet in height, erected in the year 1714, to commemorate the victories of John Duke of Marlborough, and to fix the date of the erection of Castle Howard. On the opposite side of the obelisk, facing the western avenue, is inscribed:—

If to perfection these plantations rise,
If they agreeably my heirs surprise,
This faithful pillar will their age declare,
As long as time these characters shall spare.

Nearly opposite to the grand entrance, in the north front of the house, an elegant monument commemorates the victories of Lord Nelson. Those glorious names, Aboukir, Copenhagen, and Trafalgar, inscribed on three of its sides, in large gold characters, call to remembrance the achievements of the naval hero, and testify the patriotism of the noble proprietor of this mansion. About half a mile to the eastward of the house is an Ionic temple, with four porticos and a

beautiful interior. The cornices of the door-cases are supported by Ionic columns of black and yellow marble; and in the corners of the room are pilasters.—In niches over the doors are busts of Vespasian, Faustina, Trajan, and Sabina.—The floor is disposed in compartments of antique marble of various colours, and the room is crowned with a dome, splendidly gilt.—About a quarter of a mile farther, and nearly in the same direction, stands the Mausoleum, a circular building, above 50 feet diameter, and surrounded with a handsome colonade of Doric pillars. Over the vault is an elegant circular chapel; the cornice from which the dome rises is supported by eight Corinthian columns; and the ornamental carvings are light and pleasing. The height of the structure is 90 feet, that of the inside is 68; this is in different compartments inlaid with marble.

Frederick Earl of Carlisle
George Lord Viscount Morpeth
Beal Joseph, the pedestrian
Boys John, farmer and auctioneer
Coverdale John, farmer
Elliot Isaac, gamekeeper
Kirby Ann, vict. Castle Inn

HEWORTH, in the parishes of St. Cuthbert and St. Giles, York, and wap. of Bulmer; 1 mile ENE. of York. Here is a Sunday school, supported by members of the established church. Population, 146.

Cook Robert, gentleman
Dibb Mrs. G. D. gentlewoman
Ellerbeck John, gentleman
Moore Miss Ann, gentlewoman
Sturdy Wm. gentleman
Surr Thomas, gentleman
Tomlinson John, gentleman
White William, Esq.
Wilkinson John, gentleman

*Farmers,*      Stoker Benjamin
Richardson Geo.   Todd Thomas
& cattle dealer  Wilkinson Thos.

Bewley Robert, brickmaker
Lund John, shoemaker
Robinson Wm. blacksmith
Wilkinson Sol. vict. Bull and Butcher
Wilson William, tailor
Wilson James, joiner and carpenter

*Hieldenley,* in the parish of Appleton-le-Street, and wap. of Rydale; 3 miles WSW. of Malton, a small hamlet, the residence of George Strickland, Esq. Pop. 23.

*Hiller Green,* in the parish of Hackness, wap. and liberty of Whitby Strand, 7 miles WNW. of Scarbro'.

HILTON, (P.) in the wap. and liberty of Langbargh; 4 miles ESE. of Yarm. The church is a plain, ancient small structure. The living is a perpetual curacy, in the patronage of Lord George Henry Cavendish; incumbent, the Rev. Robert Fawcett. Pop. 135.

*Farmers,*
Coates Geo.
Coates Francis
Nightingale Wm.
Preston John
Stockdale Francis
Watson Richard

Appleton Michael, tailor and draper
Appleton John, blacksmith
Preston Wm. parish clerk
Wilson Wm. vict. Fox and Hounds
Wilson Wm. jun. shoemaker
Wrightson Robert, corn miller

HINDERWELL, or HILDERWELL, (P.) in the wap. and liberty of Langbargh; 8 miles NW. of Whitby. The church, dedicated to St. Hilda, is a very ancient edifice; the living is a rectory, in the patronage of Lady M. Boynton, and the Rev. William Smith is the incumbent. In the church yard there is a well, or spring of pure water, called St. Hilda's well, near which, it is conjectured, she had an occasional retreat, which not only still retains her name, but communicates the same to the parish. Rowland thinks it probable that, in very distant ages, churches were dwelling-houses for the priests, as well as places of worship for the people; and that therefore they were generally built near a well of clear water. In the year 1603 a plague, contracted from a Turkish ship stranded on the coast, broke out in this village, and raged for six weeks, carrying off a number of the inhabitants, but fortunately did not extend its baneful influence to any of the neighbouring villages. Pop. 1483.

Van Hemmitt Rev. John, curate
White Hannah, gentlewoman

*Farmers,*
Dobson Thos.
Duell Thos.
Hill Wm.
Lewis Philip
Marshall Ann
Merry Robert
Moon Isaac, & miller
Newton John
Reed Wm.

Scarthe Isaac
Scarthe Wm.
Welford John
*Shoemakers,*
Adamson Luke
Armstrong Geo.
*Wheelwrights,*
Atkinson Wm.
Peacock Leonard
Skelton Thos.

Gibson Wm. vict. and butcher, Shoulder of Mutton
Jefferson John, tailor
Robinson Matthew, schoolmaster and parish clerk
Smallwood Wm. vict. and blacksmith, Brown Cow

*Hmlethwaite,* in the parish of Coverham, and wap. of Hang West; 6 miles SW. of Middleham, pleasantly situated in Coverdale.

HIPSWELL, in the parish of Catterick, wap. of Hang East, and liberty of Richmondshire; 3 miles SE. of Richmond. Population, 273.

Bradley Rev. James, officiating curate
Metcalfe Wm. gent. Hipswell lodge

*Farmers,*
Kirby Wm.
Metcalfe Geo. jun.
Severn Robert
Sledge Christr.

Binks Edmund, blacksmith
Gill Leonard, schoolmaster
Horner Ann, vict. Volunteer
Langstaff Anthony, wheelwright
Metcalfe Geo. corn miller

*Hole of Horcum,* a circular valley in the parish of Leavisham, wap. and liberty of Pickering Lythe; 7 miles NNE. of Pickering.

*Holme,* in the parish of Pickhill, wap. and liberty of Allertonshire; 5 miles SE. of Bedale, the residence of John Stockdale, gentleman, of Holme Lodge. Population, including Howgrave, 102.

*Holme,* (North) in the parish of Kirkdale, wap. of Rydale; 3 miles S. of Kirkby-Moor-Side. Pop. 24.

*Holme,* (South) in the parish of Hovingham, and wap. of Rydale; 7 mls. from Kirkby-Moor-Side. Pop. 66.

HOLTBY, (P.) in the wap. of Bulmer; 5 miles ENE. of York. Here is a handsome brick church, dedicated to the Holy Trinity; the living is a rectory, of which Mrs. Nelson is the patroness, and the Rev. Robert Warburton the incumbent. Pop. 170.

Appleby Thomas, gentleman
Smithson Robert, solicitor, (office, Colliergate, York)

*Farmers and yeomen* Stotwell John
Bentley John
Lund Marmaduke
Rookes David
Smithson Thos.
Taylor Jonathan
Taylor Thomas
Waud Robert
Wilson George

Archer George, shoemaker and vict. Lord Wellington
Atkinson Wm. blacksmith

*Holwick,* in the parish of Romaldkirk, wap. of Gilling West, and liberty of Richmondshire; 11 miles NW. of Barnard Castle. Pop. 201.

*Hood Grange,* in the parish of Kilburn, wap. of Birdforth, and liberty of Ripon; 6 miles ESE. of Thirsk. Population, 30.

*Hope*, in the parish of Barningham, wap. of Gilling West, and liberty of Richmondshire; 6 miles S. of Barnard Castle. Population, 44.

HOANBY, (P.) in the wap. of Hang East, and liberties of St. Peter's and Richmondshire; 5 miles NW. of Bedale. Here is a church dedicated to St. Mary; the living is a vicarage, in the patronage of the Dean and Chapter of York, and the Rev. J. Alderson is the incumbent. Hornby castle, one of the seats of his Grace the Duke of Leeds, is situated in this township. This mansion is a spacious structure of a mixed architecture, and the apartments are grand, and superbly finished. The situation is commanding, and from the battlements is seen to great advantage the rich and picturesque valley of Bedale, stretching up to the western moors, and forming a grand and imposing contrast. Hornby castle was anciently the lordship and seat of the family of St. Quintin, from whom it passed to the Conyers, and ultimately to the Osbornes. Population, 102.

Osborne, George William Frederick, Duke of Leeds, &c. Hornby castle
Pattison Rev. M. I. A. M. curate

*Farmers,*
Outhwaite Wm.
Outhwaite Richd.
Powell Christphr.
Renforth Wm.
Scaife Christopher
Stelling Anthony

M'Kenzie Dorothy, vict. Board

*Hornby*, in the parish of Great Smeaton, wap. and liberty of Allertonshire; 8 miles N. of Northallerton. The only place of worship in this village is a small Methodist chapel. The Grange in this township is the residence of Henry Howgill, Esq. Population, 238.

*Horse House*, in the parish of Coverham, wap. of Hang West, and liberty of Richmondshire; 6 miles SW. of Middleham.

HOULTBY (High) in the parish of Hornby, wap. of Hang East, & liberty of Richmond hire; 4 mls. N. of Bedale, of which Thomas Robson, Esq. is the principal inhabitant. Pop. included with Ainderby Myers.

*Houltby* (Low), in the parish of Bedale, wap. of Hang East, & liberty of Richmondshire; 3 mls. N. of Bedale.

HOVINGHAM, (P.) in the wap. of Rydale; 7 miles S. of Kirkby-Moor-Side. Anciently the seat of the great Roger de Mowbray, but now possessed by the Worsley family. In the gardens of Thomas Worsley, Esq. in 1745, was discovered a Roman hypocaust, and in another place, a small tesselated pavement. There were also found in making the gardens, considerable remains of buildings, evidently proving the spot to have been the site of a Roman villa. A charter was granted in the 36th year of the reign of Henry III. for a market, fair, &c. and renewed in the 13th of the reign of George II. 1739. The market to be held on the Thursday; the fairs to be held on the 14th, 15th, and 16th of August, for live cattle, and all kinds of English grain, merchandise, &c. The market has been discontinued a number of years. Here is a school endowed with 16l. a year, by the Rev. James Graves, of Beverley, for twelve poor children, and 20l. by Mrs. Ann Arthington, of Arthington; the interest of which was to be applied towards educating four children. The church is dedicated to All Saints; and the living is a perpetual curacy, of which the Earl of Carlisle is the patron, and the Rev. Robert Freer, the incumbent; there is here also a Methodist chapel. Population, 649.

Proud Rev. Richard
Wales John, gentleman
Worsley E. Esq. Hall

*Blacksmiths,*
Bonwell George
Mook Wm.
*Butchers,*
Audaer Thomas
Goodwill Wm.
Thompson James
*Farmers,*
Carr James
Foxton Thomas
Freer John
Gibson John
Goodul Robert
Hoggart Grace
Hornsey Thos.
Leafe Thomas
Lockey Richard
Lythe Wm.
Mercer Wm.
Mitchell Wm.

Skelton Thomas
Tindall Ralph
*Grocers,*
Banks Robert
Robson Thomas
*Joiners, &c.*
Foster George
Harrison Robert
*Shoemakers,*
Banks Robert
Banks Wm.
Jackson Thos.
*Shopkeepers,*
Foster George
Hewgill Daniel
Wilson Geo.
*Surgeons,*
Dixon Henry
Wilson James

Audaer John, stone mason
Brough William, bacon factor
Brown Peter, perfumer
Dawson Edw. plumber & glazier
Dobinson Elizabeth, straw hat mfr.
Dobson William, tallow chandler
Hessay John, watch maker
Johnson Miss, day school
Joy Richard, schoolmaster
Lockey Richard, vict. Talbot Inn
Moor John, draper and tailor
Moor Sarah, milliner
Ridsdale Thomas, saddler
Simpson Thomas, basket maker
Skelton John, vict. & maltster, New Inn
Sunlay John, cooper

Taylor Francis, vict. Lion
Watson Wm. corn miller

*Howe*, in the parish of Pickhill, &
wap. of Halikeld; 5 miles SW. of
Thirsk. Population 32. ↲

*Howe*, in the parish of Old Malton,
and wap. of Rydale; 3 miles from
Malton.

*Howgrave*, see Sutton Howgrave.

*Howlsyke*, in the parish of Danby,
wap. and liberty of Langbargh; 11
miles from Whitby.

*Howthorpe*, in the parish of Hovingham, & wap. of Rydale; 7 miles
from Malton. Population included
with Airyholme.

*Huby*, in the parish of Sutton-on-
the-Forest, wap. of Bulmer, & liberty
of Pickering Lythe; 4 miles SE. of
Easingwold. Here are Wesleyan and
Primitive Methodist chapels, and a
Friends' Meeting house. Pop. 497.

*Hudswell*, in the parish of Catterick, wap. of Hang West, and liberty of
Richmondshire; 2 miles SW. of Richmond.
There is in this township an extensive lead
mine, and also a colliery. The Chapel of
Ease is a small ancient structure, of which
the Rev. James Bradley, is curate. The
extraordinary mount, called Round Haw, is
in this township. Pop. 305.

HUMBURTON, in the parish of
Kirby-on-the-Moor, and wap. of Hali-
keld; 2 miles NE. of Boroughbridge.
The principal inhabitant is Mr. Joseph
Smith, yeoman, of Burton Grange.
Pop. with Milby, 120.

*Hunderthwaite*, in the parish of
Romaldkirk, wap. of Gilling West,
and liberty of Richmondshire; 6 miles
NW. of Barnard Castle. Pop. 313.

HUNTINGTON, (P.) in the wap. of
Bulmer, a part in the liberty of St. Peter's;
3 miles NNE. of York. Here is a church
dedicated to All Saints; the living is a vicarage; under the patronage of the College of
Vicars, York, and the Rev. J. Richardson,
A. M. is the incumbent. This village is
situated on the east bank of the navigable
river Foss. Pop. 346.

Atkinson Richard, surgeon
Darby Mrs. A. gentlewoman
Dowker Thos. Esq. Manor cottage
Smith Thos. Esq. Fosfield house
Wisker Matthias, gentleman

*Farmers & Yeomen*,    Fowler Leonard
Barron Henry    Gray Simeon
Bearpark Thos.    Hall John
Clegg Jonathan    Knapton Wm.

Land Wm.
Mosier Wm.
Mosier Edward
Phillips James
Ware Matthew
Wood James
*Land Surveyors*,
Barron Henry
Mosier John

*Shoemakers*,
Boggitt Thos.
Brown Mark
*Shopkeepers*,
Knapton Thos.
Rhodes Joseph
*Wheelwrights*,
Dunnill Wm.
Ward Wm.

Burton Robert, schoolmaster
Cass Thomas, vict. White Horse
Croft John, corn miller
Dixon Wm. vict. Hare and Hounds
Oates John, butcher
Varey John, vict. and blacksmith

HUNTON, in the parish of Patrick
Brompton, wap. of Hang West, liberties of St. Peter's and Richmondshire;
6 miles NW. of Bedale. Pop. 496.

Foster Francis, gentleman

*Blacksmiths*,    Rider Geo.
Caygill Geo.
Thompson Robt.    *Shoemakers*,
*Butchers*,    Todd Robert
Robinson Jacob    Tomlin John
Robinson Wm.    *Tailors*,
*Farmers*,    Esles Wm.
Miller Charles    Metcalf John
Thomas John
Thomas Thos.    *Wheelwrights*,
*Schoolmasters*,    Coates Geo.
Atkinson John    Richardson Geo.

Bollon Joseph, wood cutter
Carter Mary, vict. Fox and Hounds
Daggit Richard, grocer and draper
Esles Wm. vict. King's Head
Hewson Abraham, vict. Bay Horse
Owthwaite Geo. maltster & brewer
Taylor Geo. vict. New Inn

*Hurry*, in the parish of Romaldkirk, wap. of Gilling West, & liberty
of Richmondshire; 7 miles WNW. of
Barnard Castle. Population included
with Hundersthwaite.

*Hurst*, in the parish of Marrick,
wap. of Gilling West, and liberty of
Richmondshire; 3 miles NNE. of
Reeth. Pop. included with Marrick.

HUSTHWAITE, (P.) in the wap. of
Birdforth, and liberty of St. Peter's; 4
miles N. of Easingwold. The living is
a perpetual curacy, in the patronage
of Joseph Reeve, Esq.; incumbent the
Rev. John Starkey. Pop. 324.

*Blacksmiths*,    Dixon John
Robson Jesse    Hick John
Smith Jeffery    Hick Geo.
*Farmers & Yeomen*,    Nelson Thos.
Battye Richard    Smith Thos.
Burnett Timothy    Smithson Samuel
Dennison Richard    Wilkinson John

Wimp Wm.

*Joiners,*
Greenwood John
Greenwood Wm.

Burnett Joseph, wool & cattle dealer
Darley Richard, vict. Board
Gatenby John, butcher
Kendrew Christopher, shopkeeper
Mouncester Robert, schoolmaster
Mouncester Thos. wheelwright
Taylor John, vict. Black Bull
Young Wm. tailor

HUTTON, in the parish of Rudby, wap. and liberty of Langbargh; 4 miles SW. of Stokesley. An extensive, pleasant and populous village, adjacent to the small village of Rudby, wherein is situated the parish church, there being at Hutton only a Methodist chapel, and one for the Primitive Methodists lately erected. Here is likewise a Union Sunday School, capable of containing one hundred and ten children. Linen is manufactured at this place to a considerable extent. Pop. 919.

Dawson William, gentleman
Kilsey Simon, gentleman
Pulman Thomas C. surgeon
Robinson John, gentleman
Shepherd Rev. Richard, vicar
Suggitt B. D. gentleman
Thompson Brian, gentleman

*Agents.*
Graham Thomas, (to Mr. Nevill)
Oates Geo. (to Mr. Norman)
Smith James, (to Clark, Plummer & Co. Newcastle)

*Bakers,*
Jackson Nathaniel
Paterson Jane
*Bricklayers,*
Bainbridge Jas. (& brick maker)
Bainbridge John
*Butchers,*
Edwards Thos.
Goldsbrough Bart.
Tweddle Robert
*Farmers,*
Barker Joseph, (& gamekeeper)
Chapman Michael
Cristall Geo.
Harrison Cuthbert
Hutton John
Hutton John
Johnson Lewis
Johnson Richard
Low Michael
Nightingale Robt.
Shutt John
Sidgwick Wm.
Walters Joseph

Wood Wm.
*Grocers,*
Catchasides Js. jun.
Eden James, (and tallow chandler)
Honeyman Wm.
Smith James
Taylor Jonathan
Tones Sarah
*Linen Mfrs.*
Bewick Geo.
Eland James
Seamer Wm.
Sidgwick Wm.
Sidgwick Simon
Sidgwick Michael
Sidgwick Mary & Sons
Whorlton Isaac
Whorlton Joseph
*Shoemakers,*
Howe John
Imeson John
Oates Robert
Sanderson Geo.
Wright Geo.

*Tailors,*
Braithwaite Robt.
Jackson William, (draper & hatter)
*Wheelwrights,*
Burdon Simeon
Catchasides James, vict. & blacksmith, Bay Horse
Davison Thomas, hawker
Easby William, schoolmaster
Easby Wm. vict. Shoulder of Mutton
Eland Jonathan, sieve & riddle maker
Eland John, cabinet maker
Farnaby Geo. bee breeder & dealer
Meynell Edward, vict. Board
Moss Robert, vict. Black Swan
Mundale Geo. gardener
Norman Robert, coarse paper mfr.
Passman Wm. saddler
Rayney Wm. blacksmith
Richardson Robert, dog trainer
Sidgwick Charlotte, schoolmistress
Tweddle Robert, vict. Wheat Sheaf
Wood Wm. bacon and cheese factor

Hebron Samuel, (& parish clerk)
Kay John
Meynell Edward
Richardson John
Taylor Edmund

*Carriers.*
Thos. Cust to Stockton, on Wed. and to Stokesley, on Mon. Thu. & Sat.
G. Mundale to Stockton, every Wed.

HUTTON BONVILLE, in the parish of Birkby, wap. & liberty of Allertonshire; 5 miles NW. of Northallerton. The principal inhabitant is Henry Pierce, Esq. M. P. who resides at the hall. Population 107.

HUTTON BUSHEL, (P.) in the wap. and liberty of Pickering Lythe; 6 miles SW. of Scarborough. Here is a very neat church embosomed in trees, dedicated to St. Matthew, of which the Rev. G. Woolley, of Scarborough, is vicar, and Earl Fitzwilliam the patron; here is likewise a Methodist chapel. The ancestor of the ancient family of Buscel or Bushels came over with William the Conqueror, and had lands assigned him not far from Seamer; there he built a church, and married Alice, sister to William de Percy, the first abbot of that monastery, about the year 1197. In the church is a marble monument, erected to the memory of Dr. Richard Osbaldeston, son of Sir Richard Osbaldeston, of Hunmanby, in the East Riding, and Bishop of London, who died in 1764; besides some others of a more recent date. Population 419.

Smart George, surgeon

*Blacksmiths,*
Bird Robert
Hawkins James
*Farmers,*
Coulson John
Greaves Corry
Hodgson Thos.

Pearson John
Pexton Wm.
Pond Hessle
Wales Geo.
Ward John
*Shoemakers,*
Elland Wm.

Hick Matthew    Peterkin Hannah
Hobson Wm      *Tailors,*
   *Shopkeepers,*    Smith Wm.
Marflit Thomas    Spence Richard
Dawson Charles, schoolmaster
Halder Jonathan, vict. Board
Major John, wheelwright

*Hutton Conyers,* (Extra-parochial) in the wap. and liberty of Allerton-shire; 1 mile NNE. of Ripon. The property of Mrs. Lawrence. Pop. 127.

*Hutton Hang,* (High and Low), in the parish of Fingall, wap. of Hang West, and liberty of Richmondshire; 3 miles ENE. of Middleham. Pop. 25.

HUTTON-IN-THE-HOLE, in the parish of Lastingham, & wap. of Ry-dale; 3 mls. N. of Kirkby-Moor-Side. Here is a Methodist chapel. Pop. 304.

Shepherd Wm. Esq. Dowthwaite dale
   *Blacksmiths,*    Burton William
Abbey Thomas    Featherstone Wm.
Holroyd David, & Strickland Robert
   shopkeeeper    Taylor T. Ox close
*Farmers & Yeomen,*    *Wheelwrights,*
Abbey Thos. and    Pearson William
   coal dealer    Wardill John

Cooper Robert, vict. Crown
Hodgson William, shoemaker
Peacock Daniel, rope maker
Rivis Wm. corn miller, Yaudwath

*Hutton Low Cross,* in the parish of Guisborough, wap. & liberty of Lang-bargh; 2 miles SSW. of Guisborough. Population, 56.

*Hutton Magna,* (P.) in the wap. of Gilling West, and liberty of Rich-mondshire; 8 miles NNW. of Rich-mond. The living is a perpetual cu-racy, in the patronage of the vicar of Gilling; incumbent the Rev. William Heslop. Pop. with Lanehead, 248.

*Hutton Mulgrave,* in the parish of Lythe, wap. and liberty of Langbargh; 6 miles W. of Whitby. Pop. 90.

*Huttons Ambo,* (P.) in the wap. of Bulmer; 2½ miles SW. of Malton. Here is a small church, dedicated to St. Margaret; the living is a curacy, of which the Arch-bishop of York is the patron, and the Rev. J. J. Cleaver incumbent.—Here is a small Methodist chapel. The principal inhabitant is Mr. Thomas Robinson. Pop. 445.

HUTTON SAND, in the parish of Thirsk, and wap. of Birdforth; 3 miles WSW. of Thirsk. In addition to the Cha-pel of Ease, there is here a chapel for the Methodists. Pop. 273.

Atkinson Wm. gentleman
Jones Rev. Joseph, curate

Swarbreck John, gentleman
   *Farmers,*    *Shoemakers,*
Atkinson John    Clidro Wm.
Pickering Hannah Hustwaite Thos.
Taylor Wm.    *Wheelwrights,*
White Wm.    Goodrick John
White John    Lumley Thomas
Dixon John, blacksmith
Goodrick John, vict. King's Head
Metcalfe John, butcher
Milburn and Saddler, vict. Buck
Pollitt John, schoolmaster
Saddler E. cattle dlr. & vict. Bay Horse

HUTTON SAND, in the parish of Bossall, and wap. of Bulmer; 7 miles NE. of York. Here is a Chapel of Ease, of which the Rev. James Brit-ton, vicar of Bossall, has the curacy.— Population, 202.

Read Rev. Thos. Cutler Rudston, A.M. F.L.S. Sand Hutton House
   *Farmers,*    Mason Richard
Arminson John    Porter John
Coultas Thomas    Teasedale Wm.
Kidd Wm.    Topham Edward
Lazenby George, shoemaker
Seller J. vict. & blksmith, Horse Shoe

*Hutton Sessay,* in the parish of Sessay, wap. and liberty of Allerton-shire; 5 miles NW. of Easingwold. Population, 129.

HUTTON SHERIFF, (P.) in the wap. of Bulmer; 8 miles ESE. of Easing-wold. The castle here was built by Ber-tram de Bulmer, in the reign of Stephen, from whose family it passed to that of Nevil. Ralph Nevil, first Earl of Westmoreland, repaired it. Richard Nevil, Earl of War-wick, being slain at the battle of Barnett, Edward IV. seized this castle; after whose death Richard, aspiring to the throne, im-prisoned his elder brother's son, Edward Plantagenet, within this fortress, where he remained till Richard was slain at Bosworth Field, whence he was taken by Henry VII. and arraigned for high treason; supported by trifling and false pretences, he was, at the age of twenty-five, condemned, and be-headed in 1497, on Tower Hill. The Prin-cess Elizabeth, afterwards the wife of Henry VII. was also confined here. The parish church is dedicated to St. Helen; the living is a vicarage, in the patronage of the Arch-bishop of York, and the Rev. Thomas Tate is the incumbent. There are also here two chapels, one for the Methodists and the other for the Primitive Methodists; and two schools, each with a small endowment.— Population, 756.

Sagg George, surgeon
Thompson G. L. Esq. Park.

*Blacksmiths,*
Jackson John
Morley Robert
 *Bricklayers,*
Moxon Wm.
Plows John
 *Butchers,*
Bentley Henry
Saville Thos.
 *Coopers,*
Bean Wm.
Dobson Joseph
 *Corn Millers,*
Belt Susannah
Suggitt Wm.
*Farmers & Yeomen,*
Addison Thos.
Atlay John .
Atlay Robert
Barker Mary
Belt Thomas
Bowser Matth.
Brown Ferdinand
Carr John
Cattle Wm.
Cattle Timothy
Cattle Robert
Cattle Leonard
Catton Robert
Clark George
Cordeux Richard
Crispin Thomas
Etherington Geo.
Foster Geo.
Groves John
Harrison Thomas
Harper John .
Hick Richard
Hopwood Thos.
Jackson Richard
Johnson Ann
Johnson Hannah

Kendrew Christ.
Linfoot John
Lund John
Lund Benj.
Lund Richard
Morley Wm.
Pearson Geo.
Pickering Thos.
Smithson Dorothy
Stabler Thos.
Suggitt Eliz.
Tuke Samuel
Ware John
Warwick Francis
Webster Wm.
 *Joiners, &c.*
Burrell John
Clark Wm.
Clark John .
Cook Seth
Harrison J. & T. .
 *Schoolmasters,*
Dennis Wm.
Milburn Wm.
 *Shoemakers,*
Dalton Richard
Hewson Wm.
Hutchinson S.
Lund George
Pinkney Geo.
Wedgwood Francis
 *Shopkeepers,*
Hagyard Wm.
Kitchen Matth.
Pearson John
Pickering Charles
Smailes George
 *Tailors,*
Dalton George
Dalton James
Galtry Phineas
Midgley Richard

Douglass Ralph, saddler
Fawcett Robert, brewer & maltster
Hall Christr. vict. New Inn
Morley Robert, vict. Pack Horse
Saville Thos. vict. Lord Wellington
Seller Rt. vict. Blacksmiths' Arms
Stabler Robert, linen weaver

*Carriers*—John Lawson and Thomas
 Lockwood, to York Wed. and Sat.

 *Hutton-upon-Derwent,* in the parish of Huttons Ambo, and wap. of
Bulmer; 8 miles SW. of Malton.

 *Ilton,* in the parish of Masham,
wap. of Hang East, and liberty of
Richmondshire; 3 miles SW. of
Masham. Pop. including Pott, 266.

 INGLEBY ARNCLIFFE, (P.) in the
wap. and liberty of Langbargh; 8 miles
NE. of Northallerton. The church, which
is dedicated to St. Andrew, is a small, plain,
ancient structure; the living is a perpetual
curacy, in the patronage of Brign Abbes,
Esq. and the Rev. J. W. Steele is the incumbent. The village of Ingleby, which is
the only one in the parish, is small, and consists chiefly of farm-houses, neatly built.—
It stands in a retired situation, on the summit of a gentle ridge, at a little distance from
the road leading from Stokesley to Think.
A little south of the village is situated the
Cleveland Tontine Inn. Pop. 331.
 The York mail arrives daily at 1 in the
morning, northward, ret. at half-past 6 evg.
to York, leaving letters for this circuit—
Robert Turner, post-master, and posting-
house, Cleveland Tontine Inn.

Mauleverer Miss, Arncliffe Cottage
 *Blacksmiths,*  Stainthorp Thos.
Ashton John  Turnbull Robert
Burton Joseph  Wilson John
 *Butchers,*  Wilson John
Garbutt Wm.  Wright Francis
Metcalf Richard  Wright Barthw.
 *Farmers,*   *Grocers,*
Allison Thomas  Burton David
Atkinson Edward  Dawson John
Fawcett John   *Shoemakers,*
Flintoft Thomas  Hutchinson & Eeles
Flintoft John  Thompson John
Hill William   *Stone Masons,*
Russell David  Body David
Shaw Michael  Duck Thomas

Ashton Thomas, cooper
Body David, vict. Board
Duck Thomas; vict. Bell Inn

The Cleveland coach, from Redcar,
 during the season, every Mon. Wed.
 & Sat. arr. 11 mg. ret. ½ past 4 aft.

*Carrier*—Thos. Peacock, to Stockton
 Tu. & Fri. to Thirsk Mon. & Thur.

 INGLEBY BARWICK, in the parish
of Stainton, wap. and liberty of Langbargh; 3 miles NNE. of Yarm.—
Population, 175.

Meawburn Rt. lord of the manor

 INGLEBY GREENHOW, (P.) in
the wap. and liberty of Langbargh; 5 miles
ESE. of Stokesley; a small village chiefly
inhabited by farmers. The church is a
small modern structure, re-built in 1741; the
living is a perpetual curacy, in the patronage of Sir Wm. Foulis, Bart. of which
the Rev. John Dixon is the incumbent.—
Population, 158.

Sir William Foulis, Bart.
 *Farmers,*  Fell John
Blackburn Thos.  Garbutt Wm.
Braithwaite Edw.  Goulton John
Carlin Richard  Harker Joseph
Dinsley Miles  Hoggard Thomas

| | |
|---|---|
| lunt Thomas | Sherwood Samuel |
| Todd John | Sherwood John |
| Miles Wm. | Sherwood James |
| Reeston Wm. | Smith George |
| Shanelds Wm. | Watson Robert |
| Bell William, shopkeeper | |
| Redling John, wheelwright | |
| Ishson J. vict. and parish clerk | |
| Peacock Robert, schoolmaster | |
| kingle Wm. blacksmith | |
| Ripley Thomas, stone mason | |
| Watson James, vict. Fox & Hounds | |
| Watson John, butcher | |
| Watson Edward, cooper | |
| Webster John, shoemaker | |

*Irton*, in the parish of Seamer; wap. and liberty of Pickering Lythe; mls. SW. of Scarborough. Pop. 105.

IVELET, in the parish of Grinton, ownship of Muker, wap. of Gilling West, and liberty of Richmondshire; miles (NW. of Askrigg; is situated upon an minence on the northern banks of the Swale. Near Ivelet is a waterfall of fifteen or sixteen yards upon Ivelet beck, in a very secluded and romantic dell, the sides of which are well covered with wood, and the oaks which form the fall meet nearly at a point, and are fringed with the mountain ash, the hazel, &c.; a little above is another, called Yew Foxes, not quite so large as Ivelet, but from its particular situation, attracts the attention of travellers.

Keartos Joseph and Wm. yeomen

JERVEAUX ABBEY, in the parish of East Witton, wap. of Hang West, and liberty of Richmondshire; 3 miles SE. of Middleham. This once stately erection was founded in the year 1156, by Akarius, the son of Bardolph, and dedicated to the Virgin Mary. At the general dissolution, this monastery was seized, and its revenues, valued by Speed at 454*l.* 10*s.* 5*d.* granted to the King, the site being given to Maltham, Earl of Lenox. Sedberg, the late Abbot, was hanged in June, 1537, for opposing the King's measures. It is now the property of the Marquis Ailesbury. The remains of his Abbey are situated about two hundred paces from the highway leading from Middleham to Masham, and are not very visible, the view being much intercepted by trees. The name is of Norman extraction, and signifies simply Euredale Abbey, being situated on the banks of the Ure. Of all the ruins in the north of England, this has suffered the most complete demolition, considering the ample size of the building. The boundary wall, when in its pristine glory, comprehended a circuit of at least a mile. In 1806-7 the whole of this venerable ruin was

explored by order of the noble proprietor, and cleared of the briars and refuse with which, by the neglect of a succession of ages, it had been incumbered; when the Abbey church and choir, measuring 270 feet in length; with the cross aisles, the high altar, and several tombs were discovered. Further search exhibited the chapter house, 48 feet in length by 35 in width, with the marble pillars which formerly supported the roof.— The site of the Abbot's house and garden, with the kitchen and the refectory, the cloisters and the dormitory also became visible. The tesselated pavement of the great aisle, in geometrical figures, was found in a perfect state, but though the covering which had shut it out from the light of the sun had prevented its actual decomposition, the hand of time, though unseen, had been at work, and rendered the beautiful mosaic so frail, that the action of the air, and the rude blasts of winter, soon reduced it to dust. In the aisle were found several stone coffins, bearing inscriptions, in a state sufficiently perfect to be deciphered. A sunk fence, aided by a wall built for the purpose, now protects the ancient site. A neat mansion has been built near the Abbey, and is occupied as the residence of Mr. Claridge, the steward of the estate; the approach to which is by an ancient gate-way, in the style, but not of so early a date, as the Abbey.— Pop. included with East Witton.

*Kearton*, see Melbecks.

*Keld*, in the parish of Grinton, wap. of Gilling West, and liberty of Richmondshire; 8 miles NW. of Askrigg.— Here is a Calvinist chapel, erected in the year 1745, of which the Rev. Edward Stillman is minister. About one mile SE. of Keld is Kisden Force, a most beautiful waterfall: the fall is from twelve to fifteen yards high, the rocks that surround it forming a complete amphitheatre, beautifully fringed with underwood, which has a fine effect when contrasted with the barren hills and uncultivated wastes by which this place is surrounded.

*Keldholme*, in the parish of Kirkby-Moor-Side, wap. of Rydale; 1 mile E. of Kirkby-Moor-Side. There is here a flax spinning manufactory, carried on by Mr. Caleb Fletcher.

*Kelton*, in the parish of Romaldkirk, wap. of Gilling West, and liberty of Richmondshire; 13 miles W. of Barnard Castle.

*Kempswidden*, in the parish of Kildale, wap. & liberty of Langbargh; 7 miles SE. of Guisborough.

KEPWICK, in the parish of Over-

Silton, and wap. of Birdforth; 8 miles NNE. of Thirsk. Pop. 170.

Swales Rev. C. E. curate, Stayhouse

| Farmers, | Hoggart Robert, |
| Faint John | (& corn miller) |
| Faint John | Kidson Wm. |
| Hill John | Mothersill Wm. |
| Hodgson J.(&vict.) | (& butcher) |
| Hoggart Christ. | Ward John |

Cousens George, cooper
Sharp Jonathan, vict. Black Lion
Wright James, blacksmith

KETTLENESS, in the parish of Lythe, wap. and liberty of Langbargh; 6 miles NW. of Whitby. Here are very extensive alum works, belonging to Lord Mulgrave. The coast at this place is steep and rocky, and in the rocks are several large excavations, which may be entered at low water, and afford curious and romantic retreats. In the rocks here, and at Sands End, (another establishment of alum works, belonging to the same proprietor,) is frequently found Black Amber, or, Jet, by some naturalists called Gagates, which, according to Camden, was classed by the ancients among the rarest jewels.

Birks John, vict. Anchor
Mackridge Wm. agent, Alum Works
Wilson Francis, farmer

KILBURN, (High & Low) in the parish of Low Kilburn, wap. of Birdforth, & liberties of Ripon & Pickering Lythe; 7 mls. SSE. of Thirsk. Pop. 500.

Horner George, gentleman
Horner Rev. John
Quihampton Mrs. gentlewoman

| Blacksmiths, | Wood Joseph |
| Braithwaite Wm. | Shoemakers, |
| Mensforth Geo. | Burton George |
| Butchers, | Metcalf Richard |
| Cobb Joseph | Yellow James |
| Gamble Thomas | Shopkeepers, |
| Horseman Chas. | Barker James |
| Farmers & Yeomen, | Braithwaite Wm. |
| Bellwood Wm. | Gamble Thomas |
| Bolton Wm. | Kay James |
| Coates George | Stone Masons, |
| Eashalby Wm. | Ellis John |
| Horner Robert | Taylor Thos. |
| Horseman John | Tailors, |
| Kirk Wm. | Salmon James |
| Kirk Christ. | Skilbeck Thos. |
| Kirk Thomas | Wheelwrights, |
| Noaton Wm. | Elmer Robert |
| Pollard Thomas | Kemp John |
| Smith David | Manfield John |

Bosingwood Christ. linen manufr.
Kemp John, joiner
Mensforth G. vict. Hammer & Pincers
Pollard Wm. vict. Mariners' Compass

Umpleby John, vict. Black Horse

KILDALE, (P.) in the wap. and liberty of Langbargh; 6 miles S. of Guisborough. The church, which is a very ancient structure, is dedicated to St. Cuthbert, and stands in a low retired situation, at a little distance from the village, towards the south, and not far from the site of an old castle. There is nothing in the style of architecture of the present edifice that points out the era of its foundation; but, upon the authority of Domesday book, where the church is mentioned, we may conclude it to be of great antiquity, and it was probably founded at an early period of the Saxon Heptarchy. The living is a rectory, in the patronage of Robert Bell Livesey, Esq.: incumbent, the Rev. J. Holmes.    Pop. 200.

Robert Bell Livesey, Esq. Kildale hall

| Farmers, | Martin John |
| Barr Robert | Miles John |
| Clough Wm. | Skene Thos. |
| Eeles Nathaniel | Willis Peter |
| Featherston Rt. | Shoemakers, |
| Featherston Thos. | Coward John |
| Hewgill Daniel | Tate John |

Bumby A. vict. Blacksmiths' Arms
Clough Wm. butter factor
Summers Wm. wheelwright
Summers Thomas, shopkeeper
Willis Peter, bleacher and mfr.

*Kilgram Bridge*, in the parish of East Witton, wap. of Hang West, and liberty of Richmondshire; 4 miles NW. of Masham.

*Killerby*, in the parish of Catterick, wap. of Hang East, and liberty of Richmondshire; 6 miles SE. of Richmond: the residence of John Booth, Esq.    Pop. 48.

*Killerby*, in the parish of Cayton, wap. and liberty of Pickering Lythe, 6 miles WNW. of Scarborough.

*Kilmont Scar*, in the parish of Bowes, wap. of Gilling West, and liberty of Richmondshire; 3 miles S. of Barnard Castle.

*Kilton*, in the parish of Brotton, wap. and liberty of Langbargh; 7 miles NE. of Guisbro'. The castle and lordship of Kilton formerly belonged to the very ancient family of Thwengs, and then had the following hamlets belonging to them; viz. Liverton, Thorp Skelton, Easington, Skinnergrave, &c. Pop. 100.

*Kilton Thorpe*, in the parish of Brotton, wap. and liberty of Langbargh; 6 miles NE. of Guisbro'.

*Kilvington North*, in the parish of Thornton-le-Street, wap. and liberty of Allertonshire; 2 miles N. of Thirsk. Here is a Roman Catholic chapel, of which the Rev. Mr. Lawson is the priest. Pop. 68.

KILVINGTON SOUTH, (P.) in the wap. of Birdforth; 1 mile N. of Thirsk. The church here is dedicated to St. Wilfred; the living is a rectory, in the patronage of Sydney College, Cambridge. Pop. 260.

Green Rev. John, B. D. rector
Bosomworth John, yeoman
Henson John, yeoman
Waters Anthony, yeoman

| *Farmers,* | Rowell Thos. (& |
| Archbold Thos. | linen mfr.) |
| Brown John | Smails John |
| Morrell Thos. | *Shoemakers,* |
| Naylor Wm. | Palliser Thos. |
| Palliser Richard | Rymer Robert |

Brown Thomas, vict. Bay Horse
Kilvington Charles, bacon factor, and vict. Green Tree
Wright Wm. corn miller

KINGTHORPE, in the parish of Pickering, wap. & liberty of Pickering Lythe; 3 m. NE. of Pickering. Pop. 52.
Fothergill, Colonel John

*Kiplin,* in the parish of Catterick, wap. of Gilling East, and liberty of Richmondshire; 7 mls. NW. of Northallerton. Pop. 100.

*Kirkby Sigston,* see Sigston.

*Kirk Bridge,* in the parish of Bedale, wap. of Hang East, & liberty of Richmondshire; 1 m. NW. of Bedale.

*Kirkby Cold,* (P.) in the wap. of Birdforth; 5 miles W. of Helmsley. The church is an ancient edifice, in the diocese of Chester; the living is a donative in the patronage of Thos. Duncombe, Esq. of which the Rev. Geo. Dixon, is curate. Pop. 185.

KIRKBY FLEETHAM; (P.) in the wap. of Hang East, & liberty of Richmondshire; 5 miles NE. of Bedale. At Kirkby is a beautiful seat of Mrs. Lawrence, of Studley, and Fleetham is a most delightful little village adjoining. The houses are scattered round the sides of a spacious green, and interspersed with large trees. The church is dedicated to St. Mary; and the living is a vicarage in the patronage of the King. Pop. 556.

Blaister Rev. William, vicar
Kirtley John, gentleman
Strangeways Richard, gentleman

| *Butchers,* | Charge Robert |
| Hodgson Austin, (&Jackson Henry |
| vict.) Black Tot | Lintil John |
| *Pybus Henry* | Poole Wm. |
| *Farmers,* | Pybus Thos. |
| *Lowe John* | Robinson John |

*Shoemakers,* Kirton John
Burgess Wm.
Burgess Thomas, corn miller
Foss George, schoolmaster
Fryer John, veterinary surgeon
Henderson John, joiner & cabinet mkr.
Leconby Wm. blacksmith and vict.
Three Tuns
Pearson William, tailor
Plews John, common brewer
Tennant T. master of national school

KIRKBY-IN-CLEVELAND, (P.) in the wap. and liberty of Langbargh; 2 miles SSE. of Stokesley. Is pleasantly situated at the foot of a continued ridge of mountains. The ancient church, dedicated to St. Austin, was built in the form of a cross, but it was taken down, and replaced in the year 1815, by an edifice larger, and more convenient, though in a more plain and homely style. The living is a *(sinecure)* rectory, in the gift of the Archbishop of York, with a vicarage in the patronage of the rector. The Rev. L. V. Vernon, A. M. is the rector, and the Rev. W. D. Willis, A. M. the vicar. There is here a Grammar School, founded by Henry Edmunds, Esq. in the year 1663, who endowed it with a farm, at Broughton, value 50l. a year, and upwards, with a school house and garden, for ever, for the benefit of all poor children in the townships of Kirkby and Broughton; also a Sunday school established by subscription, in which 60 children are instructed under the inspection of the vicar. Here is also a parochial library for the free use of the parish, consisting of books selected from the list of the Society for promoting Christian knowledge. Pop. 168.

Hildyard Robert, Esq.
Moor Lieut. R. N.
Sanders Ann, gentlewoman
Willis Mary, gentlewoman

| *Yeoman,* | Smith William, |
| Cass Thomas | (butcher) |
| Garbutt John | *Shoemakers,* |
| Harrison Robert | Garbutt Wm. |
| Priestman Wm. | Harrison Wm. |

KIRKBY-KNOWLE, (P.) in the wap. of Birdforth; 5 miles NNE. of Thirsk. The living of the church is a rectory in the patronage of Sir T. Frankland, Bart. Pop. 138.

Smyth Mrs. Mary, lady of the manor, New buildings
Sergeantson Rev. James, rector
Foster Rev. George, curate

| *Farmers,* | Hodgson Geo. |
| Close Hannah | Rose Mary |
| Gibson Charles | Thompson Geo. |
| Hall Thomas, (& | Wilson Joseph |
| carpenter) | |

Danby James, boot and shoe maker
Nelson John, schoolmaster

KIRKBY-MISPERTON, or KIRKBY-OVER-CARR, (P.) in the wap. & liberty of Pickering Lythe; 4 miles SSW. of Pickering. The church is dedicated to St. Lawrence, and the living is a rectory, in the patronage of C. Duncombe, Esq. Here is also a Free School, salary 10l. per annum. Pop. 170.

Blomberg Rev. Dr. Kirkby hall, chaplain to his Majesty
Gray Rev. Edmund, D. D. rector

## KIRKBY, OR KIRKBY-MOOR-SIDE, (P.)

In the wap. of Rydale; 6 miles from Helmsley, 8 from Pickering, 14 from Malton, and 29 from York. This manor which formerly belonged to the Earls of Westmoreland, was forfeited; and tradition says, that Ralph, Earl of Westmoreland, by whose rebellion the estate was forfeited, in the reign of Elizabeth, made his escape from hence into Scotland, in the time of a deep snow, and eluded his pursuers by having the shoes of his horse reversed; and that the descendants of the blacksmith, who turned the shoes, enjoy at this day a house, as a reward for their ancestor's service, at the rent of a farthing a year. The manor remained in the Crown, till the reign of James I. when the favourite Duke of Buckingham, having obtained Helmsley, by his marriage with the heiress of the Earl of Rutland, is said to have begged it of the King, as a garden to that famous mansion. His son George, who married Mary, the only daughter of Thomas Lord Fairfax, after a dissolute life died in extreme want at a humble house in the Market place.* The manufacture of linen is carried on here, but not extensively. The agricultural product of the country consists of all kinds of English grain, and the mineral productions are lime, coal, and freestone. The church is dedicated to All Saints; and the living is a vicarage in the gift of the King. There are here a Methodist chapel, an independent chapel, and a Friends' Meeting house. The market is on Wednesday. Pop. 1878.

POST-MASTER, ROBERT COOPER, Crown Square.

\*\*\* A Horse Post from York & Heimsley, arr. 8 morning, dep. 12 noon.

### DIRECTORY.

Atkinson Francis, Esq. Dale end
Atkinson Mrs. gentlwmn. Market pl.
Bearcroft William, Esq. Castlegate

* See Helmsley.

Coverdale Henry, churchwarden
Eastmead Rev. Wm. Independent minister, Market place
Garbutt Lavina, gentwmn. Market pl.
Harrison Thomas, coroner of Kirkby Moor-Side
Harrison Hannah, gentwmn. West end
King Rev. Henry, West end
Petch Hannah, gentlwmn. How end
Poole James, churchwarden
Seaton Margaret, gentwn. Market pl.
Simpson Francis, gent. West end
Smyth Rev. Joseph, A. B. rect. Market place
Watson John, Esq. Jobs Hall street

*Academy, (Boarding and Day.)*
Jackson Wm. Jobs Hall street

*Attornies.*
Boys Thomas, West end
Garbutt Wm. Market place
Petch Robert, How end

*Bacon and Butter Factor,*
Potter Geo. Market place

*Blacksmiths.*
Carter Thomas, Piercy end
Garbutt Wm. Market place
Pilmer John, West end

*Boot and Shoemakers.*
Bradley John, Piercy end
Cattle James, West end
Charter John, Market place
Dobson James, Dale end
Ellerker Matthew, West end
Hebron Wm. How end
Hewerton Thomas, West end
Porteus Moses, How end
Sample James & Robert, How end
Sample John, West end

*Braziers and Tinplate Workers.*
Calvert Henry, Market place
Steward Henry, Market place

*Butchers.*
Blakelock John, Piercy end
Bower George, West end
Fisher James, West end
Fisher Charles, Castlegate
Graystock John, Castlegate
Hornsey Robert, Piercy end

*Coopers.*
Judson Brook, Dale end
Sonley Robert, West end

*Druggist,*
Lockey Wm. Market place

*Farmers and Yeomen.*
Barker Robert, West end
Fenwick Matthew, Market place
Leckonby John, Jobs Hall street
Shepherd Robert, Bowforth
Shepherd Joseph, Southfield
Sturdy John, Dale end

*Fire and Life Office,*
County, Christphr. Robinson, West end

*Flax Dressers.*
Gibson Thomas, Piercy end
Harwood Ralph, (and spirit dealer)
   Jobs Hall street
Potter Geo. Market place
Tindall Alexander, West end
Walker James, Piercy end

*Grocers and Tea Dealers.*
Ainsley Joseph, Piercy end
Cole & Frank, Market place
Dowson Thomas, Market place
Hugill Wm. Market place
Potter Geo. Market place
Sowray Thos. (& chandler) West end
Warrener Jeremiah, How end
Wood Wm. Market place

*Inns and Taverns.*
Black Swan, John Potter, (brewer &
   maltster) Market place
Crown, Peter Snowden, Crown sqr.
Dog & Duck, Richard Ransom, Mar-
   ket place
George & Dragon, Wm. Wood, Mar-
   ket place
Green Dragon, John Atkinson, Mar-
   ket place
Hare Inn, John Leng, Market place
King's Head, Henry King, Market pl.
Queen's Head, Wm. Smithies, Mar-
   ket place
Red Lion, Wm. Chapman, Crown sq.
White Horse, R. Harwood, (& post-
   ing house) West end

*Ironmongers.*
Blades John, Market place
Clark John, (rod and bar iron mer-
   chant) Crown square

*Joiners and Cabinet Makers.*
Bailey George, joiner
Clark John, (& toys) Crown square
Clark Cornelius, (and auctioneer,)
   Crown square
Potter George, Market place

*Linen and Woollen Drapers.*
Cole & Frank, Market place
Dowson Thos. (and tallow chandler)
   Market place
Fletcher Hannah, (linen) Market pl.
Haigh Geo. Piercy end
Hardy John, West end
Hill Nicholas, (linen) West end
Wood Wm. (linen) Market place

*Linen Manufacturers.*
Gill Wm. & John, Piercy end

*Plumber and Glazier.*
Dawson Thomas, West end

*Printer—Letter Press.*
Cooper Robert, Crown square

*Saddlers.*
Barwick Matthias, Market place
Webster John, Jobs Hall street

*Shopkeepers.*
Atkinson John, Market place
Charter Jeremiah, West end
Siddons James, Market place

*Stone Masons.*
Holliday John, Castlegate
Rickaby Thomas, West end

*Straw Hat Manufacturers.*
Baines Hannah, Market place
Clark Jane, Market place
Kay Elisabeth, Crown square

*Surgeons.*
Chapman Richard, Piercy end
Harrison Thomas, West end
Shepherd Joseph, How end

*Tailors.*
Coning Joseph, West end
Hall George, Piercy end
Hardy John, West end
Jackson John, Market place

*Watch and Clock Makers.*
Blades John, Market place
Ness Wm. West end

*Miscellany.*
Boys Christopher, Castlegate
Charter Wm. perfumer, Market place
Easterby Wm. gunsmith, Market pl.
Ellerker Christopher, rope maker,
   Piercy end
Ellerker Wm. gardener, Jobs Hall st.
Hall Joseph, patten maker & clogger,
   How end
Hart John, wheelwright, How end
Hugill John, surveyor of highways
Jefferson A. bookbinder, Market pl.
Newton Wm. constable
Pattison Samuel, Castlegate
Reed Thomas, exciseman, West end
Robinson John, corn miller, How end
   and Kirkby mills
Wake Geo. machine maker, How end
Wilson John, perpetual overseer

CARRIERS.

George Pearson, to Malton, Tu. and
   Sat. dep. 5 mg. ret. 6 evg.
John Pearson, (to the White Horse,)
   from Scarbro', arr. Fri. 3 aft. dep.
   6 evg. on Sat. by way of Pickering
John Wood, from Pickering, arr. Fri.
   3 aft. dep. Sat. 6 evg.
Joseph Worthy, to Malton, Tu. and
   Sat. dep. 5 mg. ret. 6 evg.
John Wrightson, to York, Thu. dep.
   1 mg. ret. Fri. 6 evg. & occasion-
   ally to Malton.

KIRKBY-ON-THE-MOOR, (P.) in
the wap. of Halikeld, and liberty of
Allertonshire; 1 mile N. of Boroughbridge. Here is a small parish church,
dedicated to All Saints; the living is a
vicarage, in the patronage of the King

and the Rev. Henry Kitchingham, A.M. is the incumbent. Pop. 190.

Hodgson Rev. Joseph, curate (academy for gentlemen)

| Farmers, | Parker George |
|---|---|
| Brotherton John | Parker George |
| Greaves James | Pick Wm. |
| Parker Wm. | Rowland James |

Brown George, blacksmith
Coates Thomas, carpenter
Coates John, parish clerk & sexton
Hanby Matthew, vict. White Horse
Pickering Grace, common brewer, maltster & vict. Blue Bell
Smithson John, schoolmaster
Walls Matthew, timber merchant

KIRKBY - RAVENSWORTH, or KIRKBY-HILL, (P.) in the wap. of Gilling West, and liberty of Richmondshire; 5 mls. NW. of Richmond. The ancient name seems to have been Kirk by Ravensworth, being the parish Church to six townships, and standing near the village of Ravensworth. The village is situated upon a hill, and the houses form a square. The church, dedicated to St. John, the Baptist, is a neat stone building, and from its white appearance, and elevated situation, seems well adapted to remind the neighbouring villagers of their great duty; it is in the diocese of the Bishop of Chester, who receives the corn tithes, and is the patron of the living. There are two Schools here, one a boarding school of some repute, for young gentlemen, the other is a Free Grammar School, founded and endowed by Dr. Dakin, Archdeacon of the East Riding, about the year 1555. It is free for as many young men and boys as may resort to it, to be instructed in grammar and classical learning; there is also an Hospital connected with the endowment, for twenty-four aged persons of both sexes, to be selected from those that were born in the parish, or have lived ten years in it. The endowment of the School, together with the Hospital, is in lands, situated principally in the parish of East Coulton, and the corn tithe arising from the parish of East Coulton, amounts to upwards of 1200l. per annum. The salary of the master is about 300l. per ann. varying however, with the rent; the usher has a third of the sum. The master must be a clergyman, in priests orders, and cannot hold any church benefice. The whole is under the management of two wardens, who, with the minister and poor people form a body corporate, and use one common seal. The office of warden is biennial, and the election, is conducted thus: the Churchwardens for the time being, with the Clergyman, nominate six householders, whose names are written upon scrolls of paper, wrapt up in balls of wax, and put in a jar or pitcher, when the minister puts in his hand and takes two out, and the persons whose names are therein written, are immediately sworn into office; they are the patrons of the living of East Coulton. The School and Hospital are dedicated to St. John, the Baptist. Cuthbert Shaw, the poet, was born at this place. Pop. 161.

A Foot Post, Mon. Thu. and Sat.

Buxton Rev. Thos. perpetual curate
Jackson Rev. Thos. master of grammar school
Wilkinson John, gent.

Bolding Wm. schoolmaster
Coates Isaac, farmer
Cuthbert A. vict. Shoulder of Mutton
Johnson John, farmer
Lambert J. usher of grammar school

KIRKBY-WISKE, (P.) in the wap. of Gilling East, and liberty of Richmondshire; 4 miles WNW. of Thirsk. Here is a church, dedicated to St. John the Baptist, patron the Duke of Northumberland. Pop. 107.

Rev. Christopher Bethel, D.D. rector

KIRKDALE, (P.) in the wap. of Rydale; 2 miles W. of Kirkby-Moor-Side. The church belonging to this village, is situated in the southern extremity of this vale, in a most sequestered but beautiful spot, surrounded with woods, and has been much noticed, on account of a very ancient Saxon inscription over the south door, which may be thus translated:—Orm, Gamal's son, bought St. Gregory's church, when it was all gone to ruin and fallen down; and he agreed with Maccan, to renew it from the ground to Christ and St. Gregory, in Edward's days, the king; and Tosti's days, the Earl. This is a draught exhibiting the time of the day, while the sun is passing to and from the winter solstice. Hawarth me made, and Brand the priest." This inscription fixes the antiquity of the church. Tosti or Tosti, the fourth son of Godwin Earl of Kent, and brother of King Harold, was created Earl of Northumberland, by Edward the Confessor, in the year 1056, and fell at the battle of Stamford Bridge, in 1066,[*] so that the erection of this church was antecedent to the Norman Conquest, a thing so rare, that there are not above three or four churches of so ancient a date in the [k]ingdom. The living of Kirkdale, after passing through a variety of patrons, came into possession of Henry Danvers, Earl of Danby, who give it to the University of Oxford, about the year 1632, when he founded the Physic

* See this Vol. page 21.

Garden there. The incumbent is the Rev. George Dixon.

*The Cave of Kirkdale.*—The fossil remains of the hyæna and other animals have been found in a cave or fissure at this place; in the year 1820, Professor Buckland examined this interesting spot with great care, and communicated the result of his inquiries to the Royal Society of London. The Professor reports, that the cave extends 300 feet into a solid white rock, and varies from 2 feet to 5 feet in height and breadth. Its bottom is covered with a layer, about a foot thick of mud, which is partially encrusted with calcsinter. It is in this mud that the fossil animal remains are found imbedded. The bones are in a nearly fresh state, still retaining their animal gelatin. They are mostly broken and gnawed in pieces, and are intermixed with teeth. The fossil remains found by Professor Buckland were of the following animals, viz. hyæna, elephant, rhinoceros, hippopotamus, deer, ox, and water rat; the four first belong to species now extinct, but of the others nothing is said. It is evident that animals having the magnitude of the elephant, or rhinoceros, could not enter a fissure so low and narrow as that at this place; and it appears probable that these bones could not have been floated into the fissure by means of water, otherwise they would not only have suffered by attrition, but would be intermixed with sand or gravel. They must therefore have been transported thither in some other way, and the Professor conjectures, that they were carried in for food by the hyænas, who appear to have been the sole inhabitants of the den.

KIRKLEATHAM, (P.) in the wap. and liberty of Langbargh; 4¼ miles NNW. of Guisbrough, situate near the mouth of the Tees, the birth-place of Sir William Turner, who was Lord Mayor of London in the year 1669; and here that gentleman erected a stately hospital, which he endowed with a valuable estate, for the maintenance of 40 poor people, namely, 10 men, the same number of women, 10 boys and 10 girls; and a sum of money was also bequeathed by John Turner, Esq. Serjeant at Law, for clothing each of the children on leaving the hospital. Lady Turner, now Vansittart, is the sole governess of this charity, which office descends on the possessor of the Kirkleatham estate for ever; and the management is committed to a chaplain, a master, and a mistress, who have handsome salaries. In the centre of the front is a small chapel, finished in a style of superior elegance. The roof is arched in compartments, and supported by four light and handsome

columns of the Ionic order; from the centre hangs a large chandelier of burnished gold, and over the altar is a window of painted glass, esteemed one of the finest in the world, representing the offerings of the Magi at the nativity of Christ. On one side is a full length figure of John Turner, Esq. Serjeant at Law, in a scarlet robe; and on the other, one of Sir William Turner, the founder, in his robes as Lord Mayor of London. In a large and commodious room, within the hospital, is the library, which is furnished with many valuable books, and several natural and artificial curiosities. In a handsome case, is a striking likeness of Sir William Turner, in wax, with the identical wig and band which he used to wear. At a short distance from the hospital is the parish church, dedicated to St. Cuthbert, a light and elegant building of stone, the roof of which is supported by six columns of the Tuscan order. In the chancel is the monument of Sir William Turner, near which he was buried, by his own desire, among the poor of his hospital; the witnesses of his piety, liberality, and humanity. The living is a vicarage, in the patronage of Lady Turner. Adjoining to the east end of the church, is a superb mausoleum of a circular form, covered with a dome, built by Cholmley Turner, Esq. in 1740, under which is the family vault. Among other monumental statues are those of that gentleman, and William Turner, Esq. executed by the famous Schemacher. The improvements made at Kirkleatham in agriculture, and planting, by the late Sir Charles Turner, rank this place amongst one of the most flourishing estates in Yorkshire. In addition to the hospital, Sir Wm. Turner bequeathed 5000*l.* for founding a Free Grammar School here, which was erected in 1709, by Cholmley Turner, Esq. his nephew, and is a large and handsome quadrangular building, near the hospital. Of the present state of this institution, Mr. Carlisle, in his "description of the endowed schools of England and Wales," published in 1818, gives the following singular account;—" The master's salary is 100*l.* and that of the usher 50*l.* but both these offices are now *sinecures*, the school having been entirely "*discontinued*" about thirty years since, by the late Sir Charles Turner. The building contained apartments for the master and usher, as well as the school-room; but *it is now occupied in tenements by various mechanics, &c. servants to Lady Turner.* Mr. John Irvine, the family *steward*, holds the *sinecure* office of *Master*, and the Rev. Mr. Shaw, the minister of Kirkleatham, that of *Usher*. The lord or lady of the manor of Kirkleatham, who is sole governor or governess of the hospital, is sole trustee for the school also. Pop. 636.

Vansittart Henry, Esq.
Shaw Rev. Edward
Bailey Charles, surgeon

| Farmers, | Smith Andrew |
| Duck Wm. | Thompson Geo. |
| King Thos. & com- | |
| mon brewer | |

Bailey Eliz. schoolmistress
Heathwaite Wm. vict. Turner's Arms
Robinson Geo. wheelwright
Wrightson Thos. schoolmaster

KIRKLEVINGTON, (P.) in the wap. and liberty of Langbargh; 2 miles SS E. of Yarm. The church, dedicated to St. Martin, is a small ancient structure. The living is a perpetual curacy, in the patronage of the Archbishop of York, of which the Rev. John Greaves is the incumbent. Here also was a castle, which anciently belonged to the family of Meinills; after passing through several other families, it was at last parcelled out to different purchasers; a circumstance hence, called Castle Hill, is the only vestige of that ancient fortress. Pop. 282.

M'Cleod John, gentleman

| Farmers, | Hilstrop John |
| Coates Wm. | Tweddle Robert |
| Elders Wm. | Wheelwrights, |
| Rickaby John | Bell John |
| Wilkinson Henry | Naggs John, & ma- |
| Shoemakers, | chine maker |
| Grear Wm. | |

Bell Wm. bailiff
Brown John, vict. & blacksmith, Crown
Greenwell Atkinson, grocer and corn miller
Hull John, tailor

KIRKLINGTON (with Upsland,) (P.) in the wap. of Hallikeld, and liberty of Richmondshire; 6 miles SSE. of Bedale.— Here is a large and handsome church. The living is a rectory, in the patronage of Lady Ormond, and the Rev. Thomas Place is the incumbent. Here is also a Free School, with a small endowment, left by Lady Ormond. This neighbourhood abounds with vestiges of antiquities, particularly the entrenchment of a Roman or Danish camp. Pop. 237.

Britain John, Esq. banker
Morley Rev. T. W. curate
Richardson Wm. gentleman

| Farmers, | Kettlewell A. |
| Appleton James | Smith Richard |
| Crook Robert | Thompson Wm. |
| Deighton Francis | Tomlington Matt. |
| Ellerton Francis | Ward Geo. |

Warrington Wm.
Wells Thos.
Shoemakers,
Hewson Abm.

Pickersgill Thos.
Tailors,
Hunter Anthony
Place Robt. & parish clerk

Bell Robert, victualler and carpenter, Royal Oak
Brown Edw. vict. Golden Lion
Deighton John, vict. Golden Lion, Leeming lane
Hunter Anthony, vict. King's Head
Kirby John, blacksmith
Lomas James, schoolmaster
Smith Wm. wheelwright
Tomlington Marmaduke, grocer

KNAYTON, in the parish of Leak, wap. and liberty of Allertonshire; 4 miles N. of Thirsk. Here is a Methodist chapel. Pop. including Brawith, 377.

Consitt Warcup, Esq. Brawith hall
Brown Miss Eliz. gentlewoman
Dunn Miss Eliz. gentlewoman
Kay Mrs. Hannah, gentlewoman
Pollard Mrs. Jane, gentlewoman
Rainton John, gentleman

| Blacksmiths, | Wilson R. E. & R. |
| Ingledew James | Wise Wm. |
| Prest Thos. | Wood John |
| Butchers, | Shoemakers, |
| Miller Wm. | Burton Wm. |
| Wise Robt. | Harland Richard |
| Farmers, | Stone masons, |
| Fawcett Joseph | Blades Thos. |
| Harland Wm. | Blades Nathan |
| Langdale Thos. | Blades John |
| Langdale John | Surgeons, |
| Nicholson John | Cowper Joseph |
| Pybus Thos. | Ripley John |
| Rawling Thos. | Tailors, |
| Shepherd Thos. | Coates Thos. |
| Wilkinson James | Edon Matthew |

Barker Thos. vict. Dog & Gun
Fisher Hannah, vict. Three Tuns
Hammond Wm. shopkeeper
Harland John, vict. Fox & Hounds
Hunter Wm. coach varnish maker
Langdale John, schoolmaster
Wass Wm. bacon and butter factor

Kneeton Under, in the parish of Middleton Tyas, wap. of Gilling East, and liberty of Richmondshire; 6 miles NNE. of Richmond.

Lackenby, in the parish of Wilton, wap. and liberty of Langbargh; 4 miles NW. of Guisborough.

Laith, see Lane Dale.

LAMBHILL, in the parish of Masham, wap. of Hang East, and liberty of Richmondshire; 2 miles SE. of Masham. The residence of Mrs. Ann Wilkinson.

*Lambhill*, in the parish of Bowes, and wap. of Gilling West; 3 miles SSW. of Barnard Castle.

*Landmoth*, in the parish of Leak, wap. and liberty of Allertonshire; 4 miles SE. of Northallerton. Population, including Catto, 59.

*Lane End*, in the parish of St. John Stanwick, wap. of Gilling West, and liberty of Richmondshire; 5 miles W. of Darlington.

*Lane Head*, in the parish of Hutton Magnum, wap. of Gilling West, and liberty of Richmondshire; 8 miles NNW. of Richmond.

*Langbargh*, in the parish of Ayton, wap. and liberty of Langbargh; 3 mls. NE. of Stokesley, a ridge of rocks, where it is supposed the wapentake courts were anciently held, and whence this wapentake is denominated.

*Langthorne*, in the parish of Bedale, and wap. of Halikeld; 2½ mls. NNW. of Bedale. Population, 135.

LANGTHORPE, in the parish of Kirby Hill, and wap. of Halikeld; ½ a mile NW. of Boroughbridge. Pop. 148.

Parker William, gentleman
Ruston Mrs. Ann, gentlewoman
Stubbs Joseph, yeoman
Yates Thomas, yeoman

Brotherton Francis, common brewer
Farmery Richard, vict. Fox & Hounds
Harker Geo. corn and coal dealer
Parker Thos. farmer, Broom house
Winoup John, vict. Red Lion

*Langthwaite*, see Arkengarthdale.

LANGTON GREAT, (P.) in the wap. of Gilling East, and liberty of Richmondshire; 6 mls. NW. of Northallerton; pleasantly situated on the banks of the Swale. The church living is a rectory, in the patronage of the Duke of Leeds, of which the Rev. Francis Drake, D.D. is the resident incumbent. Population, 116.

LANGTON LITTLE, in the parish of Great Langton, wap. of Gilling East, and liberty of Richmondshire; 5 miles WNW. of Northallerton. Red-fearn Francis, Esq. of the lodge, is the principal inhabitant. Pop. 86.

*Langwith*, or *Longwith*, in the parish of Well, wap. of Hang East, and liberty of Richmondshire; 3 miles S. of Bedale.

LARTINGTON, in the parish of Romaldkirk, wap. of Gilling West, and liberty of Richmondshire; 3 miles WNW. of

Barnard Castle, a neat rural village, the houses on one side having gardens before them, inclosed by pales, and on the other side a spacious green, shaded by lofty trees. At the foot of the village stands Lartington Hall, the seat and residence of Henry Witham, Esq. the proprietor of the village, and the lord of the manor. This is an ancient stone building, in a well wooded and pleasingly diversified park, terminating on the banks of the Tees. The Catholic chapel of the hall is one of the most handsome in the kingdom, and contains one of the best paintings in imitation of sculpture extant; it is a crucifix, executed by Le Brun, in so masterly a manner, as to deceive the most able connoisseurs. Here is a Free School, endowed with 20l. a year, by the present lord of the manor.— Population, 243.

Witham Henry, Esq. hall
Ellis Rev. Michael, Catholic priest

*Farmers,*
Bayles John
Dent Thomas
Boldron William, schoolmaster
Davison William, groom
Lawson M. agent to H. Witham, Esq.
Maddison Robert, vict. Turk's Head
Robinson John, cabinet maker
Thompson Launcelot, blacksmith

Heslop Peter, and yeoman
Parkin William

*Laskill*, in the parish of Helmsley, and wap. of Rydale; 5½ miles NW. of Helmsley. Pop. 91.

LASTINGHAM, (P.) in the wap. of Rydale; 4 miles NNE. of Kirkby-Moor-Side. Here was formerly a Benedictine monastery, founded by Cedd, Bishop of the East Saxons, about the year 648. The church is a very large and ancient structure, and has, in all probability, belonged to the monastery. The living is a vicarage, in the gift of the King, of which the Rev. W. N. Darnell is the incumbent. Here is also a Methodist chapel. Population, 225.

Blakelock Ann & Martha, gentlewomen
Kendall Rev. Henry, curate

*Laysthorpe*, in the parish of Stonegrave, and wap. of Rydale; 4 miles S. of Helmsley.

LAYTON (East), in the parish of St. John Stanwick, wap. of Gilling West, & liberty of Richmondshire; 6½ miles N. of Richmond. Is a pleasant agricultural village situated on an eminence, and commanding an extensive and beautiful prospect. Pop. 137.

Barker Thomas, Esq. Layton hall

*Farmers,*
Barker Thomas
Ellis Thomas
Harrison Henry
Thompson John

Fenwick Ralph, vict. and butcher
Pearson Michael, blacksmith
Young Christopher, wheelwright

LAYTON (West), in the parish of Hutton, wap. of Gilling West, and liberty of Richmondshire; 7 miles N NW. of Richmond. Pop. 69.

Colling John, Esq. White house
Powell Samuel, farmer
Waine George, farmer

*Lazenby*, in the parish of North-allerton, and wap. of Allertonshire; 4 miles N. of Northallerton.

LAZENBY, in the parish of Wilton, wap. and liberty of Langbargh; 5 mls. NW. of Guisborough.

Dryden Consitt, Esq.
Buckton John, gentleman

LEAK, (P.) in the wap. & liberty of Allertonshire; 6 miles ESE. of Northallerton. The church and farm house are all the remains of Leak, once a large town, but which was destroyed about the time of the Norman Conquest. The living is a vicarage, in the patronage of the Bishop of Durham, and the Rev. W. Warrington is the incumbent. Mr. William Morton, yeoman, resides at the hall. Population, 11.

LEALHOLM AND LEALHOLM BRIDGE, in the parish of Danby, wap. and liberty of Langbargh; 9 miles W. of Whitby.

| *Blacksmiths,* | Hebron George |
| Miller William | Hoggart George |
| Rodgers Richard | Lacey John |
| *Butchers,* | Mead Wm. |
| Brunton Wm. | Parks John |
| Winsper Wm. | Rigg Richard |
| *Corn Millers,* | Watson Ralph |
| Stobbart Thos. | Watson Richard |
| Stonehouse Henry | Winspear John |
| *Farmers,* | Winspear Pennick |
| Brunton John | Wood Thomas |
| Dennison Thos. | *Shoemakers,* |
| Fletcher John | Bonnus Joseph |
| Garnett Benjamin | Burrow Richard |
| Hall John | Winsby James |
| Harrison Wm. | Wood Joseph |

Bell Joseph, tailor
Gray Robert, vict. & tallow chandler
Hall Matthew, wheelwright
Joy William, blue, brown, and shop paper manufacturer
Readman Thomas, vict. Stone Gate
Snowden Michael, cooper
Yeoman William, corn miller

*Leashead*, in the parish of Whitby, wap. and liberty of Whitby Strand; 7 miles from Whitby.

LEAVINGTON CASTLE, in the parish of Kirk Leavington, wap. & liberty of Langbargh; 2 miles SE. of Yarm. Mr. John Hewitt occupies the house called the White Hall, and Mr. J. T. Sheraton the Red Hall; the mill is occupied by Mr. James Wren. Pop. 44.

LEBBERSTON, in the parish of Filey, wap. and liberty of Pickering Lythe; 4 miles N. of Hunmanby. The hall here is occupied by Mr. Robert Shepherd. Pop. 143.

*Leckby*, in the parish of Cundall, wap. of Halikeld, and liberty of Richmondshire; 5 miles NNE. of Boroughbridge. Pop. included with Cundall.

LEEMING, in the parish of Burneston, wap. of Halikeld, and liberty of Richmondshire; 2 miles ENE. of Bedale. This ancient village seems to give its name to Leeming lane, which exhibits a fine specimen of the improvements made in public roads in modern times. This road is under the management of Mr. M'Adam, whose simple but efficient system consists principally in so constructing the road as to make all parts of it equally fit for carriages, and in breaking the materials small which are used in the repairs. This road was the Herman-street of the Romans, which extended northward as far as Inverness. Here is a Chapel of Ease, of which the Rev. J. Monson, A. M. is curate. Population included with Exilby and Newton.

| *Blacksmiths,* | Spence William |
| Pybus Thomas | Sturgess John |
| Robson John, and | *Shoemakers,* |
| farrier | Elwood Mark |
| *Farmers & Yeomen,* | Miller William |
| Bell John | *Shopkeepers,* |
| Boddy John | Chapman Thomas |
| Lascelles George | Outhwaite Leond. |
| Moss William | *Wheelwrights,* |
| Ramshaw Wm. | Holmes Thomas |
| Simpson Christphr. | Wharton Wm. |

Boddy John, butcher
Harrison Wm. corn miller
Nelson George, vict. Rodney
Ramshaw Wm. brick & tile maker
Robinson Bridget, vict. Crown
Wade William, schoolmaster

*Leeming Little*, in the parish of Bedale, wap. of Hang East, & liberty of Richmondshire; 2¼ miles NE. of Bedale.

*Leighton*, in the parish of Masham, and wap. of Hang East; 4 miles W. SW. of Masham.

LEVEN BRIDGE, in the parish of Rudby, wap. & liberty of Langbargh;

2 miles ESE. of Yarm. The mill here is occupied by Mr. William Simpson, corn miller.

*Leven Grove*, see Skutterskelfe.

LEVISHAM, (P.) in the wap. and liberty of Pickering Lythe ; 5 miles N. of Pickering. Here is an ancient church, the living is a rectory, in the patronage of Mrs. Skelton, of which the Rev. Robert Skelton is the resident incumbent. There is also a free school, endowed with 12*l.* per annum. Population, 152.

## LEYBURN,

In the parish of Wensley wap. of Hang West, and liberty of Richmondshire; 3 miles from Middleham, 8 from Richmond, and 8 from Reeth. The town consists chiefly of one spacious oblong square of well-built houses, where the market is held every Friday, and where a considerable quantity of corn is weekly exposed for sale. The places of worship are a Methodist, a Calvinist, and Catholic chapel; there is here a public school, supported by voluntary subscription; and a Circulating and Subscription Library. The soil is generally very fertile, being chiefly meadow and grazing land, and the mineral productions are lead, coal, and lime. The town is pleasantly situated, and the neighbourhood presents a variety of beautifully picturesque scenery. The remarkable walk called Leyburn Shawl, which passes along the edge of one continued ridge of rocks to the village of Preston, is indisputably one of the finest natural terraces in Great Britain, and there are many views here of singular beauty. The neighbourhood abounds with objects of interest, among which may be enumerated the ruined castles of Bolton and Middleham, the remains of Jervaux and Coverham abbeys; the celebrated waterfall and cataracts of Aysgarth, and the noble mansion and pleasure grounds of Bolton Hall, most of which may be visited in the course of a day. This place is generally taken on the route to the Lakes of Westmoreland and Cumberland, by travellers from the east and south east parts of the kingdom. Population, 816.

POST-MASTER, THOMAS FALL, *Office, Market-place.*

Letters arrive every day from Bedale, at 8 o'clock, and are despatched at ½ past 2 o'clock in the afternoon for Bedale.

A post-man is despatched every Mon. Wed. Thur. and Sat. to Askrigg, departs at ½ past 7 o'clock in the morning, and returns at ½ past 2 in the afternoon.

### DIRECTORY.

Allen Wm. gent. Hill Top
Brooks Rev. George, independent minister
Clifton John, Esq. Grove house
Collier James, gentleman
Emmerson George, justice clerk, and commissioner of taxes
Sanderson Charles, gent.
Vincent Captain George
Wray James T. importer of foreign wines and spirits, timber and lead merchant, &c. &c.

*Bank.*

Hutton, Other, & Co. Wensleydale bank, on Sir P. Pole, Bart. Thornton and Co. London.

*Saving's Bank.*

Attendance every Friday from twelve o'clock till one.—James Morland, clerk ; Wm. Ware, treasurer.

*Attornies,*
Dobson Matthew
Howson Wm.
  *Blacksmiths,*
Aisken George
Nicholson R. jun.
Plewes John
  *Boot & Shoemakers,*
Anderson Edw.
Fawcett Christ.
Fishwick Wm.
M'Cullagh Thos.
Mason Wm.
Morland James
Pearson Wm.
Robinson Thos.
Robson Henry
Spence Matth.
Whitehead Geo.
  *Butchers,*
Bowes Emerson
Bowes Wm.
Peacock Matth.
  *Clock & Watch Makers,*
Bell John
Robinson Wm.
  *Drapers,*
Anderson Eliz.
Dent John
Dixon Luke
Metcalf John, (& dealer in hats)
Thackwray Wm.
Wood Thos. (& weaver)
  *Farmers,*
Anderson Henry
Blenkinsop Peter (& woolstapler)

Hayson Thos.
Ianson Wm.
Pearson Henry, How hill
  *Grocers,*
Anderson Eliz.
Dent John
Dobson John, (& tallow chandler)
Fairburn Thos.
Nicholson Rd. (& ironmonger
Orton Mary and Jane
Thackwray Wm.
  *Joiners,*
Chaploe John
Fairburn John
Wells John
Willis Christopher
Winsby Richard
Winsby John
  *Milliners,*
Anderson Eliz.
Lonsdale Grace
Spence Mary
  *Saddlers,*
Atkinson John
Dixon George
  *Shopkeepers,*
Chippindale S. & A.
Ratcliffe James
  *Stone Masons,*
Brotherton Henry
Summers James
Yeadon Thos.
  *Straw Hat Makers,*
Abbot Dorothy
Lawson Mary
Milner Eliz.

Orton Mary and Jane
Spence Mary
Willis Eliz.

*Tailors,*
Alderson Christr.
Auton Wm.
Gale George

*Surgeons,*
Edmondson Thos.
Terry John

Roper Wm.
Rountree Wm.
Rountree Richard

*Hotels, Inns, and Taverns.*

Atkinson Jonathan, Board
Blenkinsop John, Green Tree
Burton Wm. (posting-house) Bolton Arms
Coultman Richard, (excise office) King's Head
Milestone Peter, (and veterinary surgeon) Black Swan
Plewes Wm. vict. Angel Inn
Varo John, (& dram shop) Board

*Miscellany.*

Alderson Walter, schoolmaster, land surveyor, and Sun dial maker
Barker John, governor of the Poor house
Bentley Peter, officer of excise
Brotherton E. dlr. in earthenware
Butterfield William, nursery and seedsman
Day John, cooper
Deighton Henry, plumber & glazier
Coates Thomas, clerk at the Bank
Fall Thomas, (stamp office) bookseller, stationer, and printer
Holmes Leonard, bailiff & auctioneer
Horner Thomas, printer and paper hanger
Husband Wm. bleacher
Milner Geo. bread baker
Morland James, agent to the Norwich Union Fire Office
Pearson Robert, chemist & druggist
Wray John, hair dresser

---

### CARRIERS BY LAND.

William Abbott, to Leeds every Mon. dep. 2 mg. ret. on Wed. evg.
Thomas Blackburn, (waggon) from York to Hawes, arr. at 2 every Mon. ret. every Wed. at 11 o'clock forenoon.
James Cloughton, to Richmond every Thur. and Sat. departs 6 morning, and returns 6 evening; also to Bedale every Tuesday.
James Close, from Reeth to Leeds, arr. here every Sat. & ret. Thur.
James Ratcliffe, to Richmond Thur. and Sat. dep. at 6 mg. and ret. at 6 evg.; and goes to Bedale.
Anthony Thistlethwaite, to Stockton every Mon. and Thur. dep. at 8 mg. ret. on Wed. and Sat.

---

*Lilling,* or *Awbn,* (East & West) in the parish of Sheriff Hutton, and wap. of Bulmer; 9 miles NNE. of York. Pop. 208.

*Limber Hill,* in the parish of Lythe, wap. & liberty of Langbargh; 7 mh. WSW. of Whitby.

*Lingy Moor,* in the parish of Middleton Tyas, and wap. of Gilling East; 6 miles ENE. of Richmond.

*Linthorp,* in the parish of Middlesborough, wap. and liberty of Langbargh; 7 miles NNW. of Stokesley. Population, 196.

*Linton-upon-Ouse,* in the parish of Newton-upon-Ouse, and wap. of Bulmer; 7 miles S. of Easingwold. Here is a Roman Catholic chapel, and a school with a small endowment. Population, 268.

*Litherskew,* in the parish of Aysgarth, wap. of Hang West, and liberty of Richmondshire; 1 mile NE. of Hawes; a small hamlet, pleasantly situated in High Abbot side. Population, 81.

*Little Beck,* in the parish of Whitby, wap. and liberty of Whitby Strand; 6 miles from Whitby.

*Liverton,* in the parish of Easington, wap. and liberty of Langbargh; 8 miles ENE. of Guisborough. There is here a Chapel of Ease to the Parish church of Easington; curate, Rev. James Metcalfe, of Easington. Population, 251.

*Lockton,* in the parish of Middleton, wap. and liberty of Pickering Lythe; 4 miles N. of Pickering.— There is here a Chapel of Ease, and a neat Methodist chapel. Pop. 324.

*Lodge Green,* see Melbecks.

LOFTHOUSE, (P.) in the wap. and liberty of Langbargh; 9 miles ENE. of Guisborough; bounded on the north by the German ocean. It is a pleasant village, forming one continued street, or line of buildings, principally of stone; the neighbourhood abounding with stone and alum rock. The village is chiefly dependent upon the alum works here, belonging to Lord Dundas. There is a market held here on Thursday, by custom; and there is a Methodist chapel, built by subscription in 1828. The church is dedicated to St. Leonard, and the living is a rectory, in the patronage of the King. Pop. including Waplay, 1171.

Adamson Thomas, gent.
Bathgate James, gent.

Cook Paul, gent.
Childs John, gent.
Murray Rev. Wm. rector
Murray Lieut. Alexander
Smith John, gent.
Held Alexander, Esq. hall
Harper Rev. Wm. curate
Yeoman John, surgeon

*Blacksmiths,*
Robinson Henry
Thompson Isaac
*Butchers,*
Dryden Joseph
Mann Wm.
Walker Thos.
*Corn Millers,*
Bell James
Smailes Isaac
*Farmers,*
Atkinson John
Ladus Wm.
Cledson Wm.
Clsse John
Coward Joseph
Crosley Bryan
Crosley John
Crowe John,
Grange
Dryden Francis
Fawcett Nicholas
Hudson John
Leomy J. C.
Taylor Robert
Dotherd Thos.
Peters Wm.
Severs Anthony
Unthank John

Walker John
Wilkinson Mich.
*Shoemakers,*
Brown Joseph
Brown Wm.
Bryan Henry
Harbron John
Hudson Joseph
Irwin John
Watson Wm.
*Shopkeepers,*
Adamson Wm.
Adamson Robert
Langstaff John
Langstaff Eliz.
M'Naughton Geo.
Rowland Thos.
Wilkinson Jacob
*Tailors,*
Briggs Charles
Hull John
Moore Thos. (&
draper
Scarthe Robinson
*Wheelwrights, &c.*
Dobson John
Hudson Edward
Wake John

*Inns and Taverns.*

Allan John, Red Lion
Corner Robert, Angel Inn
Walker Francis, Black Bull

Adamson Thos. T. chandler
Adamson Geo. seedsman
Anderson Eliz. dress maker
Barker Ann, dress maker
Boyes William, stay maker
Barnett John, baker
Corner Robert, master mariner
Cowart Jane, straw hat maker
Dixon Wm. tinman
Fidler George, mason
Goodwill Thomas, clerk
Goodwill John, schoolmaster
Hanton Wm. alum maker
Lowsey Joseph, cooper
Iverend Thomas, slater
Patton Sarah, druggist
Shemilds Esther, straw hat maker
Simpson James, riding officer
Vase Thomas, plumber, glazier, and
tinman
Webster Richard, saddler

Wilkinson Isaac, millwright
Wilson Wm. slater

**LOFTHOUSE SOUTH.**

Burgin James, farmer
Dawson Reeves, shoemaker
Leyburn Wm. joiner
Gordon Thomas, gamekeeper
Wallace Christr. stone mason

*Carriers.*
William Boyes, South Lofthouse, to
Whitby every Fri. dep. at 9 mg.
et. 6 evg.
Thomas Cowart, carrier and post-
man, to Guisborough on Mon.
Thur. and Sat. at 8 o'clock mg.
and ret. 3 afternoon.
Thomas Johnson, passes from Guisborough to Staithes every Wed.
at 10 o'clock morning, returns at
½ past four o'clock; and passes
to Whitby from Guisborough on
Thur. at 10 o'clock morning, and
returns at 4 o'clock on Friday afternoon, to Guisborough.
Robert Naggs, from Guisborough
to Whitby every Thursday at 10
o'clock mg. and returns on Fri. at
4 o'clock aft.
Joseph Walker, to Whitby every
Mon. and Fri. at 9 o'clock mg.
ret. Tu. and Sat. at 6 evg.

**LONDONDERRY,** in the parish of
Burneston, wap. of Halikeld, and liberty of
Richmondshire; 3½ miles E. of Bedale.—
Newton-house, a hunting box, belonging to
the Right Hon. the Earl of Darlington, is
situated in this village. The above house
was sold to Lord Darlington ten or twelve
years ago; and in the latter end of the year
1821, a chimney belonging to it was blown
down, the materials of which were precipitated through the roof, and killed a young
lady in her bed. The house has since been
taken down, and re-built on the site of the
old one, leaving that part upon which the
young lady's room stood a sort of vacuum
in the middle of the house. The Countess
of Darlington educates, at her own expense,
twenty poor children in this township.

Hunton Rev. J. R. M. A. vicar of
Pickhill
Walburn Wm. gent.

*Farmers & Yeomen,* Mason Thomas H.
Dixon Wm.            Newton lodge
Foswick John         Peacock Jonathan
Kirby Jonathan       Turnbull Richard
Geldart Thomas, wheelwright
Hill John, shoemaker
Horner Mary, vict. Three Horse Shoes
Horner John, blacksmith

Mason Miles, vict. woolpack
Metcalf John, butcher
Robinson Thomas, tailor & grocer
Scott Isaac, schoolmaster
Whitelock Robert, spirit merchant
Wray Wm. joiner and machine mkr.

*Longthwaite, see* Arkengarthdale.

*Lonton,* in the parish of Romald-kirk, wap. of Gilling West, and liberty of Richmondshire ; 9 miles NW. of Barnard Castle. Mr. Charles Kaine, the bailiff of Lord Strathmore, is the principal inhabitant.

*Lowside,* or *Lowpshouse,* in the parish of Romaldkirk, wap. of Gilling West ; 4 miles W. of Barnard Castle.

*Loverome Hill,* in the parish of Kirkby, wap. and liberty of Allerton-shire ; 3¾ miles N. of Northallerton. Pop. included with Hutton Bonville.

*Low Fields,* in the parish of Bowes, wap. of Gilling West, and liberty of Richmondshire ; 5 miles SW. of Barnard Castle

*Loss Ness,* in the parish of Pick-hill, wap. of Halikeld, and liberty of Richmondshire ; 5¾ miles from Bedale.

*Low Row,* see Melbecks.

LUNE, or LUNE DALE, in the parish of Romaldkirk, wap. of Gilling West, and liberty of Richmondshire ; 7 miles W. NW. of Barnard Castle : includes the whole of Lune Dale, running westward from the river Tees to the confines of the county next to Westmoreland, and contains the following straggling hamlets ; and Chapel of Ease to the parish church, situated at Laith, hence called Laith chapel, of which the Rev. J. Thompson, A. M. is the curate.  Pop. 265.

GRASHOLMS ; 10 miles N.W. of Barnard Castle.

Alderson John, vict. Board
Elliott John, miller
Smith John, mason

LAITH CHAPEL ; 11 miles NW. of Barnard Castle.

Wallace John, farmer

BIRTLE ; 16 miles WNW. of Barnard Castle.

Allinson John, farmer
Bayles Thomas, farmer

THWINGARTH ; 12 miles WNW. of Barnard Castle.

*Farmers,*
Dent James
Dent John
Raine Joseph

WEMERGILL ; 14 miles WNW. of Barnard Castle ; the favourite shooting seat of the late Lord Strathmore.

LYTHE, (P.) in the wap. and liberty of Langbargh ; 4 miles WNW. of Whitby.  Lythe is pleasantly situated near the eastern extremity of Cleveland, about one mile distant from the sea.  *Peter de Manley* III.  In the 38th of Henry the Third, obtained a licence for a weekly market, and a fair yearly, to be held on the eve of St. Oswald, but being in the vicinity of Whitby, both the fairs and market have long been discontinued.  The lord of the manor is the Earl of Mulgrave, who resides here, in a stately mansion, which stands a little South of the village, upon the brow of a gently rising hill, commanding a pleasing and extensive prospect of the country and the sea.  The Church, dedicated to St. Oswald, is an ancient structure, but owing to a thorough repair, which it received in 1819, has rather a modern appearance at first sight.  The living is a vicarage, in the patronage of the Archbishop of York.  There is also a Methodist chapel, built in 1822.  Pop. 1134.

Letters are despatched to and received from Whitby every day at 1 o'clock.

Champion Mrs. gentlewoman
Long Rev. Wm. officiating curate
Porter Rev. Thomas, vicar
Sowerby John M. land & alum agent for Earl Mulgrave.
Stonehouse Thomas, master mariner

*Academies,*
Chapman John
Ward John
*Blacksmiths,*
Jackson John
Newbolm Wm.
*Farmers,*
Bean John
Hoggart Wm.
Humphrey Philip
Laverick Francis
Laverick Wm.
Stangbow Mrs.
Stonehouse Robt.
Taylorson Wm.
Ward John
*Grocers, &c.*
Leonard George
Duck Mary, vict. Red Lion, (post-office)
Frank John, game keeper
Hill James, weaver
Huntrodes Wm. tailor
Naggs Thomas, vict. Ship
Readman John, tailor
Tyass James, butcher

Mackenzie John
*Joiners, &c.*
Davison James
Thirlwall John
*Shoemakers,*
Elland Wm.
Leonard Geo.
Rountree John
Ward Thos.
*Stone Masons,*
Watson Leonard
Watson Richard
*Wheelwrights,*
Taylor Clement
Thompson John
Thompson Thos.

*Mains,* (High & Low) in the parish of Masham, and wap. of Hang East ; 2 miles NW. of Masham.

*Maltby,* in the parish of Stainton

wap. and liberty of Langbargh ; 3½ miles ENE. of Yarm. Mr. William Metcalf is the principal inhabitant in this village. Pop. 168.

## MALTON, (P.)

Wap. of Rydale, and part in the liberty of St. Peters ; 9 miles from Pickering ; 18 from York ; and 22 from Scarbro', one of the most ancient Brigantian fortified towns in this part of Britain. The early importance of this station is shown by the number of ancient roads which point to it. The Romans planted here one of the mumeri, or cohorts of the Legio, sexta victrix, called DERVENTRIONENSIS, and changed only the termination of its British name, to CAMVLODVNVM. This name, by abbreviation, became the Saxon MELDVN, pronounced MAIDEN, and *Maiden Greve Balk*, is at this day one of the boundaries of Malton. The river Derwent here, and at this point alone, touches the foot of the DEIRA-WOLD region ; a considerable breadth of marshy ground, formerly impassible, intervenes between the river and the Wolds in every other part of its course, and at this point was the river most readily passed by a broad but shallow ford ; at this day we know of no other ford on the northern border of the Wolds, except that named by the Saxons Stængfordes, afterwards Stængfordes brydge, now Stamford bridge. No fewer than six Roman roads may be traced by military and other remains to this station. Numerous Roman coins, both silver and copper, of various Emperors, for a long period have been and are yet found here; and on the opposite side of the river, entrenchments for the defence of this once important pass are also visible. Fragments of, and entire urns, some containing Roman coins and fine red ashes, and also many pieces of their pottery, with figures in relief, on paterae, pocula, &c. are found here. The Camulodunum of the Roman Britons became a royal villa to king Edwin in the Saxon era, and here the life of that monarch was preserved from the assassin, by his faithful Lilla. The great Earl Siward, who defeated Macbeth, was one of the lords of Malton; and after the Norman conquest, the baronial family of Vesey built here a castle and a priory for Gilbertine canons, of both which there are remains at this day. The Castle was one of those short lived structures which Henry II. demolished : but during its existence, the town was burnt down, by Abp. Thurstan, when he laid siege to it to dislodge the Scotch, and the name of New Malton commenced on the re-building of the town. On

the site of the castle, Ralph, Lord Eure, built a noble castellated mansion, which he finished at the conclusion of the 16th century; and it is remarkable, that its duration was as short as that of the castle, for his lordship's two grand daughters not agreeing respecting the property here, the mansion was pulled down, and the materials divided between them, by Henry Marwood, Esq. the High Sheriff of the County of York, in 1674; the lodge and gate-way, however, were left as a monument of the folly and vindictiveness of family feuds, or to show what the mansion had been. Mary, the youngest of these daughters, was married to William Palmer, Esq. of Linley, in this county, who in right of his wife, possessed the manor of Old and New Malton, which he, with others, conveyed to Sir Thomas Wentworth. On the 20th of May, 1728, the Hon. Thomas Wentworth, Knight of the Bath, obtained the title of Lord Malton, and six years afterwards was created Marquis of Rockingham. His lordship dying on the 14th of December, 1760, was succeeded in his title and estates by his only son, Charles Watson Wentworth, Marquis of Rockingham, who dying on the 1st of July, 1782, his nephew, Earl Fitzwilliam, succeeded to the manor of Malton, and his other principal estates. Malton was a corporate borough, and governed by two bailiffs, until the reign of Charles II. when a writ of *quo warranto*, to which the inhabitants pleaded *prescription*, deprived the burgesses of its privileges, for judgment was given in favour of the Crown, and a new charter has never been applied for; since that time, the Court Leet, and Court Baron of New Malton appoint a nominal borough Bailiff, and two Constables, and exercise the usual jurisdiction of those courts. Malton sent members to parliament so early as the reign of Edward I. ; and at that period the Prior of Malton was elected a representative, who, on his return from parliament, was arrested for debt, but, pleading a privilege of exemption in going and returning from parliamentary duty, he was liberated ; this is perhaps the earliest claim of the privilege by a member of parliament. This Borough now sends two members to parliament, elected by the householders, paying scot and lot ; the number of voters being about 500. The present representatives are, Lord Duncanon, of Margaret street, Cavendish-square, London, and of Roehampton, Surrey ; and John Charles Ramsden, Esq. of Newby park, near Boroughbridge. There are two parochial chapels here to Old Malton, one of them dedicated to St. Leonard, and the other to St. Michael ; the former of which has a tall spire, which has been left unfinished, in the form of a truncated cone. Earl Fitzwilliam is the patron, and lessee of the tithes under the See of York; the Rev. William Flower, A. M. is the incumbent, and the Rev. C. A. Binns, the assistant curate. The other places of worship are, for the Society of Friends, the Presbyterians, the Independents, and the Methodists. Here is also a Theatre, erected in 1814; besides a handsome suite of public rooms, in Yorkersgate, to which are attached a Subscription Library and News-Room. About a quarter of a mile to the SW. of New Malton, is a mineral spring, similar in its properties to those of Scarbro', and is said to be a very efficacious chalybeate. Malton is a brisk market town. The town stands on an eminence, overlooking the river which runs through a beautiful vale to the South East. A handsome stone bridge, connects this place with Norton, the river forming the boundary between the East and North Ridings. In the reign of Queen Anne an act was passed, under the authority of which, the Derwent was made navigable up to this place, and corn, butter, bacon, &c. are conveyed in large quantities from

hence to Hull, Leeds, Wakefield, and London; while from Hull are returned salt, sugar, and groceries of different kinds, and coals, and all sorts of woollens brought here from Leeds & other parts of the West-Riding in considerable quantities. The market here is held every Saturday, and is numerously attended by the families and farmers from the surrounding country to a great extent. Formerly there were two market days, the other on Tuesday, and the stone bases of two market crosses yet continue; one where the present market is held, and the other in the Low street, where fish is now generally exposed for sale. There are also five fairs annually: viz. Monday and Saturday before Palm Sunday; Saturday before Whitsuntide; Saturday before the 15th of July; on the 11th and 12th of October; and on Saturday before Martinmas day. The first is famous for the exhibition of horses, and much attended by South country dealers; and the others, on account of the great show of cattle, are frequented by a vast number of farmers and graziers. The population of New Malton, within the Borough, amounts to 4005 souls.

POST-MASTER, THOMAS ROBINSON, *Office, Market-place.*

| Places from whence Letter bags are recv'd. | Distance. | Postage | Arrival of Mails. | Departure of Mails. |
|---|---|---|---|---|
| Bridlington, ...... | 28 | 6d. | 3 o'clock mg. | 20 min. past 3 mg. |
| Driffield, ........ | 20 | 5 | ditto. | ditto. |
| Pickering, ........ | 9 | 4 | ditto. | ditto. |
| Scarbro', ........ | 22 | 6 | ditto. | ditto. |
| Whitby, ........ | 30 | 6 | ditto. | ditto. |
| York, .......... | 18 | 5 | ½ past 4 aft. | 45 min. p. 4 aft. |

### DIRECTORY.

Bartlitt Rev. John, Wheelgate
Bartindale Wm. yeoman, Wheelgate
Binns Rev. C. A. Low street
Bull Sarah, gentlewmn. Market place
Ewbank Thos. gent. Market place
Foster Jane, gentwmn. Greengate
Fox Rebecca, gentwmn. Greengate
Gibson Jane, gentwmn. Yorkersgate
Hooper Samuel, gent. Newbiggin
Hotham Eliz. gentlewmn. Market pl.
Lambert Capt. John, R. N. Low st.
Leafe Catharine, gentwn. Newbiggin
Luccock Elizabeth, gentlewoman, Old Malton gate
Nelson Wm. gent. Old Malton gate
Robinson Alice, gentwmn. Greengate
Simpson John, M. D. Wheelgate
Sootheran John, gent. Greengate
Soulby Ann, gentwmn. Market pl.
Walker John, gent. Old Malton gate

Walker John, jun. gent. Old Malton gate
Ward Henry, gent. Low street
Wilson Robert, gent. Wheelgate

*Academies.*

Carter John, (bdg.) Market place
Dearden Wm. Market place
Lotherington John, (national) Old Malton gate

*Attornies.*

Allen Wm. (& steward to Earl Fitzwilliam) Malton lodge
Atkinson Moses, Market place
Barns Joseph, Finkle street
Paul Thomas, Greengate
Rider Wm. Yorkersgate
Simpson Alfred, Yorkersgate
Smithson Rhd. & John, Yorkersgate
Stockton James, Yorkersgate
Walker Thomas, Old Malton gate

*Auctioneers.*

Boulton John and Son, (appraisers) Newbiggin
Cumber John, Yorkersgate
Masterman Thos. (& sheriff's officer) Wheelgate
Ruddock Wm. Low street

*Bacon Factors.*

Elliott Wm. jun. Wheelgate
Hesp Hannah and Son, (and cheese) Yorkersgate
Owston Robt. (& corn) Yorkersgate
Spanton Robert, Yorkersgate
Taylor Thomas, Market place

*Bakers and Flour Dealers.*

Coulson George, Greengate
Gage Thomas, Newbiggin
Gill Thomas, Old Malton gate
Jefferson John, Wheelgate
Kirby George, Newbiggin
Metcalfe James, Greengate
Proctor Wm. Market place
Stainton Matthew, Low street
Studley Wm. Wheelgate

*Bankers.*

East-Riding Bank—Messrs. Bower, Duesbery, Hall, and Thompson, Yorkersgate ; draw on Curries & Co. London.
North-Riding Bank—Messrs. Hagues, Strickland, &Allen, Market place ; draw on Barclay & Co. London.

*Basket Makers.*

Johnson James, Old Malton gate
Simpson Henry, Old Malton gate
Simpson Richard, Wheelgate

*Blacksmiths.*

Clark John, Low street
Holliday Geo. (& farrier) Finkle st.
Piercy Samuel, Market place

*Booksellers, Stationers, &c.*

Barnby Geo. (& cir. lib.) Wheelgate
Jagg George, Market place
Smithson Richard, jun. (& music dlr. and circulating lib.) Yorkersgate

*Boot and Shoemakers.*

Allison John, Low street
Birkill Thomas, Market place
Birkill Thomas, jun. Wheelgate
Ford James, Greengate
Foster Wm. Old Malton gate
Lamb Wm. & Joseph, Newbiggin
Lapish Wm. Low street
Neill George, Yorkersgate
Pennington Richard, Low street
Rontree Thomas, Savile street
Rutter Robert, Market place
Rutter Wm. Market place
Sollitt Matthias, Low street

Spavin Wm. Yorkersgate

*Braziers, &c.*

Cornwell Ann, Yorkersgate
Leafe George, Market place
Marsar John, Low street

*Brewers, Ale and Porter, and Maltsters.*

Russell & Witty, Low street
Tomlinson & Co. Low street
Walker & Dunlop, (porter) Low st.

*Butchers.*

Bell Wm. Market place
Drake John, Greengate
Foster John, Yorkersgate
Harrison Wm. Newbiggin
Ianson Timothy, Market place
Nicholson John, Old Maltongate
Nixon Isaac, Newbiggin

*Cabinet Makers and Upholsterers.*

Beverley George, Yorkersgate
Douthwaite John, Finkle street
Goodill John, Yorkersgate
Goodrick John, Market place
Jefferson John, Wheelgate
Lee John, Greengate
Lee Wm. Wheelgate
Marshall Rhd. (upholsterer) Low st.
Monkman Wm. Old Malton gate
Thompson James, Newbiggin
Wardill John, (upholsterer) Mkt. pl.

*Chemists and Druggists.*

Horsley Wm. sen. Butcher corner
Horsley Wm. jun. Wheelgate
Revis Leonard, Market place
Wrangham Joseph, Wheelgate

*Clock and Watch Makers.*

Agar John, Market place
Bartliff George, Yorkersgate
Bartliff Rbt. (& silversmith) Yorksgt.
Carr James, Low street
Skelton Coultas, Low street
Sykes George, Wheelgate

*Coal Merchants.*

Barehead George, Low street
Cleathing & Bell, Yorkersgate
Fenton Wm. Yorkersgate
Jackson W. & S. Low street
Laverack John, Low street
Monkman Wm. Low street
Ouston Robert, Yorkersgate
Rider Joseph, Yorkersgate
Russell and Witty, Low street
Shackleton G. A. Low street
Soulby Edward, Yorkersgate
Tomlinson and Co. Low street
Witty & Williamson, Low street
Woffindin Thomas, Low street

*Coopers.*

Dresser Christopher, Low street
Taylor George, Low street

### Corn Merchants.

Atkinson G. S.
Barehead Geo. Low street
Bleathing & Bell, (and wharfingers)
Yorkersgate
Dresser John, Low street
Fenton Wm. Yorkersgate
Jackson W. and S. Low street
Owston Robert, Yorkersgate
Rider Joseph, Yorkersgate
Shackleton G. A. Low street
Soulby Edward, Yorkersgate
Walker & Dunlop, Low street
Witty & Williamson, Low street
Womdin Thomas, Low street

### Curriers.

Gray Thomas, Low street
Harrison Francis & Son, Old Malton gt.
Tate and Watson, Wheelgate
Wood Preston, Newbiggin

### Dyers.

Harrison John, Yorkersgate
Williamson Edward, Yorkersgate

### Farmers.

Fawcett Wm. Greengate
Nalton John, Market place

### Fire, &c. Offices.

Atlas, John Snowball, Yorkersgate
County, Thos. Hall, Yorkersgate
Phœnix, Alfred Simpson, Swine st.
Royal Exchange, J. Smithson, York-
ersgate
Sun, Benjamin Jagger, Low street

### Gardeners, Nursery and Seedsmen.

Benton Edward, Market place
Longcaster Wm. Old Malton gate
Russell & Witty, (seedsmen) Low st.
Slater Wm. Yorkersgate
Thompson John, Newbiggin

### Glass, China, &c. Dealers.

Cleathing Christopher, Yorkersgate
Hudson Geo. Yorkersgate
Jackson Mary, Wheelgate
Tindale Thomas, Wheelgate

### Grocers and Tea Dealers.

Ainsley Wm. Market place
Beal Mary, Low street
Benton Edward, Market place
Birdsall John, (and confectioner),
Market place
Bradley John, Yorkersgate
Bradley Geo. Finkle street
Bulmer Matthew, Wheelgate
Chapman Geo. Low street
Flower John, Market place
Gray Rd. (& confectioner) Market pl.
Harrison Robert, Wheelgate
Hartley John, (and stamp distributor)
Market place
Hudson Wm. Market place
Jefferson John, Wheelgate
Jennings James, Low street

Kemp Wm. Market place
Lee John, Greengate
Marshall Ann, Low street
Metcalf James, Greengate
Pickering Robert & Son, Yorkersgt.
Rutter Wm. Market place
Shepherd John, Yorkersgate
Smith David, Market place
Spavin Robert, Old Malton gate
Stephenson Thomas, Market place
Studley Geo. Wheelgate
Studley Wm. Wheelgate
Taylor David, Wheelgate
Taylor Joseph, Wheelgate
Wilson Thomas, Low street
Wood James, Old Malton gate

### Gunsmiths.

Hudson Geo. & Sons, Wheelgate
Piercy Matthew, Newbiggin
Wightman Wm. E. (patent) Market pl.

### Hair Dressers.

Burkill Robert, Wheelgate
Hide Wm. Wheelgate
Larcum John, (& fossilist) Wheelgate
Pierson L. D. Market place
Sinclair Wm. Market place
Skelton Thomas, Wheelgate

### Hatters and Furriers.

Carr Robert, Old Malton gate
Foster Roger, Wheelgate
King Robert, Low street
Wells Thomas, Savile street

### Inns and Taverns.

Angel Inn, Wm. Bradley, Savile st.
Black Bull, Joseph Etty, Market pl.
Black Horse, John Bartindale, York-
ersgate
Blacksmiths' Arms, Francis Calam,
Wheelgate
Black Swan, John Gray, Market pl.
Blue Ball, Sarah Wood, Newbiggin
Cross Keys, Ralph Rutter, Wheelgt.
Crown & Anchor, Thomas Barehead,
Low street
Fleece, John Smith, Market place
Golden Lion, Thomas Moon, Market
place
Green Man, Geo. Spanton, Market pl.
King's Head, Geo. Nelson, Market pl.
New Globe, John Cooper, Yorkersgt.
New Talbot Inn, Edward Barton,
Yorkersgate
Old Globe, Geo. Bransby, Market pl.
Old Tabot Inn, Wm. Reed, Market pl.
Royal Oak, Eliz. Revis, Market pl.
Ship Inn, Widow Kettlewell, Wheelgt.
Shoulder of Mutton, Wm. Ruddock,
Low street
Sun Inn, John Wilson, Wheelgate
White Horse Inn, Richard Carle,
Yorkersgate
White Swan, Daniel Newton, Old
Malton gate

*Iron Founders.*

Booth James, Old Malton gate
Gibson Robert, Newbiggin
Gibson Arthur, Market place

*Ironmongers.*

Barns Wm. Market place
Gibson Arthur, Market place
Hudson Geo. & Sons, Wheelgate
Luccock James, Yorkersgate
Wright John & Geo. Wheelgate

*Joiners, &c.*

Brown Wm. Low street
Carr Joseph, Low street
Hopwood Thos. (boat builder) Low st.
Luccock Christopher, Yorkersgate
Nalton Thomas, Greengate
Spurr Hardwick, (appraiser) Low st.
Sanman Richd. (appraiser) Savile st.
Tomlinson Geo. Low street

*Linen Drapers.*

Abbott Geo. Market place
Bulmer Matthew, Wheelgate
Dunlop James, sen. Market place
Dunlop James, jun. Market place
Howson Rachael, Greengate
Merry J. and W. Yorkersgate
Pickering Robert & Son, Yorkersgate
Stubbs Robert, Market place
Tindale Thos. (& tea dlr.) Market pl.
Watson James, Butcher corner

*Painters.*

Collier John, Low street
Nicholson Geo. Wheelgate
Sunley Wm. Market place

*Plumbers and Glaziers.*

Jackson Mary, Wheelgate
Morritt John, Old Malton gate
Walter Mathers, Newbiggin

*Printers, Letter Press.*

Barnby Geo. Wheelgate
Sagg Geo. Market place
Smithson Richard, jun. Yorkersgate

*Raff and Timber Merchants.*

Kemp Jeremiah, Yorkersgate
Lee Wm. Wheelgate
Luccock Christopher, (and appraiser) Yorkersgate
Robson Benj. Low street
Smith Wm. Wheelgate

*Ropers.*

Bellerby Geo. Market place
Harrison Martin, Newbiggin
Holtby Thomas, Wheelgate

*Saddlers.*

Hall Geo. Yorkersgate
Kilvington John, Market place
Rutter Thomas, Market place
Smith Nathaniel, Low street
Thornham John, Wheelgate

*Shopkeepers.*

Brown John, Newbiggin

Ellett Ann, Newbiggin
Rigg John, Market place

*Stone Masons.*

Brown John, Newbiggin
Exley Robert, Yorkersgate
Phillis John, Newbiggin
Willoughby Geo. Low street

*Straw Hat Manufacturers.*

Brown E. Low street
Bulmer Mark, Yorkersgate
Tindale & Watson, Wheelgate

*Surgeons.*

Cobb Robert, Low street
Davye Thomas, Market place
Davye Geo. Market place
Pratt John, Newbiggin
Rymer Wm. Market place
Sagg Robert, Yorkersgate
Teasdale Thomas, Greengate
Temple John, Yorkersgate

*Tailors, &c.*

Arundale Wm. Wheelgate
Chapman C. Old Malton gate
Clement Joseph, Market place
Crawford Thomas, Wheelgate
Loft Christopher, Finkle street
Marshall Wm. Wheelgate
Simpson John, Finkle street
Sixton John, Greengate
Spencer J. H. Market place

*Tallow Chandlers.*

Elliott Wm. jun. Wheelgate
Esp & Son, Yorkersgate
Flower John, jun. Swine market
Smith David, Market place
Spanton Robert, Yorkersgate

*Whitesmiths.*

Piercy Matthew, Newbiggin
Robinson Newyear, Low street

*Wine and Spirit Merchants.*

Ask James, Yorkersgate
Etty John & Son, Market place
Gray Richard, Market place
Jagger Benj. (spirit) Low street
Richardson Thomas, Market place
Rose & Agar, Market place
Searle Robert, Yorkersgate

*Woollen Drapers,*

Dunlop James, jun, Market place
Etty John & Son, Market place
Merry J. & W. Yorkersgate
Milbourn Joseph, Finkle street
Pickering Robert & Son, Yorkersgate
Richardson Geo. Market place
Taylor Andrew, Market place

*Miscellany.*

Birdsall Thos. confectioner, Newbiggin
Booth Jas. millwright, Old Malton gt.
Boulton John, sheriff's officer, Newbiggin
Bradley Arthur, hosier, Old Malton gt.

Brown John and Son, wood turners, Newbiggin
Burrow Joseph, corn miller, New Malton mills
Cumber John, land surveyor & general accountant, Wheelgate
Ford Geo. wheelwright, Low street
Harrison Richard, stay maker, Market place
Leafe John, corn inspector, Greengt.
Lee John, glover, Newbiggin
Longfield Thos. skinner, Low st.
Potts John, sail cloth mkr. Yorkersgt.
Priestman J. & J. tanners, Low st.
Robb Charles, accountant & engraver, Newbiggin
Snowball John, land agent, Yorkersgt.
Staniland Robert, working cutler, Market place
Tindale Thomas, breeches maker, Wheelgate
Watson John, flax dresser and linen manufacturer, Wheelgate
Williamson Charles, brush manufacturer, Market place
Willoughby Geo. builder, Low street
Wright Robert, clogger and patten maker, Old Malton gate

## COACHES.

The *Mail*, from the Talbot Inn, every evg. at 5 to York; to Scarborough, every Tu. Thu. Sat. and Sun. mgs. at 3; to Whitby, every Mon. Wed. and Fri. mgs. at 3
The *True Blue*, to York every mg. at 10; to Scarborough, every day at 1 noon, (Sundays excepted) in the season only
*Diligence*, to York, every Mon. Wed. and Sat. at 3 aft. from the Black Horse, Yorkersgate

## CARRIERS BY WATER.

*Wm. Fenton's* vessels regularly to & from Hull, every week; to Leeds and Wakefield occasionally.—*C. Waterson, agent*, Yorkersgate

## CARRIERS BY LAND.

*Driffield*, Thos. Blenkinsop, (Globe, Yorkersgate) arr. Sat. 4 evg. dep. 9 Mon. mg. arr. 4 Wed. dep. 9 Thursday morning
*Driffield, Beverley and Hull*, Philemon Ashton, every Mon. and Wed. ret. Tu. and Fri.
*Helmsley*, William Howe, (Sun Inn, Wheelgate) Tu. and Fri. arrives 9 morning, departs 11
*Kirkby-Moor-Side*, George Pearson, (Blacksmith's Arms) Tu. & Sat. arr. 10 mg. dep. 12

*Kirkby-Moor-Side*, Wm. Waite, (Blue Ball, Newbiggin) Tu. & Sat. arr. 8 morning, dep. 1 afternoon
*Scarbro'*, Thomas Burneston, (New Globe, Yorkersgate) Tu. and Fri. arr. 9 night, dep. 12 night
*Scarbro'*, Thos. Larkin, (Black Horse, Yorkersgate) arr. 10 on Tu. and Fri. night, dep. 1 mg. Wed. & Sat.
*Sherburn*, Henry Clarkson, Wed. & Sat.
*Whitby*, Andrew Allen, (Black Horse) arr. 11 Wed. ngt. dep. Thu. 6 mg.
*Whitby*, Geo. Pearson, (Blacksmith's Arms) arr. 12 on Tu. night, dep. Wed. 5 morning
*York*, Thos. Burneston, (New Globe) arr. Mon. & Thu. 9 ngt. dep. 12 ngt.
*York*, Thomas Larkin, (Black Horse) arr. Mon. and Thu. 9 night, dep. Tu. and Fri. 1 morning
*York*, Andrew Allen, (Black Horse) arr. Tu. ngt. at 8, dep. 1 Wed. mg.
*York*, George Pearson, (Blacksmith's Arms) arrive Mon. 10 night, dep. 12 night

MALTON (Old), in the parish of Old Malton, wap. of Rydale, a part in the liberty of St. Peter's; adjacent to New Malton. The parish church, dedicated to St. Mary, is a very ancient structure, with the abbey-house and monastery adjoining. The living is a perpetual curacy, in the patronage of Earl Fitzwilliam, and the Rev. William Flower, A. M. is the incumbent. Here is a free school with an endowment of 100*l.* per annum. This village is much noted for its lime quarries. Pop. 1064.

Lambert David, gentleman
Milner John, gentleman
Preston Edward, gentleman
Richardson Rev. John, master of free school
Wardle Ann, gentlewoman

*Farmers,*
Frear Wm.
Humphreys John

Miller Marmaduke
Rabbit Wm.
Ruston Edward

Anderson Geo. tailor and draper
Craven John, vict. Wentworth Arms
Dunning Robert, wheelwright
Featherston Geo. basket maker
Frear Francis, shoemaker
Hardcastle John, surveyor of highways
Loft John, lime burner
Longfield Thomas, tanner
Nendick Jonathan, schoolmaster
Oliver John, tea dealer
Pickering John, blacksmith
Rountree J. and W. corn millers

*Mandale*, in the township of Thornaby, parish of Stainton, wap. and liberty of Langbargh; 1 mile S. of Stockton.

**MANFIELD, (P.)** in the wap. of Gilling East, and liberty of Richmondshire; 9 miles N. of Richmond. A parochial village; the church is an ancient structure, with a tower steeple, and is dedicated to St. Michael. The living is a rectory, in the patronage of the King. Here is a small free school, with an endowment of 10*l*. per annum. Population, 440.

Cochrane Honourable and Rev. James Arthur, rector
Sinclair Rev. J. curate

*Farmers & Yeomen,* Gibson John
Appleby Richard | Richardson Thos.
Bradley Geo. | Weatherill Wm.
Cliff Wm. | Wheelwright John
Gibson Wm. | Wright Thos.

Binks John, vict. Wheat Sheaf
Brown John, vict. Shoulder of Mutton
Carter George, mason
Dodds George, schoolmaster
Twedel Thos. blacksmith
Wright Thos. corn miller

*Manless Green,* in the parish of Skelton, wap. and liberty of Langbargh; 4 miles NE. of Guisborough.

*Marderby,* in the parish of Feliskirk, wap. of Birdforth, and liberty of Ripon; 2½ miles NE. of Thirsk.

*Marishes,* (East and West), in the parish of Pickering, wap. and liberty of Pickering Lythe; 5½ miles SSE. of Pickering. Pop. 210.

**MARRICK, (P.)** in the wap. of Gilling West, and liberty of Richmondshire; 3 miles ESE. of Reeth. Roger de Ask founded here a priory, and dedicated it to St. Mary Benedict, in the reign of King Stephen, which flourished till the general dissolution; after which it fell into ruin, and the present parish church, dedicated to the same Saint, occupies part of the site of the priory; the living is a perpetual curacy, in the gift of Josias Morley, Esq. There is an institution here, called the Duke of Bolton's charity, for the benefit of two poor widows not receiving parochial relief, which amounts to 5*l*. 12*s*. per annum. Population, including the small hamlets of Hurst, Shaw, Oxque, Owlands and Ellers, 631.

Lambert Rev. Joseph, perpetual curate
Morley Josias, Esq. Marrick park

*Blacksmiths,* | Jackson Raw
Nelson Ralph | Langstaff Thos.
Nelson Thos. | Metcalf James
*Farmers & Yeomen,* | Pickering Geo.
Blenkiron Thos. | Sherlock John
Jackson Geo. | Waggett Geo.
Jackson Joseph | Waggett Michael

Whaley Richard, White Joseph and butcher | Wilson James
Blenkiron Elizabeth, shopkeeper
Chalder George, mining agent
Hall Wm. shoemaker
Harker James, miner
Milner Robt. mason & chimney doctor
Petty Jas. schoolmaster & parish clerk
Waggett Ralph, wheelwright
Whaley Jane, vict. and shopkeeper, White Horse

*Marrisorth,* in the parish of Thornton Watlass, wap. of Hang East, and liberty of Richmondshire; 5 mls. SW. of Bedale.

*Marside,* in the parish of Aysgarth, and wap. of Hang West; 4 miles SE. of Hawes.

**MARSKE, (P.)** in the wap. and liberty of Langbargh; 6 miles N. of Guisborough. Marske Hall, one of the seats of Lord Dundas, is an ancient and commodious mansion, built by Sir William Pennyman, Bart., in the reign and according to the taste that prevailed about the time of Charles I. In the front of the building there are two shields cut in stone, bearing the arms of Pennyman and Atherton. The church, dedicated to St. Germain, stands a little distant from the village, towards the north-east, within a few yards from the sea-cliff; the spire is a conspicuous sea mark. The living is a vicarage, in the patronage of the Dundas family. Pop. 576.

Harrison Rev. Joseph, vicar
Wilkinson Rev. Joseph, curate of Upleatham
Wilson Lawrence, gentleman

*Academies,* | Metcalfe Thos.
Ainsley Stephen, | Patterson Geo.
  National School | Pierson John
Bulmer Richard | Scrafton Geo.
Bulmer Mary Ann, | Suggitt Robert
  ladies' boarding | Turner John
*Blacksmiths,* | Weatherill Wm.
Drypon Newark | *Joiners, &c.*
Farthing John | Coul John
Wilson Wm. | Dove Thomas
*Butchers,* | Herbert Thos.
Ayre Robert | *Milliners,*
Errington Thos. | Herbert Mary
*Farmers,* | Morley Eliz.
Agar Thos. | *Shoemakers,*
Ainsley Wm. | Barker Christr.
Ayre Michael | Davison Geo.
Beardshaw John | Faith Wm.
Dixon Thos. | Skelton John
Dunn Robert | Wilson Richard
Errington John | Wilson Wm.
Haigh Thos. | *Stone Masons,*
Harker Leonard | Patten Wm.
Hayes Robert | Patten Joseph

*Tailors,*
Brack Wm. and
warm baths
Green Martin
Harforth John, & bathing machine

Taylerson Wm. & grocer
Taylerson Geo.
*Weavers,*
Clark Robt.
Flintoft Wm.
King Wm.

Beadnall Cuthbt. preventive boatman
Carlisle Robert, corn miller
Clark Charles, vict. Anchor
Johnson James, gardener
King Thos. vict. Ship
Pottage Wm. grocer
Walbron Wm. road surveyor
Wilson Geo. fishmonger

MARSKE, (P.) in the wap. of Gilling West, and liberty of Richmondshire; 5 miles W. of Richmond. The church is dedicated to St. Cuthbert; the living is a rectory, in the patronage of John Hutton, Esq. incumbent the Rev. James Tate. Here is a school, erected in 1814, by John Hutton, Esq. and allowed 20*l*. per annum for the instruction of the poor children belonging to the parish. The family of the Huttons, of Marske, is the only family in the kingdom which has yielded to the church two archbishops;—Matthew, Archbishop of York, the founder of the family, died in 1605; and Matthew, first Archbishop of York, and then Archbishop of Canterbury, died in 1758, and it is recorded of them that " they were both great and good prelates." Matthew, of York, left a son, Sir Timothy Hutton, who was High Sheriff of this county in 1607.— Pop. 290.

Hick Rev. David, curate
Hutton John, Esq. Marske hall
*Farmers,*    Outhwaite John
Greathead Thos.    Place Joseph
Busby Jane, vict. Dormouse
Carter Thos. agent to John Hutton, Esq
Coates John, mason & parish clerk
Hall Thos. blacksmith
Miller Ralph, corn miller
Wilson Christopher, wheelwright

MARTIN'S ST. ABBEY, in the parish of Catterick, wap. of Hang East, and liberty of Richmondshire; 1 mile S. of Richmond. About the year 1100, Wymer, chief steward to the Earl of Richmond, gave the chapel of St. Martin, with some land near it, to the abbey of St. Mary, at York; whereupon a cell of nine or ten Benedictine monks, from that monastery, was fixed here. At the dissolution the site was granted to Edward Lord Clinton. Population, 23.
Chipendale Thos. flax manufacturer
Coates Wm. farmer

*Marton,* in the parish of Sinnington, waps. of Rydale and Pickering Lythe, a part in the liberty of St. Pe-
----'s; 4½ mls. W. of Pickering. Pop. 256.

MARTON, (P.) in the wap. and liberty of Langbargh; 7 mls. N. of Stokesley. A village ever rendered important by being the birth place of the great navigator, Captain James Cook. If any country may be proud of having produced a man who, in various ways, enlarged the bounds of human knowledge, that pride is the honourable boast of this humble village. There is scarcely a corner of the earth to which the fame of Cook has not reached; and all Europe has been unanimous in admiring, revering, and emulating this great master of his profession. Captain James Cook was one of nine children, born of honest and industrious parents, in the lowest rank of society. He was taught to read by a schoolmistress; and his father, who was a labourer, being employed to look after a farm belonging to T. Scottowe, Esq. at Ayton, near Stokesley; he was, by the liberality of that gentleman, sent to school in that village, to a master, who taught reading, writing and arithmetic. At the age of 13 years he was apprenticed to Mr. W. Sanderson, a shopkeeper at Staithes, a small fishing town near Whitby. This employment, however, did not suit his genius; and he soon quitted it for one, in which he was destined to shine with peculiar lustre. Leaving the counter, he bound himself a second time apprentice to Mr. John Walker, of Whitby, of the religious profession called Quakers, and owner of several ships in the coal trade. Here he served his apprenticeship, and after being employed some years as a seaman he was introduced into the royal navy, and by his zeal, enterprise, and intelligence, became a distinguished ornament of his profession. The remainder of his history is well known; he circumnavigated the globe three times, and fell at last a victim to the savage ferocity of the inhabitants of Owhyhee, while endeavouring to save the lives of a part of his crew. Marton church, dedicated to St. Cuthbert, is situated on rather elevated ground at the western extremity of the village, and is a small ancient edifice; the living is a vicarage, in the patronage of the Archbishop of York, and the Rev. Daniel Duck is the incumbent. Pop. 397.

Rudd Bartholomew, Esq. Marton lodge

| | |
|---|---|
| *Bricklayers,* | Robinson Geo. |
| Easton Geo. | Stoker Thos. |
| Reedman John | *Shoemakers,* |
| *Farmers,* | Atkinson Wm. |
| Carlton Robt. | Davison Geo. |
| Davison John | Ellis John |
| Garbut Joseph | Lax John |
| Harrison John | *Tailors,* |
| Jordison John | Whitfield John |
| Robinson Wm. | Whitfield Ralph |

*Wheelwrights,*   Robinson Robt.
Orde Thomas

Atkinson Wm. vict. Royal Oak
Handisides Mary, shopkeeper and
   blacksmith
Hopper John, mason
Reedman Henry, vict. Golden Lion
Stephenson Samuel, corn miller and
   flour dealer

MARTON-LE-MOOR, in the parish of Topcliffe, and wap. of Halikeld; 3 miles NW. of Boroughbridge. Here is a Chapel of Ease, under the Deanery of Ripon; the Rev. Isaac Crackelt, curate. Marton was formerly surrounded with moors, all of which are now enclosed. Agricultural distress so severely felt in other parts of the kingdom is unknown here. The township contains one thousand five hundred acres of land, the property of his Grace the Duke of Devonshire, and it supports thirteen farmers in a state of comfort, in consequence of their low rents. Pop. 901.

*Farmers,*   Marwood John
Baines Wm.   Maynard Anthony
Gilling John   Prince Ann
Hesleton Thos.   Rainforth Miles
Hesleton Wm.   Rowell Thos.
Hesleton Wm.   Spetch Thos.
Lawson Geo.   Willey John

Beeford Wm. wheelwright
Calpas Wm. vict. Holy Lamb
Newby John, shoemaker & shopkpr.
Parker Wm. blacksmith

*Marton Lordship,* in the wap. of Bulmer, and liberty of Ripon; 5 miles E. of Easingwold. Here is a small church, wherein divine service is performed once a fortnight from Easter to Michaelmas, but not at all from Michaelmas to Easter; the living is a vicarage, of which the Archbishop of York is the patron, and the Rev. D. Duck the incumbent. Pop. including Moxby, 164.

## MASHAM, (P.)

In the wap. of Hang East, and liberties of St. Peter's and Richmondshire; 6 miles from Bedale, and 10 from Ripon. The town is most delightfully situated on the western bank of the river Ure, and the adjacent country, particularly to the east, is abundantly fertile. The market is on Wednesday; but not much business is transacted. In addition to the agricultural pursuits of the place, a number of labouring men are employed in the combing of wool, and some of the females in manufacturing a kind of coarse straw platt for hats. At a distance of about half a mile from the town, on the opposite bank of the river, there is a flax mill, occupied by Mr. Prest, which affords employment to a number of men, women and children, in the spinning of flax. The church is a small stone edifice, commanding a delightful prospect, and is extremely neat and interesting within. Several of the tablets are very handsome, and the monument of Sir Marmaduke Wyvil is deservedly admired for its beauty and splendour. The living is a vicarage with the vicarage of Kirkby-Malzeard, in the patronage of Trinity College, Cambridge, of which the Rev. Wm. Lawson, M.A. is vicar. The Methodists and Anabaptists have each a small chapel here; and there is a Free School, for the education of thirty poor boys belonging to the parish. There is also a charity school, for the education of twelve poor girls, begun by the late, and continued by the present Mrs. Danby, of Swinton Park. Masham Prebend, which existed till the year 1546, was then dissolved and made a Lay Fee, by Archbishop Holgate; it consisted of the manor and rectory of Masham-cum-Kirkby Malzeard, in the deanery of Catterick, and was the richest prebend in the church of York.* The Lords Scroop, of Masham and Upsall, formerly resided here; and Henry Lord le Scroop, lord treasurer, beheaded for high treason in the reign of Henry IV. and Archbishop Scroop, who suffered the same fate in the same reign, and for a similar offence, were of that ancient family.† In the early part of the 16th century, the Scroops falling in the male line, the Burton estate came by marriage into possession of the Wyvils, and the Masham estate into possession of Sir Christopher Danby, Knt. and it is now enjoyed by Wm. Danby, Esq. of Swinton Park, whose superb mansion is within half a mile of the town, and whose highly picturesque grounds extend from the vicinity of Masham, to the margin of the moors, large tracts of which, his zeal for improvements has served to reclaim. The population of Masham amounts to 1171.

*Post-Master*—GEORGE JACKSON.
A Riding Post from Bedale to Masham, arrives every day at 8 in the morn. and returns at 2 in the afternoon.

### DIRECTORY.
Atkinson Joseph, gentleman
Bolland Joseph, Esq.
Bolland Roger, gentleman
Bowes Miss Cecilia
Burrill Rev. Joseph
Burrill Joseph, solicitor
Carter Nicholas, gentleman
Hammond Richard, gentleman

* Bacon's Liber Regis, p. 1102.
† See Vol. 11. page 27.

Hardcastle Mrs. Elizabeth
Harrison Charles Batley, Esq.
Haw Peter, gentleman
Hepple Miss Elizabeth
Heslington Wm. gentleman
Hickson Mrs. Ann
Morton Harcourt Esq.
Morton Mrs. Elizabeth
Morton Mrs. M.
Powley Mrs. Elizabeth
Raw Mrs. Lydia
Roundhill Jonathan, gentleman
Saddler Mrs.
Smith Rev. John
Spence Miss Mary
Theakstone Mrs. M.
Thompson Mrs. Elizabeth
Wilson Mrs. Ann
Wrather Samuel, Esq.
Wrather Thomas, Esq.
Wrigglesworth Mrs. A.

*Academies, &c.*
Barker Edmund,
  principal assist-
  ant at the Gram-
  mar School
Burnell James
Burrell Rev. Jph.
  curate (for young
  gentlemen)
Marsden Christr.
  assistant at the
  Grammr school
Metcalf Mw. mas-
  ter of the Free
  School
*Blacksmiths,*
Beckwith Wm.
Thos. & James
Fleetham Matt.
Mailaby Peter
Rider Thos.
*Brewers,*
Lightfoot John
Lofthouse Henry
*Butchers,*
Plews Peter
Smith Wm.
Williamson T. & W.
Windross Geo.
Wood Wm.
*Butter Factors,*
Kirkbridge Roger
Rayner Joseph
Sturdy John
*Carpenters, &c.*
Alton John
Fryer Geo.
Myers Thos.
Pullan Thos.
Siddall Benj.
*Coopers,*
Duffield Jas. sen.
Duffield Jas. jun.

*Farmers,*
Clark Thos.
Clarkson Wm.
Jeff Robert
Rider Mark
Windross John
Wintersgill Geo.
Wray Thos.
*Flour Dealers,*
Jackson Geo.
Jackson Peter
Stokel Ralph
*Grocers & Drapers,*
Blackburn Jas.
Clarkson Wm.
Coldbeck Eliz.
Durham & Carter
Metcalf Henry
*Hatters,*
Blackburn James
London Wm.
*Ironmongers,*
Jackson Geo. and
  rope maker
Terry Wm.
*Joiners and Cabinet
  Makers,*
Fisher John
Metcalf James
*Milliners and Dress
  Makers,*
Barker Mary
Hammond Jane
Welford Sarah
*Plumbers & Glazrs.*
Lee John, & tinner
Thompson James
*Saddlers,*
London James
Stott Thos.
*Shoemakers,*
Dowson Edward
Elsworth Wm.

Haste John
Leathley Wm.
Moor Joseph
Pybus Edmund
Stott James
Sturdy Francis
Towler Isaac
Towler Thos.
Wharton Thos.
*Stone Masons,*
Clarkson Mthw.
Clarkson Thos.
*Spirit Dealers,*
Barker Edmund
Grange Benj.
Lightfoot John
*Straw Hat makers,*
Barker Mary
Deighton Mary
Dixon Hannah
Duffied Jas. jun.
Thompson Betty
Urwin Jane
*Surgeons,*
Lightfoot Joseph
Lister Charles

*Tailors,*
Boynton Richard
Buckle Thos.
Burnett Thos.
London John
London Wm. (and
  draper)
Lupton Henry
Matthews Thos.
Thompson Rbt.
*Tallow Chandlers,*
Durham & Carter
Williamson T. & W.
*Watch and Clock
  Makers,*
Backhouse Benj.
Terry Wm.
*Woolstaplers and
  Combers,*
Cummins Ralph
Durham Thos.
Jackson James
Jackson W. & T.
Welford Christr.
Whitelock Joseph

*Inns and Taverns.*
Black Bull, Peter Barker
George and Dragon, Thos. Handley
King's Head, John Lightfoot, (posting
  house and excise office
Lord Nelson, Henry Lofthouse
Royal Oak, Robert Welford
Wheat Sheaf, George Ascough
White Bear, Anthony Gill

*Miscellany.*
Alton & Co. timber merchants
Ascough Henry, fellmonger
Bray Thos. linen draper
Clarkson John, hosier
Deighton John, hair dresser
Durham Thos. merchant
Durham John, linen & woollen dpr.
Grange & Imeson, iron merchants
Haste Wm. cloth manufacturer
Heslop Richd. currier & leather cutter
Husband Wm. glover
Jackson Wm. corn miller
Stokel Ralph, baker
Thwaites Richard, sieve maker

---

## CARRIERS.

*Joseph Rayner*, to Ripon and Leeds,
Mon. and Thu. departs at 9 in the
morning, and arrives at Leeds the
following morning at 8, returns at
5 the same day, and arrives at
Masham on Wed. evening at 6.—
To Middleham on Mondays, dep.
at 8 morn. and returns same day.
To Bedale on Tu. at 8 morn. and
returns same day.

*kn Sturdy*, to Leeds, on Mon. & Thu. dep. 9 mg. ret. Wed. evg. 6 o'clock, same days as Joseph Rayner. To Ripon on Thu. at 8 morn. ret. same day. To Leyburn Fri. at 6 mng. ret. same day. To Richmond on Sat. at 5 morn. return same day.

*oger Kirkbridge*, & *Joseph Towler*, to Middleham on Monday at 7 morning, returns same day.— To Bedale on Tu. at 7 morn. ret. same day. To Ripon and Leeds on Thu. at 8 morn. arrives in Leeds on Friday morn. and at Masham on Saturday evening.

*Maynby*, in the parish of Kirby Fiske, wap. of Gilling East, and liberty of Richmondshire ; 5 miles S. ſ Northallerton. Pop. 206.

MELBECKS, (township of) in the arish of Grinton, and wap. of Gilling Vest, containing the following villaes and hamlets, whose population mounts to 1726.

BARF END ; 5 miles W. of Reeth.

*Farmers & Yeomen*, Hugill John
Jemison Wm.        Spenceley Ralph
Harker John

BLAIDES ; 4 mls. WNW. of Reeth.

*Farmers & Yeomen*, Pedeldy John
Brodrick Simon        Simpson Nathaniel,
Clarkson Jas.        Smarber
Clarkson John

FEETHAM ; 3 miles W. of Reeth.

Allison Rev. John. Indep. minister
Coates Edmund, vict. Board
Hill Ralph, vict. Board
Harker Solomon, farmer
Parkin Wm. corn dealer
Parkin John, blacksmith
Raw Christopher, tallow chandler
Spenceley James, mining agent
Spenceley Thos. miner, Brockbank
Hunter Metcalf, shopkeeper
Whitehead Ambrose, blacksmith

GUNNERSIDE & LODGE GREEN ; ſ miles N. of Askrigg.

Coates Thomas, gentleman
Deakin Jonathan, gentleman
Downs Walter, gentleman
Woodward Wm. gentleman

| *Blacksmiths*, | Hunt Timothy |
| Calvert John | Remison John |
| Simpson Ralph | *Joiners and Wheel-* |
| *Farmers*, | *wrights*, |
| Buxton Thos. & | Calvert John |
| flour dealer | Close Joseph |
| Jemison Robert | Milner Ralph |
| Bates Wm. | *Shopkeepers*, |
| Deekin Joseph | Harker Christr. |

Preston James
Preston Wm.
Woodward Wm.

| | *Tailors*, |
| | Bell Michael |
| | Johnson Wm. |
| | Peacock Geo. |

Alderson James, miller, &c.
Calvert Henry, mining agent
Calvert David, vict. King's Head
Calvert James, grocer and draper
Chapman Edward, shoemaker
Coates Leonard, mining agent
Hannam Joseph, vict. Miners' Arms
Sunter Christopher, butcher

KEARTON ; 3 miles WNW. of Reeth.

Ainsley Thos. mining agent, Birch park
Birkbeck Thomas, farmer
Martin Wm. farmer, Park hall

Low Row ; 4 miles W. of Reeth.

Birkbeck John, gentleman
Harker Mary, gentlewoman
Steward Frances, gentlewoman

Hunter Wm. joiner & wheelwright
Knowles E. A. manufacturer of knit yarn hosiery
Sunter Dorothy, shopkeeper

WINTRINGS GARTHS ; 6 miles W. NW. of Reeth.

*Farmers & Yeomen*, Cantrill Ralph
Barningham L.        Raw James
Birkbeck Robert        Rutter Ralph

MELMERBY, in the parish of Wath, wap. of Halikeld, and liberty of Richmondshire ; 5 miles NNE. of Ripon. Pop. 258.

Priestley Wm. gentleman
Walker Tristram, gentleman

*Metmerby*, in the parish of Coverham, wap. of Hang West, and liberty of Richmondshire ; 4 miles SSW. of Leyburn. Pop. 112.

MELSONBY, (P.) in the wap. of Gilling West, and liberty of Richmondshire ; 5 miles N. of Richmond : a retired agricultural village. The living is a rectory, in the gift of the University of Cambridge. Here is a school for eight poor children, endowed with £21 per annum. Pop. 440.

Barnby Rev. James, A. M. rector

| *Blacksmiths*, | Pierson Cathrick |
| Mariner Wm. | Smith Joseph |
| Robson Thos. | Smith Abraham |
| *Farmers*, | Swainstone Maths. |
| Barker Edward | Weatherill Thos. |
| Dawson Wm. | Webster H. F. |
| Dennison Geo. | Wiseman Charles |
| Dent James | *Shoemakers*, |
| Lawson Robert | Barker Thos. |
| Nichol James | Best Thos. |

Pattinson Geo.        Merryweather W.
*Wheelwrights,*       Tratter Thos.
Lightfoot Wm.

Hammond John, vict. Board
Hutchinson Margaret, vict. Bay Horse
Nelson Robert, ham & bacon factor
Thompson Robert and Son, grocers, &c.
Topham Christopher, schoolmaster

*Mickleby,* a small village in the parish of Lythe, wap. and liberty of Langbargh; 7 miles WNW. of Whitby. The only place of worship here is a neat Independent chapel. Population, 147.

MICKLETON, in the parish of Romaldkirk, wap. of Gilling West, and liberty of Richmondshire; 8 miles NW. of Barnard Castle. Pop. 356.

Raine E. and B. gentlewomen

*Blacksmiths,*        Hugginson Rt.
Dawson Wm.           Kidd Robert
Langstaff John       Langstaff Thos.
*Farmers & Yeomen,*  Langstaff John
Bustin John          Langstaff Wm.
Bustin Anthony       Raine John
Dent Joseph          Raine Thos.
Dent Wm.             Wallace Richard
Dent Thomas          *Wheelwrights,*
Dent John            Bustin Anthony
Dent Christopher     Raine Thomas
Finkler John

Langstaff John, shoemaker
Sowerby Joseph, shopkeeper

MIDDLEHAM, (P.) in the wap. of Hang West, and liberty of Richmondshire; 9 miles from Leyburn, 8 from Masham, and 9 from Bedale. This is a small market town, containing a population of 880 souls. The market day is on Monday, but owing to its vicinity to the more flourishing town of Leyburn, the attendance has become very slender. As a place of trade Middleham probably never had any high interest, but its castle, even in ruins, will for ages to come attract attention :—This castle was built about A.D. 1190, by Robert, surnamed Fitz Ramulph, grandson of Ribald, younger brother of Allan, Earl of Brittany, to whom all Wensleydale was given by Conan, Earl of Brittany and Richmond. It afterwards came into the possession of Lord Robert de Nevil, who, being detected in a criminal conversation with a lady in Craven, was by the enraged husband emasculated, of which he died soon after. In the reign of Henry VI. it belonged to the Earl of Salisbury, and from hence, in the thirty-seventh year of that king's reign, he marched with 4000 men for London, to demand the redress of his son's grievances. Here, according to Stowe, the bastard Falconbridge was beheaded in 1471, after having received a royal pardon. In this castle, Edward IV. was confined, after having been surprised and taken prisoner, in his camp at Wolvey, by Richard Nevil, Earl of Warwick, surnamed the king maker, but he escaped, while taking the diversion of hunting in the extensive park, by which it was then surrounded, and afterwards vanquished, and slew Warwick, at Barnet. The estates being forfeited, Edward settled Middleham castle upon his brother of Gloucester, afterwards Richard III. who took so great a liking to it, that he raised the rectory to a deanery, and intended to build a college here, in the field called Frodingham field, but his design was frustrated by his death, Edward, the only son of Richard, was born here; but from that time to the present this castle is scarcely mentioned in history. All that is further known of it is, that in 1609 it was inhabited by Sir Henry Linley, Knight, whose effects were sold at his death, and the inventory is still extant. When it ceased to be inhabited is not ascertained.—There is a tradition, that it was reduced to ruins, by Oliver Cromwell, but it is unsupported by history. The castle stands near the town; it is a very extensive and interesting ruin, and the best view is that from the south west. Ascending from the castle towards the south, there stand, at the distance of 500 yards, two eminences, evidently raised for military purposes; and at a station about an equal distance from the castle, and these eminences, the walls afford an echo, " the most distinct and loud," says Grose, from whom we quote, " I ever remember to have heard." The castle was formerly moated round by the help of springs, and some traces of the moat are yet visible. The parish church of Middleham is dedicated to St. Mary and St. Alkild, and the living is a deanery, in the gift of the King, of which the Rev. Peter Seaimshire Wood, L. L. D. is the incumbent, and the Rev. J. Cockeroft the resident curate.—There are two dissenting chapels, one for the Methodists, and the other for the Primitive Methodists. The town is well built: it is said to have derived its name from having at one time formed the centre, or middle of a number of hamlets. About half a mile to the SW. of the town is Middleham Moor, the famous school of the turf, where so many celebrated horses have received their first training.

POST-TOWN, BEDALE.
POST-MASTER, Matthew Clarkes, *Office, Market-place.*

Letters arrive every day, at half past
o'clock morning, and are despatched at 1
clock in the afternoon, to Bedale.

### DIRECTORY.

ell John, gentleman
teare John, Esq.
uckle Mrs. Eliz. gentlewoman
layton Isaac, Methodist minister
eckcroft Rev. John, curate
ellinson Wm. gentleman
ixon Richard, gentleman
nfield Mrs. gentlewoman
wbank James, Esq.
orn Mrs. Eliz. gentlewoman
owson Alice, gentlewoman
igham John, Methodist minister
idgley Thomas, gent.
cott Christopher, gent.
nith Miss Mary, gentlewoman
ance Simon, gent.
naubensee Captain Thomas
opham Wm. gent.
opham Lupton, Esq. clerk of the
  peace for the North Riding

*Attornies,*
insdale Geo. E.
opham C. Esq.
ipham Lupton
*Blacksmiths,*
etcalf Wm.
right John
*Boot & Shoemakers,*
roft John
isher John
utchinson Thos.
ones Stephen
l'Collaugh Geo.
eacock Thos.
rest James
*Butchers,*
landley Wm.
andley John
otgan John
lace Simon
ilder George
mith Francis
mith F. jun.
*Farmers,*
earpark Matthew
laxwell Ralph,
  (& maltster)
lace Simon
mith Francis
*Grocers,*
hristian John,
  (druggist & iron-
  monger)
larkson Matth.
utchinson Jas.
  (& chandler)
ohnson Robert
*Joiners,*
shton Thomas

Hogg George
Sturdy Stephen
*Linen Drapers,*
Christian John
Digby Leonard
Handley Mrs.
Johnson Robert
*Milliners,*
Clarkson Eliz.
Handley Miss
Prest Mary
*Millwrights,*
Sayer John
Spence John
*Painters,*
Morgan Wm.
Woodward John
*Plumbers & Glaziers,*
Bowe Robert
Croft James
Deighton Wm.
*Saddlers,*
Gill Wm. J.
Horner Roger
*Stone Masons,*
Johnson Henry
Spence Peter
*Straw Hat Makers;*
Clarkson Eliz.
Jones Sarah
Metcalf Eliz.
*Stay Makers,*
Carter Jonathan
Morgan Eliz.
*Surgeons and Apo-
  thecaries,*
Edmundson Geo.
Lamb Thos. M.

*Tailors,*
Barker John
Harrison John
Harrison Wm.
Walker James

Wilson George
Winn Wm.
*Wheelwrights,*
Ashton Thomas
Willis Thomas

*Inns and Taverns.*
Black Swan, Mary Hesletine
King's Head, Richard Metcalfe
Green Dragon, Robinson Morton
Waterloo Inn, John Croft
White Swan, Wm. Swale
Bywell Wm. cooper
Croft James, race horse trainer
Handley George, baker
Heslop Thomas, exciseman
Ibbotson Thos. parish clerk
Morgan Wm. J. T. printer, and pre-
  server of birds, fish, and animals
Shields Thos. tinner and brazier
Simpson Wm. whitesmith, bellhanger,
  and tallow chandler
Tempest Thomas, hair dresser
Theakstone Christ. tanner
Wilson Wm. common brewer, Cover-
  bridge
Wood John, governor of the poorhouse

### CARRIERS.

John Walker, to Richmond every Sat.
  to Bedale on Tu.

*Middlesbrough,* (P.) in the wap.
and liberty of Langbargh; 5 miles ENE. of
Stockton. There was an ancient chapel
here, dedicated to St. Hilda, which was dependent on the church at Stainton; but, on
the grant thereof to the Abbey of Whitby,
confirmed by King Henry I. and by Thurstan, Archbishop of York, it was severed
from the mother church, and made parochial. It was certified to the governors of
the bounty of Queen Anne at 6l. per annum,
and has since had three augmentations, by
lot, laid out in lands, which produce an income of about 40l. a year: Thomas Hustler, of Acklam hall, Esq. is the patron, and,
nominates the curate. The chapel has
been long in ruins, and nothing of it now
remains: the site, together with the chapel
yard, which is still used, occasionally as a
burying place by the inhabitants, lies open,
and uninclosed from the adjoining grounds.
Population, 40.

*Middleton,* (P.) in the wap.
and liberty of Pickering Lythe; 1
mile W. of Pickering. Here is a
neat plain church; the living is a vicarage, in the patronage of the Devisees
of the Rev. J. Robinson, of which the
Rev. Michael Mackereth is the incumbent. Pop. 347.

Acton John, Esq.
Clarkson John, gentleman

Dawson John, gentleman
Dawson David, gentleman
Beal Matthew, vict. New Inn
Camplan John, bleacher, Costa mill
Frank Robert, butcher
Hood John, corn miller, Costa mill
Mintoft Robert, schoolmaster
Moorhouse Francis, cattle dealer and
  woolstapler
Pearson Robert, saddler

*Middleton Quernhow*, in the parish
of Wath, wap. of Halikeld, and liberty of Richmondshire; 5 miles N. of
Ripon. Pop. 102.

MIDDLETON TYAS, (P.) in the
wap. of Gilling East, and liberty of Richmondshire; 5 miles NE. of Richmond; the
living is a rectory, in the patronage of the
King, of which the Rev. George Burrard,
A. M. chaplain to his Majesty, is the incumbent. Population, with Kneeton, 569.

Clarke Rev. George, curate
Hartley Geo. Esq. Middleton lodge
Morley Mrs. J. gentlewoman
Pybus Robert, attorney

| *Butchers,* | Harrison Tobias |
| Raine Wm. | Ianson John |
| Robinson Christ. | Oliver Wm. |
| *Farmers & Yeomen,* | Peacock Wm. |
| Alderson Thos. | Spence George |
| Alderson John | Wilkinson Mary |
| Davison Thomas | *Wheelwrights,* |
| Dinsdale Robert | Binks George |
| Harrison Wm. | Nixon Christ. |

Gouldsbrough John, shopkeeper
Goundry Ralph, vict. Blue Anchor
Headley John, blacksmith
Hepple John, shoemaker
Martin John, schoolmaster
Robinson Christopher, vict. Shoulder
  of Mutton
Spence Geo. vict. Black Bull

MIDDLETON-UPON-LEVEN, in
the parish of Rudby, wap. and liberty of
Langbargh; 4½ miles SE. of Yarm. The
Chapel of Ease, dedicated to St. Cuthbert,
is a small modern structure; patron, the
Hon. Lady Amherst; and the Rev. Richard
Shepherd, vicar of Rudby, officiates as
curate. Pop. 111.

| *Farmers,* | Rountree Robert |
| Colbeck Henry | Rountree Wm. |
| Foster Thomas | Sligh Wm. |
| Righton Wm. | Tweddle Thos. |

Fawell Watson, vict. Chequers
Sayer Wm. bleacher & corn miller

*Milby*, in the parishes of Kirkby
Hill and Aldborough, wap. of Halikeld, and
liberty of Richmondshire; 1 mile N. of
Boroughbridge. Before the conquest, the

great north road lay through the city of
Burgh, and crossed the Ure, by a wooden
bridge, opposite to this village, some remains of which may yet be discerned when
the water is low. This hamlet is separated
from Boroughbridge by the river Ure. Pop.
included with Hum-Burton.

*Moor Cote*, in the parish of East
Witton, and wap. of Hang West; 4
miles SE. of Middleham.

*Moor House Little*, in the parish of
Haukswell, wap. of Hang West, and
liberty of Richmondshire; 2 miles
from Middleham.

*Moor Houses*, in the parish of
Helmsley, and wap. of Rydale; 4
miles from Helmsley.

*Moor Row*, in the parish of St.
John Stanwick, wap. of Gilling
West, and liberty of Richmondshire;
10 miles N. of Richmond.

MOORSOME, (Great and Little) in
the parish of Skelton, wap. and liberty of
Langbargh; 6 miles E. of Guisborough; a
long straggling village, about one mile to the
SW. of it stands the beautiful conic mountain, commonly called Freebrough hill,
which serves as a sea mark to the sailors who
frequent the neighbouring coast. Pop. 351.

| *Farmers,* | Pallister Robert |
| Agar John | Porritt Wm. & J. |
| Armstrong John | Porritt J. & Jas. |
| Askew Robert | Porritt Joseph |
| Bennison George | Porritt Robert |
| Bennison John | Robinson Thos. |
| Bulmer Geo. | Sanderson Ralph |
| Dale John | Smith Wm. |
| Dobson Wm. | Suggitt Francis |
| Ewbank Geo. | Watt Wm. |
| Hammond Wm. | *Shoemakers,* |
| Hick Mary | Cook George |
| Hodgson Wm. | Winspear Jonth. |
| Holdforth Matth. | *Wheelwrights,* |
| Howers Wm. | Dobson Wm. |
| Johnson Robert | Norman Edw. |
| Lee James | Taylor Tobias |
| Moody Wm. | |

Aysley Thomas, grocer
Charlton John, vict. Board
Cook Robinson, blacksmith
Cook Daniel, tailor
Gray John, schoolmaster
Metcalf John, clogger
Walshaw Robert, baker
Watson Robert, corn miller
Wilson Joseph, vict. Beck Hole

*Morton*, in the parish of Ormesby,
wap. and liberty of Langbargh; 4
miles W. of Guisborough. Pop. 26.

*Morton*, (Extra-parochial) in the

ap. of Birdforth; 5½ miles WNW. of elmsley ; in the constablery of Newargh. Pop. included with Newburgh.

*Morton-upon-Swale*, in the parish 'Ainderby Steeple, wap. of Gilling last, and liberty of Richmondshire ; miles WSW. of Northallerton.—opulation, 240.

*Moss Dale*, in the parish of Aysirth, wap. of Hang West, and liberty of ichmondshire; 4 miles WNW. of Hawes ; small hamlet, pleasantly situated at the stern extremity of Wensleydale, near to e source of the river Ure, and is said to we derived its name from the soil, which ounds with mossy verdure.

*Moulton*, in the parish of Middle-n Tyas, wap. of Gilling East, and erty of Richmondshire ; 4 miles NE. of Richmond. Pop. 236.

*Mount Grace*, in the parish of st Harlsey, and wap. of Birdforth ; 7 les NE. of Northallerton. Thomas Holid, Duke of Surrey, Earl of Kent, and rd Wake, founded a Carthusian Priory re, about the year 1396: but having conred against Henry IV. he was taken in ttle, and beheaded; this put a stop to the rk till Henry VI. confirmed his grants in l9, after which it flourished till the gene-dissolution, when its revenues were va-d at 382*l*. 5*s*. 11*d*. per annum. The was granted, in 1540, to James Strange-ies. The secluded situation and romantic on of this monastery seem to have been ticularly adapted to the austerities of the id order of the Carthusians placed here, l of which there were only nine houses in gland. A Gothic archway forms the en-ace into the quadrangle, the outer walls which inclose about three acres of ground, l are still standing, fantastically covered h ivy ; the inner court is surrounded by ible walls, and contained the cells of those tary monks, the doors of which, though r walled up, may be distinctly traced, and fourteen in number. A part of the build-has been converted into a farm house, of stellated form, with spacious apartments. e church, which is now in ruins, was in form of a cross; the tower, which is yet fect, rising from the centre, supported four Gothic arches. On the summit of hill that shelters the priory on the east, the ruins of an ancient building, called Lady's chapel, to which the ascent is p and difficult.

*Mowthorpe*, in the parish of Ter-gton, and wap. of Bulmer ; 7 miles ¿W. of Malton.

*Moxby*, in the parish of Marton, wap. of Bulmer, & liberty of Ripon ; 5 miles E. of Easingwold.

MUKER, in the parish of Grinton, wap. of Gilling West, and liberty of Richmondshire; 6 mls. NNW. of Askrigg. Here is a Chapel of Ease to the parish church, which is dedicated to St. Mary, and was consecrated August 3d, 1580, and of which the Rev. John Clemison is curate. This township comprises the high part of Swaledale, adjoining to Westmoreland, and is 10 miles in extent from east to west, being divided into ten divisions, or hamlets. There is at Muker a Grammar school for the education of six poor children, with an endowment of 20*l*, a year: and also a subscription library, established in 1819. The market, which has been established by custom, is held on Wednesday, and is well supplied with the necessaries of life. There is likewise an annual fair for sheep and general merchandise, held on the Wednesday next before Old Christmas day. The north side of the Dale abounds with lead mines; there is also a good vein of iron ore, with coal and lime.—The only natural curosity is the cascade, called Keasden Force, which is formed by the Swale falling over some ruggid rocks, into a very secluded and romantic dell, about two miles and a half north west of Muker. The whole population of the township amounts to 1425.

Calvert James, yeoman
Croft William, surgeon
Fidler Rev. Isaac, librarian, and offi-
    ciating curate
Grime James, yeoman
Grime Isabella, gentlewoman
Guy Richard, yeoman

| *Shopkeepers,* | Raynard Wm. (& |
|---|---|
| Alderson Richard | schoolmaster |
| Calvert George | Waistill Alex. |

Buckle John, blacksmith
Calvert James, vict. Board
Harker John, miner
Neesbarn Charles, vict. King's Head
Peacock Wm. shoemaker

*Carrier*—William Harker, to Richmond every Sat. mg. ret. same day ; and to Hawes every Tu. mg. ret. same day.

*Mulgrave Castle*, in the parish of Lythe, wap. and liberty of Langbargh ; 4 miles NW. of Whitby. Here was a castle, 200 years before the Norman conquest, which then belonged to Wade, a Saxon duke, who died about the year 800, and whose remains were interred on a high hill in the neighbourhood, between two large blocks of stone, each about seven feet high, and whom tradition represents as a giant.—After passing through various families, it became the property of Edward Lord Sheffield, who was by Charles I. created Earl of Mulgrave: and of which family it is recorded, that Sir John Sheffield, Knight, and Edmund and Philip, his brothers, were drowned, in crossing the Ouse, at Whitgift ferry, in December, 1614; William was drowned in France, and George broke his neck, in a new riding-house which his father had made of an old consecrated chapel.[*] This family became extinct in 1735; but the title was revived in the person of Constantine Phipps, a captain in the Royal Navy, and a descendant of the Anglesey family, who was created Baron Mulgrave in Ireland, in 1767, and in the year 1774, a lease of the Mulgrave estate was confirmed to him, for the sum of 30,000l. and a quit rent of 1200l. per annum. His son, Constantine John, was created a peer of Great Britain, in the year 1790. By his wife, Eliza Anne, daughter of Nathaniel Cholmley, Esq. he had a daughter, but dying without male issue, in 1792, his English title became extinct, but was revived, in 1794, in the person of his brother Henry, the present Lord, who was created Earl in 1812. The ancient Castle of Mulgrave having been garrisoned by the King's forces in the reign of Charles I. was afterwards dismantled by order of the Parliament; and there is now nothing left from which we can form any just idea of its ancient magnificence. The present seat of Lord Mulgrave, which is also known by the name of Mulgrave Castle, is in a commanding situation on the coast, at a small distance from the ancient castle. The views from the house are romantic and varied. The ground, declining to the south east, opens a fine prospect of the sea; Whitby pier, with the ships coming out of the harbour, the venerable ruins of the Abbey appearing high above the horizon, and the black Promontory of Saltwick, contrasted with the white foaming billows at its foot, compose altogether, a scene equally picturesque and interesting.

Murton, in the parish of Osbaldwick, wap. of Bulmer, and liberty of St. Peter's; 3 miles E. of York.—Here is a Chapel of Ease, and, in reality, an easy chapel, as divine service is performed only a few times in the year. Pop. 134.

*Muscoates*, in the parish of Kirkdale, and wap. of Rydale; 4½ miles S. of Kirkby-Moor-Side. Pop. 65.

**MYTON-UPON-SWALE, (P.)** in the wap. of Bulmer; 3 miles E. of Boroughbridge. Here is a very handsome church, dedicated to St. Mary; the living is a vicarage, in the patronage of the Archbishop of York, and the Rev. R. S. Thompson is the incumbent. In the year 1820, the remains of the famous Roger de Mowbray were removed from Byland Abbey, and interred here. A ferry for cattle, carriages, &c. passes over the Swale at this point, in view of the elegant mansion of M. B. Stapylton, Esq. In the year 1319, the Scots entering England, laid waste the country with fire and sword, and continuing their depredations, advanced to the walls of York; after burning the suburbs of that city, they returned northwards, on which William de Melton, Archbishop of York, immediately raised an army, composed of clergymen, monks, canons, husbandmen, labourers, and tradesmen, to the amount of 10,000 men; with this undisciplined band the Archbishop overtook the Scots at Myton; a battle ensued, the Yorkshiremen were defeated, and upwards of 3000 of them were slain. On which occasion, such a number of ecclesiastics fell, that this fight was, for a long time, called ironically, the *White Battle.*[†] Pop. 161.

Stapylton M. B. Esq.
Campbell Rev. Wm. curate
Walker Joseph, agent

*Farmers,*　　　Barnell Wm.
Britton Robert　　Calvert Wm.
Brotherton John　Marshall John
Needham I. farmer & vict. Lord Nelson

*Naby*, a small hamlet, in the parish of Romaldkirk, wap. of Gilling West, and liberty of Richmondshire; 3 miles WNW. of Barnard Castle.

**NAPPA**, in the parish of Aysgarth, wap. of Hang West, and liberty of Richmondshire; 1½ mile E. of Askrigg. This was anciently the chief seat of the family of Metcalfe, which, it is said, was, at one time, the most numerous of any in England.—Sir Christopher Metcalfe, Knight, chief of the family, being high sheriff in the year 1555, was attended by 300 horsemen, all of his own family and name, and all in the same habit, to meet the judges of assize, and conduct them to York. The village is now the property of Lord Grantham.

[*] See Dugdale's Bar. Vol. 2. p, 387.

[†] See Vol. II. p. 25.

Winn Rev. John, B. A. ball

NAWTON, in the parish of Kirkale, wap. of Rydale, and liberty of St. Peters ; 3½ miles ENE. of Helmsey. Here is a Wesleyan Methodist chapel. Pop. with Wombleton, 816.

Soon George, coal proprietor

NESS, (East) in the parish of Stonegrave, and wap. of Rydale ; 6 mls. S. of Kirkby-Moor-Side. Pop. 59.

Kendall Thomas and John, Esqrs.

*Ness*, (High) in the parish of 'ickhill, wap. of Halikeld, & liberty of Richmondshire ; 5 miles SE. of Bedale.

*Ness* (West), in the parish of Stonegrave, and wap. of Rydale ; 6 miles S. of Kirkby-Moor-Side. Pop. 65.

*Newbiggin*, in the parish of Aysgarth, wap. of Hang West, and liberty of Richmondshire ; 5 miles SE. of Askrigg ; a small hamlet, chiefly inhabited by farmers. Pop. 128.

NEWBROUGH, or Newburgh, in the parish of Coxwold, and wap. of Birdforth ; 5 miles NE. of Easingwold : was the estate of Robert de Mowbray, who was created Earl of Northumberland, by William I. in 1092 : the year following he defeated the Scots, at Alnwick, where Malcolm III. and his son Edward, were both slain : but revolting soon after from the King, he was apprehended, and kept a prisoner thirty ears in Windsor Castle, where he died. His estate was given to Nigel de Albini, whose son, Roger, assumed the name of Mowbray, and founded a priory here, for Canons regular of the order of St. Augustine, in the ear 1145. Newburgh, the famous monkish historian, was a canon regular in this priory about the year 1200. Pop. 162.

Belasyse Thos. Edw. W. Esq. Priory Hutton John, gentleman Hedley Radcliffe, Esq.

| Farmers, | Cussons Geo. and |
| Barley John | tanner |
| Bowser Joseph | Darley Thomas |
| Buckle John | Fewster John |
| Buckle Wm. | Smith John |

Asquith Francis, corn miller Bulmer John, farmer & woolstapler

*Newby*, in the parish of Scalby, wap. and liberty of Pickering Lythe ; 3 mls. NW. of Scarborough. Pop. 40.

*Newby*, in the parish of Stokesley, wap. and liberty of Langbargh ; 3 miles INW. of Stokesley. There is here a small free school, founded in 1640. Pop. 152.

NEWBY WISKE, in the parish of Kirkby Wiske, wap. of Gilling East, and liberty of Richmondshire ; 5 miles S. of Northallerton. This village, like several others similarly situated, takes its name from a rivulet called Wiske, on the banks of which it is situated, and over which it has a good stone bridge of five arches. Here is a Methodist chapel, and Sunday school instituted and supported by the Rev. Christopher Bethel, D.D. of Kirkby Wiske. Pop. 265.

Armitage John, Esq.
Henderson Edward, gentleman
Hutton John, Esq. Sobergate
Hutton Margaret, gentlewoman
Meek Sarah, gentlewoman

| *Butchers,* | Peacock John |
| Burton Robert | *Shoemakers,* |
| Wheldon George | Barnett George |
| *Carpenters,* | Robson James |
| Smith Geo. | Wainwright Ralph |
| Wright John and | *Tailors,* |
| Robert | Carter Edward |
| *Farmers,* | Davison John |
| Alderson John | Humpleby Richard |
| Hough Francis | *Wheelwrights,* |
| Kendrew James | Kirby William |
| Moore John | Smith George |

Carter Christopher, vict. grocer, flour dealer & druggist, Punch Bowl
Hutton Christ. bricklayer & builder
Merryweather Henry, vict. brewer & maltster, Maltster's Arms
Priestman Thos. blacksmith
Smith Geo. shopkeeper
Sturdy Richard, cooper
Whitfield Martin, linen and woollen draper

*New Forest*, in the parish of Kirkby-Ravensworth, and wap. of Gilling West ; 5 miles N. of Reeth. Pop. 79.

NEWHOLME, in the parish of Whitby, wap. and liberty of Whitby Strand ; 2½ miles WNW. of Whitby. Pop. including Dunsley, 259.

Mead John, yeoman

| *Farmers,* | Hasbrough James |
| Bennison Thos. | Robinson Wm. |
| Corner Wm. | Robinson Matth. |
| Emerson Robert | Whighill Mark |
| Hart George | |

Chapman Mary, vict. Board
Peacock Robert, mason

*Newport*, in the parish of Acklam, wap. and liberty of Langbargh ; 9 miles NNW. of Stokesley.

*Newsam*, in the parish of Appleton-le-Street, and wap. of Rydale ; 4 miles NW. of Malton.

NEWSHAM, in the parish of Kirkby-Ravensworth, wap. of Gilling West.

and liberty of Richmondshire ; 8 mls.
N.W. of Richmond. Pop. 511.

A foot-post from hence to Greta Bridge, every Monday, Wednesday, Thursday, and Saturday.

Hutchinson Wm. Esq. Kirkby hall
Glover Joseph, Esq.
Graham Matthew, surgeon

*Butchers,*
Glover Michael
Graham Thomas
Heslop George
Nicholson Geo.
Raine Thos.

Kirby Wm.
Lamb Wm.
Simpson Geo.
Stapleton Saml.
Wilkinson Wm.

*Farmers,*
Atkinson John
Birdy John
Dunn Wm. (and grazier
Glover Ralph
Graham James
Johnson Wm.

*Schoolmasters,*
Heslop George, (academy)
Simpson Ralph

*Shopkeepers,*
Birkit Thos.
Jackson Wm.
Lonsdale James

Atkinson Thomas, vict. Board
Hind Ralph, vict. and blacksmith, Bull
Palmer John, wheelwright
Spence Robert, miller

NEWSHAM, in the parish of Kirkby-Wiske, and wap. of Birdforth ; 3¼ miles W. of Thirsk. Pop. including Brackenbrough, 173.

Dent Rev. Wm. B. A. curate

*Farmers,*
Beck John
Gill Ingram
Langdale Richard

Oastler Thos.
Pearson John, jun.
White Robert

Pearson John, sen. blacksmith
Robinson Francis, vict. Masons' Arms

Newstead, a small hamlet, in the parish of East Witton, wap. of Hang West, and liberty of Richmondshire ; 3¾ miles SE. of Middleham.

Newton, (P.) in the wap. and liberty of Langbargh ; 5 miles NE. of Stokesley. The church is a small ancient structure, and the living a perpetual curacy, of which the Rev. John Thompson, is the incumbent. Population, 119.

Newton-cum-Rawcliffe, in the parish of Pickering, wap. and liberty of Pickering Lythe ; 4½ miles N. of Pickering. Here is a Free School, with an endowment of £20 a year. Population, 212.

Newton, in the parish of Stonegrave, wap. of Rydale, and liberty of St. Peter's ; 4 miles SSE. of Helmsley. Pop. including Laysthorpe, 72.

Newton Dale, in the parishes of ... and Levisham, wap. and liberty of Pickering Lythe ; 7 miles N. of Pickering.

Newton Grange, in the parish of Oswaldkirk, wap. of Rydale ; 3 miles SSE. of Helmsley.

Newton-le-Willows, in the parish of Patrick-Brompton, wap. of Hang East, and liberty of Richmondshire ; 3 miles WNW. of Bedale. Here is a small Methodist chapel. Pop. 250.

Newton-Morrell, in the parish of Barton, wap. of Gilling East, and liberty of Richmondshire ; 8 miles N. NE. of Richmond. Pop. 31.

Newton Mulgrave, a small hamlet, in the parish of Lythe, wap. and liberty of Langbargh ; 8 miles NW. of Whitby. Population, 124.

Newton, in the parish of Burneston, wap. of Halikeld, and liberty of Richmondshire ; 3 miles ENE. of Bedale. Pop. included with Exilby, 562.

NEWTON-UPON-OUSE, (P.) in the wap. of Bulmer ; 7 miles S. of Easingwold. Here is a handsome church ; the living is a perpetual curacy, in the patronage of Mrs. Earle, incumbent the Rev. John Gatenby. Here are also two chapels, viz. Wesleyan and Primitive Methodists. Pop. 495.

Burton Thomas, surgeon
Nords Mrs. E. gentlewoman

*Blacksmiths,*
Nicholson Geo.
Wilks Wm.

*Coal and Lime Merchants,*
Burton Thos.
Cook Wm.
Sootheran John, & maltster

*Farmers & Yeomen,*
Bell James
Brown John
Burton Michael
Carr John
Cass Wm.
Clark John
Dunnington Henry
Gibson John
Hawkin John
Musham Geo.

Parker Theakstone
Sherwood Robert
Walker John
Walkington John
Wright John

*Shoemakers,*
Anderson Joseph
Fisher Wm.
Galtres Thos.
Webster John

*Shopkeepers,*
Carriss James
Steel John

*Tailors,*
May Geo.
Moorey Thos.
Uppleby Thos.

*Wheelwrights,*
Fox Michael
Styan Seth

Bland Wm. tallow chandler and vict. Anchor
Holmes Wm. vict. George & Dragon
Kendal John ; joiner
Moorey John, bricklayer and vict. Masons' Arms
Morrill John, saddler

*Carriers by Water—*The Old Packet, George Thompson ; New Packet,

T. Morrey; The Fly, Tupman &
Burkill, to York every Saturday,
returns the same day.

*New Town*, in the township of Iu-
gleby-Berwick, and parish of Stainton,
wap. & liberty of Langbargh ; 2 miles
E. of Yarm.

NORMANBY, (P.) in the wap. of
Rydale; 5 miles SSE. of Kirkby-
Moor-Side. The church is in the
patronage of Arthur Cayley, Esq.—
Population 191.

Cayley Rev. Arthur, M. A. rector

Bean Robert, schoolmaster
Hill James, shopkeeper
Huddlestone Robert, blacksmith
Surr Thomas, farmer
Thompson George, farmer

NORMANBY, in the parish of
Ormesby, wap. and liberty of Lang-
bargh ; 4½ miles NW. of Guisborough.
Population 122.

Jackson Wm. Ward, Esq. hall
Lambton Dorothy Jane, gentlewoman

*Farmers,*     Dryden Joseph
Appleton Thos.     Easy John
Boyes Scarth     Norman John
Parkinson John, vict. Bay Horse
Robinson John, joiner

*Normanby*, (High and Low) in the
parish of Fylingdale, wap. and liberty
of Whitby Strand ; 4 m. S. of Whitby.

## NORTHALLERTON, (P.)

a the wap. and liberty of Allertonshire; 8
miles from Bedale, 9 from Thirsk, and 16
rom Richmond. This is a brisk market
wn, pleasantly situated on the side of a
ising ground, gently sloping towards the
ast. The market place is spacious, and
surrounded with very good houses: the town
, in general, well built of brick. The
market is held on Wednesday, and there are
ur fairs.* Here stood a castle, one of the
rongest fortresses in the North of England,
which was repaired and enlarged by Hugh
Pudsey, Bishop of Durham, but a quarrel
rising betwixt that prelate and Henry II.
the King ordered this castle to be rased to
the foundations. While the civil war between King Stephen and the Empress Maud
r Matilda, raged with destructive fury,
avid King of Scotland, entering the Eng-
sh territory, ravaged Northumberland,
urham, and the northern parts of York-
ire, in a merciless manner, and advancing

to the very gates of York, encamped before
that city. In this emergency, Thurstan,
Archbishop of York, who was Lieutenant Governor of the northern parts of the kingdom,
summoned the warlike nobles to the defence
of their country. The barons having assembled their followers, ranged themselves under the command of Ralph, Bishop of the
Orkney Islands, Thurstan's Lieutenant, and
Walter L'Espee, and William de Albemarle.
On hearing of this armament, the Scottish
king retired from before York, while the
barons advanced to Northallerton. On
Cuton Moor in this parish they erected
their standard, which was a tall mast, fixed
in a huge chariot, upon wheels, having at
the top a pix, with a consecrated host, and a
cross, from which were suspended the ban-
ner of St. Peter, St. John of Beverley, and
St. Wilfred. The Bishop made an oration
to the army, and at the conclusion pronounced absolution of their sins to all that
should fall in the war. The English, thus
encouraged, waited the approach of the
enemy. The Scots, relying on their superiority of numbers, rushed on to the attack;
but although the King of Scotland and his
son, Henry, gave, on this occasion, the
most astonishing proofs of valour and intrepidity, their army was totally routed, with
the loss of 10,000 men, and they were glad
to retire to their own country with the shat-
tered remains of their forces. The battle
was fought on the 23d of August, 1138,
and from the excitation produced by the
chariot-mounted banners, obtained the designation of *The Battle of the Standard.* In
the 26th of Edward I. this borough sent two
members to parliament, but for nearly four
hundred years the privilege was intermitted,
and it was not till the year 1640 that it was
again resumed, by order of the House of
Commons. Twenty years afterwards Francis Lascelles, Esq. a member of this borough,
was discharged from being a member of parliament, because he had sat as one of the
judges on the trial of Charles I. The right
of voting here is in the burgage-holders,
which amount to about two hundred in
number; the bailiff of the Bishop of Durham is the returning officer, and the patronage of the borough is in the Earl of Harewood and Henry Pierse, Esq. The present
members are the Hon. Sebright Lascelles,
and Henry Pierse, Esq. The municipal government of the town is vested in a bailiff,
deputed and authorised by the Bishop of
Durham, who is lord of the manor. The
church is dedicated to All Saints; and the
living is a vicarage, in the patronage of the
Dean and Chapter of Durham. The ancient
institutions of this place were, a hospital, de-

* See List of Fairs with Vol. I.

dicated to St. James, founded by Hugh Pudsey, Bishop of Durham, for a master, three
chaplains, four brethren, two sisters, and
nine poor persons; Richard de Moor, draper,
of Northallerton, also founded a hospital
here, in 1476, for thirteen poor men and
women, but some of its possessions have
been alienated. Here was also a House of
Carmelite White Friars, dedicated to St.
Mary; and William de Alverton gave the
Austin Friars eight acres of ground in the
town to build them a church and habitation
thereon, in the 15th of Edward III.

The manufactures of this town at present are linen cloth and leather; and the law
proceedings of the North Riding are a good
deal concentrated in this place. The Court
House is situated at the east side of the town,
where the Quarter Sessions for the North
Riding are held, and in which the Bishop
of Durham, the Chief Bailiff for the Liberty

of Allertonshire, holds his Manor and Hal-
mote Courts, and where the magistrates, sit-
ing for the division of Allertonshire, assemble
on the Wednesday weekly, to dispense justice. The Register-office of the North-riding
is here. The House of Correction, which is
the gaol of the North Riding, stands adjoining the court-house, in which are confined
from time to time from 50 to 100 prisoners.
About two years ago a corn mill called a
stepping-mill, was erected for the employment of the male and female prisoners, consisting of three pairs of stones, a dressing
mill and rollers for grinding malt which has
been found to answer the purpose intended
by this kind of labour. Mr. Thomas Shepherd (the father of the Keepers of the West
and East Riding Houses of Correction) is the
Governor, and this prison has the reputation
of being well conducted. The population of
the place amounts to 2626.

## POST-MASTER—Mr. HENRY HIRST.

| Places from whence Letter bags are recvd. | Distance. | Postage. | Arrival of Mails. | Departure of Mails. |
|---|---|---|---|---|
| London | 228 | 11d. | 20 m. past 12 A. M. | |
| York | 32 | 7 | ditto. | |
| Easingwold | 19 | 5 | ditto. | Immediately after |
| Thirsk | 9 | 4 | ditto. | the arrival from |
| Newcastle | 49 | 7 | 40 m. past 7 P. M. | the opposite |
| Gateshead | 48 | 7 | ditto. | direction. |
| Durham | 34 | 7 | ditto. | |
| Darlington | 16 | 5 | ditto. | |

### DIRECTORY.

Bailey Susan, gentlewoman
Beckett Dorothy, gentlewoman
Blanshard Richard, Esq.
Body George, gentleman
Body Jane, gentlewoman
Bowness Rev. John
Bowyer Rev. Archdeacon
Cooper Thomas, gentleman
Dighton Mrs. & Miss, gentlewomen
Dixon John, gentleman
Dowson John, gentleman
Fife Capt. 69th regiment of foot
Flower William, yeoman
Hennicott Rev. Richard, curate
Hirst Henry, solicitor, & clerk of the
general meetings of lieutenancy
Jackson Richard, gentleman
Jefferson John, gentleman
Little Robert, gentleman
Marshall Wm. architect
Metcalf Dorothy, gentlewoman
Monkhouse ——, gentlewoman
Parkins Mrs. gentlewoman
▪▪ Mary, gentlewoman

Rigge Fletcher, Esq.
Shepherd Thomas, sen. governor of
the House of Correction
Smith J. Whitney, Esq.
Wailes William, deputy clerk of the
peace
Walker Francis, gentleman
Walton J. S. deputy registrar, and
agent to the Bishop of Durham
Wasse J. M. D.
Watson Richard, gentleman
Welbank William, Esq.
Wilkinson Rev. James, lecturer, and
chaplain to the House of Correction
Wilkinson Jane, gentlewoman

*Academies, (Boarding and Day.)*

Bowness Rev. J. (endowed grammar)
Hall Jane, (ladies' day)
Mayne Richard, sen. (day)
Mitchell Mary, (ladies' boarding)
Noble John, (day)
Pallister Ann, (ladies' boarding & day)
Spivey Christopher and Margaret
(national)
York Thos. (gent.'s boarding & day)

*Banks.*

Fletcher, Stubbs, Dew, and Stott, on Sir Richard Carr Glyn, Bart. and Co.

Hutchinsons and Place, on Sir Peter Pole, Bart. and Co.

*Attornies, &c.*
Dobson Christr.
Harrison Henry
Hirst Henry
Wailes Wm.
Walton J. Sanders, steward to the Court Leet and Court Baron

*Auctioneers and Appraisers,*
Bowman Thos.
Flower Thos.
Masterman Thos.
Snowden Robert

*Bakers,*
Kingston David
Metcalf Enos
Railton Robert
Richardson Wm.
Ward John
Wardwick Alex.

*Blacksmiths,*
Garrett Robert
Meynell George
Nicholson John
Pape John
Snowball Wm.

*Boot and Shoe Makers,*
Barnett Thos. sen.
Barnett Thos. jun.
Benson John
Brown Wm.
Carver Simon
Hill Wm.
Holmes Geo.
Lambert Thos.
Metcalf John ; b.
*Brompton*
Peckitt P. Thos.
Raw David
Sayer Thos.
Smith Wm.
Thompson Robert

*Bricklayers,*
Hawman Thos.
Mudd Wm.
Mudd Richard
Peacock Abm.
Thompson Robert
Wilkinson Thos.

*Butchers,*
Dixon John
Grundy Wm.
Smith John
Wood John

*Butter and Cheese Factors,*
Hall Wm. (cheese)
Hare Rt. (cheese)
Todds S. and Co. (cheese)
Wilkinson James, (butter)

*Chain and Buckle Makers,*
Buck Wm.
Dale Henry
Dale Thos.

*Chemists & Druggts.*
Dixon Thos.
Langdale James
Robinson John

*Clock and Watch Makers,*
Hepton Wm.
Tesseyman Geo.

*Coopers,*
Carver Wm.
Chapman Roger
Smith Timothy
Tanfield John

*Curriers and Leather Cutters,*
Dixon Wm.
Hamilton Thos.
Harrison Thos.
Taylor Robert

*Fire and Life Insurance Offices,*
Globe, Wm. Wailes
London Guardian, Wm. Wellbank
Norwich Union, Thos. Dixon
Royal Exchange, Thos. Watson
Union, Jas. Langdale, stationer

*Flax Dressers,*
Russell Nathaniel

*Gardeners,*
Barnett Thos.
Bell Wm.
Robinson Thos.
Wood Geo.

*Glass, China, and Earthenware Dlrs.*
Betteney James
Jaques Thos.

*Grocers, &c.*
Airton Thos.
Buck Wm.
Clemishaw Charlt.

Elgie John, tea & coffee dealer
Geldart John
Hall Wm.
Hamilton Mary
Hare Robert
Kingston David
Langdale Mrs. (tea)
Marshall Launce.
Peacock Jonathan
Russell Nathaniel
Tanfield John
Todd S. and Co.
Wilkinson James
Wilson Thos.

*Hair Dressers,*
Flower Geo.
Gamble Thos.
Gibson Geo.
Lamb Matthew

*Iron Merchants,*
Hunter Thos.
Thompson Isaac

*Joiners, &c.*
Bowman John
Brecken Thos.
Broades Thos.
Chapman James
Metcalf John
Raw Christopher
Snowden Robert
Stokell Geo.
Tanfield Wm.
Thompson Thos.
Whytall J. R.

*Libraries, (circ.)*
Hall Jane
Langdale James
Spivey Christopher, (gent.'s subs.)

*Linen Manfrs.*
Jackson Geo.
Johnson Joseph
Russell Nathaniel

*Linen & Woollen Drapers,*
Dixon Luke
Jackson Geo.
Peacock Thos. (& mercer)
Punderson Jabez, (wholesale)

*Maltsters & Brewers,*
Hirst Francis
Peacock Jonathan
Readman John

*Milliners & Dress Makers,*
Chapman Eliz.
Cooke M. and A.
Dale Ann
Langdale Ellen
Masterman J.
Peacock Eliz.

Peckett Ann
Sowerby Mary
Stelling Mary
Weldon Jemima
Wigfield Jane
Wilson Mary

*Painters & Gilders,*
Barker Geo.
Cooper J. B.
Gibson John
Reed John

*Plumbers & Glazrs.*
Loftus Thos.
Russell Simon
Tennant James
Wood Richard

*Rope and Twine Makers,*
Best John, & curled hair manufactr.
Watson Thos.
Watson Joseph

*Saddlers, &c.*
Blackett Robert
Lunn Thos.
Masterman Geo.
Watson James

*Spirit Merchants,*
Barker Thos.
Jefferson Charles
Kemp Peter, & wine
Peacock William, and wine
Thompson Isaac

*Stone-masons,*
Humble John
Metcalf Wm.
Wallis Alice

*Straw Hat Makers,*
Dale Ann
Hill Mary
Masterman J.
Metcalf Ellen
Peckitt Ann
Shepherd Jane
Weldon Jemima
Wigfield Jane

*Surgeons, &c.*
Dighton W. B. & C.
Hodgson Robert
Oastler Wm.

*Tailors,*
Atkinson Thos.
Barnett John
Bateman Thos.
Bradley Thos.
Britton John
Hamilton Daniel
Holmes John
Stelling Thos.
Weldon Thos.

*Tallow Chandlers,*
Gibson Geo.
Hare Robert

Marshall LauncelotHobson Wm.

Tanners.
Clark John
Sedgwick H. A.
*Tinners & Braziers,*
Loftus Thos.
Russell Simeon, tinman
Tennant James
Walbran Henry
*Wheelwrights,*
GoldsbroughJonth.
Hawman Samuel

Lodge Henry & Rt.
Nelson Wm.
Pearson Thos.
*Whitesmiths,*
Calvert Mary
Nevison Wm.
Shepherd Wm.
Snowball Robert
*Wood Turners and Lime Wheel Mkrs.*
Fairburn Joseph
Flower James

*Hotels, Inns, &c.*

Black Bull, Robert Smith
Black Swan, John Simeson
Durham Ox, Robert Thompson
Fleece, William Guthrie
George & Dragon, Geo. Watson
George Inn, Dorothy Clithero
Golden Lion, Francis Hirst, (commercial Inn and posting house)
King's Arms, Charles C. Cade
King's Head, W. Scott, & posting hs.
Lord Nelson, Thos. Walker
Mason's Arms, Alice Wallis
New Inn, Wm. Humphrey
Oak Tree Inn, Thos. Masterman
Old Golden Lion, John Carls
Pack Horse, Robert Simpson
Talbot Inn, Thos. Wright
Three Tuns, John Tyreman
Victory, Thos. Robinson
Wheat Sheaf, Charles Kingston
White Horse, Wm. Grundy

*Miscellany.*

Barker Christr. veteripary surgeon
Bowman Thos. Sheriff's officer
Bray Robert, parish clerk
Broades Mary, confectioner
Chapman Ann, silk dyer
Chapman Wm. sen. perpetual overseer
Flower Thos. bailiff for the liberty of Allertonshire
Hardwick John, coach maker
Hawman Thos. glove maker, &c.
Kemp Anthony, waiter at the Golden Lion
Langdale James, printer and bookseller, chief constable for Allertonshire, and clerk of sub-division meetings of lieutenancy
Lunn Ralph, waiter at the GoldenLion
Marshall Wm. architect
Moon John, corn miller
Naisbitt Thos. hosier
Robinson Robert, reed maker
Shepherd Thos. jun. under gaoler
Soppit Robert, officer of excise
Wait Thos. clerk of indictments for North Riding
Walker Matthew, basket maker

Wigfield Jonathan, hosier, &c. and brickmaker
Wilson John, governor of workhouse, and inspector of raw hides

COACHES,
*From the Golden Lion, Francis Hirst.*

ROYAL MAIL arrives at the Golden Lion (the King's Head and Black Bull alternate months) from London at ½ past 12, and from Edinburgh, a ¼ before 8 in the evening.
The HIGHFLYER (alternate months at the Golden Lion & King's Head) arrives from York a ¾ before 12 at noon, and returns from Newcastle a ¼ before 5 evening.
The WELLINGTON, to London from Newcastle, arrives at ½ past 3 aft. and ret. to Newcastle at 2 morn.
The CLEVELAND COACH, during the season, Mon. Wed. and Sat. from Redcar to Bedale, at 11 morning, returns at 3 afternoon.

LAND CARRIAGE.

*Samuel Briggs,* at the Oak Tree, arr. from Sowerby on Mon. and Thu. and proceeds to Darlington, and ret. on Wed. and Sat.
*George Outhwaite,* at the King's Arms, proceeds to Darlington and the North on Mon. and ret. on Thu. and proceeds to York, and ret. on Saturday.
*William Pearson,* of Brompton, to Bedale and Masham every Tu. & Fri. and to Leeds, &c. every Tu.
*Pickersgill's,* at the Old Golden Lion, arrive from Darlington, Durham, Edinburgh, Sunderland, &c. on Mon. and Thu. and proceeds to York, London, &c. and ret. on Wed. and Sat.
*John Snowball,* to Thirsk on Mon. to Bedale on Tu. to Stockton on Thu. to Richmond on Sat. and to Stokesley occasionally, and returns the same evenings.
*Widow Welsh and Sons,* at the Wheat Sheaf, arr. from Leeds Mon. Wed. and Sat. and proceeds to Newcastle, and ret. on Mon. Thu. and Fri. to Leeds.

*North Cote,* in the parish of Masham, wap. of Hang East ; ½ a mile E. of Masham.

*North Fields,* in the parish of Bowes, wap. of Gilling West, and liberty of Richmondshire , 2 miles WS. W. of Bernard Castle.

*North Ings,* in the parishes of Sheriff Hutton & Dalby, and wap. of Bulmer ; 8 miles E. of Easingwold.

NORTON CONYERS, in the parish of Wath, wap. and liberty of Allertonshire ; 3 miles N. of Ripon. This was once the seat of the family of the Nortons: of whom Richard Norton was Chief Justice of England, about the year 1400: from him descended Richard Norton, who, with his sons, in 1569, engaged in the religious rebellion of the Earls of Northumberland and Westmoreland, against Queen Elizabeth, which was soon suppressed. Mr. Norton, and his sons, with many others, were executed, and the estate given to the Musgraves.

" Thee, Norton ! with thine eight good sons
" They doom'd to dye, alas ! for ruth,
" Thy reverend locks thee could not save,
" Nor them their faire and blooming
     youth !"

From the Musgraves, this estate passed to the family of Graham. Sir Richard Graham, was a very active officer, on the side of royalty ; who, after having received twenty-six wounds, in the battle of Marston-Moor, fled, when all was lost, towards his own house here, which he reached that night: and expired about an hour after his arrival. The estate still remains in the family, and is now the seat of Sir Bellingham Graham, Bart. Pop. 87.

J. Haddon Asquith, Esq.

*Norton-le-Clay,* in the parish of Cundall, wap. of Halikeld, and liberty of Richmondshire ; 3 miles NE. of Boroughbridge. Pop. 142.

*Nosterfield,* in the parish of West Tanfield, wap. of Hang East, and liberty of Richmondshire ; 3½ miles E. of Masham. There is here a small Methodist chapel.

NUNNINGTON, in the parishes of Nunnington and Stonegrave, and wap. of Rydale; 5½ miles SSW. of Kirkby-Moor-Side. This place is pleasantly situated on the banks of the Rye, and on the declivity of a hill, commanding an extensive and picturesque prospect. At the east end of the village is an ancient mansion, once the seat of Lord Viscount Preston; at a more recent date of Lord Widdrington, and now in the possession of Sir Bellingham Graham. The church is an ancient structure, dedicated to All Saints ; the living is a rectory, of which the King is patron, and the Rev. William Keary, the incumbent. Here are two handsome marble monuments erected to the memory of the Lords Preston and Widdring-

ton. There is a free-school in this village, founded by Ranold Graham, Esq. in 1678, and endowed by him with 6l. per annum for six scholars, with 4l. per annum by David Bedford, of Nunnington, for four scholars ; and twenty others are annually put to school by the voluntary bounty of Sir Bellingham Graham, besides two others educated at the expense of Mr. Peacock, of London, making a total of thirty-two scholars. Mr. George Marshall, is the present master. This charity is at present under the consideration of the commissioners of charities, as it is supposed that the original endowment was not a money payment, but rental of land. Ranold Graham, Esq. also founded and endowed an hospital here in 1678, for three poor widows and three poor widowers, with 12l. per annum, and 2l. for the repair of the building. The inmates of the hospital receive an additional sum of twelve shillings per annum, together with a new coat, stuff gown, &c. every two years, but the source from which these increased allowances arise is unknown. Population, 418.

Browne Rev. Thomas, curate
Cleaver Edward, Esq. Lodge
Moore James, gentleman

| *Farmers,* | Peacock Wm. |
|---|---|
| Audaer John | Peacock Wm. |
| Blythe Richard | *Shopkeepers,* |
| Crossby Thomes, | Harland Thos. |
| and constable | Mattison Richard |
| Harrison Wm. | Peacock John |
| Peacock John, & | Ware Wm. and |
| overseer | tailor |

Blackitt Thos. gamekeeper
Gray John, shoemaker
Peacock Richard, vict. Board
Ray Wm. cooper
Snowden Geo. blacksmith

NUNTHORPE, in the parish of Ayton, wap. and liberty of Langbargh; 3½ miles NE. of Stokesley. Nunthorpe-hall was formerly a seat of the Constables, whose arms still remain over a door at the south end of one of the out-buildings. The Chapel of Ease, dedicated to St. Mary, is a small dilapidated structure, which is at present condemned to be pulled down, and re-placed with a new one : the living was formerly only a stipendary payment of 10l. per annum. but it has lately been augmented by Queen Ann's bounty, and established a perpetual curacy ; the present incumbent is the Rev John Thompson, and the patrons, are Thos. Simpson, Esq. and Thomas Masterman. It appears from Domesday-book and other authentic records, that this place was anciently written Thorp, from the Saxon Doppe, which simply signifies a village ; and that it received its present distinguishing name from a small Cistercian Nunnery, which was first founded at Hutton, in the parish of Guisborough, by Ralph de Nevile, about the year 1162; and afterwards removed hither, when the place, from that circumstance, was called Nun-thorpe. Pop. 110.

Simpson Thomas, Esq. Hall

*Farmers & Yeomen,*  Nightingale Wm.
Barker Wm.    Sevonwell Wm.
Batty John    Skelton Andrew
Johnson Wm.    Ward Wm.
Masterman Thos.    Weatherill Wm.

Farndale Wm. wheelwright
Ingledew Geo. shoemaker
Masterman John, vict. Bay Horse
Suggitt Wm. blacksmith

*Oldstead*, in the parish of Kilburn, and wap. of Birdforth ; 7 miles N. of Easingwold.   Population included in Byland.

ORMESBY, (P.) in the wap. and liberty of Langbargh ; 6 miles W. of Guisborough.   Ormesby hall is a neat modern mansion, situated upon a gentle rising eminence, at a little distance from the village, towards the south, and commands a pleasing prospect of the winding course of the river Tees, with a view of the sea, and the southern part of the county of Durham.   The church, dedicated to St. Cuthbert, stands near the mansion, and is a small, and very ancient structure; the living is a vicarage, in the patronage of the Archbishop of York. Here is a public school, supported by voluntary contributions.   James Pennyman, Esq. was a loyalist in the time of King Charles I. and had a large sum levied upon him for his loyalty, by the sequestrators; to defray which, he was obliged to dispose of a part of his estate, at Ormesby; which was sold to Mr. Elwes, for the sum of 3,500*l*. As a proof of the rapid improvement and advance in the value of landed property in England within 50 years, it may be remarked that this estate was purchased about the year 1720, by Ralph Robinson, Esq. for the sum of 7,500*l*. and, in the year 1770, was sold by his nephew, Marshall Robinson, Esq. to the late Sir James Pennyman, Bart. for the sum of 47,500*l*.   Population, 349.

Pennyman Sir William Henry, Bart.
    Ormesby hall
Thompson Rev. James, vicar
Garbutt Richard, gentleman
Huggill Miss Mary, gentlewoman
Mowbray John, gentleman

*Farmers,*
Batty John    Fletcher John
 ̶ ̶kton John    Garbutt Wm.
    Hebron Geo.

Hymers Thos.
Jackson Robert
Jackson Ralph
Lidster Thos.
Robinson John
Sanders Thos.
Terry John

Weatherill Thos.
    *Shoemakers,*
Lindsley Robert
Lindsley Thos.
    *Tailors,*
Close Thos.
Wilkinson Thos.

Cammorin Thos. gamekeeper
Hall Thos. joiner and cartwright
Jennett John, tanner
Jennett Elizabeth, grocer
Lowther John, blacksmith & parish clerk
Morley Wm. vict. Red Lion
Ord Joseph, butcher
Weatherill Alice, vict. Black Lion
Wheatley Thos. schoolmaster

OSBALDWICK, (P.) in the wap. of Bulmer, and liberty of St. Peter's ; 2 miles E. of York.   Here is a church dedicated to St. Thomas ; the living is a vicarage, in the patronage of the Prebendary of Strensall, of which the Rev. John Ellis, is the incumbent. Population, 176.

Carlton Mrs. Ann, gentlewoman
Gossip Mrs. Eliz. gentlewoman
Hotham Wm. gentleman
*Farmers & Yeomen,*  Dalton Henry
Atkinson Samuel    Hindsley Wm.
Burrill Wm.    Robson Geo.
Croft Thos.

Barker Francis, shoemaker
Clemishaw John, gardener
Hornby Preston, keeper of the lunatic asylum
Simpson Wm. vict. Black Bull

*Osgodby*, in the parish of Cayton, wap. and liberty of Pickering Lythe ; 8 miles S. of Scarborough.   Pop. 72.

*Osgoodby*, in the parish of Kilburn, wap. of Birdforth, and liberty of Ripon ; 5 miles ESE. of Thirsk.   Population included in Kilburn.

OSMOTHERLEY, (P.) in the wap. and liberty of Allertonshire ; 7 miles NE. of Northallerton.   The parish church is dedicated to St. Peter; the living is a vicarage, in the patronage of the Bishop of Durham, and the Rev. Thomas Marshall is the incumbent.   There are besides in this parish a Catholic chapel, a meeting-house for the Society of Friends, and a chapel for the Methodists.   The market here is held on Saturday.   Population, 755.

Brown Rev. James, curate
Dibb William, surgeon
Kington Rev. Thos. Catholic minister
Milner & Co. linen cloth bleachers
Yeoman, Poynton & Co. linen mfr.

| Blacksmiths, | Joiners, |
| --- | --- |
| 'lark Matthew | Metcalfe Joseph |
| luuton John | Weighell Christ. |
| *Butchers.* | *Shoemakers,* |
| ishman Thos. | Graham Wm. |
| 'rest Wm. | Thompson Edw. |
| cott Wm. | *Stone Masons,* |
| *Corn Millers,* | Coates Geo. |
| 'undale John | Duck Robert |
| ark Richard | Duck Geo. |
| *Farmers,* | Todd Anthony |
| 'enniss Robert | *Tailors & Drapers,* |
| Vilkinson Wm. | Dobson Wm. |
| *Grocers, &c.* | Watson Thos. |
| Ingill Wm. | *Wheelwrights,* |
| iidsdale Robert | Denniss Thos. |
| 'hompson Edw. | Mitchell Barthmw. |

'harlton John, vict. Golden Lion
'oates John, dealer in paints & drugs
'ornby Charles, vict. Duke William
ishman Thos. vict. Three Tuns
litchenson N. wholesale besom maker
.gg Wm. vict. Queen Catharine

OSWALDKIRK and OSWALDKIRK QUARTER, (P.) in the wap. of Rydale; 3 iles S. of Helmsley. Here are the remains ' a very ancient building, supposed to be a onastery, begun in the ninth century, but ver completed, the establishment being re- oved to Old Byland. The church is an an- ent edifice, dedicated to St. Oswald, in the itronage of William Gray, Esq. There are me very ancient pillars at the entrance or on the south, and within the church is arch of Saxon architecture. The living a rectory. Here is a school for eight or children, endowed with 5l. a year, by n. Mary Thompson. Pop. 383.

rter Geo. chief constable for the division of Rydale
amber Rev. Thomas, A. B. rector

| *Blacksmiths,* | Carter George |
| --- | --- |
| ickson Geo. | Grey Stephen, |
| chardson Richd. | Newton grange |
| *rmers & Yeomen,* | Lazenby Robert |
| kinson Henry, | Seamour John, |
| and carpenter | Newton grange |
| itton Thos. and | Seamour John |
| tone mason | Wilson Matthew |

la Jas. maltster & vict. Malt Shovel
rbank David, shoemaker
ll Richard, schoolmaster
orp James, groom

OTTRINGTON NORTH, (P.) in wap. and liberty of Allertonshire; miles S. of Northallerton. The rch is dedicated to St. Michael; the ng is a vicarage, in the patronage of rist Church College, Oxford, of ich the Rev. T. H. Fowlds, A. M. he incumbent. Pop. 44.

Ainsley John, gentleman
Webster John, yeoman
Lambert Ann, vict. Elder Bush
Newsome John, farmer
Trowsdale Michael, farmer

Otterington South, (P.) in the wap. of Birdforth, liberties of Allertonshire and Ripon; 5 miles S. of Northallerton. There are two medieties in the rectory of South Otterington, Gamwell House and Wetherill House. The church is dedicated to St. Andrew; the living is a rectory, in the patronage of T. Bramby, gentleman, of which the Rev. Joshua Sampson, A. M. is the resident incumbent. Pop. 201.

OULSTON, in the parish of Cox- wold, and wap. of Birdforth; 3½ miles NNE. of Easingwold. Here is a Catholic chapel. Pop. 225.
*** A horse post arrives from Easingwold, at 8 morning, returns 2 afternoon.

Scott Thos. gent. land agent and chief constable for the wap. of Birdforth

| *Farmers,* | Plummer Francis, |
| --- | --- |
| Hall Wm. | and butcher |
| Harrison John, & | Winter Wm. |
| vict. Belayse's | *Joiners,* |
| Arms | Passman John |
| Jackson Eliz. | Slater Robert |
| Mitchell John | *Shoemakers,* |
| Nicholson Thos. | Winter George |
| | Winter Thomas |

Bardon Robert, tailor
Featherstone Thos. blacksmith
Feggett Wm. schoolmaster
Markham Wm. shopkeeper
Thornton Mark, cooper

Ouse (River), see Vol. I. page vii.

Overton, (P.) in the wap. of Bul- mer; 5 miles NW. of York. This was, in the Confessor's time, the Lordship of Morcar, Earl of Northumberland, who having been instrumental in subduing Earl Tosti, was, by King Edward, rewarded with many of the estates of that Earl; but afterwards rebelling against the Conqueror, and then against William Rufus, he was slain by some of his own retinue, to secure themselves from the king's displeasure. The church is dedi- cated to St. Cuthbert; the living is a vicar- age, in the patronage of Mr. Johnson and Mrs. M. Thompson, of which the Rev. J. F. Allen, is the incumbent. Pop. 59.

Ovington, in the parish of Forcett, wap. of Gilling West, and liberty of Richmondshire; 6 miles E. of Barnard Castle. A small township situated near the banks of the Tees. Pop. 1'

U U

*Oxclose House*, in the parish of West Rounton, wap. and liberty of Allertonshire; 6 miles from Yarm.

*Oxnop* (High), in the parish of Grinton, township of Muker, wap. of Hang West, and liberty of Richmondshire; 3 miles SE. of Muker.

*Oxnop* (Low), in the parish of Grinton, township of Muker, wap. of Gilling West, & liberty of Richmondshire; 2½ miles SE. of Muker.

*Oxque*, in the parish of Marrick, wap. of Gilling West, and liberty of Richmondshire; 5 miles E. of Reeth. This hamlet is known as the residence of the late Mr. Thomas Forcett, a gentleman who justly received many honourable testimonies from the Society of promoting Arts and Sciences in London, for his skill in the management of bees.

*Paradise*, in the parish of Grinton, and wap. of Gilling West; 4 miles W. of Reeth.

*Park Gate*, in the parish of Whitby, wap. & liberty of Whitby Strand; 5 miles S. of Whitby.

*Park Hall*, in the parish of Grinton, wap. of Gilling West, and liberty of Richmondshire; 3 mls. W. of Reeth. Formerly the residence of Thomas Lord Wharton. It is situated in Swaledale, in the Township of Melbecks, now occupied by a farmer.

PATRICK BRUMPTON, (P.) in the wap. of Hang East, & liberty of Richmondshire; 3½ miles NW. of Bedale. Here is a church; the living is a perpetual curacy, in the patronage of the Bishop of Chester. Here is a school endowed with about 20l. per annum. Population, 158.

Elsley Gregory, Esq.
Fall Mrs. Catharine, gentlewoman
Rigg Rev. Hugh, curate of Patrick Brumpton and Hunton

*Farmers & Yeomen*, Halton Timothy
Atkinson Wm.    Hunter George
Auton Robert,    Miller Simon
Dunn Thomas    Pybus Samuel
Edon George    Wade George
Fawcett John, joiner and carpenter
Lumley James, shoemaker
Pratt Matthew, vict. Board
Pratt John, shoemaker
Stringer Joseph, blacksmith
Wray Joseph, butcher

*Penn Hill*, in the parish of Coverham, wap. of Hang West, and liberty of Richmondshire; 4 miles. WSW. of Middleham.

## PICKERING, (P.)

In the wap. and liberty of Pickering Lythe; 8 miles from Kirkby-Moor-Side; 9 from Malton; and 18 from Scarbro'. This town belongs to the Duchy of Lancaster, having jurisdiction over several neighbouring villages, called the honour of Pickering. It is a place of great antiquity, and formerly sent two members to parliament, but it no longer retains that privilege. The town is long and straggling, but it is pleasantly situated on an eminence, at the bottom of which runs a brook, called Pickering Beck. Here is a weekly market on Monday. The church is an ancient and spacious building, with a lofty spire, dedicated to St. Peter, and the living is a vicarage, in the patronage of the Dean of York. Near the western extremity of the town stands the castle, which is now in a very ruinous state; and part of the ground within the walls is converted into gardens. The brow of the hill commands a delightful view over the vale of Pickering, celebrated for its fertility. In the reign of King Henry III. William, Lord Daere, was owner of this castle and lordship; it afterwards became the property of Edmond Plantagenet, second son of King Henry III. who was succeeded by his son, Thos. Plantagenet, Earl of Lancaster. In the tyrannic reign of Edward II. he was beheaded at Pontefract, in the year 1322. This manor and castle, with all its appendages, were afterwards given to the lady Blanch, then the wife of John of Gaunt, Duke of Lancaster. Richard II. was for some time imprisoned in the castle here, before his removal to Pontefract; as appears by the following lines, from Hardyng's Chronicle:

The kyng then sent kyng Richard to Ledis,
   There to be kepte surely in previtee
Fro thens after to Pykering went he needis,
   And to Knaresbro' after led was hee
But to Pontefrete last where he did dee.

This castle was of an irregular figure; in the first court were 4 towers, one of which was called Rosamond's tower; in the inner court were three towers, besides the keep, which stood on a circular mount, surrounded by a deep ditch. The whole of this once stupendous castle is now a mass of ruins. Pickering Forest was an appurtenance to the castle, and was very extensive. There is here a Subscription Library, and an endowed Free School, of which the Rev. Warcup Putsey is master. There is also a Calvinist, a Methodist, and a Primitive Methodist chapel, & a Friends' meeting house. The town has an ancient honour court for

:he recovery of debts, and the trial of actions, where the matter in dispute does not exceed :he value of 40s. At Keld Head, near this place, there is a spring so copious, that it is supposed to raise 500 gallons of water in a minute. Pop. 2746.

POST-MASTER, JAMES WILSTHORP, *Office, Market-place.*

| Places from whence Letter bags are recvd. | Distance. | Postage. | Arrival of Mails. | Departure of Mails. |
|---|---|---|---|---|
| York ............. | 27 | 6d. | 4 morng. daily. | ½ p. 3 aft. |
| Malton .......... | 9 | 4 | ditto. | ditto. |
| Whitby .......... | 21 | 6 | ½ p. 3 aft. | 4 morning. |

## DIRECTORY.

Adamson John, Boroughgate
Campion Mrs. Margaret, Westgate
Coultman Mrs. Eliz. Hungate
Croft Rev. Gabriel, Hall garth
Dennis Wm. gent, Eastgate
Dickinson John, gent. Eastgate
Dixon Eliz. gentlewoman, Borough-gate
Fryer Mrs. Hannah, Eastgate
Harding Mrs. Jane, Hungate
Hayes Misses C. & E. Bridge street
Hayes Matthew, Esq. Rectory house, Hall garth
Kitching Robert, gentleman, Hungate
Kitching Robert, gentleman, Borough-gate
Loy Martin Augustine, M.D. Hall garth
Lyth Robert, gentleman, Borough-gate
Mitchelson Colonel Thomas, magistrate, Hungate
Ness Ann, gentlewoman, Back lane
Oates Anthony, Esq. Potters hill
Parke Mrs. Ann, Hungate
Parke Mrs. Mary, Eastgate
Parkinson Mrs. Ann, Eastgate
Parkinson John, gentleman, Eastgate
Piper Robert, Esq. Castlegate
Ponsonby Rev. John, vicar, A. M. Vicarage, Hall garth
Richardson Mrs. Esther, Potters hill
Sidworth Mrs. Ann, Potters hill
Simpson Thomas, gentleman, Eastgate
Spenceley Mrs. Elizabeth, Smithy hill
Stockton Mrs. Catharine, Hungate
Storry Thomas, gent. Castlegate
Taft Rev. Zechariah, Hungate
Thorp Eliz. gentlewoman, Bridge street
Ward Mrs. Ann, Market place
Wells Wm. Esq. Beck hall, Potters hill
Wells Mrs. Isabella, Potters hill
Whitfield Mrs. Hannah, Eastgate
Wilson Geo. gent. Potters hill
Windle Wm. gent. Westgate
Wrangham John, gent. Castlegate

*Academies.*
Dobson John, Eastgate
Harrison Penelope and Jane, (ladies' boarding) Hungate
Hayes Francis, Eastgate
Jackson Ann, Hungate
Nares Rachael, Potters hill
Simpson John, Potters hill
Skelton Ann, (industry) Hungate
Putsey Rev. W. Castlegate
Wilson John, Eastgate

*Attornies.*
Bointon Thomas, (& chief constable for the division of Pickering Lythe) Boroughgate
Peirson Thomas, Bridge street
Watson John, Market place

*Auctioneers and Appraisers.*
Foster James, Market place
Pattinson Robert, Hall garth
Warwick Richard, Church street

*Bakers.*
Barker John, Potters hill
Champley George, Market place
Hewerdine Geo. Eastgate
Saunderson Robert, Boroughgate
Skaife John, baker
Walker Wm. Bakehouse lane

*Bankers' Agents.*
Ashton Wm. Boroughgate, (for the North-riding Bank)
Wardell Joseph, Market place, (for the East-riding Bank)

*Blacksmiths.*
Barker Thomas, Potters hill
Caward Richard, Ratten row
Rooke Richard, Eastgate

*Boot and Shoemakers.*
Appleby John, Hall garth
Bransdale Barth. Back lane
Clark John, Market place
Cole Thomas, Eastgate
Ellis John & Wm. Potters hill

Foster Thomas, Market place
Gray Caleb, Market place
Johnson Richard, Castlegate
Kidd Champley, Boroughgate
Lowther John, Hall garth
Nares Wm. Bakehouse lane
Rodgers Richard, Castlegate
Sawdon Robert, Potters hill
Sharp John, Potters hill
Stephenson Richard, Market place
Storry Christopher, Market place
Tate Mark, Potters hill
Thorp George, Potters hill
Wilson Wm. Market place

*Braziers and Tinsmiths.*
Hawson Thomas, Market place
Steward Henry & Son, Market place

*Brewers.*
Hawson George, Eastgate
Hodgson Wm. Potters hill

*Butchers.*
Cross Robert, Hall garth
Cross Thos. (& woolstplr.) Hungate
Foster John, Eastgate
Foster Robert, sen. Hall garth
Foster Robert, jun. Hall garth
Graves Thomas, Eastgate
Graystock Ralph, Castlegate
Lyon John, Castlegate
Monkman Matthew, Market place
Otterburn John, Westgate

*Chemists and Druggists.*
Ashton Wm. Boroughgate
Atkinson Wm. Market place

*Coopers.*
Hewardine George, Hall garth
Lawson John, Boroughgate

*Corn Millers.*
Harrison Wm. Bakehouse lane
Hodgson Wm. Potters hill
Pearson and Pennock, High mill
Rountree Ann, Low mill

*Curriers and Leather Cutters.*
Kirby Wm. Ratten row
Kirby Thomas, Ratten row
Marflit Thomas, Ratten row
Payler Thomas, Potters hill

*Dyers.*
Bird Thomas, Bridge street
Scales Mary, (silk) Ratten row

*Farmers.*
Boyes John, Westgate
Boyes George, Westgate
Boyes Robert, Westgate
Charles Wm. Eastgate
Coates Wm. Eastgate
Coultas James, Bridge street
Coultman Wm. Potters hill
Coultman John, Keld head
Dobson Robert, Hungate
Dobson Thomas, Eastgate

Edon Wm. Eastgate
Ellis Robert, Keld head
Glenton John, Westgate
Grayson Wm. Eastgate
Hayes Charles, Keld head
Heward John, Eastgate
Hudson John, Eastgate
Kirby John, Eastgate
Kirby George, Market place
Kirby Roger, Keld head
Kitchen Wm. Keld head
Newton Wm. Hungate
Parke Richard & Wm. Westgate
Pearson Robert, Potters hill
Robinson Wm. Eastgate
Skelton George, Boroughgate
Smidd John, Hungate
Whitfield John, Eastgate
Wilkinson Wm. Eastgate
Wilkinson George, Keld head

*Fellmongers.*
Adamson Wm. (& glover) Market pl.
Grayson Thos. (& tanner) Hungate

*Fire and Life, &c. Offices.*
Guardian, Joseph Wardell, Mkt. pl.
Norwich Union, T. Bointon, Boroughgate

*Gardeners and Seedsmen*
Dealtry John, Westgate
Gray John, Boroughgate
Kirby John, Eastgate
Wardell Joseph, (grass seeds) Market place

*Grocers and Tea Dealers.*
Ashton Wm. Boroughgate
Atkinson Wm. Market place
Coultman Robert, Market place
Grayson John, Market place
Hart Tabitha & Ruth, Market place
Jefferson Richard, Boroughgate
Salton Wm. Eastgate

*Hotels, Inns, and Taverns.*
Bay Horse, John Hayes, Market pl.
Black Swan Inn, Wm. Yeoman, (excise office, posting and commercial house) Market place
Blue Bell, Mthw. Monkman, Mkt. pl.
Board, Francis Champney, Bridge st.
Crown, Geo. Gibson, Boroughgate
George Inn, Wm. Gibson, (and horse dealer) Market place
Horse Shoe, Rhd. Rooke, Eastgate
King' Arms, Rd. Warwick, Back lane
King's Head, Thos. Vinnis, Boroughgate
Royal Oak, Thos. Edon, Eastgate
White Swan, John Harrison, (commercial Inn,) Market place
White Swan, Roger Kirby, Mkt. pl.

*Joiners, &c.*
Beilby Thomas, Boroughgate
Craike Peter, Westgate
Gray Thomas, Boroughgate

Gray John, Boroughgate
Johnson Robert, Castlegate
Kirby Thos. (& cabinet maker,) Market place
Scarr Henry, Bakehouse lane
Simpson Jonathan, Hungate

*Linen Drapers, &c.*
Atkinson Wm. (woollen) Market pl.
Coultman Robert, Market place
Dobby Ann, (& distributor of stamps) Market place
Grayson John, Market place
Hart Tabitha & Ruth, Market place

*Linen Manufacturers.*
Simpson Wm. Back lane
Simpson Wm. Smailes nook

*Linen and Woollen Drapers.*
Blanchard C. D. Boroughgate
Jefferson Richard, Boroughgate

*Linen Weavers.*
Ayres John, Westgate
Garbutt Joseph, (damask) Eastgate
Ptolomy Wm. Hungate
Sheffield Bryan, Hungate
Simpson Wm. Smailes nook
Skelton George, Hall garth
Wilson Thomas, Westgate

*Maltsters.*
Hawson George, Eastgate
Hodgson Wm. Potters hill
Parke Richard & Wm. Westgate

*Millwrights.*
Lowther Wm. Potters hill
Snowden Wm. Boroughgate

*Painters.*
Gray John, Boroughgate
Gray Thomas, Boroughgate
Johnson Robert, Castlegate

*Perfumers and Hair Dressers.*
Hodgson Wm. sen. Market place
Hodgson Wm. jun. Market place
Hutchinson John, Boroughgate

*Plumbers and Glaziers.*
Butler Thomas, Boroughgate
Mathers Thomas, Boroughgate
Salton George, Eastgate

*Saddlers.*
Robinson Wm. Market place
Walton Benjamin, Bridge street
Wilsthorp James, Market place

*Shopkeepers.*
Adamson James, Bridge street
Bean Thomas, Hungate
Clark Elizabeth, Market place
Fishbourn Thomas, Eastgate
Fletcher Matthew, Bakehouse lane
Gray Elizabeth, Market place
Hawson Wm. Eastgate
Houldgate George, Eastgate
Lomas Elizabeth, Market place

Magson Robert, Hungate
Middleton John, Bakehouse lane

*Stone Masons.*
Boulton Richard, Castlegate
Champney Francis, Bridge street
Lumley Robert, Boroughgate
Salton Wm. Eastgate
Saunderson James, Boroughgate
Scales John, sen. Hungate
Scales John, jun. Ratten row
Stockdale Robert, Boroughgate

*Straw Hat Manufacturers.*
Coultas Elizabeth, Bridge street
Haxby Mary Ann, Bridge street
Kneeshaw Margaret, Market place
Pickering Mary, Bridge street

*Surgeons.*
Birdsall Wm. Hallgarth
Carnachan T. G. Boroughgate
Paul Daniel, Market place

*Tailors, &c.*
Foster James, Market place
Hawson Wm. Eastgate
Hodgson John, Bridge street
Jackson Robert, Ratten row
Kirby Hugh, (& draper) Potters hill
Lotherington James, Church lane
Ruddock Wm. & John, Boroughgate

*Tallow Chandlers.*
Ashton Wm. Boroughgate
Greenwood Richard, Potters hill
Kirby Roger, Market place

*Watch and Clock Makers.*
Cox Robert, Boroughgate
Stephenson Robert, Market place

*Wheelwrights.*
Appleby Wm. Hungate
Craike Thomas, Potters hill
Eden Thomas, Eastgate
Newsome John, Potters hill
Rooke Mary, Hungate
Ward Thomas, Eastgate
Wilson John, Hungate

*Whitesmiths.*
Fletcher Wm. Bakehouse lane
Whitfield Robert, Eastgate

*Wine and Spirit Merchants.*
Ashton & Cross, Hall garth
Harrison John, Market place
Wardell Joseph, (& hop merchant,) Market place

*Miscellany.*
Boak Wm. book binder, &c. Market place
Brown James, wood turner, Eastgate
Burton Ralph, land surveyor, Potters hill
Buttle John, shopman at Mr. Jefferson's, Boroughgate
Chapman Geo. clog & patten maker, Bakehouse lane
Christelow Fras. flax dresser, Hungate

VVV 2

Coverdale John, excise officer, Potters hill

Ellis John, commission agent, Potters hill

Foster John, glass and china dealer, Market place

Grayson John, master mariner, Market place

Jenkinson John, worsted manufacturer, Market place

Kirby George, rope and twine maker, Market place

Kneeshaw John, purser, R.N. Eastgt.

M'Millan Peter, medicine vender, Market place

Nares Jerom, bailiff for the liberty of Pickering Lythe, Potters hill

Parke Richard & Wm. brick and tile manufacturers, Westgate

Seavers Thos. acting clerk to the magistrates, clerk to the commissioners of taxes, and deputy lieutenants, Bakehouse lane

Shipsey Wm. travelling dpr. Castlegt.

Spenceley Wm. basket maker, Potters hill

Storr John, dealer in edge tools, Ratten row

Sammersgill Robert, waiter at Black Swan, Church lane

Ward John, dealer in earthenware, Hungate

COACH,

*From Wm. Yeoman's, Black Swan, Market place.*

ROYAL MAIL, to Whitby, on Mon. Wed. and Fri. at 4 o'clock in the mng. to York, Sun. Tu. & Thu. at ½ past 3 aft.

CARRIERS.

Helmsley, John Pearson, dep. Fri. 10 mg. ret. Sat. 9 night

Helmsley, John Wood, dep. Fri. 10 mg. ret. Sat. night

Kirkby-Moor-Side, John Field, on Wed. dep. 8 mg. ret. 8 night

Kirkby-Moor-Side, John Wood, dep. Fri. 10 mg. ret. Sat. 9 night

Kirkby-Moor-Side, Wm. Walker, on Wed. and Fri. ret. same days.

Kirkby-Moor-Side, John Pearson, dep. Fri. 10 mg. ret. 9 Sat. night

Malton, John Field, dep. Sat. 7 mg. ret. 7 night

Malton, Thos. Dobson, not regular

Scarbro', John Pearson, on Wed. 9 mg. ret. Thu. night 10 o'clock

Scarbro', Thos. Carlisle, on Wed. mg. 9 o'clock, ret. Thu. night 10.

Whitby, Thomas Keddy, on Fri. 6 mg. ret. 8 Sat. evg.

Whitby, Geo. Pearson, every Thu. at 4 o'clock, ret. Tu. 7 night

Whitby, Andrew Allen, dep. Thu. at 12 noon

York, Andrew Allen, dep. Tu. 4 aft.

York, Geo. Pearson, every Tu. at 8 night, ret. Thu. 3 aft.

PICKHILL-cum-ROXBY, (P.) in the wap. of Halikeld, and liberty of Richmondshire; 7 miles SE. of Bedale. The church is dedicated to All Saints; the living is a vicarage, in the patronage of Trinity College, Cambridge, and the Rev. J. R. Hunton is the incumbent. There is also a Methodist chapel here. Population, including Roxby, 834.

Kitchen Misses J.C. & E.

*Farmers,*
Baxter Wm.
Clayton Geo.
Deighton Robt.
Dennison Robt.
Garnett Wm.
Hodgson Rhd.
Hurwood Anthy.
Law Robert
Paliser Wm.
Peverley Rhd.
Raper Elizabeth
Thackray Thos.
Walker Ralph

Wells Thos.
*Nursery & Seedsmen,*
Banning Wm.
Thompson Chpr.
*Shoemakers,*
Blakeborough B. (& shopkpr.)
Kendrew James
Robinson Geo.
*Tailors,*
Thompson Wm.
Thompson Thos.
Thompson Robt.

Butterwick John, carpenter
Dobby William
Ellis Silvester, vict. Star
Middleton Christopher, bricklayer
Prest Wm. wheelwright
Robinson John, vict. Nag's Head
Robson Thos. vict. & blacksmith, Fox and Hounds
Simpson John, blacksmith

*Pickton,* in the parish of Kirk Leavington, wap. and liberty of Langbargh; 4 miles S. of Yarm. Pop. 94.

PINCHINTHORPE, in the parish of Guisbro', wap. and liberty of Langbargh; 3 miles SW. of Guisbro', John Lee, Esq. is lord of the manor, and resides at the hall. Pop. 30.

*Farmers & Yeomen,* Orde George
Booth Isaac        Terry Wm.
Foster Thomas      Young Wm.

POCKLEY, in the parish of Helmsley, and wap. of Rydale; 2 miles NE. of Helmsley. In the year 1823, a very neat Chapel of Ease was built here by C. Duncombe, Esq. of Duncombe Park. Pop. 227.

*Farmers,*
Atkinson Thos.
Read John

Todd Sarah
Warner Rhd.

Pond-House, in the parish of Thornton Watlass, wap. of Hang East, and liberty of Richmondshire ; 3 miles WSW. of Bedale.

POTTOE, a small hamlet, in the parish of Whorlton, wap. & liberty of Langbargh ; 5 miles SW. of Stokesley. Population 207.

Wilson M. gentleman
Wilson James

*Farmers & Yeomen,* Hebron Henry
Coulbeck John    Mahon Wm.
Pavill M.

Nicholson Mary, vict. Board
Peacock James, blacksmith

PRESTON-UNDERSCAR, in the parish of Wensley, wap. of Hang West, and liberty of Richmondshire; 3 miles W. of Leyburn. There is no place of worship here, except a small Methodist chapel. This village is admired for its romantic situation ; it stands at the western extremity of that delightful walk called Leyburn Shawl, whose craggy sides are beautifully ornamented with foilage. Pop. 378.

Hammond John, gentleman
Mason Christopher, yeoman

*Blacksmiths,*    Carter John
Skelton Geo.    Hammond John
Willis Christopher  Reynolds John
*Farmers,*    Siddal Thomas
Bearpark Chpr.

Bearpark Anthony, carpenter and wheelwright
Carter George, vict. Punch Bowl
Clarkson Joseph, corn miller
Cradock Anthony, butcher
Westgarth Robert, shoemaker

Rainsdale-Graven, in the parish of Fawnby, and wap. of Birdforth ; 8 miles NNW. of Helmsley.

RAINTON, in the parish of Topliffe, wap. of Halikeld, and liberty of Richmondshire ; 4½ miles NE. of Ripon. Here is a Methodist chapel, also a Free School, built and endowed by Lord Grantham, in the year 1818. Pop. including Newby, 347.

Lamsden J.P. Esq. M.P. Newby park
Peacock Matthew, surveyor of bridges for the North Riding

*Farmers,*    Seward Wm.
Hambleton John  Seward John
Resleton Wm.    Stephenson T.
Hills Thomas    Stephenson Peter
Rainforth John  Yates George
Rainforth Samp.    *Stone-masons,*
Rainforth Miles  Blanchard Anthony
Rainforth John  Peacock Matthew
Robinson Wm.    Peacock M. jun.

Blakebrough Richard, shoemaker & shopkeeper
Blanchard John, vict. Masons' Arms
Fall Wm. shoemaker
Foster Christopher, saddle tree maker
Hamilton Eliz. vict. Holy Lamb
Metcalf Wm. schoolmaster
Pratt John, tailor
Smith Thomas, blacksmith
Spence John, bailiff to Ld. Grantham
Walls Geo. vict. Windmill, Leeming ln.

Ralph's-Cross, in the parish of Stokesley, wap. and liberty of Langbargh ; 11 miles N. of Kirkby-Moor-Side.

Ramp's-Holme, in the parish of Grinton, wap. of Gilling West ; ½ mile NE. of Muker.

Rash, in the parish of Grinton, wap. of Gilling West, and liberty of Richmondshire ; 5 miles NNW. of Askrigg.

RASKELF, in the parish of Easingwold, and wap. of Bulmer ; 3½ miles W. of Easingwold. In the year 1623, Ralph Reynard and Mark Dunn were tried for the murder of a respectable yeoman, of the name of Fletcher, who lived at or near this village; they were both convicted and executed, together with the wife of Fletcher, who was proved to have had a share in the horrid transaction. The Church, which is in the patronage of the Bishop of Chester, and of which the Rev. F. Blackburn, is incumbent, has a wooden steeple, and the whole pile is rapidly hastening to ruin. Pop. 440.

*Blacksmiths,*    Shepherd James
Lawson Joseph    Thompson Wm.
Tesseyman Wm.    Thompson Robert
*Butchers,*    Wilkinson Thos.
Shepherd John    Woodward John
Smithson Thos.    *Shoemakers,*
*Farmers,*    Moon Francis
Armstrong John  Tebb George
Armstrong Thos.    *Tailors,*
(& cattle dlr.)  Allanson Richard
Bell Thomas    Edwards James
Blackburn Thos.  Rutter John
Bosomworth Wm.    *Wheelwrights,*
Brown George    Hodgson Wm.
Kirk Charles    Knowlson Geo.
Robinson John    Robson Robert
Sadler Wm.

Brown Thomas, vict. Peacock
Gibson Robert, schoolmaster
Medcalf Edward, vict. Black Bull
Shepherd John, gamekeeper
Temple Wm. grocer

Rathwaithe, in the parish of Whitby, wap. and liberty of Whitby Strand ; 3 miles NW. of Whitby.

*Raven-Hill*, in the parish of Fylingdale, and wap. of Whitby Strand; 6 miles SSW. of Whitby. So called from the Danish General Hubba, who, after disembarking his troops in Dunsley Bay, erected his standard, with a raven pourtrayed thereon, upon this eminence, in the year 867.

RAVEN'S-SEAT, in the parish of Grinton, wap. of Gilling West, and liberty of Richmondshire; 6 miles W. of Muker.

Alderson John, yeoman
Cleasby Anthony, gentleman
Cleasby David, gentleman

RAVENSWORTH, in the parish of Kirkby-Ravensworth, wap. of Gilling West, and liberty of Richmondshire; 5 miles N. W. of Richmond. Here are the remains of an ancient castle; the time of its erection is not known, but it is said to have existed before the conquest, and at that period, together with the manor, belonged to a baron named Bardulf; who, in his old age became a monk in St. Mary's Abbey, at York: he granted to that monastery the church of Ravensworth, in pure alms. On the face of the broken tower are some large letters, but by the injuries of time they are altogether illegible. Pop. 317.

The Glasgow Mail passes here at 1 mg. and ret. ½ aft. to the South.

Allinson George, yeoman
Bell George, gentleman
Dunn Mrs. Eliz. gentlewoman
Gibson Robert, yeoman
Jackson George, yeoman
Lax Thomas, gentleman

| *Blacksmiths,* | Peat Robert |
| Allen John | *Stone-masons,* |
| Stainbank John | Parkinson John |
| *Farmers,* | Smith Ambrose |
| Fryers Robert | Smith Robert |
| Hodgson Hugh | |

Allen Robert, wheelwright
Bulmer Christopher, baker
Gibson William, victualler, Sportsman
Headley James, victualler, Fox Hall
Hind Joseph, victualler, King's Arms
Shipton John, butcher
Tennett George, shoemaker

*Rawcliffe*, in the parishes of St. Michael-le-Belfrey, and St. Olave, York, wap. of Bulmer, and liberty of St. Peter's, 2½ miles NW. of York. Population 57.

RAYDALE-SIDE, in the parish of Aysgarth, and wap. of Hang West; 4 miles S. of Askrigg. In the centre of this picturesque valley is Simmer Water, a lake of the area of 105 acres at its lowest ebb; but frequently, during heavy rains, it augments its surface to the area of 150 acres; its greatest depth is eight fathoms. The following is an enumeration of the fish and insects that are found in this fruitful lake, viz.—Bream, *Cyprinus Brama*; Roach, *Rutilus*; Minnow, *Phoxinus*; Loach, *Barbatula*; Bullhead, *Gobio Fluviatilis*; Trout, *Salmo Fario*; Eel, *Murena Anguilla*; Cray-fish or fresh water Lobsters, *Cancer Astacus*; Muscle, *Mytilus Cygneus*; Pike and Gudgeon, which have been lately introduced.— The lake is a favourite resort of water fowl. This romantic valley was the birthplace of the late celebrated Dr. John Fothergill, who was born at Carr-end, near Simmer Water, on the 8th of March, 1712; and died at his house, Harper-street, London, the 26th of December, 1780. On the North West side of this sheet of water are two beautiful cataracts, contiguous to each other, whose rocky sides are covered with a variety of trees. These romantic waterfalls are known by the names of High and Low Foss.

Thistlethwaite John, Simmerdale hs.
Thwaite James, gent. Low Foss

| *Farmers,* | Metcalf Robert |
| Barker Mark | Smith James |
| Coates Ann | Thwaite Thos. (& |
| Feasby Martin | yeoman) |
| Lambert Jane | |

Airey William, victualler, Mason's Arms

## REDCAR,

In the parish of Marske, wap. and liberty of Langbargh; 7 miles N. of Guisbro'. Formerly this was only a small fishing village, composed principally of huts, but latterly it has risen into considerable eminence as a sea-bathing place, and its fishing concerns have increased as the demand from the interior of the country has extended. There are here several good inns, and a number of commodious lodging houses, with machines and the other requisites for the accommodation of visitors; but in all parts of the year the town, near the beach, presents a somewhat dreary appearance, from the vast masses of sand which the winds of winter drift into the streets, and which are never wholly dissipated. The air of Redcar is, however, salubrious, and the surrounding country, which presents the picturesque senes of Marske, Guisbro', Skelton, Kirkleaham, is truly delightful. The population rearms of this village present an extraordinary disparity, the females exceeding the males in the proportion of upwards of 3 to 2. The returns of 1821, stand thus: males 279, females 394, total 673. The difference is accounted for by the men, who are chiefly in the sea-faring line, being obliged to emigrate, to find employment. It does not appear, however, that the progress of population is stayed by the absence of so large a portion of the males, for, notwithstanding this circumstance, there has, during the last 10 years, been an actual increase of 50 per cent. The 10 years before it was retrograde, having diminished from 431, the amount in 1801, to 411, the number in 1811. The only place of worship in the town is a neat Methodist chapel, but it has been determined to build a new church. The coast of Redcar is very rocky, and the navigation dangerous, but an excellent nautical chart, by Thompson, has lately been published, which has greatly diminished the number of shipwrecks, and the Life-boat, established here in 1802, which is very spacious and complete, renders these casualties less fatal when they do occur. It is stated on authority, that from 1800 to 1816, the number of vessels driven on shore, or lost off his coast, was on an average, five annually, but that from 1816 to 1821, the yearly average has been reduced to one and half.

Bye-post every day during the bathing season; and on Mon. Wed. Thu. and Sat. in Winter, dep. each mg. at 6, to Guisbro', in time for the Cleveland post, ret. 12 noon.

Post-Man—ROBERT WALKER.

Allanson Miss, gentlewoman
Bailey M. surgeon
Berkeley Miss, gentlewoman
Carter James, gent. Bath st.
Foster Guy, gentleman
Lewson Miss M. A. gentlewoman
Milner Jonathan, Esq.
Sabine Mrs. John, gentlewoman
Paul Rev. Thos. curate of Wilton
Walton Peter, gentleman

Those marked * are Lodging Houses.

*Academies,*
Loblin Roger
Wrightson Thos.
*Bakers,*
Barker Robert
Dove Jph. sen.
Nilson Matthew
*Baths & Bathing Machine Proprs.*
Sinner John
*Stamp Geo. (& pleasure boats)
*Billiards,*
*M'Naughton Malcolm (& Newsroom)
Newton Joseph, Red Lion
*Blacksmiths,*
*Gray Thomas

Marcea Thomas
Bookseller, &c.
Walton Thos. (& circl. liby.)
*Boot and Shoe Makers,*
*Conn John, (& tea dealer)
*Richlieu John
Simpson Robert
Wilson John, Bath street
*Bricklayers,*
Dixon Wm.
*Knaggs James
*Butchers,*
*Mothersell Thos.
*Smith Wm.
Thompson Thos. (& porter mert.)
*Confectioners,*
*Dove Jph. sen.
Richlieu Ann
Stamp Rebecca
*Drapers, &c.*
Brown Gaven, (& tea dealer)
Galbraith James & Co.
*Hall Mary
*M'Naughton Malcolm
*Moore Christphr.
*Farmers,*
Agar Thomas
*Clement Wm.
Hindson George
*Grocers,*
*Bell Thomas
*Burnicle Jane
Dove Joseph, jun.
*Hall Margaret
*Hall Mary
*M'Naughton Malcolm
*Moore Christr.
*Jewellers,*
*Bell Thomas, (& toyman)
Shewood Rbt. (& hardwareman
*Joiners, &c.*
*Richlieu Wm.
*Richlieu Robert
Sampson Nicholas

*Wilson Thomas
*Lodging Houses,*
Barnett John
Barnett Mary
Carter Ralph
Carter Ann
Darnton Easter
Darnton Ann
Dodds Grace
Eden Mrs.
Fleck Thomas
Foster Mary
Garden Zech.
Greenside Ralph
Hogg Hannah
Hudson Richard
Hudson John
Hudson Eliz.
Johnson Geo.
Leng Thomas
Mallaby Joseph
Raine Wm.
Richlieu Simon
Spurr John
Stamp Ann
Thompson T. sen.
Waister Margt.
Watson Miss
Wilkinson John
Wilson Nathan
*Milliners, &c.*
Dodds Jane
Lancaster Ann
*Pilots,*
Clark Robert
Hall Thomas
Henderson Henry
Shielden Robert
Thompson Palliser, (& author of a chart of the river Tees)
*Saddlers,*
Hildreth Wm.
Todd James
*Straw Hat Mfr.*
Wyatt Sarah
*Tailors,*
*Hutton John, (& tea dealer)
Robinson Wm. (& draper)
*Watch and Clock Maker,*
*Potts John

Hotels, Inns, and Taverns.

Crown & Anchor, Jeffery Smith
Jolly Sailor, John Harrison
Red Lion, Joseph Newton
Ship, Thomas Hall
White Swan, Joseph Tennick

*Barnett John, mariner

Bulmer Wm. painter, glazier, and tinman
*Burnicle Robert, master mariner
Carlton Prudence
Coulson Robert, corn miller
Coulson Stephen, millwright
*Lynas James, fish curer
*Walton John, master mariner
*Walton Thomas, mariner
*Watkins John, hair dresser
Younge John, custom house officer

COACH, during the season, the CLEVELAND, alternately from the Red Lion and White Swan Inns, every Mon. Wed. and Sat. to Bedale, by way of Guisbro', Stokesley, and Northallerton, dep. 7 mg. ret. ¼ past 7 evg.

*Carriers*—To Stockton, John Atkinson and Geo. Goulton, every Wed. and Sat. returns same day.

To Guisbro', Peter Kitchen, every Mon. Thu; & Sat. ret. same day.

REDMIRE, in the parish of Wensley, wap. of Hang West, and liberty of Richmondshire; 4½ miles W. of Leyburn. Here is a Chapel of Ease, dedicated to St. Mary, the living is a perpetual curacy, in the gift of the rector of Wensley; here is also a free school, with a small endowment, bequeathed by the Rev. Thomas Baynes, formerly curate of this place. A Methodist chapel was erected here some years ago.—There is in this place an excellent sulphur spring, and an open well for bathing, the water of which possesses valuable medicinal virtue in cases of rheumatism, scurvy and weakness of sight. The lead mines here are nearly exhausted, but calamine is produced in great plenty, and coals in abundance. Population 329.

Calvert Rev. John, perpetual curate
Other Thomas, Esq. banker
Robinson Henry, gentleman

*Blacksmiths*,
Nicholson Christr.
Willis John
Wood Hutchinson

Pearson John,
Wood house
Robinson Wm.
Warriner Matthew

*Butchers*,
Peacock Thos.
Waller John

*Shoemakers*,
Raw Isaiah,
Robinson J. sen.
Robinson J. jun.
Walker Other

*Farmer's*,
Calvert Henry
Heaton Tho. Driver
Hespinal Geo.
Horner Wm.
Jackson Thomas
Lambert John

*Stone Masons*,
Davy Christopher
Naylor John
Naylor Wm.
Storey Thos.

Cooper James, joiner, &c.
Dinsdale James, corn miller
Horner Leonard, tanner

Robinson James, shopkeeper
Rodgers Mary, vict. King's Arms
Storey Robert, tallow chandler
Walker Wm. parish clerk
Wood Hutchinson, vict. New Inn

## REETH,

In the parish of Grinton, wap. of Gilling West, and liberty of Richmondshire; 5 miles from Leyburn, 10 from Richmond, and 10 from Askrigg. Reeth is situated about half a mile above the conflux of the rivers Arth and Swale, upon an eminence inclining to the south, and many of the views from the town and neighbourhood are extremely beautiful and highly picturesque. There is a market on Friday, held by charter, granted by Philip Lord Wharton, in the 6th of William and Mary, and a number of fairs, for which see list of fairs. The town is irregularly built, but its form approaches to a square. The places of worship are a chapel for the Independents, erected in 1786, and another for the Methodists in 1796. There is also a school erected in 1779, in right of Marrick Abbey; and endowed with 30l. a year by Messrs. Leonard and George Raw, of the Society of Friends, the school room of which is used on first day by that community as a place of religious worship. The staple manufacture of the place is knitted stockings, of which article there is produced in the dales of Swale and Wensley, an amount of at least 50,000l. a year, which is bought up principally by the neighbouring hosiers, for exportation. The lead mines of Swaledale, Arkengarthdale and Red Hurst, serve to enrich this neighbourhood, and it is estimated that their annual produce amounts to 4000 tons. The township of Reeth consists of Reeth, Fremington and Healaugh. To the west of Healaugh, in a field called Hallgarth, are still to be seen the remains of a house said to have belonged to John of Gaunt Duke of Lancaster, who was lord of the manor.—Opposite Healaugh, is a hill called Harker, where are the remains of an entrenchment called Maiden's Castle, about one hundred yards square. Along the east of the hill there is another intrenchment, much larger than the former. There is also another entrenchment which runs in a direct line across the dale, and passes through Fremington, where some pieces of armour have been found, from which it is inferred that these works were of Roman origin. Pop. 1460.

\*\* Letters from all parts, are conveyed by John Spensley, from Richmond to Reeth, every Monday, Tuesday, Wednesday, Thursday and Saturday.

DIRECTORY.

Harland Lieutenant John
Langhorn John, gentleman
Langhorn Thomas, gentleman
Peacock Simon, gentleman
Storey Jane, gentlewoman
Underwood Rev. S. Indep. min.

**Bakers,**
Blenkison James
Hutchinson John

**Blacksmiths,**
Bowes Ralph
Littlefair Wm.
Wilkinson Thos.

**Butchers,**
Alderson Thos.
Chapman James
Cleasby David
Hird John
Ward Thos.
Wright Geo.

**Cloggers and Patten Makers,**
Bradbury John
Smith Thos.

**Drapers & Grocers,**
Coates Geo.
Dawson Thos.
Galloway James
Harker Thos.
M'Collah Richard
Smith Ralph
Stubbs John

**Farmers,**
Blenkison Thos.
Coates Thos.
Ianson Wm.

**Joiners,**
Fothergill Ralph
Fothergill Joseph

Atkinson John, vict. Buck
Bell Francis, vict. Red Lion
Cleasby John, lead carrier
Deacon Robert, miller
Galloway Thomas, painter
Joplin Cuthbert, vict. Black Bull
Lonsdale Hannah, straw hat mfr.
M'Collah Richard, druggist and spirit merchant
M'Collah Mary, dress maker
Peacock James, hair cutter
Severs Thomas, hardwareman and plumber and glazier
Tennant John, maltster
Thompson James, stocking manufctr.
Thompson Thos. schoolmaster
Thwaites John, victualler, Shoulder of Mutton
Whitell Wm. vict. King's Head

CARRIERS.

James Blenkison to Hawes, every Tu. ret. the same day

**Galloway James
Peacock John
Raine John**

**Saddlers,**
Barker John
Metcalf Wm.

**Shoemakers,**
Cleasby Robert
Emmerson Thos.
Foster Robert
Garthorn Thos.
Joplin Cuthbert
Peacock Christphr.
Peacock James
Peacock Thos.

**Shopkeepers,**
Blyth John
Fothergill Joseph
Wilson Thos.

**Surgeons,**
Bowes Thos.
Hutchinson R. E.
Robinson & Close

**Tailors,**
Ayson Thos.
Brown Geo.
Sanderson Charles
Simpson John
Turner John

**Tinmen,**
Severs Thos.
Shields John

James Close to Leeds, every Sat. mg. ars. at Leeds every Mon. evg. at the Golden Cock, Kirkgate; and ret. from thence every Tu. evg. and ars. here on Thu. night
John Spenceley, and letter carrier to Richmond, Mon. Tu. Wed. Thu. & Sat. mgs. ret. the same days

## RICHMOND, (P.)

Is situated in the wap. of Gilling West, and liberty of Richmondshire; 8 miles from Leyburn; 10 from Reeth; and 16 from Northallerton. The town stands on an eminence, boldly rising from the Swale, which winds in a semi-circular form at the foot of the castle. In the time of Leland, this was a walled town, and in the wall there had been three gates—French gate, to the north; Finkle gate, to the west; and Barr gate, leading to the Bridge over the Swale; but even then the gates were down, and their sites were marked only by vestiges. Alan Rufus, one of the adventurers who accompanied William the Conqueror, in his descent on England, and who commanded the rear guard of his army in the battle of Hastings, was the founder of this town and Castle, which, though seated on a rock, and on the verge of the moors, received the name of "Rich-mount," on account of the partiality of its lords. Alan, who was the nephew of the Conqueror, and afterwards became Earl of Bretagne, received from his uncle the title of the Earl of Richmond.—The Charter for dispossessing Earl Edwyn, the Saxon lord, of his Yorkshire estates, and conferring them upon Alan, was granted at the siege of York, in the year 1069, and is couched in these brief but comprehensive terms:—

I, WILLIAM, surnamed the Bastard, do give and grant to thee Alan, my nephew, Earl of Bretagne, and to thy heirs for ever, all the towns and lands which lately belonged to Earl Edwyn, in Yorkshire, with the Knight's fees, churches, and other privileges and customs, in as free and honourable a manner as the said Edwyn held them.
*Given from the siege before York.*

It appears from Madox's history of the Exchequer, that this grant conveyed 140 Knight's fees, each fee containing 12 plowlands, or 640 acres; and Richmondshire, the seat of these ample possessions, contains 104 parishes. This jurisdiction comprehends the five wapentakes of Halikeld,

Gilling East and Gilling West, and Hang East and Hang West. It has the Tees for its northern boundary; the Wiske to the east; the Ure to the south; and the wapentake of Claro and Staincliffe to the west.—The foundations of Richmond, and of its Castle, were laid about the year 1087, and this archdeaconry, like all the archdeaconries in the Cathedral of York, was founded in the time of Archbishop Thomas, who sat from 1070 to 1100.

In fixing upon a site for his castle, which was to serve at once for a place of residence and a station of defence, Earl Alan selected the strongest point in his domain, and laid the foundations on the almost perpendicular rock on the left bank of the Swale. To increase its security, his successors, Alan the younger, and Stephen Fergenaunt, encompassed it with a high wall, about 800 yards in length, embattled and flanked with lofty towers. To the south, the west, and the east, the fortress was rendered impregnable by the combined operation of nature and art; and on the north, which was the weakest side, Conan, the fourth Earl of Richmond, built the great square tower, or keep, in 1146, the walls of which, with their pinnacled watch towers, from their extraordinary thickness, have braved the dilapidating hand of time, and retain at this day their original dimensions, and stability. From this tower, which is 99 feet high, with walls 11 feet thick, the defenders of the castle had a commanding view of the surrounding country; and in case of attack, all the movements of their enemies became as visible to them, as if they had been made in the court yard of the fortress. To strengthen this approach, an outwork, called the Barbican, was erected, which defended the gate and the draw-bridge at the principal entrance. On the top of the walls, and on the flat roofs of the buildings, stood the defenders of the castle, and from thence discharged their arrows and missiles, according to the usages of war, before Schwartz, the German priest, had facilitated the work of destruction, by the invention of gunpowder.* A tower, about 14 feet deep, which probably served as a staircase to the Scolland, so called from the name of the high steward in the time of Earl Allan, still remains; and tradition, which is apt to deal in the marvellous, has made it the entrance to a subterraneous passage from the castle to the priory of St. Martin, under the bed of the Swale! The Earls, who were the friends, and of the family of princes, lived here in almost regal

* In 1320.

style; and the Scolland, which was a hall 72 feet long by 37 broad, was the banqueting room for the lord and his numerous officers and retainers. Happily, this castle, with almost all the other inland fortresses of England, has long since fallen into ruin.— The people want not their protection, nor the prince their aid. Rapine and hostile alarm have ceased, and the settled administration of law neither craves nor allows of these feudal auxiliaries. Richmond Castle, does not appear to have owed its destruction either to the hostile attack of an enemy, or to the dismantling enactments of a parliament, but merely to the neglect of the possessors, who, in the succession of ages, had suffered the buildings to fall into decay; and when Leland made his itinerary, in the 26th year of the reign of Henry VIII. this castle was then in ruins.* "After having stood," says the historian of Richmond, " the conflicts of the war of elements, and the depredation of man for upwards of seven centuries, nothing is now left but a poor vestige of its former strength and magnificence, and a melancholy monument of the destructive hand of time!"

At the back of French gate, a little without the walls, stood the monastery of the Grey Friars, founded in 1258, by Ralph Fitz-Randal, Lord of Middleham, and after flourishing nearly three centuries, was surrendered in 1538, by Robert Sanderson, the last warden, and fourteen brethren. Several of the families of Scroop, Plessey, and Frank, were buried here. In the time of Leland, the house, garden, orchard, and meadow, were walled in, and the edifice existed unimpaired; but there now remains only a solitary steeple, majestic and beautiful in ruins, to mark the residence and the sanctuary of that order of mendicants, called after their founder, the Franciscans. The ruins of this little monastery, and the premises, with the walls, are now the property of John Robinson, Esq. through whose public spirit the grounds have been freed from many unsightly incumbrances, and planted with shrubs and ornamental trees. To the west of the Friary was a Nunnery, but it has disappeared, and even its history is unknown.

The ruins of the Monastery of St. Martin's stand on the southern bank of the Swale, near a mile from the town. The corroding hand of time has been busy here, and, saving the situation, there is little to

* The site of this castle contains nearly six acres, and its lord is the Duke of Richmond.

admire about this ancient cell of the Benedictines. (*See Martin St. Abbey.*) On the north east side of the river, at about a mile below Richmond, the remains of the Præmonstratensian abbey of St. Agatha attract the attention of the visitor, and reward him for the time bestowed upon the inspection of his monument of baronial munificence.— The abbey, owing to its vicinity, is generally called Easby Abbey, and the date of its erection with the name of its founder are given under the name of *Easby*.

The parish church of Richmond, which is situated on the declivity of the hill, is dedicated to St. Mary; the living is a rectory, and the patron is the King. This church is provided with a fine toned organ, and within the church and the burial ground are several monuments that may serve to gratify the curious and impress the contemplative. The chapel of the Holy Trinity stands in the middle of the town, and formerly belonged to St. Mary's at York. The Rev. Mr. Atkinson, A. B. is the perpetual curate.—Divine service is performed here every Sunday morning and afternoon. The Consistory court, for the Archdeaconry of Richmond, is held in two rooms adjoining the north aisle in this chapel. This court has the institution of curates within the archdeaconry, and the care and custody of them as long as they shall be vacant; it has also the power of proving wills, granting marriage licences, letters of administration, and all other matters relating to ecclesiastical causes; but there is an appeal from the decisions of the consistory court, to the Archbishop of the province. The Rev. Francis Blackburne, archdeacon of Cleveland, and author of the Confessional," was for eight and forty years rector of the parish church of Richmond, and died here in 1787, in the eighty-second year of his age.

The Methodists have a handsome and commodious chapel in Ryder's Wynd, built 1807; The Quakers have also a meeting-house in Fryer's Wynd, but it is now otherwise appropriated. There is also a Baptist chapel. Besides these places of protestant worship, a Catholic chapel was erected in 1811, in Newbiggin, at a cost 900l. by Sir John Lawson, Bart. in the bay window of which there is a fine painting of the Crucifixion.

Richmond is a town corporate, and has been a borough ever since the erection of the castle. Indeed, a Norman castle was never without a borough,* and the term " burgess," implies merely the inhabitants who constructed their dwellings under the walls and protection of a castle. Alan III. Duke of Bretagne, made a grant to the burgesses of Richmond of his borough and land of Fonteney in Fee Farm, on condition of paying him 22l. a year, which charter was confirmed by Edward III. Queen Elizabeth afterwards incorporated the town, in the 19th year of her reign, and in the 27th of the same reign the burgesses were called upon to send members to Parliament. By a charter granted by Charles II. on the 14th of March, 1668, the government of the town was placed in the hands of the mayor and aldermen; and the corporation now consists of a mayor, a recorder,† 12 aldermen, a town clerk, 24 common council men, and two serjeants at mace. The mayor is chosen on the feast of St Hilary, and is a justice of the peace during his mayoralty, and one year afterwards. The magistrates hold their meetings every Monday morning; and a Court Leet twice in the year, namely, at Easter and Michaelmas. A Court of Record is also held here every fortnight throughout the year, before the Mayor, Recorder, or Seneschall, and three aldermen for all manner of actions, suits, and demands below 100l. The revenue of the corporation amounts to about £800. a year, and the two Chamberlains, who collect the rents, are annually chosen by the Mayor out of the Common Council.

The right of electing members of Parliament is in the owners of ancient burgages in the borough, who have also a right of pasture in a common field, called Whitecliffe pasture: the number of voters is about two hundred and seventy, of whom Lord Dundas possesses a decided majority. The mayor is the returning officer, and the present members are,—Samuel Mountain Barrett, Esq. of Carlton Hall, and the Hon. Thomas Dundas.

The town hall is a handsome and convenient structure, in which the public business of the town is transacted, and the General Quarter Sessions, both of the borough and riding are held. The corporation, to whom the town is indebted for this edifice, has had an eye on its erection to pleasure as well as business, and hence it contains a large and elegant room, 70 feet long and 24 wide, in which balls and assemblies are held, and the other public gaieties of the town enjoyed. The Duke of Leeds is the chief bailiff of the liberty and franchise of Richmond and Richmondshire.

* Dr. Whitaker's Richmondshire.

† The Recorder is nominated by the Mayor and Aldermen, and that office is filled by George Wailes, Esq. Barrister at Law.

The Gaol belongs to his Grace, who holds a court here for the trial of causes, when the amount at issue does not amount to 40s.

The following is a list of the Corporation in 1822:—

MAYOR—John Foss, Esq.

RECORDER—George Wailes, Esq.

TOWN CLERK—Ottiwell Tomlin, Esq.

ALDERMEN—William Thompson, Geo. Kay, Philip Macfarlan, William Close, Geo. Gill, Wm. S. Goodburn, Geo. Smith, Wm. Thompson, jun. Michael Brunton, Wm. Terry, Thomas Simpson, and Thomas Bradley, Esquires.

COMMON COUNCILMEN—Messrs. Simm Metcalfe, Edw. Cowling, Wm. Denham, John Cooper, Geo. Croft, P. Brackenbury, John Lowes, James Coates, John Colling, Thos. Bowman, Francis Howson, Wm. Dale, John Watkin, Michael Yarkey, Edward Mason, John Simpson, J. G. Ibbetson, Wm. Gill, Edward Macfarlan, George Smurthwaite, Thomas Lambert, George Croft, jun. John Cowling, and John Metcalfe.

" The Free Grammar School of Richmond," says our usual authority upon these subjects,* " is situated in the church yard of the low church, (St. Mary's) and was founded and endowed by the burgesses, on the 14th of March, 1568." The guardians and governors of the school and its revenues are the Mayor and Aldermen of Richmond, and in them, as the successors of the Bailiffs, the right of nominating the master is vested. The gross amount of the revenue, Mr. Carlisle states at £330. per annum, arising from land, but it happens to be within our knowledge, from an unquestionable source of information, that since his book on " Endowed Schools" was compiled, and even since the last visit of the parliamentary commissioners, the depreciation in the value of land has reduced the clear revenue of the master to a sum much below three hundred pounds a year. " All children, natives in the borough, and the children of all burgesses and other persons inhabiting in the said borough, and exercising any trade, mystery, or manual occupation therein, are intitled to be taught free in the said school." The number of boys upon the foundation seldom exceeds 20, and the average number of boarders and free scholars amounts to about 50 in the whole. The present master is the Rev. James Tate, M. A. (or as he is frequently called Dr. Tate, public estimation having conferred upon this worthy divine that honour, to which, by his learning he is well entitled.) This gentleman takes pupils at

* Mr. Carlisle.

one hundred guineas a year each for board and education, of whom the number is limited, and does not exceed those of his own children. The usher, the Rev. E. J. Lockwood, A. B. who is engaged at a salary of one hundred guineas a year, takes ten boarders, at forty-six guineas per annum. This school, which ranks among the first free grammar schools in England, has produced several eminent men, and from the estimation in which it is held at the universities, to which it yearly, (particularly to Cambridge,) sends its well qualified contributions, many more may be expected to proceed from the same source.

There are here several minor charities, which do not call for any particular enumeration: the liberality of the town also supports several Sunday schools; and the provident care of the humbler class of inhabitants has established two Friendly Societies, one for women and the other for men, from which the contributors derive assistance in sickness and old age.

From the time of the Conqueror, through several successive reigns, Richmond was a rising town, and possessed almost the exclusive trade of the shire, to which it gives its name. It had then many wealthy merchants, artificers, and other substantial inhabitants, but in the early part of the fifteenth century it had fallen into decay, and an inquisition was granted in the 18th year of the reign of Henry VI. to inquire into the causes of this reverse of fortune. From the report of the inquisitors, it appears that these causes were several—First, Richmond used to be the great mart and centre of trade, but since the time of Earl Alan, royal charters had been granted for holding markets at Masham, at Bedale, and at Middleham; second, the adjoining counties of Lancaster and Cumberland, which were formerly supplied with a considerable share of their grain from hence, had brought large tracts of their own moors and wastes into cultivation, and had, in consequence, withdrawn themselves from this market; third, the pasture of Whitcliffe had become overgrown, and no longer produced its accustomed profit to the inhabitants by the agistment of their cattle; fourth, many burgesses, artificers, victuallers, and other inhabitants of this borough had been swept away by the plague, and other epidemical diseases, and others had been obliged, in consequence of the same, to collect the fee-farm rents, to abandon their houses to desolation, and were wandering as mendicants about the country, with their wives and children. The depopulating influence of these adverse events, was probably soon checked, and Richmond large, but no larger now than it was six turies ago. Among the modern improvents in Richmond may be mentioned the rt rectilinear and level approach which been made into the town, by which the cipitous descent from the north and the p ascent into the market are avoided; coeval with this great public accommolon is the erection of a handsome bridge three arches, over the Swale, in 1789, at joint expense of the Corporation and the rth Riding.

There is here a good weekly market d on the Saturday, at which a great deal orn is sold to the corn factors and millers m Swaledale and Wensleydale, where ning is the chief pursuit of the farmer. e want of a communication for the transit merchandise by water, has operated much he disadvantage of this place, and the ty nature of the bed of the Swale, with sudden swells to which that river is le precludes the idea of navigation.— e annual fairs here are two, one of them he Saturday before Palm Sunday, and other on the feast of the Holy Cross, the h of September. According to ancient tom the men and tenants of the town of hmond were free from payment of tolls, tage, stallage, &c. these privileges were firmed by a charter granted in the 20th of ries II. and a copy of that grant signed the mayor and bearing the seal of the oration, exonerated a freeman of Richd from tolls in every part of the king-l, This right we believe still exists, but s ceased to be exercised, and like many r feudal privileges is in the present state ociety a name without a substance. The king concerns here are the Old Bank of srs. Stapleton & Co. in the Market place, draw upon Barclay & Co. London; and New Bank of Messrs. Hutton, Other, and pson, also in the Market place, who draw a Pole and Co. London. At the King's d Inn, in the Market place, there is a scription Coffee-room, at which the Lon-and country newspapers are received.

The town is abundantly supplied with r from Aislabeck Spring, which is con-d into reservoirs prepared for the pur-, by the corporation, and thence by pipes e different parts of the town. There is this spirited little town a Gas Light pany, founded in 1821, the dispersion rhose brilliant fluid serves to enliven streets and adds to the security of the bitants.

The country round Richmond is ex-ely beautiful; the valley of the Swale from the terrace of the castle appears to t advantage. This place is admired by

tourists for its romantic beauties, and by many is thought preferable to that " Rich Mount," on the banks of the Thames, to which it imparted its denomination four hundred years after the Earls of Richmond had built this castle on the Swale.

Within the last ten years the popula-tion of Richmond has increased 15 per cent. though for ages before it had been stationary, and the number of the inhabitants of the parish and the borough, which are co-exten-sive, now amount to 3,546, though according to the parliamentary returns of 1811, there were then only 3,056.

## POST-MASTER—MATTHEW CRAGGS, *Office, Finkle street.*

Letters from all parts are conveyed from Catterick to Richmond, at which latter place they arr. every day except Tues-day, at ½ past 6 morn. in Summer, and ½ past 7 morn. in Winter, and are sent off every day except Fri. at 4 aft.
There are five Walking Postmen—One for Gilling, Hartforth, & Sedbury House. One for Reeth, Marske, Marrick, Frem-mington, Grinton, Muker, and Swale-dale.—One for Kirby Hill, Washton, Newsham, Gailes, Ravensworth, and Layton.—One for Aldbrough, Melson-by, Forcett, Stanwick, and Carlton Hall.—And one for Middleton Tyas, Alnaby, and Moulton.

## DIRECTORY.

Appleby John, gent. Frenchgate
Atkinson Mrs. Newbiggin
Austin Mrs. A. gentlewoman, Low row
Bell Captain Stephen, Frenchgate
Birdsall Cottam, gent. Frenchgate
Blackburn Mrs. gentwmn. Bridge st.
Blegbrough Misses, Market place
Brackenbury Perse, gent. Newbiggin
Brockell Misses J. & A. Frenchgate
Brunton Michael, gent. Rosemary ln.
Burchall James, M. D. Newbiggin
Carter Captain James, York parade
Chadwick Elis. Market place
Clarkson Christr. Esq. Frenchgate
Close Wm. Esq. Frenchgate
Cooper John, Bargate
Cornforth Mrs. gentwmn. Newbiggin
Ellerton Mrs. gentwmn. Market place
Fisher Mrs. Ann, gentwmn. Frenchgt.
Ford Mrs. Catharine, Maison Dieu
Galloway James, adjutant, Newbiggin
Gill Wm. surveyor of taxes, Newbiggin
Goodburn Wm. gent. Newbiggin
Goodwill A.&E. gentwmn. Frenchgate
Harrison Mrs. gentwmn. Frenchgate
Harrison Wm. gent. Frenchgate
Hobson John, Esq. Millgate
Hogg Tristram, Newbiggin
Hudson Benj. Methodist minister, Pinfold green

Hunton James, gent. Frenchgate
Hunton Mrs. Eliz. gentwn. Frenchgt.
Hutton Mrs. Ann, gentwmn. Frenchgt.
Janson Thos. Esq. Prior House
Jackson Henry, gent. Newbiggin
Jackson Mrs. gentlewoman, Frenchgt.
Jefferson Mrs. Ann, Maison Dieu
Johnson Rev. Robert, Newbiggin
Langstaff Eliz. gentlewoman, Bargt.
Lawson Lady Monica, Frenchgate
Lawson Robert, Esq. Hill house
Leighton Thos. gent. Frenchgate
Lockwood Rev. Edw. B. A. Frenchgt.
Lonsdale Robert, Newbiggin
Lonsdale John, gent. Newbiggin
Moreby Mary, gentlewoman, behind
    The Friars
Murgatroyd Mrs. Alice, Frenchgt. head
Petch Margaret, gentwmn. Newbiggin
Petch Richard, gent. Pottergate
Pierse Wm. gent. Frenchgate
Plues Mark, vetern. surgeon, Prior pl.
Pringle Mrs. gentwmn. Newbiggin
Paine Mrs. Esther, gentwn. Frenchgt.
Readshaw Rev. C. Coverdale house
Reay Miss M. P. gentwmn. Low row
Robinson Mrs. O. gentwmn. Frenchgt.
Robinson John, Esq. The Friary
Scott Miss Mary, gentwmn. Frenchgt.
Simpson Mrs. Eliz. Frenchgate
Simpson Thos. Esq. Market place
Smith Geo. gent. Bargate
Stapleton Thos. Esq. Grove house
Tate Rev. James, M. A. Frenchgate
Taylor Mrs. gentlewoman, Frenchgt.
Thompson Wm. gent. Low row
Thompson Wm. Aldmn. Cornforth hill
Walker T. agt. to Lord Dundas, Bargt.
Wilson Thos. gent. Frenchgate
Wright Margaret, gentwmn. Low row
Yorke Mrs. Mary, The Friary

*Academies.*

Bowman Misses A. and M. (ladies'
    boarding) Market place
Carter Mrs. Newbiggin
Dickson Miss, (la. bdg.) Frenchgate
Firby Thos. (day school) Newbiggin
Ibbetson J. C. (drawing) Market pl.
Jameson Thos. (day school) Bargate
Lockwood Rev. Edw. B. A. second
    master of the Free grammar school
Rapier Christr. (day school) Bridge st.
Stringer Miss, (Sch. of Ind.) Finkle st.
Tate Rev. James, M. A. (master of
    the Free Grammar) Frenchgate
Wade Geo. master of the corporation
    school, Tower street
Walker Miss, (la. bdg.) Frenchgate

*Agents.*

Alderson Joseph, (to the lead mine,
    of Messrs. Hutchinson and Place)
Gill Robert, (timber yard) Newbiggin
Harland Edw. (timber) Pinfold green

*Architects.*

Foss John, behind The Friars
Foss Wm. Maison Dieu

*Artists.*

Ibbetson J. C. and drawing mast,
    Friars Wynd
Robinson Wm. engraver and drawing
    master, Cornforth hill

*Attornies.*

Allison Geo. Frenchgate
Leefe Octavius, (deputy registrar of
    the archdeaconry of Richmond),
    Frenchgate
Macfarlan Philip, Market place
Macfarlan Edw. Market place
Pratt James, Finkle street
Tomlin Ottiwell, town clerk, Low row

*Auctioneers.*

Linton Robert
Porter Ralph, Millgate
Thompson Richard, Bargate

*Bakers.*

Apedale John, New road
Barker Simon, Bargate
Carter Wm. Frenchgate
Groves John, Frenchgate
Kendall J. Waterloo street
Todd Robert, Rosemary lane
Wilkinson Henry, Castle hill
Wilson Joseph, Finkle street
Woodward John, Market place

*Bankers.*

Hutton, Other, and Simpson, Market
    place, (on Pole and Co. London)
Stapleton and Co. Market place, (on
    Barclay and Co. London)
Savings Bank's office, Bank yard,
    Market pl. open every Sat. from
    12 till 1, George Wade, clerk

*Blacksmiths.*

Atkinson Francis, New road
Atkinson John, Green
Hubbick John, Quaker lane
Miscamble Andrew, New road
Plues Mark, (farrier) Quaker lane
Stephenson John, (& farrier) Rosemary lane

*Booksellers, Binders, Printers, and
Stationers.*

Bell Mattw. (stamp office) Finkle st.
Bowman Thos. (genuine patent medi-
    cines & perfumery) Market place
Craggs Matthew, Finkle street
Macfarlan Henry, Market place
Macfarlan Leond. (printer) Market pl.

*Boot and Shoemakers.*

Alderson John, Millgate
Batchinson John, Bridge street
Britain Richard, Castle hill
Cansick Nathaniel, Bargate
Cooper and Coates, Low row
Cowling John, Rosemary lane

Barl William, Bridge street
Fletcber Wm. Tower street
Grundy John, Low row
Hurworth James, Frenchgate
Kemster John, New road
Lawson Robt. Frenchgate
Marshall John, Fryer's Wynd
Murfitt Matthew, Finkle street
Potts John, Castle hill
Robinson Peter, Market place
Sayer James, Cornforth hill
Shields Wm. Back of Shambles
Stubbs Wm. Frenchgate
Tate James, Quarry lane
Thompson Richard, Bargate
Thompson Henry, Frenchgate
Thompson George, Newbiggin
Todd Geo. Maison Dieu
Twiddle John, Frenchgate
Wilkinson Robert, Castle hill

*Braziers and Tinmen.*

Jackson George, New road
Eathead Wm. Market place
Metcalfe John, Frenchgate
Metcalfe J. D. Newbiggin
Stead Mark, Rosemary lane

*Brewer of Ale and Porter.*

Young John, Ryder's Wynd

*Bricklayers and Masons.*

Barker Thos. Newbiggin
Bullock Anthony, Frenchgate
Bullock Wm. Frenchgate
Richardson John, Newbiggin
Robinson John, Maison Dieu
Todd John, Newbiggin

*Butchers.*

Appleton Wm. Market place
Denkiron James, Bridge street
Dowling Cuthbert; Frenchgate
Harland Geo. Tower street
And Parkin, Shambles
Lewis John, Tower street
Lewis Henry, Tower street
Raageways W. & T. Tower st.
Sal Matthew, Bridge street
Wood Henry, Westfield

*Cabinet Makers.*

Bull M. M. King street
Norman Matthew, Market place
Norman James and Son, Frenchgate
Walker Wm. Frenchgate

*Chemists and Druggists.*

Hodgson Richard, Market place
Ward John and Charles, Market pl.

*Clock & Watch Makers, & Jewellers.*

Dowling Edward, Market place
Fawcett John, Finkle street
Perry Wm. Market place

*Confectioners.*

Bull M. M. King street
Brown Mrs. Coal hill

Dowdy Mrs. Low row
Harland B. (& fruiterer) Market pl.
Metcalfe Reuben, Market place
Norman Miss, Market place

*Coopers.*

Poppleton Wm. Finkle street
Poppleton Wm. Frenchgate head
Wilkinson Henry, Market place

*Corn Millers and Dealers.*

Bolland Christ. Whitecliffe mill
Robinson Geo. New road
Robinson Thomas, Castle mill
Terry Ralph, Church mill

*Curriers and Leather Cutters.*

Eeles Robert, Castle hill
Mason Henry, Bargate
Mason Edward, Castle hill

*Earthenware, Glass, and China Dealer.*

Bussey Mrs. Market place

*Fellmongers.*

Ascough John, (and woolstapler) Newbiggin
King John, Bridge end
Plewes Thomas, Green

*Fire and Life Offices.*

County, Matth. Whitelock, Market pl.
Globe, Wm. Close, Frenchgate
Norwich Union, I. Fisher, Market pl.
Phœnix, Thos. Bowman, Market pl.
Royal Exchange, Matthew Craggs, Post-office, Finkle street

*Fishmongers.*

Sweeting Richard, Back of Shambles
Ward William, Green

*Flax Dressers.*

Croft George & Sons, Millgate

*Gardeners.*

Hembleton Cuthbert, Bargate
Hembleton James, Frenchgate
Idle John, Newbiggin
Miller Thomas, Frenchgate
Miller James, Frenchgate
Todd William, St. Nicholas

*Grocers.*

Carter. William, Market place
Cook Leonard, Market place
Dinsdale Geo. Market place
Green Alice, Market place
Horn George, Finkle street
Kay George, Market place
Layfield Charles, Market place
Mason Wm. Market place
Metcalf Simm, Market place
Miller Ralph, Finkle street
Orton Benjamin, Market place
Robinson Widow, Bridge street
Smith Geo. jun. Rosemary lane
Thirlwall John, Bargate
Whitelock Matthew, (and provision merchant) Market place

*Gunsmiths, &c.*

Gill Robert, Market place
Kitchin Joseph, (to North York Regt.)

*Hardware & Furnishing Ironmongers.*

Bradley Wm. & Sons, Pinfold green
Bradwell Joseph, Pottergate
Gill George, Market place
King Mary, Finkle street

*Hat Maker.*

Musgrave Thomas, Market place

*Hair Dressers.*

Fryers Thomas, Trinity buildings
Lambert Thomas, Trinity buildings
Metcalfe Reuben, Market place
Wilkinson James, Castle hill

*Inns and Taverns.*

Bishop Blaize, Rt. Raw, Market pl.
Black Bull, Mrs. Wilkinson, Low row
Black Lion, Thos. Walker, Finkle st.
Black Swan, Thos. Cambadge, Green
Board, Wm. Walker, Frenchgate
Fleece, J. C. Ibbotson, Friars Wynd
King's Head, M. Yarker, Market pl.
Lord Nelson, F. Blades, Frenchgate
Lord Wellington, J. Foster, Market pl.
Nag's Head, Wm. Radcliff, Pinfold gr.
Punch Bowl, Jane Hall, Market pl.
Queen Catharine, John Rushforth, Low row
Red Lion, John Wilson, Finkle st.
Ship, John Clark, Castle hill
Ship, Ralph Foster, Frenchgate
Shoulder of Mutton, E. Clement, Millgt.
Talbot, Thos. Lambert, Market pl.
Three Tuns, W. D. Dawson, Bridge st.
Town Hall Tavern, T. Walker, Mkt.pl.
Turf Coffee House, Rd. Fetch, King st.
Unicorn, John Carter, Newbiggin
White Hart, Jas. Blenkiron, Bridge st.
White Swan, Rt. Brown, Frenchgt.hd.

*Iron Founders.*

Bradley Wm. & Son, Pinfold green
Bradwell Joseph, Pottergate

*Joiners and Carpenters.*

Bell Marchant, King street
Brown Robert, Frenchgate head
Greathead Matthew, Newbiggin
Harrison John, Market place
Irwin George, Newbiggin
Johnson Henry, Green
Metcalfe James, Westfield
Wharton George, Market place
Wright George, Bargate
Wright William, Castle hill

*Land Surveyors.*

Bradley Thomas, Frenchgate
Calvert Alexander, Frenchgate

*Linen and Woollen Drapers.*

Dalton C. & J. Market place
Dodsworth Miss E. Market place
Pearson Wm. Market place

Richardson Wm. & Co. Market pl.
Robinson Edward, Market place
Sanderson James, Market place
Simpson Michael, Finkle street
Westgarth Robert, Newbiggin

*Maltsters.*

Croft Geo. & Sons, Millgate
Raw Robert, Market place
Young John, Ryder's Wynd

*Milliners and Dress Makers.*

Appleby Miss, Market place
Bow Elizabeth, Market place
Burnett Ann, Trinity buildings
Dalton Mary, High row
Galleyrey Ann, Market place
Goundrey Elizabeth, Market place
Marshall Miss, Friar's Wynd
Wilson Mrs. P. Market place

*Oil Cloth Makers.*

Taylor Wm. & Thos. Bargate

*Painters and Gilders.*

Foster John, (miniature) Castle hill
Hurworth David, Market place
Newton John, Pottergate
Wanlas Wm. Pottergate
Wilson Paul, Market place

*Plasterers.*

Denham Thomas, New road
Denham Wm. Bar walk

*Plumbers and Glaziers.*

Jackson George, New road
Leathead Wm. Market place
Metcalf J. D. Bargate
Metcalf John, Frenchgate

*Rope and Twine Makers.*

Fall John, Market place
Hunter John, Waterloo street
Langstaff Thomas, Millgate

*Saddlers and Collar Makers.*

Bishoprick Robert, Market place
Deighton Christopher, Market place
Howson Francis, Market place
M'Robbie John, Market place
Wood Henry, Market place

*Shopkeepers.*

Barnaby Christopher, Bargate
Barnaby Wm. Bargate
Barningham Christopher, Bargate
Bates Elizabeth, Frenchgate
Bishoprick Mary, Newbiggin
Brown Mary, Bargate
Cowling Ann, Frenchgate
Davison Edward, Bridge street
Grundy John, Great channel
King Mary, Green
Metcalf Elizabeth, Frenchgate
Robinson Jane, Bargate
Wilson Joseph, Finkle street
Woodward John, Trinity buildings

*Spinning Wheel and Reel Mfrs.*

Vitty William, Newbiggin
Vitty William, sen. Bargate

*Stay Makers.*

awford Daniel, Market place
lam William, New road
orman Douglas, Market place
etch Mary, Market place

*Stone Masons.*

aderson M. Frenchgate
ullock William, Frenchgate
as John, (and architect) Back of
   Priory
ckson Christopher, Frenchgate head
andinson William, Castle hill
'Vay Richard, Frenchgate
adford Thomas, Newbiggin
chardson John, Newbiggin
obinson John, Maison Dieu

*Straw Hat Manufacturers.*

w Elizabeth, Market place
urwith C. (and silk dyer) Millgate
ason Anthony, Castle hill
iler Ann, Market place

*Surgeons, &c.*

wes Christopher, Market place
ckson Wm. Market place
orthwaite George, Market place
yward Peter, Market place
itchinson Wm. Frenchgate
ledew John, Frenchgate

*Tailors.*

edale Wm. Frenchgate
ll Matthew, Frenchgate
own Christopher, Castle hill
ling John A. (& draper) Market pl.
dsworth James, Millgate
tcalfe Christopher, Frenchgate
arson Edward, New road
nderson John, New road
nderson James, Market place
nderson Robert, Millgate
nderson Lawrence, Market place
tes Wm. Newbiggin
ld Wm. Bargate
ld Benj. Castle hill
itelock Christopher, Castle hill

*Tallow Chandlers.*

ter Wm. Market place
er John, Bargate
er Ralph, Finkle street
d Marmaduke, Frenchgate

*Tanners.*

on Wm. Market place
pson Stephen, Millgate
pson John, Green

*Upholsterers.*

lop Thomas, Rosemary lane
staff Francis, Market place
stone Jane, Waterloo street
lding Snowdon, Trinity buildings

*Weavers.*

inall John, Bargate
xe Richard, Green
rbray S. and Son, Back Wing
ton George, Bargate

Newton John, Maison Dieu
Pounder Richard, Bargate
Terry Vincent, Frenchgate

*Wheelwrights.*

Alderson Joseph, Newbiggin
Alderson Joseph, Maison Dieu
Harland Edw. (& timber merchant)
   Pinfold green
Metcalfe James, Newbiggin
Newton John, Maison Dieu

*Whitesmiths & Bell Hangers.*

Abdale Ralph, Rosemary lane
Bradley Joseph, Pottergate
Gatenby Wm. Newbiggin

*Wine and Spirit Merchants.*

Foster Ralph, (Ship Inn) Frenchgate
Mason John, Market place
Metcalf Elis. Frenchgate
Pratt Wm. & Co. Behind the Friars
Robling John, (and provision ware-
   house) Newbiggin
Smurthwaite Geo. Pinfold green
Whitelock Matthew, Market place

*Wool Combers & Worsted Manufactrs.*

Greenwood John, Green
Greenwood Thos. Millgate
Westgarth Robert, Newbiggin

*Miscellany.*

Abbot Edw. bailiff, Maison Dieu
Abbot Henry, basket maker, Low row
Bell Mrs. Sarah, midwife, Bargate
Bowman Thos. clerk to the commis-
   sioners of taxes, & deputy lieut.
   for Gilling West, Market place
Clarkson Thos. Serjat. Major, York pl.
Croft Wm. teadealer, Frenchgate
Crossland Chphr. governor of the poor
Deighton Christr. glover, Castle hill
Fall Wm. sheriff's officer, Market pl.
Fawcett Wm. last maker & clogger,
   castle hill
Gawford M. supervisor, Market place
Harker John, band box maker, Bargt.
Hubbick J. vetnry surgeon, Quarry ln.
Ibbotson J. M. carver and gilder,
   Fryars Wynd
Jones Wm. livery stables, Frenchgt. hd.
Parkinson Wm. gent. Maison Dieu
Peirse Thos. racing stable, Belleisle
Priestman Chpr. bank clerk, Market pl.
Reader M. toy & tea dlr. Rosemary ln.
Robinson L. horse breaker, Pinfold gr.
Robinson Joseph, horse trainer, Behind
   the Friars
Shepherd Thos. jockey, Millgate
Smith Thos. music master, Market pl.
Stevenson Wm. preserver of birds,
   fish, and animals, Market place
Taylor Joseph, working cutler & mfr.
   of surgical instruments, Market pl.
Thompson Margaret, Frenchgate
Urwin Joseph, nurseryman
Wright Robert, gaoler, Newbiggin

## CARRIERS.

PICKERSGILL's waggons every Mon. and Fri. to Leeds, London, Manchester, Liverpool, &c. and every Tu. & Sat. to Newcastle, Darlington, Durham, and Edinbro'.

*Darlington*, Robert Coltman every Tu. arr. 9 morn. dep. 3 aft. John Tweddle every Sat. arr. 9 morn. dep. 3 aft. Wm. Wilkinson every Tu. arr. 9 morn. dep. 3 aft.

*Leeds*, Christopher Pickersgill's waggon arr. Sat. 9 morn. dep. 3 aft.

*Leyburn*, James Clowton, (to Black Bull) daily. James Ratcliffe, (to Black Bull) every Saturday.

*Middleham*, John Walker, (to the Red Lion) every Thu. and Sat. arr. 9 morn. dep. 3 aft.

*Northallerton*, George Snowball, every Tu. & Sat. arr. 9 morn. dep. 3 aft.

*Reeth*, John Spenceley every day except Friday and Sunday.

*Stockton*, Thos. Ratcliff (Nag's Head) every Tu. and Thu.

*Yarm and Stockton*, John Lodge's waggon every Mon. Wed. & Fri. dep. 12 noon, arr. 8 next morning

*York*, John Fisher every Wed. ret. Sat. Christopher Pickersgill every Sat. arr. 9 morn. dep. 3 aft.

*Rievaulx Abbey*, in the parish of Helmsley, and wap. of Rydale; 2 mls. NW. of Helmsley. This beautiful monastic ruin is situated in a narrow valley, which is crowned at various parts with hanging woods The river Rye, from which the local name is acquired, winds through the vale in a stream successively deep and rapid, and is intersected by two picturesque bridges. Within this sequestered spot is the village of Rievaulx, consisting of scattered cottages, which appear amongst natural clumps of trees, with the river winding beneath, and each presents a landscape in itself. The abbey stands close by the village, from which it recedes towards a steep woody bank running nearly north and south. The principal remains are those of the church and the refectory. The former consists of the choir and part of the side aisles, with the transept and its aisle, and the commencement of the tower. This edifice ranks amongst the largest monastic churches. The choir is one hundred and forty-four feet in length, and sixty-three feet wide; and the transept is one hundred and eighteen feet long, and thirty-three wide. The probable length of the nave was one hundred and fifty feet, and the whole length of the building could not have been less than three hundred and thirty or three hundred and forty feet. This abbey,

for monks of the Cistercian order, was founded in 1131, by Sir Walter Espec, one of the commanders at "the battle of the Standard," whose only child, a son, being killed by a fall from his horse at Kirkham, the afflicted parent devoted the principal part of his large possessions to pious uses, and after building the abbies of Rievaulx and Kirkham in Yorkshire, built also the abbey of Warden in Bedfordshire. On the dissolution of the larger monasteries, Rievaulx, valued at 378*l*. 10*s*. 2*d*. per annum, was seized by the crown, and was granted in exchange by Henry VIII. to Thomas Lord Ross, Earl of Rutland, a descendant of the Espec family. From that family it came by marriage to the Duke of Buckingham, and was by the trustees of George the second duke, sold in 1695, to Sir Charles Duncombe, an ancestor of Charles Duncombe, Esq. the present proprietor. The terrace of Rievaulx, from which the ruin and the valley are seen to great advantage, is nearly half a mile in length, of ample breadth, and forming a handsome lawn. It is backed by plantations of trees, intermixed with flowering shrubs, which project forward in semi-circular sweeps, and added to the winding of the terrace impart to it an air of beauty and grandeur. At one end of this terrace is a circular temple with a Tuscan colonnade, and at the other a temple with an Ionic portico. The latter of these temples consists of a well proportioned room of large dimensions, on the ceiling of which is a copy of Guido's Aurora, with the graceful "Hours" in great brilliancy surrounding her car. In the cove of the ceiling are painted in compartments the story of Hero and Leander, the whole by the pencil of Burnice, who was brought over from Italy for the purpose. But distinguished as may be the productions of the Italian painter, the inimitable paintings of nature form the principal attractions of "Rievaulx," and the view from the Ionic temple, which presents the woody steep rising in beauteous majesty to the summit of the hills; with the monastic ruins in the vale; and the bridge beneath finely encompassed with pendant woods, disclose a combination of beauties that must be seen to be enjoyed— and once seen can never be forgot.

*Rooksby*, in the parish of Pickhill, wap. of Halikeld, and liberty of Richmondshire; 7 miles W. of Thirsk.

ROBIN HOOD's BAY, in the parish of Fylingdale, wap. & liberty of Whitby Strand; 6 miles SE. of Whitby. A small fishing town, formerly noted for being the retreat of that famous captain and his banditti; who, when closely pursued, had always in readiness at this place, a number of small fishing vessels, in which putting off to sea, he eluded the vigilance of his pursuers, and bid defiance to the whole power of the English nation, civil and military. The extensive alum mines here, and their crystalized excavations, form the principal attractions of the place. A master and seven men are now stationed here on the preventive service. Pop. included in Fylingdale.

Funer Valentine, master in the preventive service
Leassy John, gentleman

| Blacksmiths, | Schoolmasters, |
|---|---|
| Martin John | Jefferson John |
| Smallwood John | Watson Geo. |
| *Farmers,* | *Shoemakers,* |
| Booth Benj. | Abbot John |
| Jillson John | Butterwick Simon |
| Lilley Thos. (& corn miller) | Ferguson John |
| | Lamb Geo. |
| Stainthorp Geo. | Jefferson John |
| *Joiners,* | Heacock Edw. |
| Bulmer Francis | Peacock John |
| Grainger Zech. | *Shopkeepers,* |
| Thompson Thos. | Mattocks John |
| *Master Mariners,* | Newton Thomas |
| Storm Jas. sen. | Rickinson John |
| Storm Jas. jun. | *Tailors,* |
| Storm Wm. | Chapman Geo. |
| Tindall Benj. | Rickinson Rhd. |
| Tindall Joseph | Robinson John |
| | Skelton John |

Abbot Elmine, vict. Ship
Barnett Sarah, vict. King's Head
Pearson George, vict. Board, fishmonger and ham factor
Robinson Christ. vict. Mason's Arms

ROKEBY, (P.) in the wap. of Gilling West, and liberty of Richmondshire; 2½ miles SE. of Barnard Castle. Rokeby hall is described by Pennant, as an elegant house in the Italian style, built by Sir Thos. Robinson, Bart. and Dr. Whitaker says, that the oldest part of the house is indeed the work of Sir Thomas, but that it has been much enlarged by the present proprietor, J. B. Sawrey Morritt, Esq. and by his late venerable farther. It is an elegant and commodious mansion, standing on the site of the ancient manor house, but its most interesting feature is the gallery, 67 feet long, containing a profusion of statues, paintings, and sculpture; with urns, altars, and inscriptions, the productions of former times, and the admiration of the present age. The park is an angular area, of the richest soil, and shaded by luxuriant woods, bounded by the Tees and the Greta for the space of about a mile upwards from their confluences.— Mortham Tower, which is immediately be-

yond the bridge, adjoins the embattled keep of that name, and was the residence of the Rokeby's in their adversity; these objects, with the Roman statue within the park, and the near prospect of Egglestone Abbey, all conspire to constitute Rokeby hall one of the most enchanting residences in the North of England; and to form a fit retirement, and a theme for a Mason and a Scott. In the vale of the Tees and the Greta are found inexhaustible quarries of marble, which is used, though in no great quantities, to ornament the mansions of the living, and to form the monuments of the dead. The church, which is dedicated to St. Mary, is a rectory, in the patronage of the Crown, and the Rev. James Wilkinson is the incumbent. The population of Rokeby, including Eggleston Abbey, amounts to 232.

John B. S. Morritt, Esq. Rokeby hall
Bowness Rev. George, curate

| *Farmers,* | Proctor Thomas |
|---|---|
| Bustin Thomas | Proctor John |
| Fletcher John | Thompson Geo. |

Binks John, carpenter
Binks Ann, shopkeeper
Kitching James, agent to J. B. S. Morritt, Esq.
Treewitt Benjamin, blacksmith
Whitehead Wm. gardener

ROMALDKIRK, (P.) in the wap. Gilling West, and liberty of Richmondshire; 6 miles NW. of Barnard Castle. A most extensive parish, situated in Teesdale, extending from Deepdale, near Barnard Castle, to the confines of the three counties of York, Durham, and Westmoreland. This parish includes the townships of Lartington, Cotherstone, Hunderthwaite, Mickleton, Lune, Helwick, and Romaldkirk. The church is a very ancient structure, dedicated to St. Romald, and is supposed to have been built by Fitz-Hugh. The living is a rectory, in the patronage of John Hodgson, Esq. and the incumbent is the Rev. James Blackburn, A. M. In the church is a full length figure in marble, to perpetuate the memory of the founder; likewise several marble tablets to the memory of the ancient and respectable family of the Maires, of Lartington hall. Here is a hospital for six poor persons, founded by Wm. Hutchinson, Esq. of Clement's.Inn, London; and a Free Grammar school, endowed with 20l. per ann. by the Rev. Charles Parkin. St. Romald's hall, the manor house, belongs to the rector, who is also lord of the manor.— Population, 377.

Barnes William, agent to the Stockton Bank

Thompson Rev. John, A.M.
Wright Rev. M.

Dixon John, surgeon
Hugginson Anthony, Esq.

| *Farmers,* | Raine Jonathan |
|---|---|
| Barnes Wm. | *Shopkeepers,* |
| Gibson Charles | Hogg James |
| Golding John | Horn Peter |
| Waite Thos. | Raine John |
| Wrightson John | *Weavers,* |
| *Masons,* | Langerwood John |
| Raine John | Raine John |
| Waite Reginald | *Wheelwrights,* |
| Waite John | Collinson Joseph |
| *Shoemakers,* | Walker Wm. |
| Dent Wm. | Watson David |

Hind James, blacksmith
Hodgson James, butcher
Lancaster Joseph, vict. Blue Bell
Lind Wm. common carrier
Oliver Edward, miller
Robinson Thos. vict. Rose & Crown
Robson Mary, vict. Mason's Arms

ROMANBY, in the parish of Northallerton, wap. and liberty of Allertonshire; 1 mile S. of Northallerton. A
small pleasant village, which derived
its name from the Roman road passing by it. Pop. 294.
Monkhouse John, gentleman
Russell John, gentleman
Walker Robert, gentleman

*Rookwith,* in the parish of Thornton Watlass, wap. of Hang East, and
liberty of Richmondshire; 4 miles
WSW. of Bedale. Pop. 76.

*Rossberry Topping,* in the parish
of Newton, wap. and liberty of Langbargh;
3 miles S. of Guisborough; a very steep
mountain, covered with verdure from its
base to the summit; it is seen at a great distance, and serves as a land mark for sailors.
Near the top is a fine spring of excellent
water; to the north west is the beautiful
vale of Cleveland, with the county of Durham; to the east a view of the German
ocean; and to the south the prospect is
bounded by a chain of hills, rising above
each other in majestic succession. Rossberry
Topping is supposed to have been the Mars
of the Saxons, as Freeburgh hill, within
three miles of it, was said to have been their
Venus. The altitude of Rossberry Topping
is 1488 feet above the level of the sea.

*Rosedale,* (East and West side)
in the parishes of Middleton and Lastingham, waps. and liberty of Pickering
Lythe and Rydale; 7 miles NNE. of
Kirkby-Moor-Side. There was here
anciently a Nunnery of Benedictines,

dedicated to St. Mary and St. Laurence. Population of East-side 232,
West-side 179.

*Rotherford Bridge,* in the parish
of Barningham, wap. of Gilling West;
4½ miles S. of Barnard Castle.

ROUNCTON EAST, in the parish of
Rudby, wap. and liberty of Langbargh; 7 miles NNE. of Northallerton. Pop. 135.

Wailes John, Esq. Grange
Ingledew Matthew, yeoman
Kilvington John, yeoman
Smith William, yeoman

ROUNCTON WEST, (P.) in the
wap. and liberty of Allertonshire; 7
miles NNE. of Northallerton. Here
is a church, dedicated to St. James;
the living is a rectory, in the patronage of the King, as Duke of Lancaster, and the incumbent is the Rev.
Montague Wynward, of York, and the
curate is the Rev. Edmund Goldsmith.
Population, 217.

Fawcett Rev. Robert
Kendall Robert, yeoman

*Rounfield Hill,* in the parish of
Hornby, wap. of Hang East, and liberty of Richmondshire; 3 miles NW.
of Bedale.

ROUSBY, or ROXBY, in the parish of Hinderwell, wap. and liberty
of Langbargh; 11 miles ENE. of
Guisborough. There is here a small
Chapel of Ease to the Parish Church
of Hinderwell. Pop. 236.

| *Farmers,* | Welford Joseph |
|---|---|
| Booth Wm. | Welford John |
| Taylorson John | |

Bailey George, gamekeeper
Hick Wm. blacksmith
Skelton John, wheelwright
Wallace Jane, vict. Board
Wallace George, tailor

*Row,* in the parish of Grintos,
wap. of Gilling West, and liberty of
Richmondshire; 2 miles NW. of
Reeth.

*Row,* in the parish of Whitby,
wap. and liberty of Whitby Strand;
5 miles SSE. of Whitby.

*Ruckcroft,* in the parish of Grinton, wap. of Gilling West, and liberty
of Richmondshire; 2 miles NW. of
Reeth.

RUDBY, (P.) in the wap. and liberty of Langbargh; 3½ miles WSW. of
Stokesley; a small village, pleasantly situated near the banks of the Leven. The

church is an ancient plain structure, dedicated to All Saints; the living is a vicarage, in the patronage of the Hon. Lady Amherst; incumbent, Rev. Richard Shepherd. Here is a small school, with an endowment of £5. per annum, for teaching six poor children of the village. Pop. 76.

Brigham Geo. Esq. land agent and valuer, coroner for Cleveland, & chief constable for the West division of Langbargh

Barugh Jasper, farmer
Brigham Robert, yeoman
Preston Wm. schoolmaster
Robinson Robert, corn miller

*Shoemakers,*          *Weavers,*
Davison Geo.          Miller John
Milestone Thos.       Sedgwick Thos.

*Runswick,* in the parish of Hinderwell, wap. and liberty of Langbargh; 8 miles NW. of Whitby; is a small fishing village, situated on the margin of the sea, which here forms an inlet, called Runswick Bay

*Ruston,* in the parish of Wykeham, wap. and liberty of Pickering Lythe; 7½ miles SW. of Scarborough.

*Farmers,*             Williamson Wm.
Dickinson John         *Shoemakers,*
Hall Robert            Dousling Francis
Pinckney John          Dousling Henry

Hardy James, blacksmith
Jackson John, weaver
Knaggs Thomas, cooper
Willoughby Thomas, wheelwright

*Ruswarp,* in the parish of Whitby, wap. and liberty of Whitby Strand; 2 miles SW. of Whitby.—The greater part of Ruswarp adjoins Whitby. Pop. 1918.

Boulby Jane, gentlewoman
Earnshaw Mary, gentlewoman
Major Howden, gentleman
Miller Margaret, gentlewoman
Moorsom Richd. Esq. sea. Airey hill
Pennyman Miss Hannah, Ruswarp hall
Simpson H. Esq. banker, Meadow field

*Corn Millers,*        Feaster Robert
Burnard Francis        Mead John, jun.
Elgie William, &       Norman Francis
    merchant           Robson Wm.
*Farmers,*             Scott Richard
Beeforth Thos.         *Stone Masons,*
Dobson John            Robinson John
Elgie John             Robinson Robert
Bennison David, vict. Bay Horse
Booth Wm. millwright
Corner Edward, butcher & grazier
Frankland Wm. wheelmaker, &c.
Gallilee Thomas, tanner
Harrison T. collector of assessed taxes

Main Barbara, gardener
Main John, vict. Admiral Rodney
Robinson John, vict. New Inn
Weatherill Christopher, glover
Williamson James, joiner and wheelwright

*Ruswick,* in the parish of Fingall, wap. of Hang East, and liberty of Richmondshire; 4½ miles ENE. of Middleham.

*Rye,* (River) see page

*Ryton,* in the parish of Kirkby Misperton, wap. and liberty of Pickering Lythe; 3 miles N. of Malton.—Population, 212.

*Saltburn,* in the parishes of Skelton and Bretton, wap. and liberty of Langbargh; 6 miles NE. of Guisborough; situated upon the sea, near Huntcliffe, inhabited chiefly by fishermen.

*Salters Gate Inn,* in the parish of Middleton, wap. and liberty of Pickering Lythe; 8½ miles N. of Pickering.

Todd Geo. vict. Waggon & Horses

*Salton,* (P.) in the wap. of Rydale, and liberty of St. Peter's; 6 miles S. of Kirkby-Moor-Side. Here is a church, dedicated to St. John of Beverley, in the patronage of G. W. Dowker, Esq. of which the Rev. Edmund Dowker, is vicar. Pop. 148.

Dowker Geo. Woodcock, Esq. hall

*Farmers & Yeomen,* Saunderson John
Burton Thos.          Snowden Matt.
Ellerby T. & R.       Wright John
Ellerby John, Sparrow hill

Cook Eliz. vict. Black Dog
Pickard Wm. blacksmith

*Salturn* or *Satron,* in the parish of Grinton, township of Muker, wap. of Gilling West, and liberty of Richmondshire; 6 miles N. of Askrigg.

Clarkson Joseph, gentleman
Clarkson John, gentleman

*Salutation,* (High and Low) in the parish of Kirkby Fleatham, wap. of Hang West, and liberty of Richmondshire; 4 miles from Bedale.

*Sandbeck,* in the parish of Catterick, wap. of Hang East, and liberty of Richmondshire; 1½ miles S. of Richmond.

*Sand Holmes,* in the parish of Pickhill, wap. of Halikeld, and liberty of Richmondshire; 6 miles from Thirsk.

*Sand Hutton,* see Hutton Sand?

*Sand's End*, in the parish of Lythe, wap. and liberty of Langbargh; 3 miles NW. of Whitby, situated on the face of a rocky cliff near the sea. Here is an extensive establishment for making of alum, the property of Lord Mulgrave. There is also an abundance of terrace-stone, which is burnt and used for cement; the soil abounds with lime stone. In the rocks here, and other places along the coast, black amber or jet is frequently found, of which Solinus says, " In Britain there is a great store of Gagetes or Jett, a very fine stone; if you ask the colour, it is black and shining; if the quality, it is exceedingly light; if the nature, it burns in water, and is quenched with oil; if the virtue, it has an attractive power, when heated with rubbing."

*Savy Green*, in the parish of Lythe, wap. and liberty of Langbargh; 10 miles W. of Whitby.

*Sawdon*, in the parish of Brompton, wap. and liberty of Pickering Lythe; 8 mls. WSW of Scarborough. Population, 139.

*Sackleton*, in the parish of Hovingham, and wap. of Bulmer; 7 miles N. E. of Easingwold. Pop. 171.

SCALBY, (P.) in the wap. and liberty of Pickering Lythe; 3 miles N. W. of Scarborough. Here is a very ancient church, dedicated to St. Lawrence, in the patronage of the Dean & Chapter of York, of which the Rev. Thomas Preston is vicar. Pop. 446.

Baines Wm. gentleman
Brown Peter, gentleman
Dickinson Joseph, gentleman
Grundon Rev. W. S. curate
Taylor Mrs. Mary
Watson John, sen. gentleman
Wherritt Mrs. Hannah

| *Blacksmiths,* | Read Dickinson |
| Armstrong John | Richardson John |
| Hunter Thos. | Robinson Joseph |
| Monkman Geo. | Smithson John |
| *Corn Millers,* | Smithson Robert |
| Robinson Joseph | Stonehouse Saml. |
| Watson Geo. | Tindall Samuel |
| Wright Wm. | Tindall Joseph |
| *Farmers,* | Wallis Robert |
| Boddy Wm. | Watson John, jun. |
| Coates Jonathan | Waugh Abraham |
| Cockerill John | Williams Richard |
| Coveley John | Willis John |
| Craven John | Young John |
| Cross James | *Shoemakers,* |
| Frankland Wm. | Allison Geo. |
| Houson John | Hendrick Wm. |
| Newbeggin Wm. | *Stone Masons,* |
| Outhwaite Edw. | Frank Aaron |
| Pearson Wm. | Monkman Robert |

| *Tailors,* | *Wheelwrights,* |
| Cook Wm. | Tindall Wm. |
| Ridley Thos. | Weatherill Wm. |

Brown Charles, lapidary
Hodgson Jonathan, vict. Ship
Stonehouse Samuel, vict. Oak Tree
Wilson Ralph, schoolmaster

SCALBY MILL, in the parish of Scalby, wap. and liberty of Pickering Lythe; 2 miles N. of Scarborough.— A place much resorted to by the company of Scarborough, in the season, as a tea garden.

Pearson J. vict. and corn miller

*Scaling*, in the parishes of Hinderwell and Easington, wap. and liberty of Langbargh; 10 miles E. of Guisbro'.

*Scaling Dam*, in the parish of Easington, wap. and liberty of Langbargh; 10 miles E. of Guisbro', & 11 W. of Whitby, situated on the high road leading from Guisbro' to Whitby.

## SCARBROUGH, (P.)

Is situated in the wap. of Pickering Lythe, and liberty of Scarborough, in 54 degrees 17½ minutes N. latitude, and 22 minutes W. longitude, 17 miles from Pickering, 21 from Whitby, and 22 from Malton. The origin of this place is not known, but its ancient name Scearburg, is of Saxon derivation, Scear or Scar, signifying a rock, and Burgh a fortified place. The town is situated in the recess of a beautiful bay, on the shore of the German Ocean, and in a situation nearly central, between Flamborough Head and Whitby. It rises from the shore in the form of an amphitheatre, ledge towering over ledge; and the concave slope of its semi-circular bay has a very picturesque appearance. The situation, which is admired for its various beauties, is thus described by the correct and elegant historian of Scarborough. " To the east stand the ruins of the ancient castle, whose venerable walls adorn the summit of a lofty promontory. To the south is a vast expanse of ocean, a scene of the highest magnificence where fleets of ships are frequently passing. The recess of the side leaves a spacious area upon the sands, equally convenient for exercise and sea-bathing. The refreshing gale of the ocean, and the shade of the neighbouring hills, give an agreeable temperature to the air during the sultry heats of summer, and produce a grateful serenity."

Scarborough is supposed to have been one of those places which William the Conqueror reduced to a state of desolation so complete, that it is not mentioned in Domesday Book, and the first authentic record we have of it is to be found in a charter granted to the town by Henry II. In 1252 Henry III. granted a patent for making a new pier at *Scardeburgh*, as it was then called, and one of the charters of that prince mentions it as the *New Town*, in contra-distinction to Walsgrave or Walesgrif, which was the *Old Town*.

The piers, for the security of the shipping, date their origin with the time of Henry III. who, in the 36th year of his reign, granted to the bailiffs, burgesses, and inhabitants, certain duties to be taken on all merchants' ships and fishing vessels, " to make a new port with timber and stone."— Owing to the confined state of the harbour, and the insufficiency of the ancient pier, an act was passed in the 5th of Geo. II. for enlarging the pier and harbour, and a duty of a halfpenny a chaldron is imposed upon all coals laden in any ship or vessel from Newcastle or parts belonging to it, together with certain duties on imports, exports, and shipping, payable at Scarborough. Under the operation of this act the pier was extended to a length of 1200 feet in the whole. But notwithstanding this enlargement, the commissioners deemed it advisable, in order to increase the depth and capacity of the harbour still more, to build a new pier, sweeping into the sea, with a large portion of a circle. The foundations of this pier are 60 feet in breadth, and at the curvature 63 feet; it will, when finished, extend 1300 feet into the sea, and about 40 feet are completed annually. The stones used in its construction are immense, many of them weighing from 20 to 30 tons each. They are got from the White Nabb quarry, about two miles to the south of the harbour, and placed in their proper situations by a simple mechanical invention of great power, constructed for the purpose. This harbour is the only port between the Humber and Tynemouth haven where ships of large burden can find a safe refuge in the violent easterly gales which sometimes prevail on this coast. The situation of the harbour unfortunately exposes it to be warped up with sand, and the agitation of the sea, in these strong easterly gales, is the most powerful agent for keeping the port from being absolutely choaked up.

Scarborough is a borough, and sends two members to parliament. It was incorporated by charter in the reign of Henry II. which has been confirmed and extended in succeeding reigns. The corporation consists of two Bailiffs, two Coroners, four Chamberlains, and a Common Council of thirty-six members, classed in three branches of twelve each. The following is the list of the members of the body corporate, according to the appointments of the 19th of November, 1822 :—

BAILIFFS—Richard Wilson and Henry Hugall, Esquires.

CORONERS—Mr. Henry Cooke and Mr. Robert Marfitt.

FIRST TWELVE—*Mr. John Woodall*, sen. Mr. Thomas Foster, *Mr. Valentine Fowler*, sen. Mr. John Coulson, *Mr. Benjamin Fowler*, *Mr. Robert Tindall*, *Mr. Anthony Benwick*, Mr. John Travis, *Mr. Gawen Taylor*, *Mr. William Travis*, *Mr. John Woodall*, and Thomas Keld.

CHAMBERLAINS—Mr. Edward Hopper Hebden, Mr. George Woodhouse Porrett, Mr. Samuel Wharton, jun. and Mr. George Nesfield, sen. *and Church-Warden*.

SECOND TWELVE—*Mr. Joseph N. Vickerman*, *Mr. Samuel Wharton*, sen. *Mr. William Chambers*, *Mr. William Moorsom*, Mr. John Hill Coulson, Mr. Henry Byron, Mr. John Bell, Mr. John Tindall, *Mr. Jas. Cooper*, Mr. John Maling, Mr. Thomas Duesbery, and Mr. Robert Porrett.

THIRD TWELVE—Mr. Thomas Adamson, Mr. Christopher Coulson, Mr. George Harrison, jun. Mr. Valentine Fowler, jun. Mr. Thomas Parkin, Mr. Musgrave Robinson, Mr. Richard Williamson, Mr. Edward Donner, Mr. John Wharton, Mr. Thomas Staines, Mr. John Woodall, jun. Mr. George Fowler, *Church-Warden*.

Those in Italic letters have served the office of Bailiff.

LAW OFFICERS OF THE CORPORATION. His Grace the Duke of Rutland, *Recorder*. John Travis, Esq. *Deputy Recorder and Common Clerk*.

This borough sent members to parliament the 23d of Edward I. and is the only place in this county, York and Hull excepted, that regularly returned members before the time of Edward VI. The right of election is in the corporation, consisting of forty-four individuals, as stated above; the Bailiffs are the returning officers, and the patrons of the borough the Duke of Rutland and the Earl of Mulgrave. The present members are— the Rt. Hon. Chas. Manners Sutton, Speaker of the House of ·Commons, Palace yard, London; and the Hon. Edmund Phipps, 64, Mount street, London.

This place gives the title of an Earl to the noble family of Lumley, which earldom was conferred by King William III. on the 15th of April, 1690. Richard III. in 1485, changed the constitution of this borough, vesting the government in the hands of a Mayor, Sheriff, and twelve aldermen, and by the same charter " the town of Seardeburgh and the manor of Wallesgrave" was erected into a separate county, but this charter not being recited or recognised by any of the succeeding kings, the corporation returned to its ancient form, and the town and manor merged again into the County of York.

No part of the British coast can afford a situation more convenient or delightful for sea-bathing than Scarborough. The bay is spacious and open to the sea; the water pure and transparent; the sand is clean, smooth and firm, and the inclination of the beach towards the sea, so gradual as to be scarcely perceptible. No considerable river impairs the strength of the brine; and bathing may be performed at all times of the tide, and almost in all kinds of weather with security. The celebrated mineral waters which have rendered this a place of general resort, as well for persons of distinction, as for families in the middle ranks of life, were discovered so early as the year 1620, by an intelligent lady, of the name of Farrow, who having observed, that they communicated a russet colour to the stones over which they passed, conjectured that they possessed medicinal qualities, and having ascertained that fact by her own experience, recommended them to others, and soon brought them into a degree of estimation, which the test of two centuries has shown to be well founded. The spaws here consist of two wells, the north or chalybeate, and the south or saline well, situated on the sea-shore, at the foot off the cliff, a little to the south of the town, where there is a terrace adjoining the spaw-house, from whence they are dispensed.* In December, in the year 1737, these springs were overwhelmed, and for a time lost by the sinking of a large mass of the cliff, but by diligent search they were recovered, and have ever since continued to flow with their original strength, and in unimpaired perfection. These waters have been of course submitted to repeated analization, and the result appears to be, that a gallon of the south well, or purging water, contains 237 grains of solid matter; and the north well, or chalybeate water contains 233 grains in the same quantity of water :—thus

| ANALYSIS. | S. Well. | N. Well. |
|---|---|---|
| Sulphate of Magnesia | 128 grains | 98 |
| Muriate of Magnesia | 16 | 14 |
| Carbonate of Lime·· | 28 | 61.5 |
| Carbonate of Iron··. | 2.6 | 3. |
| Sulphate of Lime···. | 58.4 | 54.4 |
| Muriate of Natron·· | 4 | 2.1 |
| | 237 | 233 |

* The subscription to the spaws for the season, is 7s. 6d. each individual.

The saline water contains 98 ounce measures per gallon of Carbonic acid gas or fixed air; and the chalybeate water 100 ounce measures per gallon : and each water contains a small quantity of gas azote or phlogisticated air.* The diseases which these waters relieve or remove are various, and might be enumerated, but it is always safe for a patient to consult his medical attendant, before he puts himself under a course of medicinal waters.

Speaking generally, sea-bathing is beneficial in nervous complaints; epilepsy; palsy; St. Vitus's dance; disorders of the head; general debility; cutaneous disorders; gout; rheumatism; obstructions; scrophula; intermittents and scurvy. Healthy persons, may however bathe themselves into ill health, by going into the sea heated, or by continuing too long in the water. When the bathing does not produce a moderate glow after quitting the water; when the chilling sensation continues; when the extremities become cold, the spirits languid, the head disordered, or the appetite impaired, it may be concluded that bathing is rather doing harm than good. There are here three separate establishments where warm sea water baths may be had when required, two of them on the cliff, of which one is kept by Mr. Travis, surgeon; the other by Dr. Wm. Harland; & the third, near the Pier, by Dr. Thompson and Mr. M'Turk. There is also a General Sea Bathing Infirmary, supported by voluntary contributions, on the plan of the Margate Bethesda, where the sick poor are allowed to bathe gratis.

Of the inns and lodging-houses it is unnecessary to speak in this place, as they are enumerated with great particularity in the subjoined directory. The business of the post-office, and of the coaches and waggons, a species of information so essential to both visitors and residents, will also be found stated in detail, subjoined to the list of the inhabitants of Scarborough.

The parish church of St. Mary, originally a convent for the Cistercians, is a vicarage, in the patronage of Lord Hotham, of which the Rev. John Kirk is the incumbent. This church was formerly a spacious and magnificent structure, as the ruins at the eastern part of it sufficiently indicate, and in the time of Henry VIII. it was adorned with three ancient towers; but during the siege of the castle, a lodgment was made in it by Sir John Meldrum, and the present edfice is only a fragment of that which the Carmelites enjoyed. This is now the only church in Scarborough, though the town could once boast its three houses of "the

* Hinderwell's History of Scarborough.

pray, black, and white." The other
ses of worship here, are the Indepen-
ts, in St. Sepulchre street; the Baptists,
Westgate; the Methodists, in Church
st; the Roman Catholics, in Auborough
st; and the Quakers, in St. Sepulchre
st; on the last of whom it may be re-
rked, that the founder of their commu-
r, George Fox, was imprisoned in the
lie here, twelve months, in the time of
uries II. and the room in which he was
ped part of the time, " lying," as he
b, " much open, the wind drove in the
i so forcibly, that the water came over
bed, and ran about the room, so that I
i glad to skim it up with a platter." This
r the nature of his lodging, and of his
d he says, " A three-penny loaf lasted
three weeks, and sometimes longer, and
st of my drink was water, with an infu-
i of wormwood!"

The ancient and stupendous castle,
s the glory, and still the ornament of
rborough, was built in the reign of King
phen, by William le Gros, Earl of Al-
arle and Holderness. Here Piers de
reston, the favourite of Edward II.
ght refuge against the exasperated barons,
after a short siege, he was obliged to
render for want of supplies, and lost his
d, as already related, in the castle of
lington.* Robert Aske, the leader of the
piims of Grace, made an unsuccessful
mpt upon Scarborough Castle, in 1536.
he time of Wyatt's rebellion, in 1553, it
surprised and taken by the stratagem of
oducing a number of soldiers, disguised
peasants. This atchievement was per-
ned by Thomas, second son of Lord
fford, but his success was of short dura-
i; three days afterwards the place was re-
m by the Earl of Westmoreland, and
fford, and three other of the leaders were
veyed to London, and executed for high
son. During the civil wars, in the ca-
itous reign of Charles I. this castle was
e besieged, and taken by the parliamen-
'army. The first siege lasted for twelve
nths, and Sir John Meldrum, by whom
forces of parliament were commanded,
before the works. The command of the
eging army then devolved upon Sir
thew Boynton, to whom Sir Hugh
mley, the governor, was obliged to sur-
ier on the 22d of July, 1645. Colonel
nton, the successor of the Baronet, having
lared for the King, the castle once more
e into the hands of the royalists, but the
rison growing mutinous, the Colonel
obliged to capitulate, and on the 19th

of December, 1648, the fortress was again
surrendered to parliament, and taken possession of, in their name, by Col. Bethel.
This castle, sharing the fate of its fellows,
was dismantled by order of parliament. But
on the breaking out of the rebellion, in
1745, it underwent a temporary repair, and
when the danger was over, the present barracks, containing twelve apartments, were
erected, and will accommodate 120 soldiers.
Since that time, three batteries have been
erected for the protection of the town and
harbour, two of them at the South, and one
at the North side of the castle yard.

The ruins of the castle are situated at
the Eastern extremity of the town, on a
lofty promontory, elevated more than 300
feet on the southern, and 330 feet on the
northern side, above the level of the sea,
and presenting to the north, the east, and
the south, a vast range of perpendicular
rocks, completely inaccessible. Its western
aspect is also bold and majestic, being a high,
steep, rocky, slope, commanding the town
and the bay. The whole area, at the top of
the hill, is upwards of nineteen acres of
excellent soil, gently sloping near 20 feet
from the north to the south lines. Under
an arched vault, towards the East side of the
castle yard, near the site of the ancient
chapel, is a reservoir of water, which will
contain 40 tons, called the " Lady's Well,"
supposed to be supplied by the rain water
which falls upon the castle hill, through
subterraneous drains. The approach to the
castle is by a gate-way, on the summit of a
narrow isthmus, on the western side above
the town. Without the ditch is an outwork, which was the ancient Barbican. The
walls of the tower are 12 feet thick, cased
with square stone, and the mortar is so hard
that it is actually crystalized into spar. In
this, as in similar structures the different
stories have been vaulted, and divided by
strong arches. The area of the Ballium, in
which the tower is situated, contains half an
acre of ground; and the summit of the hill
was defended on the western side by embattled walls, flanked with semi-circular
towers, from which arrows were discharged,
but these are now falling rapidly into decay.
It is also said, that large and ponderous
pieces of timber were so placed, as to be in
constant readiness to be rolled down upon an
enemy attempting to approach the walls.
From a view of these ruins, it appears, that
before the invention of artillery, this ancient
and famous castle was absolutely impregnable.

* See Vol. I. page 401.

—— " Nature here
Exhausted all her powers.  For site she gave
A mountain, neighbour to the moon ; for walls
A pensile cliff, whence down the boldest eye
With dizzy horror looks : for moat th' abyss
Of boundless ocean, spiked with guardian rocks;
Then decked the mountains' top, a spacious mead
With ever verdant robes."——

The trade and commerce of Scarborough are on a contracted scale. The exports consist chiefly of corn, butter in firkins, hams, bacon, and salt fish ; and the imports of coals from Newcastle ; groceries from London, and timber, deals, hemp, and flax, from the Baltic, and, in time of peace, brandy and Geneva from France and Holland. The average tonnage of the port amounts to about 25,000 tons. There are here ship-building establishments, a sail cloth manufactory, and some tolerably extensive rope walks. In the Summer season, the presence of visitors imparts a stimulus to the internal trade of the place, and the shops are, for the most part, well stocked with commodities and handsomely fitted up. The fisheries are not on a large scale, but they are conducted with spirit, and not only afford a supply to the resident inhabitants and to the company who resort hither in search of health and gratification, but they also contribute to supply the interior with wholesome food, drawn from that inexhaustible store house—the Ocean

Three Steam Packets, the *James Watt,* the *City of Edinburgh,* and the *Tourist,* pass here twice a week, on their voyage between London & Edinburgh, and great facilities are thereby afforded to travellers bound either to the southern or northern metropolis. The Scarborough agents for these vessels are, Mr. Francis Hill and Mr. David Nicholson.

The markets, which are amply stocked with provisions, are held twice in the week, namely, on Thursday and Saturday; and the fairs, which are principally for cattle, on Holy Thursday and Old Martinmas day.

Messrs. Woodall and Co. whose banking concern is carried on in Queen-street, and who draw upon Sir Peter Pole, Bart. & Co. London, are now the only bankers in Scarbro'.

The public buildings are the Town-hall, Prison, the Assembly-rooms, and the Theatre, exclusive of the Baths and the Spaw-house already mentioned. The Town-hall is a spacious building, in Long Room street, where the Sessions are held and the public business of the town transacted ; the Assembly-rooms are situated in the same street; Mr. Cooke is the permanent master of the ceremonies; the subscription for the season is one guinea, and 5s. the admission fee for non-subscribers; the ball nights, during the season, are Tuesday and Friday in each week. The Theatre is a new building, in Tanner-street, neatly fitted up, and well supplied with performers and scenic decorations.

The principal charities here are, the Hospital for worn out and disabled seamen, under the government of the Trinity House, Deptford-Strand, situated on the road to the North Sands, which affords a comfortable asylum to many families and individuals, and is supported by funds arising from ships belonging to the port of Scarborough, each of which pays sixpence per month for every person on board, so long as the ship is at sea. The Amicable Society, for clothing and educating the children of the poor, established 1729, which has under its care fifty boys and twenty girls, supported by voluntary subscriptions, and by collections after sermons preached for its support at the church : a spinning school : a Lancasterian school : a School of Industry : and a number of Sunday schools.

There is also a Savings Bank in Scarborough, for receiving the savings of the humbler classes of society, and augmenting them by an annual interest of 4 per cent. paid upon all sums invested.

The population of this town is advancing gradually ; in 1811 it amounted to 7430; in 1821, to 8188; which, considering the acknowledged salubrity of the air, and the consequent longevity of the inhabitants, is not a very material increase.

The country adjacent to Scarborough is finely diversified with hills and dales, and exhibits a variety of romantic scenery—Weaponness, or *Oliver's Mount,* (so called from the improbable tradition that a battery directed against the castle was placed here, when Oliver Cromwell commanded the parliamentary armies) is little more than a mile from the town ; it is approached by an easy ascent, and presents one of the most delightful natural marine terraces in England. From this eminence, which is 500 feet above the level of the sea, there is a magnificent view of the coast, the Castle hill, and its venerable ruin ; the town, the harbour, and the piers, with the mighty expanse of the Ocean, bounded only by the horizon. Of the *Rides* about Scarborough, as they are locally called, it is unnecessary to speak here ; the places to which they extend being all described in this work under their proper heads, and it is only necessary to enumerate and refer to Hackness, Filey, Flamborough Head, Burlington, and Robin Hood's Bay

*Post-Mistress*, RACHAEL WOODALL, *Office, Palace Hill,*

Letters arrive from York, Malton, & London every morning at 7 o'clock, and depart at ¼ past 1 afternoon.

DIRECTORY.

llen Isabella, gentwmn. Newbro' st.
arnby Mrs. Castlegate
ates Ann, gentwmn. Queen st.
ean Wm. gent. out of the bar
ell John, Esq. Bell Vue
ias Mrs. Eliz. Queen street
lanchard Mrs. Sarah, Newbro' st.
ogg David, gent. Cooke's row
oldera Wm. yeoman, West Sandgate
otterill John, yeoman, Tanner st.
ottomley Rev. Saml. St. Mary's st.
ottomley Mrs. Ann, Long Westgate
reary Mrs. Harriett Ann, Queen st.
riggs John, gent. Batty's street
rown Fenwick, gent. Cooke's row
rron Henry, gent. St. Mary's st.
ipe Mrs. gentlewoman, King st.
iambers Wm. gent. Tollergate
iambers Thomas, gent. Quary st.
iambers John, gent. Quay street
ark Francis, gent. Merchant's row
ckerill Mrs. Catharine, Sand side
llins Mrs. Ann, Batty's street
ioper Mrs. Mary, Newbro' street
inlson John, gent. St. Sepulchre st.
iasins Mrs. Dorothy, Aubro' st.
vis Geo. gent. without the Bar
iughty Mrs. Jane, Newbro' street
iwker Rev. Edmund, Newbro' st.
iff Mrs. Jean, Queen st.
iers Mrs. Jane, Queen st.
itcher Mrs. Jane, St. Sepulchre st.
i Mrs. Hannah, Palace hill
iver Mrs. Catharine, Castlegate
idsbrough Mrs. Eliz. Princess st.
odrick Mrs. Eliz. Cliff
iy Mrs. Hannah, Quay street
iy Mrs. Eliz. Queen street
igh Rev. Wm. Sand side
rding Mrs. Mary, Auborough st.
rrison John, yeoman, Tanner st.
rrison Francis, gent. Batty's st.
rrison Geo. yeoman, Leaden post st.
rrison Geo. yeoman, Dumple st.
irson Robt. gent. Cooke's row
adley Thos. gent. Sand side
adley Miss Margaret, Sand side
bden Edw. Hopper, Esq. Cliff
iden Miss Grace, Queen st.
iderson Robert, gent. Cliff
iderson Mrs. Esther, Cliff
ibert Mrs. Jane, Queen street
ip Mrs. Princess street
iselwood Rt. gent. Leaden post st.
derwell Thos. Esq. Newbro' st.
igson Mrs. Cross street
igson Mrs. Mary, Sand side
uby Mrs. Mary, Long Westgate

Hudson Mrs. Sophia, Sand side
Husband Wm. yeoman, Friar's entry
Jordan Thos. gent. Princess st.
Keld Thos. Esq. Long room street
Kendal Admiral John, Auborough st.
King Mrs. Jane, Albion place
Kirk Rev. John, vicar, Long Westgt.
Lakeland Thos. gent. Tanner st.
Lord Mrs. Peggy, Newbro' street
Lund John, Esq. Princess st.
Maling Geo. gent. St. Mary's st.
Maynard David, yeoman, Tanner st.
Megson Mrs. Eliz. Auborough st.
Metcalfe Mrs. Ann, Princess street
Mills James, yeoman, Auborough st.
Morrett Ann, gentlewoman, Cliff
Neal John, yeoman, Long Westgate
Nesfield Mrs. Eliz. Auborough st.
Nightingale John, gent. Long Westgt
Oldfield Dr. J. High Westgate
Owen Chas. sen. yeoman, King st.
Owen Chas. jun. yeoman, King st.
Parkin Thos. gent. Sand side
Parkin Miss Ann, West Sandgate
Pearson Thos. gent. Princess street
Philliskirk Mrs. Ann, Queen st.
Revis Mrs. Mary, Tanner st.
Roberts Major Chas. Huntriss row
Roberts Charles, Esq. Albion place
Robinson Miss Eliz. Huntriss row
Robinson Geo. yeoman, Auborough st.
Robinson Benj. yeoman, Castlegate
Ruston Anthony, gent. Batty's street
Sargeant Rev. Geo. High Westgate
Sedman Wm. gent. Batty's st.
Shaw Miss Hannah, Castlegate
Sherwood E. gent. without the Bar
Shore John, Esq. Long room street
Smith Thomas, yeoman, Sand side
Snowball Mrs. Jane, Long Westgate
Staines Thomas, gent. Tollergate
Stephens Wm. gent. Newbro' street
Stopford Wm. gent. Albion place
Sykes Rev. John, Tollergate
Taylor Gawan, Esq. Newbro' street
Thomas Wm. gent. Cooke's row
Thompson Mrs. without the Bar
Thompson Thos. M. D. Albion place
Tindall John, Esq. Cliff
Tindall Robert, sen. Esq. High Westgt.
Tindall Wm. yeoman, Huntriss row
Todd Mrs. Jane, without the Bar
Topham Miss Mary, St. Sepulchre st.
Towse Richard, yeoman, Long Westgt.
Travis Wm. Esq. ordnance store keeper, Newbro' st.
Turner Mrs. Jane, Batty's street
Vardy Michael, yeoman, Sand side
Wellburn Mrs. Mary, Batty's st.
White Geo. yeoman, Castlegate
Whiting Richd. yeoman, Long room st.
Whittle Joshua, gent. Palace hill
Williamson Richard, gent. Albion pl.
Williamson Thos. gent. Princess st.

Willis Mrs. Eliz. Princess street
Wilson Richard, Esq. Cliff
Wilson Mrs. Ann, Sand side
Wood Wm. yeoman, West Sand gate
Woolley Mrs. Queen street
Young Mrs. Eliz. Bolts

*Academies.*
Addison Robert, Queen street
Baines Eliz. Dumple street
Beard Rev. Jas. Freeman, Queen st.
Hornsey Robert, St. Sepulchre st.
Irvin Rev. Thomas, Queen st.
Kitchingman Wm. & Ann. Newbro' st.
Kyte Mary, (la. bdg.) St. Sepulchre st.
Laube M'Roger de, (French) Friar's entry
Millburn Richard, St. Sepulchre st.
Potter Wm. King street
Simpson Wm. Cooke's row
Sleightholm Ellen, (ladies' day) Cooke's row
Stickney Jane, (ladies' boarding and day) High Westgate
Thompson Geo. St. Sepulchre st.
Wainman Nancy, Cooke's row
Wellburn Geo. Merchant's row

*Agents.*
Hill Francis, (to Edinbro' & London, steam ship, & Lloyds) Quay st.
Nicholson David, (to Edinbro' & London, steam ship) Newbro' st.
Sedman and Weddill, (lottery) Newbro' street

*Anchor Smiths.*
Cobb William and Co. Sand side
Fleming George, Bolts
March Wm. and Benjamin, Sand side

*Architect.*
Chambers Wm. Long Westgate

*Attornies and Solicitors.*
Benson C. J. F. King street
Cornwall John, Queen street
Hesp John, Tanner street
Hornby Benj. Long room street
Page Wm. Sagon, (and notary) and Nathaniel Howard Usher, Newbro' street
Robson R. S. (& notary) Newbro' st.
Shore Arthur, Long room street
Thornton W. D. Newbro' st.
Travis & Woodall, Long room st.
Wardell T. M. Newbro' street

*Auctioneers and Appraisers.*
Laybourn Thomas, Leaden post street
Mears William, Carr street
Nattriss John, (and sheriff's officer,) Batty's street
Simpson William, Cross street

*Bacon, Ham, &c. Factors.*
Boyes James, King street
Boyes William, Queen street
Galtry Matthew, Dumble street

*Bakers—Bread and Biscuit.*
Clark Daniel, Princess street

Crawford James, Quay street
Gibson William, Carr street
Hayns John, West Sandgate
Hobson Robert, West Sandgate
Nedby William, Globe street
Newton Charles, Newbro' street
Pecket Christopher, Long room street
Scott Thomas, Cross street
Shaw Benjamin, East Sandgate
Sleightholm Story, Carr street
Stonehouse Robert, Merchant's row
Waine George, Newbro' street
Ward George, Dumple street

*Bank.*
Woodall, Tindall, Cooke, & Co. (or Sir Peter Pole & Co.) Queen st.

*Baths.*
Harland William, Filey road
Thompson and Co. Quay street
Travis William, Cliff

*Billiard Tables.*
Donner Edward, Long room street
Johnson Henry, Long room st.
Keld Charles, St. Sepulchre st.
Watson Peter, King street

*Blacksmiths.*
Nicholson John, Tanner street
Reed John, Cross street

*Booksellers, Printers, Stationers, and Binders.*
Ainsworth Jane, (bookslr.) Newbro' st.
Cole John, (& paper hanging dealer) Newbro' street
Millson Richard, (binder) Cross st.
Sedman & Weddill, (& paper hanging dealers, and letter press & copper plate printers) Newbro' street
Todd Christopher & Joseph, (printers) Long room street

*Boot and Shoemakers.*
Abbey Jonathan, Long room street
Andrews John, Merchant's row
Binnington Edward, Leaden post st.
Bradshaw George, Queen street
Clark John, Long Westgate
Cranswick R. J. Newbro' street
Ellis Isaac, Long Westgate
Fox William, Merchant's row
Gibson James, Carr street
Grant Wm. St. Sepulche street
Hume Walter, Princess street
Jackson John, St. Sepulchre street
Johnson Thomas, Cooke's row
Laybourn Wm. Long Westgate
Leake F. Long room st. & Newbro' st.
Leighton Thomas, Long Westgate
Marshall Thomas, Merchant's row
Merry Joseph, King street
Nichols John, Bland's cliff
Peacock Wm. King street
Percy George, Newbro' street
Ross John, Long Westgate

Salmond Edward, Tuthill
Sellers Thomas, West Sandgate
Thompson Christopher, Cross street
Tomlinson John, Newbro' street
Vickerman Wm. St. Helen's square
Wetherill Peter, Dumple street
Wrigley John, Leaden post street

*Braziers and Tinplate Workers.*
Bye D. Newbro' street
Dale John, Newbro' street
Goodbarn Joseph, Leaden post street
Killerby Benjamin, King street
White Thomas, Carr street

*Brewers and Maltsters.*
Hammond Joseph, (maltster) Paradise
Hutchinson Wm. Tanner street
Nesfield Geo. & Son, Auborough st.
Page & Dale, Tanner street
Wellburn John, (brewer) Huntriss row

*Bricklayers and Builders.*
Barry Wm. (& brick maker) Long Westgate
Boyes James, St. Mary's street
Fryer Thomas, Long Westgate
Garnett Robert, Dumple st.
Southwell John, (and brick maker), Albion place
Thompson & Saunderson, (and brick makers,) Auborough street

*Butchers,*
Allanson Wm. St. Helen's square
Anderson John, St. Helen's square
Bailey James, St. Helen's square
Bowman Ringrose, St. Sepulchre st.
Brown Wm. Dumple street
Fenwick David, New Shambles
Leake Robert, Sand side
Meggison Stephen, Cross street
Pearson John, New Shambles
Petty Thomas, New Shambles
Read Geo. jun. St. Helen's square
Rowbotham Isaac, New Shambles
Sedman Thos. sen. Leaden post st.
Sedman Thos. jun. Leaden post st.
Sedman Wm. Leaden post street
Vazey Wm. Henry, New Shambles
Wilson Thomas, Newbro' street

*Cabinet Makers.*
Those marked thus * are Upholsterers.
*Archer Tristram, St. Sepulchre st.
*Jameson Daniel, Newbro' street
Lawson Thomas, Huntriss row
Lunn Thomas, St. Sepulchre st.
Thornton Samuel, Globe street
White Daniel, Merchant's row

*Chemists and Druggists.*
Champley John, Newbro' street
Fox John, Newbro' street
Turner & Weddill, Newbro' street

*Coach Builders.*
Potter Wm. without the Bar
Scaley M. L. top of Huntriss walk

*Coal Dealers.*
Brown Ann, St. Mary street
Owen Joseph, King street

*Confectioners.*
Beswick B. without the bar
Grayson Benjamin, Newbro' street
Newton Charles, Newbro' street
Richardson Ellen, without the bar
Waine George, Newbro' street

*Coopers.*
Chapman John, Carr street
Morwan Robert, Quay street
Watson George, Quay street

*Cork Cutters.*
Lawson Richard, Long Westgate
White George, Cross street

*Corn Factors.*
Hudson Jeremiah, Sand side
Marfitt Robert, Bland's cliff

*Corn and Flour Dealers.*
Pennock John, Newbro' street
Pitts John, Newbro' street

*Corn Millers.*
Gibson Wm. Carr street
Nesfield Guy, without the bar
Newton Charles, Newbro' street
Pennock John, Newbro' street
Pitts John, Newbro' street
Simpson Robert, Plantation mill

*Curriers and Leather Cutters.*
Adamson John, Cross street
Campion George, Cross street
Milligan P. (leather cutter) Globe st.
Thompson Samuel, Cross street
Whitehead Francis, High Westgate

*Cutlery Dealers.*
Crossby Jane, St. Sepulchre street
Howes Henry, Globe street
Mears Wm. Carr street

*Dyers.*
Hick Mary, (silk) Dumple street
Thacker John, Cross street

*Fire and Life Insurance Agents.*
Atlas, C. J. F. Benson, King street
British, Benj. Fowler, Princess street
County and Provident, Sedman and Weddill, Newbro' street
Eagle, Robert Marfitt, Bland's cliff
Globe, Robert Goodwill, Newbro' st.
Hope, W. S. Page, Newbro' street
Imperial, John Hesp, Tanner street
Newcastle, T. Hart, St. Sepulchre st.
Phoenix, Robt. Ward, Queen st.
Royal Exchange, J. Cornwall, Queen st.
Suffolk, John Rowntree, Queen st.
Sun, Timothy Hardcastle, Queen st.

*Fishmongers.*
Busfield Thomas, Sand side
Cappleman Wm. Whitehead hill
Dewsbury George, Long greece
Glenton Geo. & Co. Merchant's row
Lancaster Sarah & Co. Sand side
Potter Mary, Long greece

*Furniture Brokers.*
Jackson John, St. Sepulchre street
Lunn Sarah, St. Sepulchre street
Midgley Richard, St. Sepulchre st.
Milner Ellen, St. Sepulchre street
Rawson Elizabeth, Leaden post st.

*Gardeners, &c.*
Chatwin Robert, Dumple street
Dooker & Pinder, Weaponess
Hick John, without the bar
Nurdass Wm. Auborough street
Walshaw Thomas, King st.
Williamson John, Huntriss row

*Glass, China & Earthenware Dealers.*
Simpson Mary, Carr street
Topham George, St. Helen's square

*Grocers and Tea Dealers.*
Beeforth George, Newbro' street
Boyes James, King street
Boyes Wm. Queen street
Cass Eustace, Newbro' street
Dutchman Benjamin, East Sandgate
French Robert, Merchant's row
Henderson James, St. Mary street
Hick Mary, Princess street
Knaggs Thompson, Dumple street
Lawson John, St. Helen's square
Lord Paul, Newbro' street
Middleton Samuel, Merchant's row
Nedby Wm. Globe street
Nelson Skelton, Carr street
Pattison John, Newbro' street
Potter Charles, Newbro' street
Purcell Thomas, Newbro' street
Rowntree John, Carr street
Smith Richard, Newbro' street
Tinker Wm. Cross street
Ullathorne Wm. Newbro' street
Wellburn Z. T. (and seedsman,) Newbro' street

*Hat Warehouses.*
Brown Peter, Newbro' street
Fowler John, Newbro' street
Galbreath James, Newbro' street
Stickney Isaac, Newbro' street

*Hosiers.*
Bradshaw Joseph, Newbro' street
Broadrick & Bowler, Newbro' st.
Brown Peter, Newbro' street
Fowler John, Newbro' street
Galbreath James, Newbro' street
Hall Samuel, Leaden post street
Stickney Isaac, Newbro' street
Spurr J. (& stocking mfr.) Newbro' st.
Walker Elizabeth, Carr street

*Hotels, Inns and Taverns.*
Bay Horse, Mark Dove, Queen st.
Bee Hive, Elizabeth Bee, Sand side
Bell Inn, Richard Hopper, (posting house, Bland's cliff
Blacksmith's Arms, John Ruddock, (& posting house) Queen st.

Black Swan, Henry Johnson, Long room street
Board, Jane Ware, Quay street
Board, John Oxley, Quay street
Board, Robert Woodall, Dumple st.
Board, Eliz. Jackson, St. Sepulchre st.
Board, Eliz. Dowsling, St. Sepulchre st.
Board, Mary Harrison, Long Westgt.
Board, Thos. Huggett, Long Westgt.
Board, Dorothy Stark, East Sandgate
Board, Jeremiah Hudson, Sand side
Board, John Crooks, Quay street
Board, Wm. Burton, Quay street
Boot, James Walker, Dumple st.
Britannia, S. Pantland, Merchant's row
Bull Inn, John Howson, (posting house) without the gate
Carpenters' Arms, Jane Duncanson, Long Westgate
Dolphin, Rhd. Leaf, West Sandgate
Elephant & Castle, J. Lawson, Cross st.
Fish Cart, G. Glenton, Merchant's row
Five Men Boat, S. Holiday, Sand side
Fountain, Thomas Sedman, Leaden post street
George Inn, Ann Broomhead, Newbro' street
Golden Ball, Rt. Morwan, Quay st.
Golden Last, Fras. Goodburn, Carr st.
Grapes, Geo. Simpson, Tanner st.
Half Moon, John Wellburn, Harding's walk
Hope & Anchor, Ann New, Sand side
Hotel, Edward Donner, (assembly rooms,) Long room street
Jolly Sailors, Thos. Sollitt, Cross st.
King's Arms, John Raywood, King st.
King's Arms, Jane Halder, Sand side
King's Head, Wm. Allison, Dumple st.
King's Head, Fanny Wilson, Sand side
Lamb, Wm. Hudson, Cross street
Light Horse Man, Thos. Clark, Newbro' street
London Inn, Jas. Coates, Newbro' st.
London Packet, Stephen Gray, East Sandgate
Lord Nelson, Ann Tindall, Wharton ln.
Malt Shovel, William Gibson, Leaden post street
Mariners, Eliz. Westlake, Long room st.
Nag's Head, Rt. Miller, Newbro' st.
Neptune, Jane Martin, Cross street
New Inn, David Nicholson, Newbro' st.
Old Globe, Mary Tissiman, Globe st.
Old King's Arms, Thomas Mosey, East Sandgate
Plough, Stephen Wright, Tanner st.
Printers' Arms, Thomas Whiting, Newbro' street
Queen's Head, Francis Johnson, Palace hill
Rose & Crown, Thomas Tomlinson, Merchant's row
Sailor's Return, S. Lancaster, Sand side

Scarborough Arms, H. Lister, East
   Sandgate
Ship, Francis Boyce, West Sandgate
Ship, Ann Birch, Tuthill
Shipwrights' Arms, John Shaw, Quay st.
Smiths' Arms, John Freer, East
   Sandgate
Spaw Inn, F. Shaw, without the Gate
Spread Eagle, Eliz. Tissiman, Sand side
Star, Thomas Crossby, King street
Star and Garter, Michael Allum, St.
   Mary's street
Swan, Jonathan Read, Dumple st.
Talbot, Jane Hutchinson, Queen st.
Three Cannons, Mary Thornton, High
   Westgate
Wheat Sheaf, Wm. Tessiman, Quay st.
Wheat Sheaf, R. Pennock, Cross st.
White Bear, G. Read, St. Helen's sq.

*Ironmongers.*

Dale John, Newbro' street
Ford John and James, Newbro' st.

*Joiners,—House Builders.*

Baker Stephen, Tanner street
Bottom Robert, Princess street
Crossby Geo. West Sandgate
Easter John, Tanner street
Jordan Samuel, Dumple street
Lilley John, Merchants' row
Munn Thomas, St. Sepulchre street
Percy Robert, Tanner street
Smailes John, Tanner street
Staveley and Taylor, Bland's cliff
Stockdale John, Tanner street
Stickerman Joseph, King street
Woodall Thomas, Merchant's row

*Lapidaries.*

Brown Charles, Long room street
Carter John, Long room street
Crawford Alexander, Newbro' street
Garrison Rt. (season) Long room st.

*Libraries, Subscription & Circulating.*

Ainsworth Jane, (circulating) New-
   bro' street
Cole John, (circulating) Newbro' st.
Sodman and Weddill, (circulating)
   Newbro' street
Watson Peter, (subscription) King st.

*Linen Drapers.*

Brown Peter, (and silk mercer) New-
   bro' street
Cockerill Jane, St. Sepulchre street
Coke Daniel, Long room street
Allen Gawen, Newbro' street
Arbutt Charles, Carr street
Jones W. & Co. (season) Long room st.
Low Thomas, Carr street
Rawson John, St. Helen's square
Rewis Stephen, (season) Huntriss row
Thompson John, Merchants' row
Slathorne Wm. Newbro' street
Walker Eliz. (& mercer) Carr street

*Linen and Woollen Drapers.*

Brown Peter, (and dealer in carpets)
   Newbro' street
Fowler John, (and dealer in carpets)
   Newbro' street
Galbreath James, Newbro' street
Leadley John, Newbro' street
Mennell Isaac, Newbro' street
Smith Hodgson, Newbro' street
Stickney Isaac, Newbro' street
Stubbs Henry, (& silk mercer) New-
   bro' street

*Linen Manufacturers.*

Law Thomas, Carr street
Lownsborough John, Auborough st.

*Livery Stables,—Pony Barouches,
Gigs, Horses, Ponys, &c.*

Beecroft Matthew, (saddle horses)
   Huntriss row
Donkin Wm. (pony barouche) New-
   bro' street
Dove Mark, (barouches, &c.) Queen st.
Gleaves Thomas, (saddle horses) Tan-
   ner street
Holmes Joseph, (saddle horses) Mer-
   chants' row
Major Jonathan, (saddle horses) New-
   bro' street
Marshall Wm. (saddle horses) Tanner
   street
Peacock Wm. (barouches, &c.) Queen
   street

*Lodging and Boarding Houses.*

Those marked with a † have sea prospects.

†Banks Ann, Merchants' row
†Binnington Edward, Leaden post st.
Broomhead Ann, Newbro' street
Coates James, Newbro' street
Crossby Thomas, King street
†Donner Edward, Long room street
Goodbarn Frances, Carr street
Hodgens Elizabeth, Huntriss row
†Hopper Richard, Bland's cliff
Huntriss Ann, Huntriss row
Huntriss Hannah, Huntriss row
Hutchinson Jane, Queen street
Johnson Henry, Long room street
Linwood Charles, Leaden post street.
Miller Robert, Newbro' street
Nicholson David, Newbro' street
Ruddock John, Queen street
Sedman Thomas, Leaden post street
†Thompson Elizabeth, Sand side
Tissiman John, Globe street
†Tomlinson Thomas, Merchants' row
†Woodall John, Merchants' row

*Lodging Houses.*

Those marked with a * have sea prospects.

*Allen Richard, Merchants' row
*Allison John, Merchants' row
*Andrews John, Merchants' row

Bielby John, Leaden post street
Bradshaw Joseph, Newbro' street
*Bradshaw Ann, Merchants' row
Coates John, Huntriss row
*Cockerill Joseph, Cliff
Coulton Christiana, Long room street
*Coward Wm. Merchants' row
*Cowling Matthew, Carr street
Davison Clark, Merchants' row
*Davison Grace, Palace hill
*Dawson Wm. Long room street
*Edmonds Richard, Prospect place
*Estill Thomas, Albion place
*Featherstonehaugh Dorothy, Cliff
*Fox Wm. Merchants' row
*French Robert, Merchants' row
*Glass Ann, Cliff
*Gowland Elizabeth, Cliff
Hebden Robert, Huntriss row
*Holiday Ann, Merchants' row
Holmes Joseph, Merchants' row
Hutchinson Jane, Queen street
Hutchinson Ralph, Merchants' row
*Law Thomas, Carr street
Leadley John, Newbro' street
*Leake Francis, Long room street
*Lilley John, Merchants' row
*Lilley Richard, Bland's cliff
*Ling Christopher, Cliff
*Lister Eliz. Merchants' row
*Marshall Thomas, Merchants' row
Mason James, Merchants' row
*Moorsom John, New steps
*Newham William, King street
*Newton Charles, Newbro' street
*Nichols John, Bland's cliff
*Noel John, Long room street
*North Jane, Cooke's row
Palliser William, Huntriss row
Park Ann, Cooke's row
Parkinson Barton, St. Sepulchre st.
*Peacock Daniel, Cliff
Rawson Eliz. Leaden post street
*Rennison Charlotte, Bland's cliff
Simpson Samuel, Leaden post street
*Skelton Isaac, Cliff
*Sleightholm Ann, St. Mary's street
*Smith Isabella, Merchants' row
*Sollitt William, Cliff
*Southwell John, Albion place
*Stalker Wm. Merchants' row
Swales Christopher, Queen street
*Thompson Mary, Albion place
*Walker Francis, Albion place
*Ward Stephen, Merchants' row
Watson Ann, Long Westgate
*Westerman Joseph, Bland's cliff
*Wharton Samuel, jun. Albion place
White Thomas, Carr street
*White Eliz. Merchants' row
*Willis Richard Wingfield, Merchants' row
*Wilson Mary, Long room street
*Wood William, Cliff

*Mast, Block, and Pump Makers.*

Henry William, Sand side
Terry and Hill, Sand side

*Master Mariners.*

Allen John, Quay street
Almond Richard, Castlegate
Beswick Matthew, Long Westgate
Binney George, Quay street
Brown Geo. Fenwick, Cooke's row
Brown John, Long Greece
Chapman Wm. St. Mary's street
Crozier Francis, Castlegate
Edmonds Thomas, Castlegate
Edmonds Wm. West Sandgate
Ellington E. W. Long Westgate
Feaster Thomas, Sand side
Garbutt Richard, St. Mary's street
Goodsir Thomas, Long Greece
Grant John, Castlegate
Haigh John, Sand side
Haigh Thomas, Tuthill
Haigh Joseph, Long Westgate
Harrison John, Queen street
Hart Stephen, Long Westgate
Heckler Charles, Sand side
Helm John, Quay street
Heywood William, Tuthill
Hick Thomas, Castlegate
Hill John, High Westgate
Hudson Jeremiah, Quay street
Hudson Wm. Castle road
Husband Gregory, Quay street
Hutchinson Ralph, Merchants' row
Jackson Robert, Sand side
Jackson Fenwick, St. Mary's street
Lewens Richard, Quay street
March Cuthbert, St. Mary's street
Moorsom William, Cooke's row
Nicholson Atkinson, Quay street
Norfor Thomas, Long Greece
Outhitt Thomas, Princess street
Oxley James, Quay street
Park Robert, Castlegate
Park Joshua, Palace hill
Pennock John, Quay street
Peterson Christopher, Quay street
Pratt Thomas, St. Sepulchre street
Ripley John, Princess street
Robinson Musgrave, Princess street
Sherrington Wm. Quay street
Souter Alexander, St. Mary's street
Spouse Rawling, Princess street
Stewart John, High Westgate
Stork Thomas, Tuthill
Sutton Thomas, St. Sepulchre street
Tate Richard, Princess street
Walker Thomas B. Long Westgate
Watson John, Quay street
Williamson Richard, Tuthill
Willis John, Princess street
Wilson Robert, Sand side
Wilson Thomas, Sand side
Wilson Gowan, Castlegate

*Milliners and Dress Makers.*

Cooke Frances, Auborough street
Beighton Mary, Newbro' street
Harrison Mary, Long room street
Hayes Isabella, Long Westgate
Keld Mary, St. Sepulchre street
Labourn Mrs. Leaden post street
Ruddock Jane, Long room street
Williamson Eliz. Huntriss row

*Painters.*

Baynes Matthew, sen. Newbro' st.
Baynes Matthew, jun. (portrait and animal) Newbro' street
Gambles Geo. Princess street
Harrison Thomas, Cooke's row
Beckett John, Tollergate
Potter Charles, Newbro' street
Leightholm Thomas, Cooke's row
Todd C. and J. Long room street
Woodall John, Merchant's row

*Patten Makers.*

Bradshaw George, Queen street
Peacock Wm. (& clog boots) Queen st.
Peacock Wm. jun. (and clog boots) Queen street

*Perfumers,—Hair Dressers.*

Allinson Atkinson, Sand side
Atkinson Wm. Dumple street
Austin James, Tanner street
Brooks Samuel, (season) Cliff
Carlton Lionel, St. Sepulchre street,
Allin George, Castlegate
Griffin S. P. Newbro' street
Taylor George, Merchants' row
Todd Matthew, Newbro' street
Walker D. H. Merchants' row
Westerman Joseph, Bland's cliff

*Plumbers and Glaziers.*

Welby John, Leaden post street
Robson Abraham, Merchants' row
Woodbarn William, King street
Robinson Wm. Palace hill
Smith Edward, Globe street

*Rope and Twine Manufacturers.*

Bottomley Wm. East Sandgate
Fowler and Dickinson, Sand side
Harwood George, Castle road
Nesbit John, (white) Globe street
Higginson James, Castlegate
Walker William, Merchants' row
Walker Herbert, Sand side

*Sail Makers & Sail Cloth Mfrs.*

Fowler George, Sand side
Posey and Dale, Sand side
Barton & Armitage, (mfrs.) Sand sd.

*Saddlers.*

Frankland William, Newbro' street
Otterborn Christopher, Newbro' st.
Rice Thomas, Newbro' street
Watson Wm. Queen street

*Savings' Bank,*

Open on Thursday every other week, from 12 to 1 o'clock; and in the intervening week from 6 o'clock to 7 on Tuesdays; Thomas Smurwaite, secretary.

*Sea Bathers' Attendants.*
(Machine Owners.)

Lilley Robert, Newbro' street
Southwell John, Albion place

*Ship Builders.*

Porritt G. W. Sand side
Riby George, Sand side
Skelton John, Sand side
Smith George Dale, East Sandgate
Smith Christ. (boat) Sand side
Tindall R. W. and J. Sand side

*Ship Owners.*

Appleton John, Paradise
Batty William, Cross street
Boss Crispin, High Westgate
Bottomley Wm. East Sandgate
Cornwall Frederick, Newbro' street
Crathorne George, St. Sepulchre st.
Davison Clark, Merchants row
Edmonds Thomas, Long Westgate
Edmonds Richard, Prospect place
Fitzwilliam Thomas, Whitehead hill
Fowler Benjamin, Princess street
Fox Edward, Dumple street
Galtrey Matthew, Dumple street
Gardiner Thomas, Long Westgate
Goodwill Robert, Newbro' street
Gray Daniel, Palace hill
Hall Christiana, Queen street
Hardcastle Timothy, Queen street ]
Harland William, Newbro' street
Henry William, Queen street
Herbert Thomas, St. Mary's street
Hill Francis, Quay street
Hill Christ. High Westgate
Hudson Jeremiah, Sand side
Keathley William, Cooke's row
Kirk William, St. Sepulchre street
Knox Robert, Long Westgate
Leasley Henry, Long Westgate
Lownsborough Thos. Auborough st.
March William, sen. Quay street
Marflitt Robert, Bland's Cliff
Mosey Wm. High Westgate
Newham William, King street
Pantling Walter, Cooke's row
Parkin Thomas, Quay street
Porritt G. W. Sand side

Scott John, High Westgate
Sherwood Eleazer, Common
Smith William, Newbro' street
Smith Matthew, Long Westgate

Staines Matthew, Westgate
Stork Thomas, Sand side
Sutherland Rbt. sen. Sand side
Sutherland Rt. jun. Sand side
Taylor John, Palace hill
Tindall Robert, Westgate
Tindall W. and R. Quay street
Walker Thos. Bollison, High West gt.
Wharton Samuel, sen. Queen street
Wharton Samuel, jun. Albion place
White John, Merchants' row
Williamson Richard, Quay street

*Shopkeepers..*

Birch Ann, Tuthill
Birch Samuel, Tuthill
Cockerill Wm. St. Mary's st.
Cottam Richard, Bolts
Davison Mary, Quay street
Donkinson Wm. Merchants' row
Gibson Ann, Tanner street
Gillman John, Merchants' row
Harrison Mary, Merchants' row
Laycock Richard, Quay street
Laycock Wm. Quay street
March William, (iron merchant) Quay
  street
M'Dermot Hugh, Long Westgate
Otterborn William, Cross street
Skelton John, Dumple street
Taylor Richard, Leaden post street
Thornton Elizabeth, St. Mary's st.
Tomlinson George, (and fruiterer)
  Carr street
Traumer Matthew, Cross street
Waterhouse George, Castlegate
Woodall Thomas, Merchants' row

*Silversmiths and Jewellers.*

Cracknell Wm. Willis, Newbro' st.
Crawford Alex. jun. Newbro' street
Jacobs Israel, Long room street
Owston Michael, Newbro' street
Powell Tabitha, Harding's walk
Vassalle Jeremiah, St. Sepulchre st.

*Spirit and Wine Merchants.*

Hammond Jonas, (British wine and
  porter) Queen street
Hart Thomas, (British wine) St. Se-
  pulchre street
Hugall Henry, Queen street
Noel John (and porter) Long room
  street
Thirlwall and Vickerman, Long room
  street
Ullathorne William, Newbro' street

*Spirit Dealers,—Retail.*

Allanson Francis, Newbro' st.
Cowling Matthew, Carr street
Wrongham Henry, West Sandgate

*Stamp Office.*

Purnell Thos. (sub distbr.) Newbro' st.

*Stay, &c. Makers.*

Harker Isabella, St. Sepulchre st.
Mason James, (& draper) Merchants'
  row

*Stone Masons.*

Barry Wm. (& marble) High Westgt.
Chambers Wm. jun. Batty's street
Coulson George, Tanner street
Crossby Robert, without the Bar
Hawkswell Philip, Tanner street
Luccock Thos. St. Sepulchre st.
Sanderson Thomas, Auborough st.
Ward Wm. Long Westgate

*Straw Hat Manufacturers.*

Anderson Mary, Tuthill
Bowler Mary, Newbro' street
Breckon Joseph, Newbro' street
Cockerill Jane, St. Sepulchre st.
Holden John, Newbro' street
Jefferson Wm. Newbro' street
Sedman Margaret, Leaden post st.

*Surgeons.*

Harland Wm. (& M.D.) Newbro' st.
M'Turk Wm. Leaden post street
Travis Wm. & J. Dunn, Newbro' st.
Weddill Thomas, Newbro' street
Williams Caleb, Merchants' row
Willis Rd. Wingfield, Merchants' row

*Tailors and Drapers.*

Those marked * are Drapers.

*Allen Richard, Merchants' row
*Armstrong James, Merchants' row
Beckett George, King street
Belt John, Newbro' street
Bulmer Joseph, Newbro' street
Coulson Francis, Long room street
Davey Wm. Merchants' row
*Dobson James, Long room street
Flounders Wm. Tanner street
*Jefferson Richard, St. Sepulchre st.
*Laycock Wm. Princess street
Parkinson Barton, St. Sepulchre st.
Parkinson John, Dumple street
*Powley Jackson, Newbro' street
Ross Andrew, Leaden post street
Sedman Joseph, Long Westgate
Smith Wm. Merchants' row
Smith Thomas, Merchants' row
Stockhill Robert, Cooke's row
*Taylor John & Son, Dumple st.
Taylor Wm. Dumple street
*Tissiman Wm. Palace hill
*Woodall John, Merchants' row
Woodall Robert, Merchants' row
York Wm. Cross street

*Tallow Chandlers.*

Beeforth George, Newbro' street
Foster Richard, Cross street
Lawson John, St. Helen's square
Middleton Samuel, Merchants' row
Purnell Thomas, Newbro' street

*Tea Dealers.*

Cooper Elisa, Carr street
Harrison Wm. Newbro' street
Murray Peter, Leaden post street
Smith Isabella, Merchants' row
Smith Edward, Globe street
Wrongham Henry, West Sandgate

*Timber and Raff Merchants.*

Beswick Anthony & Son, Sandside
Terry & Hill, Sandside

*Tobacco Pipe Maker.*

Hopwood Thomas, West Sandgate

*Toy Warehouses.*

Corbett Elizabeth, Merchants' row
Griffin S. P. Newbro' street
Gritton P. R. (repository for fancy
    wares) Huntriss row
Lawson Thomas, Harding's walk
Marshall Thomas, Merchants' row
Todd Matthew, Newbro' street

*Turners in Wood, &c.*

Lamon James, Dumple street
Noble John, St. Sepulchre street

*Watch and Clock Makers.*

Bancroft Wm. Newbro' street
Bracewell Hartley, Cross street
Crawford Alex. sen. Newbro' street
Crawford Alex. jun. Newbro' street
Wston Michael, Newbro' street

*Whitesmiths.*

Dale John, Newbro' street
Love Wm. Leaden post street
Rawson Wm. Globe street
Larch Wm. Quay street
Robinson Benjamin, Quay street
Whitehead Thomas, (& bell hanger)
    King street

*Woollen Drapers.*

» See also Linen and Woollen Drapers.

Connell Isaac, Newbro' street

*Miscellany.*

Baxter John, excise officer, L. Westgt.
Arrington Wm. broom mkr. King st.
Oward Wm. hat shoe & fur cap mfr.
    Merchants' row
Dowling Matthew, flax dresser and
    paper mfr. Merchants' row
Davison Henry, dealer in marine stores,
    Tuthill
Lawson John, farmer, Tanner st.
Onkinley Thos. weaver, W. Sandgt.
Lesbury Saml. tide waiter, Sandside
Inwell Thos. farmer, Newbro' st.
Mnon Jane, midwife, Dumple st.
Scles John, parish clerk, H. Westgt.
Edmondson Thos. timber measurer,
    Tuthill
ster John, exciseman, Auborough st.
Owler John, keeper of the gaol,
    Newbro' street

Gilyard John, translator, Globe st.
Good Rachel, pastry cook, Leaden
    post street
Hardcastle Timothy, cashier at the
    bank, Queen street
Harrison George, tide surveyor, High
    Westgate
Hartley Jph. organist, Harding's walk
Hill Geo. tide waiter, Merchants' row
Holmes John, supervisor, Dumple st.
Hunter Wm. hardware dealer, St. Se-
    pulchre street
Kitson Thos. translator, Globe st.
Leamon Thos. Paradise
Levington James, farmer, Weaponness
Linn Geo. fire extinguisher, Leaden
    post street
Lyon Harris, clothes broker, Leaden
    post street
Maw Rbt. coast waiter, Castlegate
Metcalfe J. trunk mkr. Newbro' st.
Milligan Peter, leather seller, Globe st.
Nicholson Thos. farmer, Tanner st.
Nightingale Thos. serjeant at mace,
    Long room street
Osborn Mary, pastry cook, Long room
    street
Otterburn Thos. farmer, without the bar
Parkinson Robert, pawnbroker, Lead-
    en post street
Peacock Thos. traveller, Princess st.
Redhead Christopher, tide waiter,
    Long Westgate
Riddell James, millwright, Globe st.
Rous James, traveller, Harding's walk
Sanderson Wm. farmer, Weaponness
Sandwith Wm. skinner, Peaseholm
Scaling Thos. poulterer, Cross st.
Simpson Samuel, number carrier,
    Leaden post street
Stainer John, basket maker, Mer-
    chants' row
Stephenson John, clerk, Long room st.
Tessiman Wm. umbrella manufactr.
    Newbro' street
Thompson Wm. clerk, Long room st.
Thornton William, serjeant at mace,
    Tanner street
Turtle Thomas, glove & breeches
    maker, Newbro' street
Walker Dorothy, haberdasher, Carr st.
Ward Wm. gunsmith & bellhanger,
    Leaden post street
Wilkinson Wm. & Charles, linen wea-
    vers, Newbro' street
Wilson Wm. music & musical instru-
    ment dealer, Long room street

COACHES,

*From Richard Hopper's, Bell Inn,*
*Bland's Cliff.*

ROYAL MAIL, to York, on Mon. Wed.
    Fri. & Sat. at ¼ past 1 aft.

OLD TRUE BLUE, every mg. at 7, to Malton, York, Tadcaster, and Leeds, (during the season.)
DILIGENCE, every Sun. & Wed. mg. at 8 o'clock to Whitby.
WELLINGTON, every mg. at 7 o'clock (Sundays excepted) to Hunmanby, Burlington, Driffield, Beverley and Hull.

*From John Houson's, Bull Inn, without the Bar.*

OLD TRUE BLUE, every morning, at 7 o'clock to Malton, York, Tadcaster&Leeds,(during the season.)

*From David Nicholson's, New Inn, Newbro' street.*

BRITISH QUEEN, to Burlington and Hull, every Mon. Wed. and Fri. and every day during the season, (Sundays excepted.)

*From Stephen Wright's, Plough Inn, Tanner street.*

PRINCE BLUCHER, every mg. (Sundays excepted) to Malton, York, Tadcaster, Leeds and Sheffield, (during the season.)

## CARRIERS.

Burlington & Quay, Robert Owston, Star, King st. d. Mon. & Thu. 8 aft. r. Tu. and Fri.
Hull, James Doukin, Newbro' st. dep. every Mon. & Fri. at 9 mg. ret. Wed, & Sun. 6 mg.
Hunmanby & Burlington, John Johnson, King's Arms, King st. arr. Thu. 10 mg, dep. 4 aft.
Hunmanby, Driffield, Beverley and Hull, Bell and England, Cross st. dep. Mon. & Thu. 9 mg. ret. Wed. & Sat. 6 morning.
Malton and York, Thos. Burneston, dep. Mon. and Thu. 12 noon, ret. Wed. and Sat. 10 morning.
Malton and York, Thos. Larkin, Tanner st. dep. Mon. and Thu. 12 noon, ret. Wed. and Sat. 10 mg.
Malton & York, Sarah Craggs, White Bear, St. Helen's sq. dep. Mon. and Thu. 12 noon; ret. Wed. and Sat. 12 noon.
Pickering, Thos. Carlisle, Geo. Inn, Newbro' st. arr. Wed. evg. 6 o'clock, dep. Thu. 1 mg. arr. 1 Sat. nig. ret. same day 10 morn.
Pickering, John Pearson, King's Arms, King st. arr. Wed. 4 aft. ret. Thu. ½ past 1 afternoon.
Whitby, John Armin, Long room st. dep. Thu. and Sun. 10 mg. ret. evening.

Whitby, Geo. Frank, Cross st. dep. Wed. and Sat. 10 mg. ret. Thu. and Sun. 7 evg.

## SHIPPING.

*From Bland's Cliff.*—Robert Marflit, agent—To London, the Aid and Moscow, every fortnight.
R. Edmonds, agent—To London, Free Briton & Harbinger, every fortnight.
John Harrison, agent—The Commerce to Hull, every month.
J. Dale, agent—The Ribston to Hull, every three weeks summer, and every four weeks winter.
James Oxley, agent—The Fallowden, to Newcastle, not regular.
Stephen Ward, agent—The Trimmer, to Newcastle, not regular.

## STEAM PACKETS.

The CITY OF EDINBURGH, the JAMES WATT, and the TOURIST call off the port regularly to London on Thursday morning, to Edinburgh on Thursday afternoon.

*Scargill*, in the parish of Barningham, wap. of Gilling West, and liberty of Richmondshire ; 5 miles S. of Barnard Castle. Pop. 136.

*Scarth Neck*, in the parish of Aysgarth, wap. of Hang West, and liberty of Richmondshire ; 8 miles from Leyburn.

*Scarth Wood*, in the parish of Whorlton, wap. and liberty of Langbargh ; 7 miles from Stokesley.

*Scawton*, (P.) in the wap. of Rydale ; 5 miles WSW. of Helmsley. Here is an ancient church, dedicated to St. Mary, in the patronage of Mr. Worsley, of which the Rev. John Oxlee, is the rector. Pop. 154.

*Scoon Bank*, in the parish of Romaldkirk, wap. of Gilling West ; 6 miles WNW. of Barnard Castle.

SCORTON, in the chapelry of Bolton, parish of Catterick, wap. of Gilling East, and liberty of Richmondshire; 5 miles E. of Richmond.   Here is a Free Grammar School, with an endowment of 200*l.* per ann. left by Leonard Robinson, Esq.   The school house was erected in the year 1760, and the Rev. W. Bowe, officiating curate at Bolton, is the master.   There is in this township a noted spring, called St. Cuthbert's Well, (otherwise, Cuddy Kell;) it is supposed to derive its name from a monastery, dedicated to St. Cuthbert, said to have stood upon the same spot, but not a vestige of it now remains. The water is useful in the cure of cutaneous

lisease, and rheumatism; it flows into a
rook, which empties itself into the Swale,
elow Riphng, and which brook is noted for
urge fine flavoured trout. The village is
iry, and generally well built, in form rather
regular, but approaching to a square. In
se centre is a spacious green, raised three or
sur feet above the level of the road; to the
lorth side is a good Inn, and an elegant
ailding for the school; on the East the
aildings are appropriated to the purpose
? a religious Catholic community, of the
sler of St. Clair. The persons forming this
tablishment came over from Normandy, in
'95, after the French Revolution, and set-
id first at Haggerston Castle, in Northum-
riand, but removed to Scorton in 1807.
he house consists of 30 nuns, and 30
arders. Mrs. Sisson is abbess, Mrs. Innes
verness, and the Rev. Mr. Kirby priest;
d for the use of the community and
hers, a chapel is now building, which is to
dedicated to St. Clair. There is also a
all congregation of Methodists, but they
ve as yet no chapel. Pop. 496.

urker Wm. gentleman
swe Rev. Wm.
.wcett Wilson, gentleman
ankland Anthony, Esq.
cyes Mrs. M. gentlewoman
Iner Rev. James, (commercial and
   mathematical academy)
dd Ann, gentlewoman
oodhouse Henry, gent.

*Blacksmiths,* Jennings John
mpster T.&son Meynell Robt.
iger James Outhwaite Robt.
*Brick Mfrs.* Proctor Joseph
inings John Sowerby J. sen.
thwaite Robert Sowerby J. jun.
*Butchers,* *Shoemakers,*
rshall Wm. Bagley Wm.
vinson Geo. Gibson Rt. sen.
od Henry Gibson Rt. jun.
*mers & Yeomen,* *Surgeons,*
t Thos. Dinsdale P. C.
merson Jonth. Lincoln James
wer Jane *Tailors,*
wer James Bennison Philip
s Thomas Lindsey Geo.
rison Wm. Pearson Henry

pman Richard, vict. Bull Inn
rell Thomas, saddler
sr Christ. vict. Shoulder of Mutton
 Mary, cheesemonger and grocer
roth George, flax dresser
iolson James, stone mason
e Wm. clerk to the commissioners
of Gilling East
isby Mary, dress maker
isby Adam, wheelwright

Tutin Wm. grocer and seedsman
Tutin John, hop and seed merchant

Telegraph Coach, from Leeds to Newcastle, passes this place daily.
*Carriers*—John Lodge, from Stockton
   to Richmond, 3 times per week,
   and ret. same days.
Snowball Geo. to Richmond & York,
   every Saturday.

*Scotton,* in the parish of Catterick,
wap. of Hang East, and liberty of
Richmondshire; 4 miles SSE. of Richmond. Pop. 128.

*Scrafton,* (Little & West) in the
parish of Coverham, wap. of Hang
West, and liberty of Richmondshire;
4 miles SW. of Middleham. Pop. 146.

SCRUTON, (P.) in the wap. of
Hang East, and liberty of Richmondshire;
4 miles NNE. of Bedale. Here is a church,
dedicated to St. Radegund; the living is a
rectory, in the patronage of Henry Gale,
Esq. of which the Rev. Wm. Newsome,
A.M. is the incumbent. Here, in the year
1636, was born the Rev. Thomas Gale, dean
of York; and the literary labours of that
divine, and of his two sons, Roger & Henry,
will ever be highly esteemed by the scholar
and the antiquarian. Pop. 411.

Biass Mrs. Ann, gentlewoman
Gale Mrs. Mary, Scruton hall
Kettlewell Richard, yeoman

| *Bricklayers and Builders,* | *Grocers & Drapers,* |
|---|---|
| | Longtoft Mtthw. |
| Pearson Henry | Middleton John |
| Taylord Richard | *Joiners,* |
| *Farmers,* | Longtoft Mark |
| Braithwaite Rhd. | Taylor Richard |
| Busby Samuel | *Nursery and Seeds-men,* |
| Colling Wm. | |
| Fryer Leonard | Carruthers John |
| Harrison Robt. | Jackson Wm. and |
| Harrison Wm. | Co. Cross lanes |
| Kirby Wm. | Jackson Jacob |
| Middleton Geo. | Scruton grange |
| Scruton house | Kettlewell Thos. |
| Ormstone Robt. | Wells Matthew |
| Stonehouse Jph. | *Shoemakers,* |
| Cross lanes | Bowman John |
| Taylor Richard | Marlay Joseph |
| | Mitchell Geo. |

Bowman Thos. tailor & upholsterer
Cundall Wm. blacksmith
Ianson Mary, vict. Board
Kendal James, corn miller
Little Samuel, butcher
Macknay Christopher, schoolmaster
Marlay Joseph, vict. Board
*Carrier*—Joseph Blades, to Ripon,
   every Wed. ret. Fri.

z z 2

*Scugdale*, in the parish of Whorlton, wap. and liberty of Langbargh; 6 miles SW. of Stokesley; a beautiful sequestered vale, in which there is an extensive bleach yard, belonging to Mr. Wm. Boville, in great fame for its superior whitening of cloth.

*Seal Houses*, see Arkengarthdale.

**SEAMER**, (P.) in the wap. and liberty of Langbargh; 2 miles NW. of Stokesley. The church, dedicated to St. Martin, is a neat, small, plain structure, re-built in 1821, situated upon an eminence, and commanding an extensive prospect. The living is a perpetual curacy, under the patronage of Robert Greenhill Russell, Esq. M.P. Incumbent the Rev. Henry Gale. Within this township, and nearly at an equal distance, between the villages of Seamer and Newby, there is a remarkable tumulus, significantly called *How-hill*, which is not known to have ever been opened. In the fields adjoining, towards the South, on the side of a hill, are evident marks of an entrenchment; and it is reported, that in the valley or plain beneath, armour, swords, and human bones have been frequently turned up by the plough. It is difficult, perhaps, at this remote period, from the imperfect accounts we have received, to know to what people they could have belonged; but considering the nature and situation of the country, it seems probable, that this might have been the scene of action where the Saxons were overthrown by Prince Arthur, at the memorable battle of Baden-hill; which, according to Holinshed, and some other historians, is conjectured to have been fought in this neighbourhood, about the year 492. Pop. 226.

Philips Thomas, land & tithe valuer, and agent

| *Farmers,* | *Shoemakers,* |
|---|---|
| Barugh Thos. | Cornforth John |
| Hart Thos. | Ghent Geo. (& |
| Hart Robert | parish clerk) |
| Johnson Robert | Miliston Wm. |
| Nellist John | *Tailors,* |
| Philips Wm. | Garfat Wm. |
| Philips James | Marley John |
| Ronndtree Chpr. | Taylor Geo. |
| Sayer Wm. | Trotter Wm. |
| Steel Wm. | *Wheelwrights,* |
| Stockdale Chpr. | Lowther John |
| Woodhouse Rbt. | Meed Robert |
| Wright Thos. | Mothersdale John |
| | Vart Wm. |

Bainbridge Thomas, butcher
Brown Thomas, schoolmaster
Carter John, vict. Buck
Lowther John, vict. Bay Horse

Waller Thos. vict. and blacksmith, King's Head

A Carrier to Yarm and Stokesley, every Saturday.

**SEAMER**, (P.) in the wap. and liberty of Pickering Lythe; 4 miles NW. of Scarborough. This place is remarkable for a rebellion, which broke out in the year 1549, in the third of Edward VI.; the leaders were, Thomas Dale, the parish clerk, John Stevenson, and Wm. Ombler; their absurd claims were, the restoration of the old religion, the abolition of monarchy, and the extinction of all the different ranks of society. These desperadoes were soon joined by others equally desperate, and, in a few days, their number amounted to upwards of 3000; after having greatly alarmed the country, and murdered several persons, a sudden stop was put to their proceedings by the arrival of a proclamation from the King, offering pardon to the repentant, but denouncing punishment upon the contumacious; on which the greater number were wise enough to accept the proffered clemency, and to lay down their arms; but the leaders were apprehended and executed at York, on the 21st of September, 1549. The Percies were anciently lords of Seamer; it afterwards belonged to the Duke of Leeds, who sold it to William Joseph Denison, Esq. an eminent banker in London. There is here an elegant church, dedicated to St. Martin, which has the appearance of a Collegiate building; the living is a vicarage, in the patronage of W. J. Denison, Esq. and the Rev. Henry Ford is the incumbent. There is also a small, but neat Methodist chapel. A School, for boys and girls, with a dwelling-house adjoining, was built and liberally endowed by the lord of the manor, in 1814. Population, 596.

Cooke Mrs. Jane
Dowkir Rev. Edmund, curate

| *Blacksmiths,* | Stubbs Thos. |
|---|---|
| Chandler Anthy. | Taylor Wm. |
| Spencer Richard | Umpleby Geo. |
| *Farmers, &c.* | Vernon John |
| Awmack Wm. | Woodall Thos. |
| Barker John | Woodall Wm. |
| Boddis Christphr. | *Schools.* |
| Chandler Eliz. | Gibson John |
| Cook Joshua | Renaldson V. |
| Footy Wm. | *Shoemakers,* |
| Goodall Jonthn. | Buck John |
| Harland John | Davidson Robert |
| Hodgson Robert | Stephenson Thos. |
| Muschamp Rebca. | *Shopkeepers,* |
| Pennock John | Hepworth John |
| Pennock Mary | Hostler Richard |
| Smith Richard | Preston Geo. |

Villis Jonathan   Hebb Christopher
*Wheelwrights,*   Simpson Launcelot
Hobson John   Spencer John

Carlisle William, tailor
Cooper Thomas, cooper
Parker Jasper, gardener
Wikinson Robert, butcher
Yard Thos. vict. Dennison's Arms,
  brewer and maltster

SEDBURY, in the parish of Gilling, wap. of Gilling East, and liberty of Richmondshire; 3 miles N. by E. of Richmond. Pop. included with Gilling.

Bowers Henry, Esq. Sedbury hall

SEDBUSK, in the parish of Aysgarth, wap. of Hang West; 1 mile NNE. of Awes. This village is pleasantly situated on an eminence, in High Abbotside, and commands an extensive view of the western extremity of Wensleydale. Near to this place are several subterraneous caverns, commonly called, the *Maze-holes;* the roofs and sides of which are covered with beautiful trefactions and incrustations of various kinds. At the extremity of one of these caverns, there is an excellent spring of water. These rocky cavities are much frequented by visitors, and deservedly rank among the natural curiosities of a county abounding with wonderful works of nature. Pop. 123.

Alderston Wm. surgeon
Blackburn Thomas, yeoman
Prowcett Rev. Edw. perpetual curate
South Christopher, yeoman

*Simmer Water,* see Raydale.

SESSAY, (P.) in the wap. and liberty of Allertonshire; 5 miles NW. of Easingwold. Here is a church, dedicated to St. Cuthbert; the living a rectory, in the patronage of Lord Viscount Down. Pop. 364.

The Hon. & Rev. W. H. Dawney, rector

SEXHOW, a small hamlet, in the parish of Rudby, wap. and liberty of Tagbargh, 4 mls. SW. of Stokesley. Population 38.

*Farmers,*   Dinsley Joseph
Armstrong Robert,   Dinsley Henry
all   Flounders Jonas
Armstrong John   Gowland Philip

*Shaw,* see Hurst.

*Shaw and Shaw Cote,* in the parish Aysgarth, wap. of Hang West, and liberty of Richmondshire; 2½ miles N. of Hawes. Pop. 64.

*Shepherd's-hill,* in the parish of Carlton, wap. and liberty of Langbargh; 7 miles from Stokesley.

*Sheriff Hutton,* see Hutton Sheriff.

*Sherfitt-hall,* in the parish of Grinton, wap. of Gilling West, and liberty of Richmondshire; 3 mls. from Reeth.

SHIPTON, and SHIPTON SMITHY, in the parish of Overton, wap. of Bulmer, a part in the liberty of St. Peter's; 6 miles NW. of York. Here are a Methodist chapel, a chapel of Calvinistic Dissenters, and a Free School with a handsome endowment. Pop. 377.

Allen Rev. J. F. vicar of Overton

| *Farmers,* | Stewart James |
| Ambler Joseph | Styan John |
| Barker Wm. | Swales John |
| Burrill Alice | Theakstone Hanh. |
| Chapman Wm. | Tuke Thos. |
| Clarkson John | *Shoemakers,* |
| Cussons Wm. | Daniel John |
| Dawson Eliz. | Parkin John |
| Foster John | Powell Samuel |
| Garrett Thos, | *Shopkeepers,* |
| Gillah Wm. | Foster Thos. (& |
| Hobson John | bricklayer) |
| Moon Thos. | Pannett Robert |
| Parker John | |

Fenwick John, farrier, &c.
Hobson Wm. com. brewer & maltster
Jackson Wm. corn miller
Johnson Edward, blacksmith
Lund Thomas, tailor
Reynolds Jonathan, schoolmaster
Robinson Geo. fellmonger
Stabler W. carpenter & vict. Traveller
Turner John, wheelwright
Watson Wm. vict. Benningborough

*Shunnerfell,* said to be the highest hill in Swaledale, situated about 5 miles N. W. of Hawes; the land immediately surrounding this hill is very barren, owing to the rays of the sun being interrupted, and to the water from the hill in rainy seasons inundating the plain. The view from the summit is very expansive; the mountains of Westmoreland and Cumberland, the boundaries of Lancashire and Durham, and the distant wilds of Northumberland are all seen from this station.

SIGSTON-KIRBY, (P.) in the wap. and liberty of Allertonshire; 4 miles ENE. of Northallerton. The parish church is dedicated to St. Lawrence; the living is a rectory, in the patronage of Sir T. Slingsby, Bart. Pop. 131.

Fox Rev. John, rector, A. M.

*Sigston Smithy,* in the parish of Sigston, wap. and liberty of Allertonshire; 3½ mls. ENE. of Northallerton.

*Silpho,* in the parish of Hackness, wap. and liberty of Whitby Strand; 8 miles NW. of Scarborough. Pop. 96,

*Silton High* or *Over*, (P.) in the wap. of Birdforth; 6 mls. E. of North-allerton. The parish church, is a perpetual curacy, in the patronage of the Earl of Fauconberg, and the Rev. Edw. Greenwood is the incumbent. Pop. 94.

SILTON LOW or NETHER, in the parish of Leak, and wap. of Birdforth; 7 miles E. of Northallerton. Exclusive of the Chapel of Ease to the parish church, in which the vicar of Leak officiates as curate, there is here a Methodist chapel. Pop. 202.

Hickes Fowler, Esq. Silton hall

*Simonstone*, in the parish of Aysgarth, wap. of Hang West, and liberty of Richmondshire; 1½ mile N. of Hawes, pleasantly situated in High Abbotside, occasionally the seat of J. A. Stuart Wortley, Esq. M. P. lord of the manor. Pop. 41.

*Sinderby*, in the parish of Pickhill, wap. of Halikeld, and liberty of Richmondshire; 6 miles W. of Thirsk. Population 86.

SINNINGTON, (P.) in the wap. and liberty of Pickering Lythe; 4 miles WNW. of Pickering. There is here an endowment, left by Lady Lumley, for boys on going apprentice. The church living is a curacy, in the patronage of the master of Hemsworth school, and the Rev. Edward Dowker is the incumbent. There is also a Methodist chapel here. A branch of the Thornton Grammar School is established in this parish; which partakes also of the benefits of Lady Lumley's hospitals. (See Thornton.) Pop. 343.

Clarkson Wm. gentleman
Mackreth Rev. Anthony, officiating curate
Parvin Mrs. Rachael

| *Farmers & Yeomen,* | Hood Robert |
|---|---|
| Bentley Thos. | Mossley Wm. |
| Brown Eleanor | Norton Charles |
| Buckle Thos. | Petch Joseph |
| Bulman Wm. | Reed Cornelius |
| Dobson Frank | Stables Wm. |
| Dodgson Thos. | *Shoemakers,* |
| Dowkir Christr. | Jennan James |
| Gill James | Nixon Wm. |
| Goodill Robert | *Stone-masons,* |
| Grundon John | Baxter James |
| Hartas John | Baxter John |
| Hartas Thos. | *Wheelwrights,* |
| Helms David | Storr Geo. |
| Hewitt Wm. | Storr Wm. |

Brown Wm. vict. Cross Keys
Brown Geo. butcher
Close Thos. grocer, draper, and tailor
Cooper John, blacksmith
Dowker Robert, gardener

Keddy John, schoolmaster
Raine Richd. vict. Shoulder of Mutton

*Skeeby*, in the parish of Easby, wap. of Gilling West, and liberty of Richmondshire; 2 miles NE. of Richmond. Pop. 163.

*Skelderskew Grange*, in the parish of Guisborough, wap. and liberty of Langbargh; 4 miles SE. of Guisbro'.

SKELTON, in the parish of Overton, and wap. of Bulmer, a part in the liberty of St. Peter's; 4 miles NW. of York. Here is a very beautiful ancient church, built in 1227, and dedicated to St. Peter; the living is a rectory, in the patronage of Mr. Heyworth, and the incumbent is the Rev. Thomas Place. Population 273.

Drewry G. V. Esq.
Place Edward, Esq.
Thompson Mrs. Mary, gentlewoman
Thompson Henry, gentleman
Whittell Mrs. gentlewoman

| *Farmers,* | Guest Christopher |
|---|---|
| Bower J. (and butcher) | Rodwell Robert |
| | Wardman Robert |
| Bower John | Williamson Chas. |
| Busfield James | *Shoemakers,* |
| Cass John | Rigton John |
| Graves Joseph | Waterson Wm. |

Cooper G. blacksmith and victualler, Bay Horse
Hume Andrew, schoolmaster
Mountain Hannah, shopkeeper
Noble Thos. vict. Blacksmiths' Arms
Ridsdale Wm. carpenter

SKELTON, in the parish of Marske, wap. of Gilling West, and liberty of Richmondshire; 5½ miles W. of Richmond. Thomas Errington, Esq. of Clints Hall, resides in this village.

SKELTON, (P.) in the wap. and liberty of Langbargh; 3 miles NE. of Guisborough. Skelton castle was built by Robert de Brus, a Norman Baron, who accompanied William the Conqueror to England.— This nobleman, from whom some of the kings of Scotland, and the illustrious family of Bruce, Marquis of Ailesbury, are descended, was a person of such valour, and so much confided in by William the Conqueror, that he rewarded him with no less than forty-three lordships in the East and West Ridings of Yorkshire, and fifty-one in the North Riding of the county; whereof the manor and castle of Skelton were the capital of this Barony. In those days the Lords of Skelton had the privilege of a market, which, however extraordinary it may now appear, was held weekly on Sunday, when the people generally assembled in the morning to attend

vine worship, and in the afternoon to trans-
t their business, and regale themselves
th hot ale, the homely beverage of our
cestors. This market continued to be thus
ld till the 13th of Edward II. when John
rd Fauconberg obtained a license from the
ng for changing it from Sunday to Satur-
y, and also for an annual fair at Whitsun-
le; but both the market and fair have been
ng discontinued. From the Bruces this
tle passed through the families of Faucon-
rg, Neville, Conyers, and Trotter, to that
the Whartons. In the mansion, which
derwent a complete modern renovation
the year 1794, we find few traces of the
cient castle, except in the back part,
w converted into kitchen offices. It
esents an elegant extended front, situ-
d on the brink of a rivulet, which, by
ing collected into a reservoir with sloping
nks, adds greatly to the natural beauties
' the place. In the middle of the last cen-
ry, when this celebrated seat was in the
session of John Hall Stephenson, Esq.
e author of *Crazy Tales*, it was the resort
' the *literati* of the North, and Sterne,
e early and intimate friend of the proprie-
r, drew his *Eugenius* from his character.
lady of considerable worth of character,
t withal of great eccentricity, was closely
lied to this family—we allude to the late
rs. Margaret Wharton. This lady, whose
bits were of the most saving kind as far as
r own personal expenses were concerned,
ssessed a fortune of 200,000*l.* and amongst
e rest of her oddities she choose to become
r own executrix, and actually made a pre-
nt, during her life time, of 100,000*l.* to her
phew, the present worthy possessor of
telton castle.* The church of Skelton is
neat modern edifice, dedicated to All
ints; and the living, which is a perpetual
racy, is in the patronage of the Archbishop
' York. Population, 791.

tters arrive at 10 o'clock in the morning,
and the post returns at 3 in the afternoon.

lose Rev. Wm. perpetual curate
ixon Thomas, attorney
ohnson Mrs. gentlewoman
'harton John, Esq. M. P. Skelton
    castle

| *Blacksmiths,* | *Corn Millers,* |
|---|---|
| arter Thos. | Watson Robert |
| obinson Robert | Wilson Wm. |
| oung Wm. | *Farmers & Yeomen,* |
| *Butchers,* | Adamson Wm. |
| awson Wm. | Appleton John |
| 'ilkinson Isaac | Clark Thos. |
| filkinson Wm. | Cole James |

* Hutton's Trip to Coatham.

Collin James
Cooper Wm.
Emerson Stphn.
Frandale John
Gill Robert
Hall Wm.
Hall Edward
Hardon Jackson
Hutton Wm.
Johnson Sarah
Johnson John
Lockwood Wm.
Parnaby John
Rigg Thos.
Sayer Wm.
Sherwood Wm.
Taylor John
Thompson Robert
Thompson Wm.
Tiplady Robert
Wilkinson Wm.
Wilson Richard
*Grocers & Drapers,*
Appleton John
Dixon Wm.
Lynass Ralph
M'Naughton D. &
    flax dresser
Shimelds Thos.
Slater John

*Joiners, &c.*
Appleton Wm.
Dixon Leonard
Carrick Mark
Middleton Joseph
    *Schoolmasters,*
Atkinson M.
Sharp John
    *Shoemakers,*
Bell Robert
Lowis Luke
Lowis Thos.
Lynass Geo.
Steele Thos.
    *Stone Masons,*
Bryan Thos.
Pattinson John
    *Straw Hat Mfrs.*
Oliver Sarah
Shimelds Esther
    *Tailors,*
Lynass Ralph
Shimelds Thos.
Thompson Joseph
    *Weavers,*
Abelson Stephen
Dawson Thos.
Robinson John
Wilkinson Robt.

Andrew John, land agent
Bean Wm. vict. Duke William
Castley Scarth, vict. Board
Crusber James, turner in wood, &c.
Frank Thomas, gamekeeper
Gowland Wm. plumber, glasier, and
    drawn pipe manufacturer
Lawson Wm. vict. Royal George
Taylor Thomas, saddler
Wilkinson Eliz. shopkeeper

*Carriers*—Marmaduke Wilson to Guis-
    borough Tu. and Fri. dep. 8 mg.
    ret. 4 aft. Robert Wilkinson, to
    Stockton Wed. and Sat. dep. 4
    mg. ret. 8 at night ; and to Loft-
    house Mon. and Thur. dep. 9 mg.
    ret. 6 evening.

*Skelton Smithy,* in the parish of
Skelton, and wap. of Bulmer; 3 miles
NW. of York.

*Skewsby,* in the parish of Dalby,
and wap. of Bulmer; 7 miles ENE.
of Easingwold. Population included
with Dalby.

SKINNINGRAVE, in the parish of
Brotton, wap. & liberty of Langbargh ;
7 miles NE. of Guisborough. A small
hamlet situated upon the sea, in a deep
creek or bay, the lofty and rugged
sides of which entirely seclude it from
all distant view. Pop. 60.

Easterby John, Esq.
Huxton Captain David

Pearson Aaron, yeoman
Ellaby William, farmer
Patten John, coast waiter
Stonehouse Roger, vict. Board

*Skiplam*, in the parish of Kirkdale, and wap. of Rydale ; 2 miles WNW. of Kirkby-Moor-Side. Pop. 170.

SKIPTON and SKIPTON BRIDGE. in the parish of Topcliffe, and wap. of Birdforth ; 4 miles SW. of Thirsk. Population, 110.

Barstow Thomas, Esq. Skipton hall

*Farmers & Yeomen,* Watkinson Christr.
Goodrick Wm.    Watson John
Robinson John    Weatherhill Geo.

Butterfield Jane, vict. Crown Inn
Kirby Christopher, tailor
Yeates Thomas, blacksmith

SKUTTERSKELFE, or LEVEN GROVE, in the parish of Rudby, wap. and liberty of Langbargh ; 3 miles W. SW. of Stokesley. Near to this village is Folly Hill, a conspicuous sea-mark, which may be seen at the distance of twenty leagues upon the German Ocean. Pop. 32.

Hon. Lady Amherst, Leven grove

*Farmers,*    Fawcett John
Coates Robert,    Redhead John
   Tame bridge    Wrightson John

Douglass Arthur, gardener
Sidgwick John, linen manufacturer

*Slape Wath*, in the parish of Guisborough, wap. and liberty of Langbargh ; 2 miles E. of Guisborough.

*Sleddale*, in the parish of Guisborough, wap. & liberty of Langbargh ; 4 miles S. of Guisborough.

*Sledshoe*, in the parish of Lastingham, and wap. of Rydale ; 12 miles N. of Kirkby-Moor-Side.

*Sleetholme*, in the parish of Bowes, wap. of Gilling West, and liberty of Richmondshire ; 7 miles SW. of Barnard Castle.

*Sleighill* or *Holly Hill*, in the parish of Catterick, wap. of Hang West, & liberty of Richmondshire. A small hamlet near Richmond, pleasantly situated on the banks of the Swale, commanding a perspective view of Richmond castle, and the rocky sides of the mount on which it stands.

SLEIGHTS, in the parish of Whitby, wap. & liberty of Whitby Strand ; 4 mls. SW. of Whitby. There is here a very neat Chapel of Ease, and the Rev. Mr. Robertson of Whitby, is the incum-

bent, with a number of handsome monuments in the church-yard.

Bateman Mrs. Sarah, Hall
Boulby John, gentleman
Boyes John, gentleman
Boyes Mrs. Elizabeth
Coates John Campion, Esq. Esk hall
Newball George, gentleman
Wilson Mrs. Mary

| *Academies.* | Noble Geo. |
|---|---|
| Harden Rev. John | Petty Thos. |
| Marshall Thomas | *Shoemakers,* |
| *Farmers,* | Hoggarth James |
| Featherstone Peter | Speddill Jacob |

Bart Robert, cooper
Chapman Wm. joiner & wheelwright
Harrison Nathaniel, blacksmith
Hick Wm. butcher
Hill Wm. vict. Royal Oak
Noble John, vict. Board
Smith Matthew, vict. Fox.

SLINGSBY, (P.) in the wap. of Rydale ; 6 miles WNW. of Malton ; is situated on an extensive beautiful plain, and on an ancient Roman road, formerly a Roman station. This manor and castle formerly belonged to the noble family of Mowbray, who were succeeded by that of Howard : John, Lord Howard, was created Duke of Norfolk, by King Richard III. in which illustrious family the title still remains. The castle was partly re-built by Sir C. Cavendish in 1603, but not finished ; it is now the property of the Earl of Carlisle. In the woods of Earl Carlisle there are nine or ten large tumuli, showing that some severe conflict has taken place here. Here is a school for ten poor children, endowed with 5*l.* per annum by Mrs. Ann Mann, of Stokesley. There is also a church, dedicated to All Saints ; the living is a rectory, in the patronage of the Earl of Carlisle, and the Rev. John Cleaver, D. D. is the incumbent. Pop. 648.

Luccock Thomas, surgeon
Walker Rev. Wm. curate

| *Blacksmiths,* | Cooper John |
|---|---|
| Bell Thomas | Dobson Francis |
| Suggitt Thomas | Ireland Thos. |
| *Butchers,* | Linfoot Thos. |
| Coulson Jonathan | Piercy Geo. |
| Lawson Matthew | Walker John |
| *Farmers & Yeomen,* | *Shopkeepers,* |
| Bradshaw Thos. | Etty Matthew |
| Brigham Wm. | Wilson Thos. |

Burton Thomas, shoemaker
Chapman Wm. schoolmaster
Harrison Robert, tallow chandler
Mawmill M. vict. New Inn
Smith Thomas, cabinet maker and wheelwright

*Smarber,* see Melbecks.

*Smearholms,* in the parish of rneston, wap. of Halikeld, and li-ty of Richmondshire ; 4 miles from lule.

SMEATON GREAT, (P.) in the , of Gilling East, and liberty of Rich-dshire ; 7 miles N. of Northallerton. village particularly merits attention, the extent and grandeur of its pros-. The southern parts of the county of ham, Cleveland, and the fine country ; the banks of the Tees, towards Rich-d, with part of the vale of York, in con-with the black frowning mountains of eastern and western moors all in full , form a most magnificent assemblage. church is an ancient structure ; and the ; is a rectory, in the patronage of Lord leton. Pop. 250.

gill Rev. James, curate

| | |
|---|---|
| ...rs & Yeomen, | Weatherild Robt. |
| wsmith S. | Wilkinson Mthw. |
| Robert | *Schoolmasters,* |
| ...r Edward | Butterfield John |
| ...on Thomas | Williamson T. |

...h John, vict. Black Bull
...on John, surveyor of roads
...isbrough Geo. shopkeeper
...on John, saddler
...ck Benj. butcher
...pson John, cattle dealer
...dy Wm. vict. Blacksmiths' Arms
wright Wm. vict. Bay Horse

*...neaton Little,* in the parish of ?, wap. and liberty of Allerton-6 miles N. of Northallerton.—...tion, 64.

...AINTON, in the parishes of ...ton and Ebberston, wap. and of Pickering Lythe ; 8 miles E. ...ering   About a quarter of a ...om the village is Stainton New large posting house. Pop. 603.
...obert, gentleman
...ld Mrs. Mary
...homas, surgeon

| | |
|---|---|
| ...kers, | Hodgson John |
| ...ohn | Hoggard Francis |
| ...ll Hannah | Lovel Vincent |
| ...chers, | Lownsbrough Geo. |
| rough Geo. | Nesfield Richard |
| | Skelton Francis |
| ...l Peter | Skelton James |
| ...Ann | Story Thos. |
| ...l Wm. | Taylor Wm. |
| ...mers, | Ward John |
| ...i Wm. | Williamson John |
| ...Richard | *Shoemakers,* |
| ...John | Craven Wm. |
| ...ames | Donkin John |
| ...tichard | Stephenson Walter |

| | |
|---|---|
| *Shopkeepers,* | Stubbs Geo. |
| Craven Craven | Temple Martin |
| Robson Mary | *Wheelwrights,* |
| Stonehouse Geo. | Baker John |
| *Tailors,* | Beswick Anthony |
| Goodill Thos. | |

Barry Mary, vict. Peacock
Barwick James, saddler
Brown Thos. blacksmith
Coulson John, schoolmaster
Riby William, cooper
Watson Robert, vict. Plough

SNAPE, in the parish of Well, wap. of Hang East, and liberty of Rich-mondshire ; 3 miles S. of Bedale. Here is a Methodist chapel, and two free schools, one for each sex, with a liberal endowment, left by the Nevilles ; likewise an hospital or alms house for eight aged persons. The principal trade here is wool-combing, and many of the worsted spinners in the West Riding are supplied with combed wool from this place and Masham. Pop. 669.

Clark Misses, Hall
Dockeray Rev. T. vicar of Well

| *Blacksmiths,* | *Joiners, &c.* |
|---|---|
| Bradley John | Bell John |
| Bradley Wm. | Furby Christopher |
| *Butchers,* | *Schoolmasters, &c.* |
| Miller Thos. | Cowper John |
| Pearson Daniel | Lonsdale Edmund |
| *Farmers & Yeomen,* | Metcalfe Ann |
| Abel John | *Shoemakers,* |
| Auton Thos. | Cowper Richard |
| Banks Wm. | Hill John |
| Banks Edward | Oyston Joseph |
| Buckle Mary | *Shopkeepers,* |
| Dennison Richard | Baines Wm. |
| Eglin Wm. | Garthwaite Thos. |
| Eglin John | *Tailors,* |
| Gatenby Christr. | Airey Wm. |
| Hammond Wm. | Wilson John |
| Kilding John | *Woolstaplers and* |
| Lamb Thos. | *Wool-combers,* |
| Lofthouse Thos. | Cheesborough C. |
| Mudd John | Cheesborough Wm. |
| Topham Thos. | Dunn Thos. |
| Walker Thos. | Garthwaite John |
| Webster Henry | Reynard Wm. |
| Wilks Thos. | |

Crow Thos. vict. & butcher, Board
Hudle Robert, currier
Metcalf George, corn miller
Metcalf Ann, vict. Buck
Salmon Geo. vict. Sober Robin
Topham John, lime burner

*Snape Hall,* formerly a seat of the Fitz Randolph's, Lords of Middleham, Earls of Exeter, &c. but now the property of Mark Milbank, Esq. M. P. is situated in this vil-lage. This ancient house is in a dilapi-dated state, but sufficient remains to show its former extent and magnificence. It is probable, that the present mansion was built by the Latimers, not earlier perhaps than Henry VII. or VIII. but a house or castle of great extent must have before stood on the same site.

*Snayzholme*, in the parish of Aysgarth, wap. of Hang West, and liberty of Richmondshire ; 2½ miles SSW. of Hawes. A small hamlet in the township of Hawes. Population included with Hawes.

*Sneaton*, (p.) in the wap. & liberty of Whitby Strand ; 3 miles SW. of Whitby. Here is an ancient church, dedicated to St. John ; the living is a rectory, of which the King is the patron, the Rev. John Hammond, the incumbent, and the Rev. Timothy Cassley, the resident curate. Population, 251.

*Sneaton Thorpe*, in the parish of Sneaton, wap. and liberty of Whitby Strand ; 4 miles S. of Whitby.

*Snilesworth*, in the parish of Hawnby. and wap. of Birdforth ; 10 miles NW. of Hemsley.

*Sober Hill*, in the parish of Ainderby Steeple, wap. of Gilling East, and liberty of Richmondshire ; 4 miles S. of Northallerton.

*SOBER Low*, in the parish of Ainderby Steeple, wap. of Gilling East, and liberty of Richmondshire ; 4 miles SSW. of Northallerton.

Foster Miss M. gentlewoman
Meek Michael, nurseryman

*Som Leys*, in the parish of Helmsley, and wap. of Rydale ; 2½ miles NW. of Helmsley.

*South Field*, in the parish of Kirkdale, and wap. of Rydale, 3 miles S. of Kirkby-Moor-Side.

SOWERBY, in the parish of Thirsk, and wap. of Birdforth ; 1½ mile S. of Thirsk ; is a pleasant village, containing many good houses, and communicates with Thirsk by an excellent gravel walk, across the fields called the flats. This walk commands a fine view of the adjacent country, terminated by the Hambleton hills, and is the favourite promenade of the inhabitants. There is here an ancient Chapel of Ease to the church of Thirsk. Population, 748.

Bosomworth Richard, gentleman
Brook Mrs.
Cattle J. gentleman
Cayley Cornelius, Esq. magistrate
Chapman William, Esq.

Corselleis N. C. Esq. Capt. R. N.
Corselleis N. C. surgeon & apothecary
Dennison Mrs.

Kirby William, gentleman
Leafe John, Esq.
Richardson Rev. J.
Ridley Francis, gentleman
Sayers Miss
Strangeways, M.
Welbank William, Esq.
Whitewick William, Esq.
Wilkinson Rev. William
Wrighton Richard, Esq.

*Academies*,      Squires Ann
Arnit Francis      Toes Wm.
Gibbons Tho. (bdg. Waites Wm.
Gibson Chancellor Watson J.

*Bricklayers*,      *Linen Mfrs.*
Palliser James      Morrill Wm.
Palliser Charles      Ward Thos.

*Farmers & Yeomen*,      *Shoemakers*,
Bell Francis      Clarkson Joseph
Brown Thos.      Raper Thos.
Buckle Edward      *Tailors*,
Eles Thos.      Cousin Joseph
Hodge Alice      Shaw Thos.
Little Thos.

Barker James, chief constable
Bell Christopher, vict. and whip lash maker, Fox
Brensby and Court, curriers
Briggs Simon, carrier
Fox John, tallow chandler
Hardy Susannah, grocer
Harrison ——, gardener
Harwood Benjamin, blacksmith
Johnson Wm. carpenter
Kirby Thomas, joiner
Nicholson John, vict. 3 Horse Shoes

SOWERBY-UNDER-COTCLIFFE, in the parish of Kirkby Sigston, and liberty of Allertonshire ; 3 miles E. of Northallerton. Pop. 53.

*Farmers & Yeomen*, Peacock Wm.
Bell Christopher      Smith John
Herring Wm.      Tetley John
Kendall John      Topham Thos.

*Spaunton*, in the parish of Lastingham, and wap. of Rydale ; 4 miles NE. of Kirby-Moor-Side. Pop. 109.

SPENNYTHORNE, (p.) in the wap. of Hang West, and liberty of Richmondshire ; 2 miles NE. of Middleham. In this village was born and baptized on the 30th of October, 1675, the great hebraist, John Hutchinson, author of the " Principia," well known in the literary world as the advocate of the Plinian system, and the opponent of the Newtonian system (doctrine of gravitation,) and whose strenuous and particular

of thinking, relative to the principles
he Mosaic history, has attracted many
iples, and established him the founder of
ect, called the Hutchinsonians. The
rch is a neat Gothic structure, dedicated
t. Michael; the living is a rectory, in the
onage of Marmaduke Wyvill, Esq. M.P.
ulation 249.

A Mail gig arr. from Bedale, with letters every Mon. Wed. Fri. and Sat. at 3
ift. and is dispatched 7 mg. same days.
Post Office, at the Old Horn Inn.

ytor Mrs. gentlewoman
Robert, gentleman
abenzee Col. Turner
ill Rev. Wm. rector

| Farmers, | Rider Benjamin . |
| :er Thos. | Simpson Thos. |
| :n Richard | |

:es Marmaduke, blacksmith
:on George, tailor
fll Chpr. vict. Old Horn Inn

*:pittal Houses*, in the parish of
:s, wap. of Gilling West, and
y of Richmondshire; 9½ miles
ƒ. of Barnard Castle.

*:pittle Bridge Inn*, in the parish of
:e, and wap. of Bulmer; 7 miles
:f Malton. This inn, which forms
ing station, is kept by Mrs. Ann
:son.

*:ring End*, in the parish of Grin-
ap. of Gilling West, & liberty of
ondshire; 6 mls. W. of Reeth.

:ROXTON, in the parish of Helms-
nd wap. of Rydale; 1 mile S.
:ey. Pop. 67.

| armers, | Robson Wm. |
| Christ. | Robson John |
| ohn | Swales Richard |
| obert | Wilson Robert |
| r John | Wilson Richard |

*ddle Bridge*, in the parish of
:arlsey, wap. and liberty of
:shire; 7 miles from North-
.

*insacre*, in the parish of Whit-
p. and liberty of Whitby
2 miles SSE. of Whitby.—
:luded with Hawsker.

*nsby*, in the parish of Stain-
:. and liberty of Langbargh;
NE. of Yarm.

:NTON, (P.) in the wap. and
Langbargh; 4 miles NW. of
; a small pleasant village. The-
:dicated to St. Peter, is an an-
structure, but partly modernised

by having received great repairs about 14 ,
years ago. It stands on elevated ground, at
the western extremity of the village, with
the vicarage house adjoining, which is a large
and spacious mansion; the living is in the
patronage of the Archbishop of York, and
the Hon. and Rev. Henry Howard is the
incumbent. In the chancel is the ancient
sepulchre of the Pennyman family. Here
is a small school, endowed with 5*l.* per ann.
for the educating of six poor children of the
township. Pop. 356.

Gilpin Rev. John, vicar
Jeffels Rev. Wm. curate
Willis Wm. gentleman

| Farmers, | Meanburn Wm. (& |
| Fall George | parish clerk) |
| Jordison Christ. | Parnaby Wm. |
| Langdale Mary | *Schoolmasters,* |
| Sherwood John | Suggitt Thos. |
| Smith Robert | Wilson Wm. |
| Thompson John | |

Carter Thomas, vict. Black Horse
Harrison Wm. butcher
Ingledew William, blacksmith & vict.
   Anchor
Sanderson John, tailor
Sprental Robert, wheelwright
Storey Thomas, blacksmith

STAINTON, in the parish of Downholme, wap. of Hang West, and liberty of Richmondshire; 4 miles N. of
Leyburn. Pop. 54.
Naylor Henry, quarry owner

*Stainton Dale*, in the parish of
Scalby, wap. and liberty of Pickering Lythe:
8 miles NNW. of Scarborough. This
manor, about the year 1140, was granted
by King Stephen to the Knights Templar,
on condition that a chaplain should constantly be retained by them, to perform
divine service there daily, and to offer up
intercession for the kings of England.—
Population, 294.

STAITHES, in the parish of Hinderwell, wap. and liberty of Langbargh;
11 miles NW. of Whitby; a fishing village,
situated upon the coast, in a rugged creek,
surrounded by lofty hills, and so completely
is it secluded from the eye of the traveller,
that he looks in vain for the town, till he
arrives at the summit of the craggy hills by
which it is immediately encompassed. The
inhabitants live almost wholly by fishing;
during the winter and spring seasons they go
out to sea in small flat bottomed boats,
called Cobles, each carrying three men, and
so constructed as to live in very tempestu-
ous weather; in summer they go out in large
boats, of from ten to twenty tons burden,
called, "Five Men Cobles;" they generally

sail on Monday, and, if the weather permit, continue at sea the whole week; on their return, the fish is cut up and salted by the women; and after passing through the brine, it is spread out to dry on the beach.— The fishery is here carried on to a great extent, and, in the herring season, this village generally sends fifteen vessels to Yarmouth, a greater number than is sent from any other place on the Yorkshire coast. Besides fishing, the inhabitants here, and along the coast, during the summer months, are occasionally occupied in making Kelp, which is a lixivial salt, obtained by the burning of sea weeds, and consists chiefly of the fixed vegetable alkali, used in the process of making alum, glass, &c. The sea weed is cut at low water from the rocks, and when dry is burnt in heaps, being constantly stirred with an iron rake till it becomes condensed and caked together in large masses. Pop. included with Hinderwell.

Christopher Mason, post-man, to Whitby
Monday, Thursday, and Saturday.

Francillen Lieut. Thomas, Royal
Navy
Gallilee Captain Samuel

*Bakers,*
Adamson Eliz.
Dawson Thos.
Seamer Richard
Taylor James
*Blacksmiths,*
Sanders John
Smallwood Wm.
*Coopers,*
Adamson Thos.
Bell George
Lane John
*Fish Curers,*
Cole Daniel
Moore Christ.
Trattles Thos.
Trattle Thos.
*Grocers & Drapers,*
Coates Richard
Hutton Richard
Moore Christ.
Trattles Thos.

*Joiners, &c.*
Bonnes Thos.
Burton Wm.
Hudson Wm.
Rodam Thos.
Ventress Benj.
*Midwives,*
Breckon Mrs. Mary
Jackson Mrs. Jane
*Shoemakers,*
Adamson Leonard
Bell Isaac
Hudson Thos.
Jaques John
Pinder Jonathan
Robinson Thos.
Spinks James
*Tailors,*
Fletcher John
Mead Wm.
Pinder Wm.
Sayer Robert

Bonnes Thomas, vict. Golden Lion
Brown Thomas, vict. Red Lion
Brown Thomas, vessel owner
Deuil C. vict. Shoulder of Mutton
Hudson Wm. vict. Three Tuns
Morritt Isaac, stone mason
Parkes Thomas, butcher
Taylor Mark, clock maker
Trattles Matth. vict. Cod & Lobster
Waller John, vict. Fishing Boat

*Carriers.*

Robert Knaggs, to Guisbro' every Tu.

and Fri. at 4 afternoon, ret. Mon. and Thur. at 11 morning.
Thomas Johnson, to Whitby & Guisborough every Th. and Fri.
Thomas Nisbet, to Whitby every Mon. Wed. Fri. and Sat.

STAKESBY, (High and Low) in the parish of Whitby, wap. and liberty of Whitby Strand; ½ mile W. of Whitby.

Blackburn John, Esq.
Chapman Abel, Esq. banker
Ridley Edward, yeoman
Anderson Thomas and Son, corn factors and millers
Featherstone Adeline, farmer
Foster Joseph, governor of the Workhouse
Goodwill Henry, roper
Johnson John, master mariner
Waller Joseph, farmer

*Stalling Busk,* in the parish of Aysgarth, and wap. of Hang West; 5 miles S. of Askrigg; a small village pleasantly situated in Raydale. There is here a beautiful cascade, formed by a perpendicular water-fall, behind which there is a recess, excavated out of the solid rock, under which a person may walk, without being annoyed by the transparent liquid in which he seems to be immersed.

*Standard Hill,* in the parish of Northallerton, wap. and liberty of Allertonshire; 3 miles N. of Northallerton: where the English standard was placed at the battle of the Standard, in the year 1138. (See Northallerton.) The house on the hill is occupied by Mr. William Swinbourn, farmer.

STANGHOW, in the parish of Skelton, wap. and liberty of Langbargh; 3 miles ENE. of Guisborough; is pleasantly situated on an eminence, and affords a variety of beautiful scenery. The lord of the manor is J. Wharton, Esq. M.P. of Skelton Castle. Population 91.

*Farmers & Yeomen,*
Dowson Joseph
Dunn Richard
Jackson Ralph
Miller Michael
Pickering Thos.
Scarth Isaac
Scarth Wm.
Taylor James
Thompson Jph.
Watson Wm.

Lowson Thomas, vict. Crown
Story George, vict. Board

*Stank,* in the parish of Sigston, wap. and liberty of Allertonshire; 5 miles ENE. of Northallerton.

*Stapleton,* in the parishes of St. John, Stanwick, and Croft, and wap. of Gilling East and West; 11 miles NE. of Richmond. Pop. 113.

STARTFORTH, (P.) in the wap. of Gilling West, and liberty of Richmond-shire; 1 mile W. of Barnard Castle; a small irregularly built village, situated on the banks of the Tees, opposite Barnard Castle. The church, which is dedicated to the Holy Trinity, is an ancient structure; the living is a vicarage, in the patronage of the Earl of Lonsdale. Population, 460.

Fielding Mrs. gentlewoman
Hill T. W. Esq. captain & paymaster of Durham militia, Startforth hall
Preston Rev. Wm. M.A. vicar
Thompson Wm. gent.
Todd Robert, gentleman

*Farmers & Yeomen*, Thompson Rt.
Middleton Edw.    White Daniel
Teesdale Wm.
Chapman John, blacksmith
Halland John, boarding school
Garrison, Gibson, and Co. shoe thread manufacturers
Hunton George, serjeant
Jefferson Matthew, miller
Lodge Robert, shopkeeper
Thompson Joseph, vict. White Swan
Thompson John, butcher

STEARSBY, in the parish of Bransby, and wap. of Bulmer; 6 mls. NE. of Easingwold. Pop: included with Bransby.

*Farmers*,            Frank Robert
Gar Edward           Ratcliff William
Atley Thomas         Tate John
Dixon William,
Foulrice
Silvington Wm. tailor & vict. Griffin

*Stepney*, in the parish of Whitby, wap. and liberty of Whitby Strand; 1 mile W. of Whitby.

STEPNEY HOUSE, in the parish Scarborough, wap. of Pickering lythe, and liberty of Scarborough; 2 miles SW. of Scarborough.

Phillips Rev. Mr. private establishment for a select number of young gentlemen.

STILLINGTON, (P.) in the wap. Bulmer, and liberty of St. Peter's; 4 miles ESE. of Easingwold. Here is a small humble looking church, dedicated to St. Nicholas; the living is a vicarage, in the patronage of the Prebend of Stillington; incumbent, the Rev. T. H. Croft. This is one of the church livings held by the celebrated Lawrence Sterne, who resided at Coxton, in this neighbourhood. There are also a Methodist chapel and a National school in this village. Pop. 698.

A riding post from York to Helmsley passes through this village; letters from York delivered here at 7 o'clock morning, and from Helmsley at 4 evening.—William Garbutt, post-man.

Allan Robert, Esq. Captain
Croft Harry, Esq. Colonel
Croft William, Esq. Captain
Dennis Wm. surgeon
Grayson Rev. Isaac, curate
Sadler David, gentleman
Wilkinson Mrs. Mary

*Blacksmiths*,      Smith Wm.
Richardson Geo.     Snowden Wm.
Slater Jonthn.      Thompson Geo.
  *Brewers*,        Webster Thos.
Sowray Thos.        Wright Thos.
Wood C. & maltster    *Joiners, &c.*
  *Bricklayers*,    Cass John
Hall John           Cordukes John
Wood John           Halder John
Wood Thos.          Ratcliff John
  *Butchers*,       Thompson John
Brown Andrew        Thompson Wm.
Cobb Wm.              *Shoemakers*,
Wynn Noah           Cowper Christ.
*Farmers & Yeomen*, Hodgson John
Barker George       Lowther Thos.
Bell Robert         North John
Calvert John        Snowball Thos.
Farrah Robert       Wetherhill Wm.
Greenwood Thos.       *Tailors*,
Hall John           Barker Thos. (&
Jackson Thos.         draper)
Lowther John        Canby George
Morley Robert,      Robinson Geo.
Richardson Chpr.    Suggitt Wm.
Farrah Henry, grocer & draper
Gibson Robert, officer of excise
Robinson Joseph, schoolmaster
Sowray Henry, tallow chandler
Spruce Geo. plumber and glazier
Stewart Thomas, cooper
Thompson Wm. vict. Bay Horse
Wilkinson Thomas, corn miller
Wilson Matthew, vict. White Dog
Wynn Noah, vict. White Bear
*Carrier*—David Masser to York every Sat. morn. at 4, ret same day.

*Stittenham*, in the parish of Sheriff Hutton, and wap. of Bulmer; 7 miles SW. of Malton. Pop. 81.

ST. JOHN STANWICK, (P.) in the wap. of Gilling West, and liberty of Richmondshire; 8 miles N. of Richmond.—Lord Prudhoe, brother to the Duke of Northumberland, has a seat here, situated in a finely wooded park, well stocked with deer. In the park are the remains of some Roman intrenchments. The church is a very ancient stone building, dedicated to St. John, and in it are two remarkably handsome marble full length figures, to the memory of

Sir Hugh and Lady Smithson, formerly of Stanwick hall, from whom it has descended to the present proprietor. The patronage of the living is in John Wharton, Esq. M.P. the Rev. Wm. Wharton is the vicar, and the Rev. R. M. Atkinson, A. M. curate. Pop. 59.

Lax Thos. steward to Lord Prudhoe

*Farmers,*

Pearson Thomas

Todd John

Wilkin John

STOCKTON-ON-THE-FOREST, (P.) in the wap. of Bulmer, a part in the liberty of St. Peter's; 4 miles NE. of York. On the 13th of January, 1792, a meteorous appearance was observed on the forest, near this village, (by several persons of credit and respectability) resembling a large army, in separate divisions, some in black and others in white uniforms; one of these divisions formed a line that appeared near a mile in extent, in the midst of which appeared a number of fir trees, which seemed to move along with the line. These aerial troops moved in different directions, and sometimes with amazing rapidity.—(See a similar account in Clark's Survey of the Lakes, page 86.) A meteorous phenomenon, of the same kind, was seen in Heywra Park, near Harrogate, on Sunday, June 28th, 1812, between seven and eight o'clock in the evening, by Anthony Jackson, aged 45 years, and Martin Turner, a young man, the son of a farmer in the neighbourhood; both looking after their cattle, were suddenly surprised to see, at some distance, what appeared to them a large body of armed men, in white military uniforms; in the centre of which was a person of a commanding aspect, dressed in scarlet. After performing various evolutions, the whole body began to move forward, in perfect order, towards the summit of a hill, passing the spectators at the distance of about 100 yards. No sooner had this first body, which extended four deep, over an enclosure of 30 acres, attained the hill, than a second body, far more numerous than the former, dressed in a dark coloured uniform, appeared, and marched after the first, to the top of the hill, where they both joined, and passing down the opposite side of the hill, disappeared; when a column of thick smoke spread over the plain. The time, from the first appearance of this strange phenomenon to the clearing up of the smoke, the spectators suppose was little more than five minutes.

" When these prodigies do so conjointly meet, let not men say they are natural; for, I believe, they are portentous things unto the climate that they point upon.— *Julius Cæsar.*"

The church living here is a perpetual curacy, of which the Prebendary of Bugthorpe is the patron, and the Rev. William Noddins the incumbent. Here is a Methodist chapel, and a school with a small endowment, free to 10 poor children. Population, 357.

*Farmers & Yeomen,*
Atkinson Wm.
  Sanburn
Brigham John
Clark Geo. (and cattle dealer)
Dale Joseph
Jebson John, (& brickmaker)
Hawkins Edward
Milner Geo.
Nightingale Wm. (& shopkeeper)

Slaton Thos.
Staveley Benj.
  Wade John
Wade Anthony
Wardell John
Wray Ralph
  *Shoemakers,*
Lund William
Sturdy Thomas
  *Tailors,*
Hardcastle Wm.
Hodgson John

Cobb George, bricklayer
Gates John, schoolmaster
Heslegrave John, vict. Fox
Hustwick Thomas, butcher
Jebson Thos. vict. White Swan
Nightingale Matthew, blacksmith
Oxterby J. corn miller, Sanburn mill
Suggitt Christopher, carpenter
Todd Isaac, shopkeeper
Williams William; land surveyor

## STOKESLEY, (P.)

In the wap. and liberty of Langbargh; 9 miles from Guisborough; 9 from Yarm; and 16 from Northallerton. A small market town of Cleveland; consisting chiefly of one broad street, running east and west, and washed on the south by a principal branch of the river Leven, which is a remarkably fine trout stream. The buildings are neat, and for the most part in the modern style. The market is held on Saturday, and is plentifully supplied with provisions on reasonable terms. Of the fairs which are held here, an account will be found appended to the first volume. The lands near the town are chiefly in grass, and occupied in small allotments. The surrounding lands are rich and fertile, and being a fine sporting country, the situation possesses all the advantages of rural sports and agreeable retirement. The beautiful and majestic chain of mountains, called the Cleveland hills, including Roseberry Topping, range at a distance of from four to six miles from the town, with a peculiarly bold and romantic outline, and form a sort of semi-circular amphitheatre, of which Stokesley is the centre. A considerable manufacture of linen is carried on here, and that trade is likely to be extended, by a mill, which Messrs. Thomas and John Meale are now erecting, to be worked by the power of steam. In the year 1818, a Society for the promotion of Christian knowledge was established here, under the patronage of the Archdeacon of Cleveland, when a depository of books was formed in the vestry of the parish church, from which 6000 volumes have already been dispensed. The establishment of a Savings' Bank is also in contemplation. The parish church is a rectory, dedicated to St. Peter, in the patronage of the Archbishop of York. There are also three chapels; one for the Methodists, another for the Independents, and a third, on a small scale, for the Primitive Methodists. Here are also two schools, one for boys, and another for girls, in connection with the diocesan schools, and where Dr. Bell's system is adopted. The parish is of considerable extent, and comprehends an area of about 7 square miles. The population of the town amounts to 1897.

## POST MISTRESS, Mrs. Elisabeth Storey.

| Places from whence Letter bags are recvd. | Distance. | Postage | Arrival of Mails. | Departure of Mails. |
|---|---|---|---|---|
| London............ | 238 | 1 | 6 o'clock mg. | ¼ past 4 after |
| Cleveland, Ton. Inn | 8 | 4 | ditto. | ditto. |
| Guisborough...... | 9 | 4 | ¼ past 4 aft, | 6 morng. |

## DIRECTORY.

Appleton Helen, gentlewoman
Burdon Simeon, gentleman
Cunningham John, gentleman
Deason Ann, gentlewoman
Easby John, gentleman
Gibson E. gentlewoman
Greensides Misses
Healey George, Major North York militia
Hepton Nancy, gentlewoman
Hildyard Rev. H. LL.D. Manor-house, Ann grove hall
Hunt Mrs. & Miss, gentlewomen
Hutchinson & Place, bankers, draw on Sir P. Pole, bart. and Co. and Sir Wm. Curtis, bart. and Co.
Mann Thomas, gentleman
Masterman John, gentleman
Maynard Dorothy, gentlewoman
Maynard John, gentleman
Medd Esther, gentlewoman
Metcalf Robert, gentleman
Moon Wm. gentleman
Powell Wm. steward to the chief bailiff for the liberty of Langbargh
Robinson Robert, gentleman
Rookes James, gentleman
Simpson Rev. Thomas, curate
Smith Joseph, gentleman
Taylor Wm. agent to Sir Wm. Foulis, Bart.
Taylor Misses H. & D. gentlewomen
Taylerson Robert, gentleman
Turner Wm. gentleman
Watson Mary, gentlewoman
Widdowfield Richard, gentleman

*Academies, Boarding & Day Schools,*
Ibertson Mary, (ladies' day)
Grange Wm. (day)
Grammar School, Rev. J. Benson
Leng Wm. (commercial day)
Mason Thomas, (day)
National, Richard Baker, master, and Elis. Stubbings, mistress
Neasham Ann (ladies' boarding)

*Booksellers.*
Armstrong Rt. (& agt. for newspapers)
Pratt Wm. printer, agent to the Norwich Union Fire Office, circulating library, and stamp office

*Attornies,*
Appleton & Boulby
Garbutt Wm.
Powell & Harker

*Auctioneers & Appraisers,*
Johnson Wm.
Johnson Geo.

*Bakers,*
Clarke Wm.
Halton Jane
Rayner Wm.
Williamson Geo.

*Blacksmiths,*
Carling Thos.
Gill Thos.
Halton David
Rontree Robert
Storey Jonathan
Sweeting

*Boot & Shoemakers,*
Carling Christr.
Harrison Robert
Hebden Thos.
Hugill Wm.
Lee James
Newburn James

Snowden John
Stockton Christ.
Thompson John
Thurkell Robert
Ward John
Wright John, (and clogger)

*Bricklayers,*
Biggin John, (& plasterer)
Fawcett Francis
Iveson John
Waller Christr.

*Brick Makers,*
Biggins John
Richlieu Thos.

*Butchers,*
Appleton John
Biggins James
Braithwaite John
Farrow R. C. (& farrier)
Halton Geo.
Mann James
Myers Wm.
Stephenson Thos. (& cattle dlr.)

*Butter, Cheese, and Bacon Factors,*
Bowser Matthew, (bacon)
Braithwaite John
Mease John, sen.
Sawkill Robert, (butter)
  *Chemists and Druggists,*
Crummey James, (druggist)
Duck John
  *Clock and Watch Makers,*
Armstrong Robt.
Kneeshaw Robt.
Stephenson Robt.
  *Corn Millers,*
Fidler Thos.
Stonehouse Hy.
  *Corn and Flour Dealers,*
Bursey Rt. (flour)
Fidler Thos.
Oxley Jon. (flour)
Williamson Geo. (flour)
  *Carriers,*
Grey John
Stephenson John
  *Dyers,*
Havisides John & Son
Martin Thos.
  *Farmers,*
Easby Wm.
Flintoff Thos.
Hugill Thos.
Sweeting Jonth.
  *Flax Dressers,*
Mann Thos.
Stephenson S.
Watkin Christr.
  *Flax and Tow Spinners,*
Mease T. & J.
  *Gardeners, &c.*
Bowser Matthew.
Hutton Richard
Meggison Wm.
Taylor Godfrey

*Glass, China, and Earthenware dlrs.*
Barker Christr.
Calvert Sarah
Kneeshaw Robt. (glass)
Williamson Geo.
  *Grocers and Tea Dealers,*
Appleton John
Banks John

Barr John
Claxton Benj.
Crummey James
Dixon Wm.
Gill Mary, (tea)
Grange Wm.
Mease Thos.
Richardson Fras.
Taylor James
Taylerson Wm.
Turner Geo.
Winspear John
  *Hair Dressers,*
Appleton Wm.
Turner Wm.
Watkin John
  *Hat Maker, Dealer, and Furrier,*
Grey Christr.
  *Joiners, &c.*
Carter John
Coates John
Richlieu Thos. (& timber mert.)
Ward Thos.
Watkin Wm.
Watkin James
  *Linen Manfrs.*
Calvert Stephen
Cass John
Coverdale Geo.
Eason J. & J.
Garbutt John
Havisides J. & Son, (& stuffs)
Hepton Thos.
Mann Thos.
Stephenson S.
Watkin Christr.
  *Linen Merchants,*
Coverdale Geo.
Easom J. & J.
Haviside Anthony & Co. (stuffs)
  *Linen and Woollen Drapers,*
Appleton John
Barr John
Claxton Benj.
Mease Thos.
Medd Jas.
Taylor James
Taylerson Wm.
  *Maltsters, &c.*
Neasham B. & T.
  *Milliners and Dress Makers,*
Baldwin Jane
Eeles Judith.
Easby Mary
Gill Mary
Harwood Ann
Richardson Han.
Rolls Ann

Russell Ann
  *Millwright,*
Fairburn John
  *Painters & Gilders,*
Cole Thos.
Collings John
Walker John
  *Plumbers & Glazrs.*
Dennison Christr.
Gowland David
Noton Wm.
Walker John
  *Saddlers & Collar Makers,*
Taylor Wm.
Ward Wm.
Watson Ralph
  *Shopkeepers,*
Baxter Edward
Dixon Wm.
Hall Jane
Milestone Geo.
Tate Sarah
  *Spirit and Wine Merchants,*
Claxton Benj. (British wine)
Neasham B. & T. (spirit)
Winspear John (British wine)
  *Stone Masons,*
Bulmer Wm.
Dixon Wm.
Dixon Valentine
Smith Thos.
Williamson Geo.
  *Straw Bonnet mkrs.*
Easby Mary, (& tea dealer)

Fawcett Sarah
Harwood Ann
Pollitt Eliz.
Richardson Han.
Rolls Ann
Russell Ann
  *Surgeons, &c.*
Allardice James
Appleton Rhd.
Duck John, (apothecary)
Ward Wm. jun. (apothecary)
  *Tailors, &c.*
Banks John, (& draper)
Potter Robert
Rumsdale Robt.
Richardson Frs. (& draper)
Robson Robert
Shipley Thos.
Snaith John
Stephenson Thos.
Thompson Geo.
Turner Geo.
  *Tallow Chandlers,*
Stephenson Thos.
Stephenson Snowden
  *Wheelwrights,*
Carter John
Hebron John
Sunley Thos.
Walker James
  *Wood Turners, and Line Wheel mkrs.*
Appleton Rhd.
Coulson John

*Inns and Taverns.*

Angel, George Parvin
Bay Horse, Jervas Coates
Black Horse, George Johnson
Black Swan, (posting house,) John Wilstrop
Bull and Dog, John Weatherill
Bull and Punch Bowl, Hannah Smith
Chequers, Thomas Fenwick
George and Dragon, Henry Brotherton
Golden Lion, (and excise office) John Price
Greyhound, Thomas Fidler
King's Head, Sarah Peart
Masons' Arms, Thomas Smith
Race Horses, Anthony Pearson
Shoulder of Mutton, Thos. Myers
Spread Eagle, Richard Appleton
Three Tuns, Wm. Smith

*Miscellany.*

Adamson Matthew, flax dresser
Barker Christopher, glover, &c.

Bowser Matthew, parish clerk
Burnard John, rope & twine maker
Caile Joan, tinner, brazier, ironmonger and hardware man
Just Thomas, agent to J. Haviside and Son
Ilders Adam, clog & patten maker
mery James, veterinary surgeon
isher Matthew, professor of music
letcher Christ. beadle & bellman
arbutt Hannah, confectioner
all Mary, confectioner
epton Thomas, governor of workhouse
arch Lewis, officer of excise
ason Benjamin, cooper
rteus Walter, nail maker
rner Thomas, whitesmith
atson John, dog trainer
est Charles, dealer in jewellery and British lace

## COACH,

*on the Black Swan, John Wilstorp,*

CLEVELAND, three days a week from Redcar to Bedale, during the season, on Mon. Wed. and Sat. arr. at 9 morning and ret. at 5 evening.

## LAND CARRIAGE.

leton John, to Stockton, Mon. Wed. & Fri. ret. the same day.
ock Thos. & Fras. to Thirsk, on Mon. and Thur. ret. on Tu. and Fri. and to Stockton on Mon. Wed. & Fri. ret. the same day.

*try Carriers attending the Market.*
n, James Sherwood, to T. Stephenson's, every Sat. arrive at 11, return at 6.
orough, Thos. Johnson, to Three Tuns, Wed. & Sat. arr. 10, ret. 3.
allerton, John Snowball, to Bull & Dog, every Sat. arr. 10, ret. 3.
, Ralph Reed, to Three Tuns, every Sat. arr. 10, ret. 3.

tonegill Gate, in the parish of , wap. & liberty of Langbargh; from Whitby.

RONSGRAVE, (P.) in the wap. of e; 5 miles SE. of Helmsley.—hurch is a rectory of which the the patron. Pop. 177.

Rev. Mr. curate

ONESDALE, (East and West) parish of Grinton, wap. of West, and liberty of Richire; 10 miles NW. of Askrigg.

*Farmers & Yeomen,* Peacock John
Clarkson Edmund    Raw John
Clarkson James
Peacock Thomas, coal agent

*Stoneykeld,* in the parish of Bowes, wap. of Gilling West, and liberty of Richmondshire; 5¼ miles W. of Barnard Castle.

*Stoupe Brow,* in the parish of Whitby, wap. and liberty of Whitby Strand; 8 miles SSE. of Whitby. The road from Robin Hood's Bay to Stoupe Brow, is along the sandy beach, under a high and steep cliff, to which the sea flows as the tide advances; and the passage is unsafe, unless there be, when the traveller sets out, a spacious area of the sand not covered by the water, or the tide be receding. The residence of Sunderland Cooke, Esq. is at Stoupe hall, in this township. The height of Stoupe Brow is 883 feet, and few appearances in nature are more awfully grand, than the view from its summit. As the declivity of Stoupe Brow is impracticable to carriages, the main road from Whitby and Robin Hood's Bay to Scarborough lies over the moors, in some places near the edge of the cliff. On this road, in the year 1809, there happened an accident, of which the circumstances, were they not so well attested as to leave no room for doubt, would appear absolutely impossible —A lady and two young gentlemen, travelling in a post chaise to Scarborough, the driver, on some occasion, alighted, and the horses, being left to themselves, immediately struck into a gallop. Before they had proceeded far, both the horses and chaise fell over the cliff, down a tremendous precipice, of nearly one hundred feet high, and of which, about forty feet next to the bottom, is a perpendicular rock. In its fall, the chaise turned over three times, yet neither the horses, the chaise, nor the passengers suffered any injury, except that the lady received a trifling scratch on the face, and the party immediately proceeded to Scarborough.*

*Standmire,* in the parish of Hovingham, and wap. of Rydale; 8 miles from Helmsley.

*Street Houses,* in the parish of Lofthouse, and wap. of Langbargh; 1 mile NE. of Lofthouse; the residence of Mr. J. C. Liomin.

*Street Lands,* in the parish of Danby Wiske, wap. of Gilling East;

* Bigland's Yorkshire, page 342.

4 miles NW. of Northallerton. Here is the Ox Inn, kept by Mr. Luke Harrison.

STRENSALL, (P.) in the wap. of Bulmer, and liberty of St. Peter's; 6 miles NNE. of York. Here is a church, dedicated to St. Mary; the living is a vicarage, in the patronage of the Prebendary of Strensall; incumbent, the Rev. John Ellis. Population, 878.

Bosomworth Wm. gent.
Duke John, gent.
Green John, gent.
Parrott Wm. gent.

*Farmers & Yeomen,*　Tate Wm.
Agar Francis　　　　　*Shoemakers,*
Barker John　　　　　Barker Geo.
Bellerby Mathw.　　　Creaser John
Flintoff Geo.　　　　Dobson Wm.
Hammond Geo.　　　　*Shopkeepers,*
Harrison Geo.　　　　Barton Robert
Horseley John　　　　Cooper Ralph
Lazenby Geo.　　　　Nicholson Wm.
Lazenby John　　　　Wright Robert
Smailes Thos.

Heslewood Thomas, poulterer
Linfoot Ralph, joiner & cabinet mkr.
Linfoot John, bricklayer and vict. Half Moon
Spruce John, schoolmaster

*Studdow,* in the parish of Fingall, wap. of Hang West, and liberty of Richmondshire; 2½ miles E. of Leyburn.

*Suffield,* in the parish of Hackness, wap. and liberty of Whitby Strand; 4½ mls. N.W. of Scarborough. Pop. including Everley, 97.

*Sunny Cross,* in the parish of Ayton, wap. & liberty of Langbargh; 2 miles N. of Stokesley.

*Sutton Howgrave,* in the parish of Kirklington, and wap. of Halikeld; 5½ miles N. of Ripon. Here the monks of Fountain's Abbey had two oxgangs, *i.e.* 26 acres of land, with a toft, croft, and pasture for four oxen on the common. Pop. 122.

SUTTON-ON-THE-FOREST, (P.) in the wap. of Bulmer; 5 miles SE. of Easingwold. Here is a very handsome parish church, dedicated to All Saints; the living is a vicarage, in the patronage of the Archbishop of York. The celebrated Lawrence Sterne was a resident in, and the vicar of this parish; but on the destruction of the parsonage house by fire, he removed to Coxwold, of which place he was also vicar, as well as of Stillington. Pop. 443.

Harland Lady Hoare
Pellew Hon. and Rev. Geo. vicar

*Blacksmiths,*　　　Peuty Wm.
Bullock James　　　Pullan John
Roundtree Henry　　Shepherd Thos.
*Farmers & Yeomen,*　Sturdy John
Barker Thos.　　　　Thompson Thos.
Batty James　　　　Ward Geo.
Bean Geo.　　　　　Waterson John
Brotherton F.　　　*Shoemakers,*
Brown Geo.　　　　Kitchingman Geo.
Brown S.　　　　　Peuty Wm.
Coates Geo.　　　　*Shopkeepers,*
Cordeaux Rhd.　　　Clark John
Gibson Thos.　　　　Greenwood Esther
Haddleshaw Robt.　　*Tailors,*
Hodgson Robt.　　　Bell Wm.
Johnson John　　　　Wirell Edw.
Lawton James　　　Holdsworth Thos.
Leng Tabitha

Linfoot Thos. vict. Rose and Crown
Maynard Wm. vict. Blacksmith's Arms
Rowntree John, carpenter
Shepherd Mary, vict. Blackwell Ox

SUTTON-UNDER-WHITESTONE-CLIFFE, in the parish of Feliskirk, wap. of Birdforth, and liberty of Ripon; 4 miles E. of Thirsk. Here is a Calvinist chapel. Pop. 325.

Glasgow Wm. surgeon
Richardson Mrs. gentwn. Cleves
Thrush Capt. Thos. R. N. hall

*Cattle Dealers,*　　Lancaster John
Brown Geo.　　　　Shaw Matthew
Cowen Samuel　　　Sinclair Wm.
Thompson Thos.　　Steel Thos.
*Farmers,*　　　　*Shoemakers,*
Bosomworth Thos.　Astley Wm.
Brigland Joseph　　Bosomworth John
Buttery John　　　Rawling Thos.
Craven Thos.　　　*Wheelwrights,*
Holliday Thos.　　Bosomworth John
Kilvington Christ.　Kettlewell John
Kirby Thos.

Feast Wm. tailor
Pallister Wm. vict. Black Prince
Scurr Wm. stone mason
Thompson John, blacksmith
Wetherill Thos. lime dealer

*Sutton,* in the parish of Masham, and wap. of Hang East; 2 miles NW. of Masham. Pop. with Healey.

SWAINBY, in the parish of Whorlton, wap. and liberty of Langbargh; 5 miles SW. of Stokesley. There are here a Methodist chapel, and a chapel for the Primitive Methodists. An ancient religious house, founded by Hellewise, daughter of Ranulph de Glanville, in the reign of Henry II. stood here, but not a vestige of it now remains

Population, including the township of Whorlton, 583.

| Farmers, | Grocers, &c. |
|---|---|
| Baker Jacob | Cudbertson Thos. |
| Bovill Thomas | Flintoft Geo. |
| Bovill Ann | *Joiners, &c.* |
| Burton Richard | Groves John |
| Catherson Thos. | Harker Wm. |
| Eeles John | Harker Thos. |
| Hugill Jonathan | *Shoemakers,* |
| Kitchen Robert | Cowlson Thos. |
| Mitchinson Robert | Hewgill Abraham |
| Mohun Robert | *Stone Masons,* |
| Pearson James | Harland Thos. |
| Sherwood Wm. | Nelson Thos. |
| Temple John | |
| Todd John, West | |
| Lees | |

Appleton Wm. vict. Bay Horse
Brunton Thos. yarn bleacher
Burton Ann, vict. Blacksmiths' Arms
Burton Benjamin, tailor
Coulson Stephen, corn miller
Fairweather Richard, blacksmith
Farmery Thos. gardener
Feng James, schoolmaster
Sawkill John, butcher's knife, &c. mfr.

*Swainby,* in the parish of Pickhill, 3d wap. of Halikeld; 5½ miles ESE. Bedale. Population including Alrthorpe, 33.

*Swale,* (River) Page vii. Vol. I.

. *Swaledale,* and the vallies adjoining are famous for their lead mines, which may be enumerated as follows :—

*Swaledale Mines.*

The Surrender, worked by Messrs. Chaytor and Morley

The Old Gang, worked by Sir George and Thomas Alderson.

The Stands, worked by Messrs. Hopper & Co.

The Blakethwaite, worked by Messrs. Gilpin and Co.

The Earl of Pomfret is the proprietor of above mines.

*The Arkendale Mines are worked by*

| | | |
|---|---|---|
| Mr. Jaques, ......... | } | of Easby. |
| Mr. Parkinson, ... | | |
| Mr. Tomlin,..... ... | } | |
| Mr. Close, ......... | } | of Richmond. |
| Mr. Robinson, ..... | | |
| Mr. Simpson, ...... | | |
| Mr. Whitelock, of Cogden Hall | | |
| Mr. Robinson, ...... | } | |
| Mr. Thompson,...... | } | of Reeth. |
| Mr. M'Collah, ...... | | |
| Mr. Knowles, ...... | } | of Low Row. |
| Mr. Birbeck,......... | } | |

*End Mines* are worked by Messrs. Spence and Co.

*Hurst mines* are worked by Mr. Josias Morley.

*Summerlodge mines* are worked by Messrs. Robinson and Co. and a number of small miners.

And several other small mines are worked by other individuals.

The estimated produce of these works is 6000 tons a year, of which the Swaledale mines yield one moiety, and the remaining 3000 tons are obtained by the other mining companies.

The Swale was in high estimation among our Saxon ancestors, by whom it was styled the Jordan of England, owing to Paulinus, the Roman missionary, and the first Archbishop of York, having soon after the introduction of Christianity, baptized in its streams in one day, ten thousand men, exclusive of women and children.

*Swale Hall,* in the parish of Grinton, wap. of Hang West, and liberty of Richmondshire; 1½ mile SW. of Reeth; formerly the residence of a gentleman who subscribed himself " Sir Solomon Swale, of Swale Hall, in Swaledale, fast by the river Swale." This family held lands of the Crown, but had omitted for many years to renew their lease, which, being observed by a clerk in the exchequer office, he procured a grant from the crown, of this estate, for himself: many law suits ensued, but they served only to increase the misfortunes of Sir Solomon, who died a prisoner in the Fleet, in 1678, not, however, till his adversary had committed suicide.

*Swineside,* in the parish of Coverham, wap. of Hang West, and liberty of Richmondshire; 7 miles SW. of Middleham.

SWINETHWAITE, in the parish of Wensley, wap. of Hang West, and liberty of Richmondshire; 5 mls. WSW. of Leyburn. A small village, pleasantly situated in Wensleydale.

Anderson W. J. Esq.
Morland Leonard, gentleman

| Farmers, | Lodge John |
|---|---|
| Boys John | Reynolds John |
| Laidman Samuel | Russell John |

SWINTON, in the parish of Masham, wap. of Hang East, and liberty of Richmondshire; 1 mile S. of Masham; the elegant and hospitable seat of William Danby, Esq. whose beautiful gardens and pleasure grounds may vie with most in the North of England: but the improvements this gentleman h s made on the immense tracts of moors within his manor particularly call for observation. The vestiges of antiquity found in this neighbourhood are various and numerous,

Mr. Danby has preserved some of them, particularly a large golden handle, which seems to be that of a shield; and the head of a Roman battle-axe, of brass or copper, &c. Population, including Wardermask, 177.

**Danby** Wm. Esq. Swinton park
**Trumber** Henry, agent to Mr. Danby

*Farmers,*     *Shoemakers,*
Imeson Robert    Hill John
Richmond John    Hill Barnabas

Akers Benjamin, stone mason
Astwood Wm. carpenter
Imeson Geo. blacksmith & farrier
Theakston Thos. constable

*Swinton,* in the parish of Appleton-le-Street, and wap. of Rydale; 2 mls. WNW. of Walton. Here is a Chapel of Ease to Appleton-le-Street, and a Methodist chapel, Old Connexion.—Population, 834.

*Tanfield East,* in the parish of Kirklington, and wap. of Halikeld; 5 miles NNW. of Ripon. The principal inhabitants of this village are Mr. Edward Horseman, farmer, and Mr. John Jackson, corn miller. Pop. 32.

**TANFIELD WEST**, (P.) in the wap. of Halikeld, and liberty of Richmondshire; 6 miles NW. of Ripon. William the Conqueror gave this village, and East Tanfield, to Alan, Earl of Richmond: they afterwards became the property of the family of Fitz Hugh. Robert, Lord Marmion, married the heiress of this family, and succeed to these lordships. In the eighth of King Edward II. John, Lord Marmion, obtained a licence to make a castle of his house, called the Hermitage, situated in Tanfield wood, about the year 1300. In the reign of Henry VIII. the castle and manor passed by marriage into the family of the Marquis of Northampton, but by the attainder of William Parr, the Marquis, they escheated to the crown, and were conferred by James I. with other estates, on Edmund Lord Bruce, of Kinross, in right of descent from whom, they are now enjoyed by Charles Bruce Brudenell, Marquis of Ailesbury, who had a mansion in the parish, called Tanfield Hall, but which, having fallen into decay, was pulled down in the year 1816. On the banks of the Ure, which at Tanfield bridge is a fine broad expanse of water, stand the remains of Tanfield castle, but it is without history; its origin, and the time and the cause of its demolition being alike unknown. According to Grose, which information he draws from tradition, "when Tanfield castle was destroyed, the materials were purchased by several of the neighbouring gentry, and the Earl of Exeter's house at Snape, and the seat of Wandfords, at Kirklington, were built with them. Little now remains of the ruin; but a handsome parsonage house, built by the Rev. William Baines, the present rector, as an expression of gratitude to the noble patron of the living, has risen up near on the site, and adds another embellishment to this delightful valley. The church, dedicated to St. Nicholas, is a venerable edifice, and contains many curious monuments of its ancient lords; adjoining to which is the chantry, called Maud Marmion, founded in the reign of Henry III. for a master, warden, and two brothers, charged with the duty of praying for the souls of Lord and Lady Marmion, and the progenitors and successors of this family. There is in this village a Methodist chapel; and also a school with a small endowment. The population amounts to 702.

**Baines** Rev. Wm. rector
**Metcalf** Rev. James, curate

*Blacksmiths,*    Granger John
Graham George    Kildrin Mark
Smith John    Kitchin Thomas
*Butchers,*    Spence John
Bolton George    Stewart Richard
Stewart Thos.    Thompson Joseph
*Carpenters,*    Vint John
Chandler Thos.    Warrior Thos.
Walker Charles,    *Grocers,*
(& glazier)    Almack Wm. (&
*Farmers,*    tailor)
Auton John    Brown Robert
Bolton Thos.    *Shoemakers,*
Chandler Charles    Taylor Richard
Clark George    Wilson James
Edon Thomas

Geldart Christopher, vict. Bay Horse
Handley Matthew, vict. Bruce's Arms
Inchbald R. vict. Wellington
Simpson Roger, schoolmaster

*Tanton,* in the parish of Stokesley, wap. and liberty of Langbargh; 1¼ mile N. of Stokesley.

*Tees,* (River) see introduction to this volume.

*Telphit,* in the parish of Marske, wap. of Gilling West, and liberty of Richmondshire; 7 miles W. of Richmond.

**TERRINGTON**, (P.) in the wap. of Bulmer; 8 miles WSW. of Malton. Here is an elegant small parish church, dedicated to All Saints; the church living is a rectory, of which the Rev. Dr. Waddilove is the patron, and the Rev. John Caley the incumbent. Here is also a Methodist chapel.—Pop. including Wigginthorpe, 617.

ickers Miss Mary, gentlewoman
ennis Rev. Luke, curate
owerby Miss Jane, gentlewoman

| *Butchers,* | Sellers Wm. |
|---|---|
| ean Thomas | Smith Thos. |
| wan John | Teasdale Richard |
| *Carpenters,* | Thompson John |
| oodrick Robert | Warwick John |
| oodrick George | Wright John |
| oodwill James | *Schoolmasters,* |
| oodwill George | Blanchard John |
| *Coopers,* | Harrison John |
| ackson John | *Shoemakers,* |
| ackson Robert | Driffield Wm. |
| *Farmers,* | Martin Dorothy |
| ickers Robert | *Shopkeepers,* |
| ilenkhorn Richd. | Brown Ann |
| illerby John | Goodwill Robert |
| lardy John | *Tailors,* |
| lardy Phineas | Blenkin Wm. |
| lick George | Haythorn Wm. |
| loor John | Hick George |
| lortimer David | Lacy William |
| 'otter Thos. | |

gar Uriah, vict. Horse and Jockey
ordeux Wm. vict. Black Bull
lick Richard, vict. Cross Keys
toberts Wm. blacksmith

THEAKSTON, in the parish of
lurneston, wap. of Halikeld, & liberty
f Richmondshire; 3 miles SE. of
ledale. Population, 87.
larter Edmund Esq. Theakston hall
larter E. J. Esq.

*Theasby,* in the parish of Aysgarth,
rap. of Hang West, and liberty of
lichmondshire; 6 mls. E. of Askrigg.

THIMBLEBY, in the parish of
losmotherley, wap. and liberty of Al-
rtonshire; 6 miles ENE. of North-
llerton. Population, 200.
'eirse R. W. C. Esq. Thimbleby lodge

| *Farmers,* | Lightfoot Thos. |
|---|---|
| lradley John | Meggison Thos. |
| lurdon Thos. | Mothersill Robert |
| 'ooper Michael | Potter Marmaduke |
| 'owton Eliz. | Walker Isaac |
| luncalfe Robert | Wilson Wm. |

ee Robert, corn miller
lothersill Robert, woolstapler and
    worsted manufacturerer
'etch Dorothy, vict. Fighting Cocks

THIRKLEBY HIGH, (P.) in the
ap. of Birdforth; 4 miles SE. of Thirsk.
he church, which was re-built in 1722 by
ie late Sir Thomas Frankland, is dedicated
i All Saints; the living is a vicarage, in the
atronage of the Archbishop of York. The
iclent family of the Franklands has risided
ere for upwards of two centuries; and the

present baronet is lineally descended from
Oliver Cromwell, the Lord Protector, Population, 293.

Frankland Sir Thos. Bart. Hall
Barker Rev. Thomas, vicar

| *Butchers,* | Blythe Robert |
|---|---|
| Holling Christr. | Manfield Leopard |
| Manfield Geo. | Rose Leonard |
| *Farmers,* | Smith John, (and |
| Blenkhorn Stephen | miller) |
| Blenkhorn Thos. | Tose Robert |

Burton Matthew, carpenter
Masterman George, blacksmith
Waites Wm. vict. Anchor & Dolphin

*Thirkleby Low,* in the parish of
High Thirkleby, & wap. of Birdforth;
4 miles SE. of Thirsk.

*Thirlby,* in the parish of Feliskirk,
and wap. of Birdforth; 4½ miles ENE.
of Thirsk. Population, 167.

*Thirn,* in the parish of Thornton
Watlass, & wap. of Hang East; 3 mls.
N. of Masham. The residence of C.
N. Clarke, Esq. of the Hermitage.—
Population, 126.

## THIRSK, (P.)

Is a small market town, in the wap. of Birdforth; 9 miles from Northallerton, 10 miles
from Easingwold, 11 from Boroughbridge,
and 23 from York. This town is pleasantly
situated in the vale of Mowbray; and is
conjectured to derive its name from the ancient British words, Tre—a town, and Isk—
a river, or brook. The market, which is on
Monday, is well supplied with the necessaries of life, and fish is brought here from the
coast in great perfection. A great quantity
of poultry, butter, and eggs, are brought up
here by dealers, and conveyed into the populous towns of the West-Riding, where they
are re-sold. The fairs, which are numerous,
will be found stated in the list of Yorkshire
Fairs, appendant to the 1st. vol. of this work,
and they tend considerably to enrich the town
and its immediate vicinity. Of manufactures
there are none, except a few coarse linens,
owing probably to that important requisite in
manufacturing establishments—fuel, being
scarce and dear. There is here uo established
banking concern, but business is transacted
for Messrs. Backhouse & Co. Darlington, by
Mr. Story, in the Market-place; for Messrs.
Britain & Co. of Ripon, by Mr. Hansell, in
Millgate; and for Messrs. Raper, Swann,
and Co. York, by Mr. Arnett, in the Market
place. This town had formerly a strong
Castle, which stood at the south western extremity of the town. Thirsk castle claims a

high antiquity; it is said to have been built in 959, by the family to whose lordship the neighbourhood was anciently subject. The first mention of this name in history, is, however, after the conquest, when we find Robert de Mowbray, a powerful Norman Baron, created Earl of Northumberland, in 1080. The castle itself was a noble pile of building, uniting the magnificence of a royal palace with the strength and security of a baronial fortress. It was here, that Roger de Mowbray conspired with the Scotch King, and began his rebellion against Henry II. The revolt was, however, speedily suppressed, and on the 13th of March, in the year 1175, the castle was assailed by Lord de Valence, in the name of the King, and surrendered, not without the show, but without the reality of resistance. Henry, who was then at Northampton, ordered all the castles that still remained in private hands to be destroyed, and this seat of feudal magnificence shared the common lot. So complete was the demolition here, that not a vestige of the castle now remains, but a high artificial mount serves to indicate the site on which the keep formerly stood, and the place still bears the name of the Castle yard.

The church, which is a handsome Gothic edifice, at the northern extremity of the town, was, it is generally supposed, built out of the ruins of the castle. Both the exterior appearance, and the interior arrangement of this structure are deservedly admired. From the steps leading up to the altar, the view is peculiarly grand, presenting to the eye a lofty and extended vista of Gothic arches, terminated by the organ, which corresponds in its decorations with that majestic order of architecture. The internal length is 160 feet, and the length of the cross aisle 60 feet.* This church is dedicated to St. Mary Magdalen; the living is a perpetual curacy, the Archbishop of York is the patron, and Matthew Butterwick, Esq. is the lay rector. In addition to the church, the Quakers have a meeting house, and burial ground, in Kirkgate; the Independents, a chapel, near Sowerby Flats, built in 1803; and the Methodists, a handsome new chapel, in St. James's Green, built in 1816, on the site of their old place of worship.

Thirsk is a parliamentary, but not a corporate Borough. Old Thirsk, as it is called, possesses the right of sending two members to parliament, by 50 burgage holds, 49 of which belong to Sir Thomas Frankland, who has the appointment of the

bailiff, and which bailiff is the returning officer. The present members are Robert Frankland, Esq. and Richard Greenall Russel. Esq.

Old Thirsk consists of a long range of cottages on each side of the road leading to Yarm and Stockton, and of a square, surrounded by the same kind of buildings, called St. James's Green. Upon, or near this square stood an ancient chantry, founded by William de Mowbray, in the reign of Henry I. but of which time has long since swept away every vestige. Till the year 1818, a venerable Elm, the wonder and the ornament of the Green stood here; but on the night of the 5th of November, 1818, a set of luckless boys, in their mischievous sports, set fire to this piece of vegetable antiquity; sufficient was left of it to make two substantial chairs for John Bell, Esq. the lord of the manor. Under the spreading branches of this tree, the election of members of parliament for Thirsk had been conducted so long, " that the memory of man is not to the contrary;" and here, it is said, fell Henry Piercy, the fourth Earl of Northumberland, then Lord Lieutenant of Yorkshire, a victim to popular fury, raised by oppressive taxation.† The rivulet which divides the old and the new town, is called Cod-beck, over which there passes a substantial stone bridge, of three arches, of sufficient capacity to receive the floods which the heavy rains, and melting snows of winter frequently occasion. The new town stands within the precincts of the ancient castle of the Mowbrays: in the centre of the town is the Market-place, which, if the Toll-booth, now in a ruinous condition, with the Shambles, and some few dilapidated buildings were removed, would be one of the first squares for a public market in the kingdom.

The population of Thirsk has increased during the last ten years at the rate of about 15 per cent. In 1811, the total amount was 2,158, and in 1821—2,533. The air is generally considered pure and salubrious, and a fine spring of chalybeate water at a small distance from the town, resembling the Scarborough and Cheltenham waters, and used both for drinking and bathing, may contribute to the health, and consequently to the longevity, of the inhabitants. The surrounding country is rich and delightful; and all tourists concur in the opinion that the vale of Mowbray, of which Thirsk is pretty nearly the centre, is scarcely to be equalled by any tract of country in the kingdom, for fertility, expansion and picturesque scenery.

* Jefferson's History of Thirsk.    † See Topcliffe.

POST-MASTER—ROBERT PEAT, *Office, Top of North side Market place.*

| Places from whence Letter bags are recvd. | Distance. | Postage. | Arrival of Mails. | Departure of Mails. |
|---|---|---|---|---|
| York | 23 | 6*d.* | at ½ past 8 evening | ¼ before 8 evening |
| London | 219 | 11 | 20 min. past 11 evg. | 9 evening |
| Easingwold | 10 | 4 | ½ past 8 evening | ¼ before 8 evening |
| Stokesley | 19 | 5 | ¼ before 8 evening | ¼ before 11 night |
| Guisborough | 26 | 6 | Ditto. | Ditto. |
| Yarm | 19 | 5 | Ditto. | Ditto. |
| Stockton | 24 | 6 | Ditto. | Ditto. |
| Sunderland | 58 | 8 | Ditto. | Ditto. |
| South Shields | 68 | 8 | Ditto. | Ditto. |
| Bedale | 14 | 6 | ½ past 8 evening | ½ past 11 night |
| Appleby | 63 | 9 | Ditto. | Ditto. |
| Carlisle | 95 | 9 | Ditto. | Ditto. |
| Northallerton | 9 | 4 | 9 evening | 20 min. past 11 ngt. |
| Darlington | 25 | 6 | Ditto. | Ditto. |
| Newcastle | 57 | 8 | Ditto. | Ditto. |

DIRECTORY.

Addison Geo. gent. Finkle street
Bentley John, gent. S. side Mkt. pl.
Butterwick Matt. Esq. S. side Mkt. pl.
Gill Edw. gent. Paradise yd. Kirkgate
Gill Rev. Thomas, St. James's green
Gregory Rev. Benjamin, Long st.
Hildred Mrs. Eliz. S. side Market pl.
Jefferson Rev. Joseph, Kirkgate
Kendrew Mrs. Ann, Kirkgate
Kenyon Mrs. Ann, Kirkgate
Lievesey Robert Bell, Esq. Kirkgate
Maddison Col. John Thos. Ingrygate
Pick Mrs. Mary, St. James's green
Robinson Mrs. Margt. N. side Mkt. pl.
Scurr Jonah, gent. Millgate
Smith John, gent. Finkle street
Smith John, gent. Middle market
Walker Mrs. Maria, S. side Market pl.
Whitehead Mrs. Dorothy, North side Market place

*Academies (Public and Private.)*

Appleby Mary, (ladies' boarding), Kirkgate
Cornforth Ann, St. James's green
Gooding Mary, (subscription) Castle yard, Westgate
Martin Thomas, Barbeck
Metcalfe Eliz. Smith's yard, South side Market place
Mothersdale Wm. (national) Millgate
North Mary, St. James's green
Thompson Ann, Paradise yd. Kirkgt.
Winter John, Millgate; house, St. James's green

*Agents to Bankers.*

Arnitt Francis, (to Raper, Swann, & Co. York) West side Market pl.
Hansell Francis, (to Brittains and Co. Ripon) Millgate
Storey Francis, (to Backhouse & Co. Darlington) N. side Market place

*Attornies.*

Barnby Charles Wm. Long street
Richardson Thos. Kirkgate
Rider Joseph, S. side Market place
Swarbeck Thos. S. side Market place
Walker Charles Bisset, (& clerk to the magistrates for the division of Birdforth, sub-division meetings of lieutenancy, and to the trustees of the York & Northallerton road) West side Market place

*Auctioneers and Appraisers.*

Chapman Richard, (& sheriff's officer) Top of Kirkgate
Wood Benj. St. James's green

*Bakers.*

Armstrong Eliz. Kirkgate
Dodgson Thos. St. James's green
Gill Geo. Old Thirsk
Hansell Francis, Market place
Ilie John, Piper lane
Mawman John, N. side Market place
Morley Geo. Millgate
Pygass Samuel, Rawling's yard, East side Market place
Rainforth James, East side Market pl.
White Ralph, St. James's green
Young James, Rawling's yard, East side Market place

*Blacksmiths.*

Bashforth James, Middle Market pl.
Bumby John, Finkle street
Bumby Wm. Long street
Marley Matthew, Kirkgate
Taylor Robert, Westgate

*Booksellers, Binders, and Stationers.*

Hurst George, (and patent medicine vender) East side Market place

Masterman Henry, E. side Market pl.
Peat Robert, top of N. side Market pl.

*Boot and Shoemakers.*

Bainbridge Wm. N. side Market pl.
Baxter Richard, Smith's yard, S. side Market place
Bosomworth John, St. James's green
Burgess Paul, North side Market pl.
Butterwick Thos. St. James's green
Clarkson John, Westgate
Clarkson Thos. St. James's green
Dodsworth John, St. James's green
Fewster Wm. Long street
Hopper Benjamin, Smith's yard, S. side Market place
Jackson Wm. Long street
Meek John, Bentley's yard, S. side Market place
Morrell Wm. Back lane
Pratt Thos. Norby
Stockdale James, Kirkgate
Thompson Matthew, Kirkgate
Thompson Wm. top of Kirkgate
Tweedy Thos. Long street
Tweedy Thos. Millgate
Ward Ann, Finkle street
Wilkinson Thomas, S. side Market pl.
Wright Robert, Back lane

*Brandy Merchants.*

Hudson James, N. side Market place
Johnson Wm. Norby
Robinson John, N. side Market place
West Wm. North side Market place

*Breweries, Ale.*

Meek Thomas, Kirkgate
Rhodes Edward, Kirkgate

*Bricklayers.*

Fawcitt Robert, Smith's yard, S. side Market place
Fawcitt John, Kirkgate
Simison Robert, St. James's green
Wray John, Long street

*Bridle Cutters.*

Dunn Thos. Ingrygate
Harrison Robert, W. side Market pl.
Hill Wm. East side Market place
Hudson Christr. N. side Market place

*Buckle Makers.*

Goodwick Geo. St. James's green
Goothrick John, Bentley's yard, South side Market place
Mansfield Henry, Long street

*Butchers.*

Bumby John, St. James's green
Denison Thomas, Market place
Fawcett Richard, Kirkgate
Foxton John, Millgate
Gill Dinah, Long street
Goodrick John, Old Thirsk
‑‑enhill John, Kirkgate

Nelson Philip, Swarbreck's yard, S. side Market place
Nelson Richard, St. James's green

*Cabinet Makers.*

Hambleton Joseph, Kirkgate
Peacock Wm. (& upholsterer) N. side Market place
Peat Joseph, Long street
Richmond John, Kirkgate
Tindall Geo. Finkle street

*Cattle Dealers.*

Foster Geo. Kirkgate
Metcalfe Thomas, Long street

*Chemists and Druggists.*

Bingham Henry, (& dlr. in oils, paints, and colours) E. side Market place
Cass Thomas, S. side Market place
Johnson Thos. (dealer in oils & paint, and veterinary surgeon) N. side Market place

*Confectioners.*

Armstrong Elizabeth, Kirkgate
Dickinson Wm. Barbeck
Mawman John, N. side Market place
Rainforth James, E. side Market pl.

*Corn Millers.*

Armstrong James, Old Thirsk
Manfield Robert, Millgate

*Curriers and Leather Cutters.*

Bell Thomas, Finkle street
Imeson Matthew, S. side Market pl.
Morfoot Richard, Millgate
Prest Thomas, Ingrygate

*Farmers.*

Clarkson James, St. James's green
Daniels Robert, Ingrygate
Granger Wm. St. James's green
Hare Richard, St. James's green
Watson Chapman, St. James's green
Whitfield Samuel, St. James's green

*Fire, Life and Insurance Office Agents.*

Atlas, Robert Peat, top of N. side Market place
County, Geo. Hurst, E. side Market pl.
Globe, C. B. Walker, W. side Mkt. pl.
National, F. Armitt, Market place
Norwich Union, Joseph Rider, S. side Market place
Phœnix, Jacob Smith, Kirkgate
Provident Life, George Hurst, E. side Market place
Royal Exchange, John Metcalfe, Market place
Sun, Henry Masterman, E. side Market place

*Flax Dressers.*

Dunning James, Finkle street
Jackson John, Middle Market place
Smith Jacob, Kirkgate

*Gardeners.*

Bell Ralph, Ingrygate

Davison Mark, Ingrygate
Dickenson Wm. Barbeck
Rutherford Charles, St. James's green
Rutherford George, Norby
Rutherford Robert, Norby
Snowden Thomas, Barbeck
Wray Elizabeth, Back lane

*Glass, China and Earthenware Dealers.*

Metcalf John, Middle Market place
Rowntree Jane, Kirkgate
Shepherd Geo. Middle Market place

*Glove and Breeches Makers.*

Atkin Wm. Kirkgate
Bowes Thomas, St. James's green
Ransom Wm. Finkle street

*Grocers and Tea Dealers.*

Arnitt Francis, W. side Market place
Bumby John, St. James's green
Carver Wm. South side Market place
Hansell Francis, Millgate
Jackson John, Middle Market place
Lynass Wm. North side Market place
Metcalfe Joseph, E. side Market place
Metcalfe John, Middle Market place
Robinson John, N. side Market place
Routh Anthony & Robert, Kirkgate
Smith John, South side Market place
Smith Ann and Sisters, South side Market place
Smith Jacob, Kirkgate
Smithson Richard, Kirkgate
Temple John, E. side Market place
West Wm. North side Market place

*Hat Manufacturers and Dealers.*

Bates Wm. (dealer) S. side Market pl.
Hurst Geo. (dealer) E. side Market pl.
Lynass Wm. (dealer) Market place ·
Nash James, near the Beck
Metcalfe Joseph, (dealer) Market pl.
Rodgers Joseph, E. side Market place

*Hotels, Inns, and Taverns.*

Anchor and Dolphin, Matthew Fother-gill, St. James's green
Black Bull, Charles Hall, North side Market place
Black Horse, Thos. Metcalfe, Long st.
Black Lion, Wm. Faint, South side Market place
Blacksmiths' Arms, Geo. Rose, East side Market place
Blue Bell, W. Parker, St. James's green
Brewers' Arms, Ann Hutton, N. side Market place
Crown, Christopher Daniel, South side Market place
Golden Fleece Inn, George Blythe, (posting and commercial house) South side Market place
Golden Lion, John Gill, East side Market place
Half Moon, Richard Morfoot, Millgt.

King's Arms, Richard Chapman, top of Kirkgate
King's Head, Mary Hutton, Millgate
Lord Nelson, Thomas Cotham, Saint James's green
Masons' Arms, John Fawcett, Kirkgt.
New Inn, Robert Taylor, Westgate
Red Bear, William Johnson, N. side Market place
Royal Oak, James Hudson, (commer-cial) North side Market place
Star, Wm. Clayton, Westgate
Three Horse Shoes, Snowden Smith, Ingrygate
Three Tuns, Jonathan Empson, (ex-cise office, commercial & posting house) South side Market place
Three Tuns, Robert Heseltine, Finkle street
Waggon and Horses, Thomas Moon, Long street
Wheat Sheaf, Henry Atkinson, St. James's green
White Horse, Robert Seaton, St. James's green
White Swan, George Thornton, N. side Market place

*Ironmongers.*

Masterman Henry, E. side Market pl.
Peacock Wm. North side Market pl.
Russell Benj. North side Market pl.
Scurr Richard, East side Market pl.

*Jewellers.*

Russell Benj. North side Market pl.
Scurr Richard, East side Market pl.
Wylie James, Millgate

*Joiners, House Builders, &c.*

Armin John, Kirkgate
Atkinson Henry, St. James's green
Gamble William, St. James's green
Peat Joseph, Long street
Richmond John, Kirkgate
Webster Thomas, Kirkgate

*Libraries, Subscription & Circulating.*

Hurst Geo. (circulating, and librarian to the Thirsk book society) East side Market place
Masterman Henry, (circulating) East side Market place
Peat Robert, (circulating) top of N. side Market place

*Linen and Woollen Drapers.*

Barnitt Francis, S. side Market place
Metcalfe Joseph, E. side Market place
Metcalfe John, Middle Market place
West Wm. North side Market place

*Linen Drapers.*

Arnitt Francis, W. side Market place
Bumby John, St. James's green
Hansell Francis, Millgate
Lynass Wm. N. side Market place
Smith John, S. side Market place

Smith Ann and Sisters, South side Market place

*Linen Manufacturers.*
Currey Wm. & Thos. St. James's grn.
Dunning James, Finkle street
Foxton Wm. Kirkgate
Granger Wm. St. James's green
Smith Snowden, Old Thirsk

*Livery Stable Keepers.*
Johnson Wm. North side Market pl.
Seaton Robert, Long street

*Maltsters.*
Meek Thomas, Kirkgate
Rhodes Edward, Kirkgate

*Milliners and Dress Makers.*
Bales Mary, North side Market place
Cussons Ann, St. James's green
Hambleton Mary, Kirkgate
Lancaster Ann, South side Market pl.
Napier Isabella, Finkle street
Woodward Mary, Finkle street

*Music & Musical Instrument Dealers.*
Hurst Geo. East side Market place
Masterman Henry, E. side Market pl.

*Painters, (House and Sign.)*
Bickers Francis, Kirkgate
Elgie Thomas, Finkle street

*Perfumers, Hair Dressers, &c.*
Shepherd John, Swan yard, North side Market place
Shepherd Geo. Middle Market place
Wood Joshua, Rawling's yard, E. side Market place

*Plumbers and Glaziers.*
Brotherton Uriah, Kirkgate
Menill Wm. N. side Market place

*Porter Merchants.*
Adams Robert, Market place
Harrison John, Kirkgate
Johnson Thomas, Norby
Morrell Stephen, Back lane
Wood Benj. St. James's green

*Printers, (Letter Press.)*
Masterman Henry, E. side Market pl.
Peat Robt. top of N. side Market pl.

*Rope and Twine Makers.*
Clarkson John, Long street
Fothergill Matth. St. James's green
Millar John, S. side Market place

*Sacking Manufacturers.*
Raine James, Long street
Raine John, St. James's green

*Saddlers.*
Burgess Thomas, Long street
Fox Michael, (and collar maker) N. side Market place
Harrison Robert, W. side Market pl.
Hill Wm. E. side Market place
Hudson Christ. N. side Market place
Lancaster Geo. S. side Market place

Lynass W. North side Market place
Ridsdale John, West side Market pl.

*Savings' Bank.*
Open on Monday, from 12 to 1 o'clock; William Eshelby, clerk, Bentley's yard, S. side Market place

*Seedsmen.*
Armstrong James, Old Thirsk
West Wm. N. side Market place

*Shopkeepers.*
Caress William, Kirkgate
Crossby Richard, E. side Market pl.
Dinsdale Philip, N. side Market place
Dunning James, Finkle street
Edon Thomas, Long street
Horn John, N. side Market place
Ilee John, St. James's green
Jaques Wm. St. James's green
Powell Wm. Millgate
Siminson George, Norby
Smith Snowden, Ingrygate
Spence William, Long street

*Spirit and Wine Merchants.*
Foxton Thomas, Kirkgate
Heseltine Robert, Finkle street
Hudson James, N. side Market place
West Wm. N. side Market place

*Straw Hat Manufacturers.*
Dodgson Mary, Old Thirsk
Faulkner James, Finkle street
Nelson Mary, St. James's green
Stephenson Jane, Middle Market pl.
Stephenson Jane, Millgate

*Surgeons.*
Buckle John, S. side Market place
Dent Robert & John, Kirkgate
Lambert Wm. S. side Market place
Weddell John, N. side Market place

*Tailors.*
Atkin William, Kirkgate
Bales Geo. (and draper) North side Market place
Bowes Thomas, St. James's green
Ellison Charles, Long street
Gamble John, Smith's yard, S. side Market place
Gamble Wm. top of Kirkgate
Greatheed Robert, (& draper) S. side Market place
Horner James, Finkle street
Hudson John, Westgate
Ransom Wm. Finkle street
Ridsdale George, Smith's yard, South side Market place
Ridsdale Thomas, Finkle street
Rutter John, St. James's green
Scott George, Kirkgate
Scott Wm. Smith's yard, South side Market place

*Tallow Chandlers.*
Brown Geo. Middle Market place
Robinson John, N. side Market place

Rountree Hannah, Middle Market place

*Tin Plate Workers and Braziers.*
Almgill Joseph, Smith's yard, S. side Market place
Webster Robert, Kirkgate

*Watch and Clock Makers.*
Martin Thomas, Millgate
Palliser John, sen. Finkle street
Russell Benj. N. side Market pl.
Scurr Richard, E. side Market place
Wylie James, Millgate

*Wheelwrights.*
Brown Joseph, Old Thirsk
Crossby Richard, E. side Market pl.
Kirk Thomas, St. James's green
Pattinson Francis, St. James's green
Pattinson James, Old Thirsk
Raper George, Ingrygate
Smelt Henry, Westgate

*Whitesmiths.*
Harwood John, Finkle street
Palliser Michael, Jackson's yard, Kirkgate
Plews Samuel, Rawling's yard, East side Market place

*Miscellany.*
Alderwick Thos. furrier, Kirkgate
Armstrong James, corn factor, and agent, Old Thirsk
Armstrong Thomas, attorney's clerk, Millgate
Barnes John, comb manufacturer, St. James's green
Bentley Maurice, licensed teacher, St. James's green
Best Wm. fisherman, Long st.
Chapman John, thrashing and drill machine maker, Kirkgate
Coulson Joseph, chair maker, &c. Kirkgate
Dodgson John, slate merchant & stone mason, Long street
Dresser Mary & Son, bacon & butter factors, Finkle street
Eshelby Wm. commissioner for taking special bail, S. side Market pl.
Hamble Rhd. music preceptor & dancing master, St. James's green
Goodrick George, nail manufacturer, St. James's green
Oothrick John, chain maker, S. side Market place
Hall John, waiter at Blythe's Hotel, S. side Market place
Harwood John, gun maker, Finkle st.
Hudson Robert, governor of the work house, Long street
Jackson Wm. cooper, Westgate
Insley Joseph, excise officer, Westgt.
Metcalf Isaac, thong maker, St. James's green

Moorhouse Robert, blanket, &c. mfr. and woolstapler, Middle Market place
Palliser John, jun. engraver, Finkle street
Pick John and Robert, woollen drapers, S. side Market place
Stelling Geo. fellmonger, St. James's green
Varley Richard, basket maker, Westgate
Walker Thomas, drainer, St. James's green
Walker John, dyer, Market place

---

## COACHES,

*From George Blythe's, Golden Fleece Inn, S. side Market place.*

The ROYAL MAILS to London every evg. at ¼ past 8; to Newcastle & Edinburgh every evng. at ¼ past 11; to Stockton, Sunderland and Shields ¼ before 11; to York and London every evg. ¼ before 8.
The HIGHFLYER, every mg. at ¼ past 10 to Northallerton, Darlington, Durham, and Newcastle, and all parts of the North; also every evg. at 6 o'clock to York.
The WELLINGTON, every evg. at a ¼ past 8, to London, through York, Doncaster, Grantham, Stamford, and Huntingdon, arrives in London second morning at 7 o'clock; to Newcastle and Edinbro' every mg. at 1 o'clock.
The EXPEDITION, to Boroughbridge, Knaresbro', Wetherby, & Leeds, every evg. at 6 o'clock.

## CARRIERS,

*From the Blacksmiths' Arms, E. side Market place.*

Margaret Wood, to Yarm and Stockton, every Mon. and Thur. ret. Wed. & Sat. To Ripon & Leeds every Wed. and Sat. ret. Mon. and Thur.
Thomas Scafield, to Thorlby every Mon. at 8 aft.

*From the Waggon & Horses, Long st.*

Thomas Moon, to York on Tu. & Fri. ret. Thur. and Sat.
J. Peacock, to Stockton & Stokesley every Tuesday.

*From Wm. Ransom's, Finkle st.*

Pickersgill's Waggons, to York on Mon. and Thur. ret. Wed. and Sat.; to Darlington, Newcastle, &c. on Wed. and Sat. ret. Mon. and Thur.

*From the Black Bull, North side, Market place.*

Richard Fryer, to Bedale every Mon. and to Ripon every Thur. dep. 3 afternoon.

*From the White Swan, North side, Market place.*

John Jefferson, to Easingwold on Mon. and Thur. dep. 3 aft.
William Wood, to Helmsley on Mon. dep. 3 aft.

*From the Red Bear, N. side, Market pl.*

John Snowball, to Northallerton and Richmond on Mon. dep. 3 aft.

*From the King's Arms, top of Kirkgate.*

Thomas Metcalfe, to Northallerton, Bedale & Richmond, every Mon. dep. 4 aft.

*From the Crown Inn, S. side, Market pl.*

George Onthwaite, to Darlington, Easingwold and York, on Thur. dep. 2 aft.
James Hall, to Bedale on Mon, dep. 3 aft.

*Tholthorpe*, in the parish of Alne, wap. of Bulmer, and liberty of St. Peter's ; 5 miles SW. of Easingwold. Population, 238.

THORALBY, in the parish of Aysgarth, wap. of Hang West, and liberty of Richmondshire ; 4½ miles SE. of Askrigg.  Pop. 342.

Lord Morris Rokeby, Littleburn hall, near Thoralby
Sadler Miss Jane, gentlewoman
Terry Brian, yeoman
Willis James, attorney

| *Farmers*, | Wilkinson Anth. |
| Atkinson Stephen | *Shoemakers*, |
| Etherington Rt. | Drummond Daniel |
| Furniss Richard | Scott Thos. |
| Hammond Jeffery | Tennant Christ. |
| Johnson Thos. | Tomlinson Adam |
| Raw John | *Wheelwrights*, |
| Rider George | Dinsdale John |
| Thwaites James | Fawcett John |

Butterfield John, tailor
Calvert George, vict. aud corn miller, George and Dragon
Coates James, butcher
Dunn Lawson, portrait painter
Gill Peter, butter factor
Heseltine John, vict. Volunteer
Heseltine Wm. cooper
Nicholson Dorothy, grocer
Willis John, blacksmith

*Thoresby*, see Theasby

*Thormanby*, (P.) in the wap. of Bulmer, and liberty of Ripon ; 4 mls. NW. of Easingwold.  Here is a church, dedicated to St. Mary ; the living is a rectory ; patrons, Lord Vese Downe, and Sir George Cayley, Bart. alternately ; incumbent, the Hon. & Rev. W. H. Downay.  Pop. 118.

*Thornaby*, in the parish of Stainton, wap. and liberty of Langbargh ; 4 miles NNE. of Yarm.  Pop. 197.

THORNBROUGH, in the parish of West Tanfield, wap. of Hang East, and liberty of Richmondshire ; 6 miles E. of Masham.  On Thornbrough moor are three circular inclosures ; the most perfect of the these is about 540 feet in diameter.  Bishop Gibson supposes them to have been tilting circles, and gives an engraving of a similar one in Westmoreland, in his edition of Camden's Britannia, with two warriors engaging in a tournament.  Here is a small Methodist chapel.

Fox Wm. high constable of Halikeld
Heslington Thomas, yeoman
Spence John, yeoman

*Thornbrough*, in the parish of South Kilvington, and wap. of Birdforth ; 2 miles NNE. of Thirsk.  Population, 27.

*Thorney Brow*, in the parish of Scalby, wap. and liberty of Whitby Strand ; 8 miles SSE. of Whitby.

*Thorns*, in the township of Muker, parish of Grinton, wap. of Gilling West, and liberty of Richmondshire ; 8 miles NW. of Askrigg.

THORNTON, (or Thornton-cum-Farmanby), (P.) in the wap. and liberty of Pickering Lythe ; 2½ miles E. of Pickering.  There is here a Free School, built and endowed by Lady Lumley, with a salary of 40l. per annum to the master, 10l. to the usher, and 20l. for every first sermon preached by any of the persons brought up at this school.  There are also 12 charity houses, built and endowed by the same lady, for 12 poor persons, with 11l. 10s. per annum each, appertaining to the following places :— six to Sinnington, four to Thornton, one to Ellerburn, and one to Marton.  The church here is dedicated to All Saints ; the living is a rectory, in the patronage of R. Hill, Esq.  There are also chapels for the Methodists, and the Primitive Methodists.  Pop. 879.

Hill Richard, Esq. lord of the manor
Webb Rev. John, Hill, A.M. rector

*Academies*,
Mackreth Rev. Michael, master of the Free School

Schofield Rev. R. R. B. usher, and boarding house
Storr Thomas

*Blacksmiths,*
Green Robert
Maw John
Stephenson Wm.

*Bleachers,*
Coates George
Rodgers Rachael

*Butchers,*
Dixon John
Marfit Thos.

*Grocers,*
Allanson James
Humphrey Wm.

*Joiners,*
Bolton John
Brewster Wm.
Dennis Peter
Simpson Robert

*Stone Masons,*
Barnes Thomas
Bolton Richard
Spendley Wm.

*Tailors,*
Mackley John
Skelton Geo. and parish clerk

Beal George, shoemaker
Burnet Wm. flax dresser
Fell Thomas, paper box mfr.
Hoggard George, cooper
M'Goffi John, hair dresser, &c.
Nichols James, paper maker
Potter Christ. saddler and hardware dealer
Priestman Joshua, corn miller
Priestman Joseph, tanner
Richardson Thos. vict. Buck
Smith John, gardener
Vardell Francis, vict. New Inn
*Carrier,* Wm. Humphrey, to Whitby on Sat. at 4 mg. ret. 10 evg.

*Thornton,* in the parish of Stainton, wap. and liberty of Langbargh; miles NW. of Stokesley.

*Thornton Bridge,* in the parish of Rafferton, wap. of Halikeld, and liberty of Richmondshire; 4 miles NE. Boroughbridge. Pop. 43.

*Thornton-le-Beans,* in the parish North Otterington, wap. and liberty of Allertonshire; 3½ miles SE. Northallerton. The Rev. William ent resides here. Pop. 247.

*Thornton-le-Clay,* in the parish of Bolton, and wap. of Bulmer; 8 miles W. of Malton. There are here a Methodist chapel and a Friends' Meeting-house. Pop. 173.

THORNTON-LE-MOOR, in the parish of North Otterington, and wap. of Birdforth; 5 miles NW. of Thirsk. Here formerly a Chapel of Ease, which has been suffered to go to ruin, and the only part standing has been converted into a village school, without endowment. Population, 294. The principal inhabitants are—
Beckett Thomas, Esq.
...mley Thomas, yeoman
...rton John, schoolmaster
...ates Joseph, yeoman
...tson Thomas, yeoman
...son George, gentleman

THORNTON-LE-STREET, (P.) in the wap. and liberty of Allertonshire; 3 miles NNW. of Thirsk. Here is a church, dedicated to St. Leonard, in the patronage of Christ's Church College, Oxford; the Rev. T. H. Fowles, A. M. rector. Pop. 131.
Crompton Samuel, Esq. M. P. Wood End
Swift Joseph, land agent, Beal House

*Farmers,*
Allinson Wm.
Atkinson James
Atkinson Thos.

Coates Wm.
Lumley John
Morton Richard

Goulden Henry, blacksmith
Metcalfe James, miller
Pountain Mary, vict. Dog

*Thornton-on-the-Hill,* in the parish of Coxwold, and wap. of Birdforth; 5 miles N. of Easingwold. Pop. 70.

*Thornton Risebrough,* in the parish of Normanby, and wap. of Rydale; 4 miles W. of Pickering. Pop. 32.

THORNTON RUST, in the parish of Aysgarth, wap. Hang West, and liberty of Richmondshire; 2 miles SE. of Askrigg. Pop. 135.
Chapman John, gentleman

*Farmers,*
Armistead Richard
Baynes Thos.
Blakey J. R.
Chapman Henry
Gill Christopher
Mason Henry

Metcalf Richard
Mudd Robert
Pickering Robert
Tomlinson John
Tomlinson James
Turner John
Willis Matthew

THORNTON STEWARD, (P.) in the wap. of Hang West, and liberty of Richmondshire; 3 miles E. of Middleham. The church is a neat Gothic structure, dedicated to St. Oswald; the living is a vicarage, in the patronage of the Bishop of Chester. This village is pleasantly situated in Wensleydale, on the north side of the river Ure. In 1815 there was erected, by George Horn, Esq. of this place, a neat school-house, endowed with 10£. per annum, for the education of the poor children belonging to the parish. Pop. 265.
Ewbank Rev. John, vicar
Horn Captain George

*Farmers,*
Atkinson Joseph
Denison Francis
Plewes Thomas
Smith John
Thornberry Thos.

Tomlin Ottiwell
Tomlin Mrs.
Winn Christ.
*Shoemakers,*
Cooper Ralph
Cooper Richard

Brown John, grocer
Cooper Thomas, joiner
Culbert Geo. vict. No Man's Moor

Day John, vict. Board
Storey John, schoolmaster
Thornberry John, blacksmith
Winn George, vict. Board

THORNTON WATLASS, (P.) in the wap. of Hang East ; 3 miles SW. of Bedale ; a parochial village. The church, which is dedicated to St. Mary, is a rectory, in the patronage of Mark Milbank, Esq. Here is a seat of Sir Edw. Dodsworth, Bart. of Newland hall, who resides here occasionally. Pop. 180.

Dodsworth Sir Edward Bart.
Clarke C. N. Esq. Hermitage
Clark Rev. Geo. Ford, M.A. rector

*Butchers,*
Williamson Henry
Wilson Thomas
*Carpenters,*
Coates Thomas
Horner Wm.

*Farmers,*
Beck George
Boyes Joseph
Lintil George
Mitchell Jane

Beckwith Thomas, blacksmith
Duffield Abraham, schoolmaster and parish clerk
Lambert John, common brewer
Mudd Ann, vict. Stag
Naylor Francis, stone mason
Nicholson Thomas, tailor
Wright Wm. joiner and cabinet mkr.
Wright Thomas, vict. Black Horse

*Thorsby,* in the parish of Stainton, wap. and liberty of Langbargh ; 2 miles from Stokesley.

*Thorpe,* in the parish of Fylingdale, wap. and liberty of Whitby Strand ; 6 miles SSE. of Whitby. Here is a very neat Chapel of Ease, re-built 1821-2. Pop. included with Fylingdale.

Harrison Rev. James, curate

*Thorpe Field Houses,* in the parish of Topcliffe, and wap. of Birdforth ; 2 miles S. of Thirsk.

*Thorpe-under-Stone,* in the parish of Catterick, wap. of Hang West, and liberty of Richmondshire ; 4 miles W. of Richmond.

THORPE-WITH-WYCLIFFE, in the parish of Wycliffe, wap. of Gilling West ; 5 miles SE. of Barnard Castle ; a small township, situated on the banks of the river Tees. There is here a private chapel of the Catholic persuasion. Pop. 152.

Constable Sir Thomas Clifford
Headlam Rev. John, rector of Wycliffe
Sheldon Craddock, Esq. M.P.
*Farmers,*
Atkinson John
Bishoprick James
Dale Adam

Dale Robert        Young George
Waistell Wm.
Harrison Robert, miller, Wycliffe ml

*Thristoft,* in the parish of Ainderby Steeple, wap. of Gilling East, and liberty of Richmondshire ; 4 mi. W. of Northallerton. Pop. 165.

*Throxenby,* in the parish of Scalby, wap. and liberty of Pickering Lythe ; 2 miles WNW. of Scarborough. Pop. 66.

Howard Rev. Howard, curate

*Thunderbush,* in the parish of Kildale, wap. and liberty of Langbargh ; 4 miles S. of Guisborough.

THWAITE, in the parish of Grinton, wap. of Gilling West, and liberty of Richmondshire ; 7 miles NW. of Askrigg.

Butson Elizabeth, gentlewoman
Kearton William, yeoman

*Farmers,*
Calvert George
Calvert Wm.
Cleasby Edward
Guy Rd. Rash
Harker Wm.
Harker Wm. jun.
Harker Simon
Harker John
Kearton John
Kearton Christr.
Metcalf Thomas
Miller James
Pounder John

Alderson John, vict. Bull
Atkinson B. draper
Butson John, jun. carpenter
Clarke William, grocer
Hunter Jonathan, carpenter
Hutchinson John, blacksmith
Kearton William, tailor
Metcalfe Robert, shoemaker

*Thwaite Bridge,* in the parish of Aysgarth, wap. of Hang West, and liberty of Richmondshire ; 4 miles NW. of Hawes.

*Thwing Garth,* see Lunedale.

TOCKETTS, in the parish of Guisborough ; wap. and liberty of Langbargh ; 1½ mile NE. of Guisborough ; a small hamlet, inhabited chiefly by farmers, pleasantly situated, and surrounded by a variety of beautiful scenery. The lord of the manor is Robert Chaloner, Esq. Pop. 46.

*Farmers & Yeomen,*
Foster Thomas
Walker George
Weatherill Thos.

Coulson Thomas, corn miller
Pearson Geo. land agent

TOLESBY, in the parish of Marton, wap. and liberty of Langbargh ; 5 miles ENE. of Yarm.

Rudd John, Esq.

TOLLERTON, in the parish of Alne, wap. of Bulmer, and liberty of St.

Peter's; 4 miles S. of Easingwold. This village, situated on the verge of the great forest of Galtres, is supposed to be one of the places where travellers, on entering the forest, paid a certain toll, for which they were furnished with a guide, properly armed, to defend them from the attacks of robbers and wild beasts, with both of which that extensive forest is said to have abounded. Here is a Methodist chapel and Sunday school. At the western extremity of the village runs a small rivulet, which tradition says was once a navigable river, named Carr or Kyle, and, in digging for the foundation of a water mill, in 1815, part of a ship was discovered, at the depth of from ten to twelve feet below the surface. There is here a fair for sheep and cattle on the 15th of August. Population, 491.

Fawcett John, gentleman
Fawdington John, gentleman
Hodgson John, gentleman
Jackson Margaret, gentlewoman
Jackson John, gentleman
Jackson George, gentleman
Plowman Wm. gentleman
Sanderson Wm. gentleman
Vasey Richard, gentleman
Wrightson Mrs. M. gentlewoman

*Blacksmiths,*
Bowman John
Wilson James
*Farmers & yeomen,*
Bainbridge John
Bell Elisabeth
Brown Thomas
Brown Thomas
Barnett Robert
Buttery Mary
Colley Robert
Dickinson Thos.
Dunnington John
Farnhill James
Fawcett Wm.
Feather Henry
Hansell Wm.
Hodgson Thos.
Jackson John

Lowther Geo.
Lowther Thos.
Parker Mrs. M.
Plumber John
Rook John, sen.
Rook John, jun.
Saddler Wm.
Shepherd James
Stead Thomas
Stephenson John
*Shoemakers,*
Grange John
Lambert Thos.
*Shopkeepers,*
Kirk George
Reed John
Stephenson Jph.
Watson Thomas
Wentworth Thos.

Bell William, machine maker
Clark George, vict. Old Black Bull
Copley Joseph, schoolmaster
Cullingworth Benj. vict. Angel Inn, Tollerton lane
Dove Thomas, brick maker
Dunnington Chas. flax dresser & roper
Hall John, vict. Black Swan
Hodgson William, bricklayer
Morrell Robert, vict. Red Bear
Stott John, carpenter
Suggitt John and Geo. corn millers

TOPCLIFFE, (P.) in the wap. of Birdforth; a part in the liberty of St. Peter's;

4 miles SSW. of Thirsk. In the time of Leland this was "a pretty uplandish town," and here stood one of the seats of the Percy family. It is now only a village, and the few vestiges of the baronial mansion that remain are called the "Maiden Bower."— Here Henry, the fourth Earl of Northumberland, then lord lieutenant of the county, was, on St. Vitalis's day, in 1520, seised by the populace, and murdered, for enforcing a ten per cent. tax, imposed in the time of Henry VII, by the advice of Empson and Dudley. Here Thomas Percy, the succeeding Earl, conspired against Queen Elizabeth, and was beheaded at York, on the 22d of August, 1572. In this house Charles I. was a prisoner; and here the 200,000l. was paid by the Parliament to the Scotch, for quitting the country, and delivering up the King. The church, which bears evident marks of antiquity, is a vicarage, in the patronage of the Dean and Chapter of York, and is dedicated to St. Colomb; the incumbent is the Rev. R. D. Waddilove, D. D.— There is here also a Free Grammar school, founded and liberally endowed in 1849, of which Mr. William Bell is the master.— Amongst the modern buildings, which are not very numerous, may be mentioned a Methodist chapel. The population amounts to 658.

A Horse Post arrives from Thirsk every afternoon, at 5 o'clock, and proceeds immediately to Boroughbridge.

Allanson Rev. Thomas, curate
Duperoy John, gent.
Fall Ann, gentlewoman
Moyser Sarah, gentlewoman
Peate Mary, gentlewoman

*Blacksmiths,*
Gregg Christr. & farrier
Smith Henry
*Farmers & Yeomen,*
Barnett John
Fall Ann
Hawksley Christr.
Kidson James
Moyser Francis
Parler Wm.
Pickersgill Henry, West Lodge

Pickersgill Geo.
Rob Ralph, (and cattle dealer)
Walbron Thomas
Ward John
Whitaker Christr.
Yates Christr.
*Grocers & Drapers,*
Plumber G. & Jane
Slater John
*Wheelwrights,*
Fall Thomas
Kirby Richard

Adamson Edward, vict. Angel Inn
Bell William, schoolmaster
Braithwaite Christopher, bricklayer
Clarkson James, shoemaker
Dresser Joseph, corn miller
Harksley Thomas, shoemaker
Jaques Wm. cooper
Jennings Thomas, butcher
Johnson Thomas, vict. Black Bull

Seward Thos. vict. Black Horse
Shiers Henry, fishmonger
Surr Robert, vict. Red Lion
Swales G. vict. and flax dresser, Swan

Coach.—NORTH HIGHFLYER, from Leeds to Newcastle, at ½ past 10 mg. ret. ½ past 6 evg.

*Towthorpe,* in the parishes of Strensall and Huntington, and wap. of Bulmer, a part in the liberty of St. Peter's; 4¼ miles NNE. of York.—Population, 58.

*Traxmire,* in the parish of Lythe, and wap. of Langbargh; 10 miles W. of Whitby; consists of a few scattered farm houses.

*Trenholme,* a small hamlet in the parish of Whorlton, wap. and liberty of Langbargh; 8 miles SSW. of Stokesley.

*Trout's Dale,* in the parish of Brompton, wap. and liberty of Pickering Lythe; 10 miles NE. of Pickering. Pop. 45.

*Tunstall,* in the parish of Great Ayton, wap. & liberty of Langbargh; 3½ miles NE. of Stokesley.

*Tunstall,* in the parish of Catterick, wap. of Hang East, and liberty of Richmondshire; 6 miles SSE. of Richmond. A village famed for the longevity of its inhabitants. In 1808, Helen Glonton and Ann Reynolds died here within a few days of each other, the former at the age of 107 and the latter at the age of 103. Pop. 253.

*Uckerby,* in the parish of Catterick, wap. of Gilling East, and liberty of Richmondshire; 6 miles ENE. of Richmond. Pop. 52.

*Ugglebarnby,* in the parish of Whitby, wap. and liberty of Whitby Strand; 4 miles SW. of Whitby. The chapel at this place was built in the year 1137, by Nicholas, the Abbot of Whitby; the Rev. J. Robertson, of Whitby, is the perpetual curate.—Population, 428.

*Ugthorpe,* in the parish of Lythe, wap. and liberty of Langbargh; 7 miles WNW. of Whitby. There is here a Catholic chapel, built about the year 1812. Pop. 275.

*Ulshaw Bridge,* in the parish of East Witton, wap. of Hang West; 1 mile E. of Middleham.

UPLEATHAM, (P.) in the wap. and liberty of Langbargh; 3 miles NNE. of Guisborough. This village consists of a few houses, scattered irregularly on the southern declivity of a hill, and commands a pleasing view of Skelton castle, and the beautiful vale below. The hall is a neat and modern mansion, facing to the south and west, and sheltered on the east with thriving plantations; the rising grounds on the north are ornamented with clumps of trees, and the surrounding scenery presents a charming aspect of tranquillity and retirement. The chapel is a small ancient edifice, in the patronage of the Archbishop of York, and the Rev. T. P. Williamson is the perpetual curate. There is also here a small Methodist chapel. Pop. 239.

Dundas Lady Dowager, Hall
Dundas Captain George, Hall
Ingleby Rev. Henry
Pearson Rachael, gentlewoman
Smithson Richard, land agent
Wilkinson Rev. Joseph

*Farmers,*
Ainsley Wm.
Burrow Richard
Conn Thomas
Morris John
Patterson Geo.
Pybas John

Bryan Luke, blacksmith
Cowl William, vict. and cartwright, Chequers

*Upsall,* (East and West) in the parish of Ormesby, wap. and liberty of Langbargh; 3½ miles W. of Guisborough. Pop. 16.

UPSALL, in the parish of South Kilvington, and wap. of Birdforth; 4 miles NNE. of Thirsk, in an elevated situation upon the Hambleton hills.—The Mowbrays had formerly a castle here, and were succeeded by the Scroops, who were lords of Masham and Upsall. Pop. 118.

*Farmers,*
Fawcett John
Feetenby Mark
Jordison Wm.
Jordson John
Jordison Thos.

Barker Thomas, blacksmith
Lazenby Seth, vict. Hare and Hounds

*Upsland,* in the parish of Kirklington, wap. of Halikeld, and liberty of Richmondshire; 7 miles N. of Ripon. Pop. included with Kirklington.

*Upton,* in the parish of Easington, wap. and liberty of Langbargh; 8½ miles NE. of Guisborough.

*Ure,* (a river) see vol. I. page vii.

*Viewly Hill,* in the parish of Thornton-le-Street, & wap. of Allertonshire; 4 miles NW. of Thirsk.

*Wattworth,* in the parish of Catterick, wap. of Hang East, and liberty of Richmondshire; 2 miles SSW. of Richmond.

*Walburn*, a small hamlet in the parish of Downholme, wap. of Hang West, and liberty of Richmondshire; miles N. of Leyburn. Pop. 37.

*Walden*, in the parish of Aysgarth, wap. of Hang West, and liberty of Richmondshire; 7 miles SE. of Askrigg. A small township, consisting of a number of single farm-houses, scattered on the side of a hill at the northern extremity of Bishopdale. Population included with Burton.

WALLSGRAVE or FALLSGRAVE, in the parish of Scarborough, wap. of Pickering Lythe, and liberty of Scarborough; 1 mile SW. of Scarborough. A very ancient village, which, before the Norman conquest, was part of the possessions of Count Tosti, of Northumberland, and brother to Harold, king of England: in the 40th year of Henry II. it was disafforested, and annexed to the liberties of Scarborough. Pop. 345.

Bell John, Esq. Bell Vue
Hick William, yeoman
Pearson Mrs. gentlewoman

| *Farmers,* | *Sculptors,* |
| --- | --- |
| Jackson John | Coates Enos |
| Robinson Hannah | Coates George |
| *Joiners,* | *Shoemakers,* |
| Stonehouse Richd. | Cooper Wm. |
| Tindall Richard | Goodill Wm. |

Battye Susannah, vict. Board
Beech George, schoolmaster
Carlisle Joseph, vict. New Inn
Cooke George, tanner
Feaster Christopher, wheelwright
Pearson Richard, gardener
Robinson John, tailor
Wilson Matthew, vict. White Horse

*Wapley*, in the parish of Lofthouse, wap. & liberty of Langbargh; 10¼ m. E. of Guisborough.

*Warder Mask*, in the parish of Masham, wap. of Hang East, & liberties of St. Peter's & Richmondshire; miles SSW. of Masham.

WARLABY, in the parish of Ainderby Steeple, wap. of Gilling East, and liberty of Richmondshire; 2¼ mls. SW. of Northallerton. Pop. 97.

Booth Thomas, Esq.
Cooper Francis, gentleman
Foster Miss, gentlewoman
King Leonard, farmer, Warlaby grange
Meek Michael, nurseryman
Lennard George, farmer

WARTHILL, (P.) in the wap. of Bulmer, a part in the liberty of St. Peter's; 5 mls. ENE. of York. Here a church, dedicated to St. Mary; the living is a rectory, in the patronage of the Prebendary of Warthill, and the Rev. Isaac Grayson is the incumbent. Population, 153.

Agar Benjamin, Esq. Brockfield

| *Farmers,* | |
| --- | --- |
| Appleyard Wm. | Hudson Joseph |
| Brown Thos. | Hutchinson Geo. |
| Dixon Thos. | Lambert Thos. |
| Hudson Thos. | Rooks Thos. |
| Hudson Wm. | Wake John |
| | Young Leonard |

Hudson Francis
Johnson John, shopkeeper
Kirk William, carpenter
Suffield Wm. vict. Bay Horse

*Wass*, in the parish of Kilburn, and wap. of Birdforth; 6 miles SW. of Helmsley. The principal inhabitant of this place is Mr. John Bree. Pop. included with Byland.

WATH, (P.) in the wap. of Halikeld, and liberty of Richmondshire; 4 miles N. of Ripon. The church is dedicated to St. Mary; the living is a rectory, in the patronage of the Marquis of Ailesbury, and the Rev. Benj. Newton, A.M. is the incumbent. This village derives its name from its situation, there being a rivulet at each end of it, which the villagers were formerly obliged to wade or ford. There is now a good stone bridge over each. Here is a school, free to all the children of the village, for reading, writing, and accompts, founded and liberally endowed by Dr. Peter Samwaise, with lands at Bellerby. Pop. 186.

| *Carpenters,* | Whitwell John |
| --- | --- |
| Beckwith John | Wrigglesworth G. |
| Clarkson Thos. | *Grocers,* |
| *Farmers & Yeomen,* | Gatenby Mary |
| Beck John | Pearson Wm. |
| Broadwith Richd. | *Stone Masons* |
| Burnell Caleb | Busby George |
| Holridge Wm. | Gill Anthony |
| Squire Wm. | |

Coates Joseph, shoemaker
Coates John, tailor and draper
Cobb James, master of the free school
Dalton Thos. vict. George & Dragon
Steel Samuel, linen weaver
Tinsley George, blacksmith

*Wath*, in the parish of Hovingham, and wap. of Rydale; 8 miles WNW. of Malton. Pop. 22.

*Waybill*, in the parish of Romaldkirk, and wap. of Gilling West; 7 miles W. of Barnard Castle.

*Weedale*, in the parish of Brompton, wap. and liberty of Pickering Lythe; 10 miles E. of Pickering.

WELBURN, in the parish & wap. of Bulmer; 5¼ miles SW. of Malton. Population, 352.

Hodgson George, surgeon
Milburn Mrs. Ann

*Farmers & Yeomen,* Foster George
Coverdale John    Heckley Ann
Craven Richard    Nightingale Eliz.

Blake William, vict. Ship
Crawford Archibald, plumber & glazier
Gibson Thomas, blacksmith
Harrison Thomas vict. Bull
Hodgson John, shoemaker
Horner Robert, nursery & seedsman
Langdale John, schoolmaster
Sedgefield Jas. shoemkr. & shopkpr.
Simpson William, tailor
Thompson Wm. joiner & cabinet mkr.
Todd Mary, corn miller
Walkington Geo. tallow chandler
Webster Francis, wheelwright

*Welburn,* in the parish of Kirkdale, & wap. of Rydale; 1¼ mile SW. of Kirkby-Moor-Side. Pop. 112.

WELBURY, (P.) in the wap. of Birdforth; 7 miles NE. of Northallerton. There is no place of worship here except the parish church, which has lately been re-built, it is dedicated to St. Leonard, and the living is a rectory, in the patronage of the King as Duke of Lancaster. Pop. 257.

Lipscomb Rev. William, A.M. rector

*Weldale,* in the parish of Ebberston, wap. and liberty of Pickering Lythe; 7 miles ESE. of Pickering.

WELL, (P.) in the wap. of Hang East, and liberty of Richmondshire; 4 miles S. of Bedale. This village is said to derive its name from a famous well dedicated to St. Michael, which is supplied by a spring issuing from a rock, and which flows invariably at all seasons of the year. The church is an ancient edifice, dedicated to St. James; containing monuments of several of the Lords of Snape; the living is a vicarage, in the patronage of Charles Chaplin, Esq. the master of Well Hospital. Here is an hospital for sixteen poor persons, eight of Well and eight of Snape,; and two free schools, one for boys and the other for girls; all founded and very liberally endowed by the Nevilles of Snape Hall and Middleham, in the 14th century. This place also contained a monastery, of which the residence of Richard Strangeways, Esq. is the remains. Pop. 370.

Strangeways Richard, Esq.
Strangeways R. P. Esq. Holly hill.

*Farmers & Yeomen,* Todd George
Hawkswell Thos.  Walker Thomas
Johnson Richard       *Shoemakers,*
Lee John          Annill Robert
Pybus Joseph      James John
Suderby Matthew

Deighton Francis, wool comber
Duffield Francis, grocer
Lynn Thos. butcher
Masterman John, stocking manfr.
Palliser Christopher, vict. and carpenter, Well Ox
Pybus Wm. vict. Bay Horse
Scurray Joseph, blacksmith
Sivers John, vict. Board

*Wemergill,* see Lunedale.

WENSLEY, (P.) in the wap. of Hang West, and liberty of Richmondshire; 1¼ mile W. of Leyburn. Wensleydale, the valley which derives its name from this village, is of considerable width, lying between two ranges of hills, is adorned with several villages, and watered by the river Ure.—The situation of Wensley is delightful; sheltered by a long ridge of hills, alternately wood and rock to the north, and gently elevated above the bank of the Ure, it overlooks a plain of high fertility, beyond which an irregular and pleasing tract of cultivated grounds, woods and pastures, ascends before the eye, and terminates in the bold and purple form of Penhill to the south: upward the landscape is at once soft and magnificent, and the opening of Bishopdale, where it falls into the vale of Ure, affords, by its depth and mountain character, a fine contrast to the luxuriant groves and meadows of the latter. Upon the whole, Wensleydale may rank with the first of our northern vallies. Besides its natural beauties, the parish of Wensley exhibits three most interesting objects; its parish church; the castle of its ancient, and the mansion of its modern Lords. The parish church is a neat structure, dedicated to the Holy Trinity; the living is a rectory, in the patronage of Lord Bolton. Richard Scroop, Lord of Bolton, formed the design of making this church collegiate, and in the 22d of Richard II. he obtained the king's licence for this purpose; but from some cause, not explained, it is believed that the foundation, which was meant to be very extensive, never took place. The bridge at Wensley is of considerable antiquity, and is thus noticed by Leland, near three hundred years ago:—" The fayre bridge of 3 or 4 " arces that is on Ure at Wencelaw, a " mile or more above Middleham, was made " about 200 years ago and more, by one " caullyd Alwine, parson of Wencelaw." To the regret of the lovers of antiquity, but for the benefit of trade, and for the safety of the inhabitants, this venerable bridge was widened and repaired by the North Riding in 1818. Population, 317.

Costobadie Rev. Jacob, rector

Humphrey John, gentleman
Higsworth Mrs. gentlewoman

*Carpenters,*
Robinson Charles
We<sup>s</sup>tgarth Thos. (& draper)
*Corn Millers,*
Blenton Thos.
Masterman Wm.

*Farmers,*
Bell Stephen
Bell Andrew
Clarkson James
Hood Ralph
Scott James

Spencer Joseph
*Grocers,*
Johnson Jas. (& parish clerk)
Robinson Matthew
*Shoemakers,*
Collinson Geo.
Spence John
*Straw Hat Makers,*
Gaines Mrs.
Robinson Margaret
Westgarth Mrs.

Blades Isaac, groom, (racing stables)
Horner John, gardener
Kitchen Henry, bricklayer
Robinson Ann, vict. Punch Bowl
Sadler Wm. land agent
Scott Christopher, blacksmith
Ward Eliz. vict. Black Swan

*Westerdale,* (P.) in the wap. and liberty of Langbargh; 10 miles SSE. of Guisborough. The church is an ancient structure, and the living is a perpetual curacy, of which the rector of Stokesley is the patron, and the Rev. Daniel Duck, the incumbent. Pop. 281.

*Whagh,* see Arkengarthdale.

WHASHTON, in the parish of Kirky-Ravensworth, wap. of Gilling West, and liberty of Richmondshire; 4 miles NW. of Richmond. Pop. 140.

Hale Rev. Henry
Harrison Marley, gentleman

*Whenby,* (P.) in the wap. of Bulner; 8 miles E. of Easingwold. Here is a church, dedicated to St. Martin; the living is a vicarage, of which Wm. Garforth, Esq. is the patron, and the Rev. William Preston the incumbent. Pop. 129.

## WHITBY, (P.)

in the wap. and liberty of Whitby Strand; miles from Guisborough, 20 from Scarborough, 31 from Stokesley, and 47 from York; in 54 deg. 20 min. 24 sec. north latitude, and 35 min. 59 sec. west longitude. The town stands on two opposite declivities, the mouth of the Eske, by which river is divided into two parts, which are connected by a draw-bridge, so constructed as to admit vessels of 32 feet wide. The Saxon name this place, was according to Bede, *Strean-shalh,* or the Bay of the Watch Tower. It afterwards called Prestebly, or the ha-

bitation of Priests; then *Hwytby;* next *Whiteby,* (probably from the colour of the houses), and now *Whitby.* Owing to the northern aspect of the district and the rising of the land to a considerable distance into the country, the sun beams fall so obliquely on the town and its immediate vicinity, that its climate may be considered nearly on an equality with Shetland and the Orkneys. It is closely and irregularly built, though the houses of the opulent inhabitants are large and commodious; the streets in general are narrow and inconvenient, and the act obtained for paving, lighting and widening them has been very imperfectly carried into effect. Whitby owes its origin to a famous abbey, founded here in 657, by Oswy, King of Northumberland, to redeem a vow that he had made previous to the sanguinary battle of Leeds, fought in 655—that if God would grant him victory over Penda, the Pagan King of Mercia, who had invaded his dominions, he would build a monastery, and consecrate his daughter, Ethelfleda, then scarcely one year old, to the service of God, by a life of celibacy. The prayers of Oswy were heard; Panda was slain with most of his nobles, and Oswy in gratitude to heaven built the monastery of Streanshalh, for monks and nuns of the Benedictine order, appointing Lady Hilda, niece of Edwin, the first christian king of Northumbria, abbess. This lady was so famous for her sanctity, that she attained the dignity of St. Hilda, and the monastery, though dedicated to St. Peter, is generally called after her. The story goes, says Grose, that in her time, this place and its environs, were terribly overrun with serpents. These, by the prayers of St. Hilda, were deprived of their heads, and turned into stones, as the writer of her life very properly observes, to the great amazement of the beholders! In her benevolence, however, she kindly provided houses, for the snakes so petrified, all of whom are enclosed within a kind of stony matrix; these stones are still found in great quantities, in this neighbourhood, and are what the fossilists call ammonites. On the landing of the Danes at Raven's Hill, two miles to the west of Whitby, in 867, they destroyed this monastery, which lay in ruins till the conquest, when William, the Norman, assigned Whitby to Hugh de Abrincis, an expert soldier, who disposed of the place to William de Percy, by whom this monastery was refounded, and dedicated to St. Peter, and St. Hilda. In the reign of Henry VIII. this house shared the fate of the other monastic establishments, and its yearly revenues, according to Speed, were valued at 505l. 9s. 1d. The site of the abbey was granted in the 4th of Edward VI.

to John, Earl of Warwick, by whom in 1551, it was sold to Sir Edward Yorke; and in the 1st of Philip and Mary, by him to Sir Hugh Cholmeley, Knight, ancestor of the present proprietor. The ruins of this once famous abbey stand on a high cliff south-east of the town near the parish church, and the ascent to it from the town is by a flight of two hundred steps. A small distance south of the abbey Mr. Cholmeley has a splendid mansion, built probably with the materials from the monastery. This noble abbey has gone greatly to decay, but the rudest shock it received in modern times was from a storm of wind in the night of the 9d of December, 1763, when the whole western wing was overturned and thrown down to the very foundations, though supported by at least twenty strong Gothic pillars and arches, nothing being left standing thereon but the north wall of the cloisters and a part of the wall at the west end. Unlike the other great religious houses in this country, which were generally built in warm sheltered situations, Whitby abbey stands on an eminence eighty yards at least above the sea; but if the situation is bleak the prospect is commanding, and presents a view of the town and post of Whitby, with the frowning heights of the black moors, rising in the horizon in front, while in the rear is the vast expanse of the ocean, and the *tout ensemble* is truly magnificent.

When the abbey of Whitby was in the zenith of its glory, the town was little more than a small fishing station, and so late as the year 1540, it did not consist of more than from twenty to thirty houses with a population not exceeding two hundred inhabitants. At that time it is probable there was not a single chimney in the town, the abbey chimney excepted, the common way then, even in towns and cities of much greater consequence, being, to have a hearth in the middle of the room in which was made the fire, the smoke ascending and passing through a large hole at the top of the building,* after the fashion of the smoke vomitory of an Irish cabin of the present day. It does not appear during the long reign of Queen Elizabeth, that there was a single vessel deserving the name of a ship that belonged to this port; but the important discovery of the alum mines at the close of that reign raised Whitby from its obscurity, and by opening a channel of commerce, elevated the town to a degree of maritime consequence. The successful progress of the alum works, established by Mr. Chaloner at Guisborough, says Mr. Hinderwell, ex-

* Holingshed.

cited a spirit of emulation, and works of a similar kind were erected in the year 1615, near Sands end, within three miles of Whitby. This also proved advantageous, and the vicinity of Whitby abounding with alum-stone other adventurers were induced to embark in these undertakings. In consequence of these extended speculations, two great branches of trade were opened at the port of Whitby—one for supplying the works with coals, the other for conveying the alum to distant parts. This infant commerce was gradually matured; the number of vessels was increased; ship building from the oak timber which the vicinity produced was commenced, and by the industry, the enterprise, and the successful speculation of its inhabitants, the town of Whitby rose to opulence, and became a place of considerable importance. Up to the year 1632, the piers were constructed only of wood, with a few loose stones put in the framing, but during that year the stone piers began to be built, through the influence and exertions of the early benefactor of Whitby, Sir Hugh Cholmeley, who, by favour of his relation, the Earl of Strafford, procured liberty for a general contribution throughout England, by which nearly 500*l.* was collected in aid of this public work.

Since that time the piers have been progressively extending with the increase of commerce. For the support and extension of these piers, there is paid a duty of a half-penny per chaldron on all coals shipped at Newcastle or its dependencies, except in Yarmouth vessels, and the sum raised by this duty, together with the perpetual duties levied at Whitby, in virtue of the acts of 1702 and 1799, on salt, grain, and foreign goods, landed here, and on butter and fish shipped hence, amounts to 9000*l.* a year. From the funds thus provided, the harbour has been wonderfully improved, and an effectual barrier interposed to protect the town from the fury of the German Ocean. Since the year 1702, the east pier, which extends six hundred and forty-five feet into the sea, has been entirely built; and the west pier has been enlarged and improved, and now extends to the distance of one thousand eight hundred and sixty feet from the shore. Besides these outer piers others have been formed within the harbour at sufficient distances to direct the current, to break the force of the waves, and thus to give a great security both to the shipping and to the premises abutting on the harbour. Rocks that formerly obstructed the mouth of the haven have been removed, and immense beds of sand that once filled a considerable part of the harbour, and even threatened to choake up the entrance have by the projection of the piers been all cleared away. A commodious quay from Haggersgate to the west pier has been recently erected, and forms, says Mr. Young, in his excellent history of Whitby, one of the finest improvements which the town and harbour have experienced. The entrance to the harbour between the heads of the two outer piers is about ninety-two yards wide; between the Burgess pier and the Scotch head the width is seventy-two yards: but the third entrance between the Fish pier and the Coffee-house does not exceed sixty-eight yards. The depth of the water in the harbour at neap-tides is from ten to twelve feet, and at the spring tides generally from fifteen to eighteen feet. In stormy weather it is necessary for vessels to go above the bridge to escape the swell, but there is room in this inner harbour to accommodate a large fleet, and the water up to Boghall is of sufficient depth to receive them. A harbour master is appointed to direct the vessels to their proper mooring, and there are fourteen pilots belonging to the port who take charge of vessels entering into the harbour or going out to sea. The batteries are closely connected with the piers, and the cost of their outfit and support is defrayed from the same fund. When the west pier was lengthened in 1734, its circular termination was formed into a battery, with embrasures for five pieces of canon, which have since been increased to six; and since the erection of the quay, a battery, which before existed near the Scotch head, has been strongly re-built in the form of a crescent, with a small tower at each angle, and is furnished with eight eighteen pounders.

Whitby, in a commercial view, claims a superior rank among the minor ports, and, as far as the opulence of her merchants and the extent of her ship building establishments are concerned, she has some fair pretensions to aspire to the major class. The shipping of Whitby has increased amazingly during the two last centuries. In 1622, it is highly probable that the aggregate burthen of all the vessels belonging to this port did not exceed five hundred tons; in 1700, the vessels had increased to one hundred and fifteen, but their tonnage did not then exceed six thousand tons; and the number of vessels may now with safety be stated at three hundred, and their burthen at fifty-two thousand tons. These vessels are navigated upwards of two thousand seamen. The seamen of this port have long been distinguished for their courage, activity, and skill; and many of them have been eminently successful. Of one of this number, Captain

Thomas Pyeman, it is mentioned, that he was never shipwrecked or captured, nor did he ever lose so much as either an anchor or cable, during forty-five years that he was at sea! and it is proper to add, for the connection is worthy of remark—he was never intoxicated.*

The exports of Whitby to foreign parts are very limited, they consist principally of alum, whale oil, and dried fish. The imports are much more considerable; they are chiefly articles of Baltic produce, comprehending timber, deals, hemp, flax and ashes. The coasting trade is also considerable, and the shipments made hence to other parts of England consist principally of alum, sail cloth, butter, bacon, grain and leather.

The progress of the artificers of Whitby in ship building, has eminently contributed to the prosperity of the place. A number of ships have been built here for the ports of London, Liverpool, Hull, and Shields, and taken on an average, the ships built during the last twenty years may be about twenty a year. Boat building, rope making, and sail cloth manufacturing, are all carried on here, but in these departments, as well as in the demand for ships, the cessation of war has made a considerable reduction.

The Custom House here is situated in Sandgate, near the Market-place, and Christopher Coulson, Esq. is the collector. The business of the Excise Office is transacted at the Angel Inn, under the direction of John Brown, Esq. collector. Mr. George Clark, in Church street, is the distributor of stamps; and Mr. Richard Rodgers, in the Old Market place, is the post-master. The annual revenue yielded to the government by these establishments may be thus stated—

Customs.............£9,000
Excise................. 7,500
Stamps ............... 3,500
Postages ........... 3,000

One of the most lucrative branches of trade that this port has enjoyed is the whale fishery. The first ship sent from hence to Greenland was dispatched in the year 1753, by a *club* or community of enterprizing men, but it was not till the year 1772, that the beneficial effects of this branch of commerce begun to be sensibly felt, and not earlier than 1795, that they fully developed themselves. In former times a vessel was thought well fished, as it is technically called, with four or five whales, but within the last seven and twenty years the average has not been less than fifteen, yielding one hundred and twenty-seven tons of oil for each ship, and eight tons for

* Young's History of Whitby.

3 c

each fish. The number of whalers dispatched to the Greenland and Davis Straits fisheries, from this port has of late amounted to about eight annually. Their success has tended not only to benefit the owners, but also to enrich the town, as will be inferred when it is stated that each full ship is estimated before its departure and on its return to spend in the place 3000*l.* Two recent *discoveries* however useful and agreeable in other respects have tended materially to impair the prosperity of our fisheries, these are—Gas Lights and Soft Stays—the former of which have diminished the demand for oil, and the latter for whale bone. The domestic fisheries of Whitby are on a very circumscribed scale. Though both the Eske and the Ocean are at hand, and both of them ready to afford their contributions for the supply of man, the distance from and the rugged communication between this place and the large towns of the interior, preclude the possibility of fishing here to much advantage.

When it is considered that the limits of the jurisdiction of Whitby comprise about forty miles of coast, extending from Huntcliff fort contiguous to the Tees to the north, to within a mile of Scarborough castle to the south, and that within this distance here are several extensive works, it will not be thought surprising that a great deal of business is done here on Saturday which is the market day. The two annual fairs which commence on the 25th of August, St. Hilda's day; and on Martinmas day, each last three days, but all the business done at them might very well be transacted in a much shorter time. The banks here so intimately connected with trade and commerce are five in number, stable in their character, and highly conducive in their operations to the prosperity of the place; they will be found enumerated in their proper place in the subjoined directory.

The alum works, the staple trade of Whitby, which comprehend no fewer than six separate establishments, employing in the whole six hundred work people, and producing two thousand eight hundred and forty tons annually,* claim a particular notice in the history of the trade and commerce of this place. The precise period when the art of alum making was introduced into this country is unknown, but the year 1595, is the earliest period assigned. It appears that Sir Thomas Chaloner, one of the ancestors of the worthy member for the city of York, in his travels in Italy, about that period visited the alum works of his Holiness the Pope, and having ascertained that the rock from which the Italian alum was made was of

* See Vol. II. page 416.

precisely the same nature as that with which his own estate at Guisborough in the North Riding of Yorkshire abounded, Sir Thomas engaged a number of the Pope's workmen to accompany him to England, and for secrecy conveyed them on board the vessel in which they embarked in hogsheads. With the assistance of these workmen, the Knight begun his alum-works at Belman Bank, near Guisborough, and soon became a most formidable rival to the traders of the Vatican. The monopoly of the alum trade which had been enjoyed by the court of Rome for ages being thus destroyed, and a highly profitable source of revenue greatly impaired, his Holiness is said to have excommunicated not only Sir Thomas Chaloner, but also all the other persons engaged in this manufacture, and this ancient and terrible malediction may be found in Grose's Antiquities, vol. i. page 107, as well as in several other works. The profits made by Sir Thomas were more operative than the fears excited by the denunciation of the holy father, and hence several other works were set up in various parts of the country, and in time the competition became so severe that instead of alum being sold as it was in the Italian works for the sum of 53*l.* 6*s.* 8*d.* per ton, it was reduced to below one-half of that price. Up to this day the alum works on the Yorkshire coast are the principal establishment of the kind in England, and the noble Lords Dundas and Mulgrave, with three other manufacturing concerns already mentioned, are the great alum makers of England.

The neighbourhood of Whitby abounds with natural curiosities; and the various petrifactions almost every where found in the alum rocks have long excited wonder and puzzled philosophy. Besides the petrified shells of sea-fish, others have been found in the scarr or cliff on the east side of the mouth of the Eske, which cannot be arranged under any class. In the early part of the last century, Dr. Woodward, dug up on the scarr the petrified arm and hand of a man in which all the bones and joints were perfectly visible. In 1743, the Rev. Mr. Borwick found in the alum rock the complete skeleton or petrified bones of a man, and sent it, though in a mutilated state to one of our Universities to enrich their museum. After this, in the year 1758, the petrified bones of a crocodile, an animal never known in this part of the world was taken out of the rock and sent to the Royal Society, in whose transactions at —— in Vol I. Part II. it is described; and about four years after the skeleton of a petrified horse was found in the alum works at Saltwick, at the depth of thirty yards under ground, and sent as a natural rarity to the

University of Aberdeen.* The ammonitæ or snake-stones, as already mentioned, are found in almost every place where the alum rock exists, and particularly in Whitby Scarr, between high and low water mark.— The snakes are all inclosed in hard elliptical stones, which seem to have been struck within, being coiled up in spiral volutes, and every way resembling that reptile in their form and shape, save only in the head, which is always wanting. There are two different species—the round-bodied and the flat-bodied. The round-bodied are girt or encompassed from end to end with semi-circular channels or cavities: while the other have a ridge on their back, and are plated on the sides, as if they had been pressed together, the marks wherewith they are pitted, resembling the impression of a man's thumb on a soft substance. The snakes are all enclosed in hard elliptical stones, which seems to be of a different mineral from the snake itself, which may, by care, be separated from it. These ammonitæ are noticed by Camden and Leland, and both of them observe, that hame ascribes them to the power of St. Hilda's prayers. This is of course a vulgar superstition, which it is much easier to reject than it is satisfactorily to account for the phenomenon.

The parish church at Whitby, dedicated to St. Mary, is situated near the top of the hill on the eastern side of the town, near the abbey, and is approached from the bottom of the vale by one hundred and ninety stone steps. The architecture was originally gothic, but it has undergone so many modern alterations, that it retains little of its ancient form. The living is a perpetual curacy, in the patronage of the Archbishop of York, and the Rev. James Andrewes, is the incumbent. There is here also a Chapel of Ease, of the date of 1778, situated near the middle of Baxtergate, of which the Rev. Thomas

* Charlton's History of Whitby.

Holloway, is the minister, In addition to the episcopalian places of worship, there are seven meeting houses in Whitby, two belonging to the Methodists, two to the Presbyterians, of different persuasions; one to the Independents; one to the Quakers, and one to the Roman Catholics.

The benevolent institutions of this place are the Seaman's Hospital, an establishment of the same nature as that at Scarborough; the Dispensary; the Female Charity for Lying-in Women; and the Charity for clothing the aged Female Poor. There are besides Sunday Schools, and two flourishing Lancasterian Schools, the one for boys, and the other for girls. The religious societies consist of, the Whitby Auxiliary Bible Society; the Religious Tract Society; and the Missionary Societies.

The public institutions consist of a Subscription Library, in Haggersgate, commenced in 1775; a Botanic Garden, begun in 1812, and situated on the east side of Grove lane; and a News Room, in Haggersgate, built by subscription, in 1814. There is also a Subscription Theatre on a large scale, built in 1784, and situated in Skatelane, where there are dramatic performances in the winter season.

The population of Whitby, according to the parliamentary census has increased at the rate of about 20 per centum, during the last ten years. In 1811, the aggregate number of inhabitants including Ruswarp, was 8,967; in 1821, they are stated in the official returns, at 10,615.

Though the town of Whitby does not seem a desirable place of residence, its environs are romantic and beautiful, especially in the summer season, and the elegant mansions of the opulent inhabitants, mostly built on commanding situations, tend greatly to embellish the surrounding scenery, to which the shipping in the harbour and in the offing impart life and animation.

POST-MASTER, RICHARD RODGERS, *Office, Old Market-place.*

| Places from whence letter bags are recvd. | Distance. | Postage. | Arrival. | Departure. |
|---|---|---|---|---|
| London | 244 | 12d. | ¼ past 7 morng. | 12 at noon |
| Malton | 30 | 6 | ditto. | ditto |
| Pickering | 21 | 6 | ditto. | ditto |
| York | 48 | 7 | ditto. | ditto |

### DIRECTORY.

Andrewes Rev. James, Baxtergate
Andrewes Mrs. Ann, Flowergate
Barker Thomas, gent. Silver street
Barker Mrs. Ann, gentlewoman, New
    buildings
Bateman Mrs. Sarah, Baxtergate
Bedlington Mrs. Eliz. Bagdale
Blackburn Rev. Wm. New buildings
Blackburn Mary, gentwmn. Baxtergt.
Boulby Miss Elizabeth, Baxtergate
Bradekirk Margaret, gentlewoman,
    Church street
Brown John, Esq. collector of excise,
    Pier head
Bock Ann, gentlewoman, Prospect
    place, Church street
Burbanks Grace, gentlewmn. Bagdale
Burn John, gentleman, Well yard,
    Church street
Campion Thomas, gent. Flowergate
Carr Walter, gent. Bagdale
Clark Thos. Esq. Well close square
Clark Joseph, gent. Well close square
Clark Hannah, gentlewoman, Bagdale
Clarkson Wm. yeoman, Ropery lane
Cockerill Mrs. D. gentlewoman, 3,
    New buildings
Cooke Mrs. Isabella, Flowergate
Cooper Mrs. Ann, gentwmn. Routh
    buildings
Coulson Christopher, Esq. collector
    of customs, Baxtergate
Coverdale Mary, gentwmn. Flowergt.
Duck Dowson, gent. Bagdale
Emlington John, gent. Silver street
Emlington Mrs. Mary, Haggersgate
Fawcett John, gent. Bagdale
Gallilee Mary, gentlewoman, Grape la.
Gibson Wm. gent. Bagdale
Gowland Mrs. Susannah, Bagdale
Graham Jane, gentlewoman, Skinner
    street
Hall Mrs. Elizabeth, Church street
Hall Mrs. Elizabeth, Cliffe lane
Harrison Martha, gentlewoman, 12,
    New buildings
Harrison Wm. gent. 13, New buildings
Harrison Elizabeth, gentlewoman, 14,
    New buildings
Haydock Rev. Geo. Catholic pastor,
    Bagdale
Holt John, Esq. Skinner street
Holt Mary, gentlewoman, Bagdale
Hunter Thomas, insurance broker;
    house, Well close square
Hunter Hannah, gentlewoman, 8,
    New buildings
Hunter Israel, gent. 9, New buildings
Hutchinson Robert, gent. Flowergate
Jackson Richard, gent. Silver street
Jefferson Mary, gentlewoman, New
    buildings

Jefferson Mrs. Mary, Cliffe lane
Johnson Mary, gentlewoman, Old
    Market place
Knaggs Wm. gent. New buildings
Lawson Mrs. Mary, Skate lane
Marwood Isaac, gent. Well close sqr.
Middleton Wm. gentleman, 15, New
    buildings
Moorsom Isaiah, gent. Skinner st.
Moss Eliz. gentlwmn. 2, New bldngs.
Palmer Mrs. Mary, Haggersgate
Parkinson Mrs. Isabella, Church st.
Power Captain, 1, New buildings
Preswick Miss Margaret, 19, New
    buildings
Preston Robert, gent. Skinner street
Price John, gent. Church street
Richardson Mrs. Dinah, Church st.
Ripley Mrs. Hannah, Flowergate
Robertson Rev. Joseph, incumbent of
    Sleights, Ugglebarnby & Aislaby,
    Baxtergate
Rudyerd Richd. gent. St. Ann's staith
Sanders Geo. gent. 20, New buildings
Sedgwick Rev. John, Baxtergate
Simpson Rev. John, Baxtergate
Sleightholm Saml. gentleman, Skate
    lane
Smailes Mrs. Rebecca, Church street
Smith Elizabeth, gentlewoman, Well
    close square
Smith John, gent. Cliffe lane
Stephenson Robert, gentleman, Well
    close square
Steward Mrs. B. Prince's pl. Bagdale
Thompson Wm. gent. Baxtergate
Thompson Mrs. Hannah, Church st.
Thrush John, gent. Church street
Usherwood Wm. sen. gent. Bagdale
Waite Hannah, gentlewoman, Bagdale
Wardale Francis, Esq. Flowergate
Watkins Francis, gent. Bagdale
Watson John, Esq. Spring hill
Watt Mrs. Elizabeth, Cliffe lane
Wilkinson Mrs. Mary, Ropery lane
Willis William, gent. Bagdale
Yeoman Joshua, gent. Church street
Yeoman Miss Mary, New buildings
Young Rev. Geo. A. M. Cliffe lane

#### Academies.

Blackburn Alicia, (Lancasterian) Cliffe
    lane
Groves Rt. (Lancasterian) Cliffe lane
Kirkby John, Cliffe lane
Lister Mary, Little Angel yard, Flow-
    ergate
Lockwood Hannah, Flowergate
Lund Dorothy, Church street
Moffatt Rev. Robert, (classical)
    Church street
Mort Miss Sarah, Flowergate
Robinson Alice, Well yard, Church
    street

Robinson Thos. Linskill square, Baxtergate

Routh John, Routh's buildings

Rutherford Rev. James, (commercial) Skinner street

Seamer Elizabeth & Ann, Baxtergate

Smailes Thomas, Bagdale

Smith Sarah, Church street

Winter Wm. Little Angel yd. Flowergate

Winter Alice, Little Angel yard, Flowergate

### Attornies.

Belcher Henry, (and coroner for the wap. of Whitby Strand) Sandgate

Prestou and Boulby, Grape lane

Stephenson Thos. Flowergate

Walker James, Baxtergate

Wardell John, St. Ann's staith; house, Bagdale

Watson Thomas, Haggersgate

### Auctioneers and Appraisers.

Beaumont Edward, Church street

Hartley David, Baxtergate

Harwood John, West end of the Bridge

Hugill John, Grape lane

Lord Wm. (appraiser) Church street

### Bacon and Ham Factors.

Corner Edward and John, St. Ann's staith

Cowart James, Sandgate

Marwood Thos. (and butter) Flowergate

### Bakers,—Bread, and Ship Biscuit, &c.

Amos James, Church street

Atkinson John, Baxtergate

Atkinson Richard, Church street

Attley Mary, Cliffe lane

Cooke James, Cragg

Dixon John, Church street

Hamilton Joseph, Church street

Mutter James, Haggersgate

Nettleship Thomas, Church street

Readshaw Wm. Church street

Robson Rebecca, Skate lane

Scurr Wm. Baxtergate

Sleightholm Hannah, Church street

Speedy Ralph, Silver street

Stonehouse Thomas, Baxtergate

Tate Robert, Grape lane

### Banks.

Campion Robert and John, (on Sir Wm. Curtis and Co.) Church st.

Frankland John & James Wilkinson, (on Robarts, Curtis, and Co.) Church street

Richardson, Holt, and Co. (on Sir Wm. Curtis & Co.) Flowergate

Sanders Jonathan and Joseph, (on Masterman & Co.) Church street

Simpson, Chapman, & Co.(on Barclay, Tritton, and Co.) Grape lane

### Basket Makers.

Harrison Geo. St Ann's staith

Tate Sarah, Sandgate

### Blacksmiths and Farriers.

Corney Edward, Church street

M'Clachlin James, Flowergate

### Block, Mast, and Pump Makers.

Bovill John, Baxtergate

Hick and Turnbull, Baxtergate

Smales Gideon, Church street

### Boat Builders.

Falkingbridge Wm. Church street

Gale Christopher, Church street

Marshall and Copley, Church street

### Booksellers, Binders, and Stationers.

Those with a * are also Printers.

Bean Benjamin, Church street

*Clark Geo. (& stamp office) Church street

Laybourn Joshua, (binder) Baxter gt.

*Rodgers Richard, Old Market place

### Boot and Shoemakers.

Askwith Wm. St. Ann's staith

Cockburn Wm. New Market place

Cousins John, Church street

Dale Ann, Flowergate

Dalton Thomas, Flowergate

Dinsdale John, St. Ann's staith

Dixon John, Baxtergate

Elder James, Grape lane

Elder Peter, Bridge street

Gibson Henry, Flowergate

Hunter Joseph, Flowergate

Isbister John, Cliffe lane

Jackson James, Cliffe lane

Knaggs Zechariah, Church street

Meadows Henry, Cragg

Newrick Allen, Grape lane

Oates Joseph, Church street

Phillips John, Baxtergate

Robinson Joseph, Church street

Robson Thomas, Church street

Ruddock John, Church street

Summerson Ann, Flowergate

Thompson Christopher, Cliff

Wright John, Church street

Younger Thomas, Church street

### Brass and Iron Founders.

Chapman George, (and engineer) Baxtergate

Lowrie John, St. Ann's staith

Vipond Richard, Baxtergate

### Braziers and Tinsmiths.

Those with a * are also Ship Chandlers, and with a † Ironmongers.

*†Buck Gideon, Grape lane

3 c 3

*†Collier Wm. Baxtergate
Greenwell John, Flowergate
* Lowrie John, St. Ann's staith
*†Nicholson Thomas and Son, Bridge street ..
*†Skelton Richard, Grape lane
*†Wear John, St. Ann's staith

*Brewers and Maltsters.*
Akenhead and Simpson, Bagdale
Ellerby John, Cliffe lane
Stonehouse Geo. Church street

*Bricklayers.*
See Stone Masons.

*Butchers.*
Alderson Wm. New Market place
Alderson Geo. Baxtergate
Brecon Thomas, Flowergate
Coulson Richard, Church street
Cooper Thomas, Baxtergate
Cowart James, Sandgate
Duck Geo. West end of the Bridge
Harwood John, West end of the Bridge
Peacock John, New market place
Robinson Wm. St. Ann's staith
Robinson John, Old market place
Thompson Thomas, Flowergate
Trenholm Thomas, Baxtergate
Weatherill Wm. New market place

*Cabinet Makers.*
Those marked with a * are also Upholsterers
Bennison Wm. Baxtergate
*Burn Wm. Church street
*Cavillier Wm. West end of the Bridge
Dobson Thomas, Church street
*Hezlewood Moses, Flowergate
Hill Thomas, Skate lane
Hubbock Wm. Cragg
*Lord Wm. Church street
Lund Thomas, Church street
Medd Wm. Skinner street
Sedman John, Cliffe lane
Simpson David, Flowergate
Turner Edward, Church street
Weatherill George, Flowergate
Weatherill Joseph, Skinner street
Weatherill Wm. Cliffe lane

*Carpenters,—House and Ship.*
Andrew Edward, Baxtergate
Beaumont and Bovill, Baxtergate
Doughty Wm. Cliffe lane
Greenbury Ralph, Church street
Hick and Turnbull, Baxtergate
Hill Henry, Paradise row, Haggersgt.
Langdale Wm. Baxtergate
Lyth John, (& machine maker) Linskill's square, Baxtergate
Robinson Daniel, Sandgate
Simpson Thomas, Silver street
Smales Gideon, Church street
Terry Richard, Skate lane

Vasey Christopher, Baxtergate
Vasey George, Flowergate
Wright Matthew, Cliffe lane

*Carvers and Gilders.*
Bell John, Haggersgate
Hodgson John, St. Ann's staith

*Cheesemongers.—See Grocers, &c.*

*Chemists and Druggists.*
See also Grocers, &c.
Ripley Richard and John, Baxtergt.
Yeoman Thomas, Bridge street

*Clog and Patten Makers.*
Coward Robert, Church street
Elder James, Grape lane
Summerson Wm. Sandgate
Welch Thomas, Baxtergate

*Clothes Brokers and Dealers.*
Lincoln Ann, Haggersgate
Weir Elizabeth, Cragg
Wherritt Ann, Bridge street

*Confectioners, &c.*
Attley Sarah, Flowergate
Craven John, Church street
Muir Ann, Flowergate
Seaton Ann, Haggersgate
Williams Dorothy, Church street
Young Margaret, Bridge street

*Coopers.*
Anderson Charles, (and dealer in marine stores) Church street
Corner Robert, Bagdale
Donkin Robert, St. Ann's staith
Storme John, Church street; house, Paradise row, Haggersgate

*Corn Millers and Factors.*
Anderson Thomas and Son, Low Stakesby
Burnard Francis, Low Stakesby
Marwood Thomas, Flowergate
Union Mill, New Buildings

*Curriers and Leather Cutters.*
Cail Richard, Church street
Harrison George, Baxtergate
Potts John, Sandgate

*Earthenware Dealers.*
Miller John, Church street
Turner Wm. Church street
Wilson Isabella, Church street

*Fire & Life Insurance Office Agts.*
Atlas, Charles Belcher, Baxtergate
County, Richard Willis, Flowergate
Eagle, Robert Kirby, sen. Cliffe
Globe, Robert Kirby, jun. Cliffe
Guardian, Thos. Lempriere, St. Ann's staith
Newcastle, Geo. Impey, Flowergate
Norwich Union, Thomas Gibson, Flowergate
Phœnix, Thos. Johnson, Baxtergate

Royal Exchange, Geo. Clark, Church
  street
Sun, John Webster, Church street

*Flax Dressers.*

Those with a * are also Flax Spinners.
*Campion Robert, Church street
Chapman J. and W. Church street
Holt John, jun. and Co. Church street
Marshall Salton, Church street
Pennock John, Skate lane
Saunders Jonathan and Joseph, Church
  street
Smith Wm. Sandgate
*Weatherald Henry & Thos. Baxter-
  gate

*Furniture Brokers.*

Dobson Thomas, Church street
Lincoln Ann, Haggersgate
Lord Wm. Church street
Tate Thomas, Sandgate

*Gardeners.*

Bell Edward, Church street
Dawson Wm. at the Abbey
Firth Robert, Baxtergate
Pinder Jonathan, Bagdale
Willison Alexander, (and nurseryman)
  Bridge street

*Glass and China Dealers.*

Argment Thomas, Sandgate
Gardiner Alexander, Sandgate
Hartley Thomas, Church street

*Grocers and Tea Dealers.*

Those with a * are also Cheesemongers, with
  a † Druggists, with a § Spirit Dealers,
  and with a | Tallow Chandlers.
Adams Margaret, (tea) Cliffe lane
*Anderson John, Bridge street
*Anderson Joseph, Haggersgate
*Ayre Mary, Church street
Buck Gideon, (tea) Grape lane
*|Clark John, Sandgate
Close John, St Ann's staith
§Collier Dorothy, Baxtergate
§Craven John, Church street
||Dale Thomas Gallilee, Bridge street
Dickinson Robert, Baxtergate
Easterby M. and A. (tea) Flowergate
Forster Wm. Sandgate
§Foster Thomas, Baxtergate
*||Green and Pennock, Church street
*§Havelock John, Baxtergate
§Heselton George, Church street
*†Hutton H. and Co. New market pl.
Impey Geo. Flowergate
Kirk Stephen, Church street
Johnson Robert, Baxtergate
Lawson Samuel, Church street
§Lindsley Ann, Church street
Lynass George, Flowergate

Morley Wm. Church street
Nettleship John, Flowergate
*Parkinson Emanuel, Baxtergate
§Robinson Dickinson, Flowergate
†§Sanders Jonathan and Jph. Church
  street
†||Sanderson John, Church street
Tate Thomas, Sandgate
Taylor Dorothy, (tea) Church street
||Watson George, Sandgate
*Watt James, Church street
†Weatherald Henry & Thomas, Bax-
  tergate
Willis Mary, (tea) Pier head
Yeoman Knaggs, Flowergate

*Hardware Dealers.*

Bingant Robert, Church street
Langdale Wm. Baxtergate

*Hat Manufacturers and Dealers.*

Those with a * are also Furriers.
Hall Wm. (mfr.) Baxtergate
Hardcastle Peter, (dlr.) Church street
Keirsta Lars, (dlr.) Flowergate
*Kinnersley James, (mfr.) Bridge st.
Lynass Geo. (dlr.) Flowergate
*Terry James, (mfr.) New Market pl.

*Hosiers.*

See also Linen and Woollen Drapers.
Hebron Thomas, Old Market place
Limb Charles, Sandgate
Storer John, Bridge street

*Hotels, Inns, and Taverns.*

Angel Inn, Wm. Yeoman, (posting &
  commercial house) Baxtergate
Bird-in-Hand, Daniel Robinson, Sand-
  gate
Black Bull, James Sly, New Market
  place
Board, Alex. Robinson, Church street
Board, Margery Hill, Baxtergate
Brown Cow, Wm. Boult, St. Ann's
  staith
Buck, Jph. Jackson, St. Ann's staith
Buoy, Joshua Layburn, Baxtergate
Coffee House, Margaret Harrison,
  Grape lane
Cross Keys, Thomas Lund, Church st.
Crown and Thistle, Peter Cowart,
  Baxtergate
Duke of York, John Holmes, Church
  street
Fishing Smack, Michael Milner, Hag-
  gersgate
Fleece, James Whorlton, Church st.
Fleece, George Myers, Church street
Fox, Mark Weighill, Church street
Globe, Geo. Hugill, Sandgate
Golden Lion, John Cooper, Old Mar-
  ket place
Green Tree, Elizabeth Blackburn,
  Baxtergate

Greenland Fishery, John Potts, Church street

Hare and Hounds, Rebecca Appleton, St. Ann's staith

Hope and Anchor, William Tyerman, Pier head

Joiners' Arms, Wm. Hunter, Baxtergate

Jolly Butchers, Ralph Coulson, Church street

Jolly Sailors, John Carter, St. Ann's staith

King's Head, Wm. Noble, Baxtergt.

Little Angel, Wm. Surridge, Flowergate

Lord Nelson, John Marshall, Pier head

Masons Tavern, M. Creaser, Baxtergt.

Neptune, Rt. Peacock, Haggersgate

Old Buoy, Rt. Marshall Church street

Plough, Thos. Foster, Baxtergate

Raffled Anchor, Irvin Anderson, Grape lane

Red Lion, J. Harrison, St. Ann's staith

Rose and Crown, William Edwards, Flowergate

Ship, Wm. Rippon, Church street

Ship, Joseph Wardale, Church street

Ship, Jacob Johnson, Church street

Ship Launch, Peter Cato, Church st.

Ship Launch, John Clark, Baxtergate

Star, Thomas Pierson, Haggersgate

Steam Packet, Widow Erston, Henrietta street

Swan, Wm. Swan, Baxtergate

Wellington, V. Austin, Henrietta st.

Whitby Abbey, Ann Lane, Flowergt.

White Horse, Rd. Lowrie, Church st.

White Horse and Griffin, Thos. Horsman, Church street

York Minster, John Dalton, Grape ln.

*Iron Merchants.*

Barker Joseph, Baxtergate

Clarkson M. Grape lane ; h. Skinner st.

Nicholson Thomas and Son, Bridge street

*Ironmonger.*

See also Braziers and Tinsmiths.

Clarkson M. Grape lane

*Leather Dresser.*

Swales Wm. fellmonger, glover, and breeches maker, W. end of Bridge

*Lightermen.*

Bovill John, Baxtergate

Cato Peter, Church street

Lyons Joseph, Church street

Sawdon Thomas, Church street

*Linen Drapers.*

Campion Robert, Church street

Elgie Hannah, Church street

Hardcastle Peter, Church street

Hebron Thomas, Old Market place

*Linen and Woollen Drapers.*

Those marked thus * are also Hosiers.

*Burnett Wm. & silk mercer, Bridge st.

*Clarkson Wm. Church street

*Frankland, Wilkinson & Co. Church street

Hugill John, Grape lane

*Lawson John, Bridge street

Mellanby Joseph, Flowergate

*Thornhill and Cooper, Church street

*Watson, Woodwark, and Co. West end of the Bridge

*Linen Manufacturers.*

Those marked thus * are Sacking Manfrs.

Campion Robert, Church street

Hardcastle Peter, Church street

Kidd John, Flowergate

*Pennock John, Skate lane

Raine Charles, Baxtergate

Stonehouse Thos. Flowergate

*Weatherald Henry & Thos. Baxtergt.

*Linen Weavers.*

Coverdale George, Haggersgate

Jefferson Isaac, Bagdale

Thoresby Ann, Silver street

*Master Mariners.*

Agar Francis, jun. White hall

Ainsley James, Cliffe lane

Clark Geo. St. Ann's staith

Consitt Robt. Routh's buildings

Coupley Jacob, Cragg

Craig Joseph, Haggersgate

Dunbar John, Flowergate

Dunning Constable, Flowergate

Ellerington Thos. Silver street

Gales Wm. Baxtergate

Gowland Benjamin, New buildings

Harrison F. Paradise row, Haggersgt.

Hay Thomas, Church street

Hunter Thomas, Grape lane

Hutton Wm. Baxtergate

Jackson Thomas, Church street

Johnson John, Stakesby

Kearsley Wm. St. Ann's staith

Mead Wm. Prospect place, Church st.

Middleton John, Prospect pl. Church st.

Mills George, Cragg

Miller John, Church street

Naylor Jas. Prospect row, Church st.

Nicholson John, Haggersgate

Nicholson Thos. Prince's pl. Bagdale

Read James, Prospect pl. Church st.

Richardson John, Haggersgate

Robinson Alexander, Church street

Scholey Edw. Well yard, Church st.

Spence Geo. Baxtergate

Stockhill Paul, Skinner street

Thompson James, Cragg

Tindall Joseph, Prospect pl. Church st.

Willis George, Church street

Womfrey John, Pier head

Wood Wm. Baxtergate
Wray George, Ropery lane

*Milliners and Dress Makers.*
Bedlington Jane, Baxtergate
Clark Mary, Flowergate
Coupland Jane & Ann, Church st.
Coupland Mary, Church street
Dunning Elizabeth, Church street
Harrison Isabella, Flowergate
Plowman Mary, Grape lane
Skelton Hannah, Baxtergate
Smith Margaret, Cliffe lane
Taylor Christiana, Skate lane
Vasey Margaret, Flowergate
Wilson Ann, Grape lane

*Musical Instrument Dealers.*
Clark Michael, and paper hanger, Flowergate
Mercer Wm. Baxtergate

*Painters, House, Sign, and Ship.*
Copley Joseph, Church street
Croft George, Baxtergate
Ervin Christiana, Church street
Hastings and Gibson, Pier head
Hick James, St. Ann's staith
Humphrey John, Church street
Jefferson Robert and Joseph, Bennison's yard, Baxtergate
Mead Hannah, Church street
Ripley Wm. Well yard, Church st.
Sanderson Francis, Church street
Trueman George, Bridge street
Williamson Robert, Grape lane

*Pawnbrokers.*
Ainsley Jane Isabella, Cliffe lane
Brown Richard, Flowergate
Cockburn Robert, Church street
Hartley David, Baxtergate
Hugill John, Grape lane

*Perfumers and Hair Dressers.*
Bulmer John, Church street
Castle James, Bridge street
Christie Robert, St. Ann's staith
Hansen Wm. Sandgate
Jefferson John, Baxtergate
Laverack Henry, Church street
Mason Nathaniel, Flowergate
Pannett W. T. St. Ann's staith
Rayne Richard, Old Market place
Redshaw Thomas, Baxtergate
Robinson John, Church street
Souddick Richard, Church street

*Physicians.*
Borton Francis, Skinner street
Campbell William, Flowergate

*Pilots.*
Pilot Office near the Battery.
Turnbull Robert, master, Cragg
Atkinson Joseph, Cragg
Brown Thomas, Haggersgate
Burton Jacob, Cragg
Coulson Edward, Cragg

Douglass Wm. sen. Cragg
Douglass Wm. jun. Cragg
Hodgson Wm. Baxtergate
Marshall John, Pier head
Robinson Richard, Haggersgate
Wilson James, Cragg
Wilson Francis, Cragg

*Plumbers and Glaziers.*
Anderson George, Baxtergate
Andrews ——, Old Market place
Brown Joseph, Grape lane
Dale John, St. Ann's staith
Wilson Edward, Bridge street

*Porter Merchants.*
Cooper John, Old Market place
Corner Edward and John, St. Ann's staith
Gill and Brown, Flowergate
Gowland Michael, Church street
Heselton George, Church street
Hugill John, Grape lane
Johnson Jacob, Church street
Johnson Thomas, Haggersgate
Pearson Thomas, Haggersgate

*Riggers.*
Daniel Wm. Church street
Rippon Thomas, Grape lane

*Rope and Twine Manufacturers.*
Fishburn and Brodrick, Boghall
Gale John, Church street
Gibson George, Spital Bridge
Holt John, jun. and Co. Church st.
Weatherald Henry & Thos. Baxtergt.
Wray John, Ropery lane

*Saddlers, &c.*
Hall Jonathan, Church street
Morley Robt. West end of the Bridge
Wilson Richard, Baxtergate

*Sail Cloth Manufacturers.*
Campion Robert, Church street
Chapman J. and Wm. Church street
Sanders Jonathan & Joseph, Church st.

*Sail Makers.*
Addison Joseph, Church street
Chapman Wm. Baxtergate
Chilton Thos. Church street
Holt John, jun & Co. Church street

*Savings Bank.*
Open every Monday night from 7 to 8 o'clock, Haggersgate, Thomas Watson, attorney, Secretary

*Seedsmen.*
Anderson John, Bridge street
Corner Edw. & John, St. Ann's staith
Green and Pennock, Church street
Hutton H. & Co. New Market place
Marwood Thos. Flowergate
Willison Alexander, Bridge street
Yeoman Knaggs, Flowergate

*Ship Builders.*
Barrick Thos. (dock) Ship yds. Bagdale

Barrick Henry, Ship yards, Bagdale
Barry Robert, ship yards, Bagdale
Brodrick Thomas, (dock) Ship yards, Bagdale
Campion Robt. (dock) Church street
Jackson & Cato, (dock) Church street
Langborne J. & Co. (dock) Ship yds. Bagdale

### Ship Chandlers.

See also Braziers and Tinsmiths.

Clarkson M. and dealer in oils, paints, &c. Grape lane
Morley Wm. Church street

### Ship Insurance Brokers.

Ayre J. M. West end of the Bridge
Benson and Hunter, Church street
Chilton and Hunter, Church street
Gibson Thomas, Flowergate
Johnson Thomas, Haggersgate

### Ship Owners.

The names of a considerable number of Ship Owners will be found under other heads of trades.

Addison Joseph, Church street
Agar Francis, Bagdale
Akenhead Matthew, Bagdale
Appleton Robert, Baxtergate
Ayre John Martin, Well close square
Barker John, Flowergate
Barker Thomas, Skinner street
Barrick Thomas, Ship yards, Bagdale
Barry John, Bagdale
Barry Robert, Bagdale
Barry Thomas, Bagdale
Benson Wm. Church street
Boyes John, Church street
Brodrick Geo. jun. Silver street
Campion Robert, Bagdale
Campion John, Skate lane
Campion Thomas, Skinner street
Chapman Thomas, Church street
Chapman William, Skinner street
Chapman Abel, Stakesby
Chapman Edward, New buildings
Chapman W. S. New buildings
Chilton Harrison, sen. Union place
Chilton Thomas, Church street
Chilton Harrison, jun. 5, New buildings
Clark Robert, Skinner street
Clark Geo. Pier head
Dale Edward, Skinner street
Darley, William, Baxtergate
Davison Christopher, Skinner street
Dixon James, Silver street
Fishburn and Brodrick, Ship yard, Bagdale
Gowland Benjamin, Church street
Harrison Benj. New buildings
Hill William, Sandgate
Hill William, Church street
Holt John, Silver street

Holt Mary, Bagdale
Hunter Benjamin, Silver street
Hunter Thomas, Grape lane
Jameson William, Baxtergate
Johnson John, Baxtergate
Knaggs John, Well close square
Knaggs Zechariah, Church street
Kneeshaw Richard, Baxtergate
Langborne George, 11, New buildings
Langborne Wm. Baxtergate
Langborne Nathaniel, Skinner street
Lawson George, Church street
Martin Jane, Haggersgate
Marwood Thos. New buildings
Miller George, Cragg
Miller Benjamin, Church street
Moorsom Richd. jun. New buildings
Moorsom Richard, sen. Airy hill
Nettleship Edward, Church street
Potter Robert Jones, Bagdale
Richardson Christopher, Field house
Richardson Margt. 16, New buildings
Simpson Thomas, Bagdale
Skinner Wm. New Buildings
Smith George, Church street
Steward John, Flowergate
Storr John, Pier Head
Teasdale Michael, Bagdale
Trattles Seaton, Bagdale
Usherwood William, Bagdale
Usherwood Robert, Bagdale
Ward John, Ropery lane
Willis Richard, Flowergate
Willis George, Church street

### Shopkeepers, Flour, Provision, &c. Dealers.

Blades Jacob, Church street
Carter Elizabeth, Skinner street
Dixon Mary, Church street
Dring Henry, St. Ann's staith
Feaster Thomas, Church street
Fenwick Ann, Church street
Forster Wm. Sandgate
Frank Elizabeth, Flowergate
Garmison Mary, Church street
Goodill Thomas, Church street
Gordon Elizabeth, Church street
Harland Wm. St. Ann's staith
Hartley Thomas, Church street
Jackson Thomas, Church street
Jackson Eliz. Pier head
Knaggs John, Church street
Martin Robert St. Ann's staith
Neesham Jane, Church street
Nightingale Hannah, Church street
Plues Ann, West end of the Bridge
Poskitt Robert, Church street
Potts John, Church street
Robinson Richard, Cliffe lane
Robson Thomas, Church street
Selby John, Cliffe lane
Stephenson Matthew, Haggersgate
Stockton Alice, Church street
Taylor Henry, Baxtergate

Turner Edward, Church street
Walmsley Wm. Baxtergate
Waring John, Haggersgate
Wilson Isabella, Church street
Wilson Ann, Church street
Wren Elizabeth, Church street
Wren Andrew, Church street

*Silk, &c. Dyers.*
Hall J. and clothes cleaner,Haggersgt.
Hunton Thomas, Haggersgate
Ripley Wm, Well yard, Church st.

*Spirit and Wine Merchants.*
Brewster and Belcher, Baxtergate
Brown and Gill, Flowergate
Corner Edward and John, St. Ann's staith
Frankland John & Co. Church street
Hugill John, Grape lane
Hutton Henry, (British wine) New Market place
Marwood Thos. Flowergate
Stonehouse George, Church street
Watson G. (British wines) Sandgate

*Spirit Dealers, Wholesale and Retail.*
*See also Grocers, &c.*
Allinson Ann, Church street
Buck Gideon, (British wines)Grape ln.
Cooper John, Old Market place
Cowart James, Sandgate
Harrison John, St. Ann's staith
Jackson Joseph, St. Ann's staith

*Stone & Marble Masons, & Statuaries.*
Appleton Peter, Church street
Bolton John, Bagdale; h. Flowergate
Close June, Skinner street
Fewster Wm. Skate lane
Fortune Thomas, Haggersgate
Overand Thomas, (slate) Church st.
Robinson Henry, Church street
Stainthorp Richard, Flowergate
Tyerman Wm. Pier head

*Straw Hat Manufacturers.*
Elgie Hannah, Church street
Flintoft Elizabeth, Baxtergate
Foxton Mary, Flowergate
Harrison Isabella, Flowergate
Hayes Ann, Cragg
Lawson Susannah, Bridge street
Maffin Ann, Church street
Plowman Mary, Grape lane
Richardson Mary, Haggersgate
Vasey Margaret, Flowergate
Webster Margaret, St. Ann's staith

*Surgeons.*
Allen Robert, R. N. Flowergate
Boulby Mark, Baxtergate
Brecon John, New Market place
Grenside Wm. 10, New buildings
Loy John Glover, M.D. 4,New buildgs.
Mewburn John, Skinner st.
Ripley Richard, Grape lane
Ripley Richard and John, Baxtergate

Robinson John, Baxtergate

*Tailors.*
Those marked thus * are Woollen Drapers.
*Crawford Archibald & John, Church street
*Davidson James, Church street
Dotchon Thomas, Baxtergate
*Frank James, Flowergate
*Gardiner John, Church street
*Gardiner Thomas, Baxtergate
Harrison John, Ellerby lane
Havelock Thos. and mattrass maker, Baxtergate
Heselton John, Baxtergate
Hornsby Nicholas, Church street
*Jefferson Wm. Baxtergate
Johnson Robert, Baxtergate
*Jordan Leonard, Grape lane
*Keirsta Lars, Flowergate
*Lawson John, Bridge street
Martin Wm. Cliffe lane
Stewart Thomas, Skate lane
*Wilson Thomas, Flowergate

*Tallow Chandlers.*
See also Grocers and Tea Dealers.
Frankland and Wilkinson, Church st.
Gallilee Thomas, Ruswarp
Robinson Wm. St. Ann's staith

*Tanners.*
Frankland John and Co. Church st.
Gallilee Thomas, Ruswarp

*Thread Mfrs. Patent and Shoe.*
Weatherald Henry & Thos. Baxtergt.

*Tile Merchants.*
Beaumont Edw. (& brick) Church st.
Bolton John, (& brick, &c.) Flowergt.
Smales Gideon, Church street

*Timber and Raff Merchants.*
Barker Joseph, Baxtergate
Beaumont and Bovill, Baxtergate
Chapman and Simpson, Church street
Moorsom Richard, Batts
Smales Gideon, Church street

*Tobacco Manufacturers, &c.*
Chapman Wakefield Simpson, Grape lane
Cockburn Wm. (dlr.) Grape lane

*Turners in Wood, &c.*
Foster William, Wheelwright's yard, Church street
Hill Matthew, (& jeweller) Haggersgt.
Wornald William, (jet ornaments) Ruswarp

*Watch and Clock Makers, Silversmiths and Jewellers.*
Morrell John, Baxtergate
Raw Wm. West end of the Bridge
Turnbull Thos. (& lapidary) Bridge st.
Turnbull Wm. Bridge street
Webster John, Church street

*Wharfingers.*
Beaumont Thomas, Church street
Dale and Backhouse, Church street
Jackson Joseph, St. Ann's staith
Marwood and Co. Church street

*Whitesmiths.*
Boanson John, Church street
Chapman Geo. Baxtergate
Lee Wm. Haggersgate
Rose John, Church street
Vipond Richd. & shipsmith, Baxtergt.

*Woollen Draper.*
Milnes Geo. Lund's yard, Church st.

*Miscellany.*
Appleby Thos. clerk, Skinner street
Barker Wm. harbour master, Silver st.
Baxter Thos. worsted mfr. & dealer, Church street
Cartner George, supervisor, Prince's street, Bagdale
Dale Thos. Gallilee, chief constable for the wap. of Whitby Strand, inspector of corn returns & assize of bread, Bridge street
Day Mary, news room, Haggersgate
England Jas. umbrella mfr. Baxtergt.
Fewster John, clerk, Cliffe lane
Greenbury Ralph, parish clerk, Church street
Harrison and Hall, wheelwrights and machine makers, Church street
Hilton Richard, tobacco pipe maker, Baxtergate
Jackson Thos. tide waiter, Prince's place, Bagdale
King Anthony, overlooker, Haggersgt.
Kirby Robert, cashier, Cliff
Lamb Charles, gunsmith, Baxtergate
Lempriere Thomas, accountant, St. Ann's staith
Maxwell Peter, custom warehouse keeper and collector's clerk, Flowergate
Patten Wm. landing waiter, Routh's buildings
Pickernell Francis, engineer, Piers
Piercy John, clerk, Flowergate
Richardson Robert, landing waiter, Grape lane
Smith C. leather seller, Church st.
Swallwell Robt. overlooker, Bagdale
Wilson John, Church street

## COACHES.

*From Wm. Yeoman's, Angel Inn.*
ROYAL MAIL, to York every Sunday, Tu. and Thu. at 12 noon.
UNION, to Guisbro', Stockton, Castle Eden, and Sunderland every Tu. and Sat. at 6 morning.
DILIGENCE to Scarbro' every Sun. & Wed. at ¼ past 8 morning.

## WATER CARRIAGE.

*From T. Marwood and Co.'s wharf.*
Vessels to Newcastle every week, and to London & Hull every fortnight.
*From Dale and Backhouse's wharf.*
Vessels to London every week, during the Summer, & once a fortnight during the Winter.

## STEAM PACKET.

THE TOURIST, from London to Edinbro' every Thursday.—To London every Sunday.
J. Lempriere, agent, St. Ann's staith.

## LAND CARRIAGE.

*Guisbro'*, Thomas Johnson, from the King's Head, Baxtergate, arr. every Mon. and Thu. aft. ret. 9 morn. Tu. and Fri.
*Guisbro'*, John Johnson, from the White Horse, Church street, arr. daily Sat. 9 mg. ret. 4 aft.
*Guisbro'*, Robert Knaggs, from the Jolly Butchers, Church st. every Fri. mg. at 9, ret. Thu. night.
*Lofthouse*, Wm. Boyes, from the White Horse and Griffin, Church street, every Sat. mg. at 10, ret. Fri. aft. at 2.
*Pickering*, Andrew Allen, from Campion's wharf, Church st. every Tu. at 8 mg. ret. Thu. at 10 night.
*Pickering*, Thomas Keddy, from the White Horse and Griffin, Church street, every Sat. at 10 morn. ret. Fri. ½ afternoon.
*Pickering*, George Pearson, from the Jolly Butchers, Church st. every Tu. at 8 mg. ret. Thu. 8 evg.
*Robin Hood's Bay*, John Thompson, from the White Horse & Griffin, Church street, every Sat. aft. at 3, ret. at night.
*Scarbro'*, George Franks, Church st. on Wed. and Sat. at 10 mg. ret. 4 afternoon.
*Scarbro'*, Joseph Wardale, Church st. on Thu. and Sun. at ¼ past 9 mg. ret. same days, 7 evening.
*Staithes*, Thomas Nisbett, from the White Horse and Griffin, every day 3 aft. ret. 10 morning.
*Thornton*, Wm. Humphrey, from the White Horse and Griffin, Church street, every Sat. mg. at 10, ret. Fri. aft. at 2.
*York*, George Pearson, from the Jolly Butchers, Church st. every Tu. 8 mg. ret. 8 Thu. night.
*York*, Andrew Allen, from Campion's wharf, Church st. every Tu. at 8 mg. ret. Thu. night at 10.

*Whitewell*, in the parish of Catterick, wap. of Gilling East, & liberty of Richmondshire; 6¼ mls. E. of Richmond. Pop.99.

WHITEWELL, in the parish of Crambe, and wap. of Bulmer; 6 miles SW. of Malton. This village takes its name from a singular well, the water of which is nearly the colour of milk. Pop. 182.

Letters are taken in at Whitewell Inn, and forwarded by the Mail every day.

Currer Rev. D. R. Whitewell house
Reed T. Whitewell Inn & posting hs.
Tiplady Mary, vict. White Horse

*Whorlton*, (P.) in the wap. & liberty of Langbargh; 6 miles SW. of Stokesley. The church is an ancient structure, dedicated to the Holy Cross; the living is a perpetual curacy, of which the Marquis of Ailesbury, is the patron; the Rev. William Deason, the incumbent, and the Rev. Thos. Brown, the officiating curate. Here are the remains of a castle supposed to have been erected about the time of Richard II.; little now remains of the ancient fortress, except the lofty gateway tower, on which may yet be seen the arms of D'Arcy, Meynell, and Gray; who seem to have been successively lords of this mansion. —Thomas, the son of Edward Bruce, of Kinloss, was created Lord Bruce, of Whorlton, by King Charles I. in whose reign this estate came into the possession of the ancestors of the Marquis of Ailesbury, the present possessor. The church is remarkable for a beautiful ivy tree, which extends its branches along the interior in a curious and ornamental manner, covering nearly the whole of the east window. Population, 583.

WIDDALBFELL, in the parish of Ayswarth, wap. of Hang West; 2 mls. SW. of Hawes.
Lodge Ottiwell, vict. Newby Head

WIGGINTHORPE, in the parish of Terrington, wap. of Bulmer, 8 miles NE. of Easingwold.
Garforth William, Esq.

WIGGINTON, (P.) in the wap. of Bulmer, and liberty of St. Peter's; 4 miles N. of York. Here is a church, peculiar of Alne and Tollerton; the living is a rectory, in the patronage of the crown. Pop. 309.

Dealtry Rev. F. W.
Smith Charles, Esq. Plainville house
Barker Thomas, gentleman
Lockey Mrs. Sarah

*Wilden Grange*, in the parish of Coxwold, wap. of Birdforth, and liberty of Ripon; 7 miles ESE. of Thirsk. Pop. 29.

*Wilton*, in the parish of Ellerburn, wap. & liberty of Pickering Lythe; 4 mls. E. of Pickering. Here is a Chapel of Ease to Ellerburn. Pop. 203.

*Wilton*, (P.) in the wap. & liberty of Langbargh; 3 mls. NW. of Guisborough. At the western extremity of this village, formerly stood the ruins of Wilton castle, the baronial seat of the Bulmers, an ancient family of great reputation, and large possessions in Yorkshire, and the county of Durham, in which family this estate continued for many generations, till Sir John Bulmer, Knight, the last possessor, (of that family) engaging in "The Pilgrimage of Grace," was attainted for high treason; when this, and his other estates were forfeited to the crown. The castle has been re-built according to its ancient order of architecture, by the Hon. John Lowther, M.P. the lord of the manor, by whom it is now occupied. The church, dedicated to St. Cuthbert, is a perpetual curacy, in the gift of the lord of the manor, and the Rev. Thos. Saul is the incumbent. Pop. 405.

*Winton*, in the parish of Sigston, wap. & liberty of Allertonshire; 4 mls. ENE. of Northallerton. Pop. 188.

WITTON EAST, (Within & Without), (P.) in the wap. of Hang West, and liberty of Richmondshire; 2 mls. SE. of Middleham. There is here a very good school chiefly supported by the Marquis of Ailesbury, who is lord of the manor, and who built a school room for its use in 1817, master's salary 60l. per ann. This place is noted for its excellent quarry of free-stone, in great repute for making grind-stones. The parish church, dedicated to St John the Evangelist, is a handsome Gothic structure, built in a commanding situation at the sole expense of the late Earl of Ailesbury, in commemoration of his Majesty George III. having lived to enter on the 50th year of his reign. This church, which was commenced in 1809, was opened on the 29th of March, 1812, under the authority of a license from Dr. Spark, Bishop of Chester, and consecrated on the 1st of Oct. in the same year, by Dr. Law, Bishop of that diocese. The living, which is in the patronage of the Marquis of Ailesbury, is of the value of 100l. a year, exclusive of the vicarage and glebe. Population—parish *within*,444; parish *without*, 303 : total, 747.—Jerveaux Abbey is in this parish, for which see page 463.

Letters arrive 9 morn. return 2 afternoon.

Howson Thomas, gentleman
Jones Rev. Wm. A. M. vicar
King Samuel, gentleman

*Basket Makers,*    *Carpenters, &c.*
Hammond Thos.    Raper Harry
Irwin Wm.    Raper Reuben

3 D

Williams Richard
*Farmers,*
Ambler John
Coates Joseph
Croft Francis
Dixon John, sen.
Dixon John, jun.
Dixon Thomas
Fryer Wm.
Grayham Wm.
Kendray Geo.
Rider John
Shields Isabella

Smallpage John
Topham Thos.
*Grocers,*
Dixon Christopher
Morland Ann
*Shoemakers,*
Longcake Joseph
M'Collah Archibald
Spence Thos.
Towler Matthew
*Tailors,*
Raper James
Wilkinson Wm.

Buckton Christopher, blacksmith
Buckton Peggy, vict. Fox & Hounds
Clarke Christopher, stone cutter and dealer in grind stones
Dixon John, saddler
Leonard Joseph, schoolmaster
Reynolds Ann, vict. Blue Lion
Williams John, parish clerk
Wilson W. & R. common brewers
Wellock Wm. corn miller
Wood John, governor of poorhouse

WITTON WEST, (P.) in the wap. of Hang West, & liberty of Richmondshire; 4 miles WSW. of Leyburn. The church is a modern structure, of which the Rev. Jeffery Wood, is the curate; the living is a perpetual curacy, in the gift of Lord Bolton; here is likewise a Catholic chapel. There is immediately on the north side of this village a beautiful piece of ground, commonly called the Gill, situated on the side of a hill, surrounded by a natural walk or promenade, the highest part of which is finely sheltered by trees arising out of the rocky side of it, which have a grand and imposing appearance. About the centre is a small waterfall, which adds greatly to the beauty of the scene. Population, 519.

Billington Rev. Rbd. Catholic priest
Buckle John, gentleman
Clarkson Joseph, gentleman
Corkson John, gentleman
Cornforth Miss, gentlewoman
Furniss Misses Jane & Ann, gentwmn.
Gelder Richard, gentleman
King Henry, gentleman
Mark John, surgeon
Milner Rev. J. G. officiating curate
Simpson Edward, gentleman
Simpson John, gentleman
Tomlin George, gentleman

*Butchers,*
Close James
Wood Wm.
*Farmers,*
Bowsfield Wm.
Clark Wm.
Clarkson John
Furniss Wm.

Plewes Widow
Tennant Nicholas
*Shoemakers,*
Butterfield Jeffrey
Graham Thos. sen.
Graham Thos. jun.
Sidgwick John
Smith John

*Shopkeepers,*
Chapman Widow
Clark John
Reynold Jane
Sidgwick Elis.
*Slaters,*
Tatham John

Tatham Richard
*Stonemasons,*
Langstaff Wm.
Wilson Robert
*Tanners,*
King James
Tomlin Marmdk.

Barwick Jackson, dancing master
Chapman Thos. carpenter
Fairbank Thos. vict. Duke William
Fairbank Ellz. vict. Star
Hall C. & H. tallow chandlers
Harker Robert, blacksmith
Howe Henry, plumber & glasier
Jackson Wm. fellmonger
Jackson Wm. G. excise officer
Lye Ellen, milliner and dress maker
Milner John, schoolmaster
Sarison Thos. corn miller
Sidgwick James, parish clerk
Tatham Thos. vict. Board
Carriers—Geo. Clark & Geo. Scott, to Richmond ever Sat. John Scott, to Kettlewell daily.

*Wombleton,* in the parish of Kirkdale, wap. of Rydale, partly in the liberty of St. Peter's; 3 miles SW. of Kirkby-Moor-Side. Pop. 265.

*Woodale,* in the parish of Coverham, wap. of Hang West, and liberty of Richmondshire; 7 miles SW. of Middleham.

*Woodale Houses,* in the parish of Lythe, wap. & liberty of Langbargh; 9 miles W. of Whitby.

WOODHALL, in the parish of Aysgarth, wap. of Hang West, & liberty of Richmondshire; 1½ m. E. of Askrigg. Alderson C. A. Esq.

*Farmers,*
Baynes Oswald
Orton Ralph
Robinson Stephen

Snowden Geo.
Tennant Robert
Winn George

Knowles John, vict. King's Head
Pease John, corn miller

*Wool Knowle,* in the parish of Hovingham, and wap. of Rydale; 8 miles from Helmsley.

*Worsall* (High) in the parish of Northallerton, wap. and liberty of Allertonshire; 4 miles SSW. of Yarm. Here is a Chapel of Ease, under the vicar of Northallerton, Rev. John Graves, of Yarm, perpetual curate; the living has lately been endowed with Queen Ann's bounty, the principal inhabitant in this village is Thomas Meynell, Esq. Pop. 154.

WORSALL (Low), in the parish of Kirklevington, wap. and liberty of Langbargh; 3 miles SW. of Yarm. Pop. 217.
Hutchinson & Co. timber merchants
Wilkinson Mrs. Hannah, hall

*Worton*, in the parish of Aysgarth, w. wap. of Hang West; 1 m. SE. of Askrigg.

WRELTON, in the parish of Middleton, wap. and liberty of Pickering Lythe; 2½ miles W. of Pickering.  Pop. 193.

*Blacksmiths,*
Grundy Thos.
Wilson Wm.
*Farmers,*
Boddy Wm.
Cooke A. N.
Frank Francis
Grayson Thos.
Fox Charles, shoemaker
Graystock Thos. vict. White Hart
Hodgson Geo. cooper
Morley Aaron, stone mason
Stead Peter, butcher
Williamson Geo. vict. Red Lion
Wilson Thomas, wheelwright
Wilson Wm. vict. Buck Inn

Hardwick Wm.
Seamer Wm.
Skelton John
Smiddy Geo.
Vickerman Thos.
*Shopkeepers,*
Goodill Wm.
Graystock Thos.

*Wycliffe*, (P.) " the cliffe by the water" is in the wap. of Gilling West, and liberty of Richmondshire; 5 miles SE. of Barnard Castle. The church is an ancient edifice, re-built in the reign of Edward III. The living is a rectory, in the patronage of the lord of the manor, but the patrons being Catholics it has been repeatedly presented by the University of Cambridge; the incumbent is the Rev. John Headlam, who resides in the rectory house at Thorpe. Here, it is said, that John Wycliffe, the reformer, was born; and Dr. Thomas Zouch, the late rector of this parish, has presented an original picture of this Morning Star of the Reformation, tho' he says, was a native of this parish, to the rectors of Wycliffe, as an heirloom. Leyland says, that John Wickliffe *hæreticus*, was born at Spreswell, near Richmond; and that immediate neighbourhood is Willeliff pronounced exactly like the reformer's name, which Wycliffe is not. At all events the dispute is only about a few miles, and the claim of Yorkshire and even of Richmondshire to the birth of the Father of the Reformation is undisputed.* Pop. 152.

*Wycomb*, in the parish of Old Malton, and wap. of Rydale; 2½ miles NE. of Malton.

WYKEHAM, (P.) in the wap. and liberty of Pickering Lythe; 7 miles SW. of Scarborough, situated on the high road from Malton to York. The parish church, dedicated to St. Michael and St. Mary, is a neat and commodious structure, having been repaired and embellished by the liberality of the late Richard Langley, Esq.; the living is curacy, in the patronage of Mr. Hutchins,

*Dr. Whitaker's Richmondshire, p. 198.

and the Rev. John Cayley, is the incumbent. At this place was formerly a priory, of which some venerable Gothic ruins remain. It was founded by Pagan Fitz Osbert de Wykeham, about the year 1153, for nuns of the Cistercian order. The mansion-house, which is near the ruins of the abbey, and a little to the westward of the village, is an elegant modern building, and the plantations are judiciously dispersed. Pop. 582.

Langley Hon. Mrs. D. abbey
Pearson Henry, gentleman

*Farmers,*
Brown Moses
Hall Megginson
Hall Wm.

Glaves Edward
Pennock John
Simpkin Thos.
Webster Thos.

Fields Wm. shoemaker
Hodgson Robert, schoolmaster
Jowsey Richd. wheelwright & joiner
Marshall Peter, chief constable
Sharp Richard, vict. Black Bull
Troutsdale Wm. tailor

YAFFORTH, in the parish of Danby Wiske, wap. of Gilling East, & liberty of Richmondshire; 1½ m. W. of Northallerton. Pop. 149.

Hood William, Esq.

*Farmers & Yeomen,*
Bailey Joseph
Grafton John
Hood John
Haw Michael, vict. Board

Masterman John
Moses Wm.
Ward Leonard
Webster John

## YARM, (P.)

In the wap. and liberty of Langbargh; 4 miles from Stockton, 15 from Guisborough, 16 from Northallerton, and 44 from York. The town is situated on a low peninsula, and is nearly surrounded by the river Tees, which winds round in the form of a horse shoe, and is here navigable for vessels of sixty tons burthen. The main street runs north and south and is very spacious. There is not much trade, and no manufacture of any importance. The commerce in the place consists principally in corn, flour, cheese, butter, and bacon, which are shipped hence to London. A great deal of salmon is caught in the Tees, and this place partakes with Stockton in the advantage of the fishery. The market day at Yarm is on Thursday, but from the vicinity of this place to the rising town and port of Stockton, it had considerably declined, but is again reviving owing to the erection of several corn mills in the town and neighbourhood. The fairs, of which there are four annually, are on the Thursday before the 6th of April; on Ascension Day; on the 2d of August; and on the 19th and 20th of October. The fair of the 19th of October is for horned cattle and horses, and that on the following day for sheep and cheese. The October fair is one of the most considerable in the north of England, and brings a great influx of money into the town and its vicinity. Some idea of the extent of the business done at it may be formed from the subjoined return of the number of waggons and carts laden with cheese, exposed for sale that day for four successive years:—

On the 20th of Oct. 1818 ...... 359 ⎫
.................... 1819 ...... 367 ⎬ waggons and carts
.................... 1820 ...... 383 ⎪
.................... 1821 ...... 329 ⎭

Averaging about a ton and a half each, so that five hundred tons may be taken as the quantity sold, at each of these fairs, besides large supplies which are purchased by the merchants about the same time in the neighbourhood, and which never come into the fair. The new iron railway from Stockton to Darlington, and from thence to the collieries near Auckland, passes within a mile of Yarm, and a branch is completed from the main line to bring coals, lime, &c. down nearly to the bridge, which promises great advantages.

Owing to the peninsular situation of this town and to its slight elevation above the bed of the river, it is very liable to floods, the most memorable of which are those of the 17th of February, 1753, and the 16th and 17th of November, 1771. The inundation of 1753, was occasioned by a sudden thaw on the western hills, which laid the town seven feet deep under water in the higher parts, and which swept away great quantities of furniture, wares and live stock without occasioning the loss of any lives. The flood of 1771, at the time of the eruption of the Solway Moss in Cumberland, was more fatal and tremendous, the water in some parts of the town rose upwards of twenty feet in perpendicular height, and many of the inhabitants were taken in boats from the roofs of their houses: a great quantity of property and some lives were lost, and many more must have perished inevitably had they not been preserved by the active humanity and timely assistance of the people of Stockton and the neighbouring villages. Similar, though less awful visitations have taken place since, and in the flood of the 3d of February, 1822, the water was seven feet deep in the main street of the town.

To abate the violence of these frequent inundations, the bridge of five arches, built by Walter Skirlaw, Bishop of Durham, in the year 1400, has undergone several important alterations; the arch to the north has

been made more capacious and built in a semi-circular form, and the bridge itself has been widened and rendered a substantial structure. In 1805, an elegant iron bridge consisting of one arch one hundred and eighty feet span, cast by Messrs. Walkers and Co. of Masbrough, near Rotherham, was erected here, but owing to some defect in the abutments it unfortunately fell down about midnight on the 12th of January, 1806, when it was just on the point of being opened. This bridge is stated by Mr. Graves, in his history of Cleveland, to have cost 8000*l.* and the weight of iron contained in it was 250 tons.

The parish church of Yarm, dedicated to St. Mary Magdalen, stands at the west side of the town, and was rebuilt in 1730.— The exterior is plain and rather homely, but the interior is much admired for its neatness and good order; it is, however, chiefly remarkable for a window of painted glass, beautifully executed, by Pecket, in which is exhibited a full length figure of Moses, delivering the law on Mount Sinai. This living formerly was a rectory, but it is now only a perpetual curacy, of which the Archbishop of York is the patron. The Methodists, the Independents, the Catholics, and the Primitive Methodists, have each a chapel here, and the Society of Friends have their Meeting-house.

There is here an ancient Free Grammar School, founded and endowed in the time of Queen Elizabeth, by Thomas Conyers, of Egglyscliffe, in the county of Durham, and the benefits of which have been very essentially extended by the liberality of the late Wm. Chaloner, Esq. A National school, capable of containing 100 boys and girls, was built in 1816, by subscription, and is supported by voluntary contributions.

It appears, from Tanner's *Notitia*, that there was, " here an ancient hospital, dedicated to St. Nicholas, founded by some of the family of *Brus*, before the year 1186," which continued till the dissolution, but not a vestige of it now remains, and even the site of it is unknown. There was also a house of Blackfriars, said to have been founded by Peter de Brus the second, who died in 1240, but it has disappeared, and a commodious mansion has been erected upon the spot, called the Friargate, now the seat of Thomas Meynell, Esq. the grounds of which are delightful, and extend about a mile along the banks of the Tees. The population of the town has made a trifling advance during the last 10 years; in 1811 it amounted to 1431, and it now amounts to 1504, as appears from the parliamentary returns just published.

## POST-MASTER—MARSHALL STONEHOUSE.

| Places from whence Letter bags are recvd. | Distance. | Postage. | Arrival of Mails. | Departure of Mails. |
|---|---|---|---|---|
| London............ | 237 | 12d. | 2 o'clock morn. | 5 afternoon. |
| York.............. | 43 | 7 | Ditto. | Ditto. |
| Thirsk............ | 20 | 5 | Ditto. | Ditto. |
| Stockton.......... | 4 | 4 | 5 afternoon. | 2 morning. |
| Sunderland ....... | 31 | 7 | Ditto. | Ditto. |
| South Shields ..... | 38 | 7 | Ditto. | Ditto. |

### DIRECTORY.

Flounders Benjamin, Esq.
Fowler David Burton, Esq.
Meynell Thomas, Esq. Fniarage
Robinson Marshall, Esq. barrister
Waldy John, Esq.

Bradley Rev. John, Catholic minister
Cairns J. agent to T. Meynell, Esq.
Deuxelle George Perrot, gentleman
Flounders Mary, gentlewoman
Graves Rev. John, curate, and author of the History of Cleveland
Greame J. E. gentleman
Heslop John, gentleman
Meynell Miss, gentlewoman
Middleton R. M. gentleman
Nightingale Ann, gentlewoman
Overton Mrs. W. gentlewoman
Passman Mary, gentlewoman
Patten Masterman, yeoman
Robinson Mrs. S. gentlewoman
Taylor Mary, gentlewoman
Widdell Elizabeth, gentlewoman

*Academies and Schools.*
Clawson Thomas, (day)
Endowed Grammar, Rev. J. Graves
Longhead Jane, (day)
National, Wm. Board & Mary Stockton
Prince Jane, (day)
Rowell Mary, (day)
Taylor Jane, (day)
Weddell Elizabeth, (day)
Wright Dorothy, (day)

*Agents, Particular and General.*
Miles Richd. (for purchasing pig lead)
Stonehouse Christopher, (to Guardian Life and Fire Insurance Office)

*Attornies,*
Driver Wm.
Garbutt Wm.
*Auctioneers,*
Perkins W. J. K.
Smith John
*Bakers,*
Blakelock John
Nettleship John
Tate Thomas
Wiseman Stephen

*Blacksmiths,*
Smelt Newark
Spence John
Stainsby Mark
Wilson Wm.
Wright John
*Boot & Shoemakers,*
Burn Stephen
Calvert Thomas
Fearnley John
Loftus Thomas
Lynas John

Warwick Christ.
Willans Wm.
*Brick & Tile Mfrs.*
Dale Wm.
Greathead C.
*Bricklayers,*
Bainbridge Michael
Johnson Anthony
Johnson Robert
Weddell Thos.
*Butchers,*
Cowl George
Harker Matthew
Knowles Robert
Laidler Joseph
Leng Thomas
Wastell Thomas
*Butter, &c. Factors,*
Brittain Geo.
Emmitt & Wastell, (ham)
Miles Thomas
Reeds John
Walton Geo.
*Clock, &c. Makers,*
Sherwood James
Sherwood Thos.
Stockton Francis
*Coopers,*
Fowler John
Martin John
Stainsby Ralph
Suggitt Robert
*Corn Factors,*
Appleton Richard
Barras John
Brittain George
Emmitt & Wastell
Fawell Thomas
Miles Thomas
Reed John
*Corn Millers,*
Appleton Richard
Emmitt & Wastell
Fidler Wm.
Fidler John
Garbutt Wm.
*Curriers, &c.*
Kay Matthew
Lister and Merryweather

Terry Christopher
*Druggists,*
Dod Thomas
Jackson Wm.
Spence John
*Farmers,*
Cairns Jeremiah
Flounders Joshua
Hall Isaac
Mawlam Wm.
Maynard Richard
Stonehouse M.
Terry Christopher
*Farriers,*
Barker Francis
Wilson Wm.
*Flax Dresser,*
Burdon John
*Gardeners,*
Hedley Robert
Lynas John
Rowell Dennis
*Grocers,*
Appleton Richard
Armstrong Thos.
Baker John
Dod Thomas
Jackson Wm.
Leighton Henry
Martin John
Reed F. Cuthbert
Spence John
Taylor Jane, (tea)
Temple Thomas
Vallans Isabella
Wild George
Wilkinson John
*Hair Dressers,*
Muir Andrew
Potter George
*Ironmongers,*
Stockton Francis
Todd James
*Joiners,*
Pape Richard
Smith James
Smith John
*Linen, &c. Drapers,*
Appleton Richard
Davison Thomas
Jackson James

Leighton Henry
Reed F. Cuthbert
Wigham Cuthbert, Johnson Robert

*Maltsters & Brewers*
Driver Wm.
Stonehouse Christ.

*Milliners,*
Close Rebecca
Danby Harriot
Jackson Mary
Kingston Jane
Orton Jane

*Plumbers & Glaziers,*
Barras John
Sherwood Henry

*Porter Dealers,*
Crisp George
Walton George

*Saddlers,*
Greathead John
Reed John
Todd James

*Seedsmen,*
Appleton Richard
Dod Thomas
Jackson Wm.
Spence John

*Shopkeepers,*
Blakelock John
Braithwaite Christ.
Brown Eliz.
Fortune Thomas
Hill Elizabeth
Hind Wm.
King James
Oliver John

*Spirit and Wine Merchants,*
Crisp Geo. (spirit)
Stonehouse M.
Walton George, (dealer)

*Stone Masons,*
Johnson Anth.

*Straw Bonnet Mkrs.*
Burn Mary
Close Rebecca
Orton Jane

*Surgeons, &c.*
Dale John
Green Geo. M.D.
Jameson Anthony
Muir J. S.
Young Robert

*Turners,*
May Matthew
M'Naughton Duncan & Son

*Tailors,*
Bradley Michael
Crisp Geo.
Davison Geo.
Todd Thos. sen.
Todd Thos. jun.

*Timber and Mahogany Merchant,*
Miles Richard

*Turners & Braziers,*
Barras John
Sherwood Henry

*Tobacco Pipe Mkrs.*
Marshall Robert
Roe John

*Weavers, (Linen)*
Clark Robert
Dowson Stephen
Dunning Joseph

*Welch Slate Mert.*
Miles Richard

*Wheelwrights,*
Butterwick Thos.
Harrison Robert
Henderson John
Johnson Wm.

*Inns and Taverns.*
Black Bull, Wm. Temple
Coopers' Arms, R. Stainsby
Crown, John Phillips
Dragoon, Thomas Marcer
George and Dragon, Francis Staples, posting-house, and excise office
Golden Fleece, Joseph Laidler
Green Tree, Thomas Mawlam
Greyhound, Robert Hull
Ketton Ox, Thomas Wastell
Ship, Robert Wastell
Three Tuns, George Walton
Tile Shades, W. Kilvington
Union Arms, Anthony Johnson

*Miscellany.*
Appleton R. sub-distributor of stamps
Bell Francis, wood turner
Bradley Thos. hackney cartman

Dod Thomas, tallow chandler
Graham James, governor of the workhouse
Hardy Wm. cow keeper
Harrison M. skinner & woolstapler
Hodgson J. rope maker & sacking mfr.
Holmes Mary, glover
Hugill Jonathan, carter & cow keeper
Long John, toll master
Pape Richard, clerk of the parish
Perkins W. J. K. agricultural implement maker
Reed John, salt merchant
Robinson W. organist & music master
Rowell John, pig jobber
Stainsby Ralph, sworn meter for corn
Windross James, painter

## COACH.

The MAIL, from the Greyhound Inn, to London at 5 afternoon, to South Shields at 2 morning.

## LAND CARRIAGE.

*John Baker and William Hutchinson,* to Darlington on Monday, and Stockton on Wed.

*James Proctor,* fishmonger, and carrier from Leeds to Hartlepool, arr. at the Greyhound, on Tu. and Sat. and ret. on Wed. and Sunday.

*Ralph Reed,* to Darlington on Mon.; to Stockton on Tu. Wed. Thu. & Fri.; and to Stokesley on Sat.

**Yearsley,** in the parish of Coxwold, and wap. of Birdforth; 5 miles NE. of Easingwold. Pop. 170.

*Farmers,*
Brown Anthony
Dawson Richard
Easton Wm.
Hornby John
Lund Benjamin
Rutter John
Skelton Robert
Wetherill John, Park

Gowland Marm. vict. Wynn's Arms
Hornby John, tailor & shopkeeper
Wilson Wm. shoemaker

**Yerby,** in the parish of Kirkleatham, wap. and liberty of Langbargh; 4½ miles NNW. of Guisborough.

**Yore,** in the parish and township of Aysgarth, wap. of Hang West, and liberty of Richmondshire; 4 miles E. of Askrigg. Directory included with Aysgarth.

**York Gate,** in the parish of Wath, wap. of Halikeld, and liberty of Richmondshire; 5 miles NNE. of Ripon.

**Youlton,** in the parish of Alne, and wap. of Bulmer; 5 miles SSW. of Easingwold. Pop. 56.

# PEERS OF PARLIAMENT,

## *WHO HAVE SEATS IN THE COUNTY OF YORK.*

### With the Date of their Creation.

---

*The East-Riding is indicated by a \* ; the North-Riding by a † ; and the West-Riding by a ‡.*

---

**1807** Right Reverend and Honourable Edward Venables Vernon, D.C.L. Lord ARCHBISHOP OF YORK, Primate of England, and Lord High Almoner to the King; *Bishopthorpe.*

**1483** ‡Bernard Edward Howard, DUKE OF NORFOLK, Earl of Surrey and Arundel, Hereditary Earl Marshal of England, Premier Peer and Earl, F. R. S. S. A. *Sheffield Manor,* (dismantled.)

**1694** †George Wm. Frederick Osborne, DUKE OF LEEDS, Marquis of Caermarthen, Lord Lieutenant of the North-Riding of Yorkshire, Governor of the Isles of Scilly, Ranger of Richmond-Forest, and Constable of Middleham Castle; *Hornby Castle and Kiveton Park.*

**1694** ‡Wm. Spencer Cavendish, DUKE OF DEVONSHIRE, Marquis of Hartington, Lord Lieutenant and Custos Rotulorum of Derbyshire, and High Steward of Derby; D.C.L. *Bolton Abbey,* (Sporting Residence.)

**1793** ‡Francis Charles Seymour Conway, MARQUIS OF HERTFORD, Earl of Yarmouth, Lord Conway and Killulta in Ireland, Warden of the Stannaries; *Temple Newsam,* (at present enjoyed by the Dowager Marchioness.)

**1816** ‡Francis Rawdon Hastings, MARQUIS OF HASTINGS, Earl Rawdon, late Governor General of India, Constable and Chief Governor of the Tower of London, Lord Lieutenant and Custos Rotulorum of the Tower Division, a General and Colonel of the 27th Regiment, (Earl of Moira, in Ireland) K.G. K.G.H. F.R.S. F.S.A. and M.R.I.A.; *Rawdon Hall,* (dilapidated.)

**1821** †Charles Bruce Brudenell Bruce, MARQUIS OF AILESBURY, Earl Bruce, K.T.; *Jerveaux Abbey* (occasionally.)

**1628** ‡Sackville Tufton, EARL OF THANET, Lord Tufton, hereditary Sheriff of Westmoreland; *Skipton Castle.*

**1661** †Frederick Howard, EARL OF CARLISLE, Viscount Morpeth, K.G.; *Castle Howard.*

1690 ‡Richard Lumley Saunderson, EARL OF SCARBOROUGH, Viscount Lumley, (Viscount Lumley in Ireland) *Sandbeck Park.*

1711 ‡William Legge, EARL OF DARTMOUTH, Viscount Lewisham; *Woodshall Hall.*

1746 ‡Wm. Wentworth Fitzwilliam, EARL FITZWILLIAM, Viscount Milton, High Steward of Hull, Custos Rotulorum of the Soke of Peterborough and Recorder of Higham-Ferrers, (Earl Fitzwilliam in Ireland) D.C.L. ; *Wentworth House.*

1749 *George O'Brien Wyndham, EARL OF EGREMONT, Lord Cockermouth, Lord Lieutenant and Custos Rotulorum of Sussex, F.R. A.S. *Wressle Castle,* (dilapidated.)

1754 †William Harry Vane, EARL OF DARLINGTON, Viscount Barnard, Lord Lieutenant and Vice-Admiral of the County Palatine of Durham; *Newton House,* (Sporting Residence.)

1712 *Henry Willoughby, LORD MIDDLETON, High Steward of the Royal Town of Sutton Coldfield; *Birdsall Hall.*

1812 †Henry Phipps, EARL OF MULGRAVE, Viscount Normanby, an elder Brother of the Trinity House, Lord Lieutenant, Custos Rotulorum, and Vice Admiral of the East Riding of Yorkshire, a General and Colonel, in the 31st Regiment, Governor of Scarborough, G.C.B. F.S.A. (Lord Mulgrave in Ireland); *Mulgrave Castle.*

1812 ‡Henry Lascelles, EARL OF HAREWOOD, Viscount Lascelles, Lord Lieutenant and Custos Rotulorum of the West Riding of Yorkshire ; *Harewood House.*

1448 ‡Wm. Stourton, LORD STOURTON ; *Allerton Park.*

1553 ‡Kenneth Alexander Howard, LORD HOWARD OF EFFINGHAM, a Lieutenant General and Colonel of the 70th Regiment, G.C.B. K.T.S. *Thundercliffe Grange.*

1761 ‡Thomas Philip Weddell Robinson, LORD GRANTHAM, Lord Lieutenant and Custos Rotulorum of Bedfordshire, Colonel of the Yorkshire Hussars, F.S.A. *Newby Hall.*

1776 ‡Edward Harvey Hawke, LORD HAWKE ; *Towton Hall,* and *Womersley House.*

1782 ‡William Fletcher Norton, LORD GRANTLEY, F.S.A. ; *Grantley Park.*

1794 †Lawrence Dundas, LORD DUNDAS, LL.D. and A.A. *Aske Hall* and *Markse Hall.*

1796 ‡John Christopher Burton Dawnay, LORD DAWNAY, (Viscount Downe in Ireland ;) *Danby Lodge* and *Cowick Park.*

1797 †William Orde Powlett, LORD BOLTON; *Bolton Hall.*

1797 ‡Thomas Lister, LORD RIBBLESDALE; D.C.L. *Gisburn Park* and *Malham Water.*

1816 †Algernon Percy, LORD PRUDHOE, only brother of the Duke of Northumberland, a Captain in the Royal Navy; *Stanwick Park.*

## IRISH PEERS.

1761 †John Delaval Carpenter, EARL OF TYRCONNEL, Viscount Carlingford; *Kiplin Park.*

1766 ‡John Savile, EARL OF MEXBROUGH, Viscount Pollington, *Methley Park.*

1777 †Morris Robinson, LORD ROKEBY, *Littlebourn House.*

1783 *Lowther Augustus John Pennington, LORD MUNCASTER, a Cornet in the 10th Dragoons; *Water Hall.*

1797 *Beaumont Hotham, LORD HOTHAM, a Major in the Army; M.P. for Leominster, *South Dalton Park.*

1819 ‡*John Francis Cradock, LORD HOWDEN, a General, and Colonel of the 43d Regiment, G.C.B. and K.C.B. *Grimston* and *Spaldington Hall.*

## BARONETS

### WHO HAVE SEATS IN THE COUNTY OF YORK,

ALPHABETICALLY ARRANGED, WITH THE DATE OF THEIR CREATION.

1738 ‡Sir George Armytage, D.C.L. Kirklees Hall.

1813 ‡Sir John Beckett, Gledhow, Leeds.

1618 *Sir Francis Boynton, Burton Agnes.

1661 †Sir George Cayley, Brompton House.

1814 †Sir Thomas Clifford Constable, Burton Constable

1661 ‡Sir George Cooke, Wheatly Hall

1778 ‡Sir Joseph Copley, Sprotborough

1818 †Sir John Croft, K.T.S. F.R.S. D.C.L. Cowling Hall.

1713 ‡Sir Edward Dodsworth, Newland Park

1619 †Sir William Foulis, Ingleby Manor

1660 †Sir Thomas Frankland, F.R. and L.S. Thirkleby Park

1641 ‡Sir Henry Goodrick, Ribston Hall.

1662 †Sir Bellingham Reginald Graham, Norto
1808 ‡Sir James Graham, F.S.A. M.P. Kirkstall
1805 General Sir Charles Green, Milnrow
1741 ‡Sir Henry Carr Ibbetson, Denton Park.
1781 ‡Sir William Amcotts Ingilby, Ripley,
1795 *Sir John Vanden Bempde Johnstone, Ha
1812 ‡Sir John Lister Kaye, Denby Grange.
1665 †Sir Henry Maire Lawson, Brough Hall.
1660 *Sir Thomas Legard, Ganton Hall.
1716 ‡Sir William Mordaunt Milner, Nun Appl
1611 ‡Sir Philip Musgrave, M.P. Bramham Big
1663 †Sir William Henry Pennyman, Ormesby
1813 ‡Sir Joseph Radcliffe, Campsall.
1689 ‡Sir John Ramsden, Byram.
1779 Sir William Rumbold, Ferrand.
1641 *Sir William Strickland, Boynton Hall.
1783 *Sir Tatton Sykes, F.S.A. Sledmere and Se
1628 ‡Sir Thomas Vavasour, Haslewood.
1801 *Major General Sir Henry Maghull M
      Melbourne.
1802 ‡Sir Taylor Woollaston White, Walling W
1660 ‡Sir Edmund Mark Winn, Acton Hall.
1778 *Sir George Wombwell, Wombwell.
1783 ‡*Sir Francis Lindley Wood, Hemsworth I

## BARONETS OF NOVA SCOTIA

1635 ‡Sir William Pilkington, Chevet Hall.
1638 ‡Sir Thomas Turner Slingsby, Scriven Hall

# SEATS OF THE GENTRY

## OF THE

## AINSTY OF THE CITY AND COUNTY OF YORK AND OF THE EAST AND NORTH RIDINGS.

*(For the Seats of the Peers and Baronets see preceding Lists.)*

To avoid swelling this List, Gentlemen's Villas in the Neighbourhood of large Towns are not inserted here, but will be found subjoined to the Name of their Occupiers, under their appropriate Heads.

The following enumeration comprehends a complete List of the Acting Magistrates of the East and North Ridings of Yorkshire, each of whom is indicated by an Asterisk to the left, and figures to the right of the line, the latter showing the year when the oath of qualification was taken; and to render the Magistrates' List complete, a few places, not situated in the County, are inserted.

Where a † is used it denotes a Magistrate of the Liberty of St. Peter's.

## AINSTY.

Acomb, 2¼ m. W. of York, William Hale, Conyers Gale, George Lloyd Robert Anderson, John Barstow, and Kirby Torre, Esqrs. Misses Percival and Misses Ramsay

Acomb Grange, 3 m. W. of York, John Jolly, Esq.

Askam Bryan, 4 m. SW. of York, Admiral D'Arcy Preston

Askam Hall, 5 m. SW. of York, Robert Swann, Esq.

Bilbrough, 5¼ m. SW. of York, Matthew Todd, Esq.

Bishopthorpe, 3 m. S. of York, the Rev. W. V. Vernon, A. M.

†Bolton Percy, 3 m. SE. of Tadcaster, Rev. Robert Markham, B. D. Archdeacon of York

Bolton Lodge, 3 m. SE. of Tadcaster, Mrs. C. Clement

Boston, (w. R.) 3¼ m. SE. of Wetherby, the Hon. Edward Marmaduke Stourton, and George Wilkinson, Esq.

*Chesnut Grove, 3 m. SE. of Wetherby, George Strickland, Esq. 1821

Colton, 4 miles ENE. of Tadcaster, Christopher Morritt, Esq.

†Healaugh Hall, 1 mile N. of Tadcaster, Benjamin Brooksbank, Esq.

Holgate, 1 m. SW. of York, Lindley Murray, Esq.

Hutton Hall, 6 m. N. of Tadcaster, Mrs. Willoughby

Marston, 6 m. N. of Tadcaster, the Rev. Dr. Crigan

Middlethorpe Manor House, 1¼ m. S. of York, Christopher Brearey, Esq.

Middlethorpe Hall, 1¼ m. S. of York, Dowager Lady Stourton

Oxton Hall, 1 m. SE. of Tadcaster, J. W. Clough, Esq.

Poppleton Villa, 4 m. NW. of York, Isaac Spencer, Esq.

Skewkirk, 8 m. N. of Tadcaster, Henry Tennant, Esq.

Thorp Arch, 3 m. SE. of Wetherby, Colonel Randal Gossip and the Rev John Baker

Wighill Park, 4 m. N. of Tadcaster, Richard York, Esq.

## EAST RIDING.

Aldbrough, 8 m. NE. of Hedon, John Hall, gentlema:

Allerthorp, 2 m. SW. of Pocklington, (unoccupied).

Anlaby, 5 m. W. of Hull, William Voase and John Ba

Arram Hall, 3 m. NW. of Hornsea, Thomas Bainton,

*Bainton, 6 m. SW. of Driffield, John Bell, D.D. 1801

*Barmston, 3 m. S. of Bridlington, Rev. John Gilby, I

Bell Hall, 5 m. S. of York, Hewby John Baines, Esq.

Benninghelme Grange, 7 m. E. of Beverley, John Ha

Bessingby Hall, 1½ m. SW. of Bridlington, Harrington

*Beverley, Wm. Beverley, 1800, R. M. Beverley, 1820

  1813, Rev. J. Coltman, A. M. 1817, and Rev. (

Billing's Hill, 3 m. NW. of Hornsea, James Hopkinso

Bishop Burton, 8 m. W. of Beverley, Richard Watt d

Blacktoft, 7 m. SE. of Howden, William Hotham, Es

Bolton Hall, 3 m. NW. of Pocklington, John Preston,

Borees Hill, 2 m. S. of Hedon, Mrs. Susannah Stovin

*Braffords Hall, 7 m. W. of Hull, Robert Osborne, E

Brinkworth, 6 m. ESE. of York, Alexander Mather, I

Burnby, 2½ m. SE. of Pocklington, Mrs. B. Ponsonby

Burton Constable, 5 m. N. of Hedon, George Clifford,

Camerton, 3 m. SE. of Hedon, Edward Ombler, Esq.

Catwick, 7½ m. NE. of Beverley, Godfrey Park, Esq.

Cave Castle, ½ m. NW. of South Cave, Henry B. Bar

Cherry Burton, 3 m. NW. of Beverley, David Robins

Cottingham, 5 m. NW. of Hull, John William Hentl

  William Moxon, Esqrs. William Watson Will

Cottingham Castle, 1 m. W. of Cottingham, Thomas

*Doncaster, (w. a.) Edmund Denison, Esq. 1817

Dunnington Lodge, ½ m. E. of York, Edward Prest, I

Eastfield House, 4 m. E. of York, H. M. Baines, Esq.

Eddlethorp, 4 m. S. of Malton, Joseph Field, Esq.

Ella (Kirk), 5½ m. WNW. of Hull, Joseph Sykes,

  Esqrs. and Mrs. (Jane) Williamson

Ella (South), 5 m. W. of Hull, John Broadley, Esq.

*Ella (West), 6 m. W. of Hull, Rev. Richard Sykes, /

Elvington Manor House, 7 m. ESE. of York, Miss Che

*Escricke Hall, 6 m. SSE. of York, Bielby Thompson

Etton, 4 m. NW. of Beverley, Dowager Lady Lega

  Grimstone

Everingham Park, 5 m. W. of Market-Weighton, Mrs.

Fangfoss Hall, 3½ m. NW. of Pocklington, Cholmley C

Ferriby, (North) 4½ m. SE. of South Cave, Henry

  Egginton, and George Schonswar, Esqrs. an

  and Ralph Turner, gentlemen

Firby Hall, 6 m. SSW. of Malton, Rev. Thomas Harr

Fulford, (Gate) 1½ m. SSE. of York, Thomas Wilson

  Richardson, John Wormald, and William Ell

Fulford, (Water) 2½ m. S. of York, Thomas Key, Esq.
Garrow Hill, 1 m. SE. of York, Henry Bland, Esq.
*Goodmanham, 1½ m. NNE. of Market-Weighton, Rev. William Blow
*Grimston Garth, 9 m. NE. of Hedon, Charles Grimston, Esq. 1820
Gunby, 5 m. NNW. of Howden, Michael Clarkson, gentleman
*†Heslerton, 2 m. ENE. of Malton, John Robinson Foulis, Esq. 1788
Heslington, 2 m. SSE. of York, Henry Yarburgh (Hall) and Nicholas Yarburgh, Esqrs.
Hessle, 5 m. WSW. of Hull, Charles Rose, Esq. & T. B. Locke, gentleman
Hessle Wood House, 6 m. W. of Hull, Joseph Robinson Pease, Esq.
Holme-on-Spalding-Moor, 5 m. SW. of Market Weighton, the Hon. Charles Langdale
Holme House, 5 m. SW. of Market Weighton, B. J. Clarkson, jun. Esq.
Hotham Hall, 3 m. NW. of South Cave, Henry Barton Peters, Esq.
Houghton, 6 m. NNW. of South Cave, Mrs. Catharine Selby
Howden, Richard Arthur Worsop, Esq.
Howsham Hall, 8 m. SSW. of Malton, George Cholmley, Esq.
Hull Bank House, 3 m. N. of Hull, Benjamin Blaydes Haworth, Esq.
*Hunmanby Hall, 10 m. SSE. of Scarborough, H. B. Osbaldeston, Esq. 1778
Hunmanby, Rev. Francis Wrangham, A.M. F.R.S. Archdeacon of Cleveland
Kelfield Hall, 6 m. N. of Selby, Barnard Hague, Esq.
*Kilnwick Percy, 1 m. NE. of Pocklington, Robert Dennison, sen. 1793, and Robert Dennison, jun. Esqrs. 1819
Knapton House, 7 m. NE. of Malton, James Tindall, Esq.
Knedlington, 1 m. W. of Howden, Thomas Clark, Esq.
Laugton, 3½ m. S. of Malton, Norcliffe Norcliffe, Esq.
*Leaven, 6½ m. W, of Hornsea, Rev. George Sampson, 1822
Leppington Grange, 1 m. S. of Malton, Wm. Atkinson, Esq.
Lingcroft, 3 m. S. of York, William Selby, Esq.
Lowtherpe Hall, 5 m. NE. of Driffield, Wm. Thos. St. Quintin, Esq.
*Marton House, 2 m. NE. of Bridlington, Ralph Creyke, Esq. 1778
Melbourne Hall, 5 m. SSW. of Pocklington, Samuel Powell, Esq.
Melton, 4 m. SSE. of South Cave, Henry Thompson, Esq.
Melton Hill, 4 m. SSE. of South Cave, Henry Sykes, Esq. and Mrs. (John) Wilson
Metham Hall, 6 m. SE. of Howden, Philip Scholefield, Esq.
*Middleton Hall, 7 m. NE. of Market Weighton, Rev. J. Blanchard, A.M. 1817
*Moorby Hall, 5½ m. S. of York, Rev. Thomas Preston, A.M. 1792
Mount Pleasant, 2½ m. NE. of Beverley, William West, Esq.
*Naburn Hall, 4 m. S. of York, George Palmes, Esq. 1814
Neswick, 5 m. SSW. of Driffield, J. Grimstone & Henry Thorold, Esqrs.
Newbald South, 3 m. N. of South Cave, G. W. Clough, Esq.
Norton 1 m. SE. of Malton, Robert Bower, Esq.
Painthorp, 7 m. N. of Pocklington, Robert Machell, Esq.
Pockthorpe, 4 m. NW. of Driffield, William Hall, Esq.
*Rawcliffe House, 3 m. E. of Snaith, (w. r.) Ralph Creyke, Esq. 1808
*Raywell, 5 m. SSW. of Beverley, Daniel Sykes, Esq. M.P. 1816
Reighton Hall, 2½ m. SE. of Hunmanby, Arthur Strickland, Esq.
Riccall, 10 m. S. of York, Rev. William Parker

Riccall Hall, 5½ m. N. of Selby, Toft Richardson, Esq.

•Rise, 6½ m. SW. of Hornsea, Richard Bethell, Esq. Holmes, A.M. 1800

Riston Grange, 6½ m. ENE. of Beverley, Peter Jackso

•Roos, 8 m. E. of Hedon, Rev. Christopher Sykes, A.

•Rosemoor Lodge, 5 m. SSW. of Pocklington, Lient. Ge

•Rowley, 3½ m. ENE. of South Cave, Rev. Robert Crof

Rowlston, 2 m. SSE. of Hornsea, B. B. Haworth, jun.

•Saltmarshe, 3 m. SSE. of Hawden, Philip Saltmarshe

Sand Hall, 3½ m. S. of Howden, John Scolefield, Esq.

Scampston House, 6 m. NE. of Malton, Charles Thora

Scorbrough, 5 m. N. of Beverley, John Hall, Esq.

•Sculcoates, near Hull, Jonas Brown, Esq. 1801

Sewerby Hall, 1½ m. NE. of Bridlington, • John Grea Greame, Esqrs. 1820

•Sigglesthorne, 4 m. SW. of Hornsea, Rev. W. H. E.

Sigglesthorne Hall, 4 m. SW. of Hornsea, Matthew Top

Skipwith, 6 m. NNE. of Selby, Miles Atkinson, Esq.

Skirlaugh North, 9 m. NNE. of Hull, Benjamin Neasba

Sledmere Castle, 8 m. NW. of Driffield, John Evans,

Southorpe Lodge, near Driffield, Christopher Harrison,

Spring Head, 3 m. WNW. of Hull, Richard Tottie, Es

Stillingfleet Hall, 7 m. S. of York, J. Ingham, Esq.

Sunderlandwick, 3 m. SSW. of Driffield, Horner Reyn

Sutton, 3 m. NNE. of Hull, Thos. Bell, Geo. Liddell, & 

Sutton House, 1 m. SE. of Malton, George Parker, Esq

•Sutton-on-Derwent, 7 m. ESE. of York, Rev. James

Swanland Hall, 7 m. W. of Hull, Nicholas Sykes, Esq.

Thickett Hall, 9 m. SE. of York, Joseph Dunnington,

•Thorpe Brantingham, 3 m. SE. of South Cave, Rev. E.

Thorpe Hall, 5 m. W. of Bridlington, Hon. Major Gene

Thorganby Hall, 10 m. SE. of York, John Dunnington

Thorngumbald, 2 m. SSE. of Hedon, Edward Sheldon,

Tranby, 6 m. W. of Hull, James Kiero Watson, John Cooper, Esqrs. and Mrs. Barkworth

Turnham Hall, 5 m. ESE. of Selby, William Burton, E

†Ulleskelfe, 2 m. SE. of Tadcaster, (w. R.) John Shilli

•Walkington, 3½ m. SW. of Beverley, Rev. Daniel Fea

Warter House, 3 m. ENE. of Pocklington, Mrs. Jane F

•Wassand, 11 m. NE. of Beverley, Rev. Charles Const

Watton Abbey, 6 m. S. of Driffield, Mrs. Legard

Welham, 1 m. S. of Malton, Robert Bower, Esq.

Welton, 4 m. SSE. of South Cave, Chas. Whitaker & J

Welton House, 4 m. SSE. of South Cave, Robert Raike

Westow Hall, 6 m. S. of Malton, Sir Tatton Sykes

†Wheldrake, 8 m. SE. of York, Hon. & Rev. Robert El

Whitehall, near Driffield, Thomas Francis Jennings, E

Willerby, 6 m. WNW. of Hull, Clifford Pease, gentlem

•Winestead, 2 m. NW. of Patrington, Colonel Arthur M

Winestead Hall, 2 m. NW. of Patrington, Col. Hildyard

*Wold Cottage, 8 m. WNW. of Bridlington, Rev. Timothy Fish Foord
    Bowes, 1816, and Jonathan Laybourn, Esq.
Wood Hall, 6 m. N. of Hedon, Henry William Maister, Esq.
Wood Hall, 6 m. E. of Selby, Charles Reeves, jun. Esq.
Wressle Castle, 4 m. NW. of Howden, Richard Waterworth, Esq.
Wyton Hall, 4 m. N. of Hedon, Richard Harrison, Esq.
Yokefleet, 6 m. SE. of Howden, John Empson, Esq.

---

## NORTH-RIDING.

Abbey House, 1 m. E. of Richmond, Robert Jaques, Esq.
Acklam Hall, 7 m. NE. of Yarm, T. Hustler, Esq.
*Agglethorpe Hall, 3 m. WSW. of Middleham, Matthew Chaytor, Esq.
Ainderby Hall, 3 m. WNW. of Northallerton, John Wormald, Esq.
*Ainderby Steeple, 3 m. WSW. of Northallerton, Rev. J. Robson, A.M. 1822
*Airy Hill, ½ m. W. of Whitby, Richard Moorsom, Esq. 1808, and Richard
    Moorsom, jun. Esq. 1820
Aiskew, ½ m. NE. of Bedale, William Dinsdale, Esq.
Aislaby, 1½ m. NW. of Pickering, Mrs. Mary Hayes
Aislaby, 3 m. WSW. of Whitby, Mark Noble and John Benson, Esqrs.
Aldbrough Hall, 2 m. SSE. of Masham, James Henry D'Arcy Hutton, Esq.
Aldby Park, 9 m. NE. of York, Henry Darley, Esq.
Alne, 3½ m. SW. of Easingwold, Stamp Brooksbank, Esq.
Arden Hall, 7½ m. NE. of Thirsk, Darcy Tancred, Esq.
Arncliffe Cottage, 8 m. NE. of Northallerton, Miss Mauleverer
Ayton Hall, 3 m. NE. of Stokesley, Thomas Graham, Esq.
Ayton House, 3 m. NE. of Stokesley, Colonel Cookson
*Barningham Hall, 2¼ m. S. of Greta Bridge, Mark Milbank, Esq. M.P.
*Barningham, 2 m. S. of Greta Bridge, John Todd, Esq. and the Rev.
    Thomas Collins, B.D. 1818
Barton-le-Street, 5 m. WNW. of Malton, Henry Cockerill Leatham, Esq.
*Bedale, 8 m. SW. of Northallerton, Henry Pierse, Esq. M.P. Hon. and
    Rev. Thomas Monson, A.M. 1813, and Rev. J.J.T. Monson, 1821
*Belle Vue, ½ m. W. of Scarborough, John Bell, Esq. 1815
Beningbrough Hall, 8 m. NW. of York, Mrs. Margaret Earle
Benkil Grange, adjacent to Bedale, Mrs. Brooke
Bolton Hall, 2¼ m. W. of Leyburn, Hon. T.O. Powlett
*Boroughbridge, Marmaduke Lawson, Esq. 1816
Bossall, 9 m. NE. of York, Robert Belt, Esq.
Brackenbrough, 4 m. W. of Thirsk, John Leathley Armytage, Esq.
Brandsby Hall, 6 m. ENE. of Easingwold, F. Cholmley, Esq.
*Brawith Hall, 4 NNW. of Thirsk, Warcop Consett, Esq. 1786
*†Brockfield House, 5 m. ENE. of York, Benjamin Agar, Esq. 1820
Brompton Green, 8 m. SW. of Scarborough, Dowager Lady Cayley
Brotton House, 6 m. NE. of Guisborough, Robert Stephenson, Esq.
Broughton, 2 m. SE. of Stokesley, Robert Hildyard, Esq.
Burton, 6 m. SE. of Askrigg, William Purchase, Esq.
*Burton Constable, 6 m. S. of Richmond, Marmaduke Wyvill, Esq. M.P. 1820

3 E 2

Bushby Hall, 3 m. S. of Stokesley, Rev. George Marwood

•Camp Hill, 1½ m. SE. of Bedale, Wm. Rookes L. Serjeantson, Esq. 1819

Carleton High Dale, 4 m. SW. of Middleham, Anthony Buckle, Esq.

Carleton Husthwaite, 6 m. NW. of Easingwold, Valentine Kitchingham and John Welbank, Esqrs.

•Carlton Hall, 8 m. N. of Richmond, Samuel Barrett Moulton Barrett, Esq. M.P. 1815

Carr End, 3½ m. from Askrigg, William Fothergill, Esq.

Carr Hall, 3 m. SW. of Whitby, Mrs. Holt

•Catterick, 5 m. ESE. of Richmond, Ralph Hodgson and Harrison Powel, Esqrs. and Rev. Alexander John Scott, D.D. 1820

Cliffe Hall, 6 m. W. of Darlington, Henry Witham, Esq.

Clifton Castle, 2 m. N. of Masham, Timothy Hutton, Esq.

•Clifton Lodge, 3 m. N. of Masham, John Clerveaux Chaytor, Esq. 1810

Clint Hall, 5 m. W. of Richmond, Thomas Errington, Esq.

Coat Bank Lodge, near Whitby, D'Oyley Saunders, Esq.

Cogden Hall, 2 m. SE. of Reeth, Matthew Whitelock, Esq.

•Copgrove, 4 m. N. of Knaresborough, (w. r.) Thomas Duncombe, Esq.

Coverham Abbey, 3 m. S. of Leyburn, Mrs. Lister

•Coxwold, 9 m. SE. of Thirsk, Rev. Thomas Newton, A.M. 1807

•Craike, 2 m. E. of Easingwold, Rev. Powell Colchester Guise, A. M. 1820, and the Rev. W. H. Dixon, F.A.S.

•Crake Hall, (Durham) 2 m. NW. of Bedale, Colonel Henry Percy Pulleine and James Robson, Esq. 1814

Crathorne, 4 m. S. of Yarm, George Tasourgh Crathorne, Esq.

•Croft Hall, 4 m. S. of Darlington, William Chaytor, Esq. 1796

•Crosby Hall, 3 m. SE. of Northallerton, Rev. William Dent, A. M. 1807

Dalby, 7 m. ENE. of Easingwold, Mrs. Ann Leyburne

Dale End, adjacent to Kirkby-Moor-Side, Francis Atkinson, Esq.

Danby Hall, 2 m. E. of Middleham, Simon Thomas Scroope, Esq.

Danby Wiske, 4 m. W. of Northallerton, Rev. William Cust

Dinsdale Hall, 5½ m. SW. of Yarm, Miss Ann Ward

Dowthwaite Dale, 3 m. N. of Kirkby-Moor-Side, William Shepherd, Esq.

•Duncombe Park, ½ m. SW. of Helmsley, Charles Duncombe, Esq. M.P. 1790, and William Duncombe, Esq. M.P. 1821

Eastwood, 1 m. SE. of Greta Bridge, John Hanby, Esq.

•Ebberston Lodge, 6½ m. E. of Pickering, George Osbaldeston, Esq.

•Egglescliffe, (Durham) Rev. John Brewster, 1820

Egton Bridge, 8 m. SW. of Whitby, Richard Smith, Esq.

Ellingthorp Hall, 1 m. NE. of Boroughbridge, Thomas Clark, Esq.

Esk Hall, 3 m. SW. of Whitby, John Campion Coates, Esq.

•Faceby Lodge, 4 m. SW. of Stokesley, James Favell, Esq. 1819

•Field House, ½ m. W. of Whitby, Christopher Richardson, Esq. 1808

•Fingall, 5 m. E. of Leyburn, Rev. Edward Wyvill, 1822

Fleetham Kirby, 6 m. SE. of Richmond, Mrs. Lawrence

Forcett Hall, 8 m. N. of Richmond, late Charles Mitchell, Esq.

Fosfield House, 3 m. NNE. of York, Thomas Smith, Esq.

•Foston, 7½ m. SW. of Malton, Rev. Sidney Smith, A. M. 1814

Foston Hall, 7 m. SW. of Malton, the Rev. F. Simpson

Fremington, 1 m. SE. of Reeth, Lady Charlotte Dennys

Friarage, adjacent to Yarm, Thomas Meynell, Esq.

*Gilling, 3 m. N. of Richmond, Rev. Wm. Wharton, A. M. 1804, and
  Rev. Richard Mosley Atkinson, A. M. 1815

Gilling Castle, 5 m. S. of Helmsley, Charles Gregory Fairfax, Esq.

Gilling Lodge, 3 m. N. of Richmond, Mrs. (Jane) Wilson

*Grinkle Park, 11 m. ENE. of Guisborough, Robt. Wharton Middleton, Esq.

Gristhorpe Lodge, 7 m. SE. of Scarborough, Colonel George Beswick and
  William Beswick, Esq.

Grove House, adjacent to Leyburn, John Clifton, Esq.

*Guisborough, 9 m. NE. of Stokesley, John Harrison, 1795, & Rbt. Chaloner,
  Esqrs. M. P. 1807, & the Rev. Thomas Pym Williamson, A.M. 1807

Habton Hall, 4 m. NW. of Malton, Thomas Pickering, Esq.

Hallwith House, 2 m. NE. of Middleham, Thomas Place, Esq.

Halnaby Hall, 7 m. NE. of Richmond, John Peniston Milbank, Esq.

Harlsey Hall, 7 m. NE. of Northallerton, Charles John Maynard, Esq.

Hartforth Hall, 4 m. N. of Richmond, Sheldon Cradock, Esq. M. P. and
  Colonel of the North York Militia

*Haughton, (Durham) John Trotter, Esq. 1806

*Hawkswell Hall, 4½ m. NE. of Leyburn, Colonel Fletcher Lechmer
  Coore, 1820

Hemlington Hall, 4 m. N. of Stokesley, General Hall

Hermitage, 3 m. SW. of Bedale, C. N. Clarke, Esq.

Heworth, 1 m. ENE. of York, Miss Moore

Highthorne, 4 m. NNW. of Easingwold, William Hetham, Esq. 1821

Hildenley, 3 m. WSW. of Malton, George Strickland, Esq. 1819.

Hipswell Lodge, 2½ m. S. of Richmnod, William Metcalf, gentleman

Holtby House, 4 m. N. of Bedale, Thomas Robson, Esq.

Holly Hill, 3 m. S. of Bedale, Richard Purcas Strangewayes, Esq.

Hornby, 5 m. NW. of Bedale, Rev. Jonathan Alderson

Hornby Grange, 7 m. N. of Northallerton, Henry Hewgill, Esq. 1818

Hovingham Hall, 7 m. SE. of Helmsley, Edward Worsley, Esq.

Huttons Ambo, 2½ m. SW. of Malton, (unoccupied)

Hutton Bonville, 5 m. NW. of Northallerton, Wm. Battie Wrightson, Esq.

Hutton Bonville Hall, 5 m. NW. of Northallerton, Henry Pierse, Esq. M. P.

Hutton Lodge, 3½ m. SW. of Malton, General M'Leod

Hutton Sand, 7 m. NE. of York, Rev. T. C. R. Read, A.M. F.R.S. 1799

Hale Hall, 6 m. S. of Guisborough, Robert Bell Livesey, Esq.

Kexby, 1½ m. SE. of Catterick, John Booth, Esq.

Kingthorpe, 3 m. NE. of Pickering, Colonel John Fothergill

Kirkby Hall, 8 m. NW. of Richmond, William Hutchinson, Esq. 1804

Kirkby Misperton, 4 m. SSW. of Pickering, Wm. Fred. Blomberg, D.D.

Kirkleatham Hall, 4½ m. NNW. of Guisbro', Henry Vansittart, Esq. 1814

Kirklington, 6 m. SSE. of Bedale, Rev. Thomas Wilson Morley, 1817

Kirkington Lodge, 5 m. WNW. of Northallerton, Francis Redfearne, Esq.

Kirktington Hall, 2 m. WNW. of Barnard Castle, Henry Witham, Esq.

Marton Hall, 6½ m. N. of Richmond, Thomas Barker, Esq.

Kilton Menby, 5 m. NW. of Guisborough, Consitt Dryden, Esq.

Kites Hall, 2 m. NNE. of Bedale, Mrs. Arden

Kirby Green Grove, 3 m. WSW. of Stokesley, Right Hon. Dowager Lady
  Amherst, and 36, Berkeley square, London

Lofthouse Hall, 9 m. ENE. of Guisborough, Alexand

*Low Hall, 5 SW. of Scarbro', Thomas Candler, Esq.

Manor Cottage, 3 m. NNE. of York, Thomas Dowke

*Marrick Park, 4 m. ESE. of Reeth, Joshua Readsha

Marske Hall, 5 m. W. of Richmond, John Hutton, E

*Marske Hall, 6 m. N. of Guisborough, Hon. Thomas

*Marton Hall, in Westmoreland, Rev. John Rippon

*Marton Lodge, 7 m. N. of Stokesley, Bartholomew

Maunby Hall, 6 m. S. of Northallerton, Thomas Stub

Meadow Fields, ½ m. SW. of Whitby, Henry Simpson

Melmerby, 4½ m. NE. of Ripon, William Priestley,

Middleton Hall, 1 m. W. of Pickering, John Acton, E

*Middleton Lodge, 5 m. NE. of Richmond, George H

Monk End, 4 m. S. of Darlington, Charles Colling, E

Murton Hall, 3 m. E. of York, Barnard Smith, Esq.

*Myton Hall, 3 m. E. of Boroughbridge, Martin Stap

Nawton, 3½ m. ENE. of Helmsley, Thomas Whytel

Ness, (East) 7 m. SE. of Helmsley, Thomas and Joh

Newbrough, 5 m. NE. of Easingwold, Radcliffe Medl

*Newbrough Priory, 5 m. NNE. of Easingwold, Th
    Bellasyse, Esq. 1805

Newby Park, 5 m. NE. of Ripon, John Charles Rams

Newby Wiske, 5 m. S. of Northallerton, John Armita

New Buildings, 5 m. NNE. of Thirsk, Mrs. Mary Sm

New Houses, 7 m. E. of Askrigg, Robert Lodge, Es

Newsham, 8 m. NW. of Richmond, Joseph Glover,

Normanby, 4½ m. NW. of Guisborough, Mrs. Doroth

*Normanby, 5 m, SSE. of Kirkby-Moor-Side, Rev.

*Normanby Hall, 4½ m. WNW. of Guisbro', Wm. W

*Northallerton, Richard Blanchard, Esq. 1846, and
    Bowyer, 1816

Nunnington Lodge, 5¼ m. SE. of Helmsley, Edward

Nunthorpe Hall, 2½ m. NNE. of Stokesley, Thomas

Oldstead Grange, 7 m. N. of Easingwold, Thomas Pu

Oran, 5 m. ESE. of Richmond, Jonathan Walker, Es

*Oswaldkirk, 3 m. S. of Helmsley, Rev. Thomas Cos

*Otterington North, 2½ m. S. of Northallerton,
    Fowles, 1819.

*Patrick Brompton, 3½ m. NW. of Bedale, Gregory

Pepper Hall, 6 m. NW. of Northallerton, John Arde

*Pickering, 9 m. N. of Malton, Thomas Mitchelson,

Pinchinthorpe, 3 m. SW. of Guisborough, John Lee,

*Plainville House, 4 m. N. of York, Charles Smith,

Raithwaite, 3 m. from Whitby, Israel Hunter, Esq.

Redcar, 6 m. N. of Guisborough, Jonathan Milner,

Redmire, 4½ m. W. of Leyburn, Thomas Other, Esq

*Richmond, Rev. Caleb Redshaw, 1820

*†Ripon, (w.r.) Very Rev. Robert Darley Waddilo

Rokeby Hall, 1 m. N. of Greta Bridge, John B
    Esq. 1799

Romaldkirk, 6 m. NW. of Barnard Castle, Anthony Hugginson, Esq.

Rose Cottage, 4 m. NW. of York, G. N. Drury, Esq.

Rounoton Grange, 7 m. NNE. of Northallerton, John Wailes, Esq.

Rudby, 3½ m. WSW. of Stokesley, George Brigham, Esq.

Ruswarp Hall, 2 m. SW. of Whitby, Miss Hannah Pennyman

Salton Hall, 6 m. S. of Kirkby-Moor-side, Geo. Woodwick Dowker, Esq.

*Scarborough, John Woodall, Esq. 1799.

Scorton, 5 m. E. of Richmond, Anthony Frankland, Esq.

Scruton Hall, 4 m. NE. of Bedale, Mrs. (Mary) Gale

Sedbury Hall, 4 m. NNE. of Richmond, Henry Tower, Esq.

Sessay Hall, 5 m. NW. of Easingwold, Hon. & Rev. Wm. Henry Dawnay

*†Sheriff Hutton Park, 8 m. E. of Easingwold, George Lowther Thompson, Esq. 1818

Silton Hall, 7 m. E. of Northallerton, Fowler Hickes, Esq.

Sinnington Lodge, 4 m. WNW. of Pickering, Pudsey Dawson, Esq.

*Sion Hill, 4 m. WNW. of Thirsk, Edward D'Oyley, Esq.

*Skelton Castle, 3 m. NE. of Guisbro', John Wharton, Esq. M.P. 1795

Skelton Cottage, 4 m. NW. of York, Mrs. Mary Thompson

Skelton Grange, 4 m. NW. of York, Edward Place, Esq.

Skinningrave, 7 m. NE. of Guisborough, John Easterby, Esqr.

*Skipton Hall, 4 m. SW. of Thirsk, Thomas Barstow, Esq. 1818

Sleights Hall, 4 m. SW. of Whitby, Mrs. (Sarah) Bateman

Snape Hall, 3 m. NE. of Masham, Misses Clark

*Sneaton Castle, 2 m. SW. of Whitby, Colonel James Wilson, 1820

Sober Gate, 4½ m. S. of Northallerton, John Hutton, Esq.

*Sowerby, 1½ m. S. of Thirsk, Cornelius Cayley, William Chapman, 1810 John Leafe, Wm. Welbank, Wm. Whitewick, Richard Wrightson, and N. C. Cornelleis, Esqrs.

Spanton Lodge, 4 m. NE. of Kirkby-Moor-Side, Henry Darley, Esq.

*Spennithorne, 2 m. NE. of Middleham, Mrs. Chaytor, and Colonel Turner Straubenzie, 1799

*Staindrop, (Durham) John Ingram, Esq.

Stainsacre, 2 m. SSE. of Whitby, Jonathan Sanders, Esq.

*Stainton, 4 m. NNW. of Stokesley, Rev. John Gilpin; 1821

Stakesby (High) 1 m. W. of Whitby, John Blackburn, Esq.

Stakesby (Low), ½ m. W. of Whitby, Abel Chapman, Esq.

Stanghow, 4½ m. ENE. of Guisborough, Richard Scurth, Esq.

Stillington, 4 m. ESE. of Easingwold, Robert Allan, Esq. and the Rev. Witham Croft

*Stillington Hall, 4 m. ESE. of Easingwold, Colonel Harry Croft, 1818

*Stockton-upon-Tees, 5 m. N. of Yarm, Wm. Sleigh, Esq. Durham, 1807

Stoupe Brow Cottage, 8 m. SSE. of Whitby, Sunderland Cook, Esq.

*†Strensall, 6 m. NNE. of York, Rev. John Ellis, 1795

Sutton Hall, 4 m. E. of Thirsk, Captain Thomas Thrush, Royal Navy

Sutton-on-the-Forest, 5 m. SE. of Easingwold, Lady Hoare Harland

*Swinethwaite Hall, 5 m. WSW. of Leyburn, Wm. J. Anderson, Esq. 1818

Swinton Park, 1½ m. SW. of Masham, William Danby, Esq.

Theakston Hall, ½ m. SE. of Bedale, Edmund Carter, Esq.

Thimbleby Lodge, 6 m. NE. of Northallerton, Richard Wm. Christopher Peirse, Esq. 1807

Thornton House, 2¼ m. E. of Pickering, ............,
Thornton-le-Moor, 5 m. N W. of Thirsk, Thomas Beck[
Thornton Steward, 3 m. E. of Middleham, G. Horn, E[
Thorpe Hall, 8 m. ENE. of Greta Bridge, Sheldon Cra[
Thorpe Perrow, 8 m. S. of Bedale, Mark Milbank, Esq.
Tolesby, 6 m. ENE. of Yarm, John Redd, Esq.
Tynemouth (Northumberland) John Matthews, Esq.
Upleatham, 3 m. NNE. of Guisborough, Dowager Lady
        G. H. L. Dundas, M. P. and the Hon. S
        K.C.B. and K.T.S.
Upleatham Hall, 3 m. NNE. of Guisbro', Hon. & Rev.
Walworth Castle (Durham) Arthur Aylmer, Esq. 1813
Wath, 4 m. N. of Ripon, Rev. Benjamin Newton, 181[
Well Hall, 4 m. S. of Bedale, Richard Strangeways, E[
Whitby Abbey, near Whitby, George Cholmley, Esq.
White House, 7 m. NNW. of Richmond, John Colling
Whitwell House, 6 m. SW. of Malton, Rev. [
        Currer, A.M. 1817
Wigginthorpe, 5 m. W. of Malton, William Garforth, [
Wigginton, 4 m. N. of York, Rev. William Dealtry,
Wilton Castle, 3 m. NW. of Guisborough, Hon. John [
Wood End, 3 m. NW. of Thirsk, Samuel Crompton, [
Wood Hall Park, 8 m. E. of Askrigg, C. A. Alderson, E
Woodlands, 4 m. SW. of Whitby, H. W. Yeoman, E[
Worsall Hall, 3 m. SSW. of Yarm, Mrs. Hannah Wilk
Wycliffe Rectory, 2½ m. NE. of Greta Bridge, Rev. J.
Wykeham Abbey, 8 m. SW. of Scarborough, Honourab[
Yafforth, 1½ m. W. of Northallerton, William Hood, E
Yarm, 4 m. S. of Stockton, David Burton Fowler, 176
        ders, 1818, and John Waddle, Esqrs.

---

TOWN RESIDENCES OF THE MEMBERS OF PARLIA[
AND NORTH RIDINGS OF YORKSHIRE AND THE [

| | |
|---|---|
| YORK............ | Marm. Wyvill, Esq. Renton's Hote |
| | Robert Chaloner, Esq. |
| BEVERLEY ...... | John Wharton, Esq. Coulson's H[ |
| | George Lane Fox, Esq. 3, Clevel[ |
| HEDON.......... | Robert Farrand, Esq. 5, Fen cou[ |
| | Lieutenant Colonel John Baillie, |
| HULL .......... | John Mitchell, Esq. 35, Wimpole' |
| | Daniel Sykes, Esq. Bath Hotel, P |
| MALTON ........ | Viscount Duncannon, 18, Manger[ |
| | John Charles Ramsden, Esq. &c. G |
| NORTHALLERTON | Henry Pierse, Esq. 48, Harley st[ |
| | Hon. William Sebright Lascelles, |
| RICHMOND ...... | Hon. Thomas Dundas, 17, North |
| | Samuel Barrett Moulton Barrett, |
| SCARBOROUGH ... | Right Hon. Charles Manners Sutt[ |
| | Hon. Edmund Phipps, 64, Mount |
| THIRSK ........ | Robert Frankland, Esq. 35, Great |
| | Robert Greenhill Russell, Esq. : |

# PARISH CHURCH LIVINGS

## *IN THE WEST RIDING.*

r indicates Rectory; v Vicarage; c Curacy; and p c Perpetual Curacy.

| Parishes. | Tutelary Saint. | Patron. | Incumbent. |
|---|---|---|---|
| Aberford · · · · v | St. Richard | Oriel College, Oxford | Rev. James Landon |
| Ackworth · · · · r | St. Cuthbert | King as D. of Lancaster | Rev. Wm. R. Hay |
| Addingham · · · r | St. Peter | Mrs. Mary Cunliffe | Rev. John Coates |
| Addle · · · · · r | St. John Baptist | T. Arthington, Esq. | Rev. Geo. Lewthwaite |
| Addlingfleet · · · v | All Saints | The King | Rev. Isaac Tyson |
| Adwick-le-Street · · v | St. Lawrence | J. Fullerton, Esq. | Rev. L. J. Hobson |
| Aldborough · · · v | St. Andrew | Dean & Chap. of York | Rev. Robert Wirell |
| Allerton Mauleverer pc | St. Martin | Lord Stourton | Rev. James Neale |
| Almondbury · · · v | All Saints | Trustees of Clitheroe School | Rev. John F. Parker |
| Ardsley (East) · · p c | | Earl of Cardigan | Rev. W. Dixon |
| Ardsley (West) · · p c | | Earl of Cardigan | Rev. John Hepworth |
| Arksey · · · · · v | All Saints | Sir G. Cooke, Bart. | Rev. John Ramsden |
| Armthorpe · · · · r | St. Mary | The King | Rev. Thomas Wilkinson |
| Arncliffe · · · · v | St. Oswald | University Coll. Oxford | Rev. E. Norton |
| Aston · · · · · r | All Saints | Duke of Leeds | Rev. William Alderson |
| Badsworth · · · r | St. Mary | Earl of Derby | Rev. Sir T. Horton, Bart. |
| Bardsey · · · · r | All Saints | George Fox, Esq. | Rev. Francis Wilkinson |
| Barmbrough · · · r | St. Peter | Southwell College | Rev. H. Watkins |
| Barnby-on-Don · · r | St. Peter | John Gresham, Esq. | Rev. Solomon Gresham |
| Barnsley · · · · c | St. Mary | Archbishop of York | Rev. Benjamin Mence |
| Barnoldswick · · · c | St. Mary | Sir J. L. Kaye, Bart. | Rev. Adam Bray |
| Batley · · · · · v | All Saints | Lord de Gray and Earl Cardigan, alternately | Rev. Thomas Foxley |
| Bentham · · · · r | St. John Baptist | E. Parker, Esq. | Rev. Thomas Butler |
| Berwick-in-Elmet · r | All Saints | King as D. of Lancaster | Rev. William Bathurst |
| Bingley · · · · v | All Saints | The King | Rev. Rich Hartley, D.D. |
| Birkin · · · · · r | St. Mary | Devisees of the late Rev. Thomas Wright | Rev. George Alderson |
| Birstall · · · · v | St. Peter | Archbishop of York | Rev. W. M. Heald |
| Bolton-by-Bowland · r | St. Peter | C. Dawson, Esq. | Rev. Richard Dawson |
| Bolton-on-Dearne · v | St. Andrew | W. Marsden, Esq. | Rev. George Allott |
| Bracewell · · · · v | St. Michael | Lord Grantham | Rev. W. A. Wasney |
| Bradford · · · · v | St. Peter | Richard Fawcett, Esq. | Rev. Henry Heap |
| Braithwell · · · · v | St. James | The King | Rev. C. A. Stewart |
| Bramham · · · · v | All Saints | Ch. Ch. Coll. Oxford | Rev. H. B. Tristram |
| Brayton · · · · v | St. Wilfred | Hon. Edward Petre | Rev. R. Paver |
| Brodsworth · · · v | St. Michael | Archbishop of York | Rev. Roger Wilson |
| Brotherton · · · v | St. Edward | Dean & Chapter of York | Rev. John Lowe |
| Broughton · · · v | All Saints | Christ Church, Oxford | Rev. C. H. Hall, D.D. |
| Burghwallis · · · r | St. Helen | Michael Tasburgh, Esq. | Rev. W. Ewbank |
| Burnsall · · · · r | St. Wilfred | Earl of Craven | Rev. Richard Withnell |
| —— 2d Port · r | | Archbishop of York | Rev. J. Hickes |
| Burton Leonard · · v | St. Helen | Dean & Chapter of York | Rev. Robert Ellis |
| Calverley · · · · v | St. Wilfred | The King | Rev. Samuel Redhead |
| Campsall · · · · v | St. Mary Magdalen | Mr. Yarburgh | Rev. A. B. Wrightson |
| Cantley · · · · v | St. Wilfred | J. Childers, Esq. | Rev. William Childers |
| Carlton · · · · v | St. Mary | Ch. Ch. Coll. Oxford | Rev. Walter Levitt |
| Castleford · · · r | All Saints | King as D. of Lancaster | Rev. Theodore Barnes |
| Cawood · · · · c | All Saints | Prebendary of Wistow | Rev. W. J. D. Waddilove |
| Cawthorne · · p c | All Saints | John S. Stanhope, Esq. | Rev. John Bewey |
| Chapham · · · · v | | Bishop of Chester | Rev. John Halton |
| Clayton-in-the-Clay p c | All Saints | St. Andrew Ward, Esq. | Rev. William Brown |

| Parish | | Church | Patron |
|---|---|---|---|
| Collingham | - - t | St. Oswald | G. H. Wheler, Esq. |
| Conisbrough | - - t | St. Peter | Archbishop of York |
| Copgrove | - - r | St. Michael | Thos. Duncombe, Esq. |
| Cowthorpe | - - r | St. Michael | T. Stapleton, Esq. |
| Crofton | - - r | All Saints | King, as D. of Lancaster |
| Darfield | - - r | All Saints | Trinity Col. Cambridge |
| Darrington | - - r | St. Luke and All Saints | Archbishop of York |
| Darton | - - t | All Saints | G. W. Wentworth, Esq. |
| Deighton Kirk | - r | All Saints | Rev. J. Geldart, LL.D. |
| Dewsbury | - - t | All Saints | The King |
| Dinnington | - - r | St. Nicholas | The King |
| Doncaster | - - t | St. George | Archbishop of York |
| Drax | - - r | St. Peter | The King |
| Ecclesfield | - - t | St. John Baptist | Earl Fitzwilliam |
| Edlington | - - r | St. Peter | Lord Molesworth |
| Emley | - - r | St. Michael | Hon. R. L. Saville |
| Farnham | - p c | | Mrs. Ossler, &c. |
| Featherstone | - t | All Saints | Ch. Ch. Col. Oxford |
| Felkirk | - - t | St. Peter | Archbishop of York |
| Fenton Kirk | - t | | Prebendary of Fenton |
| Fewston | - - t | St. Mary Magdalen | The King |
| Firbeck | - - t | St. Peter | Prebendary of Laughton en le Morthen |
| Fishlake | - - t | St. Cuthbert | Dn. & Ch. of Durham |
| Fryston (Monk) | - t | | Prebendary of Whiston |
| Fryston (Ferry) | - v | St. Andrew | The Subchanter & Vicars Choral of York |
| Garforth | - - r | St. Mary | The Rev. J. Whitaker |
| Gargrave | - - t | St. Andrew | John Marsden, Esq. |
| Giggleswick | - - t | St. Alkald | J. Coulthurst & J. Hartley, Esqs. alternately |
| Gisburn | - - r | St. Mary | The King |
| Goldsborough | - r | St. Mary | Earl of Harewood |
| Guiseley | - - r | St. Oswald | Geo. Fox, Esq. & Trin. Col. Cambridge[*] |
| Halifax | - - t | St. John Baptist | The King |
| Hammerton, (Kirk) | c | St. John Baptist | The Rev. W. Metcalfe |
| Hampsthwaite | - t | St. Thos. a-Becket | Mr. Shann |
| Handsworth | - - r | St. Mary | Duke of Norfolk |
| Harewood | - - r | All Saints | Earl of Harewood and G. H. Wheler, Esq. |
| Harthill | - - r | All Saints | Duke of Leeds |
| Hatfield v holden as a c | | St. Lawrence | Lord Dearhurst |
| Hemsworth | - - r | St. Helen | Wm. Wrightson, Esq. |
| Hickleton | - - c | St. Dennis | G. W. Wentworth, Esq. |
| Hooton Pagnell | - t | All Saints | Governors of Wakefield School |
| Hooton Roberts | - r | St. John Baptist | Earl Fitzwilliam |
| Horton in Ribblesdale | c | | Rev. G. Holden, L.L.D. |
| Hoyland High | - t | All Saints | Earl of Mexborough |
| Huddersfield | - - v | St. Peter's | Sir J. Ramsden, Bart. |
| Hunsingore | - - t | St. John Baptist | Sir Henry Goodricke |
| Ilkley | - - - t | All Saints | L. W. Hartley, Esq. |
| Keighley | - - r | St. Andrew | Duke of Devonshire |
| Kellington | - - r | St. Edmund | Trinity Col. Cambridge |
| Kettlewell | - - r | St. Mary | R. Tennant, Esq. |
| Kildwick | - - r | St. Andrew | Ch. Ch. Col. Oxford |

[*] Trinity College has the third turn, which is t

| Parish. | Tutelary Saint. | Patron. | Incumbent. |
|---|---|---|---|
| Kippax - - - - v | St. Mary | The King | Hon. and Rev. A. H. Cathcart |
| Kirkbramwith - - r | St. Mary | King, as D. of Lancaster | Rev. Stewart Corbett |
| Kirkburton - - v | St. John Baptist | King, as D. of Lancaster | Rev. Benj. Hutchinson |
| Kirkby Malhamdale v | | Duke of Devonshire | Rev. Stephen Bland |
| Kirkby Malseard - v | St. Andrew | Trin. Coll. Cambridge | Rev. William Lawson |
| Kirkby Overblow - r | All Saints | Earl of Egremont | Hon. and Rev. Jacob Marsham, D.D. |
| Kirkby South - - v | All Saints | Rev. James Allott | Rev. George Allott |
| Kirkby Wharfe - - v | St. John Baptist | Prebendary of Wetwang | Rev. Thomas Gilpin |
| Kirkheaton - - v | St. John Baptist | T. R. Beaumont, Esq. | Rev. John Smithson |
| Knaresbrough - - v | St. John Baptist | Lord Rosslyn | Rev. Andrew Cheap |
| Laughton-en-le-Morthen - - - - v | All Saints | Chancellor of York | Rev. John Crabtree |
| Leathley - - - r | | The King | Rev. A. Hawksworth |
| Ledsham - - - v | All Saints | G. H. Wheeler, Esq. | Rev. Francis Tattersall |
| Leeds - - - v | St. Peter | 25 Patrons | Rev. Richard Fawcett |
| Linton - - - r | St. Michael | The King | Rev. Edward Coulthurst |
| Long Preston - - v | St. Mary | Ch. Ch. Coll. Oxford | Rev. Henry Thompson |
| Maltby - - - v | St. Bartholomew | Earl of Scarborough | Rev. George Rolleston |
| Marr - - - p v | St. Helen | Earl of Kinnoul | Rev. Patrick Keith |
| Marton-with-Grafton v | | St.John'sColl. Cambridge | Rev. John Foster |
| Martons both in Craven - - - - r | St. Peter | Mrs. Heber, gentlewoman | Rev. Robert Crockett |
| Melton on the Hill c | St. James | Richard F. Wilson, Esq. | Rev. Henry Ramsden |
| Methley - - - r | St. Oswald | King, as D. of Lancaster | Hon. and Rev. A. H. Cathcart |
| Mexbrough - - v | | Archdeacon of York | Rev. L. J. Hobson |
| Mirfield - - - v | St. Mary [Sts. | Sir Geo. Armytage, Bart. | Rev. Thomas Sedgwick |
| Mitton - - - v | St. Michael or All | Rev. John Wilson | Rev. John Wilson |
| Newton Kyme - - r | St. Andrew | T. L. Fairfax, Esq. | Rev. John Chaloner |
| Nidd - - - v | | King, as D. of Lancaster | Rev. H. W. Powel |
| Normanton - - - v | All Saints | Trinity Coll. Cambridge | Rev. Robert Evans |
| Nun Monkton - - c | | S. J. Tuffnell, Esq. | Rev. George Wright |
| Otley - - - v | All Saints | Lord Chancellor | Rev. Henry Robinson |
| Ouseburne Great - v | St. Mary | The King | Rev. Samuel Clapham |
| Ouseburne Little - v | Holy Trinity | Precentor of York | Rev. Anthony Watson |
| Owston - - - v | All Saints | Philip David Cooke, Esq. | Rev. J. Campbell |
| Pannall - - - v | St. Robert of Knaresbro' | Rev. R. B. Hunter | Rev. R. B. Hunter |
| Pateley Bridge - - c | St. Mary | Dean & Chap. of Ripon | Rev. James Newsham |
| Penistone - - - v | St. John Baptist | William Bosville, Esq. | Rev. Martin Naylor |
| Pontefract - - - v | St. Giles | The King | Rev. T. H. Marshall |
| Rawmarsh - - - r | St. Mary | The King | Rev. E. J. Townshend |
| Ripley - - - r | All Saints | Sir Wm. Ingilby, Bart. | Rev. George Holliwell |
| Ripon - - - dv | St. Peter and St. Wilfred | The King | Very Rev. Robert Darley Waddilove, D.D. |
| Rossington - - - r | St. Michael | Corporation of Doncaster | Rev. James Stovin, D.D. |
| Rotherham - - - v | All Saints | Lord Howard Effingham | Rev. Thomas Bailiffe |
| Rothwell - - - v | Holy Trinity | C. J. Brandling, Esq. | Rev. Ralph Brandling |
| Royston - - - v | St. John Baptist | Archbishop of York | Rev. John Fletcher |
| Ryther - - - r | All Saints | The King | Rev. John Forster |
| Sandal Magna - - v | St. Helen | The King | Rev. T. Westmorcland |
| Sandal Kirk - - r | St. Oswald | The King | Rev. John Forster |
| Saxton - - - p c | All Saints | Richard O. Gascoigne | Rev. William Crowe |
| Sedbergh - - - r | St. Andrew | Trinity Coll. Cambridge | Rev. D. M. Peacock |
| Selby - - - p c | St. Mary and St. Germains | Hon. E. Petre | Rev. Jonathan Muncaster |
| Sheffield - - - v | St. Peter | P. Gell, Esq. for this turn | Rev. Thomas Sutton |
| Sherburn - - - r | All Saints | Prebendary of Kirk Fenton in York Cathedral | Rev. William Molineux |

| Parish. | Tutelary Saint. | Patron. |
|---|---|---|
| Silkstone · · · | w All Saints | Archbishop of York |
| Skipton · · · r 4 v | Holy Trinity | Ch. Ch. Coll. Oxford |
| Slaidburn · · · | St. Andrew | J. ... |
| Smeaton Kirk · · | St. Mary | ... |
| Snaith · · · · c | St. Lawrence | C. ... Esq. |
| Spofforth · · · r | All Saints | Earl of Egremont |
| Sprotbrough · · r | St. Mary | Sir J. Copley, Bart. |
| Stainley South · p c | | Horner Reynard, Esq., late Mrs. Gilbert's ... |
| Stanton · · · · w | St. Winfred | Duke of Scarborough |
| Staveley · · · · r | All Saints | Rev. G. Ashby |
| Swillington · · · r | St. Mary | John Lowther, Esq. |
| Tadcaster · · – w | St. Mary | Earl of Egremont |
| Tankersley · · · r | St. Peter | Earl Fitzwilliam |
| Thorne · · · p c | St. Nicholas | Earl of Portmore |
| Thorner · · · · w | St. Peter | The King |
| Thornhill · · · r | St. Michael | Hon. & Rev. J. L. Savill |
| Thornscoe · · – r | St. Helen | Earl Fitzwilliam |
| Thornton, near Skip-ton · · · · r | St. Oswald or All Saints | Sir J. L. Kaye, Bart. |
| Thornton in Lons-dale · · · · v | St. Oswald | Dn. & Chap. of Worcester |
| Thorpe Salvin · · c | St. Peter | Duke of Leeds |
| Thribergh · · · r | St. Leonard | John Fullerton, Esq. |
| Tickhill · · · · v | St. Mary | G. S. Foljambe, Esq. |
| Todwick · · · · r | St. Peter and St. Paul | Duke of Leeds |
| Treeton · · · · r | St. Helen | Duke of Norfolk |
| Wadworth · · · v | St. Mary | Imp. of Wadworth, ... |
| Wakefield · · · w | All Saints | The King |
| Wales · · · · c | St. John | Chancellor of York |
| Warmfield · · · v | St. Peter | Masters of Clare Hall, Cambridge, trustees of B. Oley |
| Warmsworth · · r | St. Peter | W. Wrightson, Esq. |
| Wath-upon-Dearne w | All Saints | Ch. Ch. Coll. Oxford |
| Weston · · · · v | All Saints | The King |
| Whiston · · · · r | St. James | Lord Howard of Efffingham |
| Whitgift · · · · c | St. Mary Magdalen | Mr. Yarburgh |
| Whitkirk · · · · v | St. Mary | Trinity Coll. Cambridge |
| Whixley · · · · v | | Trustees of Tancred's charities |
| Wickersley · · · r | St. Alban | Henry Kater, Esq. |
| Wistow · · · · v | All Saints | Prebendary of Wistow |
| Womersley · · · r | St. Martin | Lord Hawke |
| Wragby · · · · c | St. Michael | Charles Winn, Esq. |

[In cases of doubt, the authorities consulted in ... Livings, have been Bacon's Liber Regis, ... and the Ecclesiastical Directory.]

## East-Riding.

### LORDS AND CHIEF BAILIFFS OF LIBERTIES.

The Hon. and Right Rev. the Lord Bishop of Durham, for Howdenshire.
Sir Thos. Constable, Bart. Burton Constable, for the Seigniory of Holderness.

### OFFICERS OF THE RIDING.

The Right Hon. Lord Mulgrave, Lord Lieutenant and Custos Rotulorum.
Richard William Johnson, Esq. Darlington, Clerk of the Peace.
John Lockwood gentleman, Beverley, Deputy Clerk of the Peace.
Samuel Hall, gentleman, Beverley, Deputy Sheriff.
John Lockwood, gentleman, Beverley, Clerk of Indictments.
Mr. William Burrell, Beverley, Crier of the Court.
Henry John Shepherd, gentleman, Beverley, Treasurer.
John Lockwood, gent. Beverley, Clerk of General Meetings of Lieutenancy.
Mr. Samuel Shepherd, Governor of the House of Correction, Beverley.
John Creyke, gentleman, Howsham, Surveyor of Bridges.

### CORONERS.

Richard Bell, Pocklington, ........
Samuel Cowling, York, ........... } For the East Riding.
Thomas Shepley, Selby, ..........
William and James Iveson, Hedon, for Holderness.
Robert Spofforth, jun. Howden, for Howdenshire.

| CHIEF CONSTABLES. | PLACES OF ABODE. | WAPENTAKES. |
|---|---|---|
| Robert Robinson.......... | Lockington............. | Bainton Beacon. |
| William Hudson......... | Howsham.............. | Buckrose. |
| Edward Ashley .......... | Molescroft ............. | Dickering. |
| Samuel Ball ............. | Hornsea.. ............. | North Holderness. |
| John Nornabell.......... | Sutton .................. | Middle Holderness. |
| William Raines .......... | Winestead ............. | South Holderness |
| Barnard Clarkson ........ | Holme on Spalding Moor | Holme Beacon. |
| James Campbell......... | Knedlington ............ | Howdenshire. |
| Robert Smelt ........... | Beverley ............... | Hunsley Beacon. |
| William Johnson ........ | Fulford................. | Ouse and Derwent. |
| George Bagley........... | Pocklington ............ | Wilton Beacon. |

### THE GENERAL QUARTER SESSIONS

Are held at Beverley, on Tuesdays in the first whole week after Epiphany; Easter; St. Thomas the Martyr; and on the first Tuesday after the eleventh of October.

## North Riding.

### LORDS AND CHIEF BAILIFFS OF LIBERTIES.

His Grace the Duke of Leeds, Hornby Castle; for Richmondshire.
The Hon. and Right Rev. the Lord Bishop of Durham; for Allertonshire.
The Rev. George Marwood, Busby Hall, Stokesley; for Langbargh.
Richard Hill, Esq. Thornton; for Pickering Lythe.
George Cholmley, Esq. Howsham; for Whitby Strand.

### OFFICERS OF THE RIDING.

George William Frederick, Duke of Leeds, Lord Lieutenant and Custos Rotulorum.
Turner Straubensee, Esq. Spennithorne; Vice Lieutenant.
Lupton Topham, Esq. Middleham; Clerk of the Peace.
William Wailes, gentleman, Northallerton; Deputy Clerk of the Peace.
Thomas Paul, gentleman, Malton; Deputy Sheriff.
Mr. Thomas Wait, Northallerton; Clerk of Indictments.
Mr. John Leafe, Malton; Crier of the Court.
Valentine Kitchingman, Esq. Carlton Husthwaite, Treasurer.
Henry Hirst, gent. Northallerton, Clerk of General Meetings of Lieutenancy.
Mr. Thomas Shepherd, Governor of the House of Correction, Northallerton.
Mr. Thomas Shepherd, jun. Under Gaoler.

3 F

George Atkinson, gent. Hagg Cottage, Richmond, Sw
Mr. Matthew Peacock, Rainton, Boroughbridge, Dep

## CORONERS.

Henry Belcher, Whitby
George Brigham, Rudby
Samuel Cowling, York

William Dinsdal
Thos. Harrison,

| CHIEF CONSTABLES. | PLACES OF ABODE. | |
|---|---|---|
| James Langdale ......... | Northallerton......... | A |
| Christopher Hudson ...... | Crosby ............... | |
| Thomas Scott ........... | Oulston............... | B |
| James Barker............ | Sowerby .............. | |
| John Plowman........... | Haxby ................ | E |
| William Ware ..:....... | Skirpenbeck .......... | |
| George Readman........ | Langton .............. | G |
| Thomas Meck...:....... | Crabtree House........ | |
| Thomas Lax ............ | Ravensworth .......... | G |
| Samuel Spedding........ | Gilling .............. | |
| George Dryden .....:..... | Aiskew................ | H |
| John Plews ............. | Colburn............... | |
| Thomas Place............ | Spennithorne ......... | H |
| Ralph Lodge............ | New Houses........... | |
| Tristram Walker......... | Melmerby ............. | H |
| William Fall............. | Wath................. | |
| George Brigham......... | Rudby ................ | L |
| Joseph Hickson........... | Guisborough .......... | |
| Peter Marshall........... | Wykeham ............. | M |
| Thomas Bolnton ........ | Pickering ............ | |
| George Carter............ | Oswaldkirk............ | M |
| John Reed............... | Stonegrave ........... | |
| Thomas G. Dale ........ | Whitby............... | W |

## THE GENERAL QUARTER SESS
Are held at Northallerton, on Tuesdays in the
Epiphany; Easter; St. Thomas the Martyr; and on ti
the eleventh of October.

Chairmen.—The Right Hon. Lawrence Lord Dr
mer and Michaelmas Sessions; and the Rev. John He
Epiphany and Easter Sessions.

## REGISTER OFFICES FOR DE
OF THE EAST, NORTH, AND WEST B

| Riding. | Name of Register. | Name of Deputy Register. | Town o Office |
|---|---|---|---|
| North | M. Butterwick.. | John S. Walton ... | Northall |
| East.. | H. W. Maister.. | Anthony Atkinson | Beverley |
| West.. | F. Hawksworth | James Stephenson | Wakefiel |

# Liberty of St. Peter's
## OFFICERS.
Henry John Dickens, Esq. Steward.
Christopher Newstead, gent. Clerk of the Peace and 1
Mr. John Brook, Chief Bailiff.
Thomas Harrison, Constable and Prison Keeper.

*⁎* For List of Magistrates and Officers of the City of York.

## MAYORS OF THE WEST RIDING F
Benjamin Sadler, Esq. Leeds
L. W. Childers, Esq. Doncaster
William Pearson, Esq. Ripon

Robert Smith, 1
Andrew Albar
Stainforth

# POPULATION

*f all the Market Towns and Boroughs in England, with the Population of the Principal Towns of Scotland and Wales. From the Census, Printed by Order of the House of Commons, on the 2d of July, 1822.*

The first Figures to the Right of each Town indicate the Distance of that Place from ondon; the initial Letters the Day on which the Market is held; and the last Figures in ie Line shew the Total Amount of the Population of that Place.

*The Towns marked thus (\*) send Members to Parliament.*

| Town | Popl. |
|---|---|
| bbotts-Bromley,129,T.1533 | |
| bbottsbury, 127, Th. | 907 |
| berford, 182, W. | 579 |
| bergavenny, 146, T. | 3388 |
| berystwith, 208, M. | 4059 |
| Abingdon, 56, M. & F. | 5137 |
| Icester, 103, T. | 2229 |
| Aldborough,94,W.&S. | 1212 |
| Aldborough, 201, S. | 735 |
| ldbourn, 71, T. | 1385 |
| ldstone, 272, S. | 4411 |
| lford, 137, T. | 1506 |
| lfreton, 140, M. & F. | 4689 |
| lnwick, 306, S. | 5927 |
| lresford, 57, Th. | 1219 |
| lton, 47, S. | 2499 |
| ltringham, 180, T. | 2302 |
| mbleside, 276, W. | 838 |
| mersham, 26, T. | 2612 |
| mesbury, 78, F. | 810 |
| mthill, 45, Th. | 1527 |
| Andover, 63, S. | 4219 |
| Appleby, 270, S. | 824 |
| Arundel, 57, W. & S. | 2511 |
| shbourne, 140, S. | 2188 |
| Ashburton, 192, T. | 3403 |
| shby de la Zouch,115,S.5957 | |
| shford, 54, T. | 2773 |
| shton U. Lyne, 186, S. | 9222 |
| skrigg, 241, Th. | 765 |
| therstone, 108, T. | 3434 |
| ttleborough, 94, Th. | 1959 |
| xbridge, 130, S. | 988 |
| rxminster, 147, S. | 1703 |
| Aylesbury, 40, W. | 4400 |
| ylesham, 120, T. | 1853 |
| Jakewell, 153, M. | 1782 |
| Jaldock, 37, Th. | 1550 |
| Jampton, 161, S. | 1633 |
| Jampton, 70, W. | 1460 |
| Banbury, 75, Th. | 3396 |
| Jarking, 7, S. | 2580 |
| Barkway, 34, — | 993 |
| Jarnard Castle, 246, W. | 3581 |
| Jarnett, 11, M. | 1755 |
| Jarnsley, 177, W. | 8284 |
| Barnstaple, 196, F. | 5079 |
| Jarton, 164, M. | 2496 |
| Jasingstoke, 45, W. | 3165 |
| Bath, 106, W. &. S. | 36,811 |
| Battle, 56, Th. | 2852 |
| Jawtry, 149, Th. | 1027 |
| Beaconsfield, 23, Th. | 1736 |
| Beaminster, 137, Th. | 2806 |
| Beccles, 109, S. | 3493 |
| Bedale, 224, T. | 1157 |

| Town | Popl. |
|---|---|
| \*Bedford, 51, T. & S. | 5466 |
| \*Bedwin, 70, — | 1928 |
| Beer Ferris, with } | 1928 |
| \*Beeralston, — } | |
| Belford, 319, Th. | 1208 |
| Bellingham, 297, T. & S. | 1154 |
| Belper, 134, S. | 7235 |
| Bere Regis, 112, W. | 953 |
| Betley, 157, T. | 932 |
| Berkhampstead, 26, S. | 2310 |
| Berkeley, 114, W. | 836 |
| \*Berwick on Twd.334,S.8723 | |
| \*Beverley, 180, W. & S. | 6728 |
| \*Bewdley, 129, S. | 3725 |
| Bicester, 55, F. | 2544 |
| Bideford, 204, T. | 4053 |
| Biggleswade, 45, W. | 2778 |
| Billericay, 23, T. | 1861 |
| Billesdon, 93, F. | 751 |
| Bilston, 128, — | 12,003 |
| Bingham, 124, Th. | 1574 |
| Bingley, 198, T. | 6176 |
| Birmingham, 110, M. T. | |
| & S. | 106,772 |
| Bishop-Auckland,284,T.2150 | |
| \*Bishop's Castle, 159, F. | 1126 |
| Bishop Stortford,30,Th. | 3358 |
| Bishop's Waltham, 65, F. | 1126 |
| Blackburn, 209, W.&S. | 21,940 |
| Blanford, 103, S. | 2643 |
| \*Bletchingley, 20, — | 1187 |
| Blyth, 151, W. | 3456 |
| \*Bodmin, 234, S. | 2902 |
| Bolingbroke, 129, T. | 753 |
| Bolsover, 145, F. | 1245 |
| Bolton, 197, M. | 31,295 |
| Bootle, 277, S. | 656 |
| \*Boroughbridge, 202, S. | 860 |
| \*Boston, 115, W. & S. | 10,373 |
| Botesdale, 86, Th. | 584 |
| Bourne, 94, S. | 2029 |
| Bovey Tracey, 188, Th. | 1685 |
| \*Brackley, 64, W. | 1851 |
| Bradford, Wilts, 102, M. | 3760 |
| Bradford, York192,Th. | 13,064 |
| Bradninch, 174, Th. | 1511 |
| Braintree, 40, W. | 2983 |
| \*Bramber, 52. | 98 |
| Brampton, 312, T. | 2448 |
| Brandon, 78, F. | 1770 |
| Brentford, New, 7, S. | 2036 |
| Brentwood, 18, Th. | 1423 |
| Brewood, 130, T. | 2263 |
| \*Bridgenorth, 140, S. | 4345 |
| \*Bridgewater,137,T.&S.6155 | |
| Bridlington, 203, S. | 4272 |

| Town | Popl. |
|---|---|
| \*Bridport, 135, | 3742 |
| Brighton, 54, Daily | 24,429 |
| \*Bristol, 119, W. & | |
| Bromley, 10, Th. | |
| Bromsgrove, 116, T. | 7519 |
| Bromyard, 125, T. | 1227 |
| Broseley, 146, W. | 4814 |
| Brough, 263, Th. | 940 |
| Bruton, 110, S. | 1858 |
| Buckenham, New, | |
| \*Buckingham, 56, | |
| Bungay, 109, Th. | 3290 |
| Burford, 73, S. | 1409 |
| Burgh, 131, Th. | 903 |
| Burnham, 121, M. | |
| Burnley, 207, M. | 6378 |
| Burslem, 151, M. & S. | 9699 |
| Burton in Kendal, 251, T. | 673 |
| Burton Stather, 165, T. | 762 |
| Burton on Trent,124,Th. | 910 |
| Bury, Lanc. 195, Th. | 10,583 |
| Bury St.Edmunds,71,W. | 9999 |
| Caerleon, 151, Th. | 1062 |
| Caistor, 153, Sat. | 1253 |
| \*Callington, 214, .W. | 1321 |
| \*Calne, 87, T. | 4549 |
| \*\*Cambridge,51,W.&S.14112 | |
| \*Camelford, 228, F. | 1256 |
| Campden, 90, W. | 1249 |
| \*Canterbury,55,W.&S.12754 | |
| \*Carlisle, 303, S. | 15,476 |
| Cartmell, 254, M. | 371 |
| \*Castle-cary, 113, T. | 1627 |
| \*Castle Rising, 102, | 343 |
| Cawood, 181, W. | 1127 |
| Cawston, 112, W. | 929 |
| Caxton, 49, T. | 406 |
| Cerne Abbas, 121, W. | 1060 |
| Chapel-en-le-Frith, 167, | |
| Th. | 3234 |
| Chard, 140, M. | 1330 |
| Charlbury, 69, F. | 2877 |
| Chatham, 30, S. | 14,754 |
| Cheadle, 146, F. | 3862 |
| Chelmsford, 29, F. | 4994 |
| Cheltenham, 95, Th. | 13,396 |
| Chepstow, 131, S. | 3008 |
| Chertsey, 20, W. | 4279 |
| Chesham, 29, W. | 5032 |
| \*Chester, 181, W. & S. | 19,949 |
| Chesterfield, 151, S. | 5077 |
| \*Chichester, 62, W. & S. | 7362 |
| \*Chippenham, 93, S. | 3201 |
| Chorley, 209, T. & S. | 7315 |
| \*Christchurch, 100, M. | 9644 |
| Chudleigh, 182, S. | 2053 |

3 F 2

Chumleigh, 191, Th. 1506  
*Cirencester, 89, M. & F. 4887  
Clare, 56, F. 1487  
Cleobury Mortimer, 157, Th. 1602  
*Clithero, 216, S. 3213  
Clun, 139, T. 732  
*Cockermouth, 305, M. 3790  
Coggeshall, 44, S. 3604  
*Colchester, 51, S. 14,016  
Coleford, 124, T. 1804  
Coleshill, 101, W. 1760  
Collumpton, 164, S. 3410  
Colne, 218, W. 7871  
Colyton, 151, Th. 1645  
Congleton, 162, S. 8205  
Corby, 103, Th. 591  
*Corfe Castle, 120, Th. 823  
*Coventry, 92, F. 21,242  
Cranborne, 93, W. 1823  
Cranbrook, 48, S. 3685  
Cray, St. Mary's, 13, W. 874  
Crediton, 180, S. 5513  
Crewkerne, 132, S. 6434  
*Cricklade, 84, S. 1635  
Cromer, 130, S. 1033  
Cromford, 142, S. 1242  
Crowland, 89, S. 2113  
Crowle, 163, M. 1961  
Croydon, 10, S. 9254  
Cuckfield, 40, T. 2385  
Dalton, 266, S. 714  
Darlington, 237, M. 5750  
Dartford, 15, S. 8303  
*Dartmouth, 203, F. 4185  
Daventry, 72, W. 3326  
Deal, 70, Th. 6811  
Debenham, 85, F. 1538  
Deddington, 79, S. 1404  
Dedham, 59, T. 1651  
Deptford, 5. 19,867  
*Derby, 127, F. 17,423  
Dereham, East, 101, F. 3273  
*Devizes, 88, Th. 4208  
Dewsbury, 184, W. 6390  
Diss, 86, F. 2760  
Dodbrook, 219, W. 885  
Doncaster, 158, S. 8544  
Donnington, 107, S. 1638  
*Dorchester, 120, S. 2743  
Dorking, 25, Th. 3812  
*Dover, 71, W. & S. 10,327  
Downham, 85, S. 2044  
*Downton, 87, 3114  
Drayton, 161, W. 252  
Driffield, 193, Th. 2303  
*Droitwich, 118, F. 2176  
Dronfield, 157, Th. 3680  
Dudley, 127, S. 18,211  
Dulverton, 164, S. 1127  
Dunmow, 38, S. 2409  
Dunstable, 34, W. 1831  
Dunster, 159, F. 895  
*Dunwich, 97, M. 200  
*Durham, 256, S. 9822  
Dursley, 109, Th. 3126  
Easingwold, 208, F. 1912  
Eastbourn, 60, S. 2607  
Eccleshall, 149, F. 1254  
Egremont, 299, S. 1741  
Elham, 66, M. 1168  
Ellesmere, 178, T. 2173  
Elsdon, 299, T. 1848  
Eltham, 8, M. 1883  
Ely, 67, S. 5079  
Enfield, 10, S. 8327  
Epping, 16, F. 1688  
Epworth, 156, T. 1763  
*Evesham, 96, M. 3487  

Ewell, 11, Th.  
*Exeter, 172, W.&S. 28,479  
*Eye, 93, S. 1832  
Fairford, 90, Th. 1547  
Fakenham, 102, S. 1616  
Falmouth, 299, Th. 4372  
Fareham, 13, W. 5677  
Farnham, 36, Th. 3152  
Faringdon, 98, 2271  
Fenny Stratford, 521  
Feversham, 47, W.&S. 5919  
Folkestone, 70, Th.  
Folkingham, 105, Th. 759  
Fordingbridge, 87, S. 2114  
Foulsham, 111, T.  
*Fowey, 229, S. 1465  
Framlingham, 87, S.  
Frodsham, 189, Th. 1558  
Frome, 104, W. & S. 12,411  
Gainsboro', 147, T.  
Garstang, 229, Th.  
Gateshead, 270, — 11,767  
*Gatton, 19.  
Gisburn, 224, M.  
Glossop Bridge, 179, Th.  
Glastonbury, 126, T.  
*Gloucester, 103, W.&S.  
Godalming, 33, S.  
Gosport, 70, S.  
Goudhurst, 44, W.  
*Grampound, 260, S.  
*Grantham, 111, S.  
Grassington, 229, F.  
Gravesend, 22, W.&S.  
Greenwich, 5, W.&S.  
*Grimsby, Gt. 164, W.  
*Grinstead, E. 32, F.  
*Guilford, 30, S.  
Guisboro', 243, T.  
Hadleigh, 61, M.  
Halesowen, 124, M.  
Halesworth, 101, Th.  
Halifax, 197, S.  
Halstead, 45, F.  
Haltwhistle, 298, Th.  
Hambledon, 72, T.  
Hanley & Shelton, 151, S.12...  
Harleston, 101, W.  
Harling, East, 95, T.  
Harlow, 24, S.  
Hartland, 217, S.  
Hartlepool, 251, S.  
*Harwich, 72, T.  
*Haslemere, 42, T.  
Haslingden, 204, W.  
*Hastings, 64, W. & S.  
Hatfield Bishop, 20, Th.  
Hatherleigh, 201, F.  
Havant, 67, S.  
Haverhill, 59, W.  
Hailsham, 56, W.  
Hawes, 246, T.  
Hawkshead, 278, M.  
*Hedon, 179, S.  
Helmsley, 218, S.  
*Helston, 274, S.  
Hemel Hempsted, 24, Th.  
Henley in Arden, 103, T.  
Henley on Thames, 22, Th.  
*Hereford, 135, S.  
*Hertford, 21, S.  
Hexham, 283, T.  
*Heytesbury, 95.  
*Higham Ferrers, 65, S.  
Highworth, 76, W.  
Hinckley, 100, M.  
*Hindon, 95, Th.

| | | | | | |
|---|---|---|---|---|---|
| Stoney Stratford, 52, F. | 1199 | *Tregony, 253, S. | 1035 | *Whitchurch, 57, F. | 141 |
| Stourbridge, 125, F. | 5090 | Tring, 32, F. | 3286 | Whitehaven, 318, T. | 12,438 |
| Stourport, 124, Tb. | 2544 | Trowbridge, 99, S. | 9545 | Wickwar, 112, M. | 919 |
| Stowe Market, 70, Th. | 2252 | *Truro, 235, W. & S. | 2712 | *Wigan, 200, F. | 17,716 |
| Stowe on the Wold, 82, Th. | 1304 | Tunbridge, 30, T. | 7406 | Wigton, 306, T. | 4051 |
| Stowey Nether, 145, T. | 773 | Tutbury, 128, T. | 1441 | *Wilton, 84, W. | 2054 |
| Stratford on Avon, 94, Th. | 3069 | Tuxford, 134, M. | 979 | Winburn Minster, 101, F. | 1357 |
| Stratton, 221, T. | 1580 | Uffcolumb, 174, W. | 1979 | Wineaunton, 108, W. | 2143 |
| Stretton Church, 159, Th. | 1226 | Ulverstone, 267, Th. | 4315 | Winchcombe, 95, S. | 2349 |
| Stroud, 101, F. | 7097 | Uppingham, 89, W. | 1630 | *Winchelsea, 66, S. | 817 |
| *St. Stephens, with Newport, 214, | 977 | Upton on Severn, 110, Th. | 2319 | *Winchester, 62, W. & S. | 7750 |
| Sturminster, Newtown, 109, Th. | 1612 | Usk, 113, M. | 989 | *Windsor, 23, S. | 5638 |
| | | Uttoxeter, 135, W. | 4658 | Winslow, 49, T. | 1222 |
| | | Uxbridge, 15, Th. | 2750 | Winster, 152, S. | 923 |
| | | Wainfleet, 128, S. | 1422 | Wirksworth, 140, T. | 6318 |
| Sutton Coldfield, 112, M. | 3466 | | | Wisbeach, 97, S. | 6515 |
| Swaffham, 93, S. | 2836 | | | Witham, 38, T. | 2578 |
| Swindon, 82, M. | 1580 | Walsham, North, 123, T. | 2303 | Witney, 66, Th. | 2827 |
| Swineshead, 109, Th. | 1696 | Wakingham, 144, Th. | 1067 | Wiveliscomb, 154, T. | 2791 |
| Tadcaster, 185, W. | 2426 | Waltham Abbey, 12, T. | 2097 | Woburn, 43, F. | 1656 |
| *Tamworth, 115, S. | 1636 | Wantage, 60, S. | 2560 | Woking, 25, T. | 1810 |
| Tarporley, 179, T. | 800 | *Wareham, 115, S. | 1931 | Wolsingham, 259, T. | 2197 |
| Tattershall, 126, F. | 126 | Warminster, 96, S. | 5612 | Wolverhampton, 123, W. | 18,380 |
| *Taunton, 142, W. & S. | 8534 | Warrington, 185, W. | 13,570 | Wooburn, 25, F. | 1831 |
| *Tavistock, 205, S. | 5483 | *Warwick, 92, S. | 8235 | Woodbridge, 77, W. | 4060 |
| Tenbury, 131, T. | 1008 | *Watford, with Cashiobury, 15, T. | 2960 | *Woodstock, 63, T. | 1455 |
| Tenterden, 56, F. | 3239 | Wallington, 46, S. | 1479 | Wooler, 316, Th. | 1850 |
| Tedbury, 99, W. | 2734 | Watton, 91, W. | 891 | Woolwich, 9, F. | 17,008 |
| *Tewkesbury, 104, W. & S. | 4962 | Wednesbury, 118, W. | 6471 | *Wootton Bassett, 87, T. | 1701 |
| Thame, 44, T. | 2472 | Weedon Beck, 84, W. | 1178 | *Worcester, 112, W. F. & S. | 17,023 |
| Thaxted, 44, F. | 2045 | Wellingbrough, 68, W. | 4454 | Workington, 312, W. | 6439 |
| *Thetford, 80, S. | 2922 | Wellington, 142, Th. | 8590 | Worksop, 142, W. | 4567 |
| *Thirsk, 214, M. | 2533 | Wellington, 119, Th. | 4170 | Worstead, 125, S. | 706 |
| Thornbury, 121, S. | 1261 | Wells, 119, S. | 2950 | Worthing, 56, Daily, | |
| Thorne, 163, W. | 3463 | **Wells, 120, W. & S. | 5888 | Wotton under Edge, 168, F. | 5004 |
| Thorney, 84, T. | 1970 | Wem, 172, Th. | 1555 | Wragby, 139, Th. | 653 |
| Thrapstone, 74, T. | 854 | *Wendover, 55, Th. | 1602 | Wrotham, 24, T. | 2357 |
| Thurrock, Grays, 21, Th. | 742 | *Wenlock Much, 148, M. | 2200 | *Wycomb, High, 29, F. | 2864 |
| Tichfield, 78, S. | 3528 | *Weobley, 145, Th. | 739 | Wye, 55, Th. | 1508 |
| Tickhill, 153, F. | 1830 | *Westbury, 100, F. | 2117 | Wymondham, 100, F. | 839 |
| Tideswell, 161, W. | 1513 | Westerham, 21, W. | 1742 | Yarm, 237, Th. | 1504 |
| *Tintagell, with Bossany, 232, Th. | 877 | *Westminster, Daily, | 182,085 | *Yarmouth, Gt. 124, W. & S. | 18,040 |
| *Tiverton, 165, T. & S. | 6712 | Wetherby, 190, Th. | 1217 | *Yarmouth (Isle of Wight), F. | 564 |
| Topsham, 170, S. | 3156 | **Weymouth, and Melcombe Regis, 128, T. & F. | 6622 | Yeovil, 122, F. | 4655 |
| Torrington, Gt. 192, S. | 2538 | Whitby, 244, S. | 8697 | *York, 196, T. Th. & S. | 22,529 |
| *Totnes, 196, S. | 3128 | Whitchurch, 161, F. | 5376 | | |
| Towcester, 60, T. | 2554 | | | | |

*Population of the Principal Towns of Scotland, including their Parishes.*

*** Those in *Italics* are Royal Burghs.

| | | | | | | | | |
|---|---|---|---|---|---|---|---|---|
| Aberdeen, Old and New | 44,796 | Banff | 3655 | Crieff | 4216 | Dunbar | 3872 |
| Aberdour | 1495 | Bathgate | 3883 | Cromarty | 2649 | Dundee | 30,575 |
| Abernethy (Fife division) | 1701 | Beith | 4472 | Comrie | 2614 | Dunfermline | 15,681 |
| Airdrie | 4860 | Bervie | 1092 | Cullen | 1452 | Dunkeld | 1364 |
| Alloa | 5577 | Berwick, North | 1694 | Culross | 1434 | Dunning | 1876 |
| Alyth | 2569 | Biggar | 1727 | Cumbernauld | 2564 | Dunse | 3775 |
| Annan | 4486 | Borrowstounness | 3018 | Cumnock, New | 1856 | Dysart | 6989 |
| Anstruther, E. | 1090 | Brechin | 5986 | Cumnock, Old | 2343 | Eaglesham | 1927 |
| Anstruther, W. | 429 | Burntisland | 2136 | Cupar Angus | 2522 | Edinburgh | 138,235 |
| Arbroath | 5817 | Callander | 2031 | Cupar Fife | 5892 | Elgin | 5008 |
| Ardrossan and Saltcoats | 3105 | Campbelton | 9016 | Dalkeith | 5169 | Ellon | 2190 |
| Auchterarder | 2870 | Carnwath and Wilsontown | 2388 | Dalmellington | 976 | Ely | 866 |
| Auchtermuchty | 2754 | Catrine | 3865 | Dalry | 3513 | Errol | 2687 |
| Ayr, with Newton | 11,482 | Ceres | 2440 | Dingwall | 2031 | Eyemouth | 1185 |
| Ayton | 1481 | Chirnside | 1189 | Dornoch | 3300 | Falkirk | 11,536 |
| Balfron | 2041 | Clackmannan | 4056 | Douglass | 2195 | Falkland | 2459 |
| | | Coldingham | 2675 | Doune | 3250 | FerryPort-on-Craig | 1461 |
| | | Coldstream | 2801 | Dumbarton | 3481 | Fochabers | 2235 |
| | | Crail | 1856 | Dunblane | 3135 | Forfar | 5091 |
| | | | | Dumfries | 11,052 | | |

| | | | | | | | |
|---|---|---|---|---|---|---|---|
| rrea | 3540 | Kilmany | 751 | Lochwinnoch | 4130 | Renfrew | 2616 |
| rtrose and Ross- | | Kilmarnock | 12,769 | Longforgan | 1514 | Rothsay | 5709 |
| arkie | 1571 | Kilrenny | 1494 | Markinch | 4661 | Rothymurchus | 585 |
| rt William | 1484 | Kilsyth | 4260 | Mauchline | 2057 | Rutherglen | 4640 |
| erburgh | 2831 | Kilwinning | 3696 | Maybole | 5204 | St. Andrews | 4899 |
| ashiels | 1545 | Kingsbarns | 998 | Meigle | 847 | St. Ninians | 8274 |
| ton | 3442 | Kincardine | 2388 | Melrose | 3467 | Sanquhar | 3006 |
| mouth | 1401 | Kinghorn | 2443 | Mid-Calder | 1410 | Seconie | 2024 |
| house | 1835 | Kinross | 2563 | Moffat | 2218 | Selkirk | 2778 |
| van | 4490 | Kintore | 1057 | Moncktown | 1744 | Stevenston | 3558 |
| mmis | 2009 | Kirkcaldy | 4452 | Monimail | 1227 | Stewarton | 3656 |
| gow | 147,043 | Kirkcudbright | 2595 | Montrose | 10,338 | Stirling | 7314 |
| aluce | 1957 | Kirkintiloch | 4580 | Muirkirk | 2647 | Stonehaven | 1797 |
| an | 19,170 | Kirkwall | 2212 | Musselburgh | 7836 | Stonehouse | 2038 |
| enlaw | 1349 | Kirremuir | 5056 | Nairn | 5228 | Stornoway | 4119 |
| nock | 22,088 | Lanark, Old, and | | Newburgh | 2190 | Stranraer | 2463 |
| dington | 5255 | New | 7085 | Newmills | 3741 | Strathaven | 5050 |
| ilton | 7613 | Langholm | 2404 | Newton-Stewart | 3090 | Strathmiglo | 1842 |
| Nick | 4387 | Largo | 2301 | Oban | 804 | Straiton | 1292 |
| tley | 3349 | Largs | 2479 | Old Meldrum | 1772 | Stromness | 2944 |
| burgh | 5251 | Lasswade | 4186 | Paisley | 26,428 | Tain | 2961 |
| rrary | 1137 | Lauder | 1845 | Pathhead | 1918 | Thurso | 4045 |
| rkeithing | 2512 | Laurencekirk | 1515 | Peebles | 2705 | Tranent | 3366 |
| rness | 12,264 | Leadhills | 1914 | Perth | 19,068 | Torryburn | 1443 |
| rarie | 1129 | Leith | 26,000 | Peterhead | 6313 | Turreff | 2406 |
| nshaven | 1406 | Lerwick | 2224 | Pittenweem | 1200 | Wemyss | 4157 |
| ne | 7007 | Leslie | 2290 | Port-Glasgow | 5262 | West Calder | 14.8 |
| th | 3926 | Leuchars | 1731 | Portobello | 3088 | Wick | 6715 |
| lo | 4880 | Linlithgow | 4692 | Postpatrick | 1818 | Wigton | 2042 |
| noway | 1649 | Linton | 1194 | Portsoy | 3245 | Whitburn | 1900 |
| archan | 4213 | Lochgilphead | 694 | Prestonpans | 2055 | Whithorn | 2361 |
| ride | 1946 | Lochmaben | 2651 | Queensferry | 690 | Yptholm | 1240 |

## TOWNS IN WALES.

| | | | | | | | |
|---|---|---|---|---|---|---|---|
| beravon | 565 | Crickeith | 530 | Llandilo | 1019 | Newtown | 3486 |
| berconway | 1105 | Crickhowel | 1008 | Llandovery | 1292 | Oystermouth | 1908 |
| berdaxon | 1254 | Denbigh | 3195 | Llanfylling | 1706 | Pembroke | 4985 |
| berfraw | 1204 | Dinas Mowddwy | 1166 | Llangadock | 2484 | Presteigne | 1387 |
| bergeley | 2517 | Dolgelly | 3588 | Llangollen | 2560 | Pwllheli | 1876 |
| berystwith | 3556 | Fishguard | 1837 | Llanidloes | 1984 | Radnor | 2136 |
| nlweh | 5292 | Flint | 1612 | Llanrwst | 2277 | Rhayader | 647 |
| la | 1163 | Haverfordwest | 4055 | Llaptrissant | 2545 | Ruthin | 1294 |
| angor | 3579 | Hawarden | 964 | Loughor | 427 | St. Asaph | 2294 |
| aumaris | 2205 | Hay | 1319 | Mackynlleth | 1585 | St. Clears | 908 |
| recknock | 4193 | Holyhead | 4071 | MerthyrTidvil | 17,404 | St. Davids | 2240 |
| alt, or Builth | 946 | Holywell | 8309 | Milford Haven | 2050 | Swansea | 10,255 |
| erwys | 952 | Kidwelly | 1733 | Mold | 6268 | Talgarth | 698 |
| rdiff | 3521 | Knighton | 1000 | Montgomery | 1062 | Tenby | 1554 |
| rdigan | 2597 | Lampeter | 847 | Narbeth | 2295 | Towyn | 2569 |
| rmarthen | 8906 | Laugharne | 1391 | Neith | 2825 | Tregarron | 709 |
| rnarvon | 5788 | Llanbadarn | 1479 | Nevyn | 1614 | Welch Pool | 4255 |
| rwen | 1742 | Llanelly | 2621 | Newpeat | 1666 | Wrexham | 4796 |
| wbridge | 1107 | Llandaff | 1138 | | | | |

## IRELAND.

| | | | | | |
|---|---|---|---|---|---|
| unties in the Province of Leinster. | | Wicklow | 115,162 | Carrickfergus, T. | 8,255 |
| | | Counties in the Province of Munster. | | Cavan | 194,880 |
| low | 81,287 | | | Donegal | 249,483 |
| gheda, Town | 18,118 | Clare | 208,896 | Down | 329,348 |
| blin | 160,274 | Cork | 702,000 | Fermanagh | 130,399 |
| blin, City | 186,276 | Cork, City | 100,535 | Londonderry | 194,099 |
| dare | 101,715 | Kerry | 205,937 | Monaghan | 178,188 |
| kenny | 157,096 | Limerick | 214,286 | Tyrone | 259,691 |
| kenny, City | 23,230 | Limerick, City | 66,642 | Counties in the Province of Connaught. | |
| g's County | 132,519 | Tipperary | 353,402 | | |
| gford | 107,702 | Waterford | 127,679 | Galway | 286,921 |
| th | 101,070 | Waterford, City | 26,787 | Galway, Town | 27,887 |
| th | 174,716 | Counties in the Province of Ulster. | | Leitrim | 105,076 |
| en's County | 129,391 | | | Mayo | 297,538 |
| tmeath | 138,042 | Antrim | 261,601 | Roscommon | 207,777 |
| ford | 169,344 | Armagh | 196,577 | Sligo | 157,878 |

# A TABLE OF THE PRINCIPAL GOLD COINS

*Now current, with their value in Sterling, according to the Mint price, viz.:— Sterling Gold £3. 17s. 10½d. per oz.*

| | £. | s. | d. |
|---|---|---|---|
| **AUSTRIAN DOMINIONS.** | | | |
| Souverain, single ... ... ... | 0 | 13 | 10 |
| Ducat, Kremnitz or Hungarian ... | 0 | 9 | 5¼ |
| **BAVARIA.** | | | |
| Carolin d'or ... ... ... ... | 1 | 0 | 9 |
| Max d'or ... ... ... ... | 0 | 13 | 10 |
| **BRUNSWICK.** | | | |
| Carl d'or ... ... ... ... | 0 | 16 | 5¼ |
| **BERN.** | | | |
| Ducat ... ... ... ... ... | 0 | 9 | 5 |
| **DENMARK.** | | | |
| Ducat, current ... ... ... | 0 | 7 | 6 |
| **EAST INDIES.** | | | |
| Mohur, or gold rupee ... ... | 1 | 9 | 11¾ |
| Star pagoda ... ... ... ... | 0 | 7 | 7 |
| **ENGLAND.** | | | |
| Guinea ... ... ... ... | 1 | 1 | 0 |
| Half-Guinea ... ... ... ... | 0 | 10 | 6 |
| Seven shillings piece ... ... | 0 | 7 | 0 |
| Sovereign ... ... ... ... | 1 | 0 | 0 |
| Half-sovereign ... ... ... | 0 | 10 | 0 |
| **FLANDERS,** *(see Austrian Dominions.)* | | | |
| **FRANCE.** | | | |
| Louis d'or, old (coined before 1786) | 0 | 19 | 11½ |
| Louis d'or, new (coined since 1786) | 0 | 18 | 9¼ |
| Napoleon, or piece of 40 franks, (new coins) ... ... .. | 1 | 11 | 8¾ |
| **GENEVA.** | | | |
| Pistole ... ... ... ... | 0 | 14 | 1½ |
| **GENOA.** | | | |
| Sequin ... ... ... ... | 0 | 9 | 5¾ |
| Genovina d'or ... ... ... | 3 | 10 | 2¼ |
| New piece, of 96-lire ... ... | 3 | 2 | 9 |
| **GERMANY.** | | | |
| Ducat *ad legem imperii* ... ... | 0 | 9 | 4½ |
| **HAMBURGH,** *(see Germany.)* | | | |
| **HANOVER.** | | | |
| George d'or ... ... ... ... | 0 | 16 | 6¼ |
| Gold guelden .. ... ... ... | 0 | 6 | 8 |
| **HOLLAND.** | | | |
| Ryder ... ... ... ... ... | 1 | 4 | 11 |
| Ducat ... ... ... ... ... | 0 | 9 | 4½ |
| **MALTA.** | | | |
| Louis d'or, double ... ... ... | 1 | 19 | 5 |
| **MILAN.** | | | |
| Doppia or pistole ... ... ... | 0 | 15 | 7 |
| **NAPLES.** | | | |
| Double ounce, or six-ducat piece ... | 1 | 1 | 3 |
| **PIEDMONT.** | | | |
| Doppia or pistole, old (coined before 1785) ... ... ... | 1 | 3 | 9¾ |
| Ditto, new (coined since 1785) ... | 1 | 2 | 7 |
| Sequin .. ... ... ... ... | 0 | 9 | 5¼ |
| **POLAND,** Ducat, *(see Germany.)* | | | |
| **PORTUGAL.** | | | |
| Joanese ... ... ... ... | 1 | 15 | 11 |
| New crusade ... ... ... ... | 0 | 2 | 6 |
| **PRUSSIA.** | | | |
| Frederick d'or ... ... ... | 0 | 16 | 6¼ |
| **ROME.** | | | |
| Sequin ... ... ... ... ... | 0 | 9 | 2¼ |
| Doppia ... ... ... ... ... | 0 | 15 | 5¾ |
| **RUSSIA.** | | | |
| Imperial of the coinage of 1763 ... | 1 | 12 | 9¾ |
| Ditto of the coinage of 1801 ... | 1 | 12 | 9½ |
| **SAXONY.** | | | |
| Auguste d'or ... ... ... ... | 0 | 16 | 3 |
| **SICILY.** | | | |
| Ounce ... ... ... ... ... | 0 | 10 | 8¼ |
| **SPAIN.** | | | |
| Doubloon or pistole, single (coined before 1772) ... ... ... | 0 | 16 | 11½ |
| Ditto (coined since 1772) ... ... | 0 | 16 | 7 |
| **SWEDEN.** | | | |
| Ducat ... ... ... ... ... | 0 | 9 | 1 |
| **TURKEY.** | | | |
| Sequin funducli of 1764 ... ... | 0 | 9 | 2¼ |
| Mahbub of 1781 ... ... ... | 0 | 5 | 9 |
| Nisfie of 1781 ... ... ... | 0 | 2 | 10½ |
| Roubbie of 1781 ... ... ... | 0 | 1 | 5¾ |
| **TUSCANY.** | | | |
| Ruspono ... ... ... ... | 1 | 8 | 6 |
| Sequin gigliato ... ... ... | 0 | 9 | 6 |
| **VENICE.** | | | |
| Sequin ... ... ... ... | 0 | 9 | 6 |
| **UNITED STATES OF AMERICA.** | | | |
| Eagle ... ... ... .. ... | 2 | 3 | 8 |

# A TABLE OF THE PRINCIPAL SILVER COINS

*now current, with their Intrinsic Value in Sterling, according to the Mint price of Silver, at 5s. 2d. per oz.*

| | s. | d. | | | s. | d. |
|---|---|---|---|---|---|---|
| **AIX-LA-CHAPELLE.** | | | Rix-dollar, specie or banco | ... | 4 | 0¼ |
| nthapruessntger ... ... ... | 0 | 7¾ | Lewendaler, or Lyondollar | ... | 3 | 9¼ |
| **USTRIA** *(see Germany)*, convention coins. | | | Goldgilder ... ... ... | ... | 2 | 8¼ |
| **BASIL.** | | | **LUBECK.** | | | |
| ix-dollar (coined since 1764) | 3 | 6¼ | Rix-dollar, current ... ... | ... | 3 | 4 |
| **BAVARIA,** *(see Germany.)* | | | **LUNEBURG.** | | | |
| **BERN.** | | | Fine piece of two-thirds ... | ... | 2 | 5¾ |
| atacon ... ... ... | 4 | 2½ | **MECKLENBURG,** *(see Hamburgh)*, mark, current. | | | |
| en-Batzes piece ... ... | 1 | 2½ | | | | |
| ive-Batzes piece ... ... | 0 | 7 | **MALTA.** | | | |
| **BOLOGNA,** *(see Rome.)* | | | Ounce ... ... ... | ... | 4 | 5¼ |
| **DENMARK.** | | | Scudo ... ... ... | ... | 1 | 9¼ |
| 3x-dollar, specie ... ... | 4 | 6¾ | **MILAN.** | | | |
| rohn, or crown, single ... | 2 | 8¾ | Filippo ... ... ... | ... | 4 | 8¼ |
| **ENGLAND.** | | | **NAPLES.** | | | |
| rown ... ... ... | 5 | 0 | Ducat ... ... ... | ... | 3 | 7 |
| lalf-crown ... ... | 2 | 6 | **PIEDMONT.** | | | |
| hilling ... ... ... | 1 | 0 | Scudo ... ... ... | ... | 5 | 8¼ |
| ixpence ... ... ... | 0 | 6 | **POLAND.** | | | |
| **EAST INDIES.** | | | Rix-dollar, (coined since 1787) | ... | 4 | 0¼ |
| tupee, Sicca ... ... | 2 | 0¼ | Double florin, Polish, id. ... | ... | 0 | 11½ |
| )itto, Bombay ... ... | 2 | 0¼ | Single florin, ditto, id. ... | ... | 0 | 6 |
| )itto, Surat ... ... | 1 | 11 | **PORTUGAL.** | | | |
| )itto, Arcot ... ... | 1 | 11½ | New crusade, (coined since 1750) | ... | 2 | 9¼ |
| )itto, Madras ... ... | 2 | 0¼ | **PRUSSIA.** | | | |
| **FLANDERS.** | | | Rix-dollar ... ... ... | ... | 3 | 0 |
| )ucatoon ... ... | 5 | 2¼ | **ROME.** | | | |
| rown ... ... ... | 4 | 7½ | Scudo ... ... ... | ... | 4 | 4¼ |
| **FRANCE.** | | | **RUSSIA.** | | | |
| cu, or crown ... ... | 4 | 9¾ | Ruble, of the coinage of 1764 ... | ... | 3 | 3 |
| ive-franc piece (new coin) ... | 4 | 0¼ | Ditto, of the coinage of 1801 ... | ... | 2 | 9¼ |
| **GENEVA.** | | | **SAXONY,** *(see Germany.)* | | | |
| cu, or patagon ... ... | 4 | 0½ | Scudo ... ... ... | ... | 4 | 2 |
| **GENOA.** | | | **SPAIN.** | | | |
| cudo d'argento, or Genovina, (full weight) ... ... | 6 | 7½ | Dollar, (coined before 1772) ... | ... | 4 | 5¼ |
| )itto, (light) ... ... | 6 | 1½ | Ditto, (coined since 1772) ... | ... | 4 | 4¼ |
| cudo di St. Giambatista ... | 3 | 4½ | **SWEDEN.** | | | |
| Horgino ... ... ... | 0 | 10½ | Rix-dollar, specie ... ... | ... | 4 | 7½ |
| Madonnina ... ... | 0 | 8½ | **ST. GALL.** | | | |
| New piece of eight-lire, of 1789 | 5 | 4 | Rix-dollar ... ... ... | ... | 4 | 4 |
| **GERMANY.** | | | **TUSCANY.** | | | |
| tix-dollar, constitution, (coined after the rate of 1566) ... | 4 | 8 | Francescone, or Leopoldone ... | ... | 4 | 6 |
| Florin, constitution, (coined after the rate of 1566) ... | 2 | 4 | Tollaro, or Scudo ... | ... | 4 | 5 |
| tix-dollar, convention, (coined after the rate of 1753) ... | 4 | 2 | **TURKEY.** | | | |
| Florin, or piece of ⅔ ditto ... | 2 | 1 | Piastre of 1780 ... ... | ... | 1 | 7½ |
| Copfstuck ... ... ... | 0 | 8½ | Ditto of 1801 ... ... | ... | 1 | 1½ |
| **HAMBURGH.** | | | **UNITED STATES.** | | | |
| tix-dollar, banco ... ... | 4 | 6½ | Dollar ... ... ... | ... | 4 | 5¾ |
| Mark, current ... ... | 1 | 2½ | **VENICE.** | | | |
| **HANOVER,** *(see Germany)*, constitution coins. | | | Scudo della croce ... ... | ... | 5 | 3 |
| | | | Giustina ... ... ... | ... | 4 | 7½ |
| **HOLLAND.** | | | Ducat ... ... ... | ... | 3 | 4¼ |
| )ucatoon ... ... | 5 | 6 | **ZURICH.** | | | |
| Three-gilder piece ... ... | 5 | 2½ | Ecu, or rix-dollar ... ... | ... | 4 | 4½ |
| Daalder ... ... ... | 2 | 7 | | | | |
| Albert's dollar ... ... | 4 | 4½ | | | | |
| Gilder, or florin ... ... | 1 | 8½ | | | | |

A TABLE

OF

**Reciprocal Distances**

OF THE

PRINCIPAL TOWNS

OF

*IRELAND.*

Find the names of the Towns wanted in the perpendicular and sloping Alphabets, and their junction of the lines will give the distance. Thus from Newry to Dundalk 10—and from Drogheda to Belfast 57 miles.

*The first column gives the distance from Dublin.*

| | Dublin | Athlone | Ballyshannon | Belfast | Cashel | Charlemont | Clonmel | Coleraine | Cork | Donaghadee | Donegal | Drogheda | Dundalk | Ennis | Enniskillen | Galway | Kildare | Kilkenny | Kinsale | Limerick | Lisburn | Londonderry | Monaghan | Mullingar | New Ross | Newry | Omagh | Philipstown | Portarlington | Roscommon | Sligo | Strabane | Tipperary | Tralee | Trim | Waterford | Wexford | Wicklow | Youghal |
|---|---|---|---|---|---|---|---|---|---|---|---|---|---|---|---|---|---|---|---|---|---|---|---|---|---|---|---|---|---|---|---|---|---|---|---|---|---|---|---|
| Athlone | | | | | | | | | | | | | | | | | | | | | | | | | | | | | | | | | | | | | | | |
| Ballyshannon | | | | | | | | | | | | | | | | | | | | | | | | | | | | | | | | | | | | | | | |
| Bandon | | | | | | | | | | | | | | | | | | | | | | | | | | | | | | | | | | | | | | | |
| Belfast | | | | | | | | | | | | | | | | | | | | | | | | | | | | | | | | | | | | | | | |
| Cashel | | | | | | | | | | | | | | | | | | | | | | | | | | | | | | | | | | | | | | | |
| Charlemont | | | | | | | | | | | | | | | | | | | | | | | | | | | | | | | | | | | | | | | |
| Charleville | | | | | | | | | | | | | | | | | | | | | | | | | | | | | | | | | | | | | | | |
| Clonmel | | | | | | | | | | | | | | | | | | | | | | | | | | | | | | | | | | | | | | | |
| Coleraine | | | | | | | | | | | | | | | | | | | | | | | | | | | | | | | | | | | | | | | |
| Cork | | | | | | | | | | | | | | | | | | | | | | | | | | | | | | | | | | | | | | | |
| Donaghadee | | | | | | | | | | | | | | | | | | | | | | | | | | | | | | | | | | | | | | | |
| Donegal | | | | | | | | | | | | | | | | | | | | | | | | | | | | | | | | | | | | | | | |
| Drogheda | | | | | | | | | | | | | | | | | | | | | | | | | | | | | | | | | | | | | | | |
| Dundalk | | | | | | | | | | | | | | | | | | | | | | | | | | | | | | | | | | | | | | | |
| Ennis | | | | | | | | | | | | | | | | | | | | | | | | | | | | | | | | | | | | | | | |
| Enniskillen | | | | | | | | | | | | | | | | | | | | | | | | | | | | | | | | | | | | | | | |
| Galway | | | | | | | | | | | | | | | | | | | | | | | | | | | | | | | | | | | | | | | |
| Kildare | | | | | | | | | | | | | | | | | | | | | | | | | | | | | | | | | | | | | | | |
| Kilkenny | | | | | | | | | | | | | | | | | | | | | | | | | | | | | | | | | | | | | | | |
| Kinsale | | | | | | | | | | | | | | | | | | | | | | | | | | | | | | | | | | | | | | | |
| Limerick | | | | | | | | | | | | | | | | | | | | | | | | | | | | | | | | | | | | | | | |
| Lisburn | | | | | | | | | | | | | | | | | | | | | | | | | | | | | | | | | | | | | | | |
| Londonderry | | | | | | | | | | | | | | | | | | | | | | | | | | | | | | | | | | | | | | | |
| Monaghan | | | | | | | | | | | | | | | | | | | | | | | | | | | | | | | | | | | | | | | |
| Mullingar | | | | | | | | | | | | | | | | | | | | | | | | | | | | | | | | | | | | | | | |
| Newry | | | | | | | | | | | | | | | | | | | | | | | | | | | | | | | | | | | | | | | |
| New Ross | | | | | | | | | | | | | | | | | | | | | | | | | | | | | | | | | | | | | | | |
| Omagh | | | | | | | | | | | | | | | | | | | | | | | | | | | | | | | | | | | | | | | |
| Philipstown | | | | | | | | | | | | | | | | | | | | | | | | | | | | | | | | | | | | | | | |
| Portarlington | | | | | | | | | | | | | | | | | | | | | | | | | | | | | | | | | | | | | | | |
| Roscommon | | | | | | | | | | | | | | | | | | | | | | | | | | | | | | | | | | | | | | | |
| Sligo | | | | | | | | | | | | | | | | | | | | | | | | | | | | | | | | | | | | | | | |
| Strabane | | | | | | | | | | | | | | | | | | | | | | | | | | | | | | | | | | | | | | | |
| Tipperary | | | | | | | | | | | | | | | | | | | | | | | | | | | | | | | | | | | | | | | |
| Tralee | | | | | | | | | | | | | | | | | | | | | | | | | | | | | | | | | | | | | | | |
| Trim | | | | | | | | | | | | | | | | | | | | | | | | | | | | | | | | | | | | | | | |
| Waterford | | | | | | | | | | | | | | | | | | | | | | | | | | | | | | | | | | | | | | | |
| Wexford | | | | | | | | | | | | | | | | | | | | | | | | | | | | | | | | | | | | | | | |
| Wicklow | | | | | | | | | | | | | | | | | | | | | | | | | | | | | | | | | | | | | | | |
| Youghal | | | | | | | | | | | | | | | | | | | | | | | | | | | | | | | | | | | | | | | |

# A TABLE

OF

# Reciprocal Distances,

OF THE

PRINCIPAL TOWNS

OF

*SCOTLAND.*

EDINBURGH from LONDON, 397½

| | Edinburgh | Aberdeen | Ayr | Banff | Berwick on Tweed | Brechin | Campbelton | Carlisle | Cupar in Angus | Cupar in Fife | Dalkeith | Dumbarton | Dunfermline |
|---|---|---|---|---|---|---|---|---|---|---|---|---|---|
| Aberdeen.... | 109 | | | | | | | | | | | | |
| Ayr.......... | 76 | 178 | | | | | | | | | | | |
| Banff........ | 165 | 43 | 217 | | | | | | | | | | |
| Berwick on T | 54 | 161 | 132 | 220 | | | | | | | | | |
| Brechin ..... | 64 | 39 | 138 | 79 | 137 | | | | | | | | |
| Campbelton.. | 170 | 241 | 137 | 280 | 231 | 191 | | | | | | | |
| Carlisle, Eng | 90 | 216 | 100 | 255 | 88 | 154 | 233 | | | | | | |
| Cupar Angus | 56 | 67 | 111 | 107 | 109 | 28 | 165 | 144 | | | | | |
| Cupar Fife... | 30 | 76 | 108 | 120 | 85 | 34 | 177 | 120 | 24 | | | | |
| Dalkeith..... | 6 | 127 | 82 | 171 | 52 | 70 | 18[illegible] | 96 | 58 | 36 | | | |
| Dumbarton... | 58 | 150 | 49 | 190 | 113 | 110 | 117 | 116 | 82 | 77 | 64 | | |
| Dunfermline. | 16 | 107 | 74 | 149 | 71 | 67 | 216 | 106 | 40 | 31 | 24 | 55 | |
| Dumfries.... | 71 | 181 | 61 | 240 | 108 | 130 | 206 | 39 | 129 | 105 | 78 | 89 | 88 |
| Dunbar...... | 27 | 148 | 103 | 192 | 27 | 91 | 203 | 115 | 79 | 57 | 27 | 86 | 43 |
| Dundee...... | 40 | 66 | 119 | 110 | 95 | 24 | 194 | 130 | 14 | 10 | 46 | 91 | 43 |
| Elgin ........ | 157 | 63 | 211 | 33 | 210 | 93 | 231 | 247 | 131 | 117 | 163 | 183 | 141 |
| Falkirk...... | 24 | 145 | 57 | 167 | 79 | 91 | 156 | 144 | 62 | 50 | 30 | 39 | 14 |
| Forfar....... | 73 | 52 | 125 | 92 | 116 | 13 | 178 | 152 | 17 | 21 | 68 | 99 | 57 |
| Glasgow..... | 43 | 144 | 34 | 183 | 99 | 104 | 132 | 113 | 76 | 74 | 50 | 15 | 40 |
| Greenock .... | 66 | 166 | 46 | 205 | 121 | 126 | 154 | 123 | 98 | 96 | 72 | 10 | 62 |
| Hamilton .... | 38 | 133 | 37 | 192 | 92 | 98 | 143 | 90 | 77 | 66 | 44 | 25 | 36 |
| Hawick...... | 47 | 168 | 89 | 212 | 43 | 111 | 226 | 42 | 99 | 77 | 53 | 91 | 63 |
| Inverary .... | 103 | 168 | 93 | 207 | 158 | 128 | 73 | 160 | 97 | 112 | 109 | 44 | 111 |
| Inverness.... | 157 | 130 | 202 | 70 | 211 | 120 | 103 | 240 | 116 | 138 | 158 | 145 | 141 |
| Jedburgh.... | 46 | 155 | 98 | 210 | 35 | 109 | 221 | 53 | 99 | 75 | 39 | 103 | 61 |
| John o' Groat | 287 | 261 | 327 | 201 | 342 | 251 | 324 | 377 | 116 | 140 | 293 | 267 | 272 |
| Kelso........ | 42 | 163 | 99 | 207 | 25 | 106 | 218 | 63 | 96 | 72 | 37 | 100 | 58 |
| Kilmarnock.. | 63 | 167 | 12 | 228 | 117 | 125 | 149 | 91 | 97 | 91 | 69 | 37 | 62 |
| Kircudbright | 100 | 207 | 64 | 266 | 134 | 165 | 230 | 67 | 155 | 131 | 101 | 113 | 117 |
| Kirkcaldy.... | 12 | 109 | 88 | 153 | 66 | 52 | 188 | 102 | 40 | 18 | 18 | 69 | 13 |
| Linlithgow .. | 16 | 137 | 60 | 155 | 71 | 75 | 164 | 106 | 70 | 46 | 22 | 42 | 10 |
| Montrose.... | 94 | 36 | 149 | 84 | 125 | 8 | 204 | 160 | 43 | 39 | 76 | 171 | 70 |
| Paisley...... | 52 | 152 | 34 | 191 | 107 | 112 | 140 | 109 | 8 | 82 | 58 | 9 | 47 |
| Peebles...... | 21 | 128 | 62 | 187 | 61 | 86 | 178 | 77 | 39 | 52 | 27 | 61 | 38 |
| Perth ........ | 40 | 82 | 96 | 121 | 95 | 42 | 151 | 130 | 14 | 26 | 46 | 68 | 25 |
| Peterhead.... | 145 | 24 | 196 | 38 | 199 | 63 | 274 | 235 | 91 | 100 | 151 | 169 | 119 |
| Port Glasgow | 62 | 163 | 43 | 202 | 118 | 123 | 151 | 120 | 95 | 93 | 68 | 7 | 59 |
| Port Patrick. | 132 | 234 | 62 | 273 | 187 | 194 | 222 | 128 | 166 | 164 | 138 | 103 | 130 |
| Stirling...... | 35 | 110 | 62 | 155 | 91 | 76 | 140 | 129 | 48 | 42 | 41 | 35 | 20 |

| | Dumfries | Dunbar | Dundee | Elgin | Falkirk | Forfar | Glasgow | Greenock | Hamilton | Hawick | Inverary | Inverness | Jedburgh | John o' Groats House |
|---|---|---|---|---|---|---|---|---|---|---|---|---|---|---|
| Dunbar...... | 99 | | | | | | | | | | | | | |
| Dundee...... | 115 | 57 | | | | | | | | | | | | |
| Elgin ........ | 93[illegible] | 184 | 108 | | | | | | | | | | | |
| Falkirk...... | 98 | 51 | 68 | 163 | | | | | | | | | | |
| Forfar....... | 126 | 89 | 14 | 80 | 86 | | | | | | | | | |
| Glasgow..... | 74 | 71 | 85 | 177 | 23 | 99 | | | | | | | | |
| Greenock .... | 96 | 93 | 107 | 199 | 45 | 119 | 22 | | | | | | | |
| Hamilton .... | 64 | 64 | 70 | 196 | 22 | 93 | 11 | 33 | | | | | | |
| Hawick...... | 24 | 73 | 87 | 204 | 71 | 109 | 76 | 98 | 65 | | | | | |
| Inverary .... | 134 | 130 | 109 | 201 | 83 | 104 | 59 | 40 | 70 | 135 | | | | |
| Inverness.... | 231 | 177 | 128 | 38 | 146 | 116 | 162 | 190 | 173 | 197 | 120 | | | |
| Jedburgh.... | 73 | 60 | 85 | 202 | 69 | 108 | 89 | 111 | 83 | 10 | 148 | 201 | | |
| John o' Groat | 362 | 314 | 259 | 169 | 293 | 247 | 293 | 315 | 304 | 241 | 251 | 131 | 333 | |
| Kelso........ | 83 | 50 | 82 | 199 | 86 | 104 | 86 | 108 | 80 | 20 | 141 | 198 | 10 | 329 |
| Kilmarnock.. | 52 | 90 | 106 | 244 | 45 | 170 | 22 | 30 | 33 | 100 | 70 | 183 | 111 | 315 |
| Kircudbright | 28 | 1[illegible]8 | 141 | 258 | 122 | 163 | 98 | 110 | 87 | 89 | 157 | 257 | 99 | 38[illegible] |
| Kirkcaldy.... | 84 | 39 | 28 | 143 | 36 | 4[illegible] | 52 | 77 | 50 | 59 | 112 | 138 | 60 | 275 |
| Linlithgow .. | 88 | 43 | 56 | 160 | 8 | 67 | 28 | 50 | 30 | 63 | 87 | 166 | 61 | 303 |
| Montrose.... | 145 | 97 | 20 | 78 | 94 | 26 | 105 | 137 | 100 | 112 | 173 | 124 | 115 | 255 |
| Paisley...... | 82 | 79 | 93 | 185 | 32 | 107 | 8 | 15 | 18 | 99 | 50 | 176 | 97 | 310 |
| Peebles...... | 53 | 48 | 62 | 179 | 46 | 73 | 46 | 88 | 35 | 68 | 105 | 184 | 41 | 30[illegible] |
| Perth ........ | 115 | 67 | 23 | 115 | 48 | 30 | 6[illegible] | 84 | 70 | 87 | 86 | 116 | 85 | 247 |
| Peterhead.... | 217 | 172 | 90 | 102 | 169 | 76 | 168 | 190 | 157 | 194 | 192 | 135 | 191 | 251 |
| Port Glasgow | 93 | 89 | 104 | 196 | 43 | 113 | 19 | 3 | 30 | 95 | 43 | 187 | 108 | 312 |
| Port Patrick. | 79 | 159 | 175 | 267 | 114 | 194 | 96 | 101 | 92 | 150 | 149 | [illegible]58 | 152 | 383 |
| Stirling...... | 102 | 62 | 57 | 192 | 11 | 71 | 27 | 45 | 34 | 100 | 78 | 13[illegible] | 81 | 265 |

| | Kelso | Kilmarnock | Kirkcudbright | Kirkcaldy | Linlithgow | Montrose | Paisley | Peebles | Perth | Peterhead | P. Glasgow | P. Patrick |
|---|---|---|---|---|---|---|---|---|---|---|---|---|
| Kilmarnock.. | 104 | | | | | | | | | | | |
| Kircudbright | 109 | 76 | | | | | | | | | | |
| Kirkcaldy.... | 54 | 75 | 113 | | | | | | | | | |
| Linlithgow .. | 58 | 50 | 117 | 24 | | | | | | | | |
| Montrose.... | 112 | 133 | 171 | 59 | 86 | | | | | | | |
| Paisley...... | 94 | 22 | 06 | 63 | 38 | 123 | | | | | | |
| Peebles...... | 3[illegible] | 50 | 78 | 33 | 38 | 92 | 54 | | | | | |
| Perth ........ | 8[illegible] | 83 | 141 | 28 | 82 | 53 | 70 | 63 | | | | |
| Peterhead.... | 187 | 183 | 146 | 133 | 161 | 60 | 176 | 167 | 106 | | | |
| Port Glasgow | 105 | 31 | 107 | 74 | 51 | 134 | 13 | 85 | 81 | 187 | | |
| Port Patrick. | 126 | 71 | 58 | 144 | 137 | 204 | 90 | 132 | 152 | 258 | 98 | |
| Stirling...... | 78 | 40 | 12[illegible] | 34 | 19 | 87 | 36 | 58 | 34 | 134 | 42 | 118 |

Sterling

[illegible]ick

# A TABLE

OF THE

# Comparative Value of the Public Funds,

*Shewing in which to Purchase to the greatest Advantage;*

**WITH THEIR RELATIVE VALUE IN LANDED ESTATES.**

| Bank Consols 3 per Cent. | South Sea Stock 3½ per Cent. | Bank Consols 4 per Cent. | Bank Navy 5 per Cent. | Bank Stock 10 per Cent. | India Stock 10½ per Cent. | Years Purchase of Land. | Ann. Interest per Cent. | | |
|---|---|---|---|---|---|---|---|---|---|
| 46½ | 54¼ | 62 | 77½ | 155 | 162¾ | 15½ | £6 | 9 | 0 |
| 48 | 56 | 64 | 80 | 160 | 168 | 16 | 6 | 5 | 0 |
| 49½ | 57¾ | 66 | 82½ | 165 | 173¼ | 16½ | 6 | 1 | 2 |
| 51 | 59½ | 68 | 85 | 170 | 178½ | 17 | 5 | 17 | 7 |
| 52½ | 61¼ | 70 | 87½ | 175 | 183¾ | 17½ | 5 | 14 | 3 |
| 54 | 63 | 72 | 90 | 180 | 189 | 18 | 5 | 11 | 1 |
| 55½ | 64¾ | 74 | 92½ | 185 | 194¼ | 18½ | 5 | 8 | 1 |
| 57 | 66½ | 76 | 95 | 190 | 199½ | 19 | 5 | 5 | 3 |
| 58½ | 68¼ | 78 | 97½ | 195 | 204¾ | 19½ | 5 | 2 | 7 |
| 60 | 70 | 80 | 100 | 200 | 210 | 20 | 5 | 0 | 0 |
| 61½ | 71¾ | 82 | 101½ | 205 | 215¼ | 20½ | 4 | 17 | 6 |
| 63 | 73½ | 84 | 105 | 210 | 220½ | 21 | 4 | 15 | 2 |
| 64½ | 75¼ | 86 | 107½ | 215 | 225¾ | 21½ | 4 | 13 | 0 |
| 66 | 77 | 88 | 110 | 220 | 231 | 22 | 4 | 10 | 10 |
| 67½ | 78¾ | 90 | 112½ | 225 | 236¼ | 22½ | 4 | 8 | 10 |
| 69 | 81½ | 92 | 115 | 230 | 241½ | 23 | 4 | 6 | 11 |
| 70½ | 82¼ | 94 | 117½ | 235 | 246¾ | 23½ | 4 | 5 | 1 |
| 72 | 84 | 96 | 120 | 240 | 252 | 24 | 4 | 3 | 4 |
| 73½ | 85¾ | 98 | 122½ | 245 | 257¼ | 24½ | 4 | 1 | 7 |
| 75 | 87½ | 100 | 125 | 250 | 262½ | 25 | 4 | 0 | 0 |
| 76½ | 89¼ | 102 | 127½ | 255 | 267¾ | 25½ | 3 | 18 | 5 |
| 78 | 91 | 104 | 130 | 260 | 273 | 26 | 3 | 16 | 11 |
| 79½ | 92¾ | 106 | 132½ | 265 | 277¾ | 26½ | 3 | 15 | 5 |
| 81 | 94½ | 108 | 135 | 270 | 283½ | 27 | 3 | 14 | 0 |
| 82½ | 96¼ | 110 | 137½ | 275 | 288¾ | 27½ | 3 | 12 | 8 |
| 84 | 98 | 112 | 140 | 280 | 294 | 28 | 3 | 11 | 5 |
| 85½ | 99¾ | 114 | 142½ | 285 | 299¼ | 28½ | 3 | 10 | 2 |
| 87 | 101½ | 116 | 145 | 290 | 304½ | 29 | 3 | 8 | 11 |
| 88½ | 103¼ | 118 | 147½ | 295 | 309¾ | 29½ | 3 | 7 | 9 |
| 90 | 105 | 120 | 150 | 300 | 315 | 30 | 3 | 6 | 8 |

EXAMPLE.—Supposing the price of 3 per Cent. Consols to be 60, then South Sea Stock should be 70—4 per Cents. 80.—and 5 per Cents. 100, and so on; but when any of the Funds are below this proportion, it is then advantageous to purchase in that Stock.

## HOLIDAYS OBSERVED AT THE PUBLIC OFFICES.

| | | |
|---|---|---|
| Jan. 1, 6, 25, 29, 30, 31 | May 1, 29 | Sept. 2, 21, 29 |
| Feb. 2, 24 | June 11, 24, 29 | Oct. 18, 28 |
| March 23, 25 | July 19, 25 | Nov. 1, 4, 5, 30 |
| April 23, 25 | August 24 | Dec. 21, 25, 26, 27, 28 |

Ash-Wednesday, Good-Friday, Easter-Monday and Tuesday, Ascension-Day, Whit-Monday and Tuesday.

N. B. At the Custom House, Stamp and Excise Offices, April 5, 23, May 29, July 19 and December 25, are the only Holidays kept. At the East India House, Good Friday and Christmas Day are the only Holidays kept.

Feb. 14, 19, March 1, April 10, 23, June 13, July 15, August 1, Sept. 14, 18, 29, Nov. 2, and 17, are also kept at the Exchequer.—Nov. 9 is kept as a Holiday at the Bank and South Sea House.

*** All Holidays that fall on a Sunday (except the Saints' Days) are kept on the Monday following.

N. B. The Holidays at the Bank, as here stated, relate to the Transfer of Stock and Payment of Dividends only: with respect to the general Business, the Holidays are the same as the Custom House, Excise and Stamp Offices.

# NEWSPAPERS

## OF THE BRITISH EUROPEAN DOMINIONS.

### LONDON PAPERS.

**DAILY MORNING.**
British Press, 127, Strand
Morning Advertiser, 127, Fleet-street
Morning Chronicle, Strand and Norfolk-street
Morning Herald, 18, Catharine-street, Strand
Morning Post, 335, Strand
New Times, 153, Fleet-street
Public Ledger, 10, Warwick-sq. Newgate-st.
Times, Printinghouse-square, Blackfriars

**DAILY EVENING.**
British Traveller, Black Horse-court, Fleet-st.
Courier, 348, Strand
General and Commercial Shipping List, General Post Office
Globe and Traveller, 127, Strand
Star, Picket-street, Temple Bar
Statesman, 291, Strand
Sun, 112, Strand

**EVENING.**
*MONDAY, WEDNESDAY AND FRIDAY.*
Evening Mail, Printinghouse-sq. Blackfriars
London Chronicle, Crane-court, Fleet-street
London Packet, 12, Warwick-square
Mercantile Chronicle, Black Horse-court, Fleet-street
*TUESDAY, THURSDAY AND SATURDAY.*
Commercial Chronicle, Crane-court, Fleet-st.
English Chronicle, Blake-court, Catharine-street, Strand
St. James's Chronicle, Union-st. Blackfriars
*WEDNESDAY.*
British Mercury, 76, Fleet-street
Moderator, Wine-office-court, Fleet-street
Nautical Register, 192, Strand
Philanthropic Gazette, 166, Fleet-street
*TUESDAY AND FRIDAY.*
Courier de Londres, Queen-street, Lincoln's-inn-fields
Lloyd's List, Royal Exchange
*TUESDAY AND SATURDAY.*
London Gazette (by Authority), Cannon-row, Westminster
*SATURDAY.*
Baldwin's Journal, Union-street, Blackfriars
County Herald, 18, Warwick-square
Domestic Chronicle, Johnson's-court, Fleet-st.
Literary Gazette, 267, Strand

Literary Chronicle, Strand
Literary Register, Bride-court
Mirror of the Times, Hind-court, Fleet-stree
Westminster Journal, 9, Lombard-street
*SUNDAY.*
British Freeholder, 76, Fleet-street
British Monitor, 291, Strand
British Luminary, Bell-yard, Temple Bar
Champion, Strand
Constitution, 291, Strand
Dispatch (Bell's), Wine-office-court, Fleet-st
Englishman, 5, Hind-court, Fleet-street
Guardian, 268, Strand
Independent Observer, 267, Strand
Life in London, 76, Fleet-street
London and Provincial Gazette, 76, Fleet-st.
Mirror, 2, Little Bridge-street, Ludgate-hill
Real John Bull, Fleet-street
Representative, 244, Strand
Sunday Advertiser, 127, Fleet-street
Sunday Monitor, 9, Lombard-street
Sunday Times, 76, Fleet-street
Thistle, 9, Newcastle-street
Town Talk, 33, Exeter-street
Weekly Intelligencer
Weekly Register, 127, Fleet-street
Wooller's Gazette, 76, Fleet-street
*SUNDAY AND MONDAY.*
British Neptune, 76, Fleet-street
Bell's Messenger, Bride-court, Fleet-street
Examiner, Catharine-street
John Bull, Johnson's-court, Fleet-street
National Register, 76, Fleet-street
News, 28, Brydges-street, Covent-garden
Observer, 169, Strand
*MONDAY.*
Christian Reporter, 22, Warwick-square
Farmer's Journal, Budge-row
*TUESDAY.*
County Chronicle
*THURSDAY.*
Law Chronicle, 113, Strand
*EVERY THIRD WEEK.*
Hue and Cry (Police Gazette), 240, Strand
*TENTH OF EACH MONTH.*
Literary Advertiser, 55, Paternoster-row
Racing Calendar, 16 Nos. in the year, Oxendon-street, Haymarket

---

## PROVINCIAL PAPERS OF ENGLAND AND WALES,

### WITH THE DAYS OF THEIR PUBLICATION.

Aylesbury (Bucks Chronicle), Sat.
Bangor (North Wales Gazette) Th.
Bath Chronicle, Th.
Bath Gazette, Wed.
Bath Herald, Sat.
Bath Journal, Mon.
Berwick Advertiser, Sat.
Birmingham Chronicle, Th.
Birmingham (Aris's) Gazette, Mon.
Blackburn Journal, Sat.
Blackburn Mail, Wed.
Boston Gazette, Tues.
Brighton Chronicle, Wed.
Brighton Gazette. Th

Brighton Herald, Sat.
Bristol Gazette, Th.
Bristol Journal (Felix Farley's), Sat.
Bristol Mercury, Mon.
Bristol Mirror, Sat.
Bristol Observer, Th.
Bury Gazette, Wed.
Bury Post, Wed.
Cambridge Chronicle, Fri.
Cambridge Huntingdon Gazette, Sat.
Canterbury Kentish Chronicle, Tues. and Fri.
Canterbury Kentish Gazette, Tues. and Fri.
Canterbury Kent Herald Th

Canterbury Kent Mercury Tues.
Carlisle Journal, Sat.
Carlisle Patriot, Sat.
Carmarthen Journal, Fri.
Carnarvon Advertiser, Sat.
Chelmsford Chronicle, Fri.
Chelmsford Gazette, Fri.
Chelmsford (Essex Herald), Tues.
Cheltenham Chronicle, Th.
Chester Chronicle, Fri.
Chester Courant, Tues.
Chester Guardian, Th.
Colchester Gazette, Sat.
Coventry Herald, Fri.
Coventry Mercury, Mon

Derby Mercury, Th.
Derby Reporter,
Devizes Gazette, Th.
Doncaster Gazette, Fri.
Durham Advertiser, Sat.
Durham Chronicle, Sat.
Exeter Alfred, Tues.
Exeter (Devonshire Freeholder), Fri.
Exeter Flying Post, Th.
Exeter Gazette, Sat.
Exeter News, Sat.
Exeter Western Luminary, Tues.
Gloucester Herald, Sat.
Gloucester Journal, Mon.
Hanley Staff. Pottery Gazette, Sat.
Hereford Journal, Wed.
Hull Advertiser, Fri.
Hull Packet, Mon.
Hull Rockingham, Sat.
Ipswich Journal, Sat.
Ipswich Suffolk Chron. Sat.
Kendal (Westmoreland Gazette), Sat.
Kendal (Westmoreland Advertiser), Sat.
Lancaster Gazette, Sat.
Leeds Mercury, Sat.
Leeds Intelligencer, Th.
Leeds Independent, Tues.
Leicester Chronicle, Sat.
Leicester Journal, Fri.
Lewes Sussex Advertiser, Mon.
Litchfield Mercury, Fri.
Liverpool Billinge's Advertiser, Tues.
Liverpool Courier, Wed.
Liverpool General Advertiser, Th.

Liverpool Mercury, Fri.
Liverpool Mercantile Advertiser, Mon.
Liverpool Saturday's Advertiser, Sat.
Macclesfield Courier, Sat.
Maidstone Gazette, Tues.
Maidstone Journal, Tues.
Manchester Chronicle, Sat.
Manchester Gazette, Sat.
Manchester Guardian, Sat.
Manchester Herald, Tues.
Manchester Mercury, Tues.
Manchester Volunteer, Sat.
Newcastle-on-Tyne Chronicle Sat.
Newcastle-on-Tyne Courant (or Hue and Cry), Sat.
Newcastle-on-Tyne Mercury, Tues.
Northampton Mercury, Sat.
Norwich (Norfolk) Chronicle, Sat.
Norwich Courier, Sat.
Norwich Mercury, Sat.
Nottingham Journal, Fri.
Nottingham Review, Fri.
Oswestry Herald, Tues.
Oxford Herald, Sat.
Oxford Journal, Sat.
Plymouth and Dock Journal, Th.
Plymouth Dock Telegraph, Sat.
Portsmouth & Portsea (Hampshire Telegraph), Mon.
Preston Chronicle, Sat.
Reading Mercury, Mon.
Rochester Gazette, Tues.
Salisbury Journal, Mon.
Sheffield Independent, Sat.

Sheffield Iris, Tues.
Sheffield Mercury, Sat.
Sherborne (Dorchester Journal), Th.
Sherborne Mercury, Mon.
Shrewsbury Chronicle, Fri.
Shrewsbury Salopian Journal, Wed.
Southampton Chronicle, Th.
Southampton Luminary, Mon
Stafford Advertiser, Sat.
Stamford Mercury, Fri.
Stamford News, Fri.
Stockport Advertiser, Fri.
Swansea (Cambrian), Fri.
Taunton Courier, Wed.
Truro (Cornwall Gazette), Sat.
Truro (West Briton), Fri.
Wakefield Journal, Fri.
Warwick Advertiser, Sat.
Weymouth Gazette, Th.
Whitehaven (Cumberland Pacquet), Mon.
Whitehaven Gazette, Mon.
Winchester (Hampshire Chronicle), Mon.
Windsor Express, Sat.
Wolverhampton Chronicle, Wed.
Worcester Herald, Sat.
Worcester Journal, Th.
York Chronicle, Th.
York Courant, Tues.
York Herald, Sat.
York (Yorkshire) Gazette, Sat.
York Pick's Racing Calendar, T. Sotheran, Coney-street.
York Racing Calendar and Turf Register, R. Johnson, Coney-street.

## DUBLIN PAPERS.

**DAILY.**
Carrick's Morning Post
Correspondent
Freeman's Journal
Saunders' News Letter
**MONDAY, WEDNESDAY AND FRIDAY.**
Dublin Journal (Faulkner's)
**MONDAY, WEDNESDAY AND SATURDAY.**
Dublin Hibernian Journal

**TUESDAY, THURSDAY AND SATURDAY.**
Dublin Evening Post
Patriot
Dublin Gazette (by Authority)
**TUESDAY AND FRIDAY.**
Dublin Evening Herald
**MONDAY.**
Mercantile Advertiser
**WEDNESDAY.**
Commercial Gazette

**SATURDAY.**
Antidote
Dublin Observer
Dublin Weekly Register
Hue and Cry
Irish Farmers' Journal
**ONCE PER QUARTER.**
Racing Calendar

## IRISH PROVINCIAL PAPERS.

Armagh Volunteer, Tues. and Fri.
Athlone Herald, Fri.
Belfast Commercial Chronicle, Mon. Wed. and Sat.
Belfast Irishman, Fri.
Belfast Mercantile Chronicle (Taggart's), Th.
Belfast News Letter, Tues. and Fri.
Carlow Morning Post, Mon. and Th.
Castlebar (Mayo Constitution) Mon. and Th.

Clonmell Advertiser, Wed. and Sat.
Clonmell Herald, Wed. and Sat.
Cork Advertiser, Tues. Th. and Sat.
Cork Mercantile Chronicle, Mon. Wed. and Fri.
Cork Constitution, Mon. Wed. and Fri.
Cork Southern Reporter, Tues. Th. and Sat.
Drogheda Journal, Wed. and

Dungannon (Ulster Chronicle) Th.
Ennis Chronicle, Wed. & Sat.
Ennis (Clare Journal), Mon. and Th.
Enniskillen Chronicle, Th.
Galway Advertiser, Sat.
Galway Chronicle, Wed. and Sat.
Galway (Connaught Journal) Mon. and Th.
Kilkenny (Leinster Journal) Wed. and Sat.
Kilkenny (Moderator), Tues. Th. and Sat.

Limerick Advertiser, Tues. and Fri.
Limerick Chronicle, Wed. and Sat.
Limerick (Evening Post) Mon. and Th.
Limerick Journal, Wed. & Sat.
Limerick Telegraph, Sat.
Londonderry Journal, Tues. and Fri.

Mullingar (Westmeath Journal), Th.
Newry Telegraph, Tues. and Sat.
Sligo Journal Wed. and Sat.
Strabane (Morning Post) Tues.
Tralee (Kerry Western Herald), Mon. and Th.
Tralee (Kerry Evening Post), Mon. and Th.

Tuam Gazette, Wed. and Sat.
Tullamore Packet, Tues. and Fri.
Waterford Chronicle, Tues. Th. and Sat.
Waterford Mirror, Mon. Wed. and Sat.
Wexford Herald, Mon. and Th.

## SCOTCH PAPERS.

Edinburgh Advertiser, Tues. and Fri.
Edinburgh Caledonian Mercury, Mon. Th. and Sat.
Edinburgh Correspondent, Mon. Th. and Sat.
Edinburgh Evening Courant, Mon. Th. and Sat.
Edinburgh Gazette (by Authority), Tues. and Fri.
Edinburgh Scotsman, Wed Sat.
Edinburgh Star, Tues. & Fri.
Edinburgh Weekly Chronicle, Wed.
Edinburgh Weekly Journal, Wed.

Aberdeen Chronicle, Sat.
Aberdeen Courier, Fri.
Aberdeen Journal, Wed.
Ayr Advertiser, Th.
Ayr and Wigtonshire Courier, Th.
Cupar (Angus) Herald, Th.
Dumfries Courier, Tues.
Dumfries Journal, Tues.
Dundee Advertiser, Fri.
Dundee Courier, Fri.
Glasgow Chronicle, Tues. Th. and Sat.
Glasgow Courier, Tues. Th. and Sat.

Glasgow Herald, Mon. and Fri.
Glasgow Journal, Fri.
Glasgow Sentinal, Fri.
Greenock Advertiser, Tues. and Fri.
Inverness Courier, Th.
Inverness Journal, Fri.
Kelso Mail, Mon. and Th.
Kelso Weekly Journal, Fri.
Leith Shipping List, Tues. and Fri.
Montrose Review, Fri.
Montrose Chronicle, Fri.
Perth Courier, Tues. and Fri.
Stirling Journal, Th.

## BRITISH ISLANDS.

Guernsey Gazette, Sat.
Guernsey Mercury, Sat.
Jersey (St. Hilliers) Constitutional, Sat.

Jersey Gazette (St. Hilliers, Mourants), Sat.
Manks' Advertiser (Douglas), Th.

Manks' Gazette (Douglas), Th.

*Days and Hours for Buying and Accepting, or Selling and Transferring*

THE SEVERAL

# STOCKS, OR GOVERNMENT SECURITIES,

And Receiving the Interest or Dividends due thereon at the Bank, India House, and South Sea House.

| STOCKS. | DIVIDENDS WHEN DUE. | TRANSFER DAYS. |
|---|---|---|
| Bank Stock - - | April 5, October 10 - - | Tuesday, Thursday, Friday |
| Navy 5 per Cents. - - | January 5, July 5 - - | Tuesday, Wedn. Th. Friday |
| 5 per Cents. 1797 and 1802 | April 5, October 10 - - | Tuesday, Thursday, Friday |
| 4 per Cent Consol - - | Ditto, Ditto - - | Tuesday, Wedn. Th. Friday |
| 3 per Cent Consol - - | January 5, July 5 - - | Tuesday, Wedn. Th. Friday |
| 3 per Cent Reduced - - | April 5, October 10 - - | Tuesday, Wedn. Th. Friday |
| 8 per Cent 1726 - - | January 5, July 5 - - | Tuesday and Thursday |
| Long Annuities - - | April 5, October 10 - - | Monday, Wednes. Saturday |
| Imperial 3 per Cents. - | { May 1, and Nov. 1, but not paid till July 5, and Jan. 5 } | Monday, Wednesday, Friday |
| Ditto Annuities - - | { paid till July 5, and Jan. 5 } | Tuesday, Thursday, Saturday |
| South Sea Stock - - | January 5, July 5 - - | Monday, Wednesday, Friday |
| 3 per Cent Old Annuities - | April 5, October 10 - - | Monday, Wednesday, Friday |
| 3 per Cent New Annuities - | January 5, July 5 - - | Tuesday, Thursday, Saturday |
| 3 per Cent 1751 - - - | Ditto, Ditto - - | Tuesday and Thursday |
| East India Stock - - | Ditto, Ditto - - | Tuesday, Thursday, Saturday |
| Irish 5 per Cent Annuities | March 25, September 25 - | Tuesday, Thursday, Saturday |
| Life Annuities - - - | Half Yearly | |

The Dividends (at the Bank) of the 3 per Cent Consols, are paid from 9 to 3 o'clock, of all the rest from 9 to 11, and 1 to 3 o'clock.

The Dividends (at the India House) are paid from 9 to 2 o'clock, Saturday from 9 to 1 o'clock,

# LIST OF THE HOUSE OF PEERS.

## PEERS OF THE BLOOD ROYAL. 6.

aHis R. H. Frederick, Duke of York
●His R. H. Wm. Henry, Duke of Clarence
●His R. H. Ernest Augustus, Duke of Cumberland
●His R. H. Augustus Frederick, Duke of Sussex
●His R. H. Adolphus Frederick, Duke of Cambridge
●His R. H. William Frederick, Duke of Gloucester

## ARCHBISHOPS. 2.

●Dr. Charles Manners Sutton, Lord Archbishop of Canterbury, 1805
●Hon. Dr. Edward Venables Vernon, Lord Archbishop of York, 1807

## DUKES. 19.

| Names. | Titles. |
| --- | --- |
| Bernard Edward Howard | Norfolk |
| Edwd. Adolphus Seymour | Somerset |
| Charles Lennox | Richmond |
| George Henry Fitzroy | Grafton |
| Henry Charles Somerset | Beaufort |
| William Beauclerk | St. Albans |
| George Wm. Fred. Osborne | Leeds |
| ●John Russell | Bedford |
| Wm. Spencer Cavendish | Devonshire |
| George Spencer Churchill | Marlborough |
| ●John Henry Manners | Rutland |
| Alexander Hamilton | Brandon |
| W. H. Cav. Scott Bentinck | Portland |
| William Montague | Manchester |
| Chas. Sackville Germaine | Dorset |
| Henry Pelham Clinton | Newcastle |
| Hugh Percy | Northumberland |
| ●Arthur Wellesley | Wellington |
| ●Richard G. C. Temple | Buckingham and Chandos |

## MARQUISES. 17.

| | |
| --- | --- |
| ●Charles Ingoldsby Paulet | Winchester |
| ●Henry Petty | Lansdown |
| ●Geo. Granv. Lev. Gower | Stafford |
| George Townshend | Townshend |
| ●James Cecil | Salisbury |
| Thomas Thyme | Bath |
| James Hamilton | Abercorn |
| Charles John Cornwallis | Cornwallis |
| Francis Ch. Seym. Conway | Hertford |
| John Crichton Stuart | Bute |
| Brownlow Cecil | Exeter |
| Charles Compton | Northampton |
| ●John Jefferies Pratt | Camden |
| ●H. W. Paget | Anglesey |
| ●G. J. Cholmondeley | Cholmondeley |
| ●F. R. Hastings | Hastings |
| Charles Bruce Brud. Bruce | Ailesbury |

## EARLS. 104.

| | |
| --- | --- |
| Charles Talbot | Shrewsbury |
| ●Edward Smith Stanley | Derby |
| Hans Francis Hastings | Huntingdon |
| ●George Aug. Herbert | Pembroke |
| Thomas Howard | Suffolk |
| John William Egerton | Bridgewater |
| Basil Percy Fielding | Denbigh |
| ●John Fane | Westmorland |
| Albemarle Bertie | Lindsey |
| George Harry Grey | Stamford |
| ●George Finch | Winchilsea |
| Geo. Aug. Fred. Stanhope | Chesterfield |

| Names. | Titles. |
| --- | --- |
| Sackville Tufton | Thanet |
| George John Montague | Sandwich |
| George Capel Coningsby | Essex |
| ●Frederick Howard | Carlisle |
| Robert Brudenell | Cardigan |
| W. F. Scott (●Buccleugh) | Doncaster |
| ●Cropley Ashley Cooper | Shaftesbury |
| Thos. Morton F. Berkeley | Berkeley |
| Montague Bertie | Abingdon |
| Other Archer Windsor | Plymouth |
| Rich. Lumley Saunderson | Scarborough |
| W. H. Nassau De Zulestein | Rochford |
| Wm. Charles Keppel | Albemarle |
| George Wm. Coventry | Coventry |
| George Villiers | Jersey |
| John Poulett | Poulett |
| Edward Hartley | Oxford |
| Robert Shirley | Ferrers |
| William Legge | Dartmouth |
| ●Charles Bennet | Tankerville |
| Heneage Finch | Aylesford |
| Frederick William Hervey | Bristol |
| Peter Leop. L. F. Cowper | Cowper |
| Philip Henry Stanhope | Stanhope |
| Philip Sherard | Harborough |
| ●George Parker | Macclesfield |
| George Fermor | Pomfret |
| Jas. Graham, (●Montrose) | Graham |
| John James Waldegrave | Waldegrave |
| George Ashburnham | Ashburnham |
| ●Charles Stanhope | Harrington |
| John Charles Wallop | Portsmouth |
| Henry Richard Greville | Brooke & Warwick |
| George Robert Hobart | Buckinghamshire |
| ●William Wentworth | Fitzwilliam |
| George O'B. Wyndham | Egremont |
| William Harcourt | Harcourt |
| Frederic North | Guilford |
| ●Philip Yorke | Hardwicke |
| Wm. Harry Vane | Darlington |
| H. Steph. Fox-Strangeways | Ilchester |
| George John West | Delawar |
| Jacob Pleydell Bouverie | Radnor |
| ●George John Spencer | Spencer |
| ●John Pitt | Chatham |
| ●Henry Bathurst | Bathurst |
| A. B. S. T. Hill (●Downsh.) | Hillsboro' |
| Thomas Villiers | Clarendon |
| Henry Neville | Abergavenny |
| Alex. Gordon (●Gordon). | Norwich |
| ●C. Chetwynd Talbot | Talbot |
| ●Robert Grosvenor | Grosvenor |
| ●John Murray, (●Atholl) | Strange |
| ●Richard Edgcombe | Mount-Edgecombe |
| Hugh Fortescue | Fortescue |
| Edward Digby | Digby |
| Algernon Percy | Beverley |
| William Murray | Mansfield, S. V. |
| Henry George Herbert | Carnarvon |
| ●Robert Banks Jenkinson | Liverpool |
| Charles H. Cadogan | Cadogan |
| ●James Edw. Harris | Malmesbury |
| James St. Clair Erskine | Rosslyn |
| William Craven | Craven |
| Thomas Onslow | Onslow |
| Charles Marsham | Romney |
| ●Thomas Pelham | Chichester |
| Thomas Grosvenor | Wilton |
| ●Edward Clive | Powis |
| Rev. Wm. Nelson | Nelson |
| Chas. Herbert Pierrepoint | Manvers |

| Names. | Titles. |
|---|---|
| Horatio Walpole | Orford |
| *Charles Grey | Grey |
| William Lowther | Lonsdale |
| *Dudley Ryder | Harrowby |
| *Henry Phipps | Mulgrave |
| Henry Lascelles | Harewood |
| G. E. M. Kynynmound | Minto |
| *Wm. Shaw Cathcart | Cathcart |
| James Walter Grimston | Verulam |
| *Charles Whitworth | Whitworth |
| John Cust | Brownlow |
| John Cragg Eliot | St. Germans |
| John Parker | Morley |
| Orlando Bridgeman | Bradford |
| Wm. Beauchamp Lygon | Beauchamp |
| *John Scott | Eldon |
| Edward Boscawen | Falmouth |
| Rd. Wm. Penn Curzon | Howe |
| John Sommers Cocks | Sommers |
| John Rous | Stradbroke |
| Charles W. Stewart | Vane |

### VISCOUNTS. 20.

| | |
|---|---|
| Henry Devereux | Hereford |
| Geo. Richard St. John | Bolingbroke |
| George Byng | Torrington |
| Augustus-Fred. Fitzgerald | Leinster |
| William Courtenay | Courtenay |
| William Ward | Dudley and Ward |
| Charles Maynard | Maynard |
| Thomas Trevor Hampden | Hampden |
| John Thomas Townshend | Sydney |
| Henry Hood | Hood |
| Robert Duncan | Duncan |
| *Robert Saunders Dundas | Melville |
| *Henry Addington | Sidmouth |
| Thomas Wm. Anson | Anson |
| Francis Gerard Lake | Lake |
| *Geo. Keith Elphinstone | Keith |
| *G.G. Hamilton (Aberdeen) | Gordon |
| *Granville Leveson Gower | Granville |
| Edward Pellew | Exmouth |
| *Richd. Hely Hutchinson | Hutchinson |
| William Carr | Beresford |

### BISHOPS. 24. With Dates of Consecration.

| | |
|---|---|
| *London, Dr. Wm. Howley | 1813 |
| Durham, Hon. S. Barrington | 1791 |
| Litchfield & Coventry, Dr. J. Cornwallis | 1781 |
| Peterborough, Dr. Herbert Marsh | 1819 |
| Worcester, Dr. F. H. Cornwall | 1808 |
| Chichester, Dr. John Buckner | 1797 |
| Bath & Wells, Dr. R. Beadon | 1802 |
| St. David's, Dr. Thomas Burgess | 1803 |
| Norwich, Dr. H. Bathurst | 1805 |
| Salisbury, Dr. John Fisher | 1807 |
| St. Asaph, Dr. J. Luxmore | 1807 |
| Carlisle, Dr. Samuel Goodenough | 1807 |
| Rochester, Dr. Walker King | 1808 |
| Bangor, Dr. H. W. Majendie | 1809 |
| Ely, Dr. B. E. Sparke | 1812 |
| Chester, Dr. G. H. Law | 1812 |
| Gloucester, Hon. Dr. H. Ryder | 1815 |
| Hereford, Dr. G. I. Huntingford | 1815 |
| Oxford, Hon. Edward Legge | 1815 |
| Llandaff, Dr. William Van Mildert | 1819 |
| Winchester, Dr. Geo. Tomline | 1820 |
| Lincoln, Hon. Dr. G. Pelham | 1820 |
| Bristol, Dr. John Kaye | 1820 |
| Exeter, Dr. William Carey | 1820 |

### BARONS. 144.

| | |
|---|---|
| Thomas Stapleton | Le Despencer |
| Edward Southwell Clifford | De Clifford |
| G. J. Thicknesse Tuchett | Audley |
| Robt. C. St. John Trefusis | Clinton |
| Thomas Brand | Dacre |
| Cecil Bisshopp | De la Zouch |

| Names. | Titles. |
|---|---|
| William Stourton | Stourton |
| Henry Verney | Willoughby de Broke |
| Kenneth Alex. Howard | Howard of Effingham |
| St. Andrew St. John | St. John of Bletso |
| Charles Augustus Ellis | Howard de Waldon |
| Wm. Fr. H. Petre | Petre |
| Gregory Wm. Twisleton | Say & Sele |
| James Everard Arundel | Arundel |
| John Bligh | Clifton |
| Robert Evelyn Dormer | Dormer |
| John Roper | Teynham |
| George Gordon Noel | Byron |
| Charles Clifford | Clifford |
| Edmund Boyle | Boyle |
| Thos. Rt. Hay-Drummond | Hay |
| Henry Willoughby | Middleton |
| Geo. Horat. Cholmondeley | Newburgh |
| Peter King | King |
| John George Monson | Monson |
| Henry Bromley | Montford |
| Frederic Ponsonby | Ponsonby |
| Lewis Richard Watson | Sondes |
| Tho. Ph. Weddell Robinson | Grantham |
| Nathaniel Curzon | Scarsdale |
| Frederick Irby | Boston |
| *Henry Richd. Fox Vassal | Holland |
| John Percival | Lovell |
| Henry Venables Vernon | Vernon |
| Thos. Reynolds Moreton | Ducie |
| Geo. Wm. Campbell | Sundridge |
| Edward Harvey Hawke | Hawke |
| George Pitt | Rivers |
| Thomas Foley | Foley |
| George Talbot Rice | Dynevor |
| George de Grey | Walsingham |
| William Bagot | Bagot |
| Charles Fitzroy | Southampton |
| William Norton | Grantley |
| George Rodney | Rodney |
| *Hen. Fred. Carteret | Carteret |
| Thomas Noel Hill | Berwick |
| John Dutton | Sherborne |
| George Gordon | Gordon |
| Henry Jas. Scott Montagu | Montagu |
| Hy. De la Pole Beresford | Tyrone |
| Henry Boyle | Carleton |
| Edward Harbord | Suffield |
| Arth. Hen. Carleton | Dorchester |
| George Kenyon | Kenyon |
| Rd. Aldw. Neville Griffin | Braybrooke |
| *William Pitt Amherst | Amherst |
| Geo. Augustus Chichester | Fisherwick |
| Archibald Douglas | Douglas |
| Henry Hall Gage | Gage |
| *Wm. Wyndham Grenville | Grenville |
| George Douglas | Douglas |
| Edward Hovel Thurlow | Thurlow |
| *George Eden | Auckland |
| George Fulke Lyttleton | Lyttleton |
| Henry John Peachey | Selsey |
| Henry Welbore Agar Ellis | Mendip |
| Lawrence Dundas | Dundas |
| Charles Anderson Pelham | Yarborough |
| Francis Stuart | Stuart |
| George Stewart | Stewart |
| *James George Stopford | Saltersford |
| John C. Burton Dawnay | Dawnay |
| George Brodrick | Brodrick |
| George G. Calthorpe | Calthorpe |
| Peter R. D. Burrell | Gwydir |
| Francis Basset | De Dunstanville |
| John Rolle | Rolle |
| John Frederick Campbell | Cawdor |
| *Richard C. Wellesley | Wellesley |
| Robert Smith | Carrington |
| Charles F. P. Townshend | Bayning |
| *James Grenville | Glastonbury |
| William Orde Powlett | Bolton |

| Names. | Titles. |
|---|---|
| John Wodehouse | Wodehouse |
| John Rushout | Northwick |
| Thomas Powis | Lilford |
| Thomas Lister | Ribblesdale |
| George Abercromby | Abercromby |
| John Fitz-Gibbon | Fitz-Gibbon |
| Charles Moore | Moore |
| John Loftus | Loftus |
| •John Joshua Proby | Carysfort |
| William Arden | Alvanley |
| •Alleyne Fitzherbert | St. Helens |
| John Hely Hutchinson | Hutchinson |
| John Freeman Mitford | Redesdale |
| Edward Law | Ellenborough |
| •Charles George Perceval | Arden |
| •G.A.F.C. Baker Holroyd | Sheffield |
| Thomas Erskine | Erskine |
| Howe Peter Browne | Monteagle |
| Archibald Montgomery | Ardrossan |
| •James Maitland | Lauderdale |
| George Forbes | Granard |
| John Crewe | Crewe |
| John Ponsonby | Ponsonby |
| Archibald Kennedy | Ailsa |
| John Campbell | Bredalbane |
| Alan Legge Gardner | Gardner |
| •Thomas Manners Sutton | Manners |
| James Gambier | Gambier |
| John Hope | Hopetoun |
| Thomas Graham | Lynedoch |
| Stapleton Cotton | Combermere |
| Rowland Hill | Hill |
| •Wm. Carr Beresford | Beresford |
| •Chas. Wm. Vane Stewart | Stewart |
| •Robt. Trench Le Poer | Trench |
| George Ramsay | Dalhousie |
| George Gordon | Meldrum |
| George Boyle | Ross |
| John Willoughby Cole | Grinstead |
| Edmund Henry Pery | Foxford |
| Peniston Lamb | Melbourne |
| Francis Almaric Spencer | Churchill |
| George Harris | Harris |
| Algernon Percy | Prudhoe |
| •Charles Abbott | Colchester |
| •William Ker | Ker |
| Henry Conyngham | Minster |
| James Wandesford Butler | Ormonde |
| Francis C. W. Douglas | Wemyss |
| Robert Jocelyn | Clanbrassill |
| George King | Kingston |
| Thomas Pakenham | Silchester |
| James Murray | Glenlyon |
| •William W. Pole | Maryborough |
| •John Foster | Oriel |
| •William Scott | Stowell |
| Thomas Henry Liddell | Ravensworth |
| Thomas Cholmondeley | Delamere |
| Cecil Weld Forester | Forester |
| Nicholas Vansittart | Bexley |

### SIXTEEN PEERS FOR SCOTLAND.

#### MARQUISES.

| Names. | Titles. |
|---|---|
| William Ker | Lothian |
| Charles Douglas | Queensberry |
| George Hay | Tweedale |

#### EARLS.

| | |
|---|---|
| Alexander Lindsay | Balcarras |
| Alex. Home Ramsey | Home |
| Thomas Erskine | Kellie |
| Archibald John Primrose | Roseberry |
| Thomas Bruce | Elgin & Kincardine |

#### VISCOUNT.

| | |
|---|---|
| John Arbuthnot | Arbuthnot |

#### BARONS.

| | |
|---|---|
| John Colville | Colville |
| James Ochoncar Forbes | Forbes |
| Francis Gray | Gray |
| Francis Napier | Napier |
| Alex. George Fraser | Saltoun |
| Charles Sinclair | Sinclair |
| Rt. Montgomery Hamilton | Belhaven |

### TWENTY-EIGHT PEERS for IRELAND.

#### MARQUISES.

| | |
|---|---|
| William O'Bryen | Thomond |
| Thomas Taylour | Headfort |
| •Henry Conyngham | Conyngham |

#### EARLS.

| | |
|---|---|
| Somerset Rich. Butler | Carrick |
| Francis Wm. Caulfield | Charlemont |
| George King | Kingston |
| Stephen Moore | Mountcashel |
| Thomas Pakenham | Longford |
| John James Maxwell | Farnham |
| John Bourke | Mayo |
| John Willoughby Cole | Enniskillen |
| John Creighton | Erne |
| Wm. Forward Howard | Wicklow |
| Richard Bingham | Lucan |
| Somerset Lowry Corry | Belmore |
| •Chas. H. St. John O'Neil | O'Neil |
| Francis Bernard | Bandon |
| •Rich. Hely Hutchinson | Donoughmore |
| Dupre Alexander | Caledon |
| •Edmund Henry Pery | Limerick |
| •Richard L. P. Trench | Clancarty |
| Laurence Parsons | Rosse |
| Archibald Acheson | Gosford |
| Charles Wm. Bury | Charleville |
| Charles John Gardiner | Blessinton |

#### VISCOUNTS.

| | |
|---|---|
| Hugh Carleton | Carleton |
| Richard Wingfield | Powerscourt |

#### BARON.

| | |
|---|---|
| James S. Blackwood | Dufferin & Claneboye |

#### IRISH REPRESENTATIVE PRELATES.

Archbishop of Tuam
Bishop of Ferns and Leighlin
Bishop of Cloyne
Bishop of Cork

English Peers, 336—Scotch, 16—Irish, 32—Total, 385.

---

## CLERKS AND OFFICERS OF THE HOUSE OF PEERS.

*Chairman of Committees, Earl of Shaftesbury.*

Clerk of the Parliaments, Right Hon. Sir Geo. Henry Rose.

Clerk Assistant, Henry Cowper, Esq.

Reading Clerk and Clerk of the Private Committees, William Stewart Rose, Esq.

Additional Clerk Assistant, Benj. Curry, Esq.

Council to the Chairman of Committees, Edward Stracey, Esq.

Clerk of Journals, Edw. G. Walmesley, Esq.

Copying Clerk, Edward Fawatt, Esq.

Clerk of Engrossments, Mr. Robt. Walmesley.

Clerk of Enrolments, Mr. Robt. Haw Strahan.

Other Clerks in the Office, Henry Stone Smith, William Walmesley.

Short Hand Writer, W. B. Gurney.

Gentleman Usher of the Black Rod, Sir Thos. Tyrwhitt, Knt.

Yeoman Usher, Robert Quarme, Esq.

Serjeant at Arms, George F. Seymour, Esq.

Deputy, Mr. William Hutt, Milbank-row.

Receiver of Fees, Mr. Charles Sutherland.

# THE HOUSE OF COMMONS,

ELECTED APRIL 21, 1820, (CORRECTED TO THE BEGINNING OF THE YEAR 1823,) THE FIRST PARLIAMENT OF GEORGE IV.

ENGLAND AND WALES, 513.

These marked thus * are Privy Councillors.

SPEAKER, *Right Hon. CHARLES MANNERS SUTTON.

*Abingdon,*
John Maberley, Esq.
*Agmondesham,*
T. T. Drake, Esq.
W. T. Drake, Esq.
*Aldborough,*
H. C. Fynes, Esq.
G. C. Antrobus, Esq.
*Aldeburgh,*
J. Walker, Esq.
James Blair, Esq.
*Andover,*
Sir J. W. Pollen, Bart.
T. A. Smith, Esq.
*Anglesey,*
Earl of Uxbridge
*Appleby,*
A. J. Dalrymple, Esq.
Thomas Creevey, Esq.
*Arundel,*
Robert Blake, Esq.
Viscount Bury
*Ashburton,*
Sir L. V. Palk, Bart.
Sir J. S. Copley, Knt.
*Aylesbury,*
Lord Nugent
Wm. Rickford, Esq.
*Banbury,*
Hon. H. Legge
*Barnstaple,*
Sir F. M. Ommaney, Kt.
Michael Nolan, Esq.
*Bath,*
*Lord John Thynne
Charles Palmer, Esq.
*Beaumaris,*
Thos. F. Lewis, Esq.
*Bedfordshire,*
Marquis of Tavistock
Francis Pym, Esq.
*Bedford,*
Lord G. W. Russell
W. H. Whitbread, Esq.
*Great Bedwin,*
*Sir John Nicholl, Kt.
J. J. Buxton, Esq.
*Beeralston,*
Lord Lowaine
Hon. Henry Percy
*Berkshire,*
Charles Dundas, Esq.

Hon. Richard Neville
*Berwick-on-Tweed,*
Sir J. Beresford
Sir Francis Blake, Bt.
*Beverley,*
G. L. Fox, Esq.
John Wharton, Esq.
*Bewdley,*
W. A. Roberts, Esq.
*Bishop's Castle,*
William Holmes, Esq.
Edward Rogers, Esq.
*Blechingly,*
Hon. E. H. E. Gower
Lord F. L. Gower
*Bodmyn,*
Davies Gilbert, Esq.
J. W. Croker, Esq.
*Boroughbridge,*
George Mundy, Esq.
Henry Dawkins, Esq.
*Bossiney,*
Sir C. Domville, Bart.
Hon. J. W. Ward
*Boston,*
G. J. Heathcote, Esq.
W. A. Johnson, Esq.
*Brackley,*
R. H. Bradshaw, Esq.
H. Wrottesley, Esq.
*Bramber,*
W. Wilberforce, Esq.
John Irving, Esq.
*Brecknock,*
Thomas Wood, Esq.
*Brecon,*
G. C. Morgan, Esq.
*Bridgenorth,*
Thos. Whitmore, Esq.
W. W. Whitmore, Esq.
*Bridgewater,*
Wm. Astell Esq.
C. K. K. Tynte, Esq
*Bridport,*
James Scott, Esq.
Sir H. D. St. Paul, Bt.
*Bristol,*
Henry Bright, Esq.
R. H. Davis, Esq.
*Buckinghamshire,*
Marquis of Chandos
Hon. Robert Smith

*Buckingham,*
Sir Geo. Nugent, Bart.
*W. H. Fremantle
*Bury St. Edmunds,*
Lord John Fitzroy
Hon. A. P. Upton
*Callington,*
Matthias Attwood, Esq.
Wm. Thompson, Esq.
*Caine,*
Hon. Jas. Abercromby
Jas. Macdonald, Esq.
*Cambridgeshire,*
Lord C. S. Manners
Lord F. G. Osborne
*Cambridge Unity.*
*Viscount Palmerston
Wm. John Banks, Esq.
*Cambridge Boro'.*
F. W. Trench, Esq.
C. M. Cheese, Esq.
*Camelford,*
Mark Milbank, Esq.
Sheldon Cradock, Esq.
*Canterbury,*
S. R. Lushington, Esq.
Lord Clifton
*Cardiff,*
Wyndham Lewis, Esq.
*Cardiganshire,*
W. E. Powell, Esq.
*Cardigan,*
Pryse Pryse, Esq.
*Carlisle,*
Sir Jas. Graham, Bart.
Wm. James, Esq.
*Carmarthenshire,*
Hon. Geo. Rice Rice
*Carmarthen,*
John Jones, Esq.
*Carnarvonshire,*
Sir R. T Williams, Bt.
*Carnarvon,*
Sir Charles Paget, Knt.
*Castle Rising,*
Hon. F. G. Howard
Lord H. Cholmondeley
*Cheshire,*
D. Davenport, Esq.
W. Egerton, Esq.
*Chester,*
Viscount Belgrave

Thos. Grosvenor, Esq.
*Chichester,*
—— Poyntz, Esq.
Lord J. G. Lennox
*Chippenham,*
W. A. Madocks, Esq.
J. R. Grosett, Esq.
*Christchurch,*
*Sir G. H. Rose, Knt.
*Hon. W. S. Bourne
*Cirencester,*
Lord Apsley
Joseph Cripps, Esq.
*Clitheroe,*
Hon. Robert Curzon
Henry Porcher, Esq.
*Cockermouth,*
J. H. Lowther, Esq.
W. W. C. Wilson, Esq.
*Colchester,*
J. B. Wildman, Esq.
Henry Baring, Esq.
*Corfe-Castle,*
Henry Bankes, Esq.
Geo. Bankes, Esq.
*Cornwall,*
Sir Wm. Lemon, Bart.
J. H. Tremayne, Esq.
*Coventry,*
Edward Ellice, Esq.
Peter Moore, Esq.
*Cricklade,*
Joseph Pitt, Esq.
Robert Gordon, Esq.
*Cumberland,*
John Lowther, Esq.
J. C. Curwen, Esq.
*Dartmouth,*
John Bastard, Esq.
Hon. J. H. Stanhope
*Denbighshire,*
Sir W. W. Wynn, Bart.
*Denbigh,*
J. W. Griffith, Esq.
*Derbyshire,*
Lord G. A. H. Cavendish
Francis Mundy, Esq.
*Derby,*
H. F. C. Cavendish, Esq.
T. W. Coke, jun. Esq.
*Devizes,*
T. G. Estcourt, Esq.

John Pearse, Esq.
*Devonshire,*
Sir T. D. Ackland, Bt.
E. P. Bastard, Esq.
*Dorchester,*
Robert Williams, Esq.
Charles Warren, Esq.
*Dorsetshire,*
W. M. Pitt, Esq.
E. B. Portman, Esq.
*Dover,*
E. B. Wilbraham, Esq.
J. Butterworth, Esq.
*Downton,*
Hon. B. Bouverie
Sir T. B. Pechel, Bart.
*Droitwich,*
Earl of Sefton
J. H. H. Foley, Esq.
*Dunwich,*
Michael Barne, Esq.
G. H. Cherry, Esq.
*Durham, County,*
J. G. Lambton, Esq.
Hon. W. J. F. Powlett
*Durham, City,*
M. A. Taylor, Esq.
Sir Henry Hardinge
*Essex,*
C. C. Western, Esq.
Sir E. Harvey
*Evesham,*
Sir C. Cockerell, Bart.
Sir W. E. R. Boughton
*Exeter,*
Wm. Courtenay, Esq.
R. W. Newman, Esq.
*Eye,*
Sir R. Gifford, Knt.
Sir M. Nightingall
*Flintshire,*
Sir T. Mostyn, Bart.
*Flint,*
Sir E. P. Lloyd, Bart.
*Fowey,*
Viscount Valletort
George Lucy, Esq.
*Galton,*
J. W. Russell, Esq.
Thomas Divett, Esq.
*Glamorganshire,*
Sir C. Cole
*Gloucestershire,*
Lord R. E. H. Somerset
Sir B. W. Guise, Bart.
*Gloucester,*
Edward Webb, Esq.
B. B. Cooper, Esq.
*Grampound,*
John Innes, Esq.
A. Robertson, Esq.
*Grantham,*
Hon. Edward Cust

Sir M. Cholmeley, Bt.
*Great Grimsby,*
C. Tennyson, Esq.
Wm, Duncombe, Esq.
*East Grinstead,*
Lord Strathaven
Hon. C C.C. Jenkinson
*Guildford,*
A. Onslow, Esq.
C. B. Wall, Esq.
*Halleston,*
Lord J. N. Townshend
H. Hudson, Esq.
*Hampshire,*
John Fleming, Esq.
G. P. Jervoise, Esq.
*Harwich,*
*Rt. Hon. G. Canning
*Rt. Hon. C. Bathurst
*Haslemere,*
*Sir Charles Long
Robert Ward, Esq.
*Hastings,*
James Dawkins, Esq.
Hon. W. H. J. Scott
*Haverfordwest,*
W. H. Scourfield, Esq.
*Hedon,*
Robert Farrand, Esq.
John Baillie, Esq.
*Herefordshire,*
Sir J. G. Cotterell, Bt.
Robert Price, Esq.
*Hereford, City*
Viscount Eastnor
R. P. Scudamore, Esq.
*Hertfordshire,*
Sir J. S. Sebright, Bt.
Hon. William Lamb
*Hertford,*
Viscount Cranborne
N. Calvert, Esq.
*Heytesbury,*
E. H. A'Court, Esq.
Henry Handley, Esq.
*Higham-Ferrers,*
Viscount Normanby
*Hindon,*
Hon. F. G. Calthorpe
John Plummer, Esq.
*Honiton,*
Hon. P. F. Cust
Samuel Crawley, Esq.
*Horsham,*
Robert Hurst, Esq.
Sir J. Aubrey, Bart.
*Huntingdonshire,*
W. H. Fellowes, Esq.
Lord John Russell
*Huntingdon,*
John Calvert, Esq.
Earl of Ancram

*Hythe,*
S. J. Loyd, Esq.
S. Majoribanks, Esq.
*Ipswich,*
Wm. Haldimand, Esq.
T. B. Lennard, Esq.
*Ivelchester,*
Sir Isaac Coffin, Bart.
S. Lushington, Esq.
*Kent,*
W. P. Honywood, Esq.
Sir E. Knatchbull, Bt.
*King's Lynn,*
Marquis of Titchfield
Hon. John Walpole
*Kingston—Hull,*
John Mitchell, Esq.
*Knaresborough,*
Daniel Sykes, Esq.
*Rt. Hon. Geo. Tierney
Sir J. Mackintosh, Knt.
*Lancashire,*
John Blackburne, Esq.
Lord Stanley
*Lancaster,*
J. F. Cawthorne, Esq.
Gabriel Doveton, Esq.
*Launceston,*
James Brogden, Esq.
Hon. P. B. Pellew
*Leicestershire,*
Lord Robert Manners
G. A. Legh-Keck, Esq.
*Leicester,*
John Mansfield, Esq.
Thomas Pares, Esq.
*Leominster,*
Lord Hotham
Sir W. C. Fairlie, Bt.
*Lewes,*
Sir G. Shiffner, Bart.
Sir J. Shelley, Bart.
*Lichfield,*
Sir George Anson
G. G. V. Vernon, Esq.
*Lincolnshire,*
Hon. C. A. Pelham
Charles Chaplin, Esq.
*Lincoln,*
Robert Smith, Esq.
John Williams, Esq.
*Liskeard,*
Hon. William Elliot
Sir W. H. Pringle
*Liverpool,*
*W. Huskisson, Esq.
Isaac Gascoyne, Esq.
*London,*
Matthew Wood, Esq.
Thomas Wilson, Esq.
Sir Wm. Curtis, Bart.
George Bridges, Esq.

*Looe East,*
T. P. Macqueen, Esq.
G. W. Taylor, Esq.
*Looe West,*
Sir Chas. Hulse, Bart.
*Rt. Hon. H. Goulburn
*Lostwithiel,*
Sir Rt. Wigram, Knt.
A. C. Grant, Esq.
*Ludgershall,*
S. Graham, Esq.
Earl of Brecknock
*Ludlow,*
Viscount Clive
Hon. Robert H. Clive
*Lyme Regis,*
John T. Fane, Esq.
Vere Fane, Esq.
*Lymington,*
Sir H. B. Neale, Bart.
Wm. Manning, Esq.
*Maidstone,*
A. W. Robarts, Esq.
John Wells, Esq.
*Maldon,*
J. H. Strutt, Esq.
Benj. Gaskell, Esq.
*Malmesbury,*
Charles Forbes, Esq.
William Leake, Esq.
*Malton,*
Viscount Duncannon
J. C. Ramsden, Esq.
*Marlborough,*
Lord Brudenell
Hon. John Wodehouse
*Great Marlow,*
Owen Williams, Esq.
T. P. Williams, Esq.
*Marionethshire,*
Sir R. W. Vaughan, Bt.
*Middlesex,*
George Byng, Esq.
S. C. Whitbread, Esq.
*Midhurst,*
John Smith, Esq.
Abel Smith, Esq.
*Milborne-Port,*
Lord Graves
Hon. B. Paget
*Minehead,*
J. F. Luttrell, Esq.
John Douglas, Esq.
*Monmouthshire,*
Sir C. Morgan, Bart.
Ld. G. C. H. Somerset
*Monmouth,*
Marquis of Worcester
*Montgomeryshire,*
*Hon. C. W. W. Wynn
*Montgomery,*
*Right Hon. H. Clive

*Morpeth,*
William Ord, Esq.
Hon. Wm. Howard
*Newark-upon-Trent,*
Sir Wm. H. Clinton
H. Willoughby, Esq.
*Newcastle un. Line,*
W. S. Kinnersly, Esq.
R. J. Wilmot, Esq.
*Newcastle-on-Tyne,*
Sir M. W. Ridley, Bt.
C. Ellison, Esq.
*Newport,*
Wm. Northey, Esq.

*Newport, (I.W.)*
Sir L. T. W. Holmes, Bt.
C. Duncombe, Esq.
*Newton,*
Thomas Legh, Esq.
Thos. Claughton, Esq.
*Newtown, (I.W.)*
Hudson Gurney, Esq.
C. C. Cavendish, Esq.
*Norfolk,*
T. W. Coke, Esq.
E. Wodehouse, Esq.
*Northallerton,*
Henry Peirse, Esq.
Hon. W. S. Lascelles
*Northamptonshire,*
W. R. Cartwright, Esq.
Viscount Althorp
*Northampton,*
Sir G. Robinson, Bart.
W. L. Maberley, Esq.
*Northumberland,*
T. W. Beaumont, Esq.
C. J. Brandling, Esq.
*Norwich,*
William Smith, Esq.
R. H. Gurney, Esq.
*Nottinghamshire,*
Ld. W. H. C. Bentick
Frank Sotheron, Esq.
*Nottingham,*
Joseph Birch, Esq.
Thos. Denman, Esq.
*Okehampton,*
Lord Dunalley
Lord Glenorchy
*Orford,*
E. A. M'Naghten, Esq.
Charles Ross, Esq.
*Oxfordshire,*
John Fane, Esq.
W. H. Ashurst, Esq.
*Oxford University,*
*Rt. Hon. Robt. Peel
Richard Heber, Esq.
*Oxford City,*
C. Wetherell, Esq.
J. L. Lockhart, Esq.

*Pembrokeshire,*
Sir John Owen, Bart.
*Pembroke,*
J. H. Allen, Esq.
*Penryn,*
Pascoe Grenfell, Esq.
Henry Swann, Esq.
*Peterborough,*
James Scarlett, Esq.
Sir R. Heron, Bart.
*Petersfield,*
Sir H. W. G. Jolliffe
Sir P. Musgrave, Bart.
*Plymouth,*
Sir W. Congreve, Bt.
Sir T. B. Martin
*Plympton-Earle,*
R. G. Macdonald, Esq.
W. G. Paxton, Esq.
*Pontefract,*
Viscount Pollington
T. Houldsworth, Esq.
*Poole,*
B. L. Lester, Esq.
John Dent, Esq.
*Portsmouth,*
John Markham, Esq.
John Carter, Esq.
*Preston,*
S. Horrocks, Esq.
Edmund Hornby, Esq.
*Queenborough,*
*Rt. Hon. J. C. Villiers
George Holford, Esq.
*Radnorshire,*
Walter Wilkins, Esq.
*New Radnor,*
Richard Price, Esq.
*Reading,*
C. F. Palmer, Esq.
J. B. Mouck, Esq.
*Reigate,*
Sir J. S. Yorke
Hon. James S. Cocks
*East Retford,*
William Evans, Esq.
Saml. Crompton, Esq.
*Richmond,*
Hon. Thomas Dundas
S. B. M. Barrett, Esq.
*Ripon,*
*Hon. F. J. Robinson
George Gipps, Esq.
*Rochester,*
*Lord Binning
Ralph Bernall, Esq.
*New Romney,*
R. E. Grosvenor, Esq.
G. H. D. Pennant, Esq.
*Rutlandshire,*
Sir G. N. Noel, Bart.
Sir. G. Heathcote, Bt.

*Rye,*
Peter Browne, Esq.
John Dodson, Esq.
*St. Albans,*
Chpr. Smith, Esq.
Sir H. W. Wilson, Kt.
*St. Germains,*
Hon. S. T. Bathurst
*Rt. Hon. C. Arbuthnot
*St. Ives,*
Lyndon Evelyn, Esq.
Sir Chpr. Hawkins, Bt.
*St. Mawes,*
Sir S. B. Morland, Bt
J. Phillimore, Esq.
*St. Michael,*
Sir G. Staunton, Bart.
W. T. Money, Esq.
*Saltash,*
William Russell, Esq.
John Fleeming, Esq.
*Sandwich,*
Joseph Marryat, Esq.
*Sir G. Warrender, Bt.
*Shropshire,*
Rowland Hill, Esq.
J. C. Pelham, Esq.
*New Sarum,*
Viscount Folkstone
W. Wyndham, Esq.
*Old Sarum,*
Jas. Alexander, Esq.
J. D. Alexander, Esq.
*Scarborough,*
*Rt. Hon. C. M. Sutton
Hon. E. Phipps
*Seaford,*
C. R. Ellis, Esq.
Hon. G. J. W. A. Ellis
*Shaftesbury,*
R. Leycester, Esq.
Hon. R. Grosvenor
*Shoreham New,*
Sir C. M. Burrell, Bt.
J. M. Lloyd, Esq.
*Shrewsbury,*
Hon. H. G. Bennet
P. Corbett, Esq.
*Somersetshire,*
Wm. Dickenson, Esq.
Sir T. Lethbridge, Bt.
*Southampton,*
Sir W. De Crespigny
W. Chamberlayne, Esq
*Southwark,*
C. Calvert, Esq.
Sir R. T. Wilson, Kt.
*Staffordshire,*
E. J. Littleton, Esq.
Sir J. F. Boughey
*Stafford,*
G. Chetwynde, Esq.
B. Benyon, Esq.

*Stamford,*
Lord T. Cecil
Hon. W. H. Percy
*Steyning,*
Lord H. T. Howard
G. R. Philips, Esq.
*Stockbridge,*
J. F. Barham, Esq.
Hon. E. G. S. Stanley
*Sudbury,*
Wm. Heygate. Esq.
C. A. Tulk, Esq.
*Suffolk,*
T. S. Gooch, Esq.
Sir W. Rowley, Bart.
*Surrey,*
G. H. Sumner, Esq.
W. J. Denison, Esq.
*Sussex,*
W. Burrell, Esq.
E. J. Curteis, Esq.
*Tamworth,*
Right Hon. Lord C.
V. F. Townshend
W. Y. Peel, Esq.
*Tavistock,*
J. P. Grant, Esq.
Viscount Ebrington
*Taunton,*
A. Baring, Esq.
J. A. Warre, Esq.
*Tewkesbury,*
J. E. Dowdeswell, Esq.
James Martin, Esq.
*Thetford,*
L. C. Fitzroy, jun.
N. W. Colborne, Esq.
*Thirsk,*
R. Frankland, Esq.
R. G. Russell, Esq.
*Tiverton,*
Viscount Sandon
*Rt. Hon. R. Ryder
*Totness,*
T. P. Courtenay, Esq.
John Bent, Esq.
*Tregony,*
Viscount Barnard
J. O'Callaghan, Esq.
*Truro,*
Sir R. H. Vivian
W. Gossett, Esq.
*Wallingford,*
W. L. Hughes, Esq.
G. J. Robarts, Esq.
*Wareham,*
J. Calcraft, Esq.
J. H. Calcraft, Esq.
*Warwickshire,*
D. S. Dugdale, Esq.
F. Lawley, Esq.
*Warwick,*
Sir C. J. Greville

Charles Mills, Esq.
*Wells,*
C. W Taylor, Esq.
J. P. Tudway, Esq.
*Wendover,*
R. Smith, Esq.
G. Smith, Esq.
*Wenlock,*
Francis Forrester, Esq.
W. L. Childe, Esq.
*Weobly,*
Lord F. C. Bentinck
Sir G. Cockburn
*Westbury,*
Sir M. M. Lopes, Bt.
P. J. Miles, Esq.
*Westminster,*
Sir F. Burdett, Bart.
J. C. Hobhouse, Esq.
*Westmoreland,*
Viscount Lowther
Hon. H. C. Lowther
*Weymouth,*
•Rt. Hon. T. Wallace
Masterton Ure, Esq.
*Melcombe Regis,*
W. Williams, Esq.
T. F. Buxton, Esq.
*Whitchurch,*
Hon. H. Townshend
Samuel Scott, Esq.
*Wigan,*
J. A. Hodson, Esq.
Lord Lindsay
*Wilton,*
Ralph Sheldon, Esq.
J. H. Penruddocke, Esq
*Wiltshire,*
John Benett, Esq.

Sir J. D. Astley, Bart.
*Winchelsea,*
Henry Brougham, Esq.
L. Concannon, Esq.
*Winchester,*
P. S. Mildmay, Esq.
J. H. Leigh, Esq.
*Windsor,*
J. Ramsbottom, Esq.
Sir H. Taylor
*Woodstock New*
J. Gladstone, Esq.
J. H. Langston
*Wootton Basset,*
Horace Twiss, Esq.
Geo. Philips, Esq.
*Worcestershire,*
Hon. H. B. Lygon
Sir T. Winnington, Bt.
*Worcester,*
Viscount Deerhurst
T. H. H. Davies, Esq.
*Wycombe High*
Sir J. D. King, Bart.
Sir T. Baring, Bart.
*Yarmouth Great*
Hon. G. Anson
C. E. Rumbold, Esq.
*Yarmouth, Isle of
Wight,*
Sir P. Pole, Bart.
T. H. Brinckman, Esq.
*Yorkshire,*
Viscount Milton
J. A. S. Wortley, Esq.
*York,*
M. Wyvill, Esq.
R. Chaloner, Esq.

*Fifeshire,*
J. Wemyss, Esq.
*Forfarshire,*
Hon. W. R. Maule
*Glasgow, &c.*
A. Campbell, Esq.
*Haddingtonshire,*
Sir J. G. Suttie, Bart.
*Haddington, &c.*
Sir H. Hamilton, Bt.
*Inverness-shire,*
•Right Hon. C. Grant
*Inverness, &c.*
Geo. Cumming, Esq.
*Kincardineshire,*
Sir A. Ramsay, Bart.
*Kirkaldy, &c.*
Sir R. C. Ferguson
*Kirkcudbright,*
J. Dunlop, Esq.
*Kirkwall, &c.*
Sir H. Innes, Bart.
*Lanarkshire,*
Lord A. Hamilton
*Linlithgowshire,*
Hon. Sir A. Hope
*Nairnshire, &c.*
Hon. G. Campbell

*Orkneys, &c.*
J. Balfour, Esq.
*Peebleshire,*
Sir J. Montgomery, B.
*Perthshire,*
J. Drummond, Esq.
*Perth, Dundee, &c.*
Hon. H. Lindsay
*Renfrewshire,*
J. Maxwell, Esq.
*Ross-shire,*
Sir J. W. Mackenzie
*Roxburghshire,*
Sir A. Don, Bart.
*Selkirkshire,*
W. E. Lockhart, Esq.
*Selkirk, &c.*
H. Monteith, Esq.
*Stirlingshire,*
H. H. Drummond,
*Straswaer, &c.*
Sir J. Osborn, Bart.
*Sutherlandshire.*
G. M. Grant, Esq.
*Wigtonshire,*
Sir. W. Maxwell, Bt.

---

## IRELAND. 100

*Antrim,*
Hon. J. B. R. O'Neil

*Armagh,*
Hon. H. Caulfield
C. Brownlow, Esq.
*Armagh, Bor.*
W. Stuart, Esq.
*Athlone,*
David Kerr, Esq.
*Bandon,*
Viscount Bernard
*Belfast,*
Earl of Belfast
*Carlowshire,*
H. Bruen, Esq.
Sir U. Burgh
*Carlow, Bor.*
Charles Harvey, Esq.
*Carrickfergus,*
Sir A. Chichester, Bt.
*Cashell,*
E. J. Collett, Esq.
*Cavanshire,*
N. Sneyd, Esq.
•Rt. Hon. J. M. Barry
*Clare,*
Sir E. O'Brien, Bart
•R. H. W.V. Fitzgerald
*Clonmel,*
J. H. M. Dawson, Esq.

*Coleraine,*
Sir J. Beresford, Bart.
*Cork,*
Viscount Ennismore
Visct. Kingsborough
*Cork,*
Hon. C. H. Hutchinson
Sir N. Colthurst, Bt.
*Donegalshire,*
G. V. Hart, Esq.
Earl of Mount Charles
*Downshire,*
Lord A. Hill
Matthew Forde, Esq.
*Downpatrick,*
J. W. Maxwell, Esq.
*Drogheda,*
W. M. Smyth, Esq.
*Dublinshire,*
Colonel White
R. W. Talbot, Esq.
*Dublin,*
Sir R. Shaw, Bart.
Thomas Ellis, Esq.
*Dublin University,*
Rt. Hon. W. Plunkett
*Dundalk,*
G. Hartopp, Esq.
*Dungannon,*
Hon. T. Knox

---

## SCOTLAND. 45

*Aberdeenshire,*
Hon. W. Gordon
*Aberdeen, &c.*
Joseph Hume, Esq.
*Argyleshire,*
W. F. Campbell, Esq.
*Ayr, &c.*
T. F. Kennedy, Esq.
*Ayrshire,*
J. Montgomerie, Esq.
*Banffshire,*
Earl of Fife
*Berwickshire,*
Sir J. Marjoribanks, Bt.
*Buteshire, &c.*
Lord P. J. H. Stuart
*Clackmannanshire,*
Robert Bruce, Esq.

*Crail, &c.*
Hon. Sir W. Rae, Bart.
*Dumbartonshire.*
J. Buchanan, Esq.
*Dunfermline, &c.*
Robert Downie, Esq.
*Dumfrieshire,*
Sir W. J. Hope
*Dumfries, &c.*
W. R. K. Douglas, Esq.
*Edinburghshire,*
Sir G. Clark, Bart.
*Edinburgh,*
•Rt. Hon. W. Dundas
*Elginshire,*
F. W. Grant, Esq.
*Elgin, &c.*
A. Farquharson, Esq.

| | | | |
|---|---|---|---|
| *Dungarvan,* | *Kinsale,* | J. Browne, Esq. | *Thralee,* |
| Hon. G. Lamb | Sir J. Rowley, Bart. | *Meathshire,* | James Cuff, Esq. |
| *Ennis,* | *Leitrim,* | Earl of Bective | *Tyroneshire,* |
| R. Wellesley, Esq. | L. White, Esq. | Sir M. Somerville, Bt. | *Right Hon. Sir J. |
| *Enniskillen,* | J. M. Clements, Esq. | *Monaghan,* | Stewart, Bart. |
| R. Magenis, Esq. | *Limerick,* | C. P. Leslie, Esq. | W. Stewart, Esq. |
| *Fermanaghshire,* | Hon. R. H. F. Gibbon | Hon. H. R. Westenra | *Waterfordshire,* |
| Hon. Sir G. L. Cole | S. O'Grady, Esq. | *Newry,* | Richard Power, Esq. |
| M. Archdall, Esq. | *Limerick City,* | Viscount Newry | Lord G. T. Beresford |
| *Galwayshire,* | T. S. Rice, Esq. | *Portarlington,* | *Waterford City,* |
| James Daly, Esq. | *Lisburne,* | D. Ricardo, Esq. | *Rt. Hon. Sir J. New- |
| R. Martin, Esq. | H. Seymour, Esq. | *Queen's County,* | port, Bart. |
| *Galway Town,* | *Londonderry,* | Sir H. Parnell, Bart. | *Westmeath,* |
| M.G. Prendergast, Esq. | G. R. Dawson, Esq. | Sir C. H. Coote, Bart. | Hon. H. R. Pakenham |
| *Kerryshire,* | A. R. Stuart, Esq. | *Roscommonshire,* | G. H. Rochfort, Esq. |
| *R.Hon. M Fitzgerald | *Londonderry City,* | Arthur French, Esq. | *Wexfordshire,* |
| James Crosbie, Esq. | *Sir G. F. Hill, Bart. | Hon. S. Mahon | R. S. Carew, Esq. |
| *Kildareshire,* | *Longfordshire,* | *New Ross,* | Viscount Stopford |
| Lord W. Fitzgerald | Viscount Forbes | Francis Leigh, Esq. | *Wexford,* |
| R. Latouche, Esq. | Sir G. R. Featherston, | *Sligoshire,* | W. Wigram, Esq. |
| *Kilkennyshire,* | *Louthshire,* | E. S. Cooper, Esq. | *Wicklow,* |
| Hon. F. C. Ponsonby | Hon. J. Jocelyn | | Hon. G. L. Proby |
| Hon. C. B. Clarke | *Rt. Hon. T. H. Skef- | *Sligo Borough,* | James Gratton, Esq. |
| *Kilkenny, Bor.* | fington | Owen Wynne, Esq. | *Youghall,* |
| *Rt. Hon. D. Browne | *Mallow,* | *Tipperary,* | James Hyde, Esq. |
| *King's County,* | W. W. Becher, Esq. | *Rt. Hon. W. Bagwell | |
| T. Bernard, Esq. | *Mayo,* | Hon. F. A. Prittie | |
| Lord Oxmantown | D. Browne, Esq. | | |

## OFFICERS AND CLERKS OF THE HOUSE OF COMMONS.

John Henry Ley, Esq. Chief Clerk

John Rickman, Esq. Clerk Assistant

Wm. Ley, Esq. Second Clerk Assistant

Thos. Dyson, Esq. Clerk of the Committees of Privileges and Elections

Mr. R. Jones, Assistant Clerk of the Committees of Privileges and Elections

John Dorington, Esq. Clerk of the Fees

Mr. J. E. Dorington, Assistant Clerk of the Fees

*Principal Committee Clerks*—Edward Stracey, Esq. John Benson, Esq. Arthur Benson, Esq. John Dorington, Esq.

*Deputy Committee Clerks*—Mr. Samuel Gunnel, Mr. Henry Coles, Mr. William G. Rose, Mr. James Robe.

*Assistant Deputy Committee Clerks*—R. Chalmers, G. Whittam, jun. G. White, and W. Hawes.

*Other Clerks, who occasionally attend upon Committees:*—T. Beeby, G. Dyson, R. Gibbons, and A. Jones.

George Whittam, Esq. Clerk of the Journals and Papers.

Edw. Stracey, Esq. } Clerks of Ingrossments.
Mr. David Jones, }

Mr. William Gunnell, Assistant Clerk of Ingrossments

Henry Gunnell, Esq. E. Johnson, T. Beeby, Clerks in Private Bill Office

*Clerks in the several offices of the Chief Clerk, according to their seniority*—E. Johnson, T. Beeby, G. White, R. Chalmers, A. Dickinson, G. Whittam, jun. W. Hawes, R. Jones, C. Gandy, S. Gunnell, jun G. Dyson, R. Gibbons, J. Gudge, C. Rowland, A. Jones, C. White.

Wm. B. Gurney, Esq. Short hand writer

Henry Seymour, Esq. Serjeant at Arms

John Clementson, Esq. Deputy Serjeant

Mr. James Mitchell, Deliverer of Votes

Mr. John Bellamy, Deputy Housekeeper & Collector of Serjeant's fees

*Messengers*—Mr. Francis Wright, Mr. Samuel Spiller, Mr. Charles Stein, Mr. Wm. Giffard.

Mr. Benjamin Spiller, Librarian

Wm. Fred. Baylay, M.A. Chaplain to the House of Commons

Edw. Phillips, Esq. Secretary to the Speaker

Mr. Wm. Rowland, Train-bearer

Luke Hansard, Esq. and Sons, Printers of the Journals, &c.

John Nichols, Esq. & Son, Printers of the Votes

# LAW DEPARTMENT.

## HIGH COURT OF CHANCERY.

Lord High Chancellor, Earl of Eldon.
Master or Keeper of the Rolls, Sir Thomas Plumer, Knt.
Vice Chancellor, Sir John Leach, Knt.
Accomptant-General, John Campbell, Esq.

## CROWN OFFICE.

Clerk of the Crown, Earl Bathurst.
Deputy, Edward Wilbraham, Esq.
First Clerk, Mr. Benjamin Pointer.
Second Clerk, Mr. Thomas Jackson.

Patentee for making out Commissions of Bankruptcy, Lord Thurlow.
Deputy, Joseph Dorin, Esq.
Clerk, Mr. Smith.

## COURT FOR RELIEF OF INSOLVENT DEBTORS.

Chief Commissioner, Henry Revel Reynolds, Esq.
Commissioners, Thomas Barton Bower, and John Greathead Harris, Esqrs.
Chief Clerk, John Massey, Esq.

## COURT OF KING'S BENCH.

Lord Chief Justice,
Right Hon. Sir Charles Abbott, Knt.
Judges. Sir John Bayley, Knt. Sir George Sowley Holroyd, Knt. Sir Wm. Draper Best, Knt.
Crown Side, King's Coroner or Attorney, Edmund Henry Lushington, Esq.
Secondary, Henry Dealtry, Esq.

Clerk of the Rules, Chas. F. Robinson, Esq. Examiner and Calendar Keeper, W. Belt. Esq.
Clerks in Court, Robt. Belt, Henry Dealtry, Benjamin Burnet, William Saml Jones, Wm. Belt, Peregrine Dealtry, Charles Francis Robinson, Esqrs.

## COURT OF COMMON PLEAS

Chief Justice, Rt. Hon. Sir Rt. Dallas, Knt.
Judges, Sir James Allan Park, Knt. Sir Jas. Burrough, Knt. Sir J. Richardson, Knt.
Office of Custos Brevium, Sir Pyers Mostyn, Bart. Sir William Eden, Bart.

Deputy, George Humphreys, Esq.
Prothonotaries, George Woodroffe, George Watlington, and Robert Ray, Esqrs.
Secondaries, George Griffith, Thomas Lodington, and Jonathan Hewlet, Esqrs.

## COURT OF EXCHEQUER.

Chancellor, The Right Hon. F. Robinson,
Lord Chief Baron, Right Hon. Sir R. Richards, Knt.
Barons, Sir Robt. Graham, Knt. Sir George Wood, Knt. Sir William Garrow, Knt.
Accomptant General, Richard Richards, Esq

Masters, Richard Richards, and Jeffries Spranger, Esqrs.
Clerk of Reports & Certificates, Mr. George Fenner.
Cursitor Baron, Francis Maseres, Esq. F.R.S.

### KING'S SERJEANTS.

Attorney-General, Sir Robert Gifford, Knt.
Solicitor-General, Sir John S. Copley, Knt.
King's Ancient Serjeant, John Lens, Esq.
King's Serjeants, John Vaughan, Arthur Onslow, Esqrs. Sir John S. Copley, Knt. and Albert Pell, Esq.

### DUCHY COURT OF LANCASTER, Somerset-Place.

Chancellor, Right Hon. Lord Bexley.
Attorney-General, William Walton, Esq.
King's Serjeant, Hon. Robert H. Eden.
King's Counsel, J. A. Roe, Esq.
Receiver-General, Charles Bathurst, Esq.
Auditors, J. Mitford & Fr. L. Holt, Esqrs.
Clerk of the Council and Registrar, Hon. Geo. Villiers.
Deputy, Robert John Harper, Esq,
Secretary, R. J. Harper, Esq.
Clerks in Court in Causes, Mr. Harper, and Mr. Minchin.

### COUNTY PALATINE of LANCASTER.

Chancellor, Right Hon. Lord Bexley.
Vice-Chancellor, Giffin Wilson, Esq.
Secretary, Robert, J. Harper, Esq.
Att.Gen. of the County, Jas. Scarlett, Esq.
King's Counsel, Wm. Walton and M.F.A. Ainslie, Esqrs.
Registrar, Examiner and First Clerk, Wm. Shawe. Esq.
Seal-Keeper, Joseph Sea Aspden, Esq.
Cursitors and Clerks of the Chancery, J.S. Aspden, Thos. Wilson, Nicholas Grimshaw, Christopher B. Walker, Esqrs.
Acting Cursitor, N. Grimshaw, Esq.
Prothonotary, • Right Hon. John Charles Villiers.
Deputy, Wm. Cross, Esq.
Clerk of the Crown, J: T. Batt, Esq.
Deputy, R. T. Hopkins, Esq.
Clerk of the Peace, Edward Gorst, Esq.
Messenger, Mr. Joseph Rose.

1. *Vicar-General's office, and Registry of the Peculiars of the Deaneries of the Arches, London, Shoreham, and Croydon.*

Vicar-General—Jas. Henry Arnold, D. C. L.
Dean of the peculiars—Right Hon. Sir John Nicholl, Knight.
Registrars, John Moore, W. M. Moore, Esqrs.
Deputy—George Jenner, Esq.

2. *Court of Arches.*

Official Principal—Right Hon. Sir John Nicholl, Knight, D. C. L.
Registrar—George Jenner, Esq.

3. *Prerogative Court.*

Master—Right Hon. Sir John Nicholl, Knight, D. C. L.

Registrars—Rev. George Moore, M.A. Chas. Moore, Esq. Rev. Robert Moore, M.A.
Deputies—Nathaniel Gosling, R. C. Creswell, George Jenner, Esqrs.
Apparitor General—G. Marshall, Esq.
Deputy—J. Thompson.

4. *Faculty-Office.*

Master—Lord Stowell, D. C. L.
Registrar—Charles Moore, Esq.
Deputy—William Moore, Esq.

5. *Consistory Court.*

Judge—Sir Christopher Robinson, Knight.
Registrar—Right Hon. Richard Ryder
Deputy—John Shephard, Esq.

# MINISTERS OF STATE.

## CABINET MINISTERS.

Earl of Harrowby, ............... President of the Council
Earl of Eldon, ................... Lord High Chancellor
Earl of Westmoreland, K. G.... Lord Privy Seal
Earl of Liverpool, K.G. ......... First Lord of the Treasury, (Prime Minister.)
F. J. Robinson, ................... Chancellor of the Exchequer.
Lord Viscount Melville, K. T. ... First Lord of the Admiralty.
Duke of Wellington, K.G. Master-General of the Ordnance.
Right Hon. Robert Peel, ......... Secretary of State for the Home Department
Right Hon. George Canning, ... Secretary of State for Foreign Affairs,
Earl Bathurst, K.G. ............... Secretary of State for the Department of Colonies.
Lord Bexley, ..................... Chancellor of the Duchy of Lancaster.
Right Hon. C. W. W. Wynne,... President of the Board of Controul for Indian Affairs.
Treasurer of Navy, and President of the Board of Trade.
Right Hon. Lord Maryborough, Master of the Mint.
Lord Viscount Sidmouth,.........

## NOT OF THE CABINET.

Viscount Palmerston, ............ Secretary at War.
Right Hon. Sir C. Long, G.C.B. Paymaster-General of the Forces.
Vice-President of the Board of Trade.
Lieutenant-General of Ordnance.
Right Hon. W. Huskisson, ...... First Commissioner of Land Revenue.
Earl of Chichester, ............... Postmaster-General.
Right Hon. C. Arbuthnot, ... } Secretaries of the Treasury.
S. R. Lushington, Esq. ....... }
Sir R. Gifford, Knight,............ Attorney-General.
Sir J. S. Copley, Knight, ......... Solicitor-General.

## PERSONS IN THE MINISTRY OF IRELAND.

Marquis Wellesley, K. G. K. C. Lord-Lieutenant.
Lord Manners, ..................... Lord High Chancellor.
Rt. Hon. Henry Goulburn, M.P. Chief Secretary.
Lord Combermere, G.C.B. ..... Commander of the Forces.
Right Hon. Sir G. F. Hill, Bart. Vice-Treasurer.
Right Hon. Wm. Plunkett, ...... Attorney-General.
Right Hon. Chas. Kendal Bushe, Solicitor-General.

3 H

# DISCOUNT TABLE.

EXAMPLE:—Required the Amount of Discount upon £804 17s. 6d. at 40 ℔ cent?

Found thus:—£800 at 40 ℔ cent, £320.—£90 do. £36.—£4 do. £1 16s.—14s. do. 6s.—2s. 6d. do. 1s.—Principal £804 17s. 6d.—Discount £356 3s.

| Principal £ | 40 ℔ cent £ s. d. | 35 ℔ cent £ s. d. | 30 ℔ cent £ s. d. | 25 ℔ cent £ s. d. | 20 ℔ cent £ s. d. | 15 ℔ cent £ s. d. | 10 ℔ cent £ s. d. | 7½ ℔ cent £ s. d. | 5 ℔ cent £ s. d. | 4 ℔ cent £ s. d. | 3 ℔ cent £ s. d. | 2 ℔ cent £ s. d. | 1 ℔ cent £ s. d. | ¾ ℔ cent £ s. d. | ½ ℔ cent £ s. d. | ¼ ℔ cent £ s. d. |
|---|---|---|---|---|---|---|---|---|---|---|---|---|---|---|---|---|
| 1000 | 400 0 0 | 350 0 0 | 300 0 0 | 250 0 0 | 200 0 0 | 150 0 0 | 100 0 0 | 75 0 0 | 50 0 0 | 40 0 0 | 30 0 0 | 20 0 0 | 10 0 0 | 7 10 0 | 5 0 0 | 2 10 0 |
| 900 | 360 0 0 | 315 0 0 | 270 0 0 | 225 0 0 | 180 0 0 | 135 0 0 | 90 0 0 | 67 10 0 | 45 0 0 | 36 0 0 | 27 0 0 | 18 0 0 | 9 0 0 | 6 15 0 | 4 10 0 | 2 5 0 |
| 800 | 320 0 0 | 280 0 0 | 240 0 0 | 200 0 0 | 160 0 0 | 120 0 0 | 80 0 0 | 60 0 0 | 40 0 0 | 32 0 0 | 24 0 0 | 16 0 0 | 8 0 0 | 6 0 0 | 4 0 0 | 2 0 0 |
| 700 | 280 0 0 | 245 0 0 | 210 0 0 | 175 0 0 | 140 0 0 | 105 0 0 | 70 0 0 | 52 10 0 | 35 0 0 | 28 0 0 | 21 0 0 | 14 0 0 | 7 0 0 | 5 5 0 | 3 10 0 | 1 15 0 |
| 600 | 240 0 0 | 210 0 0 | 180 0 0 | 150 0 0 | 120 0 0 | 90 0 0 | 60 0 0 | 45 0 0 | 30 0 0 | 24 0 0 | 18 0 0 | 12 0 0 | 6 0 0 | 4 10 0 | 3 0 0 | 1 10 0 |
| 500 | 200 0 0 | 175 0 0 | 150 0 0 | 125 0 0 | 100 0 0 | 75 0 0 | 50 0 0 | 37 10 0 | 25 0 0 | 20 0 0 | 15 0 0 | 10 0 0 | 5 0 0 | 3 15 0 | 2 10 0 | 1 5 0 |
| 400 | 160 0 0 | 140 0 0 | 120 0 0 | 100 0 0 | 80 0 0 | 60 0 0 | 40 0 0 | 30 0 0 | 20 0 0 | 16 0 0 | 12 0 0 | 8 0 0 | 4 0 0 | 3 0 0 | 2 0 0 | 1 0 0 |
| 300 | 120 0 0 | 105 0 0 | 90 0 0 | 75 0 0 | 60 0 0 | 45 0 0 | 30 0 0 | 22 10 0 | 15 0 0 | 12 0 0 | 9 0 0 | 6 0 0 | 3 0 0 | 2 5 0 | 1 10 0 | 0 15 0 |
| 200 | 80 0 0 | 70 0 0 | 60 0 0 | 50 0 0 | 40 0 0 | 30 0 0 | 20 0 0 | 15 0 0 | 10 0 0 | 8 0 0 | 6 0 0 | 4 0 0 | 2 0 0 | 1 10 0 | 1 0 0 | 0 10 0 |
| 100 | 40 0 0 | 35 0 0 | 30 0 0 | 25 0 0 | 20 0 0 | 15 0 0 | 10 0 0 | 7 10 0 | 5 0 0 | 4 0 0 | 3 0 0 | 2 0 0 | 1 0 0 | 0 15 0 | 0 10 0 | 0 5 0 |
| 90 | 36 0 0 | 31 10 0 | 27 0 0 | 22 10 0 | 18 0 0 | 13 10 0 | 9 0 0 | 6 15 0 | 4 10 0 | 3 12 0 | 2 14 0 | 1 16 0 | 0 18 0 | 0 13 6 | 0 9 0 | 0 4 6 |
| 80 | 32 0 0 | 28 0 0 | 24 0 0 | 20 0 0 | 16 0 0 | 12 0 0 | 8 0 0 | 6 0 0 | 4 0 0 | 3 4 0 | 2 8 0 | 1 12 0 | 0 16 0 | 0 12 0 | 0 8 0 | 0 4 0 |
| 70 | 28 0 0 | 24 10 0 | 21 0 0 | 17 10 0 | 14 0 0 | 10 10 0 | 7 0 0 | 5 5 0 | 3 10 0 | 2 16 0 | 2 2 0 | 1 8 0 | 0 14 0 | 0 10 6 | 0 7 0 | 0 3 6 |
| 60 | 24 0 0 | 21 0 0 | 18 0 0 | 15 0 0 | 12 0 0 | 9 0 0 | 6 0 0 | 4 10 0 | 3 0 0 | 2 8 0 | 1 16 0 | 1 4 0 | 0 12 0 | 0 9 0 | 0 6 0 | 0 3 0 |
| 50 | 20 0 0 | 17 10 0 | 15 0 0 | 12 10 0 | 10 0 0 | 7 10 0 | 5 0 0 | 3 15 0 | 2 10 0 | 2 0 0 | 1 10 0 | 1 0 0 | 0 10 0 | 0 7 6 | 0 5 0 | 0 2 6 |
| 40 | 16 0 0 | 14 0 0 | 12 0 0 | 10 0 0 | 8 0 0 | 6 0 0 | 4 0 0 | 3 0 0 | 2 0 0 | 1 12 0 | 1 4 0 | 0 16 0 | 0 8 0 | 0 6 0 | 0 4 0 | 0 2 0 |
| 30 | 12 0 0 | 10 10 0 | 9 0 0 | 7 10 0 | 6 0 0 | 4 10 0 | 3 0 0 | 2 5 0 | 1 10 0 | 1 4 0 | 0 18 0 | 0 12 0 | 0 6 0 | 0 4 6 | 0 3 0 | 0 1 6 |
| 25 | 10 0 0 | 8 15 0 | 7 10 0 | 6 5 0 | 5 0 0 | 3 15 0 | 2 10 0 | 1 17 6 | 1 5 0 | 1 0 0 | 0 15 0 | 0 10 0 | 0 5 0 | 0 3 9 | 0 2 6 | 0 1 3 |
| 20 | 8 0 0 | 7 0 0 | 6 0 0 | 5 0 0 | 4 0 0 | 3 0 0 | 2 0 0 | 1 10 0 | 1 0 0 | 0 16 0 | 0 12 0 | 0 8 0 | 0 4 0 | 0 3 0 | 0 2 0 | 0 1 0 |
| 15 | 6 0 0 | 5 5 0 | 4 10 0 | 3 15 0 | 3 0 0 | 2 5 0 | 1 10 0 | 1 2 6 | 0 15 0 | 0 12 0 | 0 9 0 | 0 6 0 | 0 3 0 | 0 2 3 | 0 1 6 | 0 0 9 |
| 10 | 4 0 0 | 3 10 0 | 3 0 0 | 2 10 0 | 2 0 0 | 1 10 0 | 1 0 0 | 0 15 0 | 0 10 0 | 0 8 0 | 0 6 0 | 0 4 0 | 0 2 0 | 0 1 6 | 0 1 0 | 0 0 6 |
| 9 | 3 12 0 | 3 3 0 | 2 14 0 | 2 5 0 | 1 16 0 | 1 7 0 | 0 18 0 | 0 13 6 | 0 9 0 | 0 7 2 | 0 5 5 | 0 3 7 | 0 1 9 | | | |
| 8 | 3 4 0 | 2 16 0 | 2 8 0 | 2 0 0 | 1 12 0 | 1 4 0 | 0 16 0 | 0 12 0 | 0 8 0 | 0 6 5 | 0 4 9 | 0 3 2 | 0 1 7 | | | |
| 7 | 2 16 0 | 2 9 0 | 2 2 0 | 1 15 0 | 1 8 0 | 1 1 0 | 0 14 0 | 0 10 6 | 0 7 0 | 0 5 7 | 0 4 2 | 0 2 9 | 0 1 5 | | | |
| 6 | 2 8 0 | 2 2 0 | 1 16 0 | 1 10 0 | 1 4 0 | 0 18 0 | 0 12 0 | 0 9 0 | 0 6 0 | 0 4 9 | 0 3 7 | 0 2 4 | 0 1 2 | | | |
| 5 | 2 0 0 | 1 15 0 | 1 10 0 | 1 5 0 | 1 0 0 | 0 15 0 | 0 10 0 | 0 7 6 | 0 5 0 | 0 4 0 | 0 3 0 | 0 2 0 | 0 1 0 | | | |
| 4 | 1 12 0 | 1 8 0 | 1 4 0 | 1 0 0 | 0 16 0 | 0 12 0 | 0 8 0 | 0 6 0 | 0 4 0 | 0 3 2 | 0 2 4 | 0 1 7 | 0 0 9½ | | | |
| 3 | 1 4 0 | 1 1 0 | 0 18 0 | 0 15 0 | 0 12 0 | 0 9 0 | 0 6 0 | 0 4 6 | 0 3 0 | 0 2 4 | 0 1 9 | 0 1 2 | 0 0 7 | | | |
| 2 | 0 16 0 | 0 14 0 | 0 12 0 | 0 10 0 | 0 8 0 | 0 6 0 | 0 4 0 | 0 3 0 | 0 2 0 | 0 1 7 | 0 1 2 | 0 0 9½ | 0 0 4¾ | | | |
| 1 | 0 8 0 | 0 7 0 | 0 6 0 | 0 5 0 | 0 4 0 | 0 3 0 | 0 2 0 | 0 1 6 | 0 1 0 | 0 0 9½ | 0 0 7 | 0 0 4¾ | 0 0 2½ | | | |

*Schedule A.*—Windows to be charged on each house per year, according to the following Table after the 5th April 1823, in England and Wales,

| No. Windows | Duty £. s. d. | No. Windows | Duty £. s. d. |
|---|---|---|---|
| 1 to 6 | 0 3 3 | 33 | 11 1 6 |
| *Ditto | 0 4 0 | 34 | 11 10 0 |
| 7 | 0 10 0 | 35 | 11 18 3 |
| 8 | 0 16 6 | 36 | 12 6 9 |
| 9 | 1 1 0 | 37 | 12 15 3 |
| 10 | 1 8 0 | 38 | 13 3 6 |
| 11 | 1 16 3 | 39 | 13 12 0 |
| 12 | 2 4 9 | 40 to 44 | 14 8 9 |
| 13 | 2 13 3 | 45 to 49 | 15 16 9 |
| 14 | 3 1 9 | 50 to 54 | 17 5 0 |
| 15 | 3 10 0 | 55 to 59 | 18 13 0 |
| 16 | 3 18 6 | 60 to 64 | 19 17 9 |
| 17 | 4 7 0 | 65 to 69 | 21 0 3 |
| 18 | 4 15 3 | 70 to 74 | 22 2 6 |
| 19 | 5 3 9 | 75 to 79 | 23 5 0 |
| 20 | 5 12 3 | 80 to 84 | 24 7 6 |
| 21 | 6 0 6 | 85 to 89 | 25 10 0 |
| 22 | 6 9 0 | 90 to 94 | 26 12 3 |
| 23 | 6 17 6 | 95 to 99 | 27 14 9 |
| 24 | 7 5 9 | 100 to 109 | 29 8 6 |
| 25 | 7 14 3 | 110 to 119 | 31 13 3 |
| 26 | 8 2 9 | 120 to 129 | 33 18 3 |
| 27 | 8 11 0 | 130 to 139 | 36 3 0 |
| 28 | 8 19 6 | 140 to 149 | 38 8 0 |
| 29 | 9 8 0 | 150 to 159 | 40 12 9 |
| 30 | 9 16 3 | 160 to 169 | 42 17 9 |
| 31 | 10 4 9 | 170 to 179 | 45 2 6 |
| 32 | 10 13 3 | 180 & upwd. | 46 11 3 |

And every House having more than 180 Windows must be charged with ONE SHILLING AND SIXPENCE for each Window above that Number, in addition to FORTY-SIX POUNDS ELEVEN SHILLINGS AND THREE-PENCE.

No window or light is exempt from the duties, by reason of its being stopt up unless it shall be effectually done with stone or brick or with the same materials whereof that part of the outside of walls of such dwelling-house chiefly consists.

Windows opened after the commencement of the year to be charged the whole year, and no abatement is to be allowed for windows stopped up after the commencement of the year.

Every house which is left to the care of a servant is liable to the window duty.

In numbering the windows in a house, all sky-lights and windows or lights however constructed in staircases, garrets, passages, and all other parts of dwelling-houses whether they are in the exterior or interior parts of the house, or in any kitchen, cellar, scullery, buttery, pantry, larder, wash-house, laundry, bake-house, and brew-house, whether within, contiguous to, or disjoined from the dwelling-house are to be included.

Every window which gives light into more rooms, landings or stories than one is to be charged as so many windows as there are rooms, landings or stories, enlightened thereby.

When windows or lights are fixed in different frames, each window or light is to be charged, whatever be the breadth of the partition or division.

When a partition or division between two or more windows or lights fixed in one frame, is, or shall be of the breadth or space of twelve inches, the window or light on each side of such partition or division is to be charged as a distinct window or light.

* Houses having less than SEVEN Windows, if charged to the Inhabited House Duty, are liable to the Duty of FOUR SHILLINGS, and if not charged to that Duty, only to THREE SHILLINGS AND THREE-PENCE.—Distinct Chambers or Apartments in any of the Inns of Court or Chancery, or in any College or Hall in either of the Universities of Oxford or Cambridge, or any Public Hospitals; also Houses divided into different Tenements, *being distinct Properties;* where the Number of Windows does not in each case respectively exceed Seven, to be charged *One Shilling and Ninepence* for each Window, where the Number of Windows exceed Seven, to be charged as if the same were an entire House.

Every window or light, including the frame, partitions and divisions thereof which shall exceed in height twelve feet; also windows which shall exceed in breadth four feet nine inches, being more than three feet six inches long, is to be charged as two windows, except windows made of greater dimensions previous to the 5th April 1785: windows in shops, workshops and warehouses: windows in the *public room* of any house licensed to sell wine, ale, &c. *such as the coffee room, tap room, &c.* and windows in farm-houses.

*Exemptions from Window Duty.*—Every public office for which the duties heretofore have been paid by his Majesty, or out of the public revenue.

Any hospital, charity school, or house provided for the reception and relief of poor persons, except such apartments therein as are occupied by the officers or servants thereof, which shall severally be assessed and subject to the same duties as an entire house.

The windows in any room of a dwelling-house, licensed according to law as a chapel for the purpose of divine worship, and used for no other purpose whatsoever.

Windows in shops or warehouses being parts of dwelling houses in the front or fronts, and on the ground or basement story; but if any such shop or warehouse, contain more than three windows, the exemption does not extend beyond three.

Windows or lights in dairies and cheese-rooms used by the occupier for keeping butter or cheese, being their own produce, for sale or private use, provided the words dairy or cheese room are painted thereon, and that the rooms are never used to sleep in, but are wholly kept for the purposes afore-mentioned.

Persons having three children born in lawful wedlock, and wholly maintained by them or at their expence, and not having more than six windows in their respective dwelling houses, which are not worth the annual rent of 5l.

Persons who receive parochial relief, or can obtain a certificate from the minister, churchwardens, and overseer of the poor of their inability to pay the duty on windows.

*House Duty, Schedule B.* — Houses worth 5l. and under 20l. a year, to pay annually in the pound, 1s. 6d. Twenty pounds to forty, 2s. 3d. Forty pounds and upwards, 2s. 10d.

These duties to be assessed on every inhabited dwelling-house which shall be of the annual value of 5l. and upwards, and in rating houses to these duties every coach-house, stable, brew-house, wash-house, laundry, wood-house, bake-house, dairy, and all other offices; and all yards, courts, and cur-

tilages, gardens and pleasure grounds, occupied therewith are also to be valued, provided that no more than one acre of such gardens and pleasure grounds shall in any case be so valued.

All shops or warehouses attached to or having any communication with the dwelling house, are to be valued together with the dwelling house and offices.

Every house let in different stories, tenements, or lodgings, and inhabited by two or more families is to be assessed to these duties as one house, and the landlord or owner to be considered the occupier and charged for the same.

*Exemptions from House Duty.*—Every hospital, charity school, or house provided for the reception or relief of poor persons.

Every farm-house occupied by a tenant for the purpose of husbandry only.

Every farm-house occupied by the owner, and *bona-fide* used for the purposes of husbandry only, which, with the household and other offices aforesaid, shall be valued at less than 11l. per annum.

Every public office, the duties of which are payable out of the public revenue.

Every house left to the care of any person who is not assessed to the rates for the church or poor, and who resides therein, for the purpose only of taking care thereof.

*Male Servants, Schedule E.*—Every person who shall have retained or employed any male person in capacity of house steward, butler, footman, coachman, groom, postillion, stable boy, or helper in the stable, gardener, park-keeper, game-keeper, huntsman, whipper-in, or by whatever name or names male persons acting in any of the said capacities shall be called, is to be charged according to the following table :—

| No. | At per Servant. | | | Total per Year. | | |
|---|---|---|---|---|---|---|
| | £. | s. | d. | £. | s. | d. |
| 1 | 1 | 4 | 0 | 1 | 4 | 0 |
| 2 | 1 | 11 | 0 | 3 | 2 | 0 |
| 3 | 1 | 18 | 0 | 5 | 14 | 0 |
| 4 | 2 | 3 | 6 | 8 | 14 | 0 |
| 5 | 2 | 9 | 0 | 12 | 5 | 0 |
| 6 | 2 | 11 | 6 | 15 | 9 | 0 |
| 7 | 2 | 12 | 6 | 18 | 7 | 6 |
| 8 | 2 | 16 | 0 | 22 | 8 | 0 |
| 9 | 3 | 1 | 0 | 27 | 9 | 0 |
| 10 | 3 | 6 | 6 | 33 | 5 | 0 |
| 11 | 3 | 16 | 6 | 42 | 1 | 6 |
| 12 | | | | 45 | 18 | 0 |
| 13 | | | | 49 | 14 | 6 |
| 14 | | | | 53 | 11 | 0 |
| 15 | | | | 57 | 7 | 6 |

## BACHELORS.

| No. | At per Servant. | | | Total per Year. | | |
|---|---|---|---|---|---|---|
| | £. | s. | d. | £. | s. | d. |
| 1 | 2 | 4 | 0 | 2 | 4 | 0 |
| 2 | 2 | 11 | 0 | 5 | 2 | 0 |
| 3 | 2 | 18 | 0 | 8 | 14 | 0 |
| 4 | 3 | 3 | 6 | 12 | 14 | 0 |
| 5 | 3 | 9 | 0 | 17 | 5 | 0 |
| 6 | 3 | 11 | 6 | 21 | 9 | 0 |
| 7 | 3 | 12 | 6 | 25 | 7 | 6 |
| 8 | 3 | 16 | 0 | 30 | 8 | 0 |
| 9 | 4 | 1 | 0 | 36 | 9 | 0 |
| 10 | 4 | 6 | 6 | 43 | 5 | 0 |
| 11 | 4 | 16 | 6 | 53 | 1 | 6 |
| 12 | ——— | | | 57 | 18 | 0 |
| 13 | ——— | | | 62 | 14 | 6 |
| 14 | ——— | | | 67 | 11 | 0 |
| 15 | ——— | | | 72 | 7 | 6 |

This Rate of Duty (1l. 4s.) is payable for every male person employed in any of the capacities, Sch. C. No. 1, and not being a servant to his employer, if the employer shall otherwise be chargeable to the above duties on servants, or for any carriage, or for more than one horse kept for riding, or drawing any carriage. And if the Employer shall not be chargeable to such other duties, then the sum of 10s. is payable for every such male person employed.

*Travellers, or Riders.*—Where one only is kept, 1l. 10s. each. Where two or more is kept, at 2l. 10s. each.

*Clerks, Book-keepers, or Office-keepers.*—Where one only is kept, at 1l. each. Where two or more is kept, at 1l. 10s. each.—† Shopmen, Warehousemen, Cellarmen, or Porters, at 1l. each. Waiters in Taverns, &c. at 1l. 10s. each. Occasional Waiters employed for the Period of Six Calender Months in any Year, to be charged 1l. each. If employed for a lesser period than Six Calender Months in any Year, 10s. each.—Any Person, (not being a Servant,) employed as an occasional waiter in any private house, not less than six times in the preceding year, 10s.

Coachmen, &c. let on Job, at 1l. 5s. each.

This Duty, by the Act of 52 Geo. III. is extended to Coachmen kept for the purpose of driving any public stage coach or carriage, and to persons employed as guards to such stage coach or carriage.

Persons chiefly retained and employed for the purpose of preserving game, as an under game-keeper, under any game-keeper, being an assessed servant, duly appointed by the lord or lady of the manor, are liable to the duty of 5s. per annum.

Persons retained for the purpose of husbandry, manufacture, or trade, and employing them in the capacity of coachman, postillion, groom, or helper in the stables, are liable to the said duties, according to the table, No. 3; if the person keep any carriage, (other than a tax-cart,) or two or more horses, chargeable with duty on horses, for the purpose of riding, &c.

*Exemptions.*—Any person having more than two parish apprentices, generally employed in the affairs of husbandry or trade, and occasionally only in the capacities of groom, coachman, postillion, helper in the stables, or footman, and not wearing livery, are exempted from the duty, in table No. 3.

Persons employed as shopmen, who are under 18 years of age, and wholly maintained and lodged in the house of their employers, and apprentices bound until 21 or upwards, are exempted from the duty on shopmen.

Traders who employ persons to travel from place to place, on foot, are exempted from the duty, for every person so employed, above four of such persons.

Every apprentice bound for the term of seven years, or upwards, and serving with his original master or assignee, where no premium or other consideration shall have been taken or contracted for, is exempted from the duty imposed upon bailiffs, overseers, clerks, shopmen, travellers, porters, and waiters.

Any officer serving in the army is exempted for one servant, provided that no more than one is employed, and that one being one of the soldiers of the regiment to which such officer shall belong. Officers in the navy are also similarly exempted.

Disabled officers on half-pay are exempted from the duty on servants, for one servant retained by him.

† This rate of duty applies to stewards, bailiffs, Overseers or managers, or clerks under them; and also to servants retained by stable-keepers, for or in expectation of profit, to take care of any horse kept for the purpose of racing or running for any plate, &c. or in training for the same.

## CARRIAGES.—SCHEDULE D.

*Duties on Carriages with Four Wheels or more.*

| Private Carriages. | | | | Carriages kept to be let to hire with Post Horses, and Carriages kept as public Stage Coaches. | | | |
|---|---|---|---|---|---|---|---|
| No. | At per Carriage. | | Total per Year. | No. | At per Carriage. | | Total per Year. |
| | £. s. d. | | £. s. d. | | £. s. | | £. s. |
| 1 | 6 0 0 | | 6 0 0 | 1 | 5 5 | | 5 5 |
| 2 | 6 10 0 | | 13 0 0 | 2 | ——— | | 10 10 |
| 3 | 7 0 0 | | 21 0 0 | 3 | ——— | | 15 15 |
| 4 | 7 10 0 | | 30 0 0 | 4 | ——— | | 21 0 |
| 5 | 7 17 6 | | 39 7 6 | 5 | ——— | | 26 5 |
| 6 | 8 4 0 | | 49 4 0 | 6 | ——— | | 31 10 |
| 7 | 8 10 0 | | 59 10 0 | 7 | ——— | | 36 15 |
| 8 | 8 16 0 | | 70 8 0 | 8 | ——— | | 42 0 |
| 9 | 9 1 6 | | 81 13 6 | 9 | ——— | | 47 5 |

And so on at the same rate for any Number of such carriages.
For every additional Body used on the same carriage is to be charged the sum of 3l. 3s.

And so on at the same Rate for any number of such carriages.
Coachmakers keeping carriages for the purpose of being let to hire without horses, to be charged 6l. for each such carriage.

### Carriages with Four Wheels, drawn by Ponies, Mules, Oxen, or Asses.

* Carriages with four wheels of less diameter than thirty inches each, built and constructed according to the regulations prescribed for taxed carts, (except as to the number of wheels) the original price, or value at any time, not exceeding 15l. and constructed without springs of any materials whatever drawn by one pony or mule under twelve hands high, or by an ox or ass, 14s. 6d. each.

* Carriages above described, constructed with a spring or springs of any materials, except iron, steel, or other metallic substance, and drawn as above described, 1l. 7s. 6d.

Carriages with four wheels of less diameter than thirty inches, constructed in any manner contrary to the regulations prescribed for taxed carts, (except as to the number of wheels) or constructed with a spring or springs of iron, steel, or any other metallic substance, the original price of which carriage, or value at any time, shall exceed 15l. drawn by one pony, &c. 3l. 5s. 0d.

Do. Do. by two ponies, &c. 4l. 10s.

And for every additional body successively used on the same carriage or number of wheels, 1l. 11s. 6d.

### On Carriages with Two Wheels.

Carriages with Two Wheels, 3l. 5s. each.—Ditto, drawn by two or more horses or mules, 4l. 10s.—For every additional body used on the same carriage, 1l. 11s. 6d.

* Taxed Carts built according to 52 Geo. III. cap. 93, with springs, not of iron, steel, or other metal or metallic composition, not exceeding the price or value of 21l. used with a covered or stuffed seat or cushion, or covered footboard or apron, 1l. 7s. 6d.

* Persons liable to be assessed for a four wheel carriage, Schedule D. No. 1, or for two servants, C. No. 1. are to be charged for such pony carriages or taxed carts to the duty on two wheel carriages above stated.

Carriages let to hire, with horses, for less than a year, to be charged 5l. 5s. each; carriages let without horses to be charged 6l. each; carriages with four wheels, kept and used as a public stage-coach or post-chaise, are liable to the duty of 5l 5s.

Coachmakers, and persons selling carriages by auction, or on commission, to pay the duty of ten shillings; and for every carriage sold with four wheels, 1l. 5s. with less than four wheels, 12s. 6d. and for every taxed cart, 3s.—Every maker of taxed carts, not being a coachmaker, is liable to the duty of 3s. and the further sum of 3s. for every taxed cart made.

*Exemptions from the before mentioned duties on carriages.*—Coaches licensed by the commissioners for hackney coaches within the cities of Westminster and London.

Carriages kept by coachmakers *bona-fide* for sale, or for the purpose of being lent to any person during the time such person's carriage shall be under repair.

Carts used wholly in the affairs of husbandry or trade are not chargeable with this duty, if used for no other purpose of riding therein than as follows, viz.—By reason of the owner, or any of his servants, riding therein, when laden ; or when returning from or going for a load in husbandry or trade; or conveying the owner or family to divine service on Sundays, Good Friday, or Christmasday ; or conveying persons to or from the elections of members to serve in parliament.

## DUTIES ON HORSES.—Schedule E.

| Horses for Riding, or drawing Carriages. | | | Horses let to hire without Post Duty, and Race Horses. | | |
|---|---|---|---|---|---|
| No. | At per Horse. | Total a Year. | No. | At per Horse. | Total a Year. |
| | £. s. d. | £. s. d. | | £. s. d. | £. s. d. |
| 1 | 1 8 9 | 1 8 9 | 1 | 1 8 9 | 1 8 9 |
| 2 | 2 7 3 | 4 14 6 | 2 | ——— | 2 17 6 |
| 3 | 2 12 3 | 7 16 9 | 3 | ——— | 4 6 3 |
| 4 | 2 15 0 | 11 0 0 | 4 | ——— | 5 15 0 |
| 5 | 2 15 9 | 13 18 9 | 5 | ——— | 7 3 9 |
| 6 | 2 18 0 | 17 8 0 | 6 | ——— | 8 12 6 |
| 7 | 2 19 9 | 20 18 8 | 7 | ——— | 10 1 3 |
| 8 | 2 19 9 | 23 18 0 | 8 | ——— | 11 10 0 |
| 9 | 3 0 9 | 27 6 9 | 9 | ——— | 12 18 9 |
| 10 | 3 3 6 | 31 15 0 | 10 | ——— | 14 7 6 |
| 11 | 3 3 6 | 34 18 6 | 11 | ——— | 15 16 3 |
| 12 | 3 3 6 | 38 2 0 | 12 | ——— | 17 5 0 |
| 13 | 3 3 9 | 41 8 9 | 13 | ——— | 18 13 9 |
| 14 | 3 3 9 | 44 12 6 | 14 | ——— | 20 2 6 |
| 15 | 3 3 9 | 47 16 3 | 15 | ——— | 21 11 3 |
| 16 | 3 3 9 | 51 0 0 | 16 | ——— | 23 0 0 |
| 17 | 3 4 0 | 54 8 0 | 17 | ——— | 24 8 9 |
| 18 | 3 4 6 | 58 1 0 | 18 | ——— | 25 17 6 |
| 19 | 3 5 0 | 61 15 0 | 19 | ——— | 27 6 3 |
| 20 | 3 6 0 | 66 0 0 | 20 | ——— | 28 15 0 |

And so on at the respective rates for any number of such horses.

Horses rode by butchers in their trade, 1*l.* 8*s.* 9*d.* each.—Where two only kept, the second at 10*s.* 6*d.*—Horses not exceeding the height of thirteen hands, 1*l.* 1*s.* each. One horse used by bailiff on a farm, 1*l.* 6*s.*

*Exemptions.*—Any farmer whose rent is less than 200*l.* per annum, and having no other income, although he does occasionally use a horse for the purpose of riding.

Any person occupying a farm, and making a livelihood solely thereby, or any person carrying on a trade, and making a livelihood solely thereby, or making a livelihood by such occupation and trade jointly ; or any ecclesiastical persons not possessed of an annual income of 100*l.* or upwards, whether arising from any ecclesiastical preferment, or otherwise, for one horse used for the purpose of drawing any taxed cart.

Any person using any horse for the purpose of carrying burdens in the course of the owner's trade or occupation, or for drawing any cart, (not chargeable with the duties on carriages) or for riding when returning from any place to which any burthen shall have been taken, or to any place from whence any burthen shall be brought back, or for the purpose of riding to procure medical assistance, or to or from market, or any place of public worship, or any election of members to serve in parliament, or any courts of justice, or meetings of the commissioners of taxes.

Horses used for the purpose of drawing any hackney coach.

All mares kept for the sole purpose of breeding.

Any officer or private serving in any corps of yeomanry or volunteer cavalry, or providing a horse for any person serving in any such corps, who shall have been returned as effective members by the certificate of the commanding officer.

Horses used in his Majesty's service by any non-commissioned officer or private.

Horses used solely in public stage coaches or post chaise.

Any rector, vicar, or curate, keeping but one horse, and actually doing duty in the church or chapel of which he is minister and not being possessed of an income of 60*l.* per annum.

*Draught Horses, Schedule F.* — For every horse, mare, gelding, or mule, (not chargeable before with any duty) if thirteen hands high of four inches to each hand, the sum of 10s. 6d.

*Exemptions.*—Horses kept and used for the purposes of husbandry.

Horses kept by persons *bonâ fide* for the occupation of farms under 200*l.* per annum, and making a livelihood solely thereby, although such horses shall occasionally be used for hire or profit.

Mules kept by persons who seek their livelihood by the carriage of ore, slate, stone, or culm, to or from the mine or pit, or the carriage of lime, sea-weed, or other manure, provided that such ore, &c. be loaded on the backs of such mules and not otherwise.

Also, see Exemptions in Schedule E.

*Dogs, Schedule G.*—Every person who shall keep any grey hound, the sum of 1*l.* for each such grey hound.

Every person who shall keep any hound, pointer, setting-dog, spaniel, lurcher or terrier, and for every other dog where two or more are kept of whatever description, (except grey hounds) the sum of 14s. for each dog.

Every person who shall keep no more than one dog, not being of the description before mentioned, the sum of 8s. for such dog.

*Exemptions from Duty on Dogs.*—Any person who on account of poverty shall be exempt from the duty on his dwelling house and having one *dog only,* the same not being a grey hound, hound, pointer, setting-dog, spaniel, lurcher, or terrier.

Persons having dogs not six months old.

*Horse Dealers, Schedule H.* — Every person who shall carry on the trade of horse dealer, whether in partnership or separately, in the cities of London and Westminster and the liberties of the same, the parishes of Mary-le-bone and Pancras in Middlesex, the weekly bills of mortality, or in the Borough of Southwark, the annual sum of 25*l.* and if in any other part of England and Wales, or Berwick-upon-Tweed, the annual sum of 12*l.* 10s.

*Hair Powder, Schedule I.*—Every person who wears it to pay annually 1*l.* 3s. 6d. This act does not extend to any of the Royal Family, or any servants serving immediately under them; nor any clergyman, dissenting minister, or any person in holy orders, not possessing the annual income of 100*l.* (however arising); nor any person serving in the navy under the rank of commander; nor any subaltern or inferior in the army; nor any officer or private in any corps of volunteers, enrolled in defence of the kingdom.

No person to pay for more than two unmarried daughters.

*Armorial Bearings, Schedule K.*—Any person keeping a coach or other carriage, and using or wearing any armorial bearing, to pay annually 2*l.* 8s. Any person not keeping a coach, &c. but liable to the house and window duty, to pay annually 1*l.* 4s. and every other description of persons 12s. annually.

*Game Certificates, Schedule L.*—Not to be altered *except making* 3*l.* 13s. into 3*l.* 13s. 6d.

Notice papers to be returned within twenty-one days from the date under the penalty of 50*l.* and if the exemptions are not claims therein they cannot be allowed.

Persons who have entered into composition for these assessed taxes are entitled to keep any number of servants or articles of the same description, as they have compounded for free of duty.

Persons who have compounded for a two wheel carriage, may keep a four wheel carriage with paying the difference between a four wheel and two wheel carriage.

# BILLS OF EXCHANGE.

A Bill of Exchange is an obligation, whereby the drawer directs the acceptor to pay a certain sum at the day and place therein mentioned, to a third party, or his order. Originally bills were drawn by a person in one country on his correspondent in another,* and they obtained the name of bills of exchange because it was the exchange, or the value of money in one place, compared with its value in another, that determined the precise extent of the sum contained in the draft. When parties to bills are of different countries, questions concerning them must be determined by the received customs of trading nations, but it is to bills of exchange drawn and negotiated in this kingdom that the following observations principally apply.

The drawer of a bill should either subscribe his name at the bottom, or it should be inserted in the body of the instrument; and it must be written either by the person purporting to be the drawer, or by some person authorised by him. If drawn or signed by an agent, it is usually signed in the following mode, " A. B. for C. D." and if such agent do not express for whom he signs, he becomes personally liable. If signed by one person of a firm, for himself and partners, it is usual, and perhaps necessary, to sign " for self and company." The obligation of the drawer to pay is absolute, and he becomes, whether the bill be drawn on his own account or that of a third person, upon its dishonour or non-acceptance, immediately,

even before the time specified for payment in such bill, liable to an action, not only for the principal sum, but likewise, in certain cases, for damages and interest; as a consequence of the bill not being honoured. Exclusive of this obligation to pay he is further bound to indemnify the acceptor, if he has not effects in his hands to the amount, from any loss he may sustain in consequence of his acceptance.

The acceptor is that party who agrees, either verbally or in writing, to pay the bill, and previous to such acceptance he is called the drawee. The contract of the acceptor being absolute, he cannot insist, as a defence, on the want of the presentment of the bill at the precise time when due, or on an indulgence to any of the other parties. In a foreign bill, where the course of exchange has altered, the acceptor will, however, only be obliged to pay according to the rate of such exchange when the bill becomes due. If the holder of a dishonoured bill sues all the parties to it at the same time, the acceptor is the only person responsible to the plaintiff for the costs of all the actions. The acceptor of an accommodation bill, if obliged to pay such bill, may sue the drawer, upon his implied contract to indemnify him. If a person write his acceptance to a bill, he is answerable, although the name of the drawer should have been forged, because his engagement has relation to his own writing.

An indorser transfers or assigns his right to another, and this may be done either simply by delivery, where the instrument is payable to bearer, or by indorsement and delivery, where it

* Bills of exchange were first introduced into the commerce of this country about the year 1381.

is payable to order. Indorsements are of three kinds, namely, in blank, in full, and restrictive. The most usual species of indorsement is in blank, where no name is mentioned but the indorser's; and although it has been adjudged that such an indorsement does not transfer the property and interest in the bill without some further act, it gives the indorsee, as well as the other persons to whom it may be afterwards transferred, the power of making himself assignee of the beneficial interest in the instrument, by filling it up payable to himself, or by writing over the indorser's name, " pay the contents," which may, when an action is brought for recovery, be done at the time of trial. An indorsement in full is that in which the name of the person in whose favour it is made is mentioned; and this is also called a special indorsement, and may restrain the negotiability of the bill. A restrictive indorsement prevents the person to whom a bill is paid from making any further transfer of it, and may be expressed in these terms—" Pay the contents to A. B. only." No form is required for an indorsement; it is sufficient that the name of the indorser is written upon the back of the bill, which is most usual, or on any other part of it, either by the party making it, or by some other person duly authorised as his agent. The forgery of an indorsement in a bill transferable by indorsement only will convey no interest, and therefore any person coming into possession of a bill by a forged indorsement, does not acquire any interest in it, although he be not aware of the forgery, and consequently the original holder may, in such case, recover against the acceptor or drawer, although the acceptor may have paid the bill; and if the person attempting to derive an interest under such indorsement sues the acceptor, he will be admitted to prove that the indorsement was not made by the person purporting to have made it. If a bill be lost, and it comes into the hand of some person who was not aware of such loss, for a valuable consideration, (and without a forgery having been committed) previous to its being due, such person, although deriving his interest in the bill from the person finding it, may recover the amount of the bill from the acceptor, or other parties to it, and the person who lost it will consequently forfeit all right of action.

The holder of a bill, whether transferable by delivery or not, ought, in all cases of loss, immediately to give notice of such accident to the acceptor and all the antecedent parties, and also to give public notice of such loss, in order to prevent any person from taking it. The holder of a bill of above £5, expressed for value received and payable after date, may, in case of loss, demand of the drawer another bill, of the same tenor with the original one, upon giving security, and indemnifying him, in case the lost bill should again be found.

The holder of a bill, either by indorsement or delivery, or both, is entitled to receive payment from the acceptor. It is in some cases necessary, and in all advisable, to present a bill for acceptance, not only because another security is thereby added to the bill, but because by acceptance only the person on whom the bill is drawn becomes debtor for the amount to the holder, and responsible to him. If the drawee refuses to accept, or, having accepted, if he refuses payment when due, the bill is dishonoured, and the holder, in case of neglect to communicate notice to the drawer or indorsers, within a reasonable time, will not be at liberty to resort to these parties, who, by that neglect, will be discharged from their respective obligations. The right of a drawer or indorser to receive notice, in case of a bill's being dishonoured, is so strong a principle of law, and in all cases so indispensable, that nothing but what has been, by the act of God, rendered impossible, can excuse the want of it. If the parties reside in the same place where the bill was dishonoured, notice should be given on the same day; and by that day's post, if the parties are resident out of that place. In inland bills, protested for non-acceptance, if the notice or protest thereof be not sent within 14 days, the drawer or indorser will not be liable for damages.

The costs on a returned bill, that can be legally demanded, are, first, the notarial fees, namely,

## NOTING.

If the acceptor reside within the city walls.................1s. 6d.

If without..................2s. 6d.

For every additional mile.....1s. 6d.

## PROTESTS.

| | Under. | Out of Stamp. In City. | City and within limits |
|---|---|---|---|
| A bill £20.......... | 2s. | 7s. 6d. | - 10s. |
| £20—£100, | 3s. | 8s. 6d. | - 11s. |
| £100—£500, | 5s. | 10s. 6d. | - 13s. |
| £500 or upward | 10s. | 17s. 6d. | - £1 |

If beyond the limits, the additional charge of noting is to be added to the protest out of the city on each kind of bill.

In addition to these, the holder of a dishonoured bill may recover postage, commission paid to a banker, and interest; but no extraordinary expenses which any of the parties may incur by travelling, or by an advantageous engagement being defeated by want of punctual payment, can be legally demanded.

Where different parties to bills or notes have become bankrupt, the holder may prove the full amount against them all, in the same manner as he may proceed in different actions at law till he has obtained a full satisfaction. The costs and charges of protesting bills, *before* an act of bankruptcy, may be proved, but those which accrue afterwards cannot; nor is the holder of a bill or note entitled to any interest accruing after the date of the commission issued. The proof of the debt, arising out of the bill or notes, is to be made before the commissioners, at their sittings, as in case of any other debt. Any bill or note given by a bankrupt as a consideration for signing his certificate, or for withdrawing a petition against it, is illegal by statute, and such instrument is null and void.

*Partnership Concerns.*—In partnership concerns, where one partner accepts a bill for himself and partners, the firm is bound to pay it if it concerns the trade; and from a decision in the case of Sheriff *v.* Wilkes, it appears to be decided that the act of one partner, in the name of the firm, is obligatory upon the others, though it may be on his own separate account, unless the persons claiming the benefit of this responsibility received the bill with the knowledge of the circumstance, that it was only the concern of one party. One partner may pledge the credit of his copartners to any amount, by an act in the way of trade and merchandize, done in the name of the firm. One partner, however cannot bind another *by deed*, without the express authority of all the parties bound. An authority given to one partner to receive all debts owing to, and to pay all debts due from the partnership, on its dissolution, does not authorize such party to indorse a bill of exchange in the name of the partnership, though drawn by him, and accepted by the debtor of the partnership *after* the dissolution. In order to render the dissolution of a partnership legal, it is indispensably necessary that notice of such dissolution should be published once in the London Gazette, with the signatures of the parties affixed; it is usual also, in the country, to advertise such notice in the provincial paper or papers published where the business has been carried on, that the persons with whom they have traded may the better be brought acquainted with that circumstance; and it is further necessary, in order that the dissolution may be brought home to the knowledge of the holder of any bill, or other negotiable instrument, in which the firm is concerned, that the partners should give notice to all their individual correspondents; otherwise, notwithstanding the notice in the Gazette, and provincial papers, they will stand responsible for all bills negotiated, by one of the former partners, in the name of the firm.

# AN UNIVERSAL INTEREST TABLE,

**For finding the Interest of any Sum of Money, at any rate per Cent. and for any number of Months, Weeks, or Days; also showing what any Estate or Income, from £1. to £1000. per annum, yields per Month, Week, or Day.**

**Rule**—First multiply the Principal by the rate per Cent. and then by the number of Months, Weeks, or Days required; cut off two figures on the right side of the product, and collect from the Table the several sums against the corresponding numbers, which, when added together, will produce the amount required.

| *Year.* | *Month.* | *Week.* | *Day.* | *Year.* | *Month.* | *Week.* | *Day.* |
|---|---|---|---|---|---|---|---|
| £. | £. s. d. | s. d. | s. d. | £. | £. s. d. | £. s. d. | £. s. d. |
| 1 | 0 1 8 | 0 4½ | 0 0½ | 60 | 5 0 0 | 1 3 1 | 0 3 3½ |
| 2 | 0 3 4 | 0 9 | 0 1¼ | 70 | 5 16 8 | 1 6 11 | 0 3 10 |
| 3 | 0 5 0 | 1 1¾ | 0 2 | 80 | 6 13 4 | 1 10 9¼ | 0 4 4½ |
| 4 | 0 6 8 | 1 6½ | 0 2½ | 90 | 7 10 0 | 1 14 7½ | 0 4 11¼ |
| 5 | 0 8 4 | 1 11 | 0 3¼ | 100 | 8 6 8 | 1 18 5½ | 0 5 5¾ |
| 6 | 0 10 0 | 2 3¾ | 0 4 | 200 | 16 13 4 | 3 16 11 | 0 10 11½ |
| 7 | 0 11 8 | 2 8¼ | 0 4½ | 300 | 25 0 0 | 5 15 4½ | 0 15 5¼ |
| 8 | 0 13 4 | 3 1 | 0 5¼ | 400 | 33 6 8 | 7 13 10 | 1 1 11 |
| 9 | 0 15 0 | 3 5½ | 0 6 | 500 | 41 13 4 | 9 12 3½ | 1 7 4¾ |
| 10 | 0 16 8 | 3 10¼ | 0 6½ | 600 | 50 0 0 | 11 10 9 | 1 12 10½ |
| 20 | 1 13 4 | 7 8¼ | 1 1¼ | 700 | 58 6 8 | 13 9 2¾ | 1 18 4¼ |
| 30 | 2 10 0 | 11 6½ | 1 7¾ | 800 | 66 13 4 | 15 7 8¼ | 2 3 10 |
| 40 | 3 6 8 | 15 4½ | 2 2¼ | 900 | 75 0 0 | 17 6 1¾ | 2 9 3¾ |
| 50 | 4 3 4 | 19 2¾ | 2 9 | 1000 | 83 6 8 | 19 4 7¼ | 2 14 9½ |

*Example*—Required the Interest of £1467. 10s. for 10 Months, at 4 per Cent.

| £. | s. | | | £. | s. | d. | |
|---|---|---|---|---|---|---|---|
| 1467 | 10 | | £500= | 41 | 13 | 4 | |
| | 4 | rate per Cent. | 80= | 6 | 13 | 4 | |
| | | | 7= | 0 | 11 | 8 | |
| 5870 | 0 | | | | | | |
| | 10 | Months. | £587= | 48 | 18 | 4 | per Ann. |
| 587 \| 00 | 0 | | | | | | |

*** If the two figures cut off be not cyphers add 2*d*. for every 10 contained in that sum when the calculation is for Months—½ for every 20, when it is for weeks—and a ¼ for every 40, when it is for Days.

# LIST OF FAIRS,

## IN ENGLAND AND WALES.

### BEDFORDSHIRE.

Ampthill, May 4, Nov 30. Bedford, 1st Tu, in Lent, April 21, July 5, Aug. 21, Oct. 11, Dec. 19 Biggleswade, Feb. 14, Sat. in Easter week, Whit Mon. Aug. 2, Nov. 8 Dunstable, Ash Wed. May 22, Aug 12, Nov 12. Elstow, May 14, Nov. 5. Harrold, Tu bf. May 13, Tu bf. July 6, Tu bf. Oct 11. Ickwell, April 5. Leighton Buzzard, Feb 5, 2nd Tu in April, Wh Tu July 26, Oct 24. St. Leonard's, Nov 7 and 17. Luton, April 18, Oct 18. Odell, Th in Whit week. Potton, 3d Tu in Jan O. S. last Tu in April, 1st Tu in July, Tu bf Oct 29. Shefford, Jan 23, April 6, May 19, Oct. 11. Silsoe, May 13, Sept 21. Toddington, April 25, 1st Monday in June, Sept 4, Nov 2, Dec 16. Woburn, Jan 4, March 23, July 13, Sept 25.

### BERKSHIRE.

Abingdon, 1st Mon in Lent, May 6, June 20, Aug 5, Sept 19, Mon bf Oct 11, Dec 11. Aborfield, Oct 5. Aldemaston, May 6, July 7, Oct 11. Bracknell, April 25, Aug 22, Oct 1. Chapel Row, July 30. Cookham, May 16, Oct 11. East Hagburn, Th bf Oct 11. East Ilsley, Wed in Easter week, and every other Wed till July, Aug 26, and 1st Wed aft Sept 29, Wed aft Oct 17, Wed aft Nov 12. Farringdou, Feb 13 Whit Tu, Tu bf and Tu aft Oct 11, Oct 29. Finchamstead, April 23. Hungerford, last Wed in April, Aug 10, Mon. bf and aft Sept 29. Lambourn, May 12, Oct 2, Dec 4. Long Cromarch, Aug 2. Maidenhead, Whit Wed. Sept 29, Nov 30. Mortimer, April 27, Nov 6. New Bridge, March 31, Sept 28. Newbury, Holy Th. July 5, Sept 4, Nov 8, Oakingham, April 23, June 11, Oct 11, Nov 2. Reading, Feb 2, May 1, July 25, Sept 21. Swallowfield, June 9. Thatcham, 2nd Tu aft Easter, week, and 1st Tu aft Sept 29. Twyford, July 24, Oct 11. Wadley, April 5. Wallingford, Tu bf Easter, June 24,

Sept 29, Dec 17. Wantage, 1st Sat in March, 1st Sat in May, July 18, Oct 10, and 17. Waltham St. Lawrence, April 10. Windsor, Easter Tu. July 5, Oct 24. Yattenden, Oct 13.

### BUCKINGHAMSHIRE.

Amersham, Whit Mon. Sept 19. Aylesbury, Fri. aft Jan 18, Sat but one bf Easter, May 8, June 14, Sept 25, Oct 12. Beaconsfield, Feb 13, Holy Th. Buckingham, Mon se'nnight aft Epiph O. S. March 7, (if Leap Year March 6,) May 6, Whit Th. July 10 Sept 4, Oct 2, Sat aft Oct 11, Nov 8. Burnham, Feb 25, May 1, Oct 2. Chesham, April 21, July 22, Sept 28. Colnbrook, April 5, May 3. Eton, Ash Wed. Fenny Stratford, April 19, July 18, Oct 11, Nov 28. Hanslop, Holy Th. Iver, July 10. Ivinghoe, May 6, Oct 17. Lavenden, Tu bf Easter. Little Brickhill, May 12, Oct 29. Merlow, May 1, 2, 3, Oct 29. Newport Pagnell, Feb 22, April 22, June 22, Aug 29, Oct 22, Dec 22. Olney, Easter Mon. June 29, Oct 21. Risborough, May 6. Stoney Stratford, Aug 2, Fri bf 10th Oct. Nov 12. St. Peter's Chalfont, Sept 4. Wendover, May 12, Oct 2. Winslow, March 20, Holy Th. Aug 21, Sept 22, 1st and 2nd Th aft Oct 11. Woobnrn, May 4, Nov 12. Wycomb, Mon bf Sept 29.

### CAMBRIDGESHIRE.

Cambridge, June 24, (for a week). Caxton, May 5, Oct 12. Ely, Ascen day, Oct 29. Ickleton, July 22. Linton, Holy Th. July 30. March, (Isle of Ely), Mon. bf Whit Sun. Whit Mon. 3d Tu in Oct. Roach, Rogation Mon. Sohabam, April 28. Sturbitch, Sept 28. Thorney, (Isle of Ely), July 1, Sept 21. Whittlesey, (Isle of Ely), Jan 25, June 13, Oct 26. Wisbeach (Isle of Ely), Sat but one bf. Easter. Wed bf Whit Sun. Sat bf Whit Sun. July 25, Aug 1 and 12.

### CHESHIRE.

Altringham, April 29, Aug 5, Nov

3 I

**22.** Budworth, Feb 3, April 5, Oct 2.
Chester, last Th. in Feb. July 5, Oct
11. Congleton, Th bf Shrove Tide,
May 12, July 13, Nov 22. Frodsham,
May 15, Aug 31. Hulton, Sept 19
Knutsford, Whit Tu. July 10, Nov 8.
Macclesfield, May 6, June 22, July 11,
Oct 4, Nov 11. Malpas, April 5, July
25, Dec 8. Middlewich, Holy Th. Aug
5, Oct 29. Namptwich, March 26, Sept
4, Dec 4. Neston & Parkgate, Feb 2,
May 1, Sept 29. Northwich, April 10,
Aug 2, Dec 6. Over, May 15, Sept 25.
Runcorn, last Fri in April & last Fri
in Oct. Sandbach, Easter Tu. 1st Th.
aft Sept 11. Stockport, March 4 & 25,
May 1, Oct 23. Tarporley, May 1, Mon
aft Aug 24, Dec 11. Winsford, May 8,
Nov 25.

### CORNWALL.
Bodmin, Jan 25, Tu & Wed. bf Whit
Sun. Dec 6. Callington, 1st Tu in
March, May 1, Sept 19, Nov 12. Cam-
born, Feb 24, June 29, Nov 11. Camel-
ford, Fri aft March 10, May 26, July 17,
Sept 5. East Looe, Feb 13, July 10,
Sept 4 Oct 11. Falmouth, Aug 7, Oct
11. Fowey, Shrove Tu. May 1,
Sept 10. Grampound, Jan 18, March
25, June 11. Helstone, Sat bf Mid
Lent Sun. Sat bf Palm Sun. Whit
Mon. July 20, Sept 9, Oct 28, Dec
20. Kellington, May 4, Sept 19, Nov 12.
Killhampton, Holy Th. June 13. Lan-
drake, July 19, Aug 24. Launceston, 1st
Th in Mar 3d Th in April, (both free)
Whit Mon. July 6, Nov 17, Dec 6. Le-
lant, Aug 15. Liskeard, Shrove Mon.
Mon bf Palm Sun. Holy Th. Aug 15,
Oct 2, Mon aft Dec 6. Lostwithiel,
July 10, Sept 6, Nov 13. Lower St.
Columb, July 9. Newlyn, Nov 8.
Northill, Sept 8, 1st Th in Nov. Pads-
tow, April 18, Sept 21. Penryn, May
12, July 7, Dec 21. Penzance, Th bf
Advent.Th aft Trin Sun. Corpus Chris-
ti. Probus, May 4, July 5, Sept 17.
Redruth, Easter Tu. May 2, July 9,
Sept 5, Oct 1. St. Austle, Whit Th
Nov 30. St. Columb, Th aft Nov 13,
Th in Mid Lent. St. Ewe, Th aft April
7, Nov 4. St.Germains, May 28, Aug 1.
St. Ives, Sat bf Advent. St. Lawrence,
Aug 10, Oct 29. St. Martin, Feb 13.
St. Mitchell, Oct 15, if Sun then Mon
aft. St. Neots, Easter Mon. May 5,
Nov 5. St Stephen's, May 12, July 31,
Sept 25. Saltash, Feb 3, July 25, Tu
bf March 25, Tu bf June 24, Tu bf Sept
29, & Tu bf Dec 25. Stratton, May 19,
Nov 8, Dec 11. Tregony, Shrove Tu.
May 3, July 25, Sept 1, Nov 6. Truro,
Wed in Mid Lent, Wed in Whitweek,
Nov 19, Dec 8. West Looe May 6.

### CUMBERLAND.
Abbey Holm, Oct 29. Alston
Moor, last Th. in May, 1st Th. in Sept
Bootle April 5, Sept 24. Brampton,
2nd Wed. aft. Whit. Sun. last Wed. in
Aug. Carlisle, Aug. 15, 26, Sept 5,
19, 1st & 2nd Sat. aft. Oct 11. Cok-
ermouth, Wed. aft. 1st Mon. in May,
& every fgt. aft. till Oct. 11; regular
fairs Whit. Mon. and Oct 11. Egremont, Sept 19. Ireby, Feb. 24, Sept.
21. Keswick, Aug 2. Kirkoswold, Th
bf. Whit. Sun. Aug 5. Longtown,
Th. aft. Whit. Sun. Th. aft. Nov. 22.
Penrith, April 25, 26, Whit. Tu. Sept
Sept. 27, Nov 11. Ravenglass, June
8, Aug 5. Roseby Hill, Whit Mon. &
every fgt. after till Sept 29. Ulpha
Mon bf. East. July 5. Whitehaven
Aug 12. Wigton, March 25. Work-
ington, Wed bf. Holy Th. Oct 18.

### DERBYSHIRE.
Alfreton, July 31, Oct 8, Nov 22
Ashbourne, 1st Tu in Jan. Feb 13, April
3, May 21, July 5, Aug 16, Oct 11, Nov 8
if Nov 29 falls on Sun. the Sat bf.
Tu in March, 3d Tu in Sept. Ashover
April 25, Oct 15. Bakewell, April 2
June 11, Aug 27, Oct 15, Nov 10. Bol-
sover, Easter Mon. May 5, June 8
Nov 1. Belper, May 12, Oct 31. Buxton, Feb 5, March 31, May 2, Sept 1
Oct 27. Chapel-le-Frith, Feb 7, Mar
24, 28, 29, April 19, 30, May 31, June
21, July 7, Aug 19, Oct 8, Nov
Chesterfield, Jan 25, Feb 28, if Sat
27, April 6, May 4, July 5, Sept
25, Nov 30, (toll free.) Critch, April
6, Oct 11. Cubley, Nov 30. Dale
Flash, May 13, Oct 27. Derby, Jan
25, March 21, 22, Fri in Easter week
Fri aft May 1, Fri in Whit week, June
25, Sept 27, 28, & 29, Fri bf Oct 11,
custom.) Dronfield, Jan 10, April
July 15, Aug 11, Sept 1. Duffield
March 1. Higham, 1st Wed aft Jan
Hope, May 12, Sept 29. Matlock, Jan
25, May 9, July 16, Oct 24. Monyash
Oct 28. Newhaven, Tu bf. 2d Wed
Sept. Oct 30. Pleasley, May 6,
29. Ripley, Easter Wed. Oct 23. Sta-
ley, Nov 12, if Sun 11. Tidswell, May
3, 2d Wed in Sept. Oct 29. Win
near Wirksworth, Feb 11, Easter
July 7, Oct 13. Wirksworth, Shr
Tu. May 12, Sept 8, Oct 4 & 5.

### DEVONSHIRE.
Alphington, 1st Th in June,
2. Ashburton, 1st Th in March,
Th in June, Aug 10, Nov 11.
minster, April 30, Wed after J
24, 1st Wed aft Oct 11. Bamp
Whit Tu last Th in Oct. Barnst
Fri bf April 21, Sept 19, 2d Fri in

Biddeford, Feb 14, July 18, Nov 12. Bishops Nympton, 3d Mon in April, Mon bf Oct 25. Bovey Tracey, Holy Th 1st Ths in July and Nov. Brent, May 13, Oct 11. Broadclift, May 3. Buckfastleigh, June 29, Aug 24. Buckland, Whit Tu Nov 2. Chudleigh, June 22, Oct 25. Chumley, last Wed in July. Collumpton, May 12, Oct 28. Crediton, May 11, Aug 21, Sept 21. Colyton, 1st Wed in May, Nov 30. Culmstock, May 21, Oct 1. Dodbrook, Wed bf Palm Sun. Ermington, Feb 2, June 23. Exeter, Ash Wed. Whit Mon Aug 1, if on Sun or Mon held on Tu Dec 6. Hartland, Easter Wed. Sept 25. Hatherleigh, May 9, June 22, Sept 7, Nov 9. High Budleigh, Good Fri.Honiton, July 20. Ilfracombe, April 14, 1st Sat aft Aug 22. Kentisbur, Whit Wed. Kingsbridge, July 20. Lifton, Feb 2, May 4, Oct 28. Milton Abbott, Easter Tu and 1st Wed in Aug. Modbury, May 4,if Sun or Mon held on Tu. Morton Hampstead, 1st Sat in June, July 18, Nov 30. North Tawton, 3d Th in April, Oct 3, Dec 18, if the last two fall on Sat Sun or Mon, held on the Th aft. Oakhampton, 2d Th aft March 11, May 17, 1st Wed aft July 5, Aug 5, when May 17 or Aug 5 fall on Sat Sun or Mon to be held Tu. Otterton, Wed in Easter week, 1st Wed after Oct 11. Ottery St Mary's, Tu bf Palm Sun Whit Tu Aug 15. Plymouth, Feb 5, Oct 2. Plympton, Feb 25, April 5, Aug 12, Oct 28. Seaton, March 1. Sidmouth, Easter Tu. Sept 2. Silverton, July 5, Sept. 4. Tavistock, Jan 17, May 6, Sept 9, Oct 11, Dec 11, if any of these days fall on Sat held on Fri. if on Sun or Mon held on Tu. Teignmouth, 3d Tu in Jan last Th in Feb. Sept 29. Thorncomb, Easter Tu. Tiverton, 2d Tu aft Trin Sun. Sept 29, if on Sun held Tu aft. Totness, 1st Tu in every month, Easter Tu. May 12,July 25, Oct 28. Uffculme, Wed bf Good Fri July 6, Aug 12. Up-Ottery, 3d Sat in March, Oct 24. Witheridge, June 24, Wed bf April 16.

### DORSETSHIRE.

Abbotsbury, July 10. Allington, July 22. Beaminster, April 4, Sept 19, Oct 9. Blandford, March 7, July 10, Nov. 8. Bridport, April 6, Holy Th. Oct 11. Broadwindsor, Trin Mon. Cerne Abbas, Mid-lent Mon April 28, Oct 2. Chardstock, Oct 11. Corfe Castle, May 12, Oct 29. Cranborne, Aug 24, Dec 6. Dorchester, Feb 14, Trin Mon July 6, Aug 6, Gillingham, Trin Mon. Sept 12. Holt Wood, Aug 5. Lyme, Feb 13, Oct

2, if on Sun on the Mon aft. Pool, May 1, Nov 2. Shaftesbury, Palm Sat June 24, Nov 23. Sherborne, May 22, July 18 and 26, if either of those days fall on Sat on Mon aft Oct 14. Stalkbridge, May 6, Sept 4. Stockland, June 12. Sturminster Newton, May 12, Oct 24. Wareham, April 17, July 5, Sept 11. Yetminster, April 23, Oct 1.

### DURHAM.

Barnard Castle, Weds in Easter and Whit weeks, July 25. Bishop Auckland, Ascen. day, Corpus Christi, and Th bf Oct 11. Cornhill, Dec 6. Darlington, 1st Mon in March, Easter and Whit Mons. Mon fort. aft Whit Mon. Nov 22, and another a fort. aft. Durham, Sat bf Feb 2, last Sat in Feb March 31, Sat bf May 12, Whit Tu Sat bf Aug 1, Sept 15, St. Cuthbert, Sat aft Oct 11, Sat bf Nov. 22. Hartlepool, May 14, Aug 21, Oct 9, Nov 27. Norham, 3d Tu in May and 2d Tu in Oct. Sedgefield, May 12. South Shields, last Weds in April and Oct 1st Weds in May and Nov. Stockton, Jan 27, July 18, Mon aft Oct 13. Sunderland, May 13, 14, Oct 11, 12. Walsingham, May 18, Sept 21.

### ESSEX.

Abridge, June 2. Althorne, June 5. Audley End, Aug 5. Aveley, near Purfleet, Easter Mon. Barfield, June 22. Barking, Sept 14, Oct 22. Belchamp St Paul's, Nov 30. Bentley, Mon aft July 15. Billericay, Aug 2, Oct 7. Bishop's Stortford, Holy Th. Th aft Trin Sun Oct 11. Blackmoor, Aug 21. Bradwell, June 24. Braintree, May 8, Oct 2, 3. Brentwood, July 11, Oct 15. Brightlingsea, near St Osyth, 1st Th in June, Oct 15. Bulmer Tye, near Sudbury, 2 days bf Holy Th. Burnham, April 25, Sept. 24. Canewedon, June 24. Canvey Island, June 25. Castle Hendingham, near Halstead, May 14, July 22, Aug 15, Oct 25. Chelmsford, May 12, Oct 12. Chesterford, July 5. Chigwell, Sept 30. Clacton (Little) July 25. Clacton (Great) July 29. Cogglesall, Whit Tu and Wed Colchester, Easter Tu July 5, 23, Oct 20. Colt, near Saffron Walden, Nov 17. Crouch, May 14. Danbury, May 29. Dedham, Easter Tu. Dunmow, May 6, Nov 8. Earl's Colne, March 25. Elmstead, May 4. Epping, Whit Tu Nov 13 Fairlop, first Fri in July. Fingeringboe, Easter Mon Fordstreet, Easter Tu Nov 1. Foulness Island, July 10. Goldanger, May 14. Grays, May 23, Oct 20. Great Baddow, May 14.

Great Holland, June 22. Great Hollingbury, near Woodside Green, Whit Tu. Great Oakley, April 26. Great Samford, Whit Mon. Great Tey, Trin Mon. Great Wakering, July 25, Sept 18. Hadleigh, June 24, Hadstock, June 28. Halstead, May 6, Oct 29. Harlow, May 13, Sept 9, Nov 28. Harwich, May 1, Oct 18. Hatfield Broad Oak, Aug 5. Hatfield Peverel, Whit Tu. High Ongar, Sept 14. Horndon, June 29. Ingatestone, Dec 1. Kelvedon, Easter Mon. Kirby, July 26. Lachinden, near Malden, June 2, Aug 27. Leigh, 2d Tu. in May. Maldon, Sept. 13, 14. Manningtree, Whit Th. Manuden, Easter Mon. Messing, 1st Tu. in July. Newport, Easter Tu. Nov 17. Ongar, Easter Tu Oct 11. Ostend, June 6. Prittlewell, July 15. Purfleet, June 13. Purleigh, Whit Tu. Ramsey, July 15. Rayleigh, Trin Mon. Rochford, Easter Tu. Wed aft Sept 29. Rumford, June 24. St Osyth, Ascen day. Salcote, Aug 24. South Ben fleet, Aug 24. South Minster, 3 days bf Easter, 9 days bf Whit Sun. Sept 29. Springfield, Whit Tu. Stanaway, April 23. Stanstead, May 12. Stebbing, July 10. Steeple, Whit Wed. Wed aft Sept 29. Stisted, Easter Tu. Tarling, Whit Mon. Tendering, Sept 21. Thaxted, Mon bf Whit Mon. Aug 10. Thorpe, Mon bf Whit Sun. Tillingham, Whit Tu. Sept 16. Tiptree Place, July 25. Tolesbury, June 29. Toleshunt Darcy, June 11. Walden Saffron, Sat aft Mid-lent Sun Nov 1. Waltham Abbey, May 14, Sept 25, 26. Walton, July 2. West Mersey, Whit Tu. Wicks, Aug 31, Sept 18. Witham, Fri and Sat in Whitsun week, June 4. Wivenhoe, Sept 4. Woodham Ferries, Sept 29, Oct 10. Writtle, near Chelmsford, Whit Mon.

## GLOUCESTERSHIRE.

Barton Regis, Sept 28. Berkeley, May 14. Bisley, May 4, Nov 12. Blakeney, May 12, Nov 12. Campden, Ash Wed April 23, Aug 5, Dec 10. Cheltenham, 2d Th in April, Holy Th Aug 5. Cirencester, Easter Tu. Mons bf and aft Oct 11, Nov 8. Coleford, June 20, Dec 5. Dursley, May 6, Dec 4. Fairford, May 14, Nov 12. Frampton, April 30. Gloucester, April 5, July 5, Sept 28, Nov 28. Hampton, Trin Mon Oct 29. Iron Octon, April 25, Sept 13. Lechlade, Aug 5, 21, Sept 9. Lidney, May 4, Nov 8. Little Dean, Whit Mon. Nov. 26. Marshfield, May 24, Oct 24. Mitchel Dean,

Easter Mon. Oct 11. Moreton, April 5, Oct 11 Newent, Weds bf East and Whit Sun Aug 12, Fri aft Sept 18. Newnham, June 11, Oct 18. Northleach, Wed. bf May 4, last Wed in May, 1st Wed in Sept Wed bf Oct 11. Painswick, Whit Tu Sept 19. Sodbury, May 23, June 24. Stonehouse, May 1, Oct 11, Nov 10. Stow-on-the-Wold, May 12, July 24, Oct 24. Stroud, May 12, Aug 21. Tetbury, Ash Wed. Weds bf and aft April 5, July 22, Weds bf and aft Oct 11. Tewksbury, 2d Mon in March, 1st Wed in April, O. S. May 14, June 22, Sept 4, Oct 11, Wed bf and aft do. 1st Wed. in Dec O. S. Thornbury, Easter Mon. Aug 15, Mon bf Dec 21. Tockington, May 9, Dec 6. Watereigh, Sept 19. Wickware, April 5, July 2. Winchcomb, last Sat in Mar. May 6, July 23. Winterburn, June 29, Oct 18. Wotton-under-Edge, Sept 25.

## HAMPSHIRE.

Alresford, last Th in July, Oct 17. Alton, Sat bf May 1, Sept 29. Andover, Tu & Sat at Mid Lent, May 13, Nov 17 & 18. Appleshaw, May 23, Fri and Sat bf Weyhill, Nov 4 & 5. Barton, July 31. Basingstoke, Easter Tu. Whit Wed. Sept 23, Oct 11. Beaulieu, April 15, Sept 4. Blackwater, Nov 8. Botley, Feb 20, May 28, July 23, Aug 20, Nov 13. Brading, May 12, Oct 2. Broughton, 1st Mon in July. Christ Church, June 13, Oct 17. East Meon, Sept 19. Eling, nr Southampton, July 5. Emsworth, April 15, July 18. Eversley, May 16, Oct 18. Fareham, June 29. Firton, May 1. Fordingbridge, Sept 9. Giles' Hill, nr Winton, Sept 12. Gosport, May 4, Oct 11. Hackfield, Good Fr. Hambledon, Feb 13, May 7, Oct 2. Hartley Row, Feb 27, June 29. Havant, June 22, Oct 17. Kingsclear, April 2, Oct 15. Liphook, March 6, June 11. Liss, May 6. Lymington, May 12, Oct 2. Magdalen Hill, Aug 2. Mattingley, Dec 4. Newport, (Isle of Wight) Whit Mon Tu & Wed. Newton, (Isle of Wight) July 22. Odiam, March 23, July 31. Overton, May 4, July 18, Oct 22, Whit Mon. Petersfield, March 5, and every other Wed. July 10, Dec 11. Portsmouth, July 10, 14 days. Post Down, July 26. Ringwood, July 10, Dec 11. Rowlands Castle, nr Havant, May 12, Nov 12. Ramsey, Easter Mon. Aug 26, Nov 8. Selborne, May 29. Southampton, Feb 17, Dec 15, May 6, Trin Mon. Southwick, April 5. Stockbridge, Holy Th. July

1st Th in Lent, Oct 7, & last Th in Oct. Sutton, Trin Tu. Nov 6. Tangley, April 15. Tichfield, March 9, May 24, Sept 25, Dec 7. Waltham, May 10, July 30, Oct 18. West Cowes, Whit Th. Weyhill, Oct 10, for 5 days. Wherwell, Sept 24, if on a Sun the Sat bf. Whitchurch, April 23, June 17, July 7, Oct 19. Wickham, May 20. Winchester, 1st Mon in Lent, Oct 24. Yarmouth, July 25.

## HEREFORDSHIRE.

Brampton, June 22. Bromyard, Th bf March 25, May 3, Whit Mon. Th bf July 25, Th bf Oct 29. Dorestone, April 27, May 18, Sept 27, Nov 18. Hereford, Tu aft Feb 2, Easter Wed. May 19, July 1, Oct 20, Dec 7. Huntington, July 18, Nov 13. Kingsland, Oct 10. Kington, or Kyneton, Wed bf Feb 2, Wed of Easter, Whit Mon. Aug 2, Sept 19, Wed bf Oct 11. Ledbury, Mon aft Feb 1, Mon bf Easter, May 12, June 22, 1st Tu in Aug, Oct 2, Mon bf Dec 21. Leintwardine, May 15, Nov 6. Leominster, Feb 13, Tu aft Mid Lent Sun. May 2, July 10, Sept 4, Nov 8, 3d Fri in Dec. Longtowne, ur Bishop's Castle, April 29, Sept 21. Orleton, April 24. Pembridge, May 13, Nov 22. Ross, Holy Th (Corpus Christi), July 20 to 25. Th aft Oct 11, Dec 11. Weobley, Holy Th. 3 weeks aft Holy Th. Wigmore, April 16, May 6, Aug 5.

## HERTFORDSHIRE.

St. Alban's, March 25, 26, Oct 11, 12. Albury Portmore Heath, July 17. Baldock, March 7, last Th in May, Aug 5, Oct 2, Dec 11. Barkway, July 20. Barnet, April 8, 9, 10, Sept 4, 5. Bennington, July 10. Berkhamstead, Shrove Mon. Whit Mon. Aug 5, Sept 29, Oct 11. Braughing, Whit Mon. Buntingford, June 29, Nov 30. Hatfield, April 23, Oct 18. Hemel Hempstead, Holy Th. 3d Mon in Sept. Hemstead, Whit Th. Hertford, Sat fort bf Easter, May 12, July 5, Nov 8. Hitchen, Easter & Whit Tus. Hoddesdon, June 29. Little Hadham, Bury Green, July 15. Much Hadham, June 24. Northall Statute, Sept 28. Preston, nr Hitchen, May 1, Oct 23. Puckeridge Statute, Sept 19. Purton, 4th Th aft April 5, th Th aft Oct 16. Redburn, 1st Wed after Jan 1, Easter and Whit Weds. Rickmansworth, July 20, Nov 24, Sat if 3d Mon in Sept. Royston, Ash Wed Easter & Whit Weds, 1st Wed in July, st Wed aft Oct 11. Sawbridgworth, April 23, Oct 20. Standon, April 25. Stevenage, 9 days bf Whit Sun. 1st Fri in Sept. Tring, Easter Mon. Oct 11.

Ware, last Tu in April, Tu bf Sept 24. Watford, March 31, Aug 31. Sept 9.

## HUNTINGDONSHIRE.

Alconbury, June 24. Earith, May 4, July 25, Nov 1. Godmauchester, Easter Tu. St Ives, Whit Mon. Oct 11. Kimbolton, Fri in Easter week, Dec 11. Leighton, May 12, Oct 5. St. Neots, Sat bf 3d Tu in Jan O. S. (toll free) Ascen day, Corpus Christi, Aug 1, Dec 17. Ramsey, July 22. Somersham, Jun 23, Fri bf Nov 12. Spaldwick, Wed. bf Whit Sun Nov 28. Stilton, Feb 16. Yaxley, Ascen. day.

## KENT.

Aylesford, June 29. Ash, April 6, Oct 11. Ashford, 1st & 3d Tu in every month, May 17, Aug 2, Sept 9, Oct 12 & 24. Benenden, May 15. Bethersden, 3d Mon in April. Boughton, Mon aft June 29. Bromley, Feb 14, Aug 5. Canterbury, Oct 11. Charing, April 29, Oct 29. Charlton, Oct 18. Chatham, May 15, Sept 19. Chilham, Nov 8. Cranbrook, May 30, Sept 29. Crayford, Sept 8. Dartford, Aug 2. Deal, April 5, Oct 12. Dover, Nov 23. East Malling, Aug 5. Eastry, Oct 2. Elham, Palm Mon. Easter & Whit Mons. Oct 20. Faversham, Feb 25, Aug 12. Folkstone, June 28. Gillingham, Easter Mon. Goudhurst, Aug 26. Gravesend, May 4, Oct 24. Greenwich, Easter & Whit Mon. & Tu. Hadlow, Whit Mon. Hawkhurst, Aug 10. Hedcorn, June 12. Horsemonden, July 26. Hythe, July 10, Dec 1. Lamberhurst, April 6. Lenham, June 6, Oct 23. Lydd, last Mon in July. Maidstone, first Tu in every month, Feb 13, May 12, June 20, Oct 17. Malling E. July 15. Malling W. Aug 12, Oct 2, Nov 17. Marden, Oct 11. Miltoutown, July 24. Minster, Palm Mon. Penshurst, June 26. Queenborough, Aug 5. Rochester, May 30, Dec 11, 4th Tu in every month. Rainham, Aug 15. Romney, Aug 26. St. Lawrence, Aug 10. Sandhurst, May 25. Sandwich, Dec 4. Seale, June 6. Sevenoaks, July 10, Oct 12, 3d Tu in every month. Sittingbourn, Whit Mon Tu & Wed. Oct 11. Staple, July 25. Stroud, Aug 26. Sutton Valence, Dec 1. Tenterden, 1st Mon in May. Tunbridge, Oct 11, 29, 1st Tu in every month. Westerham, Sept 19. Whitstable, Th bf Whit Sun. Wingham, May 12, Nov 12. Wrotham, May 4. Wye, May 29 Sept 30. Yalding, Whit Mon. Oct 15, 16.

## LANCASHIRE.

Ashton under Lyne, Mar 23, April 29, July 25, Nov 21. Bacup, Good Fri. Bartholomew, April 24, 25. Blackburn, Easter Mon May 12, Oct 17. Bolton, July 30, Sept 14, 15. Booth, Feb. 3, Whitsun Eve, Sat bf Oct 23. Broughton, Aug 1. Burnley, Mar 7, May 6, 18, July 11, Oct 11. Bury, Mar 5, May 3, 2d Th aft Whit Sun Sept 18. Cartmel, Whit Mon 1st Tu aft Oct 23. Chipping, Easter Tu Aug 24. Chorley, Mar 26, May 5, Aug 20, Sept 5. Clithero, Mar 24, July 21, Aug 1, 4th Sat aft Oct. 11, Dec 7. Cockerham, Easter Mon. Colne, Mar 7, Mar 13, 15, Oct 11, Dec 21. Dalton, June 6, Oct 23. Garstang, Holy Th, July 10, Nov 22. Haslingden, Feb 3, Easter Tu May 3, July 4, Oct 2. Hawkshead, Mon bf Holy Th. Sept 21. Hornby, June 10. Inglewhite, Tu bf Holy Th Oct 5. Kirkham, Feb 4, April 28, Oct 18. Lancaster, May 2, July 5, Aug 11, Oct 11. Littleborough, Mar 1, Oct 13, if these days fall on Sun then Mar 2 and Oct 14. Liverpool, July 25, Nov 11. Longridge, May 13, Nov 5. Manchester, Easter Mon and Tu Whit Mon and Tu Oct 1, Nov 17. Middleton, Th aft Mar 11, Th aft April 15, 2d Th aft Sept 29. Newburgh, June 21. Newchurch, April 29, Sept 30. Newton, May 17, July 15, Aug 11, 12. Oldham, May 2, July 8, Oct 13. Ormskirk, Whit Mon Sept 8. Padiham, May 8, Sept 26. Poulton, Feb 6, April 13, Nov 3. Prescot, June 12, Aug 24, 25, Nov 1. Preston, 1st Sat aft Jan 6, Mar 27, Aug 26, Sept 7. Radcliffe Bridge, April 29, 30, Sept 28, 29. Rochdale, May 14, Whit Tn Nov 7. Rufford, May 1. Standish, June 29, Nov 22. Ulverstone, Mar 29, Oct 7. Up-Holland, July 15. Warrington, July 18, Nov 30, for ten days. Weeton, 1st Th. aft Trin Sun. Wigan, Holy Th and Oct 28, June 27.

## LEICESTERSHIRE.

Ashby-de-la-Zouch, Mon bf Shrove Tu Easter and Whit Tu Sept 28, Nov 9. Belton, Mon aft Trin Week. Billesden, April 23, May 4, July 6, 25. Bosworth Husband, May 8, July 10, Oct 16. Castle Donington, Mar 18, Whit Th. Hallaton, Holy Th and Th 2 weeks aft April 30, May 21. Hinkley, 3d Mon aft Epiph. Easter Mon. Mon bf Whit Mon Whit Mon Aug 26, and Mon aft Oct 28. Kegworth, Feb 12, Easter Mon April 30, Oct 11. Leicester, Mar 2, May 12, July 5, Oct 11, Dec 8; New Fairs, Jan 4, June 1, Aug 1, Sept 13, Nov 2. Loughborough, Feb 14, Mar 23, April 25, Holy Th Aug 12, Nov 13, Mar 24, Sept 25. Lutterworth, Th aft Feb 19, April 2, Holy Th. Sept 16. Market Bosworth, May 8, July 10. Market Harborough, Jan 6, Feb 16, April 29, July 31, Oct 19, lasts 9 days; New Fairs, Tu aft May 2, Tu aft Midlent Sun Tu bf Nov 22, Dec 8. Melton Mowbray, Mon and Tu aft Jan 17, Holy Th Mar 13, May 4, Whit Tu Aug 21, Sept 7. Mountsorrel, July 29. Waltham on the Would, Sept 19.

## LINCOLNSHIRE.

Alford, Whit Tu Nov 8. Barton upon Humber, Trin Th. Belton, Sept 25. Boston, May 4, Aug 11, Town Fair Nov 30, lasts 4 days, Dec 11. Bourn, Mar 7, May 6, Oct 29, Nov 30. Brigg, Aug 5. Burgh, May 12, Oct 2. Burwell, Oct 11. Caistor, Sat bf Palm Sun, Sat aft May 12, Sat bf Whit Sun June 1, Oct 11. Corby, Aug 26, Mon bf Oct 11. Calsthorpe, April 29. Crowland, Sept 4. Crowle, last Mon in May, Nov 22. Donnington, May 26, Aug 17, Sept 4. Epworth, 1st. Tu aft May 1, 1st Th aft Sept 29, Sept 9, Oct 15. Fillingham, Th aft Easter, Nov 23. Folkingham, Ash Wed. Palm Mon May 12, June 19, July 3, Th aft Oct 11, Nov 10 and 22. Gainsborough, Tu aft Easter, Oct 20, if on a Tu held Tu aft. Grantham, 5th Mon in Lent, Sat bf Easter, Holy Th July 10, Oct 26, Dec 17. Grimsby, June 6, Sept 15. Haxey, July 5. Heckington, Th bf April 28, and Oct 11. Holbeach, May 17, Sept 17, Oct 11. Horncastle, June 22, Aug 21, Oct 28, 29. Kirton, July 18, Dec 11. Lincoln, Fri in Easter week, Tu aft April 11, July 5, last Wed in July, Oct 6, Nov 28. Louth, April 30, 3d Mon aft Easter, Aug 5, Nov 23. Ludford, Aug 2, Nov 30. Market Deeping, 2d Wed aft May 11, Wed bf Oct 11, Nov 22. Market Raisin, every other Tu aft Palm Sun Sept 25. Messingham, Trin Mon. Navenby, Aug 18, Oct 17. Partney, Aug 1 & 25, Sept 18, 19, Oct 18, 19. Saltfleet, Oct 3. Sleaford, Plough Mon Easter Mon Whit Mon Aug 1, Oct 20. Scotter, July 10. Spalding, April 27, June 29, Aug 26, Sept 25, Wed bf Dec 6. Spilsby, Mon bf Whit Mon. Mon aft do. if it falls in May, if not there is no fair, 2d Mon in July. Stamford, Tu bf Feb 13, Mon bf Mid-Lent, Mid-Lent Mon. Mon bf May 12, Mon bf Corpus Christi, July 25, O.S. St.

Simon & St. Jude, O.S. Nov 8. Stockwith, Sept 4. Stow, Oct 11. Stow Green, June 14, 15, July 3, 4. Swineshead, 3d Th in July, Oct 2. Swineshead, Mon aft Oct 11. Tattershall, May 15, Sept 25. Tidford, Mon aft Easter, Dec 6. Torksey, Whit Mon. Wainfleet, Sat aft May 21. July 5, Aug 24, Oct.24. Winteringham, July 14. Winterton, July 5. Wragby, Holy Th Sept 29.

## MIDDLESEX.

Beggars Bush, Sept 12. Bow, Th Fri & Sat in Whit week. Brentford, May 17, 18, 19, Sept 12, 13, 14 Chiswick, July 15, 16, 17. Edmonton, Sept 14, 15, 16. Enfield, Sept 28, Nov 30. Hammersmith, May 1. Hounslow, Trin Mon. Mon aft Sept 29. London, Sept 3. Staines, May 11, Sept 19. Twickenham, Holy Th Mon and Tu bf Michaelmas. Uxbridge, Mar 25, July 31, Sept 29 Oct 11.

## MONMOUTHSHIRE.

Abergavenny, May 14, June 24, Sept 25. Caerleon, May 1, July 20, Sept 24. Castletown, May 6, Aug 5, Nov 26. Chepstow, Fri in Whit week, Sat bf June 20, Aug 1, Fri bf Oct 29. Crismond, April 4, Aug 10, Oct 9. Magor, two last Mons in Lent. Monmouth, Whit Tu. Wed bf June 20, Sept 4, Nov 22. Newport, Holy Th Whit Th Aug 15, Nov 6, 3d Mon in the month. Pontypool, April 2, 22, July 5, Oct 11, last Mon in the month. Stow, 1st Th aft Whitsuntide. Usk, Mon aft Trin Oct 29.

## NORFOLK.

Acle, June 24. Aldeburgh, June 21. Attleborough, April 11, Th aft Holy Th Aug 15. Aylsham, March 23, last Tu in Sept Oct 6. Banham, June 22. Briston, May 26, Oct 11. Broomhall, Mon aft Ascen Nov 30. Brumhill, July 7. Burnham, Easter Mon Aug 1. Castle Acre, May 1, Aug 5. Cawston, Feb 1, last Wed in April & Aug. Cley, last Fri in July. Coltishall, Whit Mon. Crissingham Magna, Aug 12. Cromer, Whit Mon. Diss, Nov 8. Downham, March 3, May 8, Nov 13. East Dereham, Th & Fri bf July 6, Th & Fri bf Sept 29. East Harding, May 4, Tu aft Sept 13, Oct 24. Elmham, April 5. Fakenham, Whit Tu Nov 11. Feltwell, Nov 20. Fincham, March 3, Aug 9. Forncett, Sept 11. Foulsham, Easter Tu. Frettenham, 1st Mon in April. Fring, May 21, Dec 11. Gaywood, June 22, Oct 17, kept at Lynn Custom-house Quay.

Gissing, July 25. Gorleston, June 8. Grassinghall, Dec 6. Harleston. July 5, Sept 9, Nov 28. Harpley, July 24. Hempnall, Whit Mon. Dec 11. Hempton, Whit Tu Nov 16. Hingham, Mar 6, Whit Tu Oct 2. Hitcham, Aug 3. Hockham, Easter Mon. Hockwold, July 25. Holt, April 25, Nov 25. Horning, Mon aft Aug 2. Ingham, Mon aft Whit Mon. Kenninghall, July 18, Sept 30. Kipton Ash, Sept 4. Loddon, Easter Mon. Mon aft Nov 21. Litcham, Nov 1. Lynn Regis, Feb 14, Oct 17. Magdalen Hill, Aug 2. Martham, 1st Tu and Wed in May. Massingham, Tu bf Easter, Nov 8. Mattishall, Tu bf Holy Th. Metheld, April 23. New Buckenham, last Sats in May & Nov. North Walsham, Wed bf Holy Th. Northwould, Nov 30. Norwich, day bf Good Fri Easter and Whit Mons & Tus. Oxborough, Mar 25. Pulham St. Mary Magdalen, May 8. Reapham, June 29. Rudham, May 17, Oct 18. St. Faith's, Oct 17. Schole, Easter Tu. Scottow, Easter Tu. Shouldham, Sept 19, Oct 11. South Repps, Tu fort aft Whit Mon. Sprowston, Aug 2. Stoke, Dec 6. Stow Bridge, Sat aft Whit Sun. Swaffham, May 12, July 21, Nov 3. Thetford, May 14, Aug 2, Sept 15. Walsingham, Mon fort aft Whit Mon. Watton, July 10, Oct 11, Nov 8. Weasenham, Jan 25. Worstead, May 12. Wymondham, Feb 12, May 16, Sept 7. Yarmouth, Fri and Sat in Easter week, Sept 21.

## NORTHAMPTONSHIRE.

Boughton Green, June 24, 25, 26. Brackley, Wed. aft Feb 25, April 24, Wed aft June 22, Wed aft Oct 11, Dec 11. Brigstock, April 25, Sept 4, Nov 22. Brixworth, Whit Mon. Daventry, 1st Mon in Jan, Easter Tu June 7, Aug 3, Oct 2, Oct 27. Fotheringay, 3d Mon aft July 6. Higham Ferrers, Tu bf Feb 5, March 7 or Leap Year March 6, Th bf May 12, June 28, Th bf Aug 5, Oct 11, Dec 6. Kettering, Th bf Easter, Fri bf Whit Sun. Th bf Oct 11, Th bf Dec 21. King's Cliff, Oct 29. Northampton, Feb 20, April 6, May 4, June 19, Aug 5, 26, Sept 19, 1st Th in Nov (toll free) Nov 28, Dec 19. New Inn Road, Oct 8. Oundle, Feb 25, Whit Mon Aug 21, Oct 12. Peterborough, July 10, Oct 2. Rockingham, Sept 25. Rowell, Trin Mon, all the week. Thrapstone, 1st Tu in May, Aug 5. Towcester, Shrove Tu May 12, Oct 29.

Ashton and
17,
Fri.
Blackburn, Ec
17. Bolton,
Booth, Feb. 3
Oct 29. Brou
by, Mar 7, M
12. Bury, Bin
Whit Sun Sep
Mon lst Tu
Easter Tu Au
May 5, Aug
Mar 24, Ju
Oct. 11, Dec
Mon, Colne,
11, Dec 21. I
Gausdang, Holy
Naslington, Fe
July 4, Oct 2.
Holy Tu. Sept
Darlowhite, T
Kirkham, Feb
Lancaster, Ma
11. Littlebon.
these days fall
Oct 11. Lires
Longridge, Ma
ter, Easter Mo
Tu Oct 1, Nov
Mar 11, Tb
Sept 30. New
church, April
May 17, July 1
May 2, July
Whit Mon Sep
Sept 26. Poult
3. Prescot, Ju

RSETSHIRE.

Feb 3, March 25. Ban-
July 18. Bath, Feb 14,
up's Lydeard, April 5,
lon, Aug 30. Bridge-
in Lent, June 24, Oct 2,
Bristol, March 1, Sept 1,
ach. Bruton, April 23,
le-carey, Tu bf. Palm
Whit Tu. Chard, 1st
Aug and Nov. Chedder,
Comb St. Nicholas,
bf. Dec 11. Congers-
Crewkerne, Sept 4.
Aug 5. Dulverton, July
Dunster, Whit Mon.
Matthias day, Nov 25.
Easter Mon. Sept 19,
tspill, June 29. Ilmin-
ed in Aug. Keynsham,
Aug 15. Langport, 2nd
June 29, Oct 5, Nov 22.
Whit Sun. Aug 10, Sept
Oct 9. Midsummer Nor-
Milbourne Port, June
Mells, Mon after Trin
Milverton, Easter Tu.
Oct 11. Minehead, Whit
orlinch, Aug 20. North-
3. North Petherton, May
Nov 11. Pensford, May 6,
Decumans, Aug 24, Sept
in Mallet, Easter Mon. Aug
ton, last Mon in Jan. Palm
weeks aft. ditto, Tu six
ditto, Tu nine weeks aft.
South Petherton, July 6.
May 8, Sept 12. Stoke Go-
6, Aug 1. Stoke-under-
April 25. Stowey, Sept 7.
June 17, July 7, three days,
kept on Mon. Wedmore,
Wellington, Th, bf. Easter,
Wells, Jan 6, May 14, July
Nov 30. Weston Zoyland,
Winsham, Whit Wed. Wive-
May 12, Trin Mon. Sept 25.
June 28, Nov 17, if on Fri
Sun then on Mon.

STAFFORD

lid Lent
-under-
a Sun
Whit
rslem,
Oct
ree)
24.
1-
,

aft Oct 11 2d Mons in Jan and Feb
last Mon in June 2d Mon in Dec.
Hayward Heath, Nov 17. Holy Cross,
2d Weds in Apr and Sept. Kinfare,
May 14 Dec 14. Lane End, Feb 14
May 29 July 22 Nov 2. Leek, Wed
bf Feb 13 Easter and Whit Weds May
18 July 3, 28, Wed nearest St Luke's
day 2d Mons in Mar and Sept and the
3d Mon in Nov. Lichfield, Ash Wed
Fri aft May 12 and May 1 O S Fri
aft Oct 28. Longnor, Tu bf Feb 14
Easter Tu May 4 18 Whit Tu Aug 5
Tu bf Oct 11 Nov 12. Newcastle-un-
Lyne, Shrove Mon Easter and Whit
Mons, Mon bf July 15, Mon aft Sept
11 Nov 6. Pattingham, last Tu in
April. Penkridge, April 30 1st Mon
in Sept Oct 11. Rugeley, April 17
June 6 Oct 21. Sandon, Nov 14.
Shenstone, Feb 23. Stafford, Tu bf
Shrove Tu May 14 Sat bf and on June
29 July 10 Sept 16,17,18, Oct 2 Dec 4.
Stone, Tu aft Mid Lent, Shrove Tu
Whit Tu Aug 5. Tamworth, Jan 29
May 4 July 26 Sept 3 Oct 24. Tean,
April 10 Nov 12. Tutbury, Feb 14
Aug 15 Dec 1. Uttoxeter, Tu bf Feb
14, March 15, Th in Easter week, May
3, 6, June 3, July 4, 31, Sept 1, 6, 19,
Nov 2, 11, 27. Walsall, Feb 24 Whit
Tu. Tu bf Sept 29. Wednesbury, May
6, Aug 4. Wheaton Aston, April 20,
Nov 2. Wolverhampton, July 10. Yox
all, Sept 1.

## SUFFOLK.

Acton, July 6. Aldborough, Mar
1 May 3. Aldringham, Oct 11 Dec
11. Barrow, May 1. Beccles, Whit
Mon June 29 Oct 2. Bergholt East,
July 22. Bildeston, Ash Wed. Holy
Th. Blythborough, April 5. Botes-
dale, Holy Th. Boxford, Easter Mon
Dec 21. Boxtead, Whit Mon. Bran-
don, Feb 14 June 11 Nov 11. Bricet,
July 5. Bungay, May 14, Sept 25.
Bures, Holy Th. Bury St. Edmonds,
Easter Tu. Oct 2 three weeks, Dec 1.
Clare, Easter Tu July 26. Cooling,
July 31, Oct 17. Debenham, June
24. Dunwich, July 25. Earl's So-
ham, Aug 4. Elmset, Whit Tu. Eye,
Whit Mon. Felsham, Aug. 16. Fin-
ningham, Sept 4. Framlington, Whit
Mon. Oct 11. Framsden, Holy Th.
Glemsford, June 24. Gorleston, June
8. Great Thurlow, Oct 11. Hackes-
ton, Nov 12, Hadleigh, Whit Mon
Oct 11. Halesworth, Oct 29. Hard
ford, March 18, Aug 22. Haughley,
Aug 25. Haverhill, May 12, Aug 26.
Hinton, June 29. Horringer, Sept 4.
Hoxne, Dec 1. Hundon,
Ipswich, May 4, 18, July

Sept 25. Ixworth, Whit Mon. Kedington, June 29. Kersey, Easter Mon. Lavenham, Shrove Tu Oct 10. Laxfield, May 12, Oct 18. Lindsey, July 25. Lowestoff, May 12. Market Weston, Aug 15. Massingham, August 9. Mattishaw, Aug 9. Melford Long, Whit Tu. Mendlesham, Holy Th. Mildenhall, Oct 11. Nayland, Oct 2. Needham, Oct 28. Newmarket, Whit Tu. Orford, June 24. Polestead, June 16. Saxmundham, Holy Th Sept 23. Stradbrooke, Sept 21. Snape, Aug 11. Somerliton, July 31. Southwold, Trin Mon. Aug 24. Stanton, Whit Mon. Stoke, Feb 25, Whit Mon. May 12. Stowmarket, July 10, Aug 12. Stratford, June 11. Sudbury, March 12. July 10, Sept 4. Thandiston, July 31. Thwaite, June 30, Nov 25. Woodbridge, April 5, Oct 2, Oct 21. Woolpit, Sept 16, 19.

## SURREY.

Bagshot, July 15. Bletchingly, June 22, Nov 2. Bookham, Oct 11. Camberwell, Aug 18. Chertsey, 1st Mon in Lent, May 14, Aug 6, Sept 25. Cobham, March 17, Dec 11. Croydon, Oct 2, 3, 4. Dorking, day before Holy Th. Dulwich, Mon. aft. Trin Mon. Egham, May 30. Epsom, Aug 5. Esher, Sept 4. Ewell, May 12, Oct 29. Farnham, Holy Th. June 24, Nov. 13. Frotherheath, June 16. Godalming, Feb 13, July 10. Guildford, May 4, Nov 22. Ham, May 29. Haslemere, May 12, Sept 25. Hurdwich Court, Whit Tu. Katherine Hill, Oct 2. Kingston, Th Fri and Sat in Whit week, Aug 2, 3, and 4, Nov 13. Knaphill, Nov 9. Leatherhead, Oct 11. Lingfield, May 12. June 29, July 15, Oct 11. Limpsfield, May 22. Mitcham, Aug 12. Mortlake, July 19. Oakley, May 22. Peckham, Aug 21. Ripley, Nov 11. Ryegate, Whit Mon. Sept 14, Dec 9, 1st Wed in every month. Sydenham, Trin Mon. Thorpe, near Egham, May 29. Walton, Easter Wed. Wanbro', near Guildford, Sept 4. Wandsworth, Mon Tu and Wed in Whit wk. Woking, near Ripley, Whit Tu.

## SUSSEX.

Adversean, Sept 12. Alfriston, May 12, Nov 30. Augmering, July 30. Ardingley, May 30. Arundel, May 14, Aug 21, Sept 25, Dec 17, 2nd Tu in every month. Ashurst, Oct 16. Balcomb, June 4. Battle, Whit Mon. Nov 22, 2nd Tu in every month. Beckeley, Easter Th. Dec 26. Beeding, July 21. Billinghurst Mon. Nov. 8. Bines Green, J Blackboys, Oct 6. Bodjam, Bolney, May 17, Dec 11. B Street, Sept 21 Brede, Eas Brighton, Holy Th Sept 4. B 1st Mon aft July 7. Broadwater 22, Oct 30. Burwash, May 12, Buxtead, July 31. Catstreet, 14, June 27. Chailey, June 29. C wood, July 25. Chichester, M Whit Mon. Aug 5, Oct 10, 20, Wed in every month. Cla 5, Sept 26. Crawley, May 8, Crowborough, April 25. Cros Hand, June 22, Nov 19. Cuckl May 25, Whit Tu. Sept 16, No Dane-hill, Ascen day. Dicker, A day. Ditching, April 5, Oct 12. Bourn, Oct 10. East Dean, Oc East Grinstead, April 21, July 13, 11 Egdean, May 1. Sept 4 Ewh May 21, Aug 5. Fenden, Holy Sept 14. Fletching, Mon. bf. Wh Sun. Forest-row, June 25, Nov Franfield, June 24. Garner-Stree Aug 5. Green, Aug 12, Mon bf. Jul 5. Guestling, May 23. Hafield, Ap 14, June 27. Hartfield, Th. aft Wh week. Hastings, Whit Tu. June 2 Nov 28. Haylesham, April 5, Jun 14. Henfield, May 4, July 5, Aug Holdly, May 9. Hollington, 2nd Mo in July. Hoo, May 1. Horley, No 7. Horsebridge, May 9, Sept 2 Horsebridge-common, Sept 11. Hou sham, April 5, Mon bf. Whit Sun. Jul 18, Nov 27, last Tu in every month Horstead-Kayne, May 27, Sept 1 Hurst-Green, June 3. Hurstpierpoint May 1, Aug 10. Iventon, Easter T May 29. Lamberhurst, April 5, Ma 21. Lewes, May 6, Whit Tu. Jul 26, Oct 2. Linfield, May 12, Aug Oct 28. Longbridge, July 20. Mares field, Sept 4. Mayfield, May 30, No 13. Midhurst, April 5, Whit Tu. Oc 29. Newhaven, Oct 11. Newick June 1. Northiam, Sept 17. Nutley May 4. Old Tye Common, May 9 Peasemarsh, Th aft. Whit week, May 18. Pembury, Whit Tu. Pett, nea Hastings, May 27, July 18. Petworth Holy Th. July 29, Nov 20. Pevensey July 5. Playden, Sept 2. Pulborough, Easter Tu. Rackham, May 20, Oct 13. Riper, Aug 2. Rogate, Sept 27. Rotherfield, June 18, Oct 2. Robert's Bridge, Sept 25. Rudgwick, Trin Mon. Rushlake Green, April 22, Oct 11. Rye, Whit Mon. Aug 10. St. Leonard's Forest, Nov 17. Seaford, March 13, July 25. Shoreham, July 25. Sidley, first Mon

June 29. Silmiston, Sept 19.
ham, Easter Tu. Sliniord, Easter
. South-bourne, March 12. South
ng, first Wed in June, Oct 28.
water, July 8. Southwick, May
Steyning, June 9, Sept 19, Oct
nd Wed in every month. Stor-
ton, May 12, Nov 11, 3rd Wed in
y month. Tarring, April 5, May
Oct 2. Thakebam, May 29. Tice-
st, May 4, Oct 7. Turner's Hill,
ster Tu. Oct 16. Uckfield, May
Aug 29, Wadhurst, April 29, Nov
Warnham, Whit Tu. Warborough,
sen, June 24, Aug 1. Wellington,
nt Mon. Westfield, May 18. West
m, May 15, Sept 15. West Heath-
. Whit Mon. Wevelsfield, July
. Whitesmith, May 21, July 3.
lmington, Sept 17. Winchelsea,
y 14. Withyam, May 1, Oct. 11.
ods Corner, May 25. Worley
mmon, 2nd Wed in May.

## WARWICKSHIRE.

Alcester, Jan 22, Mar. 19, May 18,
ly 30, Oct 17, Dec 3. Allesley, May
June 15, Oct 15, Dec 9. Atherstone,
ril 7, July 18, Sept 19, Dec 4. Bid-
th, Aug 8, July 15. Birmingham,
hit Th. Sept 24, first Th in Oct.
ailes, Easter Tu. Coleshill, Shrove
on. May 6, Wed aft. Sept 29. Co-
ntry, March 1, May 2, June 7, for
ht days, Aug 30, Nov 1. Dun-
urch, Jan 12, March 23, June 29,
pt 15. Hampden, in Arden, June
Sept 7. Henley, in Arden, March
, Whit Tu. July 20, Oct 29. Kenil-
orth, April 30, Sept 30. Kineton,
n 25, Feb 2, Oct 18, Dec 16.
nowle, July 27. Nuneaton, Feb
, May 14, July 1, Oct 7, 31, if on
in the 30th, Dec 17. Rugby, 2nd
u aft. Jan 6, Feb 17, March 31, May
, July 7, Aug 21, Mon bf. Sept 29,
ov. 23, Dec 15 and 28. Solyhull,
pril 29, May 19, Fri aft Sept 9, Oct
l. Southam, Easter Mon. first Mon
Lent, July 10, first Mon in Oct.
tratford-upon-Avon, last Mon in
eb. Fri after March 25, May 14, last
on in July, Sept 25, and Fri after,
ct 12, Wed after Dec 11. Sut-
on, Trin Mon. Nov 8. Tamworth,
pril 23, Sept 23. Warwick, Jan 21,
eb 11, 23, April 1, May 13, June 3,
uly 5, Aug 12, Sept 4, Oct 12, Nov
, Dec 16.

## WESTMORELAND.

Ambleside, Wed. aft. Whit Sun.
Oct 29. Appleby, Sat bf. Whit Sun.
Whit Mon. June 10, Aug 10. Brough,
Th bf. Whit Sun. Brough Hill, Sept
30. Kendal, April 25, Nov 8, 28.
Kirby Lonsdale, Holy Th. Dec 21.
Kirby Stephen, Easter Mon. Whit Tu.
Oct 29. Milthorp, May 12. Orton,
May 2, Fri bf. Whit Sun. Shapp,
May 1.

## WILTSHIRE.

Amesbury, May 17, June 22, Dec
18. Barwick Hill, Nov 6. Bradford,
Trin Mon. Bradford Leigh, Aug 26.
Britford, Aug 12. Calne, May 6, Sept
29. Castle Combe, May 4. Chilmark,
July 30, Chippenham, May 17, June
22, Oct 29, Dec 11. Clack, April 5,
Oct 11. Collingbourn-ducis, Dec 11.
Corsham, March 7, Sept 4. Corsley
Heath, Jan 4, Aug 5. Cricklade, 2nd
Th. in April, Sept 21. Devizes, Feb
14, Holy Th. April 20, July 5, Oct 2,
20, Dilton Marsh, Sept 24. Down-
ton, April 23, Oct 2. Great Bedwin,
Aug 23, July 26, Heytesbury, May
14, Sept 25. Highworth, Aug 13,
Oct 11, 29. Hindon, May 27, Oct 29.
King's Down, Sept 23. Laycock,
July 7, Dec 21. Ludgershall, Aug 5.
Maiden Bradley, May 6, Oct 2.
Malmsbury, Mar 28, April 28, June 5.
Marlborough, July 11, Aug 22, Nov
23. Melksham, July 27. Mere, May
17, Oct 11. Norlease, April 23. North
Bradley, Sept 16. Pewsey, Sept 16.
Purton, Th. bf. May 6. Ramsbury,
May 14, Oct 11. St. Ann's hill, (De-
vizes,) Aug 6. Salisbury, 1st Tu aft.
Jan 6, Mon. bf. April 5, Whit Mon. &
Tu. Tu after Oct 10. Sherstone, May
12, Oct 2. Steeple Ashton, Sept 19.
Swindon, March 25, May 20, Sept 23,
Dec 23. Torn Hill, Aug 6. Trow-
bridge, Aug 5, 6, 7. Uphaven, Oct 29.
Warminster, April 22, Aug 11, Oct 26.
Westbury, 1st Fri in Lent, Easter &
Whit Mondays. Whitchbury, Nov 17.
Wilton, May 4, Sept 12. Wotton
Basset, April 2, May 7, Oct 8. Yar-
boro' Castle, Oct 4, 5.

## WORCESTERSHIRE.

Alvechurch, May 3, Aug 10. Bel-
broughton, first Mon in April, Mon bf.
Oct 18. Bewdley, April 23, July 24,
Dec. 10, 11. Blockley, Tu aft. Easter
week, Oct 11. Broomsgrove, June 21,
Oct 1. Droitwich, Fri in Easter week,
June 18, Sept 22, 23, Dec. 2. Dudley,
May 8, Aug 5, Oct 2. Eversham, Feb
2, Mon aft. Easter week, Whit Mon.
Sept 21. Feckenham, March 26, Sept
30. Kidderminster, Mon bf. Easter,
Holy Th. June 20, Sept 4. King's
Norton, April 25, Sept 5. Pershore,

Easter Tu. June 26, Tu bf. Nov 1. Redditch, first Mon in Aug. Sept 21. Shipston, 3rd Tu in April. Shipton, April 21, June 22, Tu aft. Oct 11, Dec 8. Stourbridge, March 29, Sept 8. Stourport, Easter Mon. Sept 13, Dec 18. Tenbury, April 27, July 18, Sept 26. Upton, 1st Th aft. Mid-lent, Whit Th July 10, Th bf. Oct 2. Worcester, Sat bf. Palm Sun. Sat in Easter week, Aug 15, Sept 19, first Mon in Dec. 2nd Mon in Feb. first Mondays in May, June, July, & Nov. (toll free.)

*For a complete List of the Yorkshire Fairs, see Distance Table of Yorkshire, in the Illustrations to Vol I. with the Fairs of the County attached.*

---

## A LIST OF THE FAIRS IN THE PRINCIPAL TOWNS OF WALES.

Aberconway, April 6, Sept 4, Oct 11, Nov 8. Aberfraw, March 7, Wed aft Trin. Oct 23, Dec 11. Abergeley, April 2, Wed bf. Holy Th. Aug 20, Oct 9. Aberystwith, Mon aft. Jan 5, Palm Mon. Whit Mon. Mon aft. Nov 11. Almwch, Nov 12. Bala, May 14, July 10, Sept 11, 21, Oct 24, Nov 8. Bangor, April 5, June 25, Oct 28. Beaumaris, Feb 13, Holy Th Sept 12, Dec 19. Brecknock, May 14, July 5, Sept 6, Nov 17. Builth, June 27, Oct 2, Dec 6. Caerwys, March 16, last Tu in April, Trinity Th. 1st Tu aft July 7, Sept 9, Nov 5. Cardiff, 2d Wed in March, April and May, June 29, Sept 19, Nov 20. Cardigan, Feb. 13, April 5, Sept 8, Dec 19. Carmarthen, April 15, June 3, July 10, Aug 12, Sept 9, Oct 9, Nov 14. Corwen, March 12, May 24, July 21, Oct 11, Dec 26. Cowbridge, 1st Tu. in Feb March 25, May 4, June 24, 1st Tu in Aug. Sept 29, 1st Tu in Dec. Crickeith, May 23, July 1, Oct 18. Crickhowell, May 12. Denbigh. May 14, July 18, Sept 25. Dinas Mowddwy, June 2, Sept 10, Oct 1, Nov 13. Dolgelly, May 11, July 4, Sept 20, Oct 9, Nov 22, Dec 16. Flint, Feb 14, June 24, Aug 10, Nov 30. Haverford West, April 14, May 12, June 12, July 18, Sept 4, 23, Oct 18. Hawarden, Oct 1, Dec 24. Hay, May 17, Aug 12, Oct 10. Kidwelly, May 24, July 22, Oct 29. Knighton, Sat aft. 1st Mon in March, Th bf Easter, May 17, Oct 2, last Th in Oct. Th bf. Nov 12. Lampeter, Jan 11, Feb 6, May 8, Whit Wed. Sat aft Aug 11 & 27, Sat aft. Sept 11 and 26, Oct 19, Sat aft. Nov 12. Llanelly, Ascen. Day, Sept 30. Llandaff, Feb 9, Whit Mon. Llandiloe, June 21. Llandovery, Wed aft. Epiph. Wed aft. Easter week, Whit Tu. July 31, Wed aft Oct 11, Nov 26. Llangadock, March 12, Ascen. Day, July 9, 1st Th in Sept. Dec 11. Llangollen, last Fri in Jan. March 17, May 31, Aug 21, Nov 22. Llanrwst, April 25, June 21, Aug 3, Sept 17, Dec 11. Merthyrtidvell, Nov 11. Mold, Feb 24, May 12, Aug 2, Nov 22. Narberth, June 4, July 5, Sept 26, Dec 11. Neath, Trin Th. July 31, Sept 12. Newport, June 27. Pembroke, May 14, Trin Mon. July 10, Sept 25. Presteigne, May 9, June 20, Dec 11. Pwllhelly, May 13, Aug 19, Sept 24, Nov 11. Radnor, Tu bf. Holy Th. 1st Tu aft Trin. Aug 14, Oct 28. Rhayader, Aug 6, 27, Sept 26, 1st Wed aft. Oct 11, Dec 3. Ruthin, March 19, Fri bf Whit Sun. Aug 8, Sept 30, Nov 10. St. Asaph, Easter Tu. July 15, Oct 16, Dec 26. Swansea, 2d Sat. in May, July 21, Aug 15, Oct 8, & two follow. Sat. Talgarth, March 12, May 31, July 10, Sept 23, Nov 3, Dec 3. Tenby, Whit Tu. May 14, July 20, Oct 29, Dec 4. Towyn, May 13. Tregarron, Mar 15, 16, 2d Tu in Oct. Wrexham, Mon & Th bf. March 23, Holy Th. June 6, Sept 9.

*•* *A considerable portion of the following Names having been received too late to be ʳᵗᵉᵈ in the Additions and Alterations at the beginning of this Volume, it has been ʳⁱᵈᵉʳᵉᵈ·pⁱoper to introduce them in this place.*

## COUNTY OF YORK.

ᵗᵉʳ Fawkes, of Farnley Hall, Esq. High Sheriff, (appointed Feb. 1, 1823.)

### YORK.

THOMAS SMITH, Lord Mayor, for 1823-4, (2nd Time.)

#### CHAMBERLAINS.

| Mr. Peter Armistead | Mr. John Rigg | Mr. George Jennings |
| Mr. George Bell | Mr. William Dawson | Mr. Richard Burdekin |

COMMON COUNCILMAN—Monk Ward. Mr. Joseph Smith.

*Aduralton,*
es Joseph, card maker

*Agbrigg,*
llito Wm. wharfinger

*Almondbury,*
ison Wm. fancy mfr.
lden Geo. carpenter

*Armley,*
wood Rt. woollen mfr.

*Barnby upon Don,*
ᵉsham Thomas, Esq.
ferson Rev.J. per. curate

*Barwick-in-Elmet,*
ain Jonth. farmer
ith T. vict. Black Swan

*Batley,*
tson Tim. blanket mfr.

*Beverley,*
hite Sir. W. Bart. Hall
atson Wm. Esq.

*Birstall,*
ercer Rev. John, (meth.)
tolton, *near Bradford,*
traclonghW. worsted mfr
awson Wm. farmer
eenhow J. worsted mfr.
odgson T. worsted mfr.

*Bowling,*
iley J. G. Esq.
olton Abm. plasterer
eaks Abm. worsted mfr.
arnside John, grocer
ied Saml. thread mfr.
att Joseph, cabinet mkr.

*Bramley,*
oldsworth J. woollen mfr
yers B.Green,wooln.mfr.
arley John, woollen mfr.

*Brighouse,*
vison John, grocer
axton Wm. tailor
*arlton, near Wakefield,*
anks Jph. vict. Unicorn

*Churwell,*
oberts Jph. grocer
earth Jas. maltster

*Clayton,*
*Worsted Manufacturers.*
entley Sam. Rhodes Thos
ershaw T. Tankard J.
ershaw Jph.

*Clayton Heights,*
Baldwin T. worsted mfr.

*Cleckheaton,*
Curry Mrs. gent. *Rawfolds*
arstow Thomas. fire-man
Blaymires Geo. card maker
Walker Benj. ironmonger

*Conisbrough,*
Hall John, gent.

*Crosland,*
Beaumont Rd. grocer
Hague Benj. wooll-n mfr.
Littlewood B. woollen mfr.
Sykes Joshua, woollen mfr

*Cullingworth,*
Craven Edw. cotton spinr.
Horsfall John, cotton spinr.
*Dalton, near Huddersfield*
Brook Jph, vict. Star Inn
Tolson John, fancy mfr.

*Darfield,*
Garland Thomas, Esq.
Harrison Thomas, *Mill*
Hodson Wm. gent.

*Deighton,*
Berry Joshua, yeoman
Jackson W. vict. Wellington
Shiers Benj. fancy mfr
Wilcock Wm. carpenter

*Dewsbury Moor,*
Smith Edw. woollen mfr.

*Earls-heaton,*
Machell Frs. woollen mfr.
Stocks John, blanket mfr.

*Elland,*
Horsfield M. excise officer
Townend D. & L. drapers
Waddington J.tal.chandler
Wooler Wm. corn dealer

*Farnley Tyas,*
Lodge David, fancy mfr.
Roberts E. T. & I W.merts
woollen mfrs. and tanners

*Farsley,*
Hardaker J. clock maker
Marshall Jph. woollen mfr.

*Finnay Bridge,*
Bowers Wm. weaver
Broadhead Matt.fancy mfr.
Spivey John, woollen mfr.

*Flockton,*
Jaques Rev. J. curate

*Foolston,*
Kay Geo. vict. White Horse
Mellor J.senr. cloth dresser
Senior John, mfr
Swires Henry, clogger

*Gildersome,*
Hartley J. woollen mfr.
Peat Wm. woollen mfr.

*Gomersall,*
Birkby Wm. card maker
Crosland J. cloth drawer
Firth Joseph, cloth dresser
Mortimer Jph. shoe maker

Scholes Wm. card maker
Seaton George, tailor

*Halifax,*
Brown Sharp, card maker
and mfr. of Iron Card.
Brass, and Bobbin Wire,
King Cross lane
Riley T.grocer,KingCrossln
*Handsworth Woodhouse,*
Birks Wm. grazier
Le Fall John. schoolmaster
Moody Benj. Beighton Mill
Potter Wm. gent. Beighton

*Hanging Heaton,*
Rhodes Saml.gent.

*Hawksworth,*
Holmes and Schofield, worsted spinners and mfrs.

*Haworth,*
Hartley Hiram, woolcombr
Pickles John, bookkeeper

*Headingley,*
Sykes Thos. dyer, Grove mill

*Heath, near Wakefield,*
Ferrand James, butler
Oliver Thomas, butcher

*Hebden Bridge.*
Ashworth Wm. grocer
Holt John, joiner
Wright J. cotton spinner

*Hebden Bridge lanes,*
Bent J cotton spnr. Bankfoot
Coates M. fustian mfr.
Wilson Jas. fustian mfr.

*Heckmondwike,*
Dauber Robert, draper
Dixon Robt. cotton mfr.
Firth Wm. vict. Wool Pack
Greenwood Daniel, gent.
Rother Thos. shoemaker

*Hemingfield,*
Webster John, farmer

*Heptonstall,*
Barritt John. linen draper
Fielding J. vict. Swan
Green John, jun. gent.
Ingham Rev. Richard
Nicholson John, joiner
Pickles Thos. grocer
Robertshaw Wm. cotton mfr.
Spencer Zech. grocer

*Hewick Lodge,*
Charnock Wm. Esq.

*High Town,*
Armitage John, cloth dresser
Brooke J. woollen mfr.
Parker Wm. card maker
Walker J. woollen mfr.

*Hipperholme.*
Turner Thos. stone mert.
*Holme on Spalding Moor,*
Calvert Rev. Thos. B.D.

*Holmfirth,*
Bailey John, woollen mfr.
Bates Jas. woollen mfr.
Boothroyd J. woollen mfr.
Dickinson W. woollen mfr.
Woodhead W. woollen mfr.

*Honley,*
France Fred. fancy mfr.
Kilner A. m. slay maker

*Hopton,*
Brook John, woollen mfr.
Wilson Joseph, fancy mfr.

*Norbury,*
Brook James, carpenter
Foster Joshua, gent.
Jackson Henry, clerk
Priestley Benjamin, surgeon

*Horsforth,*
Wood Jph. stone mason

*Horton Great,*
Drake up Saml. shuttle mkr.
Sellers Wm. size boiler

*Horton Little,*
Smith Joshua, grocer
Thornton Jph. coal mert.

*Huddersfield,*
Haigh M. woollen mfr. Marsh
Hirst J. cloth dresser, Marsh
Horsfall John, whitesmith
Richardson Wm. schoolmst
Wood Ralph, grocer

*Illingworth,*
Wigglesworth W. wrstd. mfr.

*Kirk Burton,*
Cocker Benj. white Kersey-
mere mfr. & at Huddersfd
Savage Joseph, gent.
Wilkinson Jph. fancy mfr.

*Kirk Heaton,*
Broadbent Jas. fancy mfr.
Stafford Joseph, grocer
Stainscliffe C. grocer & drpr.

*Laughton-en-le-Morthen,*
Chapman Wm. farmer
Shillito Fra. grocer, &c.

*Lindley,*
Aspinall J. woollen cord mfr.
Lindley Wm. cloth dresser

*Little Town,*
Cockell, Brook & Co. dyers

*Lockwood,*
Batty Jas. woollen mfr.
Brook Jas. cloth dresser
Kay John, carpenter

*Lofthouse, near Wakefield*
Auty G. cabinet maker

*Luddenden Foot,*
Turner Abm. carpet mkr.

*Marsden,*
Haigh Thos. woollen mfr.
Morton Thomas, bleacher

*Meltham,*
Taylor David, woollen mfr.

*Mill Bridge,*
Kay & Pool, tallow chandlers

*Mirfield,*
Eland Joseph, shoe maker
Lee Thomas, boat builder

Pearson Benj. grocer
Sheard Abraham, farmer
Webster Jph. post master

*Morley,*
Morley M. land agent

*Netherton,*
Beaumont Jph. clothier, &c.

*Newton, near Wakefield,*
Bocock John, slay maker

*Northowram,*
Brook Joseph, shopkeeper
Butterworth Saml. currier
Drake Jas. wheelwright
Wright Wm. inspector

*Okeworth,*
Broadbent W. worsted mfr.

*Ossett,*
Carr Joshua, wheelwright
Swithinbank W. King's Arms

*Ovenden,*
Barstow Saml. corn miller
Dean Wm. gent. Scausby
Eastwood John, shopkpr.
Fearnley I. worsted mfr.
Iles J. worsted mfr.
Priestley J. worsted mfr.

*Oxenhton,*
Bradshaw Chpr. grinder

*Paisley Bridge,*
Kettlewell Thomas, gent.
Metcalfe Thos. corn dealer
Parkin Thos. stone mercht.
Parke Thos. vict. Half Moon
Ward Abm. yeoman
Weatherhead J. vict. Pitcher
Weddall John, druggist
Wood C. & A. tal. chandlers

*Linen Manufacturers,*
Feasley J.    Hullah J.
Grange Wm. Hullah Thos.
Greenham W. Ingilby Jas.
Horseman G. Motley John,

*Pudsey,*
Cawood J. saddler
Cloderay J. size boiler
Hext Wm. woollen mfr.
Hyland Peter, baker
Parker Jph. schoolmaster
Sutcliffe J. woollen mfr.
Walton J. woollen mfr.

*Rawdon,*
Fox Rev. I.

*Saddleworth,*
Bostock Pet. grocer, Delph
Broadbent R. schoolmaster
Brookbank T. Nav. warehs.
Greaves Jas. Brook Bottom
Kenworthy Wm. dyer
Neal Jas. merchant, Quick
Shaw T. flour dealer, Delph
Wood J. mfr. Black bey bank

*Sheepridge,*
Wells John, mfr.

*Shelly,*
Brook Jas. Henley

*Shepley,*
---- David, woollen mfr.
---- low Jph. schoolmaster

*--- Shipley,*
---- ton G. woollen mfr.
---- chit T. grocer
---- ---- and ----,
worsted mfrs.

*Skircoat,*
Haworth Jas. --- ---
Tate Joseph, gardener

*Stainthwaite,*
Meal John, dyer
Sykes Edward, grocer

*Southowram,*
Fozard T. card maker
Howarth C. barometer mkr.
Jenkinson S. tailor

*Sowerby,*
Horsfall Jonathan, dyer,
Asquith Bottom Mill
Webster T. grocer, Triangle

*Sowerby Bridge,*
Cooper Saml. iron founder
Firth John, woollen draper
Kenworthy Wm. shopkpr.
Maude J. grocer & draper

*Stanningley,*
Wilkinson Abm. yeoman
Wilson W. tin plate mfr.

*Sutton on Derwent,*
Brown Rd. timber mert.

*Thong Upper,*
Carter John, grocer

*Thornhill,*
Bedford John, shoe maker
Buckley Jas. clothier
Fligg Mark, agent
Taylor Benj. Lee's House

*Thornton, near Bradford,*
Craven Jas. worsted mfr.
Craven Jonas, worsted mfr.
Pearson J. butcher

*Todmorden,*
Horsfall Wm. cotton spnr.

*Wadsworth,*
Ashworth Robert
Horsfall J. dimity mfr.
Mallalieu and Platts, wrsp.
mfrs. Nutclough

*Wakefield,*
Navins Jas. draper

*Wales,*
Green Thos. Bedgreave Mill
Shirt John, Esq.

*Wath upon Dearne,*
Johnson Saml. liquor mert.
Lambert Richd. farmer

*Wheatley,*
Wilde J. and L. yarn mfrs.

*Whitley Upper,*
Nussey Benj. blacksmith

*Wibsey,*
Scott J. worsted mfr.
Varley B. vict. Windmill
Yewdale J. cabinet maker

*Windhill,*
Bateson Geo. worsted mfr.
Ward Jonah, butcher

*Weston,*
Payne Rev. Saml. curate

*Wolfedale,*
Rowland John, schoolmaster

*Woodbrill Woodland,*
Bingley Wm. Esq.

*Worthley Gate,*
Bateson A. woollen mfr.

*Wyrea,*
Hodgson J. worsted mfr.

CPSIA information can be obtained
at www.ICGtesting.com
Printed in the USA
BVHW04*0017210818
525056BV00018B/2024/P